INTERNATIONAL CRIMINAL JUSTICE

To Mariella, Beatrice and Giulio

International Criminal Justice

Law and Practice from the Rome Statute to Its Review

Edited by

ROBERTO BELLELLI

Routledge
Taylor & Francis Group
LONDON AND NEW YORK

First published 2010 by Ashgate publishing

Published 2016 by Routledge
2 Park Square, Milton Park, Abingdon, Oxfordshire OX14 4RN
711 Third Avenue, New York, NY 10017, USA

First issued in paperback 2016

Routledge is an imprint of the Taylor & Francis Group, an informa business

British Library Cataloguing in Publication Data
International criminal justice : law and practice from the
Rome Statute to its review.
1. Criminal procedure (International law)--Congresses.
2. International Criminal Court--Congresses. 3. Rome
Statute of the International Criminal Court 1998--
Congresses. 4. International criminal courts--Rules and
practice--Congresses. 5. War crimes--Cases--Congresses.
6. Crimes against humanity--Cases--Congresses.
I. Bellelli, G. Roberto.
345'.01-dc22

Library of Congress Cataloging-in-Publication Data
Bellelli, Roberto.
International criminal justice : law and practice from the Rome Statute to its review / by Roberto Bellelli.
p. cm.
Includes bibliographical references and index.
ISBN 978-1-4094-0267-1 (hardback) -- ISBN 978-1-4094-0268-8
(ebook) 1. International criminal courts. 2. Criminal procedure (International law) 3. Rome Statute of the International Criminal Court
(1998) I. Title.
KZ6304.B45 2010
345'.01--dc22

2010005092

ISBN 13: 978-1-138-27705-2 (pbk)
ISBN 13: 978-1-4094-0267-1 (hbk)

Contents

The opinions contained in the present volume are those of the contributors alone and do not necessarily reflect or represent in any way the views of the States or Organizations which they are or have been associated or affiliated to.

Notes on Contributors[1]

Guido Acquaviva, Legal Officer, Special Tribunal for Lebanon; formerly Legal Officer, Appeals Chamber, ICTY.

Stefan Barriga, Legal Counsellor to the Permanent Mission of the Principality of Liechtenstein to the United Nations, New York. The author participated in the work of the Special Working Group on the Crime of Aggression and advised the Group's Chairman throughout its work, from 2003 until February 2009.

Roberto Bellelli, President of the Military Tribunal in Turin; Legal Adviser for International Criminal Law at the Italian Ministry of Foreign Affair; former member of all National Commissions for the implementation of the Rome Statute. Currently, Legal Adviser to the Embassy of Italy in The Hague. National Focal Point for the ICC, Italian delegate for the ICC since the Rome Diplomatic Conference in 1998 and at all Preparatory Commission and Assembly of States Parties sessions.

Fatou Bensouda, ICC Deputy Prosecutor.

Roger S. Clark, Board of Governors Professor, Rutgers University School of Law, Camden, New Jersey; Delegate of the Government of Samoa for all ICC related matters since 1995.

Astrid Reisinger Coracini, Lecturer, Institute of International Law and International Relations, University of Graz; Executive Director, Salzburg Law School on International Criminal Law, Humanitarian Law and Human Rights Law.

Carla Del Ponte, ICTY Chief Prosecutor (1999–2007), Swiss Ambassador to Argentina.

Paola Gaeta, Professor of International Law, University of Florence and of International Criminal Law at the University of Geneva; Co-Director, LL.M. Programme, Geneva Academy of International Humanitarian Law and Human Rights; Member of the Editorial Board of the *Journal of International Criminal Justice* and of the *European Journal of International Law*.

Edoardo Greppi, Professor of International Law, University of Turin.

Stephen Kostas, Senior Legal Officer of the Appeals Chamber and Legal Advisor to the President of the Special Court for Sierra Leone.

---

1 Titles and positions of Contributors generally refer to those held at the time of the Turin *Conference on International Criminal Justice* (14–18 May 2007) and have been updated to include the positions held at the time of editing of this book.

Claus Kreß, Professor of Criminal Law and Procedure, and of Public International Law; Chair of Criminal Law and Procedure, European Criminal and International Law, and Director of the Institute of Criminal Law and Procedure at the University of Cologne; Member of German delegation to the Rome Conference and to following negotiations on the law of the ICC; Head of the drafting committee for the ICC Regulations of the Court; sub-coordinator of the Special Working Group on the Crime of Aggression of the ICC Assembly of States Parties.

Anne-Marie La Rosa, Legal Adviser at the Advisory Service of the Legal Division of the International Committee of the Red Cross (ICRC), Geneva.

Flavia Lattanzi, *ad litem* Judge at the ICTY and formerly at the ICTR (2003–2006); Professor of International Law, University of Rome.

Chea Leang, National Co-Prosecutor, Extraordinary Chambers in the Courts of Cambodia. Formerly, Deputy in the Office of Legal Training of the Ministry of Justice and member of the Cambodian Committee for the Penal Code (1995–2002); Prosecutor in the Cambodian Court of Appeal (2002–2006).

Jürg Lindenmann, Attorney-at-Law, Ambassador, Vice-Director, Directorate of International Law, Swiss Federal Department of Foreign Affairs; Lecturer at the University of Bern.

Susanne Malmström, Legal Officer at the ICTY.

Erik Møse, ICTR President (2003–2007), Vice-President (1999–2003); ICTR Judge; Justice of the Norwegian Supreme Court.

Melika Murtezić, Legal Officer, War Crimes Chamber in the Court of Bosnia and Herzegovina, Sarajevo.

Nicola Piacente, Deputy Prosecutor, Prosecution Office of Milan, Anti-terrorism and Anti-Mafia Unit.

Fausto Pocar, ICTY President (2005–2008); ICTY Judge.

David Scheffer, Mayer Brown/Robert A. Helman Professor of Law and Director of the Center for International Human Rights at Northwestern University School of Law in Chicago, Illinois; former US Ambassador at Large for War Crimes Issues from 1997 to 2001.

Muhammad Aziz Shukri, Professor of International Law, Director General of the Arab Encyclopedia, Damascus.

Göran Sluiter, Professor of International Criminal Procedure, Amsterdam Centre of International Law, University of Amsterdam.

William Smith, International Deputy Co-Prosecutor, Extraordinary Chambers in the Courts of Cambodia, since 2006. Formerly, prosecutor and barrister in Australia; trial attorney, legal analyst and investigator at the ICTY; UNTAET Acting District Administrator of the Viqueque District (2000).

Gabriel Chavez Tafur, Legal Attaché to the Advisory Service, Legal Division of the International Committee of the Red Cross (ICRC), Geneva.

B. Don Taylor III, Associate Legal Officer, Trial Chamber II, ICTY.

Otto Triffterer, Professor of Austrian and International Criminal Law and Procedure (Emeritus) at the University of Salzburg. Awarded with the 2009 ASIL Certificate of Merit for High Technical Craftsmanship and Utility to Practicing Lawyers and Scholars by the American Society of International Law.

Renate Winter, SCSL President (March–May 2004 and since May 2008): President of the International Association of Youth and Family Court Judges.

Pål Wrange, Principal Legal Advisor, Swedish Ministry for Foreign Affairs; former delegate for the Crime of Aggression at PrepCom and until 2007 to the ASP.

Foreword

There has been a burgeoning interest in international criminal justice in recent years, reflecting both the unfilled demand for international judicial institutions and the dynamic nature of this relatively nascent field of international law. Most timely and appropriately, *International Criminal Justice* by Judge Roberto Bellelli provides a clear snapshot of an in-depth analysis of this young field at a period of remarkable transition.

The *ad hoc* tribunals for the former Yugoslavia and Rwanda as well as the Special Court for Sierra Leone, while continuing some of their most significant trials to date, are heavily focused on their completion strategies. Other mixed tribunals are performing their jurisdictions in profoundly different and challenging circumstances. The new permanent International Criminal Court is rapidly affirming its expected crucial role and attracting general interest in its worldwide field of operations. Many practical lessons have been learnt in the context of investigations and prosecutions, yet considerable challenges remain ahead. Considerable jurisprudence has emerged in relation to genocide, crimes against humanity and war crimes, but the crime of aggression, once referred to as 'the supreme crime', remains undefined. The contributors to this volume, who are among the leading scholars and practitioners of international criminal law, provide first-hand insight into the challenges and successes in all of these areas to date.

Over half of this book is devoted to the International Criminal Court and its future, a clear indication of the central importance of the Court within the broader system of international criminal justice. The Court will not replace national courts. It will only ever deal with a relatively small number of cases at a time. However, its potential influence is broad. Many states have amended their domestic legislation in light of the Court's jurisdiction. After just a few short years, national courts and academics routinely cite its legal texts and its decisions. Potential perpetrators of international crimes are now on notice that, should national courts be unwilling or unable, they may be held accountable before the Court.

This volume provides the reader with a detailed picture of the many problems confronted, the solutions adopted or still needed, and the progress made in establishing a system of international criminal justice, thus establishing a clear benchmark against which to gauge future progress. It is hoped that as time goes by the outstanding challenges identified hereafter will be addressed adequately and that the system will grow to its full potential. This will require the concerted effort and cooperation of all actors in the field. If there is one overarching lesson of the past 15 years' efforts to build a system of international criminal justice, it is that the different judicial institutions are only as strong as the support and cooperation they receive from states and other actors. It is my sincere hope that this cooperation will continue to be forthcoming, not only for the International Criminal Court but for all similar institutions. We will then look back to this transitional period, with fond memories, as a formative stage in the development of international criminal justice.

Judge Sang-Hyun Song
President of the International Criminal Court

Preface

The second half of the twentieth century has witnessed the emergence in the international community of a new awareness of its responsibilities in situations which potentially affect international peace and security. In an increasingly interdependent and interconnected world, natural and artificial borders and barriers can no longer guarantee that a crisis taking place in one state or region will not have repercussions far away, in another region of the world. Thus, the population directly affected by those events is not limited to the people living in the eye of the storm. As global challenges call for global solutions, appropriate governance must be ensured through mechanisms established and functioning beyond the national or regional level.

From this perspective, the development of the concept of the international community's responsibility to protect populations has provided a practical framework to balance rights, obligations and responsibilities as opposed to traditional doctrines based purely on sovereignty of states. In essence, the debate on the role of law and justice in building and preserving basic conditions for international stability and security revolves around the scope of state sovereignty. It is also in this ambit that the traditional prerogative of sovereign states to exercise criminal justice at a legislative and jurisdictional level has been progressively eroded by the focusing on responsibilities attached to the states' authority rather than on the authority itself. In the lengthy and complex process of the building of international humanitarian and human rights law, this different focus has represented a historical shift in the centre of gravity from states to individuals, in order to balance interests protected under international law in times of peace and armed conflict. This change of perspective, from the prerogative of states to the rights of individuals, is reflected in an unprecedented attempt by the international community to prosecute the most serious crimes of international concern, with a principled shift from total impunity to accountability.

The concept of international criminal justice developed throughout this process thus defies traditional doctrines based on the principle of state sovereignty: the protection of populations from widespread and gross violations of human rights and humanitarian law no longer depends on a state's discretion, instead it is now a positive obligation incumbent upon sovereign states. In the event that they fail to comply with this primary obligation, it is for the international community to take over the protective role. This shared responsibility includes the establishment of rules and means to fight against impunity by carrying out criminal justice at the international level or with international assistance and, thus, to deter the further commission of the most heinous crimes of international concern.

As such judicial functions of the international community are based on the capacity to provide peace and security by enhancing the protection of populations, the role of affected individuals and communities has also progressively become more apparent and – with due regard to the particularities of criminal proceedings – victims' protection, participation, representation and compensation have emerged as crucial features in the most recent international criminal procedure.

This book captures the structures, functions and challenges of international criminal justice at a turning point in its experience, when occasional and limited forms of international or mixed jurisdictions have demonstrated their potential and provided solutions in certain situations, while understandably being unable to meet all demands. At such a critical juncture, when some international and mixed jurisdictions are in the process of winding up their work, it is timely to address the issues of their legacy and of continuity through residual functions to be performed for many years in the future, as well as of the role of the permanent International Criminal Court.

It is widely understood that multiple experiences have contributed over time to the building of a system of international criminal justice. While the recent commencement of trial activity at the ICC has so far provided limited experience in terms of the implementation of a number of the Rome Statute's main innovations, substantive and procedural international criminal law provisions have been largely tested in proceedings and trials held for over 260 accused before the United Nations *ad hoc* or mandated Tribunals. This treasury of law and practice which is part of the legacy of the Tribunals will undoubtedly have an impact on the ICC as well as on national primary jurisdictions.

In 2010, at a time when the completion strategies of several international Tribunals will be well advanced, the ICC is to undergo the first review of its Statute, including a stocktaking of international criminal justice. The developments brought by the operation of other international jurisdictions will be a part of this process. The first Review Conference will follow after a seven-year experience of the actual functioning of the Rome Statute, as well as the last 11 years' experience of other international jurisdictions, since the 1998 Diplomatic Conference. The case law of the *ad hoc* Tribunals was indeed considered when adopting the Rome Statute, but at that time the Tribunals were still in their infancy and much has been achieved since then in terms of practices and policies.

These factual circumstances – law, practices and relevance of lessons learned to shed light on the future – represent the guidelines of this book: the system of international criminal justice is addressed in its dynamics rather than in its static structure, primarily focusing on substantive problems of a functional nature rather than on descriptions of the existing mechanisms, and placing the ICC and its future at the centre of possible developments of the system itself. For this reason, the review process of the legal framework of the ICC and the Review Conference of its Statute are strategically approached starting from the lessons learned in the experience of other international jurisdictions, as a reflection of the agreed inclusion in the review process of a stocktaking exercise which will also draw on the practices of the UN-established or -assisted Tribunals, including their case law on the subject matter jurisdiction.

Under this approach, the criterion informing the structure of this work is selectivity: while offering an overview on the whole system of international criminal justice, this book only deals with a selection of issues relevant to the experience of international jurisdictions and, thus, to better understand how the review process of the Rome Statute can be enriched by the lessons learned. Thus, the ability of practices to shape the possible contents for the review of the Rome Statute and its related instruments is at the core of the work. A holistic presentation of the Rome Statute system lies outside the scope of this work. For this reason, although some of its basic features are also dealt with, this is only to the extent that they appear to be relevant to an analysis of the experience thus far developed at the Court and in view of possible amendments to the law of the Statute. On the other hand, all issues related to the Review Conference of the Rome Statute are covered: this includes the concept and context of the review process, as well as the substance of amendments which appear either likely to be dealt with on the occasion of the first Review Conference or otherwise desirable in light of the lessons learned.

The Editor wishes to thank all contributors, who provide through this work their unique, invaluable and varied experience and expertise, as well as The Planethood Foundation, for its support for the project.

Roberto Bellelli

List of Abbreviations

Periodicals – Publications

Am. J. Int'l L.	*American Journal of International Law*
BEPJ	*Bro Emlyn for Peace and Justice*
B.U. INT'L L.J.	*Boston University International Law Journal*
BYBIL	*British Year Book of International Law*
Cassese, Gaeta and Jones	A. Cassese, P. Gaeta, and J.R.W.D. Jones (eds), *The Rome Statute of the International Criminal Court: A Commentary* (Oxford: Oxford University Press, 2002)
EJIL	*European Journal of International Law*
HILJ	*Harvard International Law Journal*
ILM	*International Law Magazine*
ILR	*International Law Reports*
Ind. Int'l&Comp.Law Rev.	*Indiana International & Comparative Law Review*
IRRC	*International Review of the Red Cross*
JICJ	*Journal of International Criminal Justice*
LAW	*Law Quarterly Review*
RCADI	*Recueil des Cours de l'Academie de Droit International*
RGDIP	*Revue générale de droit international public*

Acronyms

AFRC	Armed Forces Revolutionary Council
AICC	Arusha International Conference Centre
AMIS	African Union Mission in Sudan
AP I	Protocol Additional to the Geneva Conventions of 12 August 1949, and relating to the Protection of Victims of International Armed Conflicts (Protocol I), 8 June 1977
AP II	Protocol II, Additional to the Geneva Conventions of 12 August 1949, and relating to the Protection of Victims of non-International Armed Conflicts (Protocol II), 8 June 1977
ARK	Autonomous Region of Krajina
ASP	Assembly of States Parties
AU	African Union
BiH	Bosnia and Herzegovina
CAR	Central African Republic
CARICOM	Caribbean Community

CCW	Convention on Prohibition or Restrictions on the Use of Certain Conventional Weapons Which May be Deemed to be Excessively Injurious or to Have Indiscriminate Effects, Geneva, 10 October 1980
CDF	Civil Defence Forces
CFSP	Common Foreign and Security Policy
CIHL	Commission on International Humanitarian Law
CNDP	*Congrès National pour la Défense du Peuple*
CPC BiH	Criminal Procedure Code of BiH
CPK	Communist Party of Kampuchea
CPT	European Committee for the Prevention of Torture
DC-CAM	Documentation Centre of Cambodia
DK	Democratic Kampuchea
DR	Draft Internal Rules
DRC	Democratic Republic of the Congo
ECCC	Extraordinary Chambers in the Courts of Cambodia
ECHR	European Convention/Court of Human Rights and Fundamental Freedoms
FIRR	Financial Rules and Regulations
FPLC	*Forces Patriotiques pour la Libération du Congo*
FRPI	*Force de résistance patriotique en Ituri*
GA	UN General Assembly
GAOR	Official Records of the General Assembly
GCs	Geneva Conventions
GoS	Government of Sudan
HRC	Human Rights Committee
HRW	Human Rights Watch
HVO	Croatian Defense Council
IACHR	Inter-American Court of Human Rights
ICC	International Criminal Court
ICCPR	International Covenant on Civil and Political Rights
ICJ	International Court of Justice
ICRC	International Committee of the Red Cross
ICTR	International Criminal Tribunal for Rwanda
ICTY	International Criminal Tribunal for the former Yugoslavia
IHL	international humanitarian law
ILC	International Law Commission
IMT	International Military Tribunal, Nuremberg
IMTFE	International Military Tribunal for the Far East, Tokyo
IR	Internal Rules
JCE	Joint Criminal Enterprise
JNA	Yugoslav People's Army
JPK	Johnny Paul Koroma
KLA	Kosovo Liberation Army
LOTC	Law on Transfer
LRA	Lord's Resistance Army

MONUC	United Nations Organization Mission in the Democratic Republic of the Congo
NATO	North Atlantic Treaty Organization
NCOI	National Commission of Inquiry initiated by the Sudanese Government
NGO	non-governmental organization
NPT	Non-Proliferation Treaty of Nuclear Weapons
OCIJ	Office of the Co-Investigative Judges
OCP	Office of the Co-Prosecutors
OHR	Office of the High Representative
OSCE	Organization for Security and Co-operation in Europe
OTP	Office of the Prosecutor
PCIJ	Permanent Court of International Justice
PTC	Pre-Trial Chamber
PrepCom	Preparatory Commission for the International Criminal Court
R2P	responsibility to protect
RGC	Royal Government of Cambodia
RPE	Rules of Procedure and Evidence
RPF	Rwandan Patriotic Army
RUF	Revolutionary United Front
SC	Security Council of the United Nations
SCSL	Special Court for Sierra Leone
SDS	Serbian Democratic Party
SFRJ	Socialist Federal Republic of Yugoslavia
SFOR	Stabilization Force in Bosnia and Herzegovina
SLA	Sierra Leone Army
SOFA	Status of Forces Agreement
SOMA	Status of Mission Agreement
SRK	Sarajevo Romanija Corps
STL	Special Tribunal for Lebanon
SWGCA	Special Working Group for the Crime of Aggression
TC	Trial Chamber
TOC	Transnational Organized Crime Convention
TRC	Truth and Reconciliation Commission
UN	United Nations
UNCOI	United Nations Commission of Inquiry
UNGA	United Nations General Assembly
UNICRI	UN Interregional Crime and Justice Research Institute
UNSC	United Nations Security Council
UNSG	United Nations Secretary General
UNMIK	United Nations Transitional Administration in Kosovo
UNTAET	United Nations Transitional Administration in East Timor
UPC	*Union des Patriotes Congolais*
UPDA	Uganda People's Democratic Army
VRS	Army of the Republika Srpska [Vojska Republike Srpske], also Bosnian Serb Army
WCC	War Crimes Chamber in the Court of Bosnia and Herzegovina

WESU	Witnesses/Experts Support Unit
WMD	weapons of mass destruction
WVSS	Witness and Victims Support Section

PART I
Introduction

The fall of the Berlin wall and the resulting new balance of global powers have played a major role in the development of the concept of international criminal justice. The early 1990s witnessed a growing awareness in the international community of the importance that the principle of international legality and the rule of law at the domestic level have in maintaining and restoring lasting conditions for international peace and security. Inclusiveness of all relevant actors and sense of ownership have also progressively emerged as key factors for the long-run success of the means experimented with to contribute through criminal justice to conflict prevention and resolution.

The establishment of the UN *ad hoc* Tribunals for the former Yugoslavia and Rwanda is one of the most visible achievements of this process, the climax of which may be identified in the 1998 adoption of the Rome Statute of the International Criminal Court. It is from here – by establishing a permanent institutional and systematic framework for ensuring accountability for the most serious crimes of international concern – that the concept and role of international criminal justice became an irreversible feature of the efforts of the international community to produce security and stability.

The historic mission that the ICC is entrusted with will necessarily require the level of horizontal and widespread support among states that only true universality in participation and implementation may bring over time. Building in this direction is a shared responsibility for all relevant actors, including the ICC itself, whose credibility and authority will be directly affected by its practices. It is in this respect and with this objective that the permanent Court could make the best of the abundant information gathered along avenues already explored by others, in order to go smoothly on track and concentrate its resources on the factors that really make it unique as to mandate and procedure. Over 15 years of intensive, independent judicial experience of the UN *ad hoc* Tribunals and of the hybrid Special Court for Sierra Leone, in particular, has resulted in groundbreaking practice and case law that has rapidly become a reference point for all other mechanisms of international criminal justice and – not dissimilar to the International Military Tribunal at Nuremberg – will most likely continue to have such a role for a long time into the future.

It is primarily for national jurisdictions to take advantage of the legacies of the international tribunals, in order to recover their sovereign right to exert criminal justice by increasing their ability to fight against impunity under the rule of the principles of independence, impartiality and fair trial. However, at the international level, the collective exercise of the responsibility to protect by means of judicial accountability requires that practices be monitored and recorded, as well as lessons drawn, assessed and treasured in the effort to maximize the impact of international endeavours on stabilization processes, and the deterrent effect on ongoing conflicts. The international tribunals, together with the other state and non-state actors in the field, are progressively focusing their attention on this task and the Rome Statute's system would be the main beneficiary of this exercise.

An overview of the progressive institutionalization of international mechanisms for criminal accountability would, thus, enable a focus on the features of the ICC system which are most relevant to an analysis of the challenges that have so far emerged from its practices. Learning from previous experiences is a crucial step in this process and the practices of the UN *ad hoc* Tribunals, as well as of the Special Court for Sierra Leone, provide clear guidance on how to overcome recurrent issues, strengthen consensus and allow for a successful, lasting and sustainable fight against impunity for the most serious crimes of international concern.

SECTION I
Steps in History

Chapter 1
The Establishment of the System of International Criminal Justice

Roberto Bellelli

1. International Crimes as a Threat to International Peace and Security

Armed conflicts and authoritarian regimes have troubled contemporary history and continue to cause unimaginable atrocities and sufferings to civilian populations. The violation of the most basic rules that mankind has established to regulate the use of force by states, both during armed conflicts (international humanitarian law) and in time of peace (human rights law), translates into the commission of the most serious crimes of concern to the international community as a whole.

In fact, not only gross violations of the law of armed conflicts and of human rights immediately afflict the victims on the ground – whatever might be the extension of their commission on the affected territory – but also bear with them the potential of uncontrollable and expansive effects. Individual criminal conducts committed on the scale, intensity and gravity in question, even when not inscribed in a framework of illegitimate use of force, are inextricably entrenched with actions and responsibility of states, thus reverberating the issue of criminal accountability on the international order.

In this regard, the international community holds a direct and strong interest in ensuring that criminal justice is adequately dealt with by any appropriate mechanism capable of reducing the destabilizing impact and the threat posed by such crimes to international peace and security.[1] Consequently, the punishment of such crimes is a matter that goes beyond the classic approach to criminal justice, based on the principle of sovereignty.

In the aftermath of WWI and WWII the international community devoted efforts in setting up a framework of norms regulating the use of force in armed conflicts,[2] with the adoption of binding international instruments that over time have built the corpus of the existing international humanitarian law (IHL). However, in light of the traditional approach to criminal law, the effectiveness of such treaties has been left solely to the willingness of states to implement them.

---

1 '[T]he … commission of systematic, flagrant and widespread violations of international humanitarian law and human rights law in situations of armed conflict, may constitute a threat to international peace and security', SC Res. 1674, 28 April 2006, OP 26.

2 IHL establishes minimum rules applicable to all Parties to a conflict dependent on the use of force itself, with no regard to whether it is lawful – i.e., under the UN Charter – or unlawful (as for an aggressor state). For the illegality under international law of the use of force in aggressive war as an instrument to settle disputes between states, see also the Treaty between the United States and other Powers providing for the renunciation of wars as an instrument of national policy (Kellog-Briand Pact), Paris, 27 August 1928. Available at http://www.yale.edu/lawweb/avalon/imt/kbpact.htm (visited 30 September 2009).

2. Shared Responsibilities in the Suppression of Crimes of International Concern

A. The Primary Responsibility of States

Under general principles of criminal law it is a state's responsibility, as an essential feature of their sovereignty, to prevent and suppress criminal conducts, normally according to territorial or personal links.

In the aftermath of a dictatorship or of a conflict, various political reasons have often hindered, by means of delays or denial, effective punitive justice to make perpetrators accountable of horrendous crimes. Domestic political reasons may include the need to achieve stability through alternative measures, such as mechanisms for social reconciliation, including through the establishment of truth commissions and the granting of amnesties. International factors could be related to peace and include unsettled relationships at the national borders, the wider context of international agreements, or interests reaching beyond the crisis area.

Therefore, the punishment of genocide, crimes against humanity and war crimes, when left to the action of states, often results in the impunity of those most responsible for their commission, because of the absence or weakness of the rule of law, or for domestic political reasons of the territorial or national state, or because they are exempted from national justice in order to maintain occasional international compromises or, finally, because of the lack of judicial cooperation in the investigation and extradition of suspects.

B. Lessons Learnt throughout History

In this regard, significant lessons may be drawn from the otherwise very different situations originated by the military occupation of Northern Italy in 1944 and by the Democratic Kampuchea regime in Cambodia in the 1970s. In both situations, territorial states did not timely exert their primary responsibilities to prosecute international crimes either for reasons relevant to regional security or in an effort to ensure social stability and reconciliation. However, the non-applicability of statutes of limitations to serious violations of IHL enabled, in both situations (some) perpetrators to be brought to justice over lengthy periods of time and in the context of changed national and international influences.

In the first case, war crimes committed by Italian nationals during the civil war which mainly affected Northern Italy in 1944 were timely prosecuted, although sentences applied were shortly thereafter covered by amnesty laws aimed at the reconciliation of the country after the fascist dictatorship.[3] Consistently, the scope of such amnesty laws did not include war crimes committed by foreign troops on Italian soil.[4] However, the prosecution of foreigners suspected of violations of

---

3 All such amnesty laws, as drawing on the need to bring national reconciliation after the civil war, also included the most serious crimes with political motives or objectives, but were limited to the Parties of the non-international armed conflict (crimes committed by 'members of the Resistance movement or any assisting thereof' as well as by pro-fascist 'other nationals opposing the liberation movement'). Consistently, the case law has concluded that amnesties for crimes related to war do not apply to members of foreign Armed Forces involved in the international conflict. *Cassazione*, Section I, 22 February 2002, No. 15139, *Priebke*.

4 Only exceptions to the inapplicability of amnesty to foreigners in relation to the conflict were those depending on the need to support the peace or reconciliation process with the population of limited territories, e.g., for the 'territories currently outside Italian administration' and in favour of Yugoslav citizens, D.Lgs. C.P.S. (Legislative Decree of the Provisional Head of State), 8 January 1947, No. 244 and D.P.R. (Presidential Decree), 14 April 1948, No. 511.

the laws and customs of war was delayed for long time. In fact, in spite of the timely investigations conducted by the Allied Forces, suspects were allowed to leave the country and no effective action was taken to obtain their extradition.[5] The lack of institutional independence of the military judiciary before its radical reform in 1981 led to a 'provisional dismissal' of all investigations in the 1960s, upon a political decision made at the governmental level and which took into account the prevailing needs of international post-war alliance agreements. Only in the early 1990s,[6] the files containing the Military General Prosecutor's cases were 'discovered'[7] and effective investigations started in the competent territorial jurisdictions.[8]

Similarly, in the case of the crimes committed during the Democratic Kampuchea era, the agreement for their prosecution and punishment reached between Cambodia and the United Nations has only recently, and after nearly 30 years, led to the initiation of proceedings against Khmer Rouge leaders, while some of those allegedly most responsible for those crimes passed away long before.[9]

Bringing suspects to justice with a delay of more than 50 years has an impact on the stabilization process and, more generally, on the society; but it also bears some important judicial implications, including the availability of evidence and the natural ageing of suspects: when trials are finally initiated, e.g., the issue of the ability of the accused to stand trial would normally arise as well as that of a progressive deterioration of witness evidence. However, in both the aforementioned situations survivors, victims and their descendants, as well as local communities participate in proceedings. The fact that after lengthy periods of time, trials for the most serious international crimes so deeply involve victimized populations is a validation of the widespread understanding that the ascertainment of judicial truth for senior perpetrators of such crimes is an essential element of the social reconciliation process that is needed to ensure a lasting peace in a conflict area and, therefore, international security and stability.

C. The Responsibility to Protect

Included in the last consideration above, is the fact that the debate on the principle of sovereignty of states has in recent times developed the concept of a link between the right of non-intervention

5 Further investigations conducted by rogatory means in the aftermath of the war received irrelevant responses, if any at all.

6 In 1994 some 695 files concerning investigations on war crimes were discovered in the cellars at the seat of the General Military Prosecution Office in Rome, locked in a cupboard with the doors turned against the wall. The *Report of the Council for the Military Judiciary*, 23 March 1999, concluded that the cover-up was the result of inputs issued at the political level and that only a deceased military prosecutor could have been held accountable for their implementation. However, the Parliamentary Inquiry Commission on the Causes of Hindering Files concerning Nazi Fascist Crimes – established by Law 15 May 2003, No. 107 and 25 August 2004, No. 232 – in its Final Report of 9 February 2006 cleared from any responsibility whatsoever the political level and concluded that only the highest levels of the judiciary had to be blamed for the gross miscarriage of justice. Available at http://legxiv.camera.it/_dati/leg14/lavori/documentiparlamentari/indiceetesti/023/018/INTERO.pdf (visited 20 August 2009).

7 In the literature, see F. Giustolisi, *L'Armadio della vergogna* [The Cupboard of Shame] (Roma: Nutrimenti, 2004).

8 For some major trials for war crimes committed in Italy during WWII, see: www.difesa.it/Giustizia Militare/RassegnaGM/Processi (visited 20 August 2009).

9 Pol Pot (actual name Saloth Sar) died on 15 April 1998 at the age of 69. He was the leader of the Cambodian communist movement known as Khmer Rouge and Prime Minister of Cambodia during the Democratic Kampuchea (1975–1979), and whose policy resulted in the genocide of an estimated 1.7 million people.

in internal affairs, based on the principle of equal status (sovereign equality) of states, and the obligation of states to protect civilians from gross violations of international humanitarian law and human rights law.[10]

Consequently, it has been argued for the existence of a right of humanitarian intervention by the international community when states fail to act in compliance with their primary obligation because they are unwilling or unable to implement it. This has better been viewed, rather than as a right of intervention, as a responsibility to protect (R2P) civilians from the commission of genocide, crimes against humanity (ethnic cleansing) and war crimes.[11] The primary responsibility is customarily[12] attached to the state exercising jurisdiction *ratione loci* or on the basis of other relevant jurisdictional links.[13] Not complying with this primary obligation of the territorial state would, on the one hand, engage its international responsibility[14] and, on the other hand, shift the

---

10 A clear and leading stance has been taken by the European Court of Human Rights (ECHR), that affirmed the existence of a positive obligation of states under HRL to protect their citizens from serious crimes which might endanger their fundamental rights, in particular the right to life established under Article 2(1) of the 1950 Convention for the Protection of Human Rights and Fundamental Freedoms. *Pretty v. United Kingdom*, ECHR, 29 April 2002, para. 38. See R. Bellelli, 'The Law of the Statute and its Practice before the Review Conference' (hereinafter, The Law of the Statute), in this Volume, at 9(E)(3) and footnotes 256–257.

11 The current status of the evolving doctrine of the responsibility to protect is embodied in the UNSG Report *Implementing the Responsibility to Protect* (UN doc. A/63/677 of 12 January 2009), prepared with the aim of 'operationalizing the responsibility to protect' (2005 *World Summit Outcome*, UN doc. A/60/L.1, 15 September 2005, paras 138 to 139) and providing a framework based on three pillars: (i) the protection responsibilities of the state; (ii) international assistance and capacity building; (iii) timely and decisive response.

12 The existence of an obligation to prevent and suppress genocide and crimes against humanity was affirmed by the International Court of Justice (ICJ) Advisory Opinion in *Reservations to the Convention on the Prevention and Punishment of Genocide*, 28 May 1951, para. 23 and again in *Application of the Convention on the Prevention and Punishment of the Crime of Genocide, Preliminary Objections*, 11 July 1996, para. 31. As to war crimes, the ICJ also acknowledged that Common Article 3 to the 1949 Geneva Conventions has become a general principle of international humanitarian law, binding for all states (Judgement, *Nicaragua v. United States*, 27 June 1986, para. 220) and that the fundamental principles of the 1949 Conventions have become of a customary nature (Advisory Opinion, *Legality of the Threat or Use of Nuclear Weapons*, para. 79). It follows that there is a specific customary obligation to suppress the *grave breaches* of the 1949 Geneva Conventions, as also reproduced in Art. 8 of the Rome Statute of the ICC. See A. Cassese, *International Criminal Law* (Oxford: Oxford University Press, 2003), at 301–302.

13 Preamble (6) ICCS: 'it is a duty of every State to exercise its criminal jurisdiction over those responsible for international crimes.' This concept is developed in the principle of complementarity in the Rome Statute, whereby it is incumbent on states to suppress crimes under the Statute, while the Court would be called in only as a last resort. See *infra*, 4(A)(1), (C)(2) and (E)(4)(b).

14 A number of international instruments include an obligation for States Parties to take certain steps to prevent acts prohibited under the same instrument, e.g. Convention Against Torture and Other Cruel, Inhuman or Degrading Treatment or Punishment (Art. 2) of 10 December 1984; Convention on the Prevention and Punishment of Crimes against Internationally Protected Persons, including Diplomatic Agents (Art. 4) of 14 December 1973; Convention on the Safety of the United Nations and Associated Personnel (Art. 11) of 9 December 1994; International Convention on the Suppression of Terrorist Bombings (Article 15) of 15 December 1997. In *Application of the Convention on the Prevention and Punishment of the Crime of Genocide (Bosnia and Herzegovina vs. Serbia and Montenegro)*, the ICJ ruled that the duty to prevent genocide (Art. 1) for contracting states is a 'normative and compelling' legal obligation, which extends beyond the particular case where the competent organs of the United Nations (Article 8) have been called upon, as this does not relieve States Parties from taking such action as they can to prevent genocide (Judgement, *Genocide case*, 26

duty to the international community, which would be called upon to intervene with collective actions on the basis of a collective complementary obligation binding all states.[15] Such actions may be implemented either upon decisions of the Security Council (SC)[16] based on its primary responsibility for the maintenance of international peace and security,[17] or through treaty-based institutions.

On these premises, beside military action in peace-building (peacekeeping and peace-enforcement operations), the international community has progressively developed a range of measures aimed at preventing and resolving conflicts by improving the rule of law and promoting the conditions for a lasting peace through social stability and reconciliation. Such measures include a set of tools for addressing situations where peace or international security are threatened or attacked, be that in the context of Articles 39 and 41 of the UN Charter[18] or not: complex

---

February 2007, para. 427). The Court also held that such obligation is one of conduct and not of result, as it does not extend to the achievement of the prevention. The relevant test would instead be that of due diligence, which includes a *de facto* assessment of whether a state has not 'manifestly failed to take all measures to prevent genocide which were within its power, and which might have contributed to preventing the genocide' (ibid., para. 430). Under the same perspective *in concreto*, not all States Parties would be in the same position to prevent the commission of the crime, but consideration should be given to factors such as the geographical distance from the scene of the facts, links with the main actors in the events and actions permissible under international law (ibid.).

15 *2005 World Summit Outcome*, UN doc. A/60/L.1, 15 September 2005, at 31 ff., paras 138–140. The Security Council has endorsed such conclusions in SC Res. 1674, 28 April 2006, OP 4: '*Reaffirms* the provisions of paragraph 138 and 139 of the 2005 World Summit Outcome Document regarding the responsibility to protect populations from genocide, war crimes, ethnic cleansing and crimes against humanity.' See also: the previous Report of the International Committee on Intervention and State Sovereignty, *The Responsibility to Protect*; the conclusions of the High-level Panel on Threats, Challenges and Change (UN doc. A/59/565 and Corr. 1) and its report *In Larger Freedom: Towards Development, Security and Human Rights for All* (UN doc. A/59/2005).

16 For regional developments of the concept of R2P in the light of the principle of complementarity, see *infra*, 4(E)(4)(c).

17 Art 24(1) UN Charter. However, 'the failure of the Security Council to discharge its responsibilities on behalf of all Member States … does not relieve Member States of their obligations or the United Nations of its responsibility under the Charter to maintain international peace and security', and 'the General Assembly [in case of such a failure by the SC] shall consider the matter immediately with a view to making appropriate recommendations to Members for collective measures, including in case of a breach of the peace or act of aggression the use of armed force'. GA Res. 377(V) A, *Uniting for Peace*, PP 7 and OP 1.

18 P.M. Dupuy, Implications of the Institutionalization of International Crimes of States, in J.H.H. Weiler, A.Cassese and M. Spinedi (eds), *International Crimes of State: A Critical Analysis of the ILC's Draft Article 19 on State Responsibility* (Berlin: Walter DeGruyter, 1989), 170–185, at 176.

sanctions regimes,[19] temporary administration of territory,[20] assistance to national justice systems[21] and the most recent variegated experience of international criminal justice, introduced to address the unbearable atrocities committed in the context of authoritarian regimes or during bloody conflicts.

D. Protection through International Justice

Under the R2P, states are primarily obligated to afford protection to their nationals and, upon Security Council actions, to civilians of states which failed to comply with their own identical primary obligation. The triggering of the R2P through the establishment of mechanisms of international criminal justice would, thus, result in a different set of obligations for states. Although always bound by their primary responsibility, states would also be bound by such other international obligations as might be based on SC Chapter VII powers or on treaty law. In particular, this would introduce obligations for:

(a) cooperation with international tribunals,[22]
(b) implementation in national legislation.[23]

---

19 'Traditional' sanctions under Art 41 UN Charter, such as the interruption of economic relations, 'are often costly in terms of economic loss and human suffering, and affect a number of countries in addition to the actual target country'. M. Lehto, *International Responsibility for Terrorist Acts* (Rovaniemi: Lapland University Press, 2008), at 452. For some reflections on the collateral effects of indiscriminate economic sanctions, see *In Larger Freedom: Towards Development, Security And Human Rights for All*, report of the Secretary General, 21 March 2005, UN Doc. A/59/2005, para. 110. Thus, 'targeted sanctions, such as on travel, financial transfers, luxury goods and arms' may instead be used by the SC: *Implementing the responsibility to protect*, A/63/677, 12 January 2009, para. 57. For an overview on embargoes and other measures from the humanitarian perspective, see M. Bettati, *Droit Humanitaire* (Paris: Éditions du Seuil, 2000), at 236–246.

20 In Kosovo (United Nations Interim Administration Mission in Kosovo, UNMIK, 1999–2008, based on SC Res. 1244/1999) and East Timor/Timor-Leste (United Nations Transitional Administration in East Timor, UNTAET, 1999–2002), the UN has had direct responsibility for the administration of territory, including control of the police and prison services, and administration of the judiciary. The short duration of the interim administration in East Timor, however, is likely to have affected the results of efforts in the justice sector. Similar powers have been exercised in Bosnia and Herzegovina from 1996, through the Office of the High Representative (OHR) established under Article II, Annex 10 (Agreement on Civilian Implementation) of the General Framework Agreement for Peace in Bosnia and Herzegovina (Dayton Peace Agreement), finalized in *Dayton, Ohio on 21 November 1995 and signed in Paris on 14 December 1995.* Available at http://www.ohr.int/dpa/default.asp?content_id=366 (visited 20 August 2009).

21 This is the case, e.g., of the assistance provided to: Bosnia and Herzegovina in the establishment and functioning of the War Crimes Chamber in the State Court; Kosovo, with the mixed trial panels; Cambodia, with the Extraordinary Chambers in the Courts of Cambodia. See also the establishment of EU assistance to Kosovo institutions by the EU Council Joint Action 2008/124/CFSP of 4 February 2008 on the European Union Rule of Law Mission in Kosovo, EULEX KOSOVO which, building upon SC Res. 1244 (1999), recalls the 'need to prevent, on humanitarian grounds, possible outbreaks of violence, acts of persecution and intimidation in Kosovo, taking account … of the responsibility towards populations as referred to under Resolution 1674' of the SC (PP3).

22 *Infra*, at 4(F). Also see, in this Volume, N. Piacente, 'Addressing the Impunity Gap through Cooperation' (hereinafter, Impunity Gap), and R. Bellelli, 'Obligation to Cooperate and Duty to Implement', at 3 (hereinafter, Cooperation and Implementation).

23 Ibid., at 2.

Cooperation obligations would differently originate for:

(i) UN Member States (under the UN Charter), which would be bound either compulsorily – by SC resolutions establishing UN *ad hoc* Tribunals under Chapter VII powers – or voluntarily by providing assistance to hybrid tribunals established under UN authority;
(ii) States Parties (under treaty law) to relevant treaties, as for the ICC;[24]
(iii) Third States to international treaties, upon UN Agreements (e.g., for the ECCC) or any referral made by the Security Council under Article 13(b) ICCSt.

3. The Foundations of International Criminal Justice

A. Early Experiences: Nuremberg and Tokyo Trials

In order to ensure the timely punishment of those bearing the major responsibilities for genocide, crimes against humanity and war crimes, the international community has over time established various forms of super-national criminal justice, the first experiences[25] being the Tribunals of Nuremberg (1945) and Tokyo (1946), set up by the winning Powers of WWII.[26]

International Military Tribunals were successful in terms of delivering timely justice to the accused among those most responsible for crimes against peace and war crimes, but they led to the imposition of serious sentences, yet they were established after the commission of the crimes and not in response to a generally accepted model of independent justice but rather to that of victors' justice. In this regard, the Nuremberg and Tokyo Tribunals were also only 'multinational in nature,

---

24 That would also apply for any competence on serious international crimes that the African Union (AU) should decide to mandate to the African Court of Human Rights, following the report of its Commission in 2010. Assembly/AU/Dec.213 (XII), 4 February 2009, para. 9. See *infra*, 4(E)(4)(c).

25 See G. Schwarzemberger, *International Law as Applied by International Courts and Tribunals*, Vol. II, The Law of Armed Conflict (London: Stevens, 1968), at 462–464, where the earliest case of a war crime trial, which concerned Peter von Hagenbach (1474), is illustrated.

26 The International Military Tribunal (IMT) in Nuremberg was established by the 8 August 1945 London Agreement signed by the United States, France, United Kingdom, and the Soviet Union. Available at http://www.icls.de/dokumente/imt_london_agreement.pdf (visited 20 August 2009). A summary of cases is also available at http://www.law.umkc.edu/faculty/projects/ftrials/nuremberg/meetthedefendants.html (visited 20 August 2009). Military Allied tribunals in occupied Germany were also introduced by Control Council Law No. 10 of 20 December 1945. The Charter of the International Military Tribunal for the Far East (IMTFE) was established in Tokyo on 19 January 1946 by General MacArthur, Supreme Allied Commander of the Southwest Pacific. Available at http://www.stephen-stratford.co.uk/imtfe_charter.htm (visited 20 August 2009).

representing only part of the world community'.[27] However, their legacy in terms of international criminal law principles and practice was immediately recognized[28] and has been long lasting.[29]

Following or even during some of the conflicts or serious and widespread violations of human rights which took place during the second half of the past century, the United Nations intervened by establishing international criminal tribunals or lending assistance to states in order to enable the exercise of national jurisdictions. In this phase, the choice of the forms of the UN intervention was driven mainly by the assessment of the territorial states' capacity to implement basic principles of independence of the judiciary and of fair trial.

B. The UN Ad Hoc Tribunals

In the new global political environment that followed the end of the Cold War and the fall of the Berlin Wall, major developments took place in international criminal law and justice with the establishment of the *ad hoc* international Tribunals for the former Yugoslavia (1993) and Rwanda (1994).

In the UN Tribunals the legitimacy issue was overcome by the legal basis provided for under the UN Charter and, namely, through the exercise of the powers conferred on the Security Council under Chapter VII.[30] In the case of the UN Tribunals, considerations related to ongoing conflicts in the area and/or the lack of judicial capacity and professionalism made it necessary to choose an international substitutive intervention, thus depriving those states having jurisdiction under ordinary criteria of the authority to prosecute international crimes committed during those conflicts:[31] the principle of primacy[32] of international jurisdiction was affirmed in the balance, on the one hand,

---

27 ICTY, Opinion and Judgment, *Duško Tadić*, Trial Chamber I, 7 May 1997, IT-94-1-T, para. 1.

28 See GA Res. 95 (I), 11 December 1946, *Affirmation of the Principles of International Law Recognized by the Charter of the Nũremberg Tribunal*, where the General Assembly (GA) stated that the principles of the Charter and of the judgement of the IMT already existed under international law, and deserved codification. Article 6 of the IMT Charter which established (alongside with the jurisdiction and modes of criminal responsibility) the categories of crimes against peace (aggression), war crimes and crimes against humanity, has always since been recognized as customary international law. Among the others, I. Brownlie, *Principles of Public International Law* (4th edn, Oxford: Oxford University Press, 1991), at 471.

29 Nuremberg and Tokyo case law, *inter alia*, were considered during the negotiations of the Rome Statute and thereafter, the work of the Preparatory Commission (PrepCom) and of the Special Working Group on the Crime of Aggression of the Assembly of States Parties of the ICC. See, United Nations, Preparatory Commission for the International Criminal Court, Working Group on the Crime of Aggression, *Historical Review of Developments Relating to Aggression*, 24 January 2002, PCNICC/2002/WGCA/L.I and Add. 1. See also K. Dormann, *Elements of War Crimes under the Rome Statute of the International Criminal Court* (Cambridge: Cambridge University Press, 2003).

30 However, some have also argued in these cases for the implementation of a victors' justice model – both in the sense that justice is done by the winning party of a conflict and that the jurisdiction exempts the winners – as the same Allied Powers applying it at the end of WWII sit as permanent members of the Security Council establishing international tribunals under Chapter VII of the Charter. See also *supra*, 3(A).

31 Jurisprudence has held that the principle of primacy of the Tribunal over national courts is not inconsistent with the principle of the sovereignty of states under international law. The crimes within the jurisdiction of the Tribunal are universal in nature, transcending the interest of any one state and, therefore, 'the sovereign rights of States cannot and should not take precedence over the right of the international community to act appropriately'. ICTY, Decision on the Defence Motion for Interlocutory Appeal on Jurisdiction, *Duško Tadić*, Appeals Chamber, 2 October 1995, paras 59 and 77–93.

32 See also *infra*, for primacy and complementarity, 4(E)(4)(a).

of the principle of sovereignty of states and, on the other hand, of the primary role of the Security Council, acting under Chapter VII of the Charter, in the maintenance of international peace and security.

At this juncture, the experience of the *ad hoc* Tribunals may be reasonably assessed as extremely successful, also taking into account the number of judgements delivered. However, the time span between the commission of the crimes and the judicial decision has in most cases been considerable, thus affecting the main deterrent and retributive objectives of international criminal justice. The considerable delays incurred since the inception of the activity of the Tribunals have only partly been caused by the complexity of a criminal procedure system built on the human rights guidelines for an independent and fair trial. In fact, in spite of the authority deriving from the Security Council resolutions establishing the Tribunals, the major issue has always been the need to rely on cooperation of national or territorial states to deliver justice. In this regard, experience has clearly shown that only developments in the national political arena, associated with a strong international pressure, have finally contributed to achieving satisfactory responses to the Tribunals' decisions.[33]

The legacy of the twins[34] *ad hoc* Tribunals may be appreciated from different perspectives, including their groundbreaking jurisprudence and its implications on the establishment of subsequent international Tribunals or Courts[35] as well as for national jurisdictions.[36]

Although the Tribunals were not established with final terms for their activities, the high costs originated by the built-in factors of international justice, including delays for lack of cooperation, have led the Security Council to impose a deadline in 2010 for the completion strategies of the Tribunals.[37] After that, responsibility for primary jurisdiction should return to national authorities.

---

33 See, in this Volume, F. Pocar, 'The International Criminal Tribunal for the Former Yugoslavia', para. 5, and Chapter 5, C. Del Ponte, 'Reflections Based on the ICTY's Experience', para. 7.

34 The UN *ad hoc* Tribunals were established under the same Chapter VII authority and provided with similar Statutes. They were also envisaged as responding to one investigative and prosecutorial strategy, unified under a single Prosecutor, until the SC decided to provide ICTR with its own Prosecutor by virtue of SC Res. 1503, 28 August 2003, Annex, amending Art. 15 ICTRSt. Furthermore, uniformity of interpretation in the *ad hoc* Tribunals is ensured through the composition of the Appeals Chamber which serves both Tribunals.

35 The Statutes of all international jurisdictions established thereafter have abundantly drawn on the *ad hoc* Tribunals' experience, both in the definition of their substantive criminal law provisions and for organizational matters.

36 National legislation and practice, e.g., in the Balkans, has been directly influenced by ICTY's practice. See M. Murtezić, 'The War Crimes Chamber in the Court of Bosnia and Herzegovina', in this Volume, at 3.

37 As the ICTY was established while the conflict in the former Yugoslavia was still ongoing (SC/Res/808/1993, 22 February 1993), its mandate was to address crimes committed since 1991, but no determination was initially made as to the temporal end of its jurisdiction, and a deadline for investigations was only included at a later stage. See more in detail, *infra* note 47. By contrast, the late establishment of the ICTR (SC/Res/955/1994 of 8 November 1994) – at a time when genocide and other serious violations of international humanitarian had already been committed in the territory of Rwanda and in neighboring states – provided the ICTR with temporal jurisdiction only on such crimes committed between 1 January and 31 December 1994. According to the Completion Strategy for the Tribunals, investigations should have been completed by the end of 2004, trials at first instance by the end of 2008, and all the work by 2010, when the responsibility for the exercise of the primary jurisdiction would have been returned to territorial states. Adopted with S/2002/678, following endorsement by Presidential Statement (PRST), 23 July 2002, S/PRST/2002/21 and Res. 1503 of 28 August 2003, reviewed by Res. 1534 of 26 March 2004). By virtue of SC/RES/2003/1503, 28 August 2003, the Security Council further requested the Tribunals to adopt the

However, mainly because of the late surrender of fugitives and the consequent delayed start of trials, a further period of judicial activity is likely to be allowed to the Tribunals,[38] while the judicial and administrative residual functions at the time of closure will be dealt with by some form of *ad hoc* international mechanism.[39] Sensitive matters of principle may arise, however, from the closing down of a jurisdiction, in the balance between the efficiency and practical considerations deriving from the limited mandate, on the one hand, and the principles of independence of the judiciary and of fair trial, on the other.

C. The Hybrid Courts

A third-generation experience for international criminal justice has been experimented with in other cases – depending on the rule of law situation in the interested states – in an attempt to blend international supervision with local ownership and development of national capacity. Hybrid courts were thus established – when the state apparatus still enjoyed sufficient capabilities to exert judicial functions – by providing, on the basis of an agreement concluded between interested states and the UN, an international contribution consisting of the integration of international judges and prosecutors in an agreed legal and institutional framework.

---

necessary implementing measures to comply with the Strategy, while requesting the enhancement of relevant national jurisdictions and of their cooperation with the Tribunals.

38 In this regard, the Security Council '*noting with concern* that the deadline for completion of trial activities at first instance has not been met and that the Tribunals have indicated that their work is not likely to end in 2010 … emphasizes that trials must be conducted by the Tribunals as quickly and efficiently as possible', in S/PRST/2008/37, 19 December 2008, para. 4 (emphasis added). However, upon the Completion Strategy Reports of the Tribunals as of June 2009 (S/2009/252 and S/2009/247) the SC had to, *inter alia*, extend the mandate of the judges '*taking note* of the assessment by the International Tribunal … that [it] will not be in a position to compete all its work in 2010' (PP4). No position was taken at that juncture on the likely need to extend the temporal mandate of the Tribunals.

39 The SC Informal Working Group on International Tribunals is mandated to elaborate on such an '*ad hoc* international Mechanism' to carry out residual but essential functions of the UN *ad hoc* Tribunals, once they have completed their work. It is agreed that such a Mechanism will need to 'carry out a number of essential functions of the Tribunals, including the trial of high-level fugitives, after the closure of the Tribunals. In view of the substantially reduced nature of these residual functions … [there] should be a small, temporary, and efficient structure. Its functions and size will diminish over time'. Open issues are the 'options for the possible locations of the Tribunals' archives and the seat of the residual Mechanism, including the availability of suitable premises for the conduct of judicial proceedings by the residual Mechanism, with particular emphasis on locations where the United Nations has an existing presence'. S/PRST/2008/47, 19 December 2008, paras 8, 10 and 11. Following the request to the UNSG for reporting contained therein and the *Final Report*, Advisory Committee on Archives of the United Nations Tribunals for the Former Yugoslavia and Rwanda, 30 September 2008, eight out of the original 12 residual functions were identified in the *Report of the Secretary-General on the administrative and budgetary aspects of the options for possible locations of the archives of the International Tribunal for the Former Yugoslavia and the International Criminal Tribunal for Rwanda and the seat of the residual mechanism(s) for the Tribunals*, S/2009/258, 21 May 2009 (Report on Archives). Prompted by the Tribunals, the Report identifies eight out of the original 12 residual functions to fall within the scope of the Mechanism(s), which may also be recurrent issues for the other UN-assisted criminal tribunals (paras 13 and 220).

The experience of the Special Court for the Sierra Leone (2002),[40] the Special Panels for the serious crimes committed in East Timor (2000),[41] the Extraordinary Chambers in the Courts of Cambodia (2006)[42] and the Special Tribunal for Lebanon (2007)[43] shows that the main advantages, by comparison with the *ad hoc* UN Tribunals, are the maintaining of the exercise of jurisdiction in the territory, the sense of ownership of the justice process for the local communities and the reduction of the high costs of establishing *ad hoc* Tribunals by means of voluntary or mixed contributions. At the same time, and with conspicuous differences, hybrid courts have faced serious challenges depending sometimes only on the uncertainty of their funding, but in other instances also because they suffer from a reduced international presence. It should also be duly assessed that in some cases the proximity of an international court to the site were crimes were committed might not allow it to properly exert jurisdiction, especially when this might result in political turmoil or raise other security threats in the country or in the region.[44]

D. Other International Assistance in Criminal Justice

Finally, other forms of internationalization of national justice were provided where a reduced international presence appeared to be sufficient to ensure compliance with appropriate standards of justice, as for the establishment of the War Crimes Chamber of Sarajevo (2004)[45] or in the mixed trial panels in Kosovo (2000).[46] Such experiences may greatly differ one from the other – depending on a number of factors influencing the legal, political and social framework of the

40 The Special Court for Sierra Leone (SCSL) was established, following the Agreement between the United Nations and Sierra Leone on 16 January 2002, to prosecute serious violations of international humanitarian law and Sierra Leonean law committed in the territory of Sierra Leone since 30 November 1996.

41 SC Res. 1272, 25 October 1999.

42 The trial before the Extraordinary Chambers in the Courts of Cambodia (ECCC) is ruled by domestic law, as approved under the Law on the Establishment of the Extraordinary Chambers in the Courts of Cambodia for the Prosecution of Crimes Committed During the Period of Democratic Kampuchea, adopted on 10 August 2001 and as amended on 27 October 2004. Available at http://www.eccc.gov.kh/english/cabinet/law/4/KR_Law_as_amended_27_Oct_2004_Eng.pdf (visited 20 August 2009). Jurisdiction is established under Article 2 and *ratione temporis* refers to crimes committed between 17 April 1975 and 6 January 1979, *ratione personae* to 'senior leaders of Democratic Kampuchea *and* those who were most responsible' (emphasis added), and *ratione materiae* for 'crimes and serious violations of Cambodian laws related to crimes, international humanitarian law and custom, and international conventions recognized by Cambodia'. Assistance – through, *inter alia*, international judges and Prosecutors – is provided on the basis of the UN-Cambodia Agreement of 6 June 2003.

43 The Special Tribunal for Lebanon (STL) was established under Chapter VII of the Charter following SC Res. 1757 on 30 May 2007, and by virtue of which the Council decided that the Tribunal be created under its authority, should Lebanon not execute the Agreement with the UN within 11 days (OP 1(a)). As this was the case, the Agreement (Annex) and the Statute (Attachment) to the Resolution entered forcibly into force on 10 June 2007.

44 In particular, this has occurred so far at the: (a) SCSL, in the case of the Charles Taylor trial, which was moved to the premises of the ICC, in The Hague, upon a Memorandum of Understanding signed between the ICC and the SCSL on 13 April 2006; (b) Special Tribunal for Lebanon (STL), also hosted in The Netherlands.

45 See S/PRST/2002/21, 23 July 2002 and SC Res. 1534 (2004).

46 United Nations Interim Administration in Kosovo (UNMIK) Regulation 200/6 on 15 February 2000 and subsequent regulations allowing international judges, prosecutors and counsel to serve alongside domestic professionals in existing Kosovar courts.

interested states – but both offer a good example of how difficult it would be in an era of globally interconnected relationships for any state to achieve lasting peace and stability on its own and without support from the international community.

E. Common Features of UN Lead Efforts in International Criminal Justice

The common feature of all the said forms of international or internationalized jurisdictions is their establishment through an UN Security Council resolution or through negotiations between the UN and relevant states for the purpose of prosecuting crimes committed in a limited territory and within a specific timeframe. As a consequence, these limited jurisdictions are intended to exhaust their activities over time. Notably, limited internationalized jurisdictions have been mandated within parameters that, besides their different subject matter jurisdiction, include the following:

Jurisdiction	**Situation**	**Temporal jurisdiction**	**Accused**	**Completion**	**Residual issues**
ICTY	Conflicts in Balkans	Since 1 January 1991[47]	161[48]	2010[49]	International Mechanism
ICTR	Rwanda and neighbouring states	1 January 1994 31 December 1994	88[50]	2010	International Mechanism

47 Art. 1 ICTYSt. Although the SC established the ICTY by SC Res. 827 (1993) and decided that it had jurisdiction 'between 1 January 1991 and a date to be determined by the Security Council upon the restoration of peace' (operative para. 2), no such an end date to the temporal jurisdiction was thereafter decided, nor could the completion strategy's deadline of end 2004 established under operative para. 7 of SC Res. 1503 (2003) reach that far as it does not address the scope of jurisdiction. Thus, it may be argued that the SC has so far understood that the restoration of peace is not yet a completed process, although it has decided to bring to an end the activities of the Tribunal. However, under unchanged circumstances, ICTY's jurisdiction will remain active until the completion of its work, with the theoretical ability of being exerted, should the stability in the region so require. See also *supra* note 37.

48 As per indictments approved by the 2004 term for completion of investigations, as determined in S/PRST/2002/21 and SCR 1503 (2003). See *supra* note 37.

49 Although subject to developments at the Tribunals and in the Security Council, at the time of writing the status of trials and appeals suggests that judicial activities may need to continue until 2014 for ICTY, but to an earlier date for the ICTR.

50 Including 12 fugitives, as of October 2009. See also *Report on the Completion Strategy of the International Criminal Tribunal for Rwanda (as of 4 May 2009)*, S/2009/247, 14 May 2009.

51 All accused were tried in three multi-accused cases (Civil Defence Forces (CDF), Revolutionary United Front (RUF) and Armed Forces Revolutionary Council (AFRC) cases), plus the *Charles Taylor* trial, scheduled to be completed by mid 2010. Additionally, two formerly accused died before trial (Foday Sankoh and Sam Bockarie) and one remains at large (Johnny Paul Koroma).

52 As of 1 July 2009. Available at http://www.eccc.gov.kh/english/default.aspx (visited 20 August 2009).

53 However, jurisdiction *ratione temporis et personae* can be extended by the Tribunal itself, should it find that 'attacks occurred in Lebanon between 1 October 2004 and 12 December 2005, or [at] any later date ... are connected [including for criminal intent, purpose of attacks, nature of victims, *modus operandi* and perpetrators] and are of a nature and gravity similar to the attack of 14 February 2005' resulting in the death of former Lebanese Prime Minister Rafiq Hariri and in the death or injury other persons. Art. 1(1) STLSt. See *supra* note 43.

Jurisdiction	Situation	Temporal jurisdiction	Accused	Completion	Residual issues
SCSL	Sierra Leone	Since 30 November 1996	11[51]	2010	Residual Mechanism
ECCC	Cambodia (Democratic Kampuchea)	17 April 1975 6 January 1979	5[52]	n.a.	n.a.
STL	Lebanon (Rafiq Hariri and others)	14 February 2005[53]	n.a.	n.a.	n.a.

4. The International Criminal Court

A. The Rome Statute's System

1. General Features

The turning point in international criminal justice is represented by the change in perspective introduced, after lengthy proceedings,[54] by the outcome of the 1998 Rome Diplomatic Conference,[55] when some 120 states adopted[56] what has since been commonly referred to as the Rome Statute of the International Criminal Court (ICC), which, to date, has been ratified or acceded to by 111 states. While the UN-led efforts had so far resulted in occasional forms of international justice – *inter alia* limited in time (temporal jurisdiction or jurisdiction *ratione temporis*) and space (territorial jurisdiction or jurisdiction *ratione loci*), although carefully crafted on a case-by-case basis to meet the specific needs of a given post-conflict situation – the treaty-based ICC affirms a jurisdiction which is inherently permanent, independent, universal and complementary.

The ICC is not intended to deal with all crimes committed in situations relevant to its jurisdiction but, as a Court of last resort, will step in only in exceptional cases where national judicial systems have failed to bring justice because states are not willing or able[57] to investigate and prosecute those who bear the highest responsibility for the most serious crimes of concern to the international community as a whole. Through the exercise of the jurisdiction of the Court, the States Parties of the Rome Statute aim to enhance international peace and security by preventing and suppressing heinous crimes of international concern, thus contributing to the protection of populations and victims. To this end and to deliver a deterrent performance, the Court has to visibly and timely carry

54 UN works by the International Law Commission (ILC), initiated in 1949 and discontinued in 1954, were resumed in 1989 upon the initiative of Trinidad and Tobago by an UNGA decision adopted in an historical context deeply changed by the end of the Cold War in early 1990s. A succinct chronology of the ICC establishment process is available at the Court's official website: http://www.icc-cpi.int/Menus/ICC/About+the+Court/ICC+at+a+glance/Chronology+of+the+ICC.htm (visited 20 August 2009).

55 United Nations Diplomatic Conference of Plenipotentiaries on the Establishment of an International Criminal Court, with documentation available at http://untreaty.un.org/cod/icc/index.html (visited 20 August 2009).

56 Out of some 150 states participating in the Conference, on 17 July 1998, 120 voted in favour of the adoption of the Statute, seven voted against and 21 abstained, while 139 states signed the Statute thereafter.

57 On the notions of unwillingness and inability, see *infra*, 4(E)(4)(b)(i) and (ii).

out its activities, normally in situations of ongoing conflicts[58] characterized by serious challenges in terms of security, evidence collection and availability of international cooperation.

Since its adoption and through its first application, it has become apparent that the Rome Statute has established a comprehensive regime of international criminal justice and placed the ICC at the forefront of international peace and security actions. The details of the history which led to the establishment of the ICC[59] fall outside the scope of this book, but it is important to stress that a constant hurdle to the elaboration of the Rome Statute's provisions was represented by the different legal systems to be taken into account. At a time when the *ad hoc* UN Tribunals were still heavily characterized by common law influences,[60] the Rome Statute was saluted, as well as for its procedural achievements, as a balanced compromise which provided the permanent Court with a reasoned blend of tested safeguards and effective investigative and trial tools, from both the adversarial and the inquisitorial systems.[61] Well before the ICC began to actually test its procedural devices, amendments to the *ad hoc* Tribunals' Statutes – although with significant differences – followed the same approach, showing that contributions from practitioners from a wide variety of national experiences in a challenging criminal trial environment can fill substantially the gaps left open in other more formal and diplomatic settings.

2. From IHL Treaties to a System of International Criminal Law

(a) Systematic suppression of criminal conducts

Treaties containing international criminal law provisions normally pursue the progressive harmonization of the criminal legal systems of States Parties by introducing obligations or options for criminalizing certain types of conducts and obligations to establish criminal jurisdiction over serious crimes, to prosecute or extradite, and to afford mutual legal assistance in relation to certain crimes.[62]

---

58 'To have a deterrent effect during an armed conflict the prosecution of war crimes must be visible.' *European Union Guidelines on Promoting Compliance with International Humanitarian Law* (IHL), 2005/C 327/04, *Official Journal*, 23 December 2005, para. 16.

59 See A. Cassese, 'From Nuremberg to Rome: International Military Tribunals to the International Criminal Court', in A. Cassese, P. Gaeta, and J.R.W.D. Jones (eds), *The Rome Statute of the International Criminal Court: A Commentary* (Oxford: Oxford University Press, 2002), 3–65 (hereinafter, Cassese, Gaeta and Jones).

60 See F. Pocar, 'The International Criminal Tribunal for the Former Yugoslavia', in this Volume, at 2(C).

61 In a wider perspective of harmonization of legal systems, the participation of the United Kingdom in the Council of Europe and the European Union has been one of the major factors for the progressive reduction in distances from common law and civil law traditions. See J.E. Levitsky, 'The Europeanisation of the British Legal Style', *American Journal of Comparative Law*, 1994, at 347 ff., and A. Pizzorusso, *Sistemi giuridici comparati* [Compared Legal Systems] (Milano: Giuffrè, 1998), at 377 ff.

62 An indication of the different extent to which these obligations were introduced in treaty law before the adoption of the Rome Statute on 17 July 1998 – and, particularly. for the expansion of the cooperation over the last few decades – may be drawn from, e.g., the Convention on the Prevention and Punishment of the Crime of Genocide of 9 December 1948, or the four Geneva Conventions of 12 August 1949. After Rome, see in particular the wide-ranging obligations under the United Nations Convention against Transnational Organized Crime (Palermo Convention), GA Res. 55/25 of 15 November 2000, and its three supplementing Protocols relating to Human Trafficking (Protocol to Prevent, Suppress and Punish Trafficking in Persons, especially Women and Children), to Migrants (Protocol against the Smuggling of Migrants by Land, Sea and

The Rome Statute goes well beyond this perspective, no longer imposing only reciprocal obligations on states but also regulating relations between the states and the Court, and by creating a criminal legal system where prohibitions and sanctions are completed by an institutionalized jurisdictional mechanism for their application.[63] A distinctive feature of the ICC's Statute, therefore, is the introduction of a new legal system, which stands autonomously in the international order, as it is completed by an implementing mechanism for the prohibitions, sanctions and obligations it provides and entails. The Statute, in fact, includes:

- establishment and organization of an institution that has international legal personality;[64]
- substantial criminal law provisions,[65] including definitions[66] and penalties,[67] established in accordance with the principle of strict legality;[68]
- general principles of criminal law;[69] and
- procedural criminal law and cooperation provisions.[70]

One major advantage of a permanent and independent Court relying on a comprehensive and complete legal system, as detailed above, is that the existence of the international jurisdiction is assumed before any situation or case arises. This fully satisfies the need for legal certainty under the perspective of predetermined criminal provisions and sanctions (*nullum crimen, nulla poena sine lege*), as well as of a judge established and identified prior to the commission of the facts. In fact, an institutionalized international criminal jurisdiction, not dependent upon any political decision and assessment, may represent a strong deterrent to the commission or continuation of the serious

---

Air), and Firearms (Protocol against the Illicit Manufacturing of and Trafficking in Firearms, their Parts and Components and Ammunition); the United Nations Convention against Corruption (Merida Convention), GA Res. 58/4 of 31 October 2003; the International Convention for the Suppression of the Financing of Terrorism, GA res. 54/109, 9 December 1999.

63 The systematic nature of the Statute is retained in literature. See W.W. Burke-White, 'Proactive Complementarity: The International Criminal Court and National Courts in the Rome System of International Justice', 49 *Harvard International Law Journal* (1998), 53–108, at 56: 'the Statute creates a system of judicial enforcement for the prosecution of the most serious international crimes at both the domestic and international levels of governance.'

64 Art. 4(1) ICCSt. On the international legal personality of the ICC, see F. Martines, 'Legal Status and Powers of the Court', in Cassese, Gaeta and Jones, *supra* note 59, at 203–218

65 Arts 5, 6, 7, 8 and 70 ICCSt.

66 The Elements of Crimes (Art. 9 ICCSt), as applicable law (Art 21 ICCSt) and, insofar they are consistent with the Statute (Art. 9 (3) ICCSt), they qualify as primary norms, but are subordinate to the Statute. See also, *infra*, 4(A)(2)(c).

67 Art. 77 ICCSt.

68 Arts 22 and 23 ICCSt. The principle *nullum crimen nulla poena sine lege* is of general applicability to criminal liability under the Statute. In particular, the principle of legality is not affected by the current status of criminal law provisions in the Statute which, although in some cases lacking completeness, contain the conditions subject to which they would be applicable. This is true in the case of the crime of aggression, where a definition (and a procedure) in itself is still missing, thus barring the Court from exercising jurisdiction (Art. 5(1)(d) and (2) ICCSt). But it is also valid where only some elements of the definition are uncompleted, as is the case for war crimes under the 'weapons provision': weapons and other objects of criminal prohibition need to meet both the conditions of being subjected to a comprehensive prohibition and to be included in an annex to the Statute (Art. 8(2)(b)(xx) ICCSt).

69 Arts 22–33 ICCSt.

70 Arts 11–21, and 53–111 ICCSt, plus the Rules of Procedure and Evidence.

crimes that it is mandated to adjudicate upon. Realistically, the deterrent effect of the ICC should be assessed in the perspective of the pre-existing feeling of impunity that perpetrators of serious international crimes could have had. As far as deterrence is concerned, it should be appreciated that without the ICC the liability for serious international crimes would only be subject to an uncertain SC resolution establishing additional international tribunals. By contrast, the ICC makes criminal liability certain, although this may not coincide with the actual likelihood that the Court's orders are enforced, which is dependent on a number of political and factual factors, including the situation on the ground and the willingness of the international community to cooperate.

However, it is apparent that with the introduction of a wholly harmonized set of institutional, organizational, substantive and procedural provisions, the 120 founding states of the Rome Statute have headed towards systematic suppression of criminal conduct amounting to the most serious crimes of concern to the internationally community as a whole.

Although the above-mentioned features of the ICC describe it as a comprehensive legal system, this still excludes any consideration of its self-sustainability. Like the other international jurisdictions – and different to any criminal legal system established within and because of the sovereign authority of a state – the ICC is not a self-sustained system. The lack of any fiscal authority and enforcement powers of the ICC makes the institution, although judicially independent, still objectively dependent on the cooperation of states, including in its financial, political and legal dimensions.[71]

In spite of this limitation, the inherent systematic nature of the Rome Statute is further strengthened by the crucial effect of its distinctive complementarity mechanism, which inextricably links the operation of legal systems at different levels, through the integration in one comprehensive legal system of legal systems established at the national level (states) and at the international one (ICC). The result is an integrated system[72] for investigating and curbing crimes of international concern, leaving no jurisdictional lacunae and ensuring a potentially universal jurisdiction: the Court may punish what is left unpunished by states.[73]

(b) Law-making selection of crimes

While selecting and defining the conducts to be criminalized, the negotiators of the Statute adopted a strict criterion that enabled the inclusion of crimes either already provided for by customary international law, or the universal acknowledgment of which was the result of the consolidated elaboration of the jurisprudence of the *ad hoc* Tribunals, whose legitimacy is based on the *erga omnes* authority of the SC Resolutions establishing their jurisdictions.

As far as previous universally ratified conventions are concerned, only the 1949 Geneva Conventions are expressly quoted in the Statute, but their criminal law provisions relevant to the law of the Statute are incorporated in the text thereof.[74] Other conventions are also referred to,

---

71 See *infra*, 4(E) and R. Bellelli, Cooperation and Implementation, *supra* note 22, at 3(A) and (B).

72 R. Bellelli, 'Italian Implementation of the Rome Statute and Related Constitutional Issues', in R.S. Lee (ed.), *State's Responses to Issues Arising from the ICC Statute: Constitutional, Sovereignty, Judicial Cooperation and Criminal Law* (Ardsley: Transnational Publishers, 2005), at 226. The building of such system through complementarity is clearly addressed by the Office of the Prosecutor in its *Draft Prosecutorial Strategy 2009–2012* (Draft, expected to be finalized by November 2009), 18 August 2009, para. 23: 'inter-dependent, mutually reinforcing international system of justice.'

73 On the notion and scope of universal jurisdiction under the Statute, *infra*, 4(E)(3).

74 Art. 8(2)(a) ICCSt. 'grave breaches', and (c) 'serious violations of Article 3 common to the four Geneva Conventions', for non-international armed conflicts.

although only implicitly, as criminal provisions under the Statute adopt the descriptions contained therein (e.g., for the crimes of genocide[75] and apartheid[76]).

The fact that the Statute does not simply refer to other conventions to establish criminal provisions, but rather only to retain and stress the customary nature thereof, is also evidence of the independence of the Statute's provisions from those of the previous treaties explicitly or implicitly referred to. It might therefore be argued that the Statute, where it refers to earlier treaties, makes its own selection and codification of substantive provisions, which would thus exist autonomously under the law of the Statute, sometimes substantially modifying international treaty law by drawing on international criminal case law. A major effect of such autonomy of the law of the Statute is that states that are Parties to both the Rome Statute and to earlier treaties are subject to a different and independent set of obligations. As a consequence, e.g., obligations under the Geneva Conventions relating to the universal jurisdiction of states over certain crimes are only binding in implementing those Conventions while, for the same conduct criminalized under the Statute, states are bound only by the different obligations derived from the principle of complementarity (namely, arrest, surrender and assistance).

(c) The Law of the Statute

(i) Applicable law

The applicable law before the ICC is defined under the Statute with reference to internal[77] and external[78] sources. However, a hierarchy is established between these sources of law, whereby the Court shall always apply its internal norms before resorting to external law.[79] The first category includes the normative instruments established under the Law of Treaties and which are, thus, binding for States Parties in the implementation of the Rome Statute: i.e., the Statute itself and those instruments based thereon and derived therefrom, that is the Elements of Crimes and the Rules of Procedure and Evidence. As the provisions under such instruments have primacy in the normative ranking, the Court cannot discard any such provision and has to seek their full application before resorting to external sources of law. These would, thus, have secondary normative nature and their application by the Court is subsidiary and discretionary.[80] Such sources would ordinarily include norms, principles and rules of international law which govern the subject matter.[81] Only when possible gaps left open by the primary normative instruments cannot be filled under international

75 Art. 6 ICCSt. The Convention on the Prevention and Punishment of the Crime of Genocide, adopted by GA Res. 260 A (III), 9 December 1948, entered into force on 12 January 1951 and has to date been ratified by 140 states. Available at http://www.unhchr.ch/html/menu3/b/p_genoci.htm (visited 30 January 2009). The ICJ found the customary nature of the principles from which the Genocide convention stems: 'the principles underlying the Convention are principles which are recognized by civilized nations as binding on States, even without any conventional obligation.' *Reservations to the Convention on the Prevention and Punishment of the Crime of Genocide*, Advisory Opinion, 28 May 1951, ICJ Reports 1951, 15 to 69, at 23. Available at http://www.icj-cij.org/docket/files/12/4283.pdf (visited 20 August 2009).

76 Art. 7(1)(j) ICCSt.

77 Art. 21(1)(a) ICCSt.

78 Art. 21(1)(b) and (c) ICCSt.

79 Art. 21(1) ICCSt: 'The Court shall apply: (a) In the first place …; (b) In second place …; (c) Failing that …'.

80 Art. 21(1) ICCSt: 'The Court shall apply … (b) … where appropriate …; (c) … as appropriate …'.

81 E.g., the 1949 Geneva Conventions and their 1977 Additional Protocols.

law, the Court is then entitled to derive from national legislations those 'general principles of law' which might be consistent with international law.[82] However, the principle of legality retained in the Statute[83] acts as a ban to any expansion of the subject matter jurisdiction of the Court, so that criminalization of conducts under relevant treaties, other than those included in Article 5 of the Statute, cannot establish criminal liability under the Statute.

(ii) Regulations

Not all instruments mentioned in the Statute have normative status and the ranking of normative and regulatory instruments appears to be clearly defined under existing normative provisions of the Law of the Statute,[84] in line with the allocation of competencies between the States Parties and the Court. As mentioned above, a normative status pertains only to those binding instruments adopted by states at the 1998 Diplomatic Conference (the Statute) and within the Assembly of States Parties of the ICC (Elements of Crimes[85] and rules of Procedure and Evidence[86]) under its normative-setting authority.[87] Thus, applicable law under Article 21 ICCSt does not include any of the internal Regulations adopted for the functioning of the different organs of the ICC and, in particular, neither the Regulations of the Court nor those of the Registry are included.[88]

The Regulations of the Court are only intended to correctly implement the Statute's normative provisions: 'in accordance with the Statute and the Rules of Procedure and Evidence ... the

82 Art. 21(1)(c) ICCSt.

83 Art. 22 ICCSt.

84 Art. 21(1)(a) on Applicable Law, Art. 51(4) and (5) on the Rules of Procedure and Evidence, Article 9(3) on the Elements of Crimes, Art. 52 on the Regulations of the Court, Rule 14 RPE on the Regulations of the Registry.

85 Art. 9(3) ICCSt.

86 Art. 51(4) and (5) ICCSt.

87 Art. 112(2) ICCSt.

88 The Court clearly addressed the distinction between applicable law and internal rules referring, on the one hand, to 'current *law* governing the legal assistance scheme' (Art. 68(3) ICCSt and Rule 16(1)(b) ICC RPE) and, on the other hand, to '*procedure* for seeking legal assistance paid by the Court' (Regulation 84(1) Regulations of the Court and Regulation 113(2) Regulations of the Registry). ICC, Decision on the Request for the review of the Registrar's Decision of 28 March 2008 on the Application of Legal Assistance Paid by the Court Filed by Mr Keta on behalf of Victims ... under Regulation 85(3) of the Regulations of the Court, situation in the DRC, Presidency, 18 February 2009, ICC-01/04, paras 21–22 (emphasis added). However, in one instance the Court took a different view as the Presidency decided on a complaint lodged against an administrative decision of the Registrar, following a procedure established under Regulation 221 Regulations of the Registry, based on Regulation 106(2) Regulations of the Court. Decision, Mr Mathieu Ngudjolo's Complaint Under Regulation 221(1) the Regulations of the Registry against the Registrar's Decision of 18 November 2008, No. ICC-RoR-217-02/08, 10 March 2009. The Decision concluded that, based on Regulation 179(1) Regulations of the Registry, there is a positive obligation for the Court to fund family visits to indigent detainees, and stated that '[t]he Registrar shall give specific attention to visits by family of detained persons with a view of maintaining such links'. This Decision raised many legal and policy issues, among all it contradicted the conclusions reached by the Assembly of States Parties that 'according to existing law and standards, the right to family visits does not comprise a co-relative legal right to have such visits paid for by the detaining authority'. Resolution ICC-ASP/7/Res.3, *Strengthening the International Criminal Court and the Assembly of States Parties* (Omnibus Resolution), para. 17, in Official Records, ICC-ASP/7/20, at 31. See the *Report of the Bureau on Family Visits for Detainees*, 9 October 2009, ICC-ASP/8/42 and its Annexes Draft Resolution and expert's remarks.

Regulations of the Court [are] *necessary for its routine functioning*'.[89] Consequently, such Regulations cannot establish new rights and obligations, vis-à-vis those provided for under the Statute and the Rules of Procedure and Evidence (RPE). Further, the adoption of the Regulations and any amendments thereto is within the competence of the judges who, under the ICC's Statute, are not mandated to establish the normative framework of the Court, but only to regulate its functioning.

The Regulations of the Registry are provided for under the RPE 'to [only] govern the operation of the Registry'; they are prepared by the Registrar in consultation with the Prosecutor and approved by the Presidency.[90] There is no role for the Assembly of States Parties (ASP), as the policymaking and normative body of the ICC, to play in their adoption. It is for the Presidency to monitor appropriateness of these Regulations in order to direct the activities of the Registry. Consequently, these Regulations too cannot establish rights and obligations, but rather only set administrative standards and procedures.

(iii) An evolving notion

It also follows from the above considerations on the applicable law that the Law of the Statute[91] is a concept that can be defined in its minimum contents – that is the Statute, Elements of Crimes and Rules of Procedure and Evidence – including any amendment which might be adopted by the States Parties. What cannot be defined is the extension of the Law of the Statute that might stem from the jurisprudence of the Court: only the case law will define the extent to which international and national law may shape the Law of the Statute.

(d) Reservations

In order to establish an effective legal system, the Rome Statute could not have allowed differentiated regimes to operate for its States Parties and, consistently, the package compromise agreed in 1998 included a clear exclusion of any reservation.[92] Only one exception to this rule was made under Article 124 ICCSt to allow States Parties to exempt themselves from the jurisdiction of the Court over war crimes for a maximum period of seven years.[93] However, due to its purposes and transitional nature, as well as to its practice, such derogation from the principle under Article 120 ICCSt falls under the purview of a Review Conference.[94]

Reservations have been expressly ruled out by Article 120 for the purpose of maintaining the integrity of the Rome Statute in the delicate balance reached at the end of the 1998 Diplomatic Conference. The intention of the drafters of the Statute is clear: States Parties cannot 'exclude or

---

89 Art. 52(1) ICCSt (emphasis added).

90 Rule 14(1) ICC RPE.

91 For a detailed analysis, see A. Pellet, 'Applicable Law', in A. Cassese, P. Gaeta, and J.R.W.D. Jones, *The Rome Statute of the International Criminal Court: A Commentary*, Vol. II (Oxford: Oxford University Press, 2003), 1051–1084. See also M. Catenacci, *'Legalità' e 'tipicità del reato' nello Statuto della Corte penale internazionale* [Legality and Strict Construction of Crimes in the ICC Statute] (Milano: Giuffré, 2003), at 21 ff.

92 Art. 120 ICCSt: 'no reservations may be made to this Statute.'

93 Art. 124 ICCSt. See R. Bellelli, The Law of the Statute (*supra* note 10), in this Volume, at 3(C).

94 Art. 123(1) ICCSt.

modify the legal effect of certain provisions of the treaty in their application'.[95] However, the Statute does not exclude states from appending to their ratifications such declarations and understandings that are not *per se* inconsistent with the Statute, as they may specify or clarify the meaning or scope of certain provisions.[96] Declarations, understandings and provisos were, therefore, attached by some states to their ratifications, and were based on the need to deal with what such states viewed[97] as vital interests[98] and are, thus, to be assessed as part of the balance of interests which has finally resulted in the decision to ratify the Rome Statute.[99] However, under the Law of Treaties[100] the legitimacy of such statements – when intended to limit the scope of application of the Statute by, e.g., giving prevalence to national law[101] – would be questionable as, whatever their name or wording, they would still amount to reservations.[102]

B. The Subject Matter Jurisdiction

1. Core Crimes and Treaty Crimes

The mandate contained in the Rome Statute is for the ICC to fight against impunity for the most serious crimes of concern to the international community as a whole. This notion does not necessarily

---

95 Art. 2(1)(d) Vienna Convention on the Law of Treaties, 23 May 1969, United Nations, *Treaty Series*, Vol. 1155, at 331 (Law of Treaties): 'reservation means a unilateral statement, however phrased or named, made by a State, when signing, ratifying, accepting, approving or acceding to a treaty, whereby it purports to exclude or modify the legal effect of certain provisions of the treaty in their application to that State.'

96 G. Hafner, 'Article 120', in O. Triffterer, *Commentary on the Rome Statute: Observers' Notes, Article by Article* (Baden-Baden: Nomos Verlagsegesellschaft, 1999), 1251.

97 W. Schabas, *An Introduction to the International Criminal Court* (3rd edn, Cambridge: Cambridge University Press, 2007), 328–329.

98 Keeping in mind that before ratification France had to tackle the issue of its constitutional prerogatives to avail itself of nuclear weapons, and following the conclusions by its *Conseil Constitutionnel* (Decision, No. 98–408 DC, 22 January 1999), it made the following declarations: 'The provisions of Article 8 of the Statute, and in particular those of paragraph 2 (b) (war crimes in international armed conflict), exclusively concern conventional weapons and *could not regulate or prohibit the possible use of nuclear weapons* or prejudice other rules of international law that apply to other weapons which are necessary in the exercise of France's inherent right of self-defence' (informally translated from French, with emphasis added). However, in *Legality of the Threat or Use of Nuclear Weapons*, Advisory Opinion, 8 July 1996, the ICJ held that 'there can be no doubt as to the applicability of humanitarian law to nuclear weapons' (para. 85) and that 'the intrinsically humanitarian character of the [law of armed conflicts apply] to all forms of warfare and to all kind of weapons' (para. 86). Interestingly, other major nuclear powers expressed definite views during the same proceedings, e.g., 'the United States has long shared the view that the law of armed conflict governs the use of nuclear weapons – just as it governs the use of conventional weapons' (ibid., para. 86, United States of America, CR 95/34, at 85).

99 This perspective is made very clear for a possible US accession by D. Scheffer and A. Cox, 'The Constitutionality of the Rome Statute of the International Criminal Court', 98 *The Journal of Criminal Law & Criminology* (2008), 983–1068, at 1059–1064, where a number of such tools are suggested to address US constitutional concerns.

100 See *supra* note 95.

101 Article 27 Law of Treaties: 'a party may not invoke the provisions of its internal law as justification for its failure to perform a treaty.'

102 For an in depth analysis of the issue, Amnesty International, 'Declarations amounting to prohibited reservations to the Rome Statute', available at www.amnesty.org/en/library/asset/IOR40/032/2005/en/dom-IOR400322005en.html (visited 20 August 2009).

coincide with that of crimes of international concern, but is intended as a conventional concept encompassing international crimes provided for under customary international humanitarian law, as interpreted in the jurisprudence of international tribunals and retained in the Rome Statute. The ICC has competence to adjudicate (subject matter jurisdiction or jurisdiction *ratione materiae*) the following categories of 'core crimes': genocide, crimes against humanity, war crimes and the crime of aggression.[103]

While this list of crimes is a closed one, negotiations held during the Rome Diplomatic Conference in 1998 took into account the strong interest shown by a number of delegations for a possible future expansion of the jurisdiction of the ICC to also cover other international crimes. In particular, 'treaty crimes' of international drug trafficking and terrorism were recognized to be 'scourges which pose serious threats to international peace and security'.[104] As no generally acceptable definition for such crimes was reached in Rome, it was however agreed that a Review Conference could consider ('recommend') these crimes with the view to arriving at an acceptable definition and their inclusion in the list of crimes within the jurisdiction of the Court.[105]

In this regard, situations may arise where crimes – which normally affect interests belonging to and protected primarily by states – might attain a quantitative or qualitative dimension which determines a change in the nature of interests affected. Such situations may arise in relation to trafficking in illicit drugs, the effects of which create huge levels of illicit profits with the subsequent concentration of power in criminal hands and the unbalance of entire economies, leading to insecurity at the state and inter-state levels. Although such threats are serious and specific, no major developments have been reported in the field[106] since the adoption of the Statute.

Also international terrorist acts – when committed on a large scale, systematically or against certain targets – may have destabilizing effects on international peace and security,[107] thus becoming

103 Article 5(1) ICCSt. See *infra* note 224, for the definition in terms of 'universally recognized or condemned offences'. The rationale for establishing the ICC is identified in the fight against impunity in Preamble (4) and (5) ICCSt, where 'the most serious crimes of concern to the international community as a whole must not go unpunished' and determination is expressed 'to put an end to impunity for perpetrators of these crimes and thus to contribute to the prevention of such crimes'. Similarly, UNSC Res. 827, 25 May 1993, Preambular para. 5, establishing the ICTY expressed a determination 'to put an end to [flagrant violations of international humanitarian law] and to take effective measures to bring to justice the persons who are responsible'.

104 Final Act of the United Nations Diplomatic Conference of Plenipotentiaries on the Establishment of an International Criminal Court – Annex 1, Resolution E.

105 Ibid.

106 The latest international universal instrument in the field is the United Nations Convention against Illicit Traffic in Narcotic Drugs and Psychotropic Substances, Vienna, 19 December 1988. A proposal for an amendment to Article 5 ICCSt in order to include drug crimes in the jurisdiction of the Court is based on the fact that 'in the absence of an appropriate international legal framework, organized criminal networks and international drug traffickers will continue to … subvert democratically elected governments and to threaten socio-economic development, political stability and the internal and external security of States and the physical and mental security of individuals'. See R. Bellelli, The Law of the Statute (*supra* note 10), in this Volume, at 3(D)(2).

107 Significantly, SC Res. 1368, 12 September 2001, '*regards* … any act of international terrorism, as a threat to international peace and security' (OP1). For the evolution of the practice of the Security Council in considering terrorism as a threat to international peace and security, see V. Santori, 'UN Security Council's (Broad) Interpretation of the Notion of Threat to Peace in Counter-terrorism', in G. Nesi (ed.), *International Cooperation in Counter-Terrorism – The United Nations and Regional Organizations in the Fight Against Terrorism* (Aldershot: Ashgate, 2006), at 89 ff.

crimes of concern to the international community as a whole.[108] However, due to the lasting impasse in the negotiations of the Comprehensive Convention on International Terrorism,[109] delegations to the ASP have not focused preparations for the first 2010 Review Conference on including terrorism by amendments to the Rome Statute, although a proposal to that end has been presented.[110] While several definitions of terrorism exist and there is a significant number of treaties that, both at the universal[111] and regional level, address in detail both criminalization of terrorist acts and

108 Among terrorist acts that have, over the last decade, affected regional or worldwide peace, e.g., the 9/11 attacks on US soil, and the targeting of civilian objects in Israel.

109 By GA Res. 54/110 of 2000, the Assembly further elaborated on the mandate of the *Ad hoc Committee* established by its Res. 51/210 of 17 December 1996, deciding that it should have addressed means of further developing a comprehensive legal framework of conventions dealing with international terrorism, including considering the elaboration of a Comprehensive Convention on international terrorism. In 2000, the Indian delegation also formally introduced the working document entitled Draft Comprehensive Convention on International Terrorism (UN doc. A/C.6/55/1), which was a revised version of the text previously presented at the fifty-first session of the General Assembly (UN doc. A/C.6/51/6). Discussions on the draft comprehensive Convention have since continued in formal and informal settings, within the *Ad hoc* Committee, the Sixth Committee and its Working Group. However, the call of the Chiefs of State and Governments for the conclusion of negotiations during the sixtieth session of the GA, contained in the *Outcome Document of the 2005 UN World Summit*, has so far fallen short of its goal and deliberations are still ongoing.

110 New York Working Group of the Bureau, informal summary of the *Informal Consultations on the Review Conference*, 13 June 2009, at 2, General comments: delegations have initially refrained from discussing in concrete terms the possibility of putting forward formal proposals, on grounds that the Court needs not to be overburdened at an early stage with additional crimes and political sensitivities, also so as not to take time from the difficult negotiations on the crime of aggression during the first Review Conference. Such reasoning seems to match the criteria elected by the States Parties for setting the agenda of the first Review Conference. See R. Bellelli, The Law of the Statute (*supra* note 10), in this Volume, at 1(A)(1). See also ibid., at 3(D) and note 68, for an informal proposal put forward by the Netherlands on terrorism.

111 (1) Convention on Offences and Certain Other Acts Committed on Board Aircraft, Tokyo, 14 September 1963, UN doc. A/C.6/418/Corr.1, Annex II – United Nations Treaty Series, Vol. 704, 219 ff. (in force since 4 December 1969); (2) Convention for the Suppression of Unlawful Seizure of Aircraft, The Hague, 16 December 1970, UN Doc. A/C.6/418/Corr.1, Annex II – United Nations Treaty Series, Vol. 860, 105 ff. (in force since 14 October 1971); (3) Convention for the Suppression of Unlawful Acts against the Safety of Civil Aviation, Montreal, 23 September 1971, UN Doc. A/C.6/418/Corr.2, Annex III – United Nations Treaty Series, Vol. 974, 177 ff. (in force since 26 January 1973); (4) Convention on the Prevention and Punishment of Crimes against Internationally Protected Persons, including Diplomatic Agents, New York, 14 December 1973, UN Doc. A/Res/3166 – United Nations Treaty Series, Vol. 1035, 167 ff. (in force since 20 February 1977); (5) International Convention against the Taking of Hostages, New York, 17 December 1979,UN Doc. A/Res/34/146; United Nations Treaty Series, Vol. 1316, 205 ff. (in force since 3 June 1983); (6) Convention on the Physical Protection of Nuclear Material, Vienna, 3 March 1980, IAEA Doc. C/225 – United Nations Treaty Series, Vol. 1456, 101 ff. (in force since 8 February 1987); (7) Protocol on the Suppression of Unlawful Acts of Violence at Airports Serving International Civil Aviation, supplementary to the Convention for the Suppression of Unlawful Acts against the Safety of Civil Aviation, Montreal, 24 February 1988, ICAO Doc. 9518, International Legal Materials, Vol. 27, 627 ff. (in force since 6 August 1989); (8) Convention for the Suppression of Unlawful Acts against the Safety of Maritime Navigation, Rome, 10 March 1988, IMO Doc. Sua/Con/15, International Legal Materials, Vol. 27, 668 ff. (in force since 1 March 1992); (9) Protocol for the Suppression of Unlawful Acts against the Safety of Fixed Platforms located on the Continental Shelf, Rome, 10 March 1988, IMO Doc. Sua/Con/16/Rev.1, International Legal Materials, Vol. 27, 685 ff. (in force since 1 March 1992); (10) Convention on the Marking of Plastic Explosive for the Purpose of Detection, Montreal, 1 March 1991, UN Doc. S/22393/Corr.1, International Legal Materials, Vol. 30, 721 ff. (in force since 21 June 1998); (11) International Convention for the Suppression of Terrorist Bombings, New York, 15

international cooperation on the matter, the politically charged definition of terrorism is still the subject of divisive debates.

It must be noted that some understand that terrorism could already be subject to the jurisdiction of the ICC, when terrorist acts fall in the definition of Article 7 ICCSt.[112] Obviously, relevant provisions under Article 7 might include different acts, all intended to spread terror within a civilian population and with the intent of achieving a political advantage: (a) murder; (b) extermination; (e) imprisonment; (f) torture; (g) sexual violence; (h) persecution; and (k) other inhumane acts. In particular, 'other inhumane acts of a similar character intentionally causing great suffering, or serious injury to body or mental or physical health' could in some situations be key to addressing terrorist acts in the framework of the Statute.

From a factual perspective, the likelihood that terrorism would be addressed as such by the ICC seems to be rather remote, taking into account that terrorist acts in time of peace target the very essence of the public power and, thus, would often postulate the existence of a state willing and able to prosecute: although this might not always be the case, at least the territorial or passive nationality state would normally have not only jurisdiction but also a strong interest in exerting it, thus making inadmissible a case before the Court. In the possible scenario of, e.g., an event like the attacks of 11 September 2001 on the territory of the United States, it seems rather unlikely that the territorial state would not exert jurisdiction. Also, situations like the *Lockerbie* case significantly underline that a settlement between concurrent jurisdictions might be sought in several and original ways.[113]

Besides, it will be for the jurisprudence of the Court to interpret Article 7 ICCSt in light of the circumstances of the cases and to define whether the scope of acts criminalized as crimes against humanity may include conducts characterized by terrorist intent. In this regard, the Court will most likely have to take into account, on the one hand, the principle of strict legality under criminal law and, on the other hand, the intent of the parties as clarified by preparatory work and circumstances

---

December 1997, UN Doc. A/Res/52/164 (in force since 23 May 2001); (12) International Convention for the Suppression of the Financing of Terrorism, New York, 9 December 1999, UN Doc. A/Res/54/109 (in force since 10 April 2002); (13) International Convention for the Suppression of Acts of Nuclear Terrorism, New York, 13 April 2005, UN Doc. A/Res/59/290 (in force since 7 July 2007); (14) Amendment to the Convention on the Physical Protection of Nuclear Material, Vienna, 8 July 2005, IAEA Doc. GOV/INF/2005/10-GC(49)/INF/6 (not in force, as of 5 July 2009); (15) Protocol of 2005 to the Convention for the Suppression of Unlawful Acts against the Safety of the Maritime Navigation, London, 14 October 2005, IMO Doc. Leg/Conf./15/21 (not in force, as of 5 July 2009); (16) Protocol of 2005 to the Protocol for the Suppression of Unlawful Acts against the Safety of Fixed Platforms located on the Continental Shelf, London, 14 October 2005, IMO Doc. Leg/Conf./15/22 (not in force, as of 5 July 2009).

112 R. Arnold, *The ICC as a New Instrument for Repressing Terrorism* (New York: Transnational Publishers, 2004), at 276 ff.; A. Cassese, *International Criminal Law* (Oxford: Oxford University Press, 2003), at 128, and A. Cassese, 'The Multifaceted Criminal Notion of Terrorism in International Law', 4 *JICJ* (2006), at 933; L. Quadarella, *Il nuovo terrorismo internazionale come crimine contro l'umanità* [The New International Terrorism as Crime Against Humanity] (Napoli: Editoriale Scientifica, 2006), 171–178.

113 In the Lockerbie case, jurisdiction was established on the basis of both territorial and passive (for the victims on the ground) personality criteria (Scotland): while most of the victims belonged to different nationalities, the crime was committed on board a foreign aircraft (US flight, Pan Am 103), by nationals of another state (Lybia), and the trial was held under Scots law on a third state's territory (Netherlands, at the former US Air Force base of Camp van Zeist).

of the conclusion of the treaty,[114] for all of which Resolution E of the Final Act of the Rome Conference would offer arguments.

2. Crime of Aggression and Weapons Provision

The subject matter jurisdiction is not only limited by the selective approach taken in Rome, but also by the fact that jurisdiction cannot yet be exerted over some of the crimes already included in the closed list of Article 5 ICCSt.

First of all this is the case in relation for the crime of aggression, over which the Court will have actual jurisdiction only once a definition of the crime and the conditions for the exercise of jurisdiction are agreed upon[115] by means of an amendment[116] to the Rome Statute adopted by the Assembly of States Parties at a Review Conference.[117] The Special Working Group on the Crime of Aggression (SWGCA) established by the ASP devoted considerable efforts to reaching a generally acceptable definition of the individual crime of aggression – i.e., the criminal liability of the person who, be it in a civilian or military leadership position, plays a decisive role in triggering an act of aggression by a state against another state. Although the SWGCA concluded its work, informal and formal negotiations are expected to continue[118] most likely until during the Review Conference itself, as they have come to a phase where a political decision on the core issue is needed: whether an individual could be prosecuted before the ICC for a conduct amounting to an act of aggression even when the Security Council had not previously decided on the responsibility of the state for the act of aggression.[119]

In addition to the crime of aggression, in the category of war crimes the 'weapons provision' has also been left unfinished in Rome; mainly because of the inherent characteristics of the weapons of mass destruction and of the contentious issue of the legitimacy of their use,[120] no agreement was reached on the identification of the weapons 'of a nature to cause superfluous injury or unnecessary suffering or which are inherently indiscriminate in violation of the international law of armed conflict'. However, should weapons of such a nature or effects be acknowledged as the subject of a comprehensive prohibition,[121] the list of such weapons will complete the criminal provision and might be included in an annex to the Statute.[122]

114 Respectively, Art. 22 ICCSt (see *supra*, at 4(A)(2)(c)(i)) and Articles 31 and 32 Law of Treaties, see *supra* note 95.

115 Art. 5(2) ICCSt.

116 Arts 121 and 123 ICCSt.

117 Final Act, Annex 1, Resolution F, para. 7.

118 See ASP seventh session (second resumption), *Report of the Special Working Group on the Crime of Aggression*, ICC-ASP/7/SWGCA/2, 20 February 2009, Annex III, at 7.

119 See, in this Volume, Part IV, Section 2 and, on the negotiating process and its outcome in particular, Chapter 29, S. Barriga, Against the Odds: The Results of the Special Working Group on the Crime of Aggression.

120 ICJ, *Legality of the Threat or Use of Nuclear Weapons*, Advisory Opinion, 8 July 1996. See also, *supra* notes 12 and 98.

121 Art. 8(2)(b)(xx) ICCSt.

122 A proposal for an amendment to the 'weapons provision' was announced during the seventh session of the Assembly of States Parties (The Hague, 14–21 November 2008) by Belgium, and subsequently discussed in open-ended Bureau meetings. For details, see R. Bellelli, The Law of the Statute (*supra* note 10), at 3(B) and R. Clark, The 'Weapons Provisions' and its Annex: The Belgian Proposals, in this Volume.

3. The Gravity Criterion

(a) Scope

The Court is mandated to exercise jurisdiction only over 'the most serious crimes of concern to the international community as a whole',[123] that is, for 'the most serious crimes of international concern'.[124]

Thus, the gravity of the crimes is, on the one hand, the rationale justifying the derogation to the sovereignty of states in the exercise of criminal justice at the national level and, on the other hand, the quantitative limit imposed on the international jurisdiction of the ICC based on the principle of economy, taking into account the complexity and the cost of resorting to international prosecutions and trials. Consequently, the gravity of crimes of international concern may be considered as a general principle under the Statute, incorporated as the thread operating at the level of jurisdiction (subject matter), admissibility, substantive criminal law, and procedure.

(b) Crime selection

In particular, the seriousness of the crimes served as a general criterion for the selection of the crimes included in the Statute and to define its jurisdiction *ratione materiae*. In general terms, international treaties criminalizing conducts and introducing cooperation obligations use the expression 'serious crimes' to portray a category of crimes that national legal systems address with more serious penal effects, e.g., a higher maximum penalty,[125] measures at the level of proceedings,[126] sentence enforcement[127] and compensation.[128]

---

123 Preamble ICCSt: '*determined* to ... establish an [ICC] ... with jurisdiction over' (para. 9) 'unimaginable atrocities' (para. 2) that are 'grave crimes threaten[ing] the peace, security and well-being of the world' (para. 3) and, therefore, to be considered 'the most serious crimes of concern to the international community as a whole' (paras 4 and 9, and Art. 5(1) ICCSt).

124 Art. 1 ICCSt.

125 For example: '"serious crime" shall mean conduct constituting an offence punishable with a maximum deprivation of liberty of at least four years or a more serious penalty.' Art. 2(b) United Nations Convention against Transnational Organized Crime, UNGA Res. 55/25, 15 November 2000.

126 This is the case for enhanced cooperation measures between national prosecution offices – e.g., the Anti-Mafia National Direction established under Italian Law 20 January 1992, No. 8 for the coordination of proceedings under Art. 371*bis* Criminal Procedure Code in relation to crimes under 51(3)*bis* of the same Code (organized crime, drug trafficking, and others) – or at the regional level – e.g. under the Council Framework Decision on the European arrest warrant and the surrender procedures between Member States of 13 June 2000, 2002/485/JHA (in *Official Journal of the European Community* L 190/1 of 18 July 2002) applicable to an array of serious crimes, including those under the jurisdiction of the ICC (Art. 2); or under EU Council Framework Decision 2002/465/JHA, 12 June 2002, establishing joint investigative teams, replaced by the EU Convention on Mutual Assistance in Criminal Matters of 29 May 2005.

127 Differentiated (i.e., high security) regimes for persons convicted for serious crimes, e.g. terrorism or organized crime, are compatible with Human Rights Law and consist, e.g., of various degrees of isolation and other high security measures. See, e.g., ECHR, *Ganci v. Italy*, Application No. 41576/98, Section II, 20 September 2001.

128 National systems sometimes provide schemes for compensation and redress for the effects of serious crimes, including terrorism. At the international level see, e.g., Art. 8(4) of the International Convention for the Suppression of the Financing of Terrorism, *supra* note 112, but also Art. 2 European Convention on the Compensation of victims of Violent Crimes, 24 November 1983, CETS No. 116, and the Guidelines of the

(c) Threshold element

However, the gravity[129] of the crimes is also attached to the subject matter jurisdiction because it is incorporated as a threshold element for the punishment of the crimes under the Statute at the international level,[130] although it is only mandatory for crimes against humanity ('acts ... committed as a part of a widespread or systematic attack directed against any civilian population'),[131] which cannot be investigated and prosecuted by the ICC when consisting of isolated acts. However, in the case of war crimes the threshold appears to be of a discretionary nature ('*in particular* when committed as a part of a plan or a policy or as part of a large-scale commission of such crimes'),[132] thus allowing the Court to deal with isolated acts that, nonetheless, would still have to meet the gravity criterion required under the Statute in order to come within the jurisdiction of the ICC.

(d) Selection of cases

Gravity is also a crucial criterion which presides over the selection of cases which deserve the initiation of an investigation[133] and a prosecution to be carried out,[134] on the basis of relevant factors[135] including the:

(i) scale of the crimes;
(ii) nature of the crimes;
(iii) manner of commission of the crimes or *modus operandi*;
(iv) impact of the crimes.

Committee of Ministers of the Council of Europe on Human Rights and the Fight against Terrorism, 11 July 2002, at VII and XVII.

129 Preamble (4) ICCSt and Art. 5(1) *chapeau* ICCSt (most serious crimes of concern to the international community as a whole); Art. 1 ICCSt (most serious crimes of international concern); Article 17(1)(d) ICCSt (sufficient gravity to justify further action by the Court); Articles 7(1) and 8(1) *chapeaux* ICCSt (thresholds requirement); Art. 53(1)(c) and (2)(c) ICCSt (gravity of the crime as criterion for the Prosecutor to initiate an investigation or prosecuting).

130 At the national level, gravity is not required for the punishment of the same conducts criminalized under the Statute, both because of the primary duty of a state to exert criminal jurisdiction and because there is no obligation to implement substantive criminal law provisions of the Statute in national legislation, although this might make a case admissible when resulting in inability to prosecute. See R. Bellelli, Cooperation and Implementation, *supra* note 22, at 2(B)(6).

131 Art. 7(1) ICCSt.

132 Art. 8(1) ICCSt. Emphasis added

133 Art. 53(1)(c) ICCSt: '[In deciding whether to initiate an investigation, the Prosecutor shall consider whether] taking into account the gravity of the crime ... there are nonetheless substantial reasons to believe that an investigation would not serve the interests of justice.'

134 Art. 53(2)(c) ICCSt: '[If, upon investigation, the Prosecutor concludes that there is not a sufficient basis because] a prosecution is not in the interest of justice, taking into account all circumstances, including the gravity of the crime.'

135 See Office of the Prosecutor (OTP), *Draft Policy Paper on Selection Criteria*, June 2006, at II(B), page 5; also quoted in OTP, *Report on Prosecutorial Strategy*, 14 September 2006, at II(2)(b), page 5. Available at http://www.icc-cpi.int/NR/rdonlyres/699AA4B3-E8C2-4E41-9EFA-EBA503BDBF7F/143694/OTP_ProsecutorialStrategy20060914_English.pdf (visited 20 August 2009). See also the *Prosecutorial Strategy 2009–2012* (Draft), 18 August 2009, *supra* note 72.

(e) Admissibility stage

Gravity, again, comes into play as an admissibility requirement because a case which 'is not of a sufficient gravity to justify further action by the Court' would be inadmissible.[136]

(f) Other effects: Article 124 ICCSt opt-out claus

As the discretionary nature of the gravity threshold for war crimes enables the Court to decide on a case-by-case basis whether to exert jurisdiction over an incident, at the 1998 Rome Diplomatic Conference some delegations held strong concerns on the exclusion of reservations to the Statute.[137] Thus, the Article 124 derogation to the rule of non-applicability of reservation may be considered a result of the (discretionary) low gravity threshold for the prosecution of war crimes under the Statute.

C. Individual Criminal Responsibility

1. Natural Persons

The Court only deals with the individual criminal responsibility[138] of natural persons responsible for the crimes under its jurisdiction. As a criminal court, the ICC is only called upon to adjudicate conducts prohibited and criminalized under its substantive criminal law provisions, when those conducts are committed by:

> (a) nationals of a State Party or of a state that has accepted the jurisdiction of the Court, on the territory of any state;[139]
> (b) nationals of any state, on the territory of a State Party or of a state that has accepted the jurisdiction of the Court;[140]
> (c) nationals of any state, on the territory of any state, in case a referral is made by the Security Council acting under Chapter VII of the Charter.[141]

Therefore, the Court has no competence on the international responsibility of states,[142] in particular under the system established by the UN Charter. The limitation of the Court's mandate in this regard is particularly evident in the negotiations on the crime of aggression. Here, the most contentious and still unresolved issue pertains to the independence of the Court in assessing the existence of an act of aggression, versus the competence conferred on the Security Council to the determine

136 Art. 17(1)(d) ICCSt.

137 Art. 120 ICCSt. See *supra*, 4(A)(2)(d) and R. Bellelli, The Law of the Statute, *supra* note 10, at 3(C).

138 Art. 25 ICCSt.

139 Art. 12(2)(b)and (3) ICCSt.

140 Art. 12(2)(a) and (3) ICCSt.

141 Art. 12(2) *chapeau* and Art. 13(b) ICCSt.

142 Art. 25(4) ICCSt: 'No provision in this Statute relating to individual criminal responsibility shall affect the responsibility of States under international law.' See also ILC, *Responsibility of States for Internationally Wrongful Acts*, Annex to UNGA Resolution 56/83, 12 December 2001, Doc. A/56/49(Vol. I)/Corr. 4., Art. 58: 'these articles are without prejudice to any question of the individual responsibility under international law of any person acting on behalf of a State.'

the existence of an act of aggression,[143] which results in the dilemma of whether the primary responsibility conferred to the SC for the maintenance of international peace and security[144] is an exclusive responsibility or not.

In addition, although experience has shown that legal persons[145] might well play a role in the commission of crimes of international concern, principles of criminal liability under different legal systems did not allow agreement to be reached in Rome to subject legal persons to the jurisdiction of the Court.

2. Highest Responsibilities

The ICC, as a Court of last resort and due account taken also of the limited resources of an international tribunal, is intended to address only the most serious crimes committed by those bearing the highest responsibility. Thus, responsibilities at different and lower levels would necessarily need to be dealt with under the states' primary jurisdiction. Although in such cases states might occasionally be more willing to prosecute, the risk of opening an impunity gap requires that the responsibility to protect be activated and supported by other means of international assistance.[146]

(a) The seniority criterion

In line with the practice developed by other international tribunals,[147] the Court will follow a seniority criterion for investigation and prosecution[148] and not normally address low or intermediate

143 Art. 39 UN Charter.

144 Art. 24(1) UN Charter.

145 See N. Piacente, Impunity Gap, *supra* note 22, at 4.

146 See *supra*, at 2(C).

147 Articles 1 and 6 of the IMT Charter addressed the prosecution of '*major* war criminals of the European Axis' (emphasis added). Initially the *ad hoc* Tribunals also dealt with some intermediate and even low responsibilities, within a prosecutorial strategy aimed at thoroughly reflecting the criminality of a case, also charging responsibilities covering a wide range of conducts. It must also be noted that the same instance of appropriately capturing the impact of a pattern of conducts and organized criminal activities is among the rationale for a number of notions and tools under the Statute and Rules as well as in the interpretation of the ICTY's Chambers (e.g., 'same transaction', joinder of accused, joinder of charges, joint criminal enterprise). See also *infra* note 154. The definition of transaction under Rule 2(A) ICTY RPE is as follows: 'a number of acts or omissions whether occurring as one event or a number of events, at the same or different locations and being part of a common scheme, strategy or plan.' See also, e.g., ICTY, Reasons for Decision on Prosecution Interlocutory Appeal from Refusal to Order Joinder, *Milošević*, Appeals Chamber, 18 April 2002, paras 13–17, 21. It was SC Res. 1503 (2003) endorsing the completion strategy of ICTY which mandated the Tribunal to 'concentrat[e] on the prosecution and trial of the *most senior leaders suspected of being most responsible* for crimes within the ICTY's jurisdictions and [transfer] the cases concerning those who may not bear this level of responsibility to competent national jurisdictions, as appropriate, as well as the strengthening of the capacity of such jurisdictions' (PP7) (emphasis added). Thus, the SC, on the one hand, recognized that domestic capacity in the area of former Yugoslavia had increased and allowed national jurisdictions to deal with mid–low levels of responsibility while, on the other hand, it maintained a clear focus on the precarious situation of the rule of law in the region, under a yet to be finalized stabilization process.

148 *Paper on Some Policy Issues before the Office of the Prosecutor*, September 2003. Available at http://www.icc-cpi.int/NR/rdonlyres/1FA7C4C6-DE5F-42B7-8B25-60AA962ED8B6/143594/030905_Policy_Paper.pdf (visited 20 2009), at 3 and 7.

levels[149] of responsibility for crimes under its jurisdiction which, under the concurrent jurisdiction of states, are left to domestic prosecutions to address. The 'ordinary' accused before the ICC should, therefore, be individuals who are (or were) at the highest level of leadership and responsibility. This means that the Court faces a number of challenges. As individuals prosecuted at the international level hold senior positions in the political, military or police structures of their countries, they often may not be charged with direct physical perpetration of alleged crimes but rather because, by virtue of their leadership positions,[150] they are held responsible for crimes committed on a large scale. Jurisdiction over leadership crimes, therefore, entails extraordinary challenges in terms of complexity of evidence (e.g., in the reconstruction of the chain of command, which links the responsibility for the events to that of the accused), cooperation (e.g., when suspects are high officials still holding power) and overall resources needed.

Appropriate selection of cases for the jurisdiction of the ICC, therefore, requires a definition of who the 'most senior leaders' are: seniority should be assessed in the circumstances and include persons who – by virtue of both their *de iure* and/or *de facto* position and function in the relevant hierarchy – are alleged to have exercised such a degree of authority that it is appropriate to describe them as 'most senior' rather than as 'intermediate'.[151]

On similar basis the ICC has not been empowered with jurisdiction over minors.[152] Criminal responsibility for under-age persons would require substantive and procedural special rules in order to fully reflect the prevailing complex implications of socialization of minors and the wish to suppress criminal conducts at the international level.

By contrast, criminal liability is not only addressed under the ordinary modes of responsibility, that is that of the principal perpetrator and of the accomplices, facilitators or others contributing to the commission of the crime – including[153] through a joint criminal enterprise[154] – or to the attempt to commit a crime under the jurisdiction of the Court;[155] in fact, the highest levels of responsibility are not only considered in the Statute under the gravity of the crime, but also directly taken into account under the general principles of criminal law related to the official capacity and command responsibility of perpetrators.

149 For the ICTY Completion Strategy, the Security Council reiterated that the transfer to competent national jurisdictions should involve 'intermediate and lower rank accused'. SC Res. 1534 (2004), OP 6.

150 ICTY-UNICRI (eds), *ICTY Manual on Developed Practices* (Torino: UNICRI, 2009), at IX, para. 54, page 121 (hereinafter, ICTY Manual). Available at http://www.icty.org/sid/10145 (visited 20 August 2009). See also *infra*, 4(A)(2)(c).

151 ICTY, Decision on Referral of Case Pursuant to Rule 11*bis*, *Dragomir Milošević*, Referral Bench, 8 July 2005, para. 22.

152 Art. 26 ICCSt.

153 Art. 25(3)(a) to (d) ICCSt. The crime of genocide can also be committed by direct and public incitement (Art. 25(3)(e) ICCSt) in conformity with Art. 3(c) UN Convention on the Prevention and Punishment of the crime of Genocide (New York, 9 December 1948).

154 The notion of joint criminal enterprise (JCE or 'theory of common purpose') has been settled in the ICTY case law as a form of responsibility under international customary law, JCE was already formed before the conflict in former Yugoslavia. See Judgment, *Duško Tadić*, Appeals Chamber, 15 July 1999, paras 185–229, and Judgment, *Milorad Krnojelac*, Appeals Chamber, 17 September 2003, para. 29. See also *supra* note 147.

155 Art. 25(3)(f) ICCSt.

(b) Irrelevance of official capacity

The law of the Statute is equally applicable to all persons, and no discrimination for purposes of criminal liability (or mitigation of sentence) can be based on the official or private status of a person.[156] Further, no immunity of whatever nature (substantial, procedural, national or international) can bar the exercise of jurisdiction by the Court.[157]

These rules operate at the two different levels of criminal responsibility and of jurisdiction, and reflect the very basic human rights law principle of equality before the law, as well as established international law principles[158] related to crimes of international concern under the jurisdiction of the Court, and are consistent with the overall purpose of the Statute to fight impunity for such crimes.

Therefore, the jurisdiction of the Court would not be affected by any decision of national courts based on immunities relevant to the domestic legal order. Although the Statute leaves discretion to states as the to the rules applied at the national level, should immunities be granted before a domestic court, under the complementarity regime this could be considered as a case of inability or unwillingness to investigate and prosecute;[159] thus, granting of immunities in national proceedings

---

156 Art. 27(1) ICCSt: 'this Statute shall apply equally to all persons without any distinction based on official capacity … [which] shall in no case exempt a person from criminal responsibility … nor … constitute a ground for reduction of sentence.' Under Art. 7(2) ICTYSt the same rules are applicable and the Tribunal held that '[as] one of the fundamental aims of the international criminal courts and tribunals is to end impunity and ensure that serious violations of international humanitarian law are prosecuted and punished … [the] accused … can have no legitimate expectation of immunity'. Decision on Karadžić's Appeal of Trial Chamber's Decision on Alleged Holbrooke Agreement, *Radovan Karadžić*, Appeals Chamber, 12 October 2009, at para. 52. However, the Tribunal acknowledges a possible mitigating effect to *de facto* immunities, as the accused has a 'right to present trial evidence supporting allegations [of an Agreement on immunity which] could be considered for the purpose of sentencing, as appropriate'. Ibid., at para. 55. In *Bashir*, while addressing immunity in the context of jurisdiction *ratione personae*, the ICC only 'noted' that the provisions under Art. 27 ICCSt are envisaged in order to achieve the goal of fighting against impunity. Decision on the Prosecution's Application for a Warrant of Arrest against Omar Hassad Ahmad Al Bashir, Pre-Trial Chamber I, 4 March 2009, paras 42 and 43.

157 Art. 27(2) ICCSt: 'national or international law immunities or special procedural rules which may attach to the official capacity of a person … shall not bar the Court from exercising its jurisdiction over such a person.' The rule finds also authority in ICJ, Judgment, *Arrest Warrant of 11 April 2000* (*Democratic Republic of the Congo v. Belgium*), 14 February 2002, para. 61: personal immunities enjoyed by an incumbent or former state official do not represent a bar to criminal prosecution, *inter alia*, before international courts having jurisdiction. See also ICTY, Decision on Karadžić's Appeal of Trial Chamber's Decision on Alleged Holbrooke Agreement, *supra* note 156, at para. 41: the 'Holbrook agreement' – which for the defence provided assurances of immunities – was considered irrelevant on the ground that 'even if the alleged Agreement were proved, it would not limit the jurisdiction of the Tribunal [nor otherwise] be binding on the Tribunal and it would not trigger the doctrine of abuse of process'. See also Art.10 STLSt and Art. 40 ECCCSt, *infra* note 170.

158 See, e.g., ILC, *Principles of International Law Recognized in the Charter of the Nürnberg Tribunal and in the Judgment of the Tribunal*, *Yearbook of the International Law Commission*, 1950, vol. II. In particular, Principle I on equal subjection to the law, and Principle III: 'the fact that a person who committed an act which constitutes a crime under international law acted as Head of State or responsible Government official does not relieve him from responsibility under international law.' Available at http://untreaty.un.org/ilc/texts/instruments/english/draft%20articles/7_1_1950.pdf (visited 20 August 2009).

159 *Infra*, 4(E)(4)(b)(ii). For the relevance of immunities under the inability criterion for admissibility of a case before the Court according to an experts' view commissioned by the ICC, see *infra* note 281.

with the intention of providing protection to suspects would actually produce the opposite result of directly exposing the immune person to international justice.

However, exemptions from the jurisdiction of the ICC could be based on agreements containing rules for the allocation of jurisdiction between sending and receiving states[160] (e.g., Status of Forces Agreements (SOFA) or Status of Mission Agreements (SOMA)) or other instruments for legal cooperation on criminal matters (e.g., extradition). When such agreements exist, the Court would be bound not to create a conflict between obligations under the Statute and under the agreement, and cannot proceed with a request for surrender unless it can first obtain the consent of the sending state.[161]

(c) Superior responsibility

The position of a person, being a military commander or a civilian superior, able to exercise effective authority and control over subordinates is an additional ground of responsibility. Willful failure to take action to prevent, repress or punish the commission of crimes by subordinates gives rise to the liability of the superior.[162] It is a well-established principle that the *de facto* or *de iure* position of responsibility vis-à-vis some fundamental rights creates a duty to prevent (or aggravates the liability for) the commission of serious offences. In relation to international crimes, this principle has become accepted and retained in the Statutes[163] and in the case law[164] of international tribunals and courts. Thus, here the Rome Statute reflects a customary rule by introducing in Article 28 specific modes of command responsibility, in addition to the ordinary ones established under Article 25:

> (i) Military commanders would be responsible for crimes committed by forces under their control on the basis of a *culpa in vigilando*. However, the presumption of knowledge of the unlawful activities carried out under the effective command and control is challengeable, e.g., by evidence of interruption of actual communication between the subordinates and the commander.
>
> (ii) Civilian superiors who failed to properly exercise control over their subordinates would also be responsible for crimes committed by them. Responsibility on such a ground is the most likely to raise issues of immunity as it may well refer to the positions of head of state, ministers and other high officials.

---

160 Art. 98(2) ICCSt.

161 On the relationship between obligations established for States Parties under the Rome Statute and under so-called Art. 98 agreements, see the EU Council Conclusions of 30 September 2002 and its Annex EU Guiding Principles concerning Arrangements between a State Party to the Rome Statute of the International Criminal Court and the United States Regarding the Conditions to Surrender of Persons to the Court, adopted to preserve the integrity of the Rome Statute and ensure respect of obligations resulting thereof, including for full cooperation with the ICC. EU Council Conclusions. Available at http://www.consilium.europa.eu/uedocs/cmsUpload/12134_02en.pdf (visited 20 August 2009).

162 Art. 28 ICCSt.

163 Art. 7(3) ICTYSt, Art. 6(3) ICTRSt, Art. 6(3) SCSLSt, Art. 29 ECCCSt and Art. 3(2) STLSt.

164 See, e.g., IMT, *US v. Wilhelm List et al.*, Trials of War Criminals before the Nuremberg Military Tribunals under Control Council Law No. 10, vol. XI, at 1298; ICTY, Judgment, *Pavle Strugar*, 31 January 2005, 359–366, at 364.

As command responsibility is an additional mode of responsibility, it may well coexist with other grounds so that the same person can be charged for the commission of crimes perpetrated directly – as a participant, often performing a leading role in a joint criminal enterprise[165] – and because of his/her tolerance or acceptance of criminal acts committed by subordinates.

(d) Amnesties

Amnesty laws are usually adopted as part of social reconciliation processes in the aftermath of conflicts[166] or authoritarian regimes. It is normally argued that amnesties effectively contribute to social stability, but positive and negative effects can only be weighed over a lengthy period of time. The Italian post-WW II amnesty legislation, for instance, has left open wounds which, after more than 60 years,[167] are still debated in society[168] and among political parties as a determining factor of divisiveness, instability and, in the end, reduced ability to ensure governance.

No rule on amnesties is included under the Statute, nor there is any internationally binding ban on amnesties for crimes of international concern, although the jurisprudence has found that national amnesties do not apply to international prosecutions[169] and a practice of discouraging such amnesties seems to have emerged in the international community. In this regard, a clear stand was taken against the effect of amnesty laws on proceedings for international crimes at the international level under Article 6 STLSt: 'an amnesty granted to any person for any crime falling within the jurisdiction of

165 See *supra*, 4(C)(2)(a) and notes 147 and 154.

166 Most peace treaties, under traditional international law, included provisions on amnesties for war crimes. See A.M. Shukri, Individual Responsibility for the Crime of Aggression, in this Volume, at 2(A)(1).

167 See also *supra*, 3(B). The situation has not been different, e.g., in Chile or Argentina. See HRW (Human Rights Watch), *Selling Justice Short: Why Accountability Matters for Peace*, July 2009, at 115 (hereinafter, 2009 HRW Report). Available at http://www.hrw.org/node/84264 (visited 13 October 2009).

168 See *supra*, 1(B) and, e.g., G. Pansa, *Il sangue dei vinti* (Milano: Sperling & Kupfer, 2003).

169 SCSL, Decision on Challenge to Jurisdiction, *Morris Kallon, Brima Bazzy Kamara*, Appeals Chamber, 13 March 2004. See R. Winter, The Special Court for Sierra Leone, in this Volume, at 6. This is valid also for *de facto* amnesties, as it is 'well established that any immunity agreement in respect of an accused indicted for genocide, war crimes and/or crimes against humanity before an international tribunal would be invalid under international law'. ICTY, Decision on Accused's Second Motion for Inspection and Disclosure: Immunity Issue, *Radovan Karadžić*, 17 December 2008, para. 25. Also, A. Cassese, *International Law* (2nd edn, Oxford: Oxford University Press, 2005), at 208 for the argument that peremptory norms of *jus cogens* 'de-legitimize[s] any legislative or administrative act authorizing the prohibited conduct. Consequently, national measures … granting amnesty … may not be accorded international legal recognition', also citing ICTY, Judgement, *Anto Furundžija*, Trial Chamber, 10 December 1998, at 154–157. See also the *Report of the Secretary-General on the Rule of Law and Transitional Justice in Conflict and Post-Conflict Societies*, UN Doc. S/2004/616, 23 August 2004, para. 64(c), recommending that 'peace agreements and Security Council resolutions and mandates: … reject any endorsement of amnesty for genocide, war crimes, or crimes against humanity … ensure that no such amnesty previously granted is a bar to prosecution before any United Nations-created or assisted court'. However, see also: SC Res. 1325 (2000), OP 11, which 'stresses the need to exclude [serious crimes of international concern], *where feasible* from amnesty provisions'; Principle 7 of the 2001 Princeton Principles on Universal Jurisdiction, stating that 'amnesties are *generally inconsistent* with the obligation of states to provide accountability for serious crimes under international law'; and the 2007 Nuremberg Declaration on Peace and Justice, whereby 'amnesties, other than for those bearing the greatest responsibility for genocide, crimes against humanity and war crimes, *may be permissible in a specific context*', UN Doc. A/62/885, 19 June 2008, para. IV, 2, 2.6 (emphases added).

the Special Tribunal shall not be a bar to prosecution.'[170] Moreover, and in particular in light of the concept of responsibility to protect, it is debated whether amnesties may also cover leadership crimes and the highest levels of responsibility for crimes under the jurisdiction of the Court.

Under the complementarity regime of the ICC, States Parties maintain their primary jurisdiction over the crimes under the Statute, and its normative framework would allow the exercise of domestic jurisdiction through acts which, in their substance, may show unwillingness or inability to prosecute: e.g., legislative or jurisdictional acts aiming at providing impunity. Discretionary primary jurisdiction would, thus, entail that States Parties would still be free to adopt amnesties, although this might amount to making a case admissible before the ICC,[171] unless a different interpretation of 'unwilling(ness) or inability to genuinely carry out the investigation or prosecution'[172] is provided by the Court which, so far, has only incidentally considered amnesties as a factor possibly influencing admissibility.[173]

Therefore, states willing to grant an amnesty rather than to prosecute in order to enhance social stability[174] should exclude crimes under the jurisdiction of the Court from the scope of amnesty

---

170 But see also Art. 10 STLSt ('amnesty … shall not be a bar to prosecution') and Art. 40 ECCCSt, whereby 'the scope of any amnesty and pardon that may have been granted prior to the enactment of [the Statute] is a matter to be decided by the Extraordinary Chambers'. Amnesty laws also occasionally excluded from their scope war crimes, genocide and crimes against humanity, as was the case of Article 1 Décret-loi N.03-001 du 15 avril 2003 portant amnistie pour de faits de guerre, infractions politiques et d'opinion, in *Journal Officiel de la République Démocratique du Congo*, 17 April 2003. Available at http://www.unhcr.org/refworld/country,LEGAL,,LEGISLATION,COD,,47305aae2,0.html (visited 30 September 2009).

171 In the advice of the French *Conseil Constitutionel* preliminary to the ratification of the Statute and which led to the amendment of the French Constitution, it was noted that an amnesty law or the applicability of statute of limitations might in itself result in the admissibility of a case before the ICC and that, in such cases, France could be requested for arrest and surrender in relation to facts covered by an amnesty or statutes of limitations. *Conseil Constitutionnel*, Decision, No. 98-408 DC, 22 January 1999, para. 34, *supra* note 98.

172 Art. 17(1)(a) ICCSt. On admissibility, see *infra*, 4(E)(4)(b).

173 ICC, Decision on the admissibility of the case under Article 19(1) of the Statute, *Joseph Kony et al.*, Pre-Trial Chamber II, 10 March 2009, ICC-02/04-01/05, para. 50. For the relevance of amnesties under the inability criterion for admissibility of a case before the Court according to an expert's view commissioned by the ICC, see *infra* note 281. On the relationship between *ne bis in idem* and amnesties, see also C. Van den Wyngaert and T. Ongena, 'Ne bis in idem Principle, Including the Issue of Amnesty', in Cassese, Gaeta and Jones, *supra* note 39, at 726–727.

174 Under Art. 6(5) of Additional Protocol II of 1977 'at the end of the hostilities, the authorities in power shall endeavour to grant the broadest possible amnesty to persons who have participated in the armed conflict, or those deprived of their liberty for reasons related to the armed conflict'. See A.-M. La Rosa and G.C. Tafur, Implementing International Humanitarian Law through the Rome Statute, in this Volume, note 11. In the situation in the Central African Republic (CAR), the need to enforce wide-ranging amnesty laws for reconciliation purposes was set out openly as a reason for prompting an intervention of the Security Council under Article 16 ICCSt: 'aboutir à une Loi d'amnisite générale des personnes impliquée dans ces crimes' and 'afin qu'une resolution soit adoptee dans le sens selon lequel les jurisdictions centrafricaines restent compétentes pour les faits couvrant les périodes prises en compte par les lois d'amnistie.' Letter addressed to the UN Secretary General on 1 August 2008 by the Head of State, François Bozize. Also at the national level, amnesty laws should not be able to indiscriminately cover up crimes committed. 'Blanket amnesties' and 'self-amnesties' have been declared illegal, e.g., by the Inter-American Court of Human Rights in Peru in IACHR, Judgement, *Barrios Altos v. Peru*, 30 November 2001, paras 41 and 44 (case under the Fujimori regime). Also in IACHR, Judgement, *Almonacid-Arellano et al. v. Chile*, 26 September 2006, paras 129 and 152, the Court deprived the amnesty bill (cases under the Pinochet regime) of legal effect as it was found to be incompatible with the Inter-American Convention because it intended to grant amnesty for crimes against humanity.

laws if they want to: (a) retain their primary jurisdiction; (b) respect their obligations under the Statute; and (c) comply with their obligations under international law. In this regard, while it seems that whatever amnesty should address any of the Statute's crimes would not be relevant to the jurisdiction of the Court, it is apparent that an amnesty adopted by a State Party would still have effects on the jurisdiction of the Court insofar as the state would most likely find itself unable to comply with its cooperation obligations under the Statute:[175] judicial and governmental authorities would most likely directly implement amnesty provisions which, as *lex specialis* and *in favor rei*, would prevail at the internal level on implementing provisions of the Statute. In light of this and of the overall objective of the Statute to fight impunity, adopting an amnesty which does not exclude Statute crimes might raise an issue of good faith performance of obligations arising from the Statute itself.[176]

(e) Peace vs. justice dilemma

The practice of the operations of the Court in conflict-torn areas has shown the constant tension between the reasons of peace and those of criminal accountability. This 'peace versus justice dilemma' is a reality emerging from the balance of powers on the ground, where negotiations between states and armed groups in conflict, on the one hand, and with the international community, on the other, are often held hostage of the call for impunity as a pre-condition for reaching agreements.[177] While different situations may call for different solutions,[178] it seems that the collective practice of states has affirmed the principle of legality as a basis of the international order and, in this respect, the building of peace[179] cannot be detrimental to international and individual accountability established under both customary and treaty law.

175 Art. 87 ICCSt.

176 Art. 26 (*Pacta sunt servanda*) Law of Treaties: 'every treaty ... must be performed [by the parties] in good faith.' See *supra* note 95. In DRC, with Article 1 Décret-loi N.03-001 du 15 avril 2003 portant amnistie pour de faits de guerre, infractions politiques et d'opinion, in *Journal Officiel de la République Démocratique du Congo*, 17 April 2003, an amnesty was granted for acts committed in war time, political and opinion offenses, with the exception of war crimes, genocide and crimes against humanity. Available at http://www.unhcr.org/refworld/country,LEGAL,,LEGISLATION,COD,,47305aae2,0.html (visited 30 September 2009).

177 'Les arguments mettant en avant la paix peuvent être de mauvaise foi, dans la mesure où un tel processus n'existe en fait pas': FIDH, CPI – Les Premières Années del la Cour Pénale Internationale, Mars 2009, No. 516f and 'Rhéthorique contre réalité au Darfour – Les exactions continuent malgré l'offensive de charme du gouvernement', available at http://www.fidh.org/spip.php?article6074 (visited 20 August 2009). For a possible solution to ensure that peace and justice follow separate avenues and mutually respect the role of politics and law, see R. Bellelli, The Law of the Statute, *supra* note 10, at 9, in particular 9(H)(2).

178 A suggestion for 'provisional immunity in order to achieve peace first' in the situation of DRC/Ituri was contained in a letter addressed by the President of Uganda Yoweri Kaguta Museveni to the UNSG Kofi Annan on 3 July 2004. In the case of Bosco Ntaganda, formerly commander of the Laurent Nkunda's founded armed militia *Congrès National pour la Défense du Peuple* (CNDP), the accused obtained a senior position in the Congolese Government with his integration into the National Army and the interests of peace have been prioritized on the enforcement of the ICC arrest warrant.

179 See also *infra*, 4(D). In *2009 HRW Report*, *supra* note 167, the analysis of the interplay between peace and justice shows that, with the exception of Angola, the practice of *de iure* or *de facto* amnesties has damaged rather than facilitated a stable peace.

D. The Trigger Mechanism

Differently from all other previous and contemporary forms of international-ized criminal justice, the system of the Statute requires that the jurisdiction of the Court be triggered on a flexible basis: the permanent and theoretically universal nature of the jurisdiction of the ICC does not allow for situations and cases to be identified *a priori* with reference to any given conflict, period of time or accused.[180] Thus, while other international-ized jurisdictions were mandated to deal with specific situations,[181] the normative framework of the ICC leaves open the potential number of situations which might fall under its jurisdiction. The Rome Statute devises a mechanism for triggering the jurisdiction of the Court which empowers the following, based on established principles in international law:

> (i) States Parties,[182] as treaties can only bind parties thereto (*res inter alios acta tertium neque nocet neque prodest*).[183]

This seemed at first sight to be the primary option available to all States Parties to discharge collectively or separately their responsibility to protect by availing themselves of an agreed international mechanism. However, the experience of the first years at the Court shows that States Parties are not necessarily eager to refer situations not concerning their own territories or nationals, as they would rather leave the Prosecutor to analyze situations and make use of his discretion under the many facets of the complementarity principle.

In this regard, an initially unforeseen variant to the referral under Article 13(a) ICCSt has been witnessed: a state that has jurisdiction on criminal conducts committed on its territory or by its nationals deciding to resort to the jurisdiction of the Court.[184] The logic of the Statute was based on historical experiences whereby states were reluctant to exert jurisdiction on serious crimes of international concern. Thus, it was understood that a state unwilling to investigate and prosecute[185] would also have not been willing to refer cases to an international jurisdiction. However, a lesson which has been learned through the first self-referrals by States Parties is that states may be unwilling to exert their jurisdiction but at the same time be willing that the ICC steps in. In the same vein, states may argue their inability to deliver domestic justice,[186] but be able to support the jurisdiction of the Court.[187] This living notion of states' referrals may fuel different reflections.

On the one hand, the interest of a State Party in self-referring a situation in which crimes under its jurisdiction may have been committed may well not be founded on reasons of objectively verifiable 'total or substantial collapse or unavailability of its national judicial system'.[188] A political agenda – although motivated by the predominant need for ensuring the peace in a conflict-torn area

180 See P. Kirsch and D. Robinson, 'Referral by States Parties', in Cassese, Gaeta and Jones, *supra* note 59, at 619–626.

181 See *supra*, at 3(E).

182 Art. 13(a) ICCSt. See P. Kirsch and D. Robinson, Referral by States Parties, *supra* note 180.

183 Art. 34 (*General rule regarding third States*) Law of Treaties: 'A treaty does not create either obligations or rights for a third State without its consent.' See *supra* note 95.

184 Situations in Uganda (December 2003), Democratic Republic of the Congo (3 March 2004), Central African Republic (22 December 2004).

185 Art. 17(1)(a) and (2) ICCSt.

186 Art. 17(1)(a) and (3) ICCSt.

187 See *infra*, E(4)(a) and notes 272 and 279.

188 Art. 17(3) ICCSt.

by bringing justice through the, uncontroversial among parties in conflict, international legitimacy of the ICC – bears in itself a high potential for challenges to be brought to the jurisdiction of the Court, both in judicial proceedings and in the international arena, as political motives change with the situation on the ground. Practice has shown that, depending on the circumstances and mainly on the negotiations in peace processes, states willing, in principle, to support the jurisdiction of the Court might be then willing to call for an Article 16 ICCSt deferral of the jurisdiction of the Court by the Security Council acting under Chapter VII of the Charter. In cases of self-referrals, however, a reversal of such state decisions might not really be reconcilable with the principle of complementarity, unless admissibility is successfully challenged according to the Statute, ordinarily within the deadline of the commencement of the trial.[189]

On the other hand, in a system of international criminal justice totally dependent on cooperation,[190] self-referrals have the major advantage of providing a sufficiently reliable basis for the action of the ICC, at least when early and crucial decisions on jurisdiction, admissibility and investigations have to be taken. Furthermore, risks for politically motivated referrals or self-referrals are counterbalanced under the Statute's system by the powers of analysis of the Prosecutor[191] as well as at the admissibility stage.[192]

(ii) The Security Council,[193] acting under Chapter VII of the UN Charter, for its primary responsibility in the maintenance of international peace and security.[194]

The referral authority of the SC is based on its global responsibilities and executive powers recognized by all States Parties upon their common participation in the UN Charter. However, the status of the referring body, be it a State Party or the SC, does not in principle influence the independent role of the Court in assessing its jurisdiction over a situation, the admissibility of a case and, *a fortiori*, the merits of the information received. It is, on the other hand, the Article 16 ICCSt deferral power that calls into play the primacy of the Council vis-à-vis the states' responsibilities in matters of international peace and security: the additional power of the SC to defer investigations and prosecutions for renewable periods of 12 months was formally intended as a safeguard mechanism for balancing justice with the critical interests of the international community to ensure peace and security, but was in substance aimed at counterbalancing the independence of the Court and the width of its jurisdiction. Empowering the Council with deferral authority, on the one hand, explicitly recognizes the limits of judicial proceedings by themselves achieving the high expectations placed by states on the Court. On the other hand, the Security Council is a forum functioning under its own political rules, which might from time to time see prevailing different

189 Art. 19(4) ICCSt: 'In exceptional circumstances, the Court may grant leave for a challenge to be brought … at a time later than the commencement of the trial.' Interpretation of the notion of 'commencement of trial', although it normally refers to the confirmation of charges, would in practice depend on the provision to apply: ICC, Motifs de la decision orale relative à l'exception d'irrecevabilité de l'affaire (Article 19 du Statut), *Germain Katanga and Mathieu Ngudjolo Chui*, PTC II, 16 June 2009, para. 42. The decision was upheld by the Judgement on the Appeal of Mr. Germain Katanga against the Oral Decision of Trial Chamber II of 12 June 2009 on the Admissibility of the Case, Appeals Chamber, 25 September 2009.

190 See *supra*, 4(A)(2)(a).

191 Art. 15(2) ICCSt.

192 Articles 17 and 18 ICCSt.

193 Art. 13(b) ICCSt.

194 Art. 24(1) UN Charter. On the SC powers vis-à-vis the ICC, see L. Condorelli and S. Villalpando, 'Referral and Deferral by the Security Council', in Cassese, Gaeta and Jones, *supra* note 59, at 627–655.

strategies,[195] although the coming into play of veto rights together with a strong support for a credible Court may in practice act as a deterrent to the adoption of a deferral resolution.

(iii) The Prosecutor,[196] on a *proprio motu* determination, to safeguard the independence of the Court.

This can be read as the insurance that, should political considerations hinder the triggering of the Court's jurisdiction under the other legs of the mechanism, the ICC may still be able to conduct independent investigation and prosecution on a situation falling under its jurisdiction.

The power of the Prosecutor to autonomously initiate investigations is largely discretionary,[197] although not unlimited and unchecked as: it has to be based on information received on the commission of crimes under the Statute; the seriousness of such information should pass the test of providing 'a reasonable basis to proceed with an investigation';[198] the decision of the Prosecutor to initiate an investigation is subject to judicial authorization by the Pre-Trial Chamber.[199]

In spite of such safeguards from arbitrary and politicized investigation, the independence of the Court and of its Prosecutor were, both in Rome and thereafter, a concern for some states, which often referred to the 'non-accountability' of the Prosecutor as a flaw in the Statute. However, while it is historically correct that the Rome Statute – established by treaty between equally sovereign states – departs from and innovates the previous practice of international-ized tribunals and courts established under the aegis of the United Nations and of the Security Council, accountability is a built-in feature of the Rome Statute: both the judges and the Prosecutor are answerable for their conduct and compliance with duties before the Assembly of States Parties,[200] which can also provide oversight on their management functions.[201]

Furthermore, practice has shown that so far not one of the situations dealt with by the Court has been the result of a decision solely by the Prosecutor. States, and even the Security Council, have instead entrusted the Court with jurisdiction in such situations, thus showing appreciation and trust for the actions of the ICC. The fact that the Prosecutor had not to resort to his power of *motu proprio* investigation in the situations of the Democratic Republic of the Congo, Uganda, the

195 See, in this regard, the deferrals decided *in abstracto*, independently from a given situation, with the exemption from the jurisdiction of the ICC over peacekeepers under SC Res. 1422 (2002) and its roll-over in SC Res. 1487 (2003), adopted to allow the renewal of UN missions for peacekeeping operations; the enhanced exemption from the jurisdiction, both of the ICC and of third States, introduced by SC Res. 1497 (2003) for the establishment of the Multinational Force in Liberia; and the 'soft' implementation of the SC Res. 1593 (2005) referring the situation in Sudan/Darfur to the ICC. See also *infra* note 211. On the other hand, some calls or requests for deferral under Article 16 ICCSt might have not been effectively proceeded with at the Council's level. See, e.g., the request contained in the letter dated 1 August 2008 by the President of the Central African Republic, *supra* note 174. Also, in the (unsigned) Agreement on Implementation and Monitoring Mechanism, 29 February 2008, Juba/Sudan, the government of Uganda committed to seek an Article 16 deferral of cases against LRA leaders. See *Human Rights Watch Memorandum for the Seventh Session of the International Criminal Court Assembly of States Parties*, 7 November 2008, note 6. Available at http://www.hrw.org/en/node/76652/section/3 (visited 30 September 2009).

196 Art. 13(c) ICCSt. See P. Kirsch and D. Robinson, 'Initiation of Proceedings by the Prosecutor', in Cassese, Gaeta and Jones, *supra* note 59, at 619–626.

197 Art. 15(1) ICCSt: 'the Prosecutor *may* initiate investigations *motu proprio*' (emphasis added).

198 Art. 15(2) and (3) ICCSt.

199 Art. 15(3)-(5) ICCSt.

200 Art. 46 ICCSt.

201 Art. 112(2)(b) ICCSts.

Central African Republic, and Sudan does not rule out that in other situations under analysis[202] he might be compelled to do so on the basis of the abundant flow of information his Office continuously receives[203] and should states or the SC not refer themselves a relevant situation.

E. Distinctive Principles of the Court

The Rome Statute establishes an international organization of permanent nature, independent from states or other organizations, theoretically universal in participation and territorial extension of its activities, aimed at the implementation of a criminal legal system[204] focused on complementing national jurisdictions in addressing the responsibility to protect populations from the commission of serious crimes of international concern. Thus, the crucial principles characterizing the ICC are the following: permanence, independence, universality and complementarity.

1. Permanence

(a) A jurisdiction for the future

An essential feature of the rule of law is that tribunals are created to apply criminal law to the generality of unlawful conducts and with a mandate that is not limited in time. The UN-established or -agreed Tribunals and Courts have been given a mandate limited in time because they were established to bring justice for serious violations of international humanitarian law or human rights that originated from one or more specific conflicts. Therefore, their jurisdiction has been limited to the period of commission of the crimes and their existence scheduled to last only the number of years necessary to complete their mandate.[205]

By contrast, the jurisdiction of the ICC aims to put an end to such crimes 'for the sake of present and future generations'[206] and, therefore, covers the core crimes included in the Rome Statute whenever they may be committed after its entry into force (1 July 2002). Consistently, no final term is set for the activities[207] of the organization, while under customary international law no statute of limitations is applicable[208] to crimes under the jurisdiction of the Court.

The permanent Court undoubtedly offers a number of major advantages vis-à-vis *ad hoc* jurisdictions:

---

202 Situations under analysis in July 2009 include those of Colombia, Georgia, Kenya, Cote d'Ivoire and Afghanistan. Also, the Palestinian National Authority accepted the jurisdiction of the ICC under Art. 12(3) ICCSt in January 2009, although its competence to do so will have to be decided by the Prosecutor.

203 During the period from 31 March 2004 to 13 July 2009, 8,273 communications were received by the Office of the Prosecutor from governmental and non-governmental sources.

204 See *supra*, at 4(A)(2)(a).

205 See *supra*, 3(B)(C) and (E).

206 Preamble (9) ICCSt.

207 Preamble (9) and (10) and Article 1 ICCSt. The issue of permanence obviously imposes no consequences on the non-retroactivity of criminal law (Art. 24 ICCSt) as the Rome Statute is non-retrospective and binds States Parties only after its entry into force (Art. 126 ICCSt), which should make immune proceedings at the ICC from objections raised before previous international jurisdictions. On the latter point, see *supra*, 3(A) and note 30.

208 Art. 29 ICCSt.

(i) The establishment of a court before crimes are committed makes it less likely that its operations might be politically driven by the specific situation and crimes in issue, or by *ad hoc* majorities in the policymaking body.
(ii) The creation of an uniform set of substantive and procedural criminal law provisions applicable to all cases, which identifies for the first time ever a real system for the forcible implementation of international humanitarian law.
(iii) The establishment before crimes are committed of clear criteria for the allocation of jurisdiction between states and the international Court, disregarding any possible political contingency.
(iv) The existence of one judicial organization that, by contrast to many *ad hoc* or hybrid tribunals, may contribute to reducing the costs of international criminal justice and ensuring reliable funding through the assessed contributions of States Parties.

However, the main advantage of the permanence of the ICC is that since the entry into force of the Rome Statute it has existed as an institutionalized mechanism to implement international criminal law, which produces a strong deterrent against the commission or continuation of the crimes under its jurisdiction.[209] It is also self-evident that the certainty of a permanent Court no longer allows perpetrators to hope that some day it might be forced by its own mandate to complete its activities, thus leading to the impunity of successful fugitives.

(b) An irreversible choice

The permanence of the ICC also means that the establishment of further limited jurisdictions after the entry into force of the Rome Statute needs to be more strongly justified, which is also the case in light of the advantages, in terms of credible and cost-efficient action, of availing the international community of one Court.

From this perspective, Security Council Resolution 1593 (2005) for the referral of the situation in Darfur/Sudan to the ICC has a historical importance. In fact, the SC had previously only negatively acknowledged the existence of the ICC, making use of its deferral powers under Article 16 ICCSt to introduce exemptions to the Court's jurisdiction which was purportedly seen as inherently constituting a threat against international peace and security.[210] The Darfur 1593 (2005) Resolution represents a historical achievement, as for the first time ever the SC – by acknowledging a role for the ICC in conflict prevention and resolution through the rejection of an alternative proposal for the establishment of an *ad hoc* Tribunal for Sudan[211] – has also put the bases for the affirmation of a one-international-court principle.[212]

More precisely, by adopting the Rome Statute the States Parties have decided to make systematic the repression of the most serious international crimes, and this should also be appreciated as a definite and final choice vis-à-vis the further applicability of the opposite and pre-ICC model of an

209 On the establishment of a new legal system and on its deterrent effect, see also *supra*, 4(A)(2)(a).

210 See *supra*, 4(D)(ii) and note 195 for SC Res. 1422 (2002), its roll-over Res. 1487 (2003), and Res. 1497 (2003).

211 The US had originally proposed an *ad hoc* Tribunal for Sudan, but eventually abstained on the referral resolution.

212 The 'one-court principle' is a concept devised for the purpose of enhancing consistency in the Court's actions, through internal coordination of its organs and rationalization of procedures and resources, thus impacting on the credibility of the ICC, including its outreach and communications. See, e.g., *Strategic Plan of the International Criminal Court*, ICC-ASP/5/6, 4 August 2006, paras 14–16.

occasional suppression of international crimes, based on *ad hoc* or mixed international tribunals. Although participation in any treaty is not an impediment to states taking different stands and approaches to the same subject matter on different occasions[213] – provided they do not breach any treaty obligation – this issue might be looked at differently when the treaty in question contains a general regulation of a subject matter itself. Obviously, the independence of the ICC from the UN and the fact that international or hybrid tribunals are established by SC authority under Chapter VII of the UN Charter do not preclude States Parties from taking a different view instead of supporting the jurisdiction of the ICC in any given situation. However, a distinction should be made between situations arising where the jurisdiction of the Court applies because of the territoriality or active nationality criteria,[214] and situations related to crimes committed on the territory of non-States Parties or against their nationals or before the entry into force of the Statute. In situations of the Article 12 ICCSt-type – i.e., falling under the ICC jurisdictional requirements – it might be reasonably argued that States Parties to the ICC cannot support the establishment of a different jurisdiction without violating their treaty law obligation to perform the obligations stemming from the Rome Statute in good faith.[215] On the other hand, when the situation at stake falls outside the jurisdictional scope of the ICC, it would only be a policy matter for States Parties to support a referral from the Security Council under Article 13(b) ICCSt.

2. Independence

According to established human rights law standards, the principle of equality before the law requires that the judicial power be safeguarded from any interference by other powers which might affect its impartiality.

As a treaty-based institution, the ICC is not dependent upon a policymaking body where only a few states are represented (as the Security Council is) and where states are afforded unequal voting rights as a result of veto powers granted to some of them: the ICC has been established by the States Parties to the Rome Statute and the Assembly of States Parties is its policymaking body that exerts its functions with equal votes of all Parties. The ASP has variegated normative and oversight functions[216] and the ICC judges and Prosecutor are accountable to it.[217] In this regard, the independence of the ICC is a qualifier for the judicial and prosecutorial functions.[218]

However, from another perspective the notion of independence relates to the status of the organization in the international order, as external independence of the ICC from the United

213 This is, e.g., the case for States Parties to treaties prohibiting certain weapons, when such states decide not to participate in other treaties, which make different weapons illegal.

214 Art. 12 ICCSt on 'preconditions to the exercise of jurisdiction'.

215 Art. 26 (*Pacta sunt servanda*) Law of Treaties. See *supra* note 95.

216 Art. 112 ICCSt: adoption of the fundamental instruments provided for under the Final Act, Annex I(F)(4); amendments and review of the Statute at a Review Conference (Articles 121 and 123 ICCSt); overlook the settlement of disputes between States Parties relating to the interpretation or application of the Statute (Art. 119(2) ICCSt); provide management oversight and approve the budget (Art. 112 ICCSt); elect the Judges (Art. 36 ICCSt), the Prosecutor and his deputies (Art. 42(4) ICCSt) upon nomination by States Parties and decide on their removal from office (Article 46).

217 Art. 46 ICCSt.

218 External independence for the judges (Articles 40(1) and 42(1)) and for the Prosecutor and his deputies (Art. 42(5) ICCSt); internal independence of the Prosecutor, also as an autonomous organ of the Court (Art. 42(1) ICCSt).

Nations[219] stresses its non-political nature. In spite of this, the common ground between the two international organizations is apparent in their respective mandates to contribute to the maintenance of international peace and security, which has made it necessary for the ICC and the UN to be brought into a relationship[220] through a Negotiated Relationship Agreement between the United Nations and the International Criminal Court.[221]

The principle of independence from the UN gains particular momentum in light of the role played by the Security Council in the establishment of the *ad hoc* Tribunals and other international justice mechanisms under the authority of Chapter VII of the Charter, as well as with regard to the powers of referral[222] and deferral[223] of ICC proceedings attributed to the Security Council under the Rome Statute. Although this may seem to affect the independent status of the ICC, the powers acknowledged to the Security Council by the States Parties to the Rome Statute are a result of the peculiar role that the ICC is called to perform in the framework of international peace and security.

3. Universality

By their very nature, the core crimes covered by the Statute are the most serious crimes of concern to the international community as a whole.[224] As such, the fight against them is a duty for every state,[225] but also requires collective efforts that, in the case of the ICC, are implemented through the widest possible participation in the Statute. In this regard, universality refers to the context were the treaty was promoted and negotiated, and therefore to its openness to participation by all states,[226] which is possible by virtue of the non-regional nature of the treaty.[227] The contextual and

---

219 Preamble (9) ICCSt.

220 Art. 2 ICCSt.

221 Adopted by the ASP (A/58/874 of 7 September 2004), approved by the UNGA (A/RES/58/318 of 13 September 2004), and entered into force upon its signature by the UNSG and the President of the ICC on 4 October 2004.

222 Art. 13(B) ICCSt.

223 Art. 16 ICCSt.

224 Preamble (4) ICCSt. The notion of 'crimes of concern to the international community as a whole' is equated, in the ICTY jurisprudence, to the concept of 'universally recognized crimes', also with relevant consequences in terms of legality of proceedings. In *Nikolić*, where the issue of unclear circumstances of arrest – through abduction by unidentified persons and surrender to the Tribunal by the Stabilization Force in Bosnia and Herzegovina (SFOR) – was brought by the defence, the Appeals Chamber held that it is possible to exert jurisdiction over individuals illegally detained in the case of 'Universally Condemned Offences', such as genocide, crimes against humanity and war crimes. ICTY, Decision on Interlocutory Appeal Concerning Legality of Arrest, *Dragan Nikolić*, Case No. IT-94-2-AR73, Appeals Chamber, 5 September 2003, para. 24. The rationale for overcoming the otherwise inevitable consequences of illegal detentions transpires from the same Decision, para. 25: 'there is a legitimate expectation that those accused of these crimes will be brought to justice swiftly. Accountability for these crimes is a necessary condition for the achievement of international justice, which plays a critical role in the reconciliation and rebuilding based on the rule of law of countries and societies torn apart by international and internecine conflicts.'

225 Preamble (6) ICCSt. *Supra*, at 2(C) for responsibility to protect and 2(A), and 4(E)(4)(a), for primary jurisdiction of states.

226 Art. 125(3) ICCSt. Participation is also reflected in the composition of the Court, where elected officials and all the staff reflect the diversity of the regional groupings. Aiming at universality, the Court's recruitment policy is open also to non-States Parties nationals, while only judges need to be nationals of States Parties (Art. 36(4)(b) ICCSt).

227 Preamble (1), (4), (5), (6) and (9) ICCSt.

expected expansive effect of the membership of the Statute is further reinforced by the capacity of the Court to enter into agreements with any state for purposes of discharging its functions,[228] including by sitting anywhere in the world.[229]

However, the concept of universality of the Court also relates to its jurisdiction, as this is binding not only on the territory of States Parties but also on the territory of any other state having accepted it[230] and on the territory of all states in case of referrals by the Security Council;[231] although there is no explicit mention to universality of jurisdiction under the Statute, its existence may be inferred from the regime under Article 13 ICCSt.

In spite of this, the notion of universality, when jurisdiction is not triggered by the Security Council, does not coincide with the principle of universal jurisdiction, which is an exception to the general rule of the assertion of jurisdiction based on the traditional links of territoriality, nationality, passive personality or the protective principle.[232] The limitations inherent in the

---

228 See, e.g., Arts 54(3)(d) ICCSt for arrangements or agreements entered by the Prosecutor for purposes of cooperation, and Art. 87(5) ICCSt for *ad hoc* arrangements or agreements for the purposes of assistance.

229 Art. 4(2) ICCSt: 'the Court may exercise its functions and powers ... on the territory of any State Party and, by special agreement, on the territory of any other State.'

230 Arts 4(2) and 12(3) ICCSt; Rule 44 ICC RPE.

231 Art. 13(b) ICCSt.

232 Universal jurisdiction was first introduced in international customary law in the seventeenth century with regard to piracy, enabling any state to arrest and bring to justice pirates with no regard to the nationality or territoriality criteria for jurisdiction. See A. Cassese, *International Criminal Law* (Oxford: Oxford University Press, 2003), 284–286. A further step in the development of the concept of universal jurisdiction is the principle *aut dedere aut judicare*. Many international conventions are based on this concept, including the 1949 Geneva Conventions and most terrorism conventions. This principle not only grants the state in whose territory the alleged perpetrator of an international crime is to be found the power to try such person, it also creates for such state the legal duty either to try the alleged perpetrator before its own courts or to extradite the person to another state which, having jurisdiction over the case, requests the extradition. However, universal jurisdiction and *aut dedere aut iudicare* are two conceptually distinct obligations, as the first consists of the prior obligation of the state to vest its courts with competence to try criminal conducts, while the obligation to prosecute or extradite arises only once the jurisdiction has been established. See, e.g. IACHR, *La Cantuta v. Peru*, Judgement, 29 November 2006, asserting the obligation to extradite former President Alberto Fujimori to Peru. The principle of universal jurisdiction in international law is based, in one way or another, on specific provisions: (a) the four Geneva Conventions of 12 August 1949 (Art. 49 GC I; Art. 50 GC II; Art. 129 GC III; Art. 146 GC IV); (b) Additional Protocol I of 8 June 1977 (Art. 85, which qualifies as grave breaches of the Protocol acts described as grave breaches of the GC); (c) the Convention for the Protection of Cultural Property in the Event of Armed Conflict (The Hague, 14 May 1954, Art. 28); (d) the International Convention on the Suppression and Punishment of the Crime of *Apartheid* (Art. IV, GA Res. 3068 (XXVIII), 30 November 1973); (e) the Convention against Torture and other Cruel, Inhuman or Degrading Treatment or Punishment (Art. 5(2), GA res. 39/46, 10 December 1984); (f) the Convention on the Prevention and Punishment of the Crime of Genocide (GA Res. 260 (III), 9 December 1948) does not expressly provide for universal jurisdiction, although it refers to an international tribunal which, however, was never established (Art. 6). However, universal jurisdiction for genocide is generally understood as a corollary of the customary nature of the crime (ICJ, Advisory Opinion, *Reservations to the Convention on the Prevention and Punishment of the Crime of Genocide*, 28 May 1951. Available at www.icj-cij.org/icjwww/idecisions/isummaries/ippcgsummary510528.htm (visited 30 September 2009). Furthermore, the *Draft Code of Crimes against the Peace and Security of Mankind* acknowledged the existence under international law of universal jurisdiction over the crimes listed in the Draft Code, contained an obligation to establish such jurisdiction (Article 8 – Establishment of jurisdiction) and acknowledged the entitlement of a State Party to exercise jurisdiction over individuals present in its territory and allegedly responsible for crimes

temporal, geographical, personal, and subject matter international jurisdictions make universal jurisdiction an essential tool in the hands of states in the fight against impunity for crimes of international concern.[233] Thus, universal jurisdiction proper is a notion that refers only to states because territory, personality and national interests – links on which jurisdiction could be based and which are derogated by the exercise of universal jurisdiction – are only attached to states and not to international tribunals. However, the many challenges posed by the exercise of universal jurisdiction have lead to consideration that 'as a matter of policy [it should be] accord[ed] priority to territoriality as a basis of jurisdictions, since such crimes, while offending against the international community as a whole by infringing universal values, primarily injure the community where they have been perpetrated … and … it is within the territory of the state of alleged commission that the bulk of the evidence will usually be found'.[234] It is, in other words, the primary obligation of states to protect their nationals or residents that, under the general framework of the responsibility to protect, should prevail in the allocation of jurisdiction.

However, a new and peculiar notion of universality may be inferred by the Rome Statute's system, where universal jurisdiction is not dealt with directly, but instead pursued through the complementarity mechanism: conducts not punished by states can be dealt with by the Court. The complementary action of the ICC would, thus, allow it to enforce universal jurisdiction.[235] It

---

under international law (1996 UN International Law Commission (ILC), Art. 9 – Obligation to extradite or prosecute). See also http://untreaty.un.org/ilc/texts/instruments/English/commentaries/7_4_1996.pdf (visited 30 September 2009) for the relevant commentaries, in particular to Art. 8, paras 7–9 to the Draft Code, and http://www1.umn.edu/humanrts/instree/princeton.html (visited 20 August 2009) for the *Princeton Principles on Universal Jurisdiction*. On the approaches to universal jurisdiction under IHL treaties, see A.-M. La Rosa and G.C. Tafur, Implementing International Humanitarian Law through the Rome Statute, in this Volume, at para. 4 and note 53.

233 EU Council, *The AU-EU Expert Report on the Principle of Universal Jurisdiction*, No. 8672/09 16 April 2009, para. 28. Available at http://ec.europa.eu/development/icenter/repository/troika_ua_ue_rapport_competence_universelle_EN.pdf (visited 20 August 2009).

234 Ibid., para. 46, Recommendation R9. Also, '[perpetrators] shall be subject to … punishment, as a general rule in the countries in which they committed [serious crimes of international concern]', according to the *Principles of international co-operation in the detection, arrest, extradition and punishment of persons guilty of war crimes and crimes against humanity*, Principle 5. GA Res. 3074 (XXVIII), 3 December 1973. Available at www.unhcr.org/refworld/type,THEMGUIDE,UNGA,,3ae6b37114,0.html (visited 20 August 2009).

235 Along the same rationale, Rule 11*bis* RPE referrals of the *ad hoc* Tribunals allow cases to be referred to willing and able jurisdictions outside the regions affected. According to the Completion Strategy, the Tribunals should transfer cases back to the national jurisdictions and complement this with assistance in strengthening the capabilities of the national legal systems to try war crimes cases according to international standards. A referral decision makes proceedings the primary responsibility of the domestic jurisdiction in question. However, the Tribunals maintain (Rule 11*bis*(D) ICTY/ICTR RPE) monitoring powers (exerted directly by the OTP or through observers) over cases deferred to domestic jurisdictions with the objective of ensuring that proceedings are conducted properly, with the Referral Bench maintaining authority for revoking the referral at any time, before (as a result of the *ne bis in idem* principle under Art. 10 ICTYSt and Art. 9 ICTRSt) an accused is found guilty or acquitted by a national court (Rule 11*bis*(F) ICTY/ICTR RPE). See, e.g., *Bagaragaza*, *infra* notes 281, 282 and 301. Rule 11*bis* only refers to cases investigated by the Prosecutor and with indictments confirmed. In addition, the completion strategy of ICTY also concerns so-called 'Category 2' cases – investigated by the Prosecutor, but not confirmed by indictment, due to the timetable set by the completion strategy – and 'Category 3' cases or 'Rules of the Road' cases, originated from paragraph 6 of the Rome Agreement of 18 February 1996 signed by the Presidents of Bosnia, Croatia and Serbia. Available at http://www.ohr.int/ohr-dept/hr-rol/thedept/war-crime-tr/default.asp?content_id=6093 (visited 20

cannot be underestimated that delicate questions could arise from the interaction of the principle of complementarity with the principle of universal jurisdiction proper, which is 'an important measure of last resort ... to ensure that perpetrators of serious crimes of international concern do not go unpunished',[236] as these are also the nature and the objective of the complementarity mechanism.

The admissibility of a case before the Court and the surrender of an alleged perpetrator to the ICC would, therefore, provide a third alternative to the traditional *aut dedere aut judicare* principle. The state where the suspect is present (custodial state), instead of prosecuting or granting the extradition requested by another state, also has the option of ensuring cooperation with the ICC for the exercise of its complementary jurisdiction. In particular, this option would come into play when a state, due to internal tensions, external political interference, weakness of its own judiciary or any other relevant reason, is unable or unwilling[237] to exercise its own jurisdiction over a case or to make a difficult political choice concerning competing requests for extradition. In such cases, a neutral and impartial forum, perceived as such by all, would constitute an effective tool for the application of international criminal law and represent a safeguard against impunity.

4. *Complementarity*

(a) Notion

As sovereign states bear the primary responsibility to suppress violations of criminal law and, namely, serious violations of international humanitarian law, the primacy of their jurisdiction is an essential feature of sovereignty.

Similarly, the application of the principle of primacy to the UN *ad hoc* Tribunals by the Security Council acting under Chapter VII of the Charter derives from the primary responsibility of the SC in the maintenance of international peace and security.[238] At the time of the establishment of the UN *ad hoc* Tribunals, the Security Council assessed as an irrebuttable presumption that competent national jurisdictions would have not been, in the circumstances, willing or able to genuinely

---

August 2009). See *ICTY Manual*, *supra* note 150, page 4. In the case of ICTY, monitoring is carried out by the Organization for Security and Co-operation in Europe (OSCE), whose competence is derived from Annex 6: Human Rights, of the Dayton Peace Agreement (*supra* note 20): 'The parties agree to grant UN Human rights agencies, the OSCE, the International Tribunal and other organizations full access to monitor the human rights situation.' Available at http://www.ohr.int/dpa/default.asp?content_id=380 (visited 30 September 2009) and also at http://www.state.gov/www/regions/eur/bosnia/bosagree.html (visited 20 August 2009). See also, *ICTY Manual*, *supra* note 150, at pages 170–171. The revocation safety proceeding is not matched by a similar power of the Tribunals for the enforcement of sentences imposed by a national jurisdiction upon referral under Rule 11*bis*. Different from the supervisory authority under Article 27 ICTYSt maintained by the Tribunal when enforcement concerns a sentence imposed by it, and which might lead to termination of the enforcement in compliance with the relevant sentence enforcement Agreements, no provision appears to be in place for settling cases in post-verdict situations like, e.g., that of an accused escaped from detention or when the state of enforcement is not otherwise able to properly enforce a sentence. For a specific case, see the very first referral case to Bosnia and Herzegovina (BiH), that of *Radovan Stanković* who, transferred on 29 September 2005, was finally convicted on 28 March 2007 to 20 years' imprisonment by the Court of BiH Appellate Panel, but escaped under unclear circumstances from the Foča prison on 25 May 2007, and still remains at large. Available at http://www.bim.ba/en/133/10/13106/ (visited 20 August 2009).

236 EU Council, The AU-EU Expert Report on the Principle of Universal Jurisdiction, para. 39, *supra* note 233.

237 Art. 17 ICCSt. See *supra*, 4(E)(4)(b).

238 Art. 24(1) UN Charter.

prosecute, taking into account that the ongoing conflicts in the region would have reasonably hindered the implementation of principles of impartial and fair prosecutions and trials.[239]

The same factual basis was obviously not applicable to the establishment of a permanent Court with non-retrospective jurisdiction, and this had to be taken into account when devising a mechanism for allocating its jurisdiction vis-à-vis the national ones.

As the ICC has neither sovereign powers on any territory nor a primary responsibility in the maintenance of international peace and security, the system of the Rome Statute acknowledges that:

> (i) 'it is the duty of every State to exercise its criminal jurisdiction over those responsible for international crimes';[240]
> (ii) aggression, genocide, crimes against humanity and war crimes are 'grave crimes [that] threaten the peace, security [and well-being] of the world';[241]
> (iii) the system of the ICC is in line with the purposes and principles of the Charter,[242] and therefore must be 'in relationship with the United Nations system'[243] and respect the primary responsibility of the Security Council under the Charter, by acknowledging its role in the determination of a threat to international peace and security resulting from the commission of such crimes (referral)[244] or from any interference that investigation or prosecution may have on actions under Chapter VII of the Charter (deferral).[245]

Consistently, the Statute reserves to the ICC a subsidiary role in the suppression of the most heinous crimes that deeply shock the conscience of humanity,[246] with the aim of 'put[ting] an end to impunity for the perpetrators of these crimes and thus to contribute to the prevention of such crimes'.[247] This feature of the ICC is referred to under the Statute as complementarity of jurisdiction,[248] as opposed to the primacy of the jurisdiction applied to the *ad hoc* Tribunals, which entails that states normally having jurisdiction over crimes cannot exert it unless international Tribunals do not prosecute. By contrast, core crimes[249] inherent to the ICC jurisdiction – genocide, crimes against humanity, war

---

239 The concurrent jurisdiction of ICTY, e.g., was established under the principle of primacy (Art. 9 ICTYSt), but this situation has changed over time. The completion strategies of the UN Tribunals led to the introduction of Rule 11*bis* ICTY RPE and to the formal acknowledgment of the seniority criterion (see *supra*, 4(C)(2)(a)), which together transformed the primacy into complementarity, still allowing the Tribunal to intervene with revocations of referrals (Rule 11*bis*(F) ICTY RPE) and requests for deferrals (Rule 10 ICTY RPE) if national jurisdictions are unwilling or unable to genuinely prosecute the case. See *supra* note 235 and 4(E)(3). Requirements for this complementarity mechanism are very much like those applicable under Art. 17 ICCSt. Under Art. 4(1) STLSt, primacy also regulates the relationship between the Lebanese jurisdiction and that of the Special Tribunal.

240 Preamble (6) ICCSt.

241 Preamble (3) ICCSt.

242 Preamble (7) ICCSt.

243 Preamble (9) and Art. 2 ICCSt.

244 Art. 13(b) ICCSt.

245 Art. 16 ICCSt.

246 Preamble (2) ICCSt.

247 Preamble (5) ICCSt.

248 Articles 1 and 17(1) ICCSt, in relation to Preamble (10) ICCSt and Rule 51 ICC RPE.

249 Only crimes against the administration of the justice of the Court fall under the primacy rule, although the Court may still request that they be prosecuted by states (Article 70(4)(b)).

crimes, and aggression[250] – can be prosecuted under the Rome Statute only when states that would normally exert jurisdiction (territorial and active personality criteria) do not exert it because they are unable or unwilling to genuinely do so.

Complementarity has, therefore, a multifaceted meaning:

(i) substitutive complementarity, which entails the intervention of a surrogate or substitute (international) judge where there is unwillingness or inability of the state to genuinely activate its primary jurisdiction;[251]
(ii) substantial complementarity, which is the activation of the jurisdiction of the ICC only where there is an absolute lack of domestic substantive criminal law provisions that results in the inability of the domestic legal system in the absence of adaptation to the Statute (absolute lack of authority for the domestic judge);[252]
(iii) procedural complementarity, which is subordination of the organs of the Court to international judicial cooperation for investigations and enforcement of decisions.[253]

Complementarity, therefore, refers to the role of integration of any lacunae in the international community's fight against impunity for the most serious crimes of its concern:[254] no impunity is allowed for Statute's core crimes and, in case domestic punitive systems are not able to bring to justice those bearing the highest responsibilities for such crimes, the international legal system replaces them.[255] But complementarity also captures the minimal nature of the international criminal legal system as an alternative to national ones: the jurisdiction of the Court is affirmed only in the vacuum left by states' jurisdictional power in the absence of a domestic provision attributing any authority to a national criminal judge or because the public powers have collapsed or investigation and prosecution are only intended to shield the perpetrator and grant impunity.

(b) Admissibility

The principle of complementarity enables the Court to step in to prosecute and punish those who bear the greatest responsibility for the most serious conducts of genocide, crimes against humanity or war crimes in any situation where states – whether States Parties of the ICC or non-State Parties having accepted the jurisdiction of the Court, or any state upon decision of the Security Council – are unwilling or unable to do justice at the national level, as 'national judicial processes [remain] the first line of defence against impunity'.[256]

The assessment of the compliance of states with their primary responsibility to protect or 'duty … to exercise … criminal jurisdiction over those responsible for international crimes'[257] follows an

250 Art. 5 ICCSt.

251 Art. 17(2)(a) ICCSt, depending on a willful omission to genuinely investigate or prosecute or on the unavailability of public powers because, e.g., the collapse originated from internal or international conflicts, as non-exhaustively mentioned in Art. 17(3).

252 Under Art. 17(1)(a), (2)(a) and (3) ICCSt.

253 Arts 86111 ICCSt.

254 Preamble (4), (5), (6) and (10) ICCSt.

255 For the systematic nature of the complex legal system established by the Rome Statute, linking the operation of the national and of the international criminal legal systems, see *supra*, 4(A)(2)(a).

256 UNSG Report, *Implementing the Responsibility to Protect*, para. 19, *supra*, at 2(C) and notes 11 and 19.

257 Preamble (6) ICCSt.

'admissibility'[258] procedure before the Court, which is not even barred by a case that has already been adjudicated at the national level (*ne bis in idem*).[259] The approach of the Rome Statute to the admissibility of a case – i.e., the conditions required for the principle of complementarity to bring in the jurisdiction of the ICC – is necessarily a case-by-case approach: the principle of complementarity is based on a presumption of willingness and ability of sovereign states to exercise their primary jurisdiction.[260] However, such presumption is rebuttable and will stand until the Prosecutor has decided to open an investigation, subject to the rulings of the Court.[261]

In order to allow the exercise of international jurisdiction only as a last resort, challenges against admissibility may be brought by the accused and by states which have jurisdiction over a case or whose acceptance of jurisdiction is required.[262] This procedural right is balanced by the need to ensure certainty to the action of the Court through time limits and provided that the principle of *ne bis in idem* is respected. Thus, challenges on admissibility can be brought before the Pre-Trial Chamber before the decision on the confirmation of charges[263] on all grounds based on a case being: (a) investigated or prosecuted by a state that has jurisdiction and is willing or able to do so genuinely;[264] or (b) already investigated but not prosecuted by a state under the same circumstances;[265] or (c) not of sufficient gravity.[266] After charges are confirmed, such exceptions are precluded, although it will still be possible to bring *ne bis in idem* challenges. With such challenges, based on a previous genuine trial held with respect to the same conduct the accused is charged with before the Court,[267] the principle of *ne bis in idem* will come into play, together with complementarity, so that any action of the ICC – and at whatever stage of the proceedings – would be deprived of its rationale of a means of last resort to bring justice. To prevent such result, but also to avoid proceedings being hindered by baseless challenges, the Trial Chamber will be called on to assess the existence of exceptional circumstances to authorize that the challenge be brought at a late stage.[268]

In order for a case to be admissible before the ICC, the Court shall look into the conduct of states in the discharge of their investigating, prosecutorial and trial responsibilities on a case of sufficient gravity to justify action by the Court,[269] and will follow two distinct and alternative parameters, i.e., whether states are unwilling or unable to carry out a genuine national proceedings consistent with the norms of due process recognized by international law.[270] The two criteria for inadmissibility/admissibility of a case – based on the ability/inability and willingness/unwillingness of a state which has jurisdiction over it – are not mutually exclusive. Although the Statute refers

---

258 Art. 17 ICCSt.

259 Art. 20(3) ICCSt, when national proceedings were conducted for the purpose of shielding a person from criminal responsibility or otherwise not independently or impartially.

260 See *supra*, at 4(E)(4)(a) for the opposite presumption made by the SC for the establishment, once and for all their lifespan, of the primary jurisdiction of the *ad hoc* Tribunals.

261 Arts 18 and 19 ICCSt.

262 Art. 19(2) ICCSt.

263 ICC, Motifs de la décision orale relative à l'exception d'irrecevabilité de l'affaire (Article 19 du Statut), *Germain Katanga et Mathieu Ngudjolo Chui*, 16 Juin 2009, paras 47 and 49.

264 Art. 17(1)(a) ICCSt.

265 Art. 17(1)(b) ICCSt.

266 Art. 17(1)(d) ICCSt.

267 Arts 19(1)(c) and 20(3) ICCSt.

268 Art. 19(4) ICCSt.

269 Art. 17(1)(d) ICCSt.

270 Art. 17(1)(c) and Art. 20(3) ICCSt.

to a state that might be 'unwilling *or* unable'[271] (emphasis added), the admissibility of a case can be factually based on both situations existing at the same time. Such 'double admissibility' was ascertained, e.g., in the situation in Uganda for the admissibility of the case, and was based on official statements on 'Uganda's inability to arrest' and that 'the Government of Uganda [had] not conducted and [did] not intend to conduct national proceedings'.[272]

(i) Unwillingness

Unwillingness[273] may be inferred on a case-by-case basis ('in a particular case') by:

> (a) proceedings undertaken or domestic decisions made for the purpose of shielding a person from criminal responsibility;
> (b) unjustified delays inconsistent with the intent to bring the person to justice;
> (c) proceedings not conducted independently or impartially and conducted in a manner which is inconsistent with the intent to bring the person to justice.

The Court has so far accepted a quite wide notion of unwillingness, which goes beyond that of states which do not intend to bring a person to justice for the purpose of providing impunity. Although not explicit under Article 17 ICCSt, the Court's case law has accepted that a state is also to be considered unwilling – although it has no purpose of shielding perpetrators from their criminal responsibility – if, for whatever reason, it decides that they be brought before international criminal justice.[274] Such interpretation is based on the object and purpose of the Statute, i.e., to put an end to impunity through complementarity, as this basic principle aims to protect the sovereign right of states to exert jurisdiction, and the Court has concluded that states can waive such right for whatever reason they may have, provided that they fulfil their cooperation obligations under the Rome Statute.[275]

In practice, this reading of 'unwillingness' by the Court establishes that complementarity entails a right to exert a jurisdiction which can be waived. In doing so, the Court expands the notion of 'inconsistent with the intent to bring the person to justice'[276] so as to add 'before its national jurisdiction'. It seems, however, that the reasons for a state to make a self-referral might not always be as neutral, for the purposes of international criminal justice, as the decision of the Court seems to suggest. Furthermore, the acceptance of an absolute right to prosecute, which can be waived at

271 Art. 17(1)(a) ICCSt.

272 ICC, Warrant of Arrest for Joseph Kony, Issued on 8 July 2005 as Amended on 27 September 2005, Situation in Uganda, PTC II, 27 September 2005, ICC-02/04-01/05, para. 37 and, later, Decision on the admissibility of the case under Article 19(1) of the Statute, PTC II, 10 March 2009, para. 37. Similarly, in Katanga, Democratic Republic of the Congo (DRC) the Court argued for inability and unwillingness at the national level, but willingness for international prosecution. ICC, Motifs de la décision orale relative à l'exception d'irrecevabilité de l'affaire (Article 19 du Statut), *Germain Katanga et Mathieu Ngudjolo Chui*, 16 June 2009, paras 76–78.

273 Art. 17(2) and Art. 20(3) ICCSt.

274 ICC, Motifs etc., *Katanga*, note 272 *supra*, para. 77.

275 Ibid., paras 78–80.

276 Art. 17(2)(b) ICCSt.

will by interested states, might be difficult to reconcile with the 'duty ... to exercise ... criminal jurisdiction'[277] at the national level, within the framework of the responsibility to protect.

(ii) Inability

Inability[278] would be the condition of a state that, 'in a particular case', is unable to obtain the accused or the evidence or otherwise to genuinely carry out its proceedings. Thus, a state would be unable if, e.g., it has no capacity to carry out investigations and judicial proceedings as a result of a lack of implementing legislation for the crimes under the Statute or as a consequence of the collapse of its judicial apparatus. The lessons learned in various conflicts and by different international jurisdictions show that in a conflict situation a state might often be unable to execute arrests of persons considered the most responsible for international crimes, insofar they are commanders or leaders in the conflicting Party. This was the case in relation to the first arrest warrants issued by the Court for the situation in Uganda, where the admissibility had been decided and was also based on the alleged inability to arrest Lord's Resistance Army (LRA) leaders.[279]

Such assessment cannot be conducted *a priori*, on the theoretical attitude of the legal system to meet the ability test, but instead needs to take into account all specific evidentiary elements provided under a *de facto* perspective.

The object of assessment should, first of all, include the legal framework of the concerned state and, in this regard, the practice of the *ad hoc* Tribunals in implementing Rule 11*bis* RPE referrals could also be relevant as it addresses the situation – reciprocal to that under the Rome Statute – of a primary (international) jurisdiction that activates a complementary (national) one.[280]

---

277 Preamble (6) ICCSt. In this sense, C. Aptel, Discussion Paper, Domestic Justice Systems and the Impact of the Rome Statute, Consultative Conference on International Criminal Justice (UNHQ, New York, 9–11 September 2009), at 8.

278 Art. 17(3) ICCSt.

279 ICC, Warrant of Arrest for Joseph Kony Issued on 8 July 2005 as Amended on 27 September 2005, PTC II, 27 September 2005, ICC-02/04-01/05, para. 37: 'noting the statements in the "Letter of Jurisdiction" dated 28th day of May 2004, that "the Government of Uganda has been unable to arrest ... persons who may bear the greatest responsibility" for the crimes within the referred situation.' See also *supra* notes 187 and 272.

280 In ICTR, Decision on the Prosecution's Appeal against Decision on Referral under Rule11*bis*, *Idelphonse Hategekimana*, Appeals Chamber, 4 December 2008, it was clarified that the conditions for a referral under Rule11*bis* require an assessment of the competence of a state to accept a case from the Tribunal on the bases of: (a) existence of a legal framework which criminalizes the alleged conduct, provides appropriate punishment for the offences charged, an adequate penalty structure and conditions of detentions compatible with internationally recognized standards; (b) whether the accused will receive a fair trial. In *Yussuf Munyakazi*, the ICTR Appeals Chamber upheld on 8 October 2008 a decision by the Trial Chamber to denying application by the Prosecution for referral of the case to Rwanda. On the one hand, the Appeal Chamber found that the Chamber erred in upholding that Rwanda does not respect the independence of the judiciary (based on previous actions of the Government) and that the composition of the Rwandan courts does not conform with fair trial principles. On the other hand, the decision confirmed that fundamental rights of the defence (such as obtaining attendance and examination of witnesses on same conditions as Prosecution witnesses) and the penalty structure (life imprisonment in isolation) in Rwanda are not adequate for the purpose of a Rule 11*bis* referral. See also ICTR, Decision, *Idelphonse Hategekimana*, Trial Chamber, 19 June 2008, where the request for Rule 11*bis* referral was denied because, *inter alia*, 'the Chamber ... considers it possible that, pursuant to Rwandan law [the convicted person] may face life imprisonment in isolation without adequate safeguards in violation of his right not to be subjected to cruel, inhuman or degrading punishment'. A different assessment of the ability of the Rwandan penitentiary system seems to have been carried out at the SCSL, which entered into a sentence-

Substantive criminal law provisions should also be taken into account, e.g., the lack of domestic legal provisions criminalizing the conducts described under Articles 5 to 8 of the Rome Statute. In this regard, ICTR rejected for lack of jurisdiction (*ratione materiae*) the request of the Prosecutor for a referral under Rule 11*bis* RPE of a case of genocide to the jurisdiction of Norway:[281] the Norwegian Penal Code did not include any provision criminalizing genocidal conduct which, therefore, could have been only prosecuted as murder,[282] thus enabling the protection of the interest to human life but not of that to the existence of the group.[283] In other words, although serious violations of IHL may be prosecuted and adjudicated based on universal jurisdiction, ICTR found that it is not sufficient to grant a referral that a state is willing to take over jurisdiction, but that a state must also be 'adequately prepared to accept' it, taking into account the domestic legal regime

enforcement agreement with Rwanda on 18 March 2009. Available at http://www.sc-sl.org/LinkClick.aspx?fileticket=WNTKRbIUNNc%3d&tabid=203 (visited 20 August 2009). While all the five cases of transfer to Rwanda requested by the OTP since 2007 – concerning one fugitive and four accused – were denied, 'the Government of Rwanda is in the process to amending its laws in order to remove any remaining legal hurdles for the transfer of cases from the Tribunal to be heard in Rwanda [and thereafter] the Prosecutor intends to reapply for referral of cases to Rwanda'. *Report on the Completion Strategy of the International Criminal Tribunal for Rwanda (as of 4 May 2009)*, *supra*, at note 49, paras 29 and 50.

281 ICTR, Decision on the Prosecution Motion for Referral to the Kingdom of Norway, Trial Chamber III, 19 May 2006, para. 16. Norwegian reasons are included in the *amicus curiae* brief directed on 26 June 2006 to the Appeals Chamber. Norway argued before the Trial Chamber for its universal jurisdiction on the case, under condition of approval of the act of indictment by the King, and that prosecution would have been assessed on the basis of the evidence received by ICTR (ibid., para. 9). It is worth noting that Michel Bagaragaza voluntarily surrendered to ICTR, having reached an agreement with the Prosecutor, according to which his trial should have taken place before a Court of a state to be determined (ibid., paragraph 2). See also *infra* note 301. See also the *Informal Expert Paper: The Principle of Complementarity in Practice*, para. 50, ICC-OTP 2003, according to which, among the facts and evidence which may be relevant to establish inability, are the 'lack of substantive or procedural penal legislation rendering the system "unavailable"'. Available at http://www.icc-cpi.int/iccdocs/doc/doc654724.PDF (visited 20 August 2009).

282 ICTR, Appeals Chamber, Decision on Rule 11*bis* Appeal, *Michel Bagaragaza*, 30 August 2006, paras 16, 17 and 18. Available at http://69.94.11.53/ENGLISH/cases/Bagaragaza/decisions/300806.htm (visited 20 August 2009). In particular, the Appeals Chamber recalls that the power of referral under Rule 11*bis* is based on Article 8 of the ICTR Statute, affirming the concurrent nature of the international and national jurisdictions in prosecuting serious violations of IHL and, thus, limiting the power of referral only to such cases where a state is able to prosecute the same international crimes under the Statute (ibid., para. 16). The Appeals Chamber also underlined that the legal qualification of the act under national legal systems and in the Statute is at the basis of the *ne bis in idem* principle under Art. 9 ICTRSt, which allows the *ad hoc* Tribunal to prosecute for serious violation of IHL a person who has already been tried before national courts for the same acts, although only prosecuted as common crimes (ibid., para. 16). In the same case, the Trial Chamber found that Norway had no jurisdiction *ratione materiae*, as the murder offense differs in its elements and in seriousness from the crime of genocide, in particular because murder does not include the specific intention of targeting a group as such: ICTR, Decision on the Prosecution Motion for Referral to the Kingdom of Norway, 19 May 2006, paras 13, 15 and 16. A second attempt by the Prosecutor to transfer the *Bagaragaza* case was also unsuccessful. The case was referred to The Netherlands on 13 April 2007, with a specific request for monitoring on the issue of jurisdiction over the genocide counts. However, in a case involving another Rwandan national, the competent District Court in The Hague found that there was no jurisdiction of Dutch courts over genocide and the referral order was consequently revoked. ICTR, Decision on the Prosecutor's extremely urgent motion for revocation of the referral to the Kingdom of The Netherlands pursuant to Rule 11*bis* (F) & (G), Trial Chamber, 17 August 2007, paras 1 and 3.

283 ICTR, *Bagagaragaza*, Appeals Chamber, ibid., para. 17.

to be applied.[284] This would not be the case if a state brings charges for ordinary crimes, which do not sufficiently stigmatize the criminal conduct as would be the case if prosecution were brought for serious violations of IHL which are international crimes under the Statute. Similar reasoning seems fully applicable under the complementarity principle of the ICC.

Procedural law provisions would also be relevant to the ability test, e.g., rules on immunity hindering national implementation of the Article 27 ICCSt principle of irrelevance of official capacity. Amnesty laws would also impact on admissibility.

A further level of assessment would necessarily need to be conducted on the situation as it appears on the ground where, e.g., the failure of a state might have rendered unavailable the whole apparatus of public powers, judicial or other relevant organs whose contribution is crucial to carrying out or implementing judicial proceedings (e.g., police, penitentiary).[285] In this context, the existence of an ongoing conflict would obviously be a factor to be considered: an international or non-international armed conflict may affect to different extents the ability of a state to carry out judicial proceedings, depending on the impact the conflict has on the stability, structure and functioning of the public powers in the country.

However, when the impact of an ongoing conflict on the exercise of public powers is low and the judiciary retains its capacity, the mere fact that suspects cannot be arrested because they belong to a party in the conflict does not seem to be suitable for consideration as one of the circumstances of inability under the Statute. The inability of a state 'to obtain the accused' is explicitly considered under Article 17(3) ICCSt, but only as 'due to a total or substantial collapse or unavailability of its national judicial system' and not because of *de facto* situations which (occasionally) affect the absconding of suspects and amount to an inability to arrest. Admitting that inability to arrest makes a case admissible before the Court seems to contradict the relationship between complementarity and cooperation obligations and, thus, the logic itself of the role of the Court: the territorial state would, in fact, be normally the best placed to execute arrests and, consequently, the one on which the cooperation obligation with the Court would pose the heavier burden. If the state is unable to arrest, the Court would be deprived of the main possible cooperation and, in turn, be itself unable to carry out its proceedings.[286]

Although the principle of complementarity acknowledges the primary role of national jurisdictions, to make a case inadmissible before the Court national jurisdictions should be exerted in good faith and in accordance with established principles of independence and fair trial. In fact, when the ICC's jurisdiction has been triggered it is only for the Court itself to decide whether any previous or late exercise of states' jurisdiction would make a case inadmissible before it because it is or has been investigated or prosecuted by a state which has jurisdiction over it, or because the case is not of sufficient gravity.[287]

284 ICTY, Decision on Referral of Case Pursuant to Rule 11*bis*, *Radovan Stanković*, Appeal Referral Bench, 17 May 2005, paras 41–42.

285 A similar situation was the one that led to the establishment in Timor Leste/East Timor of the mixed panels for serious crimes by UNTAET; see *supra*, 2(D) and note 21.

286 For the contrary practice so far established at the ICC in the situation of Uganda, see *supra*, at 4(E)(4)(b) and notes 272 and 279. In a public statement, the Minister of Interior of Uganda also explicitly mentioned that the referral situation was decided because of the inability to apprehend the LRA leaders during the ongoing conflict. Documentary film *The Reckoning* (New York: Skylight Pictures, 2009). Available at www.thereckoningfilm.com/press (visited 30 September 2009). See UNGA Res. 3(1) Extradition and Punishment of War Criminals, 13 February 1946, at 9 and 10 for preferential extradition to states where crimes were committed.

287 Art. 17(1) ICCSt.

Consequently, when making a decision on admissibility, if the ICC finds that a person has already been tried by another court but proceedings were intended to shield that person from criminal responsibility or otherwise were not conducted independently or impartially in a manner inconsistent with an intent to bring the person to justice, the Court is not even bound[288] by any previous decision on acquittal or conviction (*ne is in idem* or prohibition of double jeopardy).[289]

The Court has, therefore, the final say on establishing its jurisdiction, which makes it clearer that it is a Court of last resort because it is called into action only for the most serious crimes,[290] the highest responsibilities and when no state is able or willing to genuinely carry out justice.

(c) Impunity gap

As the ICC can ordinarily deal only with the highest levels of responsibility for crimes under its jurisdiction, the issue of the suppression of criminal conducts at lower levels is left open, which falls squarely under the competence of states having jurisdiction over such crimes under different applicable criteria (territory, active or passive personality, universality). This impunity gap might well affect social reconciliation in conflict-torn regions and, therefore, local and international stability. Thus, it is in the interest of the international community that the ability of relevant states to uphold justice be reinforced in the framework of initiatives directed to strengthen the many facets of the rule of law.

From this perspective, a crucial role could be played by the Court using a proactive approach to complementarity (positive complementarity): first, addressing emerging situations with the aim of reducing the scope for its intervention, including by means of providing certain forms of assistance to national jurisdictions;[291] and, second, at the time when its jurisdiction has already been exerted. In this regard, as the mandate of the ICC is that of a permanent and theoretically universal Court, it deals with an indefinite number of situations which it aims to bring to a close through the complementarity mechanism, both through trials in The Hague and at the national level. Therefore,

---

288 Art. 20(3) ICCSt.

289 Art. 12(2)(a)(i) ILC, *Draft Code of Crimes Against the Peace and Security of Mankind* (1996) already provided that the *ne bis in idem* principle would have not hindered proceedings before an international criminal court when 'the act which was the subject of the judgement in the national court was characterized by that court as an ordinary crime and not as a crime against the peace and security of mankind'. The principle has often constitutional standing in domestic legislation and is, *inter alia*, affirmed in Article 4 of Protocol No. 7 to the European Convention of Human Rights, 22 November 1984 ('Right not to be tried or punished twice'): 'no one shall be liable to be tried or punished again in criminal proceedings under the jurisdiction of the same State for an offence for which he has already been finally acquitted or convicted in accordance with the law and penal procedure of that State.' For the *ne bis in idem* principle in the Tribunals' Statutes see R. Bellelli, Cooperation and Implementation, *supra* note 22, at 2(B)(5).

290 Preamble (4) and Article 5(1) *chapeau* ICCSt (most serious crimes of concern to the international community as a whole); Article 1 ICCSt (most serious crimes of international concern); Art. 17(1)(d) ICCSt (sufficient gravity to justify … action by the Court); Articles 7(1) and 8(1) *chapeaux* ICCSt (thresholds); Art. 53(1)(c) and (2)(c) ICCSt (gravity of the crime as criterion for the Prosecutor to initiate an investigation or prosecuting).

291 Positive complementarity also addresses reciprocal cooperation, with a role for the Court to promote the rule of law and the national exercise of jurisdiction aimed at filling the impunity gap: 'The Office of the Prosecutor makes particular efforts to support national authorities' initiatives to investigate allegations of crimes that would not meet the criteria for opening an ICC investigation.' *Prosecutorial Strategy 2009–2012* (Draft), para. 15, *supra* note 72. For a different, critical view on positive complementarity, see F. Lattanzi, Concurrent Jurisdictions between Primacy and Complementarity, in this Volume, at 9(B).

it could be argued that – different from the other international and limited criminal jurisdictions – the ICC needs to set up many completion strategies, one for each of the situations with which it deals, with the final aim of defeating impunity by filling the impunity gap.

In the same perspective of interplay between efforts at the international and at the national level to defeat impunity, relevant actors could well include interested regional organizations. Beside the strenuous political and financial support provided throughout the establishment and the functioning of the ICC by the European Union,[292] the activities of the Court in situations within four African states, and which impact on many more countries in the region, may over time result in an increased role for regional organizations in the fight against impunity.

In this regard, the African Union has reserved itself the 'right to intervene' in a Member State to suppress crimes of international concern[293] and is examining whether the African Court on Human and Peoples' Rights could be mandated to trying such crimes.[294] Thus, while the concept of responsibility to protect[295] is referred to the obligation of the international community to protect or to intervene[296] – within the established UN mechanisms and based on the rejection of any impunity for crimes of international concern – the AU Constitutive Act seems to approach, from a different angle, the same result of bringing justice and stability, avoiding establishing an obligation for the regional organization but granting it the 'right to protect'.

Along the same lines, an 'African option' was proposed[297] for the prosecution and trial – by Senegal, Chad or any AU member – of the former President of Chad Hissène Habré who, upon international arrest warrant issued by Belgium, was arrested in Senegal. As the latter did not grant extradition to Belgium, the AU decided that the 'crimes … fall within [its] competence'

292 The European Union considers its support for the Court in the context of its Common Foreign and Security Policy (CFSP) and clearly stated its common political commitment in Common Position 2001/443/CFSP of 11 June 2001, later renewed and reinforced with Common Positions 2002/474/CFSP, 20 June 2002, and lately 2003/444/CFSP, of 16 June 2003, Art. 1(1): '[the ICC is] an essential means of promoting respect for international humanitarian law and human rights, thus contributing to freedom, security, justice and the rule of law as well as contributing to the preservation of peace and the strengthening of international security, in accordance with the purposes and principles of the Charter of the United Nations.' Such policies – a notorious example of which were the EU Council Conclusions of 30 September 2002 on the so-called 'Article 98 Agreements' proposed with a worldwide campaign by the United States – are implemented through the Action Plan to Follow-Up the Common Position on the International Criminal Court, 4 February 2004.

293 Art. 4(h) Constitutive Act of the African Union, Lomé, 11 July 2000: right of intervention would follow a decision of the Assembly.

294 AU Assembly's Decision 213 (XII), 4 February 2009, para. 9 mandates the AU Commission to examine implications of the African Court being empowered to try genocide, crimes against humanity and war crimes.

295 See *supra*, at 2(C).

296 There is, indeed, a rather slight nuance in definitions.

297 Committee of Eminent African Jurists established by the Assembly of the AU, Assembly/AU/Dec.103 (VI).

and mandated 'Senegal to prosecute and ensure [trial] *on behalf of Africa*'.[298] In the lively debate opened by the issuance of an ICC arrest warrant for the sitting President of Sudan, Omar al Bashir, suggestions were also made for the African Court[299] to be mandated to deal with the case.

This proliferation of proposals for triggering an international criminal jurisdiction at the regional level clearly shows how strong the regional support is for contributing actively to suppressing impunity and, from this perspective, such a regional mechanism would undoubtedly enhance the complementarity role of the ICC by reducing its workload. However, some implications of a decentralization of international efforts in criminal justice matters should be considered, including whether the concept of responsibility to protect, as currently accepted, would adequately frame such efforts. Furthermore, the establishment of a third layer of jurisdiction, intermediate to those of the states and of the ICC, would be promising if an additional 'jurisdictional actor' at the regional level were to take on directly the duty of monitoring and analyzing situations for the purpose of assisting in improving the willingness and ability of states to discharge their primary responsibility for repressing serious crimes of international concern. However, the interplay of regional jurisdictions with that of the ICC would always fall within the complementarity mechanism and the ICC would still have the last word in any challenge to its jurisdiction or to the admissibility of a case. Consequently, possible diverging jurisprudence at the regional and ICC level would bear a significant potential for fuelling an undesirable politicization of criminal matters.

(d) Implementation

Under the rule of complementarity, states should have a strong interest in fully implementing the Rome Statute in order to be able to maintain jurisdiction on relevant situations.[300] Domestic substantive criminal law has, therefore, to be brought in line with the law of the Statute in order to ensure that it penalizes all conducts that are criminalized under the relevant international criminal provision.[301] The same goes for immunities or procedural rules which may attach to the official capacity of a person and that — although irrelevant before the Court (Article 27(2) ICCSt) — when applied at the national level may enhance the likelihood that the ICC steps in.[302]

States determined to join the ICC or which are already Parties to the Statute must put in place legislation which enables them both to comply with the obligations to cooperate with the Court under Part 9 of the Statute, as well as to maintain their jurisdiction when they have a link with

298 Assembly/AU/Dec.127 (VII), 2 July 2006, emphasis added. The decision was reiterated by Dec.240 (XII), 4 February 2009). The case is currently dealt with by the ICJ in *Questions relating to the Obligation to Prosecute or Extradite* (*Belgium v. Senegal*).

299 The African Court on Human and Peoples' Rights, however, although foreseen by the 1981 African Charter on Human and Peoples' Rights, has yet to be established. Available at http://www.aict-ctia.org/courts_conti/achpr/achpr_home.html (visited 20 August 2009).

300 See *supra*, at 4(E)(4)(b). See R. Bellelli, Cooperation and Implementation, *supra* note 22, at 2(A).

301 See *supra*, 4(E)(4)(b) and note 281. In particular, ICTR rejected the request of the Prosecutor to transfer a genocide case to Norway as its penal code did not include any specific provision criminalizing genocide that, consequently, should have been only prosecuted as murder. ICTR, Decision, *Michel Bagaragaza*, Appeals Chamber, *supra*, at note 281. For the scope of criminality, see R. Bellelli, Cooperation and Implementation, *supra* note 22, at 2(B).

302 Art. 27(2) ICCSt. See *supra*, at 4(C)(2)(b). However, also at the state level, immunities and other obstacles to effective prosecution granted in different forms, including through amnesties, statutes of limitations, pardons or non-genuine investigation and prosecution, should not be a bar to prosecutions. See, e.g., IACHR, *Almonacid-Arellano et al. v. Chile*, note 174 *supra*, para. 151. See note 157, *supra*, for *Bashir*.

crimes committed in a given situation. However, it could also be argued that not only states willing to ratify the Rome Statute might have an interest in keeping in line with its substantive criminal law provisions. In fact, the jurisdiction of the ICC *ratione loci* (over crimes committed in a State Party, by a national of any state) and the power of the Security Council to refer a situation to the ICC (jurisdiction over crimes committed even in non-States Parties and by anyone) makes it necessary for all states willing to preserve their right to exert primary jurisdiction – and eventually to challenge the admissibility of a case under the complementarity regime – to be able to investigate and prosecute such crimes.

The fact that the Statute reflects customary international law and the wide-ranging effects of the complementarity mechanism entail that, over time, the law of the Statute should lead to an harmonization of domestic substantive criminal law. More generally, the implementation process driven by the complementarity regime will result in the strengthening of national law and practice[303] as it also involves procedural laws – with regard to the implementation of cooperation obligations – as well as, in some instances, constitutional provisions. Notably, the Rome Statute has also exerted a driving force on other international jurisdictions which have treasured the advanced status of international law reflected in the Statute and its blend of common and civil law procedure. In this regard, it is worth stressing the appropriate lessons-learned approach taken at the ICTY, where special Working Groups of judges were established for amending the basic instruments.[304]

F. Cooperation

In light of the experience of the *ad hoc* Tribunals, it has not come as a surprise that the actual challenges for the ICC have come from the degree of cooperation[305] that, in particular, state actors are willing to afford in the fight against impunity. At the ICC, the inherent limits of an international jurisdiction totally dependent on the continuous support of the international community for performing its role – and, above all, for the execution of its decisions on personal freedom (arrest, surrender, sentence),[306] on evidence and witness protection,[307] and on assets[308] – have emerged with a strength proportional to the level of the Court's action in tackling those bearing the highest responsibilities for crimes of international concern. As a result, the threat to the smooth operations of the Court has appeared much earlier in its life and with more clarity, compared with the experience of the UN Tribunals.[309] Without the steady backing of the Security Council, the ICC has had so far

303 H. Corell, *Evalutating the ICC Regime: The Likely Impact on States and International Law*, Peace Palace in The Hague, 21 December 2000, at 13. Available at http://untreaty.un.org/OLA/media/info_from_lc/romestatute_dec00.pdf (visited 20 August 2009).

304 One example of such influence of the Rome Statute may be found in the change of requirements for defence counsel to be assigned to the suspect or accused, who were previously requested to have only 'reasonable experience' in the field of criminal law and/or international criminal law/international humanitarian law/international human rights law, will now have to 'possess … established competence in the same areas' (Rule 45(B)(ii) ICTY RPE, as amended on 28 July 2004 upon the work of the Working Group convened in May 2003), which is the same requirement applicable to ICC counsel (Rule 22 ICC RPE, adopted by the first ASP on 9 September 2002, includes the 'established competence' requirement, but only referred to 'international or criminal law and procedure').

305 See R. Bellelli, Cooperation and Implementation, *supra* note 22, at 3.

306 Arts 89–92 and Art. 103 ICCSt.

307 Art. 93 ICCSt.

308 Art. 109 ICCSt.

309 See *supra*, 3(B) and R. Bellelli, Cooperation and Implementation, *supra* note 22, at 3(C) and note 139 for issues of cooperation with some states in the Balkans.

and with mixed results to rely on a constant process of awareness and consensus-raising among states and international organizations.

Although participation in the Statute and, occasionally, resolutions of the Security Council under Chapter VII of the UN Charter are sources of obligations to cooperate, formalized remedies for incompliance are difficult to trigger and most likely inadequate to achieve the intended result. Cooperation is intrinsically a voluntary process, which can only be successfully encouraged through persuasive means, either by increasing the level of understanding for the jurisdiction or by making the option of non-cooperation disadvantageous for the state concerned. However, while the first approach has been consistently followed by interested actors,[310] efforts in the second direction are much more conditional upon concurrent political interests in a variety of fora and, therefore, cannot emerge but on a case-by-case basis.[311]

While the degree of universality of the Statute and of its implementation are not *per se* an indication of the attitude of states toward cooperation, undoubtedly an increased participation in the objective, purpose, principles and norms of the Rome Statute can only be to the benefit of the likelihood that in the future the action of the Court might be more effective. As misconceptions concerning the legal framework of the Statute and the operations of the Court are defused by the case law and practice of the Court, the number of states willing to support the Court may well play a decisive role in making the results of its decisions immediately apparent.

G. The Review of the Statute

The first Review Conference is due to take place seven years after the entry into force of the Rome Statute and it is currently scheduled to convene in the first semester of 2010,[312] with an intended and mandatory agenda mainly focused on the possible adoption of a definition and of a procedure for the actual exercise of jurisdiction on the crime of aggression, as well as on the review of the opt-out clause under Article 124 ICCSt.

Discussions among States Parties have led to the general understanding that the Review Conference should only examine proposals[313] for possible amendments of provisions of the Statute

310 States Parties, regional organizations, the ICC itself and the civil society.

311 In addition, the situation on the ground has also to be separately assessed as to its effect on the enforceability of the Court's orders. See R. Bellelli, Cooperation and Implementation, *supra* note 22, at 3(E)(1) and notes 161 (situation in Uganda), 165 (situation in Sudan), 176 (cooperation under SC Res. 1593) and at 3(E)(3), note 179.

312 Pursuant to Art. 123(1) ICCSt and according to ASP Bureau Decision of its 7 April 2009 meeting, para. 3(b), with letter addressed to all states on 7 August 2009 the Secretary General of the United Nations, Ban Ki-moon, convened the Review Conference in Kampala from 31 May–11 June 2010.

313 Such proposals should be put forward no earlier than 2 July 2009 and at least three months before an ASP meeting (Art. 121(2) ICCSt), which is currently planned to start on 18 November 2009 (8th ASP session). In fact, pursuant to Art. 121(1) ICCSt 'after the expiry of seven years from the entry into force of this Statute, any State Party may propose amendments thereto'. This means that proposals containing amendments may be not be validly put forward by States Parties before 2 July 2009 or after 18 August 2009. In this sense, see ICC-ASP/6/Inf. 3, *Review Conference: Scenarios and Options-Progress Report by the Focal Point*, 4 December 2007, para. 14, at 3. ICC-ASP/7/Res.2, para. 61 provided that 'proposals for amendments ... to be *considered* at the Review Conference should be *discussed* at the eighth session of the Assembly' (emphasis added), and with ICC-ASP/7/Res. 3, *Strengthening the International Criminal Court and the Assembly of States Parties* (Omnibus Resolution), the ASP also decided that any proposal for amendment of the Rome Statute be considered at its eight session, in November 2009. However, on 9 July 2009 the ASP Bureau decided that the formal deadline for submission of proposals for amendments be set at 30 September 2009. Available at

that have been already sufficiently tested and if proposals appear not to be controversial, that is, are likely to gather consensus.[314] Moreover, the Review Conference is likely to devote some of its sessions to an assessment of the achievements of and challenges for the ICC.[315]

However, it is a fact that at the time of the first Review Conference 12 years will have elapsed since the adoption of the Rome Statute. While the 1998 Rome Diplomatic Conference took stock of the then existing early case law of international tribunals for fine-tuning substantive and procedural criminal law provisions, the substantial developments in the field which followed the adoption of the Statute have improved the effectiveness and efficiency of other international criminal tribunals, but are not reflected in the ICC system.

In this regard, the purpose for limiting the Review Conference only to topics which 'do not risk ... affect[ing] the integrity of the Statute'[316] should be correctly defined and balanced with the need to ensure that the Rome Statute continues to stand at what in 1998 was viewed as the frontier line of international criminal justice.[317] In fact, the notion of integrity[318] of the Statute is generally referred to some core issues, which have always been at the centre of attempts to undermine the compromise reached in 1998 and which might encompass the list of crimes, the jurisdiction of the Court, its independence from the Security Council, and the powers of the Prosecutor. However, there are other provisions of the Statute the adequacy of which has been challenged in the practice

---

http://www.icc-cpi.int/iccdocs/asp_docs/ASP8/Bureau10.agenda%20and%20decisions.clean.16July09.1550.pdf (visited 20 August 2009). On the latter point, see further in R. Bellelli, The Law of the Statute, *supra* note 10, at note 25.

314 Following the approach taken by the Focal Point appointed by the ASP to deal with the issue of the preparation of the Review Conference in its Report to the fifth ASP (ICC-ASP/5/Inf.2, 21 November 2006), as well as the opinion expressed by a number of delegations during ASP5, proposals for amendments to the Rome Statute should be considered when: they are likely to gather sufficient support in the ASP; they have no potential divisive effect; they do not risk to affect the integrity of the Statute; and there has been a sufficient implementation of the relevant provisions of the Rome Statute in the practice of the Court. Thus, the ASP concluded that 'in addition to a focus on amendments that may command very broad, preferably consensual support, the Review Conference should be an occasion for a "stocktaking" of international criminal justice in 2010 ... [and] focus on a limited number of topics'. Omnibus Resolution ICC-ASP/7/Res. 3, para .62, at 35.

315 See ICC-ASP/7/Res. 3, para. 62: 'stocktaking', including but not limited to hearing from '(i) international criminal justice institutions, against the background of completion strategies well under way; (ii) national investigative and prosecution authorities with experience in transboundary cooperation consistent with the principles of the Statute, (iii) feedback from conflict areas that have benefited from the work of criminal justice institutions, with a view to identifying contributions and legacies of the latter, as well as any "lessons learned"; and (iv) considerations of the close relationship between sustainable peace and justice, for example as highlighted by social scientist and historians'. See ICC-ASP/6/Inf. 3, *Review Conference: Scenarios and Options-Progress Report by the focal point*, 4 December 2007, para. 31, at 5. In particular, the lessons learned approach, through review of the practices and achievements of the completion strategies of international jurisdictions was the core of the program, directed towards preparation for the Rome Statute Review Conference – the *Conference on International Criminal Justice*, quoted in the Progress report itself (para. 7), held in Turin (Italy) from 14–18 May 2007. All details on the Turin Conference are available at http://www.torinoconference.com/ (visited 30 September 2009). Reports available in all UN official languages at http://www.icc-cpi.int/Menus/ASP/Sessions/Documentation/6thSession/ (see ASP/6/Inf. 2, 'Turin Report') (visited 30 September 2009).

316 ICC-ASP/7/Res. 3, Omnibus Resolution, para. 62, at 35.

317 In this sense, see J. Lindenmann, Universality: Momentum and Consensus for the ICC, in this Volume, at para. 4.

318 For an analysis of this notion, see R. Bellelli, The Law of the Statute (*supra* note 10), in this Volume, at 1(B).

and is directly reflected in the timing of judicial proceedings and in the overall credibility of the institution. From this perspective, the integrity of the Rome Statute as a living instrument would seem to be better preserved through adapting its functioning to the findings of the last decade, in particular with reference to the novelties introduced in the Statutes and in the case law of other international tribunals, insofar innovations have proved to be positively productive.[319]

5. Conclusion

The *ad hoc* and hybrid Tribunals that will close down over the next few years have set the basis for the enforcement of the principle of international legality through criminal justice. Building on the experience of the UN *ad hoc* Tribunals, the ICC Rome Statute has established, through the principle of complementarity, a comprehensive and integrated system for the implementation of the responsibility to protect. At the centre of such legal system, the ICC is the permanent actor in international criminal justice called to ensure that the fight against impunity for the most serious crimes of international concern is carried out through an institution ruled by universally shared values, principles and norms.

The first steps of the ICC into actual exercise of jurisdiction have already shown that the most radical criticism of the risk of its activities being politicized is unfounded.[320] The Court has already demonstrated its deterrent impact on the perpetration of widespread and systematic atrocities, contributing to the reconciliation of conflicts involving the worst international crimes and encouraging parties to peace negotiations in Uganda, the Democratic Republic of the Congo and the Central African Republic, while stimulating the implementation of peace agreements in Sudan.

However, the strategic support of states and civil society – through various forms of cooperation and assistance – is a vital need for the ICC, as the effectiveness of its action is based on the steady consensus of the international community and of public opinion. The ratification process has been the earlier concern of all stakeholders of the ICC and the need that states enhance their efforts to participate in the shortest term to the Rome Statute and to fully implement its law in national legislation still remains vital in the perspective of universality and integrity of the Statute, as well as for the effectiveness of the Court's operations.[321] However, the very core of the issue – for a fair, effective and timely justice to be delivered – is in the willingness of States Parties to afford the ICC with the judicial cooperation required under the rule of the Law of the Statute and with the political backing needed to overcome the resistance that the institutional high profile of its action has encountered so far and will ordinarily experience in the future.

As the Court completes its first seven-year period of operation, the challenges it has encountered should also be read in light of the lessons learned and developments at the international tribunals since the adoption of the Rome Statute, so that it can be strengthened through a meaningful review process aimed at maintaining it at the forefront of international criminal justice. It is also in this

319 See in detail, R. Bellelli, ibid., in particular paras 2, 10 and 12.

320 As was demonstrated by the UN entering into the *Relationship Agreement* with the ICC, by the Security Council referral for Darfur, by the cooperation of the Court with the Special Court for Sierra Leone about holding the Charles Taylor trial in The Hague, and by the development of the US position vis-à-vis the ICC, including with reiterated offers of cooperation, although limited to specific situations and cases.

321 By the same token, early ratification of the Agreement on the Privileges and Immunity of the Court and entering into relevant cooperation agreements with the Court, including for the enforcement of its sentences and for the relocation of witnesses, are also crucial objectives to achieve.

process that state and non-state actors may play their historical role within the system of the Rome Statute: widespread and constant support to the building and functioning of a strong, permanent, independent and theoretically universal Court will represent a concrete response to the demand of justice coming from the victims of the most serious crimes that continue to deeply shock the conscience of humanity.

SECTION II
The Experience of the UN Tribunals and their Completion Strategies

Chapter 2
The International Criminal Tribunal for the Former Yugoslavia

Fausto Pocar

1. Introduction

This chapter addresses the experience of the International Criminal Tribunal for the former Yugoslavia (ICTY or Tribunal) from a 'lessons learned' perspective, particularly in light of the completion strategy and legacy. Indeed, in order to fully appreciate the accomplishments of the Tribunal, as well as the progress in international criminal law, it is equally important to look to the past and take into account the initial obstacles the Tribunal overcame. These challenges, along with the Tribunal's achievements, form the basis of the lessons which should be built upon and direct the future of international criminal justice. With this in mind, this contribution will focus on the following three themes: (i) the ICTY's establishment and its landmark developments; (ii) the ICTY's core achievements; and (iii) the issues related to the ICTY's completion strategy and its legacy.

2. Establishment and Landmark Developments

A. Significance of the Tribunal

On 25 May 1993, the Security Council passed SC Res. 827 (1993) establishing the ICTY as a response to 'the wave of horrors' that swept through the Balkans in the wake of the collapse of the former Yugoslavia, which it deemed to be a threat to international peace and security. The newly created institution was charged with the formidable task of prosecuting persons accused of serious violations of international humanitarian law committed in the territory of the former Yugoslavia since 1991. Not since the International Military Tribunals of Nuremberg (IMT) and Tokyo after World War II had an international criminal tribunal been created to prosecute individuals accused of mass atrocities. According to the Secretary-General's report presenting the draft Statute of the ICTY, 'the life-span of the international tribunal would be linked to the restoration of and maintenance of international peace and security in the territory of the former Yugoslavia, and Security Council decisions related thereto'.[1]

To the credit of the judges and lawyers involved in the actual development of the Tribunal, the ICTY not only got off the ground, but has since proved to be a genuine and credible judicial enterprise, capable of dispensing justice in a fair manner. As of early 2009, the ICTY occupies three buildings in The Hague, has 31 judges from 29 countries, employs over 1,100 staff from about 80 countries, and is hearing seven trials simultaneously in its three courtrooms. In over a decade of

1 UN Doc. S/25704 and Add. 1, para. 28.

existence, the Tribunal has indicted 161 persons: only two remain at large. Today, six accused are in the pre-trial stage, 27 accused on trial, and trial and appeal proceedings against 116 accused have been completed. However, along the way, the ICTY has had to overcome some significant challenges to become the fully functioning international Tribunal that it is today.

B. Issues Related to the Statute and the Rules of Procedure and Evidence

First of all, upon its inception, the ICTY was provided with only a skeletal statute and no provision was made for a body of rules of procedure and evidence. The skeletal nature of the ICTYSt was due partly to the assumption that the Security Council should not take on a legislative function, and partly to the time constraints under which the Statute was drafted. The ICTYSt, comprised of 34 Articles, only provides for a minimal framework, establishing the Tribunal's competence and scope of jurisdiction (subject matter, personal, temporal and territorial). The ICTYSt also provides specific instructions on the organization of the Tribunal and the conduct of trial and appellate proceedings. However, it is not a code of criminal procedure or a criminal code; it therefore provides little guidance as to the substantive and procedural law to be applied by the Tribunal. The Rules of Procedure and Evidence (RPE) had to be formulated by the newly elected judges of the Tribunal. Thus, beginning in February 1994, the ICTY judges worked them out in order to regulate the proceedings in a manner that that would ensure the fairness of international trials without compromising the need for expeditiousness. These Rules have been amended periodically as required by the developments in the Tribunal's practice.

C. The Blending of Different Legal Traditions

The second hurdle was the issue of how to effectively integrate the different legal traditions and judicial cultures brought by the judges and legal staff to the Tribunal. Not unlike the Nuremberg Tribunal, the Tribunal draws more heavily on the common law (i.e., 'adversarial') model rather than on the civil law (i.e., 'inquisitorial' system). It is largely the responsibility of the parties to develop their cases – to collect and present documentary evidence, to seek out and to examine witnesses. The judges do not conduct investigations and it is up to the Prosecutor to bring to the attention of judges the evidence supporting an indictment. Another significant common law characteristic before the Tribunal is the possibility for an accused to enter a guilty plea.

However, although the first version of the Rules of Procedure and Evidence, adopted on 11 February 1994, revealed a very strong common law influence, the extensive amendments since then show that the Rules have progressively moved away from a strict interpretation of that model and now rely more extensively on the principles of civil law systems. Thus, important civil law contributions to the system are evident as well. First of all, the fact-finders are judges, not jurors. Although judges at the ICTY play a role that is generally less active than most judges in civil law countries, they are allowed to participate rather actively in the examination of witnesses and in the pre-trial phase of the proceedings. Another striking civil law characteristic within the ICTY RPE is the provision allowing appeals by the prosecution on equal terms with the defence. In common law jurisdictions the prosecution's right to appeal is normally tightly circumscribed – prosecuting authorities do not generally have the possibility of appealing adverse factual determinations. With the continued aim of conducting trials that are both fair and expeditious, the Tribunal's proceedings are now less adversarial in character, with the judges assuming a more active role in the judicial process.

3. ICTY Core Achievements

As some of the challenges overcome by the ICTY in its development as a fully fledged international criminal court have been highlighted, the topic of the core achievements attributable to the Tribunal may be focused on four main areas.

A. Continued Challenge to Impunity

Following the historic precedent set by the Nuremburg and Tokyo trials, the ICTY has sought to fight impunity and establish individual accountability under international law for perpetrators of war crimes, genocide and crimes against humanity. This is an essential contribution of the ICTY to the international community: individuals committing what could be termed as the most heinous crimes, regardless of the rank and status, are no longer able to even suggest that the law does not bind them and that they are not criminally responsible for their conduct. Past failures to punish perpetrators, especially persons in positions of authority, only signalled to future leaders that they would also enjoy impunity. Now, the Tribunal's continued insistence on accountability has irrevocably altered a culture of impunity and has helped to prevent a recurrence of armed criminal conduct on a massive scale. Likewise, the Tribunal has strived through its action to promote reconciliation within the region of the former Yugoslavia and to bring a sense of 'closure' to the families and victims of the conflict.

B. Fair Trials before the ICTY

The ICTY has effectively implemented an international criminal justice system to ensure the highest standards of due process. The rights of the accused are respected according to, and at times beyond, the fundamental requirements of due process enshrined in universal and regional conventions. Where an accused feels that his rights have nonetheless been unduly encroached, he has the possibility of seeking a remedy on appeal.

Accordingly, for example, the ICTY has strived to strictly adhere to the legal principle of *nullum crimen sine lege*: an accused may not be convicted for acts that were not considered crimes under international humanitarian law at the time they were committed. Moreover, the Tribunal has upheld the principle of *non bis in idem*: under Article 10 of the ICTY Statute, no person may be tried before a national court and the ICTY for the same international crimes unless the national court characterized the crime as 'ordinary' or the national proceedings were not impartial or independent, were designed to shield the accused from international prosecution, or were not diligently prosecuted. Chambers remain vigilant in ensuring that accused persons receive proper notice of the charges brought against them, with adequate supporting material and a disclosure system that allows them to arrive at the trial stage prepared. Other rights of the accused related to the preparation of their defence (such as the right to have adequate time and facilities for preparation of his defence, the right to examine or have examined the witnesses against him, the right to Counsel, provision for legal aid, and protection against self-incrimination) are also protected.

In relation to the preparation of the accused's defence the ICTY has consistently faced the ongoing challenge of ensuring the expeditious disposition of cases without sacrificing the due process rights of the accused. The Tribunal has adapted to the specific requirements of international trials, adopting innovative procedures over the years. For example, aware that the length of trials at the Tribunal begins with the breadth of the indictments prepared by the Office of the Prosecutor, the judges adopted in 2003 an amendment to Rule 73*bis* ICTY RPE, which allows a Trial Chamber to invite or direct the Prosecution to select only a limited number of counts on which to proceed. This amendment was regarded as particularly necessary to ensure respect for an accused's right to a fair and expeditious trial and to prevent unduly lengthy periods of pre-trial detention.

Further examples are found in the Rules 92*ter* and 92*quater* ICTY RPE, adopted in 2006, which under certain conditions allow a Trial Chamber to consider written statements and transcripts of witnesses that go to proof of the acts and conduct of the accused in lieu of oral testimony, and to allow written statements and transcripts of witnesses that go to the acts and conduct of the accused to be introduced into evidence when a witness is unavailable.

To mention a few final examples, rules have been included to streamline pre-trial procedures, to consolidate separate indictments in order to be able to hold joint trials, and to widen the scope of judicial notice to include the recognition of identical facts already adjudicated in another case, if they do not refer to the criminal conduct of the accused.

C. International Criminal Law Developments through ICTY Jurisprudence

Third, the ICTY has developed and effectively enforced an entire body of international humanitarian law governing conflict situations put into place following World War II. When the Tribunal first commenced its judicial activities, there was little international jurisprudence available. Some guidance was provided by the interpretation of the fourth Hague Convention respecting the Laws and Customs of War on Land and its Regulations as well as the International Military Tribunal's Charter during the Nuremburg trials. However, in many instances, the Tribunal has had to determine the elements of a number of crimes under customary international law, often providing a detailed and focused examination. Consequently, the ICTY has made significant strides in clarifying the scope of fundamental concepts of international criminal law. This rich body of jurisprudence, both substantive and procedural, will be indispensable for the future enforcement of international humanitarian law in other jurisdictions. It is fair to say that no future war crimes cases will be tried without some guidance from the jurisprudence of the ICTY. I turn to highlight just a few of the ICTY's jurisprudential accomplishments.

1. Establishing the Features of Armed Conflict and the Scope of Related Protections

With the exception of the crime of genocide, a prerequisite to triggering the Tribunal's jurisdiction is, of course, the existence of an armed conflict. Through its jurisprudence, the ICTY has defined the features of armed conflict, as well as the conditions necessary to conclude whether an armed conflict of an international character has arisen.

In a related development, the Tribunal's decision in *Aleksovski*[2] clarified the meaning of 'protected persons' under Article 4 of the Geneva Convention relative to the Protection of Civilian Persons in Time of War (Fourth Geneva Convention), a further prerequisite for the Tribunal to have jurisdiction over grave breaches. The decision concluded that the phrase in Article 2 ICTYSt ('act against persons or property protected under the provisions of the relevant Geneva Convention') should be interpreted broadly to afford as much protection as possible to the civilian population and, accordingly, recognized the victimization of Bosnian Muslims by Bosnian Serbs, despite the fact that both technically shared the same nationality.

2 Judgment, *Aleksovski*, Appeals Chamber, 24 May 2000, para. 54.

2. Developing the Elements of Crimes

The ICTY has also extensively contributed to specifying the elements of crimes under its Statute. Such contributions include delineating the concept of grave breaches, the objective and subjective elements of crimes against humanity and the notion of war crimes, in particular the possibility of their commission during an internal armed conflict. The ICTY has further substantiated the definitions of specific offences, including those of extermination, enslavement, deportation, and has identified in international law a general, non-derogable prohibition against torture.[3]

3. Recognizing Gender Crimes

Furthermore, the ICTY has also made notable advances in redressing gender crimes by advancing the international law pertaining to the legal treatment and punishment of sexual violence during armed conflict. This development is seen as particularly positive since gender crimes were not addressed during the Nuremburg or Tokyo proceedings. The ICTY, along with the International Criminal Tribunal for Rwanda, have rendered judgements recognizing rape and other forms of sexual violence as crimes against humanity, war crimes, underlying acts of genocide and persecutions, and enslavement as a form of torture.[4]

4. Developing Legal Doctrines and Standards

In addition to substantiating existing international law, the Tribunal has developed legal doctrines and standards specific to international criminal tribunals.

(a) Joint Criminal Enterprise

One noteworthy example includes the development of the doctrine of 'common purpose' or 'joint criminal enterprise' (JCE) in relation to international criminal responsibility, particularly in the *Tadić*, *Kvočka*, and *Brđanin* judgements. Under this doctrine, a person can be found individually responsible for the commission of a crime, as part of 'a plurality of co-perpetrators who act pursuant to a common purpose involving the commission of a crime in the Statute'. In the course of the *Tadić* proceedings, in which the theory was first articulated, the Appeals Chamber reasoned that the very nature of many international crimes committed in wartime situations do not result from the criminal propensity of single individuals, but constitute manifestations of collective criminality.[5] Although only some members of the group materially carry out the criminal act, the participation and contribution of other members of the group is often vital to facilitating the commission of the offence, while the moral gravity of that participation would not be adequately captured by applying the mode of responsibility of 'aiding and abetting'.

In the last several years, participation in a joint criminal enterprise became the mode of responsibility most frequently applied in ICTY cases, as reflected in the *Stakić* Appeal Judgment,[6]

3 With particular reference to torture, see Judgment, *Brđanin*, Appeals Chamber, 3 April 2007, paras 244–252, where the issue of the severity of the pain inflicted is explored, rejecting the position adopted by certain States.

4 See, for instance, Judgement, *Furundžija*, Trial Chamber, 10 December 1998, paras 174–186; Judgement, *Kunarac*, Trial Chamber, 22 February 2001, paras 436–460.

5 Judgment, *Dusko Tadić*, Appeals Chamber, 15 July 1999, para. 91.

6 Judgment, *Stakić*, Appeals Chamber, 22 March 2006, para. 84.

and is often linked with the crime of persecutions. In *Brđanin*,[7] the Appeals Chamber clarified that the doctrine is perfectly adequate to describe, if all its elements are correctly understood and applied, the criminal responsibility of high-level politicians who act in concert with others to foster a criminal plan by using other individuals 'on the ground'.

(b) Standard of Review Where Additional Evidence is Admitted on Appeal

A second example is the Tribunal's development of a distinct standard of appellate review where additional evidence has been admitted on appeal. The ICTY has the power to admit additional evidence on appeal under Rule 115 ICTY RPE. The question thus arose as to what standard of review to apply on appeal where such additional evidence has been admitted. The *Blaškić* Appeals Chamber[8] reached the conclusion that, when the Appeals Chamber is itself seized of the task of evaluating trial evidence together with newly admitted evidence – in some instances even in light of a newly articulated legal finding on the elements of a crime or of a requirement for individual responsibility – before confirming a conviction on appeal it should, in the interests of justice, be convinced itself beyond reasonable doubt as to the guilt of the accused. Indeed, in such cases, if the Appeals Chamber were to apply a lower standard, neither in the first instance nor on appeal, would a conclusion of guilt based on the totality of evidence relied upon in the case, assessed in light of the correct legal standard, be reached beyond reasonable doubt.

D. The ICTY as Catalyst for Other Criminal Jurisdictions

A fourth achievement of the ICTY is that its existence has served as a catalyst for the proliferation of international and mixed criminal courts and tribunals in various parts of the world in recent years. The creation of the Tribunal marked an increased interest within the global community in the administration of international criminal justice. There is little doubt that the *ad hoc* Tribunals for the Former Yugoslavia and Rwanda accelerated the elaboration of the statute of a universal criminal court, culminating with the adoption of the Rome Statute in 1998. But it is also undeniable that the proliferation of judicial bodies supported by the international community did not end with the creation of the ICC, as demonstrated by the establishment of mixed Panels by the UN administration in Kosovo (2000), the Special Court for Sierra Leone (2002), the Special Panels for Serious Crimes for East Timor (2002) and the Extraordinary Chambers in the Courts of Cambodia (2003). The *ad hoc* Tribunals have provided invaluable guidance for the development of these judicial bodies. The proliferation phenomenon may well continue even after the ICC expands its caseload, due, for example, to the perceived need to bring perpetrators to justice for crimes committed before the Rome Statute entered into force.

4. Completion Strategy and Legacy

The third and final topic of this chapter addresses the completion strategy and the legacy of the ICTY, in a 'lessons learned' perspective in order to improve future international criminal adjudication. At this juncture in the history of the adjudication of international crimes and in the life of the Tribunal,

7 Judgment, *Brđanin*, Appeals Chamber, 3 April 2007, para. 425.
8 Judgment, *Blaškić*, Appeals Chamber, 29 July 2004, para. 23.

it is indeed extremely important to reflect on the way forward in this area of law.[9] The ICTY has accumulated a wealth of knowledge, practice and jurisprudence, which can contribute greatly to the cause of international justice. New tribunals and courts set up in the future, not to mention the international community in general, can benefit considerably from the lessons the ICTY has learned throughout its 14 years of existence.

A. Completion Strategy

1. The Meaning of the Completion Strategy

In accordance with the Tribunal's Completion Strategy, endorsed by the Security Council in Resolutions 1503 (2003) and 1534 (2004), the investigatory stage of the Prosecution's work was completed at the end of 2004 and no indictments were subsequently issued. To date, it is anticipated that all remaining trials of accused in the custody of the Tribunal will be completed in 2010, with all appellate work to be concluded within two years of the end of trials.

The Completion Strategy comprises three interrelated components as expressed in Resolution 1503 (2003): (i) the time frame for the completion of trial and appellate work; (ii) the concentration on the prosecution and trial of the most senior leaders bearing the greatest responsibility for the crimes within the Tribunal's jurisdiction; and (iii) the transferring of cases involving low- and mid-level accused to competent domestic jurisdictions. The Completion Strategy originated in an announcement[10] before the Security Council in August 2000 by the President and Prosecutor and was further developed, especially in the Report on the Judicial Status of the International Tribunal and the Prospects for Referring Certain Cases to National Courts presented to the Security Council on 23 July 2002.[11] The Tribunal has since worked consistently and creatively to meet this time frame. Of particular note is the contribution made to the Tribunal's trial capacity by Security Council Resolution 1329 (2000) which provided for the election by the General Assembly of a pool of 27 *ad litem* judges who may serve at any one time in the Trial Chambers of the Tribunal upon request of the President of the ICTY and appointment by the Secretary-General. The first election of *ad litem* judges took place on 12 June 2001 and was followed by a further election on 24 August 2005. The *ad litem* judges are elected for a term of four years, and following Security Council Resolution 1597 (2005) are now eligible for re-election.

The Security Council further supported the Tribunal in its implementation of the Completion Strategy by adopting Resolutions 1581 (2005) and 1629 (2005) which granted, respectively, the extension of terms for nine *ad litem* judges to enable them to finish the cases to which they had been assigned, and the early appointment of one *ad litem* judge as a permanent judge to facilitate her assignment to a new trial. Further, on 28 February 2006, the Security Council adopted Resolution 1660 (2006), by which it increased the number of *ad litem* judges from 9 to 12 and allowed for the assignment of *ad litem* reserve judges to appropriate trials. The possibility of appointing reserve judges was made in light of the anticipated length of the upcoming trials of multiple accused and the difficulty that could arise should one or more judges need to be replaced. The potential need, in

---

9 I have explored this issue more specifically in F. Pocar, 'Completion or Continuation Strategy?: Appraising Problems and Possible Developments in Building the Legacy of the ICTY', 6 *Journal of International Criminal Justice* (2008), at 655–665.

10 Seventh Annual Report, 26 July 2000, UN Doc. A/55/273. Available at http://www.icty.org/x/file/About/Reports%20and%20Publications/AnnualReports/annual_report_2000_en.pdf (visited 3 February 2009).

11 Appendix, press release of 20 June 2000/SB/P.I.S./512-e. Available at http://www.un.org/icty/pressreal/p512-e.htm (visited 3 February 2009).

such cases, to restart trials was seen to pose a risk to the Tribunal's ability to meet the Completion Strategy deadlines. Moreover, Resolution 1800 (2008) allowed temporary appointment of more *ad litem* judges in order for the Tribunal to be able to start more new cases even before the full completion of previous ones.

Just as key, however, to the successful implementation of the Completion Strategy is the range of new and creative measures which have been adopted and continue to be explored to improve the practice and procedure of the Tribunal's trials, particularly through the adoption of amendments to the RPE. Apart from this, on which I made separate remarks in this article, there have also been some important administrative measures taken, including the remodelling of all three courtrooms to accommodate the trials of multiple accused and their counsel, and the creation of new holding cells to accommodate the larger number of accused persons for each of the courtrooms. Greater use of the 'e-court' system – which integrates all case-related documents into a central electronic database and eliminates the need for unnecessary paper filings – has increased the accessibility of information and significantly reduced the time required to draft judgements. The Presidents of both *ad hoc* Tribunals have been regularly informing the Security Council on the progress made with the Completion Strategy and on the measures undertaken to this effect.[12]

2. Referral of Cases

Having been established by the Security Council as an *ad hoc* measure to halt and redress the serious violations of international humanitarian law being committed in the former Yugoslavia, the Tribunal was never intended to be a permanent institution or to act as a substitute for national courts. On 30 September 2002, after the Security Council had endorsed the Tribunal's strategy for the transfer of cases involving intermediary and lower-level accused to competent national jurisdictions, a revised version of Rule 11*bis* ICTY RPE was adopted in order to give effect to the broad strategy for the expeditious completion of all trial activities.

With the Security Council's endorsement, and despite the lack of an explicit legal basis for these transfers in the Statute itself, the Appeals Chamber interpreted its concurrent jurisdiction with national courts pursuant to Article 9 of the ICTYSt as providing an implicit legal basis for the transfer of lower level cases to national jurisdictions. Article 9 thus provided the legal basis for the enactment of Rule 11*bis* ICTY RPE, and Security Council Resolution 1534 (2004) formally authorized the referral of cases by the ICTY involving intermediate and lower rank accused to competent national jurisdictions.

Rule 11*bis* ICTY RPE provides that after an indictment has been confirmed, but prior to the commencement of trial, a Referral Bench appointed by the President and composed of three permanent judges may determine, after hearing the parties, that a case should be referred to the authorities of a state in which the crimes were committed, or in which the accused was arrested, or having jurisdiction and being willing and adequately prepared to accept such a case. An order for referral of an accused may be made by a Trial Chamber *proprio motu* or at the request of the Prosecutor. In determining whether to refer a case the Referral Bench must, pursuant to Security Council Resolution 1534 (2004), consider the gravity of the crimes charged and the rank and level of responsibility of the accused. In order for a referral to be granted, the judges must be satisfied

12 See the Reports from ICTY Presidents: S/2004/420 of 24 May 2004; S/2004/897 of 23 November 2004; S/2005/343 of 25 May 2005; S/2005/781 of 14 December 2005; S/2006/353 of 31 May 2006; S/2006/898 of 16 November 2006, S/2007/283 of 16 May 2007 and S/2007/663 of 12 November 2007. Available at http://www.icty.org/sections/AbouttheICTY/ReportsandPublications (visited 3 February 2009).

that the accused will receive a fair trial and that the death penalty will not be imposed or carried out. The decision of the Referral Bench may be appealed as of a right. Lastly, after a case has been referred to a national court and before the accused is convicted or acquitted, upon request of the Prosecution or *proprio motu*, the Referral Bench can revoke the referral order and formally request the deferral of the case from the authorities of the state to which the case had been transferred.

To date, the Prosecution has filed 13 referral motions involving 21 accused. The Referral Bench has granted six referrals, involving eleven accused, nine of which have been transferred to the special War Crimes Chamber of Bosnia and Herzegovina and two of which have been transferred to the authorities in Croatia for trial before its domestic courts. Let me mention a few examples. On 28 March 2007, proceedings against the first accused referred, Stanković, came to a close with the Appellate Panel of the Court of Bosnia and Herzegovina sentencing him to 20 years' imprisonment. On 25 May 2007, however, Stanković escaped from prison and is currently at large.[13] On 16 February 2007, the trial of Janković concluded with the Trial Panel finding him guilty of crimes against humanity and sentencing him to 34 years' imprisonment. On 23 October 2007, the Court of Bosnia and Herzegovina Appellate Panel upheld the Trial Panel's sentence. First-instance judgement in the case of Rasević and Todović was pronounced on 29 February 2008, finding the accused guilty of crimes against humanity and sentencing them to eight and a half years' and twelve and a half years' imprisonment, respectively. The trial in the single case referred by the ICTY to Croatia, that of Ademi and Norac, commenced on 18 June 2007 and is ongoing. In the *Kovačević* case, the only one referred to Serbia, the Belgrade District Court found on 5 December 2007 that the state of mental health of the accused temporarily prevents criminal prosecution.

The Tribunal continues to monitor the trials of referred cases in order to ensure that they are being conducted fairly and in full compliance with human rights norms. It is crucial for reasons of stability and reconciliation in the region that these national trials uphold the highest standards of due process so that justice is done and seen to be done by the victims and the rule of law becomes fully entrenched. To this end, I have asked the international community on several occasions to provide its continued and sustained support to the local judiciaries and detention facilities that will continue the historic work of the Tribunal.

I would note lastly, that the referral of cases pursuant to Rule 11*bis* ICTY RPE may be made to states beyond the former Yugoslavia through the exercise of universal jurisdiction. In fact, while the principle of complementarity, as provided for in the Rome Statute of the International Criminal Court, is never mentioned in the Statute of this Tribunal, it has nevertheless found a place in our Rules and case law through the use of the Rule 11*bis* ICTY RPE.

3. Domestic Capacity Building

Furthermore, the ICTY has actively strengthened the capacity of several domestic jurisdictions in their task of prosecuting violations of international humanitarian law. This fact is especially evident in the developing shift in focus of the Tribunal's historic work from the international to the domestic level. In fact, Rule 11*bis* ICTY RPE and referrals are only part of the solution.

The prosecution of suspected war criminals in local jurisdictions must continue long after the Tribunal closes its doors if a culture of impunity is to be eliminated and the post-war reconciliation process is to move forward. It is estimated that in Bosnia and Herzegovina alone, there remain between 5,000 and 10,000 persons to be tried. In this regard, the ICTY's role in the region of the

---

13 Information related to this case can be found at http://www.sudbih.gov.ba/?opcija=predmeti&id =159&jezik=e (visited 3 February 2009).

former Yugoslavia has not been limited to setting an example for future prosecutions. The Tribunal has been actively working to strengthen the capacity of domestic judicial systems to prosecute war crimes in accordance with international standards, particularly through its outreach programme, which has organized various capacity-building programs and working visits for legal professionals – including prosecutors and members of the judiciary – from Bosnia and Herzegovina, Serbia and Montenegro, Croatia, Macedonia, as well as from other countries. The Tribunal recognizes that strengthening the channels of communication between the local judiciaries in the Balkans and the Tribunal, so as to facilitate the transfer of knowledge, experience, and relevant material accumulated over the course of the Tribunal's mandate is essential to the development of the rule of law in the former Yugoslavia.

In this respect, the Tribunal has been working to ensure its legacy and provide a blueprint for future international courts for the transfer of war crimes cases to domestic jurisdictions through the compilation of its best practices. With the assistance of the UN Interregional Crime and Justice Research Institute (UNICRI) as facilitators, publishers and disseminators, a manual was made available in June 2009 in order to identify the challenges that judges, prosecutors and defence counsel face in the conduct of war crimes cases. Various Tribunal organs, under my chairmanship, have cooperated in the process of drafting the best practices of the Tribunal that are capable of being transferred to other international and domestic courts dealing with war crimes, crimes against humanity and genocide. The best practices project compiles the Tribunal's expertise on all aspects of the proceedings, all the way from investigations to the enforcement of sentences and may actually be followed by a digest of the ICTY's jurisprudence. Furthermore, with the assistance of the OSCE (Organization for Security and Co-operation in Europe), the ICTY is assessing its current outreach activities and training programs with a view to identifying best practices and what remains to be achieved to guarantee its lasting impact on the work of domestic courts in the region of the former Yugoslavia. These new initiatives are aimed at ensuring that the legacy of the Tribunal's work will be secured not only through proceedings carried out by domestic courts in the region, but by courts worldwide and in the jurisprudence of all Member States.

B. Upholding Due Process and Avoiding Lengthy Trials

When prosecuting individuals for violations of international humanitarian law, international tribunals must put in place a system that will ensure respect for due process and the rights of the accused at all costs. This is important not only due to the relevance assigned to the respect of fundamental human rights in criminal proceedings, but also due to the peculiarity of international jurisdictions, which cannot rely on a long tradition and therefore require, in order to act as legitimate bodies, strict adherence to the rights of the accused. Moreover, such an example is essential for the establishment of the rule of law in the states concerned, and for purposes of furthering peace and reconciliation. It is crucial that justice is done, and seen to be done.

At the same time, indictments before international criminal tribunals need to be focused to ensure expeditious adjudication at the international level. The technique of focusing indictments is part of trial management commonly used in national jurisdictions and does not impact on prosecutorial prerogatives. Moreover, international criminal tribunals will be most effective when they focus, from the start, on trying the most serious perpetrators in a given situation. International tribunals, with their costs in both financial and political terms, cannot be expected to deal with all perpetrators and all crimes. Accordingly, if at all possible, intermediate- and lower-level accused should be brought to justice within the local jurisdictions.

C. Developing Local Capacity

The work of an international criminal tribunal should be viewed in terms of its complementary function or shared responsibility with national courts in the prosecution and prevention of war crimes, crimes against humanity and genocide. Emphasis should be placed on collaboration between international and domestic jurisdictions in order to develop the capacity of national courts in post-conflict situations to assume responsibility as early as possible for the prosecution of accused persons. Furthermore, where the jurisdiction of the criminal tribunal is complementary to that of a national jurisdiction, it remains essential that there be international oversight over domestic prosecutions to ensure compliance with high standards of fair trial and due process. A special type of cooperation with domestic courts operating in the region of the former Yugoslavia is provided by the amended Rule 75 ICTY RPE, which allows direct petitioning by other judicial authorities for access to protected material in the possession of the international tribunal, and by parties in proceedings in those jurisdictions (with the authorization of the local judicial authority). This is a very powerful mechanism to avoid the strictures and delays often experienced in interstate cooperation.

D. Cooperation of States

The efficacy of the international criminal justice system depends on the cooperation of states, both those directly impacted by the conflict and the international community in general. Governments must provide (i) assistance in arresting and transferring accused persons to the international tribunals; (ii) access for investigative and evidentiary purposes; as well as (iii) ensure the appropriate protection of witnesses. States should apply continuous pressure on those governments failing to comply with their obligations to cooperate with international tribunals. Furthermore, it is important that adequate financial support be secured in order that international tribunals may fulfil their mandates.

5. Conclusion

The ICTY provides a significant benchmark of the tremendous progress made in international criminal law since World War II. Notwithstanding the considerable challenges faced by the Tribunal, its functioning and achievements demonstrate that international criminal justice is feasible: serious violations of international humanitarian law can be effectively prosecuted in the international domain. As the Tribunal winds down its activities and international criminal justice transitions to a new phase, the institutional experience, as well as the jurisprudence of the ICTY, will leave behind an impressive legacy and pave the way for future international criminal tribunals, as well as national courts, to enforce international humanitarian law and prevent impunity for war crimes, crimes against humanity and genocide.

Chapter 3
The International Criminal Tribunal for Rwanda

Erik Møse

1. Introduction

The 2007 Turin *Conference on International Criminal Justice* gathered representatives from all judicial institutions entrusted with the task of applying international criminal law, thus providing an opportunity to share experiences, exchange information and ideas, and to look ahead. This chapter includes an overview of the development and activities of the International Criminal Tribunal for Rwanda (ICTR), including its completion strategy.[1]

2. Establishment and Development

A. First Mandate[2] *(1995 to 1999)*

It is well known that the Security Council decided to set up the Tribunal in November 1994, 18 months after the adoption of the resolution establishing the International Criminal Tribunal for the Former Yugoslavia (ICTY).[3] The resolution did not determine where the ICTR should be located. The decision to place it in Arusha was made in February 1995, based on the Secretary-General's recommendation earlier that month.[4] Other alternatives, in particular Kigali and Nairobi, were considered but rejected. There was a severe shortage of premises in Kigali that could accommodate the Tribunal and serve its needs properly. It was also felt that the appearance of justice and fairness, in particular complete impartiality and objectivity, required that trial proceedings be held in a neutral country. In this connection, the Secretary-General considered that there were serious security risks in bringing the leaders of the previous regime into Rwanda.[5]

1 Useful information about the work of the Tribunal is found in its 13 annual reports to the Security Council and the General Assembly in conformity with Article 32 of the Statute. They are available on the Tribunal's website at www.ictr.org (visited 20 August 2009). See also E. Møse, 'Main Achievements of the ICTR' and 'The ICTR Completion Strategy – Challenges and Possible Solutions', *Journal of International Criminal Justice* 3 (2005), at 920–943 and 6 (2008), at 667–679, respectively.

2 Article 12*bis* (3) of the ICTR Statute provides that the judges shall be elected by the General Assembly for a term of four years, often referred to as the 'mandates' of the Tribunal. The first term of the judges started on 25 May 1995, the date of their election, followed by the second term of office from May 1999, etc. The third mandate was extended by the Security Council, see *infra*, 2(D).

3 SC Res. 808, 5 May 1993 (ICTY): SC Res. 955, 8 November 1994 (ICTR).

4 SC Res. 977, 22 February 1995; Secretary-General's report of 13 February 1995 (S/1995/134).

5 The Kenyan government ultimately decided that it would not be in a position to provide a seat for the Tribunal in Nairobi, whereas the Tanzanian government offered to accommodate the Tribunal in the Arusha International Conference Centre (AICC).

The six ICTR judges were elected for four years by the General Assembly in May 1995. One month later, they held their first plenary session. It had to take place in The Hague, as the ICTR did not have any premises in Arusha. During this meeting, the judges adopted the Rules of Procedure and Evidence (the Rules).[6] They also elected the President and Vice-President.[7] Until September 1995, they shuttled between their home countries and Arusha, in order to review indictments, issue orders and warrants of arrest, etc. Only then were they allowed by the United Nations Headquarters to take up residence in Arusha.[8]

A main challenge during the first mandate was to create a functional judicial institution under very difficult circumstances.[9] The general infrastructure in Arusha was quite rudimentary in 1995 (no tarmac roads, unstable electricity and water provisions, etc.). The Tribunal had no courtrooms, offices or prison cells. Telephone and fax lines were few and unreliable. The Registry started its activities in hotel rooms. The Tribunal could only move into its headquarters in November 1995, one year after the Security Council decided to set up the ICTR. In 1996, the United Nations Detention Facility was completed and provided accommodation for six detainees. It was built within the enclosure of Arusha prison, but the international prison is completely separated from the Tanzanian. The first accused was brought to the Tribunal in May 1996.

Building courtrooms in premises previously used for office space was not an easy task. During the construction period, pre-trial hearings were held in conference rooms. The first two courtrooms were not ready until 1997. The first trial (*Akayesu*) started on 9 January 1997, followed by other proceedings in March 1997 (*Rutaganda*) and April 1997 (*Kayishema and Ruzindana*). The third courtroom was finished in late 1998.

The ICTY Prosecutor, who had been elected in July 1994, assumed his function as the common Prosecutor of both Tribunals and carried out his dual functions from The Hague.[10] He made many visits to Rwanda and the neighbouring states in order to establish the necessary cooperation with authorities there. The recruitment of staff in Kigali was a long and complex process. As of August 1996, fewer than a dozen staff members were on board in Kigali. A new common Prosecutor of the two Tribunals took up her functions in the last quarter of 1996.[11]

In March 1998, the Prosecutor submitted a joint indictment in respect of 29 accused. The confirming judge dismissed it as inadmissible as drafted. The Prosecutor's request to appeal the decision was rejected by the Appeals Chamber. Consequently, the Prosecution had to change its strategy.[12]

---

6 The ICTR Rules were almost identical to the ICTY Rules, which had been adopted on 11 February 1994 and subsequently amended five times.

7 The six ICTR judges elected by General Assembly decision 49/324 were Laity Kama, Senegal (President); Yakov A. Ostrovsky, Russia (Vice-President); Lennart Aspegren, Sweden; Tafazzal H. Khan, Pakistan; Navanethem Pillay, South Africa; and William H. Sekule, Tanzania (listed in order of precedence after the first plenary from 26–30 June 1995).

8 The United Nations administration considered the judges as having officially taken office from 19 June 1996.

9 On 26 February 1997, the Secretary-General appointed Agwu U. Okali (Nigeria). He replaced Andronico O. Adede (Kenya).

10 By SC Res. 936, 8 July 1994, Richard J. Goldstone (South Africa) was appointed as Prosecutor for the ICTY.

11 Louise Arbour (Canada) was appointed by SC Res. 1047, 29 February 1996.

12 Decision, *Bagosora and 28 Others*, Dismissal of Indictment, 31 March 1998; Decision on the Admissibility of the Prosecutor's Appeal from the Decision of a Confirming Judge Dismissing an Indictment against Théoneste Bagosora and 28 Others, 8 June 1998. The request included three groups of persons: 11

In spite of all the challenges during the first mandate, the Tribunal rendered six judgements involving seven accused, mostly in single-accused cases. Several of them were ground-breaking, such as *Akayesu* and *Kambanda*.[13]

B. Second Mandate (1999 to 2003)

At the beginning of the second mandate it was clear that, in addition to single-accused cases, the Tribunal had to hear seven multi-accused cases, each including high-ranking personalities who allegedly participated in the same criminal transaction, such as the use of public media, or alleged crimes in certain geographical areas of Rwanda. These joint trials were *Butare* (six accused); *Cyangugu* (three); *Military I* (four); *Military II* (four); *Media* (three); *Government I* (four), which was later referred to as the *Karemera et al.* trial (three); and *Government II* (four).[14]

A main challenge for the nine judges was to make these cases ready for trial.[15] As a first step it was important to dispose of a high number of pending motions, both from the prosecution and the defence. This was facilitated through an amendment of the Rules in June 1999, which allowed the Chambers to decide motions based on written submissions.[16] In August 1999, the third Prosecutor was appointed.[17] Two multi-accused trials commenced in 2000 (*Media* and *Cyangugu*) and two in 2001 (*Military I* and *Butare*). Four single-accused trials started during the period 1999 to 2001.

The judges were anxious to bring as many cases as possible to the trial stage in order to avoid unnecessary pre-trial litigation and ensure their completion. Therefore, the three Trial Chambers

---

detainees had already appeared before a Trial Chamber at the pre-trial stage; indictments of five individuals at large had been confirmed; and 13 suspects had not yet had their indictments confirmed.

13 See also *infra*, 3(C). The judgements rendered following proceedings during the first mandate were *Akayesu* (2 September 1998); *Kambanda* (4 September 1998, guilty plea); *Serushago* (5 February 1999, guilty plea); *Kayishema and Ruzindana* (21 May 1999); and *Musema* (27 January 2000).

14 These seven multi-accused cases, involving from three to six accused, were the result of the Prosecution's need to change its strategy (see *supra*, 2(A)). Two of them are referred to by the name of the prefecture where the alleged joint criminal transaction took place: the *Butare* trial (Kanyabashi, Ndayambaje, Nsabimana, Ntahobali, Nteziryayo and Nyiramasuhuko); and the *Cyangugu* case (*Ntagerura, Bagambiki and Imanishimwe*). Other cases point to the positions of the accused: *Military I* trial (*Bagosora, Kabiligi, Ntabakuze and Nseniyumva*); the *Military II* case (*Bizimungu, Nzuwonomeye, Ndindiliyimana and Sagahutu*), and the *Government* trial (*Bizimungu, Mugenzi, Bicamumpaka and Mugiraneza*), whereas the *Media* trial (*Nahimana, Ngeze and Barayagwiza*) reflects the subject matter of the case.

15 SC Res. 1165, 30 April 1998, established a third Trial Chamber for both Tribunals (see *infra*, 3(A)). The nine judges elected for the second mandate were (in order of precedence after the June 1999 Plenary) Navanethem Pillay, South Africa (President); Erik Møse, Norway (Vice-President); Laity Kama, Senegal; Lloyd George Williams, St Kitts and Nevis; Yakov A. Ostrovsky, Russia; William H. Sekule, Tanzania; Mehmet Güney, Turkey; Pavel Dolenc, Slovenia; and Asoka de Zoysa Gunawardana (Sri Lanka). Judge Kama passed away in May 2001. On 31 May 2001, the Secretary-General appointed Andresia Vaz (Senegal) in his place. Arlette Ramaroson (Madagascar) and Winston Churchill Maqutu (Lesotho) were elected as additional judges by the General Assembly on 24 April 2001, following the Security Council's decision to increase the number of ICTR judges to 11. See *infra*, 3(A).

16 See *infra*, 3(C).

17 By SC Res. 1259, 11 August 1999, Carla del Ponte (Switzerland) was appointed Prosecutor for the two Tribunals.

conducted trials on a 'twin-track' basis.[18] Almost all judges sat in one multi-accused trial and at least one single-accused case. The purpose of this system was to use inevitable breaks during one trial to ensure progress of another case. It also enabled the prosecution and the defence to prepare for the next stage of the proceedings while the other case was heard (for instance by interviewing witnesses etc.).

This strategy resulted in the delivery of a considerable number of judgements. The number of accused who had their cases completed in the second mandate doubled to 14.[19] Two of the multi-accused trials (*Media* and *Cyangugu*) were completed. In the second half of the mandate, the Tribunal also to some extent used the so-called 'shift system', sitting in morning and afternoon sessions.[20] Many other measures were adopted to increase the Tribunal's efficiency. The productivity of the Registry continued to improve.[21]

C. Third Mandate (2003 to 2007)

At the beginning of the third mandate, it was important to start new trials and ensure the progress of the two on-going multi-accused trials, *Butare* and *Military I*.[22] The beginning of the second mandate had shown the need to plan the commencement of new trials well in advance of the following mandate. Meetings were therefore held during the last year of the second mandate by a newly established New Trial Committee, composed of representatives of Chambers, Prosecution and the Registry, to ensure an early start of trials in the third mandate. As a consequence, two single-accused trials and the two *Government* cases commenced between July and November 2003. This was facilitated by the arrival of the first four *ad litem* judges, following the election in June 2003 of a pool of 18 such judges. Three further single-accused trials and the *Military II* case,

---

18 'Twin-tracking' implies that two trials are heard in consecutive slots, for instance according to the following pattern: Trial A five weeks, trial B five weeks, trial A five weeks, etc. Defence counsel in Trial A will leave Arusha while Trial B is heard.

19 The 14 accused who received judgements following completion of proceedings during the second mandate were Ruggiu (1 June 2000, guilty plea); Bagilishema (7 June 2001); E. and G. Ntakirutimana (21 February 2003); Semanza (15 May 2003); Niyitegeka (15 May 2003); Kajelijeli (1 December 2003); Nahimana, Ngeze and Barayagwiza (the *Media* case, 3 December 2003); Kamuhanda (22 January 2004); Ntagerura, Bagambiki and Imanishimwe (the *Cyangugu* case, 25 February 2004). The most voluminous trial (238 trial days) was the *Media* case. The defence case closed on 9 May 2003.

20 The 'shift-system' means that one courtroom is used for two cases, one heard in the morning sessions and the other in the afternoon sessions. The system operates with a morning shift from, for instance, 8.45 to about 13.00, and an afternoon shift until about 18.30. In periods, some of the judges were sitting in two different trials on the same day in order to ensure rapid progress.

21 From 27 February 2001, Adama Dieng (Senegal) replaced Agwu U. Okali as Registrar of the Tribunal. His four-year mandate has subsequently been renewed.

22 The 11 ICTR judges during the third mandate from May 2007 were Erik Møse, Norway (President), Andrésia Vaz, Senegal (Vice-President), William H. Sekule, Tanzania; Lloyd George Williams, St Kitts and Nevis; Mehmet Güney, Turkey; Asoka de Zoysa Gunawardana, Sri Lanka; Arlette Ramaroson, Madagascar; Jai Ram Reddy, Fiji; Sergei Alekseevich Egorov, Russia; Inés Mônica Weinberg de Roca, Argentina; and Khalida Rachida Khan, Pakistan (replacing a judge who resigned shortly after taking office in May 2003). Judge Williams resigned with effect from 30 March 2004, and Sir Dennis C.M. Byron (St Kitts and Nevis) was appointed by the Secretary-General on 8 April 2004. Judge Gunawardana retired for health reasons by the end of June 2004 and was replaced by Asoka de Silva (Sri Lanka) by the Secretary-General's appointment of 3 August 2004. Judge Weinberg was member of the Appeals Chamber from 2003 to August 2005, when she was replaced by Judge Vaz. Judge Ramaroson was elected Vice-President from May 2005 to May 2007.

the seventh and last multi-accused case, started in 2004. The arrival of the additional five *ad litem* judges made it possible to start these trials.[23]

In August 2003, the Security Council decided that both Tribunals should complete all investigations by the end of 2004, trials in 2008, and appeals by 2010. The Council also established a separate Prosecutor for the ICTR.[24] An important part of the activities during the third mandate was to ensure progress in conformity with the Completion Strategy while maintaining the high standards of fair trial.

From June 2003 to June 2007, the Tribunal started cases involving 31 accused and continued trials involving 10 persons. The *Military I* trial was completed, whereas the other remaining multi-accused cases made considerable progress. As a consequence, a high number of judgements were rendered in 2007 and 2008.[25]

D. The Final Period (from June 2007)

In view of the Completion Strategy, the Security Council accepted a Tribunal suggestion not to elect judges for another four-year period, but to extend the term of the judges, first to 31 December 2008, and then to the end of 2009 (*infra*, 4).[26] The purpose was to ensure continuity and efficiency.

The evidentiary phase of three of the four remaining multi-accused cases (*Bizimungu et al.*, *Military II* and *Butare*) was completed in late 2008 and early 2009, followed by closing arguments and judgement writing. The situation is different in the *Karemera et al.* trial (three accused), which has a complicated history.[27] The defence commenced its case in April 2008. The evidentiary phase of this still ongoing trial required a considerable part of 2009.

---

23 See *infra*, 3(A) about *ad litem* judges in general.

24 The Security Council adopted three resolutions on 28 August 2003. Resolution 1503 contains the deadlines for completion, see *infra*, 5; Resolution 1504 establishes a separate ICTR Prosecutor, see *infra*, 3 (B); and Resolution 1505 appointed Hassan Bubacar Jallow (Gambia) as Prosecutor.

25 Judgements delivered in the third mandate include *Gacumbitsi* (17 June 2004); *Ndindabahizi* (15 July 2004); *Rutaganira* (14 March 2004, guilty plea); *Muhimana* (28 April 2005); *Simba* (13 December 2005); *Bisengimana* (13 April 2006, guilty plea); *Serugendo* (2 June 2006 guilty plea); *Mpambara* (12 September 2006); *Rwamakuba* (20 September 2006), *Muvunyi* (12 September 2006); *Seromba* (13 December 2006); *Nzabirinda* (23 February 2007, guilty plea), *Rugambarara* (16 November 2007, guilty plea); and *Karera* (7 December 2007). In *Military I*, oral closing arguments were heard from 28 May to 1 June 2007. The Chamber pronounced its unanimous judgement on 18 December 2008. Four single-accused cases which started in the third mandate resulted in judgements in 2008 and 2009, see *infra*, 2(D).

26 SC Res. 1684, 13 June 2006, and SC Res. 1717, 13 October 2006, which extended the term of office of all permanent and *ad litem* judges until 31 December 2008. With effect from June 2007, Judge Dennis C.M. Byron (St Kitts and Nevis) was elected President and Judge Khalida Rachid Khan (Pakistan) Vice-President. By SC Res. 1824, 18 July 2008, the mandate of permanent and *ad litem* judges was extended through 31 December 2009, with the exception of three judges who left the Tribunal by the end of 2008.

27 Originally referred to as the *Government I* case, the *Karemera et al.* trial (four accused) commenced on 27 November 2003. As the bench had to be reconstituted, the case started *de novo* on 19 September 2005. It now involves three accused (Karemera, Ngirumpatse and Nzirorera) because the case against the fourth person, Rwamakuba, was severed. In January 2007, one judge withdrew for health reasons. The Chamber's decision to continue with a substitute judge was appealed. After the Appeals Chamber's ruling in April 2007 and the appointment of a substitute judge in May, the trial continued in June 2007. See for details the ninth Completion Strategy report, S/2007/676, 20 November 2007, para. 57. Other problems in this case include lack of disclosure of document and ill health of one of the accused.

In this final period, it is also necessary to complete all ongoing single-accused cases. Moreover, at the end of 2008, eight detainees were awaiting trial, of whom three had been arrested recently.[28] The Prosecutor's requests that four of these cases be transferred to Rwanda were rejected in 2008 by the Trial Chambers because they were not satisfied that the accused would receive a fair trial there.[29] Another of the eight accused originally sought to be transferred to European countries, but also these efforts failed. Two transfer requests to France were successful.[30]

3. Lessons Learnt

The two *ad hoc* Tribunals were the first international judicial bodies after Nuremberg to adjudicate matters of individual criminal responsibility for serious international crimes. They were also the first Tribunals ever set up by a Security Council resolution under Chapter VII of the UN Charter. Obviously, there would have been a need to gain experience in order to deal with issues that were unforeseen or not fully appreciated and would have unfolded only through the often costly process of trial and error.[31]

In addition, the ICTR faced problems not encountered by its sister Tribunal in The Hague. Both the headquarters in Arusha and the investigation unit in Kigali were set up and had to function in towns with very limited infrastructure and in an area where there had never been any international court. In spite of these challenges, the Tribunal managed to build up a fully operational judicial institution. The proof is not only the high-tech courtrooms and the convoys of vehicles transporting the detainees to and from the proceedings every day. It follows clearly from the statistics. After the completion of cases involving seven accused during the first mandate, the number doubled to 14 in the second, and was even higher in the third mandate.[32]

Before further describing the learning experience of the Tribunal, it is important to recall some specific characteristics of international criminal proceedings compared to criminal cases at the national level. The indictees at large are hiding on many continents, although a majority of them seem to be on the African continent. Investigations are frequently carried out in states with minimal, or compromised, infrastructures. The trials are legally and factually very complex. Several of them involve multiple defendants and crimes of enormous magnitude and scale. A considerable volume of documents is required when trying alleged architects of the atrocities, including high-ranking

28 Five single-accused cases which started in the third mandate were completed in 2008 and 2009: *Nchamihigo* (12 November 2008), *Bikindi* (2 December 2008), *Zigiranyirazo* (18 December 2008), *Rukundo* (27 February 2009); and *Renzaho* (April 2009). In 2009, judgement will also be rendered in *Nsengimana* (which started in June 2007), *Kalimanzira* (May 2008) and *Setako* (August 2008).

29 See *infra*, 5D.

30 The Prosecutor's requests for transfer to national jurisdictions form part of the Tribunal's Completion Strategy, see *infra*, 5D.

31 *See*, e.g., *Report of the Expert Group to Conduct a Review of the Effective Operation and Functioning of the International Tribunal for the Former Yugoslavia and the International Criminal Tribunal for Rwanda*, submitted to the Secretary-General on 11 November 1999 (A/54/634), p. 12, para. 15: 'It cannot be overemphasized that establishing a new and unique prosecutorial and judicial institution with the task of implementing a complex and not well defined set of legal norms with respect to extraordinary events in inhospitable environments was inescapably going to involve a lengthy development period ... No system of international justice embodying standards of fairness, such as those reflected in the creation of ICTY and ICTR would, under the best of circumstances, either be inexpensive or free of the growing pains that inhere in virtually all new organizations.'

32 See *supra*, 2(B) and (C).

members of government. This documentation, often amounting to thousands of pages in just one case, is subject to disclosure and must usually be available in both English and French, the two official languages of the Tribunal.

The number of witnesses is frequently considerable, and interpretation of all testimony is required into the two official languages, as well as Kinyarwanda. Witnesses may have to be brought from a difficult environment, afforded considerable protection before and after testimony, and sometimes relocated. Staff and counsel involved in cases come from different cultures and legal traditions, and effective communication requires new skills and extra efforts. Many defence counsel need to leave the offices in their home countries for considerable periods to spend time working at the ICTR in Arusha.

The complexity of the investigation and prosecution of complex international crimes requires a comprehensive international infrastructure. As a subsidiary organ under the Security Council, the Tribunal adheres to United Nations rules and regulations, which are not always tailor-made to the activities of a court. The total number of posts includes staff across a diverse range of functions, including investigators, prosecution staff, defence teams, judges and their legal staff, interpreters and translators, court reporters, witness protection officers, security personnel and various groups of administrators. Trying cases of this nature would be difficult and expensive for any legal system.

Faced with these and other challenges, the Tribunal has amended the provisions regulating its activities and improved its working methods. Only some of these measures can be mentioned here.

A. Insufficient Number of Judges

The Statutes of both Tribunals originally provided for six judges in two Trial Chambers. Not unexpectedly, this soon proved insufficient because of the high number of accused that were apprehended and the time needed to conduct the voluminous trials. In 1997, the ICTR, followed by the ICTY, approached the Security Council with a request for a third Trial Chamber. The Security Council granted these demands and consequently established one additional Trial Chamber for each of the Tribunals.[33]

In 2000, a report prepared by the ICTY proposed the introduction of *ad litem* judges, who would be made available to serve in the Trial Chambers when needed. The purpose was to increase the Tribunal's judicial capacity. The Security Council established a pool of such judges in the ICTY in November 2000. The same resolution also enlarged the membership of the common Appeals Chambers by two judges. This reform was intended to ease its workload and would also ensure that ICTR is represented in the Appeals Chamber, which was not envisaged under the original Statutes.[34]

---

33 SC Res. 1165, 30 April 1998 (ICTR); SC Res. 1166, 13 May 1998 (ICTY). Already in SC Res. 955, 8 November 1995, the Security Council had indicated that it would 'consider increasing the number of judges and Trial Chambers of the International Tribunal if it becomes necessary'. The election of the three new ICTR judges coincided with the end of term of office of the six judges who had been elected in 1995. The election of all nine judges took place in November 1998. In February 1999, three new judges took office, the intention being to enable the third Trial Chamber to start work as soon as possible. Unfortunately, this was made impossible due to the resignation of one of the judges in this Chamber.

34 SC Res. 1329, 30 November 2000. Judges Mehmet Güney and Asoka de Zoysa Gunawardana were the first ICTR judges to serve in the Appeals Chamber.

Following a request by the ICTR, the Security Council in August 2002 accepted the creation of a pool of 18 *ad litem* judges.[35] They were elected by the General Assembly on 25 June 2003. The Security Council resolution only allowed four *ad litem* judges to take office at any one time, but pursuant to two initiatives from the ICTR in September 2003, the number was increased from four to nine in October. The Security Council also conferred on these judges the competence to adjudicate over pre-trial matters.[36] The arrival of the first four *ad litem* judges made it possible to start four new trials, to continue the *Butare* trial and to commence another two trials. The remaining five judges arrived soon thereafter.

In daily practice, the *ad litem* judges perform the same work as the permanent judges, and have contributed greatly to the work of the ICTR. As of March 2009, 14 of the 18 judges in the pool had served in Arusha, some of them for very long periods.[37]

B. Separate Prosecutor

The Statutes of the two Tribunals first provided for a common Prosecutor. This had the advantage of ensuring a uniform prosecutorial policy for the ICTR and the ICTY. In August 2003, the Security Council decided to establish a separate Prosecutor for the ICTR.[38] It was thought important to divide the comprehensive work performed by the Prosecutor as the two Tribunals entered into the crucial period of implementing their Completion Strategy. Experience has shown that this was the right decision, in particular because it has been easier for the Prosecutor to focus constantly on all activities falling under his responsibility.

C. Amendments of the Rules

The ICTR has continuously amended its Rules of Procedure and Evidence. This is done by the judges in the Plenary session, which generally takes place in May each year, sometimes twice a year. At the national level, it would be unusual if the judiciary were directly involved in legislative activities. In the *ad hoc* Tribunals, however, the judges' decision-making authority has been vital in order to ensure the necessary flexibility. Time was needed to gain experience in handling such voluminous and complex cases. It is important to note that the prosecution and representatives of the defence teams are heard before the Rules are amended.[39]

From 1998, the ICTR Trial Chambers began organizing pre-trial and pre-defence conferences, after having added Rules 73*bis* and 73*ter*, respectively. According to these provisions, the Chamber

35 SC Res. 1431, 8 August 2002.

36 SC Res. 1512, 27 October 2003. In order to meet the Completion Strategy, the Security Council in December 2008 authorized the Secretary-General to appoint additional *ad litem* judges even if the maximum number of such judges will from time to time exceeds nine. The background was the departure of two permanent and one *ad litem* judge by the end of 2008, and the indication by three other judges of their intention to leave later, once their trials were completed in late 2009. See SC Res. 1855, 19 December 2008.

37 These 14 *ad litem* judges are Solomy Balungi Bossa, Uganda; Flavia Lattanzi, Italy; Lee Gacuiga Muthoga, Kenya; Florence Rita Arrey, Cameroon; Emile Francis Short, Ghana; Karin Hökborg, Sweden; Taghrid Hikmet, Jordan; Seon Ki Park, Republic of Korea; Gberdao Gustave Kam, Burkina Faso; Robert Fremr, Czech Republic; Vagn Joensen, Denmark; Joseph Masanche, Tanzania; Mparany Rajohnson, Madagascar; and Aydin Akay, Turkey.

38 See *supra*, 2 (C).

39 The prosecution and the defence are allowed to submit proposals and comments on suggested amendments tabled by others.

may require a list of witnesses, a summary of the intended content and length of the testimony of each witness, a statement of admitted facts and law, a statement of contested facts and law, and a list of exhibits. On this basis, the Chamber can order that the number of witnesses be reduced and the length of the testimonies be shortened.

In the first mandate, all motions, irrespective of their significance, were heard orally. This meant requesting defence counsel from many parts of the world to come to Arusha, finding a suitable time for everyone involved, ensuring the availability of a courtroom, etc. In 1999, Rule 73(A) was amended to allow motions under that provision to be considered on the basis of a written procedure, thereby avoiding a hearing and the need to convoke the parties to the seat of the Tribunal. Another innovation adopted on the same date was that motions may be decided by a single judge, rather than by a Chamber. The introduction of a written procedure greatly improved the efficiency of Chambers, reduced the number of outstanding motions and reduced the Tribunal's costs.

In 2000, the judges introduced deadlines for motions to be heard orally, and a general time limit for responding to motions (Rule 73(D) and (E)). A filtering process by three judges was introduced at the appeal level (Rule 73(B)). Furthermore, an explicit provision was adopted to allow a Chamber to impose sanctions against a counsel who brings a motion that, in the opinion of the Chamber, is frivolous or an abuse of process. Such sanctions may include 'non-payment, in whole or in part, of fees associated with the motion and/or costs thereof' (Rule 73(F)). It has been used in some cases.

From 2000, judges were no longer disqualified from participating in a trial if they had confirmed the indictment against the accused in the case. It had become apparent that the disqualification clause in the Rules impeded an efficient organization of trials and that it was not really necessary in the interests of justice.

Because of the time needed to complete trials before the Tribunals, there is a greater risk than in national proceedings that persons involved in the case may fall ill. If a trial is not completed by the end of the judges' four-year mandate, the fact that a judge is not re-elected may also pose problems. At an early stage the Rules were amended to allow for short absences of up to five working days. According to a subsequent amendment, a Chamber may continue the trial in the eventuality of a judge being ill and in the event of death, resignation or a judge not being re-elected. In such situations, Rule 15 *bis* now allows cases to continue with a substitute judge, provided that certain conditions are fulfilled.

D. Interpretation and Translation

A large number of witnesses testify in Kinyarwanda. Originally, there were no Kinyarwanda interpreters in the United Nations system, and there was a need for training of interpreters. This presented problems, as some English and French words could not be translated to Kinyarwanda and vice versa. A related problem during the first and the beginning of the second mandate was the need to hear the entire answer to a question from the witness in Kinyarwanda before interpreting it into French and then English. This system of consecutive interpretation was very time-consuming. During the second mandate, simultaneous interpretation from and into Kinyarwanda became possible due to further training and was gradually introduced in all three Chambers. This has saved considerable time in the courtroom.

The need to translate masses of documents may delay the judicial proceedings. A working group found methods to reduce such problems, for instance by identifying which documents, or portions of them, are really essential. Another option may be to read certain passages into the record during the court proceedings and thereby obtain an official interpretation. In spite of such techniques to alleviate the problems, it is still necessary to establish priorities. This is not an easy task when the Tribunal's translation services works for the Appeals Chamber, the three Trial Chambers, the Prosecution and the Registry. In practice, consultation is essential to find solutions.

E. Other Measures

Pre-trial preparation ensures efficiency during trial. This is primarily the task of the Chamber responsible for the case at the pre-trial stage. The three judges, or one of them designated by the Chamber, will hold status conferences in order to move the preparations forward.[40] A useful supplement when preparing many cases for trial was the establishment in 2003 of a Trial Committee, composed of representatives of Chambers, the Registry and the prosecution. Its task was to identify and contribute to the resolution of problems that may slow down the proceedings, such as lack of disclosure, translation, availability of counsel, etc. The Committee was also in contact with the various defence teams. Its work facilitated the trial-readiness of many cases. Combined with the work of the pre-trial judges, this contributed to the high number of trials starting during 2003 to 2007.

The Prosecution has sought to develop best practices in many ways. One example is in connection with requests for confirmation of indictments. The present policy is to ensure that the case is ready for trial, in the sense that all approved identified investigations are completed, a draft pre-trial brief is prepared, together with draft exhibits and witness lists, and that disclosure searches are completed.

During trial, illness or absence of counsel may cause interruption in the proceedings. While the prosecution team is usually composed of several attorneys, the defence teams are more vulnerable to such occurrences. The Tribunal has therefore insisted that lead counsel for the defence must select a co-counsel. In many cases, the Chambers have required that the co-counsel continues the case when lead counsel is absent.

Some states require considerable time to facilitate the travel of witnesses to Arusha, in particular if they do not have travel documents. Routines have been developed to reduce these problems. Furthermore, the judges now expect counsel to have a substitute witness available in case a witness who is scheduled to testify fails to appear or falls ill. In some instances, it has been necessary to call a higher number of witnesses than can actually be heard during a certain period (overbooking) in order to avoid interruptions.

Another difficulty has been that prosecution and defence counsel request additional time for the preparation of cross-examination in situations where unexpected evidence emerges or is offered without sufficient prior notice. In order to avoid such delays, Chambers have required so-called 'will-say' statements when the counsel leading the witness discovers that new information will be provided during the testimony. This reduces the element of surprise and hence the need for adjournments.

With a high number of cases being heard simultaneously, the availability of courtrooms has been a problem. An important event was therefore the inauguration, on 1 March 2005, of a fourth courtroom. It was constructed in record time, only four weeks, and was used for trials from the day of its inauguration. This has ensured that more cases are heard in full-day sessions and has

---

40 Rule 65*bis* now contains an explicit legal basis for status conferences.

increased the judicial output of the Tribunal. The fourth courtroom has been an important element in the Tribunal's Completion Strategy, together with twin-tracking and the shift system.[41]

F. Reduced Trial Time

Following the adoption of measures to avoid delays, the time spent in the courtroom was reduced. This has been particularly noteworthy in single-accused trials. The average number of trial days in such cases was originally 62. Subsequent proceedings reflect a substantially lower number: *Ntakirutimana* (30 trial days per accused); *Niyitegeka* (35); *Gacumbitsi* (32); *Ndindabahizi* (27); *Muhimana* (34); *Karera* (33); *Renzaho* (49); *Nsengimana* (44); and *Kalimanzira* (38).[42] Although some single-accused cases still require more time, for instance because of the number of charges, it is expected that this trend of a reduced number of trial days will continue. The period required for judgement writing has varied, depending on the Chamber's overall workload.[43]

Multi-accused trials are much more time-consuming, due to extensive indictments, the number of prosecution and defence witnesses, voluminous documentary evidence and extensive cross-examination. While single-accused judgements usually consist of about 100 pages, the judgements in multi-accused cases amount to several hundred pages. It is therefore a considerable achievement that the Tribunal has now completed all but one such case.[44]

4. Other Achievements

A. Accountability for Leaders

From the outset, the Prosecutor focused on investigating and prosecuting individuals who had held important positions in Rwanda in 1994. This policy has been maintained over the years, and has since become an explicit part of the Completion Strategy for both Tribunals, as expressed in Resolution 1503 (2003). The Tribunal's focus on leadership is illustrated by the fact that the accused who have been apprehended include one prime minister, 14 ministers, six prefects, 11

41 The construction and running costs of the fourth courtroom were funded through voluntary contributions from the Norwegian and United Kingdom governments and not by the Tribunal's general budget. See *supra*, 2 (C) about twin tracking and the shift system.

42 It should be added that at the end of the first mandate, the *Musema* case required only 39 trial days. The low number of trial days is not the same as the total duration of the trial. There is usually a break between the prosecution and the defence cases, and the parties need a couple of months to produce their closing briefs, followed by oral arguments. The fastest single-accused cases so far were *Gacumbitsi* and *Ndindabahizi* (judgement in less than eleven months after the commencement of trial) and *Musema* (about one year).

43 Judgement writing in single-accused trials can be completed in about three months, but may take longer because of the complexity of the case and other work. In particular, after closing arguments in one trial, the judges usually immediately commence another case. Some judges have, at times, been involved in up to four proceedings. This will slow down judgement writing but contributes to the overall progress of the Tribunal.

44 The complexity of the multi-accused cases can be illustrated by figures: *Media* (judgement of 361 pages, 240 trial days); *Cyangugu* (215 pages, 165 trial days); *Military I* (606 pages, 408 trial days); *Government* (404 trial days), *Military II* (392 trial days before closing arguments); *Butare* (715 trial days before closing arguments); and *Karemera et al.* (so far, 207). It complicates the situation if the defence teams in a trial have conflicting interests and therefore carry out extensive cross-examination of other defence witnesses in order to challenge their credibility ('cut-throat defence'). The *Butare* trial is one example.

bourgmestres (mayors), high-ranking political, military and media personalities, as well as members of the clergy. Five persons have been acquitted. Amongst the detainees is the first female subject to international prosecution for genocide.[45]

Most of the over 70 accused persons who fled Rwanda after the genocide would probably not have been brought to justice had it not been for the Tribunal's investigations, insistence on their arrest and subsequent request for transfer to Arusha. Many states are reluctant to initiate investigations and institute criminal proceedings at their own expense against individuals who are accused of having committed crimes in other countries. Extradition is also a cumbersome process, provided that a request is at all made. The fact that the accused will receive a fair trial by the independent Tribunal in Arusha has facilitated and, in many instances, probably been a condition for transfer. Moreover, the accused do not risk capital punishment in case of conviction, as the most severe sentence in the two Tribunals is a life sentence.

There can be no doubt that the Tribunal's proceedings relating to persons in very high positions have sent a strong signal to the world, including the African continent, that the international community will not accept impunity for serious crimes.

B. Fair Trial by Impartial Tribunal

The right of the accused to a fair trial by an impartial tribunal follows from Article 20 of the ICTR Statute. The Tribunal is adamant that all trials shall be conducted in accordance with international standards of justice. In fact, one of the reasons why some cases may be time-consuming is to dispel any doubt that these norms are complied with. By conducting proceedings beyond reproach, the Tribunal has set an important precedence and contributed to the development of the international rule of law.

The Tribunals have been criticized for delays in bringing detainees to trial as well as during the proceedings. Some of this criticism may have been justified but it is important to recall the reasons why the proceedings are time-consuming as well as the measures adopted to address the challenges.[46] Furthermore, when, on rare occasions, the right of an accused has been violated, the Tribunal has not hesitated to acknowledge both the fact that a violation occurred and the right to a remedy.[47]

It should also be recalled that trials in the Tribunal have functions that are not easily comparable to those found in domestic criminal courts. Besides efficiently prosecuting a person for having allegedly committed a given crime, another result may be to establish the historical record. This requires more time and effort than would be necessary to simply obtain a conviction or acquittal.

In order for a court to be perceived as fair it is important that its proceedings are not perceived as victor's justice. During the proceedings the judges have adopted a relatively liberal attitude with regard to evidence that may be considered relevant or provide context, even if it does not fall squarely within the charges brought against the accused. This allows both sides to convey their version of the events in Rwanda.

---

45 Pauline Nyiramasuhuko was the Rwandan Minister of Family and Women's Affairs at the relevant time.

46 See *supra*, 3.

47 See, for instance, Decision, *Barayagwiza*, Prosecutor's Request for Review or Reconsideration, 31 March 2000, para. 74 (where the Appeals Chamber confirmed that Baragwiza's rights were violated, and that all violations demand a remedy. This remedy was to be given in connection with the judgement of the Trial Chamber. It should include financial compensation in the case of acquittal or a reduced sentence in the event of conviction).

All the convicted persons are Hutu, and all detainees in Arusha belong to this group. It is often argued that this may give an impression of one-sidedness. Resolution 1503 refers to 'investigations of the Rwandan Patriotic Army' (RPF). The Prosecutor has taken account of the mandate of the ICTR to investigate reports of violations by the RPF. So far, he has not issued any indictment in connection with alleged RPF crimes.[48]

C. Creating Jurisprudence

Almost all ICTR judgements have dealt with the issue of genocide. The *Akayesu* judgement was the first in which an international Tribunal was called upon to interpret the definition of genocide as defined in the Genocide Convention.[49] It has been followed by a large number of other ICTR judgements, and the ICTR Appeals Chamber has even taken judicial notice of the fact that a genocide occurred.[50] Although this crime also forms part of the ICTY Statute, the relatively few convictions for genocide in The Hague mean that the Arusha jurisprudence is a very important source for the definition and the elucidation of the legal elements of this 'crime of crimes'.

The *Akayesu* judgement was also groundbreaking for its affirmation of rape as an international crime. Apart from elucidating the elements of this offence, it is notable for the finding that rape may form part of the *actus reus* of genocide. The Chamber found that rape and sexual violence formed an integral part of the process of destruction, specifically targeting Tutsi women and contributing to their destruction and to that of the Tutsi group as a whole.[51] As sexual crimes were very widespread in 1994, it is not surprising that it is an important subject matter in the Tribunal.[52]

The ICTR was also the first international Tribunal after Nuremberg to hand down a judgement against a Head of Government. The international media have rightly stressed the significance of the trial of the former Yugoslav President Slobodan Milošević after his transfer to The Hague on 28 June 2001. The general public is less aware that, about three years earlier, the Prime Minister of Rwanda during the relevant period, Jean Kambanda, had been convicted for genocide. This judgement reaffirmed the principle, embodied in the Statutes of both *ad hoc* Tribunals, that no individual enjoys impunity for such crimes on account of their official position.[53] The *Kambanda*

48 During a Security Council meeting on 4 June 2008, the Prosecutor announced that he had, in cooperation with Rwanda, established a *prima facie* case that on 5 June 1994, RPF soldiers killed some thirteen clergymen, including five bishops and two other civilians at the Kabgayi Parish in Gitarama prefecture. Having been informed that the Rwandan Prosecutor General intended to indict and arrest four serving senior military officers of the Rwandan Army, the ICTR Prosecutor decided to hold in abeyance further action on the clear understanding that any such prosecutions in and by Rwanda should be effective, expeditious, fair and open to the public. The Prosecutor's office has been monitoring the proceedings in Rwanda, and the prosecution of these crimes in Rwanda will be without prejudice to the primacy of the ICTR jurisdiction over these crimes. On 11 June 2008, the four officers were arrested in Rwanda. Two of them pleaded guilty and were later convicted by Rwandan courts, whereas the other two were acquitted.

49 Judgement, *Akayesu*, Trial Chamber, 2 September 1998. As the Genocide Convention was adopted on 9 December 1948 and entered into force on 12 January 1951, the *ad hoc* Tribunals were *stricto sensu* the first international bodies to adjudicate the elements of that offence.

50 Decision, *Karemera et al.*, Prosecutor's Interlocutory Appeal of Judicial Notice, 16 June 2006, para. 35, where the Appeals Chamber found that the genocide in Rwanda in 1994 is a fact of common knowledge which there is no reasonable basis to dispute.

51 Judgement, *Akayesu*, Trial Chamber, 2 September 1998, paras 731–734.

52 Sexual violence was found, for instance, in *Rutaganda*, *Musema*, *Muhimana* and *Military I.*

53 Judgement, *Kambanda*, 4 September 1998.

case was also the first judgement where a Head of Government pleaded guilty to genocide and, more generally, one of the earliest sentences by the *ad hoc* Tribunals following a plea of guilty.

Another important achievement was the *Media* case, which was the first contemporary judgement to examine the role of the media in the context of mass criminality and international humanitarian law.[54] This trial drew the border line between the right guaranteed under international law to freedom of expression and incitement to serious international crimes. It was the first pronouncement on such questions by an international Tribunal since the conviction of Julius Streicher at Nuremberg.[55]

In addition to its judgements, the Tribunal has handed down thousands of written decisions. The number of oral decisions given by the bench in the courtroom is also considerable. This part of the Tribunal's jurisprudence clarifies a wealth of issues arising under the Statute and the Rules.

More than 10 years after the establishment of the *ad hoc* Tribunals it is easy to forget that when the ICTR commenced its judicial activities there was little international jurisprudence available. Guidance to the interpretation of the Statute and the Rules could be found in case law from the Nuremberg and Tokyo Tribunals, human rights bodies and the limited jurisprudence developed by the ICTY since its establishment. Solutions in national legal systems also provided inspiration. Since then, the development of substantive and procedural law has made tremendous progress. The ICTR and ICTY jurisprudence has inspired other international and hybrid tribunals, as well as the ICC.

The work at the Tribunal has confirmed that the fact that judges come from different legal systems does not create problems in the interpretation and application of international criminal law. In particular, the differences between common law and civil law play virtually no role in the everyday life of the Tribunal. Furthermore, experience has shown the usefulness that judges in international Tribunals may already have criminal trial experience at the national level, preferably as a judge.

D. Victims and Witnesses

The witnesses appearing before the Tribunal live in all parts of the world. Most prosecution witnesses come from Rwanda, whereas many defence witnesses have taken up residence in other countries. The ICTR Witness and Victims Support Section (WVSS) has ensured the availability of a very high number of witnesses from numerous countries. It establishes initial contact with them; confirms their availability to testify; assess their specific needs; ensures that travel documents, visa and tickets are issued; provides escort from their place of residence to Arusha; and places them in safe houses or other accommodation when they have arrived. While the witnesses are in Arusha, the WVSS ensures their security, looks after their welfare and transports them to and from court. After the trial, the witnesses are returned safely to their place of residence and provided with security arrangements.

Some witnesses were also victims during the 1994 events. A special project for psychological and medical support for witnesses and potential witnesses was launched in 2000. It provides technical support to the WVSS for the physical and psychological rehabilitation of witnesses,

---

54 Judgement, *Nahimana, Ngeze and Barayagwiza*, Trial Chamber, 3 December 2003; Judgement, *Nahimana, Ngeze and Barayagwiza*, Appeals Chamber, 28 November 2007.

55 Judgement of the International Military Tribunal for the Trial of the German Major War Criminals, Nuremberg, 30th September and 1st October, 1946 (London: HMSO, Cmd. 6964, Reprinted 1966), at 100–102.

including rape victims. The ICTR Medical Clinic in Kigali performs many activities, including treatment for HIV/AIDS.

E. Reconciliation

When the Tribunal was set up, the Security Council stated that the prosecution of persons responsible for serious violations of international humanitarian law would 'contribute to the process of national reconciliation'.[56] It is clear that reconciliation cannot be enforced from outside, but must emerge from within the country concerned. This being said, it is certainly an aim of the Tribunal to contribute to the process of reconciliation in Rwanda. In order to do so, it is important that the activities of the Tribunal are known by the Rwandans.

The judicial proceedings at the Tribunal represent the core element in the process of reconciliation. By conducting fair trials, listening to the parties, establishing the facts and applying the law in an objective way, the Tribunal decides on the individual guilt or innocence of the accused in respect of each of the charges against them. Whenever a judgement is delivered, an oral summary is read out by the presiding judge of the Chamber. It is simultaneously interpreted into Kinyarwanda and transmitted directly into Rwanda.

There is also reason to believe that guilty pleas, combined with expressions of remorse, contribute to reconciliation. The number of accused using this opportunity was at first low, but eight have now pleaded guilty.[57] More generally, the judgements provide a broader picture of the events in 1994 and the period preceding them. Such objective accounts can contribute to the process within Rwanda even if it is not to be expected that the Tribunal can provide a comprehensive historical record.

Even though the Tribunal conducts parts of its activities from Kigali, in particular investigations and witness protection, it would have been more visible in Rwanda if its headquarters had been there and the judicial proceedings had taken place in Kigali. As mentioned above, the Security Council did not consider this possible in the 1990s for reasons of efficiency, security and impartiality.[58] It was not a viable option to move the Tribunal later. On some occasions, Chambers have carried out *in loco* visits in Rwanda or taken depositions there. Therefore, the challenge is to disseminate information about the proceedings in Arusha to the Rwandan population.

The Tribunal's Registry has established an Outreach Programme designed to reach all sectors of Rwandan society and, secondly, the world at large. Of particular significance is the ICTR Information Centre in Kigali, which was inaugurated in September 2000. It receives around 100 visitors daily from all walks of life and carries out a wide spectrum of activities. It can safely be concluded that the Tribunal is trying, with the resources available, and within the practical possibilities, to contribute to the process of reconciliation. A total of 10 local information centres on international criminal justice are being established in Rwanda.[59]

---

56 SC Res. 955 of 8 November 1994, seventh and ninth preambular paragraphs.

57 The eight judgements based on guilty pleas are *Kambanda* (4 September 1998); *Serushago* (5 February 1999); *Ruggiu* (1 June 2000); *Rutaganira* (14 March 2005); *Bisengimana* (13 April 2006); *Serugendo* (12 June 2006); *Nzabirinda* (23 February 2007) and *Rugambarara* (16 November 2007).

58 See *supra*, 2(A).

59 The European Union has provided generous funding to the ICTR Outreach Programme.

5. Completion Strategy

A. Introduction

Security Council Resolution 1503 (2003) which adopted the two Tribunals' Completion Strategy was followed up the next year by Resolution 1534, which requested their Presidents and Prosecutors to provide reports every six months. By the end of 2008, the ICTR had submitted 11 such reports.[60] The idea of an end date was in conformity with the wishes of the Tribunals.[61]

In its second Completion Strategy report, the Tribunal indicated that it may be able to complete cases at the first instance involving between 65 and 70 persons by the end of 2008.[62] It is now clear that this was a good estimate. In late 2008, cases involving 64 accused were completed or in progress.[63] Eight detainees were awaiting trial. This brings the total number of accused to 72. In addition, two persons had been charged with contempt of court.[64] Of the eight detainees awaiting trial in Arusha, three were arrested recently, whereas the Prosecutor unsuccessfully had tried to transfer five to national jurisdictions.[65] The ICTR was therefore close to completing its work by the December 2008 deadline. In addition, 13 indictees are at large.

The remaining work of the ICTR depends on three factors: the completion of the remaining trials, the arrest of indictees at large and the transfer of cases to national jurisdictions. It is too

---

60 SC Res. 1503, 28 August 2003 (see *supra*, 3(C)) and SC Res. 1534, 26 March 2004. The 11 reports submitted by the ICTR were transmitted to the Security Council on 6 October 2003, 3 May 2004, 22 November 2004, 23 May 2005, 14 December 2005, 1 June 2006, 8 December 2006, 15 May 2007, 20 November 2007, 13 May 2008 and 21 November 2008. They are available on the Tribunal's website <www.ictr.org>. The first document indicating ways to complete the ICTR's work was submitted to United Nations Headquarters on 14 July 2003 within the context of GA Res. 57/289, 20 December 2002, which requested the proposed budget for 2004–2005 to include 'detailed information as to how the resources requested for the biennium would support the development of a sound and realistic completion strategy'. See also Jean-Pelé Fomété, 'Countdown to 2010: A Critical Overview of the Completion Strategy of the International Criminal Tribunal for Rwanda (ICTR)', in E. Decaux, A. Dieng and M. Sow (eds), *From Human Rights to International Criminal Law, Studies in Honour of an African Jurist, the Late Judge Laïty Kama* (Leiden: Martinus Nijhoff Publishers, 2007), at 345–400.

61 During a joint meeting between the ICTR and ICTY judges at Trinity College in Dublin, Ireland, from 12–14 October 2001, there appeared to be broad consensus that it was time to reflect on the time span of the two Tribunals, for instance by reviewing the prosecutorial policy or setting a target date for the filing of the last indictment. One of the suggestions made during the discussions was to set target dates for the end of the work of the Trial Chambers and the Appeals Chamber.

62 Second Completion Strategy report, S/2004/341, 3 May 2004, para. 62. The estimate was maintained in subsequent reports.

63 Of 42 persons who had received judgement by 31 December 2008, 36 were convicted and six acquitted. Three other trials involving six accused (*Renzaho, Rukundo, Government*) were at the judgement writing stage, whereas one case was awaiting oral closing arguments following the submission of written briefs (*Nsengimana*). In three trials involving 11 accused (*Butare, Military II, Kalimanzira*), the evidentiary phase was virtually completed. The Prosecution was presenting its evidence in one trial (*Setako*).

64 One witness pleaded guilty because he had committed perjury, see Judgement, *Witness GAA*, Trial Chamber, 4 December 2007. Another case involving a former defence investigator, *Léonidas Nshogoza*, is ongoing.

65 See *infra*, 5(B) and (C).

early to indicate when all ICTR appeals will be completed in The Hague, and this will not be addressed here.[66]

B. Completion of Trials

The trials of the remaining eight accused all started in 2009.[67] They are all single-accused cases and will therefore require limited time. The extension of the judges' mandates to the end of 2009 will ensure the necessary capacity and continuity, and the arrival of three new *ad litem* judges will replace those who had to leave. It would be regrettable if judges had to resign because they were not granted further leave from their positions in domestic jurisdictions. This would reduce judicial capacity and continuity. The Security Council has previously requested states to ensure that the judges remain available in the context of the Completion Strategy and the same principle should apply at the present stage.[68]

Continuity of staff is a problem. As the Tribunal's work approaches the end, staff members belonging to all professional groups are considering other options. New and qualified staff comes in, but the result is still less institutional knowledge, due to a high turnover. The Tribunal is trying to limit the effects of this tendency. Clarity and transparency about the expected duration of the various posts is important.[69] It is already clear that most staff members will be required until the end of 2009, and some may have to continue afterwards. The Tribunal has stressed that it needs the support of the Security Council and Member States to offer sufficient incentives to guarantee as much as possible that the most experienced staff will remain with the Tribunal until the completion of its work.[70]

---

66 SC Res. 1503, 28 August 2003, and SC Res. 1534, 26 March 2004, stated that the Tribunals shall complete all appeals by the end of 2010. SC Res. 1824, 18 July 2008, extended the mandate of all Trial Chamber judges to the end of 2009, whereas the mandate of the two ICTR judges in the Appeals Chamber expires at the end of 2010. The Completion Strategy for appeals is linked to the work of the ICTY, and it is therefore difficult to indicate when the common Appeals Chamber will have concluded all appeals. Consultations are ongoing between the two Tribunals. In parallel with the completion of trials in Arusha, the workload on appeals will increase. As a consequence, it is likely that the number of Appeals Chamber judges at some point will have to be increased by amending the Statutes.

67 The eight accused awaiting trial are Gatete (*bourgmestre*), Hategekimana (commander of Ngoma Camp), Munyakazi (*Interahamwe* leader), Kanyarukiga (businessman), Ngirabatware (Minister of Planning), Nzabonimana (Minister of Youth), Ntawukuriryayo (sub-prefect) and Bagaragaza (Director, National Tea Industry). In addition, Muvunyi is awaiting retrial, but this only relates to one event and will not be time-consuming. See Judgement, *Muvunyi*, Appeals Chamber, 29 August 2008. If the Prosecutor issues any RPF indictments (*supra*, 3 B), there will be additional trials in Arusha.

68 SC Res. 1684, 13 June 2006 (extending the term of 11 permanent judges) and SC Res. 1717, 13 October 2006 (extending the term of the *ad litem* judges elected in June 2003), requested States to 'make every effort to ensure that their nationals' who serve as judges of the ICTR 'remain available to serve in their positions' until 31 December 2008.

69 As one illustration, see 'The Lake Manyara Accord on the ICTR Completion Strategy', 4–6 April 2008. The aim was to assist senior and mid-level managers from all three organs of the ICTR to understand change management, develop drawdown plans and approaches to planning in uncertainty, and support staff in transition.

70 Ninth Completion Strategy report, S/2007/676, 20 November 2007, paras 45–48; 10th Completion Strategy report, paras 53–57.

C. Indictees at Large

The Prosecutor's strategy is to prosecute, before the ICTR, only those persons bearing the greatest responsibility for the crimes committed in Rwanda in 1994, and to seek the transfer of other accused to national jurisdictions. This is in conformity with Security Council resolutions on the Completion Strategy.[71] He has focused on the 18 indictees at large.[72] Of the 18, six should be tried by the ICTR, whereas the others should be transferred to national jurisdictions. Five of the eighteen have now been arrested, which means that thirteen indictees are still at liberty.

Two of the six accused whose trials should be conducted at the ICTR are among the three accused that were recently apprehended and are now awaiting trial. Consequently, four indictees are still on the run.[73] If their arrests occur after the closure of the Tribunal they should be tried by a residual mechanism.[74]

One of the four accused is Félicien Kabuga, a businessman who according to the Indictment contributed to financing the genocide and who is specifically mentioned in Security Council resolution 1534 as a fugitive who should be apprehended.[75] In spite of intensive efforts by the ICTR, as well as international pressure, he still remains at large. Most of the 13 indictees seem to be hiding in East and Central Africa. When the United Nations Secretary-General visited the ICTR on 27 February 2008, he rightly reiterated that states in the region have to increase their support in tracking down and arresting all of these fugitives.[76]

D. Transfer of Cases

Transfer of cases to national jurisdictions can take place in two ways. In relation to suspects that are not indicted by the ICTR, the Prosecutor may seek to have their case files transferred. The dossiers

---

71 SC Res. 1503, 28 August 2003, preambular para. 8, as well as para. 1; SC Res. 1534, 26 March 2004, para. 4 (Tribunal Prosecutors were requested to decide on trial or transfer) and para. 5 (Tribunals only to confirm new indictments in respect of 'the most senior leaders suspected of being the most responsible').

72 The first Completion Strategy report in 2003 indicated that 16 indictees were at large and that 26 additional suspects were subject to ongoing investigation. The maximum number of indictees at large would therefore be 42 (S/2003/946, 8 October 2003, paras 21–22). Subsequently, the Prosecutor reduced this figure of indictees at large to 18; see 6th Completion Strategy report, S/2006/358, 1 June 2006. Some files were closed due to lack of evidence and others suspects were not considered sufficiently high-ranking.

73 The six persons are Félicien Kabuga (wealthy businessman), Augustin Ngirabatware (Minister of Planning), Callixte Nzabonimana (Minister of Youth), Augustin Bizimana (Minister of Defence), Protais Mpiranya (commander of the Presidential Guard Battalion) and Idelphonse Nizeyimana (captain and second in command of the *Ecole Supérieure des Officiers* camp). Towards the end of 2007, Augustin Ngirabatware (Minister of Planning) was apprehended in Germany and Dominique Ntawukuriryayo (sub-prefect) in France. Ntawukuriryayo was brought to Arusha in June 2008, and Ngirabatware in October 2008. Callixte Nzabonimana (Minister of Youth) was arrested in Tanzania in February 2008 and arrived at the Tribunal that month.

74 See *infra*, 6.

75 SC Res. 1534, 26 March 2004, indicates the importance of apprehending and trying Radovan Karadzic, Ratko Mladic and Ante Gotovina (para. 1), as well as Félicien Kabuga (para. 2).

76 As part of the Completion Strategy, the Prosecutor has formulated a more aggressive programme for the tracking and apprehension of fugitives. He has also visited a number of states with a view to securing their political support and cooperation for the arrest and transfer of fugitives. In spite of these efforts, some of the indictees have now managed to hide for years, for instance by living in inaccessible areas or moving between countries.

may be ready for trial, or further investigations may be required before they are brought before the courts in the receiving country. The Prosecutor has transferred a total of 35 files to Rwanda and one case file to Belgium.[77] Such transfers depend on prosecutorial discretion and are administrative in nature, based on cooperation between the ICTR Prosecutor and national prosecuting authorities.

The other method requires a judicial decision. Rule 11*bis* of the Rules of Procedure and Evidence governs the referral of cases to national authorities. Its major purpose is to enable the Tribunal to transfer cases to competent national jurisdictions. It is the task of a Trial Chamber established under Rule 11*bis* to decide whether a case shall be transferred. The Chamber must be satisfied that the accused will receive a fair trial in the courts of the state concerned and that the death penalty will not be imposed or carried out.

The Prosecutor has been in contact with several states concerning both transfer of cases of indictees under Rule 11*bis*, and transfer of files of suspects. In relation to both groups, he has insisted on compliance with fair trial standards.[78] So far, only two cases have been transferred to national jurisdictions pursuant to Rule 11*bis*. Both relate to indictees at large. Wenceslas Munyeshyaka, a priest, and Laurent Bucyibaruta, a prefect, were arrested in France. In 2007, the ICTR transferred their cases to French courts.[79] No other requests for transfer to European countries are pending.

A complicating element has been lack of jurisdiction in states that are willing to receive cases. This was amply demonstrated in connection with transfer requests of Michel Bagaragaza, who was Director of the National Tea Industry in 1994. An attempt to transfer him to Norway failed.[80] The Prosecutor then contacted the Dutch authorities, who were willing to receive him, but subsequent national case law raised doubts about Dutch jurisdiction.[81] Bagaragaza was then returned from The Hague to Arusha, where he is awaiting trial.

Many of the accused and suspects are in less-developed countries where judicial systems are under strain arising from the prosecution of their own accused. The Prosecutor has stated that it is important to explore the possibility of transferring cases to African states where certain suspects are now living, despite such constraints.[82] So far, these countries have been reluctant to accept cases. The exception is Rwanda, which has abolished the death penalty and has adopted a specific Transfer Law in order to qualify for transfer.

The Prosecutor has made five referral requests to Rwanda, four in relation to detainees in Arusha and one concerning an indictee at large.[83] The defence and some non-governmental organizations

77 The Prosecution transferred 15 case files to Rwanda on 23 February 2005 and 20 files in July 2005.

78 Eighth Completion Strategy report, S/2007/323, 15 May 2007, para. 7.

79 Decision, *Munyeshyaka*, Trial Chamber, 20 November 2007; Decision, *Bucyibaruta*, Trial Chamber, 20 November 2007.

80 The Trial Chamber found that Norway did not have sufficient material jurisdiction as there was no provision against genocide and Bagaragaza would have been prosecuted only as an accessory to homicide or negligent homicide (for which the maximum penalty was 21 years). Decision, *Bagaragaza*, Trial Chamber, 19 May 2006. The result was confirmed by the Appeals Chamber. Decision, *Bagaragaza*, Appeals Chamber, 30 August 2006.

81 A request for transfer to The Netherlands was granted in April 2007. Decision, *Bagaragaza*, Trial Chamber, 13 April 2007. However, a subsequent decision by a Dutch court in another case suggested that the domestic courts did not have jurisdiction to prosecute Bagaragaza for genocide, and that jurisdiction over the war crimes counts in the indictment was uncertain. The ICTR Prosecutor therefore sought the revocation of the transfer order, and this request was granted. Decision, *Bagaragaza*, Trial Chamber, 17 August 2007.

82 Eighth Completion Strategy report, S/2007/323, 15 May 2007, para. 36.

83 The five cases (with date of the referral request to Rwanda) were *Kayishema* (11 June 2007), *Kanyarukiga* (7 September 2007), *Munyakazi* (7 September 2007), *Hategekimana* (7 September 2007) and *Gatete* (28 November 2007). The first case involves an indictee at large.

opposed transfer. Three Trial Chambers established under Rule 11*bis* denied such transfer in May and June 2008. Although Rwanda has made progress in reforming its judicial system, they were not satisfied that the accused would receive a fair trial. The main reason was that defence witnesses (in particular those residing abroad) will be afraid to testify in Rwanda, thereby raising questions about equality of arms between the prosecution and the defence.[84] The three decisions denying transfer to Rwanda were confirmed by the Appeals Chamber.[85]

The work of the Tribunal and of the possible residual mechanism afterwards will be influenced by states' willingness and ability to receive transferred cases. The Security Council has repeatedly emphasised the need for the international community to assist national judicial systems to improve their capacity to prosecute cases transferred from the two Tribunals.[86]

Several states and non-governmental organizations have contributed to projects in Rwanda. The ICTR outreach programme for Rwanda aims to contribute to national reconciliation and strengthening the Rwandan judicial system. This is part of the Tribunal's mandate to contribute to justice, stability and reconciliation.[87] The development within Rwanda, including further legislative reforms, will have an impact on the possibility of transferring cases there in the future.

6. Residual Issues

It is clear that some of the Tribunals' activities cannot terminate upon the conclusion of all trials and appeals. Failure to ensure that such functions are carried out after the ICTR and the ICTY may result in violations of the rights of victims, witnesses, accused and convicted persons. It could also undermine the long-term legacy of the Tribunals: the notion that such courts contribute to international peace, reconciliation and the rule of law, and the legitimacy of the nascent international criminal justice system.

Following consultations, the ICTY and the ICTR in April 2007 submitted a joint paper for consideration by the Security Council. The document identifies 'residual functions' and considers possible institutional mechanisms through which they could be performed. Some activities, but not judicial functions, may be delegated to other international or national bodies. They include the trial of fugitives arrested after the conclusion of appeals; future referrals and revocation of referrals under Rule 11 *bis*; preventing national courts from trying persons who have already been tried by the Tribunal (Article 9 of the Statute); review of earlier judgements when new facts are discovered (Article 25); future decisions on early release, pardon and commutation (Article 27); and support to defence counsel (e.g., through legal aid) who will be involved in the various judicial activities.[88]

84 Decision, *Munyakazi*, Trial Chamber, 28 May 2008; Decision, *Kanyarukiga*, Trial Chamber, 6 June 2008; Decision, *Hategekimana*, Trial Chamber, 20 June 2008. The three Chambers also referred to a risk of solitary confinement in case of life imprisonment. Subsequently, following the Appeals Chamber's confirmation of denial (see next footnote), the last two requests were decided. See Decision, *Gatete*, Trial Chamber, 17 November 2008; Decision, *Kayishema*, Trial Chamber, 16 December 2008.

85 Decision, *Munyakazi*, Appeals Chamber, 8 October 2008; Decision, *Kanyarukiga*, Appeals Chamber, 30 October 2008; Decision, *Hategekimana*, Appeals Chamber, 4 December 2008.

86 SC Res. 1503, 28 August 2003, 10th preambular paragraph and para. 1; SC Res. 1534, 26 March 2004, para. 9.

87 Further information is given in the eighth Completion Strategy report, S/2007/323, 15 May 2007, Annex 5, and the ninth Completion Strategy report, S/2007/676, 20 November 2007, para. 51.

88 There are several other issues. One is the need for continued support and protection of witnesses, who may face risks long after their testimony. Another is the need to maintain the archives which will support

The residual mechanism could either be centralized in one location, with responsibility for both Tribunals, or a separate capacity for each in The Hague and Arusha. Irrespective of the kind of mechanism and its precise functions, the implementation of the Completion Strategy should be seen in light of the institutional solutions to be chosen after the Tribunals.[89]

In December 2008, the Security Council, through a presidential statement, recognized the need to establish an *ad hoc* mechanism to carry out a number of essential functions of the Tribunals, including the trial of high-level fugitives, after the closure of the Tribunals. Such a mechanism should be a small, temporary and efficient structure, and its functions and size will diminish over time. It will derive its authority from a Security Council resolution and from the Statute and Rules of the ICTR and the ICTY, as modified.

The exact modalities will have to be worked out by the competent organs of the United Nations. Consultations are ongoing. The Secretary-General will submit a report on the administrative and budgetary options on the possible locations for the Tribunals' archives and the seat of the residual mechanism, including the availability of suitable premises for the conduct of judicial proceedings by the residual mechanism. Irrespective of the specific solutions to be chosen, it can safely be concluded that the Completion Strategy will not lead to a total abolition of the Tribunal's functions.

7. Conclusion

Although some work remains, it is clear that the ICTR has made a significant contribution to the development of international criminal justice. Amongst its main achievements are the arrest and prosecution of over 70 persons with a view to deciding their guilt or innocence, the creation of important judicial precedents, the building up of experience, the contribution to reconciliation and the establishment of a historical record of the genocide. In performing its tasks, the Tribunal has applied the highest standards of fair trial.

More generally, international criminal justice is moving at an incredible speed. About 15 years ago, there were no international criminal tribunals. Now they are in the focus of political decision-makers, newspaper articles, universities and the general public. New professional groups of international judges, prosecutors, defence counsel and administrators have emerged, with experience of how to handle complex international trials. There is every reason to believe that these common efforts against impunity for serious crimes will lead to a world with fewer human rights violations.

---

ongoing judicial functions and preserve documents for posterity and for the overall legacy of the Tribunals. An Advisory Committee on Archives, chaired by Justice Richard Goldstone, has considered how best to ensure future accessibility of the archives and reviewed different locations that may be appropriate for housing the materials.

89 There could be, under the auspices of the Security Council or the Secretary General, a roster of ICTY and ICTR judges. It could operate on a stand-by basis. The appointing authority would use the expertise of ICTR judges in ICTR cases, in order to preserve institutional knowledge and to ensure continuity and efficiency. Modalities will also have to be found to ensure the availability of various categories of staff to support this mechanism.

Chapter 4
The Special Court for Sierra Leone

Renate Winter

1. Introduction[1]

A. The Contribution of the Court

A brief overview of the Court's progress demonstrates its significant achievements in a relatively short period of time. The Court was established on 16 January 2002, and in the course of 2002, the Prosecutor, Registrar and the first eight Judges were appointed. A second trial chamber was added in 2005. Indictments against 13 accused have been issued by the Prosecutor and approved by a Judge. After the deaths of three accused, ten indictments remain active and all but one accused have been apprehended. The indictments were joined into four principal cases. Two of the four were finally adjudicated in 2008, in the third case the trial and sentencing judgment were recently rendered and the appeal judgement was rendered in October 2009, while the final case of Charles Taylor will be completed in autumn 2010.

In the course of setting up the Special Court, managing its day to day operations in a post-conflict setting and adjudicating its complex cases, the Court has implemented many first-of-a-kind practices that will inform future international justice mechanisms. This article describes the numerous issues arising from the Court's unique origins in a bilateral treaty, its novel and problematic financing, the use of a management committee for oversight of non-judicial activities, the streamlined number of cases (though each being among the most complex in international criminal law), the Court's extensive focus on its legacy and its focus on completion and residual issues.

B. Background

In March 1991, a group of armed men attacked a small rural village in Kailahun district in the Eastern Province of Sierra Leone, close to the Liberian border. This attack, initially thought to have been a spillover of the then ongoing Liberian war, in fact turned out to be the beginning of a ten-year violent armed conflict in Sierra Leone. The attackers, later to identify themselves as the Revolutionary United Front (RUF), were under the leadership of Foday Sankoh, an ex-corporal of the Sierra Leone army. Their self-proclaimed objective was to overthrow the one-party government of then President Joseph Momoh and to ensure a more equitable distribution of the benefits of natural resource exploitation, particularly diamonds.

Despite these purported objectives, the RUF – and subsequently, parts of the Sierra Leone Army which became known as the Armed Forces Revolutionary Council (AFRC), and a government-

1 The author wishes to thank Stephen Kostas for his research and drafting assistance, Sandy Sivakumaran and Joakim Dungel for their insightful comments, and Terry Unger and Shannon Ghadiri for editorial assistance.

sponsored militia called the Civil Defence Forces (CDF) – in fact proceeded to subject the people of Sierra Leone to some of the most brutal crimes known to humankind. Civilians in Sierra Leone were the primary victims of the atrocities committed. Villages and towns of no military or strategic importance were indiscriminately attacked, looted and burned down; unarmed civilians, especially women and children, were brutally murdered, maimed or otherwise subjected to violent crimes. Defenceless women and girls were specifically targeted; many were abducted from their families and subjected to rape, sexual slavery and other forms of sexual violence. Very often, women and girls were compelled to become 'wives' to their captors. Civilians throughout Sierra Leone were subjected to various forms of mutilation including cutting off of arms, ears, lips, and gouging of the eyes; private and public property was subjected to pillage, or wantonly destroyed without military necessity or justification; and the recruitment and use of child soldiers became normal war time practice. As a result of the war, at least 50,000 people were killed, while hundreds of thousands of others were internally displaced from their communities and livelihoods.

In view of the unprecedented gravity of the crimes, both the Government of Sierra Leone and the international community determined that those responsible should be held accountable. Therefore, upon its return to power in 1999, the Government of Sierra Leone requested the United Nations establish a strong and credible court that would bring to justice those responsible for committing serious crimes during the war.

In Resolution 1315 of 2000, the Security Council reiterated that the situation in Sierra Leone continued to constitute a threat to international peace and security, and recognized that a credible system of justice and accountability for the serious crimes committed in Sierra Leone would end impunity and contribute to the process of national reconciliation and the restoration and maintenance of peace. Furthermore, the Resolution requested the Secretary-General negotiate an agreement with the Government of Sierra Leone to create an independent Special Court.

After lengthy negotiations, on 16 January 2002, the UN concluded an agreement with the Government of Sierra Leone, thus establishing the Special Court for Sierra Leone (SCSL). The Agreement provided that the Special Court shall have its seat in Freetown, a significant departure from the post-Nuremberg international criminal tribunals established for Rwanda and the former Yugoslavia, both of which were located away from the countries in which the crimes took place. The Agreement conferred the Special Court with the mandate to prosecute 'persons bearing the greatest responsibility', not just for serious international crimes, but also for certain specified crimes under Sierra Leonean law. The Agreement also provided for the Government of Sierra Leone to appoint a minority of the Judges and the Deputy Prosecutor. This mixture of international and domestic jurisdictional competence, and international and national officials, has led some to refer to the Special Court as a 'mixed' or 'hybrid', while others still prefer the term 'nationalized international tribunals'.

Irrespective of the description applied, the fact remains that the Special Court is unlike any other post-war international tribunal. The Special Court has both international law and domestic law competence; its staff (both national and international) are selected through a domestic and international consultative process; and unlike the ICTY and ICTR, it was created through a bilateral treaty between the UN and the Government of Sierra Leone, rather than under Chapter VII of the UN Charter. This introductory section briefly addresses some of the unique attributes of the Special Court and its efforts to implement its mandate.

2. Bilateral Treaty Establishing a 'Hybrid' Tribunal

A. Established Pursuant to a Bilateral Treaty

On 12 June 2000, shortly after that return to conflict after a brief, tenuous peace, President Alhaji Dr Ahmad Tejan Kabbah wrote to Secretary-General Kofi Annan requesting the UN to assist the Government of Sierra Leone in creating 'a credible court' to try the worst offenders, 'especially the RUF leadership'.[2] President Kabbah's letter persuaded the Security Council to adopt Resolution 1315 authorizing the Secretary-General to negotiate a bilateral treaty between the UN and the Government of Sierra Leone for the establishment of the Court. Following negotiations between the Government of Sierra Leone and the UN, and discussions between the Secretary-General and the Security Council, the parties signed an agreement (Special Court Agreement) on 16 January 2002 that created the Court, and annexed to the agreement the Court's Statute, as negotiated by the parties.[3]

The establishment of the Special Court through a bilateral treaty, rather than under the auspices of the UN Security Council, was a creative way of establishing an international judicial accountability mechanism that reflects domestic resource constraints and legal and political barriers to prosecution and international political reality at the time. In 2002, the Government of Sierra Leone was theoretically willing to prosecute leaders of the principal militant factions, but lacked the resources and confidence to carry out independent and impartial domestic proceedings. The Government was also concerned that many of the worst crimes were covered by the Lomé Amnesty Agreement. At the international level, the end of the Sierra Leone war coincided with a time when political opinion had shifted against establishing *ad hoc* Tribunals based on the ICTY/ICTR model. These institutions, while primarily responsible for the resurgence of international criminal law after almost 50 years of post-Nuremberg dormancy, were at the same time viewed as too slow and expensive. Moreover, in the course of 2002, the Rome Statute establishing the ICC entered into force and states therefore saw little justification for the creation of another *ad hoc* Tribunal.

B. A 'Hybrid' Tribunal

The Special Court is a so-called 'hybrid' tribunal because its jurisdiction covers international crimes as well as national crimes; the Court's officials including the Judges, Prosecutor, Deputy Prosecutor and Registrar are, by Statute, appointed by the UN and the Government of Sierra Leone. The Court's jurisdiction over certain crimes under Sierra Leonean law has proven to be only an issue of academic interest because the Prosecutor has not brought charges under those laws. The 'mixed' composition of Chambers, Prosecution, Defence teams and the Court's staff has proven to be of far greater significance. Pursuant to the Special Court Agreement and the Statute, the Government of Sierra Leone appoints one of the three Judges of each Trial Chamber and two of the Judges of the Appeals Chamber. The Government of Sierra Leone also appoints the Deputy Prosecutor. In addition, the practice of the Court has been to hire qualified Sierra Leonean professional and general services staff in all sections of the Court, including in key leadership positions.

---

2 *Letter dated 9 August 2000 from the Permanent Representative of Sierra Leone to the United Nations addressed to the President of the Security Council*, UN doc. S/2000/786, 10 August 2000, annex.

3 *Report of the Secretary-General on the Establishment of a Special Court for Sierra Leone*, UN doc. S/2000/915, 4 October 2000, annex.

3. Fundraising and the Management Committee

Partly as a consequence of the Special Court's origins from a bilateral agreement between the UN and the Government of Sierra Leone, the Security Council initially proposed in Resolution 1315 that the Court would be financed through voluntary contributions from states and organizations. Resolution 1315, however, did not indicate how the funds would be raised or managed. In his October 2000 report on the establishment of the Special Court, the Secretary-General urged that 'a special court based on voluntary contributions would be neither viable nor sustainable'. Arguing for a mechanism that would afford 'secure and continuous funding', the Secretary-General opined that the Court should be funded from the budget of the UN. The funding of the Special Court has been a problematic and controversial matter ever since and, in the words of Professor Cassese who conducted an independent review of the Court's operations, 'the lack of stable funding has plagued the Court'.[4]

Despite the Secretary-General's view that voluntary contributions could undermine the success of the Court, the Security Council nonetheless preferred that mode of financing, and subsequently put forward the idea of a management committee:

> In order to assist the court on questions of funding and administration, it is suggested that the arrangements between the government of Sierra Leone and the UN provide for a management or oversight committee which could include representatives of Sierra Leone, the Secretary-General of the UN, the Court and interested voluntary contributors. The management committee would assist the court in obtaining adequate funding, provide advice on matters of Court administration and be available as appropriate to consult on other non-judicial matters.[5]

It was thus proposed that membership in the management committee include those states that were the largest contributors to the financing of the Court, plus the Government of Sierra Leone and the Secretary-General. It was also realized early on that operation of the Court outside the UN's bureaucratic procedures regarding budget and personnel could significantly increase the operational efficiency of the Court, particularly during the start-up phase when numerous positions in the Office of the Prosecutor would need to be staffed quickly in order to bring cases to trial in a short time frame. Quite remarkably, the Court went from being a mere proposal (with no accompanying physical structure) to commencing trials within three years.

In addition to membership requirements, the role and responsibility of the management committee also required clarification. Following consultations, the UN, the Government of Sierra Leone and the group of interested states reached an agreement on the mandate and terms of reference of the new body, which subsequently formed Article 7 of the Special Court Agreement:

> It is the understanding of the Parties that interested States will establish a management committee to assist the Secretary-General in obtaining adequate funding, and provide advice and policy direction on all non-judicial aspects of the operation of the Court, including questions of efficiency, and to perform other functions as agreed by interested States. The management committee shall

---

4 A. Cassese, *Report on the Special Court for Sierra Leone*, 12 December 2006, p. 11. Available at http://www.sc-sl.org/DOCUMENTS/OtherCourtDocuments/tabid/203/Default.aspx.

5 *Letter from the President of the Security Council Addressed to the Secretary-General*, UN doc. S/2000/1234, 22 December 2000.

consist of important contributors to the Special Court. The government of Sierra Leone and the Secretary-General will also participate in the management committee.

The management committee accordingly considers reports on the operations of the Special Court, provides policy advice and policy directions on all the non-judicial aspects of its operations, oversees the Court's annual budget and other financial reports and advises the Secretary-General on issues related to the Court's operations. Although establishment of the management committee was a thoughtful way of responding to a unique funding situation, the lack of financial security resulting from voluntary contributions may ultimately be considered an imprudent way to finance a judicial institution tasked with adjudicating 'some of the most heinous, brutal and atrocious crimes ever recorded in human history'.[6]

The Special Court has struggled to secure adequate funding for its operations since its inception. For the period from 1 July 2002 to 30 June 2005, the Court was budgeted to spend $57 million.[7] In 2004, the Court was forced to borrow against pledges for the following year in order to finish its second year of work.[8] To resolve the crisis, a one-off subvention grant in the amount of $16.7 million was issued by the UN to allow the Court to finance its third year of operations[9] and Member States said 'never again'.[10] As noted by Professor Antonio Cassese, '[o]ften donating States have provided their contributions at the last minute, thus hampering financial planning and more generally creating financial insecurity.'[11] Monies sufficient to cover annual budgets in the range of $23 million to $36 million must be raised each year, and uncertainties regarding contributions from national authorities have sometimes left the Court within only days of insufficient funding.[12] At the time of writing, the Court projected a budgetary shortfall in mid-2009 and has requested the Secretary-General's assistance to ensure the Court can complete its judicial mandate.

Ultimately, the survival of the Court has depended upon funds from a small group of key donor states. To secure these funds, key staff – principally the Registrar, Prosecutor and President – must expend substantial time, travel and energy, thus diverting valuable resources from the Court's core judicial mandate.

---

6 SCSL, Sentencing Judgment, *AFRC*, Trial Chamber, 19 July 2007, para. 34.

7 *Letter from the President of the Security Council addressed to the Secretary-General*, UN doc. S/2001/693, 12 July 2001.

8 International Center for Transitional Justice, 'The Special Court for Sierra Leone Under Scrutiny', March 2006, at 32.

9 *Resolution adopted by the General Assembly: Special Court for Sierra Leone*, UN doc. A/Res/58/284, 26 April 2004, para. 2.

10 E. Ayoola, *Second Annual Report of the President of the Special Court for Sierra Leone* (2005). Available at http://www.sc-sl.org/Documents/specialcourtannualreport2004-2005.pdf.

11 A. Cassese, *Report on the Special Court for Sierra Leone*, 12 December 2006, p. 11. Available at http://www.sc-sl.org/DOCUMENTS/OtherCourtDocuments/tabid/203/Default.aspx.

12 See E. Ayoola, *Second Annual Report of the President of the Special Court for Sierra Leone* (2005), at 27. Available at http://www.sc-sl.org/Documents/specialcourtannualreport2004-2005.pdf.

4. A Streamlined Court for 'Persons who Bear the Greatest Responsibility'

A. Those Bearing the Greatest Responsibility

The Special Court is the first court at the international level in which the Statute limits prosecutions to 'persons who bear the greatest responsibility for serious violations of international humanitarian law and Sierra Leonean law'.[13] The *travaux preparatoires* of the Statute demonstrate that this phrase was included to distinguish the Special Court from the ICTY and ICTR (which have the power to prosecute (all) 'persons responsible for serious violations of international humanitarian law') in order to limit the number of accused prosecuted by the Court.

The phrase 'persons who bear the greatest responsibility for the commission of the crimes' appears to have been first introduced by the Security Council in its resolution 1315 (2000). The Secretary-General understood the phrase 'as an indication of a limitation on the number of accused' and he proposed that 'the more general term "persons most responsible" should be used', because:

> While those "most responsible" obviously include the political or military leadership, others in command authority down the chain of command may also be regarded "most responsible" judging by the severity of the crime or its massive scale. "Most responsible", therefore, denotes both a leadership or authority position of the accused, and a sense of the gravity, seriousness or massive scale of the crime. It must be seen, however, not as a test criterion or a distinct jurisdictional threshold, but as a guidance to the Prosecutor in the adoption of a prosecution strategy and in making decisions to prosecute in individual cases.[14]

In response, the Security Council indicated that by using the language of 'greatest responsibility' rather than 'most responsible', they limited the focus of the Special Court to those who played a leadership role.[15] Although the Security Council and Secretary-General discussed the 'greatest responsibility' limitation under the heading 'personal jurisdiction', the Statute did not include that heading and instead framed the limitation on the Court's 'power to prosecute', therefore leaving it uncertain whether the limitation was intended to guide prosecutorial discretion or to restrict the Court's jurisdiction.

One of the convicted persons filed a ground of appeal arguing that the Trial Chamber erred in finding that the words 'the Special Court ... shall ... have the power to prosecute persons who bear the greatest responsibility' in Article 1(1) of the Statute is guide to prosecutorial discretion rather than a jurisdictional requirement.[16] The Trial Chamber had held that 'the greatest responsibility requirement ... solely purports to streamline the focus of prosecutorial strategy' and that the drafters of the Statute did not intend to make it 'a jurisdictional threshold which, if not met, would oblige a Trial Chamber to dismiss the case without considering the merits'.[17] On appeal, the convicted person argued that the drafters of the Statute were aware that the Special Court would have limited

---

13 Art. 1(1) SCSLSt.

14 *Report of the Secretary General on the Establishment of a Special Court for Sierra Leone*, UN doc. S/2000/915, 4 October 2000.

15 *Letter from the President of the Security Council addressed to the Secretary-General*, UN doc. S/2000/1234, 22 December 2000, para. 1.

16 See SCSL, Judgement, *AFRC*, Trial Chamber, 20 June 2007, paras 640–659.

17 SCSL, Judgement, *AFRC*, Trial Chamber, 20 June 2007, para. 653.

time and resources and therefore deliberately circumscribed the Court's personal jurisdiction through the 'greatest responsibility requirement'.

In deciding the issue, the Appeals Chamber reasoned that the Prosecutor has the responsibility and competence to determine who will be prosecuted as a result of investigations undertaken by the Prosecutor, while competence to try such persons lies with the Chambers. The Appeals Chamber therefore agreed with the Prosecution that Article 1(1) is a guide to the Prosecutor in the exercise of his prosecutorial discretion. That discretion must be exercised by the Prosecution in good faith and based on sound professional judgement. The Appeals Chamber opined that it would also be unreasonable and unworkable to suggest that the determination of 'greatest responsibility' is one that would be done by the Trial Chamber or the Appeals Chamber at the end of the trial.[18]

B. Notice Pleading and Use of a 'Case Summary'

The Rules of Procedure and Appeals Chamber jurisprudence establish a new practice in international criminal justice akin to the common law practice of 'notice pleading'. Thus, instead of having 80 or 90 page indictments, the longest indictment at the Special Court was the 20-page, 17-count original indictment of Charles Taylor (later amended to 9 pages and 11 counts). The Rules provide that the indictment is sufficient if it contains 'the name and particulars of the suspect, a statement of each specific offence of which the named suspect is charged and a short description of the particulars of the offence'.[19] The indictment must be accompanied by a 'case summary' which briefly sets out the allegations in a manner that enables the reviewing judge to determine whether the indictment charges a crime within the Court's jurisdiction and that, if the allegations in the case summary are proved, amounts to the crime or crimes particularized in the indictment.[20]

The Appeals Chamber has provided additional guidance and rationale for this approach, explaining that the indictment should contain only a list of counts with each count followed by brief particulars.[21] This does not mean that the Prosecution can omit material facts from the indictment and instead include them in the case summary. The Appeals Chamber noted the Prosecution's obligation under the Rules is to set out in the indictment 'a "short description" of the *particulars* of the offence – the time, place, reference to co-offenders and so on'.[22] The case summary accompanying the indictment forms no part of the indictment; therefore, after an accused has entered a plea, no word or phrase in the indictment can be amended without leave from the Court. The case summary, however, is not a document susceptible to amendment by the Court. Thus, the Prosecutor is not obliged to seek leave of the Court before amending the case summary, but is obliged to give full disclosure of any changes to the evidence and is obliged to alert the defence to any significant change in the way the case will be put to trial.[23]

18 SCSL, Judgment, *AFRC*, Appeals Chamber, 22 February 2008, para. 283.

19 Rule 47(C) SCSL RPE.

20 See Rule 47(E) SCSL RPE.

21 See SCSL, Decision on Amendment of the Consolidated Indictment, *Samuel Hinga Norman*, Appeals Chamber, 16 May 2005, para. 52.

22 Ibid., para. 51.

23 Ibid., para. 52.

5. Legality and Constitutionality of the Special Court

A. Background

Several defendants before the Court submitted motions challenging the constitutionality and lack of jurisdiction of the Special Court. The defendants argued that the Court was unconstitutional under the Sierra Leonean Constitution, the Government of Sierra Leone acted unconstitutionally in establishing it and, accordingly, the Court was an *ultra vires* institution. One defendant also argued that the Security Council acted *ultra vires* when it delegated its powers to the Secretary-General to conclude the Special Court Agreement and that Secretary-General did not have the power to conclude such an agreement.[24]

The defendants also contended that the Court was not competent to determine the lawfulness and validity of its establishment.[25] The matter was heard directly by the Appeals Chamber because the Statute provides that all preliminary motions challenging jurisdiction are automatically heard in that Chamber.

B. Competence and Jurisdiction of the Special Court to Decide the Legality of its Creation

In order to answer the first question, namely whether the Court had the competence and jurisdiction to determine the lawfulness and validity of its establishment, the Appeals Chamber started with the Special Court Agreement.[26] Article 1(2) of the Special Court Agreement provides:

> The Special Court shall function in accordance with the Statute of the Special Court for Sierra Leone. The Statute is annexed to the Agreement and forms an integral part thereof.

The Statute of the Special Court ('Statute'), Article 14, refers to the Rules of Procedure and Evidence of the Special Court. The Rules of Procedure and Evidence, in turn, provide that:

> Preliminary motions made in the Trial Chamber prior to the Prosecutor's opening statement which raise a serious issue relating to jurisdiction shall be referred to the Appeals Chamber, where they will proceed to a determination as soon as practicable.[27]

On the basis of these constituent instruments, the Appeals Chamber held that it was competent to decide whether or not the Special Court had jurisdiction to determine the legality and validity of its establishment.[28]

In exercising that competence, i.e., in considering whether the Special Court had jurisdiction to decide on the lawfulness and validity of its creation, the Appeals Chamber considered the *Tadić* decision of the Appeals Chamber of the International Criminal Tribunal for the former Yugoslavia

24 SCSL, Decision on Preliminary Motion on Lack of Jurisdiction Materiae: Illegal Delegation of Powers by the United Nations, *Moinina Fofana*, Appeals Chamber, 25 May 2004.

25 See SCSL, Decision on Constitutionality and Lack of Jurisdiction, *Morris Kallon, Sam Hinga Norman and Brima Bazzy Kamara*, Appeals Chamber, 13 March 2004, paras 2–28 ('Constitutionality and Jurisdiction Decision').

26 *Report of the Secretary-General on the Establishment of a Special Court for Sierra*, UN doc. S/2000/915, 4 October 2000, annex.

27 Rule 72(E) SCSL RPE.

28 Constitutionality and Jurisdiction Decision, para. 34.

(ICTY), which found that it had jurisdiction to determine the legality of its own creation.[29] Further, drawing on the Special Court Agreement as well as its Statute, the Appeals Chamber of the Special Court held that it had jurisdiction to determine the constitutionality of its establishment.[30]

C. Constitutionality of the Special Court

In addressing the defendants' arguments relating to the unconstitutionality of the Special Court, the Appeals Chamber undertook a detailed review of the process by which the Court was established. The Appeals Chamber commenced with an analysis of the Report of the Secretary-General on the establishment of a Special Court for Sierra Leone in which the Secretary-General remarked that the Special Court:

> is established by an agreement between the UN and the government of Sierra Leone and is therefore *a treaty-based sui generis court of mixed jurisdiction and composition.* Its implementation at the national level would require that the Special Court Agreement is incorporated in the national law of Sierra Leone in accordance with constitutional requirements.[31]

The Appeals Chamber also looked to general international law, drawing on the Vienna Convention on the Law of Treaties between States and International Organizations, before reaching the conclusion that the Special Court was a treaty-based and *sui generis* court.[32] Having so concluded, the Appeals Chamber then turned to the issue of the incorporation of the Special Court Agreement into the national law of Sierra Leone. An accused had argued that the incorporation in effect constituted an amendment of the Constitution of Sierra Leone, for which a referendum should have been held. He referred to section 120(2) of the Constitution, which states, in part, that '[t]he judicial power shall be vested in the Judiciary'.[33]

The Appeals Chamber noted that the Special Court is not part of the Judiciary of Sierra Leone; indeed, it is established outside the national court system. The Special Court also has the power to conclude treaties, thus distinguishing it from domestic courts. The Chamber noted further that the Special Court is not anchored in any existing system, in particular that of Sierra Leone. For these reasons, the Chamber held that the establishment of the Court under Article 1 of the Special Court Agreement met the relevant constitutional requirements and that the appropriate procedures had been followed.[34]

Finally, the Appeals Chamber turned to the issue of whether the Special Court had been 'established by law'. In order to answer this question, the Chamber considered whether the Special Court provided the necessary and fundamental safeguards for a fair trial. In particular, it had to be considered whether the Court had been established according to international criteria, had the mechanisms and facilities to dispense even-handed justice, provided guarantees of fairness and was in tune with international human rights instruments. After conducting a thorough review of the Special Court Statute and its Rules of Procedure and Evidence, the Court concluded that the

29 ICTY, Decision on the Defence Motion for Interlocutory Appeal on Jurisdiction, *Dusko Tadić*, Appeals Chamber, 2 October 1995.

30 Constitutionality and Jurisdiction Decision, para. 37.

31 *Report of the Secretary-General on the Establishment of a Special Court for Sierra Leone*, UN doc. S/2000/915, 4 October 2000, para. 9. Emphasis added.

32 See Constitutionality and Jurisdiction Decision, paras 42–43.

33 Constitutionality and Jurisdiction Decision, para. 47.

34 See Constitutionality and Jurisdiction Decision, paras 49–53.

required criteria had been observed.[35] Accordingly, in the view of the Appeals Chamber, the Special Court was lawfully and validly established.

6. Amnesty Agreement

A. Background

The Special Court is the first international court to hold that a national amnesty does not apply to international prosecutions. It has clarified that, where crimes are subject to universal jurisdiction, a state cannot deprive other states or the international community from prosecuting such crimes by granting amnesty. The international crimes under the Statute of the Special Court are subject to universal jurisdiction.

On 7 July 1999, the RUF and the Government of Sierra Leone signed a peace agreement in Lomé, Togo (Lomé Agreement).[36] The Lomé Agreement was also signed by representatives of the UN, the Organization of African Unity, the Economic Community of West African States, the Commonwealth of Nations and the Togolese government as moral guarantors of its implementation.

Under the Lomé Agreement, the Government of Sierra Leone undertook to 'grant absolute and free pardon and reprieve to all combatants and collaborators in respect of anything done by them in pursuit of their objectives', up to the time of the signing of the agreement. The Lomé Agreement further stipulated that the Government of Sierra Leone 'shall ensure that no official or judicial action is taken against any member of the RUF ..., ex-AFRC, ex-Sierra Leone Army (SLA) or CDF in respect of anything done by them in pursuit of their objectives as members of those organizations since March 1991, up to the signing of the present agreement'. Article 10 of the Statute specifically addresses the issue of amnesty, stating, '[a]n amnesty granted to any person falling within the jurisdiction of the Special Court in respect of the crimes referred to in Articles 2 through 4 of the present Statute shall not be a bar to prosecution'.[37]

The Appeals Chamber held that the Lomé amnesty does not bar SCSL prosecution of international crimes committed before July 1999.[38] The following discussion describes the reasoning behind this important holding. The defendants argued *inter alia* that the Special Court should not assert jurisdiction over crimes committed before July 1999 when the amnesty was granted under the Lomé Agreement.[39] Opposing their challenge, the Prosecution contended that, among other things, the Lomé Agreement is not an international treaty, it is limited in effect to domestic law, and Article IX does not apply to international crimes.[40] The court also heard arguments by two *amici curiae*.[41]

---

35 See Constitutionality and Jurisdiction Decision, paras 56–58.

36 Peace Agreement between the Government of Sierra Leone and the RUF of Sierra Leone of 7 July 1999, Lomé, UN doc. S/1999/777, Annex.

37 Articles 2–4 of the Statute concern crimes against humanity, violations of Common Article 3 to the Geneva Conventions and Additional Protocol II, and other serious violations of international humanitarian law. Article 5, which is not referred to in Article 10, concerns crimes under Sierra Leonean law.

38 SCSL, Decision on Challenge to Jurisdiction, *Morris Kallon, Brima Bazzy Kamara*, Appeals Chamber, 13 March 2004, paras 86–90 (Lomé Decision).

39 Lomé Decision at para. 1.

40 Lomé Decision, paras 2, 32.

41 Lomé Decision, Preamble, paras 33–35.

The Appeals Chamber's reasoning essentially focused on the status of the Lomé Agreement, the validity of Article 10 of the Statute and the limits of amnesties in international law.

B. Status of the Lomé Agreement

The defendants argued that the Lomé Agreement is an international agreement in the nature of a treaty.[42] The Appeals Chamber rejected this position on three grounds. First, it found that the parties to the Lomé Agreement were the Government of Sierra Leone and the RUF. The non-contracting signatories of the Lomé Agreement, including the UN, were mere 'moral guarantors' of its implementation in good faith. As such, they assumed no legal obligation.[43] Second, the Appeals Chamber held that an international agreement in the nature of a treaty must create rights and obligations regulated by international law; the Lomé Agreement did not do so.[44] Third, the Appeals Chamber held that an insurgent group, such as the RUF, does not have treaty-making capacity. It does not follow, the Chamber reasoned, from the mere fact that insurgents are bound under customary international law by Common Article 3 to the Geneva Conventions that they are vested with personality in international law.[45] Also, although the Government of Sierra Leone regarded the RUF as an entity with which it could enter into an agreement, no other state had granted the RUF such recognition.[46]

The Appeals Chamber held that, because the Lomé Agreement is not a treaty, it does not create obligations in international law.[47] Instead, its rights and obligations are confined to the national system of Sierra Leone and are regulated by the domestic laws of Sierra Leone. As a result, whether or not it is binding on the Government of Sierra Leone does not affect the prosecution of an accused in an international tribunal for international crimes.[48] The Appeals Chamber further opined that the grant of amnesty is an exercise of sovereign power closely linked to the criminal jurisdiction of the state granting the amnesty. Where jurisdiction is universal, such a state cannot deprive another state of its jurisdiction to prosecute the offender by granting amnesty. In the words of the Appeals Chamber, 'a State cannot bring into oblivion and forgetfulness a crime, such as a crime against international law, which other States are entitled to keep alive and remember'.[49] As such, the amnesty granted by the Government of Sierra Leone cannot cover crimes under international law that are subject to universal jurisdiction.[50]

---

42 Lomé Decision, para. 36.

43 Lomé Decision, para. 41.

44 Lomé Decision, para. 42.

45 Lomé Decision, paras 45–47.

46 Lomé Decision, para. 47.

47 Lomé Decision, para. 49. The Appeals Chamber noted that the Lomé Agreement need not be a treaty for it to create binding obligations on municipal law. Lomé Decision at para. 50. However, since the validity of Article IX of the Lomé Agreement had not been challenged based on municipal law, the Appeals Chamber did not find it of prime importance to consider its validity in the municipal law of Sierra Leone.

48 Lomé Decision, para. 86. As to the international character of the Special Court, see also SCSL, Decision on Constitutionality and Lack of Jurisdiction, *Morris Kallon, Sam Hinga Norman and Brima Bazzy Kamara*, Appeals Chamber, 13 March 2004, paras 49–53.

49 Lomé Decision, para. 67.

50 Lomé Decision, para. 71.

C. *Validity of Article 10 of the Statute*

The defendants also sought to impeach the validity of Article 10 of the Statute, which states that amnesty shall not be a bar to prosecution in respect of the international crimes under the Statute. The Appeals Chamber considered that it could not question the validity of Article 10 of its Statute unless that provision was shown to be void in the terms of Articles 53 or 64 of the Vienna Convention on the Law of Treaties or under customary international law.[51] It found that no such showing had been made.[52] In this connection, the Appeals Chamber distinguished the ICTY Appeals Chamber's decision in *Tadić*,[53] which Kallon had relied on to support that the Special Court can pronounce on the lawfulness of its own establishment.[54] The *Tadić* decision was distinguished on the grounds that the ICTY is not a treaty-based Tribunal and that the *Tadić* case did not involve the validity of provisions of a treaty, but rather the extent of the power of the Security Council, an authority established by the UN Charter.[55]

7. Head of State Immunity

An indictment and warrant of arrest were issued for Charles Taylor on 7 March 2003, when Taylor was still Liberia's head of state. The indictment contained 17 counts relating to, *inter alia*, crimes against humanity and grave breaches of the 1949 Geneva Conventions.[56] Taylor sought to quash the indictment and to set aside the warrant for his arrest on the basis that he enjoyed immunity from arrest and prosecution as Head of State. Taylor argued that he was immune from any exercise of jurisdiction on the part of the Special Court.[57] Taylor also claimed entitlement to the benefit of any immunity asserted by Liberia against the exercise of the Special Court's jurisdiction. Accordingly, the Appeals Chamber was called upon to decide whether it was lawful for the Special Court to issue an indictment and to circulate an arrest warrant in respect of a serving Head of State.

The issues raised in this appeal turned to a large extent on the legal status of the Special Court. The Appeals Chamber had previously determined, in its decision on the constitutionality of the Court, that the Special Court is not a national court of Sierra Leone and is not part of the judicial system of Sierra Leone exercising judicial powers of Sierra Leone.[58] On that basis, coupled with an analysis of the Special Court's constitutive instruments, the Appeals Chamber concluded that the Court is a truly international criminal court.[59]

The Appeals Chamber then carefully considered international jurisprudence, taking into account the views of, *inter alia*, the International Court of Justice and the House of Lords. The Appeals

---

51 United Nations, Vienna Convention on the Law of Treaties, 23 May 1969. Articles 53 and 64 essentially provide that a treaty is void if it conflicts with a peremptory norm of general international law.

52 Lomé Decision, paras 61–62.

53 ICTY, Decision on the Defence Motion on Jurisdiction, *Duško Tadić*, Appeals Chamber, 2 October 1995.

54 Lomé Decision, para. 62.

55 Ibid.

56 SCSL, Indictment, *Charles Ghankay Taylor*, Case. No. SCSL-2003-01-I, 3 March 2003.

57 SCSL, Decision on Immunity From Jurisdiction, *Charles Ghankay Taylor*, 31 May 2004, paras 6–8, 11, 15 ('Immunity Decision').

58 SCSL, Decision on Constitutionality and Lack of Jurisdiction, *Morris Kallon, Sam Hinga Norman and Brima Bazzy Kamara*. See also, Immunity Decision, paras 37–42.

59 Immunity Decision, para. 42.

Chamber held that the principle of state immunity derives from the sovereign equality of states. Therefore, it has no relevance to international criminal tribunals which are not organs of a state, but derive their mandate from the international community. As such, state immunity does not prevent a head of state from being prosecuted before an international criminal court or tribunal.[60]

The Appeals Chamber noted that it is bound by the provisions of its Statute, in so far as they are not in conflict with any peremptory norm of international law. In this regard, the Appeals Chamber observed that Article 6(2) of the Statute provides that:

> [t]he official position of any accused persons, whether as Head of State or Government or as a responsible government official, shall not relieve such person of criminal responsibility nor mitigate punishment.

After considering the statutes of other international criminal courts and tribunals, which contain similar provisions, the Appeals Chamber held that Article 6(2) was not in conflict with any peremptory norm of international law.[61] Consequently, the Appeals Chamber held that the official position of Taylor as the incumbent Head of State at the time when the criminal proceedings were initiated against him was not a bar to his prosecution by the Special Court.[62]

8. Witness Protection

The Judges' ability to effectively determine an accused's guilt or innocence depends, in great part, upon the witnesses who testify before them. Witnesses appearing in international tribunals present special needs involving their support during testimony and protection from interference. This is even more the case at the Special Court where large numbers of witnesses are often asked to testify to extremely traumatic sexual violence and/or violence they may have experienced as children. In addition, the circumstances of the conflict in Sierra Leone put witnesses in greater danger than those appearing before other courts because victims and perpetrators frequently, if not invariably, continue to live in the same villages and see each other in their daily lives.

Recognizing these unique, unprecedented needs, a section of the Court was tasked with ensuring, from the Court's inception, that witnesses are not adversely affected by their experience of testifying at the Court. Within the Registry, a specialized unit – the Witness and Victims Section (WVS) – is tasked with securing the protection and welfare of all witnesses before the Court. The reader is referred to an excellent study of the Court's exemplary witness protection programme, parts of which will be discussed briefly here.[63]

WVS works with both prosecution and defence witnesses, and is also responsible for the welfare of others put at risk as a result of testimony given by witnesses (typically the relatives of witnesses). WVS assesses the security needs of each witness and recommends to the Court if additional protective measures are necessary to ensure witnesses' security. The WVS is also responsible for developing long- and short-term plans for witness protection and support, and for ensuring that witnesses receive 'relevant support, counselling and other appropriate assistance,

60 Immunity Decision, paras 50–52.

61 Immunity Decision, paras 44–49, 53.

62 Immunity Decision, para. 53.

63 See R. Horn, S. Charters, and S. Vahidy, 'Testifying in an International War Crimes Tribunal: The Experience of Witnesses in the Special Court for Sierra Leone', 3 *The International Journal of Transitional Justice*, 2009, at 135–149.

including medical assistance, physical and psychological rehabilitation, especially in cases of rape, sexual assault and crimes against children'.[64] The Special Court is the first international tribunal to recognize in its constitutive documents the special needs of witnesses to gender-based violence crimes and crimes against children.

WVS reports directly to the Registrar and is divided into a protection, security and movement unit and a psychosocial support unit. 'The protection, security and movement unit manages all the logistical and security arrangements for witnesses, including identification and maintenance of safe houses' whereas '[t]he psychosocial unit consists of staff trained in counselling, plus two medically trained staff and one psychologist'.[65]

WVS takes a three-part approach to ensuring the safety of witnesses. First, witness identity is protected from the earliest stages such that only a witness's legal team and WVS will know the witness's identity, unless the witness chooses to testify openly. Typically, only a witness's closest relatives are aware that the individual is going to testify. Second, if there is a heightened risk to a witness, WVS places the witness in 'total protective care' which involves transferring the witness and his or her family into a safe house until the after testifying and then relocating the witness, typically within West Africa. Third, while witnesses are in the care of the Court, their basic, medical and psychological needs are provided for by professional staff.

Before testifying, each witness is briefed on the courtroom experience because many witnesses will not have been inside a courtroom before, and perhaps not inside an electrically lit, air-conditioned building. The novelty of the experience can be intimidating even without the aspect of retelling a harrowing personal story. WVS attempts to demystify the process by providing a tour of the Court, spending time with the legal teams, providing a psychosocial team member escort for witness, who is later brought in anonymity to a specialized witness waiting room and into Court. In Court, the witness will be accompanied by WVS staff, often including both a psychosocial support officer and a protection officer.

Witness identities are typically protected throughout their testimony. They testify from behind a screen in an otherwise public courtroom, they are not addressed by name and identifying information is only taken in closed session. Additional protective measures may be ordered by the Court. After testifying, WVS provides the witness with transport home and contact details of WVS staff in case they experience any problems related to their cooperation with the Court. WVS carries out follow-up visits within six months of testimony to assess the well-being of each witness. In doing so, WVS determines whether testifying has led to any negative consequences for the witness in terms of 'security, emotional well-being, social situation or financial situation'.[66] WVS intercedes if it learns that the personal circumstances of a witness have deteriorated as a consequence of their testimony (e.g., if their community learns of their testimony) and takes additional measures to ensure the witness as well as family members are protected, potentially through relocation.

9. Legacy

As the first international court situated where the crimes took place, the Court has, since its inception, understood the creation of a durable legacy as a core component of its mandate. In the Secretary-General's report on the establishment of the Special Court, he noted the 'high level

64 Art. 16, SCSLSt; see also, Rule 34 SCSL RPE.

65 R. Horn, S. Charters, and S. Vahidy, *supra* note 62, at 137.

66 Ibid., at 138.

of expectations' amongst Sierra Leoneans that the Special Court would form part of a broader undertaking dealing with impunity and developing the rule of law in Sierra Leone.[67] Responding to those expectations, in 2004 the Court established a Legacy Working Group to coordinate the work of each of the Court's sections to engage with local counterparts to leave a lasting legacy for the people and institutions in Sierra Leone. The Court's first white paper described the project as follows:

> Operating in a context such as Sierra Leone, the prosecution of individuals must be pursued along with other transitional justice strategies in order to achieve the desired objectives: the restoration of the rule of law and the development of the national legal system, which are necessary conditions for the prevention of future conflict.[68]

While the Court's jurisprudence will 'constitute the final measure' of the Court's legal success,[69] the Court has also directed substantial efforts and resources towards establishing a legacy in other terms. The Court has engaged in numerous projects aimed at local human and institutional capacity-building, transmission of legal norms and acquired skills and development of the Court's site into a facility or facilities of lasting significance to the country.

In terms of local capacity-building, the Court has conducted extensive and repeated training for local police, military recruits, prison officers, human rights and corruption investigators, prosecutors, military lawyers, criminal lawyers, jurists, interpreters, librarians, archivists and journalists. In 2008 alone, the Court conducted over 20 intensive training courses, benefiting over 1,700 external participants from a range of institutions and organizations. As the Court draws closer to completion, it is intensifying its legacy efforts to the extent that more than 20 such training sessions are planned for the first four months of 2009 in addition to capacity-building for the Court's national staff.

In addition to training those working in the national justice sector, more than half of the Court's staff are Sierra Leoneans and they have developed skills in all sections of the Court. In each section, national and international staff work side-by-side with each other, thereby sharing norms and practices of their professions.

The Court has also worked to ensure that its site, which will revert to the Government of Sierra Leone upon completion, will form a durable contribution to the development of the country's justice sector in further fulfilment of the Court's mandate. The Court sits on 11.5 acres of land complete with a state-of-the-art detention facility and courthouse. Based on the physical layout of the entire site, the land could be subdivided relatively easily into a variety of configurations based on the Government's needs. However, the annual maintenance costs make its operation by the Government difficult, if not impossible.

In light of these considerations, the Court has developed strategies for different options for the use of the site which include: forming a West African judicial training and education facility promoting the rule of law; a specialized detention facility for women or juvenile offenders; use of the courtroom by the national judiciary; relocation of a law school facility; housing for the Court's

67 *Secretary-General Report on the Establishment of a Special Court for Sierra Leone*, UN doc. S/2000/915, 4 October 2000, para. 7.

68 C. Jalloh, 'The Contribution of the Special Court for Sierra Leone to the Development of International Law', 15 *African Journal of International and Comparative Law* 165, at 184.

69 A. Cassese, *Report on the Special Court for Sierra Leone*, 12 December 2006, para. 120. Available at http://www.sc-sl.org/DOCUMENTS/OtherCourtDocuments/tabid/203/Default.aspx.

public documents and the archives of the Truth and Reconciliation Commission; and a memorial facility in the 'old courthouse'.

10. Completion Strategy

The final Special Court Completion Strategy was submitted to the General Assembly in May 2005.[70] Two phases are envisioned in the completion of the Court's mandate. Phase One involves the Court winding down its core activities by issuing final judgements against all accused in custody and transferring convicted persons to appropriate prisons in or outside Sierra Leone. This phase coincides with the downsizing of staff numbers as well as the transfer and liquidation of buildings and equipment. Phase Two is referred to as the post-completion phase during which time the Special Court will continue so-called 'residual activities', although not in its current form and capacity. The completion strategy identified a number of residual functions and stated that 'a residual mechanism, whether a restructured (miniaturized) Special Court or another institution to which has been delegated the Special Court's authority, will be needed to carry out these activities'.[71]

A brief overview of the Court's progress demonstrates its significant achievements over a relatively short period of time. The Court was established on 16 January 2002. The Prosecutor and Registrar arrived in Freetown between 22 July 2002 and 6 August 2002. On 13 November 2002, the Government of Sierra Leone appointed the Deputy Prosecutor. This was followed, on 2 December 2002, by the swearing in of eight Judges comprising the three-member Trial Chamber and the five-member Appeals Chamber, although the Appeals Judges did not take full-time status and live in Freetown until August 2007. The Acting Principal Defender was appointed in July 2003, and the Principal Defender took office in March 2004. Following a request by the President of the Special Court on 2 February 2004, three additional Judges forming the second Trial Chamber were sworn in on 17 January 2005.

To date, 13 indictments against 13 accused have been issued by the Prosecutor and approved by a Judge. In December 2003, the indictments against Foday Saybana Sankoh and Sam Bockarie were withdrawn as a result of their deaths. In May 2007, the indictment against Samuel Hinga Norman was also withdrawn as a result of his death, leaving 10 indictments still active. No additional indictments are envisaged. Of the ten accused, nine are currently in the custody of the Special Court and only Johnny Paul Koroma remains at large.

In short, the progress in the Trial and Appeals Chambers can be summarized as follows:

(a) In the CDF case, the trial began with opening statements from the Prosecution on 3 June 2004 and ended following closing arguments from all parties on 30 November 2006. The Trial Judgement was delivered on 7 August 2007 and the Sentencing Judgement on 9 October 2007. The Appeals Chamber delivered its Judgement in the CDF case on 28 May 2008.

(b) In the AFRC case, the Prosecution case-in-chief commenced on 7 March 2005 and closed on 21 November 2005. The defence case-in-chief started on 5 June 2006 and finished on 26 October 2006. The Trial Judgment was delivered on 20 June 2007 and the Sentencing

70 Special Court Completion Strategy, UN Doc. A/59/816 – S/2005/350, May 2005. Completion Strategy Updates were submitted to the Management Committee on 12 October 2005, 19 July 2006, 14 December 2006, July 2007, January 2008, July 2008 and December 2008.

71 UN Doc. A/59/816 – S/2005/350, 2005, para. 3.

Judgement on 19 July 2007. The Appeals Chamber delivered its Judgement in the AFRC case on 22 February 2008.

(c) The RUF Trial, one of the most complex cases before an international criminal tribunal, commenced on 5 July 2004 and closing arguments were made by all parties on 5 August 2008. The Trial Judgement was delivered in February 2009 and the Sentencing Judgement in April 2009. The Appeals Chamber projects that it will complete appeals in the case in October 2009.

(d) In the Taylor trial, the Prosecution began introducing evidence on 7 January 2008 and it is anticipated that the Prosecution will close its case in February 2009, the defence will close its case in October 2009 and the trial judgement and sentencing judgement, if applicable, will be delivered in March 2010 and April 2010, respectively. The Appeals Chamber projects that it would be able to deliver the Appeals Judgment approximately five months later, in October 2010.[72]

Once trials and appeals are completed, the liquidation phase of the Court begins. The draft Liquidation Plan of the Special Court details all activities involved in the physical closure of the Court. There are provisions for the archives and records management, asset disposal and the financial aspects of liquidation.

11. Residual Mechanism

At the inception of the Special Court, the Security Council affirmed that 'the international community will exert every effort to bring those responsible to justice in accordance with international standards of justice, fairness and due process of law'.[73] Legal and practical obligations will continue beyond the completion of all trials and appeals proceedings, and must be provided for in order to complete the Court's mandate in accordance with international standards of justice.

A. The 'Residual Functions'

The Special Court will be the first international court to complete its core judicial mandate and to transfer responsibility for implementation of its continuing legal and practical obligations to a residual mechanism. A stand-alone residual institution will likely be required to manage and perform 10 critical functions, which have been described by the Court as its 'residual functions', after the completion of trials.[74]

1. Maintenance, Preservation and Management of the Archive

The Special Court's voluminous records, held in Freetown and in The Hague, are in English, Mende, Temne, Krio, Limba and other languages. Much of the material must be held in confidentiality to protect witnesses or the providing entity. Therefore, a long-term plan for the Court's archive, which guarantees confidentiality and that the Court's records are safeguarded into the foreseeable

72 Special Court Completion Strategy updated December 2008.

73 UN Doc. S/RES/1315, 2000.

74 F. Donlon, *Report on the Residual Functions and the Residual Institution Options of the Special Court for Sierra Leone*, 16 December 2008, analyses in full detail the residual functions.

future, is being developed. In archiving terms, the records have primary value for the Court and its successor institution which may be required to use the records in review, contempt or other proceedings. The records have secondary value for everyone else, in particular the people of Sierra Leone. Although the records do not have the same legal significance to the people of Sierra Leone, their informational and symbolic importance as a record of the conflict is widely understood and the Court is looking into creating a memorial component with public documents and the possibility of keeping some or all of the records in Sierra Leone.

2. Trial of the Fugitive Johnny Paul Koroma

Currently, there is one outstanding Special Court indictment against the accused Johnny Paul Koroma (JPK). If JPK is arrested before the end of the Court's judicial mandate, then his trial could be conducted by the Court in Freetown. If, however, he is not captured by 2010, the Judges have revised the Rules of Procedure and Evidence to adopt a Rule 11*bis* to regulate the referral of the case to competent national jurisdictions. Since JPK is not in the custody of the Special Court, the referral bench is authorized to issue a warrant for his arrest which will specify the state to which he is to be transferred.

3. Review of Convictions and Acquittals

Pursuant to the Statute and Rules of Procedure and Evidence, judgements can be reviewed at the request of the convicted person or the Prosecutor within 12 months of the pronouncement of the Appeals Judgment. To date, the Special Court has not yet had a request for review; however, judicial capacity is required by the residual mechanism to deal with requests for review. The relevant procedures involve the judges of the Appeals Chamber determining whether the application for review has merit, and subsequently reviewing the judgement or reconvening the Trial Chamber. The Judges will consider whether to amend the Rules to streamline these proceedings.

4. Contempt of Court Proceedings

Related to the need to ensure continued protection of victims and witnesses who appeared before the Special Court is the continued need to ensure respect for, and implementation of, court orders as well as the need to sanction persons who violate them. Orders of the Special Court must continue to be respected, and consequently an ongoing capacity for contempt proceedings is required. In addition, new proceedings during the post-completion phase may generate new victims or witnesses who will require protective measures to be ordered by the residual institution.

5. Witness Protection and Support

The rules oblige the section to 'develop long- and short-term plans for the protection and support' of witnesses.[75] Long-term planning extends beyond the completion of trials and appeals. Hence, the continued protection and support of witnesses who appeared before the Special Court is a critical residual function. This was identified by the Prosecutors of ICTR, ICTY, SCSL, ECCC and ICC who have committed themselves to taking the necessary steps to 'establish a regime for the protection and support of victims providing not only physical protection, but also medical and

75 Rule 34 SCSL RPE; Art. 16 SCSLSt.

psychological support. Such a regime should continue to operate after the closure of the *ad hoc* tribunals.'[76] A distinction is drawn between judicial protective measures and measures that are more technical by nature. The Court's successor body will need the capacity to provide judicial protective measures. It will also need technical capacity to perform tasks such as monitoring relocation agreements, keeping track of protected witnesses, monitoring threat assessments and providing secure records management.

6. Defence Counsel and Legal Aid Issues

As a creation of the Registrar, the Defence Office and its head, the Principal Defender, remain under the administrative authority of the Registrar.[77] The Registrar has two main duties with respect to defence counsel: first, the Court provides legal aid for indigent defendants; and second, the Registrar must ensure that counsel meet certain standards of professionalism and ethical conduct. It is envisaged that the residual mechanism would have both oversight authority and the capacity to discipline counsel, if necessary, in the future, although this may rarely arise. It has been considered that the successor body will not require specific staff member designated to the defence unless needs arise and, consequently, that rather a roster of defence counsel based on the current list be maintained.

7. Assistance to National Prosecution Authorities

This function is critically dependent on the management and use of prosecution evidence and information, and will contribute to ongoing efforts to combat impunity for the atrocities committed during the conflict. It is anticipated that national investigation and prosecution authorities will require access to public and confidential records for domestic judicial and administrative proceedings, including forfeiture proceedings, immigration and asylum cases.

8. Prevention of Double Jeopardy

The rule regarding double jeopardy or *non bis in idem* provides, in part, that a person should not be tried twice for the same offence. Because the Court is formed by a Treaty between the Government of Sierra Leone and the UN, it lacks enforcement powers to prevent a national court outside Sierra Leone from exercising its jurisdiction. The Statute and Rules, therefore, provide that no person shall be tried before a national court of Sierra Leone for acts which he or she has already been tried by the Special Court.[78] The residual mechanism will need the capacity to respond to allegations that a court in Sierra Leone intends to prosecute a person already tried by the Court.

9. Supervision of Prison Sentences, Early Release, Pardon and Commutation

The Statute states that 'imprisonment shall be served in Sierra Leone',[79] however '[i]f circumstances so require, imprisonment may be served in a State that has reached an agreement with' the ICTR

76 See F. Donlon, *supra* note 73, at 25, citing ICTY, ICTR, SCSL, ECCC, ICC Prosecutors Roundtable Discussion on International Cooperation Agenda for Action, Arusha, Tanzania, 26–28 November 2008.

77 *Third Annual Report of the President of the Special Court for Sierra Leone*, Jan 2005–Jan 2006, at 30. Available at http://www.sc-sl.org/DOCUMENTS/SpecialCourtAnnualReports/tabid/201/Default.aspx.

78 Rule 13 SCSL RPE.

79 Rule 103(A) SCSL RPE.

or ICTY or in a State that concludes an enforcement agreement with the SCSL. In the Secretary-General's report on the draft Statute, 'the security risk entailed in the continued imprisonment of some of the convicted persons on Sierra Leonean territory'[80] was cited as an example of such a circumstance. The Office of the President of Sierra Leone has formally communicated to the Court that it does not consider the enforcement of sentences in Sierra Leone prudent. The Registrar has, therefore, concluded agreements with several states to allow enforcement outside of Sierra Leone. The Rules provide that the President shall designate the place of imprisonment for each convicted person and that transfer to the enforcing state shall be affected as soon as possible after the time limit for appeal has lapsed.[81] Once the states of enforcement are determined, the Court must provide for the supervision of the enforcement of sentences, which could continue for decades following the Court's closure. In addition, the Court must provide a mechanism to determine if a convicted person is eligible for pardon or commutation of sentence, pursuant to the law of the state in which he is imprisoned. In such a situation, the state concerned shall notify the Court and the 'residual President', in consultation with the Judges, will decide on pardon or commutation of sentence on the basis of the interests of justice and general principles of law.

10. Compensation to Victims

Finally, the Court's Rules contain a provision entitled 'Compensation to Victims' that requires the Registrar to transmit judgements finding an accused guilty of crimes that have caused injury to victims to the competent national authorities. In addition, pursuant to Article 45 of the 2002 Special Court Agreement (Ratification Act) Act, any victim of a crime within the jurisdiction of the Court may claim compensation under the national Criminal Procedure Act if the Court has found a person guilty of that crime. The Rules state that for the purposes of such a claim, 'the judgement of the Court shall be final and binding as to the criminal responsibility of the convicted person for such injury'.[82] The ICC's mechanism for victim compensation is more robust because it can order compensation to be paid. At present, no known claims have been made under this provision before a Sierra Leonean court, however, the Court's residual mechanism will require some capacity to provide information or support if required.

B. Ongoing and Ad Hoc Functions

In summary, the Special Court's residual issues report analyses that these functions can broadly be divided into two categories: ongoing functions and *ad hoc* functions. The *ad hoc* functions are those that may only be required from time to time, and may, in practice, never be required at all. The ongoing functions are those that involve ongoing day-to-day responsibilities. The *ad hoc* functions may only require a notional residual mechanism that will be called upon to perform a service as needed, which may be very rarely or in fact never performed. The Court has identified that a permanent standing mechanism needs to exist for the ongoing functions. Establishment of this mechanism or any other successor institution will require the Secretary-General and the Government of Sierra Leone to enter 'a subsequent agreement ... upon the completion of [the

80 *Report of the Secretary-General on the establishment of a Special Court for Sierra Leone*, UN doc. S/2000/915, para. 51.

81 Rule 103(B) and (C) SCSL RPE.

82 Rule 105(C) SCSL RPE.

Court's] judicial activities' as envisaged by the Secretary-General in his initial Report on the Court's establishment.[83]

12. Conclusion

Despite significant and ongoing funding problems, the Special Court has expeditiously and efficiently worked to complete its judicial mandate. Partly as a consequence of its unique situation, but also through the dogged efforts of its staff, the Court has developed numerous ground-breaking approaches to operating a international justice institution. It is one of the only courts to adjudicate cases against the leadership of all of the warring factions. Moreover, since its creation the Court has prioritized efforts to leave a lasting legacy within the justice sector in Sierra Leone. The Court has also elaborated the law with regard to many previously untested questions which will be relevant to all courts of international criminal law. As the Court nears the completion of its cases, it will again break ground as it grapples with the legal and practical questions as the first court to transition to a residual mechanism.

83 *Report of the Secretary General on the Establishment of a Special Court for Sierra Leone*, UN doc. S/2000/915, para. 28.

PART II
Investigation and Prosecution

The first testing field for any authority internationally established to bring justice for crimes of international concern is the ability to collect sufficient and reliable evidence to successfully prosecute. On the one hand, this requires organization of investigating and prosecutorial capacity in an international setting, with dramatic structural and functional differences vis-à-vis national experiences. On the other hand, the distinctive operational feature of all forms of international criminal justice is that they have no inherent sovereign authority and, thus, cannot directly enforce their decisions and orders. This lack of self-executing authority is an inherent limit on any international jurisdiction and leads to what has emerged as the major challenge for their operations, that is the degree of cooperation available from other competent international organizations, but, primarily, from a number of relevant states: where the crimes are committed; of nationality of the suspect/accused; where the suspect/accused is located; where the evidence is available; and where assets may be recovered.

Lessons learned in the distant and profoundly different situations of the Balkans, Africa and Cambodia unequivocally show that it is only by means of appropriate and strong pressure exerted by major players – be they states or universal or regional organizations – that in the most challenging circumstances reluctant states may be persuaded to arrest and surrender suspects or to create the conditions for their voluntary appearance in court, to provide evidence and contribute to its preservation.

In this process, investigators and prosecutors cannot loose sight of the impact that judicial proceedings have on the lives of those involved and, above all, on victims and witnesses. Practices in investigation and prosecution have, thus, continuously evolved in order to provide a caring environment for the concurring needs of individuals and communities – to have their rights and interests safeguarded – and of justice – to have facts adjudicated on the basis of reliable sources of evidence.

The selected experiences in investigation and prosecution of an international tribunal (ICTY), a hybrid Court (ECCC) and the permanent court (ICC) show that, although the different legal frameworks allow for different degrees of participation by victims in proceedings, investigators and prosecutors always have to take into account the impact of their operations on victims, in the perspective of achieving the overarching goal of serving the interests of justice.

Chapter 5
Reflections Based on the ICTY's Experience

Carla Del Ponte

1. Introduction[1]

Prosecutions in international and internationalized Tribunals face similar difficult challenges; and although there may be differences in structures and mandates, they share a lot in common. Thus, regular meetings between prosecutors of international criminal Tribunals – and discussion with the public on various important topics related to the development of international criminal law and the work of such Tribunals – are particularly fruitful for addressing challenges, by looking back at their respective experiences, and working out strategies for the future.

The *ad hoc* International Criminal Tribunal for the Former Yugoslavia (ICTY) and the International Criminal Tribunal for Rwanda (ICTR) were the precursors of a new generation of international prosecutors and courts. Today, we can no longer say that high-level criminals, responsible for the most atrocious crimes, can eternally hide from international justice. It is a fact: international criminal justice is now on the agenda of world leaders and brokers of peace deals.

The ICTY and ICTR are currently involved in a completion strategy which will lead to a gradual phasing down of their activities in the next few years. The Special Court for Sierra Leone will also complete its work soon, perhaps even sooner than that. Other Tribunals, such as the Extraordinary Chambers in the Courts of Cambodia, have become fully operational. A Special Tribunal for Lebanon is in the making. The ICC has been active for a few years and will need the full support of the international community. The more recently established courts and tribunals will certainly learn from the experiences of the *ad hoc* Tribunals.

The ICTY and ICTR are still very active and working at full speed to complete their work – trials and appeals – in time. A number of accused, including the most important and notorious Mladic and Kabuga, have not been brought to justice yet. Our message is clear: it is vital that they be brought to The Hague and Arusha now. But, even if they are still at large after 2010, when the ICTY and ICTR should have completed their trials and appeals, they must not escape international justice and must be tried by the ICTY and ICTR.

The following is an overview on the ICTY's experience in conducting international investigations, focusing on a number of issues related to the international investigations of very serious crimes committed on a massive scale.

1 The author, whose contribution reflects her presentation at the 2007 Turin *Conference on International Criminal Justice*, wishes to warmly thank the organizer thereof, Judge Roberto Bellelli, for his relentless efforts in bringing together in an unique opportunity all the international criminal Tribunals on that occasion, together with the other actors and observers in the field.

2. The Complexity of International Investigations

It is important to underline that the complex context wherein the international Tribunals operate appears to be very different from investigating and prosecuting organized or large-scale crimes at the national level. Though similar investigative tools may be used or similar legal concepts applied, unique challenges arise when investigating and prosecuting at the international level, such as the lack of a police force or enforcement agents, and the impact of combined common law/civil law procedures. These challenges greatly impact on the type of investigative methods, staffing and legal tools that are used and on their effectiveness.

The ICTY and ICTR were new concepts when they were established and, at that time, very few tools were available. When the ICTY began its groundbreaking work of investigating and prosecuting those accused of serious violations of international humanitarian law, the Statute simply gave the Prosecutor the authority to 'initiate investigations' and to 'question suspects, victims and witnesses, to collect evidence and conduct on-site investigations'. The Statute was silent about how these tasks were to be carried out. Adding to that challenge was the fact that procedures would require the cooperation of states often hostile to the mandates of these Tribunals.

The ICTY was established when the war was still raging in the former Yugoslavia. There were practical and operational difficulties in conducting on-site investigations as we had very difficult access to crime scenes and evidence and had to rely on the assistance of multinational forces. The political, factual and legal situation was also complex with different states opposing each other and different entities and militias also involved and sometimes changing alliances and sides. The crimes that the Office of the Prosecutor had to deal with were often massive events covering wide areas. Some lasted for many months and were highly organized. They involved regular soldiers, armed police, paramilitaries, politicians and ordinary civilians.

To understand the conflict and the political situation wherein crimes were committed and which needed to be investigated, the Tribunal had to engage experts with political, military and criminal backgrounds to study these aspects. That is why at the ICTY a Military Analyst Team and a Leadership and Research Team were established. Their functions have proven essential to our work as they provide in-house expert analysis to our teams of lawyers.

3. Engaging Experienced and Qualified Personnel

The lessons learned on the advantages of having in-house, trained human resources stresses the crucial need to hire experienced and qualified personnel; international criminal Tribunals need to attract highly skilled and experienced lawyers and investigators who can work in an international environment and adapt quickly. It is crucial that international investigations respect local customs and traditions when operating in the field. The quality of staff will impact generally on the ability of a Prosecutor's office to effectively carry out its mandate.

Engaging competent and qualified personnel, especially in the early days of the Tribunal's existence, has not been easy. As there was no pool or roster with readily available qualified staff, and due to financial restrictions, the ICTY has had to rely on *gratis* personnel seconded by governments. This was essential when investigators and lawyers had to be operational swiftly as the evidence of crimes committed on a large scale became apparent. Due to administrative and legal difficulties, the practice of engaging *gratis* personnel was stopped, but the ICTY has been in a position to attract competent staff and provide appropriate training. Today there is a substantial body of staff members and former staff members available with experience and know-how and who have worked for the different international Tribunals. As the ICTY heads towards ending its operations, and financial resources will be reduced, it is likely that the Tribunal revert to the point where it may once more need the assistance from governments to provide experienced seconded personnel.

In this regard, a roster should be created which could be kept at the UN Secretariat and which would include experienced lawyers, investigators and analysts who are ready to join these Tribunals – as well as any appropriate international investigation commissions – when called upon by them.

4. Collecting Evidence

Investigating and gathering evidence of war crimes, crimes against humanity or genocide for the purpose of international prosecutions inevitably means constructing a case after the fact. As the ICTY was established prior to the end of the conflicts in the former Yugoslavia, the ongoing nature of the conflict and the fact that the investigators of the OTP were not welcome in many areas necessarily implied that much of the gathering of evidence took place some time after the crimes were committed.

Thus, many of the ICTY's investigations began far from the crime scenes and were carried out among the thousands of refugees who had fled the conflicts to other parts of the world, even as far as New Zealand. Information was also available from states and from a number of non-governmental organizations and humanitarian agencies who were operating during the conflict. National and international media were another source of information. Nevertheless, it was vital for investigators to go directly to the victims and survivors to record their first-hand accounts.

In collecting the evidence, the ICTY had to rely on assistance provided by international armed forces, specifically in Bosnia and Herzegovina as a result of their mandate under the Dayton Peace Accord. Similarly, during the conflict in Kosovo we had to move quickly, request the assistance of states, and conduct on-site exhumations.

Along the years, we have been able to collect a massive amount of documents which are now part of our evidence collection. In total, this collection represents some 7 million documents. To organize this evidence, it was crucial to have in place the necessary modern (and sometimes expensive) electronic management tools. Given the importance of the evidence collections, for the purpose of carrying out trials, as well as for their legacy, international tribunals should invest, from their inception, in intelligent and effective evidence management systems.

5. The Protection of Threatened Witnesses

Let me now turn to another important aspect of our work, which is the question of the adequate protection of witnesses. Due to the nature of trials and the types of crimes being prosecuted, witnesses may be facing serious threats if they come to the Tribunal and testify. This is also the case for insider witnesses, who are crucial when building a case against very senior political or military officials. Proof of a complex criminal enterprise and its leadership can otherwise be extremely difficult to find and time and resource consuming. Protective measures in court proceedings – such as closed-session testimony, use of pseudonyms, facial distortion or voice distortion – assist in securing the testimony of important witnesses. For more important and at-risk witnesses, enhanced protective measures – such as relocation or insertion into a domestic witness protection programme

– may be necessary. The lack of enforcement agents, the lack of intelligence and the lack of an in-house professional witness protection programme constitute a serious challenge.

International Tribunals have had to depend on states to assist in providing the necessary protection to these vulnerable witnesses. Each Tribunal has had to make arrangements with states for the protection of witnesses. States have been particularly wary of protecting witnesses who may have a criminal background. However, it is often the case that insider witnesses do not have 'clean hands' and, therefore, they may not be accepted by other states. In this regard, the proposal to create a centralized international witness protection program, administered by an independent international organ which would negotiate such agreements should be implemented. This body would assist international criminal tribunals or international commissions seeking the assistance of states. That is a possible way, for the future, to globally and more effectively address this important issue.

6. The Selection of Suspects

The ICTY was not established to prosecute all the crimes which fall within its jurisdiction, thus the question of the selection of suspects, that is of the targets of its mandate, has been given careful consideration from the outset of the ICTY's activity. It was clear from the beginning at the ICTY that it would have not been possible to prosecute all persons responsible for international humanitarian law violations committed in the former Yugoslavia since 1991. The scale, scope and number of crimes which occurred in that period made it impractical for any judicial institution to prosecute all criminal conduct. Other international tribunals have also been confronted with the dilemma: which crimes and which offenders should be prosecuted?

The ICTY Statute limits prosecutions to serious violations of international humanitarian law. This led the OTP to focus on persons holding higher levels of responsibility. However, the number of indictments and accused tried has been influenced by a number of factors including the limited capacity to process large numbers of cases.

The need to concentrate on those with highest levels of responsibility and who are most responsible for serious violations of international humanitarian law was subsequently formalized in Security Council Resolution 1503 of 28 August 2003, whereby the ICTY was urged by the Council to 'concentrat[e] on the prosecution and trial of the most senior leaders suspected of being most responsible for crimes within the ICTY's jurisdiction and transferring cases involving those who may not bear this level of responsibility to competent national jurisdictions' (PP7, also 'recalling and reaffirming in the strongest terms' the Presidential statement of 23 July 2002 endorsing the ICTY's completion strategy – S/PRST/2002/21).

7. Cooperation with the ICTY

The importance of state cooperation and the ICTY's OTP experience in this area also deserves attention. The ICTY has had to rely heavily on the cooperation of states in the former Yugoslavia to obtain documents and the custody of suspects and accused. Despite the Tribunal's Chapter VII powers, and the deriving international legal obligation of all states to cooperate with the Tribunal, state cooperation with the ICTY has not been adequate.

Rule 7*bis* of the ICTY Rules of Procedure and Evidence offers a legal remedy in cases of non-compliance. A Chamber, Judge or the Prosecutor can raise the matter with the President who shall report to or notify the Security Council. The Rule has not always been effective. Rule 7*bis* was last used in 2004 when the President of the Tribunal brought to the attention of the Security Council a report from the OTP regarding Serbia and Montenegro's consistent failure to comply with its obligations. Though the prospect of a report to the Council may have the effect of encouraging cooperation, disappointingly, no measures were taken by the Council in reaction to this report.

The ICTY OTPs experience is that it is more successful in securing the arrest and transfer of fugitives and the provision of documents when using non-judicial measures. Our strategy has been twofold: first is to avail of incentives for the state in question to cooperate with the Tribunal, by relying on policies of conditionality imposed by the international community; second, is to work on the operational level through a tracking team and our Field Offices to engage states to do everything they can to locate and arrest fugitives.

Successes have been achieved when the US and the EU have adopted strategies requiring states in the former Yugoslavia to cooperate with the Tribunal. Milosevic was transferred to The Hague on 28 June 2001 after the US threatened to boycott a key donor's conference. The progress in the cooperation of Croatia, Serbia (to some extent), Bosnia and Herzegovina, Montenegro and the former Yugoslav Republic of Macedonia has been the result of a consistent and principled approach of the EU vis-à-vis these states. The EU decided that all Western Balkan states could join the EU provided they fulfilled a number of conditions, one of them being full cooperation with the ICTY. Most often, the level of cooperation of the concerned state was evaluated on the basis of the OTP's assessments, provided either to the EU or the Security Council.

The conditionality to start negotiations on EU membership has been the most effective tool recently vis-à-vis states failing to cooperate: 90 per cent of all accused currently on trial or awaiting their trial are in The Hague as a direct result of EU conditionality. However, this policy has been questioned in relation to Serbia. I can only call upon the EU and its Member States to firmly stick to its principled conditionality position. Without this policy, we may have never seen Karadzic and will not see Mladic being brought to justice.

8. Conclusion

Given the limited resources and rudimentary legal tools available at the start of its activities, much has been achieved by the ICTY in bringing those responsible for the most serious crimes to justice. We have developed and improved the tools that were put at our disposal and have made important achievements. But there are still important challenges ahead of us.

The ICTY and ICTR have laid down the stepping stones of the international criminal justice system. Our experience and knowledge will undoubtedly benefit the following generations of international tribunals and courts, including the International Criminal Court, the SCSL and the Extraordinary Chambers in the Courts of Cambodia.

The common goal of the various international criminal tribunals and of the other important actors and observers in the international justice system is to further strengthen this system with the aim of attempting to end impunity throughout the world.

Chapter 6
Challenges Related to Investigation and Prosecution at the International Criminal Court

Fatou Bensouda

1. Introduction

The establishment of the International Criminal Court ('the Court') represents a major triumph of concerted international efforts to combat impunity. The Court has already initiated four investigations, in the Democratic Republic of Congo, Northern Uganda, the Central African Republic, and Darfur, and is analysing several situations including Colombia, Georgia, Kenya, Côte d'Ivoire and Afghanistan. The first trial of the Court, *Prosecutor v. Thomas Lubanga Dyilo*, began on 26 January 2009. The second trial, *Prosecutor v. Germain Katanga and Mathieu Ngudjolo Chui*, is scheduled to being on the September 2009.

This chapter focuses on the principal challenges faced by the Court during the investigation and prosecution of crimes within its jurisdiction. While many of the challenges confronting the Court are common to all international courts and tribunals, unique complications have arisen in the context of, *inter alia*: (a) investigating situations of ongoing conflict; (b) the distance between the court and the situations under investigation; (c) operating in diverse cultural contexts; (d) unprecedented legal challenges; (e) cooperation; and (f) the interplay between investigations/prosecutions and conflict resolution initiatives

While drawing from the experience of all organs of the Court, this chapter will focus primarily on the challenges faced by the Office of the Prosecutor. Prior to discussing the challenges faced by the Court, it is useful to establish the structure of the Court and the main principles defining the role of the Office of the Prosecutor.

2. Structure of the Court

The Court comprises four principle organs: the Presidency, the Chambers, the Registry and the Office of the Prosecutor. The Office of the Prosecutor is further divided into the Immediate Office of the Prosecutor which directly assists the Prosecutor, and three operational divisions – the Jurisdiction, Complementarity, and Cooperation division, the Investigation Division, and the Prosecution Division.

3. Principles that Guide the Work of the Office of the Prosecutor

Three main principles define the role of the Office of the Prosecutor: (1) independence; (2) objectivity; and (3) complementarity.

A. Independence

The independence of the Prosecutor flows from the independence of the Court and is one of its main features, as it establishes one basic premise to the judicial independence of the institution. In this regard, independence is understood as a safeguard ensuring the performance of the functions of the Prosecutor from both external and internal interferences.

1. External Independence

The Prosecutor is required to make decisions regarding the scope of investigation and prosecution by identifying and selecting who (suspects) and what (situations and crimes) will be investigated and prosecuted, irrespective of the particular interests of individuals, states or organizations: the Prosecutor cannot to seek or follow instructions from any external source.[1] In this regard, independence is not a privilege, but rather an obligation for the Office of the Prosecutor. Accordingly, in all situations and circumstances the Office has strictly complied with its obligation to preserve its independence.

The Application for Summonses filed by the Office of the Prosecutor in the Darfur situation[2] illustrates the nature of this independence:

> As this application makes clear, the Prosecution has benefited greatly from the information furnished by the UNCOI [the United Nations Commission of Inquiry] and the NCOI [the National Commission of Inquiry initiated by the Sudanese Government] as well as other organisations and entities with knowledge regarding potential crimes. The Prosecution nonetheless has an obligation to conduct an independent investigation which, *inter alia*, seeks and considers evidence which might either corroborate or impugn information collected by other entities.

The same approach was adopted in the situations in Uganda, the Democratic Republic of Congo and the Central African Republic. The independence of an investigation has a significant impact on the case presented, in terms of reliability and impartiality, as well as the overall credibility of the institution.

Another key aspect of the independence of the Prosecutor is the power to investigate a situation where he believes there is a reasonable basis to proceed with an investigation in the absence of a request from a State Party to the Rome Statute, or a referral from the UN Security Council. The *motu proprio* investigative power, however, is under the Rome Statute and in practice needs to be exerted when and if states and the Security Council are not themselves active – as, on the contrary, has so far been the case – in referring situations were serious crimes of international concern are being committed.

---

1 Art. 42(1) ICCSt: 'A member of the Office shall not seek or act on instructions from any external source.'

2 Prosecutor's Application under Article 58(7), Public Redacted Version, Situation in Darfur, The Sudan, ICC-02/05, 27 February 2007, para. 14, at 27. Available at http://www.icc-cpi.int/iccdocs/doc/doc259838.PDF (visited 18 May 2009).

2. *Internal Independence*

The independence from other organs of the Court[3] derives primarily from the separation of competencies between its Office – which has exclusive responsibility for detecting, analysing, investigating and prosecuting crimes[4] – and the judiciary. Further, to ensure that the Prosecutor can achieve his mandate, he also enjoys full authority over the management and administration of the Office.[5]

B. Objectivity

Objectivity is another guiding principle of the Office of the Prosecutor. The institution aims to establish the truth and ensure that justice is done. The goal of the Office of the Prosecutor is not to secure convictions at any cost. To this end, the Prosecutor is required to '... extend the investigation to cover all facts and evidence relevant to an assessment of whether there is criminal responsibility under this Statute, and, in doing so, investigate incriminating and exonerating circumstances equally'. Hence, the principle of objectivity requires that the Office of the Prosecutor gather not only evidence which proves the guilt of an accused, but also that which may suggest his or her innocence.[6] If the Office should find, during the course of investigations, evidence that suggests the innocence of the accused, there is a duty to share this information with the defence.[7]

The Office has stated that:

> The Prosecution labours under duties imposed by the Rome Statute to conduct an independent investigation, which includes an examination of incriminating and exculpatory information and which yields evidence capable of satisfying the relevant criminal burden of proof.[8]

C. Complementarity

The principle of complementarity requires that the Office of the Prosecutor only intervenes to carry out investigations and prosecutions when countries are unwilling or unable to bring perpetrators to justice.[9] The two key elements of this principle merit further explanation:

> (a) Unwillingness. This situation arises if a country lacks the political will to try its own leaders, conducts sham trials in order to let the guilty go free, allows an unjustifiable delay

3 Art. 42(1) ICCSt: 'The Office of the Prosecutor shall act independently as a separate organ of the Court.'

4 Art. 42(1) ICCSt: 'The Office of the Prosecutor ... shall be responsible for receiving referrals and any substantiated information on crimes within the jurisdiction of the Court, for examining them and for conducting investigations and prosecutions before the Court.'

5 Art. 42(2) ICCSt: 'A member of the Office shall not seek or act on instructions from any external source.'

6 Art. 54(1)(a) ICCSt: '[The Prosecutor shall] investigate incriminating and exonerating circumstances equally.'

7 Arts 61(3) and 67(2) ICCSt.

8 Prosecutor's Application under Art. 58(7), Public Redacted Version, Situation in Darfur, The Sudan, PTC-I, ICC-02/05, 27 February 2007, para. 14, at 27. Available at http://www.icc-cpi.int/iccdocs/doc/doc259838.PDF (visited 18 May 2009).

9 Arts 17–19 ICCSt.

in bringing perpetrators to justice, or does not conduct judicial proceedings independently or impartially.[10]
(b) Inability. This situation arises, for example, when the judicial system of a country has collapsed, rendering the state unable to arrest perpetrators or gather evidence.[11] In principle, it is preferable that national courts prosecute perpetrators of serious crimes. States have a duty to investigate and, if necessary, prosecute international crimes that occur within their jurisdiction. Moreover, there are also practical reasons for the Court to step in only if states fail to do so. National authorities are closer to the scene of the crime, can collect evidence and interview witnesses and victims more easily, and encounter fewer language and communication problems. Furthermore, investigations and prosecutions can take place in a fully established and familiar legal system.

4. Principal Challenges

A. Investigating Situations of Ongoing Conflict

There are numerous challenges associated with conducting investigations in conflict situations: travelling to such areas may be impossible; local institutions may have collapsed or could be ineffective. This has a bearing on, for example, the protection of victims and witnesses, and the need to address ongoing crimes.

1. Protection of Victims and Witnesses

In the insecure and highly volatile circumstances of an ongoing conflict, the Office of the Prosecutor has to learn how to: approach the possible witnesses without exposing them; identify safe sites for interviews; secure discreet transportation for investigators and witnesses; provide for the contingency of moving witnesses to safe locations without attracting attention; and even check for possible relationships between drivers and hotel owners with the suspects.[12]

On one occasion, witness protection concerns prevented the Office from conducting investigations at the scene of the alleged crimes, and the Prosecutor stated to the Council on Foreign Relations that 'since June 2005, my Office has carried out an investigation under difficult circumstances. I have a duty to protect the persons called as witnesses and I cannot protect those living in the Sudan. Thus we had to investigate Darfur without visiting Darfur.'[13] This is not to say that such investigations are impossible, but rather, that they have necessarily to follow innovative and sometimes difficult paths. Since the start of the Sudan investigation in June 2005, the Office has collected statements and evidence during more than 105 missions in 18 countries.

---

10 Art. 17(2) ICCSt.

11 Art. 17(3) ICCSt.

12 Office of the Prosecutor, Report on the activities performed during the first three years (June 2003–June 2006), The Hague, 12 September 2006, para. 3, at 7. Available at http://www.icc-cpi.int/nr/exeres/2386f5cb-b2a5-45dc-b66f-17e762f77b1f.htm (visited 18 May 2009).

13 Prosecutor's keynote address at the Council for Foreign Relations Symposium, New York, 17 October 2008, at 3. Available at http://www.icc-cpi.int/nr/exeres/2386f5cb-b2a5-45dc-b66f-17e762f77b1f.htm (visited 18 May 2009).

Witness protection challenges also arise at the trial stage. In the *Lubanga* trial, 19 prosecution witnesses were subject to procedural measures of protection and they accordingly testified with their image and voice distorted.

Cooperation of states is crucial to achieving effective witness protection; the Court has concluded witness relocation framework agreements with 10 states. More are needed in order for the Court to have the tools necessary to protect victims and witnesses effectively. The Court is also developing another innovative solution: tripartite agreements. Here, the Court would enter into an agreement with a state that wishes to pay for another state to take on the responsibility to relocate a witness. Such a mechanism would also assist that third state to develop its witness protection programme.[14] Other international tribunals and courts which have entered into their completion phase also have their own network of relocation agreements in place. It would be useful to consider how such resources could be pooled in the future.

2. Dealing with Ongoing Crimes

In many situations, while investigations are ongoing regarding past crimes, the individuals under investigation commit new crimes. It then becomes necessary to address such crimes as well.

For example, reports indicated that on 17 September 2008 the LRA attacked Congolese villages in the Haut Uelé District of the DRC (Dungu Territory). These attacks all followed a similar method with markets surrounded and looted, students abducted from schools, properties burned and dozens of civilians killed, including several local chiefs. Tens of thousands were displaced. In the light of serious and converging information on the attacks, the Prosecutor called for renewed efforts to arrest LRA leader Kony and his top commanders.

Similarly, in Kalma camp on 25 August 2008, Sudanese government forces armed with guns attacked civilians, Furs, who sought to defend themselves with sticks and spears. At least 31 were killed, more than 65 wounded including women and children. Villages are still being bombed. Examples include the air strikes on Dairi Shagi and Oum Al-Wadi in North Darfur. The Office of the Prosecutor pursued the matter further, sending a letter to the Government of Sudan, requesting information on 'national investigations or prosecutions planned or underway in relation to the events of 25 August'. There has been no response.[15]

To address the above challenges, the Office of the Prosecutor has sought to reduce the length and scope of investigations by developing the following critical measures.

(a) Focusing on those who bear the greatest responsibility

First, the Office of the Prosecutor has adopted a policy, based on the Rome Statute, of focusing its efforts on the most serious crimes and those who bear the greatest responsibility for these crimes:

14 Statement of the Deputy Prosecutor, Fifteenth Diplomatic Briefing of the International Criminal Court, 7 April 2009. Available at http://www.icc-cpi.int/Menus/ICC/Reports+on+activities/Court+Reports+and+Statements/ at 12 (visited 18 May 2009).

15 Eighth Report of the Prosecutor of the International Criminal Court to United Nations Security Council pursuant to UNASCR 1593 (2005), 3 December 2008, para. 59. Available at http://www.icc-cpi.int/nr/exeres/2386f5cb-b2a5-45dc-b66f-17e762f77b1f.htm (visited 19 May 2009).

> ... as a general rule, the Office of the Prosecutor should focus its investigative and prosecutorial efforts and resources on those who bear the greatest responsibility, such as the leaders of the State or organisation allegedly responsible for those crimes.[16]

This approach also enables the Office of the Prosecutor to have the maximum impact with the limited resources available. It is not practical to prosecute at the international level each and every individual who has committed an offence under the Statute. The Office of the Prosecutor will prosecute only those individuals bearing the greatest responsibility, while the rest will be dealt with by domestic courts. A similar regime applies under Rule 28 of the Rules of Procedure and Evidence of the Tribunal for the Former Yugoslavia, added as part of the completion strategy relating to the *ad hoc* Tribunals.[17]

The identification of individuals who bear the greatest responsibility is based on evidence that emerges during the course of an investigation. The backgrounds of persons for whom warrants of arrest have been issued reflect this approach to case selection. These persons bear the significant responsibility for the crimes charged and held leadership positions within the state or organization involved in the crimes:

Northern Uganda
Warrants were issued for: Joseph Kony, Commander-in-Chief of the Lord's Resistance Army (LRA); Vincent Otti (then) Vice-Chairman and Second-in-Command of the LRA; Okot Odhiambo, Deputy Army Commander of the LRA; Dominic Ongwen, Brigade Commander of the Sinia Brigade of the Lord's Resistance Army; Raska Lukwiya, Deputy Army Commander of the LRA.

Darfur/the Sudan
Warrants were issued for: Ahmad Muhammad Harun, Former Minister of State for the Interior of the Government of Sudan; Ali Muhammad Ali Abd-Al-Rahman, a militia/Janjaweed leader; Omar Hassan Ahmad Al Bashir, President of the Republic of Sudan; and Bahr Idriss Abu Garda, Chairman and General Coordinator of Military Operations of the United Resistance Front.

The Democratic Republic of the Congo
Warrants were requested and obtained for: Thomas Lubanga Dyilo, Commander-in-Chief of the *Forces Patriotiques pour la Libération du Congo* (FPLC), President of the *Union des Patriotes Congolais* (UPC); Bosco Ntaganda, Deputy Chief of the General Staff of the FPLC; Germain Katanga, Commander of the *Force de résistance patriotique en Ituri* (FRPI); and Mathieu Ngudjolo Chui, former leader of the *Front des Nationalistes et Intégrationnistes*.

The Central African Republic
A warrant was issued for Jean-Pierre Bemba Gombo, President and Commander-in-chief of the *Mouvement de libération du Congo*.

Where the Office of the Prosecutor chooses not to address a particular person's conduct, it does not mean that impunity is thereby granted: the efforts of the Court are complementary to national ones, and domestic measures aimed at securing justice are strongly encouraged.

---

16 Paper on some policy issues before the Office of the Prosecutor, September 2003, para. 2.1, at 7. Available at http://www.icc-cpi.int/NR/rdonlyres/1FA7C4C6-DE5F-42B7-8B25-60AA962ED8B6/143594/030905_Policy_Paper.pdf (visited 19 May 2009).

17 Rule 28 ICTY RPE, as amended on 6 April 2004.

(b) Expeditious, focused cases representative of the range of criminality

Second, the Office of the Prosecutor strives to present expeditious and focused cases while representing the entire range of criminality. This is a difficult balancing exercise. Incidents are selected to provide a sample that reflects the gravest instances and modes of victimization. By way of example:

Northern Uganda
In *Prosecutor v. Joseph Kony et al.* the Office of the Prosecutor selected six incidents out of hundreds that occurred and charged the five top leaders of the Lord's Resistance Army with crimes against humanity (including enslavement, sexual slavery, rape and murder), and war crimes (including intentionally directing an attack against the civilian population, enlisting children and inducing rape and pillaging).

Darfur/Sudan
In *Prosecutor v. Ahmad Muhammad Harun ('Ahmad Harun') and Ali Muhammad Ali Abd-Al-Rahman ('Ali Kushayb')*, the Office focused on a limited number of attacks, on the villages and towns of Kodoom, Bindisi, Mukjar and Arawala in West Darfur between August 2003 and March 2004. In *Prosecutor v. Bahr Idriss Abu Garda*, the Office focused on one attack conducted by rebel groups against peacekeeping forces at the base of the African Union Mission in Sudan (AMIS) in Haskanita, on 29 and 30 September 2007

Democratic Republic of the Congo ('DRC')
In *Prosecutor v. Thomas Lubanga Dyilo*, initially the Office of the Prosecutor investigated a wide range of crimes allegedly committed, seeking to represent the broad range of criminality. However, the Office subsequently decided to focus its first case on the crime of enlisting and conscripting children under the age of 15 and using them to participate actively in hostilities. The decision to focus on this crime was triggered by the possible imminent release of Thomas Lubanga Dyilo, who had been under arrest in the DRC for approximately one year before he was transferred to the Court. Therefore, after careful consideration of the evidence gathered, including linkage of the accused to the crime and in accordance with the requirement to prove charges beyond a reasonable doubt, the Office decided to make a selection of charges as mentioned above.[18] In the second DRC case, the *Prosecutor v. Germain Katanga and Mathieu Ngudjolo Chui*, the Office focused on an attack on one village, and brought charges that were representative of the atrocities that took place during the attack, including the use of children under the age of 15 to take active part in the hostilities, directing an attack against a civilian population, wilful killings, murder destruction of property, pillaging, sexual slavery and rape.

Cognizant of the notoriety of international trials for being lengthy and slow, the Office of the Prosecutor is seeking to present each prosecution case in less than six months.[19] To this end, the Office plans to rely on the minimum necessary number of witnesses. In the *Lubanga* trial, this amounts to only 34 witnesses. The *Katanga and Ngudjolo* trial will feature a similar number.

---

18 Office of the Prosecutor, Report on the activities performed during the first three years (June 2003–June 2006), The Hague, 12 September 2006, para. 3, at 8.

19 Statement of the Deputy Prosecutor, Fifteenth Diplomatic Briefing of the International Criminal Court, 7 April 2009, at 5.

(c) Positive complementarity

Third, the Office takes a positive approach to cooperation and complementarity. The Office stated very early on that:

> A major part of the external relations and outreach strategy of the Office of the Prosecutor will be to encourage and facilitate States to carry out their primary responsibility of investigating and prosecuting crimes. In any assessment of these efforts, the Office will take into consideration the need to respect the diversity of legal systems, traditions and cultures. The Office will develop formal and informal networks of contacts to encourage States to undertake State action, using means appropriate in the particular circumstances of a given case.[20]

The implementation of this policy can be seen in the third investigation into crimes in the DRC. Here, we are aiming at a coordinated approach whereby national judicial authorities in the region and beyond, as appropriate, will take over cases in order to ensure that all perpetrators are prosecuted. The possibility for us to transfer information collected in the course of our investigations will depend on the development of local protection for witnesses and judges.[21] The Office is also actively working to assist in building capacities among certain cooperating states.

(d) The regulatory framework of the Office of the Prosecutor

Fourth, to ensure standardized, expeditious functioning, the Office of the Prosecutor is in the process of adopting its Regulations. More detailed forms of standardization, such as the Operations Manual, and standard operating procedures are also being finalized.

B. Distance between the Court and the Situations Under Investigation

The seat of the Court in The Hague, the Netherlands, poses significant challenges in terms of its geographical distance from the situations with which the Court is concerned. In order for successful investigations and prosecutions to take place, the Court must make careful attempts to bridge these gaps.

The geographical isolation of the court from the relevant crime scenes and witnesses creates difficulties at the investigation stage. Logistical and financial challenges arise with regard to the effective conduct of investigative activities such as inspecting crime scenes, interviewing witnesses and gathering evidence. Further challenges arise during the prosecution phase when attempting to transfer evidence to the court and bring forward witnesses to provide testimony.

An additional problem associated with the distance between the seat of the Court and the field is that it contributes to the perception that the proceedings are too far removed from victims and affected communities to assuage their sense of injustice, or to significantly impact initiatives for reconciliation and peace building. The Court attempts to meet this challenge by implementing effective external communication and outreach strategies.

---

20 Paper on some policy issues before the Office of the Prosecutor, September 2003, para. 1.2, at 5. Available at http://www.icc-cpi.int/NR/rdonlyres/1FA7C4C6-DE5F-42B7-8B25-60AA962ED8B6/143594/030905_Policy_Paper.pdf (visited 19 May 2009).

21 Statement of the Deputy Prosecutor, Fifteenth Diplomatic Briefing of the International Criminal Court, 7 April 2009, at 6.

In the context of outreach, we have a dual challenge. We have to ensure that the communities concerned are involved in and informed of the work of the Court. However, the Office must also ensure that its outreach activities do not endanger ongoing investigations, or the security of victims and witnesses.

In addition to implementing outreach strategies in situations under investigation, differently from several other tribunals, the Rome Statute provides an innovative procedure to ensure the representation of victims' interests: victims can participate in the proceedings through legal representatives. This approach is an important acknowledgement of the fact that it is principally on behalf of the victims that the Court acts. The Court must ensure that its work and methodologies remain relevant and meaningful to the victims, and strive to address their legitimate concerns.

C. Operating in Diverse Cultural Contexts

The Office of the Prosecutor is confronted with a duty to investigate and prosecute crimes which have taken place in varying cultural contexts. This poses challenges for effective communication with witnesses and victims and requires a full appreciation of the cultural context in which crimes were committed. This is especially important with regard to sexual crimes and crimes involving children, which must be investigated in a context-sensitive manner. A well-considered outreach strategy must be implemented in order to gain the trust and support of affected individuals and communities.

A particular difficulty for the Court is ensuring accurate translation and interpretation. In the three situations currently under investigation, the Office of the Prosecutor has had to effectively communicate with witnesses in different languages, some of which have no corresponding words for the legal terminology required for the interview. In Northern Uganda there are four local languages: Acholi, Lango, Ateso and Kuman. In Ituri district of the DRC there are three local languages: Lendu, Linghala and local Swahili. In Darfur, there are four languages: Fur, Zaghawa, Massalit and local Arabic. Because there are few qualified professional translators, finding persons with the appropriate skills and background required exceptional efforts.[22]

Such issues also arise in court. For example, the *Lubanga* trial which is currently underway features Swahili, French and English interpretation. The pre-trial proceedings in *Katanga and Ngudjolo* features Linghala, French and English interpretation.

D. Unprecedented Legal Challenges

In light of its unique nature and function, the Office, and the Court as a whole, face complex legal issues on a regular basis. For example, on 22 January 2009, the Palestinian National Authority lodged a declaration accepting jurisdiction of the Court in accordance with Article 12(3) ICCSt. The Office of the Prosecutor has also received 326 communications related to the situation of Israel and the Palestinian Territory. The Office of the Prosecutor stated in this context that it will examine all issues related to its jurisdiction, including whether the declaration by the Palestinian Authority accepting the exercise of jurisdiction by the Court meets statutory requirements, whether crimes

22 Office of the Prosecutor, Report on the activities performed during the first three years (June 2003–June 2006), The Hague, 12 September 2006, para. 3, at 7.

within the Court's jurisdiction have been committed and whether there are national proceedings in relation to alleged crimes.[23]

E. Cooperation

International cooperation is fundamental for the success of international courts and tribunals. Cooperation is necessary for the service and execution of arrest warrants, as it is impossible to secure the presence of an accused without the cooperation of relevant states. Cooperation is also needed for numerous measures which are the prerogative of the national authorities of a country where accused persons are present. Negotiating for cooperation is especially complex in highly charged political situations where political will is lacking.

The Rome Statute establishes a comprehensive regime for the investigation and prosecution of international crimes. However, the Court does not have an independent mechanism to enforce its decisions. Accordingly, the Court relies upon the cooperation of State parties, non-States parties, international organizations and NGOs to implement many of its decisions. The Rome Statute sets out the legal framework for the provision of assistance by States Parties and other entities, including the arrest and surrender of individuals and other forms of cooperation.

Apart from securing the presence of the accused at the seat of the Court, cooperation also includes various forms of practical and logistical support that are indispensable when conducting investigations, such as transportation, security and accommodation, as well as the performance of specific evidence-gathering measures. In order to enhance such cooperation, the Court has entered into a limited number of state-specific agreements, such as those allowing for the conduct of operations in states where the Office of the Prosecutor is carrying out investigations, such as Uganda and the Democratic Republic of the Congo. For example, a Judicial Cooperation Agreement between the Court and the DRC was signed on 6 October 2004 and cooperation mechanisms were established on the territory of the Democratic Republic of the Congo with the United Nations Organization Mission in the Democratic Republic of the Congo (MONUC) and other relevant organizations. In addition, joint field offices were established with the Registry in Kinshasa and Bunia.

Achieving the arrest and surrender of individuals remains a critical challenge for the Court. While the Court assumes responsibility for the legal aspects of arrest and surrender, it does not have a mandate to execute arrest warrants. Rather, states must ensure that suspects against whom arrest warrants are issued are subsequently arrested and surrendered to the Court. Without the assistance of states and other actors in this regard, the Court is unable to fulfil its mandate.

The surrender of Thomas Lubanga Dyilo is an example of successful and effective cooperation between the Court and a state. Although Thomas Lubanga Dyilo was detained within the DRC under national proceedings, his arrest and surrender necessitated a complex process of cooperation with the territorial state, several State Parties, and international organizations. The UN Security Council cooperated by quickly lifting the travel ban imposed on Dyilo, while the French authorities provided the aeroplane used for transporting the accused to The Hague.

The arrest and surrender of Jean-Pierre Bemba also involved complex cooperation issues. On 23 May 2008, Pre-Trial Chamber III of the Court issued a sealed warrant of arrest for Jean-Pierre Bemba, along with a request for provisional arrest to the Kingdom of Belgium. The next day,

23 See Press Release of the OTP, 13 February 2009. Available at http://www.icc-cpi.int/NR/rdonlyres/A3B77241-DEC1-4E14-9EE5-A850086A7F70/280140/ICCOTP20090213Palestinerev.pdf (visited 19 May 2009).

Bemba was arrested by the Belgian authorities. On 27 May 2008, Pre-Trial Chamber III addressed to the Portuguese Republic a decision and request to obtain the identification, localization, freezing and seizure of assets belonging to Mr Bemba. On 10 June 2008, Pre-Trial Chamber III sent a request for arrest and surrender to the Kingdom of Belgium. On 3 July 2008, Jean-Pierre Bemba was surrendered and transferred to the Court.

Cooperation may be especially difficult to obtain when an investigation is initiated following a referral from the UN Security Council, as the country whose situation has been referred might object to the referral and to the jurisdiction of the Court. The case of Sudan is a good example of a situation in which a state refuses to accept responsibility for its actions, much less cooperate with the Court. The Prosecutor[24] summarized the response of the Sudanese state to allegations of atrocities committed against civilians as follows

> Sudan, a United Nations member, has the legal obligation and the ability to arrest and surrender Ahmad Harun and Ali Kushayb. I report today that the Government of Sudan is not cooperating with the Court … the Government of Sudan is not complying with Resolution 1593. The Government of Sudan does not recognize the jurisdiction of the Court, a jurisdiction that this Council granted. As of today, and even to Security Council members in Khartoum, Sudanese officials insist that "the ICC has no jurisdiction over Sudan" … Sudanese officials protect the criminals and not the victims.

F. The Interplay between Investigations/Prosecutions and Conflict Resolution Initiatives

Apart from the lack of cooperation from states, the Court has to contend with the fact that the relationship between peace and justice is often an uneasy one. The mandate of the Court requires it to dispense justice for the victims of crimes which fall within its jurisdiction. Since many of these crimes occur in the context of an armed conflict, it is often necessary to reconcile the delivery of justice with efforts to secure peace. Victims are entitled to both justice and peace. While these are not mutually exclusive goals, each must be secured without undermining the other.

The Office policy is to maintain its own independence and pursue its mandate to investigate and prosecute, and do so in a manner that respects the mandates of other actors. In an effort to address concerns expressed by local leaders and demonstrate respect for ongoing peace talks, the Office maintained a low public profile during the investigation in Northern Uganda. At no time however, did the Office cease its investigation.[25]

The issuing of an arrest warrant against Sudan's President, Omar Al-Bashir, also highlighted the complexity of facilitating both peace and justice: after the Court's decision, Omar Al-Bashir expelled humanitarian organizations. The Office observed, in response,[26] that this is not just an aggravation of the humanitarian crisis: the expulsion of aid workers is another step in the commission

---

24 Statement by Mr Luis Moreno Ocampo, Prosecutor of the International Criminal Court, Statement to the U.N. Security Council pursuant to UNSCR 1593 (2005), 5 June 2008, at 2 and 4. Available at http://www.icc-cpi.int/nr/exeres/2386f5cb-b2a5-45dc-b66f-17e762f77b1f.htm (visited 19 May 2009).

25 Office of the Prosecutor, Report on the activities performed during the first three years (June 2003–June 2006), The Hague, 12 September 2006, at 16, para. 33.

26 Statement of the Deputy Prosecutor, Fifteenth Diplomatic Briefing of the International Criminal Court, 7 April 2009, at 7. Available at http://www.icc-cpi.int/Menus/ICC/Reports+on+activities/Court+Reports+and+Statements/ (visited 18 May 2009).

of the crime of extermination.[27] The Office pointed out that in order to prevent future crimes in Darfur, to avoid thousands of new deaths, it is necessary to act immediately. It recommended that states should implement a consistent diplomatic campaign to support the Court's decision and to deny Omar Al-Bashir any form of support. Non-essential contacts with Omar Al-Bashir should be severed. When contacts are necessary, attempts should be made first to interact with non-indicted individuals.

The Office expects similar issues to arise in most of the situations under investigation and thus to present a continuous challenge. As investigations will often take place within an ongoing conflict, the Office will be investigating and prosecuting at the same time that other actors are working to address the conflict and restore civilian livelihoods. Broadly, these conflict resolution initiatives might include efforts to provide security, humanitarian relief and peace-building, as well as justice. The mandate of the Office of the Prosecutor is to ensure accountability for those who bear the greatest responsibility, alongside national proceedings and other community initiatives. The Office recognizes that, while each actor needs to pursue its respective initiative, efforts to build long-standing stability require harmonization of these efforts. However, in order to preserve its impartiality, the Office cannot be a component of these initiatives. Accordingly, the policy of the Office is to maintain its own independence and pursue its mandate to investigate and prosecute, and do so in a manner that respects the mandates of others and attempts to maximize the positive impact of the joint efforts of all actors.[28]

5. Conclusion

As the early investigations are completed and the first trials commence, the challenges faced by the Court evolve and grow in complexity. As the Court matures, additional challenges will doubtless arise in the future. In order for the Court to succeed in its mandate, it is vital that such challenges are addressed effectively, by the Court, as well as its partners and stakeholders within the Rome Statute regime.

27 Art. 7(2)(b) ICCSt: '"Extermination" includes the intentional infliction of conditions of life, *inter alia* the deprivation of access to food and medicine, calculated to bring about the destruction of part of a population.'

28 Office of the Prosecutor, Report on the activities performed during the first three years (June 2003–June 2006), The Hague, 12 September 2006, at 16, para. 32.

Chapter 7

The Early Experience of the Extraordinary Chambers in the Courts of Cambodia

Chea Leang and William Smith

1. Introduction

Considering that the crimes being investigated at the Extraordinary Chambers in the Courts of Cambodia (ECCC) occurred at least 10 years before those currently being prosecuted in other international and hybrid criminal courts, it seems illogical that the ECCC is the newest. However, taking into account the almost-20 years of conflict in Cambodia after the Khmer Rouge was removed from power in 1979, combined with the effect that global and regional cold war politics had on Cambodia's ability to undertake this process, the long delay in the ECCC's establishment is understandable.

The purpose of this chapter is to discuss some legal and practical aspects of investigating and prosecuting international crimes in a hybrid court, as the ECCC is, from the Office of the Co-Prosecutors' (OCP) perspective. As the Court only became operational in 2006, the chapter will identify issues that present challenges to the court and some best practices that are being implemented and adapted from other international criminal courts or tribunals to deal with these issues.

2. Overview of the ECCC Goals

Article 1 of the ECCC Statute clearly states that the purpose of this court is 'to bring to trial senior leaders of Democratic Kampuchea and those who were most responsible for the crimes and serious violations of Cambodian penal law, International humanitarian law and custom, and international conventions recognized by Cambodia, that were committed during the period from 17 April 1975 to 6 January 1979'. The agreement of June 2003 between the United Nations (UN) and the Royal Government of Cambodia (RGC) leading to the establishment of the court (UN-RGC Agreement), as adopted by the UN General Assembly, recognized the legitimate concerns of the Cambodian people that the establishment of the ECCC would assist in the pursuit of justice and national reconciliation, stability, peace and security in Cambodia. The RGC and the UN also looked to the ECCC to provide a criminal justice role model for other courts in Cambodia.

It is clear from the UN-RGC Agreement that the ECCC has a number of goals. Among them, to bring justice to the victims, to punish the senior or most responsible perpetrators, to deter future offenders, and to establish the truth as to what happened during the Democratic Kampuchea (DK) period.

3. Current State of Affairs

The ECCC officially commenced its work in July 2006. From that point, key principle staff were put in place, followed over the next six months by their assisting personnel. Since then, preliminary investigations have been completed, the judicial investigations are ongoing and the first trial has begun. A major challenge of the establishing phase of the ECCC was the adoption of its Internal Rules (IR). In late 2006 a session of the plenary of ECCC judges failed to reach agreement because of dissent among national and international judges on some core principles underpinning the ECCC's Draft Internal Rules (DR). The future of the ECCC was uncertain. However, substantive agreement on the rules was later reached and an amended version of the Rules was thus adopted by the judges in 2007.[1] The adoption of the IR has provided a clear legal basis for the various organs of the ECCC to carry out their work.

Despite the initial lack of agreement on the DR, preliminary investigations were carried out by the OCP, thus enabling, shortly after the Internal Rules were passed, the OCP to forward its first investigative request (introductory submissions) to the Office of the Co-Investigative Judges (OCIJ) on 18 July 2007. The first case investigation (*Duch* case) was concluded on 15 May 2008 and the first accused was indicted,[2] following which the trial formally commenced on 17 February 2009 and is currently proceeding.

Thus, as this chapter will explain, after a difficult lead up and beginning of the establishment of the ECCC, there is a promising future and the realistic hope that justice can be delivered to the Cambodian people.

4. The Cambodian Context

To understand the challenges that the ECCC faces in Cambodia it is important to know that after the Khmer Rouge was removed from power in 1979, Cambodia found itself largely depleted of legal experience through the abolishment of the court system and the systematic killings of lawyers and other intellectuals. The Khmer Rouge regime believed in their efforts to create a classless society and saw courts and lawyers – among other intellectuals and bourgeoise – as obstacles to the implementation of their revolutionary ideals. Consequently, practically a whole generation of lawyers was eliminated.

As a result, when the then two Cambodian co-Prime Ministers sought assistance from the UN to bring to trial perpetrators of atrocities during the Khmer Rouge regime, they said 'Cambodia [did] not have the resources and the expertise to conduct this very important procedure'. Later, in its Platform for 1998–2003, the RGC emphasized the need for judicial reforms stating that 'the judicial system and the court need to be entirely overhauled. By law they ought to be independent, honest and trustworthy.' The RGC, therefore, have acknowledged that due to years of war and specific targeting of the Cambodian judiciary, like many other organs of the society, it suffered from a lack of funding, training, and resources to establish a court to deal with the Khmer Rouge crimes on an internationally acceptable standard.

---

1 Internal Rules, adopted at the Plenary Session of the ECCC on 12 June 2007, further Revisions on 1 February 2008, 5 September 2008, and 6 March 2009. Available at http://www.eccc.gov.kh/english/cabinet/fileUpload/121/IRv3-EN.pdf (visited 15 April 2009).

2 Closing Order of 8 August 2008.

5. Establishment, Structure and Process

A. Establishment

The ECCC was legally established in June 2003, by virtue of the Law on Establishment of Extraordinary Chambers in the Courts of Cambodia for the Prosecution of Crimes Committed during the Period of Democratic Kampuchea (the Statute) passed by the Cambodian parliament. This legislative act came at the end of six years of lengthy negotiations between the RGC and the UN; the two parties formally agreed to a national court with significant international involvement, from funding to staffing, as well as the application of international law and standards. These negotiations were not smooth, leading to differences of opinion as to whether the Court should be national, international, or a mixture of both with varying degrees of national or international control.

The structure of the ECCC is a negotiated compromise, with both the RGC and the UN at various times showing different amounts of satisfaction and dissatisfaction with the ever-changing proposals. There were two core issues at stake: first, that the Court should meet international fair trial standards and, second, whether the RGC or the UN should have the controlling influence over the process. At a few stages, it was likely that there would be no process at all. A solution was finally agreed which envisaged a Cambodian court with full national participation and involvement in the trials, with critical financial and other assistance in key areas from the UN Member States. This ensured that RGC had ownership of the process with guarantees of trials with internationally acceptable standards.

The complex mixed or hybrid nature of the Court can be seen in its legal establishment, financing, substantive and procedural laws and staffing. These interrelated factors directly affect the success of the Court and are all essential factors to be taken into account when adapting best practices from other courts similar to the ECCC. By law, the ECCC is a court that has been established within the existing Cambodian court structure (Article 2). However, as it is simultaneously a creature of an Act of the Cambodian parliament and an Agreement between the UN and the RGC, it can be described as a *sui generis* hybrid court, co-located in the Cambodian judiciary, with features of an international tribunal.

B. Hybrid Structure

The ECCC is primarily internationally funded. These funds are provided by UN Member States, while the RGC also makes cash and in-kind contributions. Initially, the Court had a budgeted mandate covering three years with an expectation that it would complete its work in that time frame. The budget plan as of May 2007, as endorsed by the RGC and the UN Member States under UN trust fund arrangements, was USD$56.3 million for that three-year period. The UN portion was USD$43 million and was almost fully pledged. The RGC's portion is USD$13.3 million – but as at that time pledges was short by approximately USD$4 million.

In comparison to some other international or hybrid criminal courts or tribunals, the annual budget of about USD$19 million is relatively modest; the International Criminal Tribunal for the former Yugoslavia (ICTY) and the International Criminal Tribunal for Rwanda (ICTR) each now cost over $100 million per year and the Special Court for Sierra Leone costs around USD$24 million per year. A further appeal to donors was necessary during 2008 for operations to achieve their mandated conclusion.

Substantively, the subject matter jurisdiction of the Court is predominantly international law with some core provisions of national law. The Cambodian provisions being murder, torture and religious persecution (Article 3). The international law provisions are genocide (Article 4), crimes against humanity (Article 5), grave breaches of the Geneva Conventions (Article 6), destruction of cultural property (Article 7) and crimes against internationally protected persons (Article 8). The modes of criminal liability are almost identical to those prescribed in other international criminal tribunals or courts.

Procedurally, the law to be applied at the ECCC is national law, but international law can be consulted and/or used in particular circumstances (Article 12(1) and (2) of the UN-RGC Agreement and Articles 33 and 35 ECCCSt). Guidance from international procedural rules may be sought where:

(i) Cambodian law does not deal with a particular matter;
(ii) there is uncertainty regarding the interpretation or the application of a relevant rule of Cambodian law; or
(iii) there is a question regarding consistency of such a rule with international standards.

The ECCC Statute, therefore, marries the two systems of law, giving priority to national law, but allowing for international standards in the criminal justice process to apply when necessary.

C. Civil Law Model with Alterations

As the ECCC Statute is based on national law, the ECCC has adopted the French-inspired Cambodian civil law model of criminal justice. The different roles and independence of the prosecutors and investigative judges are well defined, unlike the general international criminal law model where the prosecutor and investigator are functionally the same. However, this civil system has been altered in a way to provide dual national and international leadership in the key activities of the ECCC. In the prosecution and investigation areas, two positions of Co-Prosecutors and two positions of Co-Investigative Judges have been created (Articles 16 and 23), one national and one international in each position. Envisaging the possibility of disagreement on decisions or actions to be taken, the ECCC Statute also provides a mechanism for resolving disagreement between the two co-leaders by empowering the Pre-Trial Chamber to decide on the dispute (Articles 20 and 23).

Consequently, this system of national and international co-equal Prosecutors and Investigating Judges working together is beset with likely possibilities of situations in which the two counterparts do not agree on a possible course of action. While the ECCC Statute provides the mechanisms of dispute resolution in such cases, these processes may be time-consuming and cumbersome and may hinder the investigative and/or judicial process considerably.

Theoretically, any dispute between the Co-Prosecutors can cause them to approach the Pre-trial Chamber composed of five Judges. This may include any conceivable dispute, large or small, including the choice of suspects, decisions to prosecute, suitability of evidence, etc. This system could submit to judicial determination issues that, in normal circumstances, may lie in the exclusive domain of prosecutorial discretion. On similar lines, disagreement between the Co-Investigative Judges may also retard the judicial proceedings.

The likelihood of the disputes impeding the progress of investigation and prosecution should impel the officials of this nascent Tribunal to strive for cooperation, indeed consensus, in their decision-making. Close cooperation and solid relationships between these leaders will be the key to the success of the ECCC.

D. Chambers

The judicial component of the ECCC is divided into three chambers. The Pre-Trial Chamber, the Trial Chamber and the Appeals Chamber. In each Chamber, the national judges are in the majority. The Pre-Trial Chamber is composed of five judges (three national and two international). The Trial Chamber is composed of seven judges (four national and three international), while the Appeals Chamber is composed of nine judges (five national and four international) (Article 9 ECCCSt). The ECCC Statute encourages the Judges to arrive at unanimity in their decision-making. However, if that cannot be reached a super-majority rule applies. A super-majority requires at least one international judge within each of the three Chambers to agree with the decision. Thus, there must be at least four, five and six votes required for a decision to pass in the respective chambers. (Article 14 ECCCSt).

6. Distinctive Features

The ECCC is the newest and most nationalized of the mixed, hybrid or internationalized Courts currently investigating or prosecuting crimes under international law. In terms of best practices and learning for the future, the ECCC is likely to offer some unique and important lessons. Some lessons may have broader application; however, due to the unique nature of the ECCC, these lessons will be particularly significant for other nationalized courts that have international assistance.

There are some key differences between the ECCC and other international or hybrid courts (ICC, ICTY, ICTR, SCSL, Kosovo, East Timor and BiH War Crimes Chamber). For example, international or other hybrid courts are usually created and maintained only by international organizations, their funding comes from a more stable and predictable budget, they have combined prosecution and investigation functions, single leadership positions (for example one prosecutor), and they have a majority of international judges.

The ECCC, on the other hand, was created and is maintained by a national government and international organizations, has funding from a less stable budget which relies on voluntary contributions, has separate prosecution and investigation functions, has dual leadership positions and a minority of international judges.

These differences can be seen as strengths or weaknesses depending on what is to be achieved by the Court. Certainly, the RGC and the Cambodian peoples' ownership of the process is important in ensuring that justice is seen to be delivered for them and by them. Secondly, capacity-building that can flow from such a joint enterprise between international and national governments is extremely valuable. That said, the process that the ECCC is undertaking requires all staff, national and international, especially key leaders in the organization, to create a structure that enables consensus on issues to be achieved. In any organization characterized by stark cultural differences, such as the ECCC, creating consensus and understanding is critical for the organization's success.

7. Jurisdiction

The personal, material and temporal jurisdiction of the ECCC is limited. Its personal jurisdiction is limited to individuals who were senior leaders of DK or those who were most responsible for committing crimes under the Statute. The RGC and the UN decided that the scope of personal jurisdiction should be limited in the spirit of achieving justice, truth and national reconciliation.

Consequently, low- to middle-ranking Khmer Rouge members may not be prosecuted. In terms of numbers, this would mean that thousands of ex-Khmer Rouge soldiers would not be liable to prosecution. Individuals from foreign countries that supported or were involved with DK or individuals from countries that committed war crimes in Cambodia before 1975 are also not within the jurisdiction of the ECCC. The Court can only try individuals for crimes committed during the Khmer Rouge period.

The subject matter jurisdiction is limited to crimes under Cambodian Law such as murder, torture and religious persecution (Article 3), and international law, such as genocide (Article 4), crimes against humanity (Article 5), grave breaches of the Geneva Conventions (Article 6), destruction of cultural property (Article 7) and crimes against internationally protected persons (Article 8). Temporal jurisdiction is restricted to the reign of the Khmer Rouge from 17 April 1975 to 7 January 1979 and geographically restricted to the territory of DK.

At an international level, while customary international law recognizes the concept of universal jurisdiction in respect of serious violations of international humanitarian law, it is not anticipated that any other non-Cambodian court or international tribunal will exercise jurisdiction for the crimes within the jurisdiction of the ECCC. Regarding national crimes which are the subject of the ECCC jurisdiction under the Cambodian Penal Code of 1956, in effect, under ECCC law they have a 40-year statute of limitations. The ECCC Statute (Article 3) extended the limitation period for these crimes for an additional 30 years in addition to the 10 years that would normally apply.

Although the ECCC Statute and the UN-RGC Agreement do not grant exclusive or primary jurisdiction to the ECCC in respect of the subject matter jurisdiction, it is unlikely that other national criminal courts will assume jurisdiction over the same international crimes. There has been no express will of the RGC to do so, nor does any implementing legislation exist to try these crimes in other national courts. As the Cambodian parliament has specifically created a special court to try crimes under international law, it has been argued that it was its legislative intent that this court has the primacy, if not the exclusivity, of jurisdiction to try the crimes committed during the time of the DK.

Many issues relating to jurisdiction are expected to be raised at the ECCC. Some similar issues will have been litigated before, such as the legal establishment of the Court and the power of judges to make internal rules, as well as the legal challenges that may be made which are directly related to the specific jurisdiction of this Court. The jurisprudence relating to these and similar issues previously dealt with in the other international criminal courts will be the main primary reference source, other than any related national jurisprudence. The increased accessibility of these primary materials such as judgements, decisions, orders, motions and responses will play an extremely important role in the development of the jurisprudence at the ECCC.

8. Case Selection and Charging Policy

A. Responsibility and Challenges

Case selection at the ECCC is the responsibility of the Co-Prosecutors. After conducting preliminary investigations to determine whether there is evidence that crimes within the jurisdiction of the ECCC have been committed (IR 50), the Co-Prosecutors select a case for judicial investigation by the Co-Investigative Judges. This judicial investigation is triggered by the Co-Prosecutors sending an introductory submission to the Co-Investigative Judges where the Co-Prosecutors believe that crimes within the jurisdiction of the ECCC have been committed. The introductory submission shall contain the name of the person or persons to be charged, a summary of the facts and the types of offences charged (IR 53).

However, the filing of an indictment at the ECCC is the responsibility of the Co-Investigative Judges. Pursuant to IR 67, at the end of the judicial investigation the Co-Investigative Judges shall make a closing order, either dismissing the allegations or, alternatively, requesting that the accused be put on trial. In the latter case, the closing order becomes the indictment which, before being made by the Co-Investigative Judges, must consider a reasoned final submission from the Co-Prosecutors either to indict the charged person or to dismiss the case under IR 67. These draft rules, however, appear to be inconsistent with the ECCC Statute which states that all indictments shall be made by the two Co-Prosecutors, who shall work together to prepare indictments against suspects (Article 16 ECCCSt). It may be argued, however, that as it is the practice for the investigative judge to draft the indictment under Cambodian law, this procedural provision should apply. The Co-Prosecutors are of the view that the Statute should be followed and the Co-Prosecutors should be responsible for the drafting of the indictment in light of the size and nature of these cases.

B. Case Selection Policy

1. The Need for a Policy

Regarding case selection, the ECCC Statute limits the personal jurisdiction of the court only to senior leaders and those most responsible for crimes committed in the DK period. Even with this more restrictive group of perpetrators, due to the limited time frame in which the ECCC prosecutions are required to be carried out, it is clear that not every individual perpetrator of crimes during the DK period can be prosecuted.

For these reasons and more generally, it is viewed by the Co-Prosecutors that it is necessary to formulate a policy. In formulating its policy, the OCP recognizes that the principal objective for the establishment of the ECCC was the pursuit of justice and national reconciliation, stability, peace and security in Cambodia. The OCP also recognizes the importance of providing a true historical account of the most serious and systematic crimes committed during that period to further these objectives.

Being aware of these ECCC objectives and its limited jurisdiction, the Co-Prosecutors are continually formulating their case-selection policy, which is necessary to ensure that decisions are not made, or seen to be made, arbitrarily or under political influence, but on the basis of relevant, objective criteria, applied consistently. For the credibility of the selection process, the Co-Prosecutors are of the view that their decisions need to be independent and guided by principles of impartiality and objectivity.

2. Independence

With respect to the OCP's independence in its selection of cases, according to Article 19 ECCC, 'the Co-Prosecutors shall be independent in the performance of their functions, and shall not accept or seek instructions from any government or any other source'. This principle applies to independence not only from the RGC, but also from other states, international organizations, non-governmental organizations (NGOs) and individuals. In the Cambodian context, the long wait for the Khmer Rouge trials has created many expectations as to how the trials should be held and who should be subject to prosecution. It is, therefore, necessary that the OCP operates independently from outside influences to select cases for investigation and subsequent trial.

In its initial preliminary investigations the OCP has adopted an impartial approach in deciding which cases to select. It employed analytical and investigative methods applied equally across all individuals and groups suspected of committing crimes and applied them in a consistent manner in order to determine the reliability and probative value of the evidence. The threshold evidence level to prosecute an individual, as required under IR 53, will be the same for all cases and will not be lowered to suit any individual decision to prosecute.

3. Objectivity

In its case selection the OCP has acted, and will continue to act, in an objective manner. Where it discovers exculpatory evidence in favour of a suspect, either before or after an introductory submission is sent to the Co-Investigative Judges or at any stage of the proceedings, it shall ensure that this information is disclosed. This is required when the introductory submission is filed (IR 53). However, this responsibility is deemed to be a continuing one on the OCP throughout the whole judicial process.

4. Seniority and Leadership

In determining which specific factors should be taken into account when selecting individuals, in addition to the OCP's guiding principles, the OCP believes it is under an obligation to request for investigation and to prosecute the most responsible perpetrators, whether a senior leader or otherwise. With regards to senior leaders, the OCP is expected to only request investigation of those individuals who were in the highest political, governmental and/or military positions at the national level during the DK period and whom it believes had direct or superior responsibility for crimes committed during that time.

With regards to those most responsible, the Co-Prosecutors are likely to seek to prioritize their requests for investigation against individuals who, apart from being most responsible for chargeable crimes, participated in the crimes directly and were superiors of subordinates who committed those crimes while under their effective control. These individuals will have held positions of political, governmental, and or military leadership.

5. Gravity

In selecting the senior leaders or those most responsible, the OCP will also seek to take into account the gravity of the crimes, namely the scale of the crimes, the nature of the crimes and the manner of their commission. The case selection, hence, would take into account, among other factors, the number and vulnerability of the victims, the systematic nature of the crimes, the presence of elements of particular cruelty, as well as crimes involving discrimination.

C. Charging Policy

As stated, the responsibility for charging an accused in an indictment rests with the Co-Investigative Judges. However, the submission by the Co-Prosecutors to the Co-Investigative Judges as to what charges should be laid and against how many suspects will be guided by the evidence, as well as by an OCP charging policy. It is viewed to be necessary to have this policy to assist in ensuring that the trials are fair, efficient and expeditious. Although the policy is not formalized, the prosecution requested joint trials with multiple accused in preference to single trials with one accused. The reasons for this are all equally valid. They include constraints of time, cost, ability to arrive at the truth, and impact on witnesses. However, as to the number of criminal events, the OCP shall seek to limit these events to the most serious and only to those that provide the most serious representation of the crimes committed by the accused.

9. Character of the Crimes

A. General Features

The majority of the crimes committed in DK were committed by the reigning Khmer Rouge government against its own people within the borders of DK. After a five-year civil war against the ruling forces of Lon Nol, the Khmer Rouge secured complete control over Cambodia. The Communist Party of Kampuchea (CPK) then set about establishing a state, which they called Democratic Kampuchea. The leaders of the CPK (described as the Khmer Rouge by Prince (later King) Norodom Sihanouk) held extreme communist ideological views. They set up policies that disregarded human life and produced repression and massacres on a massive scale. The CPK leaders thought that their revolution was the only way to bring Cambodia to independence and equality. They placed no value on education. Only a few of its leaders were well educated and very few had any experience in governing a state. Most of the low-ranking cadres were illiterate.

The occurrence of large-scale crimes in DK was a result of a combination of factors, primarily the ambition of the Khmer Rouge to build a supposedly Communist state. The Khmer Rouge set out to vastly increase agricultural productivity and to industrialize the country by transforming the entire population into proletarianized, atheistic peasants, and aimed to create an agricultural surplus, which would finance industrial development. In practice, however, their policies caused catastrophic agricultural collapse, mass starvation and increasingly vicious purges. In response to the crises created by their policies, the Khmer Rouge leadership directly ordered or empowered their subordinates to carry out killings to pre-empt and repress real and imagined opposition to their vision.

The gravity of the crimes rests on the fact that they were state-sponsored acts that emanated directly from the highest levels of the government. They occurred on a large scale and can clearly be seen not to have been committed as isolated acts. High-level suspects are unlikely to deny that the crimes occurred, however, they are likely to claim that the criminal conduct was not a result of a central policy, but arose out of actions emanating at a lower more regional level, over which they had no control or of which they were unaware.

The victims of the crimes were numerous. They principally were groups considered enemies of the state, irrespective of their ethnicity. It has been estimated that approximately 1.7 million people were killed, although assessments vary. The predominant victims were men, even though it is estimated a quarter of a million women perished. Among the dead from all causes were one in seven of Cambodia's rural Khmer, one quarter of urban Khmer, half of the ethnic Chinese, more than a third of the Islamic Cham, and one in seven people amongst the country's upland minorities. Almost all ethnic Vietnamese who refused deportation were killed.

B. Categories of Crimes

The crimes within the jurisdiction of the ECCC are identified in the ECCC Statute as 'Crimes under Cambodian Law' (e.g., murder, torture and religious persecution (Article 3)), genocide (Article

4), crimes against humanity (e.g., mass murder, extermination, enslavement, deportation, torture, imprisonment, persecution on political, racial and religious grounds, rape and other crimes of sexual violence (Article 5)), war crimes (e.g., unlawful treatment of civilians or prisoners of war, attacks on civilian targets, destruction of educational and religious institutions (Article 6)), destruction of cultural property (e.g., theft or damage of historical buildings, archaeological sites, museums, art and important book collections (Article 7)) and crimes against internationally protected persons (e.g., diplomats (Article 8)).

C. Criminal Conduct

Substantially, the core criminal acts committed against the population could be described as forced movement, wanton destruction, unlawful detention, forced labour, inhumane living conditions, violence, torture, unlawful killings and other acts of persecution. As to whether the acts of the Khmer Rouge had the required special intent to commit genocide, the Co-Prosecutors are still in the process of reviewing the evidence. The nature of the core criminal acts that were perpetrated are described in greater detail below'

(i) Forced Movement

Forced movement was used as an integral part of the process of turning Cambodia into a classless society through forced social and economic change. On 17 April 1975, Khmer Rouge troops entered Phnom Penh and the government of Lon Nol's Khmer Republic collapsed. Some people initially welcomed the Khmer Rouge troops, believing that the worst was over. However, beginning that day, the entire population of Phnom Penh, approximately 2 million people, was forced to leave the city. Individuals from all sectors of society were thrown onto the streets and forcibly marched to the countryside. Foreigners were expelled from the country. From this date forward, the populations of towns and villages were moved to achieve the regime's ideological plan.

(ii) Wanton Destruction

During the process of emptying the towns and villages, the Khmer Rouge destroyed or expropriated almost all private property. The only property that people were allowed to keep was what they could carry with them, and later those belongings were gradually stripped from them. The elimination of private property was carried out as part of the Khmer Rouge's policy of forcibly creating a communist state.

(iii) Unlawful Detention, Creating Inhumane Living Conditions and Forced Labour

These acts were used as an integral part of the process of turning Cambodia into a classless society through forced social and economic change. This process began on or before 17 April 1975 and continued until after 6 January 1979, taking place throughout the country. Essentially, the entire population of Cambodia was unlawfully detained and subjected to forced labour, inhumane living conditions or enslavement.

(iv) Violence and Torture

Security centres existed throughout DK at various levels. At the very top of this pyramid was S-21, the central security centre for the whole of the DK. Torture was common at security centres and prisons and it was often used to force individuals to 'confess' to alleged 'crimes'. The confessions were then used as a reason to execute the people who had been tortured into confessing and to arrest and torture others who were named in the confessions. While torture was common at prisons and security centres, it was also used at the village and cooperative level to intimidate and coerce people. People could be imprisoned, beaten or killed for minor violations of the rules, like being late for work or complaining about the insufficiency of the food. In some cases, individuals were tortured at public gatherings. Physical violence was also used at government worksites and within ministries as a punishment for minor violations of the rules.

(v) Killings
Individuals from all sectors of society were killed in large numbers, including, *inter alia*: (a) members of disfavoured groups like doctors, lawyers, teachers, students, landowners, business people and religious leaders; (b) former officials of the Khmer Republic, including both civil servants and military personnel, and their families; (c) ethnic minorities living in Cambodia, particularly the Cham and Vietnamese minorities; (d) members of the CPK who were suspected of being disloyal; and (e) others. As a result of this policy, hundreds of thousands of men, women and children died.

(vi) Other Acts of Persecution
The Khmer Rouge plan required the elimination of racial, ethnic, political and religious differences and the conversion of the entire population into proletarianized, atheistic worker-peasants. For example, the regime decreed that Cambodian society would only have two classes: workers and peasants. This goal required the 'elimination' of all other classes, particularly the 'exploitative' classes including capitalists, feudalists and the bourgeoisie. It also required the destruction of anything else that the DK government perceived as a threat to its vision of a communist society, including all religions and evidence of ethnic differences. As a result, many racial, religious and political groups were subjected to discriminatory attacks.

10. The Perpetrators

The perpetrators who physically committed the crimes under the Khmer Rouge regime were essentially young, illiterate and rural cadres who acted under ideologically driven and secretive leadership. They committed various crimes against their own populations under the revolutionary zeal of establishing a communist utopia. To cover the panoply of the Khmer Rouge crimes, the ECCC Statute provides for individual and superior criminal responsibilities of suspects to be subject to its jurisdiction (Article 29).

A principal vehicle for perpetrating the offences was through the agency of a comprehensive security system. This system enforced compliance with the leadership's plans and policies. Torture and execution were the main forms of discipline. The crimes were committed by groups of Khmer Rouge cadres.

DK was organized in a military-like hierarchical fashion. The highest level of the hierarchy was the so-called 'Organization'. Based in Phnom Penh, the Organization consisted of the top-level apparatus of the Khmer Rouge that controlled the state and the military. All major policy decisions were made by the Standing Committee of the Central Committee of the CPK. The Standing Committee enforced its policies by means of an interlocking system of state ministries and military committees, each controlled by members of the Standing Committee.

The country as a whole was divided into zones, sectors, districts and communes. The purpose of these divisions into diminishing geographic administrative units was to ensure that the party and governmental policies were being implemented. Each administrative geographic sub-division was commanded by a small committee to implement the policies on the ground. Nonetheless, the centre had direct control over military divisions which could be brought in if any of the levels of sub-division did not cooperate adequately with policy implementation.

Crimes were committed individually or by groups of cadres, but were under the orders and direction of the central organs of the communist party. An atmosphere of institutional paranoia existed among the central power holders and throughout the country in general. Understanding that the Khmer Rouge operated in an intensely secret way, where every person was a potential informer against any potential dissident within the system, it was difficult for low-level perpetrators to refuse to kill or torture, as there was a likelihood that the same would happen to them.

The persons directing the crimes were political figures. However, many military leaders were also involved. In any case, there was a tight fusion between the political and military roles in the Khmer Rouge, so the distinction between the two hierarchies is difficult to draw. The mandate of the ECCC limits the prosecution to those perpetrators of a high level of responsibility. Only senior leaders and those most responsible for the crimes can be prosecuted. Although the crimes were perpetrated at every level, it is clear that they were directed from the top.

The evidence clearly suggests that the crimes in DK were committed as part of a joint criminal enterprise (JCE). Senior leaders of Khmer Rouge, who were the rulers of DK, and those most responsible for crimes either had the criminal intent to commit the crimes specifically or the crimes committed were a natural and foreseeable consequence of the execution of their joint criminal plan. Those leaders were aware that such a crime was a possible consequence of the execution of that enterprise and, despite such awareness, they participated in the criminal enterprise.

Evidentially, proving these crimes will require witness testimony, documentary and other evidence. As the Khmer Rouge in many cases meticulously recorded information relating to and surrounding the crimes, which has been preserved by various governments and NGOs, these documents will play a major part in the proof.

11. Procedure and Evidence

A. Challenges

Using a civil law criminal justice system to investigate the massive human rights violations, where it is estimated that approximately 1.7 million people were killed, will be a new experience in the practice of international criminal law. To date, the driving system employed has been the common law model with continual adaptations to improve the efficiency and effectiveness of the trials.

The Internal Rules of the ECCC is the primary attempt at the ECCC to adapt the civil law procedure in order to investigate and prosecute crimes of a scale not envisaged for such a process. It is expected, as with the experience of the ICTY and the ICTR, that through the daily work of the parties and communication between them at the ECCC, workable interpretations of the Statute and of the Internal Rules will be achieved.

B. Preliminary Investigations

The Co-Prosecutors have established and developed their office on the basis that their role in the ECCC process is not a substantially active investigative role (other than when conducting preliminary investigations), but a legal and analytical role. In the judicial investigation phase, witness and suspect interviews, examination of crime scenes, evidence collection and other similar investigatory matters will be the role of the Co-Investigative Judges. During the preliminary investigation phase and the investigation phase, the OCP will focus on analysis of documentary evidence that has been placed on the case file.

C. Documentary Evidence

1. Importance

Documentary evidence analysis is proving useful in preparing strong cases for trial. The Khmer Rouge regime left hundreds of thousands of documents in Phnom Penh and other places when it fled to the countryside. These documents were seized 30 years ago and, in large part, the originals are stored in various archives secured by a number of NGOs and governmental organizations. The particular importance of documentary evidence in the Khmer Rouge cases is twofold. First, the regime recorded its activities in documents which greatly assist in proving its structure, its intentions and the activities of individuals, as well as, second, providing evidence of the actual crimes themselves.

The following sections will concentrate on the documentary analysis aspect of the Co-Prosecutors' work. Understanding that documentary analysis will be critical in the success of these cases, the OCP has developed practices to maximize the efficiency and effectiveness of its documentary analysis.

The OCP has deployed its resources in areas which will avoid duplication of the work of the OCIJ. With a staff of 25, 14 national and 11 international, consisting primarily of lawyers, analysts and information management assistants, the focus of the initial preliminary investigation was on the collection and analysis of documents. The large amount of documentation in the custody of NGOs such as the Documentation Centre of Cambodia (DC-CAM) has enabled the OCP to access the material quickly.

2. Nature of the Documentary Evidence

The documents collected by DC-CAM and others are either contemporaneous or post-DK documents. The contemporaneous documents include not just those authored by DK cadres and officials, but also statements extracted from prisoners of Khmer Rouge detention units, as well as documents from foreign countries. The post-1979 documents primarily include petitions and interview transcripts from the survivors of the DK period, and mapping reports describing existing and available physical evidence.

3. Collection of Evidence

As extensive documentary evidence, which is in the possession of these respected NGOs, is available, the OCP sought to collect such material in-house in support of its filings before the Court. The OCP approach was to scan all available relevant material into its evidentiary database and leave the original documents with the supplying agency until such time as proper facilities for evidence preservation are available within the ECCC. However, in cases where the OCP feels that the holding agency will be unable to preserve the document, the OCP endeavours to take custody of the original so as to ensure its preservation. Once scanned, the documents are located in a common electronic location so as to provide simultaneous access to the OCP staff. Because the number of documents in war crimes prosecutions is usually very high, the OCP believes that scanning the documents is the only viable option.

4. Analysis of Evidence

All scanned documents are available for analysis on software that supports optical character recognition. OCP staff members are then able to conduct simultaneous searches on the evidence archives on the basis of various search criteria. Unfortunately though, while a majority of documents are in Khmer, the software does not support optical character recognition in that language. The OCP has made efforts to have software produced to recognize the Khmer script, but the cost is too high and the results are not guaranteed.

The OCP encourages continuous training of its entire staff in respect of advanced case and evidence management software so that all staff, at various levels of expertise, can participate in and contribute to the analysis of documents and evidence. To this end, the OCP has employed staff with advanced training and experience from other international tribunals to continuously be in a position to train others in the use of these modern tools. Given the constraints of time, resources and staff capacity, it is the OCP's policy to focus on a slightly macro-level analysis of a majority of documents as against a more micro-level analysis of only a few documents.

These software solutions have also acted as educational tools for staff with various backgrounds and levels of training and experience. It is expected that electronic storage of documents and information will also ease information transfer from one organ of the ECCC to the other, for example, from the OCP to the OCIJ.

5. Presentation of Evidence

The OCP trains and prepares its legal and other staff in electronic case management systems. Electronic analytical aids will assist the search for the best evidence and assist the ECCC in marshalling lengthy testamentary and documentary evidence. Further, because of the considerable time lapse, and due to the enormous research already done by scholars and journalists, there is a body of documentation already available that the OCP will use to prove its case. Thus, it shall seek to include expert evidence to prove a number of legal, jurisdictional and even factual matters.

12. Early Practices

In the preliminary investigation phases of its work, the OCP employed techniques and methods used at other international criminal tribunals and adapted them in order to suit the particular ECCC environment. Many of these practices may seem standard in larger tribunals, however in smaller courts such as the ECCC, it is critical that these are employed because of the limited budget and human resources to undertake the work. Some of the practices employed at the OCP that have been extremely beneficial for the office are outlined below.

A. Human Resources

1. Employment of Experts

The OCP has employed academic experts and other staff who have had extensive experience analyzing documentary evidence which was collected before the ECCC was established. This reduces the need to engage expensive experts or specialists during the investigation or prosecution phases. Employing core experts as staff members dramatically increases the capacity of all staff to understand the cases and find relevant and probative evidence quickly.

2. Employment of Specialist with Capacity-Building Skills

Where possible, the OCP has attempted to employ staff who have, in addition to their specialist knowledge, an ability to educate others. In the hybrid context, both national and international staff have greatly benefited from this skill transfer.

3. Continuous Staff Training and Development

Regular short training sessions on topics relevant to the current work have been held and have proven invaluable in increasing the efficiency in the OCP. This is particularly the case in the areas relating to the use of information technology to ensure that all staff members are making the best use of the resources available to them. These sessions are also expected to cover other areas such as substantive or procedural law, historical and factual overviews of different areas of the investigations, etc.

4. Employment of Interns

Over the years, international criminal Tribunals have benefited greatly from the contribution of legal interns. The ECCC is no exception. As internships are unpaid, interns from poorer countries are less likely to apply. The OCP is attempting to broaden the geographical spread of interns by seeking minimum financial assistance for these interns. There is a particular aim to attract Cambodian interns to the Office.

5. Use of Document Management and Analysis Systems

Use of modern document and case management technology enables staff to use basic search mechanisms to locate documents instantaneously in large collections. Having staff work in one case analysis programme means the individual efforts of each staff member accumulate to arrive at conclusions faster. This method also avoids repetitive recording of information relating to common attributes of documents.

6. Use of Bilingual Software

Introduction of document and case management software in Khmer and English has assisted in breaking the linguistic barrier experienced by some staff, while proving invaluable in the acceptance of more sophisticated analytical systems previously unknown to many staff members.

B. Consensus and Capacity Building Issues

1. Joint Responsibilities and Partnering

National and international staff members are given joint responsibilities such as leading small analysis teams, interviewing witnesses, speaking at outreach forums and representing the OCP at meetings with outside groups, government officials or NGOs. It is important that the process is executed by both national and international staff. Failure to work closely together is likely to end in misunderstandings which can lead to disagreements between the Co-Prosecutors, thus slowing and making the process less effective.

2. Communication

(a) Daily and Weekly Management Meetings

Weekly meetings are vital to the smooth running of the Tribunal, as well as the close working relationships that the OCP aims to create with its staff. It is also important that the Co-Prosecutors and Deputy Co-Prosecutors meet with their counterparts daily, if possible, but at least once a week as a group. The OCP has found that this is the best way to ensure that the Co-Prosecutors are jointly satisfied with the direction of the investigations and prosecutions;

(b) Management-Staff Communication and Interaction

Regular and joint management-staff communication is critical to the cohesive functioning of the OCP. Regular small-scale social events provide informal opportunities for staff to interact outside the work environment.

3. External Relations with Evidence Providers

As a substantial amount of documentary evidence is provided to the OCP by external organizations, it is essential that regular contact is maintained with them. These organizations and the documents they provide are a valuable resource to the ECCC.

13. Victims and Witnesses

A. Relevance

The support and protection of victims and witnesses before any court should be one of its primary concerns. Without victims and witnesses, the courts have little chance of success. Without safeguarding their interests, the ECCC's reason for being is undermined. The overall challenges of delivering adequate witness support and protection at the ECCC are similar to other Tribunals. However, the Cambodian context presents a unique set of issues, which are being addressed. The success of the ECCC in protecting its victims and witnesses will significantly depend on the willingness and ability of the RGC and UN Member States to continue to address these issues both financially and through other assistance throughout the mandate of the ECCC. NGO assistance has been and is likely to be a significant component leading to the ECCC's success in providing support and protection to witnesses. However, due to their limited mandates, their assistance must be accompanied by substantial national and international involvement and assistance.

B. Legal Provisions

Other than measures that would include but not be limited to 'the conduct of in camera proceedings and the protection of the victim's identity', no other responsibilities are established under the ECCC law for the protection of victims and witnesses during the trial process at the ECCC. However, the IRs include sufficient provisions to ensure that the ECCC and its subsidiary offices are aware of their legal obligations to protect and take into account the needs of victims and witnesses throughout the proceedings. The rules allow for the ECCC, of its own volition or at the request of the parties, to seek appropriate measures to protect victims and witnesses whose appearance before the ECCC is likely to place their life or property or their family members or close relatives in danger. They are likely to allow for appropriate judicial guarantees and/or physical protection in Cambodia or overseas.

Importantly, the IRs allow the ECCC to sanction any person who knowingly or wilfully interferes or incites or attempts to interfere with the administration of justice, including any person who threatens, intimidates, causes any injury or offers a bribe to, or otherwise interferes with a witness, or potential witness.

C. The Witnesses/Experts Support Unit

1. Structure

In readiness to provide this support and protection, the ECCC Office of Administration established in July 2006 a witness section, the Witnesses/Experts Support Unit (WESU), which currently comprises one international staff member, serving as the Coordinator of WESU, two national staff members, serving as WESU Officers; and two additional staff members, one national and one international, serving as WESU Assistants. The WESU is responsible for three main areas regarding witness care: Operations, which consists of organizing and arranging the logistical requirements and witness protection; Support, which consists of providing social and psychological counselling and assistance to witnesses, and; Protection, which consists of coordinating responses to the security requirements. The WESU has drafted a comprehensive set of internal policies and guidelines, which also outlines the functions of each WESU staff member and each area of witness care.

2. WESU Assistance

At the moment, the assistance provided to victims and witnesses from the RGC has been limited. The most significant service provided by the RGC is the Cambodian Taskforce Police, which will provide witness protection services to all ECCC witnesses. As stated in Article 23 of the Agreement between the UN and the RGC, the latter is responsible for the 'safety and security of all persons referred to in the Agreement', which includes victims and witnesses. The WESU is currently preparing a memorandum of understanding and guidelines to implement this Agreement. Additionally, the WESU has submitted a request to the RGC to initiate negotiations with other countries to establish relocation programmes for particularly threatened witnesses, though these negotiations have yet to begin.

3. Witness Protection

Not surprisingly, the most important concerns for victims and witnesses at the ECCC are for their health and safety. Some witnesses have expressed their desire to keep their identities, as well as those of their family members, hidden from the public, particularly through in-court identity protection measures as described in Article 33 of the ECCC Statute. There will be some witnesses who will require psychological counselling throughout the process. Some will also be interested in possible relocation either within or outside Cambodia. There have also been several requests from survivors for information regarding the rights and entitlements of victims, and many more are expected as trials proceed. Each of these concerns will be dealt with as thoroughly as possible by WESU and the emerging Victims Claim Unit.

WESU is also serving as an advisor to a Phnom Penh-based NGO, which is preparing a witness protection training course for the Cambodian Taskforce Police officers. This training course is being funded by the European Union and by some NGOs. Through this course, approximately 120 Taskforce Police officers will be trained to become the country's first witness protection officers. About 30 of these officers are to be deployed for WESU purposes.

4. Witness Support

In the area of general witness support, the WESU has submitted proposals requesting additional staffing to the unit, but limited funding requires WESU to rely heavily on services offered by external entities, particularly NGOs, in order to perform its duties adequately. The WESU has established a working relationship with four NGOs. A Memorandum of Understanding has been prepared between WESU and two NGOs, both of whom will be available to provide professional psychological counselling services to witnesses before, during and after their interview and testimony. By utilizing their provincial networks and offices, these NGOs will also be able to provide post-testimony counselling to witnesses living in regions outside Phnom Penh. WESU has also been approached by another NGO for a project specifically designed to provide legal support to victims and witnesses who wish to become involved with the ECCC.

5. Victims' Rights and Victims Unit

The rights of the victims have been adequately addressed in the Internal Rules. Under IR 23, a civil party action by the victims is provided for, so as to facilitate their participation in the criminal proceedings against those responsible for the crimes and also to enable the victims 'to seek collective and moral reparation'. The IRs provide that the court may award non-financial collective and moral reparations, subject to the availability of funds from the accused, the UN, the RGC, NGOs or any other sources. Such awards may take, *inter alia*, the following forms:

(i) construction of memorials and organizing commemoration ceremonies;
(ii) provision of collective, medical, psychological or social services;
(iii) verification of facts or full public disclosure about the truth;
(iv) an official declaration or a judicial decision restoring the dignity or the rights of the victims;
(v) public apologies, etc.

The rights of victims in the proceedings before the ECCC include the appearance of the civil party, or their lawyer in the proceedings (IR 23 and 83) and a specific judgement on the claims of the civil party (IR 100).

A Victims Unit has also been established, with the mandate to ensure a proper representation of the interests of the victims before the judicial organs of the Court (IR 12). The Section, among other tasks, shall:

(i) assist in the legal representation of victims before the Court by maintaining a list of foreign and national lawyers to represent the victims and victims associations before the ECCC and ensure training of these lawyers;
(ii) assist the Co-Prosecutors in receipt, verification and registration of complaints;
(iii) assist the Co-Investigative Judges in registering the civil party petitions;
(iv) assist, in general, in the protection of the rights of the victims;
(v) provide information to civil society and victims associations regarding victim participation in the ECCC.

14. Cooperation with States, International Organizations and NGOs

Good cooperation with states, international organizations and NGOs is as essential for the ECCC as with all other international or hybrid tribunals.

A. The Government of Cambodia

As the ECCC is a court located in Cambodia where the crimes occurred, cooperation with the RGC is the most critical of all relationships to ensure its success. It is expected that, because the ECCC Statute is an Act of the Cambodian parliament, all the agencies of that government, particularly its law enforcement and investigative agencies, shall aid and assist the organs of the ECCC in implementing its mandate. It is imperative that the ECCC gets full cooperation from the RGC, as without this support the ECCC cannot realistically succeed.

The importance of this relationship is specifically reflected in Article 25 of the UN-RGC Agreement: '[the RGC] shall comply without undue delay with any request for assistance by the co-investigating judges, the co-prosecutors and the ECCC or an order issued by any of them', including but not limited to (1) identification and location of persons; (2) service of documents; (3) arrest or detention of persons; and (4) transfer of an indictee to the Court. This cooperation is expected, therefore, in these and other areas relating to the effective functioning of the Court, such as the maintenance and security of the Court building, the security of staff in Cambodia, access to documents, crime sites, witnesses and other evidence.

Article 23 of the Statute codifies these types of obligations where it states that 'in carrying out the investigations, the Co-Investigating judges may seek the assistance of the Royal Government of Cambodia, if such assistance would be useful to the investigation, and such assistance shall be provided'. Further codification of the RGC's commitment to its cooperation with regards to the apprehension of accused persons is seen in Article 33 where it is stated that 'the judicial police will be assisted by other law enforcement agencies of Cambodia, including its armed forces, in order to ensure that the accused persons are brought into the court's custody immediately'. With such provisions, it is the view of the Co-Prosecutors that the ECCC, being a creature of an Act of the Cambodian parliament, any request, order, direction, decision or judgement of the ECCC shall be legally binding within the territory of Cambodia.

In addition to specific assistance from the RGC, the ECCC expects cooperation, in general, to realize its mandate efficiently and effectively. The ECCC also expects from the Government sustained financial support, non-interference in its mandate and assistance in securing international cooperation. For example, the RGC owns and runs most of the important modes of mass dissemination of information in the country. The ECCC would also expect cooperation from the RGC in its outreach programmes. The purpose of this assistance is to disseminate relevant and timely information about the Court to the victim groups who, in this case, effectively constitute the whole of the population of Cambodia.

Up until now, in the short life of the ECCC, the RGC has been supportive of its work. After the adoption of the IR, the filing of introductory submissions, the commencement of the judicial investigation phase of the proceedings, and the start of the ECCC's first trial, the continued cooperation of the RGC is essential to establish the ECCC as a credible, functioning court delivering justice to a high standard both nationally and internationally.

B. Other States

As some UN Member States are the core voluntary financiers of the ECCC, their continued support and cooperation is equally essential to the success of the ECCC. As such, the ECCC is heavily reliant on these select Member States if it is to deliver a standard of justice which is both nationally and internationally acceptable. This pre-condition by the international donor community is clearly addressed by the power of the UN to terminate its cooperation under the terms of Article 28:

> should the Cambodian government change the structure or the organization of the ECCC or otherwise cause them to function in a manner that does not conform with the terms of the present Agreement, the United Nations reserves the right to cease to provide assistance, financial or otherwise, pursuant to the present Agreement.

This condition reflects the constant pressure on the RGC for the trials to meet international standards for the ECCC to continue its work.

In other ways it is expected that the ECCC may require the assistance of certain donor countries and/or multilateral agencies to exercise its mandate effectively. This may happen, for instance, in a number of ways such as the:

(1) loaning of expert staff;
(2) provision of evidence and intelligence information;
(3) facilitation of investigative work in country;
(4) location and relocation of witnesses;
(5) location and arrest of suspects;
(6) provision of expertise and related project funding.

In such situations, it is expected that the ECCC shall, at the first instance, seek this assistance through the good offices of the RGC where necessary. It is legitimately expected that the donor countries and/or multilateral agencies shall respond to these requests and assist the ECCC. Indeed, there are already examples of this cooperation and support. This expectation is predicated on the reasoning that the establishment of the ECCC reflects the collective will of the international community in that the Court was, *inter alia*, founded by the UN-RGC Agreement which was approved by an overwhelming majority of the General Assembly of the United Nations that authorized the Secretary General to enter into this Agreement.

To date, states have been supportive to the requests or needs of the ECCC generally, reflecting the will of the international community that justice should finally be brought to the people of Cambodia. This support will not be a constant unless the work of the ECCC is perceived as being efficient and effective by the donor states who currently fund and assist it.

C. International and National Non-Governmental Organizations

Due to the limited funding of the ECCC, it is likely that the Court will rely heavily on the assistance of international and local NGOs to realize some of its mandates. The OCP has received significant assistance from respected NGOs in collecting evidence and resource materials in aid of its mandate. This is particularly helpful as it saves ECCC resources and time and avoids duplication of work, considering the length of time that has elapsed since the commission of the indictable crimes. The ECCC is receiving significant assistance from national and international NGOs in training both its staff and staff working within the Government of Cambodia who are necessary to complete the ECCC mandate.

The ECCC shall increasingly solicit the assistance of the NGOs in the above-noted areas and also, very importantly, in its outreach programme to inform the Cambodian people of its mandate and performance. Many NGOs in Cambodia and around the world are interested in the Khmer Rouge trials and wish to be supportive in different ways. Support is being provided in diverse areas, for example, in psychological counselling of the victims and witnesses. Other organizations will report on the proceedings of the trials or assist in providing training or legal advice and representation. Accepting support from NGOs is an important method of allowing the Cambodian civil society to have some ownership of the process that is established for them. It is important, however, that the ECCC not rely on this support to such a degree that it does not control the quality and direction of the process.

15. Conclusion

A. ECCC's Unique Contribution

It is far too early to tell what the ultimate contribution of the ECCC will be to international investigation and prosecution practices. Nonetheless, the very fact that the ECCC has commenced operation and the OCP and OCIJ have been investigating international criminal law abuses in partnership with Cambodian lawyers and analysts is a unique contribution in itself. Being an internationalized national court, the acceptance of international criminal law as a legitimate source of law and the application of international standards is a significant achievement. The transfer of this knowledge to Cambodian judges, lawyers and investigators has enabled Cambodia to enter the arena of international criminal law understanding and practice.

B. Evaluating Results or Improving Output

At the ECCC, there has been no internal practice or procedure for evaluating the results achieved or for improving its output at this stage. It is too early to do so. It has been agreed across all organs of the ECCC that the initial staff structure and budget were insufficient to sustain international standards as required in the ECCC Statute. Consequently, other financing options are being explored to ensure that these standards can be attained. Outside experts in the field of international criminal law from organizations such as the ICC, ICTY, the State Court of Bosnia and Herzegovina, and others have provided assessments to ensure the ECCC meets the necessary international standards.

C. Influence from Other National or International Jurisdictions

Within the OCP, we have directly borrowed work practices and jurisprudence, especially from the ICTY and SCSL, and applied them to the ECCC Statute. This in turn has led the OCP to develop a system that is sustainable and workable. The ECCC has bought and implemented the same information management technology as the ICTY. This has proven to be very successful. In short, the influence of the other national and international jurisdictions has been crucial to the OCP's early establishment issues.

D. Seeking Outside Experience

Other than employing key staff with international experience, the OCP has engaged with the other international organizations and universities to assist with its work. On a secondment or consultancy basis, for short periods of time, experts from the internationalized courts, such as the ICTY, ICC, ICTR, the State Court of Bosnia and Herzegovina, have come to the ECCC to share their knowledge. NGOs have been of great help in providing funding for training and conferences. For example, in October 2006 a one-week training session was funded by a respected international NGO for the OCP, OCIJ and the Defence Support Office in the core aspects of Cambodian and international criminal law. This NGO brought academic experts and international criminal law practitioners to impart their knowledge. Another NGO trained investigators and lawyers at the ECCC in 2006 and 2007 in best practice investigative techniques. On the technological side, trainers in analytical software applications and legal research tools have been engaged to build technical skills of staff. It is the OCP's view that any training sought from outside must be supportive of and complementary to the in-house training provided.

E. Importance of Transferring Lessons Learned

It is important for the development of international criminal law that the lessons learnt from activities of courts such as the ECCC be transferred to other bodies and authorities. Good practices, however, do not develop or are not passed on as a matter of course. The work and knowledge required to investigate and prosecute is simply too time consuming to develop without reference to prior best practices, and efforts must be made by all tribunals to learn from each other. Other than the general benefit to international criminal law, the lessons learned at the ECCC will benefit national governments, courts, as well as other similarly situated organizations.

PART III
Jurisdiction and Case-Law

The most visible footprint of any jurisdiction is represented by the impact it has on adjudication of facts and responsibilities, and on the development of the law through its case law and practice. International criminal jurisdictions are mandated to establish individual criminal responsibility for conducts that customary and treaty law, as well as their evolving jurisprudence, have contributed to identifying as crimes of international concern.

In this process and for such purpose, the interplay between relevant jurisdictions at the domestic and at the international level is characterized by criteria aimed at preventing conflicts (primacy/complementarity) while preserving the sovereignty of states, in order to maintain momentum on the fight against impunity. It is from this perspective that the practice in the performance of obligations of implementation and cooperation, and remedies for the incompliance thereof, are at the very centre of the degree of success of international criminal justice. It is in the same direction that full use should be made of both horizontal and vertical cooperation under all available international instruments, in order to fill the impunity gap that is left open by political, legal and organizational limits of the relevant jurisdictions. When cooperation is attained, the result achieved is apparent in the completion of proceedings and, eventually, in the case law of international-ized courts.

Some of the most significant jurisprudential contributions to the development of international criminal law and to the ascertainment of facts in conflict situations are captured in the selected practices included in this Part. Their legacy, as notably exemplified by the impact of the ICTY's jurisprudence on the case law of the War Crimes Chambers in the Court of Bosnia and Herzegovina, is expected to represent a guideline for domestic jurisdictions in the affected regions, but also a benchmark for other international jurisdictions.

SECTION I
Jurisdiction Over International Crimes

Chapter 8

The History and the Evolution of the Notion of International Crimes

Paola Gaeta

1. The Emergence of Prohibitions of Conducts Amounting to International Crimes

At the international level, the criminalization of individual conducts is a recent phenomenon that evolved in the early 1990s. Until that time, international law was instrumental in allowing states to better organize the joint repression of certain criminal offences, more specifically those that damaged their collective interests and had a strong transnational dimension. In other words, international law was used by states to achieve stronger cooperation in judicial matters to oppose transnational criminality. During the first decades of last century, treaties, for the repression of crimes such as counterfeiting, slavery and the trafficking of women and children, began to emerge and continued to appear throughout the twentieth century up until the present day, for example to fight terrorism, money laundering, corruption and so on. All these treaties follow the same pattern: they contain an agreed definition of the prohibited conduct, oblige contracting states to criminalize that conduct within their legal systems (i.e., to adopt the necessary national criminal legislation to repress the conduct), provide for certain heads of criminal jurisdiction and ensure the mutual extradition of alleged offenders.

One clear example of the instrumental role international law plays in repressing such crimes is the customary rule on piracy. Due to a well-established rule of customary international law, each state is authorized to seize pirate vessels and arrest pirates on the high seas and bring them to trial, regardless of whether the pirates had attacked one of their ships. This age-old customary rule does not itself prohibit or criminalize piracy: it merely provides that acts of violence on the high seas amounting to piracy can be repressed by *any* state that has captured the perpetrators on the high seas. International law, here, helps states to realize a more effective criminal repression of a crime which puts in jeopardy safety at high sea.

Interestingly, it is this approach that inspired states to tackle a different form of criminality, namely ‘state criminality’, that is crimes perpetrated by state officials in their official capacity or backed by the apparatus of the state, or within the context of widespread and collective violence (such as wars and armed conflicts in general). With the exception of the Nuremberg and Tokyo Tribunals, which were created to take an innovative approach to the repression of such unique forms of criminality, states applied the traditional methods to cope with this form of criminality. While debating the establishment of a permanent international criminal court, they drafted treaties or treaty provisions for the prosecution and punishment of crimes, such as genocide, grave breaches of the Geneva Conventions (GCs), torture, apartheid; these treaties ‘simply’ enjoined contracting states (i) to criminalize those conducts within their own legal orders and (ii) to punish the responsible persons (or, in the case of grave breaches, to extradite them to another contracting state). In other words, also with regard to crimes perpetrated within the context of state criminality or state violence, the international community reacted by resorting to the traditional institutional framework of specific treaties or treaty rules aimed at imposing on states a duty to criminalize the prohibited conducts, and organizing judicial cooperation for their repression. Again, international law was used as a tool for the coordination of the exercise of criminal jurisdiction by states.

Unfortunately, this traditional institutional framework was not well suited to the job at hand, and consequently was seldom employed by contracting states. Some of them even failed to pass the necessary implementing criminal legislation; or, when they did possess all the necessary legal requirements for the exercise of their criminal jurisdiction, they simply failed to make use of it. For a long time the scheme, under which it was up to national criminal jurisdictions to deal with forms of state criminality, committed either 'at home' or abroad, simply proved unworkable (and to some extent still is today). This should come as no surprise. The method was originally conceived of to react to forms of 'private' transnational criminality that states, moved by selfish but shared interests, wanted to repress by enhancing their judicial cooperation. Things are radically different concerning crimes committed by state officials on behalf of, or with the support of, their state. Here, when those crimes are committed abroad, a 'negative' comity of nations comes into play: it forces states not to interfere with the internal or external affairs of other states, although – faced with mass-scale crimes – international law allows (and in some cases even obliges) them to act. When crimes are committed 'at home', various reasons can stand in the way of prosecution: if the crimes are perpetrated under an authoritarian regime, prosecutors and judges have to wait for its toppling; however, when this occurs, amnesty laws are normally passed 'for the sake of' national reconciliation, or immunities or the statute of limitation are urged by the culprits, or other political and legal hurdles are relied upon.

The establishment of the International Criminal Tribunal for the Former Yugoslavia (ICTY) and of the International Criminal Tribunal for Rwanda (ICTR) by the UN Security Council (UNSC) was the start of a new era. For the first time in history, truly international criminal tribunals were set up to prosecute and punish genocide, crimes against humanity and war crimes, i.e., the so-called 'core crimes'. Their creation paved the way to the establishment of the International Criminal Court (in 1998) and of a group of mixed criminal tribunals (or internationalized courts), some of them with a strong international component as with the Special Court for Sierra Leone. All these international or mixed criminal tribunals exercise their jurisdiction over individuals who may be indicted on account of criminal rules of a truly international nature. Those rules are provided for in their constitutive instruments: they describe the prohibited conducts and indicate what criteria must be applied for sentencing. In addition, they are normally supplemented by other international rules, chiefly customary rules, and by general principles of law common to national legal orders. These international and mixed criminal tribunals, in particular the two *ad hoc* Tribunals for the former Yugoslavia and Rwanda, have spawned copious case law, thus contributing to the emergence of new international customary rules supplementing those which already existed. Finally, and more importantly, their functioning, although not flawless, has contributed to disseminating the idea that there are criminal conducts that should not go unpunished, and that individuals responsible for them must be brought to justice.

The international community has therefore begun to enforce its criminal prohibitions through international or quasi-international courts and tribunals that apply international criminal rules directly. In a nutshell, with regard to the core crimes the *jus puniendi* has ceased to be an exclusive state prerogative. Furthermore, it is exercised at the international level on behalf of the international community as a whole. Plainly, states can still prosecute and punish individuals who engage in those criminal conducts. However, the current exercise of national criminal jurisdiction in this field can better be described as a judicial activity performed for the international community as such, rather than as a modality of exercise of a sovereign power. One could go so far as to say that, with respect to the core crimes, the new approach has reversed the traditional one briefly described above: now it is national criminal law and national criminal jurisdictions that constitute the instrument enabling the international community to repress such crimes. These are crimes directly criminalized at the international level. As few international mechanisms have been set up to prosecute and punish the responsible individuals, national judges, if and when they step in and exercise their criminal jurisdiction over those crimes, also act as judicial organs of the international community thereby accomplishing a sort of *dédoublement fonctionnel*, a phenomenon well known to international lawyers[1] and of which some national courts seemed to have been fully aware.[2] It is as though the international community, still a *communitas imperfecta*, availed itself of national criminal courts to enforce its criminal prohibitions.

Be that as it may, we can however conclude that in the field of core crimes there now exists a branch of international law comprising a truly international criminal law.

2. The Notion of International Crimes Proper

As is clear from the previous discussion, international law directly criminalizes only a few conducts belonging to the much broader notion of international crime. This is a notion which encompasses both crimes belonging to what I have described above as 'state criminality' and crimes that are taken into account by international law only because of their transnational dimension. The criminalization by international law of the former class of crimes seems to be undisputable. It has its roots in the gradual emergence of a set of '*supra*-national' values, proper to the international community as a whole, that must be safeguarded against those states that – through their individual organs or their whole apparatus – disregard them. It is on account of the values they protect that these crimes are truly international; it is because of the importance of these values that the international community directly criminalizes them, striking at the fabric of state in one of the most sacrosanct pillars of its sovereignty, the monopoly in criminal matters. The international criminalization of each of these crimes has its own rationale and has followed its own path.

1 On the theory of the *dédoublement fonctionnel*, see the work of G. Scelle quoted by A. Cassese, 'Remarks on Scelle's Theory of "Role Splitting" (*dédoublement fonctionnel*) in International Law', 1 *EJIL* (1990), at 210, note 1.

2 See the Judgment of the Israeli Supreme Court of 29 May 1962 in *Eichmann*, where the Court stated: 'Not only do all the crimes attributed to the appellant bear an international character, but their harmful and murderous effects were so embracing and widespread as to shake the international community to its very foundations. The State of Israel therefore was entitled, pursuant to the principle of universal jurisdiction and *in the capacity of a guardian of international law and an agent for its enforcement*, to try the appellant. That being the case, no importance attaches to the fact that the State of Israel did not exist when the offences were committed' (emphasis added). The judgement is available at http://www.nizkor.org (visited 20 August 2009). See also 36 *ILR* (1968), 304. In the same vein see the decision of 31 October 1985 of a US Court in *Demjaniuk*, where the Court states the following: 'The underlying assumption is that the crimes [of which Demjaniuk was accused] are offences against the law of nations or against humanity and that the *prosecuting nation is acting for all nations*. This being so, Israel or any other nation, regardless of its status in 1942 or 1943, may undertake to vindicate the interest of all nations by seeking to punish the perpetrator of such crimes' (776 F.2d 57, 1985, § 21, emphasis added). See also the *Yunis* case (concerning the hijacking of an aircraft), decided on 12 February 1988 by the District Court of Columbia, where it noted: 'Not only is the United States *acting on behalf of the world community to punish alleged offenders of crimes that threatened the very foundations of world order*, but the United States has its own interest in protecting its nationals' (681 F.Supp. 896, D.D.C., 1988, at 903, emphasis added).

As for war crimes, it is at least since the eighteenth century that national criminal codes and military manuals have provided for the right of a belligerent to prosecute and punish his own soldiers for violations of the laws of war.[3] As for war crimes committed by enemy personnel or civilians, it would seem that the power of a belligerent to exercise his criminal jurisdiction was initially limited to the time of the armed conflict and, in any case, only within occupied territories.[4] WWI abruptly launched the discourse on war crimes in the international arena. Article 228 of the Peace Treaty of Versailles constitutes the first clear international recognition of the right of a belligerent party to bring to justice persons belonging to the other belligerents for violations of the laws and customs of war after the end of hostilities.[5] The path towards criminalization of war crimes developed (leaving aside the exception of the Nuremberg and Tokyo Tribunals) following the aforementioned traditional pattern, through the adoption of the provisions on grave breaches in the 1949 Geneva Conventions and Additional Protocol I, and a set of criminal provisions contained in a few other treaties of international humanitarian law.[6]

As for other classes of war crimes, the process culminated in the creation of the *ad hoc* criminal Tribunals, and with the further developments mentioned above. The rationale behind the international criminalization of conducts involving serious violations of the rules of international humanitarian law is clear. It lies in the need to ensure – also by way of a threat of criminal sanctions – that some elementary principles and considerations of humanity are respected in warlike situations, so as to reduce as much as possible the suffering and misery caused by war.

The case of crimes against humanity and genocide is slightly different. The path towards their international criminalization is not rooted in national criminal legal systems, as is the case with war crimes, but started at the international level with the adoption of the Statute of the International Military Tribunal (IMT) and the Nuremberg trial. The story is well known: the Allies had to find a way to come to terms with odious crimes committed by the Nazis against Germans, or against the civilian population of the Allies of the Third Reich. These crimes did not fall under the notion of war crimes (that can be committed only against an enemy population or enemy combatants). Moreover, under traditional international law the treatment by a state of its own citizens or those of allied countries was a matter pertaining to the 'internal and external affairs' of states and no interference from other states was envisaged or allowed. Crimes against humanity were therefore conceived of as a sort of 'umbrella' notion, to be applied if necessary to fill the lacunae left by the notion of war crimes, subject however to an important limitation: these crimes had to be linked to the perpetration of war crimes or crimes against peace, i.e., they had to be connected with war. However, after these truly international first steps, the notion of crimes against humanity remained dormant for a long time, and the process of its international criminalization never went through the traditional mechanism of criminal repression, as was the case in war crimes such as grave

3 M. Bothe, 'War Crimes', in A. Cassese, P. Gaeta and J. R.W.D. Jones (eds), *The Rome Statute of the International Criminal Court* (Oxford: Oxford University Press, 2002), Vol. I, at 382.

4 See UN War Crimes Commission, *History of the UN War Crimes Commission and the Development of the Laws of War* (1948), at 29 to 30. It was envisaged that armistice or peace treaties could contain a clause whereby the victorious belligerent imposed upon the defeated states the obligation to surrender alleged war criminals for trial (ibid.).

5 Art. 228 of the Treaty of Versailles provided as follows: 'The German Government recognizes the right of the allied and associated powers to bring before military tribunals persons accused of having committed acts in violation of the laws and customs of war …'.

6 See for instance Article 28 of the 1954 Hague Convention for the Protection of Cultural Property in the Event of Armed Conflict, and Chapter 4 of the 1999 Second Protocol to the 1954 Hague Convention for the Protection of Cultural Property in the Event of Armed Conflict.

breaches of the Geneva Conventions. In other words, states never felt it necessary to conclude an international treaty by which they obliged themselves both to criminalize these crimes within their legal systems and to coordinate their efforts in the field of criminal repression. On the contrary: the notion of crimes against humanity was by some national courts conceived of as strictly connected to WWII and the punishment of German and Japanese criminals, as if there were no international rule prohibiting crimes against humanity except for the one that had evolved from the Nuremberg Charter.[7]

Genocide, which was punished at Nuremberg as part of the wider notion of crimes against humanity in the form of persecution or extermination, took a different route. Its international prohibition was solemnly incorporated in the 1948 Genocide Convention. This Convention, on the one hand, applied the traditional scheme of repression, by requesting contracting states to criminalize genocide and obliging the territorial state to punish genocide within its legal orders; on the other hand, it went so far as to envisage the future establishment of an international criminal court endowed with jurisdiction over acts of genocide. The Genocide Convention was rapidly ratified by a large number of states, and the general revulsion against this crime quickly gave rise to a customary rule contemplating genocide not only as an individual crime, but also as a very serious international wrongful act of state. This explains why, when the SC established the ICTY and ICTR, the definition of genocide was taken verbatim from the Genocide Convention without much discussion, and again inserted in all subsequent instruments instituting international or mixed tribunals for the repression of international crimes. By contrast, at the time of the adoption of the ICTYSt and ICTRSt the notion of crimes against humanity was still highly controversial, as the subsequent Rome negotiations for the ICC made abundantly clear.

One can speculate on the reasons why the process of international criminalization of these two classes of international crimes was different from that relating to war crimes. Arguably, for war crimes the national origin of their international criminalization can be explained by taking into account that states had a sort of 'selfish' interest in their criminal repression within their national legal systems. Whatever the humanitarian reasons behind the birth and development of the laws of war, it is a fact that these laws could apply solely within the context of an interstate relationship (i.e., were conceived to regulate international armed conflicts), and hence were synallagmatic in nature. For a long time, no humanitarian reason was strong enough to force or convince states to regulate civil strife as well. The notion of war crimes served various purposes: when it applied to national military servicemen, repression of violations of the laws of war served to impose military discipline and to protect the honour of armed forces, with regard to enemy combatants, such repression constituted an effective tool to discourage breaches of the rules of warfare by the belligerent enemy. The notions of crimes against humanity and genocide were born from a totally different seed: the concept that states are not the absolute owners of the lives and human dignity of their citizens, but that individual's and groups' fundamental rights must be respected. At Nuremberg, for the first time, the right of the international community was proclaimed to lift the veil of state sovereignty and to interfere in the relationship between the state and its citizens when it is the state that systematically tramples upon their basic human rights. This was an unexpected revolution. True, the drafters of the Nuremberg Charter carefully tried to confine the notion of crimes against humanity to the historical events of World War II, to avoid future interferences by the international community in their internal affairs as regards the treatment of their citizens. Two US Military Tribunals sitting at Nuremberg even asserted that the notion of crimes against

7 See the *Boudarel* case (*Wladyslav Sobanski v. George Boudarel*) decided on 1 April 1993 by the French Court of Cassation, in *RGDIP* (1994), at 471–474.

humanity could apply to extermination through euthanasia only if the victims were foreigners![8] A similar cautious development can be seen in the UN Charter; for example, the powers of the new organization in matters of human rights were originally limited to the adoption of general resolutions, while the passing of resolutions condemning a state for violating human rights fell within the remit of domestic jurisdiction under Article 2(7) of the Charter. Notwithstanding these and other sophisticated attempts to avoid undesirable developments, the seeds of the human rights doctrine had been sown. In the 1990s, this doctrine was embedded enough in the 'conscience' of the international community to allow the notion of individual criminal responsibility for large-scale violations of human rights to flourish. The Rome negotiations for the ICCSt and the adoption of Articles 6 and 7 of this Statute (on genocide and crimes against humanity) are the finish line of a process that started and developed, with some stops (for crimes against humanity), entirely at the international level.

3. The Uncertain Status of the Crimes of Aggression, Torture and Terrorism

Notwithstanding Nuremberg and Tokyo, it does not seem that international law rules on the criminalization of aggression have evolved. Undoubtedly, aggression constitutes a very serious international wrong. However, the chance that a rule of international law will provide for the criminalization of acts of aggression seems seriously undermined by the alleged connection between aggression as a crime and aggression as a serious wrongful act of state. For, on the one side, the profound legal uncertainties surrounding the definition of aggression as a wrongful act of state will inevitably have repercussions on the basic legal ingredients of aggression as a crime; on the other side, the strong defence of the prerogatives of the UN SC by some great powers collides with the very idea that a national or an international court may find the senior political or military leader of a particular state criminally responsible for acts of aggression.

As for torture as a discrete crime, as defined in the 1984 UN Convention against torture, some authoritative judicial decisions assert that its prohibition is also entrenched in customary international law.[9] The exact purport of this proposition is not entirely clear. If it means that the UN Convention definition of torture as a crime to be punished within national legal systems as an 'ordinary' offence (i.e., not different from other ordinary criminal offences committed by state officials in the exercise of their functions, such as embezzlement or graft is also customary in nature) one can perhaps agree. By contrast, if it means that there exists a customary international law rule that criminalizes torture as a crime *per se*, i.e., that under international law every single instance of torture, although episodic, entails the personal criminal responsibility of the perpetrator, then that view goes too far. Such a view would not only be unsupported by international practice. One would also fail to see the rationale behind the international criminalization of torture as a discrete crime, i.e., regardless of whether it is part of a state practice (and therefore punishable as a crime against humanity) or perpetrated in wartime against protected persons (hence constituting a war crime). Why should international law be concerned with single instances of criminal behaviour by a state official, especially if his state does not condone or tolerate such misconduct?

8 See in this regard the cases reported in A. Cassese, *International Criminal Law* (Oxford: Oxford University Press, 2003), at 88–89.

9 ICTY (IT-95-17/1), Trial Chamber II, *Furundžija*, 10 December 1988, para. 146. See also the decision of 24 March 1999 of the House of Lords in the *Pinochet* case, in *ILM* (1999), at 581.

Things are changing fast with regard to acts of so-called international terrorism. It is well known that until the tragic attacks of 11 September 2001, states were still conceiving these crimes as belonging to a very dangerous form of transnational criminality. They therefore adopted a series of international treaties to enhance their international cooperation for the repression of certain offences that, for one reason or another, could be classified as acts of terrorism. After 11 September, however, it was clear that some acts of terrorism can be so egregious and of such a magnitude that they can seriously jeopardize international peace and security. Moreover, the political goals of the terrorist groups connected to so-called Islamic terrorism are such that terrorist attacks are and may be planned worldwide. This has forced the UNSC and the General Assembly to consider terrorism as a threat to international peace and security, and to adopt a host of resolutions against it. In the meantime, some states have adopted new criminal legislation to contrast international terrorism and are intensively negotiating the text of a Comprehensive Convention against international terrorism. The contention can therefore be made that, in international law, there is a clear trend towards the criminalization of acts of terrorism that are committed outside a war context and select their victims at random in the territory of a state where no armed conflict is fought.[10]

4. The Relevance of the Notion of International Crimes

A. International Crimes Proper and Treaty-Based Crimes

Apart from the theoretical importance of the direct criminalization of some individual conducts at an international level, what are the practical consequences of such criminalization?

Before answering this question, it needs clarifying that individual conducts are criminalized in international law only by virtue of general rules that are directed at individuals. These general rules, which in international law can be either customary or based on general principles of law, may be applied by international or mixed criminal tribunals (to the extent that their statutes allow them to do so),[11] or by those national criminal courts that are empowered, within their own legal systems, directly to apply general international law in criminal matters. The criminalization of a given conduct through treaties, i.e., the fact that a certain number of states decide that that conduct is punishable as an international crime within their legal systems (or even by an international tribunal instituted by them), does not necessarily mean that one is faced with a international crime 'proper'. As I noted above, a crime can be held to be truly international only if it offends against the values that the international community aims to protect by means of criminal rules directed at individuals. An example can help clarify this point.

Let us imagine that some states enter into an international agreement which deems the use of nuclear weapons during an armed conflict a punishable offence amounting to a war crime. Let us also imagine that they set up an international tribunal vested with criminal jurisdiction over

---

10 The view according to which international terrorism in peacetime is already criminalized by international law has been forcefully put forward by A. Cassese, 'The Multifaceted Criminal Notion of Terrorism in International Law', 4 *JICJ* (2006), at 933.

11 This is not the case for the ICC. The ICC can exercise its jurisdiction only over the crimes listed in its statute and cannot rely upon customary international law to expand or limit its subject matter jurisdiction. This is made clear in Art. 22 ICCSt: 'A person shall not be criminally responsible under this Statute unless the conduct in question constitutes, at the time it takes place, a crime within the jurisdiction of the Court.' According to Art. 22(3), 'this article shall not affect the characterization of any conduct as criminal under international law independently of this Statute'.

such a crime. In this scenario, one can assert that the use of nuclear weapons is 'internationally criminalized' by the states party to the treaty in question; this criminalization, however, is not truly 'international' unless: (i) the prohibited conduct is also proscribed by a general rule of international law; and (ii) it is regarded by the international community as a whole as a conduct deserving to be criminally sanctioned, on account of the community values it breaches. If these two conditions are not met the use of nuclear weapons would have to be labelled a treaty-based crime, not an international crime proper. This would entail a few relevant consequences, as we will see below.

B. What the International Criminalization of Individuals' Conduct Entails for States in the Area of Criminal Law

States are free to criminalize within their legal orders whatever individual conduct they choose, and are also free to conclude treaties whereby they mutually agree that a conduct constitutes a crime. However, their power to *enforce* criminal prohibitions is not unfettered. This power encounters restrictions under international law. As the Permanent Court of International Justice (PCIJ) clearly stated in the well-known *Lotus* case, 'the first and foremost restriction imposed by international law upon a State is that – failing the existence of a permissive rule to the contrary – it may not exercise its power in any form in the territory of another State'.[12] In other words, the ambit of the so-called jurisdiction to enforce (that also comprises the so-called jurisdiction to adjudicate) is territorial, unless there exists a rule to the contrary. By contrast, the power of states to legislate (i.e., the so-called jurisdiction to prescribe) can extend to acts performed outside the territory of the state. However, as the PCIJ put it in *Lotus*, international law '[f]ar from laying down a general prohibition to the effect that States may not extend the application of their laws and the jurisdiction of their courts to persons, property and acts outside their territory, … leaves them a wide measure of discretion which is only limited in certain cases by prohibitive rules; as regards other cases, every State remains free to adopt the principles which it regards as best and most suitable'.[13]

What are the main prohibitive rules of international law that limit the freedom of states in this area? It can be maintained that for criminal offences that do not constitute international crimes proper, a clear prohibition stems from the principle of not interfering in internal affairs and the principle of respect for the sovereignty and independence of states. With regard to conduct abroad, and unless states consent to a permissive rule to the contrary in their mutual relationships, it is generally contended that a state may not assert its criminal jurisdiction unless the criminal act was performed by one of its nationals or against the interest of the state. Other grounds of extraterritorial jurisdiction are instead considered at odds with the two aforementioned principles. This is true not only for the so-called universality of jurisdiction, but also with regard to the passive nationality head of jurisdiction, whose application with regard to 'ordinary crimes' is strongly opposed by states of common law tradition.

Things are different with international crimes proper. On the one hand, they are unlikely to be prosecuted by states on the basis of the two undisputed titles of criminal jurisdiction (the territoriality principle and the active personality principle). These crimes – being an expression of a sort of 'state criminality' – are normally perpetrated with the acquiescence, tolerance or support of the authorities of the state on whose territory they are committed, or where they are committed by its officials.

---

12 PCIJ, *The Case of the S.S. Lotus*, in *Publications of the Permanent Court of International Justice*, Series A, No. 10, 2 ff., at 18. The judgement is also available at http://www.icj-cij.org/pcij/serie_A/A_10/30_Lotus_Arret.pdf (visited 20 August 2009).

13 Ibid., at 19.

Think of genocide, crimes against humanity or war crimes in internal armed conflict committed by a state, on its territory against its own population (as is always the case with war crimes in internal armed conflict, and as is often the case with genocide and crimes against humanity). The possibility of having these crimes prosecuted by national authorities depends on a change of government and on the lack of amnesty laws or other legal impediments. As for war crimes in international armed conflict, states seldom exercise their criminal jurisdiction over members of their armed forces who commit such crimes abroad, for they tend to 'protect' their own military personnel and deny they violated the rules of war.[14] As for war crimes committed by a belligerent on the territory of the enemy, the territoriality principle is more likely to apply, as evidenced by the war crimes trials held in France, the Netherlands and Italy after World War II. However, political reasons (above all, the need to restore peaceful relations after the war) can easily lead to the issuance of amnesties, or even to covering up past crimes (as occurred in Italy, with regard to the criminal prosecution of German alleged war criminals).[15] In such circumstances, reliance upon the principles of territoriality and active personality for the prosecution of international crimes by national courts is plainly not the best way to enforce the rule of law and throw out impunity.

This helps to explain why, alongside general rules criminalizing international offences, a customary rule allowing states to exercise extraterritorial (prescriptive) jurisdiction to repress such crimes has also emerged. In addition to contemplating the active personality principle, customary international law not only does not prohibit, but clearly permits states to assert their criminal jurisdiction over international crimes on the basis of the passive personality principle and, according to most commentators, also on the basis of the universality principle. This development has a clear theoretical foundation: the principles of non-interference in internal affairs of other states and

14 The criminal trials conducted in Germany, by the Supreme Court of Leipzig (*Reichsgericht*), in the aftermath of WWI constitute the first notable exception. By virtue of a Law of 18 December 1919, this Court was given jurisdiction over war crimes committed by German nationals during the war. It was a 'political' manoeuvre to show France and Great Britain that the application of Art. 228 of the Versailles Treaty (quoted *supra* note 5) was unnecessary, since Germany had already adopted the necessary internal measures to punish its war criminals. As is well known, this manoeuvre proved to be successful and Art. 228 was never applied. Germany was authorized to try 45 individuals out of the long list of suspected war criminals prepared by the Allied Commission for War Crimes; however, in the end, the Court of Leipzig tried only 16, all of them low-ranking state officials. See C. Lombois, *Droit pénal international* (2nd edn, Paris: Dalloz, 1979), at 132–135. Other exceptions are the trials for war crimes conducted in Germany after World War II (It seems that, up to 1996, more than 9,000 individuals have been tried, and around 6,500 were found guilty: see A. Marschik, 'The Politics of Persecution: European National Approaches to War Crimes', in T.H.L. McCormack and G.J. Simpson, *The Law of War Crimes: National and International Approaches* (The Hague: Kluwer Law International, 1997), 74–76; and the trials by the US court martials for war crimes committed in the Philippines (see G. Mettraux, 'US Courts-Martial and the Armed Conflict in the Philippines (1899–1902): Their Contribution to National Case Law on War Crimes', in 1 *JICJ* (2003), 135) and for war crimes in Vietnam, see, for instance, the well-known *Calley* case: for references, A. Cassese, *Violence and Law in the Modern Age* (Oxford: Polity Press, 1988), at 105–106 and 137–139).

15 Towards the end of the 1960s, thousands of dossiers concerning war crimes allegedly committed by the Germans in Italy were covered up, both to allow the re-establishment of peaceful a relationship with Germany in view of its participation in the North Atlantic Treaty, and because the Italian requests to try German alleged war criminals were at odds with the refusal by the Italian government to accept similar requests made by Yugoslavia with regard to war crimes allegedly committed by Italians in this country. See F. Focardi, 'La questione della punizione dei criminali di guerra in Italia dopo la fine del Secondo conflitto mondiale', 80 *Quellen und Forschungen aus italienischen Archiven und Bibliotheken* (Bollettino dell'Istituto italo-germanico di Roma) (2000), at 543.

of respect for their sovereignty and independence cannot have any bearing on the prosecution of conducts that the whole international community regards as deserving criminal sanctioning. It is one thing to extend the applicability of one's own national criminal law to ordinary crimes committed abroad (for instance, to assert criminal jurisdiction over theft, armed robbery, drug-dealing or any other conduct criminalized by the national legal system if committed abroad), it is quite another to prosecute someone who is accused of a crime under international law (such as genocide, crimes against humanity or war crimes), whatever the *locus commissi delicti* or the nationality of the alleged perpetrator. Clearly, in the latter case national courts simply enforce international prohibitions directed at individuals. This also holds true where national courts, not being empowered by their national legal systems to apply customary international law in criminal matters, apply their own national criminal law implementing international prohibitions. In sum, in the field of international crimes, general international law authorizes the exercise of extraterritorial jurisdiction beyond the limits that apply with regard to 'national' offences.

The second prohibitive rule of international law that restricts states' freedom in criminal matters rests on the doctrine of immunity *ratione materiae*. Under this doctrine, a state may not call before its own courts foreign state officials for acts performed in the exercise of their duties. This doctrine, which can apply – to a certain extent – to ordinary national crimes,[16] does not affect the prosecution of international crimes proper; clearly, the irrelevance of the official capacity is the necessary postulate of the entire edifice of personal criminal liability under international law. Indeed, the whole system of international criminal accountability mainly addresses crimes perpetrated by state officials in the exercise of their official functions or by others but with their support, tolerance or at least acquiescence. Leaving aside a contrary *obiter dictum* of the ICJ in the *Arrest Warrant* case,[17] it would seem that the inapplicability of the doctrine of immunity *ratione materiae* also takes into account former senior state officials, such as former heads of state or government, or former ministers of foreign affairs. To hold the contrary view would lead to preposterous results: national judges would be authorized to prosecute and punish the physical perpetrators of international crimes, while the most responsible persons would be sheltered from criminal responsibility forever because they acted in their official capacity. The absurdity of this outcome is all the more evident if one considers that, had these persons not wielded power, perhaps the crimes perpetrated under their authority would not have been committed![18]

Another consequence follows from the 'truly' international criminalization of individual conduct. It concerns the possibility for states to freely decide upon the applicability of the defence of obedience to orders. It is common knowledge that national criminal systems normally provide that – for crimes committed by subordinates who are legally bound to obey orders of their superiors and may not challenge the lawfulness of such orders – the defence of superior orders may be successfully raised within certain limits. However, for international crimes this possibility is precluded by a rule of customary international law. The reason is self-evident: since these crimes are normally perpetrated in the context of state criminality (i.e., they are ordered, tolerated or condoned by the supreme authorities of the state), to admit the possibility of successfully pleading this defence would amount to saying that only the supreme authorities of the state bear criminal responsibility. Here the result would be as preposterous as to contend that the doctrine of immunity

16 As for criminal conducts perpetrated on the territory of a state, this doctrine seems to apply only if the foreign state official was duly authorized to exercise its mandate by the territorial state and in relation to crimes perpetrated in the exercise of the official function.

17 ICJ, Judgment of 14 February 2002, para. 60.

18 See in this respect the apposite remarks of A. Cassese, 'When May Senior State Officials Be Tried for International Crimes? Some Comments on the *Congo v. Belgium Case*', 13 *EJIL* (2002), at 853.

ratione materiae protects senior state officials while it does not apply to low-ranking state agents: the perpetrators of abhorrent crimes could escape justice by simply pleading that they had merely obeyed orders!

A third consequence pertains to the superior responsibility. A rule of customary international law provides for the possibility to call to account military superiors for failing to prevent and repress crimes committed by their subordinates, and also for dereliction of their supervisory duties when they had information that crimes were about to be committed by their subordinates and failed to prevent them. Together with the rule establishing the irrelevance of acting in an official capacity and the rule establishing the unavailability of the defence of superior orders, the so-called doctrine of command responsibility ensures that state officials, at whatever level, can be held responsible for the system of state criminality they contributed to putting in place.

C. The Inconsistency of Some Traditional Legal Constructs with the International Criminalization of Individuals' Conduct

While the notion of personal criminal responsibility for international crimes has affirmed itself with the consequences outlined so far, this innovative notion still has to display all its potentialities in other traditional areas of international law.

One of them is the doctrine of foreign state immunity: while in criminal matters individuals who have committed an international crime in the exercise of their official functions may not claim immunity *ratione materiae* to evade justice, there still exists a trend in national case law to recognize immunity from national jurisdiction when victims of international crimes bring claims for compensation against a foreign state.[19] Here one fails to understand, from a theoretical point of view, why one can admit the possibility that a foreign state official can be tried before a national court for the conduct he performed in his official capacity, and at the same time contend that the state to which that official belongs may not be sued for compensation in relation to the illegal conduct of its organs, because it enjoys immunity from jurisdiction.[20]

In addition, it is worrying to see that in a recent case the ECHR held, in *Marković*, that the victims of the alleged unlawful bombing by NATO forces on the Serbian Radio-Television station in 1999 had no right to claim individual compensation since the combat rules embodied in Protocol Additional to the Geneva Conventions of 12 August 1949, and relating to the Protection of Victims of International Armed Conflicts (Protocol I), 8 June 1977 (AP I) only regulate relations between states and cannot therefore provide the foundation for such a claim. This statement is blatantly at odds with the notion that under international law individuals are responsible for serious violations of the laws of warfare, as is the case with the violations of the rules of AP I that are also customary in nature. How is it possible to assert that, under international law, individuals are criminally

19 See the Judgment of the ECHR in *Al-Adsani*, of 21 November 2001. Although the case concerned claims for compensation against the Sheikh and the Government of Kuwait in respect of acts of torture, the Court took a stand that is open to debate when it states that, although 'the prohibition of torture has achieved the status of a peremptory norm in international law … the present case does not concern … the criminal liability of an individual for alleged acts of torture, but the immunity of a State in civil suit for damages in respect of acts of torture within the territory of that State. Notwithstanding the special character of the prohibition of torture in international law, the Court is unable to discern in the international instruments, judicial authorities or other materials before it any firm basis for concluding that, as a matter of international law, a State no longer enjoys immunity from civil suit in the court of another State where acts of torture are alleged' (para. 61).

20 See on this issue Cassese, *Int. Crim. Law*, at 105–108.

accountable for breaching the rules on the conduct of warfare and contend, at the same time, that the victims of those breaches have no right to seek compensation, because of the exclusive interstate nature of such rules?

5. Conclusion

As is clear from the last two examples, international law still has to come to terms with some basic contradictions that have emerged from the process of international criminalization of individual conduct. Unfortunately this process – it would seem – will take a long time.

Chapter 9

Concurrent Jurisdictions between Primacy and Complementarity

Flavia Lattanzi

1. Introduction

The international community has long been aware that international peace may not be attained till the coexistence at the national level is disrupted by heinous crimes committed systematically and on large scale, with the direct involvement or complicity of individuals holding high positions in state apparatus, including that of those managing international relations.

Consequently, the repression of such crimes is of concern to the international community, in particular to states more involved in pursuing international peace and security, in spite of the uninterestedness or even opposition of police states, not concerned at all about the well-being of their people.

Until the end of WWI, the international community considered that the repression of these crimes could be left in the hands of states' jurisdictions. It is unquestionable that states represent the 'natural' context where the punitive function can be better allocated, since they are the only entities holding the coercive power instrumental to public and legitimate administration of justice. Moreover, 'national institutions are in the best position to do justice, for they normally constitute *forum conveniens*, where both the evidence and the alleged culprit are to be found'.[1]

Consequently, the repression of war crimes – the oldest crimes among the core crimes of international concern – was for long time left to the enemy state in time of war, according to the principle of reciprocity and the practice of blanket amnesties under peace treaties. At the international level, it was only a question of international responsibility of states for war, which was punished by the annexation of territories by the victorious state to the detriment of the vanquished state.

The practice of amnesties for war crimes came to a turning point at the end of WWI, as the Versailles Treaty acknowledged the international responsibility of individuals having committed those crimes as well as the crime of aggression, and provided different means for punishing them. But, the special tribunal envisaged for prosecuting the Head of the German Empire – a joint repressive body of the victorious Allied and Associated Powers – did not eventually come into existence. As provided by Article 228, the other German war criminals were to be brought before military tribunals of the victors, 'notwithstanding any proceedings or prosecution before a tribunal in Germany or in the territory of her allies', thus explicitly excluding the applicability of *ne bis in idem*. By such a provision, the Versailles Treaty intended to confer to the victorious Powers

1 A. Cassese, 'The Statute of the International Criminal Court: Some Preliminary Reflections', 10 (1) *European Journal of International Law*, 1999, 158 ff.

an exclusive jurisdiction on war crimes, thus imposing their primacy over the jurisdictions of Germany and its allies.[2]

The reality of the international community is always far from the ambitious claims of certain states, in particular those of victors. Germany did not cooperate in handing over the suspects 'to the Allied and Associated Powers, or to such one of them as shall so request', as provided by the Versailles Treaty. Rather, through a subsequent agreement, in 1920, it obtained the recognition of its right to try these persons. This agreement was a natural consequence of concurrent national jurisdictions and, at the same time, of the difficulty or even impossibility of prosecuting criminals without the cooperation of the state where the crimes were committed or the authors were detained. It recognized, in fact, a certain priority to the jurisdiction of the state of nationality of the alleged perpetrators.

The Allied and Associated Powers reserved their right to try the suspect criminals before their jurisdictions if not satisfied with the justice administered in German courts. This was the first formulation at the international level of the principle of complementarity in interstate relations. Out of the original list of 901 suspects prepared by the victors, only 45 suspects were indicted and 20 among them stood trial, while only 13 were convicted of lenient sentences ranging from six months to four years. Among all the criminals sentenced in Germany, whether or not prosecuted based on such list, some were released before having served the sentence and several escaped from prison and were also publicly congratulated for that. Yet, national courts of the Allied and Associated Powers did not 'complement' the German courts. This weakness was one of the root causes of WWII and of its horrors.

After WWII the situation was different. Not only did the Allied Forces succeed in creating two joint military Tribunals for the prosecution of major war criminals of Axis Powers, but they continued operations after the war with the joint military occupation of Germany and, for a shorter time, of Japan and other vanquished or liberated countries. These two factors allowed the declaration that 'nothing in this Agreement shall prejudice the provisions established by the Moscow Declaration concerning the return of war criminals to the countries where they committed their crimes'[3] 'in order that they may be judged and punished according to the laws of these liberated countries and of free governments which will be erected therein'.[4] It was also provided that 'nothing in this Agreement shall prejudice the jurisdiction or the powers of any national or occupation Court established or to be established in any allied territory or in Germany for the trial of war criminals'.[5] This means that the joint Tribunals, the national jurisdictions of the victorious and occupying Powers and those of the liberated countries which had chosen a free government were in concurrent relations, with priority for the territorial jurisdictions.

Furthermore, the Statute of the Nuremberg Tribunal annexed to London Agreement – which provided also for the criminalization of a group or organization – stated that 'any person convicted by the Tribunal may be charged before a national, military or occupation Court ... with a crime other than of membership in a criminal group or organization and such Court may, after convicting him, impose upon him punishment independent of and additional to the punishment imposed by the Tribunal for participation in the criminal activities of such group or organization'. So,

2 A historical perspective on the relationship between national and international criminal jurisdictions in P. Benvenuti, 'Complementarity of the International Criminal Court to National Criminal Jurisdictions', in F. Lattanzi and W. A. Schabas (eds), *Essays on the Rome Statute of the International Criminal Court* (L'Aquila: Il Sirente, 1999), 21 ff.

3 Art. 4 London Agreement, 8 August 1945 (hereinafter, London Agreement).

4 Statement on Atrocities, Moscow Conference, 30 October 1943, para. 3.

5 Art. 6 London Agreement.

implicitly, it partially acknowledged the principle of *ne bis in idem*, eliminating a possible conflict of jurisdictions and judgments.

Unfortunately, the majority of states disregarded their duty to prosecute the perpetrators of Nazi-fascist crimes. So, numerous Axis crimes remained unpunished (Italy is still dealing with this problem), as well as, according to the logic of victors' justice, some crimes committed by the Allied Forces and rebel entities having courageously fought for the liberation of their countries. Such indifference continued in respect of war crimes committed during the few international and the numerous internal conflicts of the Cold War period. This negative approach to the duty to end impunity was generalized among the countries of both sides of the 'divided' world, in spite of the adoption in 1948 of the Genocide Convention and of the four 1949 Geneva Conventions on international humanitarian law.

The Genocide Convention places the obligation to suppress the crime of genocide only on the territorial state, although it might have not taken any step – especially when directly or indirectly implicated in the commission of genocide through its agents – to prevent and punish perpetrators thereof. But, this very naïve provision can be understood in the light of the further conventional provision envisaging the institution and competence of an international criminal court. Yet, during the Cold War this old dream of the international community appeared impracticable. Thus, the delegations of states at the Geneva Conference, prompted by the ICRC, considered that a solution might have been found in imposing the responsibility to repress war crimes on all states, according to the principle of universal jurisdiction. They too optimistically believed that the concurrent jurisdictions of all States Parties (and very soon almost all states acceded to these conventions) could have solved the *impasse*.

However, international rules providing an obligation to prosecute and imposing jurisdictional criteria are not self-executing in domestic systems, as specific incorporation is needed for their application at national level. Yet even states whose legal systems are inspired by fundamental humanitarian values fail to implement the mandatory Geneva obligation on territorial jurisdiction, as well as on suppressing war crimes according to the jurisdictional links freely chosen in their own legislation. Consequently, instead of a positive conflict of jurisdictions among all States Parties, we are still dealing with negative conflicts of jurisdictions, except for the vain attempt made by a few states – e.g., Belgium and Spain – to apply universal jurisdiction.

The resulting feeling of dissatisfaction of some peace-loving states and of international civil society (NGOs) led to updating the project of an international criminal court which, however, was only possible after the 1989 fall of the Berlin Wall.

As a matter of fact, when the world was divided in two adverse blocks, the international community agreed to create international tribunals competent on interstates disputes, and to give the UN a limited governance in emergency situations for international peace and security. Domestic affairs in normal situations were left to domestic jurisdictions.[6] The divided international community agreed on some common values in the field of human rights, but only few states assumed at universal treaty level some limited obligations allowing individuals under their jurisdiction to claim before an international body in order to protect their own rights infringed by a state party. However, the assessment of alleged violations made by the Committee on human and civil rights is only contained in a report, rather than in a binding decision.[7]

6 Art. 2(7) UN Charter.

7 The Optional Protocol to the International Covenant on Civil and Political Rights entitles individuals to claim before the Human Rights Committee, provided that the individual is under the jurisdiction of a state having explicitly accepted the competence of the Committee.

Only at the regional level, in Europe and Latin America, did states accept the competence of an international court to make an assessment of human rights violations by a decision that is binding on 'accused' state.[8] Even so, such courts are only competent to interpret the conventional rules of the relevant international pact and ascertain any violations by parties thereto, as no competence was delegated to replace state organs in their relations either with the victims of the violations or with other state organs. Thus, these regional courts can not implement the reparations they decide or override national legislation considered not in conformity with conventional rules. States' organs maintain their prerogatives to remedy violations by national means – before the victim or another state party has resorted to the Court – so as to provide victims with reparations decided at international level and to conform the domestic system to international standards, if necessary. Again only at the regional level, in particular in Europe, states accepted certain limitations of their sovereign prerogatives by transferring some national competencies to supranational bodies, e.g., law-making in specific fields, interpreting the law, ordering the domestic organs to apply it directly or to conform the domestic legal system to it, rendering judicial decisions directly applicable to national public institutions and private entities. The subject matter competencies of the European bodies are continuously increasing, but there is a very limited supranational role in criminal matters, which essentially remains an issue of interstate cooperation, although a progressively enhanced one.

As a matter of fact, criminal law is still conceived by states as a matter of domestic jurisdiction, strictly linked with sovereign choices made to protect national interests. The dogma of sovereignty is particularly strong in this field as administration of justice is an original prerogative of states and not a right conferred by international law. The statement of the Permanent Court of International Justice (PCIJ) is still appropriate for illustrating this status: 'international law does not prohibit a state from exercising jurisdiction in its own territory in respect of any case which relates to acts which have taken place abroad, and in which it cannot rely on some permissive rule of international law. All that can be required of a state is that it should not overstep the limits which international law places upon its jurisdiction; within these limits its title to exercise jurisdiction rests in its sovereignty.'[9] Such a limit might be represented, for instance, by the official position of the accused, internationally acknowledged as barring a foreign criminal jurisdiction. Unfortunately, this limit was considered by the International Court of Justice (ICJ) as applicable even with respect to core crimes of international concern,[10] though in absence of a different specific treaty provision. The PCIJ statement means that international customary law does not play a role in the allocation among states of their respective competencies to administer justice, nor does it prohibit a state from exercising this sovereign prerogative on infractions committed abroad; it is silent on this because it is not able to organize the exercise of sovereign domestic prerogatives, which is to some extent possible through an international agreement.

Even if we follow the different assumption that a state would be limited by general international law in choosing criminal jurisdictional criteria, such a limitation might not affect the interest and discretion of a state to exercise its jurisdiction with respect to core crimes of international concern, even by choosing the universal criterion. Precisely because of this interest, some international agreements impose on states parties the exercise of their criminal jurisdiction with respect to

8 Indeed, the European Court of Human Rights and the Inter-American Court on Human Rights are competent to assess the violations of the respective Conventions on Human Rights upon claims either by an individual under the jurisdiction of a State Party having accepted the competence of the Court or by a State Party.

9 PCIJ, Judgement No. 9, The Case of S.S. 'Lotus', 7 September 1927, *Publications*, Series A, No. 10, at 19.

10 ICJ, Judgement, *Congo v. Belgium* (*Yerodia* case), 14 February 2002.

some of these crimes according to relevant jurisdictional links, including the universal one, which automatically results in a concurrence between states' jurisdictions.

States are used to assuming obligations with respect to ordinary offences, in particular when a transnational element is present, by means of international multilateral and bilateral agreements on assistance in criminal matters. Such treaties give some responses to the issue of concurrence between national jurisdictions through the principle of *ne bis in idem* and/or *aut iudicare aut dedere*, which are the norms as regards treaty-based crimes[11] and core crimes of international concern. These principles might not solve all the problems of concurrence between national jurisdictions (horizontal concurrence) and much less when an international jurisdiction is implicated (vertical concurrence). Indeed, starting from 1993 and in the context of the present analysis, international instruments have created some supranational criminal bodies charged with the task of 'supplementing' state organs in the exercise of their punitive powers in respect to the most serious crimes of concern to the international community.

The UN Security Council, by its decisions establishing the two *ad hoc* international criminal Tribunals – ICTY and ICTR – authoritatively imposed some limitations on states' punitive powers in this respect, although with some differences under the two Statutes. Agreements between the UN and a state on whose territory core crimes have been committed have also provided for the obligation of the territorial state to vest an internal/international hybrid tribunal with jurisdiction.[12] Furthermore, by ratifying the Rome Statute a state freely accepted – on the condition of their acceptance by the other 59 states – even broader limitations on sovereign prerogatives, transferring to the ICC their sovereign power to administrate justice on core crimes. Had this transfer been final – that is to the exclusive jurisdiction of the Court, without complementarity[13] – every problem of concurrence of jurisdictions, whether horizontal or vertical, would have been solved at least vis-à-vis States Parties. The deference paid to state sovereignty leaves open the concurrence between jurisdictions, even the actual possibility of a conflict of jurisdictions.

Given the silence of international customary law in this matter, some solutions as to the relations between national and international jurisdictions might be found only in the specific statutory rules of international (and 'hybrid') criminal tribunals, read in the light both of the original sovereign prerogative of every state to exercise its punitive powers and in the spirit and purpose of the specific Statute. As a general, overall guidance in the present analysis it will be assumed that – if every state is entitled, if not obliged, to exercise its jurisdiction with respect at least to core crimes of international concern – no state is entitled to assert its exclusive exercise of jurisdiction for the investigation and prosecution of such offences.

For reasons of good administration of justice, however, it might still be more convenient for a state rather than for another to exercise sovereign jurisdiction with respect to any specific crime and accused. In particular, territorial, national or custodial states would be 'closer' to the crime, as it would be easier to collect evidence and to administer fair and efficient justice there. If international law does not provide a criterion for selection, the issue has to be solved on a case-by-case basis. Thus, in theory, concurrence would be automatic between different national jurisdictions or between them and international tribunals.

---

11 On this notion see R. Bellelli, 'The Establishment of a System of International Criminal Justice', Chapter 1 in this Volume, at 4(B)(1) (The System).

12 On the notion of hybrid tribunal, ibid, at 3(C).

13 The exclusive jurisdiction of ICC, according to the universality criterion, was proposed during the preparatory works of the Statute for genocide, but the large majority of States opposed it. On the principle of complementarity, see also R. Bellelli, The System, *supra* note 11, at 4 (E)(4) and *passim*.

As a matter of fact, the Statutes of the two *ad hoc* Tribunals, as well of 'hybrid' criminal tribunals and the ICC do not deal directly with jurisdictional criteria applicable by states in their legal systems. They only presume or reiterate in their respective Preambles the obligation of states to suppress crimes by their domestic means, which is considered as an obligation under general international law, irrespective of jurisdictional criteria to be applied. The Statutes only regulate the jurisdiction *ratione materiae*, *ratione personae* and *temporis* of the relevant tribunal, as well as general relations with domestic criminal jurisdictions, in some instances also dealing with the *ratione loci* jurisdiction (ICTY and ICTR). Thus, both the principles of concurrent jurisdiction and primacy under the ICTY and ICTR Statutes, as well the principle of complementarity under the ICC Statute, leave open the possibility of a conflict of jurisdictions.

All these considerations are relevant to a correct understanding of the actual role of the ICC in its relations with national jurisdictions, as it appears in the light of the principle of complementarity and in comparison with the different roles assigned to ICTY and ICTR.

2. Concurrence and Primacy of UN *Ad Hoc* Tribunals

Article 9(1) ICTYSt provides that the Tribunal and national courts 'shall have concurrent jurisdiction to prosecute persons for serious violations of international humanitarian law committed in the territory of the former Yugoslavia since 1 January 1991'. Article 8(1) ICTRSt has, *mutatis mutandis*, the same content: this Tribunal and national Courts 'shall have concurrent jurisdiction to prosecute persons for serious violations of international humanitarian law committed in the territory of Rwanda and Rwandan citizens for such violations committed in the territories of neighbouring states, between 1 January 1994 and 31 December 1994'.

Under the same Articles, in paragraphs 2, both Statutes provide that 'the International Tribunal shall have the primacy over national Courts' ('over the national Courts of all States', in ICTRSt). As an application of the primacy, the Statute points out that 'at any stage of the procedure, the International Tribunal may formally request national Courts to defer to the competence of the International Tribunal'. The primacy of the two *ad hoc* international Tribunals also results from the identical wording of Article 10 ICTYSt and Article 9 ICTRSt, which prohibits double jeopardy (*ne bis in idem* principle): 'no person shall be tried before a national Court for acts constituting serious violations of international humanitarian law under the present Statute, for which he or she has already been tried by the International Tribunal.' Paragraph 2 of those same Articles limits the prohibition of double jeopardy, adding that a person who has been tried by a national court for acts constituting serious violations of international humanitarian law may be subsequently tried by the international tribunal only if: '(a) the act for which he or she was tried was characterized as an ordinary crime; or (b) the national Court proceedings were not impartial or independent, were designed to shield the accused from international criminal responsibility, or the case was not diligently prosecuted.' This means that the *ne bis in idem* principle plays only in one direction: to the detriment of national jurisdictions and in favour of the international one. The decision of national jurisdictions with respect to the international one are considered in paragraph 3 only with respect to the conviction of a person for a crime under the Statute: 'the International Tribunal shall take into account the extent to which any penalty imposed by a national Court on the same person for the same act has already been served.'

Pursuant to Rule 9(iii) ICTY Rules of Procedure and Evidence (RPE), the Prosecutor may propose a formal request for deferral when the case under scrutiny of any national court 'is closely related to, or otherwise involves, significant factual or legal questions which may have implications for investigations or prosecutions before the Tribunal'. The content of the similar Rule 9 ICTR RPE is more detailed, though also more restrictive:

> Where it appears to the Prosecutor that crimes which are the object of investigations or criminal proceedings instituted in the Courts of any State:
>
> (i) are subject to an investigation by the Prosecutor;
>
> (ii) should be the subject of an investigation by the Prosecutor considering, *inter alia*: a) the seriousness of the offences; b) the status of the accused at the time of the alleged offences; c) the general importance of the legal questions involved in the case;
>
> (iii) are the subject of an indictment in the Tribunal, the Prosecutor may request the Trial Chamber designated by the President to issue a formal request that such Court defer to the competence of the Tribunal.

It could be argued that, by virtue of the authoritative source of the two Statutes – UN Charter Chapter VII coercive powers of Security Council – the aforementioned statutory provisions should enjoy direct applicability in domestic legal systems. However, national systems generally consider that – for the provisions of the Statute to have legal force – implementing legislation is needed, thus refusing an exception to the traditional concept of an international legal system based on the sovereignty of states and on a clear distinction between the international and the national legal orders.[14] Consequently, the principle of primacy receives no direct enforcement either.[15] It is for states to render primacy effective, by taking any measure necessary under their domestic law when an international court formally requests national courts to defer a case and by applying the *ne bis in*

14 The duty to conform the domestic jurisdiction to the statutory rules is envisaged in SC Res. 827(1993), para. 4. Even the ICTY, in the Decision in *Tadic* excluded the direct applicability of the principle of the primacy posed by Article 9(2) ICTYSt. In fact, the Chamber in rejecting the arguments of the defence in alleging the violation of both the German and the Bosnian sovereignty did not rely directly on Art. 9 ICTYSt, but on the specific consent expressed by states involved at the different stages of proceedings (the territorial state and the detaining state) and on their cooperation on the transfer of the dossier and of the accused. The Chamber did not refer to Bosnian or German legislation.

15 This approach is affirmed by the content of some national laws implementing the ICTY and ICTR Statutes. Some of these laws, by providing for the possibility of a national judge to challenge the jurisdiction of the International Tribunal, refuse to acknowledge the direct primacy of the Tribunal. The Italian law implementing ICTY Statute, for instance, provides for the transfer of criminal proceedings at the request of the Tribunal, but only if some conditions are satisfied: a) the International Tribunal must proceed with respect to the same facts as the Italian judge is proceeding; b) the fact must fall within the territorial and temporal jurisdiction of the International Tribunal. Similar provisions are also included in the German (para. 2(3)), Dutch (s. 4(3)) and French (Art. 4) implementing laws. The Spanish law seems to comply, *prima facie*, with the principle of primacy; actually, it states that national tribunals have jurisdiction over a case under the international jurisdiction only if the Tribunal doesn't forbid it. But it also provides that the prohibitory order can be rejected by the High National Court when the crime doesn't fall within the competence *ratione temporis* or *ratione loci* of the International Tribunal. All these laws conflict with the principle *kompetenz-kompetenz*, universally recognized at international level. On the other hand, the Bosnian implementing law does not provide for a procedure to verify the condition for the deferral, being so fully in line with Art. 9. The Danish (Arts 1–3), Swedish (s. 13), Norwegian (s. 5) and Finnish laws have the same approach.

idem principle.[16] The only possible way for the *ad hoc* Tribunals to coercively impose the primacy of their own decisions is to ask an intervention by the Security Council through the enforcement measures that it may adopt pursuant to Chapter VII of the UN Charter.

The swift establishment of the *ad hoc* Tribunals was the consequence of the inability of the states involved in the conflicts to suppress the crimes which were being committed in Rwanda and in the former Yugoslavia, and the fact that they were totally incapable of restoring peace. Pursuant to the Completion Strategy decided by the Security Council for the two *ad hoc* Tribunals, the investigations were terminated at the end of 2004 and the activities of the two Tribunals should close at the end of 2010 (but a further extension will be needed). Thus, not all persons accused at ICTY and ICTR will be tried before the international jurisdictions. The temporary nature of the two Tribunals – inherent to the SC-established purpose and to their mandate – and the consequent completion strategy decision led to the adoption of a common Rule 11*bis* RPE (with some differences between the two Statutes). This Rule allows, on certain conditions, the transfer of an accused, and their dossier, by the Tribunal to national jurisdictions available to prosecute. Thus, it could be argued that these Tribunals now accept the principle of complementarity, though always in the rationale of the primacy of the international jurisdiction vis-à-vis the national ones (and not priority of these latter ones). Indeed, the transfer decision remains under the full unilateral judicial control of the Tribunal, without a dialectic approach to the state that is claiming the transfer or that is simply available – upon request by the Prosecutor or the defence – to receive the accused and prosecute him. It is interesting to note that, in the application of Rule 11*bis*, the Tribunals do not exclude the possibility of a transfer to a state only endowed, in respect of the crime charged in the indictment, with a universal criterion of jurisdiction. Such an open approach is implicit in the ICTR decision refusing the transfer to Norway of an accused of genocide.[17] The reasoning was that the Norwegian legal system does not include any jurisdictional criterion for genocide, and not that the crime under the specific indictment was not linked to it, from the point of view of the territoriality or nationality criteria (and it was not linked at all, given that the accused was in the custody of ICTR).

3. Complementarity in Preparatory Works of the ICC Statute

International society is indeed still organized in a horizontal rather than vertical structure, even though it is based on some common fundamental values, which justifies the expression 'international community'. International law-making may not disregard this reality and the Rome Diplomatic Conference did not. States, with their sovereign attributions, have been the first element to take into account in setting out the conditions for the Court to exercise its jurisdiction.

The principle of complementarity, as a key element of the jurisdiction of the Court, had been inserted in the different drafts of the statute prepared either by the Commission of International Law (Geneva, 1994) or the *ad hoc* Committee (New York, 1995) or the Preparatory Committee (New York, 1996–1998). The principle was never seriously questioned *per se*, either during these

16 F. Lattanzi, 'The Complementary Character of the Jurisdiction of the Court With Respect to National Jurisdictions', in F. Lattanzi (ed.), *The International Criminal Court, Comments on the Draft Statute* (Editoriale Scientifica: Napoli, 1998), at 4.

17 ICTR, Decision on the Prosecution Motion for Referral to the Kingdom of Norway, Trial Chamber III, 19 May 2006, and Decision on Rule 11*bis* Appeal, *Michel Bagaragaza*, Appeals Chamber, 30 August 2006.

works or the Rome Diplomatic Conference,[18] while the determination of complex concepts like 'unwillingness' and 'inability' – crucial to the application of the principle as conditions to be satisfied for allowing the Court to exercise its jurisdiction – were very carefully and thoroughly discussed. It was clear from these discussions that sensitive questions were involved in the relationship between the would-be Court and the states represented by their delegations at preparatory meetings and at the Conference.

A compromise was reached in the Preparatory Committee on the actual wording of Article 17. The subsequent 1998 Rome negotiations were very linear on this wording, with all states being fully in agreement on the 'complementary' role of the Court vis-à-vis their jurisdictions and on the concepts of 'unwillingness' and 'inability' defined in Article 17.

However, at the Rome Conference – an environment more sensitive to the claims coming from states which, differently from what happened during the preparatory meetings, were represented by delegations composed not only of technicians – the United States' suggestion that a preliminary procedure on admissibility be added, received general consent and was thus approved under current Article 18. This preliminary procedure on admissibility takes place at the stage of the decision to open an investigation and represents a further obstacle for the Court to deal with crimes committed or being committed in a situation referred by a state or *proprio motu* under scrutiny of the Prosecutor. While the admissibility procedure was introduced to address 'a case', it is applicable to 'a situation' and, therefore, results in an enhancement: it is an enhancement of the Prosecutor's discretion to decide to open an investigation, and allows him to open a dialogue with states instead of opening an investigation. It is a further filter in deference to the sovereignty of states that, as it has been said, is a double key for opening the door of the Court to crimes under its competence. Thus, the likelihood of an inadmissibility outcome is increased vis-à-vis the previous Geneva and New York drafts.

4. Complementarity in the Preamble to the ICC Statute

The Preamble of the Statute makes it apparent that the Court has not been conceived as a criminal mechanism with an exclusive jurisdiction that automatically replaces state courts in prosecuting selected serious crimes. Its role is not even characterized as concurrent with domestic courts, as it is the case for ICTY and ICTR. If the *ad hoc* Tribunals enjoy a certain primacy with respect to national ones, the latter have a conditional priority in the exercise of their punitive powers with respect to the jurisdiction of the Court. The primary responsibility for punishing crimes lies with states. After all, according to general international law, all states are obliged to ensure the fundamental values of international concern in the exercise of their 'territorial' and 'personal' sovereignty. Only the correct exercise of sovereignty can exempt states from international responsibility for unlawful conducts: the establishment of an international criminal court does not release states from their positive and negative obligations as regards the prevention and suppression of crimes of international concern. This primary responsibility is clearly illustrated by the wording of the Preamble of the ICC Statute: 'the most serious crimes of concern to the international community must not go unpunished and ... their effective prosecution must be ensured by taking measures at the national level and by

18 On the debates in the Preparatory Committee and in Rome, see J.T. Holmes, 'The Principle of Complementarity', in R. Lee (ed.), *The International Criminal Court. The Making of the Rome Statute. Issues, Negotiations, Results* (Kluwer Law International: The Hague/London/Boston, 1999), at 45 ff.

enhancing international cooperation',[19] while 'it is a duty of every State to exercise its criminal jurisdiction over those responsible for international crimes'.[20]

The primary responsibility of states to suppress crimes of international concern finds a general manifestation, first of all, in the choice to provide the Court with a subject matter jurisdiction limited to core crimes and not extended to all crimes of international concern, as was proposed during the Statute's preparatory works. The Statute provides that the ICC is intended to exercise jurisdiction only over the most serious crimes of concern to the international community as a whole. The role played by national jurisdictions in this area appears also in the choice to leave with those jurisdictions the prosecution of underage persons: '[t]he Court shall have no jurisdiction over any person who was under the age of 18 at the time of the alleged commission of a crime.'[21]

It could be argued that the ICC is endowed with a 'substantial' exclusive jurisdiction vis-à-vis the major perpetrators, who enjoy international immunities for their official tasks. Given that ICJ also applies these immunities with respect to prosecutions for core crimes of international concern, in the absence of a specific treaty exception, the only possibility that those bearing the major responsibility do not go unpunished remains in the hands of ICC, whose Statute provides such an exception. Indeed Article 27(2) ICCSt reads: 'immunities or special procedural rules which may attach to the official capacity of a person, whether under national or international law, shall not bar the Court from exercising its jurisdiction over such a person'.

The principle of complementarity is enshrined in Preamble (10) ICCSt: 'the International Criminal Court ... shall be complementary to national criminal jurisdictions.' It is further reaffirmed in Article 1 that the ICC 'shall be a permanent institution and shall have the power to exercise its jurisdiction over persons for the most serious crimes of international concern ... and shall be complementary to national criminal jurisdictions'. However, what states wanted to achieve by devising such feature for the Court can be understood only from Articles 17, 18 and 19 ICCSt, which specify the content and regulate the applicable procedures for the principle to become operative at the investigative and trial stages.

The application of the principle of complementarity in the relations between the Court and national jurisdictions poses many interpretative problems with regard to several provisions in the Statute and the Rules. Only the most relevant issues will be dealt with in the following paragraphs.

5. Conditions of Admissibility

In application of the principle of complementarity under Preamble (10) and Article 1 ICCSt – to which Article 17 (Issues of admissibility) refers in the chapeau – the Court may not deal with a case before overcoming the admissibility issue, which is the first obstacle in its prosecutorial task. In reality, the issue is considered in Article 17 as one of inadmissibility rather than admissibility, unless certain conditions are satisfied; this is a typical approach aimed at putting the emphasis once again on the presumption of the priority of national jurisdictions.

Article 17(1) ICCSt establishes four conditions to be satisfied for a case to be admissible. The first two directly concern the question of unwillingness and inability:

19 Preamble (4) ICCSt.
20 Preamble (6) ICCSt.
21 Art. 26 ICCSt.

1. 'the case is being investigated or prosecuted by a State which has jurisdiction over it, but this State is unwilling or unable genuinely to carry out the investigation or the prosecution';[22]
2. the case 'has been investigated by a State which has jurisdiction over it and the State has decided not to prosecute the person concerned, but such decision resulted from the unwillingness or inability of the State genuinely to prosecute'.[23]

The third condition is posed with reference to the exception of the *ne bis in idem* principle provided in Article 20(3) ICCSt: a person who has been tried by a national court for a conduct constituting a crime of genocide, a crime against humanity or a war crime, shall be tried by the ICC with respect to the same conduct if the proceedings in the national Court: '(a) were for the purpose of shielding the person concerned from criminal responsibility for crimes within the jurisdiction of the Court', or '(b) otherwise were not conducted independently or impartially in accordance with the norms of due process recognized by international law and were conducted in a manner which, in the circumstances, was inconsistent with an intent to bring the person concerned to justice'.[24] Thus, these provisions on *ne bis in idem* entail some elements of the definition of unwillingness, including that of due process.

Even when a negative assessment of the willingness and ability of a national jurisdiction to prosecute has been made, the Court has still to ascertain whether 'the case is not of sufficient gravity to justify further action by the Court'.[25]

Some wording of Article 17(1), like 'genuinely',[26] 'the purpose of shielding', 'unjustified delay',[27] 'intent to bring to justice', remain too generic and ambiguous under the Statute without the clarification which might only be offered by the jurisprudence of the Court. Article 17 attempts to clarify the meaning of the terms 'unwillingness' and 'inability', but these concepts would also benefit from the Court's judicial interpretation. Until now, the Pre-Trial Chambers have not provided such clarifications as they only rule on the admissibility of a case in the context of decisions on arrest warrants, confirming decisions taken by the Prosecutor at different stages of his prosecutorial activity.

A. Unwillingness

Article 17(2) ICCSt provides that, in order to determine unwillingness in a particular case, the Court shall have 'regard to the principles of due process recognized by international law' (chapeau), and assess whether one or more of the following factors are present: (i) 'the proceedings were or are being undertaken or the national decision was made for the purpose of shielding the person concerned from criminal responsibility for crimes within the jurisdiction of the Court referred to in

22 Art. 17(1)(a) ICCSt.

23 Art. 17(1)(b) ICCSt.

24 Art. 17(1)(c) ICCSt.

25 Art. 17(1)(d) ICCSt.

26 'Genuinely' was preferred to other terms, such as 'effectively', 'diligently', 'in good faith', because it was apparently more objective.

27 This wording also is linked with the issue of state sovereignty, in particular with the need for a dialogue between the state and the Court. It was preferred to 'undue delay' as it implies the right of states to explain any delay before the Court determines that a case is admissible, while a Court assessment on undue delay could have occurred without any views expressed by the states concerned. See Holmes, *supra* note 18, at 54.

Article 5'; (ii) 'there has been an unjustified delay in the proceedings which in the circumstances is inconsistent with an intent to bring the person concerned to justice'; and (iii) 'the proceedings were not or are not being conducted independently or impartially, and they were or are being conducted in a manner which, in the circumstances, is inconsistent with an intent to bring the person concerned to justice'.

The focus of 'unwillingness' is on the intent not to bring to justice the person concerned, which is inconsistent with the aim pursued by establishing the Court, that is to end impunity. Therefore, in the light of this general objective, the willingness or unwillingness of a state to bring a suspect to justice is the first relevant element to be considered. In furtherance of this aim and in the context of admissibility procedures, according to the 'unwillingness' factor the core question for the Court is the following: did or does the state intend to shield the accused from his criminal responsibility or is it willing to bring him to justice?

Under Article 17(2) ICCSt the assessment of a state's willingness/unwillingness is to be carried out on the conduct of a specific judicial organ vis-à-vis the culpability of the accused. This means that in the willingness/unwillingness assessment there is no room for other considerations, except from the general point of view of the due process of law. Other issues, including fair trial and rights of the accused, are only relevant, under some conditions, in the context of assessing the state ability/inability to genuinely carry out the investigation or prosecution. The reference to principles of due process recognized by international law – that is the rule of law system inspired by international standards – adds some ambiguities as regards the relevance to be given to the functioning as a whole of the judicial system. According to the ICC's Prosecutor, 'the legal test [of admissibility] is specific to the cases selected for prosecution, and not the state of the Sudanese justice system as a whole'.[28] It seems that these views of the Prosecutor can be shared, to a limited extent, with regard to the stage of proceedings on cases, where indeed the willingness/unwillingness is certainly more a question of the conduct of the specific case by a specific domestic judicial organ. On the other hand, at the stage of a situation under scrutiny by the Prosecutor a judicial system enshrining 'the principles of due process recognized by international law' could represent a rebuttable presumption of willingness of a state, as a judicial system not generally respecting these principles might be presumed unwilling.

This appears to be the only clear reading of Article 17(2) chapeau because 'principles of due process of law' does not mean principles of fair trial.[29] In short, if the state system is not organized according to the due process principles, it is much easier for the Court to assess the admissibility of an investigation/prosecution because of the structural unwillingness of the state to bring to justice the perpetrators of crimes. This reading of the reference to due process of law as a general context relevant for the assessment of unwillingness obviously benefits 'ripe' democracies, as well as the contexts of inability; but this is what states wanted at the Rome Conference.

---

28 Address to the United Nations Security Council, New York, 13 December 2005.

29 See, on due process of law, the following judicial statement in a state where the concept originated: '[I]t is objected, that by Mag. Chart. c. 29, no man ought to be taken or imprisoned, but by the law of the land. But to this I answer, that lex terrae is not confined to the common law, but takes in all the other laws, which are in force in this realm; as the civil and canon law … By the 28 Ed. 3, c. 3, there the words lex terrae, which are used in Mag. Char. are explained by the words, due process of law; and the meaning of the statute is, that all commitments must be by a legal authority.' *Regina v. Paty*, 92 Eng. Rep. 232, 234 (1704) reprinted in *Reports of Cases Argued and Adjudged in the Courts of King's Bench and Common Pleas: In the Reigns of the Late King William, Queen Anne, King George the First, and King George the Second*, Volume 2, 1792, at 1105 and 1108.

B. Inability

Article 17(3) specifies that 'in order to determine inability in a particular case, the Court shall consider whether, due to a total or substantial collapse or unavailability of its national judicial system, the state is unable to obtain the accused or the necessary evidence and testimony or otherwise unable to carry out its proceedings'. This assessment is more complex than the willingness/unwillingness since the definition of inability under Article 17(3) ICCSt is more ambiguous in its wording and numerous elements have to be interpreted. Likewise, the definition of unwillingness refers to the due process of law context, Article 17(3) indicates, first, some general contexts (causes) of inability and then the different forms of inability.

1. Causes of Inability

Inability, in its different forms, is not conceived in Article 17(3) as an absolute factor of admissibility which the Court could consider *in abstracto*, to screen the degree of 'ability' of any judicial system. It is assumed instead as related to specific judicial systems, the 'critical' systems, to which the scrutiny appears to have been reserved. Indeed, the assessment of a state's ability to investigate or prosecute has to be made only 'due to the total or substantial collapse or unavailability of a judicial system'. This means that the Court cannot confine its evaluation to the different forms of inability indicated in the last wording of the provision without at the same time assessing the judicial system as totally or substantially collapsed or unavailable. The concrete inability 'to obtain the accused or the necessary evidence and testimony or otherwise ... to carry out its proceeding' appears as a consequence of one of these factors rather than as the main factor of admissibility. This approach represents a further manifestation of the deference given to state sovereignty, but only for states whose judicial systems appear to be sound and available.

Moreover, even if the definition of inability is focused on contexts where there is a more or less serious weakness of the judicial system and not of the state system as such, a judicial system cannot be scrutinized separately from other branches of a state system. The judicial system applies and interprets the existing domestic law, as well the internal law implementing the international rules: the judicial system is the mirror of the state system. Thus, in the context of the assessment of ability/inability, the overall system could well come under scrutiny by the Court.

The difficulty the Court faces in evaluating a judicial system according to the qualification of its total or substantial collapse or unavailability is also caused by the lack of details in the Statute. While the total collapse could be considered more 'factual' and thus easier to determine, the substantial collapse might appear more 'legal', subject to a more complex interpretation.

To some extent, it will be easier for the Court to assess the total collapse of a judicial system when the entire state organization is totally collapsing, as is the case for many countries raged by internal conflicts. This is a factual situation, often ascertained by the UN Security Council pursuant to Chapter VII, where many events show clearly that the judicial system is one among the most important branches of the state apparatus to collapse. But a total collapse of the judicial system can also easily be assessed in situations of a judiciary being under the threat of powerful criminal organizations, as is the case in some countries, where the state apparatus does not appear to collapse but can stand only with the complicity of these criminal organizations.

The qualification as substantial collapse represents a compromise with respect to the first proposal tabled in Rome, that of a 'partial' collapse,[30] raising the threshold of the inability context, again in favour of states' jurisdictions. Even in a strong state apparatus the judicial system might be considered as substantially collapsed, as would be the case in a police state where the judiciary is not independent from the political power – formally it works, but substantially it is a fake judicial system.

In any case, the reference to a total or substantial collapse of a judicial system was intended to limit the situations of inability from the point of view of its causes. An attempt was made to correct such a limitation by adding the reference to the generic concept of 'unavailability' of a judicial system as a further possible context of inability. This third context only adds uncertainty rather than widening admissibility. Indeed, even if very broad, this third source of inability still refers to the unavailability of a judicial system as such and not only to its malfunction in a specific case. Thus, it seems always to imply an essential reference to both: an overall 'critical' judicial system – as, for instance, would be a judiciary totally lacking independence and impartiality – as well as, implicitly, the overall state apparatus when, e.g., lacking a democratic organization.

Yet, 'ripe democracies', where the overall judicial system works independently and impartially, also very often do not act properly in repressing crimes within the Court's subject matter jurisdiction as addressed above. It does not seem that the intent of the states present at the Rome Conference was that inability in such situation could be assessed by the Court pursuant to Article 17(3) ICCSt, in particular with reference to the unavailability context. However, the interpretative rules under Article 31 and 32 of the Vienna Convention do not allow an interpretation contrary to the fundamental principles of equality between sovereign states[31] and, thus, an assessment of concrete forms of ability/inability only vis-à-vis some states and not others. The reference to the generic concept of 'unavailability' could assist the Court in this direction. On this question the ICC should also find guidance in the jurisprudence of the European Court of Human Rights, which very often adjudicates on violations of fundamental human rights committed by European states of 'ripe democracy', notwithstanding the overall organization of the state apparatus and judicial system pursuant to the rule of law.

2. Forms of Inability

The first form of inability under Article 17(3) ICCSt refers to the apprehension ('obtain') of the accused, a very specific condition although not always easy to assess. When the custodial state claims jurisdiction through deferral, there is no question. But if the admissibility issue arises in a non-custodial state, its ability to obtain the extradition of the suspect/accused from another state is problematic even if an extradition agreement binds the two states: extradition is a judicial-administrative-executive procedure which could encounter many obstacles before achieving its objective.

30 See Holmes, *supra* note 18, at 55: 'it raised the threshold criterion higher, but seemingly avoided the situation where part of a State's judicial apparatus was incapacitated but significant portions remained intact.'

31 Vienna Convention on the Law of Treaties, 1969. The general rule of interpretation under Art. 31 reads: 'A treaty shall be interpreted in good faith in accordance with the ordinary meaning to be given to the terms of the treaty in their context and in the light of its object and purpose' (para. 1). But the treaty must be interpreted also in the light of 'any relevant rules of international law applicable in the relations between the parties' (para. 3(c)).

It might be easier to assess an inability to obtain evidence and testimony, in particular in the case of a state other than the territorial and national ones, which would not be in the best position for collecting the evidence. However, the custodial state, although it has the person in question, might not be ideally placed to obtaining the evidence.

The fact that the Statute does not provide a criterion to allow one state to be preferred over another is the manifestation, on the one hand, of the ambiguity accompanying every difficult compromise during diplomatic negotiations and, on the other hand, of the awareness that only a case-by-case assessment is possible. This also means that the Court enjoys in this field a very large discretion, much more than in criminal matters. In fact, here the Court faces a mixed judicial/political task, not a judicial/criminal one.

The discretion of the Court is even greater when assessing when a state is 'otherwise unable to carry out its proceedings'. Under this third general form of inability – interpreted in the context of the unavailability of a judicial system according to the broad meaning suggested above – the jurisdiction of the Court would be admissible in many situations: when a state did not endorse the international definitions of crimes under the Statute or international standards on defence rights,[32] or even if its legal order does not provide a participation of victims to proceedings.[33]

An issue on which there are divergent views in literature concerns the effect on admissibility of amnesties, pardons and commutation of sentences. This issue is not directly addressed by the Rome Statute since many delegations resisted to the adoption of a provision on this point. The idea was that 'the Statute should not permit the Court to intercede in the administrative (parole) or political decision-making process (pardons, amnesties) of a State ... Finally, there were some who argued that the proposal was not absolutely necessary, as the provision on admissibility could give the Court sufficient breadth to examine cases of pardons or amnesties made in bad faith'.[34] The solution is, again, a diplomatic compromise in the face of opposing positions. Thus, the reply to the specific question was left to the ICC's jurisprudence. In this matter, it seems that the Court is not bound by national legislations on amnesties and that such legislations should come under the scrutiny of the Court in the context of admissibility procedures, in particular in the case of 'blanket amnesties'.

In short, to be able to conduct the proceedings using this broad meaning of the expression 'unavailability of a judicial system', states simply need to endorse the Rome Statute's standards of conducting criminal investigations and trials, at least against those accused of genocide, war

32 On ICC Statute implementation see F. Lattanzi, 'L'intégration du Statut de Rome aux ordres juridiques étatiques', in S. Perrakis (ed.), *International Criminal Court. A New Dimension in International Justice. Questions and Prospects for a New Humanitarian Order. Proceedings of Santorini Colloquium* (Athens: Sakkoulas Publishers, 2002), at 213 ff.

33 The fair trial principle also includes the rights of victims to participate in the proceedings, in a way which would not correspond exactly to the ICC standards, but would essentially allow the victims to collaborate to a correct assessment of the evidence.

34 Holmes, *supra* note 18, at 59 ff. See also B. Broomhall, 'The International Criminal Court: A Checklist for National Implementation', *Nouvelles études pénales*, Vol. 13 quarter, 1999, at 144: '[W]hile a "blanket amnesty" could possibly be considered a form of inaction giving rise to the admissibility of a case before the Court, it is also conceivable that an amnesty granted in the context of a "truth commission" process could be considered an "investigation" followed by a *bona fide* decision not to proceed for purposes of Art. 17(1)(b). Whatever the situation with regard to pre-conviction amnesties, it is reasonably clear that post-conviction measures, such as parole, pardon or commutation of sentence, when following a conviction secured in accordance with the standard of fairness and good faith foreseen by the Statute, are beyond the scope of Art. 17(1)(c) and Art. 20 of the Statute.' On the issue of amnesty in the ICC Statute, see also R. Bellelli, *supra* note 11, at 25 ff.

crimes and crimes against humanity. This can be done by implementing the Statute at the domestic level, not only with the objective of cooperating with the Court, but to allow the complementarity principle to work in favour of domestic jurisdictions. This is the revolutionary potential of the Rome Statute, which also operates with respect to non-States Parties.

A determination of inability by the Court, based on these grounds, could easily lead to a conflict of jurisdictions with a state claiming the application of complementarity in its favour and refusing to comply with the Court's decision on admissibility, in particular in the case of a non-State Party.

For each of these factors of inability, as in the assessment of factors of unwillingness, only well-established ICC jurisprudence might provide guidance for solving possible conflicts of jurisdictions in specific cases, avoiding future conflicts and limiting the discretion of the Prosecutor and of different Chambers. In any case, clarification on these matters should not be left to the discretionary and individual power of the Prosecutor.

C. Sufficient Gravity of the Crime

The third factor of inadmissibility does not pertain to unwillingness or inability, but rather to considerations of opportunity for the Court to proceed in the interest of justice: a case may be inadmissible based on its gravity. Given the primary responsibility of states to suppress crimes of international concern and in order not to overload the Court with too many proceedings, it was decided that the Court would enjoy discretion, on a case-by-case basis, in deciding whether to leave with national courts the competence for cases of lesser gravity.

In reality, when the issue of admissibility comes before the Court the gravity criterion has already been considered and positively decided by the Prosecutor in assessing the reasonable basis for opening an investigation pursuant to Article 53 (see next paragraph). It is true that the gravity criterion was considered at that stage only *prima facie* and for the purpose of investigating a situation. However, the reference to the gravity criterion for assessing both the reasonable basis for investigating and admissibility provides the Court with a double possibility of avoiding proceeding with the case.[35] This double key – as well the discretion left to the Prosecutor to renounce an investigation and to the Chambers not to proceed based on the insufficient gravity of a situation/case, without giving any criterion for such an assessment – still reflects the deference for states' primary responsibility to suppress the crimes. As a matter of fact, the Court has a very residual task: to intervene only for suppressing the most serious crimes among very serious crimes, as core crimes of international concern certainly are. This approach is traditional, when in international relations individuals are concerned, and is reflected by the old rule of first exhausting domestic remedies, with the same finality of the principle of complementarity: that is, to allow the internationalization of a claim only after all domestic remedies have been exhausted.[36]

But, these principles can only be applied in favour of national jurisdictions insofar domestic remedies work correctly and efficiently – otherwise the purpose is frustrated. This means that the principle of complementarity applies in favour of the international jurisdiction only in critical

35 In theory, the element of gravity could come under consideration by the Prosecutor three times at the stage of investigations: two in the context of the preliminary examination of the reasonable basis (Art. 53) and one in the context of the preliminary ruling on admissibility (Art. 18)!

36 In another perspective, the same finality is also reflected by the principle of subsidiarity applicable in the relations between European and state organs.

situations, when states have failed to correctly exert sovereignty, 'when horrendous crimes have been committed with the collusion or impotence of national authorities'.[37]

This inherent role of complementarity also has an impact on the assessment of the sufficient/insufficient gravity, which could not be evaluated as a factor isolated and completely independent from the availability/unavailability of a national jurisdiction to deal efficiently with a situation/case. There is no doubt that the gravity degree of a crime is also related to whether it is acutally punishable. Thus, the unwillingness/willingness and/or inability/ability of a state to deal with a crime shall also have be relevant in the evaluation of the gravity of a situation/case.

6. Admissibility at the Stage of Investigations

A. The Reasonable Basis

As indicated in the preceding paragraph, the admissibility issue first arises when the Prosecutor decides whether there would be a reasonable basis to commence an investigation upon referral by a State Party or the Security Council or *motu proprio*. Pursuant to Article 53, the following elements are to be evaluated by the Prosecutor in assessing the reasonable basis for opening an investigation:

> (a) the information available to the Prosecutor provides a reasonable basis to believe that a crime within the jurisdiction of the Court has been or is being committed;
> (b) the case is or would be admissible under Article 17; and
> (c) taking into account the gravity of the crime and the interests of victims, there are nonetheless substantial reasons to believe that an investigation would not serve the interests of justice.

Thus, the ICC Prosecutor must preliminarily assess, *prima facie*, whether crimes under the Statute are alleged to have been committed on the territory of a State Party or by a national of a State Party, or on the territory or by a national of a state which accepted *ad hoc* the ICC's jurisdiction.

He must also verify, again only *prima facie*, whether some conditions for admissibility established in Article 17 are satisfied. In fact, not all conditions of admissibility are applicable at the stage of such a preliminary examination, since some of them may only be considered at the stage of a case relating at least to a suspect. This is the case of the conditions addressing a 'person' under Article 17(1)(b) and (c), envisaged by reference to the *ne bis in idem* principle. Furthermore, the Prosecutor could not need to evaluate the gravity as a factor of admissibility in the context of Article 53, given that he must consider it as an autonomous element of the reasonable basis, together with the interests of the victims. Indeed, notwithstanding a possible *prima facie* assessment of jurisdiction and admissibility, the Prosecutor must further consider if opening an investigation is in the interests of justice in the light of the gravity of the crime and interests of victims.

Thus, the preliminary examination of a reasonable basis for opening an investigation is totally in the hands of the Prosecutor, who has only the duty to inform the Pre-Trial Chamber (PTC) should the negative determination of the reasonable basis be based solely on the gravity of the crime.

---

37 L. Arbour, Statement on Establishment of an International Criminal Court, NATO, 10 December 1997, *M2 Presswire*, at 1.

B. Preliminary Ruling

At the Rome Conference, states did not wish to leave to the Prosecutor the unilateral assessment of admissibility at the very early stage of the determination of a reasonable basis for opening an investigation. Consequently, states assumed a direct role in a further procedure on admissibility, in a dialectic relationship with the Prosecutor.

Indeed, according to Article 18, if the Prosecutor – after having determined a reasonable basis for opening an investigation *motu proprio* or upon a state referral – decides to commence an investigation, he must inform 'all States Parties and those States which, taking into account the information available, would normally exercise jurisdiction over the crimes concerned'. The addressees of this information could be several non-States Parties, not just the territorial or national or custodial state. It depends only on the jurisdictional links that states might provide for in their legislations for suppressing the crimes scrutinized by the Prosecutor and on the information received about these links. It means that the Prosecutor shall notify every state in the world theoretically/normally able to exert its jurisdiction on crimes concerned by the referral or in the *notitia criminis*, even on the basis of the universality principle. The Prosecutor may not make a subjective selection of these states.[38] This 'universal' notification does not mean, automatically, that all states informed by the Prosecutor and claiming their jurisdiction could equally benefit from the principle of complementarity (see below, in this paragraph).

Within one month, one or more among all States Parties and some non-States Parties may inform the Prosecutor about ongoing or concluded investigations in their jurisdiction 'with respect to criminal acts which may constitute crimes referred to in Article 5 and which relate to the information provided in the notification to States' and request the deferral of the investigation. The Prosecutor shall defer to the state, 'unless the Pre-Trial Chamber, on the application of the Prosecutor, decides to authorize the investigation'.[39]

At this stage, the admissibility/inadmissibility assessment by the Prosecutor will be based on more information on national proceedings, if any, rather than on the information that he had before, at the stage of the preliminary examination of the reasonable basis. Furthermore, while the preliminary examination was made unilaterally – even though on the basis of information received from many different sources – at the stage of the preliminary ruling on admissibility the specific unwillingness or inability of national jurisdictions in repressing crimes will be verified by the Prosecutor through a direct relationship with the state/s claiming jurisdiction. This dialectic relationship can even start again after the deferral: pursuant to Article 18(3) '[t]he Prosecutor's deferral to a State's investigation shall be open to review by the Prosecutor six months after the date of deferral or at any time when there has been a significant change of circumstances based on the State's unwillingness or inability genuinely to carry out the investigation'. This

38 In the situation of Northern Uganda, the Prosecutor notified the decision to open an investigation to all states 'concerned' (statement of 29 January 2004). It is not clear whether these states were all those who would have had jurisdiction over the crimes under the would-be investigation, or only states involved in the situation, like Sudan and Congo (where the suspects at large seem to hide, and which could be endowed by a custodial link). In the situation of Congo originated by a March 2004 self-referral, no public information was made available by the Prosecutor on any Art. 18 notification to states, as the OTP only communicated that 'in September 2003 the Prosecutor had informed the Assembly of States Parties that he would be prepared to seek authorisation from a Pre-Trial Chamber to start an investigation under his *proprio motu* powers, but that a referral and active support from the DRC would facilitate the work of the Office of the Prosecutor'. *Press release*, 19 April 2004, on ICC website.

39 Art. 18(2) ICCSt.

rule entails a dynamic assessment of willingness and inability and was inserted in order to verify their continued presence after the initial deferral decision, with the possibility of reviewing it in favour of admissibility. Further, according to Article 18(5), in case of deferral of the investigation the Prosecutor may request that the state concerned provides, without undue delay, periodical information on the progress of its investigations and any subsequent prosecutions.

The Statute does not provide for a dynamic assessment that allows the Prosecutor to delay his decision to open an investigation or for the state to prepare its legal order to investigate and prosecute as seems to be the practice of the ICC's Office of the Prosecutor (OTP).[40]

As a matter of fact, the preliminary procedure on admissibility is very sensitive given the risk that states, in affirming the priority of their courts, only intend to delay or even nullify the ICC's role, thus abusively invoking the principle of complementarity in their own favour; the fair outcome of such procedure depends both on the good faith of states and on the capacity of the Prosecutor to understand without ambiguities whether a state claiming jurisdiction is actually willing and able to proceed.

Pending a preliminary ruling on admissibility, or at any time when the Prosecutor has deferred an investigation, preservation of evidence is safeguarded through the 'unique opportunity' procedure: the Prosecutor may, on an exceptional basis, seek authority from the PTC to pursue necessary investigative steps when there is a unique opportunity to obtain important evidence or there is a significant risk that such evidence may not be subsequently available.[41] However, this provision may prove inadequate 'when one is faced with a state bent on shunning international jurisdiction and therefore unwilling to cooperate in the search for and collection of evidence, or even willing to destroy such evidence to evade justice'.[42]

The preliminary procedure on admissibility raises some problems of interpretation, in particular as it concerns states that benefit from the complementarity principle. It is not immediately clear if the principle of complementarity has to apply in favour of every state, whether Party or non-Party, on the basis of any possible jurisdictional criterion adopted by national legislations, including the universal one. The obligation of the Prosecutor to notify 'those States which, taking into account the information available, would normally exercise jurisdiction over the crimes concerned' can be subject – due to the ambiguity of the term 'normally' – to a wider or a stricter interpretation. Would a state utilizing, for instance, the universal criterion of jurisdiction with respect to war crimes – for which this criterion is mandatory according to the Geneva Conventions – exercise it 'normally'? Or where 'normally' includes only the territorial, nationality or custodial criteria? It might seem a convincing reading that confines the application of the principle only in favour of those national jurisdictions directly linked to the criminal conduct or the accused, as may reasonably be presumed to be the best placed to collect relevant evidence.

40 This is, e.g., the case in the Ugandan situation, notwithstanding the four warrants of arrest, all addressed only to rebels leaders. Delaying further investigations, which should be extended in every direction and not only towards the rebels, may appear fruitless, perhaps even harmful from the point of view of collecting evidence on crimes committed by both sides of the conflict.

41 Art. 18(6) ICCSt.

42 See A. Cassese, *supra* note 1, at 159. Further, 'complementarity could lend itself to abuse. It might amount to a shield used by states to thwart international justice. This may happen with regard to those crimes (genocide, crimes against humanity) which are normally perpetrated with the help and assistance, or the connivance or acquiescence, of national authorities. In these cases, state authorities may pretend to investigate and try crimes, and may even conduct proceedings, but only for the purpose of actually protecting the allegedly responsible persons'. Ibid., at 158.

At any rate, the 'absolute universal' criterion is very rare in domestic jurisdictions and, thus, claims on this criterion will not represent a problem for admissibility procedures. However, some problems might be raised by the 'relative universal' criterion based on the custody of the accused.[43] Applying the principle of complementarity in favour of the custodial state, when it is not the state on which territory the crimes were committed, might allow an effective prosecution of the accused only on the condition that the territorial state is available to cooperate, while applying the principle of complementarity in favour of the territorial state not detaining the accused could impede effective prosecution if the custodial state refuses extradition. On the other hand, the ICC could take advantage of the surrender and cooperation obligations imposed by the Statute on States Parties (or, in case of a Security Council referral, on all UN Member States). Because of this, in deciding the deferral the Prosecutor might prefer a State Party with a weaker link to the crime rather than a non-State Party with a stronger link to it. Should the principle of complementarity be applied with regard to any possible basis of jurisdiction, without cautious evaluation in the light of the Statute and specific circumstances, there would be a risk of thwarting the essential aim of the creation of a criminal international jurisdiction.

The question can not be solved in abstract, but only on a case-by-case basis in favour of the main aim of the Rome Statute: to avoid perpetrators of crimes of international concern going unpunished. As Article 17 is the main source for this assessment, the Prosecutor may defer only if the state is effectively willing and able to proceed according to factors provided in this Article. In order to verify that willingness exists, it is probably necessary to also take into account the requirements of Article 19, which reads that challenges to admissibility may be made, *inter alia*, by 'a State which has jurisdiction over a case, on the ground that it is investigating or prosecuting the case or has investigated and prosecuted'.[44] In other words, 'it is not enough that a State had instituted or wants to institute national proceedings, it must establish to the Court that it has jurisdiction in the case. This addition was intended to forestall situations where a State could delay an investigation on the ground that it was investigating when in fact the investigation could not bring to a prosecution because the State lacked jurisdiction.'[45]

The same evaluation must be made if several states claim jurisdiction, by comparing the different possibilities of an actual willingness and ability to proceed and then selecting the *forum conveniens*. Even in the case of concurring jurisdiction, the Prosecutor, if correctly applying the principle of complementarity, might decide not to defer to any state.

The assessment by the Prosecutor of the inadmissibility of the investigation will be definitive, while the opposite assessment is subject to judicial review. Indeed, according to Article 17, for the deferral decision the Prosecutor is the sole *dominus* of the evaluation of the inadmissibility, while for initiating an investigation he needs the authorization of the PTC. The concurrent claims of the Prosecutor and the state/s will be presented to the Chamber only by the Prosecutor, since a state has no *locus standi* in the procedure. However, the ruling of the PTC, denying or allowing the Prosecutor's investigation, may be challenged before the Appeals Chamber either by the Prosecutor or the state.[46]

---

43 On the distinction between absolute and relative universal criterion, F.Lattanzi, 'Quelques réflexions sur le "principe de juridiction universelle"', in G. Venturini and S. Bariatti (eds), *Droits individuals et justice internationale, Liber* Fausto Pocar (Milano: Giuffré, 2009), at 461 ff.

44 Art. 19(2)(b) ICCSt.

45 Holmes, *supra* note 18, p. 67.

46 Art. 18(4) ICCSt. If a state has challenged the ruling of the Pre-Trial Chamber under this provision, it may subsequently challenge the admissibility of a case under Art. 19 only on the grounds of additional significant facts or significant change of circumstances (Art. 18(7)).

It is therefore evident that during the investigation phase the application of the complementarity principle in the direction of deferral remains in the exclusive and discretionary control of an individual and non-judicial organ of the Court. Conversely, whenever the Prosecution's scrutiny on complementarity concludes in favour of international prosecutorial activity, the Chambers have the last word on different steps: in the context of the authorization procedure and of a possible procedure on appeal against the pre-trial decision on authorization, as well as for further proceedings if the investigation arrives at the arrest warrant, confirmation of charges and trial stages. Furthermore, the Court always has, at any stage of the case, the power to rule on admissibility on its own motion.[47]

This means that the most serious and delicate problem regarding the application of the principle of complementarity concerns the early phase of investigations, when the Prosecutor is faced with the issue of concurrent jurisdictions of the state and the Court. The discretion of the Prosecutor finds some guidance in the definitions of unwillingness and inability under Article 17. However, such discretion appears without limit or guidance in the application of the third factor of complementarity, that is, that of the sufficient gravity.

In the likely event that the Prosecutor is confronted with some incertitude when the determining the admissibility of a situation/case, it seems appropriate that he should avail himself of the possibility of requesting an Article 19(3) ruling by a Trial Chamber (TC). This would be in the interest of justice, of efficient and expeditious proceedings, and resources saving. Seeking a judicial ruling on the admissibility issue is particularly necessary when the Prosecutor intends to defer an investigation to a state, given that this decision, in addition to not being subject to a review by a judicial organ of the Court, is also not challengeable by states, individuals concerned by investigations and/or victims considered in the *notitia criminis*: states and individuals concerned may only challenge the admissibility of a case (and not the inadmissibility of a situation/case).[48]

This means that in the case of a deferral to 'the State' or to 'a State' a conflict of jurisdiction between the state and the Court will not arise, while a conflict between two or more states claiming jurisdiction will be directly solved by the Prosecutor himself. Conversely, if the Prosecutor does not intend to defer, the TC will face a conflict between the international jurisdiction and one or more national ones. In particular, the territorial and the national ones are the jurisdictions most likely to be in conflict with each other. The TC does not intervene directly in such a conflict – due to its competence to only decide whether or not to authorize the investigation by the ICC Prosecutor – but in exercising this competence it evaluates the willingness/unwillingness and ability/inability of one or more states, in contrast with the Prosecutor's position.

The TC will give a decision that, without any doubt, binds both the State Party and the Prosecutor, while its binding effect with respect to a non-State Party is questionable. While the Statute is silent on this issue, it seems that the decision is binding also for a non-State Party claiming jurisdiction before the Prosecutor on the basis of the statutory conditions of Article 17. By claiming jurisdiction, such state would recognize to some extent the authority of the Court and submit itself to its authority. But what about the effect of an authorization by the PTC to open an investigation if the non-State Party has even challenged the Article 18 notification by the Prosecutor questioning the 'legitimacy' of the ICC's complementarity with respect to non-States Parties jurisdictions? The real problem in this event is the cooperation of the non-State Party with the Court for the

47 Art.19(1).

48 According to Art. 19(2), admissibility may be challenged: (a) by an accused or a person for whom a warrant of arrest or summons to appear has been issued by the ICC; (b) by a state that has jurisdiction over a case, on the grounds that it is investigating or prosecuting the case or has investigated or prosecuted; and (c) by a state from which acceptance of jurisdiction is required under Article 12 as a precondition to the exercise of jurisdiction.

purpose of collecting evidence and transferring the suspect. Upon an authorization given by the PTC the Prosecutor may certainly proceed, but, if at any stage there is lack of state cooperation, the proceedings will inevitably come to an halt.

This is the biggest challenge the Court faces and is due to the involvement in the preliminary procedure on admissibility under Article 18, also to non-States Parties. The rationale of such involvement, in particular the obligation of the Prosecutor to notify these states as well as defer to them, is again the deference to national sovereignty. However, what is missing is any counterbalance with an obligation to respect a TC decision on admissibility against the deferral and to cooperate with the Court for its implementation.

In any case states – Parties and non-Parties – have some duties to respect when conducting this Article 18 dialogue with the Prosecutor. Indeed, every state is obliged to respect the principle of good faith in international relations, which also applies in respect of relations with the ICC. As a result, states have to act in good faith in asserting the primary responsibility of their courts, in order to avoid complementarity leading to an unjustified delay of the proceedings before the international jurisdiction, which would result in making it ineffective. An unjustified delay in the repression of a crime under the ICC Statute, caused by a non-State Party, could entail its international responsibility for violation of its obligation to repress the crime. Unfortunately, such a violation is subject to the weak means of the international community to react to infractions of international law.

7. Inapplicability of Article 18 to Referrals by the Security Council

The Court may also exercise its jurisdiction whenever 'a situation in which one or more [of the Statute's] crimes appears to have been committed is referred to Prosecutor by the Security Council acting under Chapter VII of the Charter of the United Nations'.[49] By its referral, the SC not only utilizes the ICC – an instrument created by states – as an *ad hoc* Tribunal, but even confers on the Court the jurisdiction on crimes linked with the situation ascertained pursuant to its coercive powers and, thus, the ICC does not need any acceptance of jurisdiction by the territorial or national state.

As a consequence of the exercise of the SC's authority under Chapter VII of the UN Charter, no preliminary procedure on admissibility is needed. The Council is entitled to intervene in domestic affairs of states in order to restore international peace and security and, thus, when the Prosecutor is proceeding upon a SC referral there is no need for yet another filter aimed at protecting states' sovereignty.

As a result, the Prosecutor is not obliged to inform the states indicated in Article 18 about his intention to open an investigation, nor to initiate a dialogue with them. It might also be argued that the Prosecutor must not open such a dialogue because it is the same determination of a threat to or violation of peace according to Chapter VII that includes an assessment of the unwillingness or inability of states to suppress the crimes. This does not mean that the question of admissibility can not be raised any more before the Court, as is held by some. The Court is still competent to assess the admissibility – as it appears evident by the possibility that the SC itself challenges it – but, at the investigative stage there is at least a 'universal' presumption of admissibility. This means that the SC, before referring a situation to the ICC – as it did for the Sudan/Darfur situation – evaluates the situation according to Chapter VII, but also in light, at least *prima facie*, of the principle of complementarity inherent to the system to which the referral belongs. This is the reason why Article 18 does not apply to the SC referral.

---

49 Art. 13(b) ICCSt.

Such presumption, however, does not prevent states with jurisdiction over the crimes related to the situation referred by the Security Council from informing the Prosecutor that their authorities are investigating or prosecuting the case or have already done so. The Prosecutor may be aware of this upon information received for the determination of the existence of a reasonable basis to proceed pursuant to Article 53(1) of the Statute, which is also applicable to a SC referral.[50]

In the situation in Darfur, Sudan notified the Prosecutor that it had 'established a new special Court to deal with crimes committed in Darfur' and the OTP stated that 'before deciding whether to start an investigation Prosecutor Moreno-Ocampo is obliged under the Rome Statute … to assess the admissibility of the situation in Darfur'.[51] He did not mean a one-off scrutiny, as he also declared that 'the admissibility assessment is an ongoing process and [that the OTP] will follow the work of this tribunal and any other national proceedings'. Actually, the Prosecutor seemed to assess admissibility in the context of the Article 18 procedure, rather than limiting himself to a determination of whether there was a reasonable basis to proceed (and, in this context, to assessing the admissibility only *prima facie*).[52]

In *Darfur* the Prosecutor was also forced to recognize:

> the continuing insecurities in Darfur do not allow for an effective system of victim and witness protection. This has forced my Office to investigate outside Sudan and represents a serious impediment to the conduct of effective investigations in Darfur by national judicial bodies as well. Up to this point, the work of the Special Court does not suggest that cases likely to be prosecuted before the International Criminal Court would be inadmissible in terms of Article 53(2)(b) of the Statute. My Office will continue to follow closely all national proceeding.

This statement proves that the assessment given by the Security Council was based on strong foundations and that, upon a SC referral, a long Article 18 dialogue between the Prosecutor and the state on admissibility is excluded. After all, a long dialogue in the absence of a strong decision by the Prosecutor on admissibility/inadmissibility would only prevent a request for a review of the

50 At the Rome Conference, states, very judiciously, also provided for the SC to seek a review by the PTC of a decision of the Prosecutor not to open the investigation or not to prosecute. Art. 53, 3(a) ICCSt.

51 PTC II, *Registration in a record of proceedings of Statement by Luis Moreno-Ocampo, Fourth Session of the Assembly of States Parties*, The Hague, 28 November 2005.

52 The long dialogue between the Prosecutor and Sudan is also evidenced by the following subsequent statements made by the Prosecutor, although the SC decision according to Chapter VII had been issued not in a vacuum, but after many assessments of a threat to international peace coming from this situation: 'my Office continues to gather and assess information relating to the various mechanisms established by the Sudanese authorities in relation to crimes allegedly committed in Darfur, including the Special Court for Darfur established by decrees issued on 7 and 11 June 2005. In November 2005 a decree is reported to have been issued establishing two new Special Courts to sit in Geneina and Nyala. Additional prosecutors and judges have been appointed to staff these Courts. The jurisdiction of the Court is also reported to have been expanded to consider allegations of violations of international humanitarian law and the Government of the Sudan has renewed its commitment to allow access to the AU and other international monitors. In addition, various other mechanisms and committees have been established to look at aspects of the crimes in Darfur, including the centres for the elimination of violence against women and an attorney office for Crimes against Humanity. The Government has also pointed to efforts to promote tribal reconciliation and to the proposed Darfur Conference to take place in December 2005 as efforts towards a comprehensive solution to the conflict.' The investigative activity of the Prosecutor was delayed, with some risk for the potential witnesses and victims, by the Sudanese behaviour and statements intended to prepare the ground for challenging the admissibility of the case. Relations between the Court and Sudan progressed accordingly.

Prosecutor's decision according to Article 53(3), which seems highly unfair, also with respect to the victims' expectations that justice be done.[53]

8. Self-Referrals

The Statute is silent about the self-referral of a situation. This is evidence of the inability of a theoretical approach in negotiating international instruments to capture the complexity stemming from their implementation in the practice of international relations. Thus, as the Rome Statute not even implicitly exclude it, the self-referral practice was prompted by the ICC itself.

In the circumstances of a self-referral, where the territorial or national state itself gives an assessment of its own inability – when unwillingness is not in question, otherwise it would not refer the situation to the Court – there is a presumption of a 'relative' admissibility, that is only vis-à-vis the referral state, while in the case of a SC referral there is a presumption of admissibility at least vis-à-vis all UN Member States.

In all cases of self-referral the Prosecutor has to notify all states, Parties and non-Parties, having ordinarily jurisdiction on the crimes, of his intention to initiate an investigation, as these states could investigate the situation on the basis of criteria other than territoriality or nationality. Indeed, the Prosecutor applied Article 18 to the Ugandan referral, while having already taken into account – for the determination of a reasonable basis for investigations – the inability of the territorial states to investigate, as ascertained by the referring state itself.[54]

A related issue is whether a referring state might thereafter review its position and challenge the admissibility. However, the estoppel rule should act as a bar to such possibility.

9. ICC's Direct Repressive Role

A. Alternative Forms of Justice

The relationship between the principle of complementarity and the so-called alternative forms of justice represents another very delicate issue the Court faces when implementing complementarity. In fact, alternative forms of justice could come under ICC consideration in the context of the factor of the interest of justice.[55] However, it is appropriate to remember that the notion of justice for the Court is primarily to 'bring to justice' perpetrators. Some interesting comments on the issue argue

53 See on this approach some interesting reactions, for example, that of J. Mendez, Special Advisor of the UN General Secretary for the prevention of genocide: 'United Nations official slams Darfur crimes court', *Reuters*, 26 September 2005. Available at http://www.alertnet.org (visited 20 September 2009).

54 The letter of referral of 16 December 2003 from the Attorney General of the Republic of Uganda, appended as Exhibit A to the Prosecutor's application, was sent confidentially and its entire content was never rendered public. But, it was indicated by the OTP that in this self-referral Uganda mentioned its inability to apprehend the Lord's Resistance Army leaders. See R. Bellelli, The System, *supra* note 11, notes 279 and 286. Reference to this letter, 'by which the "situation concerning the Lord's Resistance Army" in northern and western Uganda was submitted to the Court' is contained in ICC, Warrant of Arrest for Joseph Kony Issued on 8 July 2005 as Amended on 27 September 2005, PTC II, 27 September 2005, para. 30.

55 This was also fully evident from what the Prosecutor himself had the opportunity to declare: 'In addition to admissibility I am also required by the Rome Statute to consider whether a prosecution is not in the interests of justice. In considering this factor I will follow the various national and international efforts

in favour of the primacy of the prosecutorial aim of the ICC, which entails the need to proceed at the international level if the domestic one does not properly prosecute. Others favour a primacy of the international aspiration to restore international peace through national reconciliation. Some of the arguments raised by one or other of the opinions are well founded, but the key question is overlooked.

Nobody can deny that, as it was conceived in Rome and enshrined in the Statute, the ultimate goal of the ICC is the promotion of international peace and security, as crimes of concern to the international community were appropriately qualified as a threat to this fundamental and shared value. However, the Rome legislators decided to pursue that ultimate objective by creating a body endowed with punitive powers. The ICC was not created as an international reconciliation tool, but as a criminal tribunal having – as any other criminal jurisdiction has – a prosecutorial task. Obviously, such task was mandated with the final goal of pacifying the world, while domestic tribunals aim to contribute to the maintenance of public order and peaceful coexistence in a national community. While this does not exclude the same objective from also being pursued by means of reconciliation mechanisms, reconciliation is not the function of the ICC. Besides, national reconciliation is not yet international peace.

Further, the complementarity principle involves two parallel systems, the primary and the complementary. Such a parallelism cannot exist between, on the one hand, any domestic or international reconciliation mechanism and, on the other hand, the ICC's repressive mechanism.

To clarify this issue, it could be useful to recall that many reconciliation activities were performed after WWII, within or outside the UN framework. The UN Charter devotes the entire Chapter VI to devising peaceful means for settling disputes, to be used as a preventive action to maintain international peace and security in cases where there is an existing risk. However, no other Chapter in the Charter has worked, and is still working, so poorly as VI. Unfortunately, the hundreds of conflicts which followed WWII, during the Cold War and thereafter, could not be avoided because those peaceful means have not been successful and are still failing in the majority of conflict situations.

On the other hand, Chapter VII of the Charter envisages and regulates emergency situations for international peace and security which arise whenever the recourse to peaceful means cannot avoid a shifting from a mere risk for peace to an actual threat to or the violation of peace or to an aggression. For such situations, the Charter even envisaged a world government in the hands of the Security Council: a common military body and a common military force under both the political and operative control of the Security Council. It is well known how this system failed to be properly implemented, as a common army was never established due to the Member States' (especially the permanent ones') refusal to put at the complete disposal of the SC and its operative military body an army that – whenever one of the three above-mentioned situations were to arise – would be able to automatically intervene – that is without an *ad hoc* consent by the states sending and receiving military intervention – in the territory of a state and even against it with a view to imposing peace by use of heavy weaponry. As a substitute for a 'UN army', Member States decided to put peacekeeping contingents at the disposal of the SC, although only *ad hoc* and *ex post facto*, for concrete situations and based on the consent of the state were the situation arises and often even of the rebel groups partly in control of the territory. UN peacekeepers are lightly armed and legally and physically unable to impose peace over the parties in conflict, as well as never endowed with a coercive mandate vis-à-vis a state. As they represent more a peaceful tool than a coercive one,

to achieve peace and security, as well as the views of witnesses and victims of the crimes.' L.M. Ocampo, *Address to the United Nations Security Council*, 13 December 2005, at 4.

in many situations peace forces failed to contribute to restoring or maintaining peace in domestic societies and at the international level.

With reference to situations relevant to the suppression of crimes of international concern that imply a threat to international peace and security, it suffices to recall how UN peacekeepers were unable to avoid the egregious crimes committed in Rwanda and in the former Yugoslavia. Contrary to one opinion, this did not happen because of the unwillingness of the UN to stop such crimes, but because of the unwillingness of states to endow peacekeeping operations with an actual coercive military mandate.

States could not but acknowledge the frequent failure of peaceful means and that even the regained formal unity of the world after the fall of the Berlin Wall did not lead to the establishment of the UN Army that was too optimistically envisaged in 1945. As states may act criminally only through individuals – in particular those who have military and political responsibilities at the top of a state apparatus – in 1993 and 1994, the SC created two international criminal Tribunals for restoring international peace and security by coercive measures directly applicable vis-à-vis individuals who violated fundamental humanitarian values.

However, the SC's Permanent Members, with the political and military cooperation and assistance of the majority of non-permanent Members, also adopted the questionable decision to undertake coercive multinational military measures against states, considered as collective entities.[56] Whether this approach is a viable contributor to national reconciliation and international peace should be assessed against experiences such as those of Somalia, Afghanistan and Iraq.

If armed interventions against states involved in heinous and systematic massacres and even acts of international terrorism are not able to contribute efficiently to restoring international peace; if peaceful means vis-à-vis collective entities, including states and rebel groups, are often inadequate or impracticable or failing; if the international community has until now been divided in seeking global social and economic solutions to conflict and crisis situations, then the step made in Rome through the establishment of a repressive mechanism against individuals for ending the impunity of heinous criminals as a means for attaining world peace may not be reversed.

Furthermore and while knowledge of local alternative justice effectively working in African communities can always be improved, alternative ways of justice – ceremonies of pardon and other methods – are utilized for infractions of local customs of minor gravity and not for criminal conducts as serious as those covered by the ICC's jurisdiction.[57] In those societies, alternative

56 To perform this task in situations particularly serious for international peace, the SC devised the practice of authorizing multinational armed forces (sometimes even uni-national, as it was for the 1994 French 'Opération Turquoise' in Rwanda) to intervene to impose the peace both on the rebels and the governmental warring parties. Such a procedure is not contemplated by the Charter, but it is compatible with the spirit and main objective of Chapter VII if it maintains its inherent preventive feature and is only aimed at protecting the civilian population (so-called humanitarian intervention). However, states could not legitimate *ex post*, through a Security Council measure under Chapter VII, a military intervention by a state, as some commentators seem read the *ex post* decision of the 1999 NATO bombing of Belgrade during the Kosovo war. The legality of such attack is questionable, even on grounds of humanitarian intervention to protect the Albanian ethnic group in Kosovo. The SC itself did not go so far as to legitimate it *ex post*. Acting under Chapter VII, the Council only decided some measures for addressing the factual situation which followed the attack, that is the threat to international peace which some might even consider was aggravated by the military intervention.

57 It needs to be recalled that the Truth and Reconciliation Commission of South Africa did not work to make a *tabula rasa* of what occurred in the apartheid era, but only for the determination, through investigations and confessions, of the truth. This was also achieved by some degree of threat of criminal prosecution posed to those allegedly responsible, should they not have cooperated in the determination of the truth. In spite of this, many South Africans are not satisfied by the approach taken to reconciliation; some also question whether

forms of justice coexist with the state's punitive justice and with international standards for the administration of justice, as these states are under an obligation to also organize themselves in accordance with UN values. Punitive justice in African countries is widely acknowledged to be usually strong and, supported by general consent, it even provides the death penalty for crimes not as serious as those of international concern. For local communities it should instead be a priority to call in forms of alternative justice in these situations, so as to avoid the death penalty – the rationale for which is strongly disputable and contested at the international level – being further applied.[58]

There is no dissent whatsoever on the right, duty and need of states, for the purpose of ensuring the security of their society, to punish perpetrators of ordinary crimes. Thus, such right, duty and need cannot be reasonably challenged when the focus is on crimes that 'deeply shock the conscience of humanity'.[59]

Renouncing international investigations in favour of alternative forms of justice – essentially pardon and amnesty – does not represent the way to implement the complementarity principle. It must be possible to pursue the way of national reconciliation in parallel with the prosecutorial activity against the perpetrators of all sides of a conflict. Independent prosecution of all those responsible for crimes represents one of the possible ways to achieve national reconciliation between groups whose members must be equal before justice, irrespective of their allegiance.[60]

B. Proactive Complementarity

The above line of reasoning also makes questionable the approach that suggests a proactive role for the Court vis-à-vis national jurisdictions, to the detriment of its expeditious and efficient repressive role that is the so-called ICC proactive complementarity.[61]

Rather than commencing an investigation *proprio motu*, which would *ipso facto* imply an intervention of the PTC in the context of the authorization procedure, the ICC's Prosecutor often

---

it led to actual reconciliation. A more in-depth and dispassionate analysis of the Truth Commission would enable a better understanding of the current South African situation, which still involves issues in the relations between the different communities.

58 It seems that – rather than devoting efforts to trying to assert a presumed primacy of alternative forms of justice over the punitive task of ICC – focus and attention should be put on improving consideration for human life by some states or local communities, including with additional care for detainees who suffer inhuman treatment when in detention on remand or convicted and sentenced to a low penalty.

59 Preamble (2) ICCSt.

60 In the name of reconciliation pursued by Ugandan authorities, nothing seems to have occurred at the Court after the issuance of the arrest warrants against five rebel leaders – all of them being at large in Uganda's neighbouring states (one dead, which the consequent withdrawal of the arrest warrant against him). Hundreds of individuals continued to be actively involved in crimes in Northern Uganda, even among the Uganda People's Democratic Army (UPDA), as alleged in information received by the ICC Prosecutor from different authoritative sources. The situation came to a stalemate due to the ongoing negotiations between the Ugandan government and the rebels, including the main leader of the rebels, Joseph Kony, who was participating in the negotiations, even if physically represented by his deputy. A reconciliation agreement, it seems, could even entail a substantial blanket amnesty for everyone. The Prosecutor does not seem to have extended the investigations over crimes committed by military and civilian governmental officials. Some also contend that after the self-referral, the government might no longer be interested in international proceedings because the Court formally did not accept limiting the investigations to rebels' acts, as Uganda indicated in its referral.

61 On this approach, see W.W. Burke-White, 'Proactive Complementarity: The International Criminal Court and National Courts in the Rome System of International Justice', 49 *Harvard International Law Journal* 1 (2008), at 53 ff.

engages in an activity – certainly important although seemingly going beyond his responsibilities – aimed at encouraging and domestic proceedings whatsoever by situation states, irrespective of self-referrals and referrals by the SC. While complementarity captures the competing international and national jurisdictions, the Prosecutor instead asserts that 'rather than competing with national systems for jurisdiction, we will encourage national proceedings wherever possible'.[62]

It seems hard to see why a state involved for years in a conflict where heinous crimes are committed by all warring parties – in total disregard of its political, military and even judicial authorities – would suddenly be willing, able and ready to embark on ending impunity only because the *notitia criminis* arrived at the Court that, rather than investigating, tries to trigger domestic procedures.

ICC complementarity does not mean the OTP's assistance to states to upgrade their legal systems to international criminal law norms so as to allow complementarity to play in favour of national jurisdictions. It is through means other than the ICC that the international community must work towards enabling national legal orders to adapt to the Rome Statute's standards if they want domestic jurisdictions to prevail under the rule of complementarity. Some NGO's also provide some states with effective assistance.[63]

A proactive complementarity approach also seems unhelpful for future efficient activity of national jurisdictions. In order to make a prosecution possible, a state often needs new legislation, new tribunals with competence in international humanitarian and human rights law, often even training for domestic judges who probably have no experience in international criminal law. It is therefore a process that could last for years, rather than months, and that would run the risk of leading to an inappropriate solution from the complementarity point of view. This is particularly true in situations of ongoing conflicts, where the admissibility issue could rise again during the trial or at its end.

In such situations a *de facto* presumption exists that the state is either unwilling – normally also because its governmental forces are involved in the crimes – or unable, because the government lost control of that state's apparatus, territory and community. Therefore, proactive complementarity in such situations could only lead to postponing justice, seriously threatening the preservation of evidence and, overall, missing the crucial objective of a timely justice. The main aim of complementarity is not to defer a case to a state, but the proper administration of justice, mainly in time of conflicts. The Court is called upon to deal with a situation or case by implementing both faces of complementarity, that is, by favouring the states' primary responsibility as well as the ICC substitutive role when needed, in the overall interest of justice, which is the main avenue by which to achieve peace.

10. Conclusion

The practice of the ICC has so far explored in few situations the implications of the structural and functional characters of the principle of complementarity. Within this limited experience, admissibility proceedings have been tested marginally and the case law has still to fully develop on the leading requirements of inability and unwillingness, as well as on their scope.

---

62 L.M. Ocampo, *Building a Future on Peace an Justice*, address at the International Conference in Nuremberg (25–27 June 2007).

63 Among these, Parliamentarians for Global Action is very active in the promotion of ratifications of the Statute and its implementation in domestic legislations.

However, practice has shown the ICC the difficult task of impartially conducting its proceedings in situations where the cooperation of situation countries might be more dependent on national interests rather that on the interests of international justice. This difficult balance is a core challenge for the Office of the Prosecutor and, in this regard, any acceptable development of the notion of positive complementarity might request clarification of the respective roles of the states and of the ICC.

In this perspective, insight into the future of the Court might lead to revisiting the argument that 'if complementarity works, then the ICC will have no cases'. This would be true in an ideal world if domestic systems were to function correctly in suppressing crimes under the Rome Statute. As this is unfortunately not the case, the argument would instead be that, if complementarity works, then the ICC will have numerous cases.

Chapter 10

Obligation to Cooperate and Duty to Implement

Roberto Bellelli

1. Responsibility to Protect and Complementarity

The Statute of the International Criminal Court (ICC) addresses the implementation of the primary responsibility of states to protect civilians from the commission of crimes of international concern by means of the principle of complementarity: the Court is called to discharge the complementary responsibility of the international community to intervene when states fail to comply with the responsibility attached to their sovereignty.[1]

Under the comprehensive and integrated legal system[2] established by the Rome Statute, the 'duty of every State to exercise its criminal jurisdiction over those responsible for international crimes'[3] is maintained and stressed, while failure to perform such functions does not hinder the fight against impunity to be carried out at the international level, but instead establishes new obligations for States Parties. As under the complementarity principle the Court steps in only when states fail to genuinely exert their jurisdiction,[4] there is an inextricable link between the conditions, modalities and means for national proceedings and the coming into operation of the ICC through the admissibility of a case[5] as well as with the obligations to cooperate.

The responsibility to protect incumbent on all states entails that, when it comes to the exercise of criminal jurisdiction, under international law states are normally faced with two traditional options, that is either to prosecute or to extradite (*aut dedere aut iudicare*).[6] The presence of an alleged offender on its territory triggers an obligation[7] for the custodial state to ensure – by taking all necessary and reasonable steps to apprehend and bring him/her to justice – that the individual is prosecuted either before its own or another competent jurisdiction. Consequently, the custodial state has the choice between two alternative courses of action: prosecuting in its own national courts or granting a request for extradition. However, under the Rome Statute's regime a third option has become available, as states not willing to bring a person before national justice (by

---

1 For the notion of responsibility to protect and its implementation, including through the various forms of international-ized criminal justice, see R. Bellelli, The Establishment of the System of International Criminal Justice, in this Volume, at 2(C) and (D) (hereinafter, The System).

2 Ibid., at 4(A)(2)(a).

3 Preamble (6) ICCSt.

4 R. Bellelli, The System, at 4(E)(4)(a). See *supra* note 1.

5 Ibid., at 4(E)(4)(b).

6 Ibid., at 4(E)(3) and note 230.

7 The physical presence of the alleged offender on its territory provides sufficient basis for the exercise of jurisdiction by a custodial state, beyond any jurisdictional link it may have. The International Court of Justice (ICJ) is currently seized with the case *Questions relating to the Obligation to Prosecute or Extradite* (*Belgium v. Senegal*) originated by the arrest of the former President of Chad, Hissène Habré, in Senegal. See R. Bellelli, The System, *supra* note 1, at 4(D)(4)(c).

prosecution or extradition) might still be willing to cooperate with the ICC and, when a case is admissible before it, would also be subject to an obligation to do so.[8]

Thus, the exercise of the primary national jurisdiction and of the complementary jurisdiction of the Court requires two distinct sets of actions by States Parties: implementation of the Rome Statute, on the one hand, and cooperation with the ICC, on the other hand. However, there is no alternative choice for States Parties to both implement and cooperate, as the full cooperation required by the general obligation to cooperate with the Court[9] requires full implementation too.[10] It is, therefore, apparent that – although not the subject of an obligation *stricto sensu* – implementation is required by the Statute in order to avoid, as a minimum, incompliance with cooperation obligations.

2. Implementation

A. A Mandatory Option

The importance of implementation in domestic legal systems and the possible consequences for the lack of compliance with the obligations deriving from the Statute[11] cannot be compared with precedent records[12] in national implementation of Conventions containing provisions of international criminal law.

As the Statute establishes a comprehensive legal system,[13] a full implementation of the obligations introduced by its substantive criminal law and cooperation provisions is unavoidable. While incompliance with obligations to implement established under other Conventions also introducing criminal law provisions could not have entailed legal consequences of practical significance, the absence in domestic criminal legal systems of any of the crimes under the Statute would raise an Article 17 ICCSt issue of admissibility: the state might be found 'unable to carry out its proceedings'[14] and the Court establish its complementary jurisdiction on specific cases.[15] In other words, the lack of a domestic provision attributing to a national criminal judge whatsoever authority would shift, *ipso iure*, the jurisdiction to the international Court.

While the Rome Statute has envisaged that the Assembly of States Parties (ASP) could have carried out oversight 'for inspection, evaluation and investigation on the Court',[16] for any further

8 R. Bellelli, The System, ibid. See also International Law Commission (ILC), Draft Code of Crimes against the Peace and Security of Mankind, in the *Report of the International Law Commission on the Work Carried out during its 48th Session*, 6 May–26 July 1996, UN Doc. Suppl. No. 10, A/51/10, para. 8, at 32 (Draft Code). Available at http://untreaty.un.org/ilc/documentation/english/A_51_10.pdf (visited 20 August 2009).

9 Art. 86 ICCSt.

10 See *infra*, 3(1).

11 For an obligation to implement the crimes under the Statute, see M. Roscini, 'Great Expectations: The Implementation of the Rome Statute in Italy', 5 *JICJ* (2007), 493–512.

12 Y. Sandoz, 'Implementing International Humanitarian Law', in UNESCO (ed.), *International Dimensions of Humanitarian Law* (London: Martinus Nijhoff, 1988), 259–282.

13 See R. Bellelli, The System, *supra* note 1, at 4(A)(2)(a).

14 Art. 17(3) ICCSt.

15 Art. 19(1) ICCSt.

16 Art. 112(4) ICCSt. Such function has so far been performed with extreme caution and without establishing the 'mechanism' which would have contributed to the effectiveness of such a role. The ASP is currently committed to setting up an appropriate subsidiary body, an Oversight Mechanism, which, however, will initially begin to perform investigative functions concerning disciplinary matters. See ICC-ASP/4/Res.4,

evaluation[17] related to the performance of the Statute – including in its implementation by States Parties – it has relied on vague provisions[18] to build a role for the ASP. So far, this has resulted in a monitoring based on reporting from states,[19] while no overall verification mechanism for the fulfilment of obligations exists under the Statute.[20]

Thus, the only binding authority in assessing implementation is the judicial one of the Court, during its admissibility procedure, but within the limits of the specific situation and case. The establishment of the complementary jurisdiction of the Court would not be applicable *in abstracto*, once and for all situations and cases, when lacunae are found in national substantive criminal law provisions. The Court has no judicial oversight on the ability as such of national legal systems to conform to the principle of complementarity *in abstracto* and once and for all, but it is instead empowered to assess *in concreto*, on a case-by-case basis,[21] the ability and willingness to prosecute

---

the latest *Report of the Bureau on the establishment of an independent oversight mechanism* (ICC-ASP/8/2 of 15 April 2009 and Add. 2 of 29 July 2009), and R. Bellelli, The Law of the Statute and its Practice before the Review Conference, in this Volume, at 13 and note 55 (hereinafter, The Law of the Statute).

17 The notion of evaluation, here, is exclusive of the ICC's mechanisms for ensuring compliance with cooperation obligations in specific cases, as detailed *infra*, at 2(E).

18 Under Art. 112(2)(c) ICCSt, the ASP is called to 'consider the reports and activities of the Bureau ... and take appropriate action in regard thereto' and (g) to 'perform any other function consistent with this Statute'. See also Art. 123 for the Review of the Statute. On the latter point, see R. Bellelli, The System, at 2(B), *supra* note 1.

19 This is allowed by the 2006 *Plan of action for achieving universality and full implementation of the Rome Statute*. See ICC-ASP/5/Res.3 of 1 December 2006, Annex I (Plan of action), ICC-ASP/6/Res. 2 of 14 December 2007, and ICC-ASP/7/Res. 3 of 21 November 2008. Under para. 6(h) of the Plan of Action, States Parties provide yearly information relevant to, *inter alia*, full implementation of the Statute. Available at http://www2.icc-cpi.int/iccdocs/asp_docs/Resolutions/ICC-ASP-ASP5-Res-03-ENG.pdf (visited 20 August 2009).

20 The establishment of such a mechanism for the implementation of an international instrument would apparently foster a wider participation of states and their ratification process through confidence building, information sharing, awareness raising and technical assistance. However, the inclusion of a verification mechanism in a treaty is rather a rare occurrence, as states' interest is in maintaining their sovereign right to keep under control the means, procedure and timing of implementing international law provisions in accordance with national interests. Examples of effective verification mechanisms for the implementation of treaty obligations are available in the field of disarmament, e.g.: the 'safeguard system' under the 1968 Treaty on the Non-Proliferation of Nuclear Weapons (NPT), as revamped by the 1997 Model Additional Protocol; the comprehensive and robust 'verification' system established by the 1993 Convention of the Prohibition of the Development, Production, Stockpiling and Use of Chemical Weapons and on their Destruction.

21 Art. 17(1)(a) and (3) ICCSt: 'in order to determine *inability in a particular case*' (emphasis added). This does not preclude the Court monitoring of the status of implementation of the Statute in national legal systems and of their ability to exert jurisdiction over situations which arise out of communications received. The Office of the Prosecutor is understood to cover this task through its Division on Jurisdiction, Complementarity and Cooperation, in line with the guidelines of the Office contained in the *Paper on Some Policy Issues before the Office of the Prosecutor*, September 2003. Available at http://www.icc-cpi.int/Menus/ICC/Structure+of+the+Court/Office+of+the+Prosecutor/Policies+and+Strategies/ (visited 20 August 2009). However, the Prosecutor clarified, e.g., in the Sudan/Darfur situation, that 'the Office is not mandated to assess the Sudanese judicial system as a whole, or to monitor judicial proceedings in the Sudan'. *Eight Report of the Prosecutor of the International Criminal Court to the UN Security Council Pursuant to UNSCR 1593 (2005)*, 3 December 2008, para. 67.

at the national level.[22] In this regard, the Court is the sole judge of the Law of the Statute,[23] not only because it decides what the applicable law[24] is, but because it makes final decisions on issues of admissibility and jurisdiction.[25]

This peculiar and effective judicial role under the complementarity principle entails that the lack of adaptation of the internal legal system to the crimes under the Statute would not result in the usual – in historical precedents – effect of hindering the implementation of international criminal law,[26] but only in that of depriving a state of the primary jurisdiction reserved to it under the Statute. Such effect would follow, in particular, also in case of a lack of implementation of the general principles establishing the irrelevance – as a result of the general principle of equality before the Law of the Statute[27] – of official capacity and immunities,[28] as well as of the responsibility of military and civilian commanders[29] for all the crimes under the Statute including, for civilian superiors, that for war crimes.[30]

Complementarity, therefore, entails that although the Statute does not impose an obligation to criminalize (with the exception, under Article 70(4)(a) ICCSt, of the crimes against the administration of justice), States Parties have the option either to incorporate the facts criminalized under the Statute into domestic law or relinquish their own jurisdiction.

As a consequence, national legislators have to carry out a particularly scrupulous effort in order to grant full protection under domestic criminal law provisions to the same interests protected by crimes under the Statute, so as to safeguard national sovereignty in the application of criminal law. There is no real alternative to filling the lacunae in national substantive criminal law resulting from the lack of crimes corresponding to the international ones or from a different scope of criminality.

---

22 ICTR, Decision on the Prosecution Motion for Referral to the Kingdom of Norway, *Bagaragaza*, Trial Chamber, 19 May 2006, found that while the Tribunal has no authority to determine which of a number of national criminal provisions has to be applied, it is competent to assess whether a domestic provision exists which contains an 'appropriate legal qualification in accordance with the Statute' (para. 15), to establish or exclude the jurisdiction of the state (para. 16). See also ICTY, Decision on the Motion of the Defence Filed pursuant to Rule 64 of the Rules of Procedure and Evidence, *Tihofil a.k.a. Tihomir Blaškić*, President, 3 April 1996, para. 6: 'unless expressly or implicitly authorized to the contrary by an international legal rule, international judges cannot interpret national laws in lieu of national courts or administrative bodies.'

23 See R. Bellelli, The System, *supra* note 1, at 4(2)(A)(c).

24 Art. 21 ICCSt.

25 Arts 17, 18 and 19 ICCSt, and Rules 52 and from 57–62 ICC RPE. It would be for the Court itself whether to declare the case admissible (depending on the inability of the state), based on the criteria under Art. 17, the gravity threshold and the existence of a reasonable basis to proceed with an investigation under Art. 15(3) ICCSt. For the notion of gravity, see R. Bellelli, The System, *supra* note 1, at 4(B)(3).

26 However, such preclusive effect might still be produced in the limited case of offences against the administration of justice, should the Court decide not to exert its primary jurisdiction and to refer the case to the national jurisdiction competent under territorial or active personality jurisdictional links (Art. 70(4)(b) ICCSt. and Rule 162 ICC RPE). Had the State Party failed to comply with the obligation to extend its criminal laws penalizing offences against the integrity of its own investigative or judicial process to those committed against the administration of the justice of the Court (Art. 70(4)(a) ICCSt.) on its territory or by a national, the exercise of the complementary jurisdiction of the state would be precluded and, thus, not only the Court would be unable to refer to such a state the case, but the state would also find itself in violation of international obligations which are incumbent on it as a Party to the Statute.

27 Art. 27(1) ICCSt.

28 Art. 27(1) and (2) ICCSt.

29 Art. 28 ICCSt.

30 Arts 27(1) and 8 ICCSt.

B. The Scope of Criminality

1. Identical Elements of Crimes

Differently from many other international conventions on criminal matters, the Rome Statute does not include any obligation for States Parties to criminalize in domestic law conducts penalized at the international level or to establish jurisdiction over such conducts.[31]

The permanent and institutionalized legal system for the enforcement of serious violations of international humanitarian law (IHL) and human rights law established under the Law of the Statute[32] is fully independent from states.[33] However, states are left with discretion to identify the means[34] to implement – in their different national legal systems – the duty to fight against impunity for crimes of international concern. In fact, according to the principle of complementarity and under an established principle of customary international law,[35] it is also incumbent on States Parties to suppress within their own national jurisdictions, and with primacy over the ICC jurisdiction, the crimes under the Statute

The notion of repression of the crimes of international concern falling under the jurisdiction of the ICC goes beyond the penalization of the generic conducts that have produced the harm to a protected interest or the threat thereof. To assess whether there has or has not been suppression of criminal conducts (i.e., establishment of such conducts as criminal offences) in the fight against impunity for the most serious crimes of international concern and as required by the principle of complementarity, it is relevant to ascertain whether investigation, prosecution, trial and eventually punishment at the national level has or not taken place by enforcing criminal law provisions which reflect the identical scope of criminality of the provisions penalizing a conduct at the international level. That is, that substantive criminal law provisions applied before domestic jurisdictions need to incorporate all the constitutive acts and elements of the international crimes as retained in the Statute. Such conclusions are unequivocally supported by the evidence provided under international and national law and practice, as detailed in the following sub-paragraphs.

2. National Case Law

The case law of national courts has adjudicated on the relationship between, on the one hand, customary and treaty law provisions and, on the other hand, the exercise of national jurisdiction.

31 See D. Robinson, 'The Rome Statute and its Impact on National Law, in A. Cassese, P. Gaeta, and J.R.W.D. Jones (eds), *The Rome Statute of the International Criminal Court: A Commentary* (Oxford: Oxford University Press, 2002), at 1860 (hereinafter, Cassese, Gaeta and Jones); B. Broomhall, *International Justice and the International Criminal Court between Sovereignty and the Rule of Law* (Oxford: Oxford University Press, 2004), at 86; G. Werle, *Principles of International Criminal Law* (The Hague: TMC Asser Press, 2005), at 75.

32 R. Bellelli, The System, *supra* note 1, at 4(A)(2)(c).

33 Ibid., at 4(E)(2).

34 For a review of implementation techniques, see A. Cassese, *International Law* (2nd edn, Oxford: Oxford University Press, 2005), at 224–231.

35 R. Bellelli, The System, *supra* note 1, note 12.

Jurisprudence ruled out that obligations to criminalize contained in international criminal law provisions can be performed at the state level in the absence of national implementing legislation.[36]

3. International Law Commission

The 1996 ILC Draft Code of Crimes against Peace and Security of Mankind included the possibility of retrial before an international criminal court in case 'the act which was the subject of the judgement in the national court was characterized by that court as an ordinary crime and not as a crime' of international concern.[37] In such situation, the second trial for the same conduct would have been justified because 'the individual has not been tried or punished for the same crime but for a "lesser crime" that does not encompass the full extent of his criminal conduct'.[38]

4. International Case Law

International criminal case law requires that the national criminal law provision covers the same criminality as the international criminal law one and be identically categorized. In *Bagaragaza*[39] the issue of lack of a national substantive criminal law provision penalizing genocide as such arose and resulted in the lack of jurisdiction *ratione materiae* of a state. The Tribunal denied to refer the case under Rule 11*bis* Rules of Procedure and Evidence (RPE) holding that, by charging the conduct as murder,[40] national prosecution would have only allowed the violation of the protected interest of the human life but not that of the integrity of the group, to be addressed.[41]

5. The Ne Bis in Idem Principle in the Statutes

The *ne bis in idem* principle (or prohibition of double jeopardy) is applicable in internal law, as a fundamental human rights guarantee to protect an individual from multiple prosecutions or

36 See A. Cassese, *International Criminal Law* (Oxford: Oxford University Press, 2003), at 303–306 for a review of case law of Switzerland, France and Australia. The dualistic approach in the relationship between international and national legal systems – only domestic law is applicable internally by the state – means that non-implemented international law remains inapplicable and without effect. This position is unchallenged, e.g., in Italian jurisprudence. See, e.g., *Cassazione*, S.U., 22 March 1972, No. 867.

37 See *supra* note 8, para. 10 at 38 and *infra* note 49.

38 Art. 12(2)(a)(i) Draft Code.

39 See R. Bellelli, The System, *supra* note 1, at 4(E)(4)(ii).

40 ICTR, Appeals Chamber, Decision on Rule 11*bis* Appeal, *Michel Bagaragaza*, 30 August 2006, paras 16, 17 and 18. Available at http://69.94.11.53/ENGLISH/cases/Bagaragaza/decisions/300806.htm (visited 20 August 2009). The Trial Chamber had found that Norway had no jurisdiction *ratione materiae*, as the murder offence differs in its elements and in seriousness from the crime of genocide, in particular it does not require the specific intention of targeting a group as such. ICTR, Decision on the Prosecution Motion for Referral to the Kingdom of Norway, 19 May 2006, paras 13, 15 and 16.

41 ICTR, *Bagagaragaza*, Appeals Chamber, ibid., para. 17, and also R. Bellelli, The System, *supra* note 1, at note 282. See also ICTR, Decision on the Prosecution's Appeal against Decision on Referral under Rule11*bis*, *Idelphonse Hategekimana*, Appeals Chamber, 4 December 2008, where it was clarified that the conditions for a referral under Rule 11*bis* ICTR RPE require an assessment of the competence of a state to accept a case from the Tribunal, including an assessment of the bases of the existence of a legal framework which criminalizes the alleged conduct and provides appropriate punishment for the offences charged.

punishments by a state for the same crime.[42] However, there is no obligation under international law[43] to extend the effect of the principle in interstate relations: in this area, the implementation of the *ne bis in idem* falls within the matter of respect by one state for the final judgements of another.[44]

In international trials, the safeguard from multiple prosecutions does afford protection from genuine prosecutions – i.e., meeting the necessary standards of independence and impartiality – while not from sham trials aimed at shielding perpetrators from international accountability.[45] Sham trials cannot qualify as lawful trials, held for the purpose of implementing constitutional guarantees and, therefore, would logically have no effect on international trials. This result is achieved by including under the Tribunals' Statutes an unidirectional or relative *ne bis in idem* principle[46] which establishes an absolute or irrebuttable presumption (*iuris et de iure*) that a different legal characterization of criminal conducts under domestic legal systems translates into substantive impunity for crimes of international concern.[47] To prevent the purpose of the Statutes being defeated, the national final decision (*res iudicata*) cannot be opposed to the international jurisdiction[48] when it is the result of charges brought under domestic criminal law provisions characterizing the facts as ordinary crimes instead of serious violations of IHL.[49]

The unidirectional *ne bis in idem* principle contributes – together with provisions on jurisdiction and admissibility – to ensuring that the international jurisdiction prevails in the repression of crimes of international concern, by reserving to it the authority to establish the lawfulness of the performance of national jurisdictions, even after a final decision is taken at the domestic level (*res iudicata*). This legality test is a prerogative of international jurisdictions, whatever is the

---

42 Art. 14(7) International Covenant on Civil and Political Rights; Art. 4 Protocol No. 7 to the Convention for the Protection of Human Rights and Fundamental Freedoms, Strasbourg, 22 November 1984; Art. 8(4) American Convention on Human Rights, San José, 22 November 1969.

43 Unless this is established under treaty law by states. See *infra* note 44.

44 See, e.g., European Convention on the Transfer of Proceedings in Criminal Matters, Strasbourg, 15 May 1972, ETS No. 073; Convention on the Transfer of Sentenced Persons, Strasbourg, 21 March 1983, ETS No. 112; Additional Protocol to the Convention on the Transfer of Sentenced Persons, Strasbourg, 18 November 1997, ETS No. 197. Available at http://conventions.coe.int/Treaty/Commun/ListeTraites.asp?CM=8&CL=ENG.

45 See the ILC 1996 Draft Code, *supra* note 8, at 72.

46 For an analysis of the *ne bis in idem* in the Rome Statute, C. Van den Wyngaert and T. Ongena, '*Ne bis in idem* Principle, Including the Issue of Amnesty', in Cassese, Gaeta and Jones, *supra* note 31, at 705729; J.P. Pierini, 'Il principio del *ne bis in idem* nello Statuto della Corte' [The *ne bis in idem* principle in the Court's Statute], in G. Lattanzi and V. Monetti (eds), *La Corte penale internazionale* [The International Criminal Court] (Milano: Giuffrè, 2006), at 1362 ff.

47 Art. 10(2) ICTYSt, Art. 9(2) ICTRSt, Art. 9(2) SCSLSt, Art. 5(2) STLSt and Art. 20(3) ICCSt.

48 Final decisions may also be reversed under national law, as is the case in review proceedings, or in cases of violations of fundamental human rights, where individual action is allowed before an international court, for example, the European Court of Human Rights.

49 Art. 10(2)(a) ICTYSt and Art. 9(2) ICTRSt: 'A person who has been tried before a national court for acts constituting serious violations of international humanitarian law may be subsequently tried by the International Tribunal … only if: (a) The act for which he or she was tried was characterized as an ordinary crime.' The same case (different legal characterization) is not considered under Art. 5 STLSt, due to the different subject matter jurisdiction of the STL, which is limited to Lebanese criminal law provisions concerning illicit associations, crimes of terrorism, against life and personal integrity (Art. 2 STLSt). See also R. Bellelli, The System, at 3(E). See *supra* note 1. See also R. Winter, The Special Court for Sierra Leone, in this Volume, at 11(A)(8).

principle regulating the relationship between international and national jurisdictions, that is: (a) primacy, as is the case of the UN *ad hoc* or other assisted Tribunals (ICTY, ICTR, SCSL, STL); or (b) complementarity, as is the case for the ICC. At the earlier stages, the relationship between concurrent jurisdictions is regulated by the Statutes of international jurisdictions either by establishing a predetermined criterion[50] or by categorizing the jurisdictional spheres with reference to the time of commission of the crime (*tempus commissi delicti*) and/or to specific facts.[51] Consequently, the rationale of the unidirectional *ne bis in idem* principle is to be found in the very purpose of international criminal justice: to prevent impunity for crimes of international concern. Thus, impunity is presumed under the Statutes when proceedings before national courts lack independence or impartiality and, therefore, are designed to shield the accused from criminal liability.[52] Although the Statutes use a different wording, it can be understood that the situation where the national judicial decision resulted in an acquittal because 'the case was not diligently prosecuted'[53] equates to that of 'proceedings … undertaken for the purpose of shielding the person concerned from criminal responsibility' under the Rome Statute.[54]

6. *Criminality and Admissibility*

(a) Inability and unwillingness

Under the Rome Statute's admissibility criteria for a case, a diverging scope in the criminality of international and national offenses may be relevant either as a case of inability or of unwillingness.

The inability of a state to investigate or prosecute[55] or otherwise carry out its proceedings[56] may depend on 'a total or substantial (collapse or) unavailability of its national judicial system'.[57] Thus, the inability of a state, which may result in the admissibility of a case before the Court, may depend either on a:

> (i) *de facto* situation, consisting of the lack of such minimal structures as they are needed for the functioning of the rule of law; or on a
> (ii) *de iure* situation, depending on the absence of criminal law provisions covering the same criminality of international law provisions penalizing conducts.[58]

---

50 Art. 17 ICCSt, for the admissibility based on willingness or ability.

51 Arts 1 and 8 ICTYSt and Arts 1 and 7 ICTRSt for limitations of these jurisdictions in space and time; Arts 1 and 4 STLSt, limiting jurisdiction to the attacks against Prime Minister Rafiq Hariri, those committed between 1 October 2004 and 12 December 2005 or that, although committed thereafter, are connected to them. See R. Bellelli, The System, at 3(E), *supra* note 1.

52 See *infra*, 2(B)(6)(a) and R. Bellelli, The System, at 4(E)(4)(i).

53 Art. 10(2)(b) ICTYSt, Art. 9(2)(b) ICTRSt, Art. 9(2)(b) SCSLSt and Art. 5(2) STLSt.

54 Art. 20(3)(a)ICCSt.

55 Art. 17(1)(a) ICCSt.

56 Art. 17(3) ICCSt. See R. Bellelli, The System, *supra* note 1, at 4(E)(4)(b)(ii).

57 Art. 17(3) ICCSt.

58 D. Robinson, *supra* note 31, at 1860–1862, addresses the risks for states trying to implement complementarity based only on ordinary legislation. See also B. Broomhall, *supra* note 31, at 91 for the risk, as an incentive for a punctual implementation in domestic law, of states losing their jurisdiction in the case of a failed complementarity test. Also, F. Lattanzi, Il principio di complementarietà [The principle of

Investigating a suspect for or charging an accused with domestic offenses incorporating a criminality which does not reflect that of the crimes under Article 5 ICCSt is equated to unwillingness and to the purpose of shielding a person from 'criminal responsibility for crimes within the jurisdiction of the Court'.[59]

The same conclusion can also be reached drawing on the UN *ad hoc* and assisted Tribunals' Statutes, whereby national proceedings have to bring an accused to justice for *international criminal responsibility*.[60] Thus, ensuring only a *national criminal responsibility* for crimes of international concern is not sufficient for a state to discharging its duty to prosecute.

(b) The scope of criminality: Elements and interests

Although a state might be genuinely willing to perform its duty to protect by exerting jurisdiction over conducts amounting to international crimes – while utilizing national criminal provisions originally intended to protect different interests[61] – this can only be done in accordance with international criminal law if its same substantive protected interests are also incorporated in the criminality of the national criminal law provision.

As a consequence, to satisfy the (in)admissibility criteria it is not sufficient that implementing criminal law provisions are actually introduced[62] under domestic law; should such provisions be drafted more restrictively than the international corresponding provisions – by penalizing a reduced scope, as to the protected interests – a substantial impunity would be granted for acts falling within the jurisdiction of the Court. This would also happen when domestic criminalizing provisions only indirectly address the interests protected by the international criminal law provision, especially when the latter has translated into law developments which (only) took place in international criminal case law as, e.g., is the case for the crimes against humanity of forced pregnancy or enforced disappearances.[63] In all such instances, the result would be a conflict between national provisions and the purpose itself of the Statute – that is the fight against impunity for the crimes under the ICC jurisdiction[64] – and, thus, such reduced implementation would amount to a breach of international obligations.[65]

The triggering of the complementary jurisdiction of the Court as a result of the inability of a state to exert its primary one is a conventional mechanism for the enforcement of the general responsibility of the state for the correct implementation of international treaties by means of internal

complementarity], in G. Lattanzi and V. Monetti, *supra* note 46, at 193: 'the lack of implementation could ... result in inability to conduct proceedings.'

59 Art. 17(2)(a) ICCSt. See R. Bellelli, The System, *supra* note 1, at 4(E)(4)(b)(i). Identical wording is used under Art. 5(2) STLSt: 'to shield the accused from criminal responsibility for crimes within the jurisdiction of the Tribunal.'

60 Art. 10(2)(b) ICTYSt, Art. 9(2)(b) ICTRSt, Art. 9(2)(b) SCSLSt (emphasis added).

61 For such a situation in *Bagaragaza*, see *supra* notes 22, 39 and 40. See also R. Bellelli, The System, *supra* note 1, at notes 235, 281, 282 and 301.

62 See *infra*, at 2(B)(6)(c). See also *infra* note 80.

63 Art. 7(1)(g) and (i) ICCSt. As to sex-based war crimes, identical definitions are included, respectively for international and non-international armed conflicts, under Art. 8(2)(b)(xxii) and (e)(vi) ICCSt.

64 Preamble (5) ICCSt.

65 According to Arts 26 and 31 Vienna Convention on the Law of Treaties, 23 May 1969, United Nations, *Treaty Series*, Vol. 1155, at 331 (Law of Treaties), international treaties 'must be performed in good faith' and 'interpreted in the light of their object and purpose'.

law.[66] Such responsibility requires that the result aimed at by the international law provision is attained,[67] while the means for such implementation would normally not be relevant. Consequently, the assessment of the conformity of national law to international law cannot disregard the ability of the domestic provision to be applied by a national court within the same context of the definition introduced by the international provision.[68] Such ability will be lacking when domestic law does not protect the same interests as are protected by international law and by means of correspondent elements of crimes.

The above entails that – in order to ensure the exercise of national jurisdiction on crimes which could amount to those falling within the ICC jurisdiction – it is not sufficient that default provisions are in place to cover, by means of ordinary criminal law provisions (e.g., murder, serious bodily harm, damaging), the generic criminality of a conduct which is harmful to a protected interest defined in general terms (e.g., life, personal integrity, property). Instead, the national legal system has to cover the specific criminality resulting from all the elements of the international crime (e.g., extermination, torture, attacks against protected objects)[69] within its relevant category (genocide, crimes against humanity or war crimes). In this regard, it is of significance that a number of criminal legal systems chose to implement criminal law provisions of the Statute by introducing internal provisions reproducing the international ones[70] although, in other cases, differently defined and/or worded.[71]

Therefore, although legal definitions that are to some extent different between domestic criminal law and the Statute are still possible[72] – and justified by the distinct characters of the legal elements of crimes as known under national legislation and developed in established national case law – such differences cannot translate into a diverging characterization of facts. Such situation appears to be very similar to that which originated the notion of 'double criminality' in extradition procedure: judicial cooperation and assistance can be lawfully refused on the ground of absence of dual criminality[73] in order to protect the sovereign right of states to exert jurisdiction (and extradite) only for acts constituting crimes in their own legal system.[74] However, under the ICC Statute the same criminality becomes the criterion regulating jurisdictions, as it is the criminal relevance of a conduct under the Statute that becomes the basis for allocating jurisdiction: in the absence of dual criminality, a case is admissible before the Court.

---

66 Based on the principle of prevalence of international law on domestic legislation, Art. 27 Law of Treaties provides that 'a party may not invoke the provisions of its internal law as justification for its failure to perform a treaty'. See *infra* note 77.

67 See, e.g., P. Vivaldi, L'adattamento al diritto internazionale [Implementation to International Law], in S. Baratti et al. (eds), *Istituzioni di diritto internazionale* (Torino: Giappichelli, 2003), at 126. For the result, fighting impunity, to be achieved, see *infra*, at 2(B)(6)(c).

68 See *Cassazione*, 24 June 1968, n. 2106.

69 See the reasoning of A. Cassese, *supra* note 36, at 305307 for some practices in treaty law implementation.

70 See, e.g., in the UK, the International Criminal Court Act 2001, Sec. 50 ff. Available at http://www.opsi.gov.uk/acts/acts2001/ukpga_20010017_en_1 (visited 20 August 2009). Also, for South Africa, the Implementation of the Rome Statute of the International Criminal Court Act 27 of 2002. Available at http://www.info.gov.za/acts/2002/a27-02/index.html (visited 20 August 2009).

71 See, e.g., for Germany, the Code of crimes against international law. Available at http://www.iuscomp.org/gla/statutes/VoeStGB.pdf (visited 20 August 2009).

72 G. Werle, *supra* note 9, para. 218.

73 Although double criminality is inapplicable for the European arrest warrant regime. See *infra*, at 3(D)(3).

74 Extraditable offences usually are serious offences. See I. Bantekas and S. Nash, *International Criminal Law* (2nd edn, London: Cavendish Publishing, 2003), at 181ff. See also *infra*, 3(D)(2) and (3).

(c) Fighting impunity: A result to be achieved

The Statute – differently from other international instruments containing criminalization provisions – does not explicitly include an obligation for states to criminalize prohibited conducts, as the Statute's whole new system for the suppression of the most serious crimes of international concern is instead based on the cooperation of states. From this perspective, rather than an obligation to criminalize, the Statute requires a result to be achieved – that is the fight against impunity. Obviously, 'achievement' is here referred to having in place the means for fighting against impunity, not that impunity is effectively defeated by eradicating criminal conducts, a result which goes well beyond what can be required of any state.[75] The situation is in this regard different for the UN *ad hoc* Tribunals and for the ICC. The authority of Security Council (SC) action under Chapter VII of the Charter made incumbent on all states an obligation of conduct to pass implementing legislation, including in order to be able to cooperate with the Tribunals.[76] As a result, failure to implement the *ad hoc* Tribunals' Statutes results *per se* in a breach of an international obligation,[77] even before the actual need to cooperate arises.[78] This approach was necessitated by the primacy of jurisdiction for the UN Tribunals vis-à-vis national jurisdictions. Under the Rome Statute's system the reverse primary role of states in fighting impunity is affirmed. As a consequence, the Statute does not require the adoption of any criminal provision with specific contents but the achievement of the result, by showing objective willingness and ability to fight against impunity (investigate and prosecute crimes at the national level). Should this result not be achieved, as a state is unwilling or unable, this would amount to attaining the threshold of admissibility before the international jurisdiction.

Therefore, while ratification of or accession to the Statute which is not prepared, accompanied or followed by substantive criminal law implementing provisions does not *per se* amount to incompliance with an international obligation, such approach by a state would be unsustainable in the longer term[79] because the implementation of the Statute in the relevant domestic legislation is subject, in specific situations and for admissibility purposes, to the final assessment of the ICC.

In turn, the notion of 'achievement' is based on effectiveness: implementing legislation which can be considered to satisfy the duty of states must be actually in place and not only the subject of ongoing drafting and or parliamentary procedures. The ICC case law has already found that the

---

75 For the different implications of the obligations to prevent crimes under the responsibility to protect and in the case law of the ICJ, see R. Bellelli, The System, *supra* note 1, at 2(C) and note 14. The ICJ stressed the importance of diligence in the prevention of genocide (conduct) rather than of achieving prevention (result). See ICJ, Judgment, *Application of the Convention on the Prevention and Punishment of the Crime of Genocide (Bosnia and Herzegovina vs. Serbia and Montenegro)*, 26 February 2007, paras 427–430.

76 SC Res. 827 (1993), OP 4 for ICTY and identical SC Res. 955 (1994), OP for ICTR: '*decides* that all States cooperate fully with the International Tribunal … and that consequently all States shall take any measures necessary under their domestic law to implement the provisions of … the Statute … including the obligation of States to comply with requests for assistance and orders issued' by the Tribunal. The obligation is repeated under identical Art. 29 ICTYSt; and Art. 28 ICTRSt: 'States shall cooperate' (para. 1) and 'comply without undue delay with any request of assistance or an order issued by a Trial Chamber' (para. 2).

77 Under general international law, lacunae in national legislation cannot be pleaded as a valid reason to absolve a state of its obligations under international law. The principle of prevalence of international law on domestic legislation is embodied in Art. 27 Law of Treaties, *supra* note 65: 'a party may not invoke the provisions of its internal law as justification for its failure to perform a treaty.' See also *supra* note 66.

78 ICTY, Decision on the Motion of the Defence Filed pursuant to Rule 64 of the Rules of Procedure and Evidence, *Tihofil a.k.a. Tihomir Blaškić*, President, 3 April 1996, para. 8.

79 G. Werle, *supra* note 9, para. 227.

actual adoption of national implementing legislation to the Statute[80] is relevant to the admissibility of a case so that a mere political intent or the establishment of any accountability mechanism may well prove to be insufficient. The same should be applicable when implementing legislation is adopted after the Court has ruled on admissibility, also on the occasion of a *motu proprio* review[81] of the inability/unwillingness.

(d) The final test

Under the Statute's regime of the unidirectional application of the *ne bis in idem* principle,[82] the national *res iudicata* established on a case, including crimes falling within the subject matter jurisdiction of the ICC, is still subject to the willingness and ability test before the Court.

As a consequence, should the ICC find that national proceedings were carried out for the purpose of granting impunity to the person concerned,[83] what is a final decision under internal law would be ineffective in the international order and cannot bar the exercise of the jurisdiction of the Court[84] where a new trial can take place for the same facts.[85]

Once the Court's jurisdiction is triggered, only the Court can interpret and apply the provisions governing the complementarity regime and decide on admissibility.[86] As a result of the authority of any jurisdiction to determine the limits of its own jurisdiction and competence (*kompetenz-kompetenz* principle), 'the Court shall determine that a case is admissible'[87] and 'shall satisfy itself that it has jurisdiction in any case brought before it'.[88] Thus, whatever might be the initiatives taken by a state to show ability and willingness, the Court has the 'ultimate authority to determine the admissibility of the case'.[89]

3. Cooperation

The interest of states to a provide for a substantially full implementation of the Rome Statute in order to avoid possible interference with the authority of the Court to establish its own ambits of jurisdiction and admissibility also holds true when the issue is approached in the positive

80 ICC, Decision on the admissibility of the case under Article 19(1) of the Statute, *Joseph Kony et al.*, Pre-Trial Chamber II, 10 March 2009, ICC-02/04-01/05, pages 25–27, at paras 48 and 49 (Decision on Ugandan Admissibility): 'no formal legal text relating to the Special Division is available and … draft legislation implementing the Statute is pending before the Ugandan Parliament' and '*the Chamber will* only be in a position to *assess the* envisaged *procedural and substantive laws* in the context and for the purposes of Article 17 of the Statute *after they are enacted and in force*. In this respect, *the contents of the envisaged legislation regarding the substantive and procedural laws* to be applied by the Special Division, as well as the criteria presiding over the appointment of its members, *will be critical*' (emphasis added).

81 Art. 19(1) ICCSt.

82 See *supra*, at 2(B)(5).

83 Art. 20(3)(a)ICCSt: 'shielding … from criminal responsibility.'

84 Art. 20(1) and (3)ICCSt. Right to the contrary, following the trial before the ICC, the *ne bis in idem* effect is fully operational for national jurisdictions, based on Art. 20(2) ICCSt. For a more detailed analysis, R. Bellelli, The System, *supra* note 1, at 4(E)(4)(ii).

85 See also *supra*, at 2(B)(2),(3) and (4).

86 Decision on Ugandan Admissibility, *supra* note 80, para. 45.

87 Art. 17 *chapeau* ICCSt.

88 Art. 19(1) ICCSt.

89 Decision on Ugandan Admissibility, *supra* note 80, para. 51.

perspective of the undisputed need to implement the cooperation obligations under the Statute,[90] rather than in the one of the formal absence of an obligation of implementing substantive criminal law provisions.

A. International Cooperation Proper

1. The Importance of Cooperation

As the Court has no sovereign powers on any territory, it also does not enjoy any autonomous enforcement capacity and has to rely on international cooperation for enforcing its decisions. Although this is a common feature of international jurisdictions, some remarkable differences result from the choice of states to establish the ICC as an organization independent from the United Nations.[91]

The relationship between the UN *ad hoc* Tribunals and the Security Council results in the Tribunals' legitimacy resting on the *erga omnes* binding Security Council's resolutions adopted under the authority of Chapter VII of the UN Charter. As subsidiary bodies of the Security Council,[92] the Tribunals enjoy the strong mandatory nature of the obligation to cooperate with them.[93] Due to the vertical[94] relationship established with states, the arrest and surrender orders of the *ad hoc* Tribunals – assisted by the binding nature of the measures under Chapter VII – cannot be disregarded without exposing states to the systematic consequences of breaching an obligation established under the UN Charter.[95]

On the other hand, the treaty-based ICC has to rely on a weaker requests-based cooperation system,[96] assisted (only) by the binding effect of the Statute between its States Parties.[97] It is in the light of this that the 'full cooperation' required of States Parties in line with the practice of many

90 Arts 86–93 ICCSt.

91 For the multifaceted meanings of independence, see R. Bellelli, The System, *supra* note 1, at 4(D)(2).

92 *Report of the Secretary-General pursuant to paragraph 2 of Security Council Resolution 808 (1993)*, UN Doc. S/25704, 3 May 1993, para. 28 (1993 UNSG Report).

93 In particular, the obligation of states to cooperate with the UN *ad hoc* Tribunals is based on Art. 24(1) UN Charter, whereby UN Member States 'confer on the Security Council primary responsibility for the maintenance of international peace and security'.

94 ICTY, Judgement on the Request of the Republic of Croatia for Review of the Decision of Trial Chamber II of 18 July 1997, *Tihomir Blaskić*, Appeals Chamber, 29 October 1997. See also A. Cassese, 'On the Current Trends towards Criminal Prosecution and Punishment of Breaches of International Humanitarian Law', 9 *EJIL* (1998), at 13.

95 The cooperation obligation for states in the enforcement of arrest warrants is restated in Rules 56 (Cooperation of States) ICTY/ICTR RPE, while the effects of incompliance are addressed under Rules 7*bis* (Non-Compliance with Obligations), 11 (Non-Compliance with a Request for Deferral) and 59 (Failure to Execute a Warrant or Transfer Order) ICTY/ICTR RPE.

96 The difference in strength between cooperation obligations of the Tribunals and of the ICC is stressed in J.R.W.D. Jones and S. Powles, *International Criminal Practice* (3rd edn, Oxford: Oxford University Press, 2003), at 837, para. 11.1.5.

97 The disadvantages of the establishment of an international tribunal by means of a treaty rather than a Security Council resolution, in terms of effectiveness of cooperation, were detailed in the 1993 UNSG Report, *supra* note 92, paras 22 and 23. For the sanctions related to non-compliance by States Parties or non-States Parties, see *infra*, 3(E)(1) and (2).

multilateral treaties[98] – by the general obligation to cooperate[99] appeared to be insufficient to such crucial procedural steps as ensuring the presence of the accused before the Court,[100] the taking of evidence, and other forms of cooperation. Thus, for these specific obligations, the Statute[101] enhances the legal effects of the obligations by using the notion of compliance.[102] As a result, the unavailability under national law of appropriate procedures for allowing cooperation cannot constitute a ground for excusing incompliance and less than full cooperation:[103] States Parties have no alternative than implementing in their legal systems such provisions as may be needed to grant cooperation to the Court.

As the judicial independence of the international jurisdiction cannot be matched by autonomous coercive powers, investigation, enforcement of orders and of sentences[104] are heavily dependent

---

98 See. e.g., A. Lanciotti, Rapporti tra l'attuazione del mandato d'arresto europeo e la giurisdizione della Corte penale internazionale [Relationship between the implementation of the European arrest warrant and the ICC's jurisdiction], in G. Pansini and A. Scalfati, *Il mandato europeo d'arresto* [The European arrest warrant] (Napoli: Jovene, 2005), at 188.

99 Art. 86 ICCSt.

100 As, under Art. 63(1) ICCSt, trials *in absentia* are not allowed.

101 The difficult experience of ensuring cooperation with ICTY in the former Yugoslavia has shown that concrete initiatives on the part of some states, and regional or international organizations to pressurize others for compliance were much more effective than the deterrent effect of any possible consequence deriving from breaches of international obligations under the UN Charter and SC resolutions. For the influence of cooperation experiences of ICTY on the definitions of the cooperation obligations under the ICC Statute, see W. Bourdon, *La Cour pénale internationale-Le statut de Rome* (Paris: Éditions de Seuil, 2000), at 240 ff. See also *infra*, 3(E)(3).

102 Art. 89(1) ICCSt: 'States Parties shall ... comply with requests for arrest and surrender'; Art. 93(1) ICCSt: 'States Parties shall ... comply with requests ... to provide the following assistance.' Similarly, for the *ad hoc* Tribunals, see *supra* note 76.

103 Art. 88 ICCSt: 'States Parties shall ensure that there are procedures available under their national law for all of the forms of cooperation which are specified under this Part' 9. See Arts 86–102 ICCSt.

104 The Court is building a network of agreements to ensure that its final sentences can be enforced in states (Arts 103–111). Agreements between the Court and states and organizations are published in the *Official Journal* of the ICC and are available at http://www.icc-cpi.int/about/Official_Journal.html (visited 20 September 2009). So far, these include agreements with Austria (27 October 2005, entered into force on 26 November 2005) and with the UK (8 November 2007, entered into force on 8 December 2007). It must be noted that, as for the enforcement of their sentences, the *ad hoc* Tribunals had diverging experiences and regulatory frameworks, as Art. 26 ICTRSt expressly contemplates that sentences might be enforced in Rwanda, while – lacking such a provision in the ICTYSt – the UN Secretary General directed that the enforcement of ICTY's sentences should take place outside the territory of the former Yugoslavia. 1993 UNSG Report, *supra* note 92, para. 121.While the Report responded to the need to avoid inadmissible risks deriving from the ongoing conflict in the Balkans, as well as to doubts about the functioning of a regular prison regime and judicial supervision of detention conditions, a different situation on the ground has thereafter lead to the adoption of Rule 11*bis* ICTY RPE, the rationale of which seems hard to reconcile with such limitation for sentence enforcement: 'if it is legally possible to refer an entire case to the territory of the former Yugoslavia, including the enforcement of the sentence in the event of a conviction, it can be concluded, *a maiore ad minus*, that the States on the territory of the former Yugoslavia can now be entrusted with the enforcement of sentences.' ICTY, Decision, *Pavle Strugar*, Dissenting Opinion of Judge Shomburg, para. 27. Along the same lines is the *Report of the Secretary-General on the administrative and budgetary aspects of the options for possible locations of the archives of the International Tribunal for the Former Yugoslavia and the International Criminal Tribunal for Rwanda and the seat of the residual mechanism(s) for the Tribunals*, S/2009/258, 21 May 2009 (Report on Archives), para. 75: 'fifteen or sixteen years later it might be argued that the judicial capacity of these

upon cooperation by the international community and other actors. These include all subjects that may have contracted an obligation to cooperate with the Court (including through the specific arrangements or agreements concluded with the Organs of the Court) or are bound under the relevant provisions of the UN Charter, as well as those willing to cooperate on an *ad hoc* basis because they share the purposes and objectives of the Rome Statute.

2. Cooperation of States

Members of the international community able to exert sovereign powers within their jurisdictions are naturally best placed to be in the frontline of cooperation providers for the ICC. These comprise states, including States Parties, states having accepted its jurisdiction and those that, although not party to the Statute, entered into special agreements or arrangements with the Court 'or on any other appropriate basis'.[105] Additional and special cooperation is required under the Statute to the Host State and regulated through a specific agreement.[106] Under international law, states may also be obliged to cooperate with the Court when a situation is referred by the Security Council acting under Chapter VII of the Charter.[107] The scope of cooperation in these instances is, however, different, as in the first category of cases – where the obligation to cooperate is voluntarily contracted, although on different bases, by a state – it is defined strictly under Part 9 of the Statute: while States Parties 'shall … cooperate fully with the Court in its investigation and prosecution'[108] and, further, 'shall … comply with a request for arrest and surrender',[109] non-States Parties are only bound to 'cooperate',[110] including for the execution of arrest and surrender.[111] In the second category – obligations imposed under the authority of Chapter VII of the Charter – the requested cooperation would normally be characterized as a 'full cooperation'.[112]

As to the contents of such binding cooperation, i.e., the scope of the obligation, this cannot but be interpreted restrictively, based on the specific obligations set forth under Part 9 of the Statute. The general obligation under Article 86 ICCSt cannot be read as a residual obligation to cooperate in situations other that those addressed by specific obligations.[113] In this regard, the scope for cooperation and judicial assistance under the Rome Statute is different from that under the *ad hoc*

countries has moved forward and it is therefore possible to consider transferring to them functions relating to proceedings before the Tribunals.' However, for *Radovan Stanković*, the very first referral case which also resulted in the escape of the convicted person, see R. Bellelli, The System, *supra* note 1, at 4(E)(3) and note 233. See also at http://www.bim.ba/en/133/10/13106/ (visited 20 August 2009).

105 Art. 87(5)(a) ICCSt.

106 Headquarter Agreement between the International Criminal Court and the Host State, adopted on 7 June 2007 and entered into force on 1 March 2008. Available at http://www.icc-cpi.int/NR/rdonlyres/99A82721-ED93-4088-B84D-7B8ADA4DD062/277525/ICCBD040108ENG.pdf (visited 16 February 2009).

107 Art. 13(b) ICCSt. In the only situation resulting so far from a referral by the SC, Res. 1593 (2005), 31 March 2005, OP 2, sets up an obligation ('*decides*') that 'the Government of Sudan and all other parties to the conflict in Darfur, *shall* cooperate fully', while *urging* 'all States and concerned regional and other international organizations to cooperate fully' (emphasis added).

108 Art. 86 ICCSt.

109 Art. 89(1) ICCSt.

110 Art. 87(5)(b) ICCSt.

111 Art. 89(1) ICCSt.

112 SC Res. 1593 (2005), OP 2: 'cooperate fully.'

113 B. Swart, 'General Problems', in Cassese, Gaeta and Jones, *supra* note 31, at 1595; C. Kress, 'Art. 86', in O. Triffterer (ed.), *Commentary on the Rome Statute of the International Criminal Court: Observers' Notes, Article by Article* (Baden-Baden: Nomos Verlagsgesellschaft, 1999), at 1053.

Tribunals' Statutes, where the assertion of their primacy over national jurisdictions requires that '*any* request for assistance or an order issued by a Trial Chamber' be complied with.[114] Therefore, other forms of cooperation, beyond those explicitly addressed in any of the obligations under the Statute, would only arise on a voluntary basis[115] and, thus, could be treated according to practices of prior consultations well established at the *ad hoc* Tribunals, although the case law of the Court does not seem to have yet fully explored the implications thereof.[116]

---

114 Art. 29(2) ICTYSt and Art. 28(2) ICTRSt: 'States shall comply without undue delay with *any* request of assistance or an order issued by a Trial Chamber, *including, but not limited* to ...' (emphasis added).

115 See *infra* note 121 and 3(B) and, for the settlement of disputes on requests of cooperation, at 3(E).

116 In ICC, Decision on the Interim Release of Jean-Pierre Bemba Gombo and Convening Hearings with the Kingdom of Belgium, the Republic of Portugal, the Republic of France, the Federal Republic of Germany, the Italian Republic, and the Republic of South Africa, *Jean-Pierre Bemba Gombo*, Pre-Trial Chamber II, 14 August 2009 (Decision), the Single Judge granted provisional release for the suspect, although all the six States Parties indicated in the request for release by the applicant had refused to accept him on their soil in the event of release. The Decision affirms that possible guarantees proposed by states 'are not a prior indispensable requirement for granting interim release; rather they provide assurance to the Single Judge' (para. 88) although 'cooperation of States is essential in these proceedings' (para. 89). The defence took the stand that accepting a person for purposes of interim release would fall (at least) under the general obligation to cooperate (Art. 86 ICCSt), recalling the obligation of States Parties under Art. 88 ICCSt to make available procedures in their national law for all forms of cooperation under Part 9 of the Statute. Réplique de la Défense conformément à la Décision de la Chambre Péliminaire II du 14 août 2009 et Requêtes Incidentes de la Défense, 24 August 2009, para. 9. While the Decision did not directly address the issue of whether the availability and guarantees requested of a State Party fell under an obligation to cooperate, the Single Judge made the effects of the release conditional on the identification of a state for the release, and convened hearings to hear additional arguments from states on several grounds. Under Art. 60(2) ICCSt, the PTC 'shall release' the person if it is satisfied that the conditions for arrest (Art. 58(1) ICCSt) are no longer met. Further, Rule 119(3) ICC RPE requires the PTC to hear the views of any relevant state only 'before imposing or amending any conditions restricting the liberty'. The acceptance by a state of the person on its territory can be considered as a sort of pre-condition for the release, at least because in its absence 'the arrest of the person appears necessary to ensure the person's appearance at trial' under Art. 58(1)(b) ICCSt. The need for such condition to be in place before deciding on the change of the condition of detention or on release is also undisputed in domestic jurisdictions, where granting house arrest or early release would be precluded if the detainee faced similar circumstances, i.e., homeless or otherwise where their whereabouts in the case of release would be undefined. As neither the Statute nor the Rules explicitly make conditional the interim release upon the acceptance by a state, the interpretation provided by the proceeding Chamber is widely discretionary and may produce unprecedented effect. In particular, the *Bemba* Decision produced the effect of granting release while its execution was made impossible by the lack of the necessary consent from states. The Court appears to overturn the findings of the ICTY's jurisprudence on the matter – that there is no absolute right to provisional release – also with the arguments put forward in the Draft *Report of the Court on international cooperation* (Report on cooperation), ICC-ASP/8/44, 20 October 2009, paras 58–60, where it made the point that, failing the ability for the Court to provisionally release detainees in the absence of states willing to accept them, 'the Court may be not able to fully enforce judicial guarantees of fair trial', at para. 60. In fact, under the *ad hoc* Tribunals' Statutes similar Rules 65(B) ICTY/ICTR RPE (provisional 'release may be ordered ... only after giving the ... State to which the accused seeks to be released the opportunity to be heard') jurisprudence has constantly held that the burden of identifying a suitable and willing state for the release is on the accused, and has consistently rejected release when such an agreement (guarantee) between the applicant and a state was not in place beforehand and when such a state had no legislation in place for cooperation with the Tribunal or did not have positive records of cooperation. See, e.g., ICTY, Decision on Milan Lukić's Motion for Provisional Release, *Lukić et Sredoje Lukić*, Appeals Chamber, 28 August 2009 9 (para. 5, for guarantees from Serbia not obtained by the accused at the time of the decision); Decision on

3. Cooperation of Other Actors

Other actors called by their mandate and field of operations to interact with the ICC include non-state actors, such as international or intergovernmental organizations[117] and civil society.[118] Under the Statute they may assist the Court in the fight against impunity, e.g., by providing information conducive to the exercise of jurisdiction and investigations[119] or the various forms of support discussed in the following paragraph.

Lazarević Motion for Temporary Provisional Release, *Milan Milutinović et al.*, Trial Chamber, 9 February 2009 (paras 16 and 27 for guarantees issued beforehand by a state); Decision on Motion for Provisional Release, *Dragan Zelenović*, Appeals Chamber, 21 February 2008 (para. 6 for prior guarantees of the state); Decision on Defence Request for Provisional Release, *Stanislav Galić*, Appeals Chamber, 23 March 2005 (para. 17 for prior guarantees form the state); Order for Provisional Release, *Beqë Beqaj*, Trial Chamber, 4 March 2005; Order on Motion for Provisional Release, *Rahim Ademi*, Trial Chamber, 20 February 2002 (para. 24 for the need for cooperation of states for the enforcement, and para. 34, for guarantees provided before a decision is taken on the release); Decision rejecting a request for provisional release, *Tihofil a.k.a. Tihomir Blaškić*, Trial Chamber, 25 April 1996. For the factors to be taken into account in the balance of interests to grant provisional release, see Order on Miodrag Jokić's Motion for Provisional Release, *Jokić*, Trial Chamber, 20 February 2002, paras 19–25 and Decision on Request for Pre-Trial Provisional Release, *Halilović*, 13 December 2001. Negative and positive preconditions for modified conditions of detention during trial were also considered in Decision on the Motion of the Defence Filed Pursuant to Rule 64 of the Rules of Procedure and Evidence, *Blaškić*, President, 3 April 1996, paras 20–24. See also the requests of the accused for release, in ICTY, Defence Motion for Temporary Release with Annexes A and B, *Dragan Zelenović*, 30 January 2008 (para. 15 for guarantees issued from a state beforehand); Defence Motion for Provisional release, *Mile Mrkšić et al.*, 23 February 2005 (paras 26 and 27 for guarantees issued beforehand by states); Guarantees from Government of Republic of Serbia and Council of Ministers of Serbia and Montenegro in Support of Mr Milutinović's Second Motion for Provisional Release Filed on 17 December 2004, *Milan Milutinović et al.*, 24 February 2005; Proposal for a Provisional Release from Prison for the Defendant Jokić Dragan, *Dragan Jokić*, 10 January 2002 (page 19 for prior guarantees provided by a state: 'following the request of the defendant Jokić's attorney, RS Government has presented guarantees'). The Pre-Trial Chamber II's decisions in *Bemba* was finally reverted by the ICC, Judgment on the appeal of the Prosecutor, Appeals Chamber, 2 December 2009, which *inter alia*, found that 'a State willing and able to accept the person concerned ought to be indentified prior to a decision on conditional release' (para. 106).

117 Article 87(6) ICCSt. These would include: the UN (Negotiated Relationship Agreement between the International Criminal Court and the United Nations, adopted on 4 October 2004 and immediately entered into force), including through its peacekeeping operations (Memorandum of Understanding with MONUC); regional organizations like the European Union (Agreement between the International Criminal Court and the European Union on Cooperation and Assistance, adopted on 10 April 2006 and into force since 1 May 2006) or others (Memorandum of Understanding between the International Criminal Court and the Asian-African Legal Consultative Organization of 5 February 2008, immediately entered into force); international Courts (Memorandum of Understanding regarding Administrative Arrangements between the International Criminal Court and the Special Court for Sierra Leone, adopted on 13 April 2006 and immediately entered into force).

118 Agreement between the International Criminal Court and the International Committee of the Red Cross on Visits to Persons deprived of Liberty Pursuant to the Jurisdiction of the International Criminal Court (29 March 2006, entered into force on 13 April 2006).

119 The Prosecutor may initiate investigations *proprio motu* on the basis of unqualified information provided by any source, including 'organs of the United Nations, intergovernmental or non-governmental organizations, or other reliable sources that he or she deems appropriate' (Arts 13(c) and 15(1) and (2)) that is, also individuals. It must be noted that the achievement of the objectives within each goal is assessed by the Court itself, as no independent oversight is provided.

B. Cooperation at Large

The notion of cooperation proper, as strictly construed in relation to the obligations established under Part 9 of the Statute, should not be confused with other obligations deriving from the Statute (e.g., to pay assessed contributions and to observe the treaty) or with any support the Court might need or avail of on different and voluntary bases. Under this concept of cooperation at large fall a number of different issues, vital for the success of the ICC.

1. Agreements

In the wider meaning of cooperation at large, including support to the establishment and mandate of the Court, an important role is played by States Parties and organizations through the negotiation and implementation of agreements with the Court, such as general or specific cooperation agreements[120] envisaged under the Statute for the relocation of witnesses, the enforcement of sentences and the release from the custody of the Court.[121] As there is no legal obligation under the Statute to provide such cooperation, states may decide whether to voluntarily assume additional obligations by entering into such agreements which would, therefore, need to widely defer to national legislations as a source of applicable law,[122] while reserving a role of supervision for the Court[123] in order to preserve the purposes of its judicial or protective decisions.

Cooperation of states under the supervision of the Court does not preclude an important role being performed by other organizations or structures that – as in the case of monitoring of the condition of detention of prisoners, similarly to other international jurisdictions which have developed established practices in a significant number of cases of detention on remand or upon

120 See *supra* note 117 for various agreements in force. However, closely related arrangements and agreements might also cover, e.g., the situations of interim release of accused. See *supra* note 116 and *infra* note 121. A clear distinction between 'mandatory cooperation' and 'supplemental agreements' under Part 9 is drawn in the *Report on Cooperation*, *supra* note 116, paras 12 and 14, and Annexes I and II.

121 Rule 16(4) ICC RPE for 'agreements on relocation and provision of support services' of witnesses. Views expressed by the Court on the subject sometimes seem to understand that relocation of witnesses may also be the subject of cooperation obligations. See S. Arbia, Discussion Paper, *The Three Year Plan & Strategies of the Registry in Respect of Complementarity for an effective Rome Statute System on International Criminal Justice*, Consultative Conference on International Criminal Justice (UNHQ, New York, 9–11 September 2009), page 4. Art. 103(1)(a) ICCSt: 'a sentence of imprisonment shall be served in a State designated by the Court from a list of States which have indicated to the Court their *willingness to accept* sentenced persons' (emphasis added). See also Rule 189 ICC RPE. Under Rule 185 ICC RPE, voluntary cooperation is also addressed for 'release of a person from the custody of the Court other than upon completion of a sentence', to a state 'which agrees to receive' that person. Such regime is applicable to '*any* other reason', which seems clearly to include early or provisional release. On this point, see *supra* note 116.

122 Art. 106(2) ICCSt: 'the conditions of imprisonment shall be governed by the law of the State of enforcement.'

123 Art. 106(1) ICCSt: 'the enforcement of a sentence of imprisonment shall be subject to the supervision of the Court.' See also Rule 211 ICC RPE. Similarly, Rule 104 ICTY RPE provides that 'all sentences of imprisonment shall be supervised by the Tribunal or a body designated by it'.

conviction[124] – may provide reliable and independent external contributions to maintain institutional credibility and public confidence in the ICC.[125]

2. Funding and Supporting Activities

The support provided for the purposes and aims of an international jurisdiction by states or regional organizations could also be framed as cooperation at large. This, e.g., may include the provision of funds for training[126] and project-related activities. As to the latter, both under the ICC complementarity system and under different allocation of concurrent international and national jurisdictions, improvement of the rule of law in situation countries is crucial to the achievement of a permanent jurisdiction as well as to the completion strategy of a limited tribunal. Therefore, enhancement of local conditions for exerting jurisdiction at the domestic level falls squarely within the mandate of an international jurisdiction, while international organizations involved in the maintenance of peace and security would naturally be well placed to support justice-related activities in the field aimed at developing a culture of justice, including by disseminating the legacy of international jurisdictions.[127] Similarly, contributions to the Victims' Trust Fund, established under Article 79 ICCSt, can be framed as support at large for the Court since the related programmes assist in redressing victimized populations.

3. Diplomatic and Political Support

Voluntary support to the ICC can be provided by States Parties through active campaigns of démarches and other initiatives for the universality of the Court (ratification and implementation) or for upholding its principles and values and to protect the integrity of the Rome Statute. Meanwhile NGOs are also extremely active in a number of activities in the field, which include awareness-raising initiatives, outreach and assistance to facilitate the access of victims to the proceedings.

The involvement of States Parties and observers, including civil society, in discussions and oversight mechanisms on the administration of the Court is also vital to ensure a sense of ownership by the international community. In this regard, the Court itself is responsible for the implementation of its Strategic Plan[128] as an instrument of self-management intended to enhance

---

124 Supervision of sentence enforcement is conducted by the ICTY, depending on enforcement states, through inspections carried out mainly by the International Committee of the Red Cross (ICRC), but also by the European Committee for the Prevention of Torture (CPT) or, in some cases, by a joint Parity Commission composed by state and ICTY officials. ICTY-UNICRI (eds), *ICTY Manual on Developed Practices* (Torino: UNICRI, 2009), at XII, para. 35, at 59 (hereinafter, ICTY Manual). See also, including for the list of sentence enforcement agreements, the 2009 Report on Archives, *supra* note 104, para. 39 and note 14. Similar agreements for the Tribunals also involve the monitoring of referred cases by the OSCE and the African Commission on Human and Peoples' Rights, ibid., para. 82.

125 Ibid.

126 E.g., support to the ICC's Internship and Visiting Professional Programmes.

127 Among other such activities, the promotion of the legacy, e.g., of the ICTR is implemented through Information and Documentation Centres in Rwanda, which are being opened at the offices of 10 of the Intermediate Courts of Instance (in Nyamagabe and Muhanga Districts, in Southern Province; at Gasabo, in Gasabo District of Kigali City; and in Nyagatare, Rusizi, Karongi, Ngoma, Musanze, Rubavu and Gicumbi) with the support of the European Union. The role of such information centres is also acknowledged in the 2009 UNSG's Report on Archives, *supra* note 104, paras 235–237.

128 See *Revised strategic goals and objectives of the International Criminal Court for 2009–2018*, ICC-ASP/7/25, Annex, where the three main goals of the ICC have been set: (1) a Model of International

the effectiveness of the organization. However, as the credibility of the Court also directly depends on the appearance of its action to match its goals and objectives, all external stakeholders need to play an important role by providing open contributions to the overall administrative functions of the ICC.

The mandate of the ICC – to address the highest levels of criminal responsibility for conducts threatening international peace and security[129] – bears with it the fact that the Court is normally called to operate under highly politicized circumstances. This means that its activities involve discussions in a number of political fora and organs, at the national and international levels, both in bilateral and multilateral settings. The operations and the decisions of the Court require follow-up by a number of actors in the international arena, including Security Council – based on it role under the Rome Statute and in conformity with the UN Charter – and relevant regional and international organizations. In addition, a positive complementarity[130] approach brings the Court into the field of the promotion of the rule of law, thereby requiring necessary coordination by, or at least interaction with, a number of relevant actors in the field.[131]

A role for States Parties and other states is, in this context, crucial in order to obtain cooperation and the consequent achievement of common goals of criminal accountability for the purpose of international stability. Even when structured and overall political support for the ICC's operations might be hindered for contingent and divisive political reasons, states may well continue to assist in defusing misconceptions about the Court and with supporting its related matters in the political dialogue.[132]

C. Challenges for Cooperation

The dependence of the ICC on international cooperation implies that cooperation issues that characterized the activities of international *ad hoc* and hybrid Tribunals were not overcome in the ICC system which cannot even rely on a steady and strong support by the Security Council.

However, the failure of a state to provide due cooperation to the ICC does not hinder its jurisdiction, although trials require the presence of the accused[133]and only the confirmation of charges hearing can be held *in absentia*.[134] Besides, if a person sought by the Court is not

---

Criminal Justice; (2) a Well Recognized and Adequately Supported Institution; and (3) a Model of Public Administration.

129 Preamble ICCSt: '*determined* to … establish an [ICC] … with jurisdiction over' (para. 9) 'unimaginable atrocities' (para. 2) that are 'grave crimes threaten[ing] the peace, security and well-being of the world' (para. 3) and, therefore, to be considered 'the most serious crimes of concern to the international community as a whole' (para. 9).

130 R. Bellelli, The System, *supra* note 1, at 4(E)(4)(c).

131 'The contribution of the AU and the Arab League and others to the promotion of accountability mechanisms in the Sudan is essential'. *Eighth Report of the Prosecutor of the International Criminal Court to the UN Security Council Pursuant to UNSCR 1593 (2005)*, 3 December 2008, para. 67. See also *supra* note 21.

132 Under Art. 2(4) Council Common Position 2003/444/CFSP of 16 June 2003 on the International Criminal Court, 'the Union and its Member States shall coordinate political … support for the Court with regard to various States or groups of States'. Available at http://www.consilium.europa.eu/uedocs/cmsUpload/l_15020030618en00670069.pdf (visited 20 August 2009). See also the Action Plan to Follow-Up on the Common Position on the International Criminal Court, 4 February 2004. Available at http://www.consilium.europa.eu/uedocs/cmsUpload/ICC48EN.pdf (visited 20 August 2009). See also *infra* note 142.

133 Art. 63(1) ICCSt.

134 Art. 61(2) ICCSt.

surrendered to it, the arrest warrant still produces the effect of substantially modifying the legal status of the person sought and isolating the accused by restricting their freedom of movement within the borders of the state of residence or other non-cooperating states and establishing what has been referred to as a status of international pariah: free circulation abroad would be restricted under the threat of the execution of the international arrest warrant.

An example of the practical implications of incompliance with cooperation obligations can be drawn from the Italian experience with the delayed adoption of implementing legislation for cooperation with the ICTR:[135] when requested to arrest and surrender a person sought for heinous international crimes and who was located on its territory, Italy was neither able to execute the provisional custodial measures nor to proceed with the surrender to international justice.[136] The case clearly shows that, when dealing with serious international crimes, the parameters of territorial jurisdiction and of the proximity of crime scenes to national borders[137] have little significance, if any.

As the effective exercise of the ICC's jurisdiction requires the full cooperation of states, it will be of the utmost importance that the territories where a person sought by the Court can find safe haven be as limited as possible. This would require, on the one hand, that states which would normally have jurisdiction (territorial or personal) be genuinely willing to exert their primacy by carrying out criminal proceedings in their own courts of justice and, on the other hand, that states which would not normally have jurisdiction over the case be neither unwilling to cooperate with the Court nor unable to do so because, e.g., they have not fulfilled their treaty obligations by implementing the Statute in their domestic law. The existence or lack of these two conditions would affect the extension of the area of territorial impunity for the accused.[138]

The challenges of cooperation become more and more evident when considering that to faithfully apply its own mandate the Court needs to be present and active on crime scenes in highly volatile situations, where civil wars and international conflicts are still ongoing and military, social, political and economic tensions make the collection and preservation of evidence, including witness protection, extremely challenging.

Furthermore, it is apparent that ongoing conflicts and investigative and judicial activity involving persons still sitting at the top of the pyramid of national power creates a politically charged and sometimes volatile climate surrounding ICC cases, as it has been the case for the other international-

135 The cooperation law for ICTR was finally enacted in Italy by Law 2 August 2002, n. 181 (in *Official Journal*, No. 190 of 14 August 2002). The cooperation law for ICTY had been enacted promptly with Law 14 February 1994, No. 120 (in *Official Journal*, No. 43 of 22 February 1994), Provisions concerning the cooperation with the Tribunal competent for serious violations of humanitarian law committed in the territories of the former Yugoslavia (ratifying the Decree Law No. 544 of 28 December 1993). See also *infra* note 137.

136 The case concerned a Catholic priest, Father Athanase Seromba, wanted for genocide and crimes against humanity by the ICTR Prosecutor and eventually convicted thereof. As the accused was reportedly continuing his religious duties in the district of Florence after the cooperation request was notified on 10 July 2001, the issue was only sorted out by the voluntary surrender of the accused to the ICTR, in Arusha, on 6 February 2002. ICTR, Judgement, *Athanase Seromba*, Trial Chamber, 13 December 2006, para. 13. See also ICTR, Judgement, *Seromba*, Appeals Chamber, 12 March 2008.

137 In this regard, e.g., Italian cooperation law was enacted in 1994 for the 1993 established ICTY, while only in 2002 upon the 1994 SCR establishing ICTR. See *supra* note 135.

138 For the interesting position of Member States of the European Union before the Court, with reference to the binding reciprocal obligations of enhanced cooperation established under Community Law, see *infra*, 3(D)(1) and (3).

ized[139] jurisdictions. Issues concerning the execution of arrest warrant flow, in particular, from the power which the accused is able to exert, gathering consensus and support both at the national and international levels, thereby using the pressure of political and diplomatic strategies on the international community. Consequently, in such cases the enforcement of arrest warrants would normally be likely only under two sets of circumstances: (a) the accused looses his/her power at the national level, and surrender is a viable political option for the custodial state; (b) the international community is able to use its options under Chapter VI and VII of the UN Charter.

On the other hand, positive inferences could also be made from the fact that the adverse influence that a political climate or an unsettled conflict may exert on the exercise of an international jurisdiction may be reduced if not cancelled over time. In this regard, the permanent nature of the ICC is an advantage with respect to the negative impact that the same factors exert(ed) on other international jurisdictions. While substantial delays may still happen in the administration of international justice, the threat posed to impunity of perpetrators by the permanence of the ICC's jurisdiction – together with the non-applicability of statute of limitations[140] – could exert its assumed deterrent effect without any risk that artificial deadlines might affect accountability and a final adjudication of facts and responsibilities.

D. Indirect Cooperation

1. Peculiarities for the EU Member States

The suppression at the state level of the crimes under the Rome Statute is required under the principle of complementarity, but the obligation to cooperate for the effective functioning of the ICC is also strengthened for the EU Member States by instruments specific to the ICC[141] or relevant to fighting impunity[142] and indirectly implemented through the European arrest warrant regime. The

139 This applies, e.g., to the: ICTY, for a number of issues of cooperation with some states in the Balkans; SCSL, for the transfer of the Charles Taylor trial to The Hague, on grounds of a possible destabilization in the region; ECCC, for the continued delays in the establishment and start of its activities. In the experience of the ICTY, and from this perspective, reference could also be made to several consequences of the continuing instability in the area, including for the enforcement of sentences passed by the ICTY, which was excluded from taking place in the territory of the former Yugoslavia. See 1993 UNSG Report, *supra* note 92, para. 121. For further analysis on the point, see *ICTY Manual*, *supra* note 124, at XII, para. 23, at 156.

140 Art. 29 ICCSt: 'the crimes within the jurisdiction of the Court shall not be subject to any statute of limitations.'

141 See the latest Council Common Position 2003/444/CFSP of 16 June 2003 on the International Criminal Court, and its implementing Action Plan, *supra* note 132. See also the Agreement between the International Criminal Court and the European Union on Cooperation, *supra* note 117. R. Bellelli, The System, at 4(E)(4)(c) and note 292.

142 In the EU Justice and Home Affairs field a number of instruments have the objective of fighting against impunity for serious international crimes, or are relevant to that objective. See: Council Decision 2002/494/JHA of 13 June 2002, setting up an European network of contact points in respect of persons responsible for genocide, crimes against humanity and war crimes, 2002/494/JHA, *Official Journal* L 167, 26.06.2002; Council Framework Decision 2002/465/JHA, 12 June 2002, establishing joint investigative teams, replaced by the EU Convention on Mutual Assistance in Criminal Matters of 29 May 2005; Council Decision 2003/335/JHA of 8 May 2003 on the investigation and prosecution of genocide, crimes against humanity and war crimes, *Official Journal* L 118/12, 14 May 2003; Council Framework Decision of 13 June 2002 on joint investigative teams, 2002/465/JHA, *Official Journal* L 162/1, 20 June 2002; Joint Action of 29 June 1998 adopted by the Council on the basis of Article K.3 of the Treaty on European Union, on good

interaction of these two layers of Treaty and Community Law on obligations incumbent on States Parties of the ICC that are also Member States of the European Union may provide alternative means to ensure that the fight against impunity be pursued even if lacunae exist in implementing legislations of such states.

2. Dual Criminality in Extradition Law

According to the double criminality requirement, extradition or mutual legal assistance may only be sought if a conduct is criminalized in the legal systems of both the requesting and of the requested state. The principle of double criminality is applied in all bilateral agreements and is also repeated in the most recent multilateral Conventions concerning serious crimes.[143]

However, the principle of dual criminality no longer has any meaning in relation to cooperation between the States Parties and the ICC, because states which have not criminalized the conduct constituting core crimes under the Statute are under an obligation to allow the Court to exercise its complementary jurisdiction and, therefore, to surrender unconditionally.

The scope of the principle of double criminality is also partially different in the EU's perspective of direct mutual legal assistance, as the lines of judicial cooperation between Member States are directed towards simplified and accelerated forms: e.g., although the principle is preserved in its general scope, it is excluded – that is, cannot be opposed as a justified ground for refusing extradition – in a limited number of cases under the extradition Conventions.[144]

3. The European Arrest Warrant

Dual criminality is a fading requirement in the more developed forms of cooperation for the purpose of transfer between Member States of persons sought on the basis of arrest warrants. It is no longer applicable – for a set of crimes including, *inter alia*, Rome Statute's crimes – since the establishment of the European arrest warrant regime,[145] which has successfully replaced the extradition procedure

practice in mutual legal assistance in criminal matters, 98/427/JHA; Joint Action of 29 June 1998 adopted by the Council on the basis of Article K.3 of the Treaty on European Union, on the creation of a European Judicial Network, 98/428/JHA, *Official Journal* L 191, 7 July 1998; Joint Action of 22 April 1996 adopted by the Council on the basis of Article K.3 of the Treaty on European Union, concerning a framework for the exchange of liaison magistrates to improve judicial cooperation between the Member States of the European Union, 96/277/JHA, *Official Journal* L 105, 27 April 1996; Council Decision of 28 May 2001 setting up a European crime prevention network, 2001/427/JHA, *Official Journal* L 153/1, 8 June 2001.

143 E.g., Art. 18(9) Convention against Transnational Organized Crime, New York, 15 November 2000; Art. 18(1)(f) Convention on Laundering, Search, Seizure and Confiscation of the Proceeds from Crime, Strasbourg, 8 November 1990. The latter, however, allows for the refusal of assistance in the absence of the required double criminality only in the limited case of a request of assistance entailing coercive acts.

144 This applies with respect to the crimes of association to commit crimes or conspiracy, when directed to the commission of any of the crimes under Arts 1 and 2 European Convention on the Suppression of Terrorism of 27 January 1977. See Convention on simplified extradition procedure between Member States of the EU in case of consent of the requested person for extradition, Brussels, 10 March 1995, in *Official Journal*, C 78, 30 March 1995, at 2–10; Extradition procedure between Member States of the EU in the case of consent of the requested person for extradition, Dublin, 27 March 1996. See also the European Convention on Extradition, Paris, 13 December 1957, ETS 24.

145 The European arrest warrant introduced by the Council Framework Decision of 13 June 2002 on the European arrest warrant and the surrender procedures between Member States is intended to progressively substitute between EU Member States all the precedent extradition conventions (e.g., extradition provisions of

with direct surrender which is aimed at removing the political[146] phase needed for extraditions, and by the establishment a strictly judicial procedure for surrender.[147]

---

the 1977 European Convention for the suppression of terrorism; 1995 Brussels Convention for the simplified procedure of extradition; 1996 Dublin Convention on the extradition procedure) and this result is being progressively and steadily achieved, with a growing number of warrants and requests issued and successes in their execution and in surrender. All instruments and Reports available at http://ec.europa.eu/justice_home/doc_centre/criminal/extradition/doc_criminal_extradition_en.htm (visited 20 August 2009). See the second *Report of the Commission on the implementation since 2005 of the Council Framework Decision of 13 June 2002 on the European arrest warrant and the surrender procedures between Member States*, SEC(2007)979, 11 July 2007, para. 3 (Second Report). Available at http://eur-lex.europa.eu/LexUriserv/site/en/com/2007/com2007_0407en01.pdf (visited 20 August 2009).

146 I.e., the ministerial procedure. However, in implementing the 2002 Framework Decision, some Member States have designated an executive body as the competent judicial authority. See first *Report from the Commission based on Article 34 of the Council Framework Decision of 13 June 2002 on the European arrest warrant and the surrender procedures between Member States*, SEC(2005)267, 23 February 2005, para. 2.1.2. (First Report) and *Second Report, supra* note 145, at 2.2.3.

147 The term 'extradition' is understood to be used only to address state-to-state relations. Art. 102 ICCSt gives a clear indication of the use of terms: 'surrender', as the delivering up of a person by a state to the Court, pursuant to the Statute; 'extradition', as the delivering up of a person from one state to another, as provided by a treaty, convention or national legislation. These definitions reflect the different nature of the acts and were already well used in precedents having as their common denominator the transfer of accused persons by states to entities established with jurisdictional functions under international law, as is the case of the UN *ad hoc* Tribunals. See Art. 29(2)(e) ICTYSt and Art. 28(2)(e) ICTRSt. Surrender is also a term used when referring to cooperation between states when, in the context of a reciprocal waiver of sovereign prerogatives, enhanced cooperation comes under consideration. This applies, e.g., in Europe, in addition to the European arrest warrant regime, for the surrender provided under the 1995 Brussels Convention (see *supra* note 145), which is only applicable when the requested person has voluntarily consented to the delivering up to another jurisdiction. Surrender is also used in Art. 3 Treaty between the Italian Republic and the Kingdom of Spain for the prosecution of serious crimes through the replacement of extradition in a common area of justice, Rome, 28 November 2000. This agreement was the precedent limited to two EU Member States of the surrender mechanism later introduced by the 2002 Framework Decision on the European arrest warrant. Similarly, surrender is the form used within NATO member states, in their SOFAs, as Art. VII of the Convention between the states participating in the North Atlantic Treaty on the Status of their Armed Forces (London, 19 June 1951) provides the criteria for allocating the jurisdiction between the sending and the receiving state, and (para. 5) for the surrender to the state which has jurisdiction over the case. In all these surrender situations, the common denominator is the transfer of a person to an international judge or to a judge or authority of another state, pursuant to international customary or treaty law. Therefore, it can be argued that the international norm has widened (through reciprocal waivers to states' sovereignty) the traditional limits of national jurisdictions, by adding explicitly established organs (international Tribunals) or by acknowledging homogeneity of other national jurisdictional organs. As far as the ICC is concerned, this would mean that the international permanent criminal jurisdiction may be appreciated as an extension of the national jurisdiction and, consequently, that none of the substantive or procedural grounds of the constitutional prohibition for extradition is applicable to a judge of the same nature as the national judge. Drawing on the differences between extradition and surrender based on the intention expressed by states by ratifying the treaties, on the explicit definitions in the Statute and on the homogeneity of the jurisdictions involved, it can be concluded on this point that constitutional provisions on extradition are not applicable to surrender. See R. Bellelli, 'Italian Implementation of the Rome Statute and Related Constitutional Issues', in R.S. Lee (ed.), *State's Responses to Issues Arising from the ICC Statute: Constitutional, Sovereignty, Judicial Cooperation and Criminal Law* (Ardsley: Transnational Publishers, 2005), 231–235.

The enhanced cooperation regime established between the EU Member States results in a differentiated regime vis-à-vis that applicable for interstate cooperation addressing crimes of international concern. In fact, in the absence of a national substantive criminal law provision containing all the elements of the international provision, the principle of double criminality would hinder judicial cooperation and assistance between third states. However, between EU Member States, the list of offences for which an European arrest warrant can be issued and surrender procedures take place without verification of the double criminality of the act includes all the 'crimes within the jurisdiction of the International Criminal Court'.[148] Consequently, for arrest and surrender procedures between the EU Member States[149] – limited to the European arrest warrant, and since the entry into force of that regime[150] – the double criminality requirement should no longer be applicable for serious crimes of international concern.[151]

This strengthened arrest and surrender procedure between Member States of the EU could provide a default mechanism to ensure cooperation with the ICC, in case any EU Member State finds itself in the position of being unable to cooperate directly with the Court for the enforcement of its arrest warrants because, e.g., it has not adopted any cooperation legislation or incorporated in its national legislation any of the crimes under the Statute. In such a situation, an EU Member State's arrest warrant for a crime under the jurisdiction of the Court, but for which such state has also primary jurisdiction, could well douple the arrest warrant issued by the Court, although this would raise issues of complementarity as the case would have normally already been provisionally ruled as admissible before the ICC.[152] Beside any challenge brought by such state to the admissibility of

148 Art. 2(2) Council Framework Decision of 13 June 2002 on the European arrest warrant and the surrender procedures between Member States, 2002/584/JHA, in *Official Journal L* 190 of 18 July 2002, at 1 to 20. Available at http://eur-lex.europa.eu/smartapi/cgi/sga_doc?smartapi!celexapi!prod!CELEXnum doc&lg=EN&numdoc=32002F0584&model=guichett (visited 20 September 2009). The list also contains international crimes which might be of relevance for ICC's operations, such as trafficking in human beings, illicit trafficking in weapons, corruption, laundering of the proceeds of crimes, terrorism, participation in a criminal organization. See N. Piacente, Addressing the Impunity Gap through Cooperation, in this Volume, at 2(D), (E)(6) and (7).

149 The dual criminality requirement still remains valid and applicable in extradition procedures between EU Member States and other states.

150 From 1 January 2004, although the arrangements were applied for some states with delays up to April 2006. See the *First Report*, *supra* note 148 at 2.1.1. and the *Second Report*, *supra*, 145, at 2.1.2

151 However, some national legislation implementing the Framework Decision on the European arrest warrant did, in their substance, reintroduce a double criminality criterion by a mandatory requirement that the national legislation of the requested state criminalizes conducts (falling under the ICC jurisdiction and) identical to those which are the subject of the request contained in the request of execution of an arrest warrant by another Member State. *Second Report*, *supra* note 145, para. 2.2.3. See also Art. 8(1)(ii) Italian Law 22 April 2005, No. 69: 'Disregarding the double criminality, surrender is executed on the basis of the European arrest warrant for … crimes falling under the jurisdiction of the ICC.' However, the following Art. 8(2) provides that 'the Italian judicial authority ascertains what is the definition of the offenses for which the surrender is requested … and whether the same corresponds to the offenses under para. 1', thus making it necessary that the same elements of the crimes are included in the criminalization of conducts both in the requesting and in the requested state. As a consequence, the following Art. 8(3) concludes that 'should the act not be criminalized under Italian law, the surrender of an Italian national is not proceeded with', if he/she was unintentionally unaware of the requesting state's criminal law provision on which the arrest warrant was issued.

152 Art. 19(1) ICCSt. E.g., in Decision on the Prosecution Application under Article 58(7) of the Statute, *Ahmad Muhammad Harun ('Ahmad Harun') and Ali Muhammad Al Abd-Rahman ('Ali Kushayb')*, Pre-Trial

the case,[153] the EU Member State identically requested both by the Court and by another Member State for execution of competing arrest warrants and surrender requests would find itself in a situation of competing requests under Article 90(2) ICCSt.

The EU Member States and State Parties to the ICC are bound by two different obligations to cooperate, the one towards the other Member States and the other towards the Court. Thus, a Member State of the Union finding itself unable to grant an ICC request for cooperation because of the lack of implementing legislation would breach the cooperation obligation under the Statute, but still be subject to an obligation under the 2002 Framework Decision towards the other EU Member States. Not complying with the latter obligation would then make such Member State accountable under Community law.[154]

However, in the assumption that the requested state is unable to cooperate with the Court, it could be argued that – rather than being non-compliant under Articles 86–90 ICCSt – the requested state could grant the request of the EU Member State for arrest and surrender and in this way indirectly cooperate with the Court. In fact, when the requesting state is not in a similar situation of inability to cooperate with the Court, such solution would ensure that the obligation to arrest and surrender to the Court is followed up after the completion of the procedure under the 2002 Framework Decision; the receiving state would be in turn obliged under Article 90 ICCSt to comply with the prevailing request of the Court and the effect of enabling the ICC to further its proceedings would be reached with the mediation of a state different from the originally requested one.

E. Remedies for Incompliance

Remedies for the lack of compliance with an obligation to cooperate with the ICC depend on the source of the obligation itself (Statute or UN Charter), which also affects the act adopted by the Court to trigger the liability of the state (referral or information).

1. States Parties and States Having Accepted the Jurisdiction of the Court

The obligation to cooperate of states – that have voluntarily and in full accepted the jurisdiction of the Court, either through ratification or by acceptance of jurisdiction[155] – is inherent in the binding nature of the treaty between Parties,[156] and the violations thereof fall within the competence of the policymaking body of the ICC, that is the Assembly of States Parties; in case of failure to comply with a request of the Court for cooperation, 'thereby preventing the Court from exercising its functions and powers under [this] Statute, the Court may make a finding … and refer the

Chamber I, 27 April 2007, para. 25, ruled that 'without prejudice to any challenge to the admissibility of the case under Article 19(2)(a) and (b) … [it] appears to be admissible'.

153 Art. 19(2)(b) ICCSt.

154 The same conduct would also entail political responsibility within the EU, taking into account the high profile that the Union has consistently maintained in supporting the Court. See R. Bellelli, The System, *supra* note 1, at 4(E)(4)(c).

155 Art. 12(3) ICCSt: 'if the acceptance of a State which is not Party to this Statute is required under paragraph 2, that State may, with declaration lodged with the Registrar, accept the exercise of jurisdiction by the Court with respect to the crime in question. The accepting State shall cooperate with the Court without undue delay or exception in accordance with Part 9.'

156 Art. 26 (*Pacta sunt servanda*) Law of Treaties, *supra* note 65: 'every treaty in force is binding upon the parties to it.'

matter' to the ASP.[157] However, the Court would refer the matter to the Security Council, when the jurisdiction was activated upon initiative of the latter,[158] as the obligation to cooperate would originate in Chapter VII powers.

As failure to cooperate is considered relevant to trigger such referral procedure only when it results in disruption of the 'functions and powers' of the Court, it seems that not all violations of the obligation to cooperate would necessarily lead to a referral to the ASP or to the Security Council, but only those violations that, for their gravity and impact on the proceedings, may be considered serious violations as they amount to disruption of the functions and powers of the Court. This should necessarily be the case for the failure to surrender in execution of an arrest warrant[159] which – as it would determine an absolute impediment to proceed with the trial in presence of the accused[160] would affect the very judicial function. However, it will still be a matter for the Court to assess whether such a failure is due to unwillingness to cooperate or, instead, to inability of the requested state(s) to arrest persons sought by the Court because, e.g., an ongoing conflict makes an arrest within the adversary field dependent on circumstances beyond the control of a state, such as the balance of the forces on the ground.[161] Other such cases might be inferred reasonably from the experience of the *ad hoc* UN tribunals,[162] where persistent lack of cooperation in the 'provision of records and documents'[163] has also been a matter for referral before the Security Council.

157 Art. 87(7) ICCSt.

158 Ibid.

159 Art. 89(1) ICCSt: 'States Parties shall ... comply with requests for arrest and surrender.' See also SC Res. 1207, 17 November 1998, for action taken by the SC upon request of the ICTY President following a refusal by one state to execute arrest warrants.

160 See, for proceedings *in absentia* only at the Pre-Trial stage, R. Bellelli, The Law of the Statute, *supra* note 16, at 9(B).

161 In the situation of Uganda, arrest warrants issued under seal on 8 July 2005 by Pre-Trial Chamber II for five leaders of the Lord's Resistance Army (LRA) were unsealed on 13 October 2005, but are still to be executed as regards Joseph Kony, Vincent Otti, Okot Odhiambo and Dominic Ongwen. Uganda's inability to arrest LRA leaders has been considered a reason for admissibility: 'noting the statements in the "Letter of Jurisdiction" dated 28th day of May 2004, that "the Government of Uganda has been unable to arrest ... persons who may bear the greatest responsibility" for the crimes within the referred situation.' ICC, Warrant of Arrest for Joseph Kony Issued on 8 July 2005 as Amended on 27 September 2005, Pre-Trial Chamber II, 27 September 2005, ICC-02/04-01/05, para. 37. The execution of arrest warrants in a conflict situation raises a number of technical issues, including verification of rumours, which might be spread on purpose, about the possible death of persons sought by the Court. In this regard, proceedings against the LRA leader Raska Lukwiya were terminated only upon ascertainment of his death, by Decision ICC-02/04-01/05-248, PTC II, 11 July 2007. Available at http://www.icc-cpi.int/Menus/ICC/Situations+and+Cases/Situations/Situation+ICC+0204 (visited 20 August 2009).

162 Rule 7*bis* ICTY RPE (non-compliance with obligations) provides that the President of the ICTY shall 'report' to the SC the matter of the failure of a state to cooperate, when it is so advised by a Trial Chamber or a permanent judge (para. A), or that the President shall 'notify' the SC when he is so satisfied by the Prosecutor (para. B). Rule 7*bis* ICTY RPE was used, e.g., in the case of persistent failure to cooperate with the ICTY by Serbia and Montenegro, but without major actions by the Security Council. On this point, see C. Del Ponte, Reflections Based on the ICTY's Experience, in this Volume, at 7.

163 Art. 93(1)(i) ICCSt. See the annual *Report of the International Tribunal for the Former Yugoslavia*, 4 August 2008, S/2008/515, containing information on the cooperation and failure thereof for, e.g., 'crucial documents and information', paras 72–85, at para. 79.

It must also be noted that the notion of a 'finding' to be made by the Court for referring the matter to the ASP or the Security Council implies a judicial activity by the competent Chamber,[164] under Article 87(7) ICCSt.[165] However, such referral procedure could still be prevented depending on the outcome of appropriate consultations[166] or – in case of failure thereof certified by the requesting body – of any challenge successfully brought by the requested state to the legality of a request of cooperation.[167] Should such alternative means not lead to a settlement of the matter, the judicial referral phase may be initiated by the Prosecutor or *proprio motu* by the Chamber itself through a procedure where the requested State Party is to be heard[168] and, upon the finding, the President refers the matter to the ASP or to the SC.

Although being competent for 'consider[ing] … any question relating to non-cooperation',[169] it does not seem that the ASP may impose any sanction, other than through the adoption of resolutions containing official reprimands of the conduct of the state found in contravention of its obligations. It cannot, however, be excluded that violations of the obligation to cooperate may result also in disputes between States Parties (e.g., in the implementation of obligations concerning competing requests for cooperation, under Article 90), which may lead to a referral by the ASP itself to the ICJ.[170] In cases where it is the Security Council to decide on matters of non-cooperation of States Parties upon referral of non-compliance of their obligations,[171] the Council may avail itself of the sanctions and other measures[172] under Chapter VII of the Charter to enforce cooperation.

2. Third States

For non-States Parties that entered into *ad hoc* arrangements or agreements with the Court,[173] or where a situation concerning Third States has been referred to the Court by the Security Council, the obligation to cooperate would not stem from the Statute – as this is *res inter alios acta* and,

164 The UN *ad hoc* Tribunals' regime establishes the competence of the President for deciding on non-compliance, on its own motion (Rule 13 ICTY RPE) or upon advise or request by a Chamber, a permanent judge or the Prosecutor (Rules 7*bis*, 11 and 13 ICTY RPE), or decision of a Trial Chamber (Rules 59(2) and 61(E) ICTY RPE).

165 In *Bashir*, Pre-Trial Chamber I found that the Government of Sudan (GoS) systematically refused to cooperate with the Court since the first two arrest warrants in the Darfur situation were issued on 2 May 2007 for Ahmed Harun, Minister of Humanitarian Affairs, and Ali Kushayb, regional Janjaweed militia leader. The PTC concluded that, 'if the GoS continues failing to comply', it would refer the matter to the Security Council, under Art. 87(7) ICCSt. ICC, Decision on the Prosecution's Application for a Warrant of Arrest against Omar Hassan Ahmad Al Bashir (Decision), Pre-Trial Chamber I, 4 March 2009, paras 228 and 248.

166 Art. 93(3) ICCSt.

167 Regulation 108(1) and (2) Regulations of the Court.

168 Regulation 109 Regulations of the Court.

169 Art. 112(2)(f) ICCSt.

170 Art. 119(2) ICCSt.

171 Art. 87(7) ICCSt and Article 17(3) of the UN-ICC Relationship Agreement: 'the Court shall … refer the matter to [the Security Council].'

172 The practice of the SC also includes the imposition of measures of progressive political pressure, with condemnation of a failure to comply with an obligation and specific requests to cooperate. See, e.g., also SC Res. 1207, 17 November 1998, by which the Council 'condemns the failure to date … and demands the immediate and unconditional execution', at OP 3.

173 Art. 87(5) ICCSt: '(a) The Court may invite any State not party to this Statute to provide assistance under this Part on the basis of an *ad hoc* arrangement, an agreement … or any other appropriate basis.' Such arrangements and agreements are either 'setting out a general framework for cooperation on matters within

therefore, not binding on non-Parties[174] – but directly from a bilateral agreement or the binding authority of the SC referral resolution adopted under Chapter VII of the Charter, in the performance of the role of the SC in the maintenance of international peace and security.[175] Consequently, when a Third State to the Statute fails to comply with an obligation established by the SC,[176] the latter is competent to assess the situation and draw any inference as to further actions to be taken and on the possible responsibility of the state.

Consistently, the Court – once it concludes that a Third State has not complied with its obligations – is entitled to take no action other than informing the Security Council.[177] In particular, it would not be possible for the Court to make a judicial finding of non-compliance because this is a procedure explicitly envisaged only for the lack of cooperation by States Parties, as it implies the exercise of authoritative powers which cannot be exerted on non-Parties to the treaty. The Security Council, once seized of the matter, would again[178] be able to avail itself of the measures under Chapter VII and, in particular, of Articles 41 and 42 of the Charter.[179]

3. Political Remedies

As judicial cooperation proper entails relationships between national sovereignties, it is normally a process characterized by a crucial political phase,[180] although afforded within established legal frameworks.[181] Policy matters would, therefore, normally[182] play an important role in determining

---

the competency of more than one organ of the Court' (Regulation 107(1) Regulation of the Court), or only fall within the competencies of one organ (e.g., the Prosecutor, under Art. 54(3)(d) ICCSt).

174 The rule on privity of treaty is customary in international law (*pacta tertiis nec nocent nec prosunt*) and is incorporated in Art. 34 (*General rule regarding third States*) Law of Treaties, *supra* note 65: 'A treaty does not create either obligations or rights for a third State without its consent.'

175 Art. 87(5)(b) and (7) ICCSt. In fact, under SC Res. 1593 (2005) referring the situation in Sudan to the ICC, the SC 'recalling Article 16 of the Rome Statute' (PP2) clarifies that it is 'acting under Chapter VII of the Charter' (PP 6).

176 It is worth noting that under SC Res. 1593, 31 March 2005, OP 2 a cooperation obligation was established for 'the Government of Sudan and all other parties to the conflict in Darfur', while states not Parties to the Rome Statute and other international organizations were only 'urged' to cooperate fully, as they were acknowledged as not bound by a cooperation obligation under the Statute. However, the SC seems to have adopted here two diverging criteria: on the one hand, it has maintained its authority under Chapter VII powers to establish obligations upon any member of the international community (in this case, Sudan) while, on the other hand, it has not established similar cooperation obligations for states that are not Parties to the Rome Statute. These being the facts, cooperation obligations in the situation in Darfur/Sudan now exist only for Sudan, under SC Res. 1593 (2005) and for the States Parties to the Rome Statute, under the latter instrument.

177 Art. 87(5)(b) ICCSt: 'the Court may so inform … the Security Council', and Article 17(3) UN-ICC Relationship Agreement: 'the Court shall inform the Security Council.'

178 Art. 87(5)(b) ICCSt and Art. 17(3) UN-ICC Relationship Agreement: 'the Security Council … shall inform the Court … of action, if any, taken by it under the circumstances.'

179 The ICC recalled expressly the powers of the SC under Articles 41 and 42 of the UN Charter (peaceful and armed actions). Decision, *Bashir*, PTC I, 4 March 2009, para. 248.

180 See *supra* note 146.

181 Multilateral and bilateral treaties and/or agreements, as well as national provisions for rogatory procedures.

182 With the exception of the various forms of direct cooperation between judicial authorities. See *supra*, 3(D)(3).

the degree of cooperation between states on specific situations and this appears to be the practice also when cooperation is requested by international Tribunals.

Due to the inherent weakness of the enforcement mechanism of cooperation proper available to international jurisdictions, it is instead at the political level that cooperation has been achieved in some of the most contentious or challenging cases. In this regard, experience has clearly shown that only developments in the national political arena, associated with a strong international pressure, have finally contributed to achieving satisfactory responses to the Tribunals' decisions.[183]

International practice seems, therefore, to clearly suggest that it is important to focus on the voluntary rather than on the compulsory dimension of cooperation. Experience in the field has shown that cooperation is an inherently voluntary process, which can only be successfully shouldered through persuasive means, either by increasing the level of understanding for the international jurisdiction or by making the option of non-cooperation disadvantageous for the state concerned.

4. Conclusion

Although the Rome Statute does not make explicit an obligation to implement its substantive criminal law provisions, States Parties have accepted that the responsibility to protect by judicial means is to be enforced collectively through the ICC in situations where states are unable themselves to discharge their primary duty. Thus, the principle of complementarity, on the one hand, deprives States Parties of any substantial discretion in the choice of whether or not to implement the Statute, as a minimum to avoid the admissibility of a case before the Court; on the other hand, the lack of implementing legislation or a different scope thereof vis-à-vis criminalization of conducts as contained under the Statute would, *inter alia*, hinder cooperation and, thus, result in a breach of explicit obligations under Part 9 of the Statute.

Even when implementing provisions are included in municipal law, full cooperation with the ICC may depend on the interplay of national and international interests with that of fighting impunity. Consequently, while legal remedies are formally in place to address non-compliance with the obligations under the Rome Statute, the practice both of the UN *ad hoc* Tribunals and of the ICC shows that international criminal justice has to pragmatically rely on the level of political backing that its independent decisions are able to gather in any given situation and case. This is the main challenge for the international community in making a success out of its commitment to fight against impunity.

183 See, in this Volume, F. Pocar, The International Criminal Tribunal for the Former Yugoslavia, at 5, in particular (C). C. Del Ponte, Reflections Based on the ICTY's Experience, at 7. See *supra*, at 3(A)(1) and note 101.

Chapter 11
Addressing the Impunity Gap through Cooperation

Nicola Piacente

1. Introduction

Instruments introducing obligations for the international cooperation of states in criminal matters may criminalize conducts which are often instrumental to the commission of serious crimes of international concern falling within the jurisdiction of international and international-ized tribunals. It has, so far, been scarcely explored whether, by means of implementing such instruments, states may afford international cooperation to the international or mixed criminal jurisdictions, from the perspective of an effective fight against impunity for international crimes.

2. The Complementary Jurisdiction of the ICC

A. General Features

The jurisdiction of the International Criminal Court (ICC) is based on the principle of complementarity, which allows states to retain their primary jurisdiction and hold perpetrators locally accountable for their crimes, provided that such states are able and willing to bring perpetrators to justice. Complementarity is not defined in the ICC Statute, although there are definitional provisions in some of its Articles.

An analysis of the provisions of the Rome Statute on admissibility shows that complementarity does not mean concurrent jurisdiction. By contrast with the *ad hoc* international Tribunals for the former Yugoslavia (ICTY) and for Rwanda (ICTR) the Court may exercise jurisdiction only if:

(i) national jurisdictions are unwilling or unable to do so;
(ii) the crime is of a sufficient gravity; and
(iii) the person has not already been tried for the conduct in question.

The preconditions for the exercise of ICC jurisdiction are set in Article 12 of its Statute, whereby the jurisdiction of the Court is automatically accepted once a state becomes party to the Rome Statute.

The Court can only exert its jurisdiction when either the territorial state or the active nationality state[1] are Parties to the Statute or have accepted its jurisdiction.[2] The jurisdiction of the ICC is, therefore, complementary to the jurisdiction of the following categories of states:

1 Art. 12(2) ICCSt.
2 Art. 12(3) ICCSt.

(1) the state of commission, that is the state on whose territory the conduct in question occurred or, if the crime was committed on board a vessel or aircraft, the state of registration of that vessel or aircraft;
(2) the state of which the person accused of the crime is a national.

It must be highlighted that among the preconditions to the exercise of ICC jurisdiction no mention is made of the state where the individual who allegedly perpetrated the crime resides, or to the state of nationality of the victims of the crimes.

According to Article 13 of the Statute, the ICC jurisdiction is triggered by three possible mechanisms:

(a) referral by a State Party;
(b) referral by the Security Council acting under Chapter VII of the Charter of United Nations, in which case the Court may initiate the investigation even if the national and territorial states have not accepted the Court's jurisdiction;
(c) initiation of an investigation by the Prosecutor, on his or her own initiative.

At the 1998 Rome Diplomatic Conference an overwhelming majority of states favoured universal jurisdiction over genocide, crimes against humanity and war crimes for the International Criminal Court. However, as a result of a decision taken in an attempt to convince certain states not to oppose the Court, the Rome Statute only includes universal jurisdiction for the ICC when acting upon a referral by the Security Council. Article 12 limits the Court's jurisdiction to crimes committed within the territory of a State Party or on board its ships and aircraft and to crimes committed by the nationals of a State Party, unless a non-State Party makes a special declaration recognizing the Court's jurisdiction over crimes within its territory, on its ships or aircraft or by its nationals. However, the Security Council – acting pursuant to Chapter VII of the UN Charter to maintain or restore international peace and security – may refer to the Court a situation involving crimes committed in the territory of a non-State Party.

B. Existing Lacunae Under the Principle of Complementarity

Despite the creation of the ICC and of *ad hoc* international Courts such as the ICTY, the ICTR, and the Special Court for Sierra Leone (SCSL), vast gaps still remain in the ability to bring to justice persons accused of the gravest international crimes: genocide, crimes against humanity, and war crimes. With limited resources, international courts and mixed internationalized tribunals can only try a relatively small number of perpetrators for crimes committed in specific territories and conflicts. Even with the establishment of the International Criminal Court, it is expected that there will remain an 'impunity gap unless national authorities, the international community and the ICC work together to ensure that all appropriate means for bringing other perpetrators to justice are used'.[3]

Addressing the impunity gap in the aforementioned situations also requires consideration of whether there is a role for international binding instruments, other than the ICC Statute. In this

3 *Paper on Some Policy Issues Before the Office of the Prosecutor* (Policy Paper), ICC-OTP, September 2003, at I, page 3. Available at http://www.icc-cpi.int/library/organs/otp/030905_Policy_Paper.pdf (visited 22 May 2009).

regard, the ICC complementarity regime makes it apparent that the ICC jurisdiction cannot be triggered when:

(a) the crime falling under the jurisdiction of the ICC is committed in a non-State Party and by nationals of a non-State Party;
(b) the relevant situation is not referred by the Security Council, and the non-State Party where the crime has been perpetrated or the perpetrators are nationals of is unwilling and/or unable to prosecute.

In addition, prosecution of serious crimes under the Rome Statute is also not available when crimes:

(i) were committed before the entry into force of the Rome Statute;[4]
(ii) were committed by middle- or low-level perpetrators;[5]
(iii) were committed by perpetrators under the age of 18;[6]
(iv) involve the liability of legal persons;[7]
(v) are not of sufficient gravity to justify further action by the Court.[8]

As the ICC was established taking advantage of a number of precedent experiences and of existing international judicial mechanisms, the Prosecutor has publicly announced[9] that his interpretation of the principle of complementarity will lead to seeking prosecution according to the seniority criterion, that is to investigate and prosecute only those suspected of being most responsible for the most serious crimes under the jurisdiction of the ICC. Such a policy would help to maintain the caseload at a reasonable level for the Court, thus complying with principles of timely and affordable justice.

Another challenging field for the functioning of the jurisdiction of the ICC is the level of implementation of the Rome Statute in national jurisdictions. The lack of implementing legislation to ensure prosecution before national courts of serious crimes falling under the jurisdiction of the ICC is relevant twofold:

(1) at the stage of admissibility it can result in the inability of a state; and
(2) any time an investigation at the ICC is not or cannot be triggered, as such non-availability of domestic legislation would open the impunity gap.

C. Ensuring Complementarity through Universal Jurisdiction and International Cooperation

In combating impunity for grave human rights violations a critical role remains for national courts and tribunals through the exercise of the so-called universal jurisdiction. Universal jurisdiction can be defined as an extraterritorial jurisdiction whereby a state adopts legislation and provides that

4 Art. 11(1) ICCSt: 'The Court has jurisdiction only with respect to crimes committed after the entry into force of this Statute.'

5 *Policy Paper*, at 3 and 7, *supra* note 3.

6 Art. 26 ICCSt: 'The Court shall have no jurisdiction over any person who was under the age of 18 at the time of the alleged commission of a crime.'

7 Art. 25 ICCSt: 'The Court shall have jurisdiction over natural persons pursuant to this Statute.'

8 Art. 17(1)(d) ICCSt: 'a case is inadmissible where … is not of sufficient gravity to justify further action by the Court.'

9 *Policy Paper*, at 7, see *supra* note 3.

its jurisdiction will be competent to apply such legislation without any factor connecting it to that state.[10] Universal jurisdiction refers to the competence of a national court to try a person suspected of a serious international crime even if neither the suspect nor the victim are nationals of the country where the court is located ('the forum state'), and the crime took place outside that country. The exercise of universal jurisdiction is commonly allowed or even required by national legislation and/or by some international conventions to which the state is a party. For example, the 1984 UN Convention against Torture and Other Cruel, Inhuman or Degrading Treatment or Punishment (Torture Convention) and the Grave Breaches provisions of the 1949 Geneva Conventions both mandate the exercise of universal jurisdiction. Since the Second World War, more than a dozen states have conducted investigations, commenced prosecutions and completed trials based on universal jurisdiction, or arrested suspects with a view to extraditing the persons to a state for purposes of prosecution.[11]

When the ICC Statute mentions the jurisdiction of states, it does not refer to universal jurisdiction.[12] However, any time a crime under the Statute is inadmissible for the ICC, the exercise of jurisdiction by a state is in substance a form of cooperation with the ICC, although the Statute confines the notion of cooperation of states to the Court's investigation and prosecution.[13]

Article 29 ICTYSt and Article 28 ICTRSt bind states to cooperate, without undue delay, with any request for assistance or order issued by a Trial Chamber, including, but not limited to:

(a) identification and location of persons;
(b) taking of testimony and production of evidence;
(c) service of documents;
(d) arrest or detention of persons;
(e) surrender or transfer of the accused.

However, none of those Statutes makes reference to cooperation between the ICC and the *ad hoc* Tribunals in maintaining the case load for international jurisdictions at a reasonable level or in filling the other above mentioned gaps.

D. Tribunals' Statues and Serious Crimes Established Under the Relevant Conventions

Some serious crimes included or mentioned in the ICC and in the *ad hoc* Tribunals' Statutes are contemplated by international binding instruments:

(a) serious violations of the Geneva Conventions;
(b) genocide;
(c) apartheid;
(d) discrimination;
(e) rape;
(f) forced disappearances;

---

10 See O. De Shutter, *Extraterritorial Jurisdiction as a Tool for Improving the Human Rights Accountability of Transnational Corporations*, Report to the 3–4 November 2006 Seminar (Brussels) in collaboration with the UN High Commissioner for Human Rights, at 10, note 42.

11 For an updated perspective on implications of universal jurisdiction in the operations of the ICC, see R. Bellelli, The Establishment of a System of International Criminal Justice, in this Volume, para. 4(D)(3).

12 Arts 12, 17, and 18 ICCSt.

13 Arts 86 and 93 ICCSt.

(g) trafficking of human beings;
(h) smuggling of migrants.

It must be wondered whether the relevant rules on jurisdiction within these international binding instruments may bind States Parties to fill the above mentioned gaps in the exercise of the jurisdiction of the ICC, bearing in mind that most of these conventions were adopted before the entry into force of the Statutes of the *ad hoc* Tribunals and of the ICC. Filling those gaps through international instruments or national legislation would in fact amount to an effective cooperation with mechanisms of international justice.

E. Jurisdiction of States Parties Under Existing Binding Instruments

The existing binding instruments introducing provisions on cooperation in criminal matters may be divided into the following categories, according to the criteria adopted to establish the jurisdiction of states:

(i) state of commission;[14]
(ii) state where the crime has been perpetrated and/or the perpetrator and/or the victim is a national and/or of the state in whose territory the alleged offender is, when that country refuses to extradite him/her;[15]
(iii) state where the crime has been perpetrated, and/or the state where the perpetrator and/or the victim is a national, or the state in the territory of which the alleged offender is, when that country refuses to extradite him/her, together with the criterion provided by the Transnational Organized Crime (TOC) Convention: a crime is committed outside of the State Party with a view to the commission of an offence established in accordance with Article 61(a)(i) or (ii) or (b)(i), of the Convention within its territory;
(iv) state where the legal person for whose benefit the crime was committed is located;
(v) state where the institution of the European Union against which the crime was committed is located.[16]

Therefore, not all such international instruments establish the jurisdiction of States Parties based only on the criteria under Article 12 ICCSt, that is territory and active nationality.

1. The Genocide Convention

The 1948 UN Convention on the Prevention and Punishment of the Crime of Genocide (Genocide Convention)[17] provides strict criteria to set up the jurisdiction of States Parties,[18] including

14 Art. 6 UN International Convention on the Elimination of All Forms of Racial Discrimination; Art. 6 Genocide Convention.

15 Art. 5 Torture Convention.

16 Art. 9 of the Council Framework Decision of 13 June 2002 on combating terrorism, 2002/475/JHA in *Official Gazette* No. L.164 of 22 June 2002.

17 GA Res. 260 A(III), 9 December 1948. Available at http://www.unhchr.ch/html/menu3/b/p_genoci.htm (visited 29 January 2009).

18 In their understandings of the Convention the US stated: '… (3) That the pledge to grant extradition in accordance with a state's laws and treaties in force found in article VII extends only to acts which are

jurisdiction *ratione loci* or the jurisdiction of an international Tribunal.[19] Therefore, combining the criteria under the ICC Statute and the Genocide Convention the ICC jurisdiction is complementary to the jurisdiction of states where genocide has been perpetrated, unless the legislation of other states provides rules based on the principle of universal jurisdiction.

According to Article VI of the Genocide Convention, it can be assumed that the UN failed to give their support to universal jurisdiction to try crimes of genocide, but expressly provided that, in the absence of an international criminal tribunal, those accused of this crime shall be tried by 'a competent court of the country in whose territory the act was committed'. This issue was dealt with by the Israeli Court that tried Adolf Eichmann.[20] According to *Eichmann*, provisions under Articles VI and VII of the Genocide Convention are not intended to ensure a universal repression of the crime of genocide by an obligation imposed on all states to cooperate with the state of the *loci delicti*. Those provisions do not impose on states an obligation to prosecute other than on the state on whose territory the crime has been committed (jurisdiction *ratione loci*), although the provisions do not exclude the possibility that other states, for instance the state of the nationality of the alleged perpetrator, may prosecute.[21]

---

criminal under the laws of both the requesting and the requested state and nothing in article VI affects the right of any state to bring to trial before its own tribunals any of its nationals for acts committed outside a state.'

19 Article VI Genocide Convention: 'Persons charged with genocide or any of the other acts enumerated in article III shall be tried by a competent tribunal of the State in the territory of which the act was committed, or by such international penal tribunal as may have jurisdiction with respect to those Contracting Parties which shall have accepted its jurisdiction.'

20 District Court of Jerusalem, *Eichmann*, Criminal Case No. 40/61. Eichmann was charged with the 'crime against the Jewish People' defined on the pattern of the conduct of genocide, as defined in the 1948 Genocide Convention. Crimes against humanity and war crimes are defined on the pattern of crimes of identical designations defined in the Charter of the International Military Tribunal – IMT (which is the Statute of the Nuremberg Tribunal) annexed to the Four-Power Agreement of 8 August 1945 on the subject of the trial of the principal war criminals (the London Agreement), and also in Law No. 10 of the Control Council of Germany of 20 December 1945. The offence of 'membership of a hostile organization' is defined in the judgment of the Nuremberg Tribunal, according to its Charter, declaring the organizations in question to be 'criminal organizations', and is also patterned on the Control Council Law No. 10.

21 The Jerusalem Court stated: 'in order to answer this objection, we must direct attention to the distinction between the rules of customary and the rules of conventional international law, a distinction which also found expression in the Advisory Opinion of the International Court of Justice (ICJ) with respect to the Convention in question. That Convention fulfils two roles simultaneously: In the sphere of customary law it re-affirms the deep conviction of all peoples that "genocide, whether in times of peace or in times of war, is a crime under international law" (Article 1). That confirmation which, as stressed in the Advisory Opinion of the International Court of Justice, was given "unanimously by fifty-six countries" is of "universal character", and the purport of which is that "the principles inherent in the Convention are acknowledged by the civilized nations as binding on the country even without a conventional obligation (ibid.). ... It is clear that Article 6, like all other articles which determine the conventional obligations of the contracting parties, is intended for cases of genocide which will occur in future, after the ratification of the treaty or adherence thereto by the country or countries concerned. It cannot be assumed, in the absence of an express provision in the Convention itself, that any of the conventional obligations, including Article 6, will apply to crimes perpetrated in the past. It is of the essence of conventional obligations, as distinct from the confirmation of existing principles, that unless another intention is implicit, their application shall be *ex nunc* and not *ex tunc*. Article 6 of the Convention is a purely pragmatic provision and does not presume to confirm a subsisting principle. Therefore, we must draw a clear line of distinction between the provision in the first part of Article 1, which says that "the contracting parties confirm that genocide, whether in times of peace or in times of war, is a crime under international law", i.e., a general provision which confirms the principle of customary

However, some argue that, since all states have an obligation to cooperate in the repression of the crime of genocide imposed on them, they should be considered obliged to provide in their domestic legislation for the possibility of prosecuting and trying a person accused of genocide, either where no state requests the extradition of that person or where, for whatever reason, the extradition request cannot be honoured. This would enhance cooperation among states in the suppression of the crime of genocide as well as cooperation of states with international Courts. Such conclusions seem to follow from the views adopted by the International Court of Justice on the nature of the 1948 Genocide Convention.

2. The Convention against Discrimination

The principle of *locus commissi delicti* has also inspired the rules on jurisdiction contained in the International Convention on the Elimination of All Forms of Racial Discrimination,[22] under which States Parties, under Article 3, particularly condemn racial segregation[23] and apartheid and undertake to prevent, prohibit and eradicate all practices of this nature in territories under their jurisdiction. Currently, there are 173 States Parties to the Convention, but some of them have not ratified the Rome Statute.

3. The 1973 UN Principles

Under the Principles of International Cooperation in the Detection, Arrest, Extradition and Punishment of Persons Guilty of War Crimes and Crimes Against Humanity[24] it is an objective of the international community that serious crimes of international concern be effectively investigated and perpetrators tried: 'war crimes and crimes against humanity, wherever they are committed, shall be subject to investigation and the persons against whom there is evidence that they have committed such crimes shall be subject to tracing, arrest, trial and, if found guilty, to punishment' (Principle 1). These principles insist on the need for international cooperation in this regard. They even state that 'persons against whom there is evidence that they have committed war crimes and crimes against humanity shall be subject to trial and, if found guilty, to punishment, as a general rule in the countries in which they committed those crimes. In that connection, states shall co-operate on questions of extraditing such persons' (Principle 5).

international law that "is binding on all countries even without conventional obligation", and the provision of Article 6 which is a special provision in which the contracting parties pledged themselves to the trial of crimes that may be committed in future. Whatever may be the purport of this obligation within the meaning of the Convention (and in the event of differences of opinion as to the interpretation thereof the contracting party may, under Article 9, appeal to the International Court of Justice), it is certain that it constitutes no part of the principles of customary international law, which are also binding outside the contractual application of the Convention.'

22 GA Res. 2106 (XX), 21 December 1965. Entered into force on 4 January 1969. Available at http://www.unhchr.ch/html/menu3/b/d_icerd.htm (visited 22 May 2009).

23 Article 1: '1. In this Convention, the term "racial discrimination" shall mean any distinction, exclusion, restriction or preference based on race, colour, descent, or national or ethnic origin which has the purpose or effect of nullifying or impairing the recognition, enjoyment or exercise, on an equal footing, of human rights and fundamental freedoms in the political, economic, social, cultural or any other field of public life. 2. This Convention shall not apply to distinctions, exclusions, restrictions or preferences made by a State Party to this Convention between citizens and non-citizens.'

24 GA Res. 3074 (XXVIII), 3 December 1973. Available, on the UNHCR website, www.unhcr.org/refworld/type,THEMGUIDE,UNGA,3ae6b37114,0.html (visited 22 May 2009).

Thus, the primary responsibility for repression lies with the state where the crime was committed. It is clear however that, where the state of the *loci delicti* remains passive – that is, unwilling or unable to investigate and prosecute the crime – the other states (in particular the state where the perpetrator is found) are under an obligation to contribute to such repression; any other understanding would run counter to the overarching objective of the international community as expressed through these principles, which is to ensure adequate repression not only of war crimes – for which the Geneva Conventions already provide for the principle *aut dedere, aut judicare* – but also of crimes against humanity.[25]

4. The Apartheid Convention

The International Convention for the Suppression and Punishment of the Crime of Apartheid (Apartheid Convention)[26] indicates other criteria for states to establish their own jurisdiction, as under Article IV the States Parties undertake:

> To adopt legislative, judicial and administrative measures to prosecute, bring to trial and punish in accordance with their jurisdiction persons responsible for, or accused of, the acts defined in article II of the present Convention, whether or not such persons reside in the territory of the State in which the acts are committed or are nationals of that State or of some other State or are stateless persons.

Therefore, states are bound to adopt measures to prosecute, bring to trial and punish persons responsible for acts of apartheid – regardless that such persons reside in the territory of the state in which the acts are committed or are nationals of that state or are stateless persons – and, pursuant to Article V:

> Persons charged with the acts enumerated in articles II of the present Convention may be tried by a competent tribunal of any State Party to the Convention which may acquire jurisdiction over the person of the accused or by an international penal tribunal having jurisdiction with respect to those States Parties which shall have accepted its jurisdiction.

---

25 Indeed, this would correspond to the trend as illustrated in other soft law instruments, which provides at least indicia about the expectations of the international community concerning the contribution of each state to the repression of international crimes. For instance, when in its Draft Code of Crimes against the Peace and Security of Mankind in 1996 (1996 Draft Code), the International Law Commission (ILC) proposed (Article 8) that 'without prejudice to the jurisdiction of an international criminal court, each State Party shall take such measures as may be necessary to establish its jurisdiction over the crimes set out in Articles 17, 18, 19 and 20 [genocide, crimes against humanity, crimes against United Nations and associated personnel, and war crimes], irrespective of where or by whom those crimes were committed. Jurisdiction over the crime set out in Article 16 [crime of aggression], shall rest with an international criminal court. However, a state referred to in Article 16 is not precluded from trying its nationals for the crime set out in that article.'

26 Adopted by GA Res. 3068, 30 November 1973. Entered into force on 18 July 1976. Available at http://www.anc.org.za/un/uncrime.htm (visited 12 February 2009).

It cannot be ignored that the definition of apartheid pursuant to the UN Apartheid Convention[27] is much wider than the definition under the ICC Statute,[28] as it also includes elements of other crimes contemplated in the ICC Statute, such as genocide (deliberate imposition on a racial group or groups of living conditions calculated to cause its or their physical destruction in whole or in part) and other crimes against humanity. It also cannot be ignored that some of the States Parties to the Rome Statute have not yet ratified the Apartheid Convention, as is the case for Canada, France, Germany, Italy and UK, while the US has neither ratified the Apartheid Convention nor the Rome Statute.

---

27 International Convention on the Suppression and Punishment of the Crime of Apartheid, New York, 30 November 1973, Article II:

'The term "the crime of apartheid", which shall include similar policies and practices of racial segregation and discrimination as practised in southern Africa, shall apply to the following inhuman acts committed for the purpose of establishing and maintaining domination by one racial group of persons over any other racial group of persons and systematically oppressing them:

(a) Denial to a member or members of a racial group or groups of the right to life and liberty of person:

(i) By murder of members of a racial group or groups;
(ii) By the infliction upon the members of a racial group or groups of serious bodily or mental harm, by the infringement of their freedom or dignity, or by subjecting them to torture or to cruel, inhuman or degrading treatment or punishment;
(iii) By arbitrary arrest and illegal imprisonment of the members of a racial group or groups;

(b) Deliberate imposition on a racial group or groups of living conditions calculated to cause its or their physical destruction in whole or in part;

(c) Any legislative measures and other measures calculated to prevent a racial group or groups from participation in the political, social, economic and cultural life of the country and the deliberate creation of conditions preventing the full development of such a group or groups, in particular by denying to members of a racial group or groups basic human rights and freedoms, including the right to work, the right to form recognized trade unions, the right to education, the right to leave and to return to their country, the right to a nationality, the right to freedom of movement and residence, the right to freedom of opinion and expression, and the right to freedom of peaceful assembly and association;

(d) Any measures, including legislative measures, designed to divide the population along racial lines by the creation of separate reserves and ghettos for the members of a racial group or groups, the prohibition of mixed marriages among members of various racial groups, the expropriation of landed property belonging to a racial group or groups or to members thereof;

(e) Exploitation of the labour of the members of a racial group or groups, in particular by submitting them to forced labour;

(f) Persecution of organizations and persons, by depriving them of fundamental rights and freedoms, because they oppose apartheid.'

28 Art. 7(2)(h) ICCSt: '"The crime of apartheid" means inhumane acts of a character similar to those referred to in paragraph 1, committed in the context of an institutionalized regime of systematic oppression and domination by one racial group over any other racial group or groups and committed with the intention of maintaining that regime.'

5. Geneva Law and Torture Convention

The four 1949 Geneva Conventions and Article 5 of the 1984 UN Convention against Torture and Other Cruel, Inhuman or Degrading Treatment or Punishment (Torture Convention) extend the jurisdictional criteria,[29] as States Parties will establish their jurisdiction when:

(a) the relevant crimes are committed within the territory of that state;
(b) the alleged offender is a national of that state; or
(c) the victim is a national of that state;
(d) the alleged offender is in a territory under the jurisdiction of that state and that state refuses to extradite him or her.

6. The Convention Against Transnational Organized Crime

Taking into account the mentioned Conventions, for the prosecution of the crimes of Apartheid, Torture and Other Cruel, Inhuman or Degrading Treatment or Punishment, the ICC jurisdiction is complementary to that of a wider category of states. At the same time, inertia by the state where the crime was committed or that of which the alleged offender is a national (if both of them are not States Parties of the Rome Statute) shall not prevent the alleged perpetrators from being prosecuted by other countries.

Cooperation in prosecution of war crimes and crimes against humanity may also be achieved through the prosecution of other crimes that can be deemed as instrumental to the crimes falling within the jurisdiction of the ICC and of the *ad hoc* Tribunals. Other binding instruments, such as those relevant in the fight against organized crime must be taken into account. The 2000 United Nations Convention Against Transnational Organized Crime (TOC or Palermo Convention)[30] – which establishes obligations for the prosecution of serious organized crimes – is in this regard undoubtedly relevant, as crimes established under the Convention and its supplementing Protocols are often instrumental to the perpetration of crimes falling under the jurisdiction of the ICC.

---

29 The ICC Statute contemplates a wider and less detailed definition of torture than the UN Torture Convention. Article 1 of the Torture Convention provides: 'For the purposes of this Convention, the term "torture" means any act by which severe pain or suffering, whether physical or mental, is intentionally inflicted on a person for such purposes as obtaining from him or a third person information or a confession, punishing him for an act he or a third person has committed or is suspected of having committed, or intimidating or coercing him or a third person, or for any reason based on discrimination of any kind, when such pain or suffering is inflicted by or at the instigation of or with the consent or acquiescence of a public official or other person acting in an official capacity. It does not include pain or suffering arising only from, inherent in or incidental to lawful sanctions. This article is without prejudice to any international instrument or national legislation which does or may contain provisions of wider application.'

Under Art. 7(2)(e) ICCSt:

'"Torture" means the intentional infliction of severe pain or suffering, whether physical or mental, upon a person in the custody or under the control of the accused; except that torture shall not include pain or suffering arising only from, inherent in or incidental to, lawful sanctions.'

30 Arts 5, 6 and 8 United Nations Convention against Transnational Organized Crime, UNGA Res. 55/25, 15 November 2000. Available at http://www.unodc.org/documents/treaties/UNTOC/Publications/TOC%20Convention/TOCebook-e.pdf (visited 10 May 2009).

All crimes under the jurisdiction of the international tribunals also fall within the definition of serious crimes of the Palermo Convention. Most of the crimes included in the Statutes of international Tribunals and Courts are in fact usually perpetrated by an organized or structured group[31] and, based on Article 2 TOC, can be considered transnational in nature. One of the lessons learned at the *ad hoc* international Tribunals is in fact that war crimes, genocide and crimes against humanity are – at the highest political and military level – planned, financed and instigated by groups of people acting with strategies that are very similar to those of criminal and terrorist organizations.

The 2000 TOC – the Parties to which include states which have not ratified the Rome Statute, such as China, India, Israel, and the US – specifically mentions in its supplementing Protocols the following crimes:

(i) trafficking in persons, especially women and children;[32]
(ii) smuggling of migrants;[33]
(iii) illicit manufacturing of and trafficking in firearms, their parts and components and ammunition.[34]

In particular, trafficking in women and children are crimes which are already included in the ICC Statute,[35] while smuggling of migrants can apply to situations of international displacement of persons during armed conflicts.

---

31 See Art. 2 TOC: '"Organized criminal group" shall mean a structured group of three or more persons, existing for a period of time and acting in concert with the aim of committing one or more serious crimes or offences established in accordance with this Convention, in order to obtain, directly or indirectly, a financial or other material benefit ...; "Structured group" shall mean a group that is not randomly formed for the immediate commission of an offence and that does not need to have formally defined roles for its members, continuity of its membership or a developed structure ...'.

32 Protocol to Prevent, Suppress and Punish Trafficking in Persons, especially Women and Children, supplementing the United Nations Convention against Transnational Organized Crime, GA Res. 55/25, 15 November 2000 (Human Trafficking Protocol). Art. 3: '(a) "Trafficking in persons" shall mean the recruitment, transportation, transfer, harbouring or receipt of persons, by means of the threat or use of force or other forms of coercion, of abduction, of fraud, of deception, of the abuse of power or of a position of vulnerability or of the giving or receiving of payments or benefits to achieve the consent of a person having control over another person, for the purpose of exploitation. Exploitation shall include, at a minimum, the exploitation of the prostitution of others or other forms of sexual exploitation, forced labour or services, slavery or practices similar to slavery, servitude or the removal of organs; (b) The consent of a victim of trafficking in persons to the intended exploitation set forth in subparagraph (a) of this article shall be irrelevant where any of the means set forth in subparagraph (a) have been used; (c) The recruitment, transportation, transfer, harbouring or receipt of a child for the purpose of exploitation shall be considered "trafficking in persons" even if this does not involve any of the means set forth in subparagraph (a) of this article; (d) "Child" shall mean any person under eighteen years of age.'

33 Protocol against the Smuggling of Migrants by Land, Sea and Air, supplementing the United Nations Convention against Transnational Organized Crime, GA Res. 55/25, 15 November 2000 (Migrants Protocol). Art. 3: '(a) "Smuggling of migrants" shall mean the procurement, in order to obtain, directly or indirectly, a financial or other material benefit, of the illegal entry of a person into a State Party of which the person is not a national or a permanent resident.'

34 'Protocol against the Illicit Manufacturing in Firearms, their parts and Components and Ammunition, supplementing the United Nations Convention against Transnational Organized Crime', GA Res. 55/255, 31 May 2001 (Firearms Protocol).

35 Art. 7(2)(c) ICCSt: '"Enslavement" means the exercise of any or all of the powers attaching to the right of ownership over a person and includes the exercise of such power in the course of trafficking in persons, in particular women and children.'

Trafficking of weapons is a crime which is often instrumental to the perpetration of crimes included in the Statutes of the ICC and *ad hoc* Tribunals. The relevance of cooperation among states on this issue is therefore vital to prevent those crimes from being committed. In this regard, the 2001 Firearms Protocol supplementing the TOC establishes specific duties for exchange of information, following the general provision of Article 7 TOC. Parties shall exchange among themselves, consistent with their respective domestic legal and administrative systems, relevant information on matters such as:

> (i) organized criminal groups known to take part or suspected of taking part in the illicit manufacturing of or trafficking in firearms, their parts and components and ammunition;
> (ii) the means of concealment used in the illicit manufacturing of or trafficking in firearms, their parts and components and ammunition, and ways of detecting them;
> (iii) methods and means, points of dispatch and destination and routes customarily used by organized criminal groups engaged in illicit trafficking in firearms, their parts and components and ammunition.

Thus, the TOC provides States Parties with legal tools to exercise their own jurisdiction and to prosecute a wide range of serious crimes that might include some of the crimes mentioned under the ICC Statute, and also includes very specific rules on the jurisdiction of states (Articles 4[36] and 15[37]),

---

36 Art. 4 (Protection of sovereignty): '1. States Parties shall carry out their obligations under this Convention in a manner consistent with the principles of sovereign equality and territorial integrity of States and that of non-intervention in the domestic affairs of other States. 2. Nothing in this Convention entitles a State Party to undertake in the territory of another State the exercise of jurisdiction and performance of functions that are reserved exclusively for the authorities of that other State by its domestic law.'

37 Art. 15 (Jurisdiction):

'1. Each State Party shall adopt such measures as may be necessary to establish its jurisdiction over the offences established in accordance with articles 5,6, 8 and 23 of this Convention when:

(a) The offence is committed in the territory of that State Party; or

(b) The offence is committed on board a vessel that is flying the flag of that State Party or an aircraft that is registered under the laws of that State Party at the time that the offence is committed.

2. Subject to article 4 of this Convention, a State Party may also establish its jurisdiction over any such offence when:

(a) The offence is committed against a national of that State Party;

(b) The offence is committed by a national of that State Party or a stateless person who has his or her habitual residence in its territory; or

(c) The offence is:

(i) One of those established in accordance with article 5, paragraph 1, of this Convention and is committed outside its territory with a view to the commission of a serious crime within its territory;

although the establishment of the jurisdiction of one state may also result from the agreement of some States Parties.[38]

Consequently, in light of the specific advantage offered by the many tools available under the TOC, appropriate consideration should be given to the prosecution of serious crimes falling under the ICC Statute pursuant to the TOC, if transnational and/or perpetrated by an organized or structured group. States Parties would be able to exercise their jurisdiction if the criteria under Articles 14, 15 and 21 TOC are met. Moreover, Article 18 TOC calls on states to strict and effective judicial cooperation,[39] and identifies specific investigative techniques, such as electronic or other forms of surveillance, undercover operations and controlled delivery,[40] while similar investigation techniques are not contemplated in the Statutes of the ICC and of the *ad hoc* Tribunals.

(ii) One of those established in accordance with article 6, paragraph 1(b)(ii), of this Convention and is committed outside its territory with a view to the commission of an offence established in accordance with article 6, paragraph 1(a)(i) or (ii) or (b)(i), of this Convention within its territory.

3. For the purposes of article 16, paragraph 10, of this Convention, each State Party shall adopt such measures as may be necessary to establish its jurisdiction over the offences covered by this Convention when the alleged offender is present in its territory and it does not extradite such person solely on the ground that he or she is one of its nationals.
4. Each State Party may also adopt such measures as may be necessary to establish its jurisdiction over the offences covered by this Convention when the alleged offender is present in its territory and it does not extradite him or her.'

38 Art. 16 (Extradition): 'A State Party in whose territory an alleged offender is found, if it does not extradite such person in respect of an offence to which this article applies solely on the ground that he or she is one of its nationals, shall, at the request of the State Party seeking extradition, be obliged to submit the case without undue delay to its competent authorities for the purpose of prosecution. Those authorities shall take their decision and conduct their proceedings in the same manner as in the case of any other offence of a grave nature under the domestic law of that State Party. The States Parties concerned shall cooperate with each other, in particular on procedural and evidentiary aspects, to ensure the efficiency of such prosecution.' Art. 21 (Transfer of criminal proceedings): 'States Parties shall consider the possibility of transferring to one another proceedings for the prosecution of an offence covered by this Convention in cases where such transfer is considered to be in the interests of the proper administration of justice, in particular in cases where several jurisdictions are involved, with a view to concentrating the prosecution.'

39 Ibid., Arts 16 and 21.

40 Art. 20 (Special investigative techniques):

'1. If permitted by the basic principles of its domestic legal system, each State Party shall, within its possibilities and under the conditions prescribed by its domestic law, take the necessary measures to allow for the appropriate use of controlled delivery and, where it deems appropriate, for the use of other special investigative techniques, such as electronic or other forms of surveillance and undercover operations, by its competent authorities in its territory for the purpose of effectively combating organized crime.
2. For the purpose of investigating the offences covered by this Convention, States Parties are encouraged to conclude, when necessary, appropriate bilateral or multilateral agreements or arrangements for using such special investigative techniques in the context of cooperation at the international level. Such agreements or arrangements shall be concluded and implemented in full compliance with the principle of sovereign equality of States and shall be carried out strictly in accordance with the terms of those agreements or arrangements.
3. In the absence of an agreement or arrangement as set forth in paragraph 2 of this article, decisions to use such special investigative techniques at the international level shall be made on a case-by-case basis and may, when necessary, take into consideration financial arrangements and understandings with respect to the exercise of jurisdiction by the States Parties concerned.

7. European Cooperation in Criminal Matters

States Parties to the 1959 European Convention on Mutual Assistance in Criminal Matters[41] can request judicial cooperation also with reference to investigations and prosecutions of crimes under all the mentioned UN Conventions, as well as under the Statutes of the ICC and the *ad hoc* Tribunals.

Moreover, the second Additional Protocol to the 1959 said Convention[42] provides for cooperation in special investigation techniques (e.g., cross-border observations) also for crimes, such as murder, rape, trafficking in human beings, which may well fall under the ICC's and the UN *ad hoc* Tribunals' jurisdictions.

8. Terrorism Instruments

Similar rules on jurisdiction are also contemplated in other relevant Conventions, such as under Article 7 of the 1999 UN International Convention for the Suppression of the Financing of Terrorism (Financing Convention), which might also be considered relevant, taking into account that acts of terrorism may fall within the jurisdiction of an UN *ad hoc* tribunal (e.g., Article 4 ICTRSt on 'acts of terrorism').

Exchange of information among states, similar to that under the TOC instruments, is also provided for under the Financing Convention, whereby cooperation among states in conducting inquiries includes providing information on the identity, whereabouts and activities of persons in respect of whom reasonable suspicion exists that they are involved in such offences, and on the movement of funds relating to the commission of such offences.[43] Under the Financing Convention a terrorist act is defined as:

> [an] act intended to cause death or serious bodily injury to a civilian, or to any other person not taking an active part in the hostilities in a situation of armed conflict, when the purpose of such act, by its nature or context, is to intimidate a population, or to compel a government or an international organization to do or to abstain from doing any act.[44]

This definition recalls the criminal conduct of an 'attack directed against any civilian population', which under Articles 7 and 8 ICCSt falls within the categories of crimes against humanity and of war crimes. Prosecuting acts of terrorism on the basis of the wide jurisdictional criteria of the Financing Convention would, therefore, imply an effective prosecution and an effective action aimed at detecting assets bound for financing the perpetration of serious crimes of international concern.

---

4. Decisions to use controlled delivery at the international level may, with the consent of the States Parties concerned, include methods such as intercepting and allowing the goods to continue intact or be removed or replaced in whole or in part.'

41 European Convention of Mutual Assistance on Criminal Matters, Strasbourg, 20 April 1959, ETS No. 30. Available at http://conventions.coe.int/Treaty/en/Treaties/Word/030.doc (visited 17 March 2009).

42 Art. 17, Second Additional Protocol to the European Convention on Mutual Assistance in Criminal Matters, ETS No. 182 Strasbourg, 8 November 2001.

43 Art. 18(3)(b) Financing Convention.

44 Art. 2(1)(b) Financing Convention.

Furthermore, under Article 1 of the EU Framework Decision on combating terrorism,[45] states are bound to considering, among other things, the following criminal offences which may also fall under the grave breaches provisions of the Geneva Conventions:

> (a) attacks upon a person's life which may cause death;
> (b) attacks upon the physical integrity of a person;
> (c) kidnapping or hostage taking;
> (d) causing extensive destruction to a government or public facility, a transport system, an infrastructure facility, including an information system, a fixed platform located on the continental shelf, a public place or private property, and likely to endanger human life or result in major economic loss;
> (e) seizure of aircraft, ships or other means of public or goods transport;
> (f) manufacture, possession, acquisition, transport, supply or use of weapons, explosives or of nuclear, biological or chemical weapons, as well as research into, and development of, biological and chemical weapons;
> (g) release of dangerous substances, or causing fires, floods or explosions the effect of which is to endanger human life;
> (h) interfering with or disrupting the supply of water, power or any other fundamental natural resource the effect of which is to endanger human life;
> (i) threatening to commit any of the acts listed in (a) to (h);
> (j) directing a terrorist group;
> (k) participating in the activities of a terrorist group, including by supplying information or material resources, or by funding its activities in any way, with knowledge of the fact that such participation will contribute to the criminal activities of the terrorist group.

3. Jurisdiction of States Parties Under Some International Instruments

Wide criteria to establish the jurisdiction of states are also contemplated in many EU framework decisions, which should be taken into account even though they are only binding on EU Member States. The most relevant Framework Decisions provide a new criterion for establishing the jurisdiction of states with reference to serious crimes such as terrorism and trafficking of human beings. The state where the legal person for the benefit of which the crime has been perpetrated is established.

Pursuant to the EU Framework Decisions against terrorism (Article 9)[46] and on combating trafficking in human beings (Article 6):[47]

> Each Member State shall take the necessary measures to establish its jurisdiction over the offences … where:
>
> (a) the offence is committed in whole or in part in its territory. Each Member State may extend its jurisdiction if the offence is committed in the territory of a Member State;

45 Council Framework Decision of 13 June 2002 on combating terrorism, 2002/475/JHA in *Official Gazette* No. L.164 of 22 June 2002, 3–7.

46 Ibid.

47 Council Framework Decision on combating trafficking in human beings, 2002/629/JHA, 19 July 2002, in *Official Journal*, L.209 of 1 August 2002.

(b) the offence is committed on board a vessel flying its flag or an aircraft registered there;

(c) the offender is one of its nationals or residents;

(d) the offence is committed for the benefit of a legal person established in its territory;

...

Furthermore, Article 9(1)(e) of the Framework Decision against terrorism includes the other criterion of an offence committed against the institutions or people of the Member State in question or against an institution of the European Union or a body set up in accordance with the Treaty establishing the European Community or the Treaty on European Union and based in that Member State. A Member State may establish its jurisdiction on offences concerning trafficking in human beings for the purposes of labour exploitation or sexual exploitation[48] anywhere the crime has been committed, when the offender is one of its nationals or when the offence is committed for the benefit of a legal person established in the territory of that Member State.

Some crimes under the ICC Statute have a financial dimension, such as the war crimes of: extensive destruction and appropriation of property, not justified by military necessity and carried out unlawfully and wantonly;[49] destroying or seizing the enemy's property unless such destruction or seizure be imperatively demanded by the necessities of war;[50] destroying or seizing the property of an adversary unless such destruction or seizure be imperatively demanded by the necessities of the conflict.[51] The perpetrators of such crimes could also be investigated and prosecuted on the basis of the 1990 European Convention on Money Laundering, the 2000 TOC and the 2005 Council of Europe Convention on Laundering, Search, Seizure and Confiscation of the Proceeds from Crime and on the Financing of Terrorism.[52]

With reference to the jurisdiction of States Parties, Article 6 of the 1990 Convention on Laundering, Search, Seizure and Confiscation of the Proceeds from Crime provides that:

> it shall not matter whether the predicate offence was subject to the criminal jurisdiction of the Party; it may be provided that the offences set forth in that paragraph do not apply to the persons who committed the predicate offence.

And, pursuant to Article 6(2)(c) TOC:

> predicate offences shall include offences committed both within and outside the jurisdiction of the State Party in question. However, offences committed outside the jurisdiction of a State Party shall constitute predicate offences only when the relevant conduct is a criminal offence under the

---

48 Convention on Laundering, Search, Seizure and Confiscation of the Proceeds from Crime, Council of Europe, Strasbourg 8 November 1990, ETS. 140. Available at http://conventions.coe.int/Treaty/en/Treaties/Word/141.doc (visited 22 May 2009).

49 Art. 8(2)(a)(iv) ICCSt.

50 Art. 8(2)(b)(xiii) ICCSt.

51 Art. 8(2)(e)(xii) ICCSt.

52 Convention on Laundering, Search, Seizure and Confiscation of the Proceeds from Crime and on the Financing of Terrorism, Council of Europe, Warsaw 16 May 2005, ETS. 198. Available at http://conventions.coe.int/Treaty/EN/Treaties/Word/198.doc (visited 5 May 2009).

domestic law of the State where it is committed and would be a criminal offence under the domestic law of the State Party implementing or applying this article had it been committed there.

It can be concluded that the higher the number of international binding instruments for the suppression of crimes falling under international criminal jurisdictions and the wider the criteria establishing the jurisdiction of states over those crimes, the greater the contribution that states can give to international justice.

4. Cooperation in Corporate Liability

The aforementioned international binding instruments at the EU level have specific rules on jurisdiction and introduce the additional jurisdictional criterion of the state of establishment of the legal person for whose benefit the crime is committed. However, liability of legal entities is not contemplated by the Statutes of the ICC and of the *ad hoc* international Tribunals: 'Crimes against international law are committed by men, not by abstract entities, and only by punishing individuals who commit such crimes can the provisions of international law be enforced.'[53] Neither organizations nor legal persons nor states can be brought to trial before international criminal tribunals, as proceedings can be instituted only against individuals. The concept of collective liability is increasingly yielding to the notion of individual responsibility in international humanitarian law. Participation in war crimes and crimes against humanity, at the level of suppliers and financers, is usually implemented through a corporate shell rather than in the individual names of the perpetrators.[54] Thus, it may be of interest to establish the liability of the corporation itself, particularly when it holds substantial assets that may be subject to seizure, forfeiture and use for compensation. However, international law in this area is relatively underdeveloped.

The Security Council did not include criminal organizations or legal persons within the *ratione personae* jurisdiction in the Statutes of ICTY and ICTR. Proposals to the same effect during the negotiations leading to the Rome Statute were also unsuccessful. The French delegation at the 1998 Rome Diplomatic Conference argued strongly that criminal liability of legal or juridical persons should also be covered by the Statute, insisting that this would be important in terms of restitution and compensation orders for victims. But because many states did not provide for such a form of criminal responsibility in their domestic law, there were awesome and ultimately insurmountable problems of complementarity,[55] so that no consensus was possible and draft provisions to that effect were, in the end, dropped.

As a result, the Statutes of *ad hoc* Tribunals and of the ICC contemplate only the liability of natural and not of legal persons.[56] This is a significant limitation affecting international criminal

53 Trial of the Major War Criminals before the International Military Tribunal, Nüremberg, 14 November 1945–1 October 1946, 1947, at 223.

54 In many ICTY cases (*Milan Martic, Goran Hadzic, Jovica Stanisic, Franko Simatovic, Vojislav Seselj*) the accused allegedly financed paramilitary or special police forces. According to the OTP theory of the case, the accused committed the alleged crimes by participating in a joint criminal enterprise. This participation included the formation, financing, supply and support of the special units.

55 For the Committee of the Whole drafts, see the 1998 UN Conference of Plenipotentiaries on the establishment of the ICC, *Official Records*, Volume III, Reports and other documents. Available at http://untreaty.un.org/cod/icc/rome/proceedings/E/Rome%20Proceedings_v3_e.pdf (visited 5 May 2009).

56 E.g., Art. 25(1) ICCSt.

jurisdictions, since many international instruments[57] often call on states to contemplate in domestic legislation the liability of legal persons for the most serious crimes.[58]

This lacuna in the Statutes of the international Tribunals and Courts is particularly relevant in light of the lessons learned in cases of radio or TV broadcasting companies inciting the commission of genocide, as has already happened in Rwanda with the broadcasts of Radio Milles Collines, a company financing paramilitary groups responsible for widespread and systematic crimes against civilians.[59] The lack of any concurrent or complementary jurisdiction over legal persons under the Statues entails that in similar situations legal persons responsible for serious crimes of international concern might only be held accountable under domestic legislation (when it exists) of the relevant state. It may well be that these lacunae can be partially corrected by national legal systems implementing international instruments. Those states which allow for corporate criminal liability will be in a position to prosecute legal persons in the same manner they would prosecute individuals. Of course there are theoretical issues relating to the mental element of a business corporation, but national practices have developed a range of acceptable approaches.

As international jurisdictions only extend over natural persons, domestic courts may have to deal with cases involving legal persons liable for complicity in the perpetration of international crimes committed by individuals being prosecuted before international courts. This possibility imposes tight bilateral cooperation between domestic and international jurisdictions in order to facilitate exchange of information between prosecution offices and to expedite cooperation and consistency in the prosecutorial strategies of the prosecution offices. This implies that international Courts not only require but also provide domestic jurisdictions with judicial cooperation.

None of the international instruments before the 2000 TOC were drafted to address the criminal liability of legal persons. It would therefore not be plausible to derive from them an obligation, for instance, for states where a company is incorporated to launch an investigation against that company, leading possibly to the imposition of effective sanctions, if it appears on the basis of reliable information that the company has taken part in the commission of international crimes.

57 TOC and Terrorism Financing, as well as the EU Framework Decisions against terrorism, against enslavement and trafficking of humans.

58 Not all states have accepted the concept of criminal liability of corporate bodies – although the international crimes discussed above call, per definition, for sanctions of a criminal nature. At most therefore, the *aut dedere aut judicare* principle – established in order to ensure that the natural persons who are authors of international crimes will not be allowed to seek impunity because of the obstacles facing their extradition – may imply that the imposition by a state of certain sanctions (for instance, the confiscation of assets or the imposition of financial penalties) against a corporation 'present' under that state's jurisdiction, even when the corporation is not considered under the law of the forum state to have its 'nationality', should be considered allowable, if it is determined that the corporation has indeed committed or is an accomplice in an international crime: it should not matter that the crime was committed abroad and that is not connected in any way to the forum state except by the 'presence' of the corporation on its territory. But this does not bring us any further than the principle of universality itself as a basis for the optional exercise of extraterritorial jurisdiction. It states a mere *possibility*, which states may wish to exercise or not: it does not impose an obligation. One provision should be added, however. In imposing the principle *aut dedere, aut judicare*, the instruments cited in fact draw precise conclusions from a broader principle, which is the obligation of international cooperation in combating international crimes. See O. de Schutter, *Extraterritorial Jurisdiction as a Tool for Improving the Human Rights Accountability of Transnational Corporation*, background report to the seminar organized in collaboration with the Office of the High Commissioner for Human Rights, Brussels, 3–4 November 2006. Available at http://www.business-humanrights.org/Links/Repository/775593 (visited 5 May 2009).

59 ICTR, Judgment, *Simon Bikindi*, Trial Chamber III, 2 December 2008, ICTR 01-72. Available at http://69.94.11.53/default.htm (visited 5 May 2009).

According to the UN Principles of International Cooperation in the Detection, Arrest, Extradition and Punishment of Persons Guilty of War Crimes and Crimes Against Humanity:[60]

> States shall co-operate with each other on a bilateral and multilateral basis with a view to halting and preventing war crimes and crimes against humanity, and shall take the domestic and international measures necessary for that purpose [and] shall assist each other in detecting, arresting and bringing to trial persons suspected of having committed such crimes and, if they are found guilty, in punishing them.

Similar references to strengthening international cooperation are also found in the Preamble of the Rome Statute of the ICC.[61]

The implications of the requirement of international cooperation would be very difficult to deal with if the difficulties the host state may encounter where it seeks to engage the criminal liability of the corporation operating within its territory are not taken into account. This might happen when, for instance, the corporation is a foreign corporation or belongs to a multinational group led by a parent corporation domiciled abroad. Legal persons such as corporations cannot be extradited, when found to be present on one state's territory, in order to face prosecution in another state. The risk is therefore high that they will be left unpunished even in cases where their criminal liability could be engaged under the laws of the host state. For instance, the imposition of financial penalties may require that assets of the corporation be seized, but the assets present on the territory of the host state may not be sufficient. In this case, a judicial winding-up order or the placement of the corporation under judicial supervision will require the cooperation of the state of incorporation. But such cooperation is extremely problematic because of diverging approaches of states, not only to the principle of criminal liability of corporations, but also on the nature of the legal sanctions applicable to any offence which is relevant to the case.

The number of international binding instruments that expressly provide for the liability of legal entities is limited:

(i) Article 10 TOC (Liability of legal persons):

> 1. Each State Party shall adopt such measures as may be necessary, consistent with its legal principles, to establish the liability of legal persons for participation in serious crimes involving an organized criminal group and for the offences established in accordance with articles 5, 6, 8 and 23 of this Convention.
>
> 2. Subject to the legal principles of the State Party, the liability of legal persons may be criminal, civil or administrative.
>
> 3. Such liability shall be without prejudice to the criminal liability of the natural persons who have committed the offences.

60 *Supra* note 24, GA Res. 3074 (XXVIII), 3 December 1973, paras 3 and 4.

61 Preamble (4) ICCSt: 'effective prosecution must be ensured … by enhancing international cooperation.'

> 4. Each State Party shall, in particular, ensure that legal persons held liable in accordance with this article are subject to effective, proportionate and dissuasive criminal or non-criminal sanctions, including monetary sanctions.

(ii) under EU law, pursuant to Article 7 of the Terrorism Framework Decision[62] and Article 4 of the Human Trafficking Framework Decision,[63] Member States:

> shall take the necessary measures to ensure that legal persons can be held liable for any of the offences referred to in those decisions, committed for their benefit by any person, acting either individually or as part of an organ of the legal person who has a leading position within the legal person, based on one of the following:
>
> (a) a power of representation of the legal person;
>
> (b) an authority to take decisions on behalf of the legal person;
>
> (c) an authority to exercise control within the legal person.
>
> Each Member State shall take the necessary measures to ensure that legal persons can be held liable where the lack of supervision or control by a person referred to in paragraph 1 has made possible the commission of any of the offences related to terrorism and human trafficking.

With reference to penalties for legal persons, both the above mentioned EU Framework Decisions provide that Member States must take the necessary measures to ensure that a legal person held liable is punishable by effective, proportionate and dissuasive penalties, which shall include criminal or non-criminal fines, but may also include other penalties, such as:

(a) exclusion from entitlement to public benefits or aid;
(b) temporary or permanent disqualification from the practice of commercial activities;
(c) placing under judicial supervision;
(d) a judicial winding-up order;
(e) temporary or permanent closure of establishments which have been used for committing the offence.

(iii) other international instruments which deal with the issue of liability of legal persons, include the United Nations Convention against Corruption[64] and the 2005 Council of Europe Terrorism Financing Convention.[65]

Finally, it should be noted that Security Council Resolution 864 (1993) establishing a sanctions regime for Angola required states 'to bring proceedings against persons and entities violating the

---

62 See *supra* note 45.

63 See *supra* note 47.

64 Art. 26. See GA Res. 58/41, 31 October 2003 (entered into force on 14 December 2005, with 129 States Parties), Doc. A/58/422.

65 Art. 10 of the Convention on Laundering, Search, Seizure and Confiscation of the Proceeds from Crime and on the Financing of Terrorism, 8 October 1990, ETS No. 141 (entered into force on 1 September 1993, with ratification by all Council of Europe Member States).

measures imposed by the present resolution and to impose appropriate penalties'. Besides criminal sanctions other measures may be considered, such as confiscation and forfeiture of proceeds of crimes.

5. Confiscation and Seizure

Cooperation of states with international Courts is crucial for the detection, forfeiture and confiscation of the proceeds of international crimes. The ICTY (Article 24) and ICTR (Article 23) Statutes provide that 'in addition to imprisonment, Trial Chambers may order the return of property and proceeds acquired by criminal conduct, including by means of duress, to their rightful owners'. At the SCSL, the Trial Chamber may order the forfeiture of the property, proceeds and any assets acquired unlawfully or by criminal conduct, and their return to their rightful owner or to the state of Sierra Leone. There are similar provisions for the Extraordinary Chambers in the Court of Cambodia.[66]

These rules only provide the restitution to victims of the assets and properties illegally acquired. Victims are not entitled to be compensated for all the damages suffered from the perpetration of the crimes. Freezing the assets of alleged war criminals is only possible if these assets were illegally acquired, or as a provisional measure in order to prevent the escape of an accused, pursuant to Rule 40 ICTY RPE.

Article 77(2) ICCSt provides that:

> In addition to imprisonment, the Court may order:
>
> (a) A fine under the criteria provided for in the Rules of Procedure and Evidence;
>
> (b) A forfeiture of proceeds, property and assets derived directly or indirectly from that crime, without prejudice to the rights of bona fide third parties.

The list of items subject to forfeiture and indicated in the ICC Statute includes items derived indirectly from the perpetration of statutory crimes, such as assets purchased through money laundering of the proceeds of such crimes, and implies the necessity for the ICC to carry out financial investigations and request the judicial cooperation of States Parties. In this regard, it seems that for purposes of the implementation of fines and forfeitures under the Rome Statute,[67] the 1990 Convention on Laundering, Search, Seizure and Confiscation of the Proceeds from Crime, and the 2000 TOC or the 2005 Council of Europe Financing of Terrorism Convention can be used.

Financial investigations and judicial cooperation must always be considered relevant when dealing with international crimes. Investigations should focus also on those who financed the crimes falling within the jurisdiction of international Courts and on the assets that financed those crimes. These investigations can make it possible to identify those who financed the crimes falling within the jurisdiction of international Courts and prosecute them as co-perpetrators. In fact, proceeds and assets derived from the perpetration of crimes such as trafficking of drugs, cigarettes, weapons and stolen cars were used in the past to finance military and paramilitary groups that were responsible

66 Art. 19 SCSLSt and Art. 39 ECCCSt.

67 Arts 77(2) and 109 ICCSt.

for serious crimes. Financing these crimes is also qualified as a conduct relevant under Article 7(1) ICTYSt, as it was found in *Tadic*:[68]

> The Statute does not confine itself to providing for jurisdiction over those persons who plan, instigate, order, physically perpetrate a crime or otherwise aid and abet in its planning, preparation, or execution. The Statute does not stop there. It does not exclude those modes of participating in the commission of crimes which occur where several persons having a common purpose embark on criminal activity that is then carried out either jointly or by some members of this plurality of persons. Whoever contributes to the commission of crimes by the group of persons or some members of the groups, in execution of a common criminal purpose, may be held to be criminally liable ... Although only some members of the group may physically perpetrate the criminal act (murder, extermination, wanton destruction of cities, towns or villages, etc.), the participation and contribution of the other members of the group is often vital in facilitating the commission of the offence in question.

Not many international binding instruments can assist States Parties and international Courts in filling the existing lacunae in the Statutes on the subject matter. One of them is the Palermo Convention, as Article 12 TOC extends confiscation to the following assets:

> (i) property, equipment or other instrumentalities used in or destined for use in offences covered by the TOC;
> (ii) property into which proceeds of crime have been transformed or converted;
> (iii) property with which proceeds of crime have been intermingled shall also be liable to the measures referred to in this article, in the same manner and to the same extent as proceeds of crime.

Furthermore, Article 3 of the 2005 Council of Europe Convention on Laundering, Search, Seizure and Confiscation of the Proceeds from Crime and on the Financing of Terrorism provides for the confiscation of instrumentalities and proceeds or property the value of which corresponds to such proceeds and laundered property.

Other relevant provisions can be found in the TOC, in the 1990 Convention on Laundering, Search, Seizure and Confiscation of the Proceeds from Crime and in the II Additional Protocol Supplementing the European 1959 Convention on Mutual Assistance in Criminal Matters,[69] which also allow for specific investigation techniques to be activated by the relevant authorities of States Parties and included in a request for judicial assistance.[70]

---

68 ICTY, Judgement, *Tadic*, Case No. IT-94-1-A, Appeals Chamber, 15 July 1999, paras 190–191.

69 Art. 7 of 1990 Convention on Laundering, Search, Seizure and Confiscation of the Proceeds from Crime provides under the heading 'General principles and measures for international co-operation' that: 'The Parties shall co-operate with each other to the widest extent possible for the purposes of investigations and proceedings aiming at the confiscation of instrumentalities and proceeds.

Each Party shall adopt such legislative or other measures as may be necessary to enable it to comply, under the conditions provided for in this chapter, with requests: for confiscation of specific items of property representing proceeds or instrumentalities, as well as for confiscation of proceeds consisting in a requirement to pay a sum of money corresponding to the value of proceeds; for investigative assistance and provisional measures with a view to either form of confiscation referred to under a above.'

70 See Art. 20 TOC and Arts 17, 19 and 20 of the II Additional Protocol Supplementing the European 1959 Convention on Mutual Assistance in Criminal Matters.

6. Conclusion

The arrest and conviction of individuals responsible for crimes falling within international jurisdictions, as well as for any serious crime, is not the ultimate purpose of justice, be it domestic or international.

The strategy for a successful fight against the most serious crimes must be twofold:

> (a) perpetrators must be prosecuted and convicted, and legal entities involved in the perpetration of international crimes should also be held criminally liable thereof;
> (b) assets and proceeds derived from the crimes committed or that financed those crimes must be frozen, seized and confiscated, either by international or by national jurisdictions. In this perspective, Prosecution Offices at either the international and domestic level should expand and strengthen mutual judicial cooperation.

Serious organized crimes entail that each criminal conduct is a segment of a widespread and systematic criminal activity and is committed in execution of a precise criminal design. Therefore, the investigation of a single segment of the whole criminal pattern of conduct should focus on identifying the criminal network each criminal act is related to.

Serious crimes might differ from each other with reference to their nature and their complexity, be they of an international or non-international character. What they have in common is that behind each serious crime there is a precise strategy, a group of people sharing, planning and implementing this strategy, and assets financing that crime. For this reason, investigation and prosecution of serious crimes require a holistic approach, through the appropriate investigation of criminal strategies and criminal plans behind each crime.

The freezing, seizure and confiscation of the assets derived from the crimes or of the assets that financed those crimes, as well as the prosecution of legal entities involved with individuals in the perpetration of serious crimes of international concern, should be perceived as major objectives, and not less important than the arrest and the conviction of the perpetrators. The confiscation of the proceeds of crimes and of the assets that were instrumental is also vital, in national and international jurisdiction, to neutralize the criminal enterprises that were responsible for such serious crimes and to give more credibility to justice.

SECTION II
Select Practice

Chapter 12
Genocide Case Law at the ICTY

Susanne Malmström*

> The United Nations was founded as a reaction to the horrors of the Second World War. Even so, the international community has too often failed to stand up to mass atrocities. Let us pledge ourselves to even greater efforts to prevent genocide and crimes against humanity.
>
> *Kofi Annan*

1. Introduction

A. The ICTY's Scope of Jurisdiction

Termed the 'crime of crimes', genocide is most commonly understood as the mass killing of a group, with the intent to destroy that particular group.[1] This overview focuses on the genocide case law of the Trial and Appeals Chambers of the International Criminal Tribunal for the former Yugoslavia (ICTY). The International Criminal Tribunal for Rwanda (ICTR) also has extensive case law on genocide which is not reflected directly in this overview.[2]

The ICTY was given the jurisdiction to prosecute individuals for genocide pursuant to Article 4 of the ICTY Statute, which was adopted by the Security Council in 1993.[3] Article 4 provides:

Genocide

> 1. The International Tribunal shall have the power to prosecute persons committing genocide as defined in paragraph 2 of this article or of committing any of the other acts enumerated in paragraph 3 of this article.
>
> 2. Genocide means any of the following acts committed with intent to destroy, in whole or in part, a national, ethnical, racial or religious group, as such:
>
> (a) killing members of the group;
> (b) causing serious bodily or mental harm to members of the group;
> (c) deliberately inflicting on the group conditions of life calculated to bring about its physical destruction in whole or in part;
> (d) imposing measures intended to prevent births within the group;
> (e) forcibly transferring children of the group to another group.

---

* The author is most grateful to Lisa-Claire Hutchinson, Oliva Go and John Oh for their extensive assistance.

1 See for example, Judgement, *Stakić*, Trial Chamber, 31 July 2003, para. 502; Judge Wald's separate opinion in Judgement, *Jelisić* Appeals Chamber, 5 July 2001, at 69, para. 2.

2 The author is conscious of the fact that there are instances where this article refers to the ICTY as having taken a particular legal point that may have first been reflected in the ICTR case law.

3 SC Res. 808, 22 February 1993, para. 1.

3. The following acts shall be punishable:

(a) genocide;
(b) conspiracy to commit genocide;
(c) direct and public incitement to commit genocide;
(d) attempt to commit genocide;
(e) complicity in genocide.[4]

Article 4(2) and (3) of the ICTY Statute reproduce verbatim Article II and III of the Convention on the Prevention and Punishment of the Crime of Genocide adopted by the UN General Assembly on 9 December 1948.[5] It is widely recognized that these provisions of the Genocide Convention reflect customary international law, and that the prohibition of genocide constitutes a peremptory norm or *jus cogens*.[6] Accordingly, objections of retroactivity and non-recognition in customary international law, which have been submitted with regard to other crimes, have not been raised in relation to genocide.

B. Outcome of Indictments

The Prosecutor of the ICTY has indicted 19 individuals for genocide.[7] As of January 2009, the cases against 11 individuals were concluded.[8] The trials against five are ongoing,[9] two accused are at the pre-trial stage[10] and one is still at large.[11]

The accused were acquitted of genocide in two cases following the Trial Chamber's decisions that there was 'no case to answer' for the accused, pursuant to Rule 98*bis* of the ICTY's Rules of Procedure and Evidence. This rule provides that at the close of the Prosecution's case, the Trial

4 Art. 4 ICTYSt.

5 UN General Assembly, *United Nations Convention on the Prevention and Punishment of the Crime of Genocide*, 9 December 1948. United Nations, Treaty Series, Vol. 78, at 277.

6 See *Advisory Opinion Concerning Reservations to the Genocide Convention*, 28 May 1951, ICJ Reports 23. See also Secretary General's Report, S/25704, 3 May 1993, para. 45.

7 The following individuals have been charged with genocide: Goran Jelisić (IT-95-10), Duško Sikirica (IT-95-8), Slobodan Milošević (IT-02-54), Radoslav Brđanin (IT-99-36), Milomir Stakić (IT-97-24), Momčilo Krajišnik (IT-00-39), Biljana Plavšić (IT-00-39 & 40/1), Momir Nikolić (IT-02-60/1), Dragan Obrenović (IT-02-60/2), Radislav Krstić (IT-98-33), Vidoje Blagojević (IT-02-60), Vujadin Popović (IT-05-88), Ljubiša Beara (IT-05-88), Drago Nikolić (IT-05-88), Ljubomir Borovčanin (IT-05-88), Vinko Pandurević (IT-05-88), Ratko Mladić (IT-95-5/18); Radovan Karadžić (IT-95-5/18) and Zdravko Tolimir (IT-05-88/2).

8 Goran Jelisić (Judgment, *Jelisić*, Trial Chamber, 14 December 1999); Duško Sikirica (Judgment, *Sikirica et al.*, Trial Chamber, 13 November 2001); Slobodan Milošević (Deceased on 11 March 2006, proceedings terminated on 14 March 2006); Radoslav Brđanin (Judgment, *Brđanin*, Trial Chamber, 1 September 2004); Milomir Stakić (Judgment, *Stakić*, Trial Chamber, 31 July 2003); Momčilo Krajišnik (Judgment, *Krajišnik*, Trial Chamber, 27 September 2006); Biljana Plavšić (Judgment, *Plavšić*, Trial Chamber, 27 February 2003); Momir Nikolić (Judgment, *Nikolić*, Trial Chamber, 2 December 2003); Dragan Obrenović (Judgment, *Obrenović*, Trial Chamber, 10 December 2003); Radislav Krstić (Judgment, *Krstić*, Trial Chamber, 19 April 2004); and Vidoje Blagojević (Judgment, *Blagojević and Jokić*, Trial Chamber, 17 January 2005).

9 The trial against Vujadin Popović, Ljubiša Beara, Drago Nikolić, Ljubomir Borovčanin, Vinko Pandurević, for genocide and conspiracy to commit genocide in Srebrenica is at the time of writing ongoing.

10 *Radovan Karadžić* (IT-95-5/18) and *Zdravko Tolimir* (IT-05-88/2).

11 *Ratko Mladić* (IT-95-5/18).

Chamber 'shall enter a judgement of acquittal on any count if there is no evidence capable of supporting a conviction'.

The first genocide case ever heard before the ICTY was against Goran Jelisić, who referred to himself as 'the Serbian Adolf'. He was charged with genocide, specifically for killings in the Luka detention facility in Brčko, north-eastern Bosnia and Herzegovina.[12] After the Prosecution had presented its case, the Trial Chamber found that Jelisić had no case to answer and acquitted him of genocide.[13] The Prosecution's appeal was not successful.[14] Duško Sikirica, Commander of Security in the Keraterm detention facility at the outskirts of Prijedor, in north-western Bosnia and Herzegovina, also was initially charged with genocide and complicity to commit genocide.[15] However, the Trial Chamber found pursuant to Rule 98*bis* that he had no case to answer with regard to the genocide charges and thereafter acquitted him.[16] An appeal was not filed.

In three cases the genocide charges were modified following plea agreements with the Prosecution.[17] The pleas were made before the cases had reached the Rule 98*bis* stage. Biljana Plavsić, a senior politician and member of the Supreme Command of the Bosnian Serb Army (VRS), was charged with genocide and complicity to commit genocide in Bosnia and Herzegovina,[18] for acts in the areas of Bosanski Novi, Brčko, Kljuc, Kotor Varoš, Prijedor, and Sanski Most.[19] However, following a plea agreement, the genocide charges were removed and Plavsić pleaded guilty to persecution and was subsequently sentenced to 11 years' imprisonment.[20]

In the cases of Momir Nikolić and Dragan Obrenović, charges of genocide and complicity in genocide for the 1995 killings of Bosnian Muslims in Srebrenica, Eastern Bosnia and Herzegovina, were also abandoned.[21] Momir Nikolić was the Assistant Commander and Chief of Security and Intelligence of the Bratunac Brigade in the Bosnian Serb Army, and Dragan Obrenović was the Chief of Staff and Deputy Commander of the Zvornik Brigade in the Bosnian Serb Army.[22] Following plea agreements with the Prosecution, they both pleaded guilty to persecution and the genocide charges were not pursued.[23] The Trial Chamber sentenced Momir Nikolić to 27 years,[24]

---

12 Second Amended Indictment, *Goran Jelisić and Ranko Česić*, 19 October 1998, para. 14.

13 Judgment, *Jelisić*, Trial Chamber, 14 December 1999, para. 138.

14 Judgment, *Jelisić*, Appeals Chamber, 5 July 2001, paras 22–77.

15 Second Amended Indictment, *Sikirica et al.*, 3 January 2001, paras 26–34.

16 On 27 June 2001, the Trial Chamber issued an oral decision grating Sikirica's motion pursuant to Rule 98*bis* with regard to genocide and complicity to commit genocide, with the written judgement being issued on 3 September 2001, Judgement on Defence Motions to Acquit, *Sikirica et al.*, Trial Chamber, 3 September 2001. See also, Sentencing Judgement, *Sikirica et al.*, Trial Chamber, 13 November 2001, para. 10.

17 Plea Agreement, *Plavšić*, Trial Chamber, 30 September 2002; Decision on Motion to Dismiss Charges Against Accused Momir Nikolić, *Blagojević et al.*, 12 May 2003; Plea Hearing, *Blagojević et. al.*, 21 May 2003.

18 Amended Consolidated Indictment, *Momcilo Krajišnik and Biljana Plavšić*, Trial Chamber, 7 March 2002, paras 4, 15–16.

19 Ibid., para. 16.

20 Plea Agreement, *Plavšić*, Trial Chamber, 30 September 2002; Judgment, *Plavšić*, Trial Chamber, 27 February 2003, para. 4.

21 Amended Joinder Indictment, *Vidoje Blagojević, Dragan Obrenović, Dragan Jokić, Momir Nikolić*, Trial Chamber, 27 May 2002, at 1.

22 Ibid.

23 Judgment, *Nikolić*, Trial Chamber, 2 December 2003; Judgment, *Obrenović*, Trial Chamber, 10 December 2003.

24 Judgment, *Nikolić*, Trial Chamber, 2 December 2003.

which was subsequently reduced to 20 by the Appeals Chamber.[25] Dragan Obrenović received a sentence of 17 years from the Trial Chamber,[26] which was not appealed.

All other of the six genocide cases have passed the Rule 98*bis* stage.[27] Of these cases, one was terminated due to the death of the accused – Slobodan Milošević. He was charged with genocide and complicity to commit genocide in Bosnia and Herzegovina,[28] but following his death the case was terminated and no verdict was passed.[29] In the cases of Radoslav Brđanin,[30] Milomir Stakić[31] and Momcilo Krajišnik,[32] the Trial Chambers did not find that the crime of genocide had been proved as such and the accused were acquitted.[33] All three cases involved high-level Bosnian Serb politicians charged with genocide and complicity to commit genocide in the areas of Krajina and Prijedor in Bosnia and Herzegovina. The Trial Chambers were satisfied that certain acts met the standard of the required *actus reus* for genocide, but in each of the cases found that the specific genocidal intent had not been established.[34]

The ICTY has found that genocide occurred in two cases: *Krstić* and *Blagojević*.[35] Both cases relate to the killings of Bosnian Muslim men in Srebrenica, Bosnia and Herzegovina.[36] Krstić was sentenced to 46 years imprisonment by the Trial Chamber, subsequently reduced to 35 years by the Appeals Chamber.[37] In *Blagojević*, the Trial Chamber found the accused guilty of aiding and

25 Judgment, *Nikolić*, Appeals Chamber, 8 March 2006.

26 Sentencing Judgment, *Obrenović*, Trial Chamber, 10 December 2003.

27 Decision on Motion for Judgement of Acquittal, *Milošević*, Trial Chamber, 16 June 2004, para. 316; Decision on Motion for Acquittal Pursuant to 98*bis*, *Brđanin*, Trial Chamber, 19 March 2004; Decision on Motion for Acquittal Pursuant to 98*bis*, *Krajišnik*, Trial Chamber, 19 August 2005; Judgment on Motions for Acquittal Pursuant to Rule 98*bis*, *Blagojević et al.*, Trial Chamber, 4 April 2004). Krstić did not file a motion for acquittal pursuant to Rule 98*bis*, Scheduling Order, *Krstić*, Trial Chamber, 12 September 2000. On 3 March 2008, the Trial Chamber made an oral ruling, pursuant to Rule 98*bis*, in the ongoing cases against Popović, Beara, Nikolić, Borovčanin and Pandurević that there was a case to answer. T. 21461-21474.

28 Amended Indictment, *Bosnia and Herzegovina*, *Milošević*, Trial Chamber, 22 November 2002, para. 32.

29 Order Terminating the Proceedings, *Milošević*, Trial Chamber, 14 March 2006.

30 Sixth Amended Indictment, *Radoslav Brđanin*, Trial Chamber, 9 December 2003. Radoslav Brđanin was a prominent politician in the Autonomous Region of Krajina (ARK) and held important positions at the municipal, regional and republic levels, including that of First Vice-President of the ARK Assembly, President of the ARK Crisis Staff, and acting Vice-President of the Government of the Republika Srpska.

31 Fourth Amended Indictment, *Milomir Stakić*, Trial Chamber, 10 April 2002. From 30 April 1992 until 30 September 1992, Milomir Stakić was President of the Serb-controlled Prijedor Municipality Crisis Staff and Head of the Municipal Council for National Defence in Prijedor, in north-western Bosnia and Herzegovina.

32 Amended Consolidated Indictment, *Momcilo Krajišnik and Biljana Plavsić*, Trial Chamber, 7 March 2002, Momcilo Krajišnik was a senior politician in the Bosnian Serb leadership, member of the main board of the Serbian Democratic Party (SDS) and President of the Bosnian Serb Assembly, and one of the negotiators for the Bosnian Serb leadership in the Dayton peace negotiations.

33 Judgment, *Krajišnik*, Trial Chamber, 27 September 2006, para. 1181; Judgment, *Brđanin*, Trial Chamber, 1 September 2004, paras 867–869, 1125; Judgment, *Stakić*, Trial Chamber, 31 July 2003, at 560–561.

34 Judgment, *Brđanin*, Trial Chamber, 1 September 2004; Judgment, *Stakić*, Trial Chamber, 31 July 2003; Judgment, *Krajišnik*, Trial Chamber, 27 September 2006.

35 Judgment, *Krstić*, Trial Chamber, 19 April 2004; Judgment, *Blagojević and Jokić*, Trial Chamber, 17 January 2005.

36 Ibid.

37 Judgment, *Krstić*, Trial Chamber, 2 August 2001, at 255; Judgment, *Krstić*, Appeals Chamber, 19 April 2004, at 87.

abetting complicity in genocide, but the Appeals Chamber overturned those findings and acquitted him completely of genocide.[38]

2. Definition of the Crime of Genocide

Article 4(2) of the ICTY Statute enumerates five acts or *actus reus* by which genocide can be perpetrated:

> (a) killing members of the group;
> (b) causing serious bodily or mental harm to members of the group;
> (c) deliberately inflicting on the group conditions of life calculated to bring about its physical destruction in whole or in part;
> (d) imposing measures intended to prevent births within the group;
> (e) forcibly transferring children of the group to another group.

At the time of writing, no case at the ICTY has considered whether particular acts constitute the *actus reus* of (d), imposing measures intended to prevent births within the group, or (e), forcibly transferring children of the group to another group.

For a finding of genocide, the *actus reus* must be coupled with the mental element or *mens rea* of the underlying act, as well as an additional mental element often referred to as 'special' or 'specific intent' (*dolus specialis*) or genocidal intent.[39] The intent referred to is the 'intent to destroy, in whole or in part, a national, ethnical, racial or religious group, as such'.[40] It is this intent that distinguishes genocide from crimes against humanity such as extermination.

A. Actus Reus

1. Article 4(2)(a) – Killing Members of the Group

In the case law of the ICTY, killing members of the group has been interpreted to mean wilful killing or murder.[41] In addition, the killing has to be committed against members of a protected group.[42]

In both *Krstić and Blagojević*, the Trial Chambers considered the July 1995 killings of between 7,000 and 8,000 Bosnian Muslim men in the area of Srebrenica in Eastern Bosnia and Herzegovina to satisfy Article 4(2)(a).[43] The *Brđanin* Trial Chamber also found that the *actus reus* of killing members of the group was established.[44] Its finding was based on the killings of at least 1,669

---

38 Judgment, *Blagojević and Jokić*, Appeals Chamber, 9 May 2007.

39 Judgment, *Jelisić*, Appeals Chamber, 5 July 2001, para. 45; Judgment, *Blagojević and Jokić*, Trial Chamber, para. 665, note 2082; Judgment, *Stakić*, Trial Chamber, 31 July 2003, para. 520.

40 Art. 4 ICTYSt.

41 Judgment, *Blagojević and Jokić*, Trial Chamber, 17 January 2005, para. 642; Judgment, *Krajišnik*, Trial Chamber, 27 September 2006, para. 859; Judgment, *Brđanin*, Trial Chamber, 1 September 2004; para. 689; Judgment, *Stakić*, Trial Chamber, 31 July 2003, para. 515.

42 Judgment, *Brđanin*, Trial Chamber, 1 September 2004, para. 739.

43 Judgment, *Krstić*, Trial Chamber, 2 August 2001, paras 486, 543; Judgment, *Blagojević and Jokić*, Trial Chamber, 17 January 2005, para. 643.

44 Judgment, *Brđanin*, Trial Chamber, 1 September 2004, paras 738–740.

Bosnian Muslim and Bosnian Croat non-combatants by Bosnian Serb forces.[45] The killings occurred in municipalities, civilian/military camps and in detention facilities.[46] The *Stakić* Trial Chamber found that killings in the Omarska, Keraterm and Trnopolje camps and other detention centres, as well as those occurring during the attacks by the Bosnian Serb army on the predominantly Bosnian Muslim villages and towns throughout the Prijedor municipality, met the standard of Article 4(2)(a).[47] In *Krajišnik*, the *actus reus* was satisfied by killings perpetrated in connection with attacks on towns and villages as well as in detention centres.[48] It found that approximately 3,000 Muslims and Croats were discriminatorily killed in 30 municipalities[49]

2. Article 4(2)(b) – Causing Serious Bodily or Mental Harm to Members of the Group

Acts causing serious bodily or mental harm to members of the group were legally defined in *Stakić* and *Brđanin* to include: torture, inhumane or degrading treatment, sexual violence including rape, interrogations combined with beatings, threats of death, and harm that damages health or causes disfigurement or serious injury to members of the targeted national, ethnical, racial or religious group.[50] The *Krajišnik* Trial Chamber found 'causing serious bodily or mental harm to members of the same group, by cruel or inhumane treatment, including torture, physical and psychological abuse, and sexual violence' to satisfy the *actus reus* of genocide.[51]

In order to meet the requisite *mens rea* of 4 (2)(b), the harm must be inflicted intentionally.[52] The *Krstić*, *Blagojević*, *Stakić* and *Brđanin* trial judgments all held that the harm inflicted need not

45 Ibid., para. 739.

46 Ibid., paras 465, 738–740. The Trial Chamber was persuaded by a number of incidents, including on 20 July 1992, in the village of Biščani hundreds of Bosnian Muslim residents were rounded up and executed; at a school in Velagići at least 77 civilians were lined up against a wall and killed on 1 June 1992; and there were also numerous killings by beatings at the hands of guards at the Trnopolje camp. Ibid., paras 407–409, 427, 450.

47 Judgment, *Stakić*, Trial Chamber, 31 July 2003, para. 544.

48 Judgment, *Krajišnik*, Trial Chamber, 27 September 2006, para. 860. 'The Chamber finds that some of the crimes described earlier in part 5 meet the requirements of the *actus reus* for genocide. This is the case with regard to all of the crimes of murder and extermination, described above in part 5.2.2, as well as some instances of cruel or inhumane treatment, discussed above in part 5.4.2. The Chamber does not find, however, that any of these acts were committed with the intent to destroy, in part, the Bosnian-Muslim or Bosnian-Croat ethnic group, as such.' Ibid., para. 867.

49 Ibid., para. 792. For example, in Zvornik, on different dates ranging from April to June 1992, various groups, totalling 70 Muslim detainees, were killed as well as dozens of men, women and children during an attack; during the summer of 1992 approximately 200 non-Serb civilians, mostly Muslims were killed in Višegrad; and on 14 June 1992 in Novi Grad (Sarajevo) 47 detainees were killed using grenades and automatic weapons. Judgment, *Krajišnik*, Trial Chamber, 27 September 2006, para. 718.

50 Judgment, *Brđanin*, Trial Chamber, 1 September 2004, para. 690; Judgment, *Stakić*, Trial Chamber, 31 July 2003, para. 515. See also ICJ, Judgment, *Application of the Convention on the Prevention and Punishment of the Crime of Genocide (Bosnia and Herzegovina v. Serbia and Montenegro)*, 26 February 2007 (Bosnia Judgment), para. 319. The ICJ found that systematic 'massive mistreatment, beatings, rape and torture causing serious bodily and mental harm during the conflict and, in particular, in the detention camps' satisfied Article II(*b*) of the Genocide Convention, which is reproduced in Art. 4(2)(b) of the Statute.

51 Judgment, *Krajišnik*, Trial Chamber, 27 September 2006, para. 859.

52 Judgement, *Blagojević and Jokić*, Trial Chamber, 17 January 2005, para. 645; Judgment, *Brđanin*, Trial Chamber, 1 September 2004, para. 690.

be permanent and irremediable.[53] *Blagojević* added that the harm must inflict 'grave and long-term disadvantage to a person's ability to lead a normal and constructive life',[54] and *Brđanin* that the harm 'needs to be serious.'[55]

In its factual application of Article 4(2)(b), the *Brđanin* Trial Chamber found that in relation to a large number of camps and detention facilities serious bodily or mental harm was inflicted intentionally upon the detainees.[56] For example, '[a] Bosnian Muslim man suffered broken ribs and cuts to his face, whilst another broke a few teeth and still bears the marks of strangulation'.[57] In the Manjača detention camp, approximately 3,640 men were detained and subject to regular beatings,[58] and in the Trnopolje camp male detainees were interrogated and beaten unconscious.[59] Detainees were subjected to electroshocks[60] and made to run through gauntlets where they would be beaten with baseball bats, rifle butts and batons.[61] With regard to sexual violence including rape, the Trial Chamber found that Bosnian Muslim and Bosnian Croat detainees were raped, and in some instances forced to perform sexual acts with each other, including *fellatio*, and that such acts satisfied Article 4(2)(b).[62]

The *Krajišnik* Trial Chamber found that Bosnian Muslim and Bosnian Croat detainees in many detention centres were both physically and psychologically attacked.[63] More specifically it found that detainees were subjected to electroshocks and forced to beat one another, while others were beaten up to three times a day.[64] Sexual abuse was rampant in the detention centres, ranging from the raping of young women to forcing male detainees to perform sexual acts on one another.[65] These acts were found to result in serious injuries, mental and physical suffering constituting cruel or inhumane treatment, and thereby satisfied Article 4(2)(b).[66]

The *Stakić* Trial Chamber found that

> [T]housands of persons who were detained in the camps were subjected to inhumane and degrading treatment, including routine beatings. Moreover, rapes and sexual assaults were committed at some of these facilities. Detainees were given little more than a subsistence diet. In addition, Bosnian

53 Judgment, *Stakić*, Trial Chamber, 31 July 2003, para. 516; Judgment, *Brđanin*, Trial Chamber, 1 September 2004, para. 690; Judgment, *Krstić*, Trial Chamber, 2 August 2001, para. 513; Judgment, *Blagojević and Jokić*, Trial Chamber, 17 January 2005, para. 645.

54 Judgment, *Blagojević and Jokić*, Trial Chamber, 17 January 2005, para. 645. The *Krajišnik* Trial Chamber worded it slightly differently, holding that 'a fair and consistent construction of this clause alongside the four other types of *actus reus* is that, in order to pass as the *actus reus* of genocide under [4 (2)(b)], the act must inflict such "harm" as to contribute, or tend to contribute, to the destruction of the group or part thereof. Harm amounting to "a grave and long-term disadvantage to a person's ability to lead a normal and constructive life" has been said to be sufficient for this purpose.' Judgment, *Krajišnik*, Trial Chamber, 27 September 2006, paras 861–862.

55 Judgment, *Brđanin*, Trial Chamber, 1 September 2004, para. 690.

56 Ibid., para. 744.

57 Ibid., para. 746.

58 Ibid., paras 747–751.

59 Ibid., para. 856.

60 Ibid., para. 772.

61 Ibid., para. 822.

62 Ibid., paras 824, 835, 847, 856.

63 Ibid., para. 798.

64 Ibid.

65 Ibid., para. 799.

66 Ibid., para. 803. See *supra* note 48.

> Muslims who had lived their whole lives in the municipality of Prijedor were expelled from their homes. Bosnian Muslims were discriminated against in employment, e.g. by arbitrary dismissals, their houses were marked for destruction, and in many cases were destroyed along with mosques and Catholic churches.[67]

While the *Stakić* Chamber found that Article 4(2)(b) was established,[68] it is not evident which of the above cited acts it considered under Article 4(2)(b), as opposed to those acts it believed to satisfy the requirements of Article 4(2)(c) – 'deliberately inflicting on the group conditions of life calculated to bring about its physical destruction in whole or in part'.[69]

Both the *Krstić and Blagojević* Trial Chambers found that the injuries and trauma suffered by the few victims who survived the mass executions constituted serious bodily and mental harm within the meaning of Article 4 of the Statute.[70] Further, the *Blagojević* Trial Chamber held that 'the forced displacement of women, children, and elderly people was itself a traumatic experience, which, [reached] the requisite level of causing serious mental harm under Article 4(2)(b) of the Statute'.[71] The Appeals Chamber has stated that forcible transfer 'does not constitute in and of itself

67 Judgment, *Stakić*, Trial Chamber, 31 July 2003, para. 544.

68 Ibid., para. 556.

69 Ibid., paras 545–561. See also Judgment, *Stakić*, Appeals Chamber, 23 March 2006, para. 47.

70 Judgment, *Krstić*, Trial Chamber, 2 August 2001, paras 507, 514, 543; Judgment, *Blagojević*, Trial Chamber, 17 January 2005, para. 647. The *Blagojević* Trial Chamber specified that '[t]he fear of being captured, and, at the moment of the separation, the sense of utter helplessness and extreme fear for their family and friends' safety as well as for their own safety, is a traumatic experience from which one will not quickly – if ever – recover'. Furthermore, the Trial Chamber found that 'the men suffered mental harm having their identification documents taken away from them, seeing that they would not be exchanged as previously told, and when they understood what their ultimate fate was. Upon arrival at an execution site, they saw the killing fields covered of bodies of the Bosnian Muslim men brought to the execution site before them and murdered. After having witnessed the executions of relatives and friends, and in some cases suffering from injuries themselves, they suffered the further mental anguish of lying still, in fear, under the bodies – sometimes of relative or friends – for long hours, listening to the sounds of the executions, of the moans of those suffering in pain, and then of the machines as mass graves were dug.' Ibid., para. 647.

71 Judgment, *Blagojević*, Trial Chamber, 17 January 2005, para. 648. It considered the Bosnian Muslim population fleeing from Srebrenica, leaving their homes and possessions after a five-day military offensive, while being shot at as they moved to Potočari in search of refuge and '[u]pon arrival in Potočari, the Bosnian Muslim population did not find the refuge they were seeking: rather they found UNPROFOR unable to provide the assistance they needed: DutchBat was woefully unprepared for the mass influx of people to its base. After months of having its supply convoys searched or blocked, it did not have adequate supplies of food, medicine or even water for the thousands of Bosnian Muslims who arrived.' The Trial Chamber continued '[a]s the brutal separations began under the watchful eye of the Bosnian Serb forces and the abuse of the population became more widespread, particularly during the "night of terror", the Bosnian Muslims were terrified – and helpless' and as the Bosnian Muslim population 'boarded the buses, without being asked even for their name, the Bosnian Muslims saw the smoke from their homes being burned and knew that this was not a temporary displacement for their immediate safety. Rather, this displacement was a critical step in achieving the ultimate objective of the attack on the Srebrenica enclave to eliminate the Bosnian Muslim population from the enclave.' Ibid., para. 648.

a genocidal act'.[72] Nonetheless, this holding does not preclude a Trial Chamber from relying on this evidence when inferring genocidal intent.[73]

3. Article 4(2)(c) – Deliberately Inflicting on the Group Conditions of Life Calculated to Bring About its Physical Destruction in Whole or in Part

This *actus reus* was not charged or considered in the *Krstić* and *Blagojević* cases.[74] In the *Krajišnik* case it was charged, but the Trial Chamber appears not to have been satisfied that the requirements were met.[75] Two Trial Chambers, *Brđanin* and *Stakić*, elaborated on the circumstances which are relevant to this *actus reus*, holding it to include 'methods of destruction apart from direct killings such as subjecting the group to a subsistence diet, systematic expulsion from homes and denial of the right to medical services'.[76] Also listed were circumstances 'that would lead to a slow death, such as lack of proper housing, clothing and hygiene or excessive work or physical exertion'.[77] In contrast to Article 4(2)(a) and 4(2)(b), the *actus reus* in Article 4(2)(c) does not require a specific result to prove its occurrence.[78]

Both the *Brđanin* and *Stakić* Trial Chambers listed in the applicable law of Article 4(2)(c) lack of proper housing and clothing as a method of destruction.[79] Nevertheless, these methods were ultimately not applied to the facts. Also, 'systematic expulsion from homes' has been listed as an Article 4(2)(c) method of destruction,[80] which the *Stakić* Trial Chamber qualified by stating that '[i]t does not suffice to deport a group or a part of a group. A clear distinction must be drawn

72 Judgment, *Blagojević*, Appeals Chamber, 9 May 2007, para. 123; Judgment, *Krstić*, Appeals Chamber, 19 April 2004, para. 33. The International Court of Justice has held that neither the intent to render an area ethnically homogenous nor operations to implement the policy 'can as such be designated as genocide: the intent that characterizes genocide is to "destroy, in whole or in part", a particular group, and deportation or displacement of the members of a group, even if effected by force, is not necessarily equivalent to destruction of that group'. ICJ, Bosnia Judgment, para. 190.

73 Judgment, *Krstić*, Appeals Chamber, 19 April 2004, para. 33.

74 Judgment, *Krstić*, Trial Chamber, 2 August 2001, para. 543; Judgment, *Blagojević*, Trial Chamber, para. 641.

75 Judgment, *Krajišnik*, Trial Chamber, 27 September 2006, para. 867. The Chamber found that 'some of the crimes described earlier … meet the requirements of the *actus reus* of genocide. This is the case with regard to all the crimes of murder and extermination … as well as some instances of cruel or inhumane treatment … The Chamber does not find, however, that any of these acts were committed with the intent to destroy, in part, the Bosnian-Muslim or Bosnian-Croat ethnic group, as such.' The Trial Chamber's silence with regard to the *actus reus* of 'deliberately inflicting on the group conditions of life calculated to bring about its physical destruction in whole or in part' is interpreted to mean that it was not satisfied that the requirements of this *actus reus* were met.

76 Judgment, *Brđanin*, Trial Chamber, 1 September 2004, para. 691; Judgment, *Stakić*, Trial Chamber, 31 July 2003, para. 517. See Judgment, *Stakić*, Trial Chamber, 31 July 2003, para. 518 stated by referring to UN Doc. A/C.6/217; UN Doc. A/C.6/SR.82 that '[t]he words "calculated to bring about its physical destruction" replaced the phrase "aimed at causing death" proposed by Belgium in the UN General Assembly's Sixth (Legal) Committee'.

77 Judgment, *Brđanin*, Trial Chamber, 1 September 2004, para. 691; Judgment, *Stakić*, Trial Chamber, 31 July 2003, para. 517.

78 Judgment, *Brđanin*, Trial Chamber, 1 September 2004, para. 691; Judgment, *Stakić*, Trial Chamber, 31 July 2003, para. 517. See *Eichmann*, Jerusalem District Court Judgement, para. 196.

79 Judgment, *Stakić*, Trial Chamber, 31 July 2003, para. 517; Judgment, *Brđanin*, Trial Chamber, 1 September 2004, para. 691.

80 Ibid.

between *physical destruction* and *mere dissolution* of a group.'[81] As stated above, the Appeals Chamber has held that 'forcible transfer does not in itself constitute a genocidal act.'[82]

The *Brđanin* Trial Chamber only considered whether acts satisfied Article 4(3)(c) once it had already found them not to amount to the *actus reus* under Article 4(2)(b).[83] The Chamber was satisfied that conditions to bring about physical destruction were inflicted deliberately upon the Bosnian Muslim and Bosnian Croat detainees.[84] The detainees were kept in crowded stables normally used for livestock,[85] where all they could do was lie or sit down.[86] There were no shower or bath facilities and no running water, and there was an infestation of lice that combined to create an atmosphere where it was difficult to breathe because of the stench.[87] Water came from a lake and created intestinal and stomach problems.[88] The detainees also had to perform heavy physical work.[89] One group of 120 individuals was crammed into a garage for several days during intense heat,[90] and had to beg for water by singing Serbian songs.[91] The daily food ration consisted of one serving of bread, stew and spoiled cabbage.[92] Food was so insufficient that some detainees resorted to eating grass.[93] Water rations were not fit for human consumption.[94] These factors, in addition to deficient hygienic conditions, resulted in a lot of health problems, but medicine was not readily available.[95] In its determination, the *Brđanin* Trial Chamber analysed the *mens rea* of 'deliberately inflicting on the group conditions of life calculated to bring about its physical destruction' separately from the genocidal intent, and focused on 'the objective probability of these conditions leading to the physical destruction of the group in part'.[96] It assessed factors including the nature of the conditions imposed, the duration of exposure and the characteristics of the victims, such as vulnerability.[97]

The *Stakić* Trial Chamber also found that the acts satisfied Article 4(2)(c), though it is not clear precisely which of the acts it considered in relation to 'deliberately inflicting on the group conditions of life calculated to bring about its physical destruction in whole or in part'.[98] It further

---

81 Judgment, *Stakić*, Trial Chamber, 31 July 2003, para. 519 (emphasis added).

82 Judgment, *Blagojević*, Appeals Chamber, 9 May 2007, para. 123; Judgment, *Krstić*, Appeals Chamber, 19 April 2004, para. 33. Expulsion is an act of forcible transfer, Judgement, *Krnojelac*, Appeals Chamber, paras 211, 224.

83 Judgment, *Brđanin*, Trial Chamber, 1 September 2004, para. 905.

84 Ibid., para. 909.

85 Ibid., para. 910.

86 Ibid.

87 Ibid., para. 911.

88 Ibid., para. 913.

89 Ibid., para. 914.

90 Ibid., para. 931.

91 Ibid.

92 Ibid., para. 932.

93 Ibid., para. 912.

94 Ibid., para. 933.

95 Ibid., para. 934.

96 Judgment, *Brđanin*, Trial Chamber, 1 September 2004, para. 906.

97 Ibid.

98 Judgment, *Stakić*, Trial Chamber, 31 July 2003, paras 544, 557. The Trial Chamber held that 'thousands of persons who were detained in the camps were subjected to inhumane and degrading treatment, including routine beatings. Moreover, rapes and sexual assaults were committed at some of these facilities. Detainees were given little more than a subsistence diet. In addition, Bosnian Muslims who had lived their whole lives in the municipality of Prijedor were expelled from their homes. Bosnian Muslims were discriminated against

found that the genocidal intent had not been proven in relation to this *actus reus* arguing that 'in this context, deporting a group or part of a group is insufficient if it is not accompanied by methods seeking the physical destruction of the group'.[99] The Prosecution appealed, arguing that the Trial Chamber should have considered whether, in addition to the genocidal intent, the *mens rea* of 'deliberately inflicting on the group conditions of life calculated to bring about its physical destruction in whole or in part' was satisfied. The Appeals Chamber held this was not specifically discussed at trial, but was satisfied that the Trial Chamber's analysis in relation to the accused's genocidal intent with regard to Article 4(2)(a) and 4(2)(b) 'was equally applicable to all of the alleged genocidal acts, including the imposition of intolerable living conditions pointed to by the Prosecution'.[100]

B. Mens Rea

1. 'Destroy in Whole or in Part, a National, Ethnical, Racial or Religious Group, as Such'

(a) Identity of the group

The *Krstić* Trial Chamber noted that what constitutes a 'national, ethnical, racial or religious group' is not defined in the Genocide Convention or in the Statute.[101] It further stated that European human rights instruments use the term national minorities, while international instruments use terms such as ethnic, religious or linguistic minorities, but that the two concepts 'appear to embrace the same goal' and that 'to attempt to differentiate each of the named groups on the basis of scientifically objective criteria would thus be inconsistent with the object and purpose of the [Genocide] Convention. A group's cultural, religious, ethnical or national characteristics must be identified within the social-historic context which it inhabits'[102] and the relevant group is identified 'by the perpetrators of the crime, on the basis of its perceived national, ethnical, racial or religious characteristics'.[103]

Applying this reasoning to the facts of the case, the Trial Chamber held that 'the Bosnian Muslims were recognised as a "nation" by the Yugoslav Constitution of 1963' and that 'the highest Bosnian Serb political authorities and the Bosnian Serb forces operating in Srebrenica in July 1995 viewed the Bosnian Muslims as a specific national group'.[104] The *Krstić* Trial Chamber concluded that 'no national, ethnical or religious characteristic makes it possible to differentiate the Bosnian Muslims in Srebrenica … from other Bosnian Muslims'[105] and found that the protected group was the Bosnian Muslims.[106] In addition, it stated that 'It is doubtful that the Bosnian Muslims residing in the enclave at the time of the offensive considered themselves a distinct national, ethnical, racial

in employment, e.g. by arbitrary dismissals, their houses were marked for destruction, and in many cases were destroyed along with mosques and Catholic churches. The Prosecution relies upon these events in Prijedor municipality in 1992 in their totality as being the *actus reus* for genocide under Article 4 (2) (a) to (c) of the Statute.' Ibid., para. 544.

99 Ibid., para. 557.

100 Judgment, *Stakić*, Appeals Chamber, 23 March 2006, para. 47.

101 Judgment, *Krstić*, Trial Chamber, 2 August 2001, para. 555.

102 Ibid., para. 556.

103 Ibid., para. 557.

104 Ibid., para. 559.

105 Judgment, *Krstić*, Trial Chamber, 2 August 2001, para. 559.

106 Ibid., para. 560.

or religious group among the Bosnian Muslims'.[107] Following similar reasoning, the *Brđanin* Trial Chamber found that 'no national, ethnical, racial or religious characteristic makes it possible to differentiate the Bosnian Muslims and Bosnian Croats residing in the [geographical area of] ARK [Autonomous Regions of Krajina] ... from the other Bosnian Muslims and Bosnian Croats'.[108] It further stated that the geographical location of the Bosnian Muslims and Bosnian Croats of ARK was the only defining or differentiating characteristic, and this was 'not a criterion contemplated by the Genocide Convention'.[109] The *Brđanin* Trial Chamber found that the Bosnian Muslims and Bosnian Croats were the protected groups and that the Bosnian Muslims and Bosnian Croats in ARK constituted a part of the protected group.[110]

One debated issue has been whether a group can be defined on the basis of a 'negative criteri[on]', in that individuals are targeted on the basis of non-membership of a group (e.g. non-Muslims or non-Serbs).[111] The *Stakić* Appeals Chamber rejected such a possibility, holding that the targeted group should be defined 'positively', by virtue of what it includes, and not what it excludes.[112]

(b) Destruction of the group, in whole or in part

The term 'destroy' has been interpreted in ICTY case law to include physical or biological destruction, and to exclude cultural or sociological destruction.[113] Attacks on cultural and religious property and symbols of the targeted group often occur alongside physical and biological destruction, and may be considered as evidence of an intent to physically destroy the group.[114]

107 Ibid., para. 559.

108 Judgment, *Brđanin*, Trial Chamber, 1 September 2004, para. 734.

109 Ibid.

110 Ibid., paras 735–736.

111 The *Stakić* and *Brđanin* Trial Chambers disagreed with the 'negative approach' taken in the *Jelisić* Trial Chamber and held that 'a targeted group may be distinguishable on more than one basis and the elements of genocide must be considered in relation to each group separately, e.g. Bosnian Muslims and Bosnian Croats.' Judgment, *Stakić*, Trial Chamber, 31 July 2003, para. 512; Judgment, *Brđanin*, Trial Chamber, 1 September 2004, paras 698–700. *Cf. Jelisić*, Trial Chamber, 14 December 1999, para. 82.

112 Judgment, *Stakić*, Appeals Chamber, 22 March 2006, paras 9–28.

113 Judgment, *Krstić*, Appeals Chamber, 19 April 2004, paras 25–26. See also ICJ Bosnia Judgment, para. 344. The ICJ Judgment interpreted Art. II(c) of the Genocide Convention, which is identical to Art. 4(2)(c) of the Statute. The ICJ ruled that 'the destruction of historical, cultural and religious heritage cannot be considered to constitute the deliberate infliction of conditions of life calculated to bring about the physical destruction of the group'. See also Report of the International Law Commission, UN Doc, A/51/10, at 90–91, and for different view, the *Jorgić* ECHR Judgment, which held that the interpretation by German courts of genocidal intent as extending beyond biological and physical destruction to include destruction of the group as a social unit 'could reasonably be regarded as consistent with the essence' of the crime and 'reasonably be foreseen', paras 18, 23, 27, 36, 106, 108, 112–113.

114 Judgment, *Krstić*, Trial Chamber, 2 August 2001, para. 580. The Trial Chamber considered 'as evidence of intent to destroy the group the deliberate destruction of mosques and houses belonging to members of the group'. Judge Shahabuddeen in his separate opinion in the *Krstić* Appeals Judgement stated that '[a] group is constituted by characteristics – often intangible – binding together a collection of people as a social unit. If those characteristics have been destroyed in pursuance of the intent with which a listed act of a physical or biological nature was done, it is not convincing to say that the destruction, though effectively obliterating the group, is not genocide because the obliteration was not physical or biological'. Separate Opinion by Judge Shahabuddeen, in *Krstić*, Appeals Chamber, 19 April 2004, at 105, para. 50.

Article 4 refers to the destruction 'in whole' or 'in part', which has been discussed in several cases. A finding of intent to destroy in 'in part' carries with it a substantiality requirement:[115] evidence must prove that the accused 'intended to destroy at least a substantial part of the protected group'.[116] The substantiality requirement reflects both 'genocide's defining character as a crime of massive proportions' and 'the impact [which] the destruction of the targeted part will have on the overall survival of the group'.[117] Evaluation of the substantiality requirement involves a number of considerations 'including but not limited to: the numeric size of the targeted group – measured not only in absolute terms but also in relation to the overall size of the entire group – the prominence within the group of the targeted part of the group, and the area of the perpetrator's activities and control as well as the possible extent of their reach'.[118] The Appeals Chamber has held that '[t]he applicability of these factors, as well as their relative weight, will vary depending on the circumstances of a particular case'.[119]

With regard to the numeric size of a group, it is not necessary for a finding of genocide that a large number of individuals are killed.[120] Trial Chambers must ask itself 'how much of a group a perpetrator ... *intend[ed] to destroy* in order to meet the legal requirement of genocide'.[121] The *Sikirica* Trial Chamber found that genocidal intent could be inferred from the killing of 1,000–1,400 Bosnian Muslims out of a total of about 49,000, which constituted between 2 and 2.8 per cent of the Bosnian Muslims group in the Prijedor municipality.[122] The *Brđanin* Trial Chamber found that out of approximately 2.2 million Bosnian Muslims and 800,000 Bosnian Croats living in Bosnia and Herzegovina, about 230,000 Bosnian Muslims and 60,000 Bosnian Croats lived in the relevant targeted areas. Numerically speaking, these relevant targeted areas were found 'on their own, [to constitute] a substantial part, both intrinsically and in relation to the overall Bosnian Muslim and Bosnian Croat groups in [Bosnia and Herzegovina]'.[123]

The *Krstić* Trial Chamber held, and the Appeals Chamber agreed, that the part of the targeted group was the Muslim population in Srebrenica, as a part of the greater Muslim population in Bosnia and Herzegovina.[124] The size of this targeted group was approximately 40,000 people, comprising not only Bosnian Muslims from the Srebrenica municipality but also refugees from the surrounding areas.[125] The Appeals Chamber held that '[a]lthough this population constituted only a small percentage of the overall Muslim population of Bosnia and Herzegovina at the time, the importance of the Muslim community of Srebrenica is not captured solely by its size'.[126]

115 Judgment, *Krstić*, Appeals Chamber, 19 April 2004, paras 8–11.

116 Ibid., para. 12.

117 Ibid., para. 8.

118 Judgment, *Brđanin*, Trial Chamber, 1 September 2004, para. 702, summarizing the Judgment, *Krstić*, Appeals Chamber, 19 April 2004, paras 12–14.

119 Judgment, *Krstić*, Appeals Chamber, 19 April 2004, para. 14. See also Judgment, *Brđanin*, Trial Chamber, 1 September 2004, para. 702.

120 Judgment, *Stakić*, Trial Chamber, 31 July 2003, para. 522.

121 Decision on Motion for Judgement of Acquittal, Slobodan Milošević, 16 June 2004, para. 127 (emphasis added). See also Judgment, *Brđanin*, Trial Chamber, 1 September 2004, para. 964.

122 Judgement on Defence Motions to Acquit, *Sikirica*, Trial Chamber, 3 September 2001, paras 72–75.

123 Judgment, *Brđanin*, Trial Chamber, 1 September 2004, para. 967.

124 Judgment, *Krstić*, Trial Chamber, 2 August 2001, paras 560, 561; Judgment, *Krstić*, Appeals Chamber, 19 April 2004, paras 15, 19.

125 Judgment, *Krstić*, Appeals Chamber, 19 April 2004, para. 15.

126 Ibid., para. 15.

The Appeals Chamber in *Krstić* also considered factors such as the strategic importance of the targeted location for achieving the goals of the perpetrators,[127] and the significance of Srebrenica in 'the eyes of both the Bosnian Muslims and the international community' as '[t]he town of Srebrenica was the most visible of the "safe areas" established by the UN Security Council in Bosnia'.[128] Further, in *Krstić* it was found that the Main Staff of the Bosnian Serb Army 'extended throughout Bosnia, [while] the authority of the Bosnian Serb Forces charged with the take-over of Srebrenica did not extend beyond the Central Podrinje region'[129] – the area where Srebrenica is located.[130] The Appeals Chamber held that '[f]rom the perspective of the Bosnian Serb forces alleged to have had genocidal intent ... the Muslims of Srebrenica were the only part of the Bosnian Muslim group within their area of control'.[131] Finally, the Appeals Chamber also held that 'if a specific part of the group is emblematic of the overall group, or is essential to its survival, that may support a finding that the part qualifies as substantial within the meaning of Article 4'.[132] Accordingly, the Appeals Chamber was satisfied that the intent of the Main Staff of the VRS was found to satisfy the requisite of substantiality.[133]

Following this reasoning, the *Blagojević* Trial Chamber found, without any analysis, that the targeted group, the Bosnian Muslims of Srebrenica, was a 'substantial part of the Bosnian Muslim group'.[134]

(c) 'As such'

The phrase 'as such' requires that the intent is to destroy the targeted group as a separate and distinct entity.[135] The ultimate victim is the group, as opposed to an accumulation of isolated individuals within it, although the group's destruction necessarily requires the commission of crimes against individuals.[136] This is consonant with the 1946 UN General Assembly Resolution 96(I), which defined genocide as 'a denial of the right of existence of entire human groups'.[137]

127 Ibid.

128 Ibid., para. 16.

129 Ibid., para. 17.

130 Ibid., paras 35–37.

131 Ibid., para. 17.

132 Judgment, *Krstić*, Appeals Chamber, 19 April 2004, para. 12. See also Judgment, *Jelisić*, Trial Chamber, 14 December 1999, para. 82; Judgment on Defence Motions to Acquit, *Sikirica et al.*, Trial Chamber, 3 September 2001, para. 77; Judgment, *Stakić*, Trial Chamber, 31 July 2003, para. 525.

133 Ibid., paras 6–23.

134 Judgment, *Blagojević and Jokić*, Trial Chamber, para. 673.

135 Judgment, *Stakić*, Trial Chamber, 31 July 2003, para. 521; Judgment, *Brđanin*, Trial Chamber, 1 September 2004, para. 698; Judgment, *Blagojević*, Trial Chamber, para. 665.

136 Judgment, *Brđanin*, Trial Chamber, 1 September 2004, paras 698–700; Judgment, *Blagojević*, Trial Chamber, para. 665; Judgement on Motions to Acquit, *Sikirica*, Trial Chamber, 3 September 2001, para. 89; Judgment, *Stakić*, Trial Chamber, 31 July 2003, para. 521; Judgment, *Jelisić*, Trial Chamber, 14 December 1999, para. 79. See also Judgment, *Jelisić*, Trial Chamber, 14 December 1999, para. 108. The Trial Chamber found that, even though Jelisić had singled out Bosnian Muslims as his victims, he killed arbitrarily and he did not possess the intent to destroy the Bosnian Muslim group.

137 GA Res. 96 (I), 11 December 1946.

2. Inferring Genocidal Intent

Absent direct evidence, the intent to destroy 'may be inferred from a number of facts and circumstances, such as the general context, the perpetration of other culpable acts systematically directed against the same group, the scale of atrocities committed, the systematic targeting of victims on account of their membership of a particular group, or the repetition of destructive and discriminatory acts'.[138] The Appeals Chamber has held that all of the evidence, taken together, should be considered in determining whether genocidal intent might be inferred rather than considering separately whether an accused 'intended to destroy the group through each of the genocidal acts specified by Article 4(1)(a), (b), and (c)'.[139]

The *Blagojević* Appeals Chamber held that 'the forcible transfer operation, the separations, and the mistreatment and murders in Bratunac town are relevant considerations in assessing whether the principal perpetrators had genocidal intent' as it was evidence of 'other culpable acts systematically directed against the same group'.[140] The *Krstić* Appeals Chamber ruled that the scale of the killing in the area of Srebrenica, 'combined with the VRS Main Staff's awareness of the detrimental consequences it would have for the Bosnian Muslim community of Srebrenica and with the other actions the Main Staff took to ensure that community's physical demise', together confirmed the inference that some members of the VRS Main Staff had genocidal intent.[141] While a plan or policy is not a requisite element of the offence, the existence of such a plan or policy may be an important factor in inferring genocidal intent.[142] So too can proof of the requisite mental state in committing the underlying acts be used to support the inference of genocidal intent.[143]

The ICTY Appeals Chamber has further held that 'the existence of a personal motive does not preclude the perpetrator from also having the specific intent to commit genocide'[144] and that the reason why an accused sought to destroy the victim group 'has no bearing on guilt'.[145]

The *Stakić* Appeals Chamber held in relation to an accused's derogatory statements and propaganda that while it demonstrated 'ethnic bias, however reprehensible, [it] does not necessarily prove genocidal intent'. Nonetheless, such statements could be used as evidence for inferring genocidal intent even if they 'fall short of express calls for a group's physical destruction; a perpetrator's statements must be understood in their proper context'.[146] It concluded that '[i]n the

138 Judgment, *Jelisić*, Appeal Chamber, 5 July 2001, para. 47. See also Judgment, *Krstic*, Appeals Chamber, 19 April 2004, paras 33–35.

139 Ibid., para. 55. 'Nonetheless, it does not appear that the Trial Chamber's piecemeal approach had any effect on its conclusion. The reasons it gave with respect to Article 4 (1)(b) and (c) simply cross-referenced its analysis of mental state with respect to Article 4 (1)(a), in which it concluded that there simply was no evidence in the record (including, for example, the Appellant's statements) that proved that the Appellant sought to destroy the Muslim population. In reaching this conclusion, it must be assumed, the Trial Chamber was obviously aware of its own factual findings, but found them insufficient to establish intent beyond a reasonable doubt.'

140 Judgment, *Blagojević and Jokić*, Appeals Chamber, 9 May 2007, para. 123.

141 Judgment, *Krstić*, Appeals Chamber, 19 April 2004, para. 35.

142 Judgment, *Jelisić*, Appeal Chamber, 5 July 2001, paras 48, 66–68.

143 Judgment, *Krstić*, Appeals Chamber, 19 April 2004, para. 20.

144 Judgment, *Jelisić*, Appeals Chamber, 5 July 2001, para. 49. On motives generally see Judgment, *Tadić*, Appeal Chamber, 15 July 1999, paras 268–269.

145 Judgment, *Stakić*, Appeal Chamber, 22 March 2006, para. 45.

146 Ibid., para. 52.

context of events such as those occurring at Prijedor, ethnic slurs and calls for ethnic cleansing might reasonably be understood as an implied call for the group's destruction'.[147]

In the *Stakić* case the Trial Chamber considered whether anyone else on a horizontal level (to *Stakić*) had the *dolus specialis* for genocide by killing members of the Muslim group.[148] On appeal, the Prosecution argued that these statements improperly focus on the mental state of other perpetrators.[149] The Appeals Chamber stated that in this context it was clear that 'the Trial Chamber did not suggest that genocidal intent on the part of others was a prerequisite to convicting an appellant for genocide'[150] and found no error, in that the Trial Chamber considered whether the apparent intentions of others 'could provide indirect evidence of the Appellant's own intentions when he agreed with those others to undertake criminal plans'.[151]

The *Krstić* and *Blagojević* cases provide further illustration of how the ICTY infers genocidal intent. Krstić, the commander of the Drina Corps of the VRS in 1995, was charged with genocide for the killings of an estimated 7,000 Bosnian Muslim men in Srebrenica in July 1995. The Trial Chamber inferred that Krstić committed genocide, and that both he personally and the VRS Main Staff possessed the specific genocidal intent to destroy in whole or in part a national, ethnical, racial or religious group, as such.[152] The decision was appealed.

On appeal, the Chamber held that genocidal intent may be inferred, even where the individuals to whom the intent is attributable are not precisely identified or tried.[153] It was found that 'Krstić was aware of the intent to commit genocide on the part of some members of the VRS Main Staff, and with that knowledge he did nothing to prevent the use of the Drina Corps personnel and resources to facilitate those killings'.[154] The Appeals Chamber found that the genocidal intent could be attributed to members of the Bosnian Serb Army (VRS) Main Staff, but not Krstić himself.[155] In ICTY case law, responsibility for aiding and abetting of a crime with a specific intent requires knowledge of that specific intent – here being knowledge of the genocidal intent.[156] Having overturned the Trial Chamber's finding that Krstić personally possessed genocidal intent, the Appeals Chamber held that 'Krstić had knowledge of the genocidal intent of some of the Members of the VRS Main Staff'[157] and was 'aware that the Main Staff had insufficient resources of its own to carry out the executions' and that 'without the use of Drina Corps resources, the Main Staff

---

147 Ibid.

148 Judgment, *Stakić*, Trial Chamber, 31 July 2003, para. 555. More specifically the Trial Chamber held that 'Simo Drljača, Prijedor Police Chief, played an important role in establishing and running the camps, and was portrayed by the evidence as being a difficult or even brutal person, but the Trial Chamber is not satisfied that Drljača pulled the Crisis Staff into a genocidal campaign'.

149 Judgment, *Stakić*, Appeal Chamber, 22 March 2006, para. 39, referring to Prosecution Appeal Brief, paras 3.119–3.121.

150 Ibid., para. 40.

151 Ibid.

152 Judgment, *Krstić*, Trial Chamber, 2 August 2001.

153 Judgment, *Krstić*, Appeals Chamber, 19 April 2004, para. 143, referring to Judgment, *Vasiljević*, Appeal Chamber, 25 February 2004, para. 142.

154 Judgment, *Krstić*, Appeals Chamber, 19 April 2004, para. 134.

155 Ibid., para. 143.

156 Judgment, *Krstić*, Appeals Chamber, 19 April 2004, para. 143. Judgment, *Vasiljević*, Appeal Chamber, 25 February 2004, paras 142–143; Judgment; *Blagojević and Jokić*, Appeals Chamber, 9 May 2007, para. 127; Judgment, *Simić*, Appeal Chamber, 28 November 2006, para. 86; Judgment, *Krnojelac*, Appeals Chamber, 17 September 2003, para. 52.

157 Judgment, *Krstić*, Appeals Chamber, 19 April 2004, para. 137.

would not have been able to implement its genocidal plan'.[158] It concluded that by allowing the use of Drina Corps resources, Krstić made 'a substantial contribution to the execution of the Bosnian Muslim prisoners'[159] and found Krstić liable as an aider and abettor of genocide.[160]

In the most recent case on genocide, Vidoje Blagojević, Commander of the Bratunac Brigade of the VRS, was convicted by the Trial Chamber of aiding and abetting complicity to commit genocide.[161] It was found that the elements of genocide were established by virtue of individuals in the VRS Main Staff possessing the requisite genocidal intent.[162] The Trial Chamber inferred that Blagojević had knowledge of the genocidal intent of those individuals of the VRS Main Staff based on his knowledge of some so-called opportunistic killings (that is, killings which are not organized killings), and of the forcible transfer of women, children and elderly out of Srebrenica.[163] Blagojević appealed.

On 9 May 2007, the Appeals Chamber overturned his conviction in part, acquitting him of aiding and abetting complicity to commit genocide.[164] The Appeals Chamber found that the Trial Chamber's inference of Blagojević's knowledge of the genocidal intent was in error. Forcible transfer alone or coupled with opportunistic killings and mistreatment was an insufficient base from which to infer knowledge of genocidal intent.[165] Further, knowledge of '"opportunistic killings" by their very nature provide a very limited basis for inferring genocidal intent'.[166] The Appeals Chamber did not, however, overturn the Trial Chamber's finding that genocide had occurred in Srebrenica.[167]

3. Conclusion

Apart from the *Krstić* Trial Chamber – which was overturned by the Appeals Chamber – the ICTY has not found that any accused has personally possessed the requisite genocidal intent. The findings of genocide in *Krstić* and *Blagojević* were premised not on the intent of persons tried before those Chambers, but rather on findings of the intent of other individuals in the VRS Main Staff. The International Court of Justice (ICJ) in its case on genocide in Bosnia and Herzegovina found that genocide had occurred in Srebrenica in 1995. It relied on the findings in *Krstić* and *Blagojević*, holding that it had no reason to depart from the ICTY's determination that the necessary genocidal intent had been established.

158 Ibid.

159 Ibid.

160 Ibid.

161 Judgment, *Blagojević and Jokić*, Trial Chamber, 17 January 2005.

162 Ibid., paras 671–677.

163 Ibid., paras 783–787.

164 That finding was mainly based on the fact that the Trial Chamber had not found that Blagojević had knowledge of the mass killings. The Appeals Chamber found that Blagojević's knowledge of the opportunistic killings provides very little basis for inferring genocidal intent and that without his knowledge of the mass killings, Blagojević's knowledge of other factors such as the forcible transfer does not show that he had knowledge of the genocidal intent. Judgment, *Blagojević and Jokić*, Appeals Chamber, 9 May 2007.

165 Judgment, *Blagojević and Jokić*, Appeal Chamber, 9 May 2007, para. 123.

166 Ibid.

167 Ibid.

Chapter 13
Crimes Against Humanity in the Former Yugoslavia

B. Don Taylor III

1. Introduction

The beginning point for any discussion of crimes against humanity in the former Yugoslavia is Article 5 of the Statute of the International Criminal Tribunal for the former Yugoslavia (ICTY). Article 5 provides:

> The International Tribunal shall have the power to prosecute persons responsible for the following crimes when committed in armed conflict, whether international or internal in character, and directed against any civilian population:
>
> (a) murder;
> (b) extermination;
> (c) enslavement;
> (d) deportation;
> (e) imprisonment;
> (f) torture;
> (g) rape;
> (h) persecutions on political, racial and religious grounds;
> (i) other inhumane acts.

The definition of crimes against humanity found in Article 5 is unique to the ICTY, and various differences are to be found when comparing Article 5 to the statutes of other international criminal courts and tribunals. Thus, for example, Article 3 of the Statute of the International Criminal Tribunal for Rwanda (ICTR) includes a discriminatory element in the chapeau not found in the ICTY Statute,[1] while Article 2 of the Statute of the Special Court for Sierra Leone (SCSL) includes

---

1 Art. 3 of the ICTR Statute provides (emphasis added):

'The International Tribunal for Rwanda shall have the power to prosecute persons responsible for the following crimes when committed as part of a widespread or systematic attack against any civilian population *on national, political, ethnic, racial or religious grounds*:

(a) Murder;
(b) Extermination;
(c) Enslavement;
(d) Deportation;
(e) Imprisonment;
(f) Torture;
(g) Rape;

additional forms of sexual violence beyond rape.[2] Finally, Article 7 of the Rome Statute of the International Criminal Court (ICC) differs in several significant respects.[3]

(h) Persecutions on political, racial and religious grounds;
(i) Other inhumane acts.

2 Art. 2 of the SCSL Statute provides (emphasis added):

'The Special Court shall have the power to prosecute persons who committed the following crimes as part of a widespread or systematic attack against any civilian population:

(a) Murder;
(b) Extermination;
(c) Enslavement;
(d) Deportation;
(e) Imprisonment;
(f) Torture;
(g) Rape, sexual slavery, enforced prostitution, forced pregnancy and any other form of sexual violence;
(h) Persecution on political, racial, ethnic or religious grounds;
(i) Other inhumane acts.

3 Art. 7 of the ICC Statute provides (emphasis added):

'1. For the purpose of this Statute, "crime against humanity" means any of the following acts when committed as part of a *widespread or systematic attack directed against any civilian population*, with knowledge of the attack:

(a) Murder;
(b) Extermination;
(c) Enslavement;
(d) Deportation or forcible transfer of population;
(e) Imprisonment or other severe deprivation of physical liberty in violation of fundamental rules of international law;
(f) Torture;
(g) Rape, sexual slavery, enforced prostitution, forced pregnancy, enforced sterilization, or any other form of sexual violence of comparable gravity;
(h) Persecution against *any identifiable group or collectivity on political, racial, national, ethnic, cultural, religious, gender as defined in paragraph 3, or other grounds that are universally recognized as impermissible under international law, in connection with any act referred to in this paragraph or any crime within the jurisdiction of the Court*;
(i) Enforced disappearance of persons;
(j) The crime of apartheid;
(k) Other inhumane acts of a similar character intentionally causing great suffering, or serious injury to body or to mental or physical health.

2. For the purpose of paragraph 1:

(a) "Attack directed against any civilian population" means a course of conduct involving the multiple commission of acts referred to in paragraph 1 against any civilian population, *pursuant to or in furtherance of a State or organizational policy to commit such attack*;
(b) "Extermination" includes the intentional infliction of conditions of life, inter alia the deprivation of access to food and medicine, calculated to bring about the destruction of part of a population;

2. Crimes Against Humanity (Article 5 ICTYSt)

A. Jurisdictional Prerequisite: Armed Conflict

Unlike the other *ad hoc* international criminal Tribunals, and unlike the ICC, the enumerated crimes in Article 5 of the ICTY Statute are only punishable when committed in armed conflict.[4] Additionally, the Tribunal has found that customary international law does not require a link to armed conflict.[5] Accordingly, the chapeau of crimes against humanity for purposes of the ICTY Statute requires proof of a unique element, which has generally been described as a *jurisdictional* prerequisite.[6] Whether the armed conflict is international or internal in character is immaterial.

Armed conflict 'is a resort to armed force between States or protracted armed violence between governmental authorities and organised armed groups or between such groups within a State'.[7]

(c) "Enslavement" means the exercise of any or all of the powers attaching to the right of ownership over a person and includes the exercise of such power in the course of trafficking in persons, in particular women and children;

(d) "Deportation or forcible transfer of population" means forced displacement of the persons concerned by expulsion or other coercive acts from the area in which they are lawfully present, without grounds permitted under international law;

(e) "Torture" means the intentional infliction of severe pain or suffering, whether physical or mental, upon a person in the custody or under the control of the accused; except that torture shall not include pain or suffering arising only from, inherent in or incidental to, lawful sanctions;

(f) "Forced pregnancy" means the unlawful confinement of a woman forcibly made pregnant, with the intent of affecting the ethnic composition of any population or carrying out other grave violations of international law. This definition shall not in any way be interpreted as affecting national laws relating to pregnancy;

(g) *"Persecution" means the intentional and severe deprivation of fundamental rights contrary to international law by reason of the identity of the group or collectivity*;

(h) "The crime of apartheid" means inhumane acts of a character similar to those referred to in paragraph 1, committed in the context of an institutionalized regime of systematic oppression and domination by one racial group over any other racial group or groups and committed with the intention of maintaining that regime;

(i) "Enforced disappearance of persons" means the arrest, detention or abduction of persons by, or with the authorization, support or acquiescence of, a State or a political organization, followed by a refusal to acknowledge that deprivation of freedom or to give information on the fate or whereabouts of those persons, with the intention of removing them from the protection of the law for a prolonged period of time.

3. For the purpose of this Statute, it is understood that the term "gender" refers to the two sexes, male and female, within the context of society. The term "gender" does not indicate any meaning different from the above.'

4 Art. 5 ICTYSt.

5 Judgment, *Stakić*, Trial Chamber, 31 July 2003, para. 567 ('While the Appeals Chamber has held that "customary international law may not require a connection between crimes against humanity and any conflict at all", Article 5 imposes a jurisdictional requirement limiting the Tribunal's jurisdiction to crimes against humanity "when committed in armed conflict".')

6 Judgment, *Kunarac, Kovač, and Voković*, Appeals Chamber, 12 June 2002, para. 83 ('[T]he requirement contained in Article 5 of the Statute is a purely jurisdictional prerequisite which is satisfied by proof that there was an armed conflict'). See also Judgment, *Limaj, Bala and Musliu*, Trial Chamber, 30 November 2005, para. 180; Judgment, *Brđanin*, Trial Chamber, 1 September 2004, para. 133.

7 Judgment, *Kunarac, Kovač, and Voković*, Appeals Chamber, 12 June 2002, para. 56. See also Judgment, *Brđanin*, Trial Chamber, 1 September 2004, para. 122.

Although there must be a geographic and temporal link between the acts of the accused and the armed conflict, proof of a nexus between the acts of the accused and the armed conflict is not required;[8] the only nexus required is between the acts of the accused and the attack on the civilian population – one of the general elements of Article 5 dealt with below.

B. General Elements

The general elements of Article 5 have been described as follows:

> To qualify as crimes against humanity the acts of an accused must be part of a widespread or systematic attack "directed against any civilian population". It is established in the jurisprudence of the Tribunal that the general elements required for the applicability of Article 5 of the Statute are that: (i) there must be an attack; (ii) the acts of the perpetrator must be part of the attack; (iii) the attack must be directed against any civilian population; (iv) the attack must be widespread or systematic; and (v) the perpetrator must know that his or her acts constitute part of a pattern of widespread or systematic crimes directed against a civilian population and know that his or her acts fit into such a pattern (i.e. knowledge of the wider context in which his or her acts occur and knowledge that his or her acts are part of the attack).[9]

Thus, five general elements can be discerned.

1. There Must be an Attack

To qualify as crimes against humanity under Article 5, the acts of the accused must be part of a widespread or systematic attack directed against a civilian population. 'Attack' in this context has been defined as a course of conduct involving the commission of acts of violence.[10] Importantly, although the attack may be part of the 'armed conflict', this is not required.[11] The attack on the civilian population general element and the armed conflict jurisdictional prerequisite are not synonymous.[12]

The attack in the context of a crime against humanity under Article 5 is not limited to the use of force.[13] Rather, it encompasses any mistreatment of the civilian population.[14] '[T]he relevant conduct need not amount to a military assault or forceful takeover; the evidence need only demonstrate a "course of conduct" directed against the civilian population that indicates a widespread or systematic reach.'[15]

8 Judgment, *Limaj, Bala and Musliu*, Trial Chamber, 30 November 2005, para. 180; Judgment, *Kordić and Cerkez*, Trial Chamber, 26 February 2001, para. 33.

9 Judgment, *Limaj, Bala and Musliu*, Trial Chamber, 30 November 2005, para. 181 (citing Judgment, *Kunarac, Kovać, and Voković*, Appeals Chamber, 12 June 2002, para. 85.

10 Judgment, *Blagojević and Jokić*, Trial Chamber, 17 January 2005, para. 543.

11 Judgment, *Kunarac, Kovać, and Voković*, Appeals Chamber, 12 June 2002, para. 86 ('[T]he attack could precede, outlast, or continue during the armed conflict, but it need not be a part of it').

12 Judgment, *Limaj, Bala and Musliu*, Trial Chamber, 30 November 2005, para. 182.

13 Judgment, *Galić*, Trial Chamber, 5 December 2003, para. 141 ('In the context of a crime against humanity, "attack" is not limited to armed combat. It may also encompass situations of mistreatment of persons taking no active part in hostilities, such as of a person in detention').

14 Judgment, *Kunarac, Kovać, and Voković*, Appeals Chamber, 12 June 2002, para. 86.

15 Judgment, *Limaj, Bala and Musliu*, Trial Chamber, 30 November 2005, para. 194.

Additionally, it is irrelevant which party to the conflict started the hostilities or whether the other side has also committed atrocities against its opponent's civilian population. 'Each attack against the other side's civilian population would be equally illegitimate and crimes committed as part of such an attack could, all other conditions being met, amount to crimes against humanity.'[16]

2. The Acts of the Accused Must be Part of the Attack

The acts of the accused must form part of the attack on the civilian population. As previously noted, this entails proof of a nexus between the accused's acts at issue in the indictment and the attack – as opposed to a nexus with the armed conflict jurisdictional requirement. This means that the acts must be *related* to the attack; 'it must be established that the acts of the accused are not isolated, but rather, by their nature and consequence, are objectively part of the attack'.[17] This excludes single, random or limited acts from the reach of Article 5.[18]

As to timing, the acts of the accused need not be committed in the midst of, or at the height of, the attack. Indeed, the acts of the accused might conceivably occur several months after the main attack.[19] The acts must, however, be sufficiently connected to the main attack.[20] As to proximity, it has also been noted that crimes committed several kilometres away from the main attack could still be part of the attack – if sufficiently connected otherwise.[21]

3. The Attack Must be Directed Against a Civilian Population

In order to constitute a crime against humanity, the acts of the accused must be part of a widespread or systematic attack directed against a civilian population. An attack is 'directed against' a civilian population if the civilian population is the primary object of the attack.[22] This does not mean that the entire population of a given geographic area must have been subjected to the attack. Rather, '[i]t is sufficient to show that enough individuals were targeted in the course of the attack, or that they were targeted in such a way as to satisfy the Chamber that the attack was in fact directed against a civilian population rather than against a limited and randomly selected number of individuals'.[23]

---

16 Judgment, *Brđanin*, Trial Chamber, 1 September 2004, para. 131. See also Judgment, *Galić*, Trial Chamber, 5 December 2003, para. 145 ('Evidence of attack by opposing forces on the civilian population to which the accused belongs may not be introduced unless it tends to prove or disprove an allegation made in an indictment, such as the Prosecution's contention that there was a widespread or systematic attack against a civilian population. A submission that the opposing side is responsible for starting the hostilities is not relevant to disproving the allegation that there was an attack on the civilian population in question').

17 Judgment, *Limaj, Bala and Musliu*, Trial Chamber, 30 November 2005, para. 189; Judgment, *Simić, Tadić and Zarić*, Trial Chamber, 17 October 2003, para. 41, quoting Judgment, *Kunarac*, Appeals Chamber, para. 100 ('Isolated acts are defined as those acts "so far removed from that attack that, having considered the context and circumstances in which it was committed, it cannot reasonably be said to have been part of the attack"').

18 Judgment, *Limaj, Bala and Musliu*, Trial Chamber, 30 November 2005, para. 194.

19 Judgment, *Brđanin*, Trial Chamber, 1 September 2004, para. 132.

20 Judgment, *Limaj, Bala and Musliu*, Trial Chamber, 30 November 2005, para. 189.

21 Judgment, *Brđanin*, Trial Chamber, 1 September 2004, para. 132.

22 Judgment, *Kunarac, Kovać, and Voković*, Appeals Chamber, 12 June 2002, para. 91; Judgment, *Limaj, Bala and Musliu*, Trial Chamber, 30 November 2005, para. 185.

23 Judgment, *Kunarac, Kovać, and Voković*, Appeals Chamber, 12 June 2002, para. 90; Judgment, *Blaskić*, Appeals Chamber, 29 July 2004, para. 105; Judgment, *Naletelić and Martinović*, Trial Chamber, 31 March 2003, para. 235.

Although not a strictly necessary condition, it has been noted that attacks directed primarily at the civilian population will most often occur at the behest of a state.[24] Any analysis necessarily involves balancing the evidence, and Chambers of the Tribunal have looked at various criteria in reaching a conclusion as to whether an attack is truly 'directed against' a civilian population. Factors which have explicitly been considered include:

(i) the means and methods used in the attack;
(ii) the status of the victims;
(iii) the number of victims;
(iv) the discriminatory nature of the attack;
(v) the nature of the crimes committed in the course of the attack;
(vi) the resistance to the assailants at the time of the attack; and
(vii) the extent to which the attacking force attempted to comply with the precautionary requirements of the laws of war.[25]

This last factor seems especially salient, and the Appeals Chamber has noted that the laws of war provide a benchmark against which to assess the nature of the attack.[26]

To say that an attack must be directed against a civilian population is a fine beginning point. However, determining whether any given population is civilian in character requires further definition and a sifting of the facts on the ground. The term 'civilian' refers to persons not taking part in hostilities, including members of armed forces who have laid down their arms and those placed *hors de combat* by sickness, wounds, detention or any other cause. Such persons are protected from attack as a principle of customary international law.[27] Indeed, this prohibition against targeting civilians is absolute.[28]

It is to be expected that in the conflict areas in which crimes against humanity are likely to be perpetrated, complete and easy dividing lines between combatants and civilians are unlikely to

24 Judgment, *Limaj, Bala and Musliu*, Trial Chamber, 30 November 2005, para. 191 ('Being the locus of organized authority within a given territory, able to mobilise and direct military and civilian power, a sovereign State by its very nature possesses the attributes that permit it to organise and deliver an attack against a civilian population; it is States which can most easily and efficiently marshal the resources to launch an attack against a civilian population on a widespread scale, or upon a systematic basis'). Note, however, that it has also been held that targeting a number of political opponents does not satisfy the requirements of Art. 5. Ibid., para. 187.

25 Judgment, *Kunarac, Kovać, and Voković*, Appeals Chamber, 12 June 2002, para. 90; Judgment, *Kordić and Cerkez*, Appeals Chamber, 17 December 2004, para. 96; Judgment, *Galić*, Trial Chamber, 5 December 2003, para. 142.

26 Judgment, *Blaskić*, Appeals Chamber, 29 July 2004, para. 106. See also Judgment, *Galić*, Trial Chamber, 5 December 2003, para. 144 ('[W]hen considering the general requirements of Article 5, the body of laws of way plays an important part in the assessment of the legality of the acts committed in the course of an armed conflict and whether the population may be said to have been targeted as such').

27 See e.g., Judgment, *Blagojević and Jokić*, Trial Chamber, 17 January 2005, para. 544. Those expressly excluded from civilian status include members of the armed forces, members of militias or volunteer corps forming part of such armed forces, and members of organized resistance groups, provided they are commanded by a person responsible for his subordinates, that they have a fixed distinctive sign recognizable at a distance, that they carry arms openly, and that they conduct their operations in accordance with the laws and customs of war. See Judgment, *Blaskić*, Appeals Chamber, 29 July 2004, para. 113 (reading together Art. 50 of Additional Protocol I and Art. 4A of the Third Geneva Convention).

28 Judgment, *Limaj, Bala and Musliu*, Trial Chamber, 30 November 2005, para. 186.

exist. How is the nature of the population to be characterized, for example, when combatants are to be found within the non-combatant population?

The Chambers of the Tribunal have answered this question in a highly practical manner. A population may qualify as civilian in character even if non-civilians are among it, as long as the population is 'predominantly' civilian.[29] Here, the Chambers have noted two additional principles. First, noting the requirement of Article 50, paragraph 1 of Additional Protocol I – which has been construed as reflecting customary international law[30] – that in cases of doubt as to status, persons are to be considered civilians, the Chambers have held that the burden of proof as to whether a person is a civilian rests squarely with the Prosecution.[31] At the same time, however, Chambers have noted that the term 'civilian population' must be interpreted broadly if it is to comport with the object and purpose of the general rules and principles of international humanitarian law.[32]

Determining whether the presence of combatants deprives a population of its predominantly civilian character requires examining the number of combatants within the population, as well as whether they are on leave.[33] So long as the presence of combatants does not amount to 'fairly large numbers', this will not alter the predominantly civilian character of the population.[34]

Finally, there is no requirement that the targeted civilian population be linked to any particular side of the conflict.[35] Thus, Article 5 protects any civilian population including, if a state takes part in the attack, that state's own population.[36]

4. The Attack Must be Widespread or Systematic

In order to come within the scope of Article 5, the acts of an accused must be part of a widespread or systematic attack. This requirement is disjunctive rather than cumulative.[37] Proof of either will

29 Judgment, *Limaj, Bala and Musliu*, Trial Chamber, 30 November 2005, para. 186; Judgment, *Simić, Tadić and Zarić*, Trial Chamber, 17 October 2003, para. 41 ('Both the primary object of the attack and its victims must be "any civilian population", a phrase that pertains to any predominantly civilian population, notwithstanding the presence of non-civilians'); Judgment, *Brđanin*, Trial Chamber, 1 September 2004, para. 134 ('It is not required that every single member of that population be a civilian – it is enough it if is predominantly civilian in nature, and may include, e.g. individuals *hors de combat*').

30 Judgment, *Kordić and Cerkez*, Appeals Chamber, 17 December 2004, para. 97.

31 Judgment, *Blaskić*, Appeals Chamber, 29 July 2004, para. 111 (referring to Art. 50, para. 1 of Additional Protocol I and noting that 'the imperative "in case of doubt" is limited to the expected conduct of a member of the military. However, when the latter's criminal responsibility is at issue, the burden of proof as to whether a person is a civilian rests on the Prosecution').

32 Judgment, *Kupreskić et al.*, Trial Chamber 14 January 2000, para. 547 ('It would seem that a wide definition of civilian and population is intended. This is warranted first of all by the object and purpose of the general principles and rules of humanitarian law, in particular by the rules prohibiting crimes against humanity. The latter are intended to safeguard basic human values by banning atrocities directed against human dignity').

33 Judgment, *Blaskić*, Appeals Chamber, 29 July 2004, para. 115 (quoting the International Committee of the Red Cross Commentary that 'in wartime conditions it is inevitable that individuals belonging to the category of combatants become intermingled with the civilian population, for example, soldiers on leave visiting their families ... provided that these are not regular units with fairly large numbers, this does not in any way change the civilian character of the population').

34 Judgment, *Brđanin*, Trial Chamber, 1 September 2004, para. 134.

35 Judgment, *Limaj, Bala and Musliu*, Trial Chamber, 30 November 2005, para. 186.

36 Judgment, *Vasiljević*, Trial Chamber, 29 November 2002, para. 33.

37 Judgment, *Kunarac, Kovać, and Voković*, Appeals Chamber, 12 June 2002, para. 97.

suffice. Note, however, that this requirement applies only to the attack, not to the individual acts of the accused.[38]

(a) Widespread

The term 'widespread' refers to the large-scale nature of the attack and the number of victims.[39] Additionally, it has been held that a crime may be considered widespread by the 'cumulative effect of a series of inhumane acts or the singular effect of an inhumane act of extraordinary magnitude'.[40]

(b) Systematic

The term systematic refers to the organized nature of the acts of violence and the improbability of their random occurrence.[41] This is often expressed through patterns of crimes, 'in the sense of the non-accidental repetition of similar criminal conduct on a regular basis'.[42]

(c) Factors to be considered

Chambers have identified factors that can be taken into consideration in determining whether an attack qualifies as widespread or systematic. These include:

(i) the consequences of the attack upon the targeted population;[43]
(ii) the number of victims;[44]
(iii) the nature of the acts;[45]
(iv) the possible participation of officials or authorities;[46]
(v) the existence of identifiable patterns of crimes;[47]
(vi) the existence of an acknowledged policy targeting a particular community;[48]
(vii) the establishment of parallel institutions meant to implement this policy;[49]
(viii) the employment of considerable financial, military or other resources;[50]
(ix) the repeated, unchanging and continuous nature of the violence.[51]

38 Judgment, *Kordić and Cerkez*, Appeals Chamber, 17 December 2004, para. 94.
39 Judgment, *Limaj, Bala and Musliu*, Trial Chamber, 30 November 2005, para. 183.
40 Judgment, *Blagojević and Jokić*, Trial Chamber, 17 January 2005, para. 545.
41 Judgment, *Kordić and Cerkez*, Appeals Chamber, 17 December 2004, para. 94.
42 Judgment, *Blagojević and Jokić*, Trial Chamber, 17 January 2005, para. 545.
43 Ibid.
44 Ibid.
45 Ibid.
46 Ibid.
47 Ibid.
48 Judgment, *Jelisić*, Trial Chamber, 14 December 1999, para. 53.
49 Ibid.
50 Ibid.
51 Ibid.

This list is, of course, non-exhaustive. As previously noted, these factors describe the attack, not the act or acts of the individual accused. Thus, even a single act of an accused, if linked to a widespread or systematic attack, potentially comes within the ambit of Article 5.[52]

Finally, the existence of a plan or policy to carry out the attack is not a legal element of a crime against humanity under Article 5.[53] Neither does customary international law require proof of such an element.[54] Of course, proof of the existence of such a plan or policy may be evidentially relevant in proving that the attack was directed against a civilian population and that it was widespread or systematic.[55]

5. The accused must have knowledge

The *mens rea*, or mental element, of crimes against humanity under Article 5 is satisfied when the accused possesses:

> (i) the intent to commit the underlying offence or offences with which he is charged;
> (ii) the knowledge that there is an attack against the civilian population; and
> (iii) the knowledge that his acts comprise part of the attack.[56]

As noted, it is crucial that the accused be shown to have knowledge of the attack against the civilian population and that his acts comprise part of the attack. As one Trial Chamber has noted: 'Part of what transforms an individual's acts into a crime against humanity is the inclusion of the act within a greater dimension of criminal conduct; therefore an accused should be aware of this greater dimension in order to be culpable thereof. Accordingly, actual or constructive knowledge of the broader context of the attack … is necessary to satisfy the *mens rea* element of the accused.'[57]

Although the accused must know of the wider context in which his acts occur, and that his acts comprise part of the overall attack on a civilian population, there is no requirement that the accused be aware of the details of the overall attack.[58] The accused does not have to 'approve of

52 Judgment, *Simić, Tadić and Zarić*, Trial Chamber, 17 October 2003, para. 43 ('Provided that the acts of the individual are sufficiently linked to the widespread or systematic attack, and are not found to be random or isolated, it is possible that a single act could be found to be a crime against humanity'); Judgment, *Kupreskić et al.*, Trial Chamber 14 January 2000, para. 550 ('[I]n certain circumstances, a single act has comprised a crime against humanity when it occurred within the necessary context. An isolated act, however – i.e. an atrocity which did not occur within such a context – cannot').

53 Judgment, *Blaskić*, Appeals Chamber, 29 July 2004, para. 120.

54 Judgment, *Brđanin*, Trial Chamber, 1 September 2004, para. 137.

55 Judgment, *Limaj, Bala and Musliu*, Trial Chamber, 30 November 2005, para. 212 ('The existence of a plan or policy can be indicative of the systematic character of offences charged as crimes against humanity. The existence of a "policy" to conduct an attack against a civilian population is most easily determined or inferred when a State's conduct is in question; but absence of a policy does not mean that widespread or systematic attack against a civilian population has not occurred. Although not a legal element of Article 5, evidence of a policy or plan is an important indication that the acts in question are not merely the workings of individuals acting pursuant to haphazard or individual design, but instead have a level of organizational coherence and support of a magnitude sufficient to elevate them into the realm of crimes against humanity').

56 Judgment, *Brđanin*, Trial Chamber, 1 September 2004, para. 138.

57 Judgment, *Kordić and Cerkez*, Trial Chamber, 26 February 2001, para. 185.

58 Judgment, *Kunarac, Kovać, and Voković*, Appeals Chamber, 12 June 2002, para. 102; Judgment, *Limaj, Bala and Musliu*, Trial Chamber, 30 November 2005, para. 190.

the context in which his or acts occur'.[59] Nor is it required that the accused share the purpose or the goal behind the attack.[60] Indeed, the motives of the accused are generally irrelevant, and a crime against humanity under Article 5 may be committed for purely personal reasons.[61] Finally, it does not matter whether the accused intended his acts to be directed against the targeted population or merely against his victim.[62]

3. Conclusion

As previously noted, the following acts fall within the purview of Article 5 ICTYSt when the above discussed elements have all been satisfied:

(a) murder;
(b) extermination;
(c) enslavement;
(d) deportation;
(e) imprisonment;
(f) torture;
(g) rape;
(h) persecutions on political, racial and religious grounds;
(i) other inhumane acts.

It is the inclusion of these acts 'within a greater dimension of criminal conduct'[63] that transforms them into crimes against humanity.

---

59 Judgment, *Limaj, Bala and Musliu*, Trial Chamber, 30 November 2005, para. 190.

60 Judgment, *Kordić and Cerkez*, Appeals Chamber, 17 December 2004, para. 99.

61 Judgment, *Limaj, Bala and Musliu*, Trial Chamber, 30 November 2005, para. 190; Judgment, *Kordić and Cerkez*, Appeals Chamber, 17 December 2004, para. 99 ('[T]he motives of the accused for taking part in the attack are irrelevant and a crime against humanity may be committed for purely personal reasons'). See also Judgment, *Krnojelac*, Appeals Chamber, 17 September 2003, para. 102, quoting Judgment, *Jelisić*, Appeals Chamber, 5 July 1991, para. 49 ('"The personal motive of the perpetrator of the crime of genocide may be, for example, to obtain personal economic benefits, or political advantage or some form of power. The existence of a personal motive does not preclude the perpetrator from also having the specific intent to commit genocide." It is the Appeals Chamber's belief that this distinction between intent and motive must also be applied to the other crimes laid down in the Statute').

62 Judgment, *Kordić and Cerkez*, Appeals Chamber, 17 December 2004, para. 99.

63 Judgment, *Kordić and Cerkez*, Trial Chamber, 26 February 2001, para. 185.

Chapter 14
War Crimes at the ICTY: Jurisdictional and Substantive Issues

Guido Acquaviva

1. Introductory Remarks

This chapter discusses some aspects of the law of war crimes under customary international law as developed and applied by the International Criminal Tribunal for the former Yugoslavia (ICTY). It begins with general remarks on the legal requirements of war crimes and then analyses two specific areas of the laws of war that bear specific interest in the contemporary world: the protection of cultural property during armed conflicts (*Jokić* and *Strugar* cases), as well as the attack against civilians and the terrorization of the civilian population (as exemplified in the *Galić* case).

2. War Crimes in Historical Perspective

Despite having evolved throughout many centuries, until only a few years ago war crimes remained a vague concept for most people, even for scholars. It is true that, at Nüremberg, certain individuals were charged and tried for war crimes; only a few years later, however, when drafting the texts of what would become the four Geneva Conventions of 1949, states were reluctant to use this expression and resorted to a list of 'grave breaches', which only refers to some war crimes. It was only in 1977, at the time of the drafting of Protocol Additional to the 1949 Geneva Conventions and relating to the protection of victims of international armed conflicts (Additional Protocol I), that states agreed to insert an explicit clause according to which 'grave breaches of these instruments shall be regarded as war crimes'.[1]

Moreover, in the last decades of the twentieth century, scholars and commentators have more and more resorted to this expression, which traces its origins back to the Middle Ages and before, to discuss the importance of the concept of serious violations of the laws or customs of war in the conduct of hostilities.[2]

1 Protocol Additional to the 1949 Geneva Conventions and Relating to the Protection of Victims of International Armed Conflicts (1979), 1125 UNTS 3, Art. 85(5).

2 In general, see L. Green, 'International Regulation of Armed Conflicts', in C. Bassiouni (ed.), *International Criminal Law*, Vol. 1 (Ardsley: Transnational Publishers, 1999), 355–363. See also T. Meron, *Henry's Wars and Shakespeare's Law, Perspectives on the Law of War in the Later Middle Ages* (Oxford: Clarendon Press, 1993). Other examples of 'early' war crimes trials have been suggested: G. Maridakis, 'An Ancient Precedent to Nuremberg', in 4 *Journal of International Criminal Justice* (2006), 847 (for an example of 'international' trial in Ancient Greece); G. Schwarzenberger, *International Law*, Vol. 2 (London: Stevens, 1968), 462–466 (for an account of the trial of Peter van Hagenbach in 1474 by an 'international' tribunal).

Therefore, unlike crimes against humanity, which are essentially a creation of a very specific historical and political situation,[3] war crimes are a product of a long and complex evolution. Suffice it to say for the purposes of this chapter that, having definitively abandoned the idea that each and every violation of the laws or customs of war amounts to a war crime,[4] it is now generally recognized that only some – egregious – violations of the law of armed conflict amount to war crimes proper. Among war crimes, 'grave breaches' are those that attract universal jurisdiction and impose on every state an obligation to investigate and, if need be, prosecute.

3. War Crimes before the ICTY

In the early 1990s, after having considered as a threat to peace and security the conflicts in the territory of the former Yugoslavia and that of Rwanda, the United Nations set up two *ad hoc* Tribunals, the ICTY and the International Criminal Tribunal for Rwanda (ICTR), in order to prosecute and try individuals suspected of having committed breaches of international humanitarian law. Both the ICTY and the ICTR were established by the Security Council, which enacted their Statutes through Resolutions pursuant to its authority under Chapter VII of the UN Charter. It is relevant to note that, despite being separate entities, their respective Appeals Chambers are composed of the same judges; this is a structure intended to coordinate the law applied within those two – otherwise distinct – jurisdictions. This chapter will only focus on the relevant provisions and their interpretation by the ICTY, which is the institution that has contributed more to the development of the concept of war crimes.[5]

Two substantive articles of the ICTYSt[6] deal with war crimes, that is Articles 2 and 3.

Article 2 reads:

Grave breaches of the Geneva Conventions of 1949

> The International Tribunal shall have the power to prosecute persons committing or ordering to be committed grave breaches of the Geneva Conventions of 12 August 1949, namely the following acts against persons or property protected under the provisions of the relevant Geneva Convention:
>
> (a) wilful killing;
> (b) torture or inhuman treatment, including biological experiments;
> (c) wilfully causing great suffering or serious injury to body or health;
> (d) extensive destruction and appropriation of property, not justified by military necessity and carried out unlawfully and wantonly;
> (e) compelling a prisoner of war or a civilian to serve in the forces of a hostile power;
> (f) wilfully depriving a prisoner of war or a civilian of the rights of fair and regular trial;

---

3 See G. Acquaviva and F. Pocar, *Crimes against Humanity*, in R. Wolfrum (ed.), *Max Planck Encyclopedia of Public International Law* (Oxford: Oxford University Press, 2008–2010).

4 *See*, for example, *Field Manual: The Law of Land Warfare* (US Department of Army, 1956), 178.

5 A. Zahar and G. Sluiter, *International Criminal Law* (Oxford: Oxford University Press, 2007), 110–113, 154.

6 Statute of the International Tribunal for the Former Yugoslavia established by Security Council Resolution 827, as amended by SC Res. 1166 (1998), SC Res. 1329 (2000), SC Res. 1411 (2002), SC Res. 1431 (2002), SC Res. 1481 (2003), SC Res. 1597 (2005), SC Res. 1660 (2006).

(g) unlawful deportation or transfer or unlawful confinement of a civilian;
(h) taking civilians as hostages.

Article 3 reads:

Violations of the laws or customs of war

The International Tribunal shall have the power to prosecute persons violating the laws or customs of war. Such violations shall include, but not be limited to:

(a) employment of poisonous weapons or other weapons calculated to cause unnecessary suffering;
(b) wanton destruction of cities, towns or villages, or devastation not justified by military necessity;
(c) attack, or bombardment, by whatever means, of undefended towns, villages, dwellings, or buildings;
(d) seizure of, destruction or wilful damage done to institutions dedicated to religion, charity and education, the arts and sciences, historic monuments and works of art and science; (e) plunder of public or private property.

As should be evident from the headings of the two Articles in question, the distinction between these two articles echoes the different sources from which their respective provisions stem. In brief, Article 2 is a codification of the grave breaches regime mentioned above, derived from the criminalization, in the aftermath of the World War II, of certain extremely serious conducts through the Geneva Conventions of 1949 (Geneva law). For this reason, and as confirmed by the ICTY Appeals Chamber in its seminal decision on jurisdiction, this provision only applies to international armed conflicts.[7] Article 3, as interpreted by the ICTY Appeals Chamber, is instead aimed at covering a whole range of other violations of the laws or customs of war which trace back their source to the 1907 Hague Convention IV Respecting the Laws and Customs of War on Land and to its application in international criminal proceedings during the Nüremberg trials.[8] As will be more thoroughly discussed below, criminal prosecution for violations of the latter category of war crimes may occur not only when such violations are committed in international armed conflict, but also when they took place during a non-international armed conflict – what historically has been defined as 'civil war'.

4. Armed Conflicts

On the basis of the foregoing, it is clear that two concepts are essential to understand and apply the law of war crimes: the concept of 'armed conflict' and the related notion of 'international vs. non-international armed conflict'. Unsurprisingly, therefore, the case law of the ICTY has devoted a fair amount of attention to these issues, relying on previous elaborations by scholars and other courts, but also developing an interesting approach to deal with the multifaceted realities of the events in the former Yugoslavia.

7 Decision on the Defence Motion for Interlocutory Appeal on Jurisdiction, *Tadić*, Appeals Chamber, 2 October 1995 (hereafter, *Tadić* Jurisdiction Decision), para. 79–85.

8 Ibid., para. 85–137.

In this respect, a trier of fact should first of all analyse a specific situation, as described by the evidence on the record, in order to distinguish mere domestic disturbances or riots from an armed conflict proper. Some indications on this distinction are suggested by Protocol Additional to the Geneva Conventions of 12 August 1949 and relating to the protection of victims of non-international armed conflicts (Additional Protocol II).[9]

Article 1 of Additional Protocol II states:

> This Protocol ... shall apply to all armed conflict ... which take place in the territory of a High Contracting Party between its armed forces and dissident armed forces or other organized armed groups which, under responsible command, exercise such control over a part of its territory as to enable them to carry out sustained and concerted military operations and to implement this Protocol [and] shall not apply to situations of internal disturbances and tensions, such as riots, isolated and sporadic acts of violence and other acts of a similar nature, as not being armed conflicts.

The *Tadić* Jurisdiction Decision stated that:

> an armed conflict exists whenever there is a resort to armed force between States or protracted armed violence between governmental authorities and organized armed groups or between such groups within a State.[10]

An interesting application of this concept and of its two corollary requirements ('intensity' and 'organization') was provided by the Inter-American Commission on Human Rights in its report on the *Tablada* case.[11] The case involved an attack by 42 armed individuals on military barracks of the Argentinean armed forces in 1989; the attack developed into clashes lasting more than one day and resulting in the deaths of 29 of the attackers as well as of several soldiers. In its report the Commission examined in detail whether it was competent to apply international humanitarian law directly. The Commission remarked:

> 154. Based on a careful appreciation of the facts, the Commission does not believe that the violent acts at the La Tablada military base on January 23 and 24, 1989 can be properly characterized as a situation of internal disturbances. What happened there was not equivalent to large scale violent demonstrations, students throwing stones at the police, bandits holding persons hostage for ransom, or the assassination of government officials for political reasons – all forms of domestic violence not qualifying as armed conflicts.
>
> 155. What differentiates the events at the La Tablada base from these situations are the concerted nature of the hostile acts undertaken by the attackers, the direct involvement of governmental armed forces, and the nature and level of the violence attending the events in question. More particularly, the attackers involved carefully planned, coordinated and executed an armed attack, i.e., a military operation, against a quintessential military objective – a military base. The officer in charge of the La Tablada base sought, as was his duty, to repulse the attackers, and President

9 Additional Protocol II, of 8 June 1977 (1979), 1125 UNTS 609.

10 *Tadić* Jurisdiction Decision, para. 70.

11 *IACHR Report No. 55/97*, Case No. 11.137, Argentina, OEA/Ser/L/V/II.97, Doc. 38, October 30, 1997 (*Abella v. Argentina*), paras 147–156.

> Alfonsín, exercising his constitutional authority as Commander-in-Chief of the armed forces, ordered that military action be taken to recapture the base and subdue the attackers.
>
> 156. The Commission concludes therefore that, despite its brief duration, the violent clash between the attackers and members of the Argentine armed forces triggered application of the provisions of Common Article 3, as well as other rules relevant to the conduct of internal hostilities.

One might argue that this kind of 'armed conflict' is at the low end of the spectrum, while the type of clashes that the ICTY has had to deal with so far entail more protracted armed violence on a scale that is hardly comparable to the one analysed in the *Tablada* case. However, the ICTY has also dealt with low-intensity conflicts, such as the one in Kosovo before the campaign launched in 1999 by some NATO countries against Yugoslavia.

For example, the Trial Chamber in the *Limaj* case found that, in order to establish the existence of an armed conflict, 'there must be the opposition of armed forces and a certain intensity of the fighting' (*intensity* requirement).[12] Consequently, the Trial Chamber took into account all the facts relevant to ascertain the level of violence and the intensity of the armed clashes between the Kosovo Liberation Army (KLA) and Serbian forces during the indictment period.[13] Such relevant facts include, in the opinion of the Trial Chamber: the involvement of the UN Security Council;[14] the geographical scope; the seriousness, and the increase over time of the armed activities;[15] the number and type of government forces participating;[16] the kind of weapons used by the parties.[17] As far as the requirement that both armed forces involved in the conflict be organized (*organization* requirement), the *Limaj* Trial Chamber held that the establishment of *some* degree of organization is sufficient[18] and engaged in a very meticulous analysis of the structure of the KLA in this respect.[19]

However, as will be made clearer below, it is not enough to ascertain the existence of an armed conflict to find that a war crime was committed. Various persons accused before the ICTY have raised the issue of whether a specific conduct should be considered a war crime or, on the other hand, an ordinary crime committed in the course of an armed conflict. The *Kunarac* Appeal Judgement attempted to shed some light on this distinction. The Appeals Chamber stated:

> What ultimately distinguishes a war crime from a purely domestic offence is that a war crime is shaped by or dependent upon the environment – the armed conflict – in which it is committed. It need not have been planned or supported by some form of policy. The armed conflict need not have been causal to the commission of the crime, but the existence of an armed conflict must, at a minimum, have played a substantial part in the perpetrator's ability to commit it, his decision to commit it, the manner in which it was committed or the purpose for which it was committed. Hence, if it can be established, as in the present case, that the perpetrator acted in furtherance of or

12 Judgement, *Limaj et al.*, Trial Chamber III, 30 November 2005, para. 89. These findings were not disturbed by the Appeal Judgement (Judgement, *Limaj et al.*, Appeals Chamber, 27 September 2007). A further application of these principles can be found in Judgement, *Haradinaj et al.*, Trial Chamber, 3 April 2008.

13 Ibid., paras 135–170 and 172.

14 Ibid., para. 90.

15 Ibid., paras 90, 135–163.

16 Ibid., paras 90, 164–165.

17 Ibid., paras 159, 164–166.

18 Ibid., para. 89.

19 Ibid., paras 94–134.

> under the guise of the armed conflict, it would be sufficient to conclude that his acts were closely related to the armed conflict.[20]
>
> In determining whether or not the act in question is sufficiently related to the armed conflict, the Trial Chamber may take into account, *inter alia*, the following factors: the fact that the perpetrator is a combatant; the fact that the victim is a non-combatant; the fact that the victim is a member of the opposing party; the fact that the act may be said to serve the ultimate goal of a military campaign; and the fact that the crime is committed as part of or in the context of the perpetrator's official duties.[21]

This reasoning has been consistently applied by the Tribunal in dealing with the allegations by accused persons that at least some of the crimes charged against them were not related to the armed conflict, but were, rather, mere ordinary (sometimes defined 'domestic') crimes. For instance, in a recent appeal judgment,[22] the appellant Radoslav Brđanin had suggested that, in order to prove torture as a grave breach of the Geneva Conventions, it was not sufficient simply to demonstrate that a war was going on at the time the crime was occurring.[23] The Appeals Chamber remarked:

> When concluding that the members of the Bosnian Serb police and the VRS [i.e., the Bosnian-Serb Army] committed rapes [which amounted to torture, in this case] in Teslić municipality, the Trial Chamber cited witnesses who described rapes associated with weapons searches. The Appeals Chamber considers that the Trial Chamber clearly established the existence of an international armed conflict and furthermore reasonably concluded that the rapes in Teslić, committed as they were during weapons searches, were committed in the context of the armed conflict, and were not "individual domestic crimes" as suggested by Brđanin. *Crimes committed by combatants and by members of forces accompanying them while searching for weapons during an armed conflict, and taking advantage of their position, clearly fall into the category of crimes committed "in the context of the armed conflict"*.[24]

The case law, as well as the interpretation of treaty and customary law related to this issue, broadly supports this type of findings – although it is admittedly sometimes difficult to establish whether a crime is sufficiently related to an armed conflict in certain borderline situations. I would like to mention in this respect at least one example that suggests a radically different approach, contradicting the rule that 'a war crime is shaped by or dependent upon the environment – the armed conflict – in which it is committed'. The case is the one of Emden Wolfgang Lehnigk and Kurt Arthur Werner Schuster, in which the *Corte di assise* of Santa Maria Capua Vetere (Italy) issued its judgement on 25 October 1994.[25]

The two accused in this case were both officers in the German armed forces in October 1943, stationed around Caiazzo (in southern Italy) – an area where, on one occasion, German soldiers killed 22 civilians who were hiding in a country house. The court explained that a civilian court had

20 Judgement, *Kunarac*, Appeals Chamber, 12 June 2002 (hereafter, *Kunarac* Appeal Judgement), para. 58.

21 *Kunarac* Appeal Judgement, para. 59.

22 Judgement, *Brđanin*, Appeals Chamber, 3 April 2007 (hereafter, *Brđanin* Appeal Judgement).

23 *Brdjanin* Appeal Brief, para. 264, cited in *Brđanin* Appeal Judgement, para. 253.

24 *Brdjanin* Appeal Judgement, para. 256 (footnotes omitted and emphasis added).

25 The text of this judgement is available online in its original (Italian) version at http://www.difesa.it/GiustiziaMilitare/RassegnaGM/Processi/Lehnigk-Emden-Schuster/c-assise-smcv.html (visited 20 August 2009).

jurisdiction over this crime because, although Lehnigk and Schuster were military officers accused of killing innocent civilians during a war operation,

> war crimes are characterised by an objective link with war necessities, that is, on account of their military nature; killings lacking such a link, and only broadly related with the war, fall into the category of common murders.

In order for an act to be considered a violation of the laws or customs of war, in the view of the judges, violence must be 'the result, the effect, the product of a military operation'. The court found that the crimes had been committed due to 'hatred against the Italian people' (*intolleranza e astio ... nei confronti del popolo italiano*) and for reasons unrelated to the war operations (*i motivi ... trascendevano la logica della guerra*) – thus questionably assigning relevance to motives rather than to objective circumstances. This is an interpretation of the applicable rules that is at the very least dubious in light of the law that I have discussed above.

As mentioned above, the present state of the law does not limit the analysis to the issue of whether certain clashes reach the level of 'an' armed conflict. Depending on the war crime charged, it might be necessary to explore the issue of the nature of the armed conflict (that is, international vs non-international). This is so because grave breaches of the Geneva Conventions (punishable under Article 2 of the ICTYSt) are only applicable in international armed conflicts, while other violations of the laws or customs of war (punishable under Article 3 of the ICTYSt) might be applicable both in international and in non-international armed conflicts. This distinction was reaffirmed by later practice as well as recent military manuals.

In approximation, one could say that an international armed conflict exists in at least three cases: (i) where there is an armed conflict between different states; (ii) where there is an internal armed conflict with one or more foreign states (or intergovernmental organization) intervening; (iii) where there is a struggle for independence in the form of a war of national liberation.[26]

Two main issues arise in this respect for the jurisprudence of the ICTY. One is the determination of the exact moment when a republic (formerly a member of Federal Yugoslavia) becomes a new state, thus making it necessary to qualify certain armed clashes as an international armed conflict. Due to the pleading practice of the Prosecution, which has hardly ever charged crimes under Article 2 of the Statute, this issue has not arisen often.[27] The second issue, which also calls for a careful assessment of the ICJ decisions related to this matter, regards the degree of intervention by a foreign country necessary to turn a non-international armed conflict into an international one.[28] This is also a very interesting topic, but is beyond the scope of this chapter.

---

26 For a slightly different perspective, see E. David, *Principes de droit de conflits armés* (Bruxelles: Bruylant, 2002), 131 ff.

27 See, for example: Judgement, *Strugar*, Trial Chamber II, 28 January 2005 (hereafter, *Strugar* Trial Judgement), para. 216, considering it unnecessary to reach a conclusion on the nature of the conflict (with respect to the date of independence of Croatia) due to the fact that all charges related to Art. 3 of the ICTYSt; Judgement, *Galić*, Trial Chamber I, 5 December 2003 (hereafter, *Galić* Trial Judgement), para. 22, making (*rectius*, failing to make) the same determination as to the conflict in and around Sarajevo between 1992 and 1993.

28 This is the contentious issue of 'overall control test' (Judgement, *Tadić*, Appeals Chamber, 15 July 1999, in particular paras 130–145) vs the 'effective control test' (*Military and Paramilitary Activities in and Against Nicaragua (Nicaragua v. United States of America)* (Merits), Judgement, ICJ Reports (1986), at 14; *Genocide Case* (*Bosnia and Herzegovina v. Serbia and Montenegro*) (Merits), Judgement of 26 February 2007, paras 402–406.

I will now spend a few words on two interesting areas of the law of war crimes developed by the ICTY in the past few years. In both cases, I will deal with conducts criminalized under Article 3 of the ICTYSt.

5. *Jokić* and *Strugar*: The Destruction of Cultural Property

Although destruction of civilian property occurs in every conflict and can be therefore considered a 'normal' (albeit illegal) occurrence, it is in relation to war-related devastation that the very idea of protecting cultural property emerged.[29] The ICTY has provided some interesting insights into the criminalization of this type of conduct, in particular in its judgments issued on the shelling of the Old Town of Dubrovnik on 6 December 1991.[30]

In October 1991, during the conflict which arose between Federal Yugoslavia and Croatia for the independence of the latter, Miodrag Jokić was appointed Yugoslav commander of the Ninth Naval Sector (VPS) in Boka, Montenegro. In this capacity, from 8 October through 31 December 1991, he conducted a military campaign directed at the area around the territory of Dubrovnik, which was in the hands of Croatian forces.[31] On 6 December 1991, Yugoslav forces – under the command of Jokić, Strugar, and others – unlawfully shelled the Old Town of Dubrovnik. Notwithstanding the fact that the forces shelling the Old Town were under Jokić's *de jure* control, the Prosecution expressed its position that the unlawful attack had not been ordered by him.[32] Miodrag Jokić pleaded guilty as a commander to six counts, including the destruction of protected cultural property within the Old Town of the ancient Croat city. By his own admission, Jokić was aware of the Old Town's status, in its entirety, as a UNESCO World Cultural Heritage site pursuant to the 1972 Convention for the Protection of the World Cultural and Natural Heritage and that many buildings were marked with the symbols mandated by the 1954 Hague Convention on the Protection of Cultural Property in the Event of Armed Conflict.[33]

On the other hand, Pavle Strugar, a general during the same military operation and who was charged essentially with the same crimes, did not plead guilty. His trial started on 16 December 2003 and was concluded by the Trial Judgment issued on 31 January 2005. The case is still under appeal.

The Trial Chamber in that case found Strugar to have had 'material ability to prevent an attack on Dubrovnik by the Yugoslav People's Army (JNA) forces deployed in the region'[34] and therefore

29 On this issue, see recently T. Scovazzi, 'Le patrimoine culturel de l'humanité', in Académie de Droit International de La Haye, Centre d'Etudes et de Recherche de Droit International et de Relations Internationales, *Le patrimoine culturel de l'humanité* (Leiden: Martinus Nijhoff, 2007), at 19.

30 The judgements are: Sentencing Judgement, *Jokić*, Trial Chamber I, 18 March 2004 (hereafter, *Jokić* Sentencing Judgement), confirmed on appeals, and the *Strugar* Trial Judgement. For an analysis of the protection of cultural property by international tribunals, see H. Abtahi, 'The Protection of Cultural Property in Times of Armed Conflict: The Practice of the International Criminal Tribunal for the Former Yugoslavia', in 14 *Harvard Human Rights Journal* (2001), 1–33; Y. Gottlieb, 'Criminalizing Destruction of Cultural Property: A Proposal for Defining New Crimes under the Rome Statute of the ICC', in 23 *Penn State International Law Review* (2005), 857–96; C. Forrest, 'The Doctrine of Military Necessity and the Protection of Cultural Property During Armed Conflicts', 37 *California Western International Law Journal* (2007), 177.

31 *Jokić* Sentencing Judgement, paras 19–21.

32 *Jokić* Sentencing Judgement, para. 26.

33 *Jokić* Sentencing Judgement, paras 8 and 23.

34 See, for example, *Strugar* Trial Judgement, para. 398.

convicted him under the doctrine of superior responsibility for destruction or wilful damage done to institutions dedicated to religion, charity and education, the arts and sciences, historic monuments and works or art and science, as well as for attack on civilians.[35] In relation to the crime enshrined in Article 3(d) of the ICTYSt (destruction or wilful damage done to institutions dedicated to religion, charity and education, the arts and sciences, historic monuments and works or art and science), the *Strugar* Trial Chamber stated:

> Article 3(d) of the Statute is a rule of international humanitarian law which not only reflects customary international law but is applicable to both international and non-international armed conflicts.[36]

The *Jokić* Trial Judgment also elaborated on the rationale underlying the special protection afforded to cultural property. It stated that '[t]he shelling attack on the Old Town was an attack not only against the history and heritage of the region, but also against the cultural heritage of humankind',[37] adding that '[r]estoration of buildings of this kind, when possible, can never return the buildings to their state prior to the attack'.[38]

The Trial Chamber in *Strugar* also clarified the elements of this crime, establishing that the conduct is criminal if: (i) it has caused damage to property which constitutes the cultural or spiritual heritage of peoples; (ii) the damaged property was not used for military purposes at the time when the acts of hostility took place; and (iii) it is carried out with the intent to damage the property in question.[39] It is important to note that, despite a previous split within the jurisprudence of the ICTY, the *Strugar* Trial Chamber found that:

> The special protection awarded to cultural property itself may not be lost simply because of military activities or military installations in the immediate vicinity of the cultural property.[40]

This appears to be a very important statement, in light of the problems faced by armies and soldiers when engaged in urban warfare, in particular within town and cities with a rich cultural heritage.[41]

6. *Galić*: Attack Against Civilians and Terrorization of the Civilian Population

A. Introductory Notes

In *Galić*, the Trial Chamber was faced with the charge of attacks on civilians; the indictment in this case related to the long period (23 months) of the siege of Sarajevo by Bosnian-Serb forces.

35 For a more thorough analysis of this judgement, see F. Lagos-Pola and E. Carnero Rojo, 'The *Strugar* Case before the International Criminal Tribunal for the Former Yugoslavia', in 18(2) *Humanitäres Völkerrecht* (2005), at 139–45.

36 *Strugar* Trial Judgement, para. 230.

37 *Jokić* Sentencing Judgement, para. 51.

38 *Jokić* Sentencing Judgement, para. 52.

39 *Strugar* Trial Judgement, para. 312.

40 *Strugar* Trial Judgement, para. 310.

41 These findings were essentially confirmed on appeal (see Judgement, *Strugar*, Appeals Chamber, 17 July 2008).

Another difference between this case and *Strugar* was that, despite the presence of monuments expressing the rich cultural heritage of the city of Sarajevo, the Prosecution chose not to charge, in the *Galić* Indictment, any crime specifically related to the protection of cultural property.

Stanislav Galić was the commander of the Corps in charge of operations within and around Sarajevo (the Sarajevo Romanija Corps or SRK); his immediate superior was the Chief of Staff of the Army of the Bosnian-Serb Republic (*Republika Srpska*), General Ratko Mladić.[42] Galić was charged with conducting a campaign of shelling and sniping against civilian areas of Sarajevo between 10 September 1992 and 10 August 1994, thereby inflicting terror upon its civilian population; a protracted campaign of sniper attacks upon the civilian population of Sarajevo, killing and wounding a large number of persons of all ages and both sexes; and a coordinated and protracted campaign of artillery and mortar shelling of civilian areas of Sarajevo, resulting in thousands of civilians being killed or injured.[43]

The case posed numerous challenges to the parties and to the judges. The Trial Judgement was issued on 5 December 2003, while the Appeal Judgement was issued on 30 November 2006. Remarkably, the Appeals Chamber concluded that the Trial Chamber did not err on any legal issue, but modified the original sentence (20 years' imprisonment) into life sentence for General Galić.[44]

The crime of attack against the civilian population was charged as a grave breach of the Geneva Conventions (common Article 3 to the Geneva Conventions, which stipulates minimum guaranteed protections in cases of non-international armed conflicts), punishable under Article 3 of the ICTYSt. The Appeals Chamber in this case recalled that customary international law makes offences under Article 3 of the ICTYSt (including the crime of attacks on civilians) applicable to all types of armed conflicts, whether internal or international.[45] The crime charged in this case was found to be constituted of the following elements: (i) acts of violence; (ii) wilfully directed against the civilian population or individual civilians not taking direct part in hostilities; and (iii) causing death or serious injury to body or health within the civilian population.[46]

The crime of 'acts or threats of violence the primary purpose of which is to spread terror among the civilian population', as the Appeals Chamber defined it,[47] charged under Count 1 of the Indictment, was also based on Article 3 of the ICTYSt, encompassing the prohibition of Article 51(2) of Additional Protocol I and Article 13(2) of Additional Protocol II. These Articles provide, in their relevant parts, that:

42 Judgement, *Galić*, Appeals Chamber, 30 November 2006 (hereafter, *Galić* Appeal Judgement), para. 2.

43 *Galić* Appeal Judgement, para. 3.

44 On this case and, more generally, on the war crime of 'terror', see: H. Gasser, 'Prohibition of Terrorist Acts in International Humanitarian Law', in 26 *International Review of Red Cross* (1986), at 200; D. Kravetz, 'The Protection of Civilians in War: the ICTY's *Galić* Case', in 17 *Leiden Journal of International Law* (2004), 521; G. Acquaviva, 'Il diritto umanitario nella giurisprudenza del Tribunale penale per la ex-Jugoslavia: l'attacco contro i civili nei casi *Strugar* e *Galić*', in T. Scovazzi and I. Papanicolopulu (eds), *Quale diritto nei conflitti armati?* (Milano: Giuffrè, 2006), 149; W. Fenrick, 'Riding the Rhino: Attempting to Develop Usable Legal Standards for Combat Activities', in 30 *Boston College International & Comparative Law Review* (2007), 111 (with various references to the *Galić* Trial Judgement); M. Sossai, 'Il crimine di "terrore": il caso *Galic*', in G. Calvetti and T. Scovazzi (eds), *Il Tribunale per la ex-Iugoslavia: attività svolta e prospettive in vista del suo scioglimento* (Milano: Giuffrè, 2007), 210.

45 *Galić* Appeal Judgement, para. 120.

46 *Galić* Trial Judgement, para. 62 (confirmed on appeal).

47 *Galić* Appeal Judgement, para. 69. In this paper, the term 'terror' will be used for ease of reference.

> [t]he civilian population as such, as well as individual civilians, shall not be made the object of attack. Acts or threats of violence the primary purpose of which is to spread terror among the civilian population are prohibited.

With respect to the *actus reus* of the crime in question, the Appeals Chamber made the following determination:

> The Appeals Chamber has already found that the crime of acts or threats of violence the primary purpose of which is to spread terror among the civilian population falls within the general prohibition of attacks on civilians. The definition of terror of the civilian population uses the terms "acts or threats of violence" and not "attacks or threats of attacks". However, the Appeals Chamber notes that Article 49(1) of Additional Protocol I defines "attacks" as "acts of violence". Accordingly, the crime of acts or threats of violence the primary purpose of which is to spread terror among the civilian population can comprise attacks or threats of attacks against the civilian population. The acts or threats of violence constitutive of the crime of terror shall not however be limited to direct attacks against civilians or threats thereof but may include indiscriminate or disportionate [sic] attacks or threats thereof. The nature of the acts or threats of violence directed against the civilian population can vary; the primary concern, as explained below, is that those acts or threats of violence be committed with the specific intent to spread terror among the civilian population. Further, the crime of acts or threats of violence the primary purpose of which is to spread terror among the civilian population is not a case in which an explosive device was planted outside of an ongoing military attack but rather a case of "extensive trauma and psychological damage" being caused by "attacks [which] were designed to keep the inhabitants in a constant state of terror". Such extensive trauma and psychological damage form part of the acts or threats of violence.[48]

The *mens rea* of the crime is the specific intent to spread terror among the civilian population.[49] These issues have been aptly discussed in scholarly papers,[50] but two related matters have not received proper attention. First, the jurisdictional issue: is it necessary to find that terror was criminalized under customary international law in order to punish the perpetrators? Second, a matter of method: how should prosecuting authorities go about in trying to prove the crime of terror beyond reasonable doubt? To this, of course, is linked the impact of the ICTY findings on future courts that will deal with similar problems. The two matters will be discussed separately.

B. Jurisdictional Issues

According to the *Tadić* Jurisdiction Decision mentioned above, offences that are not explicitly enumerated in Article 3 of the ICTYSt must meet the following criteria in order to fall within the ICTY's jurisdiction (so-called '*Tadić* conditions'): (i) the violation must constitute an infringement of a rule of international humanitarian law; (ii) the rule must be customary in nature or, if it belongs to treaty law, the treaty must bind the parties at the time of the offence and not be in conflict with or derogate from a peremptory norm of international law; (iii) the violation must be serious, that is to say, it must constitute a breach of a rule protecting important values, and the breach must

48 *Galić* Appeal Judgement, para. 102.

49 *Galić* Appeal Judgement, para. 104.

50 See, for example, S. Jodoin, 'Terrorism as a War Crime', 7 *International Criminal Law Review* (2007), at 77–115.

involve grave consequences for the victim; and (iv) the violation of the rule must entail, under customary or conventional law, the individual criminal responsibility of the person breaching the rule.[51] Considering that the crime of 'terror' is not explicitly set out in Article 3 (but, as mentioned before, is derived from Article 51(2) of Additional Protocol I), the Trial Chamber was obliged to engage in such an analysis in order to determine whether it had subject matter jurisdiction.

One feature of the *Galić* case was that the evidence on the record showed that the parties to the conflict in and around Sarajevo (identified as: Bosnian Serbs, i.e., the SRK; Bosnian Croats; and Bosnian Muslims) had signed a series of agreements under the auspices of the International Committee of the Red Cross in order to protect the civilian population. The first of these agreements, signed on 22 May 1992 (22 May Agreement), was aimed at bringing into force, *inter alia*, Articles 35 through 42 and 48 through 58 of Additional Protocol I.[52] The 22 May Agreement specified the steps each warring party would undertake when informed of allegations of violations of international humanitarian law. Thus, each party agreed, *inter alia*:

> to open an enquiry promptly and pursue it conscientiously, and to take the necessary steps to put an end to the alleged violations or prevent their recurrence *and to punish those responsible in accordance with the law in force*.[53]

On this basis, the Trial Chamber came to the conclusion that, whether or not 'terror' was a crime under customary international law, the 22 May Agreement was enough to provide subject matter jurisdiction in this respect.[54] The Appeals Chamber, for the reasons detailed below, did not need to discuss the matter. However, had there been any doubt on whether the formal requirements for entry into force of the 22 May Agreement were met, attention could have been paid to the subsequent agreements signed by the parties. These subsequent agreements, which develop and detail the obligations enshrined by the original (22 May) Agreement, clearly rely on it and show that the parties intended it to apply provisionally amongst themselves until its formal entry into force. This would seem a reasonable application of the rule according to which a treaty is applied provisionally pending its entry into force if the negotiating parties have in some manner so agreed.[55]

The Appeals Chamber decided that it did not need to address the issue because, in the Appeals Chamber's own assessment, 'terror' had become a crime under general international law by 1992.[56] Such a finding, coupled with the Appeals Chamber's conclusion that the ICTY always ascertains that a treaty provision relating to a crime is also declaratory of custom,[57] rendered it moot

---

51 *Tadić* Jurisdiction Decision, paras 94 and 143.

52 *Galić* Trial Judgement, para. 22.

53 *Galić* Trial Judgement, paras 22–25 (emphasis added).

54 *Galić* Trial Judgement, in particular paras 124–129. The Trial Chamber ascertained that the 22 May Agreement had not only been signed, but had actually entered into force among the parties (*Galić* Trial Judgement, para. 23). This finding was challenged on appeal (see *Galić* Appeal Judgement, para. 79).

55 See, for example, Art. 25(1)(b) of the Vienna Convention on the Law of Treaties (1155 UNTS 331).

56 *Galić* Appeal Judgement, paras 87–98.

57 *Galić* Appeal Judgement, para. 85 ('However, while binding conventional law that prohibits conduct and provides for individual criminal responsibility could provide the basis for the International Tribunal's jurisdiction, in practice the International Tribunal always ascertains that the treaty provision in question is also declaratory of custom'). This statement could have been qualified, however, since in at least one case (the *Galić* Trial Judgement itself), a Chamber had not actually made such an assessment. In general on the issue of customary law in ICTY jurisprudence, see *inter alia* T. Meron, 'Reflections on the Prosecution of War Crimes

to discuss the import of the 22 May Agreement for purposes of the ICTY's jurisdiction over the crime in question.

Despite some criticism,[58] and absent any finding on the customary nature of 'terror', the Trial Chamber appears to have been right in applying the binding precedents to the circumstances of this case.[59] The *Tadić* conditions require Chambers to assess not just that a specific rule (in this case, the prohibition of terror) was binding upon the parties at the relevant time, be it by virtue of custom or of valid treaty in force (see above, under (ii)). The next step must be that of ascertaining that individual criminal responsibility for violation of that rule was provided for by international law at the time of the conduct (see above, under (iv)). *Tadić* explicitly said that such prohibition may stem from customary international law or from conventional law, i.e., a valid and binding treaty.

The warring parties in this case were armed forces in the territory of Bosnia-Herzegovina, originally one of the republics composing Federal Yugoslavia, which had ratified Additional Protocols I and II. It is settled that parties to an armed conflict can, by agreement, bring into force provisions of Additional Protocol I, regardless of the nature of the conflict.[60] Since the Trial Chamber had found that certain parts of Additional Protocol I, including Article 51 thereof, applied to the armed conflict in Sarajevo during the relevant time, it considered that the rule in question (prohibition of 'terror') had been brought into effect *at least* by virtue of the 22 May Agreement. This agreement not only incorporated the second part of Article 51(2) by reference, but repeated in the Agreement proper the very prohibition: '[a]cts or threats of violence the primary purpose of which is to spread terror among the civilian population are prohibited.'[61]

Considering this finding and the fact that the 22 May Agreement explicitly also contained the understanding that the parties to the conflict intended to prosecute alleged cases of violations of international humanitarian law ('to open an enquiry promptly … *and to punish those responsible in accordance with the law in force*'[62]), the Trial Chamber was warranted in asserting jurisdiction on the crime of terror under Tadić.[63] The Tadić condition under (iv) above was clearly met since the parties to the conflict had agreed by treaty to prosecute and punish persons responsible for violations of applicable humanitarian rules.[64]

---

by International Tribunals', 100 *American Journal of International Law* (2006), 551–579 (in particular, at 576–577).

58 See, for example, G. Mettraux, *International Crimes and the* ad hoc *Tribunals* (Oxford: Oxford University Press, 2005), 129 ('The reasoning of the Trial Chamber in relation to this offence appears flawed in that it seems to conflate the illegality of a conduct with its criminal character … the Trial Chamber in this case relied upon treaty law alone, in the absence of accompanying customary law, to convict the accused, thereby going beyond the Tribunal's jurisdiction and infringing upon the principle of legality').

59 Under the regime in force, ICTY Trial Chambers are bound to follow precedents set by the ICTY Appeals Chamber. See Judgement, *Aleksovski*, Appeals Chamber, 24 March 2000, paras 112–113.

60 This principle is reflected in Common Art. 3 to the Geneva Conventions and Art. 96 of Additional Protocol I. See *Galić* Trial Judgement, para. 23.

61 *Galić* Trial Judgement, para. 96.

62 *Galić* Trial Judgement, para. 124 (emphasis added).

63 The Trial Chamber also engaged in an additional exercise to establish its jurisdiction at paras 127–129.

64 One might even argue that the legality principle (with its tenets of accessibility and foreseeability) is better served when individual criminal responsibility for specific conduct is enshrined in a treaty – which specifies in writing the elements of the crime so that each person may be presumed to be aware of them. See the reflections on this issue and the bibliography cited in R. Cryer, *Prosecuting International Crimes – Selectivity and the International Criminal Law Regime* (Cambridge: Cambridge University Press, 2005), 238–241.

The requirement that 'the violation of the rule must entail, under customary or conventional law, the individual criminal responsibility of the person' may not be read as requiring that a violation of the prohibition of 'terror' should entail, according to the text of the treaty in question, individual criminal responsibility *before an international tribunal*, lest this condition be rendered completely meaningless.[65] In addition, an analysis in good faith of the 22 May Agreement makes it clear that the law in force clearly comprised, *inter alia*, applicable rules of international humanitarian law recalled by the agreement itself, which, as set out before, undoubtedly included the prohibition of terror. Thus, an agreement providing for the criminal prosecution of violations of the laws or customs of war, such as the 22 May Agreement, may undoubtedly serve as a basis for asserting jurisdiction by an international tribunal like the ICTY. There appears to be no strict requirement to identify a separate jurisdictional basis on customary international law.

Apart from the text of the agreement in question, there is arguably no reason to deny ICTY jurisdiction in cases where domestic courts in the states that arose on the territory of the former Yugoslavia (in this case, Bosnia-Herzegovina) could have prosecuted individuals for the same crimes based on domestic implementation of international law, whether conventional or customary. In this respect, it is interesting to note that the Trial Chamber also cited one relevant case before a municipal court in the territory of the former Yugoslavia. In May 1997, the Split County Court in Croatia convicted various Bosnian Serb soldiers pursuant to provisions including Article 33 of Geneva Convention IV, Article 51 of Additional Protocol I, and Article 13 of Additional Protocol II, for, *inter alia*, 'a plan of terrorising and mistreating the civilians', which had taken place during the period covered by the *Galić* Indictment.[66]

This case supports the conclusion that the *nullum crimen sine lege* principle is not breached by alleging individual criminal responsibility for the crime of terror against an accused from the former Yugoslavia. In light of the fact that the ICTY was established also 'to take effective measures to bring to justice the persons who are responsible' for widespread and flagrant violations of international humanitarian law[67] in substitution for courts within the territory of the former Yugoslavia, this is arguably a relevant consideration in assessing whether the exercise of the ICTY subject matter jurisdiction for this crime is properly within the authority bestowed upon it by the Security Council.

C. How to Prove the Crime of Terror

Another interesting feature of the *Galić* case is how the Prosecution set out to prove the existence of this campaign of terror by the SRK against the civilian population in and around the besieged city.

The judges were satisfied that the Prosecution had proven many incidents of sniping and shelling of civilian targets. These incidents, considered in their context, provided evidence

---

65 One treaty which does mention criminal responsibility with jurisdiction vested in an international tribunal prior to the ICC Statute is the Convention on the Prevention and Punishment of the Crimes of Genocide, adopted by GA Resolution 260 (III)A, 9 December 1948 (entered into force on 12 January 1951). Not even this treaty, however, would seem to satisfy such a strict understanding of the above-mentioned requirement, since its Art. 6 merely holds: 'Persons charged with genocide or any of the other acts enumerated in article III shall be tried by a competent tribunal of the State in the territory of which the act was committed, or by such international penal tribunal as may have jurisdiction with respect to those Contracting Parties *which shall have accepted its jurisdiction*' (emphasis added).

66 *Galić* Trial Judgement, para. 126; *Galić* Appeal Judgement, para. 97.

67 GA Res. 827, 25 May 1993.

beyond reasonable doubt of a general campaign to target civilians, orchestrated by the top military leadership in and around Sarajevo. Such a campaign, which lacked the characteristics of 'military necessity', was characterized by thousands of casualties among the civilian population of Sarajevo.[68] Many United Nations observers on the ground, as well as foreign journalists and other 'objective' witnesses, described the campaign as clearly devoid of any rational military objective. On the contrary, they stated before the Trial Chamber, this type of attacks appeared designed to instil terror within the civilian population, possibly with the ultimate aim of putting pressure on local political authorities to surrender.[69] Thus, the Trial Chamber took an interesting approach, building upon small individual incidents in order to provide the broad picture of the longest and bloodiest siege in contemporary times, without ever losing sight of the overall impact of fighting activities on the civilians suffering under those circumstances. The merits of such an approach were confirmed by the Appeals Chamber.[70]

Another related issue was the question of whether General Galić had actually ordered the campaign of terror. The main problem facing the Trial Chamber was that, while the Prosecution had charged General Galić with having 'planned, instigated, ordered, committed or otherwise aided and abetted in the planning, preparation or execution of' the crimes listed in the indictment,[71] there was no direct proof of a written, or otherwise explicit, order issued by the accused to commit any such crime. However, the Trial Chamber remarked, orders 'may be inferred from a variety of factors, such as the number of illegal acts, the number, identity and type of troops involved, the effective command and control exerted over these troops, the logistics involved, the widespread occurrence of the illegal acts, the tactical tempo of operations, the *modus operandi* of similar acts, the officers and staff involved, the location of the superior at the time and the knowledge of that officer of criminal acts committed under his command'.[72]

In light of these factors, and after an extensive analysis of the evidence adduced at trial, the Trial Chamber concluded that the only reasonable conclusion was that Galić had ordered the campaign with the primary purpose of spreading terror within the civilian population of Sarajevo. The evidence to reach this finding included proof that: (i) Galić had absolute control over his subordinates and frequent access to the fighting positions; (ii) his subordinates obeyed his orders and they continued the sniping and shelling of Sarajevo over 23 months; (iii) the intensity of fire changed depending on pressures by the international community on Galić and his staff; (iv) most of the artillery attacks appeared to be very carefully coordinated; and (v) Galić had repeatedly failed to prevent the crimes even after he was explicitly made aware of local and international complaints about the actions of his subordinates.[73] On the basis of the foregoing, the Trial Chamber concluded that:

> the evidence impels the conclusion that General Galić, although put on notice of crimes committed by his subordinates over whom he had total control, and who consistently and over a long period of time (twenty-three months) failed to prevent the commission of crime and punish the perpetrators

68 *Galić* Trial Judgement, paras 210–225, 578–586.

69 *Galić* Trial Judgement, paras 566–577.

70 *Galić* Appeal Judgement, paras 216–219. For a comment on the approach taken by the Trial Chamber in assessing the single incidents of sniping and shelling in light of the law on targeting, see M. N. Schmitt, 'Targeting and Humanitarian Law: Current Issues', in 34 *Israel Yearbook on Human Rights* (2004), at 59–104.

71 Art. 7(1) of the ICTY Statute; *Galić* Trial Judgement, para. 167.

72 *Galić* Trial Judgement, para. 171.

73 *Galić* Trial Judgement, paras 603–748.

> thereof upon that knowledge, furthered a campaign of unlawful acts of violence against civilians through orders relayed down the SRK chain of command and that he intended to conduct that campaign with the primary purpose of spreading terror within the civilian population of Sarajevo.

The approach taken by the ICTY in this case was remarkable because it did not limit itself to trusting the victims with their accounts of what had happened to them and their families in Sarajevo during the siege. The Trial Chamber instead sought confirmation of their testimonies in the most 'independent' sources available at the time in order to reach a conclusion that could truly be considered 'beyond reasonable doubt'. While this is of course a general requirement for international (and domestic) judges, one wonders whether a less independent tribunal, such as the military commissions that are often charged with assessing the criminal responsibility of foreigners in times of war, would be so cautious and careful in evaluating the single incidents that make up an overall 'campaign of terror' and would actually require independent corroboration on the impact of the military strategies employed to besiege a city. The ICTY has, in this case, undoubtedly gone to a great length in order to ensure that General Galić was not convicted for a crime that did not exist or of which he was not otherwise aware (*nullum crimen* principle) and that the evidence against him clearly pointed to his responsibility.

It should be mentioned that recent judgements by another UN-sponsored judicial institution, the Special Court for Sierra Leone, have applied and developed the legal findings reached by the ICTY in the *Galić* case. In the so-called AFRC (Armed Forces Revolutionary Council) Judgement, that Court held that the crime of terror against the civilian population encompasses the *actus reus* of acts of violence against property, as long as the special intent of spreading terror is there.[74] Thus, not only violence or threats against persons appear to be encompassed, but also shelling or other types of destruction of property. The issue, of course, is more a matter of factual and evidentiary analysis.

7. Conclusion

In its almost 15 years of judicial activity, the ICTY has contributed to the development and codification of many aspects of the laws applicable to armed conflict, not only with respect to crimes against humanity and genocide, but also in relation to war crimes. It has clarified in numerous decisions the definition of armed conflict by applying it to the armed clashes in the territory of the former Yugoslavia, and will likely continue to do so in future cases. It has shed some light on the difference between international and non-international armed conflict, trying to bridge the gap between the rules of customary law applicable in these two types of situation. Moreover, it has discussed in detail numerous important crimes and tested their application in landmark proceedings and decisions. In *Strugar* and *Jokić*, the ICTY has dealt with serious allegations of destruction of cultural property, clarifying many aspects of the law which had hardly been applied before in international criminal proceedings. In *Galić*, both the Trial Chamber and the Appeals Chamber have dealt with the law related to the attacks against civilians and to the terrorization of the civilian population, applying it to the extremely complex circumstances of that case, which involved urban warfare. In doing so, they also addressed interesting issues related to the subject matter jurisdiction of the *ad hoc* Tribunal and to the burden of proof beyond reasonable doubt in confused war situations.

---

74 Judgement, *Brima et al.*, 20 June 2007, para. 670 (confirmed on appeal).

Chapter 15

Gender-Based Violence Offences and Crimes Against Children at the SCSL

Renate Winter and Stephen Kostas*

1. Introduction

The armed conflict in Sierra Leone contained astonishingly brutal and large-scale crimes against civilians. Women and girls were targeted specifically on the basis of their gender. Thousands of women and girls all over the country were victims of rape, sexual violence, sexual slavery and 'forced marriage'. Children were abducted from their homes, villages or places of hiding and forced to kill or mutilate their kin and recruited into the combatant groups. This chapter will examine the Special Court's response to these crimes.

In addition to the Special Court for Sierra Leone (SCSL), several fact-finding investigations have attempted to document the scope of violence perpetrated against women. Notable amongst these have been the studies by the UN Assistance Mission in Sierra Leone sponsored studies by Physicians for Human Rights,[1] the Sierra Leone Truth and Reconciliation Commission[2] (TRC), and the UN Special Rapporteur on Violence Against Women, its Causes and Consequences.[3] The TRC determined that 32 per cent of the human rights violations it recorded were perpetrated against women.[4] It also recorded 800 statements reporting rape, while 58 per cent of the raped victims suffered multiple rapes.[5] According to the UN Special Rapporteur, 90 per cent of the abducted women were raped or subjected to sexual slavery; more than 8 per cent were forced to marry their abductors.[6] Women and girls of all ages were abused, as known victims range from four to sixty years old; 50 per cent of the rape victims were 18 years old or younger and 25 per cent of them under the age of 13.[7]

---

* The authors wish to thank Sandy Sivakumaran and Joakim Dungel for their insightful comments, and Terry Unger and Shannon Ghadiri for editorial assistance.

1 See C. Reis, 'Documenting Sexual Violence among Internally Displaced Women: Sierra Leone', in C. Beyrer and H. Pizer (eds), *Public Health & Human Rights* (Baltimore: Johns Hopkins University Press, 2007); Physicians for Human Rights, 'War-Related Sexual Violence in Sierra Leone: A Population-Based Assessment' (2002), available at http://physiciansforhumanrights.org/library/documents/reports/sexual-violence-sierra-leone.pdf (visited 8 May 2009).

2 Report available at http://www.trcsierraleone.org/drwebsite/publish/index.shtml (visited 21 February 2010).

3 *Report of the Special Rapporteur on Violence Against Women, its Causes and Consequences*, UN doc. E/CN.4/2002/83/Add.2, 11 February 2002 ('Report of the Special Rapporteur on Violence Against Women').

4 'Women and the Armed Conflict in Sierra Leone', Vol. 3(b), *Final Report of the Truth & Reconciliation Commission of Sierra Leone*, Chapter 3, para. 203 ('TRC Report on Women and the Armed Conflict').

5 TRC Report on Women and the Armed Conflict, at para. 283.

6 Report of the Special Rapporteur on Violence Against Women, at para. 44.

7 TRC Report on Women and the Armed Conflict, at para. 283.

Children formed another prominent civilian group subject to violence. They were frequently targeted for 'amputation, mutilation, displacement and torture'[8] and frequently recruited into the armed forces or groups of one of the parties to the conflict. There are no accurate figures on how many children were conscripted, enlisted or used by the warring factions, however, various submissions to the TRC put the figure at somewhere between 5,000 and 10,000 children.[9] The TRC found that all the armed factions forcibly enlisted and used child soldiers.[10] Often under the influence of drugs or through coercion, children also committed grave crimes against civilians while serving as child soldiers. As a result, these children were effectively both victims and perpetrators of crime, and in court these children also become witnesses. They therefore fulfil the criteria of all three functions of an individual who appears before a penal court. Numerous questions surround the appropriate treatment of these children, not least of which involves the protections afforded to them. The Special Court has been faced with the significant task of striking a balance between ensuring justice for victims and their families on the one hand and holding perpetrators accountable on the other.

With these conditions in mind, the Government of Sierra Leone and the UN drafted the Special Court's Statute (Statute) and the Rules of Procedure and Evidence (Rules) of the Special Court to contain specific provisions to provide for the prosecution of those who conscripted or enlisted children or used them to participate actively in hostilities. The Statute and Rules also ensure the care for child victims and witnesses. The following discussion describes the relevant provisions of the Statute and Rules and how they have been applied in particular cases involving children.

The constitutive documents of the Special Court are specifically tailored to address the scale and diversity of crimes committed against children and based on gender during the decade-long armed conflict in Sierra Leone. The Statute contains provisions adopted from the ICC's Rome Statute to provide jurisdiction over the recruitment of children into armed groups and their use to participate actively in hostilities. It also grants jurisdiction over a much broader range of gender-based crimes than the statutes of the ICTY and ICTR. The Rules are also shaped to address the specific needs of witnesses of crimes.

All but one of the cases before the Special Court includes charges for gender-based violence, and all of the cases include charges for recruitment of child soldiers. To date, six persons have been convicted for gender-based violence crimes, including the first convictions in international criminal law for the crimes against humanity of 'forced marriage' as an 'other inhumane act' as well as sexual slavery. In addition, for the first time in international criminal law, five persons have been convicted for recruitment or use of child soldiers. In the process of adjudicating these cases, the Special Court has made important clarifications with respect to these crimes and the underlying law.

This chapter proceeds in three principal parts. Following this introduction, the second part discusses the Court's jurisprudence on questions of first impression in the area of gender-based violence. The third part examines the Court's case law regarding the recruitment and use of child soldiers and the several questions of law the Court has begun to delineate. In both categories of crimes, the Special Court is distinguished from the *ad hoc* Tribunals in terms of having similar subject matter jurisdiction as in the Rome Statute, and having underlying facts similar to other

---

8 'Children and the Armed Conflict in Sierra Leone', Vol. 3(b), *Final Report of the Truth & Reconciliation Commission of Sierra Leone*, Chapter 4, para. 7 ('TRC Report on Children and the Armed Conflict').

9 TRC Report on Children and the Armed Conflict, at para. 9.

10 TRC Report on Children and the Armed Conflict, at para. 126.

recent and ongoing conflicts. The Court is well-positioned, therefore, to establish jurisprudence that will be of assistance to future tribunals.

2. Gender-Based Violence

A. Provisions of the Statute and Rules that Address Gender-Based Violence

1. Gender-based Offences in the Statute

The Statute of the Special Court, drawing upon the Rome Statute, presents several innovations relative to the statutes of the ICTY and ICTR and, specifically, takes into account gender-based violence by providing for its broad criminalization. For example, whereas the statutes of the ICTY and ICTR only expressly provide jurisdiction over one gender-based violence crime (rape), the Statute enumerates rape, sexual slavery, enforced prostitution, forced pregnancy and any other form of sexual violence as crimes against humanity in Article 2.[11] The Statute also grants the Court power to prosecute the war crimes of 'outrages upon personal dignity, in particular humiliating and degrading treatment, rape, enforced prostitution and any form of indecent assault'. As a so-called hybrid court with mixed subject matter jurisdiction, the Court also has the power to prosecute persons for offences relating to the abuse of girls under Sierra Leone's Prevention of Cruelty to Children Act of 1926, although none of the indictments filed by the Prosecution contained charges under this offence.

As discussed below, additional statutory provisions that do not exclusively pertain to sexual violence have been used to try persons for gender-based violence. Most significantly, the Prosecution charged acts of 'forced marriage' as 'other inhumane acts' a crime against humanity listed in Article 2(i) of the Statute. These are the first such prosecutions in international criminal law. Sexual violence has also been accepted as part of the crime base establishing the crimes of 'outrages upon personal dignity', the first such treatment by an international criminal court.

2. Procedures Regarding Evidence of Gender-based Violence

Collecting and introducing evidence of alleged crimes under the Statute often requires victims to participate in investigations and to testify about the acts committed against them, which can be a difficult experience. In an attempt to address these difficulties, the Statute and the Rules specifically require that victims of gender-based violence are interviewed, assisted and counselled by personnel with expertise in gender-based violence.[12] In addition, particular principles of evidence apply in

11 This article is taken from the corresponding provision in the Statute of the International Criminal Court, Article 7(1)(g). In contrast, the statutes of the UN *ad hoc* Tribunals for the former Yugoslavia and Rwanda, include only rape as the sole act of a gender-based nature that expressly qualifies as a crime against humanity. Article 5(g) ICTYSt; Article 3(g) ICTRSt.

12 Article 15(4) of the Statute, related to 'The Prosecutor' provides: 'Given the nature of the crimes committed and the particular sensitivities of girls, young women and children victims of rape, sexual assault, abduction and slavery of all kinds, due consideration should be given in the appointment of staff to the employment of prosecutors and investigators experienced in gender-related crimes and juvenile justice.' Article 16 of the Statute provides that the Witnesses and Victims Section 'shall include experts in trauma, including trauma related to crimes of sexual violence and violence against children'. Rule34(A)(iii) of the Rules states: '[The Witnesses and Victims Section] shall ensure that [witnesses and victims] receive relevant

cases of sexual assault. For example, consent cannot be inferred from any words or conduct of a victim where coercion undermined the victim's ability to give voluntary and genuine consent, or from the silence of, or lack of resistance by, a victim of alleged sexual violence.[13]

B. Gender-Based Violence in the Cases of the Special Court

In three of the four principal cases before the Special Court, the accused were charged with gender-based violence crimes. In the course of the trials, numerous victims of sexual violence testified. To date, judgments on appeal have been entered in two of the four cases, the so-called Armed Forces Revolutionary Council (*AFRC*) and Civil Defence Forces (*CDF*) cases, and the trial judgment has been rendered in the so-called Revolutionary United Front case (*RUF*). The judgments in these cases elaborate and develop the legal protections available for women and girls under international criminal law and will hopefully significantly contribute to ending impunity for violence against them. The following section, takes a closer look at the legal and factual findings in the principal cases that have been completed at the Special Court.

1. The AFRC Case

The Prosecution charged the three AFRC[14] accused with responsibility for widespread gender-based violence committed against women and girls, including the crimes against humanity of rape, sexual slavery and any other form of sexual violence, and 'forced marriage' as an 'other inhumane act'. In addition, or in the alternative, the Prosecution charged 'outrages upon personal dignity', a violation of Article 3 common to the Geneva Conventions and of Additional Protocol II under Article 3 of the Statute. The Prosecution alleged that members of the AFRC (often acting in concert with RUF combatants) raped and abducted an unknown number of women and girls, used them as sex slaves, forced them into marriages and subjected them to other forms of sexual violence in numerous locations throughout the country. The crime base for these gender-based violence allegations was substantial and, arguably, greater than in any prior international trial.

(a) Rape

Brima, Kamara and Kanu were charged with rape as a crime against humanity and each was convicted of superior responsibility for rapes committed by their subordinates.[15] No novel legal developments accompany these convictions. They are, nonetheless, notable in that they represent one of the few instances in international criminal law in which a superior is held responsible for rapes committed by a subordinate, including occasions where the superior is not present at the scene of the crime.

---

support, counselling and other appropriate assistance, including … physical and psychological rehabilitation, especially in cases of rape, sexual assault and crimes against children.' Rule 34(B): 'The Section personnel shall include experts in trauma, including trauma related to crimes of sexual violence and violence against children.'

13 Rule 96 SCSL RPE.

14 SCSL, Judgment, Alex Tamba Brima, Brima Bazzy Kamara, and Santigie Borbor Kanu, Trial Chamber, 20 June 2007 (*AFRC* Trial Judgment).

15 *AFRC* Trial Judgment, para. 2104.

(b) 'Sexual slavery and any form of sexual violence' and 'outrages upon personal dignity'

Brima, Kamara and Kanu were also charged in a single count with 'sexual slavery and any form of sexual violence' as crimes against humanity. In a holding that may be significant for the ICC because the Courts have similar relevant statutory provisions, the Trial Chamber held that the count was duplicitous because it charged multiple crimes in the same count. The Trial Chamber, therefore, struck the count in its entirety.[16] However, the Trial Chamber considered that because the Prosecution had presented sufficient evidence of sexual slavery during the course of the trial, it was in the interest of justice to consider this evidence under the count charging 'outrages upon personal dignity' as a war crime.[17]

The Trial Chamber set out the following elements of sexual slavery:

> (1) The perpetrator exercised a power attaching to the right of ownership over a person; (2) he or she caused the person to engage in one or more acts of a sexual nature; and (3) he or she intended to engage in the act of sexual slavery or in the reasonable knowledge that it was likely to occur.

Based on these elements, the Trial Chamber found that sexual slavery was an act of humiliation and degradation so serious as to be generally considered an outrage upon personal dignity.[18] Referring to the case law of the ICTY that 'performing subservient acts' and 'endur[ing] the constant fear of being subjected to physical, mental, or sexual violence'[19] in detention camps constituted the crime of outrages upon personal dignity, the Trial Chamber held that 'sexual slavery, which may encompass rape and/or other types of sexual violence as well as enslavement, entails a similar humiliation and degradation of personal dignity'.[20] The Trial Chamber entered a conviction against the three accused under Count 9, finding the accused guilty of outrages upon personal dignity as a war crime, based on the same underlying acts for sexual slavery.

(c) Forced Marriage

As discussed above, multiple provisions in the Statute give jurisdiction over multiple gender-based violence crimes. Two examples are Article 2(g) which gives the Court power to prosecute 'rape, sexual slavery, enforced prostitution, forced pregnancy and any other form of sexual violence' and Article 2(i), which gives the Court power to prosecute 'other inhumane acts'. In *Brima et al.*, the Prosecution charged the accused with 'other inhumane acts' as a crime against humanity under Article 2(i) of the Statute for the act of 'forced marriage'. The allegation presented several novel legal questions. First, is 'forced marriage' an 'other form of sexual violence' chargeable under Article 2(g)? If 'forced marriage' was determined to be a form of sexual violence, then arguably it should have been charged under Article 2(g) rather than Article 2(i). Moreover, as argued by one

---

16 *AFRC* Trial Judgment, paras 94–95. The Appeals Chamber affirmed the duplicity of Count 7. However, it held that the Trial Chamber should have: (1) proceeded on the basis that the offence of sexual slavery had been properly charged in Count 7; (2) returned an appropriate verdict on that count with respect to the crime of sexual slavery; and (3) struck out the charge of 'any other form of sexual violence'. *AFRC* Appeals Judgment, at para. 109.

17 *AFRC* Trial Judgment, at para. 713.

18 *AFRC* Trial Judgment, at para. 719.

19 ICTY, Judgment, *Kvočka et al.*, Appeals Chamber, 28 February 2005, para. 173, as referenced in *AFRC* Trial Judgment, at para. 719.

20 *AFRC* Trial Judgment, at para. 719 (emphasis added).

of the accused, inclusion of 'any other form of sexual violence' in Article 2(g) could be read to restrict the scope of offences chargeable as 'other inhumane acts' pursuant to Article 2(i). Second, is 'forced marriage' distinct from sexual slavery? If it is, then convictions could be entered for both crimes, even for the same underlying acts.

At trial, the Prosecution contended that 'forced marriage' involves conduct distinct from sexual acts and was, therefore, not an 'other form of sexual violence' because it forces a person into a relationship with the appearance of marriage. Even if forced marriage usually involves sex, the Prosecution asserted, it has its own distinctive features and is sufficiently serious to qualify as an 'other inhumane act'.[21] Thus, sexual slaves are not necessarily obliged to pretend they are the spouse of another, and may not be obliged to perform conjugal duties.

On the second question, the Prosecution argued at trial that although 'forced marriage' as an inhumane act may include sexual slavery, a separate offence under the Statute, it involves distinct elements as well. The Prosecution claimed that 'forced marriage':

> consists of words or other conduct intended to confer a status of marriage by force or threat of force or coercion, such as that caused by fear of violence, duress, detention, psychological oppression or abuse of power against the victim, or by taking advantage of a coercive environment, with the intention of conferring the status of marriage.[22]

A majority of the Trial Chamber disagreed, however, and found first that '[i]n light of the exhaustive category of sexual crimes particularized in Article 2(g) of the Statute, the offence of "other inhumane acts", even though residual, must logically be restrictively interpreted as applying only to acts of a non-sexual nature amounting to an affront to human dignity'.[23] As a consequence, according to the majority, 'forced marriage' could only be charged as an 'other inhumane act' if it did not constitute a form of sexual violence. Regarding the second question, the majority of the Trial Chamber found that 'the totality of the evidence adduced by the Prosecution as proof of "forced marriage" goes to proof of elements subsumed by the crime of sexual slavery'.[24] The majority considered that the evidence demonstrated that women and girls had been abducted and forced to become 'wives' of 'individual rebels' and that this relationship of ownership involved the exercise of control by the perpetrator over the victim, including the victim's sexuality, movement and labour. The majority considered that the use of the term 'wife' by the perpetrator in reference to the victim was indicative of 'the intent of the perpetrator to exercise ownership over the victim, and not an intent to assume a marital or quasi-marital status with the victim in the sense of establishing mutual obligations inherent in a husband wife relationship'. Based on these observations, the majority concluded that 'the evidence adduced by the Prosecution is completely subsumed by the crime of sexual slavery and that there is no lacuna in the law which would necessitate a separate crime of "forced marriage" as an "other inhumane act"'.[25] The majority, therefore, dismissed the count charging 'other inhumane acts' as redundant with the count charging 'sexual slavery'.

In Justice Doherty's dissenting opinion, she extensively analyzed the evidence adduced at trial and concluded that the conduct described as 'forced marriage' is distinguishable from the crime of sexual slavery. She examined the nature of the relationship between the 'bush husband' and 'bush wife' and the roles expected of the bush wife. Justice Doherty stressed the numerous non-

21 *AFRC* Trial Judgment, at para. 701.
22 *AFRC* Trial Judgment, at para. 701.
23 *AFRC* Trial Judgment, at para. 697.
24 *AFRC* Trial Judgment, at para. 711.
25 *AFRC* Trial Judgment, at para. 713.

sexual acts which the bush wives were compelled to perform, and which she considered to be part of the criminal conduct. Justice Doherty also focused on the 'serious psychological and moral injury' caused to the victims, and distinguished forced marriage from sexual slavery in part on the basis that victims of sexual slavery were not in exclusive relationships and, therefore, had no protection from rape by other rebels. However, unlike victims of forced marriage, the victims of sexual slavery did not suffer the stigma of being 'rebel wives' or bush wives. Concluding that the totality of the conduct inflicts great suffering of a gravity similar to the enumerated crimes against humanity in the Statute, Justice Doherty held that the *actus reus* and *mens rea* for 'other inhumane acts' were satisfied by the conduct termed 'forced marriage' and would have entered convictions for that crime.

The Appeals Chamber reversed the Trial Chamber's legal holding, finding instead that inclusion of the phrase 'any other form of sexual violence' in Article 2(g) of the Statute does not necessitate a restrictive interpretation of the offence 'other inhumane acts' in Article 2(i) such that the latter could not include sexual violence crimes.[26] The Appeals Chamber reiterated that 'other inhumane acts' was intended to be residual so as to punish acts not specifically recognized as crimes against humanity, but which, in context, are of comparable gravity to the enumerated crimes against humanity.[27] Further, the Appeals Chamber found the majority of the Trial Chamber had erroneously considered 'forced marriage' to be subsumed by the crime of sexual slavery.[28] The Appeals Chamber found that this was not supported by the trial record, and, moreover, erroneous in law. The Appeals Chamber observed that:

> While "forced marriage" shares certain elements with sexual slavery such as non-consensual sex and deprivation of liberty, there are also distinguishing factors. First, "forced marriage" involves a perpetrator compelling a person by force or threat of force, through the words or conduct of the perpetrator or those associated with him, into a forced conjugal association with a another person resulting in great suffering, or serious physical or mental injury on the part of the victim. Second, unlike sexual slavery, "forced marriage" implies a relationship of exclusivity between the "husband" and "wife", which could lead to disciplinary consequences for breach of this exclusive arrangement. These distinctions imply that "forced marriage" is not predominantly a sexual crime.[29]

The Appeals Chamber ultimately considered that the conduct of 'forced marriage' amounted to an 'other inhumane act', a crime against humanity. It reasoned that acts of 'forced marriage' were of similar gravity to other underlying acts of crimes against humanity that are enumerated in the Statute, such as enslavement, imprisonment, torture, sexual slavery and sexual violence. To clarify the distinctions between 'forced marriage' and sexual slavery, the Appeals Chamber found that in the context of the Sierra Leone conflict,

> "forced marriage" describes a situation in which the perpetrator through his words or conduct, or those of someone for whose actions he is responsible, compels a person by force, threat of force, or coercion to serve as a conjugal partner resulting in severe suffering, or physical, mental or psychological injury to the victim.[30]

26 SCSL, Judgment, *AFRC*, Appeals Chamber, 22 February 2008, para. 186 (*AFRC* Appeals Judgment).

27 *AFRC* Appeals Judgment, at para. 183.

28 *AFRC* Appeals Judgment, at para. 188.

29 *AFRC* Appeals Judgment, at para. 195.

30 *AFRC* Appeals Judgment, at para. 196.

In so ruling, the Special Court is the first tribunal to recognize that acts of 'forced marriage' committed as part of a widespread or systematic attack against a civilian population may constitute a crime against humanity. The Appeals Chamber's finding that *'forced marriage' can constitute 'other inhumane acts' as a crime against humanity* is a significant pronouncement for the victims of these crimes, and more generally for the development of international criminal law. Notably, co-lawyers for civil parties at the Extraordinary Chambers in the Courts of Cambodia have now requested that Court to open a new supplemental investigation into the role of Tuol Sleng prison chief Kaing Guek Eav (alias 'Duch') in planning and ordering 'forced marriages',[31] and commentators have urged the ICC prosecutor to expand investigations of this offence in situations before that court.[32]

2. The CDF Case

Some critics of international Tribunals have rightly observed that trials have often failed to contain charges and evidence of sexual violence in cases alleging superior responsibility, and that they suggest the exercise of prosecutorial discretion to bring charges of murder, but not rape, for example, when both charges were apparently warranted.[33] At the Special Court, substantial procedural irregularities in the *CDF* case[34] resulted in the 'silencing sexual violence',[35] and no findings regarding gender-based violence.[36]

In *Prosecutor v. Fofana and Kondewa*, no charges for gender-based violence crimes were contained in the original indictment. However, before the trial began the Prosecution filed a motion[37] seeking leave to amend the original indictment in order to add counts of gender-based crimes, namely: rape, as a crime against humanity under Article 2(g) of the Statute; sexual slavery and any other forms of sexual violence as a crime against humanity under Article 2(g) of the Statute; other inhumane acts, as a crime against humanity under Article 2(i) of the Statute; and

31 Extraordinary Chambers in the Courts of Cambodia. Civil Parties' Co-Lawyers' Request for Supplementary Preliminary Investigations, 001/18-07-2007-ECCC/TC, 9 February 2009, available at http://www.eccc.gov.kh/english/cabinet/courtDoc/258/E11_EN.pdf (visited 21 February 2010); See also N. Jain, Forced Marriage as a Crime Against Humanity, 6 *J. Int'l Criminal Justice* (2008), 1013–1032, at 1022–1025.

32 See K. Carlson and D. Mazurana, Forced Marriage within the Lord's Resistance Army, *Uganda, Report* (Feinstein International Centre, Tufts University, May 2008) available at http://www.reliefweb.int/rw/RWB.NSF/db900SID/AMMF-7F3D3A?OpenDocument (visited 21 February 2010); Institute for War and Peace Reporting, ICC Investigative Strategy Under Fire, 17 October 2008, available at http://www.iwpr.net/pdf/IWPR_NL_DRC_special_102008.pdf, at 8–14 (visited 21 February 2010)).

33 See, e.g., C.A. MacKinnon, The ICTR's Legacy on Sexual Violence, 114 *New Eng. J. Int'l & Comp. L.* 101, 104.

34 SCSL, Judgment, *Moinina Fofana and Allieu Kondewa*, Trial Chamber, 2 August 2007 (*CDF* Trial Judgment). Samuel Hinga Norman was prosecuted jointly with Fofana and Kondewa, however Norman died on 22 February 2007 after the Judges heard closing arguments and while they were in deliberations pending their judgment. The Trial Chamber decided to terminate the proceedings against Norman and held that the trial judgment would be rendered only against Fofana and Kondewa on the basis of the entirety of the evidence adduced during the trial.

35 M.S. Kelsall and S. Stepakoff, 'When We Wanted to Talk About Rape': Silencing Sexual Violence at the Special Court for Sierra Leone, 1 *Int'l J. Transitional Justice* (2007), 355–374.

36 V. Oosterveld, The Special Court for Sierra Leone, Child Soldiers, and 'forced marriage': Providing Clarity or Confusion?, 45 *Canadian Yearbook of International Law* (2007); Kelsall and Stepakoff, ibid.; see also *CDF* Appeals Judgment, Partially Dissenting Opinion of Honourable Justice Renate Winter.

37 SCSL, Request for Leave to Amend the Indictment, *Norman et al.*, 9 February 2004.

outrages upon personal dignity as a war crime under Article 3(e) of the Statute. On 20 May 2004, the majority of the Trial Chamber denied the Prosecution's motion on the ground that granting the amendment would have prejudiced the accused and violated their right to be tried without undue delay and would constitute an abuse of process.[38] The Prosecution's application for leave to appeal the Trial Chamber Decision was denied by the majority of the Trial Chamber.[39]

In the course of the trial, the Prosecution requested the Trial Chamber to allow sexual violence evidence to be admissible for the proof of 'other inhumane acts', a crime against humanity, and cruel treatment, a war crime.[40] The Trial Chamber ruled, by majority, however, that evidence of sexual violence was not admissible under existing counts in the indictment.[41] The Prosecution's application for leave to appeal this decision was also denied by the majority of the Trial Chamber.[42]

On final appeal, the Prosecution filed two grounds of appeal against the Trial Chamber refusal to allow amendment of the indictment and failure to allow evidence on gender violence. The majority of the Appeals Chamber denied the Prosecution appeal against the decision on leave to amend the indictment.[43] The Appeals Chamber considered that the Prosecution in effect did not request a remedy within the Court's authority since it neither requested the Appeals Chamber to substitute an additional conviction or to order any further trial proceedings.[44] Further, the Appeals Chamber reasoned that the alleged error of law did not relate to any existing count in the indictment and as such did not affect the trial verdict.[45] However, the majority of the Appeals Chamber granted the Prosecution's appeal against the decision on admissibility of evidence of sexual violence.[46] The Appeal Chamber held that the Trial Chamber erred in denying admissibility of evidence on the basis that sexual violence charges were not included in the indictment,[47] because sexual violence may constitute the underlying acts for 'other inhumane acts' as well as 'cruel treatment' which were charged.[48] The Appeals Chamber accordingly held that evidence of sexual violence was relevant and the Trial Chamber erred in prospectively denying the admittance of such evidence.[49]

38 SCSL, Decision on Prosecution Request For Leave to Amend the Indictment, *Norman et al.*, Trial Chamber, 20 May 2004.

39 SCSL, Majority Decision on The Prosecution's Application for Leave to File an Interlocutory Appeal Against the Decision on the Prosecution Request for Leave to Amend the Indictment, *Norman et al.*, Trial Chamber, 2 August 2004.

40 SCSL, Urgent Prosecution Motion for a Ruling on the Admissibility of Evidence, *Norman et al.*, 15 February 2005.

41 SCSL, Decision on Urgent Prosecution Motion Filed on 15 February 2005 for a Ruling on the Admissibility of Evidence, *Norman et al.*, 22 June 2005, para. 19.

42 SCSL, Majority Decision on Request for Leave to Appeal Decision on Prosecution Motion for a Ruling on Admissibility of Evidence, *Norman et al.*, Trial Chamber, 9 December 2005.

43 *AFRC* Appeal Judgment, paras 410–427.

44 *AFRC* Appeal Judgment, paras 425–426.

45 *AFRC* Appeal Judgment, para. 426.

46 *AFRC* Appeal Judgment, paras 428–451.

47 *AFRC* Appeal Judgment, para. 450.

48 *AFRC* Appeal Judgment, para. 441.

49 *AFRC* Appeal Judgment, para. 446.

3. The RUF Case

The Trial Judgment[50] was rendered in February 2009 and the parties are expected to appeal the judgment; therefore this case is in effect *sub judice* and, thus, it is only possible to briefly restate the allegations by the Prosecution and the Trial Chamber's verdicts. According to the Prosecution, widespread sexual violence was committed against women and girls, including brutal rapes, often by multiple rapists, and 'forced marriage'. The Prosecution alleged that members of AFRC/RUF raped and abducted an unknown number of women and girls, used them as sex slaves and or forced them into 'marriages' and/or subjected them to other forms of sexual violence in numerous districts of Sierra Leone and Freetown. Sesay, Kallon and Gbao were charged with rape, sexual slavery and any form of sexual violence, and 'other inhumane acts', as crimes against humanity under Article 2 of the Statute. In addition, or in the alternative, the Prosecution charged 'outrages upon personal dignity', a violation of Article 3 common to the Geneva Conventions and of Additional Protocol II under Article 3 of the Statute. The Trial Chamber found all three accused guilty of numerous acts of gender-based violence pursuant to joint criminal enterprise liability, including rape, sexual slavery, 'forced marriage' as an 'other inhumane act', and outrages upon personal dignity.

4. The Taylor Case

At the time of writing, no findings have been made by the Court with respect to the allegations in the Special Court's last case.[51] The Prosecution alleges that members of RUF, AFRC, AFRC/RUF Junta or alliance and/or Liberian fighters raped and abducted an unknown number of women and girls and used them as sex slaves in numerous locations in several districts in Sierra Leone. Based on the allegation that the accused is responsible for the crimes of these actors, he is charged with rape and sexual slavery, as crimes against humanity, and in addition, or in the alternative, with outrage upon personal dignity, a violation of Article 3 common to the Geneva Conventions and of Additional Protocol II.

3. Offences Involving Children

A. Provisions of the Statute and Rules Regarding Juvenile Justice and Child Soldiers

1. Crimes Committed Against Children

Pursuant to Article 4(c) of the Statute, the Special Court has the power to prosecute persons who conscripted or enlisted children under the age of 15 years into armed forces or groups. Under the same Article, the Special Court also has the power to prosecute persons for using children under the age of 15 years to participate actively in hostilities. The Statute classifies these offences as 'other serious violations of international humanitarian law'.

Article 5(a) of the Statute, containing crimes under Sierra Leonean law, authorizes the Special Court to prosecute persons for:

---

50 SCSL, Judgment, *Issa Sesay, Morris Kallon, and Augustine Gbao*, Trial Chamber, 25 February 2009 (*RUF* Trial Judgment).

51 SCSL, *Charles Ghankay Taylor*.

Offences relating to the abuse of girls under the Prevention of Cruelty to Children Act, 1926 (Cap. 31):

i. Abusing a girl under 13 years of age …;
ii. Abusing a girl between 13 and 14 years of age …;
iii. Abduction of a girl for immoral purposes ….

2. Crimes Committed by Children and Juveniles

In addition to the provisions relating to crimes committed against children, the Statute includes provisions on crimes committed by children. In this regard, Article 7(1) of the Statute provides that the Special Court does not have jurisdiction to prosecute a person who was under the age of 15 years at the time of the alleged commission of the crime. Article 7(1) of the Statute provides that where a person, who was between the ages of 15 and 18 years at the time of the alleged commission of the crime, comes before the Special Court, the Special Court shall treat the individual with dignity and a sense of worth, having regard to the age of the individual as well the desirability of rehabilitating and reintegrating him or her into society.

Additionally, pursuant to Article 19(1) of the Statute, the Special Court may not imprison juvenile offenders. Instead, it may make a series of orders geared towards promoting their rehabilitation and reintegration into society such as counselling, care guidance and supervision orders, correctional, educational and vocational training programmes and foster care.[52] Article 15(5) of the Statute qualifies the Special Court's jurisdiction over juvenile offenders by requiring the Prosecution, when prosecuting juvenile offenders, to ensure that the child soldier rehabilitation programme[53] is not placed at risk and that, where appropriate, resort should be had to alternative truth and reconciliation mechanisms, to the extent of their availability.

Although these Statutory provisions represent new developments in international criminal law, they remain untested because the Prosecution did not press charges against any juvenile offenders.

3. Child Victims and Witnesses

The Statute and Rules contain specific provisions on victims and witnesses who are children in order to cater for their particular situation. Under Article 16(4) of the Statute, the Registrar of the Special Court has established a Victims and Witnesses Unit responsible for providing protection and security for witnesses and victims who appear before the Special Court and who may be vulnerable to external influence on account of their testimony. The Victims and Witnesses Unit also offers various services to witnesses and victims, including that of counselling. Rule 34(A)(iii) of the Rules specifically provides that counselling and other forms of assistance are to be provided especially in cases involving crimes against children.

The Rules also tailor the provision of testimony by children to their particular situation. Thus, Rule 90 of the Rules provides that:

> A child shall be permitted to testify if the Chamber is of the opinion that he is sufficiently mature to be able to report the facts of which he had knowledge, that he understands the duty to tell the truth, and is not subject to undue influence. However, he shall not be compelled to testify by solemn declaration.

52 Article 7(2) SCSLSt.
53 See SC Res. 1270 (1999), para. 18.

Protective measures such as a pseudonym, and facial and voice distortion are also available to these victims when they testify, as long as the measures are consistent with the rights of the accused.[54] In practice, the Trial Chambers have also ordered that child witnesses be allowed to testify with the aid of closed-circuit television, which may be observed by the defence, the defendant, the Prosecution and the Trial Chamber, but not the public.[55]

The Statute also establishes that judges and staff should have expertise in working with children and juveniles. Article 13 of the Statute states that 'in the overall composition of the Chambers, due account shall be taken of the experience of the judges in ... juvenile justice'. Under Articles 15(4) and 16(4) of the Statute respectively, Special Court staff, particularly in the Office of the Prosecutor and the Victims and Witnesses Unit, should include experts in trauma, violence against children and juvenile justice.[56]

B. Case Law on Child Soldiers

All of the accused persons at the Special Court have been charged with the crime of conscripting or enlisting children under the age of 15 or using them to participate actively in hostilities, pursuant to Article 4(c) of the Statute. The Court's jurisprudence has elaborated legal protections available for children under international humanitarian law and will hopefully contribute to mechanisms that reduce or eliminate violence committed against them during armed conflict. The following section takes a closer look at the legal and factual findings in each of the principal cases.

1. The Norman Child Recruitment Decision

The issue of child soldiers was addressed by the Special Court for the first time on 31 May 2004, in the case of *Prosecutor v. Samuel Hinga Norman*. The accused, Samuel Hinga Norman (subsequently deceased), was charged together with Moinina Fofana and Allieu Kondewa of the CDF with, *inter alia*, child enlistment and the use of child soldiers under Article 4(c) of the Statute. Norman challenged the jurisdiction of the Special Court to prosecute him for this crime, arguing that Article 4(c) violated the principle of *nullum crimen sine lege* because child recruitment was not a crime under customary international law at the time alleged in the indictment, that is, from 30 November 1996.[57] As a preliminary motion regarding jurisdiction, the matter was referred to the Appeals Chamber for determination.

The Appeals Chamber noted that the original proposal for the Statute submitted by the UN Secretary-General referred to the crime of 'abduction and forced recruitment of children under the age of 15 years into armed forces or groups for the purpose of using them to participate actively in hostilities'. In his report on the establishment of a Special Court the Secretary-General explained that his proposed formulation of the crime was based on his doubt as to the customary nature

---

54 Rule 75 SCSL RPE.

55 See, e.g., SCSL, *Issa Sesay, Morris Kallon, and Augustine Gbao*, Decision on Prosecution Motion for Modification of Protective Measures for Witnesses, Trial Chamber, 5 July 2004, discussing *Maryland v. Craig*, 497 U.S. 836 (1990) (holding that the use of closed circuit television does not violate the constitutional right of an accused to confrontation if it is necessary in the opinion of the Court to protect a child witness from psychological harm).

56 See also Rule 34(B) SCSL RPE.

57 SCSL, Decision on Preliminary Motion Based on Lack of Jurisdiction (Child Recruitment), *Sam Hinga Norman*, 31 May 2004 ('*Norman* Child Recruitment Decision'), paras 1, 3.

of formulation in the ICC Statute.[58] The original proposal of the Secretary-General reflected, according to the Appeals Chamber, 'some uncertainty as to the customary international law nature of the crime of conscripting or enlisting children'.[59] Nonetheless, the Secretary-General's proposal was subsequently changed by the Security Council to reflect the ICC Statute's formulation of the crime as 'conscripting or enlisting children under the age of 15 years into armed forces or groups or using them to participate actively in hostilities' (referred to collectively as 'child recruitment').[60] The question therefore was whether enlistment (i.e., when a child *voluntarily* joins an armed force or armed group) constituted an offence in international law at the relevant time.

The Appeals Chamber, therefore, needed to satisfy itself that the crime as set out in Article 4(c) of the Statute was recognized as a crime entailing individual criminal responsibility under customary international law at the relevant time. The Appeals Chamber undertook a thorough review of relevant treaties, including the 1949 Geneva Conventions, the 1977 Protocols Additional thereto, and the Convention on the Rights of the Child, before concluding that treaty law prohibited child recruitment.[61] The Appeals Chamber similarly found that child recruitment was prohibited in customary international law in the period prior to 1996, having ascertained the relevant state practice and *opinio juris*.[62]

Having so concluded, the Appeals Chamber turned to the issue of whether the prohibition on child recruitment also entailed individual criminal responsibility at the time in question. In answering in the affirmative, the Appeals Chamber pointed to, *inter alia*, extensive domestic legislation that criminalized child recruitment prior to 1996. Accordingly, a majority of the Appeals Chamber held that child recruitment was criminalized by November 1996 – the relevant time for the purposes of the indictment – in a considerable number of states of different legal traditions (e.g., common law, civil law, Sharia law).

2. The AFRC and CDF Cases

To date, the Special Court has completed proceedings in two cases involving prosecutions for the offence of child recruitment. In June 2007, Trial Chamber II delivered the first judgment in international criminal law convicting persons of child recruitment. In the case against the three members of the AFRC, the Prosecution had charged the three *AFRC* accused with, *inter alia*:

---

58 The Secretary-General's letter states: 'while the prohibition on child recruitment has by now acquired a customary international law status, it is far less clear whether it is customarily recognized as a war crime entailing the individual criminal responsibility of the accused. Owing to the doubtful customary nature of the ICC Statutory crime which criminalizes the conscription or enlistment of children under the age of 14, whether forced or "voluntary", the crime which is included in Article 4(c) of the Statute of the Special Court is not the equivalent of the ICC provision.' *Report of the Secretary-General on the establishment of a Special Court for Sierra Leone*, UN doc. S/2000/915, 4 October 2000, paras 17–18.

59 *Norman* Child Recruitment Decision, para. 8.

60 See *Letter dated 22 December 2000 from the President of the Security Council addressed to the Secretary-General*, UN doc. S/2000/1234, 4 October 2000, at 5.

61 *Norman* Child Recruitment Decision, paras 10–16.

62 *Norman* Child Recruitment Decision, paras 17–24.

> CONSCRIPTING or ENLISTING children under the age of 15 years into armed forces or groups, or USING them to participate actively in hostilities, an other serious violation of international humanitarian law, punishable under Article 4.c of the Statute.[63]

Several months later, in August 2007, Trial Chamber I delivered its judgment in the case against Fofana and Kondewa, the two members of the CDF. In *CDF*, the Prosecution phrased the count differently, charging the CDF accused instead with:

> ENLISTING children under the age of 15 years into armed forces or groups or USING them to participate actively in hostilities, an other serious violation of international humanitarian law, punishable under Article 4.c of the Statute.[64]

These two cases are the first international criminal law judgments involving these crimes, and therefore they are the first to elaborate the application of the law to facts presented in a case. The Trial Chambers adopted somewhat varying approaches to the elements of the crimes.

In *AFRC*, Trial Chamber II adopted the ICC elements of crimes[65] in interpreting Article 4(c) of the Statute, namely: (i) the perpetrator conscripted or enlisted one or more persons into an armed force or group or used one or more persons to participate actively in hostilities; (ii) such person or persons were under the age of 15 years; (iii) the perpetrator knew or should have known that such person or persons were under the age of 15 years; (iv) the conduct took place in the context of and was associated with an armed conflict; and (v) the perpetrator was aware of the factual circumstances that established the existence of an armed conflict.[66]

In *CDF*, Trial Chamber I, however, concluded that the elements of the crime of 'enlisting' children under the age of 15 years into armed forces or groups are: (i) one or more persons were enlisted, either voluntarily or compulsorily, into an armed force or group by the accused; (ii) such person or persons were under the age of 15 years; (iii) the accused knew or had reason to know that such person or persons were under the age of 15 years; and (iv) the accused intended to enlist the said persons into the armed force or group.[67] On the issue of 'using' children under the age of 15 years to participate actively in hostilities, Trial Chamber I considered the elements to be: (i) one or more persons were used by the accused to actively participate in hostilities; (ii) such person or persons were under the age of 15 years; (iii) the accused knew or had reason to know that such person or persons were under the age of 15 years; and (iv) the accused intended to use the said persons to actively participate in hostilities.[68]

Both Trial Chambers and the Appeals Chamber have considered Article 4(c) of the Statute to contain one crime, the *actus reus* of which can be satisfied in three different ways: by conscripting children under the age of 15, by enlisting them or by using them to participate in hostilities.[69]

63 SCSL, Further Amended Consolidated Indictment, *AFRC*, 18 February 2005, Count 12 (emphasis added).

64 SCSL, Indictment, *CDF*, 5 February 2004, Count 8 (emphasis added).

65 Art. 8 (2)(b)(xxvi) ICC EC.

66 SCSL, Judgment, *AFRC*, Trial Chamber, 20 June 2007, para. 729 (*AFRC* Trial Judgment).

67 SCSL, Judgment, *CDF*, Trial Chamber, 2 August 2007, para. 195 (*CDF* Trial Judgment).

68 *CDF* Trial Judgment, para. 196.

69 *AFRC* Trial Judgment, para. 733; *CDF* Appeal Judgment, para. 139.

(a) Conscription and enlistment into an armed force or group

Adopting language from the *Norman* Child Recruitment Decision, Trial Chamber II considered that '"[c]onscription" implies compulsion, in some instances through the force of law'. It encompasses 'acts of coercion, such as abductions and forced recruitment, by an armed group against children, committed for the purpose of using them to participate actively in hostilities'.[70] This formulation of conscription as 'forcible recruitment' has been followed by an International Criminal Court (ICC) Pre-Trial Chamber in the *Prosecutor v. Thomas Lubanga Dyilo*.[71]

By contrast, 'enlistment' was defined by Trial Chamber II as 'accepting and enrolling individuals when they volunteer to join an armed force or group'. This definition of the crime thus excludes consent on behalf of the child as a valid defence.[72] Trial Chamber I commented, in a statement that blurs the line between conscription and enlistment, that reference to 'enlistment' in the indictment 'could encompass both *voluntary* enlistment and *forced* enlistment into armed forces or groups, forced enlistment being the aggravated form of the crime'.[73] In the view of Trial Chamber I, 'the distinction between voluntary enlistment and conscription is somewhat contrived. Attributing voluntary enlistment in armed forces or groups to a child under the age of 15 years, particularly in a conflict setting where human rights abuses are rife, is ... of questionable merit.'[74] Trial Chamber I preferred instead that forced enlistment should be treated as 'the aggravated form of the crime'.[75]

The findings of the Trial Chambers are instructive for their treatment of factual situations that help demonstrate some of the difficulties in drawing sharp lines between enlistment, conscription and use. In *AFRC*, the Trial Chamber examined evidence of children who were abducted from their villages, forced to march with combatants, to fetch water and to carry their rice and luggage. Upon arrival at their headquarters camp, the children were 'forced to undergo military training' during which they were given daily doses of narcotics including 'injections and tablets of drugs which he believed to be cocaine'.[76] Following training, some children were forced to enter battle while others continued to carry the property of older fighters.[77] The Trial Chamber considered that each of these children had been conscripted into the AFRC. The Trial Chamber also described a girl child soldier who was abducted, forced to 'marry' her captor, and subsequently 'forced to undergo military training', after which she remained sexually enslaved to her 'husband' and was forced to participate in combat.[78]

In *CDF*, the majority of Trial Chamber I found Kondewa criminally responsible for enlisting a child into the Kamajor society, which comprised part of the fighting force (discussed in greater detail below). Trial Chamber I noted that initiation into the Kamajor society did not necessarily

70 *AFRC* Trial Judgment, para. 734.

71 ICC, *Thomas Lubanga Dyilo*, ICC-01/04-01/06, 29, January 2007, para. 246, citing *Norman* Child Recruitment Decision, Dissenting Opinion of Justice Robertson.

72 *AFRC* Trial Judgment, para. 735.

73 CDF Trial Judgment, para. 192. See also ICC, *Joseph Kony et al.*, ICC-02/04-01/05, Pre-Trial Chamber II, Warrant of Arrest for Joseph Kony issued on 8 July 2005 as amended on 27 September 2005, 27 September 2005, at 13 (charging 'enlisting, through *abduction*') (emphasis added).

74 *CDF* Trial Judgment, at para. 192. See also: *CDF* Appeal Judgment, at para. 140: 'where a child under the age of 15 years is allowed to voluntarily join an armed force or group, his or her consent is not a valid defence.'

75 *CDF* Trial Judgment, para. 192.

76 *AFRC* Trial Judgment, paras 1254, 1256.

77 *AFRC* Trial Judgment, paras 1255, 1256.

78 *AFRC* Trial Judgment, para. 1260 discussing protected witness TF1-085.

amount to enlistment, and that children were initiated for other reasons. However, the Trial Chamber examined evidence that a child was initiated into the CDF along with around 20 other young boys, and that Kondewa told the boys that they would be made powerful for fighting and gave them a potion to rub on their bodies before going into battle.[79] The Trial Chamber also observed that initiates were subsequently given military training, and that following training, initiates were sent into battle. In light of these findings, Trial Chamber I found that through initiation the children 'had taken the first step in becoming fighters'.[80] Consequently, although holding that initiating children is not *per se* an international crime, Trial Chamber I considered that 'evidence of "initiation" may be of relevance in establishing liability' for child recruitment.[81] Trial Chamber I held that the initiation performed by Kondewa was an act analogous to enlistment.

On appeal, the Appeals Chamber clarified that child recruitment may be committed irrespective of the number of children recruited by an accused. However, the majority of the Appeals Chamber overturned Kondewa's conviction. The Appeals Chamber explained that the child in question had already been enlisted into the CDF prior to his initiation by Kondewa, therefore Kondewa could not have enlisted him. In arriving at this conclusion the Appeals Chamber considered evidence demonstrating that the witness was forced to carry looted property by the CDF after he had been captured by them, but before Kondewa had initiated him.[82] Thus, the Appeals judgment could be understood to provide that forced attachment to an armed group, even in the absence of military training, can amount to enlistment.

Aspects of the definition of an armed group are also suggested by the treatment of the Kamajor society in *CDF*. The Kamajor society comprised traditional Mende hunters, predominantly in chiefdoms of the southern province of Sierra Leone, who were later organized for community defence purposes and eventually into a fighting force called the Civil Defence Forces. Trial Chamber I followed the definition of 'armed groups' given in the *Tadic* Appeal Judgement:

> One should distinguish the situation of individuals acting on behalf of a State without specific instructions, from that of individuals making up *an organised and hierarchically structured group*, such as a military unit or, in case of war or civil strife, armed bands of irregulars or rebels. Plainly, an organised group differs from an individual in that the former normally has a structure, a chain of command and a set of rules as well as the outward symbols of authority. Normally a member of the group does not act on his own but conforms to the standards prevailing in the group and is subject to the authority of the head of the group.[83]

Additional questions did not arise on appeal and remain to be addressed, such as what constitutes an armed group in the context of dual/multi-purpose groups, and whether conscription or enlistment of a child into a non-military part of the group constitutes recruitment into an armed group.

---

79 *CDF* Trial Judgment, para. 968.

80 *CDF* Trial Judgment, para. 970.

81 *CDF* Trial Judgment, para. 198.

82 *CDF* Appeal Judgment, paras 142–145. The looted property consisted of tape, used clothing and seed rice. See SCSL Transcript, *CDF*, Trial Chamber, 2 November 2004, at 33–35.

83 *CDF* Trial Judgment, at para. 194 citing *Tadić* Appeal Judgment, para. 120 (emphasis in original); see also *AFRC* Trial Judgment at para. 738. (Trial Chamber II stated similar requirements in slightly different terms: 'The elements of "armed forces or groups" entail that the armed forces or groups must be under responsible command, which entails a degree of organization which should be such as to enable the armed groups to plan and carry out concerted military operations and to impose discipline within the armed group.')

The Special Court Appeals Chamber has held that: 'for enlistment there must be a nexus between the act of the accused and the child joining the armed force or group. There must also be knowledge on the part of the accused that the child is under the age of 15 years and that he or she may be trained for combat. Whether such a nexus exists is a question of fact which must be determined on a case-by-case basis.'[84] Furthermore, the Appeals Chamber reasoned that, in situations in which 'the armed group is not a conventional military organization, "enlistment" cannot narrowly be defined as a formal process. The Appeals Chamber regards "enlistment" in the broad sense as including any conduct which evidences acceptance of the child as a part of the militia. Such conduct would include making him participate in military operations.'[85] In a partially dissenting opinion to the CDF Appeal judgment, Judge Winter noted that often the facts do not allow for facile differentiation of the modes of perpetration, particularly

> in the situation where there are no formal or informal processes for enlisting individuals, especially children, the "use" of a child to participate actively in hostilities may amount to enlistment. However, where the evidence demonstrates the existence of a process that contributes to the enrolment and acceptance of a child into an armed force or group, logic dictates that "use" of a child cannot constitute enlistment.[86]

(b) Use to participate actively in hostilities

Both Trial Chambers have adopted the interpretation of 'using them to participate actively in hostilities' contained in a footnote to the draft ICC Statute which purports to distinguish 'active participation' from 'direct participation':[87]

> The words "using" and "participate [actively]" have been adopted in order to cover both direct participation in combat and also active participation in military activities linked to combat such as scouting, spying, sabotage and use of children such as decoys, couriers or at military checkpoints. It would not cover activities clearly unrelated to the hostilities such as food deliveries to an airbase or the use of domestic staff in an Officer's accommodation. However, use of children in a direct support function such as acting as bearers to take supplies to the front line or activities at the front line itself would be included within the terminology.

The ICRC commentary on the Rome Statute reflects this distinction between active and direct participation in largely similar terms[88] and the expansive definition of active participation was

84 *CDF* Appeal Judgment, para. 141.

85 *CDF* Appeal Judgment, para. 144.

86 *CDF* Appeal Judgment, Dissenting Opinion of Justice Winter, para. 13.

87 *AFRC* Trial Judgment, paras 736–737; CDF Judgment, para. 193; *Draft Statute for the International Criminal Court, Report of the Preparatory Committee on the Establishment of an International Criminal Court*. UN doc. A/CONF.183/2/Add.1, 14 April 1998, at 21, n. 12.

88 BRCS and ICRC, *Customary International Humanitarian Law*, Vol. 2, part 2 (Cambridge: Cambridge University Press, 2005), para. 599, stating that active participation includes taking a 'direct part in the fighting and active participation in related activities, such as reconnaissance, espionage, and sabotage. The same applies to the use of children as decoys, as messengers or at military checkpoints.'

explicitly adopted in the *Lubanga* case.[89] In *AFRC*, Trial Chamber II applied an instrumentalist interpretation of using children to 'participate actively in hostilities' stating that:

> the use of children to participate actively in hostilities is not limited to participation in combat. An armed force requires logistical support to maintain its operations. Any labour or support that gives effect to, or helps maintain, operations in a conflict constitutes active participation.[90]

Applying this test to the facts of the case, the Trial Chamber ruled that because the underlying conflict involved the mining of diamonds to raise revenue for the war effort, using children to guard diamond mines constituted use of the child pursuant to Article 4(c) of the Statute.[91] The Trial Chamber also separately found that 'forcing children to undergo military training in a hostile environment constitutes illegal use of children pursuant to Article 4.c'.[92] Trial Chamber II found the three AFRC accused individually criminally responsible for planning the use of child soldiers, and these convictions were upheld on appeal.

3. The RUF and Taylor Cases

In each of the two remaining cases, the Prosecution has charged the accused with, *inter alia*:

> CONSCRIPTING or ENLISTING children under the age of 15 years into armed forces or groups, or USING them to participate actively in hostilities, an other serious violation of international humanitarian law, punishable under Article 4.c of the Statute.[93]

The Trial Chamber convicted Issa Sesay and Morris Kallon for planning the use of child soldiers to participate actively in hostilities and acquitted Augustine Gbao of the charge. It is expected that the parties will file appeals in the case in May 2009. The *Taylor* case is currently at trial.

4. Conclusion

The jurisprudence of the Special Court on the issues of gender-based violence and child soldiers is part of a much broader international effort to combat these problems. Human rights organizations, agencies within the UN, and other international courts are all focusing increasing and much needed – attention on these crimes.

As the first international court to prosecute and convict individuals for sexual slavery, 'forced marriage' as an 'other inhumane act', and recruiting and using child soldiers, the Special Court begun to elaborate the underlying prohibitions and the criminal responsibility for violating those prohibitions. It is hoped that this jurisprudence will assist future courts to adjudicate these complex questions of law.

---

89 ICC, Decision on the Confirmation of Charges, *Lubanga*, Pre-Trial Chamber, 29 January 2007, paras 259–264.

90 AFRC Trial Judgment, at para. 1266; See also *Norman* Child Recruitment Decision, Dissenting Opinion of Justice Robertson, at para. 5(c).

91 AFRC Trial Judgment, at para. 1267.

92 AFRC Trial Judgment, at para. 1278.

93 SCSL, Corrected Amended Consolidated Indictment, *RUF*, 2 August 2006, Count 12; SCSL, Prosecution's Second Amended Indictment, *Taylor*, Case No. SCSL-2003-01-PT, 29 May 2007.

Chapter 16

The War Crimes Chamber in the Court of Bosnia and Herzegovina

Melika Murtezić

1. Introduction

Domestic courts in Bosnia and Herzegovina (BiH) made an effort to try war crimes during and immediately after the conflict in the territory of BiH (1992–1995). Many factors influenced these proceedings – such as the lack of skilled members of the legal profession and judiciary, physical destruction and lack of proper equipment or facilities – and considerably disadvantaged the ability of courts to deliver justice. The situation did not improve after the end of the hostilities because of the complexities of the legal framework, with two separate entities,[1] and at the same time with distinct legal systems, ministries of justice, police forces, as well as different approaches to the prosecution of war crimes.

In this context, the War Crimes Chamber (WCC) was established within the Court of Bosnia and Herzegovina (Court of BiH) in early 2005. The creation of the WCC was considered necessary to enable effective war crimes prosecutions in Bosnia and was part of an overhaul of the national justice system by the High Representative for BiH.[2] Such overhaul included numerous reforms of Bosnian criminal law, among them the introduction in 2003 of the state-level Criminal Code and Criminal Procedure Code of BiH, the former of which established the State Court's jurisdiction over war crimes.

The WCC has both Trial and Appeals Chambers. Section I for War Crimes has five first-instance court panels composed of three judges each, two international and one national. Section I of the Appellate Division consists of one second-instance court panel composed of three judges, two international and one national. This panel decides upon the appeals lodged against the decision of Section I of the Criminal Division. As a rule, the national judge is the president of the panel both in first instance and in the appellate proceedings. The support staff of the panels is also international and national in its composition.

The *raison d'être* of the international presence is to ensure that rule of law and international human rights standards are applied in proceedings, in light of the fact that the entire legal system has been rebuilt in view of the sensitivity and the complexity of the cases being prosecuted. However, it is anticipated that the international presence may be replaced in its entirety by 2010, assuming that the state and the national judiciary system will by then be fully capable of trying war crimes suspects by taking advantage of the many positive years of international assistance and presence.

1 Federation of Bosnia and Herzegovina and Republika Srpska, as established under Annex 4 of the General Framework Agreement for Peace in Bosnia and Herzegovina (Dayton Peace Agreement), signed on 14 December 1995 in Paris.

2 The Office of the High Representative (OHR) was established under the Dayton Peace Agreement.

The goal is to build on the existing expertise of local professionals within the justice sector to ensure a sustainable domestic capacity to address war crimes cases after international involvement has ceased.

As part of the Court of BiH, the WCC exercises supreme jurisdiction over the most serious war crimes cases in Bosnia. First, the WCC is trying the cases of the lower- to mid-level perpetrators that are referred to it by the ICTY pursuant to Rule 11*bis* of the ICTY Rules of Procedure and Evidence (RPE). Therefore the WCC is crucial for the completion strategy of the ICTY. In addition to Rule 11*bis* cases, the WCC is responsible for those cases submitted to the Prosecutor's Office of BiH by the Office of the Prosecutor (OTP) of the ICTY, when investigations have not been completed.

As a mark of the progress made by the WCC in its establishment phase, the ICTY Appeals Chamber referred the first-ever case to it on 1 September 2005. In doing so, it confirmed that the WCC was fully capable of providing the accused, Radovan Stanković, with a fair trial. In accordance with that decision, Stanković was physically transferred to Bosnia on 29 September 2005, to stand trial before the WCC on charges of crimes against humanity, including enslavement and rape. The ICTY has since referred other cases, including those of Gojko Jankovic, Zeljko Mejakic and others, Pasko Ljubicic, Savo Todovic and Mitar Rasevic to the WCC. On 14 November 2006, the Court pronounced the first instance verdict, found the accused Radovan Stanković guilty of crimes against humanity and sentenced him to 16 years imprisonment. On 28 March 2007, the Appellate Panel of Section I for War Crimes of the Court BiH handed down the final verdict in the case of Radovan Stanković, modifying the sentence handed down by the Trial Panel from 16 years to 20 years long-term imprisonment.

The WCC also has jurisdiction over Rules of the Road cases. The Rules of the Road procedure was first established in response to the widespread fear of arbitrary arrest and detention immediately after the conflict in Bosnia. Under this procedure, the relevant authorities in Bosnia were required to submit every war crime case proposed for prosecution in Bosnia to the OTP of the ICTY, to determine whether the evidence was sufficient by international standards before proceeding to arrest. The principal aim of this procedure was to ensure freedom of movement for returnees throughout BiH in order to prevent arbitrary arrest, detentions and harassment of ethnic groups. The ICTY ceased reviewing cases on 1 October 2004. The Rules of the Road cases are handled in two ways. According to Article 449(2) of the Criminal Procedure Code of BiH (CPC BiH), cases falling within the competence of the Court which are pending before other courts or prosecutor's offices and where the case has not led to a legally effective or confirmed indictment shall be finalized by these courts unless the Court, *ex officio* or upon the reasoned proposal of the parties or defence attorney, decide to take on such a case. If, however, the indictment has been legally effective or confirmed prior to the entry into force of the CPC BiH (1 March 2003), the cases shall be finalized by these courts according to Article 449(1) CPC BiH, so that the case remains with the relevant cantonal or district court to complete the proceedings.

2. Application of Substantive Law

A. General Features

During the 1992–1995 conflict in the territory of BiH, the 1976 Criminal Code (CC) of Socialist Federal Republic of Yugoslavia (SFRJ) was in force as it had been adopted as the law of the Republic of Bosnia and Herzegovina. The CC SFRY contains relevant provisions recognizing genocide and war crimes as criminal offences, so the application of the Criminal Code of BiH to these criminal offences creates no problem. However, crimes against humanity and the concept of command responsibility as such were not codified in the laws that were in force at the time of commission of the criminal offences, which is often used by the defence to raise objections in the proceedings.

Nevertheless, despite the fact that crimes against humanity were not precisely defined in the laws of BiH which were in force in the relevant period, individual criminal offences included in Article 172 of the 2003 Criminal Code of BiH (Crimes against Humanity)[3] were provided by laws in force in the relevant time period. The fact that criminal legislation in the territory of Bosnia and Herzegovina was changed on several occasions in the period 1992–2003 additionally burdens the

---

3 Art. 172, Crimes against Humanity, CC BiH:

(1) Whoever, as part of a widespread or systematic attack directed against any civilian population, with knowledge of such an attack perpetrates any of the following acts:

a) Depriving another person of his life (murder);
b) Extermination;
c) Enslavement;
d) Deportation or forcible transfer of population;
e) Imprisonment or other severe deprivation of physical liberty in violation of fundamental rules of international law;
f) Torture;
g) Coercing another by force or by threat of immediate attack upon his life or limb, or the life or limb of a person close to him, to sexual intercourse or an equivalent sexual act (rape), sexual slavery, enforced prostitution, forced pregnancy, enforced sterilization or any other form of sexual violence of comparable gravity;
h) Persecutions against any identifiable group or collectivity on political, racial, national, ethnic, cultural, religious or sexual gender or other grounds that are universally recognized as impermissible under international law, in connection with any offence listed in this paragraph of this Code, any offence listed in this Code or any offence falling under the competence of the Court of Bosnia and Herzegovina;
i) Enforced disappearance of persons;
j) The crime of apartheid;
k) Other inhumane acts of a similar character intentionally causing great suffering, or serious injury to body or to physical or mental health;
shall be punished by imprisonment for a term not less than ten years or long-term imprisonment.

(2) For the purpose of paragraph 1 of this Article the following terms shall have the following meanings:

a) *Attack directed against any civilian population* means a course of conduct involving the multiple perpetrations of acts referred to in paragraph 1 of this Article against any civilian population, pursuant to or in furtherance of a State or organizational policy to commit such attack.
b) *Extermination* includes the intentional infliction of conditions of life, especially deprivation of access to food and medicines, calculated to bring about the destruction of part of a population.
c) *Enslavement* means the exercise of any or all of the powers attaching to the right of ownership over a person, and includes the exercise of such power in the course of trafficking in persons, in particular women and children.
d) *Deportation or forcible transfer of population* means forced displacement of the persons concerned by expulsion or other coercive acts from the area in which they are lawfully present, without grounds permitted under international law.
e) *Torture* means the intentional infliction of severe pain or suffering, whether physical or mental, upon a person in the custody or under control of the accused; except that torture shall not include pain or suffering arising only from, or being inherent in or incidental to, lawful sanctions.

situation. The Criminal Code of Bosnia and Herzegovina (CC BiH) was passed by decision of the High Representative on 24 January 2003, and entered into force on 1 March 2006.[4]

B. The Principles of Legality and of Favor Rei

The Court of BiH had initially to provide its interpretation on the basic issues of compliance of the applicable substantive criminal law with the principles of legality and of *favor rei*. In *Stanković*, the Court found[5] that Article 172 CC BiH introducing crimes against humanity was applicable

f) *Forced pregnancy* means the unlawful confinement of a woman forcibly made pregnant, with the intent of affecting the ethnic composition of any population or carrying out other grave violations of international law.
g) *Persecution* means the intentional and severe deprivation of fundamental rights, contrary to international law, by reason of the identity of a group or collectivity.
h) *Enforced disappearance of persons* means the arrest, detention or abduction of persons by, or with the authorization, support or acquiescence of, a State or a political organization, followed by a refusal to acknowledge that deprivation of freedom or to give information on the fate or whereabouts of those persons, with an aim of removing them from the protection of the law for a prolonged period of time.
i) *The crime of apartheid* means inhumane acts of a character similar to those referred to in paragraph 1 of this Article, perpetrated in the context of an institutionalized regime of systematic oppression and domination by one racial group over any other racial group or groups and perpetrated with an aim of maintaining that regime.

4 Art. 256 CC BiH.

5 Verdict, *Radovan Stanković*, Trial Panel, 14 November 2006, No. X-KR-05/70, pp. 32–33: 'As regards the substantive law to be applied given the time of the perpetration of offense, the Court has accepted the legal qualification of the charges and sentenced the accused for the criminal offense of Crimes against Humanity, in violation of Article 172 paragraph 1 item c), e), f) and g) of the Criminal Code of Bosnia and Herzegovina.

Given the time of the perpetration of the offense and the substantive law in effect at that time, the Court finds relevant the principle of legality and the principle of time constraints regarding the applicability of the criminal code:

Article 3 of the CC of BiH stipulates the principle of legality according to which no punishment or other criminal sanction may be imposed on any person for an act which, prior to being perpetrated, has not been defined as a criminal offense by law or international law, and for which a punishment has not been prescribed by law. Article 4 of the CC of BiH (Time Constraints Regarding Applicability) stipulates that the law that was in effect at the time when the criminal offense was perpetrated shall apply to the perpetrator of the criminal offense, and if the law has been amended on one or more occasions after the criminal offense was perpetrated, the law that is more lenient to the perpetrator shall be applied. The principle of legality is also stipulated in Article 7(1) of the ECHR which supersedes all national legislation of BiH (Article 2.2 of the BiH Constitution). The said Article of the ECHR reads: "No one shall be held guilty of any criminal offense on account of any act or omission which did not constitute a criminal offense under national or international law at the time when it was committed. Nor shall a heavier penalty be imposed than the one that was applicable at the time the criminal offense was committed". Thus, a heavier penalty than the one that was applicable at the time the criminal offense was committed is prohibited. Therefore, this provision bars the imposition of a heavier penalty without prescribing mandatory application of the law that is more lenient to the accused in comparison with the penalty applicable at the time of the perpetration of criminal offense. Article 7(2) of the ECHR stipulates that: "This article shall not prejudice the trial and punishment of any person for any act or omission which, at the time when it was committed, was criminal according to the general principles of law recognized by civilized nations".

Article 15 (1) of the International Covenant on Civil and Political Rights (hereinafter: ICCPR) stipulates: "No one shall be held guilty of any criminal offense on account of any act or omission which did not constitute

to conducts committed in 1992, before its entry into force, despite the general provisions under Articles 3 and 4 of the same Code. Such conclusion was reached drawing on the superseding effect of Article 7(2) ECHR, which allows for penalization of conducts on the basis of the

---

a criminal offense, under national or international law, at the time when it was committed. Nor shall a heavier penalty be imposed than the one that was applicable at the time when the criminal offense was committed if, subsequent to the commission of the offense, provision is made by law for the imposition of a lighter penalty, the offender shall benefit thereby."

Article 15 (2) of the ICCPR prescribes that "nothing in this article shall prejudice the trial and punishment of any person for any act or omission which, at the time when it was committed, was criminal according to the general principles of law recognized by the community of nations."

Finally, Article 4a) of the CC of BiH stipulates that Articles 3 and 4 of the CC of BiH shall not prejudice the trial and punishment of any person for any act or omission which, at the time when it was committed, was criminal according to the general principles of international law, whereby provision of Article 7(2) of the ECHR has actually been adopted enabling a significant departure from the principles of Article 4 of the CC of BiH, as well as a departure from the mandatory application of a more lenient law in proceedings conducted for acts which are criminal according to international law, which is exactly the case in the proceedings against the accused, because this is exactly an incrimination which includes a violation of international law. This is the position so far taken in the Court of BiH case law.

The State of Bosnia and Herzegovina, as a successor to the former Yugoslavia, ratified the ECHR and the ICCPR. Therefore, these treaties are binding on the State of Bosnia and Herzegovina and they must be applied by the authorities of BiH. Therefore, Article 4a) of the CC of BiH is only a domestic legal reminder, as it would not be necessary for the application of these treaties. For the same reason, all the courts in BiH are bound by the mentioned treaties and a provision like Article 4a) of the CC of BiH is not needed for its application.

Article 172 of the CC of BiH prescribes Crimes against Humanity like Article 5 of the ICTY Statute (Article 5 of the ICTY Statute defines Crimes against Humanity as specific individual acts "when committed in armed conflict, whether international or internal in character, and directed against any civilian population"). At the critical period, Crimes against Humanity were not explicitly prescribed by the criminal legislation in Bosnia and Herzegovina.

Customary status of punishability of Crimes against Humanity and individual responsibility for its commission in 1992 has been confirmed by the UN Secretary General, International Law Commission, as well as the jurisprudence of ICTY and the International Criminal Tribunal for Rwanda (ICTR). These institutions found that the punishability of crimes against humanity represents an imperative standard of international law or *jus cogens*, therefore, it appears to be beyond dispute that in 1992 Crimes against Humanity were part of International Customary Law. That conclusion was confirmed by the Study on Customary International Humanitarian Law of the International Committee of the Red Cross. According to that Study "serious violations of international humanitarian law constitute war crimes" (Rule 156), "individuals are criminally responsible for war crimes they commit" (Rule 151) and "States must investigate war crimes allegedly committed by their nationals or armed forces, or on their territory, and, if appropriate, prosecute the suspects. They must also investigate other war crimes over which they have jurisdiction and, if appropriate, prosecute the suspects" (Rule 158).

Article 4a) of the CPC of BiH mentions "general principles of international law". Article 7(2) of the ECHR is about "general principles of law recognized by civilized nations" and Article 15(2) of the ICCPR is about "general principles of law recognized by the community of nations". As neither the ECHR nor the ICCPR recognize a term identical to that one used by Article 4a) of the CPC of BiH, the used phrase is then a combination of the "principles of international law", as recognized by the UN General Assembly and the International Law Commission on the one hand, and the "general principles of the rights recognized by a community of nations, as recognized by the Statute of the International Court of Justice and Article 7 (2) of the ECHR and Article 15 (2) of the ICCPR" on the other hand.

criminalization contained in 'general principles of law recognized by civilized nations', as well as for the international customary law nature of crimes against humanity.[6]

Principles of international law as recognized by the General Assembly Resolution 95(I) (1946) and the International Law Commission (1950) are related to the "Nuremberg Charter and Judgment of the Tribunal", and therefore to the crimes against humanity as well. Principle VI.c. of the "Principles of the International Law Recognized in the Charter of the Nuremberg Tribunal and in the Judgment of the Tribunal" adopted by the International Law Commission in 1950 and submitted to the General Assembly, sets out crimes against humanity as a crime punishable under international law. Principle I stipulates that: "Any person who commits an act which constitutes a crime under international law is responsible therefore and liable to punishment." Principle II stipulates that: "The fact that internal law does not impose a penalty for an act which constitutes a crime under international law does not relieve the person who committed the act from responsibility under international law." The case law of the European Court of Human Rights stresses the application of the provision of Article 7(2) in relation to the application of Article 7(1) of the ECHR in several similar cases which discuss the existence and punishability of Crimes against Humanity as a criminal offense. What is more, in the case of *Kolk and Kislyiy v Estonia*, the European Court "recalls that the interpretation and application of the national in principle fall within the competence of national courts ... This is also applicable in cases when national law is related to the rules of general international law or international agreements".

Therefore, the criminal offense of Crimes against Humanity can, in any case, be classified under "general principles of international law" under Article 4a) of the CC of BiH. Thus, regardless of whether it is seen from the aspect of international customary law or the "principles of international law", it is beyond dispute that Crimes against Humanity represented a criminal offense in the critical period, i.e. that the principle of legality has been satisfied.

The fact that the criminal acts set forth in Article 172 of the CC of BiH can also be found in the law which was in effect at the critical time period – at the time of the perpetration of the offense, specifically under Articles 134, 141, 142, 143, 144, 145, 146, 147, 154, 155 and 186 of the CC of SFRY, or, in other words, that the criminal acts were punishable under the criminal code then in effect, additionally supports the inference of the Court regarding the principle of legality. Finally, as regards Article 7 (1) of the ECHR, the Court notes that the application of Article 4a) is further justified by the fact that the imposed punishment is definitely more lenient than the death penalty applicable at the time of the perpetration of the offense, which satisfies the principle of time constraints regarding applicability, or, in other words, the application of a "law more lenient to the perpetrator".'

6 Verdict, *Radovan Stanković*, Appellate Panel, 28 March 2007, No. X-KRŽ-05/07, pp. 13–14: 'The arguments of the appeal contesting the application of the substantive law are also ungrounded. That is, he states that the first instance panel, instead of the SFRY CC, which as deemed by the appellants was the law in force at the time of commission of the criminal offense and which was more lenient to the perpetrator both from the aspect of existence of the criminal offense concerned as such and the punishment foreseen, erroneously applied the BiH CC. Thus, the appeal alleges it violated both the principle of legality and of time constraints regarding applicability referred to in Article 3 and 4 of the Criminal Code of Bosnia and Herzegovina.

In other words, it is indisputable that at the time of commission of the acts the accused is charged with and which constitute all the elements of the criminal offense of Crimes against Humanity, the said criminal offense, as such, was not stipulated by the Criminal Code of SFRY which was the applicable substantive law at the time of commission of the criminal offense.

It is also indisputable that, pursuant to the principle of legality, no punishment or other criminal sanction may be imposed on any person for an act which, prior to being perpetrated, has not been defined as a criminal offence by law or international law, and for which no punishment was prescribed by the law (Article 3 of the BiH CC), while, pursuant to the principle of time constraints regarding applicability, the law that was in effect at the time when the criminal offence was perpetrated shall apply to the perpetrator of the criminal offence and if the law has been amended on one or more occasions after the criminal offence was perpetrated, the law that is more lenient to the perpetrator shall be applied (Article 4 of the BiH CC). The principle of legality is

C. Case Law

The appellate panel of the Court of Bosnia and Herzegovina rendered four final verdicts by May 2007. In three cases the accused were charged with the criminal offence of Crimes against Humanity under Article 172 of the CC of BiH and one accused was charged with the criminal offence of War Crimes against Civilians under Article 173 CC BiH.

---

also stipulated under Article 7(2) of the ECHR and Article 15(1) of the International Covenant on Civil and Political Rights (hereinafter: the ICCPR).

However, Articles 4a) of the BiH CC which the first instance Verdict correctly refers to regulates that Articles 3 and 4 of the Code shall not prejudice the trial and punishment of any person for any act or omission which, at the time when it was committed, was criminal according to the general principles of international law. Thus, the provisions of Article 7(2) of the ECHR and Article 15(2) of the ICCPR have practically been adopted, therefore providing for departure from the mandatory application of a more lenient law in proceedings conducted for acts which are criminal according to international law. It is stated that this is the case in the proceedings against the accused because this is exactly an incrimination which includes a violation of international law. In other words, as correctly reasoned in the contested Verdict, in the period relevant to the Indictment, Crimes against Humanity indisputably constituted a criminal offense both from the aspect of international customary law and from the aspect of the general principles of international law. The detailed and comprehensive arguments corroborating such conclusion presented by the first instance panel are absolutely valid and correct, and therefore also accepted by this Panel as a whole.

Further, international customary law and international treaties signed by the Socialist Federative Republic of Yugoslavia automatically became binding on Bosnia and Herzegovina, either during the time when it was part of the Socialist Federative Republic of Yugoslavia or after it became a successor to the former Socialist Federative Republic of Yugoslavia. The 1978 Vienna Convention on Succession of States in respect of Treaties, ratified by the Socialist Federative Republic of Yugoslavia on 18 April 1980, in Article 34 stipulates that a treaty in force at the date of the succession of States in respect of the entire territory of the predecessor State continues to be in force in respect of each successor State so formed unless the States concerned agree otherwise. In addition to the above mentioned, on 10 June 1994, Bosnia and Herzegovina declared that it recognized all the international treaties which were binding on the former Yugoslavia. Article 210 of the Constitution of the Socialist Federative Republic of Yugoslavia, indeed, stipulates that international treaties are automatically implemented and applied from the day of entry into force without the adoption of implementing regulations.

The foregoing results in the correct position of the first instance panel that Bosnia and Herzegovina, as a successor to the former Yugoslavia, ratified the ECHR and the ICCPR, therefore, these treaties are binding on it. Given that they regulate the obligation to try and punish any person for any act or omission which, at the time when it was committed, was criminal according to the general principles of international law, which is definitely the case with Crimes against Humanity pursuant to the above mentioned, it is indisputable that the arguments of the appeal claiming the opposite are entirely ungrounded and as such refused.

As regards the objections indicating that the SFRY CC was more lenient to the perpetrator in respect to the imposed criminal sanction, the Appellate Panel notes that at the time of commission of the crime the accused is charged with, it was possible to pronounce a death penalty, because as correctly stated by the Defense Attorney Dragica Glušac, it was abolished after the ratification of Protocol 13 of the ECHR on 29 July 2003. That is, by the said Protocol, the signatory countries committed not to prescribe the death penalty in their criminal laws. Prior to that, the death penalty was removed from the criminal laws of Bosnia and Herzegovina by adoption of the Criminal Code of the Federation of BiH (1998), Criminal Code of Republika Srpska (2000) and Criminal Code of the Brčko District (2000), and the 2003 Criminal Code of BiH. Therefore, it follows that the Law which does not envisage pronouncement of such penalty, meaning the Criminal Code of BiH, is in any case more lenient law to the perpetrator.'

The accused, Abduladhim Maktouf, was charged with the criminal offence of War Crimes against Civilians under Article 173(1)(e) CC BiH.[7] As alleged in the indictment, on or about 18 October 1993, in Travnik, together with Al Mujahid soldiers, the accused illegally arrested, detained and took five Croat civilians hostage. As it is further alleged, Abduladhim Maktouf drove one of two vehicles used to carry the prisoners and participated in the planning, carrying out and aftermath of the abduction operation.

On appeal, the Court referred to the ICTY case law as binding[8] in defining the existence of an international conflict that was undergoing in 1993 between Bosnian Croats and Bosniaks in

---

7 Art. 173, War Crimes against Civilians, CC BiH:

(1) Whoever in violation of rules of international law in time of war, armed conflict or occupation, orders or perpetrates any of the following acts:

a) Attack on civilian population, settlement, individual civilians or persons unable to fight, which results in the death, grave bodily injuries or serious damaging of people's health;
b) Attack without selecting a target, by which civilian population is harmed;
c) Killings, intentional infliction of severe physical or mental pain or suffering upon a person (torture), inhuman treatment, biological, medical or other scientific experiments, taking of tissue or organs for the purpose of transplantation, immense suffering or violation of bodily integrity or health;
d) Dislocation or displacement or forced conversion to another nationality or religion;
e) Coercing another by force or by threat of immediate attack upon his life or limb, or the life or limb of a person close to him, to sexual intercourse or an equivalent sexual act (rape) or forcible prostitution, application of measures of intimidation and terror, taking of hostages, imposing collective punishment, unlawful bringing in concentration camps and other illegal arrests and detention, deprivation of rights to fair and impartial trial, forcible service in the armed forces of enemy's army or in its intelligence service or administration;
f) Forced labour, starvation of the population, property confiscation, pillaging, illegal and self-willed destruction and stealing on large scale of property that is not justified by military needs, taking an illegal and disproportionate contribution or requisition, devaluation of domestic money or the unlawful issuance of money, shall be punished by imprisonment for a term not less than ten years or long-term imprisonment.

(2) The punishment referred to in paragraph 1 of this Article shall be imposed on whomever in violation of rules of international law, in the time of war, armed conflict or occupation, orders or perpetrates any of the following acts:

a) Attack against objects specifically protected by the international law, as well as objects and facilities with dangerous power, such as dams, embankments and nuclear power stations;
b) Targeting indiscriminately of civilian objects which are under specific protection of international law, of non-defended places and of demilitarized zone;
c) Long-lasting and large-scale environment devastation, which may be detrimental to the health or survival of the population.

(3) Whoever in violation of the rules of international law applicable in the time of war, armed conflict or occupation, orders or carries out as an occupier the resettlement of parts of his civilian population into the occupied territory, shall be punished by imprisonment for a term not less than ten years or long-term imprisonment.'

8 See Arts 3 and 4 of the Law on Transfer of Cases, *infra* note 11.

Central Bosnia.[9] Further, it referred to: Article 3 of IV Geneva Convention for identifying victims as civilians; the 1979 Convention against the taking of hostages, to qualify as hostages such civilians; the role performed by the accused to assess his mode of responsibility for the assistance to perpetrators.[10]

9 Verdict, *Abdouladhim Maktouf*, Appellate Panel, 4 April 2006, No. KPŽ-32/05: 'It is indisputable that at the time of the event in question in 1993, in the territory of Travnik in Bosnia and Herzegovina, an international conflict between Bosnian Croats and Bosniaks was underway in Central Bosnia. This has been established by the ICTY Judgements number IT-95-14/02 of 17 December 2004 and of 26 February 2001 in the *Prosecutor v. Dario Kordić and Mario Čerkez* case which the Panel accepts pursuant to Article 4 of the Law on the Transfer of cases from the ICTY to the Prosecutor's Office of B-H and the Use of Evidence Collected by the ICTY in the Proceedings Before the Courts in B-H, stipulating acceptance of the facts established by the legally binding decisions of the ICTY, which the parties have made indisputable as well.'

10 Verdict, *Abdouladhim Maktouf*, Appellate Panel, 4 April 2006, No. KPŽ-32/05: 'However, disputable circumstances refer to the perpetration of the criminal offences – War Crimes against Civilians and elements constituting subject matter of this criminal offense, in other words, whether a criminal offense and criminal responsibility of the Accused exist as well as whether the abducted persons were civilians and hostages. First, Article 3 of the IV Geneva Convention stipulates: "(1) Persons taking no active part in the hostilities, including members of armed forces who have laid down their arms and those placed *hors de combat* by ... shall in all circumstances be treated humanely, without any adverse distinction founded on race, color, religion or faith, sex, birth or wealth, or any other similar criteria. To this end the following acts are and shall remain prohibited at any time and in any place whatsoever with respect to the above-mentioned persons ... (b) Taking of hostages";

In respect to status of the captured persons, according to testimony of ..., the relevant evening he was with ... in his apartment, in civilian clothes and unarmed. Article 3 of the IV Geneva Convention protects persons considered civilians and these are persons who: "... taking no active part in the hostilities, including members of armed forces who have laid down their arms and those placed hors de combat by ...". Therefore, broader interpretation of this Article indicates that it's irrelevant whether at that moment these persons were members of the [Croatian Defense Council] HVC, as the defense tries to present it. The relevant facts which indisputably indicate that these were civilians are the facts that in the moment of abduction these persons were not in the zone of combat activities, they were not uniformed and they were not armed.

Also, the issue is whether the abducted persons could be considered hostages, which is an important element of this criminal offence. According to the international convention against the taking of hostages from 1979, that is, Article 1, of the Convention, hostage is any person seized or detained or threatened to be killed, to be injured or continually detained by another person in order to compel a third party, namely, a state, an international intergovernmental organization, a natural or juridical person, or a group of persons, to do or obtain from doing any act as an explicit or implicit condition for the release of the hostage. So, it raises beyond doubt that the persons who were taken from the apartment of ... that night were hostages within the meaning of the said convention because they were taken by a group of persons-members of the Al Mujahid Unit in order to force the other group, HVO members, to release the captured members of the Al Mujahid Unit.

Furthermore, Article 31 of CCB-H stipulates that accessory in commission of criminal offence is, among other things, supplying the perpetrator with tools for perpetrating the criminal offence and removing obstacles for the perpetration of criminal offence. Accessory for which this penal deems the accused criminally responsible is that he got the list of persons that he was supposed to take as hostages, the relevant evening, that he knowingly and willingly used his knowledge of the place of residence of the persons on the list, that he drove his van to the building were the said persons lived and that, after they were abducted and placed into the vehicle, he drove the vehicle transporting them to Orašac camp. It raises beyond dispute that when the accused carried out this activity, he acted with direct intent until completion of the pre-planned activity, thus fully contributing to perpetration of this criminal offence. Therefore, the panel deems him criminally responsible for this criminal offence. The panel accepts this fact as established, because it is absolutely indisputable and realistic to believe that the accused, being a citizen of B-H and Travnik for many years, has sufficient

3. Procedural Connections with the ICTY

A. Acceptance of Facts Established by the ICTY

There is a significant connection between war crimes cases before the Court of BiH and cases which were tried or are on trial before the ICTY, as both sets of cases are based on almost identical facts to be established and evidence on which such facts are to be proven. This connection is additionally impressively expressed by Rule 11*bis* ICTY RPE and by the *lex specialis* established in the Law on the Transfer of Cases from the ICTY to the Prosecutor's Office of BiH and the Use of Evidence Collected by ICTY in proceedings before the Courts in BiH (Law on Transfer).[11] Such provisions had an impact on the operations of the Court, due to the specificities adjudicated before the ICTY, such as acceptance of facts. Article 4 of the Law on Transfer provides the basis for the possibility of accepting as proven the facts established by the ICTY decisions and, in particular

> at the request of a party or *proprio motu*, the courts, after hearing the parties, may decide to accept as proven those facts that are established by legally binding decisions in any other proceedings by the ICTY or to accept documentary evidence from proceedings of the ICTY relating to matters at issue in the current proceedings.

The commission of the criminal offences at issue are characterized by specific circumstances, especially considering:

(a) the general framework of events and the mass character of crimes which constitute the violation of the highest values protected by international law;
(b) that the majority of the offences were committed at the same time, in the same place and against the same protected values.

---

knowledge of the area of Travnik and its citizens. Given that Travnik is a smaller town, it is possible to expect that he knew where the mentioned persons resided, which supports the belief that he really committed the criminal offence charged with by the Indictment of the Prosecutors Office of B-H. In respect to tools for commission of the criminal offence, the testimonies of all the witnesses result in the fact that a dark green vehicle participated in the offence. The Witness stated that the Accused owned a dark green Volkswagen van in which he frequently rode with the accused and that this was the vehicle in which the abducted persons were taken to the camp in Orašac. The fact that the accused is the owner of the Volkswagen vehicle was not disputed in any moment during the trial before this panel. Witness … describes it in his testimony as an all-terrain vehicle similar to Lada Niva. However, given that it is reasonable that witness … at the moment when he was taken away was afraid for his security and life, it is not realistic to expect that he could be interested to see what type of vehicle it was and he could not be decisive in respect to type of the vehicle in question, therefore, the panel, establishes based on the testimony of the Witness, that it was a dark green Volkswagen van owned by the accused. The accessory in commission of the criminal offence ends for the accused at the moment when he drove the vehicle with the abducted civilians to the entry of the Orašac camp. The presented evidence does not prove in any manner the involvement of the accused in the mistreatment of civilians in the camp, thus, he cannot, by any means, be linked with the death of …, who was murdered on the relevant evening. It also rises from the presented evidence that two persons – … and … – were in the vehicle of the accused. Equally, contrary to the allegations of the Indictment, the panel did not find with certainty based on the evidence presented, especially testimony of witness …, that … had been transported by the vehicle concerned driven by the accused to the Orašac camp. Therefore, the panel rendered the decision accordingly.'

11 *Official Gazette* of Bosnia and Herzegovina, No. 61/04, 46/06, 53/06, 76/06.

Consequently, facts established in ICTY judgements represent an important starting point in proving individual criminal responsibility and, in the jurisprudence of the Court, they constitute presumption. However, neither the *lex specialis* nor the CPC of BiH provide for criteria to have such facts accepted by the Court of BiH. Thus, the case law of the Court has so far ordinarily applied the criteria established by the ICTY for acceptance of facts as proven in its own proceedings.

In *Stanković*, the Court found that facts established by ICTY decisions originate a presumption which, however, is challengeable,[12] thus complying with fair trial guarantees.[13] Criteria established by ICTY to supplement Rule 94(b) ICTY RPE on judicial notice, which have been consistently applied at the Court,[14] require that judicial notice may be taken of an adjudicated fact when:

---

12 Decision, *Radovan Stanković*, Trial Panel, 13 July 2006, No. X-KR-05/70: '... the acceptance of a fact established by an ICTY decision only creates a grounded yet refutable presumption as to the accuracy of this fact, which therefore does not have to be proven again at trial but which, subject to that presumption, may be challenged at that trial, in compliance with the rights of the Defense as guaranteed under Articles 3 and 5 of the CPC and under Article 6 paragraph 2 and 3 of the European Convention of Human Rights.'

13 Verdict, *Radovan Stanković*, Appellate Panel, 28 March 2007, No. X-KRŽ-05/70: 'The arguments given in the appeal, filed by both Defense Attorneys and the accused himself, that the decision of the court to accept as proven the facts established by the ICTY judgments, represents a violation of the provision of criminal procedure, that is, the principle of immediacy and contradiction are also ungrounded. In other words, in the hearing held on 13 July 2006, having heard the Prosecutor and the Defense Attorneys, the first instance panel granted the Motion of the Prosecutor's Office of BiH number KT RZ/05 to accept, as proven, the facts established in the ICTY first instance and the Appeals Panel Judgments in the case against *Kunarac et al.* number IT-96-23-T and IT-96-23/1-T and to also agree and accept the Decision on Judicial Notice of the ICTY Trial Chamber dated 16 May 2003.

In rendering this decision, the first instance panel, as deemed by the Appellate Panel, fully complied with the provision of Article 4 of the Law on Transfer of Cases from the ICTY to the Prosecutor's Office of BiH and the Use of Evidence Collected by the ICTY in Proceedings Before the Courts in BiH, which as a *lex specialis*, in such cases, provides for departure from the said principles. Therefore, the objection of the defense in that sense is not grounded. The facts accepted by the first instance panel as proven are clear and concrete, do not include legal qualifications, and at the same time constitute a part of the Verdict which was adjudicated in the appeals procedure. Furthermore, they do not establish the criminal responsibility of the accused but the concrete act of perpetration is placed in a wider context of the war events, that is, the context of the existence of a widespread and systematic attack against non-Serb civilians in the said territory and at the time relevant to the Indictment. Their acceptance, as also concluded by this Panel, in no way influenced the right of the accused to a fair trial'.

14 Verdict, *Nedjo Samardžić*, Appellate Panel, 13 December 2006, No. X-KRŽ-05/49: 'Article 4 of the LOTC [Law on Transfer] prescribes that, after hearing the parties, at the request of a party or *proprio motu*, the court may decide to accept as proven those facts that are established by legally binding decisions in any other proceedings by the ICTY. As the LOTC does not prescribe criteria which must be met in order for a certain fact to be considered "adjudicated", the Panel, examining the facts relevant for adjudication in this legal matter, and bearing in mind the obligation to respect the principle of the right to a fair trial guaranteed by the European Convention on Human Rights and Fundamental Freedoms (ECHR), as well as by the CPC BiH, applied to them the criteria which the ICTY established in that regard in the decision of 28 February 2003 in the case *Prosecutor v. Momčilo Krajišnik.*

Under mentioned criteria which supplement Rule 94(b) (Judicial Notice) of the ICTY Rules of Procedure and Evidence, judicial notice may be taken of an adjudicated fact provided it is: distinct, concrete and identifiable, restricted to factual findings and does not include legal characterizations, contested at trial and forms part of a judgment which has either not been appealed or has been finally settled on appeal or contested at trial and now forms part of a judgment which is under appeal, but falls within issues which are not in dispute on appeal. Furthermore, it must not confirm the criminal responsibility of the accused or be the subject of

(a) it is distinct, concrete and identifiable;
(b) it is restricted to factual findings;
(c) it does not include legal qualifications;
(d) it is part of a decision which, at least for such facts, has become final;
(e) it does not establish criminal responsibility of the accused;
(f) it is not based on plea agreements.

B. Use of Evidence Collected at ICTY

The use of evidence collected by ICTY has been regulated in the Law on Transfer, where the general principle is that: 'evidence collected in accordance with the ICTY Statute and RoPE may be used in proceedings before the courts in BiH.'[15]

The Law on Transfer, however, was envisaged as *lex specialis* to remove the risk of inadmissibility under the CPC of the evidence collected by the ICTY: specialty qualifies the Law on Transfer, as its special regulations have priority over the CPC in terms of the substance (evidence collected by the ICTY) and area of application (rules on admissibility and use). As *lex specialis*, the Law on Transfer of Cases either deviates from and supersedes the CPC when the CPC is not in compliance with the Law on Transfer, or it invokes the CPC on issues not specifically covered by the Law on Transfer.[16]

The Law on Transfer sets forth the procedure for transferring cases to the Prosecutor's Office of BiH, but also regulates procedures and conditions for the use of the evidence before other courts. As Article 3(1) of the Law on Transfer provides for the use of evidence collected by the ICTY in proceedings before the courts in BiH, its application goes beyond cases transferred from the ICTY and allows for ICTY-originated evidence to be used in any proceeding under the BiH jurisdiction, regardless of whether the proceeding concerns Rule 11*bis* ICTY RPE or domestic cases of war crimes.

(reasonable) dispute between the parties in the case and it may not be based on plea agreements in previous cases and affect the right of the accused to a fair trial.

Since the above cited facts from final ICTY judgments entirely meet the mentioned criteria, the Panel, after the defense stated its position, granted the Prosecution motion to accept them as proven, as it was correctly established also by the first instance Verdict of this Court. ... Assessing the above mentioned evidence in relation to accepted facts, the Panel established that in the area of the municipalities of Foča, Gacko and Kalinovik, in the period from April 1992 until the end of March 1993, the army and police of the so-called Serb Republic of BiH carried out a number of acts of violence, which were extensive and resulted in a large number of victims.

Bearing in mind the pattern of committed crimes which took place in the mentioned period, multiple rapes, taking away, killings, pillaging and destruction of property, the Appellate Panel concludes that the acts of violence were organized and systematic and that they were directed solely against Bosniak civilian population.

It follows from the above-mentioned that, in the period from April 1992 until the end of March 1993, there was a widespread and systematic attack by the army and police of the so-called Serb Republic of BiH directed against Bosniak civilian population of the Foča Municipality.

Therefore, this Panel assesses as unfounded the defense claim that a widespread and systematic attack did not exist in the area of Miljevina because there were no war operations there, as the concept of "attack" is not limited to the hostilities but encompasses situations in which persons not taking any active part in the hostilities are mistreated, and humanitarian law is applied on the entire territory under the control of one side, which was indisputably the case in the entire territory of the Municipality of Foča, including Miljevina.'

15 Art. 3(1) Law on Transfer.

16 Art. 1(2) Law on Transfer.

The court may decide to use evidence collected by the ICTY at the request of parties or defence counsel for the accused. In proceedings before the Court of BiH, evidence collected by the ICTY is in most cases used upon the motion of the Prosecutor's Office of BiH. Such evidence consists mainly of statements of witnesses who testified before the Tribunal, expert witnesses' findings, but also reports of investigators of the OTP.

Objections raised by the defence on the use of such evidence mostly address the specific guarantees set forth under Article 6 of ECHR, especially the right of the accused to summon and hear witnesses and the right to directly present evidence in the proceedings.

Authentication of evidentiary material appears as a separate issue in this problem area. A large number of documents is certified by the ICTY and delivered to the Prosecutor's Office electronically, which leads to the defence objecting to the authenticity of such evidentiary material because in a certain number of cases 'verification' of documents consists of the ICTY stamp which certifies that any specific document is a copy of the document in possession of ICTY. For that purpose, the Law on Transfer of Cases has been amended in order to have ICTY-originated evidence treated as if it were obtained by national authorities.[17]

4. The Right of the Accused to Present his Own Defence

Pursuant to Article 7 CPC BiH,[18] the right of the suspect or of the accused to have material and formal defence provided throughout criminal proceedings shall be guaranteed. The right of the suspect/accused to present his defence encompasses all procedural activities related to the challenge of any element charged under the indictment. Article 45 CPC of BiH[19] identifies the circumstances when

17 Art. 8(1) Law on Transfer: 'Original documents, certified copies, certified electronic copies and copies authenticated as unaltered in comparison to their originals and forensic evidence collected by the ICTY shall be used in proceedings before the courts and shall be treated as if they were obtained by competent national authorities.'

18 Article 7, Right to Defense, CPC BiH: '(1)The suspect or accused has a right to present his own defense or to defend himself with the professional aid of a defense attorney of his own choice. (2) If the suspect or accused does not have a defense attorney, a defense attorney shall be appointed to him in cases as stipulated by this Code.'

19 Article 45, Mandatory Defense, CC BiH:

(1) 'A suspect shall have a defense attorney at the first questioning if he is mute or deaf or if he is suspected of a criminal offense for which a penalty of long-term imprisonment may be pronounced.
(2) A suspect or accused must have a defense attorney immediately after he has been assigned to pretrial custody, throughout the pretrial custody.
(3) After an indictment has been brought for a criminal offense for which a prison sentence of ten (10) years or more may be pronounced, the accused must have a defense attorney at the time of the delivery of the indictment.
(4) If the suspect, or the accused in the case of a mandatory defense, does not retain a defense attorney himself, or if the persons referred to in Article 39, Paragraph 3, of this Code do not retain a defense attorney, the preliminary proceeding judge, preliminary hearing judge, the judge or the Presiding judge shall appoint him a defense attorney in the proceedings. In this case, the suspect or the accused shall have the right to a defense attorney until the verdict becomes final and, if a long-term imprisonment is pronounced for proceedings under legal remedies.
(5) If the Court finds it necessary for the sake of justice, due to the complexity of the case or the mental condition of the suspect or the accused, it shall appoint an attorney for his defense.

the suspect or the accused must have a defence attorney – that is, cases of mandatory defence are envisaged. The appointment of a defence attorney regardless of the will of the suspect/accused is justified on fair trial grounds when s/he is unable to defend appropriately himself/herself. However, also when counsel is appointed to the suspect *ex officio*, professional defence shall not exclude the right to carry out material defence, which is the right of the suspect/accused to present his/her own defence. In *Stanković*, the Court has faced a request for self-representation filed by the accused in a case where the requirements for the mandatory defence were met.

The Court dismissed the request and assigned a lawyer *ex officio* to the accused, considering:

- the lack of qualification of the accused to defend himself;[20]
- the mandatory defence provided for under Article 45 CPC BiH to be in line with human rights law;[21]
- the complexity of the case;
- the need to balance the rights of the accused with those of protected witnesses;[22]
- the ICTY denied self-representation to the accused;[23]
- the right to defence cannot be waived, and that pursuant to Article 45(1) CPC BiH the Court is under an obligation to ensure equality of arms with the Prosecution by providing adequate professional assistance in cases where a long-term imprisonment sentence may be imposed.[24]

---

(6) In the case of appointing a defense attorney, the suspect or the accused shall be asked to select a defense attorney from the presented list himself. If the suspect or the accused does not select a defense attorney from the presented list himself, the defense attorney shall be appointed by the Court.'

20 Decision, *Radovan Stanković*, Trial Panel, 6 April 2006, No. X-KR-05/70: '…the Accused Stanković has no professional qualifications required to defend himself in person adequately in such a complex case, in which, as deemed by the Court, it is an absolute priority and duty of the Court to provide the Accused with high-standard defense, that is, defense requiring particular legal expertise, considering the right of the accused to defense in terms of the Criminal Procedure Code of Bosnia and Herzegovina and Article 6 of the European Convention on Human Rights and Fundamental Freedoms…'.

21 Ibid.: 'according to the jurisprudence of the European Court of Human Rights there is no violation of Article 6 of the Convention if the Court appoints defense attorney against the will of the accused, if it is done in the interest of justice and adequate defense (See *Croissant v Germany*, judgment of 25 September 1992).'

22 Ibid.: 'in the concrete case the Indictment proposes witnesses-injured parties who should testify in respect to the huge number of rapes and other humiliating treatments. In reference to that fact, the European Court of Human Rights recognized in its jurisprudence the need to balance the rights of the accused and witnesses-victims, in particular in sexual crimes cases, for which the European Court concluded that certain measures must be taken by the Court in order to protect victims of these crimes, for example referring to the control of method of questioning witnesses under threat (See *Accardi et al. v Italy*, judgment of 20 January 2005). Given that in the concrete example the case concerned is the one in which the Court has to take into account this balance and the need to protect the rights of the accused to adequate defense as well as rights of the witnesses under threat, a certain number of whom are protected witnesses, the Court is of the opinion that due to these reasons it is necessary for the Accused to be represented by persons qualified for the job, that is, by lawyers.'

23 Ibid.: 'the Trial Chamber I of the ICTY, by its decision dated 19 January 2005, refused the request of the Accused Stanković for self-representation, in other words, he was not allowed to waive his right to professional assistance.'

24 Verdict, *Radovan Stanković*, Appellate Panel, 28 March 2007 No. X-KRŽ-05/70: 'the right [to a defense] is not a right which can be waived voluntarily but that it is the duty of the court, according to the law, to provide the accused adequate professional assistance in prescribed cases, therefore, equality of arms in respect to the Prosecutor's Office as the other party to the proceedings.'

5. Cases when the Accused Refuses to Appear

One of the novelties in criminal proceedings before the courts of Bosnia and Herzegovina is certainly the ban of trials *in absentia* under Article 247 CPC BiH: an accused may never be tried *in absentia*. However, the question arises as to how to define the term *in absentia*, i.e., whether it includes the absence of an accused at trial or at any specific hearing s/he is summoned to:

- because s/he is not physically attainable to the court;
- when s/he is attainable but makes it clear that s/he does not wish to attend the trial, i.e., when s/he explicitly waives the right to be present in the course of the proceedings conducted against him/her.

'Trial *in absentia*' can be interpreted as an accused being fully unattainable in the proceedings, e.g., when fleeing or hiding, but it mostly relates to cases when it is not possible to ensure his presence in the course of the proceedings because his whereabouts are unknown or there are other obstacles to ensuring his presence. It is important to note that the CPC BiH also prescribes the actions the court might take in case the accused is attainable, i.e., when his presence in the proceedings has been ensured by one of the measures to ensure the presence of the accused. Article 246(1) CPC BiH provides for the apprehension of the accused in case he refuses to appear at the hearing and fails to justify his absence.

However, the situation is entirely different when it comes to proceedings taking place *without the presence* of the accused, when such presence has been previously ensured by a measure ensuring the accused's presence in the course of the proceedings. The provisions of the Criminal Procedure Code of BiH do not refer in detail to all situations which might arise in the proceedings, but clearly allow for exceptions when proceedings take place without the presence of the accused, as proceedings do when the President of the Panel orders that the accused be excluded from the courtroom.[25]

In *Stanković*, the accused was removed from the courtroom for improper conduct and contempt of the Court, subsequently refusing to appear at trial and stating that, if brought there by force, he would appear in underwear and continue with improper conduct.[26] Considering that such conduct was aimed at delaying and preventing continuation of the proceedings, the Court held that the ban of trials *in absentia* under the CPC BiH and under fair trial guarantees of Article 6 ECHR is complied

---

25 Art. 242(2) CPC BiH.

26 Verdict, *Radovan Stanković*, Appellate Panel, 28 March 2007, No. X-KRŽ-05/70: 'at the hearings held on 23 February 2006 and 6 June 2006 the accused, having received multiple warnings from the Presiding Judge, had to be removed from the courtroom for the reason of improper conduct and contempt of the court. After that, as it can be seen from the official notes of the authorized officers of the Detention Unit of the Court of BiH, on 16 June 2006 and 4 July 2006, he refused to appear at the continuation of the main trial stating that he could only be brought in there with the use of force and announcing that he would continue with improper conduct by coming to the Court in his underwear. The first instance panel resolved the resulting procedural situation by rendering the decision that in case of further unjustified refusal by the accused to appear at the scheduled trial to which he was duly summoned the trial should be held even without his presence and noted that the accused should have the right to appear before the Court at all times, that his Defense Attorneys would be present at the trials held without his presence and that he would be informed about the course of the proceedings by serving the accused with the recording of the entire trial the same day the session was held. Such actions, contrary to the arguments of the appeal, neither violated the principle of ban of trial *in absentia* nor prevented the accused from following and participating in the main trial.'

with when the accused is detained upon order of the Court, is duly informed of and summoned to the hearings scheduled, and is represented by counsel in the proceedings.[27] Consequently, any subsequent refusal to appear in person at hearings is a conscious and voluntary choice which does not affect proceedings and needs not be addressed by the use of force, which may also result

27 Decision, *Radovan Stanković*, Trial Panel, 7 July 2006, No. X-KR-05/70: 'The accused Radovan Stankovic has been informed that criminal proceedings are underway against him, for the criminal offense of Crimes against Humanity under Article 172, paragraph 1 items c), e), f) and g) of the Criminal Code of Bosnia and Herzegovina.

The custody was ordered against the accused in order to, *inter alia*, secure his presence. The accused is currently in the Detention Unit of the Court of Bosnia and Herzegovina. By this, his presence at the criminal proceedings against him is secured – the Ban of Trial in Case of Absentia prescribed under Article 247 of the CPC BiH is thus not brought in question. Until now, the accused has been duly informed of all the hearings scheduled in the criminal proceedings against him. His defense attorneys were present at all the hearings and took adequate defense actions in order to protect the procedural rights of the accused.

The overall conduct of the accused, including his refusal to appear before the Court BiH, led the Court to conclude that this is a conscious conduct with the aim to hinder and delay the criminal proceedings. The defendant's failure to appear at the scheduled hearings is nothing but the wayward decision by the accused himself not to attend the trial.

The forceful apprehension of the accused who was duly summoned pursuant to Article 246, paragraph 1 of the CPC BiH refers to the situation when the accused is not in custody and its purpose is to inform the accused of the criminal proceedings conducted against him.

Therefore, the Court believes that forceful bringing in and the use of force are not an appropriate way to let the accused know that the trial will continue without his presence. Furthermore, bringing the accused to the Court in his underwear with the use of force, according to the position of the Court, might actually represent the inhumane treatment of the accused and at the same time it would undermine the authority and the dignity of the Court. Besides, bearing in mind the conduct of the accused at the previous sessions, it is reasonable to expect that bringing him in with the use of force would only contribute that the accused repeats the conduct which results in his exclusion from the courtroom.

The Court, therefore, rather than using force, finds it more purposeful in this particular case to duly inform the accused that the trial shall continue even without him present, and inform him that he may attend the Court when ever he wishes to do so.

This position of the Court is known in the international court practice. For example, the International Criminal Tribunal for Rwanda (ICTR) in the case against *Jean-Bosco Barayagwiza* (case number ICTR – 97-19-T) with regard to the choice of the accused not to attend the sessions, if the accused is duly informed about the trial, the proceedings may be conducted in the absence of the accused, because in that case it does not constitute a violation of the ICTR Statute or violation of his human rights.

The Ban of Trial in Absentia prescribed by the International Covenant on Civil and Political Rights, Article 14, and the European Convention for the Protection of Human Rights and Fundamental Freedoms (ECHR), Article 4, is also not absolute.

The European Court of Human Rights primarily finds that, although it is not explicitly stated under Article 6, paragraph 1 of the ECHR, the subject and the objective of this Article, if regarded as a whole, indicate that the person "charged with a criminal offence" has the right to participate in the criminal proceedings. In addition, specific items, c), d) and e) under paragraph 3 guarantee that "anyone charged with the criminal offence" has minimum rights whose exercise is hard to imagine if the accused does not participate in the trial (see *Colozza*, Judgment of 12 February 1985, paragraph 27).

However, in the cases related to the criminal proceedings in which the accused did not personally attend the trial, in terms of Article 6 of the ECHR, the court finds the following circumstances relevant:

- whether or not the accused was informed about the charges against him in the language he understands;

in inhumane treatment and undermine the authority and dignity of the Court itself. The Court concluded that in cases of such a waiver of the right of the accused to be present, it is adequate for him to follow proceedings by being provided with the records at the end of each hearing.[28]

- whether or not the accused was duly summoned to the trial;
- whether or not the absence of the accused is unjustified, or whether the accused has beyond any doubt and by his own will waived the right to attend the trial (see the Judgment of the Court in the case *FCB v Italy* dated 28 August 1991, paragraphs 29–36).

In this case, as stated earlier, there is no dilemma as to whether or not the accused was informed about the charges against him in the language he understands. It is also obvious that the accused was duly summoned to all the sessions scheduled, as well as that the accused voluntarily decided and explicitly stated that he does not whish to attend the trial, which can be seen from the mentioned official notes and earlier submissions.

In relation to all of the above, the Court finally observes that, pursuant to Article 239 and Article 241 of the CPC BiH, it is the duty of the presiding judge to ensure that everything delaying the proceedings and does not contribute to the clarification of the issue in case be eliminated, and to ensure the maintenance of order in the courtroom and the dignity of the Court.'

28 Verdict, *Radovan Stanković*, Appellate Panel, 28 March 2007, No. X-KRŽ-05/70: 'The objections of the appeal, indicating that the decision of the first instance panel to conduct the main trial even outside the presence of the accused violated the provision of Article 247 of the BiH CPC, thus preventing him from following the course of the main trial and actively participating in it, are also ungrounded.

The said Decision of the first instance panel was rendered and explained at the main trial held on 4 July 2006, and made in writing, and as such it was submitted to the parties to the proceedings and Defense Attorneys. The first instance panel also gave a detailed explanation of the reasons for rendering the Decision in the contested Verdict. Based on the above mentioned it arises that at the hearings held on 23 February 2006 and 6 June 2006 the accused, having received multiple warnings from the Presiding Judge, had to be removed from the courtroom for the reason of improper conduct and contempt of the court. After that, as it can be seen from the official notes of the authorized officers of the Detention Unit of the Court of BiH, on 16 June 2006 and 4 July 2006, he refused to appear at the continuation of the main trial stating that he could only be brought in there with the use of force and announcing that he would continue with improper conduct by coming to the Court in his underwear. The first instance panel resolved the resulting procedural situation by rendering the decision that in case of further unjustified refusal by the accused to appear at the scheduled trial to which he was duly summoned the trial should be held even without his presence and noted that the accused should have the right to appear before the Court at all times, that his Defense Attorneys would be present at the trials held without his presence and that he would be informed about the course of the proceedings by serving the accused with the recording of the entire trial the same day the session was held. Such actions, contrary to the arguments of the appeal, neither violated the principle of ban of trial in absentia nor prevented the accused from following and participating in the main trial.

Absence of the accused as regulated by Article 247 of the BiH CPC implies a situation in which it is not possible to provide for the presence of the accused at the main trial because he is hiding or on the run or if there are other difficulties in informing him about the proceedings. Considering that the accused was in custody during the entire course of main trial and that he consciously refused to appear at the hearings to which he was duly summoned, the Appellate Panel is of the opinion that it cannot be considered that he was absent pursuant to Article 247 of the BiH CPC.

The continuation of the trial outside the presence of the accused, considered within the context of the guarantees of Article 6 of the ECHR, is also possible. That is, the standards set by Article 6 of the ECHR applicable to the concrete procedural issue require the accused to be informed promptly, in a language which he understands and in detail, of the nature and cause of the accusation against him, which was indisputably done during the hearing before the Preliminary Proceedings Judge and by delivery of the Indictment, holding of the guilty or not guilty plea hearing and opening of the main trial by reading the Indictment. Furthermore, he is entitled to examine or have examined the witnesses against him and to obtain the attendance and

6. Protection of Witnesses

Protection of witnesses before the Court of BiH is enforced pursuant to the Law on Protection of Witnesses Under Threat and Vulnerable Witnesses (Law on Protection of Witnesses), which:[29] recognizes two categories of witnesses[30] – witnesses under threat and vulnerable witnesses; defines protected witnesses (in terms of protective measures that may be granted to witnesses under threat); foresees a number of protective measures to be ordered for a witness who falls within either of the two categories. Measures range from the mildest, such as securing psychological, social and other types of professional assistance, and alterations in the order of presentation of evidence at the main trial, up to the most restrictive measure for the hearing of protected witnesses pursuant to the provisions set forth in Articles 15 through 23 of the Law on Protection of Witnesses.

---

examination of witnesses on his behalf under the same conditions as witnesses against him. However, the said right of the accused which would also imply his presence is not an absolute right in the light of the fact that the accused can actually waive the right. Taking into consideration the fact that at all times the accused was aware of the charges against him, that he was timely informed and summoned to the scheduled hearings, that he was capable to attend them, that his Defense Attorney was always present throughout the main trial and that each time the accused would waive his right to attend the trial clearly, voluntarily and explicitly, the Appellate Panel is of the opinion that he was in no way prevented from attending, following and participating in the main trial, but that he waived the right voluntarily, thus accepting continuance of the main trial even without him. Although the BiH CPC does not explicitly regulate such a procedural situation, based on the provision of Article 242 (2) of the BiH CPC, it can be seen that it is possible to remove the accused from the courtroom if the accused persists in disruptive conduct after being warned by the Presiding Judge and that the proceedings may continue during this period if the accused is represented by counsel. Thus, the conclusion of the first instance panel that the mere fact that the accused is not physically present in the courtroom does not automatically mean that the trial cannot continue is additionally supported. And above all, it was noted that the purpose of the constant improper conduct of the accused was obviously to prevent continuation of the proceedings and delay it, as correctly concluded by the first instance panel. Considering the alternative measure which could be applied in the concrete case, that is, forceful bringing of the accused to the courtroom in spite of his will, regardless of the threats to appear in his underwear, as proposed by the Defense Attorney Pantić in his appeal, the first instance panel concluded correctly that such treatment would represent the inhumane treatment of the accused, undermining the physical integrity of the accused and authority and the dignity of the Court. Besides, except for the physical presence of the accused he could not be forced to follow the course of the proceedings and respect procedural discipline in his own interest. Taking into account the foregoing, the decision of the panel, following the end of each hearing, to serve the recording to the accused, in order for him to be able to be informed about the course of the proceedings, represents an adequate manner to provide for the possibility to follow the course of the main trial without undermining his physical integrity by forcefully bringing him to the courtroom.'

29 In *Official Gazette* of BiH 3/03, as amended in 21/03, 61/04, 55/05.

30 Article 3 – Witnesses under threat and vulnerable witnesses:

(1) A witness under threat is a witness whose personal security or the security of his family is endangered through his participation in the proceedings, as a result of threats, intimidation or similar actions pertaining to his testimony.

(2) A vulnerable witness is a witness who has been severely physically or mentally traumatized by the events of the offence, or otherwise suffers from a serious mental condition rendering him unusually sensitive, and a child and a juvenile.

(3) A protected witness is a witness heard according to the provisions of Articles 14 through 23 of this Law.

Measures predominantly applied in the Court of BiH include:

- testimony by technical means for transferring image and sound (Article 9);
- limitation of the right of an accused and his defence attorney to inspect files and documentation (Article 12);[31]
- additional measures for non-disclosure of the identity of the witness (Article 13); and
- witness protection hearing (Article 15).

Every day's practice reveals some discrepancies emerging from different interpretations and application of the measures under Articles 12 and 13 of the Law on Protection of Witnesses, as well as from the adaptation and extension of protective measures ordered by the ICTY in cases transferred in accordance with Rule 11*bis*.

A first issue concerns the application of the limitation of the right of an accused and his defence attorney to inspect files and documentation under Article 12(1), which stipulates that such measure should apply to witnesses under threat, but it is most suitable to be applied to vulnerable witnesses (victims of rape, for instance) since is normally intended to protect witnesses' privacy from the public, but not from the defence. The practice at the Court of BiH is to make use of general provisions of the Law on Protection of Witnesses under its Articles 3 and 4, which define witnesses under threat and vulnerable witnesses and stipulate that the most lenient measures be ordered in accordance with the principle of proportionality.[32] Article 12(8)

31 Article 12 – Limitation of the right of the accused and his defence attorney to inspect files and documentation:

(1) In exceptional circumstances, if revealing some or all of the personal details of a witness or other details would contribute to identifying a witness, and would seriously endanger the witness under threat, the preliminary proceedings judge may, upon the motion of the Prosecutor, decide that some or all of the personal details of the witness continue to be kept confidential even after the indictment is issued.
(2) The prosecutor shall immediately notify the accused and his defense attorney of the submission of the motion referred to in Paragraph 1 of this Article.
(3) If possible, the preliminary proceedings judge shall hear the accused and his defense attorney prior to making the decision referred to in Paragraph 1 of this Article. The decision of the preliminary proceedings judge must be made within 72 hours following the day the motion is received.
(4) No appeal shall be permissible against the decision referred to in Paragraph 1 of this Article.
(5) If the preliminary proceedings judge was unable to hear the accused and his defense attorney prior to the decision referred to in Paragraph 1 of this Article, the Court shall hear them immediately upon receiving the indictment.
(6) The Court may revoke the decision referred to in Paragraph 1 of this Article, either *ex officio* or upon the motion of the accused or his defense attorney.
(7) Upon the motion of the Prosecutor, the Court shall revoke the decision referred to in Paragraph 1 of this Article.
(8) The Court shall always bear in mind the need to release, as soon as possible, the information to which the decision referred to in Paragraph 1 of this Article pertains. Sufficient details shall be released for the defense to prepare for examination of the witness. The information must be released at the latest when the witness testifies at the main trial.

32 Article 4 – Application of witness protection measures:

The Court may order such witness protection measures provided for by this Law as it considers necessary, including the application of more than one measure at the same time. When deciding which of the witness

also poses a question of interpretation since it stipulates that sufficient details shall be released, at the latest when the witness testifies at the main trial, in order that the defence can prepare for the examination of a witness.

The maximum confidentiality measure of full anonymity of a witness under threat may also apply:[33] the Court of BiH has rendered decisions in several cases so as to apply this protection measure and ordered full confidentiality of data for a period of 30 years after the decision became final, so that only the judges would know the identity of witnesses.

In *Stanković,* pseudonyms previously assigned at ICTY were changed and anonymity granted.[34] In the same case, the Court also defined[35] the conditions for the application of the limits to the value

---

protection measures is to be applied, the Court shall not order the application of a more severe measure if the same effect can be achieved by the application of a less severe measure.

33 Article 13 – Additional measures to provide for the anonymity of a witness:

(1) In exceptional circumstances, where there is a justified concern that the personal security of a witness or his family would be seriously endangered if some or all of the personal details of the witness are released, and that the danger would persist even after the testimony is given, the Court may, either *ex officio* or upon the motion of the parties or the defense attorney, decide that the personal details of the witness shall remain confidential for such a period as may be determined to be necessary, but in any event not exceeding thirty years after the decision has become final.
(2) The Court may, after hearing the parties and the defense attorney, decide that the anonymity of the witness be preserved by allowing the witness to testify behind a screen or utilizing electronic voice or image distortion device, or both the image and the voice, by using technical means for image and sound transmission.
(3) The Court may, at any time, revoke the decision under Paragraph 1 of this Article, either *ex officio* or upon the motion of the parties or the defense attorney.

34 Verdict, *Radovan Stanković*, Trial Panel, 14 November 2006, No. X-KR-05/70*:* 'By the Decisions (3 decisions) number X-KRO-05/70 dated 28 November 2005, the Court ordered protection measures for 14 witnesses in total in these proceedings, while a certain number of them were already granted protection measures in the proceedings against the accused Radovan Stanković before the ICTY. By these decisions all the personal details of the protected witnesses, real names and surnames and other personal data were declared confidential, while during the proceedings the witnesses were enabled to testify behind a screen or utilizing electronic distortion of the voice of the witness or the image of the witness, or both the image and the voice, by using technical means for transferring image and sound. On 5 June 2006, the Court rendered the Decision on changing the previously assigned pseudonyms for increased and more appropriate protection of personal data and identity of the witnesses.

During the proceedings, the protected witnesses were enabled to testify from another room, utilizing electronic distortion of voice or image; however, this possibility was used only by the protected witnesses with pseudonyms A. and H., while the other protected witnesses testified in the courtroom without electronic distortion of voice or image, in a manner that those present in the courtroom could directly see and hear them. They made such a decision after they were informed by the Court that the public was excluded from the main trial and that the accused Radovan Stanković was not present in the courtroom. The reasons for the absence of the accused from the main trial during the evidentiary procedure are explained in the Decision of the Court dated 4 July 2006 and elaborated hereinafter.

The Court was mindful of the protection of identity of the protected witnesses during the entire proceedings, making sure that no identity data would be mentioned, so even in the Verdict these witnesses are not fully named but are mentioned under assigned pseudonyms, while the complete data on the protected witnesses are included in the court case file which is also specially protected.'

35 Verdict, *Radovan Stanković*, Appellate Panel, 28 March 2007, No. X-KRŽ-05/70: 'Furthermore, the position of the appellants is wrong in claiming that the contested Verdict is based on the evidence on which, pursuant to the provisions of the Law on Protection of Witnesses Under Threat and Vulnerable Witness, it could not be based. The reason is that contrary to the arguments of the appeal, the witnesses who were

of evidence provided by protected witnesses, as under Article 23 Law on Protection of Witnesses the sentencing verdict cannot be based solely or to a decisive extent on evidence provided by reading records of the testimony given by protected witnesses.

7. Conclusion

The foregoing is a short overview of the judicial reforms and early days of the War Crimes Chamber of the Court of Bosnia and Herzegovina – the first attempt ever to establish a national, permanent, but temporarily international-ized judicial body. The War Crimes Chamber faces important challenges which will likely result in the processing of a remarkable number of war crimes cases. The jurisprudence of this Court is expected to be unique, since full application is made not only of substantive criminal law provisions of BiH, but also of the provisions of the European Convention for the Protection of Human Rights and Fundamental Freedoms, as well as of the relevant case law of the European Court of Human Rights in Strasbourg.

---

granted the measures of protection in a form of protection of identity data and enabled to testify with the use of electronic device for distortion of voice or image of the witness were not granted the status of "protected witnesses" pursuant to the provision of Article 14 through 22 of the Law on Protection of Witnesses Under Threat and Vulnerable Witness (hereinafter: Law on Protection of Witnesses). In that case, the records on their hearing would only be read out at the main trial, pursuant to Article 21 of the said Law, therefore, pursuant to Article 23 of the Law on Protection of Witnesses, the sentencing verdict could not be based solely or to a decisive extent on evidence provided in that way. Contrary to the above mentioned, the witnesses under pseudonyms "A", "B", "C", "D", "E", "I", "J", "G", and "K" personally attended the main trial, as indicated by the Defense Attorney in the appeal, and gave their testimonies directly before the court panel, they were subjected to cross-examination by the defense for the accused pursuant to the provision of Article 262 of the BiH CPC thus the said restriction referred to in Article 23 of the Law on Protection of Witnesses does not apply to these witnesses. Based on the foregoing, it is clear that the objection of the Defense Attorney is ungrounded and as such refused.'

PART IV
The ICC and its Future

Inherent temporal limits are the natural framework for the activity of international-ized jurisdictions bound to exert their mandate over specific situations, definite in time and space. Scaling down and, eventually, closing the operations of such jurisdictions is, therefore, a normal occurrence for which completion strategies need to be devised in a timely fashion in order to ensure smooth and efficient transfer of their residual functions and legacies to other, international or national, actors.

The permanent nature of the ICC and its potentially universal territorial jurisdiction, however, entails that the focus of forecasts for its future is not on the conclusion of its operations, but rather on the progressive strengthening of the context needed for the Court to discharge its mandate. In this perspective, the practice of the ICC, as well as of its precursors and co-existing international-ized jurisdictions, provide the factual contributions for developing updated legal and practical tools. In the complex and comprehensive legal system established with the ICC, the Law of the Statute cannot be frozen at the stage of development that international criminal law and justice reached at the time of the adoption of the Rome Statute or at any time thereafter. To achieve its overarching goals of fighting impunity in order to contribute to international peace and justice, the Law of the Statute has to be seen as a living instrument: the multiplicity of situations where the Court operates and the conspicuous and variegated experience of other international-ized jurisdictions, as well as of national ones, provide substantial lessons to be treasured in order to enhance the efficiency and effectiveness of the ICC.

Three main layers of challenges have so far emerged in the early life of the Court:

(a) Political. This could be captured under a concept of universality at large of the Rome Statute, that is, the need for expanding the acceptance of the Court in the international community. Important players appear still to hold reservations on the benefits that an independent court could have for international peace and stability, and sometimes seem to make implicitly conditional their support to specific actions or inactions of the Court. Ratification, accession and implementation remain the primary instruments for achieving participation and translating generic support into facts to be asserted through compliance with cooperation obligations.

(b) Legal. The first years of operations of the Court have been characterized by an important organizational activity, as the institution has been building its own structures and practices. Due to the reduced number of judicial proceedings, a more limited, although still significant, experience has been made in implementing procedural and regulatory provisions. In this regard, some of the provisions under the Statute and the Rules of Procedure and Evidence have already revealed shortcomings which seem to affect the ability of the Court to perform its mandate in an efficient and economic manner, while fully respecting established fair trial standards.

(c) Organizational. The build-up of structures and functions within the ICC has produced a result which appears to be unique in international criminal justice. This has opened delicate issues concerning the respective roles of the Court and of the Assembly of States Parties, in

> light of the scope of the principles – both fundamental and interrelated under the Statute – of independence and of accountability before a policymaking body. A growing awareness has emerged that an appropriate oversight has to be seen as a normal instrument for ensuring ownership and preservation of momentum. The reality of the first years of the Court's life has, thus, witnessed states becoming progressively involved in a number of processes, including the budget cycle, administration and practice.

All these layers of challenges – political, legal and organizational – produce experiences that need to be monitored, categorized, studied, selected and translated into lessons learned, in order for the ICC to refine its ability to achieve realistically and effectively its final goal to fight against impunity. The Rome Statute includes provisions for the review of its law and has called since its adoption for some amendments to complete provisions which were left unfinished or considered transitional in Rome. This peculiarity of a first review, focused since the beginning on some potentially controversial items, has so far deterred relevant actors from capturing the importance of a review process aimed at keeping always updated and functional the legal machinery of the Court, a process which is well experimented and successful at other international-ized tribunals.

In this perspective, the first Review Conference of the Rome Statute may be an opportunity for all actors to increase their awareness of the real needs of the system established in 1998, in the light of the many lessons learned, achievements and unresolved issues of the last 10 years. In the same context, the feasibility of amendments foreseen since the adoption of the Statute will involve discussing some of the provisions which were the subject of the final compromise package. In particular, the complex negotiations on the crime of aggression will come under scrutiny and the political choices that states will be able or not to make are likely to deeply affect the life of the Court and of its Statute in the years to come.

SECTION I
The Review Conference

Chapter 17
The Object of Review Mechanisms: Statutes' Provisions, Elements of Crimes and Rules of Procedure and Evidence

Otto Triffterer

1. Introduction: Scope, Present Importance and Starting Positions

(A) When dealing with the Review Conference of the Rome Statute there are, indeed, good reasons to deal not only with the Statutes provisions, but also with the Elements of Crimes, the Rules of Procedure and Evidence, as well as to limit it to these three bodies of law.[1]

Part 13 of the Rome Statute, headed Final Clauses, in Article 121 refers only to the Statute, as a possible subject of amendments. Article 123, Review of the Statute, also only deals with 'amendments to this Statute'. But there is nevertheless a narrow connection between the three above-mentioned bodies of law: the Statute itself expressly mentions in Article 21 the Elements and the Rules as 'in the first place' applicable law in addition to its own provisions, and, thus, as 'amendments' to the Statute. Therefore, they should be considered in the context of this chapter as well. In addition, for the Elements, Article 9[2] provides a special competence for the Assembly of States Parties to amend these guidelines and for the Court to interpret and implement Articles 6, 7 and 8. Given this competence and as amendments to the Elements can be adopted by a regular Assembly, they can also be reviewed by the first Review Conference as well.[3]

A similar situation is described in Article 51(1) for the Rules. Amendments to the Rules should, therefore, also be dealt with together with the Statute.[4] However there is good reason not to include the Regulations of the Court in our consideration. They, according to Article 52, merely 'shall be circulated to States Parties for comments', after they have been adopted by an absolute majority of the judges; and they shall remain in force as long as – and permanently if – no objections from a majority of States Parties are raised. Even though there is no reason, why the States Parties may not themselves propose new or different Regulations at the first or a later Review Conference, for

---

1 This chapter draws on the presentation delivered by the author at the 2007 Turin *Conference on International Justice*.

2 Articles and paragraphs referred to without any further identification are those of the Rome Statute.

3 With respect to the Elements of Crimes in general see R. Clark and E. Gadirov, 'Article 9 – Elements of Crimes, in O. Triffterer' (ed.), *Commentary on the Rome Statute of the International Criminal Court – Observers' Notes, Article by Article* (1st edn, Baden-Baden: Nomos Verlagsgesellschaft, 1999; 2nd edn, Oxford: Hart Publishing, 2008), at 505 ff.; see also O. Triffterer, 'Kriminalpolitische und dogmatische Überlegungen zum Entwurf gleichlautender "Elements of Crimes" für alle Tatbestände des Völkermordes', in B. Schünemann et al. (eds), *Festschrift für Claus Roxin zum 70. Geburtstag am 15 Mai 2001* (Berlin: de Gruyter, 2001), at 1415–1446.

4 See for details B. Broomhall, 'Article 51 – Rules of Procedure and Evidence', in O. Triffterer (ed.), *Commentary*, *supra* note 3, at 1033 ff.

practical reasons this possibility ought to remain the exception because, corresponding to Article 52, the judges have to make the final decision as to which Regulations they wish or need immediately and should be presented to the Assembly of States Parties merely for approval. In addition, since the Regulations by their scope and notion deal exclusively with those issues 'necessary for [the] routine functioning' of the Court, the initiative for these internal affairs should remain with the judges and not be acquired by the States Parties.[5] Therefore, this alternative will not be included in our considerations.

(B) The current importance of the topic we have to deal with is revealed by the fact that (already!) a Review Conference in 2009 is provided for by the Statute. The Rome Statute entered into force on 1 July 2002; and Article 123 provides that seven years 'after' (and not any time before) that date, the General Secretary of the UN has to convene a Review Conference. He should have adequate time to invite all States Parties, all other states and members of the international community 'interested' in the Court, to attend this Conference. But since the date is fixed already, the Conference has to be convened at the beginning of July 2009.

However, this does not mean that the first Review Conference ought to take place in July 2009. Even though the participants can already start to get prepared it is preferable to give ample time and to have the Conference at one of the usual dates of the Assembly of States Parties, which means by the end of 2009 or perhaps even at the beginning of 2010, depending on the demands of the majority of States Parties for getting adequately prepared, but equally on the urgency of the relevant topics.

With regard to this predictable timetable there is sufficient time available to get prepared for the Conference. Correspondingly this preparation already started, for instance with the Salzburg Retreat, The Future of the International Criminal Court, in May 2006,[6] and the Eighth Summer Session of the Salzburg Law School on International Criminal Law, Humanitarian Law and Human Rights Law, in August 2006.[7] It was continued in May 2007 by the Turin *Conference on International Criminal Justice*[8] and in August 2007 by the Ninth Session of the Salzburg Law School.[9] The preparatory work continued in Meran[10] and The Hague.[11] Another highlight was the Tenth Session of the Salzburg Law School, entitled Reviewing the First Review Conference in

5 See for details H. Behrens and C. Staker, 'Article 52 – Regulations of the Court', in O. Triffterer (ed.), *Commentary*, *supra* note 3, at 1053 ff.

6 For details about the 'Salzburg Retreat, The future of the International Criminal Court' see the Report thereto . Available at www.sbg.ac.at/salzburglawschool/Retreat.pdf (visited 20 August 2009). Published also by the Austrian Federal Ministry for Foreign Affairs and Salzburg Law School on International Criminal Law, Humanitarian Law and Human Rights Law in 2007, and therein see, in particular, O. Triffterer, 'Concluding Remarks', at 19 ff.

7 Details about the Salzburg Law School on International Criminal Law, Humanitarian Law and Human Rights Law are available at www.sbg.ac.at/salzburglawschool/ (visited 20 August 2009).

8 For the Report of the Conference see R. Bellelli (ed.), *Conference on International Criminal Justice* (2008). The Report is also available at www.icc-cpi.int/asp/documentation/doc_6thsession.html, as well as at www.torinoconference.com (both visited 20 August 2009).

9 See *supra* note 7.

10 The Conference took place on 26 and 27 October 2007. The various presentations are printed in G. Fornasari and R. Wenin (eds), *Aktuelle Probleme der internationalen Strafjustiz, Akten des XXVII. Internationalen Seminars deutsch-italienischer Studien, Meran 26–27 Oktober 2007* (Trento: Università degli Studi, 2009).

11 The Conference took place on 30 and 31 October 2008.

Advance – Preparing Special Amendments to the Statute, the Elements and the Rules (Sunday 3 to Friday 15 August 2008).[12]

All these early activities demonstrate that the diplomatic procedure to find an agreement at the Conference is evaluated as being rather time-consuming. The States Parties, the only voters at this Conference, in principle need, according to past experience, a year to get sufficiently prepared, in particular to communicate with other member states, non-States Parties and also with members of the governmental and non-governmental organizations or their coalitions. The success of this Review Conference, and perhaps the future of the Court, will depend on how well issues are prepared which ought to be (perhaps) discussed and clarified at this Review Conference. This aim justifies not only the above-mentioned preparatory conferences, but also the scope of this chapter.

(C) However, before addressing the details, the following aspects should be kept in mind. To review means to check up, to control, for instance the effectiveness of the Statute and its organs, to question and discuss the clarity of definitions as well as the value and practicability of regulations, institutions, etc. Review, therefore, by covering all aspects which may play a role, in particular in the future, describes the broader notion compared with amending.

To amend, however, also has no narrow concept. It means not only to add, but also to change, eliminate, improve in any way certain objects. It is thus focused more on results to be achieved, while the notion of 'to review' merely emphasizes collection and consideration of all aspects that might be of relevance for the future; or even evaluation or only criticism of the application of the law and the procedures used by the Court in the first years of its operation, with or without making any specific proposals for improvement.

Anyhow, both approaches – to review and to amend – are independent from each other and equally valuable for the future interpretation and application of the three groups of provisions concerned, because, independent of what will finally be adopted by the majority, considerations and proposals that are not adopted may play a role in the future of the Court as *travaux preparatoires*.

(D) Reviewing and/or amending is in principle possible at the discretion of the Assembly of States Parties, as long as the voting majority keeps in mind that they have no comprehensive legislative competence for all issues of importance for the future activities and functioning of the Court. International criminal law is by its concept and notion a rather theoretical, narrowly structured subject matter and, therefore, not completely at the disposal of any specific legal or political institution because there may be inherent limits of the material with which the Statute deals.

Article 5 paragraph 2, for instance, demonstrates these limits very clearly. Aggression is already a crime for which individual persons are punishable directly under international law.[13] The Assembly of States Parties therefore does not have to create and cannot abolish this punishability. It only has the task of defining what is generally accepted and establishing the conditions under which the Court may exercise its jurisdiction over these crimes. The decision about the definition of aggression has to be (merely!) a confirmation and precision of already existing law, not more and not less, but not a manifestation of a legislative power of the Assembly of States Parties.

This body has legislative competence in relation to some other issues, such as when it comes to 'setting out the conditions under which the Court shall exercise jurisdiction with respect to this crime'. But there is no such power as far as the creation of crimes or the aggravation of penalties is

12 See *supra* note 7.

13 See A. Zimmermann, 'Article 5 – Crimes within the jurisdiction of the Court', in O. Triffterer (ed.), *Commentary*, *supra* note 3, margin Nos. 16 ff.

concerned; though, with respect to the latter, the Assembly of States Parties may decide indirectly what penalties should not be applicable, as was demonstrated by not mentioning the death penalty in Article 80.[14] With regard to the formulation of these conditions and the role of the Security Council, I will refer to my contribution in the Report of the Turin Conference and to 4B and C below.[15]

2. Amendments Barred Under International Criminal Law

Each legal system has some basic pillars as its foundation. They cannot be changed without changing the whole character, scope and notion and, thereby, the system as such. This is true also for international criminal law.[16]

A. Penal Provisions as an Inherent Part of the Law of Nations

Criminal law is typically an inherent part of every legal system in the world. This is true also for the law of nations – the legal system of the international community as a whole. Its criminal law is shaped by its assignment to this legal system; and since its object is to 'handle' criminal behaviour 'through' law, it is characterized equally by those principles which establish criminal responsibility according to the rule of law.[17] In this context it has to be differentiated from 'lawless' practice or rather vague regulations, which leave it at the discretion of some freely established institutions to decide without a precise legal basis what – at least according to their opinion – ought to be right or wrong, or for what behaviour persons should be responsible for and liable to punishment.

To avoid such free-floating chaos, international criminal law is structured by two affiliations: by the foundations, possibilities and limits inherent to the law of nations, the system which it is a part of; and by the object shaping its substance, namely to investigate and prosecute exclusively in accordance with the existing law especially grave violations of legally protected values of the community to which it belongs.

The Rome Statute deals with such issues by enforcing the existing international criminal law which should govern the procedures before the Court. This leads to some consequences for the admissibility of amendments to the Statute, the Elements and the Rules.

B. Sources

In principle, for instance, all sources of international law listed in Article 38 ICJ Statute are permissible and suitable to define crimes falling within the jurisdiction of the Court. But since one of the basic pillars of criminal law is the principle *nullum crimen, nulla poena sine lege*, there are limits for the creation of new crimes. Their definition, for instance, must be according to Article 22 'strictly construed'. This leads to the consequence that general principles in the sense of Article

14 For further details see R.E. Fife, 'Article 80 – Non-prejudice to national application of penalties and national laws', in O. Triffterer (ed.), *Commentary*, *supra* note 3, margin Nos. 4 ff.

15 See my Summary there, *supra* note 8.

16 See O. Triffterer, 'Preliminary Remarks to Part 1: The Permanent International Criminal Court – Ideal and Reality', in O. Triffterer (ed.), *Commentary*, *supra* note 3, margin Nos. 14 ff.

17 The Rule of Law is the principle that governmental authority is legitimately exercised only in accordance with written, publicly disclosed laws adopted and enforced in accordance with established procedure.

38(c) ICJ Statute are not suitable to serve as a source of international law for establishing new crimes. Such principles may define single aspects of criminal behaviour or their evaluation. They, therefore, are mentioned in Article 21(1)(b), but, in general, do not deal with the criminality as such, because principles do not contain with the required certainty descriptions sufficiently 'strictly construed' to shape and create a definition of a crime.[18] The same limitation follows with regard to the well-established opinion of legal experts mentioned under Article 38(d) ICJ Statute.

Both sources, however, may contribute to establish well-accepted basic decisions for a General Part, like 'creating' the punishability of an attempted crime, admitting defences or demanding personal guilt (whatever that may mean) as a prerequisite for the punishability. New crimes or more severe punishment, therefore, can only be established by the first two sources of Article 38 ICJ Statute, namely conventions and customary international law. If such crimes should be included in the Rome Statute, the Assembly of States Parties cannot create them, but merely has to decide whether the punishability of such behaviour is already established by one of the two major sources of international law, and what definitions of such crimes correspond with the (already) acknowledged existing law and, of course, whether they should fall within the jurisdiction of the Court.

If international criminal law ought to stay as it is, namely independent as one branch of international law and fulfilling the demands of criminal law, it has to obey these foundations and principles of both international and criminal law. This has the consequence that no amendment concerning the creation of new crimes (not the establishment of an additional competence of the Court for already existing crimes) or the abolition of one of those principles is at the discretion of the Assembly of States Parties. Such a discretion, however, exists and consequently corresponding amendments are admissible, if amendments deal with a definition or the application of already existing laws, in particular when giving the Court an additional new competence to investigate and prosecute, for what is and even may have been a crime directly punishable under international law before the Statute was adopted or entered into force. Of course, such a competence could then only be exercised in accordance with Articles 11 (jurisdiction *ratione temporis*) and 24 (non-retroactivity *ratione personae*).

Such discretion for extending or narrowing the competence of the Court has, however, to be handled with extreme care because the present jurisdiction of the Court has been assigned to this body by 121 states adopting the Rome Statute on 17 July 1998 and confirmed by the 111 States that have up till now ratified this Statute. We will come back to this issue later, when dealing with concrete examples under 4 below.

C. Addressees

With respect to the addressees of international criminal law, the situation is similar but a little different. Criminal law, in principle, focuses on the responsibility of natural persons and on individual liability for punishment. Nüremberg and Tokyo were based on the assumption that crimes are only committed by natural persons and not by abstract entities. This also is at least the basis for the present structure of the Rome Statute.[19]

---

18 See B. Broomhall, 'Article 22 – *Nullum crimen sine lege*', in O. Triffterer (ed.), *Commentary, supra* note 3, margin Nos. 36 ff.

19 See O. Triffterer, 'Preliminary Remarks', in O. Triffterer, *Commentary, supra* note 16, margin Nos. 25 ff.

However, in national law as well as in international law, there has been since then a tendency to hold non-natural persons responsible. Correspondingly, state responsibility is still an open question, as expressly described by Article 25(4). This provision does not contain a decision as to whether there is a criminal responsibility of states acknowledged in international law. But equally, it does not exclude this possibility, in particular, for the future. It is, therefore, for a Review Conference to decide whether there is already a generally acknowledged criminal responsibility of states or whether their responsibility should continue to be limited to non-penal liability.[20]

Whatever the decision at a Review Conference may be, there is already now in national legislation a tendency to slowly open international law towards a criminal responsibility of states, and such a tendency appears appropriate. Occupation or peacekeeping missions by using armed forces quite often already results in a sort of sequestration, a sanction with an at least penal character, as well known in national law, for instance against companies violating the environment.[21] Therefore, one day it may well become the position that financial compensation or other reparations follow the criminal responsibility of states for committing crimes, as well as for retribution, which are comparable with, but do not fulfil, the strict criteria for penal sanctions.[22]

D. Scope and Notion of Responsibility

Under Articles 25 and 28, the Rome Statute limits individual criminal responsibility to certain categories of persons. These can be summarized as committing a crime as principle perpetrator, soliciting or inducing, as well as aiding and abetting, or the failing of superiors to control properly and, in addition, not preventing the crimes which they have caused by their failure and which are committed by their subordinates.[23]

1. Participation and Attempted Crimes

Such extensions or narrowing of the direct commission, in whatever direction this may be interpreted, may well be at the discretion of the Assembly of States Parties when it comes to decide whether the Court should have jurisdiction, or keep jurisdiction, over certain zones of the mentioned modalities. But since these modalities are not equally shaped and limited in all legal systems, the decision, what is and what is not within its jurisdiction of the alternatives mentioned in the Rome Statute, should be left to the Court under the framework of Article 21.

There are, however, variations which perhaps are not so easily subsumed into one of the groups, such as aiding or abetting or otherwise assisting by neutral behaviour, for instance, by buying products of a merchant who uses, as the consumer knows, all his profits to support terrorism. Such alternatives may nevertheless play a role in practice. The case *Prosecutor v. Seselj*, started on 7 November 2007 before the ICTY, demonstrates that inspiring political speeches may perhaps amount to participation in the sense of Article 7(1) ICTY Statute. But since such an interpretation

---

20 For further details see K. Ambos, 'Article 25 – Individual Criminal Responsibility', in O. Triffterer (ed.), *Commentary*, *supra* note 3, in particular margin No. 42.

21 See O. Triffterer, 'Vorbemerkung zu §§ 169–187', in O. Triffterer et al. (eds), *Salzburger Kommentar zum Strafgesetzbuch Vol. 3* (19th edn, Wien: LexisNexis Verlag ARD Orac, 2007), in particular margin Nos. 12 ff.

22 See H. Kelsen, 'Collective and Individual Responsibility in International Law with Particular Regard to Punishment of War Criminals', 31 *Cal. L. Rev.* (1943), at 530 ff.

23 For further details see Articles 25 to 28 and the commentaries thereto in O. Triffterer (ed.), *Commentary*, *supra* note 3, at 743 ff.

of the law described in Articles 25 and 28 needs to be generally accepted in order to be applied by the Court, the decision should be left to the Court under the framework of Article 21, as already mentioned. However, and once more, when it comes to the decision whether the Court should continue to have jurisdiction over certain modalities, like superior responsibility according to Article 28, or get an additional competence for new, well-acknowledged modes, the Assembly of States Parties may decide, because to decide in principle about the 'amount' of competence of the Court falls within the competence of the Assembly.

The situation is similar, but also a little different with respect to the punishability of an attempt; whether an attempt should trigger responsibility according to Article 25(3)(f) or not may be an open question in international criminal law. But the situation, as open as it may well be without a provision like paragraph (3)(f) regulating the issue, must be clearly described in the Statute to fulfil the demands of the rule of law. Therefore, the competence of the Assembly of States Parties includes the possibility of deciding whether attempted crimes should no longer fall within the jurisdiction of the Court, because it may, in general, be too difficult to prove such attempted crimes. But this competence of the Assembly does not include the interpretation of the definition of an attempt as given in Article 25(3)(f) as interpretation, in accordance with Article 21, is an exclusive competence of the Court.

2. Participation and its Mental Element

For participation, in any of its alternatives, the situation is similar. There is a kind of double intent required though this does not always have to be a complete mental element as for the principal perpetrator. The principal perpetrator needs to have the intent to commit a crime, which means he wants to be successful and to realize all its material elements according to Article 30. His 'mental element' has to also include – as far as there is for 'purpose crimes' – the additional intent to realize the purpose, as in Article 6 the genocidal intent to destroy a protected group 'in whole or in part', even though the completion of the crime does not depend on the realization of this 'purpose' (intent).[24] An initiator of a crime needs to intend that his behaviour causes the addressee to commit a crime. This requires a double intent, namely to act and to be 'successful', in the sense that someone who after being inspired builds the intent to complete the crime he or she was inspired to. In cases of purpose crimes, the completion depends on the particular intent of the inspired person, not on the realization of this intent. The purpose of the first perpetrator may well be to inspire someone to commit a purpose crime and he may himself act also with respect to the realization of this purpose. But it is sufficient he intends that the addressee 'builds' such a particular intent, while his behaviour is dominated by other purposes.[25]

It falls out the competence of the Assembly of States Parties to decide whether this interpretation is correct according to the present international criminal law. It concerns an interpretation within the framework of Article 21 and, therefore is in the competence of the Court. Of course, the Assembly of States Parties at the Review Conference may discuss this question and, as a kind of amendment to the Statute, propose a certain interpretation to the Court and express the opinion that this would

24 For such purpose crimes see O. Triffterer, *Österreichisches Strafrecht – Allgemeiner Teil* (2nd edn., Wien: Springer-Verlag, 1994; unchanged reprint 2002), Chapter 6, margin Nos. 35 ff. and, for the intent of the initiator or abettor, Chapter 16, margin Nos. 77 ff. as well as 103 and 104.

25 See O. Triffterer, 'Kriminalpolitische und dogmatische Überlegungen', in B. Schünemann et al. (eds), *Festschrift*, *supra* note 3, at 1421 ff. and, to the scope and notion of the requirement of a 'double intent' see *supra* note 24.

be preferable. But the Assembly of States Parties is well advised not to do so in order to avoid the slightest suspicion it intends to interfere with the independence of the Court.

E. Irrelevance of Official Capacity and the List of Crimes

The examples considered so far in this chapter mirror the situation in general with respect to the objects of reviewing and amending, the possibilities and limits of these two approaches, as well as the different modalities available and their relation to the authority of the Court to decide certain issues independent of the Assembly of States Parties. The broadness of the notions of review and amendments can also be demonstrated by dealing with the relationship between Article 27, '[i]rrelevance of official capacity', and Article 98, '[c]ooperation with respect to waiver of immunity and consent to surrender',[26] and, in addition, by looking at the exclusiveness of the list of crimes within the jurisdiction of the Court contained in Article 5.

1. Relationship between Articles 27 and 98

Article 27(1) provides that '[t]his Statute shall apply equally to all persons without any distinction based on official capacity'. This means that the Statute with all its substantive and procedural rules and regulations remains applicable, independent of the official capacity in which the perpetrator may have acted. Article 27(1) further continues in the second sentence that any such capacity 'shall in no case exempt a person from criminal responsibility'. This means, under all circumstances, the responsibility remains and the official capacity is irrelevant.

Both provisions, defining and confirming direct criminal responsibility of persons, acting in their official capacity, under international law are not disputed, neither in principle nor in detail. This means that when the Court does not need more evidence or a surrender – because it has all relevant documents and witnesses available, as well as the suspect in custody at the Court or in a state willing to surrender – the Court may proceed through all stages of a criminal case. The clear language of Article 27(1) is underlined by the following paragraph 2. It states that '[i]mmunities or special procedural rules which may attach to the official capacity of a person, whether under national or international law, shall not bar the Court from exercising its jurisdiction over such a person'. This means that the Court may start preliminary proceedings, in particular investigation and prosecution, but also enter the trial phase, because all this is 'exercising its jurisdiction'.

Therefore, only if the Court needs the presence of the suspect, such as for the trial, and does not have him or her 'available', Article 98 may play a role. But even then, the state concerned may decide itself and by its exclusive competence whether to use the possibility given to it by Article 98 or whether to fulfil its obligations according to Part 9 of the Statute to fully cooperate with the Court, as triggered by a request received by the Court and, thereby, violate a bi- or multilateral treaty with other states.

Such '[i]mmunities or special procedural rules' attached to an official capacity, as mentioned in Article 27 and presupposed, in principle, also by Article 98, however may bar national jurisdictions. But in such cases the states concerned are obliged to adapt their laws to implement the obligations they have under the Statute, as established in Part 9. In addition, such an implementation is

26 The relation between these two Articles is also dealt with by O. Triffterer, 'Irrelevance of Official Capacity – Article 27 Rome Statute undermined by Obligations under International Law or by Agreements, Article 98?', in I. Buffard et al. (eds), *International Law between Universalism and Fragmentation: Festschrift in Honour of Gerhard Hafner* (The Hague: Martinus Nijhoff Publishers, 2008), at 571–662.

required to exercise their primary jurisdiction according to the complementarity regime of the Rome Statute.

However, Article 98 contains a procedural exception, adopted as a concession to some States Parties and a few non-States Parties by the Rome Conference and accepted without any discussion so far by the Assembly of States Parties.[27] But now, at the first Review Conference, the Assembly has the opportunity to consider whether Article 98 ought to be changed by the Assembly or even abolished, with all its consequences for those states that may insist on this privilege. Because Article 98 is not a constituent pillar of the proceedings before the Court, an exception of this type may be withdrawn more easily. However, when considering this possibility the Assembly has to keep in mind that there has so far been no reason to demand that Article 98 be abolished, as it has not yet had any remarkable importance in practice; and, in addition, it contains sufficient space for the Court to try to solve such a tension by negotiations that lead to a mutual agreement. If this cannot be achieved, but sufficient evidence is available for an indictment, the Court may proceed because an indictment is not as strong as a request for surrender, although it is still a contribution to the prevention of crimes, as is demonstrated by the *Mladic* and *Karadzic* cases, still pending before the ICTY.[28]

2. Limits of the Article 98 Exception

This interpretation of Article 27 is supported, in addition, by a comparison with Article 5(2) dealing with aggression, which provides a different approach compared with Article 27.

According to Article 5(2) the Court shall exercise its *ius puniendi* only 'once a provision is adopted ... defining the crime and setting out the conditions under which the Court shall exercise jurisdiction with respect to this crime'. This formulation emphasizes that the Court can not even investigate a situation which is referred to it only for the purpose of finding out whether there is reasonable ground to believe that an aggression could have been committed because, as stated above, investigating already amounts to the exercise of jurisdiction and thus is only permissible once crimes against peace are defined in accordance with international law and accepted by the Assembly of States Parties.[29]

With regard to Article 27 the situation is different. In relevant cases the Court shall not be barred 'from exercising its jurisdiction over such a person'. This means the Court has the competence to start an investigation and prosecution in order to find out whether there is reasonable ground for a suspicion against an individual person because only such an investigation may clarify whether there is a specific suspicion for a certain crime falling within the jurisdiction of the Court and whether, in the case where there is, the suspect may have acted in an official capacity.

Only when during these preliminary proceedings or later, when evidence or the surrender of the suspect is needed and the question of the applicability of Article 98 arises, the relationship between these two provisions has to be clarified. But even then a decision is only needed in such cases where, for instance, as already mentioned above, the evidence is not otherwise available or

27 For details to these aspects see O. Triffterer, 'Article 27 – Irrelevance of Official Capacity' and C. Kreß and K. Prost, 'Article 98 – Cooperation with Respect to Waiver of Immunity and Consent to Surrender', both in O. Triffterer (ed.), *Commentary*, *supra* note 3.

28 See Indictment, *Mladic*, 11 October 2002 and Indictment, *Karadzic*, 31 May 2000; see also D.D. Cattin, 'Outline of the presentations of David Donat Cattin – 9th Salzburg Law School on International Criminal Law (2007)', on file with the author; see also O. Triffterer, 'Article 27', in O. Triffterer (ed.), *Commentary*, *supra* note 27, in particular margin Nos. 14 and 29 ff.

29 See O. Triffterer, 'Article 27', in: O. Triffterer (ed.), *Commentary*, *supra* note 27, margin Nos. 29 ff.

the Court does not yet have the suspect in custody or the suspect is about to be surrendered to the Court by another state.

In such situations the custodial state should, according to Article 98, not be obliged to surrender or assist when this would be inconsistent with its other obligations under international law. Whether this is or is not the case is a question of law and, therefore, to be decided by the Court.[30]

For such a situation Article 98 provides a *lex specialis* in comparison to Article 119, demanding that both sides have to seek a settlement[31] but leaving no space for a direct involvement of the Assembly of States Parties. Therefore, perhaps the only task left to the Assembly is to give an opinion at the Review Conference, such as recommending the States Parties and non-Parties not try to bar the Court from exercising its power to investigate and prosecute.

For States Parties such a barring would anyhow be a *venire contra factum proprium*, at least as far as those states have made such agreements with other states after the Statute entered into force, independent of whether the respective state has already signed the Statute before or after it entered into force. For states who ratified before 1 July 2002, the situation is the same because if they took no due notice of Article 27 before entering an agreement in the sense of Article 98, they can be blamed for not properly and completely studying the Statute. Only those who had relevant obligations existing before they accepted the Statute may claim, subject to the approval of the Court, that they could not fulfil their duty to cooperate with the Court without breaking an international obligation.

3. Inherent Limits to the Expansion of the Article 5 List

The above-mentioned conclusion on the role of the Assembly and on how to proceed may be valid *mutatis mutandis* and *cum grano salis* also for other issues. In particular, with respect to the jurisdiction of the Court it remains an open question whether there is an inherent limitation which, at the present time, prevents including within the jurisdiction of the Court specific forms of international terrorism and international drug trafficking as further examples of 'the most serious crimes of concern to the international community as a whole'; or whether this competence of the Court should also be extended to ('very') serious crimes of concern to this community. I have dealt with this issue in more detail in my Summary for the Report of the Turin Conference.[32] But before coming back to this issue under 4(B) and (C), I will briefly recall three decisive aspects for this decision:

- All crimes within the jurisdiction of the Court violate those legally protected values inherent to the international community as a whole as enumerated in para. 3 of the Preamble of the Rome Statute, namely 'the peace, security and wellbeing of the world'.
- Terrorism and drug offences directly threaten 'only' national legal values. This is demonstrated by the extremely intensive and well-functioning horizontal cooperation between those states which are concerned in specific cases or, in particular, are more endangered than others.
- In addition, if there is need for an engagement of the international community as a whole, such situations or cases may be well covered by the scope and notion of crimes against humanity and war crimes, as defined in Articles 7 and 8. Such expressions as 'enduring

30 For details see *supra* note 27.

31 For details see R. Clark, 'Article 119 – Settlement of Disputes', in O. Triffterer (ed.), *Commentary*, *supra* note 3, at 1727 ff.

32 See *supra* notes 6 and 8.

freedom' or 'war against terrorism' have no legal importance. But they symbolize underlying structures, which at least come close to fulfilling the elements needed to establish one of the crimes defined in Articles 6, 7 and 8.

This is not the place to deal with international terrorism and drug offences and the necessity to, perhaps, limit so far well-established rights. But at least up till now both these categories of crimes are not (yet) threats to legally protected values belonging to the international community as a whole. States and the coalition of interested or threatened states appear strong enough to deal with it by horizontal cooperation. The *Lockerbie* case is an example of a Court not internationalized, but strongly influenced by the demands of an effective cooperation between states for the prevention of future terrorism.[33]

3. Modalities for Reviewing and Objects of the Review Conferences

When considering the inherent structures of international criminal law and the establishment of the Court, we have already briefly touched upon a few modalities for reviewing and/or amending the Statute, and the Elements and the Rules. But in order to demonstrate the variety of the relevant spectrum of possibilities there is need for a few additional examples.

A. Possible Additional Scope of the Review Conference

When dealing with the mechanisms for reviewing the Statute it became obvious that such activities may, or could well, be undertaken to demonstrate a certain political line or even be abused for such purposes. This should be prevented in order not to degrade the Assembly of States Parties to a political forum and, at the same time, not to endanger the reputation of the Court, one of the highest independent and impartial judicial organ of the world.

But a Review Conference may well serve as a forum to present legal considerations to the 'international public', including 'potential perpetrators'. This may contribute to the prevention of such crimes. It may also help to draw an comprehensive picture which mirrors the opinion on present and future perspectives of the ICC and on international criminal law and justice in general. It may thus contribute to making everybody more acquainted with the Court, its function and its task, its possibilities and its limits. A Review Conference may thus have a certain 'advertising effect' and perhaps may inspire non-States Parties to accept the Rome Statute or at least to participate by supporting the investigations and prosecutions of the Court.

It also has to be kept in mind that proposals for amendments cannot only be brought before the Assembly of States Parties '[a]fter the expiry of seven years' (Article 121(1)), but also, when referring 'to provisions of an institutional nature ... at any time' (Article 122(1)).[34] The fact that no such initiative has been taken so far clearly demonstrates that up till now the member states and all other states and organizations involved have seen no reason to become active in this direction. This may be evaluated, with all due reservations, as a sign that they all are content with the institutional

33 The trial and appeal judgements of the *Lockerbie* case are available at http://www.scotcourts.gov.uk/library/lockerbie/index.asp (visited 24 February 2009).

34 For details to these provisions see R. Clark, 'Article 121 – Amendments', margin Nos. 6 ff. and 'Article 122 – Amendments to Provisions of an Institutional Nature', margin Nos. 3 ff., both in O. Triffterer (ed.), *Commentary, supra* note 3.

nature and its details regulated in the Statute of the Court. However, there is an exception I will deal with later, under 4(I)(1).

B. Optional and Obligatory Issues to be Considered. Articles 5(2) and 124

An analysis of the wording used in the Statute leads to the conclusion that there are different modalities for reviewing, some of which are optional and others are obligatory. With regard to the first Review Conference, Article 123(1) requires that the Secretary General 'shall convene' such a conference. The Conference is open to all issues and therefore 'may include but is not limited to, the list of crimes contained in Article 5'. Any time after this first Conference the Secretary General 'shall, upon approval by a majority of States Parties, convene a [second] Review Conference', even if only one state requests such a meeting. He has no discretion or choice, but has to react.

With regard to the agenda for such conferences the Statute contains only a few hints. Concerning the crime of aggression, there is no deadline provided in the Statute. Article 5(2) merely refers to activities of the Court 'once a provision is adopted in accordance with Articles 121 and 123'. These regulations thus include the possibility for any draft to be discussed at the first Review Conference, but also 'at any time thereafter'.

The only deviation from Article 123(2) is that it does not need 'the request of a State Party' to put this issue on the agenda. The Secretary General is obliged to observe the situation and – as far as the presentation of a draft is predictable and in accordance with the results of the Special Working Group – has to convene the Review Conference, while it is for the Assembly of States Parties (ASP) Bureau to define the Agenda and to include 'aggression' in it. The Secretary General has then to wait to find out what the Assembly of States Parties will decide in this respect and whether drafts presented may lead to an agreement on a definition of elements 'strictly construed' and on the conditions under which the jurisdiction shall be exercised. If there is no such agreement, the issue ought to be placed on the next agenda. Only if at least one or two crimes against peace are defined and adopted by the Assembly of States Parties at a Review Conference and the conditions established, the Court can exercise its jurisdiction.

The situation is different with regard to the transitional provision in Article 124. This exception from Article 120 ('no reservations may be made to this Statute') triggers the necessity that after 'a period of seven years ... the provisions of this Article shall be reviewed at a Review Conference'. Without any doubt, this has to be the first Review Conference, which takes place exactly after such period of time. With regard to this issue, the Conference perhaps has only to decide whether Article 124 has meanwhile become obsolete and should therefore be deleted. But such a decision may be overhasty because there may be one or more relevant crimes committed within the seven-year period which have not yet been detected or referred.

The question of whether Article 124 can be 'prolonged', perhaps for a limited and shorter period of time, may be reviewed in the sense of being discussed by the Assembly of States Parties. Although the wording of the provision does not prejudice such a decision in one direction, it does not exclude such a prolongation. However, the drafting history does: Article 124 regulates one of the compromises to increase the acceptance of the Statute, and part of this compromise was the acceptance of an exception from the jurisdiction of the Court for war crimes, but only within a certain time limit, for those states who had made this 'reservation'. This reservation, however, was made by only very few states, including France. So far, no opinion has been published in favour of a prolongation. But with all due respect for the drafters of the Rome Statute, whether a prolongation is possible and desirable is at the discretion of the Assembly.[35]

C. The 'Settlement of Disputes' Under Article 119

With regard to the '[s]ettlement of disputes' (Article 119) the Court has the exclusive competence to decide 'any dispute concerning the judicial functions of the Court'; but for 'any other disputes between two or more States Parties relating to the interpretation or application of this Statute, which are not settled through negotiations within three months of their commencement', the Assembly is competent. In case its attempt to settle the dispute or to 'make recommendations on further means of settlement' is not successful, the Assembly may refer the situation to the International Court of Justice.

For the interpretation of this Article it has to be kept in mind that other provisions may be insofar *leges speciales*. For instance, the Elements shall merely assist the Court in 'the interpretation and application of Articles 6, 7 and 8' (Article 9). Therefore, Article 119 is not relevant to a dispute concerning the interpretation or the application of the Elements. But nevertheless, since the adoption of the Statute and the Elements is, in any event, within the competence of the Assembly, it may well solve a conflict by amending the Statute, as far as this is within its competence (*supra*, 2(A) and (E)), or by amending the Elements for which the Assembly has competence, since the Elements are merely guidelines for the Court.

The same is true, though with some differences, with regard to Article 21 which provides that the Court 'may apply' certain provisions or laws. Interpretation of the applicable law is, thus, in principle with the Court and, although the Assembly is in principle free to consider and give an opinion on applicable law in general, it may be well advised not to do so for due respect to the competence of the Court. In particular with regard to cases pending before the Court the Assembly should abstain from so doing because this could give the impression that it is interfering with the independence of the Court.

D. Article 10 Open Doors to Developments of International Law

The considerations above also give reason to remember that according to Article 10 a lack of agreement concerning amendments to the Statute, the Elements or the Rules, shall not bar the development of international criminal law outside these documents. Therefore, an agreement in substance on issues of international criminal law and its jurisdiction may well deal with new laws on other fields, such as horizontal cooperation between states. Thus the development of international criminal law aside from those provisions applicable according to the Statute may be improved and promoted by a Review Conference as well. Article 10 opens the door for such developments.[36]

E. The (Limited) Law-Making Power of the Court

In addition, the question may well be raised whether the law-making power of the judiciary – here the Court – may also have such an effect for issues outside the Statute. The Court has no power

35 For the states having made use of Article 124 and for Article 124 in general see A. Zimmermann, 'Article 124 – Transitional Provision', in O. Triffterer (ed.), *Commentary, supra* note 3, at 1767 ff.

36 Only as far as the Assembly has adopted 'new provisions' by the Statute, the Elements or the Rules, it may take the opportunity at the Review Conference to amend these provisions. For details on this issue see *supra* under 3(A).

to create crimes and it cannot even include crimes not mentioned in Article 5 into its jurisdiction because the latter competence is exclusively with the Assembly of States Parties. But by interpreting and applying the law, the Court has the power to give its binding opinion on what is the law to be applied in cases falling within its jurisdiction. It may be considered that by doing so the Court may decide by an *obiter dictum* that the investigation and prosecution deals with a serious crime of concern to the international community as a whole, but not with one of the 'most serious' crimes. Such a statement, however, has no binding force beyond the negative effect for the cases pending before the Court, but it may well have an influence on national laws and their jurisdiction, as well as on the development of international criminal law in general, because the Rome Statute covers only part of this branch of law, although the most important one. Review Conferences and any other Assembly of States Parties have to keep both aspects equally in mind when considering, discussing and voting on any substantive and procedural international criminal law issue.

4. Common Guidelines on How to Proceed, and Examples Promising to be Effective

The following considerations try to structure the different possibilities for reviewing and amending the Statute, the Elements and the Rules, by means only of a few examples, and not even all of them in detail.

A. Reviewing the Relevant Documents and Proposing Amendments

When dealing with the question of how to make the first (and all coming) Review Conference(s) most effective in the sense of achieving justice and peace for the victims, the suspects, the local social community and the international community as a whole, it is helpful to remember that a request for a Review Conference opens the broadest possibilities for dealing with various issues: everything is possible within the borders described above. However, issues other than those concerning the Statute, the Elements or the Rules are not, at least in principle, 'on the table' of the Assembly of States Parties. But such issues may, when nevertheless raised, lead to desirable side effects, for instance by achieving new and additional agreements in respect to horizontal cooperation, such as for the investigation and prosecution of international terrorism and certain drug offences. Since, as already been mentioned above, specific proposals for amendments may perhaps be the easiest and most effective way to achieving changes, we will deal with a few examples in order to demonstrate this assumption. However, such amendments do not necessarily require additional regulations or changes of the Statute or the other provisions mentioned. They may, for example, merely confirm the *status quo* by explaining convincing reasons to continue the line as it started after the Rome Conference and the entry into force of the Statute.

B. Importance of the Final Act of the 1998 Rome Conference

In order to evaluate the effectiveness of any initiative at any Review Conference or at an ordinary Assembly, it has to be carefully investigated, first, whether such an initiative concerns provisions defining and acknowledging already existing law or those created by the States Parties to regulate 'new issues', as far as the competence of this organ includes such power. Taking due consideration of these aspects we have to first look at – in addition to what has been already mentioned above under 2(E) and 3(B) – the Final Act and at the Statute to see whether there are certain obligations or recommendations already provided for the Assembly of States Parties.

The Rome Statute and the Final Act differentiate, with regard to the crimes falling within the jurisdiction of the Court, between two categories.

1. Aggression: Crimes Against the Peace

Aggression – crimes against peace – already falls within this jurisdiction, though its exercise and, thus, the investigation of such crimes can only commence after the Assembly of States Parties has accepted a definition and set out 'the conditions under which the Court shall exercise jurisdiction with respect to this crime'.

With regard to international terrorism and international drug-trafficking the situation is different. The Final Act merely recommends that the Assembly of States Parties consider whether these two groups of crimes should be included in the Rome Statute. The same or a similar recommendation is given with respect to (other) treaty-based crimes, such as those concerning the most serious disturbances of air traffic.

Correspondingly, Article 123(1) already provides for the first Review Conference to consider whether 'the list of crimes contained in Article 5' should be changed, in whatever direction. With regard to aggression I can refer to what has been written above and in my presentation to the Turin Conference.[37] To promote the exercise of jurisdiction over the crime of aggression it is only important that initially at least one or two special crimes out of this group are strictly construed in order to start with. This appears, at the moment, to be the most urgent task of the Assembly.

In addition, the conditions triggering the possibility of starting an investigation should not be formulated in a way which requires a resolution of the Security Council to start the Court doing its duty with regard to a relevant situation. For the Court to start or to continue an investigation or prosecution it should be the other way round, as provided by the 'Singapore Clause' used in Article 16: only when there is a majority resolution by the Security Council can an investigation on aggression be blocked. The formulation then may also resemble the one used in Article 80 and which appears acceptable because it excludes a single veto blocking the whole situation.[38]

2. International Terrorism and Certain Drug Offences

With regard to international terrorist acts and certain drug offences, I would like to underpin a few amending aspects: the question whether (international or state) terrorism and international trafficking of illicit drugs should be included in the list of crimes in Article 5 is not only disputed, but is also difficult to answer. The Final Act, in Annex I resolution F paragraph 7, only refers to the definition of aggression 'for inclusion in this Statute'. This means that there is no choice: such an inclusion has to happen one day, whenever that day may be.

With regard to terrorism and international drug-trafficking, resolution E of the Final Act recognizes that these are 'very serious crime[s], sometimes destabilizing the political and social and economic order in States'. But the Final Act makes a difference, since these crimes are not yet listed in the Statute. It recommends only 'that the Review Conference ... considers the crime of terrorism and drug crimes with a view of arriving at an acceptable definition and their inclusion in the list of crimes within the jurisdiction of the Court'. This means that the inclusion has to be merely considered, with the objective to find out whether such crimes can be defined 'strictly

37 See *supra* note 8.

38 Ibid.

construed' and ought to be accepted as an additional group of the so-called 'core crimes' and, therefore, should fall within the jurisdiction of the Court.

This raises the question of whether the existing crimes in the Article 5 list have some characteristics which shape them all and, therefore, need to be fulfilled also by additional crimes before they can be included in the Statute. One of the typical elements of the 'most serious crimes of concern to the international community as a whole' is that they are all directly punishable under international law. But this is only a formal criterion. Decisive is, however, that such crimes have been developed and accepted to protect legal values inherent to the international community as a whole, in particular the 'peace, security and well-being of the world' as mentioned in paragraph 3 of the Preamble of the Rome Statute.

Terrorism and international trafficking of illicit drugs threaten individuals and states worldwide, but they also violate values which primarily belong to national legal systems. The international cooperation to fight terrorism and drug offences demonstrates clearly that the need for such a horizontal cooperation is in the interest of many states. This cooperation functions best between states which are individually or 'on block' threatened by these crimes because such states have similar interests. Expressions like 'enduring freedom' and 'war against terrorism' address these interests very clearly. But perhaps it is too early, and hopefully it is not needed at all, to develop in this respect a legal value or interest of the international community as a whole to be protected by this community as such and not only by the national legal systems. In addition, the *Lockerbie* case has demonstrated that with regard to those crimes, such values are, or may be, sufficiently protected at the national level.[39]

It may be a challenge to the Assembly to deal with these questions. Hopefully not, but perhaps one day it has to be decided whether in practice and in theory the two groups of crimes mentioned – terrorism and drug offences – amount to a serious threat for the inherent legal values of the international community as a whole and, therefore, need to be included into the group of the most serious crimes of concern to the international community.[40]

3. *Treaty-Based Crimes*

The same is true with regard to other treaty-based crimes, such as corruption, as defined in the 2003 United Nations Convention against Corruption. To include, in addition to the most serious crimes, those which are 'only' very serious, carries the danger of diminishing the concentrated power of the Court which has the competence to call all persons acting in an official capacity to criminal responsibility. Such a step should, however, not be taken for the reason mentioned above. In addition, it easily could lead to an overload of situations referred to the Court and, perhaps, to corresponding attempts to politically influence the Court, which is something that has to be avoided. As for international terrorism and drug-related offences, interests protected by all treaty-based crimes may still be adequately addressed by national jurisdictions.

C. The Ius Puniendi of the International Community and Enforcement Mechanisms

This just-mentioned limitation appears to be not only required for practical reasons, but is also necessary because the Court is based on and exercises an inherent *ius puniendi* of the international community as a whole. The competence of the Court is not delegated by states, though the

39 See *supra* note 33.

40 See also *supra*, 3A.

establishment of the Court depended on a certain number of States Parties. The difference in comparison with national jurisdictions is that the *ius puniendi*, for instance of the ICTY and ICTR, has not been created, but only expressed and delegated by the Security Council which has empowered these Tribunals for certain 'situations', limited by time and territory, to exercise and execute jurisdiction on behalf of and instead of the international community as a whole. National jurisdictions, therefore, are something different even if they deal with crimes which have, for some reason, an international character.

When states, however, exercise their primary jurisdiction within the complementarity regime of the Rome Statute, they execute jurisdiction on behalf of and instead of the international community's *ius puniendi* – though under the control of the Court – through their national criminal justice system. The Review Conference, therefore, may be well advised not to include additional crimes in the list of Article 5 without due consideration and careful investigation on basic structures and practical agreement on the punishability of these crimes. To deal with such crimes at the Conference may nevertheless perhaps be helpful for clarification of the concept and of certain limits to generally well-accepted procedural rights.

D. Superior Responsibility: An Extension of Article 25 or a Crime Sui Generis?

The Review Conference might also find it desirable to shed light on the structural settings of provisions criminalizing relevant conducts – as an example, the responsibility of superiors with regard to the question of whether this extension of the modalities of participation needs an intentional failure to control. If this is agreed, the question would arise as to whether the requirements for triggering responsibility ('knew or should have known' or 'consciously disregarded information') narrow the original broader concept by a certain objective condition or whether they describe personal guilt in the sense of negligence.

There is also need to clarify whether command responsibility for genocide needs a genocidal intent on the part of the superior, which is a concept which would not correspond with the general notion of participation to which superior responsibility belongs.[41] The reason for this 'assignment' of accountability is that superior responsibility cannot be interpreted as a separate crime of 'superiors merely violating their pre-established legal duties' to properly control their subordinates because the Article 5(1) list of crimes falling within the jurisdiction of the Court is a closed one. This exclusiveness is also demonstrated by Articles 71 and 72, both of which do not presuppose or create (establish) such an extension, but merely give the Court the power to sanction, in a different direction, certain behaviour.[42]

Equally difficult is the differentiation between 'should have known' and 'consciously disregarded information'. This state of mind may be called 'unconscious negligence' as in Article 28(a)(i), or 'conscious negligence' as in Article 28(a)(ii). Such a differentiation, however, comes

41 For details see *supra* 2(D) and O. Triffterer, 'Command Responsibility, Article 28 Rome Statute, an Extension of Individual Criminal Responsibility for Crimes Within the Jurisdiction of the Court – Compatible with Article 22, *nullum crimen sine lege*?', in O. Triffterer (ed.), *Gedächtnisschrift für Theo Vogler* (Heidelberg: C.F. Müller Verlag, 2004), 213–262; see also O. Triffterer, 'Command Responsibility – *crimen sui generis* or Participation as "Otherwise Provided"'?, in O. Lagodny et al. (eds), *Festschrift für Albin Eser* (München: Beck Verlag, 2005), 901–924; see also O. Triffterer, 'Command Responsibility', in C. Prittwitz et al. (eds), *Festschrift für Klaus Lüderssen* (Baden-Baden: Nomos Verlagsgesellschaft, 2002), at 437–462.

42 See for details O. Triffterer, 'Article 71 – Sanctions for Misconduct Before the Court', margin Nos. 4 ff. and R. Dixen, H. Duffy and C. Hall, 'Article 72 – Protection of National Security Information', both in O. Triffterer (ed.), *Commentary*, *supra* note 3, at 1361 ff.

close to the difficulties arising when the relation and borderlines between recklessness and *dolus eventualis* have to be drawn. The first requires an intentional behaviour which 'in the ordinary course of the event' will cause a certain criminal harm. For the second, it is sufficient that such a consequence clearly came to the knowledge of the perpetrator and he or she, nevertheless, did not abstain from starting or continuing the dangerous behaviour. In the struggle to prevent impunity for those crimes, both issues should be clearly defined, which easily could be done by the Court when using its power according to Article 21. Therefore, such a clarification does not need an amendment to Article 30 and the Assembly's reviewing role may only be that of pointing out aspects for arguing in one or other direction.

E. 'Collateral Damage' and 'Friendly Fire' under Article 8(2)(b)(iv)

The Review Conference should also discuss the scope, notion and differentiation between 'collateral damage' and 'friendly fire' and their common overlapping elements. Both equally describe situations where in armed conflicts persons or other 'objects' are endangered or violated and which, according to the military plan, should not have been attacked or otherwise made objects of a violation of the laws and customs of war. The difference is that 'collateral damage' is characterized as an 'incidental' loss of persons or objects of the adversary not aimed at, whereas 'friendly fire' typically hits the own combatants either by an error in choosing the object, holding it erroneously to belong to the adversary, or because the attack and its consequence deviate from the original plan to hit the enemy and thus the actual loss is equally incidental. With regard to the former, Article 8(2)(b)(iv) defines the 'war crime of excessive incidental death, injury or damage'. This heading under the Elements of Crimes, underlines that this crime deals with collateral damage and under which conditions such a loss amounts or does not amount to a war crime. Typically, the protected target is not aimed at, though finally endangered or even violated. But it is an open question as to what mental elements are required for the perpetrator 'intentionally launching an attack' which causes 'collateral damage'. Has he to be aware merely of the 'factual circumstances' that make an 'incidental loss' appear to 'be clearly excessive in relation to the concrete and direct overall military advantage anticipated'? Or has he to be aware (not only) that his attack could cause loss, but also that such a loss 'would be clearly excessive', which means, has he to evaluate the situation correctly in order to be criminally responsible for the 'collateral damage'? The latter requirement would imply that a wrong evaluation – assessing a possible loss as 'proportional', while it was not – would exempt him from punishment.

When we apply the general regime of Article 32 to this situation, the suspect has to know only the factual circumstances which make the military advantage anticipated 'excessive'. The conclusion – that because of these objective circumstances the 'collateral damage' would be 'clearly excessive' – is left to the organs of the Court and eventually to trial judges.[43]

Deviating from this rule, the opinion is that such an evaluation has to be made by the suspect to trigger his or her accountability and not (only) by the Court.[44] An error of the suspect based on the correct awareness of the factual circumstances but, nevertheless, drawing the wrong conclusions from these facts (namely that the loss is not excessive compared with the military advantage anticipated) would then exempt him or her from criminal liability. This appears as an unacceptable

43 See O. Triffterer, 'Article 32 – Mistake of Fact or Mistake of Law', in O. Triffterer, *Commentary*, *supra* note 3, margin Nos. 49 ff.

44 See M.J.D. Reynolds, 'Collateral Damage on the 21st Century Battlefield: Enemy Exploitation of the Law of Armed Conflict, and the Struggle for a Moral High Ground', 56 *The Air Force Law Review* (2005), 1–108, at 72 ff.

result,[45] above all because whether the possible loss would be disproportionate compared to the 'advantage anticipated' depends on, and, therefore, can only be explained by, the military itself: the higher they put or claim to be the value of the military advantage anticipated, the greater could be the lawful incidental loss on protected targets; and, further, because the 'collateral damage' still may remain 'proportional' – in the sense of not 'clearly excessive', and thus *per se* does not trigger criminal responsibility – at least as long as such loss is not caused intentionally. To accept and require that such an evaluation needs to be made by the perpetrator himself and not only by the Court would, therefore, come close to granting impunity, though the perpetrator has acted with 'full intent' and merely erred in evaluating proportionality, or at least claims to have done so. Therefore, a clarification at the Review Conference could be helpful, in particular since the Elements of Crimes to this provision can, at least, be misleading or leave the question open as to whether criminal liability requires mere knowledge of the factual circumstances or, in addition to that, a correct legal evaluation.

In this context, some assistance could be found in the wording of Article 51 Additional Protocol I of 1977 to the 1949 Geneva Conventions: 'may be expected to cause incidental loss of civilian life, injury to civilians, damage to civilian objects, or a combination thereof, which would be excessive in relation to the concrete and direct military advantage anticipated.' Protocol I thus offers one of the earliest definitions of collateral damage. But equally, it does not answer the question of whether the above-mentioned evaluation has to be made by the perpetrator. In the Commentary to the Additional Protocols it is merely stated that those who plan an attack must determine whether its effects could be excessive. They have to base their decision on '(1) the foreseeable extent of incidental or collateral civilian casualties or damage, and (2) the relative importance of the military objective as a target'. Because both aspects 'involve a balancing of different values which are difficult to compare, the judgment must be subjective'.[46]

Since this question concerning value judgements also has relevance for many other crimes within the jurisdiction of the Court, a few further considerations on these issues are justified, in particular with regard to the armed conflicts in the Near East, where quite often more civilians are violated than military personnel or objects.

Collateral damages are incidental losses which, in connection with an intentionally launched military attack, violate certain protected targets. Such an attack triggers responsibility for a war crime only under the conditions mentioned above. Therefore, it would be dangerous to accept as a defence the perpetrator's argument that he had (with the best of his knowledge about the factual situation) evaluated possible incidental loss as (still) not excessive, and that he had been motivated, in particular, by this evaluation of the facts to launch the attack and take the risk of causing collateral damage; had he known that his attack could cause disproportionate or excessive 'collateral damage' he would not have launched or would have at least stopped the attack immediately when becoming aware of such a danger. This interpretation appears as an effective defence, at least when in practice the perpetrator makes a reliable impression on judges – the Court may then be convinced that the perpetrator really 'believed' in the 'proportionality' of the incidental loss.

---

45 See *supra* note 43.

46 See with regard to this issue O. Triffterer, 'Ius in bello: Eskalation durch ‚Kollateralschäden' wie durch Kriegsverbrechen – Beweisbarkeit und Vermeidbarkeit?', in R. Moos et al. (eds), *Festschrift für Roland Miklau* (Wien: Studienverlag Innsbruck-Wien-Bozen, 2006), 559–584. With regard to Article 51 of the 1977 Additional Protocol I see W.A. Solf, 'Article 51 – Protection of the Civilian Population', in M. Bothe et al., *New Rules for Victims of Armed Conflicts – Commentary on the Two 1977 Protocols Additional to the Geneva Conventions of 1949* (The Hague: Martinus Nijhoff Publishers, 1982), at 296–318.

In addition, looking at the Elements to Article 8(2)(b)(iv), some inconsistencies become obvious, and which do not fit in with the general principles accepted in international criminal law. And, because this field is, in substance, criminal law, it is as such bound by the basic foundations of criminal law. The wording of Article 8(2)(b)(iv) – 'in the knowledge that such attack will cause incidental loss' – is misleading as when I know that my attack will cause this result the loss is, for me, no longer 'incidental'. This lack of clarity is perpetuated in Element 3, where knowledge that the attack 'would cause' does not fit in with 'incidental death' either, because the perpetrator then knows what 'will' indeed happen. 'Will', 'would' and 'incidental' instead exclude each other. A more correct wording should instead be the knowledge that the attack 'could cause' or 'may be expected to cause' and then, if this happens, it 'would be incidental', as appropriately expressed in Article 51 Additional Protocol I.

A similar inconsistency exists with regard to the required knowledge. 'Knew' refers not only to the possibility of causing incidental death, but by the wording of Element 3 ('and') it also refers to the further Element that 'such death ... would be of such an extent as to be clearly excessive in relation to the concrete and direct military advantage anticipated'.

What is required for the mental element, in this case, is only that the perpetrator is aware of the factual circumstances which establish the basis for this evaluation. This interpretation can be demonstrated and is confirmed by the fact that everywhere else in the Elements the formulation 'was aware of factual circumstances' is used to describe a mental element different from and 'otherwise provided', with regard to the general requirements under Article 30.

With regard to the war crime of collateral damage or incidental damages under Article 8(2)(b)(iv), this aspect is underlined by the fact that according to Element 5 the 'factual circumstances' for the international character of the armed conflict do not even have to be known by the perpetrator. The perpetrator has only to be 'aware of factual circumstances that establish the existence of an armed conflict'. This limitation is convincing because the international character of the armed conflict may not even come to the knowledge of the perpetrator, e.g., in cases where foreign troops support the other side in such a conflict without any announcement or visibility of their status.

With regard to other elements, since a perpetrator does not have to establish the juridical evaluation of a legal definition, but only has to know the factual circumstances on which such an evaluation is based and its social relevance for the situation, this 'amount' of knowledge ought to be sufficient also with respect to the 'disproportionality'. Otherwise, as already mentioned, the mere defence that the perpetrator has evaluated possible collateral damage as not being clearly excessive compared with the military advantage anticipated would risk to lead to impunity.

This interpretation is confirmed by Article 8(2)(c) where Element 3 requires only that the perpetrator 'was aware of the factual circumstances that established this status'. What is meant is the status of being placed *hors de combat* by the 1949 Geneva Conventions. And again, war crime under Article 8(2)(b)(xxi) 'outrages upon personal dignity', needs not even awareness, as long as this 'violation' is of such degree as to be generally recognized as an outrage upon personal dignity (Element 2).

The above interpretation of the war crime of excessive 'incidental' damages (iv) is further supported by war crime (xxiii) of using protected persons as shields. The status of the victims, being 'other persons protected under the international law of armed conflict', needs no evaluation by the perpetrator as it is sufficient that the perpetrator be aware of the factual circumstances that give these persons a special protection, even though he may believe that such a protection is not established in international law or that there is not such a protection at all.

The notion of 'friendly fire' is not precisely defined, but is to a certain degree self-evident. It describes a military attack which hits persons or objects from the group launching the attack, mainly combatants, but in principle independent of whether they are combatants or civilians or objects belonging to one of these groups. Such loss may be caused by an intentional attack on these objects because the attacker erroneously believed the target aimed at belonged to the adversary while in reality it was assigned to his own group. But the expression 'friendly fire' also covers the situation of an attack aimed at foreign civilians or protected property that incidentally causes, exclusively or in addition, a loss of the own party. At first sight the competence of the Court would extend only to cases where such loss of the 'enemy' is actually caused. In all other cases the competence seems to fall exclusively within the disciplinary or military penal law of the respective party. But this impression is not convincing.

Collateral damage as a war crime under (iv) and loss caused by friendly fire may in some instances overlap. 'War crimes committed by friendly fire' seems to be, at first sight, a contradiction in itself. Nevertheless, a relationship is not only conceivable, but convincing, because war crime (iv) already by its wording does not require a result at all, neither intentionally on military targets aimed at nor (incidentally) on protected targets (not aimed at). It is instead sufficient that the attack launched violates military targets and results in 'clearly excessive loss' of protected targets. Launching such an attack is *per se* a completed crime, as is the directing of intentional attacks against protected targets in war crimes (i), (ii) and (iii). Attacking protected targets should be prevented even if no violation occurs. And war crime (iv) is applicable even if there is a *per se* permitted military attack because of the dangerousness of such attacks in the acceptance of their risk for protected targets. Such risk constitutes the harm to the interests protected by the criminal provision and, thus, forms the basis for criminal responsibility. In cases of friendly fire, the attacker has agreed to widen this risk through an *ex ante* assessment of the dangerousness of his conduct and, therefore, triggers his responsibility independently of whether the risk amounts to a violation of protected targets or not. This result cannot be changed when *ex post* the whole attack fails and causes no violations at all. Therefore the risk appears *ex post* as danger for, or a violation of, values of the attacker, as in cases of 'friendly fire'. This is the reason why such a constellation should trigger responsibility under (iv).

This is the only convincing interpretation of the wording of war crime (iv). And it is acceptable also for practical reasons, because otherwise the defence could be raised that in fact the attack as such was erroneously aiming 'only' at targets of the own side and could have caused loss only there. The included attempt – to hit the enemy and consequently causing incidental loss only there – would then go unpunished, even if such loss is or would have been 'clearly excessive'. Therefore 'friendly fire' by erroneously believing to attack the adversary – and thereby accepting the risk to cause 'clearly excessive' loss on his protected targets, while in reality aiming at the own people – is an (attempted) war crime (iv), even if neither the attacker nor its adversary has suffered loss on protected or military targets.

F. Employing Weapons Listed in an Annex to the Statute. Article 8(2)(b)(xx)

While the question of interpretation and application of the law (also considered under E) has to be left to the Court, the application of Article 8(2)(b)(xx) '[e]mploying weapons … which are of a nature to cause superfluous injury or unnecessary suffering' is exclusively within the competence of the Assembly. Because this definition contains a 'reservation' that it can be only applied after 'a comprehensive prohibition' and thereby relevant weapons, etc., 'are included in an annex to this Statute'. Every annex within the meaning of this definition is an amendment to the Statute and, therefore, left at the discretion of the Assembly, which has to accept and deal with all reviews and any proposals for amendments or for a complete annex. However, the competence of the

Assembly is only to define what is in any event acknowledged and accepted by the law of nations as 'dangerous weapons'.[47]

G. Using Certain Protected Persons as Shields. Article 8(2)(b)(xxiii)

This war crime covers '[u]tilizing the presence of a civilian or other protected person to render certain points, areas or military forces immune from military operations'. The conduct of the perpetrator must concern civilians 'or other persons protected under international law of armed conflict' as mentioned in Element 1 to this provision. But the Elements do not say anything with regard to the question of whether such a conduct should be intentional in the sense of the perpetrator knowing that he is using targets 'protected under the international law of armed conflict'. However, this is obvious because otherwise the purpose of shielding an own military object from an attack launched by the adversary could not be achieved.

But a defence could argue that the perpetrator did not believe that a certain person was 'protected under international law in armed conflict' and therefore this definition would not be fulfilled. Also for this situation it should, therefore, be clarified that the perpetrator has only to be aware of factual circumstances and is not required to make the evaluation that his behaviour is a violation of international law. Thus, an incorrect legal evaluation in this respect does not exempt him from punishment.

H. Supporting Impunity by Proposing Elements to Narrow the Definitions of Crimes?

Some of the Elements considered above do not correspond to the law described by the relevant definition. A further example of that is to be found under war crime Article 8(2)(b)(xii), 'denying quarter', in the Elements of which the 'will be given' wording of the Article was changed into 'shall'. The Elements also propose a specific intent, though such a requirement is not based on the actual wording of Article 6. The following aspects should, therefore, be taken into consideration at the Review Conference in case any of the definitions of the crimes and/or their elements are placed on the agenda:

- The Elements of Crimes shall 'assist the Court in the interpretation and application of Articles 6, 7, 8'. These Elements are thus mere guidelines clarifying or only confirming material and/or mental requirements of the crimes concerned.
- The wording of the law is in general, and in particular with respect to the definitions of crimes, the indispensable borderline for every interpretation of acknowledged descriptions. Elements proposed to deviate from the wording, therefore, violate the basic criminal law principle of legal certainty which requires all definitions of crimes to be 'strictly construed' (Article 22(2)).
- As far as the Elements deviate from the wording of definitions of crimes contained in Articles 6, 7 and 8, they all propose to narrow responsibility. This 'uniformity' appears suspicious and raises the doubt that the drafters may have intended to limit the competence of the Court and thus extend impunity.
- Though clarification and confirmation of material and mental requirements of the crimes by the Court are demanded by the rule of law and, therefore, are in the interest of justice,

47 A first step could be the ratification of the Convention on Cluster Munitions and the insertion of this Convention in an annex to Article 8(2)(b)(xx).

such a procedure may not respect the Statute and creates legal uncertainty. This is not in the interest of anybody, in particular the suspect, the victim and the international community as a whole, which have a right that the Court finds out whether crimes as defined in the Statute have been committed. In case these premises are accepted, the Assembly should, either directly or by establishing a Commission, clarify whether the Elements remain in the framework of the definition.

- Although the Court is independent enough to have its own opinion on all these questions, there is a task for the Assembly as well, since it has to be avoided that the Court or – under the complementarity regime – national jurisdictions be overloaded with cases which would finally be dismissed because of an unsound legal basis. In particular, narrowing Elements may lead to impunity and thus prevent the world's awareness about what is described in the Statute as criminal behaviour.

Though the Court is entitled to express an opinion on such questions, it can only do so within pending judicial proceedings on situations or cases. The Assembly, however, may use its forum to express not only a legal opinion, but also to recall the overarching policy goal set under the Statute, that is to prevent the most serious crimes of concern to the international community as a whole going unpunished. Article 6 is a good and further example of this danger and for the need to clarify these matters.[48]

I. Rules to be Amended?

Aspects similar to those considered for the Elements may come into consideration for reviewing the Rules of Procedure and Evidence and be placed on the agenda of the Review Conference. Here are three examples.

1. The Defence as an Independent Organ of the International Criminal Justice System?

It is discussed, whether the rights of the defence – as established in Articles 55 '[r]ights of the persons during an investigation', Article 66 '[p]resumption of innocence', and Article 67 '[r]ights of the accused', corresponding to the relevant Rules 20 RPE *et seq.* – describe and guarantee the position of the defence in a clearly enough structured manner that contains all aspects of practical importance. Rule 20, for instance, merely gives the Registrar the responsibilities for issues 'relating to the rights of the defence'.

These provisions appear neither sufficiently detailed nor attached to an organ of the Court which is close enough to the daily legal problems of the defence. Therefore, it does not come as a surprise that a private opinion within the Court promotes the idea of establishing the defence as an independent organ of the Court and providing via the Registry a training programme for defence counsel,[49] which is a worthwhile idea to consider even though there may be considerable

48 See O. Triffterer, 'Genocide, its Particular Intent to Destroy in Whole or in Part the Group as Such', 14 *Leiden Journal of International Law* (2001), at 399–408. See also O. Triffterer, 'Can the Elements of Crimes Narrow or Broaden Responsibility for Criminal Behaviour Defined in the Rome Statute?', in C. Stahn and G. Sluiter (eds), *The Emerging Practice of the International Criminal Court* (Leiden: Brill Publishers, 2009).

49 Corresponding proposals were made by Mark Dubuisson, Director Court Management, ICC, at the Conference of the Amsterdam Center for International Law, 'The ICC at Five Years: A Look at the Court's

disagreement about the detail.[50] However, the proposed establishment as an organ of the Court is perhaps not the best option. In some states the defence has a standing as an inherent organ of the administration of justice, not as an organ of the Court in the sense of Article 34. This affiliation with the judiciary appears to be strong enough because it already gives the defence the right and the duty to argue exclusively in favour of the accused and to carry out investigations on its own initiative unless the suspect consents otherwise. The main important aspect in this context is to guarantee the independence of the defence from all organs of the Court in order to fully implement its duty as a party in criminal proceedings to guarantee the rule of law and a fair trial, and to monitor deviations in proceedings before any organ of the Court as soon as they become obvious.[51]

For these reasons, training defence counsel at the Court does not only appear to be the non-optimal solution, but is also not advisable. In order to guarantee the function of the defence, its independence and neutrality from of all organs of the Court has to be the basis for any action. Differently from all other organs of the Court, the defence is the only organ within the judicial system that is not only permitted, but has a specific duty, to be partial in favour of its client, while the Court, the Prosecutor and the Registry have to be impartial. However, the defence has to take action exclusively in the interest of its client, as long as its argumentation and other activities remain within the rule of law. For instance, the defence is not permitted to present unfavourable results of its own investigations to the Court without the express consent of its clients. Partiality is required even if the interests of justice may be disturbed, as long as the defence counsel does not use unlawful means. This position is currently not guaranteed by the Statute or by the Rules or by the relevant Regulations 19 and 20 of the Court, which only cover the functional aspects of the defence. After the original idea of the international organization of defence counsel in The Hague to be, at least partly, financed by the Court has been rejected, there may be sufficient reason to believe that a clarifying statement by the Assembly could be helpful and perhaps lead in the near future to guarantee the defence more independent standing in the administration of the international judicial system by putting corresponding provisions either in the Statute or at least in the Rules.

2. Protecting the Independence of Judges

Article 41 opens the possibility of 'excusing and disqualification of judges', but grounds for these are not provided either there or in the relevant Rules 33–35 RPE. However, it would make sense to allow for a judge to be excused because he is a national of a state involved in a situation he has to adjudicate. Only at the ICJ and, for instance, at the European Court of Human Rights, where 'the state is on trial', a judge appointed by the state 'on trial' has to sit on the bench, if necessary by special appointment (as in *Congo v. Belgium*). But this structure and function is not comparable with the proceedings before the Court, which is dealing with individual criminal responsibility: here, the state is not directly and openly 'attacked', even though it may be indirectly blamed for what has been committed by one of its organs or other persons acting in an official capacity.

With regard to the Court, the situation, therefore, is shaped by the fact that the judges can be nominated exclusively by States Parties. When a nomination has been made successfully by a state the judge is a national of, he or she should not sit when an organ or another person acting

Emerging Practice', 6 October 2007. Available at http://www.grotiuscentre.org/files/ConferenceICCProgramme.pdf (visited 20 August 2009).

50 The question whether the defence should be an independent organ of the Court is also dealt with by J. Temminck Tuinstra in her *Defence Counsel in International Criminal Law* (Cambridge: Cambridge University Press, 2009).

51 See O. Triffterer, 'Preface', in J. Temminck Tuinstra, ibid.

in an official capacity of his/her own state is suspected of having committed a crime within the jurisdiction of the Court. The same would be true with regard to the position of the victim and the nationality of the judge.

In such situations, for various reasons, not least the pressure exerted by the expectation of a nomination by his or her state for a second term of office,[52] a judge's 'impartiality might be reasonably doubted'. This wording in Article 41(2)(a) 'on any ground', repeated in Article 42(7) together with other grounds, makes it desirable to expect that the judges in such situations ask to be excused. Therefore, the Assembly of States Parties does not have to take action on this issue. The initiative in such cases can be clearly left to the President or the Presidency, as it is at least a moral obligation of the judges to apply to be excused. Should this not be the case, the danger exists that one of the parties will raise the issue in the proceedings before the Court, with possible damage for the reputation of the Court.

3. Obligations and Modalities for Cooperation

Part 9 of the Statute deals with one of the most important subject matters for the practical enforcement of the Statute. It regulates primarily vertical cooperation bottom-up and top-down between the Court and the states. But, in addition, horizontal cooperation between states – quite common with regard to the protection of national interests by mutual assistance in criminal matters – must equally be guaranteed in order that justice can be done according to the task and function of the Court. It is, therefore, the second basis for an effective enforcement of international criminal law within the framework of the Statute.

With its missing structure for the different categories of cooperation, Part 9 has been explained as 'there was not enough time at the end of the negotiations to bring the Articles in an all together logical order'.[53] Rules 176 to 197 RPE have tried to fill this lacuna but, being dependent on the Articles in Part 9, the task has not been finished yet. Perhaps it may be advisable to review Part 9 by taking into consideration the experience so far developed, not only at the ICC, but mainly at the two UN *ad hoc* Tribunals over the last decade. However, it should be clarified in advance whether the Assembly may be in the position to find a solution, perhaps by a generally accepted common agreement, or whether the issue needs a Preparatory Commission for amending the Statute and the Rules at a later conference.

On the open issues an agreement should, in principle, be possible, in particular when it is considered that Article 98, '[c]ooperation with respect to waiver of immunity and consent to surrender', may be of lesser importance than originally expected. The *Slobodan Milosevic and others* case clearly demonstrates that political pressure combined with economic sanctions may create an atmosphere for international agreements which at least helps to overcome the difficulties. But an exchange of ideas and considerations of possible amendments may be helpful to improve further vertical and horizontal cooperation, the latter perhaps also with those states not yet parties to the Statute.

The demand for the future is that since the Court and the States Parties are exercising equally the *ius puniendi* of the international community as a whole and, therefore, since all states are members of this community, independently from their ratification of the Rome Statute they should equally be interested in the protection of the international community using criminal law as *ultima ratio*.

---

52 When applicable, under Article 36(9)(c).

53 See C. Kreß, K. Prost and P. Wilkitzki, 'Preliminary Remarks to Part 9', in O. Triffterer (ed.), *Commentary*, *supra* note 3, margin No. 4.

5. Conclusion

This collection of different topics and regulations to be reviewed or amended at the Review Conference should not be closed without daring a prognosis for the future development of international criminal law and its jurisdiction: does this rather new field of law and the Court have a future at all, in the sense of being one day accepted and applied everywhere around the globe and thereby contributing to the prevention of the most serious crimes of concern to the international community as a whole?

A. Unpredictable Developments as a Challenge to the Court

When the Statute was adopted in 1998, and even after the Court had been established on 1 July 2002 by the Statute entering into force, everybody believed that the enforcement of this substantial international criminal law instrument with its 'complementarity regime' would have started from the 'primarily competent' national level. The 'international community as a whole' was prepared to carefully observe this situation, where national jurisdictions were called in to exercise of the *ius puniendi* on its behalf.

The international community, with its subsidiary jurisdiction based on the complementarity regime, was entrusted with the task of finding out for every single situation and case whether the competent state was able and willing to execute this right at all and, in case it was, if it would do so properly, for instance by applying the general standards of a fair trial and of the rule of law.

Surprisingly, the implementation of the complementarity regime took a different, unexpected direction. Not one or even a few of States Parties started, either silently or publicly, to exercise their rights and duties within the complementarity regime. Nor did a non-States Party to the Rome Statute make any use of its inherent right to apply international criminal law according to the indirect enforcement model, which means as applicable law in the legal system with or without implementation, depending on the law in their legal system.

Instead, the first situations unexpectedly came to the Court: a 'state which is not a party to the Statute … by declaration lodged with the Registrar, accept[ed] the exercise of jurisdiction by the Court with respect to the crime in question', under Article 12(3) (Ivory Coast); around the same time, a 'situation in which one or more of such crimes appears to have been committed is referred to the Prosecutor by a State Party in accordance with Article 14' (Democratic Republic of the Congo, Uganda, Central African Republic); and a third competence of the Court was established by the Security Council acting under Chapter VII of the Charter of the United Nations, by referral of a situation 'in which one or more of such crimes appears to have been committed … to the Prosecutor' (Darfur/Sudan). In all such situations the Court, and not a state, had to start and then continue to exercise the *ius puniendi* entrusted to it by the international community as a whole under the complementarity regime, where such subsidiary exercise of this jurisdiction by the Court is normally triggered only after the states have not fulfilled their duties properly.[54]

The Court, in principle, has to accept such referrals even though it may later come, and with 'a closer sight', to the conclusion that there is not sufficient ground for further investigation. In this context, when taking over such referrals, the Court, by whatever organ, has to decide whether political reasons were the causes for such referrals. The Security Council as a political organ of

---

54 For details concerning this development see http://www.icc-cpi.int/cases.html (visited 20 August 2009). See also 'Lady ICC: A Play about the Court takes Ivory Coast by Storm', 34 *The Monitor: Journal of the Coalition for the International Criminal Court* (2007), at 18.

the UN has in itself sufficient guarantees to avoid a merely political referral triggering a criminal investigation. The fact that political motives may play a role at all does not, and should not, bar such a referral. What has to be avoided is such a referral being abused for political purposes by bringing organs of a state or other persons acting in official capacity into discredit. There may be such situations, as for instance in Burma in autumn 2007, calling for an 'intervention' of the Court. But whenever there is a referral, it has to be carefully observed, investigated and decided whether there is a competence of the Court. With regard to genocide and crimes against humanity, there is no limitation for such a referral. But according to its lit. (f), Article 8 '[p]aragraph 2 (e) applies to armed conflicts not of an international character and thus does not apply to situations of internal disturbances and tensions, such as riots, isolated and sporadic acts of violence or other acts of a similar nature. It applies to armed conflicts that take place in the territory of a state when there is protracted armed conflict between governmental authorities and organized armed groups or between such groups'. Paragraph 3 of Article 8 continues that '[n]othing in paragraph 2(c) and (e) shall affect the responsibility of a Government to maintain or re-establish law and order in the state or to defend the unity and territorial integrity of the state, by all legitimate means'. With regard to this limitation, referrals are to be handled with great sensitivity, skill and due care. As discussed above, although political purposes might always be present, referrals have to be based on genuine situations, because a state being suspected of having committed crimes or of silent tolerance of such crimes may easily have its reputation endangered in and outside the Assembly. Thus the Court's investigative organs bear a great responsibility and have the duty to remain impartial. This is even more vital in situations where criminal conduct appears on a purely state level, where it may be difficult to prove that such a referral was motivated by political reasons and not to prevent grave violations of the international legal order.

B. International Criminal Law and Enforcement of Human Rights

The last statement under (A) above brings us to an issue which, in general, characterizes international criminal law where crimes are committed mainly by abuse of power, though not exclusively. As perpetrators of international crimes are normally persons in power who quite often dominate their national legal system or can influence its criminal jurisdiction, it is well established and, by now accepted, that the international community as a whole is required to deal with those violations of basic human rights.

The question of whether international criminal law could be used as *ultima ratio* to abolish starvation, hunger, poverty and similar intolerable forms of social injustice in the world should also be raised. In this direction stands the guarantee of equal minimum living conditions as social rights for all human beings.

Obviously, such a high objective could not be achieved at the first Review Conference, but perhaps one day – when the Court is well established and has proven its independence, impartiality and neutrality in more than a few cases – the law may develop in this direction. Hopefully, we may not need such an *ultima ratio* judicial means in order to abolish hunger and avoid thousands of people dying every day while the rest of the world has enough financial and human power to immediately stop starvation all over the world. That such a combined action is possible very quickly has been demonstrated by the worldwide reactions to the financial crises. In addition, we should not forget that the widespread forms of injustice mentioned above are causes not only of international terrorism and drug offences, but also of abuse of power, which is a common denominator of all the core crimes within the jurisdiction of the Court, which makes it necessary to act for their prevention.[55]

55 See also O. Triffterer, 'Diskussionsbeitrag: Zum Beachtungsanspruch des Völkerstrafrechts in staatlichen Rechtssystemen', in Landesgruppe Österreich der Internationalen Strafrechtsgesellschaft (AIDP) und Österreichischer Juristenverband (eds), *Internationale Strafgerichtshöfe und Menschenrechte* (Wien: Bundesministerium für Justiz, 2007), 69–114, in particular 112 ff.; see also O. Triffterer, 'Die gesellschaftspolitische Verpflichtung als Herausforderung der heutigen Juristen?' Festrede zur Eröffnung des 13. Österreichischen Juristentages 1997, in Schriftenreihe des Österreichischen Juristentages (1999), 25–72; see also The Pontifical Academy of Social Scienes, XV Plenary Session on Catholic Social Doctrine and Human Rights (1–5 May 2009).

Chapter 18
Universality: Momentum and Consensus for the ICC

Jürg Lindenmann

1. The Road from the Rome Statute

The period from the adoption of the Rome Statute in 1998 until now has been remarkable. Up to and including the Rome Conference, the whole negotiation process was based on consensus. Given the enormous political and technical complexity of establishing an international organization like the International Criminal Court (ICC), this is quite admirable. It may be interesting to recall that the document forming the basis for the discussions at the Rome Conference, the so called Zutphen-Draft, contained some 1,600 square brackets and 100 options, most of which were resolved, during the five-week Rome Conference, by consensus. This consensus-based approach was only interrupted on 17 July 1998, unfortunately, with the two votes relating to the adoption of the Rome Statute itself.

Votes sometimes tend to estrange those who have been defeated as a minority from those whose position has been upheld by the majority. It is therefore remarkable that the process after 1998 and up until now has remained inclusive and consensus-driven. States that have not been favourable to the adoption of the Rome Statute have nonetheless shown interest in the process, have continued to be involved and have participated actively in the Preparatory Commission (PrepCom).

All the instruments supplementing the Rome Statute – the Elements of Crimes, the Rules of Procedure and Evidence, the Financial Regulations and Rules, the Rules of the Assembly of States Parties, to mention just a few – have indeed been prepared and adopted as a draft by the PrepCom on the basis of consensus, consensus including those states who had (and may still have) reservations with respect to the Statute itself. I find that quite extraordinary.

This spirit also prevailed after the entry into force of the Rome Statute on 1 July 2002, in the meetings of the Assembly of States Parties (ASP). Article 112 of the Rome Statute provides that states not party to the Rome Statute but that have signed either the Statute or the Final Act of the Rome Conference may be observers in the ASP. The Rules of the ASP go further, however. They provide that states which have signed neither document may nonetheless be invited to participate in the meetings of the Assembly.[1] And this the Assembly has done regularly since its very first meeting in September 2002; careful to maintain an atmosphere of inclusiveness, it always extended invitations to all states.

A second example is the decision of the ASP with respect to the venue of the Special Working Group on the Crime of Aggression. The Assembly decided that those discussions should take place in New York. I think there are two reasons for that: first, a substantive reason, given the thematic interrelation between the crime of aggression and the UN Charter. But there is also a second reason, more procedural in character, related to the issue of inclusiveness: the Assembly was mindful of the fact that not all states are represented in The Hague and that some of those states might be particularly interested in participating actively in the discussions on the definition of the crime of aggression.

1 Rule 94 of the Rules of Procedure for the Assembly of States Parties.

This spirit of inclusiveness prevails even in activities undertaken *outside* the Assembly of States Parties. Both in New York and in The Hague, a Group of Friends of the International Criminal Court meets on a regular basis in order to inform each other and informally exchange views on subjects relating to the ICC. This group is open not only to States Parties to the Statute, but to all states that can identify themselves with a few underlying principles of like-mindedness. It is my understanding that at least some meetings are even open to *all* states, including states which take an interest in the ICC but – for whatever reason – may not be ready to subscribe to such principles.

In short, since 1998, states have been careful to maintain an open, transparent, inclusive and consensus-driven process. This is, of course, in order to prepare the ground with a view to achieving growing support for the Court.

2. A Representative Court

An institution that aims to be universal must, from its inception, reflect the world's communality and the world's diversity.

The Rome Statute mirrors that imperative in a number of ways: the crimes for which the Court may exercise jurisdiction are *universally* recognized as being the worst crimes. The principle of complementarity may be called a *universally* recognized factor for ordering international relations. The Statute reflects *diversity* in its procedural law, where features of different legal systems and traditions, including common law and civil law, have been assembled into a one workable solution. The Statute also reflects *diversity* in its provisions for the election of judges, in particular with respect to regional and gender balance.

I think it is fair to say that from 1998 and up until now, all actors – the PrepCom, the ASP and the Court itself – have been mindful of the fact that representativeness and balance are important in all functions and at all levels: within the three organs of the Court, but also within the ASP and the Trust Fund for Victims. Indeed, if the Court is to become universal over time, it is key that all those joining may have a sense that they are part of the Court and that the Court is part of them.

3. Toward a Universally Accepted Institution

As is well known, the ICC does not exercise jurisdiction on the basis of universal jurisdiction. It only deals with crimes committed on the territory or by a national of a State Party.[2] This limitation may seem somewhat astonishing at first sight, given the fact that states are allowed (and perhaps in some instances held) to exercise (subsidiary) universal jurisdiction for the crimes under the jurisdiction of the Court within their own jurisdiction. However, in drafting the Rome Statute, states were careful not to violate the principle that an international treaty can only affect States Parties to it and cannot have any legal effects on states which are not parties.[3]

The result of the limitations provided for in Article 12 of the Rome Statute and its complementarity regime is the following: if the fight against impunity is to become truly universal, it must be ensured that the ICC will, over time, be supported universally. It is therefore important that awareness,

2 Art. 12(2) of the Rome Statute. Only based on a referral of a situation by the Security Council in accordance with Art. 13(b) ICCSt and Chapter VII of the UN Charter may the Court's jurisdiction reach further.

3 Arts 34–38 of the Vienna Convention on the Law of Treaties of 23 May 1969.

knowledge and acceptance of the Statute are promoted worldwide and that sufficient information made available as to what the Court can do and, just as importantly perhaps, what it cannot be expected to do.

Many states have put the promotion of the Rome Statute high up on their political agenda, and some have adopted programmes and funds to support such activities. Apart from the efforts undertaken by governments and international organizations, the efforts undertaken by non-governmental organizations are particularly noteworthy. Without their commitment, that continued to be strong after 1998, I do not think that there would be as many ratifications, and the level of implementation would be lower.

I think that these efforts, undertaken since 1998 by governments, international organizations and non-governmental organizations, are quite remarkable. And it is important that they continue.

4. The Future of the Court: Conclusions

What can be done to keep up the political momentum? I would like to formulate two sets of expectations.

The first is addressed to the Court.[4] Obviously, the Court is fully established today and 'on track'. The three referrals by Uganda, the Democratic Republic of Congo and the Central African Republic, as well as the referral by the Security Council of the situation in Darfur, prove that the ICC responds to a real need and that it has become part of the international security architecture.

The Court very much depends on states' support for it. In order to continue to be successful, the Court must therefore meet the expectations of the States Parties in the long run. The question then is: what is it that states expect from the Court? The answer is actually quite easy: I believe that states want the Court to fulfil its mandate under the Rome Statute. Nothing more and nothing less.

Of course, the Court must be aware – and there is no doubt that it is acutely aware – of the fact that it acts in a sometimes highly charged political environment. It must not, however, let itself be derailed by political considerations from fulfilling its tasks. The ICC must do what a court of law does: apply the law in a consequential, unpartisan, objective and well-reasoned manner. With this, it continues to act predictably and credibly and remains the well-respected institution it is today. I say this because there have been voices claiming that the Court has been interfering with political processes. I believe the opposite is true: the Court would interfere if it were to base its activities on what does or does not appear to be politically opportune at any given moment.

A second set of expectations is addressed to the states. What can they contribute to keep up the momentum?

> (a) Within the ASP, the representatives of States Parties must continue to maintain an inclusive, transparent and consensus driven process.
> (b) We must act credibly ourselves. We must respect the Statute and maintain its integrity. We must also act credibly in implementing decisions that we have taken earlier. I think of the definition of the crime of aggression here, where we must make – as we certainly do – serious efforts to achieve progress in accordance with the requirements of the Final Act.

---

4 In doing so, I do not wish to appear to be patronizing or giving advice to the Court: I simply try to frame in words what I believe to be the expectations of the international community towards the Court.

We must also take seriously our obligations under the Statute with respect to such issues as cooperation or payment of assessed contributions.
(c) We must understand and appreciate that international criminal justice is very much a learning process. While the Statute has proven to be operative, it is not inscribed in stone. Rather, it is a text open for adaptation over time, in order to reflect, at every moment of history, the 'state of the art' in international criminal law and international criminal jurisdiction.
(d) We should be careful, on the other hand, to adopt modifications based on sufficient practical experience only. With respect to the next Review Conference, we must keep in mind in this regard that, in some fields, there is not very much experience as of yet.
(e) Unless there are compelling reasons to do so, States Parties should avoid adopting amendments that might make it more difficult for states not yet parties to the Rome Statute to join at a later time.[5]
(f) Finally, we must be aware that the Review Conference is not a meeting that takes place *en famille*, that is to say within the family of States Parties only, but that the Conference is of interest also to states not yet parties to whom we would like to reach out.

---

5 One would have to be careful to avoid that any amendments adopted in accordance with Art. 121(3) of the Rome Statute, in particular those falling under the procedure described in Art. 121(5) ICCSt, deploy unwanted discriminatory effects between states that are parties to the Statute at the time of the adoption of an amendment and states not yet parties. While the former have the possibility to 'opt out' by refusing to ratify the amendment, it may be doubtful under the wording of Art. 121 ICCSt whether the latter also have the faculty to make such a choice. If they do not, the amendment might be have a disincentive effect with respect to future ratifications.

Chapter 19

The Law of the Statute and its Practice Under Review

Roberto Bellelli

1. The Scope of the Review Conference

A. The Preparatory Process

1. Agreed Assumptions

Preparations for the 2010[1] first Review Conference of the Rome Statute within the Assembly of States Parties (ASP) of the International Criminal Court (ICC) have been dealt with by the appointment of a focal point on general issues such as timing, venue, duration and scope, while a separate mandate was given to a member of the Bureau[2] for the definition of the Rules of Procedure of the Review Conference and for collecting possible proposals for amendments. The consultation process was carried out through bilateral meetings, diplomatic briefings and open-ended meetings of the Bureau, while light was shed on some objectives of the Review Conference through the organization of thematic international conferences.[3]

Preparatory works for the Review Conference have so far stressed three levels of its scope:

---

1 Art. 123(1) ICCSt requests ('shall') that the first Review Conference be convened 'seven years after the entry into force' of the Statute by the UN Secretary General (UNSG). As the Statute entered into force on 1 July 2002, at first glance the date of the Review Conference was understood by many to be set somewhere at the beginning of July 2009. However, the interpretation prevailed that the obligation set under Art. 123(1) ICCSt referred only to the issuance of invitations by the UNSG, not to the date for actually having the Review Conference convened. See *Review Conference: Scenarios and Options – Preliminary paper by Mr. Rolf Einar Fife* (Preliminary Paper), 21 November 2006, ICC-ASP/5/INF.2, para. 4, at 2. Confirmed in *Review Conference: Scenarios and Options – Progress Report by the focal point, Mr. Rolf Einar Fife* (Progress Report), ICC-ASP/6/INF.3, 4 December 2007, paras 11–12, at 2. Furthermore, preparations for the Review Conference were focused for long time on the choice of a proper venue, with the offer from the Government of Uganda to host the Conference in Kampala only accepted by the ASP at its seventh session, in November 2008. See *Venue of the Review Conference*, ICC-ASP/7/Res. 2. The ASP also decided that any proposal for amendment of the Rome Statute be considered at its eighth session, in November 2009: *Strengthening the International Criminal Court and the Assembly of States Parties* (Omnibus Resolution), ICC-ASP/7/Res. 3. The first Review Conference is scheduled to take place from 31 May to 11 June 2010. See ASP Bureau Decision at its 7 April 2009 meeting, para. 3(b).

2 Sivuyle Maqungo, Legal Adviser to the Permanent Mission of South Africa to the UN.

3 *Progress Report*, note 1 *supra*, at 7, acknowledges, *inter alia*, the contribution provided to the process by the *Conference on International Criminal Justice*, organized by R. Bellelli and held in Turin on 14–18 May 2007. Documentation available at http://www.torinoconference.com and on the ICC website in all UN languages http://www.icc-cpi.int/Menus/ASP/Sessions/Documentation/6thSession (visited 13 May 2009).

(a) Amendments. Consideration has been given to the 'mandatory issues arising from the Rome Statute and the Final Act of the Rome Conference', identified in the following:[4]

(i) the transitional provision under Article 124 on the seven-years deferred acceptance of the jurisdiction of the Court for war crimes;
(ii) the outcome of the work of the Special Working Group on the Crime of Aggression;[5]
(iii) international drug trafficking and terrorism.[6]

However, in the categorization of 'mandatory issues', a nuance is offered to states for consideration, when the review of Article 124 is still defined as 'the only *legally* mandatory review to be carried out at the first Review Conference'.[7] Furthermore, it was indicated that consideration of other potential amendments, like the Belgian initiative related to Article 8(2)(b)(xx), should take place within the Bureau;[8]

(b) Outreach, including 'projecting to the outside world an image of the present stage of development of the Court and of the continued existence of a consensus among States Parties with regard to international criminal justice',[9] with a view to 'actively contribute to promoting and achieving universality of the Rome Statute'.[10]

---

4 Informal discussions between 2006 and 2009 have led to an evolution in the definition of the scope of 'mandatory issues', as the first approach of the focal point was to consider that the review of the opt-out clause in Article 124 was the 'only one mandatory review to be carried out at the first Review Conference', Preliminary Paper, note 1 *supra*, at 7. See also *infra* note 6 and text.

5 Resolution F(7), in Annex I of the 'Final Act of the United Nations Diplomatic Conference of Plenipotentiaries on the Establishment of an International Criminal Court' (Final Act) provides that '[the Commission] shall submit [proposals for a provision on aggression] to the Assembly of States Parties at a Review Conference'.

6 Final Act, Resolution E only 'recommends' that not necessarily the first but 'a Review Conference consider the crimes of terrorism and drug crimes with a view to arriving at an acceptable definition and their inclusion in the list of crimes within the jurisdiction of the Court'. The *Report of the Working Group on the Review Conference* at the seventh session of the ASP (The Hague, 14–22 November 2008) stresses that 'due consideration would need to be given to substantive issues that are to be discussed at the Conference' and that 'delegations [are] invited to *consider primarily* the provision contained in article 124 ... as well as the issues raised in resolutions E and F' (emphasis added). Annex II to ICC-ASP/7/20, *Official Records*, Vol. 1, at 46, para. 6. Dealing with drug and terrorism crimes is also addressed in the report on the informal consultations conducted at the first resumption of the seventh session of the ASP, on 22 January 2009, para. 4 and from the 9 February 2009 *Non-paper on the scope of the Review Conference submitted by the focal point. Mr. Rolf Einar Fife* (Non-paper), ICC-ASP/7/20/Add. 1, at the second resumption of the seventh session of the ASP. However, Final Act, Resolution E only 'recommends' that not necessarily the first but 'a Review Conference consider the crimes of terrorism and drug crimes with a view to arriving at an acceptable definition and their inclusion in the list of crimes within the jurisdiction of the Court'.

7 New York Working Group of the ASP Bureau, Informal consultations on the Review Conference of 11 March 2009, minutes of 31 March 2009, at 9(i)(a). See also *supra* note 3 (emphasis added).

8 See *infra,* at (C) and note 35.

9 Ibid., at 12 and also in the 4 December 2007 *Progress Report*, note 1 *supra*, at 29.

10 *Report of the Working Group on the Review Conference* at the seventh session of the ASP, Annex II to ICC-ASP/7/20, *Official Records*, Vol. 1, at 46, para. 5.

(c) 'Stocktaking' of international criminal justice, including developments brought by the completion strategies of ICTY, ICTR and SCSL.[11]

However, the approach to and discussions about amendments have definitely been of a low profile, likely depending on the substantial uncertainties of the outcome of the negotiations on the crime on aggression or on the need to avoid amendments carrying the potential of opening the Pandora's box of discussions settled with the package agreed upon in Rome on 17 July 1998. The success of the first Review Conference appears, therefore, to be attached primarily to its side-scope (outreach and stocktaking), rather than to its substance (amendments),[12] with the objective of 'strengthening the Court and protecting the integrity of the Rome Statute'.[13] On these premises the Assembly agreed that proposals for amendments should be considered when they 'command very broad, preferably consensual support'.[14]

The status of discussions has clarified that States Parties are tentatively willing to only deal with such amendments that:

(a) are likely to gather consensus;
(b) have no potentially divisive effect;
(c) do not risk to affect the integrity of the Statute;[15]
(d) address provisions that have received sufficient implementation in the practice of the Court.[16]

---

11 *Preliminary Paper*, note 1 *supra*, at 12, *Progress Report*, note 1 *supra*, at 29 and, lastly, *Strengthening the International Criminal Court and the Assembly of States Parties* (Omnibus Resolution), ICC-ASP/7/Res. 3, 21 November 2008, at 62, which has labelled the Review Conference as 'an occasion for a "stocktaking" of international criminal justice in 2010'. This was, thus, also recommended by the focal point in its *Non-paper*, *supra* note 6, Annex III, at 39: 'in addition to a focus on amendments that command a very broad, preferably consensual, support, consideration should also be given to a stocktaking of international criminal justice in 2010.'

12 'The key *success criteria* for the Conference may therefore *have less to do with amendments* to the Statute *than with* what *kind of overall message* is conveyed to the international community at large about international criminal justice' (emphasis added). *Preliminary Paper*, note 1 *supra*, at 13 and *Progress Report*, note 1 *supra*, at 30. Also 'not [to have] an exclusive focus on amendments, the number of which should have no bearing in determining the success of the Conference', *Progress Report*, at 28.

13 Ibid. at 9 and also at 27, 'preserving the integrity of the Statute is deemed primordial'.

14 ICC-ASP/6/Res. 2, *Strengthening the International Criminal Court and its Assembly of States Parties* (Omnibus resolution), at para. 54 and identically in ICC-ASP/7/Res. 3, at 62. See also the focal point *Non-paper*, *supra* note 6, Annex II, at 39.

15 'Deep commitment by States Parties to the aims and integrity of the Rome Statute' (*Non-paper*, at 39) and 'there is broad support for the proposed goals of the Review Conference of strengthening the Court and protecting the integrity of the Statute' (*Progress Report*, note 1 *supra*, para. 9).

16 'The Court has yet to complete a full cycle of a trial' and, Ibid., at 10: 'Key procedures have not yet been implemented. This has limited the empirical basis for any discussion of amendments in important areas.' *Progress Report*, note 1 *supra*, para. 23.

2. Procedure for Amendments

Amendments may be proposed only as of 1 July 2009,[17] but nothing forbids the prior circulation of draft amendments, as any possible proponent might be willing to preliminarily assess whether a proposal might gather sufficient consensus.[18] This has been the case of the Belgian proposal on the 'weapons provision' of Article 8, announced at the seventh session of the ASP[19] and circulated during its second resumption (New York, 9–13 February 2009).[20]

Although there is no provision in the draft rules of procedure of the Review Conference[21] for a cut-off date for submission of proposed amendments,[22] the focal point recommended that guidelines be issued to have any proposed amendment considered at the 2009 eight session of the ASP in order to ensure that such proposals may enjoy the broadest possible support.[23] The ASP, therefore, decided that 'proposals for amendments to be considered at the Review Conference should be discussed at the eighth session [of the ASP] in 2009, with a view to promoting consensus and a well prepared Review Conference'.[24] On these lines, the Bureau went further by anticipating that 'any proposed amendments ... will have been identified *by* the eight session' of the ASP (emphasis added) and proposing 30 September 2009 as deadline for presentation of amendments.[25]

---

17 Art. 121(1) ICCSt: 'after the expiry of seven years from the entry into force of this Statute, any State Party may propose amendments thereto.'

18 It is in this spirit that the proposal on the weapons provision by Belgium and others (see *infra*, 3(B)(1)) makes it clear that 'it is the intent of the sponsors not to insist for amendments to be transferred by the Assembly to the Review Conference if they do not attract an overwhelming support', at para. 5. 'Prior consideration of any proposals for amendments may also be particularly useful with a view to refining or streamlining proposals'. *Progress Report*, note 1 *supra*, para. 15.

19 'One delegation indicated that it was considering circulating a text for an amendment to the list of war crimes in article 8 of the Rome Statute, specifically regarding the use of certain weapons, prior to the next session of the Assembly.' *Report of the Working Group on the Review Conference*, 21 November 2008, ICC-ASP/7/WGRC/1, at 7.

20 See Roger Clark, 'The "Weapons Provisions" and its Annex: The Belgian Proposals', in this Volume.

21 The 'draft rules of procedure of the Review Conference' are contained in the *Report of the Bureau on the Review Conference*, 16 October 2007, ICC-ASP/6/17 and were only endorsed by the ASP at its sixth session ICC-ASP/6/Res. 2 *Strengthening the International Criminal Court and its Assembly of States Parties* (*Omnibus resolution*), at para. 58 and Annex IV.

22 Rule 49 deals with 'consideration and adoption of amendments to the Statute'.

23 *Progress Report*, note 1 *supra*, at 17–18.

24 ICC-ASP/6/Res. 2, *Omnibus resolution*, at para. 53 and identically in ICC-ASP/7/Res.3, at 61.

25 New York Working Group of the ASP Bureau, Informal consultations on the Review Conference of 11 March 2009, minutes of 31 March 2009, at 4. The Bureau 'agreed that States would require sufficient time to consider proposals in advance of the eighth session of the Assembly and decided to propose 30 September 2009 as the deadline for the formal submission of proposals for amendment to the Rome Statute', while 'the dates for [such submissions] would be communicated to States by the President of the Assembly'. Tenth ICC-ASP Bureau Meeting, 9 July 2009, Agenda and Decisions, para. 1(b). As a result, the ASP President reminded States that 30 September 2009 '*should be the deadline* for formal submission of amendment proposals to the Secretary-General of the United Nations' (emphasis added). Letter to states, ASP President, ASP/2009/139, 15 September 2009. While such deadline needs to be approved by ASP/8 itself, the possible issue of respect of the three months required under Art. 121(2) ICCSt between the notification of proposed amendments and the date of the ASP might also be addressed by, e.g., having the first day of the Review Conference convened as an ASP in the meaning and for the purposes of the said provision of the Statute. However, the Bureau has further clarified that 'the 30 September deadline was not of a legal nature, yet it was the expectation that all

B. The Integrity of the Rome Statute

1. Notion

While there is consensus among States Parties on the need to protect the integrity of the Rome Statute, the scope of this principle has never been clearly defined.

The Rome Statute was adopted upon a compromise package: individual provisions and key features of the Statute were accepted only in the context of the package which, thus, has since been understood as an achievement to be protected in its totality. However, if this agreement has inspired since 1998 all the supporters and stakeholders of the ICC and the need to protect the integrity of the Statute has arisen, it is only insofar as the consensus in Rome was painfully achieved on that package and some states remained outside of or unconvinced by that consensus.[26] Thus, one could argue that only principles/provisions that formed the subject of that compromise fall squarely within the core concept of the integrity to be protected.

Therefore, the notion of integrity seems to relate only to what makes the Rome Statute unique and, on the one hand, crucial to the perspective of the like-mined actors supporting it, while, on the other hand, criticized by those who held strong reservations and have consistently campaigned against its implementation. This uniqueness may be summarized in the peculiarities of the Rome Statute, identifiable in the principles of permanence, independence and complementarity.[27] In this context, provisions – among other things, on jurisdiction and admissibility, triggering mechanism, powers of the Prosecutor – could be easily identified as the subjects of the protection to be afforded under the integrity principle. Controversial initiatives proposed, but finally rejected, during the PrepCom sessions – in particular during the elaboration of the Rules of Procedure and Evidence (RPE) – might also offer reasonable ground for identifying integrity-sensitive issues.

Beyond that, the Rome Statute system includes a number of organizational and procedural provisions which do not characterize the Statute under its peculiar principles (permanence, independence and complementarity), although they play a systematic role in effectively achieving the judicial mandate of the Court in the fight against impunity. This category of non-integrity-related provisions should, therefore, not fall within the agreed assumptions for the Review Conference.[28]

2. From Static to Dynamic Protection

The notion of integrity, however, should not only be confined to its traditional and formal notion, which aims to protect the final compromise reached in Rome, that States Parties acknowledge to be an untouchable balance. This 'static protection' or passive role of protecting the structural harmony of the Statute by means of avoiding amendments to its crucial provisions entails, e.g., that proposals or suggestions to dilute the Statute in order to gain possible support of some major players in the Security Council were in the past rejected: circumstances do not influence the law.

States would respect the deadline which they had all concurred with, since no request for an extension thereto had been raised'. Thirteenth ICC-ASP Bureau Meeting, 12 October 2009, Agenda and Decisions, para. 1(a).

26 Out of some 150 states participating in the Rome Diplomatic Conference on 17 July 1998, 120 voted in favour of the Statute, 7 against and 21 abstained. However, 139 states have signed thereafter the Statute, thus reducing to 10 states the potential for substantial dissent on the scope and contents of the Statute.

27 See R. Bellelli, 'The Establishment of the System of International Criminal Justice', in this Volume, at 4(D) (hereinafter, The System).

28 See *supra*, at 1(A)(1).

However, beyond this 'static integrity' there is also a functional notion of integrity of the Statute, that reflects the obligation of States Parties under the Law of Treaties to protect and ensure that the Statute can attain its object and fulfil its purpose.[29] This concept of integrity 'in-motion' or 'dynamic protection' of the Rome Statute captures, on the one hand, the proactive role to be played by stakeholders willing to protect the Statute against its functional failure, and, on the other hand, a reactive approach: change what is needed in the circumstances.

It is widely agreed, in fact, that the success of the Court does depend on the way it is able to establish its jurisdiction through cooperation of States Parties and the international community at large. From this perspective, although independence is afforded to the largest extent possible to the ICC judiciary and to its Prosecutor,[30] not only the establishment of the ICC, but also its future, is based on a consensus-driven process. A permanent Court needs the sense of ownership of its stakeholders to be maintained unchanged over time, with no regard to any specific case it is dealing with, and that its authority not be challenged on its very substance. Furthermore, only willing cooperation and support of the activities of the Court are able to provide it with the means for its routine functioning, as well as for the peaks of its judicial and organizational activities. In this regard, although under the Statute there are means for enforcing and sanctioning the lack of compliance with the obligations of states,[31] these are limited in scope and their effect would mainly depend on the deterrence they might perform.

Therefore, conclusions should be consistently drawn from the otherwise widely agreed understanding that it is of the utmost importance to preserve consensus throughout the life of the Court.[32] In this regard, it is apparent that the challenges the ICC has been facing, since it publicly started its operational phase with the issuance of the first arrest warrants, have an impact not only on the immediate reactions of states, but also from the perspective of long-term consensus. With this in mind, stakeholders should care about avoiding that well-founded criticism can support otherwise arbitrary claims against the performance of independent functions of the Court, that are only expected to become more frequent as the actions of the Court intensify.[33]

Defusing threats to the stability of the ICC system should, thus, entail a manifold approach: on the one hand, preservation of the credibility of the Court, including in its growing managerial complexity and the devising of a transparent process of verification, through the establishment of an objective and external mechanisms of oversight; on the other hand, procedural tools that are suggested by lessons learned should not be discarded as a matter of principled position.[34]

From this perspective, the formal notion of integrity should be implemented by protecting the Statute, but rather than from any amendment, only from those that would alter its hard core of

---

29 Art. 31(1) Vienna Convention on the Law of Treaties, 23 May 1969, United Nations, *Treaty Series*, Vol. 1155, at 331 (Law of Treaties): 'a treaty shall be interpreted in good faith and in accordance with the ordinary meaning to be given to the terms of the treaty in their context and *in light of its object and purpose*' (emphasis added).

30 On this point, see R. Bellelli, The System, *supra* note 27, at 4(D)(2).

31 Ibid., para. 4(E)(3).

32 See *supra*, at 1(A)(1).

33 *Infra*, at 9(A), (G)(2),(3) and (7)(c)), and 12(D). See also R. Bellelli, The System, *supra* note 27 at 4(E)(4)(a) and (b)(ii), and R. Bellelli, 'Obligation to Cooperation and Duty to Implement', in this Volume, at 3(C) and (E)(i).

34 Along these lines, see J. Lindenmann, 'Universality: Momentum and Consensus for the ICC', in this Volume, at 4(c): 'international criminal justice is very much a learning process [and] the Statute ... is not inscribed in stone.'

substantial and procedural provisions representing the magical blend of the 1998 compromise that brought the ICC into existence.

C. Transparency and Inclusiveness of the Process

It is widely acknowledged that the success of the ICC depends on many factors, both internal and external to the proper functioning of the Statute's mechanisms. In this regard, the sense of ownership that a theoretically universal Court should promote needs to take into account all the driving forces in the development and implementation of international criminal justice. Among other things, this concerns the role of the civil society – including Academy – the multifaceted contribution of which cannot be disregarded, but instead should be addressed with appropriate in-depth reflections. Similar reasoning applies to possible substantial contributions of international organizations relevant in the field and, in particular, other international-ized Tribunals and Courts.

Although the ASP position is that 'the preparatory process will be conducted in a transparent and inclusive manner',[35] the aforementioned categories of qualified and possible contributors to the assessment of the status of international criminal justice have no standing to access the official working format for the preparations.[36] One could, therefore, wonder whether the best use of the enormous human and scientific resources available among non-state actors is only to be officially involved at the late stage of the actual holding of the Review Conference – mainly for outreach/ dissemination purposes – or, rather, as a source of inspiration and discussion in preparation of the substance for the Review Conference itself.

D. Nature of and Competence for Amendments

As to the scope of the Review Conference from the perspective of the instruments subject to review, the Statute appears to be rather open, as there is no normative impediment that a Review Conference also deals with all matters falling within the competence of the Assembly of States Parties, while for the Assembly there are preclusions to deal with some amendments reserved to the Review Conference.

Any conclusion on this point requires that the notion of Review Conference under the Statute be clarified. Articles 121 to 124 ICCSt devise a system whereby:

(a) one Review Conference only is compulsorily provided for, to be convened by the Secretary General of the United Nations (UNSG) 'seven years after the entry into force' of the Statute, to consider 'any amendments' thereof, included but not limited to the list of crimes contained in Article 5;[37]
(b) additional Review Conferences are to be convened 'at any time' after the first Review Conference, by the UNSG but only

(i) at the request of a State Party;
(ii) for the purposes of considering amendments to the Statute;

35 *Non-paper on the scope of the Review Conference*, ICC-ASP/7/20/Add. 1, Annex I, at 39.

36 Ibid.: 'This process … will be conducted in the framework of the New York Working Group of the Bureau. All substantive suggestions and proposals for the Review Conference should be coordinated informally within this framework and with the assistance of the joint facilitators appointed by the Bureau for this purpose.'

37 Art. 123(1) ICCSt.

(iii) upon approval by a majority of States Parties;[38]

(c) amendments to the Statute can be dealt with both by the Assembly of States Parties and the Review Conference.[39] It is for the ASP to decide whether

(i) to 'take up the proposal' for an amendment and, in this case;
(ii) to 'deal with the proposal directly'; or
(iii) to 'convene a Review Conference if the issue involved so warrants'.[40]

Furthermore, the need to fully test over a reasonable period of time the Statute's provisions adopted in Rome entails that no amendment can be proposed before the expiry of seven years from the entry into force of the Statute.[41] However, amendments 'which are of an exclusively institutional nature ... may be proposed at any time'.[42] Consequently:

(i) Amendments of an institutional nature can be (could have been) proposed since the entry into force of the Rome Statute, on 1 July 2002. Importantly, such amendments 'shall be adopted by the Assembly of States Parties or by a Review Conference'.[43]
(iii) Amendments of a non-institutional nature – i.e., on any other provision of the Statute different from those under Article 122 – can be proposed from 1 July 2009, to be dealt with either by the Assembly of States Parties or by the first or any other Review Conference.

Both the Assembly of States Parties and a Review Conference are, therefore, equally entitled to deal with any kind of amendments, either of institutional or non-institutional nature. However, it is for the ASP to decide whether to take up any such proposal and who – the ASP or the Review Conference – has to deal with it. Such a decision is taken by the ASP depending on the importance of the issue ('if the issue involved so warrants') and, thus, it should be clarified what are the issues that request attention by a Review Conference, rather than by the Assembly. In this regard, the role of a Review Conference is only partially clarified by its own mandate, that is, to 'review' the Statute, because this role is further detailed as intended 'to consider any amendments' to the Statute.[44] Therefore, the issue of the qualitative difference between amendments is left open, which makes only some issues warrant attention by a Review Conference.

38 Art. 123(2) ICCSt.

39 Art. 121(1) ICCSt: amendments cannot be proposed before seven years from the entry into force of the Statute have expired, and have to be proposed by at least one State Party and circulated by the UNSG to all Sates Parties.

40 Art. 121(2) ICCSt.

41 Art. 121(1) ICCSt.

42 Art. 122(1) ICCSt, where the closed list of provisions of the Statute open to amendments of an institutional nature is contained: Art. 35 (Service of judges); Art. 36 para. 8 (representation criteria in the election of judges) and para. 9 (differentiated term of office at the first election); Art.37 (judicial vacancies); Art. 38 (Presidency); Art. 39 para. 1 (organization in divisions) para. 2 (composition and functions of the Chambers) and para. 4 (limited interchangeability of judges); Art. 42 paras 4–9 (election and disqualification of the Prosecutor and its Deputies, and OTP advisers); Art. 43 para. 2 (subjection of the Registrar to the authority of the President) and para. 3 (qualification of the Registrar and its Deputy); Art. 44 (staff); Articles 46, 47 and 49 (removal from office, disciplinary measures, and remuneration of elected officials).

43 Art. 122(2) ICCSt.

44 Art. 123(1) ICCSt.

The wording of the Statute is clear on the nature of amendments that can be considered at a Review Conference, that is, 'any amendments', including those of an:

(a) institutional nature, that involve issues warranting to be dealt with a Review Conference;
(b) institutional nature, that involve issues that would normally be dealt with by an ASP;
(c) non-institutional nature.

On the other hand, the nature of amendments that can be considered at an ASP include those of:

(i) institutional nature, that involve issues not warranting to be dealt with by a Review Conference;
(ii) non-institutional nature.

To establish the amendments involving issues that warrant being dealt with by a Review Conference, the Statute provides only one guideline, that is that it ought to be an issue which cannot be dealt with 'directly' by the ASP. This does not preclude that whatever provision is the object of an amendment proposal it cannot be dealt with by an ASP. Amendments to Articles 5, 6, 7 and 8 of the Statute – which are the only ones to be reserved a limited (as to entry into force) separate regime[45] – could be considered to be of such importance that only a Review Conference can deal with them. However, this might not always be the case as it is theoretically possible that such amendments do not involve an issue that warrants attention by a Review Conference when, e.g., the agreement on amending the list or categories of crimes under Article 5 subject to the ICC jurisdiction is appreciated as universal.

It is, therefore, a matter of extended discretion for the Assembly to assess what are the amendments to be dealt with directly or only by convening a Review Conference.[46]

However, as it does not seem disputable that all the amendments that can be dealt with by an ASP can also be dealt with by a Review Conference – and that the function of the latter is to 'review' the functioning of the Statute – an additional inference would be that there are no reasons for limiting the functions of a Review Conference only to part of those of the ASP. The Review Conference is open to all States Parties and to observers, with the same rights they exert during an ASP[47] and, thus, the legitimacy of a Review Conference to adopt any decision falling within the competence of the Assembly would be unquestionable: *a Review Conference is nothing else than the Assembly of States Parties itself*, although convened with a specific mandate. This conclusion is confirmed by:

45 Art. 121(5) ICCSt: 'shall enter into force for those States Parties which have accepted the amendment one year after the deposit of their instruments of ratification or acceptance. In respect of a State Party which has not accepted the amendment, the Court shall not exercise its jurisdiction regarding a crime covered by the amendment when committed by that State Party's nationals or on its territory.'

46 The Assembly's focal point on the Review conference captured the same concept when saying that 'the real question here is what States Parties … believe would be helpful for the Court and for the interests of international criminal justice'. *Preliminary Paper*, note 1 *supra*, at 11. However, 'what States Parties believe' does not identify a criterion applicable *ex ante* for selecting proposals suitable for a Review Conference, but rather would only allow *ex post* to understand the reasons why any proposal might have been adopted by the Assembly for further consideration.

47 Art. 123(1) ICCSt, last sentence: 'the Conference shall be open to those participating in the Assembly of States Parties and on the same conditions.'

(a) the wording of the Final Act of the 1998 Rome Diplomatic Conference ('the Assembly of States Parties at a Review Conference');[48]
(b) the organizational structure of the Review Conference, as under its draft rules of procedure the Bureau of the ASP is also the Bureau of the Review Conference;[49]
(c) the fact that the scope of the Review Conference, as it was pictured in the 2006–2009 preliminary work conducted by the facilitator on the issue,[50] includes in a possible agenda for the first Review Conference not only amendments to provisions of the Statute,[51] but additional items which – while undoubtedly pertaining to the activities of the Court – are in part related to an assessment of the functioning of the Statute, but also in part unrelated to that (lessons learned by other international jurisdictions and outreach).

Unless this wider approach taken by the ASP is to be appreciated as only eagerness to celebrate a further anniversary of the entry into force of the Rome Statute – which does not seem to be the case – it should consistently lead to the conclusion that the Review Conference is the proper context to deal with any issue identified over a period of functioning of the Rome Statute. This would obviously include substantial developments in international criminal justice – as developed through the practice and case law of other international jurisdictions – but also issues that have arisen within the Rome Statute's system, that is not only within the Statute itself, but also under the rule of its related instruments.[52]

The RPE and Elements of Crimes are, therefore, suitable in their own right to become the subjects of proposals for amendments at a Review Conference, while their exclusion from such process cannot be agreed on the basis of their secondary normative ranking under the Statute.[53] In fact, any amendment on substantive criminal law provisions of the Statute – e.g., crime of aggression and weapons provision – may normally entail that RPE are amended (e.g., for the crime of aggression), and Elements of Crimes amended or introduced (*idem*).

---

48 Final Act, Resolution 7 '[the Preparatory Commission] shall submit such *proposals to the Assembly of States Parties at a Review Conference*' (emphasis added). The same conclusions – that the Review Conference could deal with amendments also of the RPE, Elements of Crimes and Regulations – is shared in O. Triffterer, 'The Object of Review Mechanisms: Statutes' Provisions, Elements of Crimes and Rules of Procedure and Evidence', in this Volume, at 1(A).

49 ICC-ASP/6/17, at Rule 1: 'For the purposes of these Rules: ... "Bureau" means *the Bureau as defined in article 112, paragraph 3(a)* of the Statute, which *shall be the Bureau of the Conference*' (emphasis added). See *supra*, at 1(A)(2) and note 21.

50 Ambassador Rolf Fife, Director General of the Legal Department of the Royal Norwegian Ministry of Foreign Affairs.

51 Crime of aggression, Art. 124 option, and any other 'potential amendment'. See *supra*, at 1(A)(1)(a).

52 The Law of the Statute is generally understood as including the applicable law under Art. 21 ICCSt, that is both the Statute and the normative instruments derived thereof (Rules of Procedure and Evidence and Elements of Crimes), as well as other binding instruments adopted before or after the Statute as far as they are recalled by the Statute (e.g., 1949 Geneva Conventions and 1977 Additional Protocols) or otherwise compatible with the purposes and object of the Statute, subject to the interpretation developed under the ICC's own jurisprudence (Art. 21(1)(b), (c) and (2) ICCSt). In this Volume, see R. Bellelli, The System, *supra* note 27, at 4(A)(2)(c). See also M. Catenacci, *'Legalità' e 'tipicità del reato' nello Statuto della Corte penale internazionale* [Legality and strict construction of crimes in the ICC Statute] (Milano: Giuffré, 2003), at 21.

53 Art. 9(3) ICCSt, 'The Elements of Crimes and amendments thereto shall be consistent with this Statute'; Art. 51(5) ICCSt, 'In the event of conflict between the Statute and the Rules of Procedure and Evidence, the Statute shall prevail; Art. 21(1) ICCSt, 'The Court shall apply (a) in first place, the Statute, Elements of Crimes and its Rules of Procedure and Evidence'.

The same applies to the Regulations of the Court: such regulations cannot establish new rights and obligations, vis-à-vis those established under the Statute and the RPE, but are needed to correctly implement Statutes provisions.[54] Consequently, amendments of the Regulations of the Court might be prompted by the ASP within the Review Conference when discharging its oversight role on the Court.[55] Although the adoption and amendments of the Regulations is within the competence of the judges,[56] States Parties' consent is a requisite for their permanent validity[57] and, therefore, it can be argued that objections from a majority of States Parties circulated after the entry into force of the Regulations would be a viable procedure for prompting amendments by the judges.[58]

---

54 Art. 52(1) ICCSt: 'in accordance with the Statute and the Rules of Procedure and Evidence ... the Regulations of the Court [are] *necessary for its routine functioning*' (emphasis added). Similar reasoning applies also to the Financial Rules and Regulations (FIRR) which, based on Art. 113 ICCSt and subject to the Statute, govern financial matters related to the Court and ASP meetings. The need to keep the Regulations updated to ensure sound financial governance has been never called into question and FIRR, adopted by the ASP on 9 February 2002, were subject to six amendments with ICC-ASP/3/Res. 4, Annex of 10 September 2004, ICC-ASP/4/Res. 10 of 3 December 2005, and with ICC-ASP/7/Res. 5 on 14 December 2007. Available at http://www.icc-cpi.int/Menus/ICC/Legal+Texts+and+Tools/Official+Journal/Financial+Regulations+and+Rules.htm (visited 20 August 2009).

55 Art. 112(2)(b) ICCSt: [The Assembly shall] provide management oversight to the Presidency ... regarding the administration of the Court.' Also, 'In urgent cases, the Presidency, on its own motion ... may submit proposals for amendments ... for ... consideration in a plenary session'. Such oversight role of the ASP is, however, not yet channelled through established mechanisms which could hopefully avoid basic misunderstandings on its relations with the principle of independence of the Court. For an occasion where the exercise of oversight by the ASP was referred to by the Court itself as an attempt to encroach on the independence of the Court by 'outside actors', and the States Parties concerns were considered 'external concerns on administrative issues', see *infra*, at 5(C) and note 160. The ASP is currently committed in setting up an appropriate subsidiary body, an Oversight Mechanism, which, however, will initially only have the task of performing investigations to be conducted on disciplinary matters, although developments are envisaged for additional functions of evaluation and inspection. See ICC-ASP/4/Res. 4, the latest *Report of the Bureau on the establishment of an independent oversight mechanism* (ICC-ASP/8/2 of 15 April 2009 and Add. 2 of 29 July 2009) and *infra* note 332. The growing awareness of the ASP on the need to exert appropriate management oversight is reflected by the ASP President C. Wenaweser, Discussion Paper, The Assembly of States Parties of the Rome Statute: Perspectives on the Years Ahead, Consultative Conference on International Criminal Justice (UNHQ, New York, 9–11 September 2009), where criteria for the ASP oversight functions are identified in: dialogue and channels of communications, avoiding micromanagement, respecting judicial independence and creating a culture of accountability. Available at http://www.internationalcriminaljustice.net/papers/Session4.pdf (visited 25 September 2009).

56 Art. 52(1) ICCSt: 'The judges shall ... adopt ... the Regulations of the Court.'

57 Art. 52(3) ICCSt: 'The Regulations and any amendments thereto shall take effect upon adoption unless otherwise decided by the judges. Immediately upon adoption, they shall be circulated to *States Parties for comments. If* within six months *there are no objections from a majority of States Parties, they shall remain in force*' (emphasis added).

58 Issues have, e.g., arisen for Regulation 84(2) of the Regulations of the Court as far as the scope of the means relevant to the determination of the indigence of an accused for purposes of legal assistance paid by the Court are concerned. It has been argued that the exclusion of assets owned by the dependants of the accused in the assessment of his/her indigence does not correspond to the exclusion of the family obligations from the disposable means of the accused which is the basis for calculation of indigence. Thus, family links would be relevant only to maintenance obligations, but not in the reciprocity deriving from the solidarity between family members, according to established principles of mutual contribution to the family budget proportional to members' income and assets. Besides, abusive practices of fictitious assets cannot be ruled out under the existing system, while recovery of sums unduly paid by the Court would follow the uncertain path

On the other hand, any need for amendments to the Regulations of the Registry should take into account their nature and, thus, the different procedure envisaged for their adoption. As such Regulations are only provided for under the RPE 'to govern the operation of the Registry', they are prepared by the Registrar in consultation with the Prosecutor and approved by the Presidency.[59] Thus, while there is no role for the ASP – as the policymaking and normative body of the ICC – to play in setting these Regulations, it is for the Presidency to monitor their appropriateness to direct the activities of the Registry. However, the ASP would always be entitled to exert its oversight role on any related matter by providing appropriate guidance – under its Article 112(2)(b) authority – on the management exercised by the Presidency.[60]

---

of cooperation. Also, practice at the other international Tribunals does not support such system. See *Report on different legal aid mechanisms before the international criminal jurisdictions*, ICC-ASP/7/23; *Report on the principles and criteria for the determination of indigence for purposes of legal aid*, ICC-ASP/6/INF.1; *Report on the operation of the Court's legal aid system and proposals for its amendment*, ICC-ASP/6/4/Annex I. Although the practice of other international Tribunals include the assets of members of the household, the Court maintains the point that 'it would be an unfair burden on the finances of … dependants [should their assets be included] as funds which might serve to ensure representation of the applicant' (para. 25), *Report of the Court on legal aid: Alternative models for assessment of indigence*, ICC-ASP/8/24, 18 September 2009, paras 21–26 and Annex II, Recommendation 2. See its Annex III for the practice of other international jurisdictions. See also the *Report of the Bureau on family visits for detainees*, ICC-ASP/8/42, 9 October 2009, with the annexed expert's advice on some possible precedential effects.

59 Rule 14(1) ICC RPE.

60 An issue related to the Regulations of the Registrar emerged with the Decision, Mr Mathieu Ngudjolo's Complaint Under Regulation 221(1) the Regulations of the Registry against the Registrar's Decision of 18 November 2008, No. ICC-RoR-217-02/08, 10 March 2009, whereby the Presidency decided on a complaint lodged against an administrative decision of the Registrar, following a procedure established under Regulation 221 of the Regulations of the Registry, based on Regulation 106(2) of the Regulations of the Court. The Decision concluded that there is a positive obligation for the Court to fund family visits to indigent detainees, based on Regulation 179(1) of the Regulations of the Registry, stating that '[t]he Registrar shall give specific attention to visits by family of detained persons with a view of maintaining such links'. Such Decision opened many issues, including on its nature (administrative or judicial), on its findings (positive obligation and correspondent right, based on Regulations) and on its contradiction to the conclusions reached by the ASP that 'according to existing law and standards, the right to family visits does not comprise a co-relative legal right to have such visits paid for by the detaining authority': Resolution ICC-ASP/7/Res. 3, Strengthening the International Criminal Court and the Assembly of States Parties (Omnibus Resolution), para. 17, in Official Records, ICC-ASP/7/20, at 31. Apparently, 'judicial functions' in the Court are only exercised by the judges when composing the Chambers (Art. 39(2)(a) ICCSt) and not as members of the Presidency, unless some 'quasi-judicial' functions are explicitly delegated, as is the case under Rule 199 ICC RPE for the Presidency's sentence enforcement competencies under Part 10 of the Statute. The Decision of the Presidency was, therefore, taken in its managerial capacity – as the complaint procedure is an administrative one – and, as the Regulations of the Registry cannot establish rights and obligations, it is for the ASP to exert its oversight rather than normative functions under Article 112 ICCSt. The Committee on Budget and Finance (CBF) at its first subsequent session suggested a role for the ASP in amending Regulation 179(1) of the Regulations of the Registry to clarify that a right to have family visits funded cannot be established under the Regulations. Report of the Committee on Budget and Finance on the work of its twelfth session, ICC-ASP/8/5, 13 May 2009, para. 96. As explained in the text, however, the ASP is not entitled to draw or amend the Regulations of the Registry. However, should Art. 21(1) ICCSt not be considered sufficient to avoid interpretations that lead to attribute creation of rights and obligations to the Regulations, clarification of the matter could be achieved through amending Rule 14 ICC RPE, which provides for such Regulations, or by introducing a more general Rule on the exclusion of normative value both to Regulations of the Court and of the Registry.

Over the last seven years or so, States Parties have witnessed sufficient developments in some areas or the Rome Statute, of the Rules of Procedure and Evidence, and of the Regulations of the Court, so that reasonable experience has been gained in order to draw conclusions as to whether or not some relevant provisions should be amended.

Although one of the assumptions[61] for the first Review Conference has been that the Court might not take the initiative by introducing amendments until a 'full judicial cycle' (that is, from investigation to final judgment) is completed,[62] this approach seems to be in open contradiction with the wider perspective the Assembly has already taken by opening the Review Conference to an assessment of the overall functioning of the Law of the Statute.

If consistent conclusions had been drawn from the ASP approach, States should not have waited for any possible future ASP or additional Review Conference to deal with issues that had identified under the Law of the Statute as deserving some sort of amendments. As a Review Conference, including the first one, is the appropriate venue and occasion to ensure that the applicable rules and provisions appropriately safeguard the functioning of the Statute and the ability of the Court to fulfil its mandate, this opportunity should have been seized. This is even truer for issues which have emerged as insurmountable for the Court under the existing legal framework and, thus, for amendments which should have received priority consideration to preserve the image and functionality of the institution.

2. Developments Since 1998

A. Law and Practice

The Rome Statute was drafted taking account of the status of international criminal justice in 1998, including substantive, procedural, and institutional provisions.

More than a decade after the 1998 Rome Diplomatic Conference, substantial developments have taken place in the field, as the experience of the international and international-ized Tribunals and Courts has provided useful lessons. This relates not only to jurisprudence – with its bearing on the definition and on the scope of the subject matter jurisdiction – but also to the wider perspective of the practices which resulted, *inter alia*, in the adoption of amendments and new provisions under the relevant Statutes and Rules of Procedure and Evidence. These instruments – under the normative powers of the Tribunals to deal with their own Rules – have been the subject of a continuous revision process in order to meet pragmatically the challenges of the Tribunals' activity.[63]

There is a wide understanding in the international community that, in particular, the completion strategies of the international tribunals have contributed to developing procedural tools which – sometimes allowing for a more balanced position between adversarial and inquisitorial systems – have proven very successful in terms of solving some outstanding issues of criminal procedure before international courts.

61 See *supra*, at 1(A)(1)(a) to (d).

62 Ibid., at (d) and note 16. See also, *Progress Report*, note 1 *supra*, at 23.

63 At the ICTY, the Statute adopted on 25 May 1993 was amended seven times, from 13 May 1998 to 28 February 2008. The RPE, adopted on 11 February 1994, were amended 44 times, from 5 May 1994 to 28 February 2008. At the ICTR, the RPE adopted on 29 June 1995 were amended 17 times, from 12 January 196 to 14 March 2008.

This is particularly true in relation to the length of criminal proceedings at the trial stage, and for the consequences on:

(i) The right to a fair trial. In particular, as ICC trials can only be held in the presence of the accused[64] and this is normally ensured through arrest and consequent detention on remand, the expeditiousness of the trial impacts greatly on the rights of the accused.[65]
(ii) The rights of victims. Among other considerations, the timeliness of a judicial decision affects the effectiveness of redress.
(iii) The rights of witnesses. The burden imposed by the interests of justice on witnesses – especially for the retraumatizing effect of interviews and depositions, as well as for the impact of protective measures on individual and family lives – should be kept as low as possible.
(iv) The costs of justice. Lengthy proceedings at different stages and, in particular, protracted depositions at the seat of the Court during multiple hearings have relevant financial implications on different budget Sections (for, e.g., witnesses and defence).
(v) The contribution to international peace and security. The deterrent effect of the ICC – and its contribution to stability processes throughout situation countries and regions affected by conflicts – is dependent upon judicial proceedings conducted not only with the appearance of a credible justice, but also in an effective manner, which includes reasonably expeditious decisions and implementation thereof.

B. Detection or Stocktaking

A review exercise of the normative framework of the Law of the Statute should, therefore, have as a starting point an informed preparation focused on uncontroversial lessons learned through the law and practice in international criminal justice. This would allow the detection of:

(i) provisions which proved successful in their implementation;
(ii) provisions, the interpretation of which has not improved their implementation;
(iii) provisions which were amended, and how amendments met expectations.

The importance of stocktaking has been acknowledged by the ASP,[66] but it should also be stressed that monitoring of the practices of states is equally crucial to improve the effectiveness of the Rome Statute system. In this perspective, consideration should also be given, e.g., to:

---

64 While this is not requested at the pre-trial confirmation of charges stage (Arts 60 and 61(2) ICCSt and Rules 125–126 ICC RPE), the presence of the accused has to be ensured through voluntary appearance (Art. 58(7) ICCSt) or arrest and surrender (Art. 58(1) ICCSt) in order to proceed further to the trial stage ('the accused shall be present during the trial' – Art. 63(1) ICCSt).

65 In particular, Art. 67(1)(c) ICCSt, 'to be tried without undue delay', which reflects the language of Art. 14(3)(c) ICCPR, as one of the established facets of the right to a fair trial. See, also Art. 6(1) ECHR: 'in the determination of … any criminal charges against him, everyone is entitled to a fair and public hearing within reasonable time.'

66 See *supra*, at 1(A)(c) and note 11.

(a) practices of states and international organizations in their cooperation with the Court;
(b) implementing legislation adopted by states, both for cooperation and substantive criminal law;
(c) practice as to declarations at the time of ratification.[67]

3. The Scope for Amendments

A. Issues Under Review

Among the issues relevant to the Review Conference and that have been considered to a different extent within the established framework of the ASP, this paragraph addresses some general remarks to those amendments which have, so far, been the subject of some – although sometimes limited – discussion (weapons provision and opt-out clause). Issues which have been tabled for discussion or have otherwise become the subject of formal proposals for amendments are also briefly examined here. These include international terrorism and drug trafficking, which played a role in the compromise reached at the 1998 Rome Conference.[68] However, the crime of aggression is not addressed here as it is dealt with extensively in Part IV of this Volume. On the other hand, and on the premises of the agreed assumptions for the Review Conference (detailed above at paragraphs 1(A)(1)(a) to (d)), additional items scarcely if at all explored so far, but which appear suitable as objects for other possible proposals, will be analysed in greater details in the following paragraphs.

B. The Weapons Provision

Besides the crime of aggression, Rome also left unfinished the war crime dealt with in the so-called 'weapons provision'; mainly because of the inherent characteristics of the weapons of mass destruction and of the contentious issue of the legitimacy of their use,[69] no agreement was reached on the identification of the weapons 'of a nature to cause superfluous injury or unnecessary suffering or which are inherently indiscriminate in violation of the international law of armed conflict'. However, should weapons of such a nature or effects be acknowledged as the subject of a comprehensive prohibition,[70] the list of such weapons will complete the existing criminal provision and might be included in an Annex to the Statute.

1. Belgian and Others Proposal

A proposal for an amendment to the weapons provision was announced during the seventh session of the Assembly of States Parties (The Hague, 14–21 November 2008) by Belgium, subsequently discussed informally during Bureau meetings consultations and formally submitted to the UNSG with the co-sponsorship of several States Parties (hereinafter, Belgian proposal).

---

67 See R. Bellelli, The System, *supra* note 27, at 4(A)(d).

68 On drug and terrorist crimes, see R. Bellelli, The System, *supra* note 27, at 4(B)(1) and in this Chapter, *infra*, (D). See also O. Triffterer, The Object of Review Mechanisms: Statutes' Provisions, Elements of Crimes and Rules of Procedure and Evidence, in this *Volume*, at 4(B)(2).

69 ICJ, Advisory Opinion, *Legality of the Threat or Use of Nuclear Weapons*, 8 July 1996, is still the only available authority on the issue.

70 Art. 8(2)(b)(xx) ICCSt.

The Belgian proposal was the first to be presented of several proposals which touch upon a substantial criminal law provision of the Statute, which is assumed to fall within the concept of the integrity to be protected.[71] Thus, a sceptical approach would consider that at a crucial juncture of the early life of the ICC, the opening of a negotiation on the definition of crimes other than aggression could risk spreading the discussion to issues that for different reasons may be controversial and divisive. In this respect, a basic and agreed assumption for any amendment proposal to be introduced at the Review Conference is that it should serve the interests of strengthening the Court,[72] with due account taken of the experience so far developed. Completing the weapons provision may not appear *prima facie* as a priority for strengthening the Court: although the interests protected by the unfinished provision are different from those addressed by other war crimes in Article 8, employing weapons prohibited under international humanitarian law (IHL) is not a distinctive character of the low-tech armed conflicts currently under ICC scrutiny, investigations and prosecutions, as well as of those dealt with by the ICTY (with some exceptions), ICTR and SCSL.

However, it cannot be underestimated that, on the one hand, it is a basic characteristic of normative provisions not to be drafted to address only specific cases which might occur in situations at stake, but instead with a far-reaching perspective and for the generality of possible situations. On the other hand, the prohibition of weapons inherently disproportionate and indiscriminate is an essential feature of IHL, insofar it addresses the limitation to otherwise unbearable sufferings, both of combatants and civilians, conditions which may appear in any conflict.

In this regard, the Belgian proposal undoubtedly has the merit of again putting on the agenda of States Parties the very essence of the technical objectives of the Statute, that is, ensuring protection of actual and potential victims by implementing IHL through a binding judicial mechanism.

While originally Belgium circulated a text suggesting the adoption of the Annex called for by Article 8(2)(b)(xx) plus several amendments,[73] a revised proposal includes draft amendments which would:

> (a) extend to armed conflicts not of an international character the criminalization[74] of weapons already prohibited under the Statute, but only in the context of international armed conflicts (poison or poisoned weapons; asphyxiating, poisonous or other gases, and all analogous liquids, materials or devices; bullets which can expand or flatten easily in the human body, etc.);
> (b) criminalize, both when committed in international or non international armed conflicts:

---

71 On the notion of integrity, see *supra*, at 1(B)(1). The other proposals referred to – on nuclear weapons, terrorism and drug crimes – are dealt with *infra*, in this paragraph.

72 See *supra*, at 1(A)(1).

73 Draft of 9 February 2003.

74 New Art. 8(2)(e)(xiii), (xviii) and (xix).

(i) the use[75] of chemical[76] and biological[77] weapons, and landmines,[78] which have become the subject of an universally agreed prohibition due to the large number of States Parties to the relevant Conventions;
(ii) the use[79] of Non-Detectable Fragments and Blinding Laser in violation of the relevant Protocols[80] to the 1980 Certain Conventional Weapons Convention,[81] and its Protocols, although these instruments have so far been ratified by a lower number of states, in order that the weapons they address are considered 'the subject of a comprehensive prohibition'.[82]

The scope of such proposals is, thus, focused on two substantive issues:

(1) overcoming the distinction between international and non-international armed conflicts, insofar the prohibition of use of some weapons is concerned;
(2) criminalizing the use of only those weapons whose use can be understood as illegitimate under international customary law.

With these limits and objectives …, the Belgian proposals – although still open to improvements – seems to fully reflect the status of IHL, the normative selection criteria adopted in Rome[83] and the agreed assumptions for the Review Conference.[84]

2. The Mexican Proposal

An informal proposal on nuclear weapons was introduced by Mexico at the informal consultations on the Review Conference held by the New York Working Group of the Bureau of the ASP at the UNHQ on 10 June 2009 and was formally deposited with the UNSG.

75 New Art. 8(2)(b)(xxvii), (xxviii) and (xxix), in international conflict, and Art. 8 (2)(e)(xiii), (xiv) and (xv), in non–international armed conflicts.

76 Convention on the Prohibition of the Development, Production, Stockpiling and Use of Chemical Weapons and on their Destruction, Paris, 13 January 1993: 188 States Parties as of 6 May 2009.

77 Convention on the Prohibition of the Development, Production and Stockpiling of Bacteriological (Biological) and Toxin Weapons and on their Destruction, London, Moscow and Washington, 10 April 1972: 163 States Parties as of 6 May 2009.

78 Convention on the Prohibition of the Use, Stockpiling, Production and Transfer of Anti-Personnel Mines and on their Destruction, Ottawa, 18 September 1997: 156 States Parties as of 6 May 2009.

79 New Art. 8(2)(b)(xxx) and (e)(xvi).

80 Protocol on Non-Detectable Fragments (Protocol I), Geneva, 10 October 1980: 107 States Parties on 7 May 2009; Protocol on Blinding Laser Weapons (Protocol IV), Vienna 13 October 1995: 94 States Parties as of 6 May 2009.

81 Convention on Prohibition or Restrictions on the Use of Certain Conventional Weapons Which May Be Deemed to be Excessively Injurious or to Have Indiscriminate Effects (CCW), Geneva, 10 October 1980: 109 States Parties as of 6 May 2009.

82 The original first draft of the Belgian proposal also included the criminalization of the weapons covered by: the CCW Protocol on Prohibitions or Restrictions on the Use of Mines, Booby-Traps and Other Devices (Protocol II), Geneva 10 October 1980, and Protocol on Prohibitions or Restrictions on the Use of Incendiary Weapons (Protocol III), Geneva 10 October 1980; the Convention on Cluster Munitions, Dublin, 30 May 2008, which has not yet entered into force.

83 On this point, see R. Bellelli, The System, *supra* note 27, at 4(B), (C).

84 *Supra*, 1(A)(1)(a) to (d).

The proposal addresses and Amendment to Article 8 of the Rome Statute of the International Criminal Court Regarding the Use of Nuclear Weapons and reads: 'Add to article 8, paragraph 2, b), the following: *(...) Employing nuclear weapons or threatening to employ nuclear weapons*'. The background mentioned in the proposal includes:

(a) GA Res. 1653 (XVI), Declaration on the Prohibition of the Use of Nuclear and Thermo-Nuclear Weapons, 24 November 1961, OP 1(b): 'the use of nuclear and thermonuclear weapons would exceed even the scope of war and cause indiscriminate suffering and destruction to mankind and civilization and, as such, is contrary to the rules of international law and to the laws of humanity';
(b) the wording of Art. 8(2)(b)(iv) ICCSt: 'intentionally launching an attack in the knowledge that such attack will cause incidental loss of life or injury to civilians or damage to civilian objects or widespread, long-term and severe damage to the natural environment which would be clearly excessive in relation to the concrete and direct overall military advantage anticipated';
(c) various international treaties, e.g., Comprehensive Nuclear-Test-Ban Treaty; Treaty for the Prohibition of Nuclear Weapons in Latin America (Treaty of Tlatelolco); Treaty on the Non-Proliferation of Nuclear Weapons; Treaty Banning Nuclear Weapon Tests in the Atmosphere, in Outer Space and Under Water; Treaty on the Prohibition of the Emplacement of Nuclear Weapons and Other Weapons of Mass Destruction on the Seabed and the Ocean Floor and in the Subsoil Thereof'; and
(d) the ICJ Advisory opinion on the Legality of the Threat or Use of Nuclear Weapons, 8 July 1996.

The Mexican proposal addresses the criminalization of the conduct of using or threatening to use nuclear weapons in a structural approach similar to that of the Belgian proposal, i.e., adding such specific acts to the list of the 'other serious violations of the laws and customs' of armed conflicts. The choice of this solution in alternative to the inclusion of nuclear weapons in an annex to the Statute following Article 8(2)(b)(xx) ICCSt would also theoretically allow a different evidentiary regime for the threat or use of nuclear weapons vis-à-vis the one applicable under the 'weapons provision', as the elements of the crime under the latter would not need to be met (ability to cause superfluous injury or unnecessary suffering, inherent indiscrimination, violation of international law of armed conflict, object of a comprehensive prohibition).

The issue of criminalization of the use of nuclear weapons is, *per se*, contentious and calls into question a number of legal and political, including strategic, questions, among them the legality of certain weapons of mass destruction, the limited access to nuclear weapons by only a small group of states and the basis itself for strategic military deterrence. This complex dimension of the issue clearly represents a challenge for the ASP, in order that all aspects involved are scrutinized with sufficient authority, preparation and analysis within its time-limited framework. In this regard, it seems that additional actors and procedures would have still to be involved and triggered before delegations at an ASP and a Review Conference might take the same main legislative approach followed in Rome for other war crimes; that is, to agree on the existence of a customary rule prohibiting the use of nuclear weapons and, consequently, on the criminalization of such use.

C. The Opt-Out Clause

As the assessment of the discretionary gravity threshold for war crimes is left to the Court, concerns were raised in Rome in relation to the exclusion of reservations to the Statute (Article 120). Therefore, the compromise solution reached in the Statute provides that States Parties can opt-out from the jurisdiction of the Court over war crimes for a period of seven years (Article 124). The opt-out clause – which is an exception to the jurisdiction of the Court over States Parties or third states accepting such jurisdiction[85] – is the only derogation to the exclusion of reservations under the Statute, and reservations made under the term of validity of the clause are only of a temporary nature and in essence self-expiring.[86] The clause is also temporary in another meaning, as states can only avail themselves of this exemption from jurisdiction 'on becoming party' to the Statute, that is when they deposit their instruments of ratification, acceptance, approval or accession.[87] The opt-out clause, originally intended to facilitate ratification for some states,[88] has so far received limited application[89] and, due to its purposes and transitional nature, the Statute itself makes it the subject of a mandatory[90] review at a Review Conference.[91]

Once again, any change to the Statute has to be assessed realistically in terms of its effect on strengthening the Court and expanding its membership towards universal participation. From this perspective, amendments or deletion of Article 124 should be dealt with in a very pragmatic way; while resort to the reservation contained in the opt-out clause has been so far largely unutilized, the potential negative impact of the clause appears to be overestimated.

85 Art. 124 ICCSt, which refers to Art. 12(1) and (2) ICCSt on the 'preconditions to the exercise of jurisdiction'.

86 Such mechanisms are normally conceived, when introduced at the time of their adoption, to facilitate the entry into force of treaties by widening participation through allowing exemptions to specific regimes which might be of particular concern for a potential Party. However, at the stage of treaty implementation, the number and extension of reservations might hinder the proper functioning, e.g., of a cooperation regime and make it necessary to revert on the issue by means of amendments to the treaty. This has been, e.g., the case of the incentive to the withdrawal of reservations with their limited temporal validity and the subsequent expiration without explicit renewal, as introduced by Art. 38(1) and (2) of the Council of Europe *Criminal Law Convention on Corruption*, Strasbourg, 27 January 1999, CETS. 173; Art. 16(5) and (6) of the of the *European Convention on the Suppression of Terrorism*, Strasbourg, 27 January 1977, CETS. 190, amended by Art. 12(7) of the *Protocol Amending the European Convention on the Suppression of Terrorism*, Strasbourg, 15 May 2003, CETS. 190; Art. 20(5) and (6) of the *Council of Europe Convention on the Prevention of Terrorism,* Warsaw, 16 May 2005, CETS. 196.

87 Art. 125(2) and (3) ICCSt.

88 During the negotiation of the Statute, Art. 124 ICCSt was conceived essentially to meet the concerns raised by France. See H.-P. Kaul, 'Preconditions to Exercise of Jurisdiction', in A. Cassese, P. Gaeta and J.R.W.D. Jones (eds), *The Rome Statute of the International Criminal Court: A Commentary* (Oxford: Oxford University Press, 2002), 583–616, at 604 (hereinafter, Cassese, Gaeta and Jones).

89 Out of 111 States Parties, only two, France and Colombia, driven by considerations of a different nature, have made a declaration under Art. 124 ICCSt at the time of the deposit of their instrument of ratification. However, France subsequently decided to withdraw its declaration with effect from 15 June 2008 (Art. 124 states that 'a declaration under this article may be withdrawn at any time'). The declaration itself would have otherwise naturally expired on 1 July 2009, seven years after the entry into force of the Statute and for the first 60 States which ratified it. As Colombia deposited its instrument of ratification on 5 August 2002, the Statute entered into force on 1 November 2002 for it (Art. 126 ICCSt), and its declaration expired on 31 October 2009.

90 See also *supra* notes 75 and 76.

91 Art. 123(1) ICCSt.

As Article 124 is an exception to the general principle of non-admissibility of reservations under Article 120, the case of the opt-out clause is, in the eyes of many, that of a breach of the strength of the Statute. However, the drafting history of Article 124[92] clearly shows that its purpose and objectives are fully in line with the overall design pursued by the Statute: accommodate the needs of some delegations in order to facilitate the achievement of consensus at the Rome Conference. Thus, as a tool for enhancing the universality of the Statute, Article 124 is an integral part of the Rome compromise and of the integrity of the Statute and should be assessed in the balance between rigour and integrity.

Consistent with the assumptions for the Review Conference,[93] the crucial question to be answered in the process of reviewing the Statute is whether the amendment or deletion of a 1998 adopted provision would strengthen the ICC. In the circumstances of Article 124, such question could be expressed through the following other: whether the opt-out clause ever hindered or facilitated the participation in the Rome Statute. A response to such question can be provided by answering the following two questions on the relevant practice of states:

> (i) Has the opt-out clause been useful in increasing the ICC membership? The affirmative response is in the records, as two states availed themselves of Article 124 at the time of ratification.[94]
> (ii) Has the opt-out clause withheld any state from ratification of the Statute? Again, no state has ever argued that its concerns vis-à-vis the Rome Statute depended on Article 124.

These considerations seem to shed light on the scope of the mandatory review of the opt-out clause. The fact that 'the provisions of [Article 124] shall be reviewed at the [first] Review Conference' only entails that a review has to take place, while the content of the review is apparently open to the following alternative outcomes:

Option 1 – Delete Article 124

This should be based on the understanding that either its purposes no longer exist or that its provisions are counterproductive to the overall goal of strengthening the Statute. However, the proven usefulness and harmless nature of the opt-out clause would seem to contradict such conclusions.

---

92 See, e.g., F. Lattanzi, 'The Rome Statute and State Sovereignty. ICC Competence, Jurisdictional Links, Trigger Mechanism', in F. Lattanzi and W.A. Schabas (eds), *Essays on the Rome Statute of the International Criminal Court* (Teramo: Il Sirente, 1999), at 55–56. Among the reasons for the choice to opt-out for war crimes was also indicated the extension of the Court's jurisdiction to isolated acts, under Art. 8(1) ICCSt ('*in particular*...when committed as a part of' (emphasis added)). See for a critical position on the point, W. Bourdon, *La Cour pénale internationale. Le statut de Rome* (Paris: Éditions du Seuil, 2000), at 297–300.

93 See *supra*, at 1(A)(1)(a) to (d).

94 Consequently, it cannot be excluded that Art. 124 could assist accession of other states in the future. In this sense, see W. Schabas (Co-rapporteur) for the findings of International Law Association, *Third Report on the International Criminal Court at the Rio De Janeiro Conference* (2008), at 15. Available at http://www.ila-hq.org (visited 30 June 2009).

Option 2 – amend Article 124 in its first and last sentences so that a new text would read (additions in italics):

> 'Notwithstanding article 12, paragraphs 1 and 2, a State, on becoming a party to this Statute *after the Review Conference convened in accordance with article 123*, may declare that, for a period of [*x*] [delete "seven"] years after the entry into force of this Statute for the State concerned, it does not accept the jurisdiction of the Court with respect to the category of crimes referred to in article 8 when a crime is alleged to have been committed by its nationals or on its territory. A declaration under this article may be withdrawn at any time. The provisions of this article shall be reviewed at *any* [delete "the"] Review Conference convened in accordance with article 123' [delete 'paragraph 1'].

Such amendments would reduce the seven-year term to a shorter one, applicable only to states that will ratify or accede to the Rome Statute in the future and after the first Review Conference takes place. This is based on the consideration that, within the rationale of the opt-out clause, there is a substantial difference in position between, on the one hand, states that ratified prior to the entry into force of the Statute (1998–2002) and the first investigative and judicial activities of the Court (2003–2010), and, on the other hand, states that will ratify or accede only after the Review Conference. The advantage for the latter states is that they have already had the benefit of roughly a seven-year period (2003–2010)[95] to observe the functioning of the Statute and, through an assessment of its decisions, be objectively reassured of the impartiality of the Court. Meanwhile, monitoring of these provisions would be left open to any following Review Conference.

Option 3 – amend Article 124 only in the last sentence, so that it would read:

'The provisions of this article shall be reviewed at any [delete 'the'] Review Conference convened in accordance with article 123' [delete 'paragraph 1'].

This approach would preserve the current structure of the opt-out clause while pragmatically ensuring that its deletion can be scheduled any time in future Review Conferences and that the item of its review is kept as a mandatory for each of the Review Conferences held after 2010.

D. Treaty Crimes

Terrorist acts and international trafficking of illicit drugs were discussed at the 1998 Rome Diplomatic Conference, but, in the end, there was no consensus on their inclusion in the ICC's Statute. However, under Resolution E of the Final Act of the Conference, treaty crimes of 'terrorism and drug crimes' were acknowledged to be (not 'the most' but still) 'serious crimes of international concern' and referred to in a recommendation for being considered at 'a Review Conference ... with the view to arriving at an acceptable definition and their inclusion in the list of crimes within the jurisdiction of the Court' (paras 3 and 8).

95 The judges were elected at the first session of the ASP (first and second resumptions) on 4–7 February 2003 and sworn in on 11 March 2003, while the Prosecutor was elected on 21 April 2003 and pledged his solemn undertaking on 16 June 2003. However, the first referral to the OTP (situation in Uganda) dates from December 2003.

1. Terrorism

While negotiations on the Comprehensive Convention on International Terrorism seem still far from a conclusion on the crucial issue of the definition of terrorism, the Netherlands circulated an 'Informal proposal for the inclusion of the crime of terrorism in the Rome Statute' during the informal consultations on the Review Conference held in the New York Bureau Working Group, on 11 September 2009, and suggested following the same approach for terrorism as that adopted in Rome for aggression. A formal proposal was thereafter filed with the UNSG, which would entail amending Article 5(1) to include 'the crime of terrorism' (new letter (e)) and deferring the actual jurisdiction of the Court to when 'a provision is adopted ... defining the crime and setting out the conditions' for the exercise of jurisdiction of the Court (new Article 5(3)). The proposal also suggests that further possible amendments needed as a result of the introduction of the crime of terrorism should be dealt with by an informal working group of the Review Conference.

Discussions on such proposal will necessarily have to include legal issues, but the political ones on which the emphasis is still placed during the UN negotiations seem overwhelming. It must also be noted that the unconditional exercise of the jurisdiction of the Court on aggression has been hindered by causes different from those which now stand in the way of the jurisdiction on terrorism as such. Furthermore, some might consider the mechanism chosen for bringing into operation the jurisdiction on the crime of aggression as an exceptional one, inextricably linked to the balanced compromise reached in Rome and not necessarily an example to follow in the future. At the same time, according to an opinion, the Court would already have jurisdiction on acts of terrorism matching relevant definitions of crimes against humanity under Article 7 ICCSt (see Chapter 1, above para. 4(B)(1)). With this in mind, however, the proposal seems to deserve attention as a basis for a wider exercise of assessment of the legal means of which the international community might avail itself in fighting against terrorism.

2. Drug Crimes

No informal draft was circulated before a joint proposal on drug trafficking was officially presented by Trinidad and Tobago and Belize, a draft that along structural lines was similar to the one on terrorism, but which would have immediate effect on the Court's jurisdiction. In particular, amendments have been suggested so that Article 5(1) should include 'the Crime of International Drug Trafficking' (new letter (e)) and Article 5(2) contain the definition of the conduct criminalized, subject to the threshold that: 'crimes involving the illicit trafficking in narcotic drugs and psychotropic substances mean any of the following acts, but only when they pose a threat to peace, order and security of a State or region.' A definition of the illicit conducts is provided in the list of acts under the new Article 5(2), which includes:

> (a) conducts criminalized by the relevant 1961 Single Convention on Narcotic Drugs, the 1961 Single Convention on Narcotic Drugs, as amended, the 1971 Convention on Psychotropic Substances and the 1988 United Nations Convention against Illicit Traffic in Narcotic Drugs and Psychotropic Substances, subject that such acts are 'committed on a large scale and involving acts of a transboundary character';
> (b) attacks against the person or liberty in furtherance of acts under (a);
> (c) violent attacks upon premises 'with the intention of creating fear or insecurity within a State or States or disrupting their economic, social, political or security structures', when committed in connection with acts under (a).

Thresholds are carefully introduced in the proposal in relation to the different acts criminalized, including the gravity of drug crimes ('large scale'), their transnational nature ('transboundary'), as well as the *dolus specialis* required for the punishment of acts directed against private or public facilities ('intention of creating fear or insecurity … or disrupting … economic, social, political or security structures'). The most interesting threshold, however, is the one contained in the chapeau: 'acts [that] pose a threat to peace, order and security of a State or region' is apparently a high requirement to satisfy, but some remarkable differences in substance exist with the 'most serious crimes of international concern' (Article 1 ICCSt), which ought to be 'of concern to the international community as a whole' (Article 5(1) ICCSt) because they 'threaten the peace, security and well-being of the world' (Preamble (3) ICCSt). However, the reference to state or regional peace and security and, *a fortiori*, to the 'order' should also raise interesting questions from the perspective of international assistance to national capacities to fight serious crimes of international concern. This includes the role of the permanent jurisdiction of the ICC (and of a positive complementarity approach), which might at some point in the future be elected by the international community as the only means to further stability through criminal justice.

E. Sentence Enforcement

Differently from those provisions for which amendments to the Statute were called on by a specific mandate or expectation since the Rome Conference, an amendment, proposed by Norway on 30 September 2009 to Article 103(1)(a) ICCSt, provided the preparations for the first Review Conference with interesting material drawn from lessons learned in international criminal justice. The proposal is based on the experience in sentence enforcement developed at the international tribunals, with a reduced number of states either willing or able to accept, in their national prison facilities, persons internationally convicted. The Norwegian draft amendment anticipated that at the ICC the issue might not be different and suggests that execution of sentences might be subsidized, so that states might improve their detention standards and become eligible to be designated for the purpose.

The proposal includes an unqualified reference to possible prison facilities made available to a state by 'an international or regional organization, arrangement or agency'. In this regard, the proposal seems to follow an emerging trend to enhance support for international criminal justice and, in general, for capacity building efforts. The mechanism proposed seems also to rely mainly on assessed contributions of international or regional organizations, although such resources are formally explained as 'voluntary financial contributions'. The wide mandate, in particular in the field of international peace and security, of some such organizations might offer sufficient means to respond to requests for assistance by states willing to enforce ICC sentences. However, on the one hand, security and political implications of such a solution might also suggest that enforcement responsibilities could be taken by any such states within a framework of regional support, if not mandate. On the other hand, upgrading prison facilities in any given country is a task which might reasonably require thorough reforms in the criminal justice field. In this regard, it might also prove useful to look into the lessons learned from situations (e.g., Afghanistan) where commitments of the international community have already addressed such complex issues.

Whatever the level of support that the Norwegian proposal is able to gather, in its late form of a resolution, it has undoubtedly the merit of adding to the review process of the Statute the first 'non-traditional' item based on experience and on effectiveness, rather than on the hard core of jurisdiction and criminality of the Statute.

This vision is shared, in the spirit of addressing the needs for the Court, by the approach taken in the following paragraphs to other possible amendments.

F. The Object of Other Possible Proposals

Based on the premises of the agreed assumptions for the Review Conference,[96] the current scope for proposals of amendments which might be considered by a Review Conference goes beyond amendments that are dealt with within an established framework of the ASP (aggression) or that have already been the subject of discussions and proposals (e.g., weapons provision', Article 124 and, to some extent, terrorism and drug trafficking).

Any amendment of a purely technical nature which – also taking into account established and successful practices developed over the last decade in other international tribunals – might strengthen the effectiveness of the judicial institution and improve the functioning of the ICC, at a juncture when practical challenges have become to emerge through both its first judicial proceedings and its administrative experience, should also be pragmatically considered. As such issues are intensifying with the increasing activity of the Court and could potentially impact negatively on the image of the institution and on its ability to reach its objectives, such amendments have to be considered as a matter of urgency: challenges insurmountable by the Court under its existing framework should have been addressed by the first Review Conference and not any one thereafter or the ASP as such.

Other provisions of a transitional nature might also need minor changes as they become outdated on the expiration of their built-in terms.

From this perspective, the following considerations refer both to developments of the Law of the Statute suggested by its practice and functionality, and also to other possible amendments that, for various reasons, it might not be appropriate to consider at an early stage of the ICC's experience. The issues below and possible solutions are listed in the order of the relevant Articles of the Statute, without prejudice to the appropriateness for review at the first Review Conference, at a later one or during an ASP.

4. Age Limit and Term of Office for Elected Officials (Article 36(3))

The status of elected officials[97] under the Statute includes rules related to age limits and health conditions which differ substantially from those applicable to the staff of the Court. However, the status of elected officials is not *per se* incompatible with the rules governing the employment of staff of the Court, as the ASP has acknowledged when requiring that the Registrar fulfils for its election criteria established under the staff rules.[98]

96 See *supra*, at 1(A)(1)(a) to (d).

97 Elected officials only include those at the USG (judges and Prosecutor) and ASG (Deputy Prosecutors and Registrar) elected by the ASP or the judges.

98 *Recommendation concerning the election of the Registrar of the International Criminal Court*, 14 December 2007, Recommendation 1, ICC-ASP/6/20, *Official Records*, at 80. See *infra*, at 8(B)(2) and note 207. Under Art. 13 ICTYSt judges must 'possess the qualifications required in their respective countries for appointment to the highest judicial offices'. The case law has, however, concluded that the rationale of the provision is to ensure that only essential qualifications for judges coming from a variety of legal system do not differ. Consequently, the distinction has been established between essential qualifications (e.g., impartiality, integrity, experience) and local qualifications (nationality, age). ICTY, Judgement, *Zejnil Delalic, Zdravko Mucic (aka "Pavo"), Hazim Delic and Esad Landžo (aka "Zenga")*, Appeals Chamber, 20 February 2001

A number of elections of ICC officials took place since 2002 and some of the judges terminated their mandate for reasons relevant to the aforementioned provisions: such provisions have, thus, been already tested and their functioning might be reasonably assessed at this juncture.

A. Features and Interpretation of the Regime

The practice so far at the ICC has revealed some shortcomings of a regime for elected officials whereby no age limit and/or scrutiny of the physical suitability for a long term of office is provided for, as:

(a) states are free to nominate candidates, whatever is their age;[99]
(b) no age limit applies during the term of office; and
(c) no medical checks/clearances whatsoever are required prior to taking office.

The lack of age limits, as well as of any relevance of health conditions, appear to be distinctive, but not logically based features of the requirements for elected officials at the Court, because these features would normally apply to all the staff.[100] However, these could only be understood as negative requirements, meaning that the Statute or the Regulations are silent on this point.

As far as the age limit is concerned, undoubtedly the absence of limits under the Statute cannot be interpreted but in the sense that States' ability to nominate candidates of their choice cannot be limited for reasons of the age of the chosen person. On the other hand, for the medical conditions of candidates, interpretation of the lack of any provisions is less unequivocal, as physical suitability for public offices might be seen as a prerequisite for the recruitment of any official, whatever their mandate might be. This possible alternative interpretation of the implicit requirement of appropriate good health of elected officials would not be based on any provision regulating the status of elected officials under the Statute and has not been endorsed by the Court in its practice.

In particular, the exercise of jurisdictional and administrative functions at the Court dramatically differs from those exerted in other international jurisdictions. For the very nature of the subject matter and theoretically universal jurisdiction of the ICC, its elected officials are regularly called upon to travel extensively in uneasy and stressful conditions, while the Court itself can sit and exercise its functions, when desirable, in any country.[101] Issues concerning, e.g., the composition of a Chamber might arise in case it has to be displaced far away from the Seat of the Court and it includes judges with precarious health conditions. It would not make much difference whether only a hearing or the entire trial were to be held away from the Seat of the Court. As the jurisdiction of the Court has so far been seized with situations all located in states included in the LDC/ODC

(hereinafter, Čelebići), para. 659. Consequently, a judge whose age limit under national legislation would have expired during the mandate at the ICTY was elected. Ibid., para. 661. See also ICTY, *Decision on Motion to Recuse Judge Baird and Report to Judge Güney*, 20 October 2009, paras 9–21.

99 This also applies, *mutatis mutandis*, for the nomination by the Prosecutor of candidates for the positions of Deputy Prosecutor (Art. 42(4) ICCSt) and for the election of the Registrar and its Deputy by the judges (Art. 43(4) ICCSt).

100 Regulation 9.5 Staff Regulations: 'Staff members shall not be retained in active service beyond the age limit of sixty-two years.' Staff Regulations for the International Criminal Court, Resolution ICC-ASP/1/Res. 10, adopted under Art. 44(3) ICCSt.

101 Art. 3(1) and (3) ICCSt: 'The Seat of the Court shall be established at The Hague … the Court may sit elsewhere, whenever it considers it desirable.' Art. 4(2) ICCSt: 'The Court may exercise its functions and powers … on the territory of any State Party and, by special agreement, on the territory of any other State.'

list[102] and most of the States Parties belong to the same categories,[103] it is reasonable to argue that site hearings or even site visits would pose particular strain on any official and, most likely, would not be compatible with less-than-good health conditions, let alone with any disability.

It cannot be underestimated that the fact that elected officials do not undergo any medical clearance – as they are not required to provide a medical statement on the condition of their health before taking office – also has a bearing on the procedure for finding that they are unable to perform their duties, as permanent health and ability permanent conditions which negatively affect a judge or other elected official are only assessed *ex post* of his or her taking office. The disability pension regime for judges itself is based on a rather basic procedure[104] which, in the absence of any objective and *ex ante* statement on the good health of judges prior to taking office, does not allow the Court to take into account whether any illness or disability existing prior to taking office would give rise to the right to the disability pension, at least to the full amount currently foreseen.[105] Thus, the disability pension would normally be granted under discretion of the Presidency only, and based on the alleged illness or disability and on an additional medical opinion sought by the Court.[106]

B. The ICC Practice

On this matter, three cases have been dealt with so far by the Court and the ASP, both concerning the invalidity or inability or death of judges:

(a) Among the judges elected at the 2003 first election[107] and who were selected by lot to serve for a term of six years,[108] one – who at the time of the election was 65 years old – was found by the Court to be unable to perform his duties since early August 2007 because of his

102 Least Developed Countries (LDC) and Other Developing Countries (ODC) which, for the International Monetary Fund (IMF), fall within the category of Emerging and DevelopingEconomies (EDE). Comprehensive IMF October 2008 World Economic Outlook list of 153 states. Available at http://www.imf.org/external/pubs/ft/weo/2008/02/weodata/groups.htm#oem (visited 8 April 2009).

103 Out of 111 States Parties of the Rome Statute, 76 are currently included in the LDC/ODC list and 25 qualify as LDC. The list of LDC is available at www.un.org/special-rep/ohrlls/ldc/list.htm (visited 8 April 2009).

104 *Conditions of service and compensation of judges of the International Criminal Court*, Annex to ICC-ASP/3/Res. 3, *Omnibus resolution*, Appendix 2, *Pension scheme regulations for judges of the International Criminal Court.* Art. II 'Disability Pension', is based on the rules applicable to the ICJ and ICTY judges for whom, however, even the basic double medical statements are not required. The 'Proposal regarding conditions of service and compensation of judges and elected officials' prepared by the Presidency of the ICC gives account that the said mechanism (Article II(2)) was 'added by the ICC to prevent potential abuse and to set forth clear procedures to be followed'). ICC-ASP/3/12, 10 August 2004, at12.

105 Art. II(2) *Pension Scheme*, ibid., para. 3. See also *infra* note 116.

106 However, the Committee on Budget and Finance (CBF) did not make any observation or recommendation on the procedure and merits in the precedent quoted below sub (B)(a) in the text, but only addressed technicalities on the transfer of funds to Major Programme I of the budget (Judiciary) to allow overspending. *Report of the Committee on Budget and Finance on the work of its tenth session*, 26 May 2008, ICC-ASP/7/3, para. 26.

107 First resumed session of the first session of the ASP, New York 4–7 February 2003.

108 Art. 36(9)(b) ICCSt.

health conditions. Consequently, his judicial vacancy had to be filled through new elections, which were also convened to fill additional two vacancies.[109]
(b) A judge elected at the third election in 2009[110] for a regular nine-year term – aged 78 at the time of election – resigned before taking his office[111] and new elections had to be convened in 2009 to cover this judicial position.[112]
(c) A judge elected in 2008 and further re-elected in 2009 to serve a full term – aged 65 at the time of the election – sadly passed away shortly after,[113] and elections were also called for in 2009.[114]

C. Consequences of the Regime

Early retirement of elected officials and, in particular, of judges has manifold implications:

(a) On the one hand, some important financial consequences would flow from:

(i) Any disability pension, which is equal 'to the amount of the retirement pension … payable … had he or she, at the time of leaving office, completed the term for which he or she had been elected.'[115] This means that a judge who is sworn in for the usual nine-year term – in the unfortunate event s/he is subsequently found by the Court 'unable to perform his or her duties because of permanent ill-health or disability' – would be entitled to a full-term pension, although s/he might have served for one day only. As external insurers do not cover disability risk after the age of 65, the entire cost of such benefit would be born by the budget of the Court.[116]

---

109 Elections held on the occasion of the sixth session of the ASP (New York, 30 November–3 December 2007).

110 First resumption of the seventh session of the ASP, New York, 19–23 January 2009.

111 Resignation for 'personal reasons' on 16 February 2009. ICC-ASP-20090218-PR391, 18 February 2009. Available at http://www.icc-cpi.int/NR/exeres/45E2E2C4-E409-4852-9CB1-0BCF4EE495D0.htm (visited 1 March 2009).

112 The President of the Court, on 23 March 2009, informed the President of the ASP 'that the Court wished for the vacancy … to be filled as soon as possible'. However, on 7 April 2009, the ASP Bureau decided to hold elections to fill that vacancy during the regular eighth session of the ASP (The Hague, 18–26 November 2009), including for reasons of the additional costs for a special session that could have been convened prior to that date. Seventh ICC-ASP Bureau Meeting, 7 April 2009, Agenda and Decisions, para. 1.

113 See Press Release, ICC-CPI-20090424-PR407, 24 April 2009. Available at http://www.icc-cpi.int/NR/exeres/DA77F323-4CFC-4A73-975A-481DD453AD13.htm (visited 5 May 2009).

114 Decision of the ASP Bureau of 7 May 2009, communicated by Note Verbale, ICC-ASP/8/S/20, 13 May 2009.

115 Art. II(1) and (3) of the 'Conditions of service and compensation of judges of the International Criminal Court', Annex to ICC-ASP/3/Res. 3 *Strengthening the International Criminal Court and the Assembly of States Parties* (Omnibus Resolution), third session 2004, *Official Records*, 315–322, at 320. But judges forced to stop working due to disability 'will immediately receive the full pension that they would have been entitled to if they had served a full nine year term. This benefit is without any age limit.' *External Auditor's Report 2006*, ICC-ASP/6/20, *Official Records*, Vol. II, 283–284, at 44.

116 An annual disability pension payable to a former judge has an annual financial impact of €90,000 which, in the only case so far experienced (see *supra*, at 4(B)(a)) is payable through funding an external insurer of the judges' pension scheme, with a disability premium of €1,407,179. This happens because the insurers 'do not insure people against disability after they have reached retirement age' and for judges over

(ii) Costs associated with new elections to be convened to fill a judicial vacancy,[117] especially when the situation arises well in advance of a scheduled electoral resumed session of the ASP and depending on such circumstances as the number of vacancies, workload at the Court and 'contamination' of other judges.

(b) On the other hand, additional implications would be related, e.g., to:

(i) the respect for balanced regional representation; and
(ii) ongoing proceedings and the need, if no alternate judge has been appointed, to start a trial anew.

D. Towards an Age Limit

The setting of an age limit is an exercise which, although largely discretionary, is normally influenced by consideration of relevant factors, such as the suitability to perform the specific functions, similar age limits for similar positions, and sustainability of the pension scheme in the long run.

Further, it must be noted that at the ICC the age limit for staff is set by the Staff Regulations[118] at a rather low level – 62 years[119] – although this may be extended on a discretionary basis, but only in exceptional cases and with reasoned decisions.[120]

An additional factor relevant to ICC judges may be inferred from their own qualifications under lists A and B in Article 36(3)(b), taking into account that the same rationale for an age limit in national systems attached to such qualifications would seem valid also at the international level.

An age limit for elected officials could be introduced, in the following options, as a:

(a) requirement for the nomination of candidates, in which case the limit should take into account the term of office of the elected officials;[121] or
(b) deadline for the term of office, so that nominations could still be made at any date prior to the age limit, provided that this limit would still operate by severing the office at any date after the election, even if the term of office has not yet expired. The possible inconvenience attached to the need to fill a vacancy left by a judge elected when less than a full nine-

65 the ICC has to 'manage the disability risk in the absence of insurance cover, and bear the cost of benefits'. *External Auditor's Report 2006*, ICC-ASP/6/20, *Official Records*, Vol. II, 284, at 45–46.

117 Art. 37 ICCSt.

118 Staff Regulations for the International Criminal Court, ICC-ASP/1/Res. 10, adopted under Art. 44(3) ICCSt.

119 The age limit is drawn from that applicable to the UN staff: 'Staff members shall not be retained in active service beyond the age of sixty years or, if appointed on or after 1 January 1990, beyond the age of sixty-two years. The Secretary-General may, in the interest of the Organization, extend this age limit in exceptional cases.' Regulation 9.5 UN Staff Regulations.

120 Staff Regulation 9.5: 'Staff members shall not be retained in active service beyond the age of sixty-two years. The Registrar or the Prosecutor, as appropriate, may in the interest of the Court, extend that age limit in exceptional cases.'

121 Respectively, nine years for the judges (Art. 36(9) ICCSt), the Prosecutor and its Deputies (Art. 42(4) ICCSt); five years for the Registrar and its Deputy (Art. 43(5) ICCSt).

year term of office is remaining before the age limit would be compensated by the regular holding of elections every three years.[122]

Assuming that option (b) might be considered desirable, a possible new provision on the age limit for ICC elected officials should appear under:

(i) Article 36(3) new letter (d), for the Judges;
(ii) Article 42(3) new additional last sentence, for the Prosecutor and the Deputy Prosecutors; and
(iii) Article 43(3) new additional last sentence, for the Registrar and its Deputy.

Drawing on the provision applicable to the judges of the European Court of Human Rights (ECHR),[123] such a provision could read: 'The term of office of the [Judges/Prosecutor and Deputy Prosecutors/Registrar and Deputy Registrar] shall expire when they reach the age of [xx].'

5. Lists of Candidates (Article 36(3) and (5)) and the Composition of Divisions and Chambers (Article 39(2), (3)(b) and (4))

A. Qualifications of Judges

The ICC was established to adjudicate facts involving individual criminal responsibility for the most serious crimes of international concern. Thus, the Statute provides for a composition of the Court which takes into account the need to have judges who possess either:

(a) 'established competence in criminal law and procedure';[124] or
(b) 'established competence in … international law';[125] or
(c) both such competences.[126]

Consequently, candidates may appear in:

(i) List A, if qualified in criminal law and procedure; or
(ii) List B, if qualified in international law; or
(iii) List A and B, if they have sufficient qualifications for both Lists.

122 Art. 39(3)(b) ICCSt. It must be noted that 'a judge must *remain* qualified … throughout his or her term of office'. ICTY, Judgement, *Čelebići*, note 98 *supra*, para. 655.

123 Art. 23(6) ECHR: 'The terms of office of judges shall expire when they reach the age of 70.'

124 Art. 36(3)(b)(i) ICCSt: [Every candidate for the election to the Court shall have] 'established competence in criminal law and procedure, and the necessary relevant experience, whether as a judge, prosecutor, advocate or in other similar capacity, in criminal proceedings.'

125 Art. 36(3)(b)(ii) ICCSt: [Every candidate for the election to the Court shall have] 'established competence in relevant areas of international law such as international humanitarian law and the law of human rights, and extensive experience in a professional legal capacity which is of relevance to the judicial work of the Court.'

126 Art. 36(5) ICCSt, last sub-paragraph, first sentence: 'A candidate with sufficient qualifications for both lists may choose on which list to appear.'

While the Statutes of the *ad hoc* Tribunals do not detail the required background qualifications for judges, the Rome Conference did consider the need to ensure prevailing criminal trial expertise among judges by establishing a proportion of judges who are qualified under the two lists: the Statute sets a minimum requirement of nine judges elected under list A and five under list B.[127]

B. Issues and Criteria in the Composition of Divisions

1. Emerging Issues

As the Court has entered into operation and the first pre-trial, trial and appeal proceedings have begun, however, this proportion as well as the current regime for the composition of, and the term of service in, the different divisions[128] do not seem to solve all the challenges that a criminal Court has to tackle. In this regard, issues may arise:

(a) in the assignment of judges to various functions – including as a single judge at the pre-trial stage,[129] a duty judge[130] or as a Presiding judge in any Chamber[131] – where established competence, *inter alia* in criminal procedure and in the conduct of criminal judicial proceedings, is reasonably required;
(b) depending on the non-applicability to judges assigned to the Appeals Division of the principle of rotation for the term of service in divisions[132] and of their exclusive service in the Appeals Chamber.[133]

2. Discretion of the Court and Binding Criteria

To some extent, these issues may be addressed through an appropriate discretion in relation to the composition of the divisions which, however, under the Statute falls within the sole responsibility of the judges: 'as soon as possible after the election of the judges, the Court shall organize itself into the divisions.'[134]

Any discretionary authority, however, calls for limits, and the Statute states very clearly the compulsory criteria to be followed in the composition of the Divisions, as 'the assignment of judges ... *shall* be based on':[135]

---

127 Art. 36(5) ICCSt, last sub-paragraph, second last and last sentences: 'At the first election to the Court, at least nine judges shall be elected from list A and at least five judges from list B. Subsequent elections shall be organized as to maintain the equivalent proportion on the Court of judges qualified on the two lists.' Identical Art. 13 ICTYSt and Art. 12 ICTRSt provide only that judges 'possess the qualifications required in their respective countries for appointment to the highest judicial offices'. This language is retained also in Art. 36(3)(a) ICCSt where it does not address competencies of candidate judges, detailed for list A and B in Art. 36(3)(b)(i) and (ii). However, the case law at the ICTY has also included in the meaning of 'qualifications' under Art. 13 ICTYSt the background experience of the candidate in criminal law and international law. ICTY, *Čelebići*, note 98 *supra*, Appeals Chamber, para .659.

128 Art. 39(3)(a) and (b) ICCSt.

129 Art. 39(2)(b)(iii) ICCSt.

130 Regulation 17 Regulations of the Court.

131 Regulation 13 Regulations of the Court.

132 Art. 39(3)(a) and (b) ICCSt.

133 Art. 39(4 ICCSt.

134 Art. 39(1) ICCSt.

135 Ibid. (emphasis added).

(i) 'the nature of the functions to be performed';
(ii) 'the qualifications and experience of the judges';
(iii) 'an appropriate combination of expertise in criminal law and procedure and in international law';
(iv) the prevalence 'of judges with criminal trial experience' in the Trial and Pre-Trial divisions.

Such criteria are cumulative and, thus, have to be read and interpreted each in the context of the others. It follows that the binding minimum requirements for the Court when organizing its divisions are:

(a) no division may be composed exclusively with judges qualified and experienced only in criminal law and procedure or in international law; and
(b) the majority of judges in the Trial and Pre-Trial Divisions need to possess criminal trial experience.

Furthermore, it is crucial to correctly define the notion of qualifications required under Article 39(1), which does not coincide with that of the requirements applicable for election purposes under Article 36(3)(b). For the inclusion of nominees in List A or B, the Statute retains a 'formal notion' of qualifications in criminal law and procedure or in international law, leaving to the discretion of candidates and nominating States to decide under which list a candidate should appear. On the other hand, for the composition of the divisions it is a 'substantive notion' of the same definitions (criminal law and procedure or international law) that is considered in order to enable the Court to perform properly its judicial functions.

Elections are held by sovereign States Parties in the ASP, for purposes and under principles and rules that aim to ensure fair representation. On the other hand, the composition of the divisions is run by the Plenary[136] – a session of judges[137] – and for ensuring the efficient organization[138] of the divisions, that is, discharging its judicial functions in the best interest of justice: competing with a number of requirements for winning an election appears to be totally different in substance than deciding who is doing what at the different stages of judicial proceedings.

Literal and systematic arguments also allow a different interpretation of the same definitions (criminal law and procedure or international law). In this regard, when considering the organization into divisions under Article 39(1), the Statute calls for a substantive notion of the same qualifications, which are here indicated as 'expertise' and without any reference to the election regime under Article 36: had the Statute intended the same requirements and formal notion under Article 36(3)(b) to be also applicable for the composition of the divisions, it would have used the same references and techniques used in Article 36(5), where the inclusion in Lists A and B is referred to 'qualifications specified in paragraph[s] 3(b)(i) [and] (ii)'.[139]

---

136 Under Art. 34 ICCSt, only the Presidency, the divisions, the OTP and the Registry, are 'organs of the Court'.

137 Rule 4 ICC RPE: 'The judges shall meet in plenary session [to] assign judges to divisions.'

138 Art. 39(1): 'the Court shall *organize* itself into the divisions ... *based on the functions to be performed*' (emphasis added).

139 Art. 36(5) ICCSt: 'For the purposes of the election, there shall be two lists of candidates:
List A containing the names of candidates with the qualifications specified in paragraph 3 (b) (i): and
List B containing the names of candidates with the qualifications specified in paragraph 3 (b) (ii).'

3. Rotation vs. Permanent Service

While service in Pre-Trial and Trial Divisions is subject to the principle of rotation – as judges assigned to these divisions will serve there for a term of three years[140] – 'judges assigned to the Appeals Division shall serve in that division for their entire term of office'.[141] This provision – as well as the one prohibiting judges of the Appeals Division serving in any other division[142] – is intended to avoid contamination of judges at the appellate stage by any judicial function performed at the pre-trial and trial stage, and vice versa, but it is confronted with the many issues it originates and that were already addressed in the practice of the *ad hoc* international Tribunals.

The issue of 'contamination' of judges by the performance of functions in different stages of proceedings is an ordinary occurrence in any jurisdiction, where management tools have to be used often to enable the number of judges available in house be sufficient to address all the workload. Although this issue is well known and dealt with at the national level, reference to international jurisdictions where the matter has been addressed because of their workload is more appropriate. In this regard, the ICTY's experience shows[143] that appropriate management allows for one Chamber to hold more than one trial or appeal at a time, and for judges to be assigned to more than one case, thus making the full and best possible use of courtroom time and space. This may be achieved by means of rotating panels in one courtroom in morning and afternoon hearings and including the same judge in different benches of several Chambers (shift system).[144] Similar practice is also well established at the ICTR.[145]

The ICTY addressed the challenge posed by contamination of judges in the Appeals Chamber by amending its RPE to allow rotation of judges between the Trial and Appeals Chambers.[146]

It is open to interpretation whether under the currently applicable ICC law the Appeals Chamber, when some of its judges are contaminated, may function by means of temporary attachments of judges from the Pre-Trial and Trial Divisions. In fact, while Article 39(4) ICCSt makes clear that 'judges assigned to the Appeals Division shall serve only in that division' and that judges from the Pre-Trial and the Trial Divisions can be subject to temporary attachment among such divisions, it does not directly address the possibility of such attachment to the Appeals Division. It could, in this regard, be argued that the only limit to such attachment would stem from a judge having been involved in a judicial capacity at the previous stages of the same proceeding (Article 41(2)(a)), which is made explicit for attachments in a Trial Chamber of judges who heard the same case

140 Art. 39(3)(a) ICCSt.

141 Art. 39(3)(b) ICCSt.

142 Art. 39(4) ICCSt: 'Judges assigned to the Appeals Division shall serve only in that division.'

143 The composition of the ICTY Chambers is available on the official Tribunal's website at http://www.icty.org/sections/TheCases/AssignmentofCases (visited 10 May 2009).

144 In this regard, one option available for the ICC, taking into account the reduced number of trials foreseeable at this stage, would be to consider assigning further trials to Trial Chamber I, so that judges in Trial Chamber II are available for attachment to the Appeals Chamber.

145 See E. Møse, 'The International Criminal Tribunal for Rwanda', in this Volume, at 2(B) and note 20: 'The shift-system means that one courtroom is used for two cases heard in morning and afternoon sessions. The system operates with a morning shift from, for instance, 8.45 to about 13.00, and an afternoon shift until about 18.30. In periods, some of the judges were sitting in two different trials on the same day in order to ensure rapid progress.'

146 Rule 27(A) ICTY RPE was amended on 12 April 2001 and now reads: '(A) Permanent Judges shall rotate on a regular basis between the Trial Chambers and the Appeals Chamber. Rotation shall take into account the efficient disposal of cases.' The following (C) also provides that: 'The President may at any time temporarily assign a member of a Trial Chamber or of the Appeals Chamber to another Chamber.'

at the pre-trial stage (Article 39(4), last sentence). However, on the one hand, the argument *a contrario* (*ubi lex voluit dixit, ubi noluit tacuit*) and, on the other hand, consideration that both Article 39(3)(b) and (4) – establishing the exclusive service of judges of the Appeals Division – are exceptions meant to avoid contamination of judges in the Appeals Division, should lead to the conclusion that temporary attachment from other divisions to the Appeals Division is not allowed, because the regime for the latter provides that the Appeals Division is:

(a) to be composed by uncontaminated judges;
(b) understood as preserved from any contamination through the provisions on the privileged exclusive assignment of appeal judges under Article 39(3)(b) and (4).

It is worth noting that the Presidency has so far expressed the opposite opinion that contaminated judges 'will have to be replaced on every appeal by other judges of the Pre-Trial or Trial Divisions ... every time an appeal arises from any of the cases they sat in prior to their assignment to Appeals Division'.[147] This conclusion is likely to be based on the text of Regulation 12 of the Regulations of the Court, which allows the Presidency, 'in the interests of the administration of justice, [to attach] on a temporary basis a judge from either the Trial or Pre-Trial Division' to the Appeals Chamber. Such Regulation has, in substance, applied requirements introduced by the RPE for the replacement of judges in order to make possible the attachment of judges to the Appeals Chamber, which is not foreseen under Article 39(4). However, the status of the Regulations[148] vis-à-vis the provisions of the Statute and of the Rules of Procedure and Evidence which establish the regime for attachments[149] and replacements[150] raises serious doubts about the compatibility of Regulation 12 with the applicable law: if 'in the event of conflict between the Statute and the Rules of Procedure and Evidence, the Statute shall prevail',[151] *a fortiori* the Regulations of the Court cannot conflict with the Statute and the RPE by establishing a new regime for the composition of the Court. In practical terms, this might well lead to the Court being called upon to adjudicate on the observance of the principle of legality during its proceedings, by means of requests for disqualification of judges.[152] Whatever might then be the decision taken by a majority of the judges of the Court[153] on the consistency of Regulation 12 with the law of the Statute, the fact itself that such issue arises appears to be likely to impact on the credibility of the Court.

147 Additional information to the CBF from the Judiciary, informal paper from the Presidency, 21 April 2009, last paragraph, produced to the CBF and cited in Report of the Committee on Budget and Finance on the work of its twelfth session, ICC-ASP/8/5, 13 May 2009, para. 107.

148 See R. Bellelli, The System, *supra* note 27, at 4(2)(c): 'The Regulations of the Court are only intended to implement correctly Statute's normative provisions: "in accordance with the Statute and the Rules of Procedure and Evidence ... the Regulations of the Court necessary for its routine functioning" [Art. 52(1) ICCSt]. Consequently, such regulations cannot establish new rights and obligations, vis-à-vis those established under the Statute and the RPE. Further, the adoption and amendments of the Regulations is within the competence of the judges, who are not mandated under the ICC's Statute to establish the normative framework for the Court, but only to regulate its functioning.' See *supra* note 27.

149 Art. 39(4) ICCSt.

150 Rule 38 ICC RPE.

151 Art. 51(5) ICCSt. See also Art. 51(4) ICCSt: 'The Rules of Procedure and Evidence ... shall be consistent with this Statute.'

152 Art. 41(2)(a) and (c) ICCSt and Rule 34 ICCRPE.

153 Art. 41(2)(c) ICCSt.

As the situation originated by the current composition of the Appeals Division addressed below indicates, the strict legal regimes of non-applicability of rotation and attachment for judges of the Appeals Division may lead – over the time needed for a sufficient number of cases to come to the Trial and Appeals stages – to a shortage of judges who would be uncontaminated and able to sit in a case.

C. The Recent Practice

The competent body to make assignments of judges to the divisions is the 'Court'[154] in its Plenary session of judges,[155] while it is for the Presidency to constitute Chambers and decide the assignment of judges, within a division, to one Chamber or the other.[156]

Following the swearing in of five newly elected judges on 11 March 2009, the Plenary of judges decided on a composition of the divisions which lead to the Appeals Division being composed only of judges possessing substantive qualification in international law ('substantive notion', at 5(B)(2) *supra*). Unfortunately, two of these judges also appeared to be unable to sit in cases which might be heard by the Appeals Chamber as they were previously involved[157] in the same cases at different stages of the proceedings and, thus, appeared to be contaminated.

On its side, the CBF 'expressed concern with the financial implications ... in terms of amount of work the two "contaminated" judges may be able to engage in over the next few years, as well as the impact on any legal officers working with these judges'.[158]

While the Bureau of the ASP requested the Court reconsider such composition because of its likely impact on the output of the Court,[159] the Plenary decided to follow the first of the options which seemed to be available to it:

---

154 Ibid.: 'the Court shall organize itself.'

155 Rule 4(1)(b) ICC RPE.

156 Arts 39(4) and 61(11) ICCSt.

157 Art. 41(2)(a) ICCSt, applicable to two judges moved to the Appeals Chamber from their previous assignments to Pre-Trial Chamber I and II, hearing cases in the situations, respectively, of Sudan and Democratic Republic of the Congo, and of Uganda and Central African Republic. 'Since the new composition of Chambers, three interlocutory appeals have been filed before the Appeals Chamber in Kony, Katanga-Ngudjolo and Al-Bashir cases [and] Judges Kuenyeja and Ušaka [were] excused from the entirety of the two appeals on the basis of their previous involvement in the pre-trial phases of those cases.' *Report of the Court on the new composition of the Appeals Division and the excusal of judges*, ICC-ASP/8/31, 17 September 2009, para. 10 (Report on Composition of Appeals).

158 See *Report of the Committee on Budget and Finance on the work of its twelfth session*, ICC-ASP/8/5, 13 May 2009, para. 108, expressing 'concern with the financial implications ... in terms of the amount of work' that contaminated 'judges may be able to engage in over the next few years'. In response, the Court, while noting that the contaminated judges will not be able to work on appeals resulting from two of the four current situations, suggests that such judges could also be employed in 'many of the Court's activities outside the courtroom: outreach, speaking to high-level visitors, sitting on recruitment panels, induction for new staff, heading Chambers working groups, and representing the Judiciary on various inter-organ working groups'. *Report on Composition Appeals*, para. 14, *supra* note 157.

159 Following a decision taken by the Bureau, the President of the ASP conveyed to the President of the Court 'the concern at the manner in which the Appeals Division has been composed. It would appear that reconsidering these assignments would help alleviate the burden placed on the Court and enhance its ability to exercise its functions as expeditiously and efficiently as possible'. Seventh ICC-ASP Bureau Meeting, 7 April 2009, Agenda and Decisions, para. 1 and letter ASP/2009/111, dated 9 April 2009.

(a) In Plenary session, maintain unchanged the composition of the Appeals Division. In this case, it would seem that some reasoning had to be provided on the conformity of such solution with the criteria limiting the Court's discretion when deciding on the assignment of judges to the divisions. However, the Plenary rather focused on the possibility of enabling the functioning of the Appeals Chamber through temporary attachments of judges from the other divisions, which in turn raises issues under the Law of the Statute.[160]

(b) In Plenary session, change the composition of the divisions.

(c) The Presidency, acting on its own authority, could have replaced at least one of the (other) four judges (in addition to the President himself) composing the Appeals Division.[161] The replacement of one or more judges is, in fact, to take place for any 'objective and justified reason[s]',[162] which seems to be the case when obligatory criteria are provided for under the Statute.

While the decision by the Court formally closed the matter, the real issues raised above are still open and seemingly producing effects on the daily work of the Court.

D. Proposed Solutions

The different sets of issues identified in the composition of the divisions and Chambers – depending on the qualification of judges and on the service and term of office in each division – call for different amendments of the relevant provisions of the Statute.

1. Alternative Review of List Qualifications or Minimum Requirements

Whatever may be the solution in the specific case concerning the composition of the Appeals Division, the issue remains that the number of judges strictly qualified under List A may not be sufficient to discharge the judicial functions of a Court which has by now entered into the active phase of its operations.

The Statute provides for a proportion of List A and List B qualified judges, with prevalence of the former, while the number of candidates on List A has been increasing over the last elections.[163] However, the cited case of the Appeals Division composition clearly shows that the minimum requirement of five judges to be elected under List B is potentially creating situations which might affect the functionality of the Court.

In this regard, prompt consideration should be given to a review of the Statute which could alternatively insist either on the substance of qualifications or on the proportion of judges qualified under the two lists:

160 On this point and on the legality of Regulations 12 and 15 of the Regulations of the Court, see *supra*, 5(B)(3). In response to the concern expressed by the ASP (*supra* note 159), at its 8 June 2009 meeting, the Plenary also expressed concern about 'outside actors' attempting to encroach on the independence of the Court. Letter of the President of the Court to the ASP President, 2009/PRES/269/SHS/PD, 23 June 2009, and *Report on Composition of Appeals*, para. 1, *supra* note 157. See also *supra*, at 1(D) and note 55.

161 Regulation 15(1) Regulations of the Court: 'The Presidency shall be responsible for the replacement of a judge pursuant to rule 38 and in accordance with article 39.'

162 Rule 38(1) ICC RPE.

163 At the third election convened (New York, 19–20 January 2009) for six judicial vacancies, out of 21 candidates 13 nominations were on List A and 8 on List B. See ICC-ASP/7/33/Add. 1.

(a) Option 1 – Qualifications of judges

Improving criminal-law-based qualifications amongst the judges of the Court, under this approach, would mean that this should be a basic and common qualification, to which established competence in international law should be added. Actually, this solution is already applied when considering that candidates who would have been qualified under List B because of their national professional careers as scholars or diplomats, after adequate service in an international criminal tribunal would be also considered as qualified under List A. Thus, from this perspective, joining qualifications of Article 36(3)(b)(i) and (ii) would only mutually apply the upgrading in qualifications – as is currently granted for List B original candidates – to those candidates who currently may only apply under List A. Joining List A and List B would, therefore, offer the advantage of selecting candidates based on a double requisite of established competence, both in criminal and international law.

The new Article 36(3)(b) may thus read (addition in italics):

> 'Every candidate for the election to the Court shall:
>
> (i) have established competence in criminal law and procedure, and the necessary relevant experience, whether as judge, prosecutor, advocate or in other similar capacity, in criminal proceedings, [delete "or"] *and*
> (ii) have established competence in relevant areas of international law such as international humanitarian law and the law of human rights [delete "and extensive experience in a professional legal capacity which is of relevance to the judicial work of the Court"].'

A further amendment entailed would be that Article 36(5), dealing with the election procedure and establishing List A and List B, would need to be deleted.

On the other hand, the Article 39(1) requisite that 'each division shall contain an appropriate expertise in criminal law and procedure and in international law' could be preserved as it would still allow the weighing of the different background of judges under the relevant qualifications.

(b) Option 2 – Proportion of judges qualified under list A and B

A different avenue would be enhancing the List A component of judges, thus altering the existing proportion with List B. This could be achieved, e.g., by raising the minimum number of judges under List A (from nine to *xx*) and removing the minimum requirement under List B (from five to zero), so that the last three sentences of Article 36(5) would read (replacement in italics):

> 'A candidate with sufficient qualifications for both lists may choose on which list to appear. [Delete: "At the first election to the Court"]. At least [*xx*] judges shall be elected from list A' [delete: 'and at least five judges from list B. Subsequent elections shall be organized as to maintain the equivalent proportion on the Court of judges qualified on the two lists'].

2. Composition of the Divisions and Appeals Chamber

Some of the issues that have emerged in the practice at the Court depend on provisions of the Statute that are of an institutional nature and which were agreed in Rome, but adopted subject to their early testing in the first years after the entry into force of the Statute. Such provisions are open to review 'at any time, notwithstanding' the general admissibility term for amendments is set after a seven-year test time.[164]

This applies to existing provisions which under Article 39: (a) mandate the Plenary for the composition of the divisions (Article 39(1), first sentence); (b) hinder that the Appeals Chamber be composed of less than all members of the Division (Article 39(2)(a)); (c) preclude that appeals judges be moved (Article 39(3)(b)) or temporarily attached to hear cases dealt with by the Pre-Trial or Trial Division (Article 39(4)). In the medium term, these provisions are likely to result in a number of contaminated judges, which would possibly justify a proposal for an increase of the overall number of judges under Article 36(1) and (2).[165]

(a) Decision for the composition of the divisions (Article 39(1))

While Article 39(1) provides that is for 'the Court' to organize itself into the divisions, this procedure might lead to a complex balance of interests within the Court that, in the end, could result in solutions difficult to reconcile with the criteria established under the same Article. The composition of the divisions is, after all, an organizational issue that involves assessment of qualifications of human resources – the judges – available to the Court. In this regard, the composition of the divisions – as well as that of the Chambers – is a management function, which should be exerted by the appropriate authority.

As the management of judges is a function which relates to the role of the Presidency,[166] it is instead this organ[167] that could efficiently ensure consistent composition of the divisions. To this objective, Article 39(1) should be amended as follows (additions in italics):

> 'As soon as possible after the election of the judges, the *Presidency* [delete "Court"] shall organize [delete "itself"] *the* Court ...'.

(b) Composition of the Appeals Chamber (Article 39(2)(a))

Under Article 39(2)(a) all the five judges of the Appeals Division compose the Appeals Chamber, which carries out its judicial functions in this composition. This 'plenary' composition of the Appeals Chamber would exacerbate, over time, the issue of availability of uncontaminated judges. The experience at the *ad hoc* Tribunals, in this regard, is different because only at the ICC the pre-trial stage puts additional strains on the management of judicial human resources. However, it is exactly the existing regime for the exercise of the pre-trial functions by a panel or a single judge[168] that can provide guidance and precedent for an appropriate solution, within the framework of the Rome Statute. In this regard, a bench of five appeal judges seems to provide the appearance of additional reliability of a decision. However, the same structure of the bench does not seem to be

164 Art. 122(1) ICCSt, with reference to Art. 121(1) ICCSt. See *supra*, at 1(D)(i).

165 See *Additional information to the CBF from the Judiciary*, para. 4, at 1–2, cited *supra* note 147, and *infra* note 182, where shortage of judges is already considered as an issue: 'the Court is faced with a major problem because of its heavy workload and the limited availability of several judges.'

166 See, e.g., Art. 38(3)(a), 'The Presidency is responsible for the proper administration of the Court'; Art. 36(2)(a) and (c)(ii), proposal for increase/decrease of the number of judges; Art. 39(4), Art. 61(11) and Rule 130 ICC RPE, composition and establishment of the Chambers; Art.74, designation of alternate judges; Art. 41(1), excusing of judges; Rule 30(1) ICC RPE, decision on disciplinary measures.

167 Art. 34 ICCSt: 'The Court shall be composed of the following organs: (a) The Presidency.'

168 Art. 39(2)(a)(iii) ICCSt.

strictly required whatever may be the nature of the proceedings involved, either at pre-trial or at the appeals stage. In particular, appeals against decisions other than those on criminal responsibility and sentence[169] – that is, interlocutory appeals under Article 82 – could well be heard by an Appeals panel composed by a reduced number of three judges. Thus, full use of the maximum number of judges could be improved by means of an amendment to Article 39(2)(b)(i), which could read (additions in italics):

> '*The functions of* the Appeals Chamber shall be [delete "composed of"] *carried out either by three or by* all the judges of the Appeals Division, *in accordance with this Statute and the Rules of Procedure and Evidence.*'

(c) Introducing rotation and continuation in office (Article 39(3)(b) and (4))

The following amendments would appear to be able to prevent the further negative impact of the current provisions under Article 39(3)(b) and (4).

Amendment 1 – Extended rotation – Article 39(3)(b)

The application of the principle of rotation also to Appeals judges may be achieved through an amendment to Article 39(3)(b), which would read (addition in italics):

> 'Judges assigned to the Appeals Division shall serve in that division for *a period of three years*' [delete 'their entire term of office'].

Amendment 2 – Continuation in office – Article 39(4)

As judges moved to the Appeals Division from the other divisions may have been involved in proceedings which are still ongoing in their division of origin, but for which they are contaminated in the Appeals Division, these judges should continue to serve until completion of such cases in the Pre-Trial or Trial Divisions. This does not require exclusive service, so that such judges of the Appeals Division would also serve as required in this Division, while it will be a matter of management of resources for the Presidency to balance their limited availability with appropriate temporary attachments from the other divisions.

To this purpose, an amendment of Article 39(4) would read (addition in italics):

> 'Judges assigned to the Appeals Division shall serve only in that division, *but shall continue to serve also in Pre-Trial or Trial Divisions in circumstances under paragraph 3 (a) of this article.*'

6. Future Elections of Judges (Article 36(9))

For the first election of judges, a provision to avoid the mandates of all judges expiring at the same time – and, thus, to maintain continuity in the organization and in the jurisprudence – was established: Article 36(9)(b) differentiated the time of service for the judges of the Court, a third

169 Arts 74 and 81(1) and (2) ICCSt.

of which where upon election selected by lot to remain in office for a term of three, six or nine years.[170] These different terms of office for judges elected in the first election affect the composition of the Court and the election procedure, which will be necessarily held roughly once every three years, unless vacancies require additional elections to be convened. However, at some point the system is bound to equalize the duration of office for all judges, which is the regular mandate of nine years.[171]

As the end of the differentiated provisional terms of office approaches, consideration might be given, on the one hand, to deleting Article 36(9)(b) – which provides for the selection by lot for the differentiated term – and Article 36(9)(c), which contains the exception (for the three-year-term selected judges) to the rule of exclusion of re-election.[172]

On the other hand, the basic positive rule on the term of office (nine years) and the negative rule on the re-election (non-eligibility), as currently contained in Article 36(a), will become the ordinary and only regime applicable for future elections. Accordingly, consideration should be given to amending Article 36(a) in order to remove references to the other subparagraphs no longer useful and to be deleted as suggested above.

A new Article 36(9) might, therefore, consist of only one subparagraph left and read as follows:

> '*Judges shall hold office for a term of nine years and shall not be eligible for re-election.*'

As to the procedure, amendments to Article 36(9) are considered 'of an exclusively institutional nature' and 'may be proposed at any time … by any State Party',[173] that is even immediately after the entry into force of the Statute. Although such amendments are not subject to the terms and conditions set for amendments of different nature under Article 121, they may be dealt with either by the Assembly of States Parties or at a Review Conference.[174] However, in order to avoid misinterpretations, it might be appropriate that the suggested amendments be not considered before the whole provisional system is in effect, that is at least until the last judge who was originally elected for a nine-year term in 2003 is still in office, i.e., not before 2012.

---

170 Art. 36(9)(b) ICCSt: 'At the first election, one third of the judges elected shall be selected by lot to serve for a term of three years; one third of the judges elected shall be selected by lot to serve for a term of six years; and the remainder shall serve for a term of nine years.'

171 This might be a long term of office, especially in light of the eligibility for re-election that characterized the first elected judges who were selected to serve for a three-year term. Other international jurisdictions may have a shorter term of office, but would then allow for a second mandate: Art. 23(1) ECHR: 'the judges shall be elected for a period of six years. They may be re-elected.' The ICC system is, in this regard, a hybrid one, as its nine-year term is drawn on the one of the ICJ, while the latter allows for a second full mandate, as under Art. 13(1) ICJSt 'the members of the Court shall be elected for nine years and may be re-elected'.

172 Art. 36(9)(c) ICCSt: 'A judge who is selected to serve for a term of three years under subparagraph (b) shall be eligible for re-election for a full term.'

173 Art. 122(1) ICCSt. For the nature of amendments, see *supra*, at 1(D).

174 Art. 122(2) ICCSt. See ibid.

7. Term of Office for Judges and Composition of the Chambers (Article 36(10))

A. The Legal Framework

Relevant provisions under Article 36 for determining the maximum number of judges of the Court while allowing for the judgment to be delivered by the same bench that heard the case provide that:

> 1. There shall be 18 judges of the Court [with the exception of increases in the number of judges approved by the ASP upon request of the Presidency].
>
> [...]
>
> 9. (a) Judges shall hold office for a term of nine years [with the exception of the mandates for 3 and 6 years].
>
> [...]
>
> 10. Notwithstanding paragraph 9, a judge assigned to a Trial or Appeals Chamber ... shall continue in office to complete any trial or appeal the hearing of which has already commenced before that Chamber.

B. The Practice at the Court

The experience so far developed at the ICC has shown that some additional guidance may be needed in a normative framework to ensure that the composition of the Chambers be at any time consistent with the overall number of judges of the Court.

The very first trial at the ICC started in *Lubanga* on 26 January 2009 before a Trial Chamber including a judge whose six-year term was expected to expire on 10 March 2009, while the elections to fill his judicial vacancy had already been successfully carried out on 19 January 2009. As at the date of expiration of his mandate the 'hearing [of the trial had] already commenced before [the] Chamber'[175] to which that judge was assigned, he was called to continue in office until completion of the trial.

C. Management Powers of the Presidency

Both in international and national jurisdictions the terms and conditions of the mandate of a judge are not dictated by the characteristics of any trial (length, complexity, accused), but rather by circumstances under the law (age limit, term of office), its will (resignation, application for a different position), disciplinary measures (removal from office, movement to a different position), *force majeure* (pregnancy, illness, disability, death, termination of the jurisdiction/office). Thus, as many circumstances may interfere with the performance of judicial functions, and in order to protect the interests of justice, legal systems resort to administrative measures to minimize these potential negative effects.

---

175 Art. 36(1) ICCSt.

As in national legal systems, the Statute also provides for the Presidency of the Court to avail itself of managerial tools suitable to prevent situations which might impact on the sound administration of the Court, thus allowing for the protection of the interests of justice in a number of ordinary circumstances which might interfere with the judicial functions. In this regard, it must be recalled that the right to a fair trial entails, for the accused, the right to have his/her case decided on the merits by the same judge who heard the evidence. Thus, the Statute provides that one of the 'requirements for the decision' is that: 'All the judges of the Trial Chamber shall be present at each stage of the trial and throughout their deliberations.'[176] Consequently, if one of the judges on the panel sitting in a trial or appeal is no longer available because of illness, disability, disqualification or resignation, the lack of one of the requirements for the judicial decision entails that proceedings would need to start anew.

It is for this kind of ordinary but potentially harmful situation that the Presidency has the authority and management responsibility to use any of the following tools:

> (a) Change the composition of a Chamber, where a judge whose mandate is expiring in the near future should be a member of a Trial panel.[177] Moving judges from one to another Chamber is a power that does not seem to have any limitation, beyond the workload of the judge himself/herself (both in the sense that this is not excessive and that the judge is not removed from any case that was assigned to him/her), which seems a factor not suitable for consideration in the current situation at the Court and with due account taken of the multiple trials in which judges, e.g., at the ICTY, participate.[178]
> (b) Designate an alternate judge[179] for the same Trial Chamber where a judge, whose term expires during a proceeding, is serving, thus allowing his/her replacement in the panel at the regular term of office without any adverse effect on the trial.
> (c) Defer the initiation of a trial or an appeal, when
>
> > (i) the mandate of one of the judges composing the relevant Chamber would expire soon;
> > (ii) a short postponement of the proceedings would not substantially affect the interests of justice; and
> > (iii) remedies under (a) or (b) above are not applicable.[180]

---

176 Art. 74(1) ICCSt.

177 The rule of continuation in office under Art. 36(10) ICCSt does not apply to judges in the Pre-Trial Chamber, who do not have to take decisions on the evidence that would affect the responsibility and sentence.

178 On this point and the rotation mechanism, see *supra*, 5(B)(3).

179 Art. 74(1) ICCSt: 'the Presidency may, on a case by case basis, designate, as available, one or more alternate judges to be present at each stage of the trial and to replace a member of the Trial Chamber if that member is unable to continue attending.' Rule 39 ICC RPE provides that an alternate 'shall sit through all proceedings and deliberations of the case, but may not take part therein and shall not exercise any of the functions of the members of the Trial Chamber hearing the case, unless and until he or she is required to replace' one of such members 'unable to continue attending'. See also Regulation 16 Regulations of the Court, 26 May 2004, *Official Documents*, ICC-BD/01-01-04, whereby 'the Presidency [shall take into account] first ... the availability of judges from the Trial Division and thereafter from the Pre-Trial Division'.

180 The designation of an alternate judge, e.g., requires that judges are available from the Pre-Trial and Trial Division. It would, obviously, be a matter of discretion and good management to identify the precise contours of this availability. In this regard, it could be noted that *the same judges at the ICTY have been sitting in up to three trials at the same time* and, thus, the fact that one judge is already assigned to any proceeding should not be an obstacle to having the same judge as an alternate in other proceedings.

In this regard, it must be noted that in *Lubanga* the trial had to be adjourned from 8 April to 5 May 2009, taking into account the spring judicial recess and other bank holiday,[181] all circumstances which appear to be of an institutional nature and, thus, foreseeable well in advance and, namely, at the time the decision to start the trial was made (*supra*, at (B)). As the period of adjournment was approximately of the same length of that of the trial (26 January–10 March) before the term of office for the mandate of one of the judges expired, no major consequences would have resulted for the length of trial if this had instead started on 11 March, even with a newly elected judge.

The aforementioned discretionary tools are most useful in order to grant the Presidency sufficient freedom to address any particular case, taking into account both the overall workload of the Court and that of the judges, as well as any other relevant interest, so that the risk of a shortage of judges in the short to medium term is avoided.[182]

D. Composition of the Court

1. The Rule and its Exception

The composition of the Court is a matter regulated under Article 36 with the clear intention of the States Parties to have an ICC composed of a maximum number of 18 judges at any time: 'there shall be 18 judges of the Court'.[183]

This number is subject to increase, on a temporary basis, only by way of a decision of the ASP, depending on the workload of the Court, upon consideration of strict requirements (the increase has to be 'necessary and appropriate') and under a detailed and reinforced procedure (proposal of the Presidency, decision of the ASP adopted by a two-thirds majority of States Parties, subsequent regular election procedure).[184] Any increase is of a temporary nature and, thus, reversible by the same procedure – although aimed at a reduction in the number of judges – when 'the workload of the Court justifies it'.[185]

Therefore, it appears that there is a relationship between Article 36(1) and (10), which establishes a hierarchy between the two provisions, with priority for the application of Article 36(1).

The provision under Article 36(10) allowing for the continuation in office of a judge assigned to a trial or appeal is an established safeguard for the independence of the judiciary against arbitrary removal from office and for the right of the accused to have his/her case decided by the same judges who heard it. Such provision is, therefore, of an exceptional nature and only applicable when no other lawful and appropriate remedies assist the Court to have a trial or appeal heard in complete respect of the fair trial principle. This entails that, under the Statute, remedies for addressing cases where the mandate of judges would expire during a proceeding have to follow a precise, logical and strict order: first, the Presidency should consider using any of the tools under its managerial authority and, only when these would not be applicable, should it resort to requesting a judge to remain in office beyond his or her term. Thus, Article 36(10) would only be the *ultima ratio* of

181 Press release, ICC-CPI-200900408-MA38 of 8 April 2009.

182 In the absence of appropriate actions within the Court, the possible need for an increase of judges is implicit in the issue arising out of the inclusion of contaminated judges in the Appeals Division. In this regard, the Court's own assessment is that 'the Court is faced with a major problem because of its heavy workload and the limited availability of several judges'. See *supra* note 143, *Additional information to the CBF from the Judiciary*, para. 4, 1–2.

183 Art. 36(1) ICCSt.

184 Art. 36(2)(a), (b) and (c)(i) ICCSt.

185 Art. 36(c)(ii) ICCSt.

the system, applicable to the case when all other tools have been unsuccessfully exhausted. In this regard, the policy guidance for the Presidency under the Statute is undoubtedly clear: continuation in office, as it alters the number of judges, is an undesirable result/situation to be avoided through careful management.

Useful elements can also be drawn from the law and practice regulating the UN *ad hoc* Tribunals. In this regard, both the *ad hoc* Tribunals and the ICC have a policymaking body to which they are answerable: the Security Council and the ASP, respectively.

Any change in the number of judges of the *ad hoc* Tribunals has always been previously authorized by the Security Council. That goes for the number of permanent and *ad litem* judges,[186] the extension of their term of office and other similar modifications,[187] but also for the continuation in office until completion of a case.[188]

2. Added Clarity

The correct implementation of the rule on the composition of the Court is a matter which is highly relevant for the policy role of States Parties. An increase in the number of judges which takes place outside the circumstances (workload) and the procedure (decision of the ASP) under Article 36(2), and is not prevented by appropriate use of administrative remedies, is a serious risk for the credibility of the Court. Thus, and based on the experience referred to above, States Parties may wish to provide additional and clearer guidance for the management of relevant situations, by adopting an amendment along the lines of the following wording for adding a new sub-paragraph (2) to Article 36(10):

> '*A judge assigned to a Trial or Appeals Chamber shall not commence an hearing before that Chamber when his term of office may expire during a trial or appeal. Judges whose term of office expire within two years shall be moved to a Pre-Trial Chamber.*'

E. Meaning of 'Continuation in Office'

An additional issue related to the continuation in office of a judge who has not completed a trial or appeal proceeding is whether his/her status would remain unchanged or would, to some extent, be limited by the functions he/she is further called to perform.

In this regard, the Statute is silent, although Article 36(10) refers to continuation 'in office' and, similarly, paragraph 9 says that judges 'hold office'. On the other hand, paragraph 10 clearly sets out the reasons for continuation in office – 'to complete any trial or appeal the hearing of which has already commenced' – while paragraph 1 admits only 18 judges in the Court and only includes exceptions to that number under paragraph 2 (proposal of the Presidency approved by the ASP) and not under paragraph 10. Thus, there are two possible readings, one focusing on the literal and formal interpretation of the term 'office' and the other on the functional and systematic reading.

186 SC Res. 1849, 12 December 2008; SC Res. 1855, 19 December 2008.

187 SC Res. 1684, 13 June 2006; SC Res. 1717, 13 October 2006; SC Res. 1824, 18 July 2008; SC Res.1837, 29 September 2008; SC Res. 1800, 20 February 2008.

188 See, e.g., SC Res. 1705, 29 August 2006: 'Decides [to] authorize [name of the judge] to continue to serve as a judge in the [title of the case] case until its completion'; SC Res. 1668, 10 April 2006: 'Decides … to confirm that Judge … can continue to sit in the [name of the] case … and see the case through its completion.'

The similar provision for the judges of the ECHR appears to be somewhat clearer as it provides that 'they shall ... *continue to deal with such cases* as they already have under consideration' (emphasis added).[189] Differences in formulation might depend on the difference in procedure for a criminal trial (with long oral hearings) from that of a proceeding based only on documentary evidence and for the interpretation of international treaties, with limited involvement of the parties in public hearings. However, the reference to 'cases' seems to clearly address only the judicial functions exerted in specific cases.

Useful elements of interpretation could also be provided by the difference between permanent and *ad litem* judges in the UN *ad hoc* Tribunals, as the office of the latter judges is specifically motivated to the individual trials they are assigned to. There is, therefore, a functional relationship between the office of an *ad litem* judge and any given proceeding.[190]

8. Election of the Deputy Registrar (Article 43(4))

A. The Deputies' Role Under the Statute

The Rome Statute provides for Deputies to ICC Principals, both in the case of the Prosecutor[191] and that of the Registrar.[192]

Although the Statute explicitly provides that the Deputy Prosecutors are mandated to 'assist'[193] the Prosecutor and that they are 'entitled to carry out any of the acts required of the Prosecutor',[194] no similar provision is envisaged for the Deputy Registrar. However, some indications on its functions are to be found in the establishment of the position of Deputy Registrar only 'if the need arises and upon recommendation of the Registrar'[195] and in the possibility that its election be 'on the basis that the Deputy Registrar shall be called upon to serve as required'.[196] Apparently, these provisions establish a functional relationship between the functions performed by the Registrar and those required of its Deputy. Thus, the establishment itself of the position of the Deputy seems to respond to the otherwise rather obvious principle that a Deputy Registrar is also called to 'assist' the Registrar.

In addition to the obvious difference in role and functions of the Deputy Prosecutor and of the Deputy Registrar, in both cases the relationships between Deputies and Principals are characterized

---

189 Art. 23(7) ECHR: 'The judges shall hold office until replaced. They shall, however, continue to deal with such cases as they already have under consideration.'

190 The *ad litem* judges benefit from the same terms and conditions as the permanent judges; however, they are not eligible for election as President or the Presiding Judge of a Trial Chamber. In addition, *ad litem* judges do not have the power to adopt Rules of Procedure and Evidence, although they are consulted before the adoption of any new Rules. They also do not have the power to review an indictment or to consult with the President in relation to the assignment of judges to the various Chambers or in relation to a pardon or commutation of a sentence. According to Security Council resolution 1660 (2006), *ad litem* judges may also be appointed as reserve judges to be present at each stage of a trial and to replace a judge that is unable to continue sitting.

191 Art. 42(2) ICCSt, whereby there might be 'one or more Deputy Prosecutors'.

192 Art. 43(4) ICCSt, whereby only 'a Deputy Registrar' may be elected, 'if the need arises'.

193 Art. 42(2) ICCSt: 'the Prosecutor shall be assisted by [...] Deputy Prosecutors.'

194 Ibid.

195 Art. 43(4) ICCSt.

196 Art. 43(5) ICCSt.

by their 'assistance' role, including thorough substitution in the role of the Principal. However, while the Deputy Prosecutors are mandated by the Statute itself to 'carry out any of the acts required of the Prosecutor',[197] the Deputy Registrar, in the absence of a similar provision, would only be entitled to carry out acts that might be specifically mandated to him/her by the Registrar.

B. The Choice of Deputies

1. Functions and Selection of Deputies

As Deputies – whatever their functions – seem to have in common the duty to assist their Principal also through substitution, the relationship between the former and the latter seems to be characterized by the common need for confidence. However, in this regard the Statute is much clearer for the election of the Deputy Prosecutors than for the Deputy Registrar: 'Deputy Prosecutors shall be elected [by the ASP] from a list of [three] candidates provided by the Prosecutor.'[198] However, the Deputy Registrar is elected by the judges 'upon recommendation' of the Registrar.[199]

The lack of clarity is more evident when the procedure for the election of the Deputy Registrar is considered together with the provision for the election of the Registrar, as Article 43(4) provides that:

> The judges shall elect the Registrar by an absolute majority by secret ballot, taking into account any recommendation by the Assembly of States Parties. If the need arises and upon recommendation of the Registrar, the judges shall elect, in the same manner, a Deputy Registrar.

2. The Role of the ASP

As to the role of the ASP in the procedure, one reading – which was officially endorsed by the ASP[200] – would be that in both cases the ASP plays a role in that it makes recommendations for the election of the Registrar and its Deputy. This is based on the interpretation of the wording 'upon recommendation of the Registrar' as referring only to the establishment of the position of Deputy, i.e., the identification of 'the need' that might arise. At the same time, 'in the same manner' would be understood as requiring, as for the election of the Registrar, a recommendation of the ASP.

Also, the recommendation of the Assembly is required for the election of the Registrar because it is the 'principal administrative officer of the Court'[201] and one of the functions of the ASP is to 'provide management oversight to … the Registrar regarding the administration of the Court'.[202]

Thus – if there were no recommendation by the ASP for the election of the Deputy Registrar – should the Deputy be called to substitute for the Registrar in case his/her its resignation or removal from office,[203] there would be no relationship of confidence between the acting-Registrar and the

197 Art. 42(2) ICCSt.

198 Art. 42(4) ICCSt.

199 Art. 43(4) ICCSt.

200 See Decision of the Bureau at its 17th meeting, 14 December 2007: 'the Assembly's recommendations concerning the election of the Registrar should also be taken into account by the judges when electing the Deputy Registrar.' See also the letter of the Coordinator of The Hague Working Group of the ASP Bureau to the President of the Court, ASP/2007/156, 15 November 2007 presenting these views.

201 Art. 43(2) ICCSt.

202 Art. 112(2)(b) ICCSt.

203 Art. 46(1) and (3) ICCSt.

Assembly. In particular, this might become a serious issue for the performance of crucial duties of the Registrar that are inextricably linked with the authority of the ASP as policymaking body.[204]

Further, the practice of the ASP stresses that the policymaking body of the ICC has no interest in making recommendations on individual candidates as it is mindful that 'the Registrar shall exercise his or her functions under the authority of the President of the Court',[205] thus requiring a special relationship to be established between the electing body of the judges and the Registrar. Consistently, at the first election of the Registrar in 2003, the Assembly only recommended that 'the judges proceed to elect the Registrar on the basis of the list submitted by the Presidency'.[206] At the 2007 second election, with due account taken of the experience so far acquired on the complexity of the duties required to the Registrar, the ASP additionally recommended that judges 'in considering the list of candidates ... take into account ... elements, which include criteria governing the employment of staff of the Court provided in the Rome Statute'.[207]

Against this legal framework, reasoning and practice of the ASP, the practice of the Court has followed a different interpretation of Article 43(4), denying any role to the ASP in the election of the Deputy Registrar. The interpretation of the Court has focused on a reading of 'in the same manner'[208] which relates exclusively to the election procedure before the Plenary of the judges, that is, 'by an absolute majority by secret ballot'.[209]

3. The Role of the Registrar

Under Article 42(4) the ASP proceeds to the election of a Deputy Prosecutor on the basis of a shortlist of three candidates selected by the Prosecutor. This allows the latter to focus the attention of the ASP on a limited number of candidates proposed by him/herself. On the other hand, the Registrar is not allowed to suggest a list of candidates as he/she may only make a recommendation to the judges.

---

204 As indicators, the preparation of the budget and the responsibilities for the construction of the permanent premises seem to fall in this category of major implications.

205 Art. 43(2) ICCSt.

206 *Recommendation concerning the election of the Registrar of the International Criminal Court*, 23 April 2003, Recommendation 1, ICC-ASP/1/3/Add. 1, Official Records, part II. A, at 12.

207 *Recommendation concerning the election of the Registrar of the International Criminal Court*, 14 December 2007, Recommendation 1, ICC-ASP/6/20, *Official Records*, at 80. Elements and criteria included: (a) highest standards of efficiency, competency and integrity, as in Art. 44(2); (b) criteria under Art. 36(8) applicable to the election of judges but also for employment of staff, namely representation of the principal legal systems of the world, equitable geographical representation, gender balance, legal expertise; (c) managerial skills; (d) diplomatic skills; (e) State Party's nationality; (f) different nationality/regional group from the Deputy Registrar; (g) qualifications according to the vacancy announcement; (h) ability to work in cooperation and to lead a team.

208 See also Rule 12(5) ICC RPE: 'The Deputy Registrar shall be elected by the Court, meeting in plenary session, in the same manner as the Registrar.'

209 The President of the Court replied by letter of 16 November 2007 to the letter by the Coordinator of The Hague Working Group denying any role of the ASP in the election of the Deputy Registrar, arguing that for its election under the RPE the 'process is distinct ... and falls into the responsibility of the Registrar, who will submit a list of candidates directly to the plenary of Judges'. See, *supra*, 8(B)(2).

4. An Amended Procedure

These inconsistencies in the regime of selection of the Deputy Registrar may be addressed through an amendment which harmonizes the selection procedure to that applicable to the Deputies of the Prosecutor, both for the role of the Principal and of the ASP.

An amended Article 43(4), second sentence, would thus read (additions in italics):

> 'If the need arises, *a Deputy Registrar shall be elected in the same manner by the judges*, upon recommendation of *and from a list of candidates submitted by the Registrar, also taking into account any recommendation of the Assembly of States Parties*.'

9. Trials *In Absentia* (Article 63)

A. Impossible Trials

International criminal jurisdictions – whatever the authority they derive from and their scope – share the common goal of contributing to peace and security by bringing to timely justice those most responsible for serious crimes of international concern. As far as international criminal justice has to complement other means available to the international community for the maintenance or restoration of peace, it needs to be carried out while situations are ongoing where crimes are being committed. Thus, serious challenges will arise and have repeatedly arisen when international tribunals and Courts have exerted jurisdiction during ongoing conflicts and addressed criminal responsibilities incurred for conducts committed in the exercise of public or *de facto* powers by persons who might still be holding such authority, be they vested official positions or not.

As a general principle of applicable criminal law, the Rome Statute addresses the issues of the official capacity and of immunities which may be attached to a person by denying any relevance on criminal liability or ability to bar the jurisdiction of the Court.[210] While these provisions are based on customary international law[211] their implementation is always problematic, insofar it often results in a confrontation between law and power. Similar issues may also arise at the interstate level for the exercise of jurisdiction – be it universal or on other grounds – on foreign officials exercising representative functions on behalf of their state.[212]

In this respect, common denominators for national and international jurisdictions are:

---

210 Art. 27(1) and (2) ICCSt.

211 See also the ICJ, Judgment, *Arrest Warrant of 11 April 2000* (*Democratic Republic of the Congo v. Belgium*), 14 February 2002, para. 61, where the Court held that personal immunities enjoyed by an incumbent or former state official do not represent a bar to criminal prosecution, *inter alia*, before international courts having jurisdiction. On functional and personal immunities under Art. 27 ICCSt, see P. Gaeta, 'Official Capacities and Immunities', in Cassese, Gaeta and Jones, *supra* note 88, Vol. I, at 990–1001.

212 See the diverging views expressed on the issue of universal jurisdiction allegedly exerted by some EU Member States in: (a) the *Report of the Commission on the Use of the Principle of Universal Jurisdiction by some Non-African States as Recommended by the Conference of Ministers of Justice/Attorneys General*, Assembly/AU/14 (XI), Assembly of the African Union, Eleventh ordinary session, 30 June–1 July 2008 (Sharm El-Sheikh, Egypt); (b) the *AU-EU Expert Report on the Principle of Universal Jurisdiction*, EU Council, 16 April 2009, No. 8672/09 (AU-EU Report).

(i) the resulting limit to the enforcement of arrest warrants issued for persons holding official positions and sometimes sitting at the highest level of the state's hierarchy; and
(ii) the political tensions originated by conflicting views on assertions of jurisdictions or denial of immunities.

The impact of such tensions might have deep and long-lasting effects on basic and historically achieved mutual understandings, with negative implications both for peaceful and constructive relationships between states or groups of states[213] and for the preservation of critical consensus on established mechanisms of international criminal justice.[214]

In the experience so far developed under the ICC's jurisdiction such tensions have already emerged twice (Uganda and Sudan situations) at the stages of requests and issuance of arrest warrants and, as they continue to be unsolved and accused remain at large, have effectively hindered the continuation of proceedings in the presence of the accused. As the allocation of powers originating such situations continue unchanged, most important trials (also) at the ICC might be revealed to be impossible to carry out in a timely manner.

B. International Criminal Procedure

Relevant provisions of the Statute allow only the pre-trial phase to be held *in absentia* of the accused.[215] In order to further proceed to the trial stage after the confirmation of charges[216] the rule, with no exception, is that 'the accused shall be present during the trial',[217] while his presence may

213 *AU-EU Report*, para. 37: 'Indictments issued by European states against officials of African states have the effect of subjecting the latter to the jurisdiction of European states, contrary to the sovereign equality and independence of states. For African states, this evokes memories of colonialism.'

214 See, e.g., in the ICC situation of Sudan/Darfur, the *Al-Bashir* case, for the positions expressed by: (a) the Organization of the Islamic Conference ('the ICC action targeting … Al-Bashir … would … undermine the ongoing efforts [for bringing peace in Sudan and] also lead to destabilization of the country and the region [and] affect the credibility of the international legal system'), Final Communique of the expanded meeting of the executive Committee of the OIC, 27 March 2009, at 2 and 3; (b) the OIC, the African Group, the Arab Group and the Non-Aligned Movement with the 25 February 2009 request to the President of the Security Council to defer ICC proceedings under Art. 16 ICCSt to avoid destabilizing effects for Sudan and the entire region.

215 Art. 61(2) ICCSt: 'The Pre-Trial Chamber may, upon request of the Prosecutor or on its own motion, hold a hearing in the absence of the person charged to confirm the charges on which the Prosecutor intends to seek trial when the person has: (a) Waived his or her right to be present; or (b) Fled or cannot be found an all reasonable steeps have been taken to secure his or her appearance before the Court and to inform the person of the charges and that a hearing to confirm those charges will be held. In that case, the person shall be represented by counsel where the Pre-Trial Chamber determines that it is in the interests of justice.' Under Rule 125(1) ICC RPE 'the Pre-Trial Chamber shall decide whether there is cause to hold a hearing on confirmation of charges in the absence of the person concerned, and in that case, whether the person may be represented by counsel', while in the latter case, under Rule 126(2) ICC RPE, 'the counsel shall have the opportunity to exercise the rights of the person concerned'.

216 Arts 60 and 61 ICCSt.

217 Art. 63(1) ICCSt. However, under Art. 83(5) ICCSt, 'the Appeals Chamber may deliver its judgement in the absence of the person acquitted or convicted'.

be ensured through voluntary appearance[218] or arrest and surrender.[219] Similar provisions are also built-in in the Statutes of the *ad hoc* and hybrid international Tribunals.[220]

This approach under international procedural law is well rooted in domestic legislation shaped by common law and takes into account that trials *in absentia* potentially encroach upon the accused's right to defend himself in person and to examine witnesses against him.[221] At the same time, scepticism around trials *in absentia* is fuelled by the remark that they are often used by authoritarian regimes for politically motivated prosecutions and trials of political opponents abroad.[222]

However, 'grounds militating against trials *in absentia* at the national level do not apply to international criminal trials, particularly when they are not based on full acceptance of adversarial model [and as they] are conducted under a spotlight – the close scrutiny of the whole international community – which would not tolerate any abuse, bias or unfair treatment'.[223]

As a matter of fact, early international criminal procedure enshrined in the Charter of the International Military Tribunal of Nüremberg provided for *in absentia* trials and the trial against Martin Bormann was held in his absence.[224]

C. Lessons Learned at the Ad Hoc International Tribunals

Experience in the *ad hoc* Tribunals[225] has proven that:

> (i) trials in the presence of the accused might not, in practice, be viable when the persons at large still gather political and social support in the territorial states;

---

218 Art. 58(7) ICCSt: 'As an alternative to seeking a warrant of arrest, the Prosecutor may submit an application requesting that the Pre-Trial Chamber issue a summons for the person to appear.'

219 Art. 58(1) ICCSt: 'At any time after the initiation of an investigation, the Pre-Trial Chamber shall, on the application of the Prosecutor, issue a warrant of arrest of a person.'

220 Art. 21(4)(d) and (e) ICTYSt; Art. 20(4)(d) and (e) ICTRSt; Art.17(4)(d) and (e) SCSLSt; Art. 35(d) and (e) ECCCSt.

221 See Art. 14(3)(d) the International Covenant on Civil and Political Rights (ICCPR); Art. 8(2)(d) and (f) American Convention on Human Rights; Art. 6(3)(c) and (d) European Convention on Human Rights (ECHR).

222 STL RPE, *Explanatory Memorandum by the Tribunal's President*, para. 35 (hereinafter, Explanatory Memorandum). Available at http://www.stl-tsl.org/sid/112 (visited 30 August 2009).

223 Ibid., para. 36.

224 Ibid., also for some implications of *Bormann*. Art. 12 IMT Charter, annexed to the London Agreement of 8 August 1945: 'The Tribunal shall have the right to take proceedings against a person charged with crimes set out in Article 6 of this Charter in his absence, if he has not been found or if the Tribunal, for any reason, finds it necessary, in the interests of Justice, to conduct the hearing in his absence.'

225 At ICTY, accused are still at large in the *Ratko Mladić* and *Goran Hadžić* cases, while in *Karadzic* the accused – the former President of the Republika Srpska, formerly Serbian Republic of Bosnia and Herzegovina – remained at large for 13 years, from 25 July 1995 to 21 July 2008, before the arrest warrant was executed by the Serbian authorities. See, also ICTY-UNICRI (eds), *ICTY Manual on Developed Practices* (Torino: UNICRI, 2009), at V, para. 26, at 41–42 (hereinafter, ICTY Manual). Not dissimilarly, 13 accused are still at large at ICTR, absconding in many continents, but mainly in Africa: E. Møse, 'The International Criminal Tribunal for Rwanda', in this Volume, paras 3 and 5(A). Also, at the SCSL one accused (Johnny Paul Koroma) remains at large, and the closing in of the completion date for the Court has led to the introduction of a Rule 11*bis* SCSL RPE upon the conclusion that jurisdiction on this case will need to be referred back to the territorial state. See R. Winter, 'The Special Court for Sierra Leone', in this Volume, at 11(A)(2).

(ii) delaying indefinitely such trials can seriously affect the credibility of international justice by suggesting that political considerations prevail on the principles of legality and of equality;
(iii) although international crimes under the Statutes of the *ad hoc* Tribunals are not subject to any statute of limitations, applicable time limits to the existence of the jurisdiction (i.e., the UN Security Council-approved completion strategy) might be perceived as a hope for effective impunity for accused still at large when business is closed.[226]

D. Practice and Issues at the ICC

Obviously, as the jurisdiction of the ICC is permanent in nature, the length of the time span between the issuance of a warrant of arrest and its execution might be considered irrelevant. However, an excessive delay in the arrest and surrender of an accused to the Court might twofold adversely affect the functioning of the ICC because of the impact on the following key factors:

(i) Deterrence. The deterrent effect of the proceedings would be lost if those most responsible for the crimes are able to escape justice for a long period of time.
(ii) Timely justice. The ICC would not be able to tackle ongoing conflicts, addressing at trial the responsibility of high officials still holding power and, therefore, not likely to be surrendered by the very same state apparatus over which they exert *de iure* or *de facto* control.

In existing situations before the Court, experience has shown that, in spite of pledges for cooperation of competent states, including those self-referring, cooperation actually provided might be far from perfect and leave open possibilities for a conflict between the obligation to execute arrest warrants and the interest in impunity provisions relevant to reaching peace agreements.

In the Uganda situation, the four Lord's Resistance Army leaders sought by the Court with the 2005 arrest warrants are still at large and the theoretical possibility for a political agreement on their fate is hanging over the credibility of the results so far achieved by the efforts of the Office of the Prosecutor (OTP) to conduct an effective and expeditious investigation and prosecution.

In the Darfur situation, the first two arrest warrants issued[227] were already being challenged by the systematic and absolute lack of cooperation,[228] and cooperation does not seem likely to be obtained in the future, due to the stand taken by the territorial state. The third arrest warrant – issued on 4 March 2009 against the Sudanese sitting President Omar Al-Bashir – has formally opened an issue of non-compliance with SC Resolution 1593 (2005), as this specifically required

226 The establishment of any International Mechanism that the Security Council might decide for dealing with a number of residual issues, including the trial of remaining fugitives, would only to some extent address this concern as the arrest and surrender of major accused is highly dependent on the pressure that the international community can exert on states were the person sought is absconding. On the importance of the support of the international community for the enforcement of the decisions of international tribunals, see R. Bellelli, The System, *supra* note 27, at 4 (E). It is doubtful whether after the closure of the Tribunals such pressure – which would have not been enough to result in arrest and surrender until the Tribunals were holding the agenda of the SC – would still be sufficiently consistent as to produce the desired result.

227 On 2 May 2007, PTC I had issued arrest warrants against Ahmed Harun, Minister of Humanitarian Affairs, and Ali Kushayb, regional Janjaweed militia leader.

228 ICC, Decision on the Prosecution's Application for a Warrant of Arrest against Omar Hassan Ahmad Al Bashir (Decision), Pre-Trial Chamber I, 4 March 2009, paras 228 and 231.

that 'the Government of Sudan … shall cooperate fully with and provide the necessary assistance to the Court and the Prosecutor'.[229]

It is also apparent that an excessively delayed trial would run against basic needs of preservation of evidence. This, in particular, goes for witnesses who might have gone through long social and mental processes to cope with their past experiences related to the crimes suffered. Also, those witnesses who needed to be relocated and/or protected might find it difficult to live in such situations without the prospect of a trial being completed in reasonable time, while the number of contempt cases before the *ad hoc* Tribunals has made clear that – in spite of all the protective measures that might be put in place – the risk of intentional disclosure of the identity of witnesses intensifies over time and may result in permanent damage to protective efforts.[230] Again, this protracted situation would need a revision of the capability of the Court to offer protective measures to all persons concerned, with unforeseeable consequences, including for the budgetary sustainability.

E. Trials in Absentia Under Human Rights Law

1. Right to Public Trial

The right of the accused to be tried in his/her presence is strictly linked with the right to a public trial[231] which, however, has a much wider scope and is afforded – mainly to protect the accused against the arbitrary conduct of the proceedings – by allowing the fairness of trial to be publicly verifiable in open hearings.[232] However, the right to a public trial is not an absolute one[233] and in the balance with other values and interests, public trial safeguards are reduced (e.g., video/teleconference, voice and/or image distortion),[234] trial sessions can also take place in the total

---

229 SC Res. 1593, 31 March 2005, OP 2. The same cooperation obligation was established for 'all other parties to the conflict in Darfur', while states not Parties to the Rome Statute and other international organizations were only urged to 'cooperate fully', as they were acknowledged as not bound by a cooperation obligation under the Statute. On the extent of such obligation, see R. Bellelli, The System, *supra* note 27, at 4(E)(b).

230 This has been particularly evident in the many contempt cases originated through the duration of proceedings and trials at the ICTY through the divulgation of the identity of witnesses committed in violation of orders granting protective measures, with details of such identities published in books (*Vojislav Šešelj*, case IT 03-67-R77.2; *Florence Hartmann*, case IT 02-54-R77.5), in the press (*Josip Jović*, cases IT 95-14 & 14/2 R77; *Baton Haxhiu*, case IT 04-84-R77.5; *Ivica Marijaćić* & *Markica Rebić*, case IT 95-14-R77.2) and on the Web (*Domagoj Margetić*, case IT 95-14-R77.6).

231 Art. 6(1) ECHR; Art. 14(1) ICCPR; Art. 64(7) ICCSt: 'the trial shall be held in public'; identical in Rules 78 ICTY and ICTR RPE: 'all proceedings … shall be held in public, unless otherwise provided.'

232 'Article 6, paragraph 1 protects litigants against the administration of justice in secret with no public scrutiny … by rendering the administration of justice visible, publicity contributes to the achievement of the aim of Article 6, paragraph 1, namely a fair trial, the guarantee of which is one of the fundamental principles of any democratic society'. ECHR, Judgment, *Pretto and others v. Italy*, 8 December 1983, Series A No.71, at 11–12, paras 21–22.

233 'The Convention does not make this principle an absolute one, since … the press and public may be excluded from all or part of the trial in the interests of morals … where the … protection of the private life of the parties so require[s], or … where publicity would prejudice the interests of justice.' ECHR, Judgment, *Diennet v. France*, 26 September 1995, Series A No. 325-A, para. 33.

234 On this point, see *infra*, at 12 and notes 313 and 316.

absence of public (closed sessions),[235] and motions, as well as evidence, can be presented in written form (written testimony[236] and motions[237]).

2. Limitations to the Right to be Present

The principle of the trial in presence of the accused is well established within the context and for the purpose of an effective fair trial.[238] However, the possibility of holding trials *in absentia* is not discarded under human rights law (HRL),[239] when non-appearance:[240]

(a) depends on the accused seeking to evade trial;[241] or

235 See, e.g, Art. 64(7) ICCSt, when 'special circumstances require that certain proceedings be in closed session for [witnesses and victims protection] or to protect confidential or sensitive information to be given in evidence'. The exception to public trial is much wider under identical Rules 79 ICTY and ICTR RPE, as it is extended to reasons of public order or morality, victims or witnesses protection, or to 'the protection of the interests of justice'.

236 See *infra*, para. 12(B).

237 Rule 73(A) ICTY RPE, amended in 1997, thus allowed the reduction of trials' costs, as was the case of the similar Rule 73(A) ICTR RPE. See E. Møse, 'The International Criminal Tribunal for Rwanda', in this Volume, at 3(C).

238 Art. 6 ECHR does not explicitly state the right to be present, but the European Court of Human Rights has acknowledged that it flows from the object and purpose of the right to a fair trial. ECHR, Judgment, *Brozicek v. Italy*, 19 December 1989, Series A No.167, para. 45. See also, Judgment, *Colozza v. Italy*, 12 February 1985, Series A, No. 89, para. 27. On the same point, in *Sejdovic*, Grand Chamber, para. 81, the ECHR held: 'Moreover, [Article 6] sub-paragraphs (c), (d) and (e) of paragraph 3 guarantee to "everyone charged with a criminal offence" the right "to defend himself in person", "to examine or have examined witnesses" and "to have the free assistance of an interpreter if he cannot understand or speak the language used in court", and it is difficult to see how he could exercise these rights without being present' also quoting *Colozza*, para. 27; *T. v. Italy*, para. 26; *F.C.B. v. Italy*, para. 33; and *Belziuk v. Poland*, 25 March 1998, para. 37, *Reports* 1998-II. In *Sejdovic*, para. 92, it is also added that: 'it is of capital importance that a defendant should appear, both because of his right to a hearing and because of the need to verify the accuracy of his statements and compare them with those of the victim – whose interests need to be protected – and of the witnesses.' Also quoting *Krombach*, paras 84, 89 and 90; Judgment, *Van Geyseghem v. Belgium*, Grand Chamber, No. 26103/95, para. 34, and *Poitrimol v. France*, 25 November 1993, Series A No. 277-A, para. 35.

239 According to the jurisprudence of the European Court of Human Rights (ECHR), trials *in absentia* are admissible when held in full respect for the rights of the accused. See, e.g., ECHR, Judgement, *Krombach v. France*, 13 February 2001; Judgment, *Sejdovic v. Italy*, 1 March 2000. This is also recognized by the ICTY: 'Trials *in absentia* are not provided for under ICTY regime although they are acknowledged in International Law and are compatible with Human Rights Law.' *ICTY Manual*, at note 225 *supra*, VIII, para. 74 and note 160, at 94–95.

240 The Human Rights Committee (HRC) has clarified that the reasons for the absence of the defendant have to be taken into account in *Mbenge v. Zaire*, Doc. A/38/40, 134.

241 ECHR, Judgment, *Medenica v. Switzerland*, No. 20491/92, para. 55.

(b) is attributable to a waiver of the right be present at trial that, although implicit, is informed[242] and unequivocal,[243] and provided that sufficient minimum guarantees are afforded to the accused,[244] including

(i) an effective notice of the pending proceedings (awareness);[245]
(ii) representation by a lawyer;[246] and
(iii) the possibility of retrial[247] upon appearance after conviction.

---

242 Before an accused can be said to have implicitly, through his conduct, waived an important right under Article 6 of the Convention, it must be shown that he could reasonably have foreseen what the consequences of his conduct would be. ECHR, Decision, *Jones v. the United Kingdom*, No. 30900/02, 9 September 2003 and *Sejdovic*, para. 87.

243 'Neither the letter nor the spirit of [Article 6] prevents a person from waiving of his own free will, either expressly or tacitly, the entitlement to have his case heard in public ... . However, a waiver must be made in an unequivocal manner.' ECHR, *Håkansson and Sturesson v. Sweden*, 21 February 1990, Series A No. 171-A, at 20, para. 66. Also, ECHR, *Poitrimol v. France*, 23 November 1993, Series A No. 277-A, paras 31and 56, and Decision, *Kwiatkowska v. Italy*, No. 52868/99, 30 November 2000. Furthermore, a waiver to appear at trial and defend him/herself cannot be inferred by the status of fugitive of a person who was not notified in person of criminal charges brought against him/her: *Colozza*, para. 28.

244 ECHR, Judgment, *Poitrimol v. France*, 23 November 1993, Series A No. 277-A, para. 31.

245 'To inform someone of a prosecution brought against him is a legal act of such importance that it must be carried out in accordance with procedural and substantive requirements capable of guaranteeing the effective exercise of the accused's rights; vague and informal knowledge cannot suffice.' ECHR, Judgment, *Sejdovic v. Italy*, Grand Chamber, 1 March 2006, para. 99. See also ECHR, *T. v. Italy*, 12 October 1992, Series A No. 245-C, para. 28 and *Somogyi v. Italy*, No. 67972/01, para. 75. Under United States law, similar rules apply, as held in Arizona Supreme Court, *State v. Whitlet*, 85 P.3d 116 (2004): 'a voluntary waiver to the right to be present requires true freedom of choice [and] a defendant's absence from trial is voluntary and constitutes a waiver if the defendant had personal knowledge of the time of the proceeding, the right to be present, and had received a warning that the proceeding would take place in their absence if they failed to appear.' Therefore, if the defendant has been given proper and actual notice of the proceedings, his/her absence may be held to amount to a waiver of its right to be present in Court. Trial *in absentia* is then allowed, provided that (under the ECHR) the defendant is represented by a lawyer who must be fully entitled to speak in his/her name and submit arguments for his/her defence.

246 See, e.g., ECHR, Judgment, *Lala v. Netherlands*, Series A 297-A, 22 September 1994 and, for an analysis of its impact on the Dutch legal system and practice, E.F. Stamhuis, '*In absentia* Trials and the Right to Defend: The Incorporation of a European Human Rights Principle into the Dutch Criminal Justice System', 32 *Victoria University of Wellington Law Review* (2001), at 715–728.

247 Under Art. 6 ECHR, the right to retrial would entail 'to obtain from a court which has heard [the person convicted *in absentia*] a fresh determination of the merits of the charge, in respect of both law and fact, where it has not been established that he has waived his right to appear and to defend himself (ECHR, *Colozza*, paras29–30; Decision, *Einhorn v. France*, No. 71555/01, para. 33; *Krombach v. France*, No. 29731/96, para. 85; and *Somogyi v. Italy*, No. 67972/01, para. 66) or that he intended to escape trial (Judgment, *Medenica v. Switzerland*, No. 20491/92, para. 55). The right to a new trial would, thus, be lost in case of waiver of the right to be present or when a person intended to escape trial. The intention to escape trial extinguishes the right of a person convicted *in absentia* to a new trial because the inability to appear has been the accused's own fault and the accused did not provide any valid excuse for his absence. Presumption to evade justice is always rebuttable by explanations of unawareness of proceedings or legitimate impediments (*Sejdovic*, Grand Chamber, 1 March 2006, para. 63). See also, Council of Europe, Committee of Ministers, Resolution 11/1975, para. 1 'Nul ne peut être mis en jugement s'il n'a été au préalable attaint effectivement par une citation remise en temps utile pour lui permettre de comparaître et de preparer sa défense, sauf s'il est établi qu'il s'est soustrait volontairement à la justice'; and para. 6, where terms for seeking remedy against a judgment

Under these conditions it is well established that trials *in absentia* are not inevitably against human rights[248] and, on the contrary, 'prohibiting all trials *in absentia* could paralyse the conduct of criminal proceedings'.[249]

Practice has shown that main problems with *in absentia* trials under HRL arise in circumstances when the awareness of the defendant cannot be presumed because s/he has not been personally served with the formal notification, which, most of the time, is when an accused is absconding. However, the ECHR[250] has also affirmed that the awareness of proceedings and the intention not to defend oneself is fully proven[251] under certain circumstances, which include written or public statements of the accused or the accused evading an attempted arrest.

3. Balancing the Rights of Accused and Victims, and Preserving Evidence

That a person charged with serious crimes remains at large is a rather common situation in national jurisdictions, as well as in international ones, when common features of domestic and international crimes and of the context thereof play a facilitating role in ensuring that power, protection and consensus continue to support fugitives.

In this regard, organized crimes – either at the national or at the transnational level – may offer a contextual basis similar to that of serious crimes of international concern falling within international jurisdictions. In such situations, persons at large would normally receive substantial financial and other material assistance from large and organized groups exerting control over wide

---

in absentia would lapse from the moment of actual knowledge by the convicted of the judgment, unless it is proven that he/she has voluntarily escaped justice.

248 HRC, *Ali Maleki v. Italy*, para. 9.3: 'a trial in absentia is compatible with article 14 [ICCPR] when the accused was summoned in a timely manner and informed of the proceedings against him'; Communication No. 699/1996, U.N. Doc. CCPR/C/66/D/699/1996, 27 July 1999. Available at http://www1.umn.edu/humanrts/undocs/session66/view699.htm (visited on 20 April 2009). Identically, in HRC, *Mbenge v. Zaire*, U.N. Doc. A/37/40, para. 14.1: 'article 14 (3) [ICCPR] and other requirements of due process enshrined in article 14 cannot be construed as invariably rendering proceedings in absentia inadmissible irrespective of the reasons for the accused person's absence. Indeed, proceedings in absentia are in some circumstances (for instance, when the accused person, although informed of the proceedings sufficiently in advance, declines to exercise his right to be present) permissible in the interest of the proper administration of justice'; Communication No. 16/1977, Views of 25 March 1983. Also, see ECHR, 'Proceedings that take place in the accused's absence will not of themselves be incompatible with the Convention if the accused may subsequently obtain, from a court which has heard him, a fresh determination of the merits of the charge' (*Colozza*, 12 February 1985, para. 29; *Poitrimol*, para. 31, and *Medenica*, para. 54); 'proceedings that take place in the accused's absence are not of themselves incompatible with Article 6', *Sejdovic*, Grand Chamber, para. 81.

249 ECHR, *Sejdovic*, Grand Chamber, para. 79, where the Court argued that should trials *in absentia* be always prohibited, the result could be, e.g., the dispersal of evidence, expiry of the time allowed for prosecution or a miscarriage of justice. See identically in Judgment, *Colozza v. Italy*, 12 February 1985, para. 29.

250 An analysis of ECHR Case law in N. Lettieri, 'Articolo 175 comma 2 – Processo in contumacia' [Art. 175(2) – Trial in Absentia], in G. Tranchina (ed.), *Codice di Procedura Penale* (Milano: Giuffrè, 2008).

251 'Certain established facts might provide an unequivocal indication that the accused is aware of the existence of the criminal proceedings against him and of the nature and the cause of the accusation and does not intend to take part in the trial or wishes to escape prosecution. This may be the case, for example, where the accused states publicly that he does not intend to respond to summonses of which he has become aware through sources other than the authorities, or succeeds in evading an attempted arrest … or when materials are brought to the attention of the authorities which unequivocally show that he is aware of the proceedings pending against him and of the charges he faces.' ECHR, *Sejdovic*, Grand Chamber, paras 99–100.

territories, in some cases even in a state capacity.[252] The experience of national jurisdictions – where fugitives have been able to abscond for life-long periods of time[253] – is coupled with some of the most notorious cases in international jurisdictions where, e.g., Ratko Mladić's continued absence from the ICTY courtroom since 1995 is an open defiance to the *ius puniendi* of the international community.

On a factual ground, the fact that an accused with a leadership position in organized crime or serious crimes of international concern (which have similar characterization of organization)[254] remains at large allows him/her to continue exerting his/her role, thus perpetuating the pattern of criminal conduct and jeopardizing the preservation and acquisition of evidence.[255] In this regard, it should be stressed that HRL not only provides safeguards to individuals in the position of suspect/accused from possible abuses of public powers, but also balances individual and collective rights, imposing on states positive obligations[256] to protect their citizens from serious crimes which might endanger fundamental rights.[257] Thus, an approach to the principle of trial in presence of the accused that discarded – under any of the circumstances considered in HRL as interpreted by international Courts on human rights – the holding of trials *in absentia* would, in itself, be a selective one and not in line with the aforementioned objective to protect the fundamental rights of actual and potential victims of a perpetrator at large.

252 On this point, see N. Piacente, 'Addressing the Impunity Gap through Cooperation', in this Volume, at 2(E).

253 The Italian Mafia boss Bernardo Provenzano remained at large for a record period of over 40 years, while many other members of mafia-type organizations have absconded for decades.

254 On the similarities between international crimes and organized crime, see N. Piacente, *supra* note 252, at 2(E).

255 Special proceedings for the preservation of evidence for trials of fugitives who might be eventually arrested is under consideration for amendments to the ICTR RPE: although this is explicitly not framed as an *in absentia* trial, the fact remains that the envisaged appointment of counsel by the Trial Chamber to provide adequate fair trial guarantees exactly matches with the scope and conditions for a trial *in absentia* under current international case law. See *Report on the Completion Strategy of the International Criminal Tribunal for Rwanda (as of 4 May 2009)*, S/2009/247, transmitted to the President of the UN Security Council on 14 May 2009, para. 51. Available at http://www.ictr.org/default.htm (visited 30 June 2009).

256 'States are under the obligation to take the measures needed to protect the fundamental rights of everyone within their jurisdiction against terrorist acts, especially right to life.' Guidelines of the Committee of Ministers of the Council of Europe on Human Rights and the Fight against Terrorism, 11 July 2002, Guideline I. Available at www.coe.int/t/e/legal_affairs/legal_co-operation/fight_against_terrorism (Docs/Adopted Texts) (visited 24 March 2009).

257 Regarding the right to life under Art. 2(1) of the 1950 Convention for the Protection of Human Rights and Fundamental Freedoms, in *Pretty v. the United Kingdom*, 29 April 2002, para. 38, the ECHR indicated that 'the first sentence of Art. 2 para. 1 enjoins the State not only to refrain from the intentional and lawful taking of life, but also to take appropriate steps to safeguard the lives of those within its jurisdiction (see the Judgment, *L.C.B. v. the United Kingdom*, 9 June 1998, Reports of Judgments and Decisions 1998-III, at 1403, para. 36). This obligation … may also imply in certain well-defined circumstances a positive obligation on the authorities to take preventive operational measures to protect an individual whose life is at risk from the criminal acts of another individual' (Judgment, *Osman v. the United Kingdom*, 28 October 1998, para. 115; Application, *Kiliç v. Turkey*, ECHR, No. 22492/93, paras 62 and 76).

F. The Precedent of the Special Tribunal for Lebanon

These principles may well apply also to international criminal jurisdictions, as it has been proven by the Agreement between the United Nations and the Lebanese Republic on the establishment of a Special Tribunal for Lebanon (STL):[258] a mixed jurisdiction were trials *in absentia* are possible, subject to certain conditions which carefully reflect the requirements set under HRL for trials to be held not in the presence of the accused, including the right to retrial or the re-opening of the trial.[259]

Article 22 of the Statute of the Special Tribunal for Lebanon attached to the Agreement takes into account the relevant case law of the European Court of Human Rights and reads (emphasis added):

> 1. The Special Tribunal shall conduct trial proceedings in the absence of the accused, if he or she:
>
> (a) Has expressly and in writing *waived his or her right* to be present;
>
> (b) *Has not been handed over to the Tribunal* by the State authorities concerned;
>
> (c) *Has absconded* or otherwise cannot be found and all reasonable steps have been taken to secure his or her appearance before the Tribunal to inform him or her of the charges confirmed by the Pre-Trial Judge;
>
> 2. When hearings are conducted in the absence of the accused, the Special Tribunal shall ensure that:
>
> (a) The accused *has been notified, or served with the indictment*, or notice has otherwise been given of the indictment through publication in the media or communication to the State of residence or nationality;
>
> (b) The accused has designated a *defence counsel* of his or her own choosing, to be remunerated either by the accused or, if the accused is proved to be indigent, by the Tribunal;
>
> (c) Whenever the accused refuses or fails to appoint a defence counsel, such counsel has been assigned by the Defence Office of the Tribunal with a view to ensuring full representation of the interests and rights of the accused.
>
> 3. In case of conviction in absentia, the accused, if he or she had not designated a defence counsel of his or her choosing, shall have the *right to be retried* in his or her presence before the Special Tribunal, unless he or she accepts the judgement.

---

258 *Report of the Secretary-General on the establishment of a special tribunal for Lebanon*, S/2006/893, 15 November 2006. On the 'forceful' entry into force of the Agreement establishing the STL, see R. Bellelli, The System, *supra* note 27, at 3(C) and note 43.

259 See, e.g., ECHR, Judgment, *Somogyi v. Italy*, No. 67972/01, para. 86 and ECHR, Judgment, *Stoichkov v. Bulgaria*, No. 9808/02, 24 March 2005, paras 56 and 81. See also in greater details *supra*, (E)(2) and note 247.

As to the right to retrial, the Rules of Procedure and Evidence of the STL provide for two different situations where the accused tried *in absentia* appears:

> (a) During proceedings. In this case the proceedings would start anew in the presence of the accused, unless the accused explicitly refuses a new trial,[260] but results of the proceedings *in absentia* could still be utilized upon the consent of the defence.[261]
> (b) After the sentencing. The accused would be granted the right to retrial or appeal.[262]

Although the STL is not an international jurisdiction proper, but rather an internationalized one,[263] its precedent makes clear that *in absentia* trials are a viable option when the situation where the crimes were committed or the nationality and quality of the accused so demand.

G. Contempt Cases in Absentia at the ICTY

The same human rights principles are also implemented in the contempt proceedings *in absentia*, which are allowed at the ICTY and ICTR. The RPE of the *ad hoc* Tribunals do not address proceedings for contempt by referring to an accused, but only to a 'person' or 'party', thereby avoiding calling into play the right of the accused 'to be tried in his presence'.[264]

Under the amended regime of Rules 77 ICTY/ICTR RPE, 'any person indicted for or charged of contempt shall … be assigned counsel'[265] and, if 'not present or represented when the decision was pronounced', entitled to appeal within a time limit running from the date of notification to him/her of the first instance decision.[266]

H. The Interests of Justice at the ICC

In the balance between a trial fully in the presence of the accused or, under strictly limited circumstances, even in the accused's absence, the driving consideration should be whether or not prosecution in the absence of the accused might serve the interests of justice. In this regard, factors which appear relevant to a thorough assessment of the appropriateness of the current system of trial in presence of the accused under the ICC Statute include the following.

1. Final Goal

The essence of the Rome Statute's system, established to defeat impunity, is to send a clear message to perpetrators: they will not escape justice on political grounds. Whatever is their ability to exploit their leadership within a given historical and territorial context, they will be held personally liable before the ICC. In highly sensitive cases this liability may remain a theoretical doctrine – in case

260 Rule 108(A) STL RPE.

261 Rule 108(B) STL RPE.

262 Rule 109 STL RPE.

263 The STL applicable criminal law is Lebanese (Art. 2 STLSt), but its jurisdiction was established based on an international agreement and thanks to the assistance of the international community. See R. Bellelli, The System, *supra* note 27, at 3(C).

264 Art. 21(4)(d) ICTYSt.

265 Rule 77(F) ICTY RPE, as amended on 13 December 2001. See identical Rule 77(F) ICTR RPE.

266 Rule 77(J)(i) and (K)(i) ICTY RPE, as amended on 12 July 2002 and identical Rules for ICTR.

of persistent lack of cooperation in the arrest and surrender of suspects – or can be effectively implemented in a timely manner, even in the absence of the accused.

2. Peace vs Justice Dilemma

Efforts of the Court to deliver timely justice – i.e., carry out proceedings while situations are ongoing – in order to allow for the full deployment of the potential deterrent effect of its action, have so far clashed with repeated objections and obstacles raised on international peace and security grounds. Arrest warrants issued against militia leaders (Lord's Resistance Army, in the Democratic Republic of the Congo situation) or government officials (Sudan situation) have been starkly argued as being an impediment if not the cause for the failure of peace negotiations or agreements. Although blatantly unfounded, these positions reflect the reality of a difficult relationship between justice and politics, between law and power, where law and justice are – at least historically – doomed by political agreements which, in turn, may entail wide-ranging amnesties or other forms of impunity. Therefore, severing this relationship between justice and politics, by identifying separate avenues for performing their respective roles, would seem a viable solution to ensure that the fight against impunity goes hand in hand with all the tools that politics can put in place to achieve social reconciliation and stability.

Respect for the different roles of justice and politics is key in order not to make the justice process conditional upon the peace process: trials should be assured full independence from the political agenda of states. This result cannot be achieved insofar trials need political backing in order to proceed.

3. Cooperation

The jurisdiction of the ICC stems from the historical experience of the failure of states to address justice on various political grounds related to conflicts. The lack of cooperation is, therefore, inherent to the ICC competence to address ongoing conflicts as governments are often either unwilling to hand over their own officials (Sudan) or unable to secure those of the other parties in conflict (Uganda). In this regard, the Rome Statute has not dramatically improved the situation existing in, e.g., the UN *ad hoc* Tribunals, as it has not established an independent and self-executing system of enforcement of the Court's orders, but, instead, it has linked trials to the political will of states to support each single investigation and trial. This unavoidable feature of the ICC has revealed itself as a major shortcoming for the effectiveness of the Rome Statute system, as the Court has immediately been called on to operate in ongoing conflict situations and face so serious cooperation challenges that its own existence might be put at risk.[267]

4. Judicial Review

The fair trial remedies – provided for under the Statute at all stages of proceedings and throughout trial and appeal stages – allow for further strengthening the factual and legal basis upon which an indictment and an arrest warrant are issued. If lack of cooperation does not allow the execution of an arrest warrant in time to enable the trial to start in the presence of the accused, a judgment

267 'Without targeted efforts [cooperation] to advance the ICC's objectives, this court will fail', in Human Rights Watch, Memorandum for the Sixth Session of the International Criminal Court Assembly of States Parties, at 5. Available at www.hrw.org/en/node/76660/section/3 (visited 20 August 2009).

in absentia passed at trial or even at the appeal stage would make it more compelling for states to execute arrest warrants, as the case would have undergone further justice instances and the bias for politically motivated initiatives would correspondingly loose strength among relevant national and international actors.

5. Judicial Economy and Rights of the Accused and Witnesses

Capturing the complexity of crimes committed within a situation sometimes makes it necessary to indict several persons with charges either identical to or conditional upon the others. Proceedings with multiple accused enhance the likelihood that not all of them are surrendered at the same time. In particular, fugitives accused of crimes committed within a 'same transaction'[268] may be apprehended at different times, sometimes when proceedings for co-accused have reached a different trial stage or even a final decision. The identity of transaction would normally lead to a joinder of accused within the same trial[269] as a means for avoiding separate trials on the same facts and with the same evidence. Although joinder of accused is rooted in reasons of judicial economy and efficient justice, if not all accused involved in the same transaction are at the Seat of the Court within a reasonable time frame, joining them would not be feasible in order to ensure, *inter alia*, respect for a reasonable length of detention on remand. In the case of separate trials for accused who may potentially be joined, the consequences might be burdensome, both for the additional resources needed and for the duplication of evidence. In particular, witnesses would need to go through a multiple testimony process, providing the same evidence in separate trials, with risks of re-trauma, contradictory depositions, witness fatigue and even resentment.[270]

6. Effectiveness

Under the system of the trial in the presence of the accused, a perpetrator who is at large might never be tried. On the other hand, a sentence issued *in absentia* may also never be enforced if the accused or convicted is not apprehended. The purpose of a prosecution is to make perpetrators accountable for their criminal conducts by bringing them to justice. However, while the enforcement of a sentence is crucial to the accomplishment of goals of domestic justice (including respect for legality, punitive retribution for individual conducts, compensation for victims), international criminal justice has additional objectives related to it being instrumental to the maintenance of international peace and security. In this respect, a substantial contribution for the cause of national and international pacification and stability may well be unrelated to the actual enforcement of a sentence and flow from the very act of the judgment, with its authority to shed light on the historic reality of facts.

This situation is not dissimilar to the one of an accused that, although tried in his or her presence, becomes permanently unfit to stand trial because of illness, disability or death. When the responsibility of such an accused is intertwined with that of others by, e.g., participation in criminal

268 Rule 2(A) ICTY RPE and Art. 25(3)(d) ICCSt. On this notion and on joint criminal enterprise see R. Bellelli, The System, *supra* note 27, at 4(C)(2), in particular at note 117.

269 Rule 136(1) ICC RPE: 'persons accused jointly shall be tried together unless … separate trials are necessary, in order to avoid serious prejudice to the accused, to protect the interests of justice or because a person jointly accused has made an admission of guilt.'

270 Further on this point *ICTY Manual*, at note 225 *supra*, V, para. 22, at 41 and at XIV, para. 120, last bullet, at 200.

activities or joint criminal enterprise,[271] the judgment passed on the responsibility of the (other) participants or of the group may obviously only be executed in relation to them, although the role of the (former) accused unable to stand trial would still sometimes need to be called into question (e.g., when his or her role is relevant to the allocation of responsibility to the other participants or members of the group).[272]

Beyond the need to define the scope and structure of individual participation in criminal conducts, judicial ascertainment of facts and conducts contributes to healing the wounds of individuals and populations victimized, usually on a mass scale, by the commission of crimes under international jurisdictions and, thus, to achieving the goal of long-lasting peace and security through stabilization of social, ethnical, religious and political factors. In this regard, it should be stressed that timely justice is part of a 'timely and decisive response' of the international community:[273] timing is crucial to deterrence[274] and, thus, to preventing the further aggravation of a destructive chain of events which unfolds tragically on the lives of victims.

7. Preservation of Evidence

Due to the lengthy periods during which accused who are absconding may remain at large,[275] the situation existing at the time of an indictment and of an arrest warrant and that at the time (if any) of the actual start of a trial in the presence of the accused may radically change because:

(a) spontaneously deteriorating factors – such as the aging of witnesses and traditional documentation – would affect the evidence available both to the prosecution and to the defence cases;
(b) influence on the reliability of witness statements may be exerted by accused who remain at large,[276] either directly or through their support networks;

---

271 Art. 25(3)(d) ICCSt: 'a group of persons acting with a common purpose.' On the notion of joint criminal enterprise in international law, see R. Bellelli, The System, *supra* note 27, para. 4(C)(1).

272 This has been the case of the ICTY Judgment, *Milutinović et al.*, Trial Chamber, 26 February 2009, where judges found that the President of the Federal Republic of Yugoslavia Slobodan Milošević – deceased at the United Nations Detention Centre in The Hague on 11 March 2006 while in custody of the ICTY – was the 'Supreme Commander', responsible for abuses committed by the military forces operating in Kosovo in 1999 (ibid., Vol. 1, paras 441 and 451) with a leading role (e.g., ibid., Vol. 3, paras 293, 300, 308, 427) and directly involved in criminal activities (e.g., ibid. Vol. 2, para. 1356). The judgment clearly attributes to Milošević membership with a leading contribution in a JCE with the convicted (co-)accused (ibid., Vol. 3, para. 466).

273 UNSG Report on *Implementing the Responsibility to Protect*, A/63/677, 12 January 2009, paras 49–55.

274 Ibid., paras 18 and 53–54. This includes the need for a credible support to the enforcement of international arrest warrants. For examples where such deterrent effect has been manifest, see Human Rights Watch, *Selling Justice Short: Why Accountability Matters for Peace*, July 2009, at 123–127. Available at http://www.hrw.org/node/84264 (visited 13 October 2009).

275 See *supra*, at (E)(3) and note 253.

276 Preservation of evidence is one of the conditions for the issuance of an arrest warrant itself. Art. 58(1)(b)(ii) ICCSt, 'to ensure that the person does not obstruct or endanger the investigation or the court proceedings'. Thus, when an arrest warrant issued on grounds of evidence preservation is not executed, the danger for the evidence exists *per se*.

(c) traceability of witnesses, in the highly volatile security and political climate characterizing an ongoing situation, may be drastically reduced over time as witnesses move or re-settle over wide territories and beyond boundaries.

For purposes of evidence preservation the ICTY Statute includes a 'review *in absentia*'[277] under Rule 61 ICTY RPE: in case of a warrant of arrest not executed within reasonable time, the Trial Chamber may examine witnesses and issue an international arrest warrant. Although this procedure provides an additional tool by which to pressurize states to execute arrest warrants,[278] some might still question if evidence recorded in the absence of the accused could be fairly used at a subsequent trial in his/her presence, without allowing the appropriate defence challenge on the evidence acquisition (reopening). Similar needs – number of indictees-at-large and the increasing loss of witness evidence over time – have also recently led to the introduction of Rule 71*bis* ICTR RPE (Preservation of Evidence by Special Deposition for Future Trials), allowing evidence to be secured for a future trial by deposition recorded before a single judge in case the accused is not present at the Tribunal and the arrest warrant has not been executed within a reasonable time or pending the arrest and surrender procedure.

I. Implications for the ICC

In light of the factors analyzed above, adapting the relevant provisions[279] of the Law of the Statute dealing with the trial in the presence of the accused to also allow trials *in absentia* with all the safeguards due under HRL[280] would offer the following major advantages:

(a) Ensure timely justice through expeditious trials, by reducing the gap between the time of commission of the crime and a judicial decision on the case. The possible challenge to such decision through retrial or reopening of the trial would not reduce the effectiveness of the system, as such right of the accused or convicted would still be subject to its appearance before the Court.
(b) Preserve the evidence from any lengthy lapse of time between the pre-trial and the trial phase.
(c) Reinforce the deterrent effect of the jurisdiction of the Court, through the authority and legal certainty created by its judgment.
(d) Reduce the possibility of political interference in the execution of arrest warrants. Proceedings would continue after the issuance of arrest warrants under the exclusive responsibility of the Court, so that judgments would be delivered whatever the political climate surrounding any specific case, and States Parties and other relevant actors would still be bound to cooperation in the execution of the judgment.
(e) Increase the isolation of persons sought by the ICC upon conviction, thereby reinforcing the conditions for the execution of its arrest warrants.

277 C.J.M. Safferling, *Towards an International Criminal Procedure* (Oxford: Oxford University Press, 2003), at 244.

278 If the 'failure to effect personal service was due in whole or in part to a failure or refusal of a State to cooperate … the Trial Chamber shall so certify [and] the President shall notify the Security Council'. Rule 61(E) ICTY RPE.

279 Art. 63(1) ICCSt and RPE. See also *supra*, at 9(B).

280 See *supra*, at (D)(1) and (2) and notes.

10. Functions and Powers of the Trial Chamber. Subpoena Powers (Article 64)

A. Only Willing Witnesses Appear at the ICC

Although witnesses are obliged to testify before the ICC[281] – unless the confidentiality of the information at stake is protected under the Statute[282] – the scope of such an obligation and its relevant sanctions include only the actual provision of testimony by witnesses appearing before the Court[283] and the truthfulness of their deposition:[284] should they choose to appear, they have an obligation to testify and to tell the truth.

However, as there is no obligation for the witnesses to appear at the Seat of the Court, their presence cannot be compelled on the basis of an order of the Court, as the general obligation of States Parties to cooperate[285] with the Court only entails that assistance provided by States Parties should not go beyond 'facilitating the *voluntary appearance* of persons as witnesses or experts before the Court'.[286] Therefore, attendance and testimony of witnesses required by the Trial Chamber cannot form the basis of an enforceable order and for penalties in case of non-compliance thereof: in case of the refusal of a witness to appear before the Court, no sanction whatsoever is applicable.

B. National Legislation and Practice

To ensure that the duty to testify is complied with, national legislations provide for an obligation to appear and for coercive orders, subpoenas, to be issued by judges. A subpoena is an order issued by a judge, requiring a witness to personally appear in court in order to give testimony. In the case of a failure to appear without valid justification, the subpoena is enforceable by issuance of an arrest warrant for contempt and a penalty (usually a fine) may be imposed. The rationale for a subpoena is, therefore, the disruption of judicial proceedings caused by non-appearance of a witness and the need to ensure evidence and judicial economy and to avoid hearing time not being fully and appropriately used.

Experience at the domestic level shows that it is good practice to ensure that the witnesses are well informed about the consequence of their failure to appear before a court in response to a validly issued subpoena. Whether or not the contempt proceeding would then have a bearing on the

---

281 Art. 64(6)(b) ICCSt: '[the Trial Chamber may] require the attendance and testimony of witnesses.'

282 Art. 69(5) ICCSt: 'The Court shall respect and observe privileges on confidentiality as provided for in the Rules of Procedure and Evidence.' See Rules 73 (privileged communications and information), 74 (self-incrimination by a witness), and 75 (incrimination by family members) ICC RPE.

283 Rule 65 ICC RPE: 'a witness who appears before the Court is compellable by the Court to provide testimony.' Deliberate refusal to comply with an order of the Court to provide testimony amounts to a misconduct, punishable with a fine, under Rule 171(1) and (5) ICC RPE. The dissuasive nature and effectiveness of a monetary sanction can also be an issue, when account is taken of the frequent absolute indigence of witnesses, who travel and are assisted at the expense of the ICC.

284 For the obligation to tell the truth, see Art. 69(1) ICCSt: 'Before testifying, each witness shall, in accordance with the Rules of Procedure and Evidence, give an undertaking as to the truthfulness of the evidence to be given.' Also, Rule 66 ICC RPE. For the liability, see Art. 70(1) ICCSt: 'The court shall have jurisdiction over the following offences against its administration of justice when committed intentionally: (a) Giving false testimony when under an obligation pursuant to article 69, paragraph 1, to tell the truth.'

285 Art. 86 ICCSt: 'States Parties shall … cooperate fully with the Court.'

286 Art. 93(1)(e) ICCSt (emphasis added).

overall length of trial depends on the regulatory framework and, namely, on whether the trial has to be suspended to proceed for contempt or not. In the former case, the uncertainty that the proceeding might produce the evidence that is being sought might be overwhelmed by the delays resulting from the suspension of the trial. On the other hand, if the contempt proceedings are conducted independently of the trial, their deterrent effect has no implication at all on the expeditiousness of the trial and, therefore, should be assessed as an additional opportunity to obtain the evidence.

Non-appearance of witnesses in court may or may not depend on their will. In the latter case, valid justifications include all situations of *force majeur*, most frequently, proven health reasons, but also threat or other interferences with the administration of justice.

When witnesses are unwilling to appear in court in unjustified situations, the use of subpoenas produces the appearance of the witness, but does not necessarily satisfy the need to have his/her deposition. In addition to cases when subpoenas cannot be enforced (e.g., because of proven illness), in other cases, upon appearance the witness would be able to justify a previous non-appearance because of prevailing conflicting obligations (e.g., appearance in hearings of a different trial); sometimes a witness compelled to appear in court would not provide a fully cooperative contribution to the trial. Additionally, the enforcement of subpoenas is not cost neutral as it requires the use of police forces, travel, at least, if not detention expenses.

However, these shortcomings may be addressed and compensated by appropriate judicial management, e.g., by medical examination ordered by the judge upon failure of a witness to appear in court and before issuance of a subpoena or in conjunction with it, or by suspending the execution of the subpoena for the first hearing to which it applies.[287]

C. International Practice

Not differently from the experience of subpoenas at the domestic level, the practice at the ICTY[288] has shown their usefulness as a tool of last resort for obtaining testimony. Although results were mixed – and mostly dependent upon the cooperation of the state of residence of witnesses to enforce an arrest warrant issued for failure to appear at the seat of the Tribunal – in some cases subpoena orders led to the appearance before the Tribunal and testimony.[289]

In the ICC's system, like for the *ad hoc* Tribunals, cooperation of states would be a key factor in ensuring both voluntary and – should subpoenas be introduced – forcible appearance of witnesses.

However, the case may well occur that witnesses have a victim status, whatever right is attached thereto. This is both true before any national or international jurisdiction, but, in the latter case, the specificity of the participative role of victims under the Rome Statute system may to some extent differentiate the terms of the problem with the *ad hoc* Tribunals. The problem is further aggravated under the Statute because no provision addresses the possible conflicting interests borne by a victim who might be called to provide evidence at trial, thereby limiting the admissibility of the testimony

287 Whereby the witness is warned that in case of further non-compliance he/she will be forcibly accompanied and an additional fine imposed, as well as any additional costs incurred would be covered by him/her. The pressure put on reluctant witnesses by such measures would be highly effective and, in some domestic experiences, has attained a rate of success close to 100 per cent.

288 Rule 54 ICTY RPE allows a Chamber to issue 'orders, summonses, subpoenas, warrants and transfer orders as may be necessary for purposes of an investigation of for the preparation or conduct of the trial'.

289 *ICTY Manual*, at note 225 *supra*, VIII, paras 26, 28 and 32, at 84 (hereinafter, ICTY Manual). In *Haradinaj et al.*, two witnesses were arrested and transferred to the ICTY, and gave testimony before initial appearance in their own contempt cases.

of a victim/witness. On the other hand, this issue was taken into account in the Rules of Procedure and Evidence of the Special Tribunal for Lebanon,[290] providing that 'a victim participating in the proceedings shall not be permitted to give evidence unless a Chamber decides that the interests of justice so require'.[291]

The situation of a victim/witness refusing to appear before the ICC may appear as a rather theoretical one as a victim successfully applying for participation in proceedings will normally also be strongly motivated to contribute substantially to the proceedings and to the ascertainment of the judicial truth. However, victims participate into the proceedings at the Court only through their representatives[292] and do not need to appear personally before the Court to exert their statutory rights. Thus, it may well occur that the same person, while exerting his/her rights under the status of victim, may also not serve the interests of justice by omitting to appear for a deposition under his/her status of witness. In this regard, it does not seem that under the Statute there are established mechanisms allowing the relevant Chamber to revoke the admission of participation of a victim, unless his/her failure to appear is interpreted as 'prejudicial to or inconsistent with the rights of the accused and a fair and impartial trial'.[293]

Furthermore, a witness in an international criminal trial would often be under protective measures,[294] which are conditional upon the testimony of a witness, but are also applicable to victims.[295] The issue may, therefore, arise of a victim–witness under protection who subsequently is unwilling to appear before the Court, in which case it would seem that protection might only be lifted insofar it is exclusively attached to the status of witness.

In weighing the extent to which subpoenas may improve the functioning of the Law of the Statute, it should, on the one hand, be considered that in case of appearance at the Seat of the Court as a result of a subpoena order and of its subsequent arrest warrant, the cost of the deposition would possibly be – when appropriately proactive management practices such as those under (B) above are not applied – substantially increased for travel and security expenses, including for accompanying security officers, travel and detention. On the other hand, when the evidence to be provided orally is key to the prosecution or defence cases, the alternative would be not to prove the case at all. In particular, from the perspective of fair trial guarantees, and although the Court has

290 Adopted on 20 March 2009, STL/BD/2009/01.

291 Rule 150(D) STL RPE. In *Explanatory Memorandum*, para. 20 (*supra* note 222), it is clarified that 'a victim must decide at the outset whether he or she wishes to be (i) a participant in the proceedings, or (ii) a witness. Nonetheless, since the situation may change and, for example, parties may realize later in the proceedings that a victim might be important as a witness, an application may be made to the appropriate Chamber to solve the quandary'.

292 Art. 68(3) ICCSt and Rules 90 to 93 ICC RPE.

293 Art. 68(5) ICCSt.

294 Early 2009 ICC statistics show that in the seven existing cases – for which only the *Lubanga* trial had commenced – as many as 80 per cent of witnesses have been subjected to protective measures, making a total of 55 protection cases involving 307 individuals. However, ICTY data for the entire life span of the Tribunal up to the same time express an opposite experience as – out of 101 cases (83 of which concluded) dealing with 161 indictees – 71.46 per cent of witnesses have not been subject to any protective measure. These discrepancies, however, need to be analysed in the light not only of the different scope and stage of applicability of protective measures, but also depending on the categories of witnesses testifying in court (expert witnesses, state officials, insider witnesses, victims, etc.).

295 Art. 68(1) ICCSt.

not yet dealt directly with the issue,[296] the absence of subpoena powers are likely to impact on the rights of defence.[297]

Therefore, the real question here seems to be whether the interests of justice are better served by forcing the appearance of witnesses or by merely relying on their voluntary contribution to trials. In this sense, and when other tools to obtain the voluntary appearance of witnesses (see (B) above) are no longer viable, subpoena powers would be an additional and complementary instrument at disposal of a judge.

11. Victims' Participation (Article 68)

The system envisaged under the Statute for participation of victims in proceedings has already been widely tested, so some shortcomings of statutory provisions may be already considered as well established.

In particular, the number of case-related victims continues to appear disproportionate, vis-à-vis the reality of mass-victimization,[298] while the current legal framework poses challenges to the actual possibility of having them all represented in the Court's proceedings.

At the same time, the costs deriving from the participation of victims at the Seat of the Court, including assistance and legal representation, have considerably grown. In this regard, it should also be considered that in the experience of the *ad hoc* international Tribunals – where there are no costs at all associated with the representation of victims – financial resources allocated for legal aid amount to an average of above 20 per cent of the annual budget.

Therefore, efforts are needed to reconcile these two factors of the current system of victims' representation before the ICC:

(a) afford all victims identical opportunities to be represented and, thus, have them all participating in proceedings;
(b) have a sustainable financial impact of victims' representation.

296 ICC, Motif de la décision orale relative à l'exception d'irrecevabilité de l'affaire (article 19 du Statut), *Germain Katanga et Mathieu Ngudjolo Chui*, Trial Chamber II, 16 June 2009, paras 83–85. The Court rejected the exception raised by the defence on the consequences of the lack of *subpoena* powers for the fair trial as not relevant for the purpose of admissibility, including because Art. 17 grounds of inadmissibility do not include violations of the rights of the accused (ibid., para. 85). The Court also used the argument that international criminal trials are ruled by procedural conditions which necessarily depart from those under national legislation (ibid., para. 84). The last argument, however, seems to be necessarily confined within the purpose and the object of the Decision, as the need for compliance of both national and international criminal procedure with basic human rights guarantees is otherwise undisputed. The decision was upheld by Judgement on the Appeal of Mr. Germain Katanga against the Oral Decision of Trial Chamber II of 12 June 2009 on the Admissibility of the Case, Appeals Chamber, 25 September 2009.

297 Art. 6(3)(d) ECHR: '[everyone charged with a criminal offence has the following minimum rights] to examine or have examined witnesses against him and *obtain the attendance* and examination *of witnesses* on his behalf under the same conditions as witnesses against him' (emphasis added).

298 According to early 2009 ICC data, out of 1,599 applicant victims, 405 were authorized by the relevant Chamber to participate in the proceedings. Of these, participation in the situations amounted to 196 in DRC, 21 in Uganda, 11 in Darfur and 54 in CAR; while participation in the cases was at 97 in *Lubanga*, 57 in *Katanga and Ngudjolo Chui* and 57 in *Kony et al.*

International practice is of limited guidance – as the ICC is peculiar, to the extent it allows victims to participate in proceedings – although some relevant provisions can be found in the systems of:

(i) ECCC, where there are provisions for a civil party action to 'seek collective and moral reparation';[299]
(ii) STL, where participation roughly follows the lines of the Rome Statute.[300]

The experience developed in domestic legal systems where participation of victims is known and established, although with a different scope, may assist in an effort to identify procedural tools to address these concerns by finding an acceptable balance. In particular, victims' associations have proven an effective means for representation of the interests of victims when their number is high or various circumstances (e.g., conflicts, migration, elapse of time from the crime) may have dispersed or made it hard to trace the victims or their survivors.

Grouping victims in associations or other organizations – which might also allow to enlisting affected communities as such – is a process that *per se* would not involve any judicial proceedings at the Court, while the relevant Chamber would need to retain its discretion in the assessment, e.g., of whether the applicant association is actually representative of the victims of a case. Thus, participation of victims in collective instances appears a process more manageable than grouping individual victims as their applications are filed under the current regime, including – through the appointment of one common legal representative at the time when the collective application for participation is made – in the reduction of controversial issues resulting from the choice of several legal representatives by the victims[301] or by the filling-in of complex forms by illiterate applicants.

It should also be noted that the Court is not allowed, under the existing regulatory framework, to establish the indigence of applicant victims on the basis of an absolute presumption.[302] On the other hand, should associations be allowed to represent the interests of individual victims, presumptions could reasonably be inferred by the non-profit status of such organizations. At the same time, the cost level of the legal aid provided to an association representing a large number of victims would be the same as the representation of one victim.[303]

The issue could be addressed at the level of the Rules of Procedure and Evidence, by a new provision under the relevant Rule 89 RPE on the 'Application for participation of victims in the proceedings'. A new paragraph (5) may, thus, read:

---

299 Rule 23 Internal Rules of ECCC. See also victims' rights under Rules 83 and 100. See C. Leang and W. Smith, Investigation and Prosecution in the Early Experience of the Extraordinary Chambers in the Courts of Cambodia, in this *Volume*, at 13(C)(6).

300 Rule 86 STL RPE.

301 This is the controversial case of the implementation of the Rule 90(2) ICC RPE on the common legal representation of victims in *Lubanga,* where seven lawyers representing 93 victims were grouped in two teams, so that all remained involved in the proceedings. See *Interim report of the Court on legal aid: Legal and financial aspects for funding victims' legal representation before the Court*, ICC-ASP/8/CBF.1/2, 26 March 2009, para. 13.

302 The Presidency confirmed such approach of the Registry in *Reasons for the Decision of the Presidency*, ICC-01/04/559, 18 February 2009.

303 Report of the Court on legal aid: Legal and financial aspects for funding victims' legal representation before the Court, ICC-ASP/8/25, 17 September 2009 at para. 64 and Annex II.

'The Chamber may admit non-profit organizations or associations to represent collectively the interests of victims.'

12. Written Testimony (Article 69(2))

A. Implications of Witness Personal Appearance

Under the Rome Statute, the principle of public hearing[304] entails that, at trial,[305] witnesses have to be heard in person[306] before the Court – unless protective measures are applied and testimony is taken by other means[307] – including in cases of proceedings on an admission of guilt by the accused.[308] The authorized 'introduction of documents or written transcripts' is not a substitute for the personal appearance and deposition of the witness.[309]

Trials at the ICC are likely to normally involve a relatively large number of witnesses, both for the prosecution and defence cases, with time-consuming hearings and a number of implications for the personal well-being of witnesses and of their families (security and re-trauma), and for the budget of the Court (preventive measures, assistance, travel and prolonged stay at the Seat of the Court).

Although a witness is under a legal obligation to provide his/her testimony in open trial,[310] the rationale of the system of protective measures[311] is an acknowledgment that it is not in the interest of justice to ascertain the truth through acquisition of all possible oral evidence, whatever might be the cost. In the balance between the personal safety and security, on the one hand, and the right of the accused to a fair trial, on the other hand, protective measures are a compromise which allows for still challengeable witnesses while affording a degree of secrecy for their identity. This compromise has been achieved, first, in national legal systems and then progressively introduced in the international tribunals' rules as a result of the lessons painfully learned at the expense of the lives and well-being of witnesses and of persons related to them. The resulting witness-protection regime is, thus, in itself the proof that practice has rejected any heroic notion of testimony[312] whereby a witness obligation to contribute publicly in the interest of justice (including the rights of the accused to have a witness challenged and cross-examined) requires a drastic change in the lifestyle of witnesses and often of all the persons related to them.

304 Art. 67(1) chapeau ICCSt.

305 Art. 68(5) ICCSt.

306 Art. 67(1)(e) ICCSt and 69(1). Rule 140 ICC RPE.

307 Arts 69(2) and 68(2) ICCSt: 'by electronic or other means.'

308 Art. 65(1)(c)(iii) and (4)(a) ICCSt.

309 Art. 69(2) ICCSt.

310 Art. 64(6)(b) ICCSt. See *supra*, at 10(A).

311 Protective measures are addressed under the Rome Statute by Arts 68 and 54(3)(f), 56(2)(e) and (f), 57(3)(c), 64(6)(e), 69(2) and Rules 67–68, 81, 87–88 ICC RPE.

312 Under the Rome Statute, the absence of an obligation to appear at the Seat of the Court (only obligation is to testify, under Art. 69(1) and Rules 65 and 66 ICCRPE) and of any subpoena power (see, e.g., Rule 54 ICTY RPE) is also an indicator of the focus on the principled willing to contribution of witnesses. See, *supra*, at 10(A) and (C).

B. The Practice at ICTY

The experience at the ICTY – where the complexity of the evidence admitted at trial is similar to that of the ICC – has shown that live testimony can be, in a wide range of circumstances, partially or totally avoided without impinging on the rights of the accused.

Although in its early stages, the procedure at the ICTY was heavily characterized as adversarial and did not allow for derogations to the oral depositions, amendments introduced to the ICTY RPE from 2000 to 2006 have allowed for the admissibility of written statements in place of live testimony and without cross-examination[313] when:

> (a) the evidence 'goes to proof of a matter other than the acts and conduct of the accused'.[314] This allows uncontested issues not to be dealt with orally;
> (b) the evidence also 'goes to proof of the acts and conduct of the accused', provided that the witness is present at court, available for cross-examination and questioning, and s/he attests that the written statement contains what s/he would say if examined;[315]
> (c) the witness is no longer 'available' – because he/she is dead or untraceable or unable for mental or physical conditions to testify – and the evidence is reliable, depending on the circumstances in which the statement was made and recorded.[316]

The ICTY Chambers have increasingly relied on written statements, with beneficial effects on the duration of both the prosecution and defence cases. In particular, the combined use of the tools under the relevant Rules[317] allows for documentation to be used instead of oral depositions in a gradual range of solutions, from reducing through conciseness (Rule 92*ter* ICTY RPE) to avoiding at all *viva voce* testimony (Rule 92*quater* ICTY RPE). This has proven particularly helpful for the purposes of judicial economy, by reducing the time needed for presentation of evidence dealing with factual portions of a case, evidence relating to sites where crimes occurred and historical, sociological and statistical evidence.

Some shortcomings of this regime – however, only limited to the admissibility of evidence going to the acts and conduct of the accused, but which cannot be challenged at trial (Rule 92*quater* ICTY RPE) – might be considered relevant for the adversarial nature of the investigations at the ICTY, in particular with reference to statements obtained without safeguards for the impartiality of the process and in the absence of a duty for the Prosecutor to seek potentially exculpatory evidence).

The trend of increasing appreciation for the usefulness of written statements under strict circumstances and safeguards is also apparent in the consideration currently given by the Rules Committee of the Tribunal to the 'adoption of a Rule to allow the admission of written statements of witnesses who are kept away from trial through fear or intimidation'.[318]

---

313 Rule 89(F) ICTY RPE: 'A Chamber may receive the evidence of a witness orally or, where the interests of justice allow, in written form' (amended 1 and 13 December 2000).

314 Rule 92*bis* (A) ICTY RPE. Similarly in Rule 92*bis* ICTR RPE and Rule 155 STL RPE.

315 Rule 92*ter* ICTY RPE. Similarly, Rule 156 STL RPE.

316 Rule 92*quater* ICTY RPE. Also Rule 158 STL RPE allows written statements of 'unavailable persons' to be admitted, under discretion of the Chamber.

317 Rules 89(F), 92*bis, ter* and *quater* ICTY RPE.

318 Presentation of President Robinson to the Diplomatic Seminar, The Hague, 28 May 2009, at 3.

C. The Limits of the ICC Legal Framework

The aforementioned shortcomings do not even appear relevant in the different procedural context of the ICC where the Prosecutor is under an obligation to 'investigate incriminating and exonerating circumstances equally'.[319]

At the ICC, 'the introduction of previously recorded audio or video testimony of a witness, or the transcript or other documented evidence of such testimony', is admissible provided that:

> (a) the Parties had both – at the time of recording – the opportunity to examine a witness who is not present at trial; or
> (b) the witness – present at trial – does not object to the submission of the recorded testimony and is available for examination.[320]

The latter (b) situation appears to reflect to a large extent the scope of Rule 92*ter* ICTY RPE,[321] while Rule 92*bis* ICTY RPE[322] issues (agreed facts other that on conduct) – although with some differences – are also addressed under Rule 69 ICC RPE.[323]

On the other hand, the opportunities offered under Rule 92*quater* ICTY RPE ('Unavailable Persons')[324] seem not to be captured under the Rome Statute, with the result that, should a witness not appear[325] at trial, his/her contribution to the interests of justice would be lost without remedy.

D. Enhancing the Preservation of Deposition

The appropriateness of a regime concerning 'unavailable persons' should be assessed in light of the established experience of situation countries where security issues relating to ongoing conflicts, to difficult reconciliation processes and to the displacement and consequent difficult traceability of persons may result in the loss of some of the evidence the parties relied upon before trial. These concerns have to be appropriately addressed by means of protective measures whenever circumstances so suggest, *inter alia*, because of the uniqueness of the witnesses and the importance of the evidence they can provide. However, in other instances, affording protective measures may often appear disproportionate when due account is taken of, e.g., the number of available witnesses or their expected contribution. In these cases, allowing for written testimony – although with appropriate safeguards – may reasonably increase the preservation of evidence through a sensitive

319 Art. 54(1)(a) ICCSt. Such obligation is not included under the ICTYSt, but under Rule 68 (i) ICTY RPE the Prosecutor still has to disclose to the defence 'as soon as practicable … any material which in [its] actual knowledge … may suggest the innocence or mitigate the guilt of the accused or affect the credibility of Prosecution evidence'.

320 Rule 68 ICC RPE.

321 See *supra*, at 12(B) and note 315.

322 See *supra*, at 12(B) and note 314.

323 Rule 69 ICC RPE: 'The Prosecutor and the defence may agree that an alleged fact, which is contained in the charges, the contents of a document, the expected testimony of a witness or other evidence is not contested and, accordingly, a Chamber may consider such alleged facts as being proven, unless the Chamber is of the opinion that a more complete presentation of the alleged facts is required in the interests of justice, in particular the interests of the victims.'

324 See *supra*, at 12(B) and note 315.

325 On non-appearance of witnesses and subpoena powers, *supra*, 10(A) and G. Sluiter, 'Appearance of Witnesses and Unavailability of Subpoena Powers for the Court', in this Volume.

reduction of the risk of witnesses suffering retaliations, while avoiding trials to be delayed and limiting protection-related costs.[326]

Thus, it might be appropriate that a rule similar to Rule 92*quater* ICTY RPE be introduced at the ICC so that written testimony is admitted also when witnesses, in limited circumstances, may not actually appear before the Court, but their testimony is appreciated as reliable by the Court. Such text could appear under Rule 68 new (c) ICC RPE[327] and read:

> '(c) *if the witness who gave a reliable previously recorded evidence subsequently died, cannot be traced or has become unable to testify because of bodily or mental condition.*'

13. From the PrepCom to the Subsidiary Bodies of the ASP (Article 112(2)(a))

Under Article 112(2)(a) ICCSt. the Assembly shall 'consider and adopt, as appropriate, recommendations of the Preparatory Commission'.

The Preparatory Commission for the International Criminal Court (PrepCom) was established under the Final Act of the 1998 Rome Conference, which provided for the mandate of the Commission and that it 'shall remain in existence until the conclusion of the first meeting of the Assembly of States Parties'.[328]

As the work of the PrepCom was successfully completed by 12 July 2002[329] and the first ASP session was held in the same year,[330] the PrepCom mandate expired and it no longer exists, so that its unfinished business related to the crime of aggression had to be taken over by a newly ASP-mandated – under Article 112(2)(a) – subsidiary body, the Special Working Group on the Crime of Aggression.[331] Thus, the wording in Article 112(2)(a) ICCSt referring to the PrepCom became outdated in 2002 and is no longer applicable.

However, the Assembly still needs to conduct its work with adequate preparation and assistance through the establishment of 'such subsidiary bodies as may be necessary',[332] which would normally

326 See *supra*, at 10(C) and note 294 for dramatically divergent data of 80 per cent of ICC witnesses currently under protective measures, while only 71.46 per cent have been under such measures during the entire life span of the ICTY.

327 Rule 68 ICC RPE: 'Prior recorded testimony – When the Pre-Trial Chamber has not taken measures under article 56, the Trial Chamber may, in accordance with article 69, paragraph 2, allow the introduction of previously recorded audio or video testimony of a witness, or the transcript or other documented evidence of such testimony, provided that: (a) If the witness who gave the previously recorded testimony is not present before the Trial Chamber, both the Prosecutor and the defence had the opportunity to examine the witness during the recording; or (b) If the witness who gave the previously recorded testimony is present before the Trial Chamber, he or she does not object to the submission of the previously recorded testimony and the Prosecutor, the defence and the Chamber have the opportunity to examine the witness during the proceedings.'

328 United Nations Diplomatic Conference of Plenipotentiaries on the Establishment of an International Criminal Court, held in Rome 15 June–17 July 1998. See Final Act, Resolution F, paras 1 and 5–9.

329 See *Report on the work of the PrepCom at its tenth session*, PCNICC/2002/2 and Add. 1–3.

330 New York, 3–10 September 2002, *Official Records*, ICC-ASP/1/3.

331 Resolution ICC-ASP/1/Res. 1.

332 Art. 112(4) ICCSt. While the ASP is currently committed to setting up an appropriate Oversight Mechanism for investigations to be conducted on disciplinary matters (ICC-ASP/4/Res. 4; latest Report ICC-ASP/8/2; and *supra* note 55), several such bodies were established over time: the Special Working Group on the Crime of Aggression (ICC-ASP/1/Res. 1), the Committee on Budget and Finance (ICC-ASP/1/Res. 4), and the Oversight Committee on the Permanent Premises (ICC-ASP/6/Res. 1, para. 5 and Annex II).

provide their output in the form of recommendations for further action by the Assembly. In this regard, recommendations of such subsidiary bodies would trigger the same competence previously attributed under Article 112(2)(a) to recommendations of the PrepCom.

Therefore, the first Review Conference should have updated the current text of the relevant provision by deleting the existing wording – 'Preparatory Commission' – and inserting in its place a reference to such subsidiary bodies. The new Article 112(2)(a) ICCSt may, thus, read (addition in italics):

> 'The Assembly shall:
>
> (a) Consider and adopt, as appropriate, recommendations of *any subsidiary bodies established pursuant to paragraph 4 of this article*.'

14. Review of the Statute after the First Review Conference (Article 123)

Article 123 'Review of the Statute', reads:

> 1. Seven years after the entry into force of this Statute the Secretary General of the United Nations shall convene a Review Conference to consider any amendments to this Statute. Such review may include, but is not limited to, the list of crimes contained in article 5. The Conference shall be open to those participating in the Assembly of States Parties and on the same conditions.
>
> 2. At any time thereafter, at the request of a State Party and for the purposes set out in paragraph 1, the Secretary-General of the United Nations shall, upon approval by a majority of States Parties, convene a Review Conference.
>
> 3. The provisions of article 121, paragraphs 3 to 7, shall apply to the adoption and entry into force of any amendments to the Statute considered at a Review Conference.

Paragraph 1 provides for the first Review Conference to be convened 'seven years after the entry into force of [the] Statute' and further details its object and participation thereto. As the first Review Conference takes place, the temporal clause of such provision would be outdated and, thus, it should be deleted. However, the rest of the same provision would still maintain its objective, although it should be reshuffled within the following paragraph 2, dealing with all future Review Conferences.

As a result, Article 123 might be amended and its paragraphs renumbered as to delete in paragraph 1 the wording 'seven years after the entry into force of this Statute' and, in paragraph 2, its opening wording 'at any time thereafter' [the first Review Conference], so as to read:

> '1. *At any time and at the request of a State Party the Secretary-General of the United Nations shall, upon approval by a majority of States Parties, convene a Review Conference to consider any amendments to this Statute. Such review may include, but is not limited to, the list of crimes contained in article 5. The Conference shall be open to those participating in the Assembly of States Parties and on the same conditions.*

2. *The provisions of article 121, paragraphs 3 to 7, shall apply to the adoption and entry into force of any amendments to the Statute considered at a Review Conference.*'

15. Conclusion

It is widely agreed that the ICC is a fully operational judicial institution, as by 2010 it has not only completed the setting-up of organizational instruments and structures, but has also developed its own practices in a variegated array of issues and on the basis of the Law of the Statute. Such practices have brought to the attention of the international community a number of challenges which cannot be fully addressed under the existing applicable normative instruments.

As unsolved issues may result in reduced effectiveness and, at the end, in threats to the credibility of Court, the legal bases which left open such issues should be addressed in a timely manner. In this regard, it is a responsibility of States Parties to the Rome Statute to provide the Court with the means needed for it to function properly. This not only concerns judicial cooperation, but also political support, which includes the exercise of the legislative authority of States Parties in updating the Law of the Statute.

According also to the experience developed at the international criminal Tribunals, amendments and modifications of the normative and regulatory framework is an ongoing process which has to be lived with as a regular and non-traumatic event. On the other hand, amendments of the Statute and of the Rules of Procedure and Evidence are to be firmly and consistently based on experience and, as such, inherently motivated by the need to strengthen the ability of the judicial institution to reach its objectives.

In this spirit, and to preserve the substantive integrity of the Rome Statute, the Assembly of States Parties as such, or under its Review Conference format, should consider to introducing some amendments to only those provisions – mostly concerning the organization of the institution – that have already been sufficiently tested at the Court.

Chapter 20
Appearance of Witnesses and Unavailability of Subpoena Powers for the Court*

Göran Sluiter

1. Introduction

One of the most puzzling aspects of the ICC's legal edifice is the lack of subpoena powers in relation to witnesses. This lack of any such powers is also referred to as the principle of voluntary appearance. One can indeed wonder how any criminal court could function with a permanent and structural absence of subpoena powers. The importance of compulsory process in international criminal proceedings has been amply demonstrated by international criminal tribunals with longer experience than the ICC, such as the ICTY. It is as good as certain that the ICC will be highly dependent upon (eye)witnesses giving testimony and it is likely that many witnesses – because of security concerns, for example – will be reluctant to testify. There can be no doubt that legitimate fears must be accommodated, for example by means of protective measures, but any such accommodation must always be understood and approached against the background of a clear duty to give evidence in the interests of justice. Although initially not used often in practice, the mere availability of subpoena powers at the ICTY and ICTR may have had important effects on witnesses' decisions to testify. It may be the mere threat of criminal prosecution that convinces witnesses to appear in court. One notices a recent increase in the application of compulsory process; in the *Haradinaj* case no less than 18 subpoenas were served, of which 13 were complied with.[1] This illustrates the growing importance of this instrument.

This chapter's objective is to challenge the lack of subpoena power in the ICC legal framework and to explore the potential harm this may occasion. The central question is whether under the current circumstances a fair and good quality trial can be provided to the accused and the international community.

In order to address this issue it is necessary to first explore briefly the three different dimensions of the subpoena power in international criminal proceedings. Then, I will move to the legislative history of the ICC Statute on this point; why did the drafters not endow ICC judges with a subpoena power? Next the current legal regime will be analysed, especially the question whether the lack of subpoena powers is absolute and whether witness enjoy – under the Statute – a right not to appear before the Court to give testimony. In light of this analysis, I will address the pivotal question of the consequences for trials at the ICC. The chapter ends with a conclusion and recommendations for future reform.

---

* This chapter is an adapted version of a paper submitted for publication in the *New Criminal Law Review* and part of the research project 'Law of International Criminal Procedure: In Search of General Rules and Principles', financed by the Netherlands Organization for Scientific Research (NWO).

1 ICTY, Judgement, *Haradinaj et al.*, Trial Chamber I, Case No. IT-04-84-T, 3 April 2008, para. 22.

2. Dimensions of Subpoena Powers in International Criminal Justice

As a legal notion, a 'subpoena' can be described as a court order requiring somebody under the threat of penalty to appear in court. The purpose of appearance may differ. When the purpose is the giving of testimony this is referred to by the Latin words *subpoena ad testificandum*.

As a specific term, subpoena is part of the common law tradition and is unknown in the continental or civil law criminal justice systems. However, it can be safely said that whatever the terminology employed, all national criminal justice systems have in common the availability of compulsory process to ensure the attendance of witnesses, except for exceptions recognized by law. These exceptions tend to include public official immunity, privilege against self-incrimination and other privileges. A distinction, however, must be drawn between the duty to appear as a witness and the duty to answer questions. Privileges, in principle, only concern the latter. But it would be a waste of the court's time to subpoena a witness who enjoys a testimonial privilege and will use it.

Among national criminal jurisdictions, the two key dimensions to subpoenas are the following.

First, there is a power to impose a direct obligation on a witness to appear, with a view to assisting in the administration of justice. Hence, a direct obligation towards the court is created. The creation of such obligation, and the ensuing consequences of failure to comply with this obligation, infringes upon rights and liberties of the witness. Therefore it is only natural that imposition of an obligation to appear is subject to conditions. Most importantly, the judge will review whether the prospective testimony is relevant and material. The precise standard may differ among national criminal jurisdictions, just like the method of taking testimony. In civil law systems the taking of testimony may – and often does – also take place outside the courtroom, by a pre-trial judge (*juge d'instruction*), whereas in common law systems such testimony must be produced at trial. Undeniably, the current law related to subpoena powers is to a large degree influenced by human rights law, notably the right for a defendant to call witnesses.[2] For the proper administration of justice, accurate fact-finding, and duties imposed on witnesses are already indispensable, but added to this is a fair trial element, which will be explored in more detail below.

The second dimension of duties imposed on witnesses concerns the enforcement of the duties. As always, the strength of a duty to appear depends upon likelihood and degree of enforcement. Also in this second dimension, national criminal jurisdictions differ in approaches, but they all share the common purpose of taking failure to comply with an obligation to appear very seriously. When examining national approaches, it is not always possible to distinguish between the duty to appear and the duty to answer questions. In common law systems it seems that both failures are encapsulated in the law on contempt.[3] Those held in contempt can be liable to severe sanctions. In other systems, failure to comply with an obligation to appear as a witness may be met by direct enforcement action, namely bringing the witness by force before the court. This is, for example, the case in the Netherlands.[4] In that country subsequent failure to answer questions submitted to the witness by participants in the proceedings may result in deprivation of liberty of the witness, in principle until he or she is prepared to respond.[5] In other countries, like Russia, the refusal to attend hearings as a witness is penalized as an autonomous criminal offence.[6]

2 See S. Trechsel, *Human Rights in Criminal Proceedings* (Oxford: Oxford University Press, 2005), at 291–326.

3 On the law of contempt, see N. Keijzer, *Contempt of Court* (Deventer: Gouda Quint, 2000).

4 Art. 287(3)(b) of the Dutch Code of Criminal Procedure.

5 Art. 294 Dutch Code of Criminal Procedure.

6 Art. 307 Russian Criminal Code.

It can thus be concluded that the methods of enforcing subpoenas may vary among criminal jurisdictions. As will be further explored below, international criminal tribunals should have the flexibility to either directly seek to enforce subpoenas themselves or to make use of assistance by states in enforcing subpoenas, either by physically bringing the witness before the court or by enforcing sanctions imposed on the individual by the court.

This brings us to the third dimension of subpoena law in criminal proceedings and this concerns the cooperation of states. It is self-evident that witnesses residing outside the court's own jurisdiction cannot be subjected to the same powers as witnesses within its jurisdiction. Domestic criminal jurisdictions have certainly had difficulties in ensuring the appearance of witnesses residing abroad; as will be explored below, the sovereign equality of states is a serious obstacle in imposing and enforcing any obligation to appear on witnesses outside domestic territory. Whereas this concerns only a very small percentage of witnesses in domestic criminal proceedings, we must bear in mind that in international criminal proceedings *every single* witness is outside the international tribunal's jurisdiction. Hence, in relation to every witness, state cooperation – or the cooperation of other entities – is inevitable. Such cooperation consists of (a) serving summonses or subpoenas upon the witness; (b) bringing the witness by force before the competent international tribunal; or (c) enforcing the sentences imposed by the competent tribunal for failure by the witness to attend the hearing.

The vital question is what degree of cooperation from both witnesses and states may be expected in respect of international criminal proceedings. An interesting element in the discussion is to what degree the witness should be subject to the jurisdiction of the prosecuting international criminal tribunal. As far as national prosecutions are concerned, it is clear that fundamental rules of international law, notably those based on sovereign equality of states, put clear limitations on what can be done in respect of witnesses residing abroad. But should such limitations carry any force in the relationship between states and international criminal tribunals? And should, just like individuals who are suspected of having committed international crimes, the relevant witnesses not be subjected to the jurisdiction of international criminal tribunals?

3. The ICC Legislative History

The aforementioned third dimension of subpoena law in international criminal proceedings produced significant troubles for the drafters of the ICC Statute. They had at their disposal two possible approaches.

First, it is general knowledge that in traditional interstate cooperation law, it has been a long-standing rule that witnesses residing abroad cannot be the object of subpoena powers, in the sense that the subpoena cannot have legal effect outside the state's territory.[7] This tradition finds its basis in protection of a state's nationals and its sovereignty and in the practical consideration that for a subpoena to produce legal effect it needs to be served on the individual concerned – for this the cooperation of foreign authorities is required. The freedom of choice for the witness residing abroad can thus be regarded as an important unwritten rule of interstate cooperation; sometimes it has been codified in legal assistance treaties.[8] Clearly, once a witness enters the trial forum's

7 A. Klip, *Buitenlandse getuigen in strafzaken* [Foreign witnesses in criminal proceedings] (Arnhem: Gouda Quint, 1994), at 268.

8 See, e.g., Art. 8 of the European Convention on Mutual Assistance in Criminal Matters, 20 April 1959, ETS No. 30.

jurisdiction and is served there he is fully subject to subpoena powers. Exceptions to the territorial limits to subpoena powers exist in a few legal assistance regimes between countries which closely cooperate in other areas as well.[9]

It is general knowledge that a considerable number of negotiating states at the diplomatic conference favoured a cooperation regime based on interstate experiences in this field. As commentators and participants in the negotiations observed:

> Throughout the negotiations there was a basic opposition between the adherents of a (more) horizontal and the proponents of a (more) vertical approach. The first group of delegations emphasized state sovereignty … and often referred to the UN Model Treaties on extradition and mutual assistance in criminal matters. The opposed camp started from the assumption that only a cooperation regime that is essentially distinct from traditional inter-state concepts in that it attaches greater weight to the community interest in an international criminal prosecution, fully corresponded to the specific relationship between States Parties and the Court.[10]

Second, the alternative approach towards subpoena law is based on the model of cooperation developed by the *ad hoc* Tribunals, especially the ICTY. The relevant rules of this model were essentially judge-made and highly favoured – from the perspective of the ICTY – effective cooperation, without much consideration for national interests and sovereignty.[11] Interestingly, at the origin of the ICTY's law on cooperation lies a dispute between Croatia and the ICTY over a subpoena issued by the Trial Chamber to one of Croatia's Ministers. The crucial ICTY Appeals Chamber decision in *Blaškić* was handed down at the end of 1997.[12] Bearing in mind the ICTY's aspiration for effective cooperation, the subpoena power was inferred from the ICTY's mandate:

> the International Tribunal's power to issue binding orders to individuals derives instead from the general object and purpose of the Statute, as well as the role the International Tribunal is called upon to play thereunder. The International Tribunal is an international criminal court constituting a novelty in the world community. Normally, individuals subject to the sovereign authority of States may only be tried by national courts. If a national court intends to bring to trial an individual subject to the jurisdiction of another State, as a rule it relies on treaties of judicial cooperation or, if such treaties are not available, on voluntary interstate cooperation. Thus, the relation between national courts of different States is "horizontal" in nature. In 1993 the Security Council for the first time established an international criminal court endowed with jurisdiction over individuals living within sovereign States, be they States of the former Yugoslavia or third States, and, in addition,

---

9 See Art. 34 of the legal assistance treaty between the Netherlands, Belgium and Luxemburg (1962) pursuant to which a witness who fails to respond to a summons from the trial forum is, in the requested state, liable to the usual sanctions for non-cooperative witnesses in that state; one should also mention the arrangement between the Nordic countries, where a witness who fails to comply with a summons may be fined (example from A. Klip, *Buitenlandse getuigen in strafzaken* [Foreign witnesses in criminal proceedings] (Arnhem, Gouda Quint, 1994), at 276.

10 C. Kress and K. Prost, 'Part 9 – Preliminary Remarks', in O. Triffterer (ed.), *Commentary on the Rome Statute of the International Criminal Court* (Munich: C.H. Beck Verlag, 2008), at 1507.

11 See on the differences between the horizontal and vertical cooperation models in more detail, G. Sluiter, *International Criminal Adjudication and the Collection of Evidence – Obligations of States* (Antwerp: Intersentia, 2002), at 3.

12 ICTY, Judgement on the Request of the Republic of Croatia for Review of the Decision of Trial Chamber II of 18 July 1997, *Blaškić*, Case No. IT-95-14-AR108*bis*, Appeals Chamber, 29 October 1997.

> conferred on the International Tribunal primacy over national courts. By the same token, the Statute granted the International Tribunal the power to address to States binding orders concerning a broad variety of judicial matters (including the identification and location of persons, the taking of testimony and the production of evidence, the service of documents, the arrest or detention of persons, and the surrender or transfer of indictees to the International Tribunal). Clearly, a "vertical" relationship was thus established, at least as far as the judicial and injunctory powers of the International Tribunal are concerned (whereas in the area of enforcement the International Tribunal is still dependent upon States and the Security Council). In addition, the aforementioned power is spelt out in provisions such as Article 18, paragraph 2, first part, which states: "The Prosecutor shall have *the power to question suspects, victims and witnesses*, to collect evidence and to conduct on-site investigations"; and in Article 19, paragraph 2: "Upon confirmation of an indictment, the judge may, at the request of the Prosecutor, issue such orders and warrants for the arrest, detention, surrender or transfer of persons, *and any other orders as may be required for the conduct of the trial*."[13]

It was also established that the ICTY possesses a power to enter directly into contact with witnesses, when necessary under the circumstances.[14] Furthermore, the Appeals Chamber ruled that the ICTY judges were vested with an inherent power to prosecute witnesses who refuse to comply with a subpoena for contempt of court, including holding trials in their absence.[15]

The *Blaškić* subpoena decision was – in the absence of a strong statutory basis – quite revolutionary. Subsequent case law was aimed at consolidating this vertical legal assistance model, which in relation to the UN *ad hoc* Tribunals, was never really challenged by states.[16] It is therefore interesting that the vertical model was not fully embraced at the Rome Diplomatic Conference, as the ICC Statute adopts a less effective cooperation model in a number of areas. One factor capable

13 Ibid., para. 47 (emphasis added).

14 Ibid., para. 55: 'It is therefore to be assumed that an inherent power to address itself directly to those individuals inures to the advantage of the International Tribunal. Were it not vested with such a power, the International Tribunal would be unable to guarantee a fair trial to persons accused of atrocities in the former Yugoslavia'; para. 56: 'the International Tribunal may enter into direct contact with an individual subject to the sovereign authority of a State. The individual, being within the ancillary (or incidental) criminal jurisdiction of the International Tribunal, is duty-bound to comply with its orders, requests and summonses.'

15 Ibid., paras 58 and 59: 'The Appeals Chamber holds the view that, normally, the International Tribunal should turn to the relevant national authorities to seek remedies or sanctions for non-compliance by an individual with a subpoena or order issued by a Judge or a Trial Chamber. Legal remedies or sanctions put in place by the national authorities themselves are more likely to work effectively and expeditiously. However, allowance should be made for cases where resort to national remedies or sanctions would not prove workable. This holds true for those cases where, from the outset, the International Tribunal decides to enter into direct contact with individuals, at the request of either the Prosecutor or the defence, on the assumption that the authorities of the State or Entity would either prevent the International Tribunal from fulfilling its mission (see *supra*, paragraph 55) or be unable to compel a State official to comply with an order issued under Article 29 (see *supra*, the case mentioned in paragraph 51). In these cases, it may prove pointless to request those national authorities to enforce the International Tribunal's order through national means. … The remedies available to the International Tribunal range from a general power to hold individuals in contempt of the International Tribunal (utilizing the inherent contempt power rightly mentioned by the Trial Chamber) to the specific contempt power provided for in Rule 77.'

16 See G. Sluiter, 'Cooperation of States with International Criminal Tribunals', in A. Cassese et al. (eds), *The Oxford Companion to International Criminal Justice* (Oxford: Oxford University Press, 2009), at 189.

of explaining this discrepancy is timing. The *Blaškić* subpoena decision was handed down at the end of 1997 and its impact and importance for cooperation law regarding international criminal tribunals may not have been fully grasped by the vast majority of delegations drafting the Rome Statute in the summer of 1998.

The commentaries on the Rome Statute do not inform us much about the nature of the discussions regarding subpoena powers. As with many other matters, the issue was divided over more than one working group. There were the external cooperation dimension of the subpoena power, the mandate of the Working Group on Part 9, and the internal aspect, the necessary powers for Chambers to ensure effective and fair trials, covered by the Working Group on Part 6, the trial. The separate negotiation processes in these working groups explain some of the inconsistency in the handling of the subpoena powers, which will be further explored *infra* 4.

As mentioned above, the issue of subpoena powers in international criminal justice implies regulations regarding the power to impose an obligation to appear, regarding the enforcement of this duty via state cooperation, and regarding the direct enforcement of the duty via contempt proceedings. In the very rudimentary 1994 International Law Commission (ILC) Draft Statute for the ICC the starting point may seem to have been some duty for witnesses to appear, given the power attributed to the Trial Chamber to require the attendance and testimony of witnesses.[17] This power has not been significantly changed or challenged throughout the negotiating process and appears to have found codification without significant controversy in Article 64(6)(b) of the Statute.[18]

The cooperation Part in the 1994 Draft paid no specific attention to legal assistance by states in enforcing the subpoena power. However, the general draft provision on cooperation and judicial assistance, Article 51, seemed broad enough in scope to ground a duty to bring witnesses by force to the Court to testify.[19] As to direct enforcement, the 1994 Draft contained no provisions on contempt, but one could have regarded this as an inherent power, as was the ruling of the ICTY Appeals Chamber in the *Blaškić* case, cited above. While the 1994 Draft Statute appears to allow for an approach as adopted by the ICTY in *Blaškić*, thus inspired by a vertical cooperation relationship, and by implication rejecting the interstate approach, the subsequent negotiations revealed significant reservations. Looking at the legislative history regarding cooperation and contempt power (offences against the administration of justice), one notices an increasing reluctance to impose an obligation on witnesses to appear.

As was already mentioned above, the power of the Trial Chamber to require the attendance of witnesses remained unchallenged and unchanged from the time of the 1994 ILC Draft until its final adoption as Article 64(6)(b) of the Statute. But the vital developments took place in the Part 9 Working Group. The imposition of an obligation upon citizens to testify at the seat of the Court met with strong opposition by a number of delegations. It seems to me – and follows from the official record – that the absence of subpoena powers was easily sacrificed, possibly as bargaining chip in respect to matters deemed at that time more important by certain delegations, such as grounds for

17 Art. 38(5)(b) of the 1994 Draft Statute (Report of the International Law Commission on the work of its forty-sixth session, 2 May–22 July 1994, UN Doc. A/49/10, at 110).

18 See for an overview of the evolution of Art. 64, C. Bassiouni, *The Legislative History of the International Criminal Court: An Article-by-Article Evolution of the Statute* (Ardsley, NY: Transnational Publishers, 2005), at 458–474.

19 *Report of the International Law Commission on the work of its forty-sixth session*, 2 May–22 July 1994, UN Doc. A/49/10, at 129. The provision was modelled on Art. 29 of the ICTY Statute and thus offered a strong basis for a variety of legal assistance requests. The references to 'taking of testimony' and 'arrest of persons' could be sufficient to oblige states to arrest and transfer witnesses to the seat of the Court.

refusal, surrender and on-site investigations. The essential question is how the word 'voluntary' came to be inserted in the final text of Article 93(1)(e) and how the detained witness came to have a right to free and informed consent regarding his transfer with a view to taking testimony at the ICC (Article 93(7)). Going through the evolution of Article 93 since the 1994 ILC Draft, one notices that the word voluntary did not appear in any draft prior to the Rome Conference, nor was there any provision regarding transfer of detained witnesses to the Court.[20] However, this is not to indicate that an obligation to enforce subpoenas by the Court was strongly envisaged prior to the Rome Conference because text proposals of Part 9 in its entirety were full of options allowing states to refuse cooperation.[21] No other conclusion can be drawn that subpoena powers had to be sacrificed with a view to significantly eliminating, from Part 9, grounds for refusal. That this was at the time not a highly controversial sacrifice seems to follow, in my view, from the Report of the Working Group on Part 9 to the Plenary of the Conference.[22] What is clear from this report is that the present Article 93(1)(e) – which refers to 'facilitating voluntary appearance' – means exactly this. A footnote to this section reads as follows:

> This includes the notion that witnesses or experts may not be compelled to travel to appear before the Court.[23]

Neither the footnote nor the text of the provision conditions or qualifies in any way this principle of voluntary appearance. The principle of voluntary appearance was further strengthened in Part 9 by the inclusion of Article 93(7), which attributes to the detained person a right to 'informed consent' as a condition to transfer with a view to testifying at the ICC. It is not entirely clear to me at what time and under which circumstances this archaic and unnecessary provision was introduced. Participants in the negotiations refer to wording 'that was too hastily copied from tradition inter-State vocabulary'.[24]

It thus seems that the principle of voluntary appearance was firmly established relatively early in the diplomatic conference – the report of the Part 9 Group was dated 1 July and the final text was adopted 17 July – which raises the question as to why the relationship between Part 9 and Part 6 was not clarified. Indeed, the power to require the attendance of witnesses remained in Part 6. The puzzling thing is that within this same Part 6 – thus the same Working Group – provisions regarding offences against the administration of justice and misconduct were negotiated which are totally silent about sanctions or enforcement measures in case of failure to respond to a summons to appear as a witness. Regarding the evolution of Article 70 of the Rome Statute, the failure to comply with an order by a Trial Chamber to attend hearings as a witness has not really managed to impose itself as a serious option for inclusion in that provision.[25] However, mention must be made of the draft Article 44*bis* that emerged from the Preparatory Committee at its December

20 Bassiouni, *supra* note 18, at 680–700.

21 See ibid.

22 See United Nations Diplomatic Conference of Plenipotentiaries on the Establishment of an International Criminal Court, Rome, 15 June–17 July 1998, OR Vol. III (UN Doc. A/CONF.183/13), at 325–326, where the Working Group explains what provisions were amended.

23 Ibid., at 329.

24 C. Kress and K. Prost, 'Article 93', in O. Triffterer (ed.), *Commentary on the Rome Statute of the International Criminal Court* (Munich: C.H. Beck Verlag, 2008), at 1576.

25 For an overview, see Bassiouni, *supra* note 18, at 523–529.

1997 session and which penalizes 'obstructing the functions of the Court'.[26] Arguably, this could have been a basis for prosecution of non-compliance with a subpoena, although it is lacking in precision.

The absence of any mechanism to directly enforce an 'order to appear as a witness' raises the question as to what should then be understood by the power to require the appearance of witnesses, as contained in Article 64(6)(b) of the Statute. It seems to me to have essentially – or only – internal effect, namely among parties, because no sanction can be imposed *on the witness* for failure to appear. It should thus be understood as requiring parties to undertake their best efforts to ensure the appearance of witnesses; and the Trial Chamber could issue orders to that effect. One can thus envisage on the basis of Article 64(6)(b) that a party is ordered to seek the appearance of a certain witness, but – in light of other provisions in the Statute, or absence thereof – a direct obligation to appear cannot be imposed on the witness.

4. Is there a Right for Witnesses Not to Appear before the Court?

Witnesses have a right not to be compelled to testify before the ICC; as regrettable as this may be, this implies that states cannot compel them to appear, even if Part 9 can be regarded as imposing only *minimum* obligations upon states.[27] Others have opposed this interpretation and would favour an interpretation allowing states to bring by force witnesses before the Court, if these states would be prepared to do so.[28] The argument has also been made that Article 93(1)(l) of the Statute would allow the Court to request states to use compulsory process as another form of assistance and, when not prohibited by national law, states would have to give effect to it.[29]

I would be the first to recognize the importance of and need for compelling witness to attend ICC hearings in the interests of justice, but there is no basis for it in the law of the ICC, even not in respect of states who would be prepared to be of more assistance than required under the Statute. I therefore maintain that witnesses have a right under the Statute not to be compelled to appear before the ICC, whether the compulsion is imposed by the Court or by national authorities.

As far as the use of Article 93(1)(l) is concerned, it is my view that this provision, as a residual, or 'catch-all', clause, cannot be used to circumvent the specific provision of Article 93(1)(e). It would be inconsistent with the object and purpose of Article 93(1)(l) to strengthen Article 93(1)(e) and thereby create two forms of facilitating appearance of witnesses, one of a voluntary nature, covered by Article 93(1)(e), and one of a non-voluntary nature, to which Article 93(1)(l) should then apply. An additional problem is that in respect of the detained witness, Article 93(7) sets out a closed regime which cannot be 'repaired' by Article 93(1)(l); this would then create the bizarre situation that non-detained witnesses could be compelled, using Article 93(1)(l), to testify, but for the detained witness free and informed consent remains required. Finally, the wording of Article 93(1)(l) militates against its use to compel the attendance of witnesses. The provision refers to 'any other *type* of assistance' (emphasis added). However, 'facilitating the non-voluntary appearance

26 Ibid., at 526.

27 Sluiter, *supra* note 16, at 254.

28 B. Broomhall and C. Kress, 'Implementing Cooperation Duties under the Rome Statute: A Comparative Synthesis', in C. Kress et al. (eds), *The Rome Statute and Domestic Legal Orders, Volume II: Constitutional Issues, Cooperation and Enforcement* (Baden-Baden: Nomos, 2005), at 529; Kress and Prost, *supra* note 24, at 1576

29 R. Rastan, 'Testing Cooperation: The International Criminal Court and National Authorities', 21 *Leiden Journal of International Law* (2008), at 436.

of witnesses' is exactly the same type of assistance as 'facilitating the voluntary appearance'. These may be different modalities, but within the same type of assistance, namely regarding the assistance related to appearance of witnesses. Clearly, the drafters have dealt with this type of assistance, namely in Article 93(1)(e), and decided it had to be voluntary, thereby leaving no room for Article 93(1)(l). This view finds support in the literature, where 'facilitating the non-voluntary appearance of witnesses' has never been mentioned as an example of a type of assistance covered by Article 93(1)(l).[30]

The other argument in favour of some possibility of compelling witnesses to give evidence is the wording of Article 64(6)(b), attributing the power to Chambers to require the attendance of witnesses; it is argued that this inconsistency with Part 9 should not be widened and that Article 64(6)(b) could very well be the basis for an international obligation of witnesses towards the Court to appear.[31] Also, it is submitted by a commentator to this provision that Chambers can still summons witnesses, but that it follows from Part 9 simply that a State Party is not under an obligation to compel the witness's appearance before the Court.[32]

This is not convincing. First, the language of Article 64(6)(b) is not clear. It does not follow from it that a direct obligation towards witnesses is envisaged. 'Requiring the attendance' is not identical to 'ordering' or similar language. One must therefore construe this wording in light of other relevant provisions. Second, this brings us to Part 6 as a whole, still leaving aside the obligation to cooperate under Part 9. It is symptomatic that within Part 6 the provision on offences against the administration of justice (Article 70) does not include the failure of a witness to respond to a request or summons from a Trial Chamber to appear; nor has there ever been adopted any enforcement provision in the Rules of Procedure and Evidence. It means nothing other than that the ICC itself has no direct enforcement powers and, while this is not determinative regarding the existence of a direct obligation towards the Court, it is nevertheless very strong evidence that simply no obligation was intended at the Rome Conference. This makes perfect sense in light of the language of Part 9. Third, it would be wrong to view Part 9 in its entirety as merely imposing only minimum obligations upon states. There are many aspects of Part 9 which set out procedural arrangements going beyond the mere question of state cooperation and which contain direct obligations for the Court.[33] From the legislative history, as outlined earlier, it follows in my view that the reference to voluntary appearance in Article 93(1)(e) entails a general prohibition of compulsion, whether by the ICC or by states. Article 93(7) is a procedural arrangement – that one may dislike very much or think was hastily adopted, but this does not reduces its legal effect – that gives an already detained witness a right not to be brought before the Court. As this is an exclusive arrangement it applies to every detained witness at the national level and precludes more progressive arrangements. It accords with the apparent wish of the drafters not to compel witnesses in any way to appear before the Court as witnesses. *A fortiori*, I maintain my view that witnesses who are not detained should have at least the same rights towards the Court as detained witnesses and cannot be compelled in any way to testify. Fourth, it would be particularly damaging to leave the matter of compulsory process to states. It may very well be the case that one state is more cooperative than another. In principle, there is nothing wrong with this, but not when the liberty of individuals is at stake. Compelling witnesses to testify at the ICC may in practice trigger temporary deprivation of liberty, as well as criminal sanctions. These invasive and serious consequences of failing to comply with a

30 See, for example, Kress and Prost, *supra* note 24, at 1579.

31 Kress and Prost, *supra* note 24, at 1576–1577.

32 G. Bitti, 'Article 64', in O. Triffterer (ed.), *Commentary on the Rome Statute of the International Criminal Court* (Munich: C.H. Beck Verlag, 2008), at 1213.

33 Arts 87, 91, 93(8), 96, 98, 99(4) and 100 ICCSt.

subpoena should not differ depending upon a state's willingness to cooperate, but should be subject to a uniform regime. This was, in my conviction, also the intention of the drafters – namely to codify a general regime of voluntary appearance, going beyond the mere question of state cooperation. Voluntary appearance can thus not be contravened by 'enhanced cooperation', on the basis of which some states would compel witnesses to appear at the seat of the Court and others won't.[34] There is no basis in the drafting history for this view, whereas there is for the contrary position, as explained above. While it is understandable that supporters of a strong ICC use all creativity to repair in some way the damage, this cannot be done without properly observing the rules and principles of treaty interpretation.

5. Fairness and Proper Administration of Justice

It may seem self-evident that the principle of voluntary appearance negatively affects the functioning of any criminal court. The question that needs to be addressed is how serious this really is in the particular context of the ICC. In particular, it needs to be explored whether the lack of subpoena powers could violate the accused's right to a fair trial or damage the proper administration of justice. I will confine myself to a few observations.

It must be acknowledged that the lack of subpoena powers can hurt both the Prosecutor and the defence side and, as such, conforms to the principle of equality of arms. Yet, the accused has been granted a number of inalienable rights which apply unconditionally and occupy the highest position in the hierarchy of applicable law, as provided for in Article 21(3) of the ICC Statute. Article 67(1)(e) of the Statute is the most important one to examine in the framework of this paper, granting the accused the right

> to examine, or have examined, the witnesses against him or her and to obtain the attendance and examination of witnesses on his or her behalf under the same conditions as witnesses against him or her.

The first part of this provision is an independent right, whereas the second part builds upon the principle of equality of arms, in the sense that in obtaining attendance and examining witnesses the accused should not be in a worse position than the Prosecutor is in relation to his witnesses. The lack of subpoena powers, making no distinction between the parties, does thus not seem to be problematic from this particular perspective. In respect of the first part, the right to examine or have examined witness *à charge*, the absence of subpoena powers may be more problematic. Schabas, in relation to this, has submitted the following: 'Nothing in the Statute provides for compellability of witnesses, for example by issuance of subpoena or similar orders to appear before the Court. Although this may create hardship for the defence, it does not seem that it can argue that the right to a fair trial is being denied because of the impossibility of obtaining witnesses and compelling their attendance in court.'[35]

I am not fully convinced. I acknowledge that the right allows for interpretation according to which incriminating witness testimony may also be taken elsewhere than in the courtroom and that in that procedure the accused may be allowed to either examine the witness or have examined

34 This difference in treatment has in fact been proposed by Kress and Prost, *supra* note 24, at 1577.

35 W. Schabas, 'Article 67', in O. Triffterer (ed.), *Commentary on the Rome Statute of the International Criminal Court* (Munich: C.H. Beck Verlag, 2008), at 1265.

– for example, by a national judge – the witness. Case law of human rights courts seems to accept this as an alternative to the examination of witnesses at trial.[36] The ICC Rules furthermore contain an additional safeguard. According to Rule 68, prior recorded testimony is only admissible when both parties have had the opportunity to examine the witness.[37] Consequently, the right seems to be respected as unchallenged evidence cannot be used against the accused. Yet, I remain in doubt. The absence of any subpoena power is so strikingly peculiar for the ICC, as I know of no system where criminal courts lack this power as a general rule. Of course, domestic courts may be in need of some foreign witnesses in a small number of cases, but they rarely are the only witnesses. Simply, no human rights court has ever been called upon to assess the fairness of a trial where in relation to *every* witness the court – and thus, ultimately, the accused – *ab initio* lacked the power to compel attendance. It makes one wonder how human rights courts and organs would respond to this unique situation.

My doubts have gained in strength since ICTR Trial Chamber and Appeals Chamber decisions concerning the transfer of cases from the ICTR to Rwanda.[38] The ICTR Trial Chamber, in the case of Mr Kanyarukiga, concluded that his case could not be transferred to Rwanda because it cannot be ensured that he will receive a fair trial in Rwanda. A significant factor was that witnesses residing outside Rwanda could not be compelled to testify before Rwandese courts, given the absence of subpoena powers to that end. This contributed to the situation where he would not be able to call witnesses residing outside Rwanda to the extent and manner that would ensure a fair trial.[39] This was confirmed on appeal:

> [the accused] would still face significant difficulties in securing the attendance of witnesses who reside outside Rwanda to the extent and in a manner which would jeopardize his right to a fair trial.[40]

How to interpret and apply these findings in relation to the ICC? If the situation in Rwanda may jeopardize the accused's right to a fair trial – because a large number of witnesses residing outside Rwanda cannot be compelled to testify before Rwandese courts – this is even more so the case at the ICC where *no* witness can be compelled to testify. At least in Rwandese proceedings, witnesses residing in Rwanda can be compelled, without any problem, to testify.

---

36 Cp. S. Trechsel, *Human Rights in Criminal Proceedings* (Oxford: Oxford University Press, 2005), at 307–308.

37 Rule 68 ICC RPE reads as follows: 'When the Pre-Trial Chamber has not taken measures under Article 56, the Trial Chamber may, in accordance with Article 69, paragraph 2, allow the introduction of previously recorded audio or video testimony of a witness, or the transcript or other documented evidence of such testimony, provided that:

> (a) If the witness who gave the previously recorded testimony is not present before the Trial Chamber, both the Prosecutor and the defence had the opportunity to examine the witness during the recording; or
> (b) If the witness who gave the previously recorded testimony is present before the Trial Chamber, he or she does not object to the submission of the previously recorded testimony and the Prosecutor, the defence and the Chamber have the opportunity to examine the witness during the proceedings.'

38 ICTR, Decision on Prosecutor's Request for Referral to the Republic of Rwanda, *Kanyarukiga*, Case No. ICTR-2002-78-R11bis, T. Ch., 6 June 2008; ICTR, Decision on the Prosecution's Appeal against Decision on Referral under Rule 11bis, *Kanyarukiga*, Case No. ICTR-2002-78-R11bis, A. Ch., 30 October 2008.

39 See Decision ICTR Trial Chamber, *supra* note 38, paras 104, 80 and 81.

40 Decision ICTR Appeals Chamber, *supra* note 38, para. 34.

These are disconcerting findings – coming from an ICTR Trial Chamber and the ICTR Appeals Chamber – seemingly disqualifying the ICC procedure from a fair trial perspective. Of course, from the ICC perspective it may be said that these concerns are still premature as they have not (yet) materialized in practice. But a similar argument could be said to apply to the ICTR transfer decisions and prospective proceedings in Rwanda; still, both Trial Chamber and the Appeals Chamber found the mere risk too significant to allow transfer. The situation at the ICC is not only not different, but it is even worse, raising the legitimate question of whether the absence of subpoena powers is a risk capable of producing similar effects, namely that we should not allow trials to take place without subpoena powers being available. There is a precedent at the ICC on staying proceedings because of fair trial concerns; in the *Lubanga* case the question also arose whether a trial could start under conditions making it impossible to ensure fairness. The Trial Chamber took the courageous and right decision that it could not allow the trial to start under such conditions.[41] A similar question could be raised in respect of the lack of subpoena powers. Of course, a vital difference is that contrary to the *Lubanga* disclosure situation, the Prosecutor cannot be blamed in any way for the lack of subpoena powers and is likely to suffer from the lack as well. Irrespective of the origin of the problem, it is legitimate, even obligatory, for a Trial Chamber to inquire whether all reasonable conditions allowing a fair trial to be conducted have been satisfied.

The ramifications of the lack of subpoena powers go beyond the strict notion of a fair trial. There are, of course, also the interests of the quality of the administration of justice. The impact of a complete absence of subpoena powers still remains to be properly assessed.

The most obvious concern regarding the lack of subpoena power is that the ICC may not have at its disposition important evidence. Witnesses who do not wish to come to the Court may not always be heard by alternative means, such as the taking of testimony by national courts, as provided for in Article 93(1)(b).[42] This may be the case when there is no properly functioning national court structure. Even when witnesses are heard by alternative means, the requirements of the already mentioned Rule 68 may constitute an obstacle to admissibility of the evidence because it may not always be possible to satisfy the presence of all parties and allow for proper cross-examination. Of course, one can argue that in the situation where the national court structure is not available or defective it is also not very likely that subpoenas would be properly executed. While I acknowledge that in the 'failed state' scenario the issuance of a subpoena is not likely to have great effect, there are at least two distinctive advantages of the subpoena in this regard. First, while a properly functioning national justice system is indispensable for taking testimony in a domestic court, a subpoena could also be enforced by entities other than national law enforcement agencies, such as UN peacekeeping forces. Second, a subpoena enables the Court to 'get hold' of a witness when he/she is travelling; this is likely to be less problematic to organize than taking testimony in

---

41 ICC, Decision on the consequences of non-disclosure of exculpatory materials covered by Article 54(3)(e) agreements and the application to stay the prosecution of the accused, together with certain other issues raised at the status conference on 10 June 2008, *Lubanga Dyilo*, Case No. ICC-01/04-01/06, T. Ch. 1, 13 June 2008; parts of paras 91 and 93 are especially worth quoting: 'If, at the outset, it is clear that the essential preconditions of a fair trial are missing and there is no sufficient indication that this will be resolved during the trial process, it is necessary – indeed, inevitable – that the proceedings should be stayed. It would be wholly wrong for a criminal court to begin, or to continue, a trial once it has become clear that the inevitable conclusion in the final judgment will be that the proceedings are vitiated because of unfairness which will not be rectified' and '... the trial process has been ruptured to such a degree that it is now impossible to piece together the constituent elements of a fair trial'.

42 Art. 93(1)(b) ICCSt reads as follows: 'The taking of evidence, including testimony under oath, and the production of evidence, including expert opinions and reports necessary to the Court.'

a domestic court in the country where the witness happens to be present, which requires a specific cooperation request to that end.

Even when the Court succeeds in taking testimony elsewhere and when this is done in accordance with the requirements of Rule 68, it is submitted that the quality of the administration of justice still significantly suffers from the absence of a witness in the courtroom. In any criminal justice system, most evidentiary weight tends to be attributed to live testimony in the courtroom. It is regarded of such weight that 'direct evidence' does not require corroboration.[43] Witness testimony taken elsewhere means that the decision-maker is unable to observe the witness during examination-in-chief and cross-examination, and to submit questions, either prepared beforehand or in light of the testimony given. The direct perception and interaction between the decision-maker and the witness is in and of itself ground enough to reject the absence of subpoena powers as a ridiculous thought.

In addition to these concerns, there are other negative sides to the absence of subpoena powers which may jeopardize the quality and accuracy of fact-finding. We have to acknowledge that failing subpoena powers, the witness is in an incredibly strong bargaining position towards the Court. Taking as a starting point that the witness is aware of his right not to appear before the Court – in my view he should be adequately informed of his legal position – there is an increasing risk that his prospective testimony is used as a bargaining chip in obtaining a variety of benefits, such as financial compensation or (far-reaching) protective measures. The question indeed arises as to what incentive there is for a witness to come to testify at the ICC, besides his desire to assist in the administration of justice. Failing any threat of a subpoena, it is possible that witnesses may try to get the best bargain for their testimony, and when that happens they regard their testimony as a *quid pro quo* which may seriously jeopardize that testimony's credibility. In practice, when a witness views his/her testimony as a *quid pro quo*, just as may be the case in respect of a plea arrangement including giving testimony as part of the arrangement, there is the risk that the testimony is regarded as keeping one's part of the bargain rather than as just revealing the truth. This may seem speculative and is certainly not my biggest problem with the absence of subpoena powers, but it is something to be reckoned with when assessing the probative value of witness testimony.

6. Conclusion and Recommendations

For a criminal lawyer one of the most puzzling aspects of the ICC Statute is that it rules out the use of compulsory process in respect of witnesses. The analysis of both the legislative history and the final outcome of the Rome Statute reveals that this vital tool for fair and effective criminal proceedings was quite easily sacrificed. While we may very much regret that now, I don't see how we can repair it under the Statute in its current form. The power attributed to the Trial Chamber in Article 64(6)(b) of the Statute to 'require the attendance of witnesses' is severely hampered by the non-availability of sanctions for witnesses who fail to appear and the provisions in Part 9 which underline that appearance must be voluntary.

The absence of subpoena powers seriously jeopardizes both the accused's right to a fair trial and the quality of the administration of justice. The ICTR has recently ruled – in the context of Rule 11*bis* – that proceedings cannot be fair when courts cannot subpoena a significant number of defence witnesses. This begs a response from the ICC, even if this reproach was not immediately

43 See ICTY, Judgement, *Aleksovski*, Case No. IT-95-14/1-A, Appeals Chamber, 24 March 2000, paras 62–64.

directed to it. In addition to these fairness concerns, it must be acknowledged that the quality of fact-finding may be in jeopardy when the decision-maker is not directly confronted with a witness or when testimony becomes too much the object of negotiations.

I do not claim that the attribution of subpoena powers to ICC judges will solve all problems regarding witness testimony. But it should be there to illustrate that the ICC's mandate is extremely important and that it cannot be allowed to be frustrated by an individual's decision to assist the Court or not. I strongly recommend amending the Statute on three points.

First, Article 64 should provide in less ambiguous terms that the Trial Chamber can directly order a witness to appear before it and to give testimony. It should be clear that such an order creates a direct obligation for the witness. This power should be available in case of a witness present on the territory of a State Party and a witness who is the national of a State Party or any other state having accepted the jurisdiction of the Court. Hereby the jurisdictional regime of Article 12 is followed.

Second, Article 70 should include as an offence against the administration of justice the deliberate non-compliance by a witness with an order to appear.

Third, Article 93 should be amended, to the extent that states must comply with requests relating to compelling the appearance of witnesses, including the use of compulsory process to that end. More concretely, the word 'voluntary' must be deleted from Article 93(1)(e), and 'facilitating' replaced by 'ensuring'. Furthermore, Article 93(7) should be deleted in its entirety; the witness in the proposed amended Article 93(1)(e) also includes the detained witnesses. Arrangements regarding continuing detention and return of the detained witness are not a matter for regulation in the Statute.

While these proposed amendments radically abolish the regime of voluntary appearance for witnesses, they are indispensable for a fair and effective Court. It can be expected that among the States Parties the importance of these amendments is recognized, especially since the protagonists of the principle of voluntary appearance are in my view not (strongly) represented in the Assembly of States Parties.

Chapter 21
Implementing International Humanitarian Law through the Rome Statute

Anne-Marie La Rosa and Gabriel Chavez Tafur

1. Introduction

Despite the valuable contribution of the *ad hoc* international Tribunals, and most recently the establishment of the International Criminal Court (ICC or Court), the repression of serious violations of international humanitarian law (IHL) remains primarily the responsibility of states. Based on grounds of efficiency (access to evidence, a judicial apparatus in place) and justice (proximity to the victims and increased dissuasive and preventive effect of holding a trial where the crime was committed), this responsibility derives most importantly from states' obligation to 'investigate war crimes allegedly committed by their nationals or armed forces, or on their territory, and, if appropriate, prosecute the suspects'.[1] It is also on states' actions that the effective application of the ICC's complementarity principle relies.

Such role of states is obviously not performed in a vacuum, as it is but one stage in a cycle of constant interplaying between the development and application of international and domestic law: a phase where implementation of IHL – the incorporation of international obligations into the domestic system of states – fulfils an essential role. It is such states' practice – including through their domestic courts – that feeds the development of custom, which then is recognized internationally and codified into treaties, or applied directly, restarting this cross-feeding cycle. As shall be discussed later, the process can present many challenges; the aim remains, however, to achieve a common set of rules regarding war crimes and their punishment that is enforced everywhere by domestic courts.

To attain such an integrated criminal system, few recent developments have provided greater momentum toward the repression of IHL violations – and, in particular, of grave breaches of the Geneva Conventions – than the adoption of the Rome Statute.[2] The result of truly multilateral negotiations, the Treaty remains the first and most comprehensive multilateral attempt to establish a code of international crimes.[3] However, Article 8 of the Statute, which codifies war crimes committed in both international and non-international armed conflicts falling under the Court's jurisdiction, is far from perfect. Authoritative voices have criticized some of its provisions for not appropriately reflecting customary law, or even as representing a step backward in its development,

---

1 J. Henckaerts and L. Doswald-Beck, *Customary International Humanitarian Law* (Cambridge: Cambridge University Press, 2005), Rule 158, at 607–611 (hereinafter, CIHL).

2 The Treaty was adopted on 18 July 1998 at the United Nations Diplomatic Conference of Plenipotentiaries on the Establishment of an International Criminal Court. It entered into force on 1 July 2002.

3 Efforts to create such a code have a long history. For developments following the Second World War, refer for instance to the work of the International Law Commission (ILC) in 1954 (ILC Yearbook, 1954, Vol. II, at 112–123) and its extensive discussions and work on this issue in 1996 (ILC Yearbook, 1996, Vols I and II).

regardless (or perhaps precisely because) of the inevitably politicized multilateral environment in which they were adopted.[4]

With this in mind, the purpose of this chapter is to analyze the process(es) that might improve the implementation at domestic level of mechanisms aimed at repressing serious violations of IHL and explore what role Article 8 ICCSt, with its strengths and weaknesses, might play in this regard. It shall do so in four parts: first, it will briefly discuss how the repression of serious violations of IHL may be incorporated into domestic law, as the first and most important step in the cycle to combat impunity; secondly, it shall review the contribution to such implementation process by the Rome Statute's provisions on serious violations of IHL, as enshrined in Article 8; this shall lead to, thirdly, an analysis of how states could – at the domestic level – best approach implementation of war crimes into their domestic systems, favouring, but not limited to, Article 8. A fourth section will briefly analyse how the upcoming ICC Review Conference, scheduled for 2010, could possibly serve as an opportunity – this time at the international level – to strengthen the rules available for the repression of serious violations of IHL by domestic courts.

It should be noted that, for the purposes of this chapter, the expressions 'war crimes' and 'serious violations of IHL' shall be used interchangeably and referred to the definition provided by the ICTY Appeals Chamber in *Tadić*, namely any act involving a serious infringement of an international rule protecting important values, involving grave consequences for the victim(s), belonging to the corpus of customary law or to an applicable IHL treaty, and the violation of which entails the individual criminal responsibility of the perpetrator.[5]

2. Incorporating Serious Violations of IHL into Domestic Legislation

International humanitarian law sets out detailed rules that seek to limit the effects of armed conflicts.[6] In particular, it protects those who are not, or no longer, taking a direct part in the fighting and sets limits on the means and methods of warfare. It also provides for the criminalization of specific acts, attaching individual criminal responsibility to their perpetrators. Implementing such war crimes (or other international crimes) into the domestic legislation of states – that is, making such prohibited conduct an offence within the penal system of states and, thus, punishable by their judiciary – may be achieved in a number of ways, as shown by states' practice.[7]

A first approach consists of applying the military or ordinary national criminal law already in force, and relying on those domestic crimes (such as murder, torture, grievous bodily harm and other common offences) which are closest to the conduct in question. Such approach – fairly common during the trials that followed World War II – has been and continues to be adopted in more recent cases involving international crimes. Examples could include the court martial of

4 For detailed commentary on the drafting of the Statute see O. Triffterer (ed.), *Commentary on the Rome Statute of the International Criminal Court – Observers' Notes, Article by Article* (1st edn., Baden-Baden: Nomos Verlagsgesellschaft, 1999); R. Lee (ed.), *The International Criminal Court* (Alphen aan den Rijn: Kluwer Law International, 1999); A. Cassese, P. Gaeta and J.R.W.D. Jones (eds), *The Rome Statute of the International Criminal Court: A Commentary* (Oxford: Oxford University Press, 2002).

5 ICTY, Decision, *Duško Tadić*, Appeal Chamber, 10 October 1995, para. 94.

6 ICRC, *What is International Humanitarian Law?* ICRC Advisory Service on IHL, July 2004. Available at http://www.gva.icrc.priv/web/eng/siteeng0.nsf/htmlall/5kzf5n?opendocument (visited 8 June 2009).

7 ICRC, *Method of Incorporating Punishment into Criminal Law*, ICRC Advisory Service on IHL, January 2004. Available at http://www.gva.icrc.priv/Web/Eng/siteeng0.nsf/htmlall/5XDJ4G/$File/Kit_national_enforcement.pdf (visited 8 June 2009).

Lieutenant William L. Calley, charged in the US with murder under the Uniform Code of Military Justice for the My Lai massacre (1970)[8] and, more recently, US military personnel tried before courts martial for crimes committed in Iraq (allegations of widespread use of torture against Iraqi detainees in 2004): in both cases the conduct charged could have amounted to war crimes or crimes against humanity.[9] In April 2009, the Peruvian Supreme Court sentenced former president Alberto Fujimori for murder, serious bodily harm and kidnapping, while recognizing that the acts under scrutiny could have also fallen under the international definition of crimes against humanity.[10]

While prosecuting international crimes using penalization for common crimes has the advantage that no major modifications of the law are necessary, practice shows at least six potential shortcomings:

> (a) Crimes under penal codes will always fail to cover the whole range of conduct amounting to a war crime. In particular, violations of the laws on the conduct of hostilities obviously cannot be found in codes covering offences committed by civilians in peace time.
> (b) Such practice can result in substantive and procedural setbacks, as many times there will be no appropriate definition of the crime as a war crime (thus lacking some of the required objective elements), nor will the *mens rea* determined under international law be present.
> (c) Resorting to common crimes may lead to punishment of behaviour perfectly lawful under IHL, further jeopardizing non-state actors' (the most expected to be subjected to state prosecutions) attitude to comply with humanitarian law.[11]
> (d) Common crimes may also be subject to restrictions no longer accepted for international crimes, such as statutes of limitations or amnesty provisions.
> (e) The criminal code may also ignore modes of liability, such as command responsibility, or allow defences not admitted under international criminal law, such as unconditionally accepting superior orders.
> (f) Legislation for common crimes does not generally provide for extraterritorial jurisdiction, an obligation which is attached to prosecution of certain war crimes.[12]

---

8 *US v. Calley*, 46 C.M.R 1131, 1138 (1973), cited in W. Ferdinandusse, *Direct Application of International Criminal Law in National Courts* (T.M.C. Asser Press: The Hague, 2006), at 19. For another example where, even after the adoption of an ICC implementing legislation, it was felt necessary to also refer to common crimes, see the proceedings of the UK General Court-Martial in the case of Donald Payne and others (7 September 2006 to 30 April 2007). In that case, out of seven members of the UK armed forces indicted, only one (D. Payne) was sentenced to one-year imprisonment for inhumane treatment, after having pleaded guilty.

9 On this, see W. Ferdinandusse, *supra* note 8, at 18–19.

10 Corte Suprema de Justicia de la República, *Alberto Fujimori Fujimori*, 7 April 2009, Exp. No. A.V. 19-2001.

11 While states shall always retain the right to punish those who take arms against them, Art. 6(5) of Additional Protocol II of 1977 encourages authorities to 'grant the broadest possible amnesty to persons who have participated in the armed conflict, or those deprived of their liberty for reasons related to the armed conflict …'. Any such amnesty would not, however, cover the commission of war crimes. See A. La Rosa and C. Wuerzner, 'Armed Groups, Sanctions and the implementation of International Humanitarian Law', *International Review of the Red Cross*, Vol. 90, No. 870, June 2008, at 335–336; and ICRC, *Increasing Respect for International Humanitarian Law in Non-International Armed Conflicts*, February 2008. Available at http://www.gva.icrc.priv/Web/eng/siteeng0.nsf/htmlall/review?OpenDocument (visited 8 June 2009).

12 Particularly 'grave breaches', as defined in the four 1949 Geneva Conventions (Arts 50, 51, 130 and 147, respectively).

A second option for implementation is criminalization of serious violations of IHL through a general reference to treaties the state is a party to,[13] to international law in general, or, most commonly, to the 'laws and customs of war', followed by a range of penalties, as may be found in a number of penal codes.[14] This approach, as the first one, is relatively simple to adopt and can easily cover all serious breaches of IHL, including (or excluding) those found in custom. Further, no new legislation is needed should the treaties in question be amended, new custom developed or new obligations arise as the state becomes a party to a new treaty.

Unfortunately, such simple procedure may also prove insufficient in certain domestic systems in view of the interpretation given to the principle of legality (in particular, under the variations *nullum crimen sine lege scripta* and *sine lege certa*), which requires the predictability of the punishment for any conduct. Such approach may also oblige the national judge to determine the law applicable domestically in light of the provisions found in treaties, international custom and case law, leaving the judiciary with considerable room for manoeuvre (and confusion). Such task may be made even more difficult by the fact that the language and structure used to typify war crimes in international instruments may not correspond to that used in a state's domestic legislation, forcing judges to work around unfamiliar wording or concepts.

A third option consists of incorporating into domestic law a list of specific crimes, corresponding to those found in the relevant IHL treaties. This may be achieved by: making a direct reference to specific articles in a treaty; transcribing the whole list of crimes into national law, using the treaty's exact wording and adding only the relevant penalties applicable to each crime or category of crimes; incorporating each crime individually, rewording it to better suit the overall penal texts. Evidently, such specific criminalization may prove to be a major task for the legislating body, requiring that considerable efforts be spent on research and drafting, with the added risk of substantial modifications to the definitions of crimes. It could also entail extensive revision of existing penal legislation, making the process long and cumbersome, and potentially subject to being affected by a perceived opportunity by legislators to amend other unrelated sections of the code. Should the criminalization become too specific and detailed, it could also lack the flexibility available under the other options when adaptation to new developments in international law is needed.

The upside, of course, is that incorporating detailed provisions into the criminal codes results in clearer and specific texts, providing the sufficient degree of predictability of what has to be considered as a criminal conduct and, thus, is subject to punishment. Obviously, such predictability facilitates both deterrence of potential perpetrators and correct application of the law by judges to specific cases. This was a favoured approach in the practice of implementation of the 1949 Geneva Conventions' 'grave breaches' provisions, as well as of the Genocide Convention.[15] The same approach is used by states willing to incorporate Rome Statute's substantive criminal law

---

13 See Venezuela, Article 156(3), *Código Penal de Venezuela*, 1964. Available at http://www.gva.icrc.priv/ihl-nat.nsf/WebLAW!OpenView (last visited on 8 June 2009).

14 For example, Costa Rica, Law No. 8272, 2002, inserting Arts 378 and 379 into the Penal Code; El Salvador, Article 362, Código Penal de El Salvador, 1997, before the 1998 amendments; Switzerland, Article 109, Code Pénale Militaire, 1928, on 'Violations of the Laws of War'; the Netherlands, Art. 8(1), War Crimes Act (repealed).

15 See, for instance: UK, Article 1, Geneva Conventions Act 1957 (as amended); India, Article 3(3), Geneva Conventions Act, 1960. On repressing genocide, see: Bolivia, Article 138, Penal Code; Honduras, Article 319, Penal Code,; Peru, Article 319, Penal Code; Brazil, Law No. 2889/1956.

provisions: while some have essentially introduced the whole treaty into their codes,[16] others seized the opportunity to adjust the definitions of crimes to their previous practice.[17]

Fourthly, implementation may follow a mixed approach, achieving criminalization both through a generic reference to IHL, combined with the explicit and specific incorporation of certain serious crimes (often genocide) in the penal codes.[18] Such method, often found in state practice before the

---

16 See, for example: Australia, International Criminal Court Act (Consequential Amendments) 202, No. 42 (2002); Samoa, International Criminal Court Act 2007; Burundi, Law No. 1/004, 08 May 2003; Argentina, Law No. 26/200 on the Implementation of the ICC Statute (2007); Cyprus, Law 23 (III)/2006; Denmark, Act No. 342 (2001) on the International Criminal Court; Ireland, International Criminal Court Act 2006; Malta, Criminal Code as amended by International Criminal Court Act 2003; New Zealand, International Crimes and International Criminal Court Act 2000; Trinidad and Tobago, International Criminal Court Act 2006; UK, International Criminal Court Act 2001; Nigeria's Rome Statute of the International Criminal Court (Ratification and Jurisdiction) Act, as well as an amendment of the Penal Code of the Democratic Republic of Congo, both still in bill form, also follow this same approach.

17 Examples could include France, whose Art. 212 (1) of the Code Pénal altered the currently accepted definition of crimes against humanity (replacing widespread *or* systematic with widespread *and* systematic). Other examples include Croatia, Criminal Code of 1997, Chapter XIII, 'Criminal Offences against Values Protected by International Law', as amended in 2003; Estonia, Criminal Code, Division 4 on War Crimes (para. 94 and following), 2002; Georgia, Law of Georgia on Amendments to the Criminal Code of Georgia, 2003; Germany, Code of Crimes Against International Law, 2002; Mali, Criminal Code, Book III, Art. 31, 2001; the Netherlands, International Crimes Act 2003; Nicaragua, Penal Code, Law No. 641, 2008, Title XXII; Romania, Criminal Code, the Special Part, Title I, Chapter I, 2003. On 7 May 2009, Chile's lower house of parliament approved a bill inserting all ICC crimes in their penal code, drafted with the distinct intention to conform their domestic law with international norms.

18 For practice previous to the adoption of the ICC Statute, see Bangladesh's International Crimes (Tribunal) Act 1973, which lists 'war crimes: namely, violation of laws or customs of war which include, but are not limited to [a list of offences]'. China's Criminal Law of the PRC 1997, Art. 9, reads: 'This Law shall be applicable to crimes which are stipulated in international treaties concluded or acceded to by the People's Republic of China and over which the People's Republic of China exercises criminal jurisdiction within the scope of obligations, prescribed in these treaties, it agrees to perform.' The Czech Republic (Criminal Code, Act No. 140/1961 as amended, Part II: Special Provisions; Chapter X: Crimes Against Humanity), Poland (Arts 121 ff., Penal Code, Law of 6 June 1997, Chapter XVI,), Slovenia (Arts 373 ff., Penal Code 1994,), and Hungary (Criminal Code of 1978, paras 155–164) include in their codes specific war crimes, but add the requirement that the act must be carried out 'in violation of rules of international law'. Guatemala penalizes genocide following a standard definition, but also considers an offence to 'violate duties, laws or treaties on POWs or *war hostages*, wounded during battle ...' (Art. 378, Penal Code, 1973).

For provisions adopted or left unmodified following an amendment process after the adoption of the ICC Statute, see, for instance: Ukraine, Art. 438 of the Penal Code (2001), on 'Violation of Laws and Customs of War', provides for a list of offences, while at the same time it prohibits the '... use of means of warfare prohibited by international law, other violations of laws and customs of war recognized by international treaties, consent for binding force of which was granted by the Supreme Council of the Ukraine'. The same would apply to South Africa, whose Implementation of the Rome Statute of the International Criminal Court Act 2002, although it includes a schedule with the relevant ICC crimes, commands domestic courts to consider and, where appropriate, apply conventional and customary international law (Art. 2). Azerbaijan's Criminal Code (2000) also provides for punishment of, *inter alia*, pillage and abuse of protected signs, but also 'violations of the laws and customs of war' (Art. 115) and 'violations of the norms of international humanitarian law in time of armed conflict' (Art. 116). A similar provision citing violations 'within the established framework of international law' may be found in Congo's Genocide, War Crimes and Crimes against Humanity Act 1998, Article 4. Canada's Crimes Against Humanity and War Crimes Act 2000 defines a war crime according to 'customary international law or conventional law applicable to armed conflicts,

adoption of the Rome Statute, allows for treaty obligations to be carried out fully, while having in place the appropriate differentiation of individual crimes. However, this solution could require judges to interpret both international and domestic law, and the often confusing interplay between the two.[19]

Finally, IHL may be implemented via the direct application of international law domestically, without any express reference in national legislation. This is normally allowed by a law of constitutional rank or a provision in the Constitution, by which international law (either written or customary, or both) is either recognized as a source of criminalization, or is assigned a superior rank to that of domestic law.[20] The uncertainty attached to such approach is undeniable, as evidenced by contradictory domestic case law.[21]

Whatever the method preferred, implementation of IHL domestically involves taking into account a few additional considerations. First, it should be noted that rules prohibiting conduct carried out during armed conflicts are to be found not only in one, but in numerous international instruments, not all of which have attained customary status. Similarly, the scope of such prohibitions also vary, covering in some cases the protection of special categories of protected

---

stating thereafter that the crimes as defined in the ICC Statute (annexed as schedule) shall be considered to be customary law. Finland's Penal Code (amended up to 2003), although defines other international crimes (genocide), provides in the case of war crimes for any act that '... violates the provisions of an international agreement on warfare binding on Finland or the generally acknowledged and established rules and customs of war under public international law' (Chapter 11, Section 1). Latvia's Criminal Code (amended in 2004) makes reference to 'violating provisions and customs regarding the conduct of war forbidden by international agreements binding upon the Republic of Latvia' (Section 74). The amended Penal Code of Belgium (in particular with regards to international crimes in 2003) recognizes as a war crime offences found directly in different IHL treaties and the ICC Statute, followed by a detailed list of crimes (Art. 136 quarter). Chapter XVII of Bosnia's Penal Code (2003), dealing with international crimes, lists numerous offences, but always with the chapeau 'Whoever, in violation of the rules of international law in the time of war or armed conflict ...'. Similar wording may be found in the Penal Codes of Bulgaria (Section II, Art. 410 and following, with amendments up to 2005), Colombia (Penal Code – Law 599 of 24 July 2000 promulgating the Penal Code, Book II), Lithuania (Criminal Code as amended up to 2008, Chapter XV, Arts 99 and following), Montenegro (Criminal Code, No. 70/2003, corrected 2004, Arts 428 and following), Panama (Penal Code, law No. 14/2007, Title XV, Chapter II), Serbia (Criminal Code, 2005, Chapter 34, Arts 372 and following), and Macedonia (Criminal Code 1996, amended up to 2004, Chapter 34, Arts 404 and following). Niger's Law No. 2003-025 penalizes specific conduct carried out against 'persons or goods protected by the conventions signed in Geneva on 12 August 1949 and the protocols I and II additional to such conventions...'. A similar provision may be found in Portugal's Law No. 31/2004 adapting the Criminal Code to include ICC crimes, as well as in Art. 608 of Spain's Penal Code (with amendments up to 2007), Senegal's Law No. 2007-02 Modifying the Penal Code, and Uruguay's Law No. 18.026 (2006). Norway's new Chapter 16-1 of the Penal Code (amended in 2008) includes detailed provisions on war crimes, but also a residual clause penalizing 'any other means of warfare that is in violation of international law' (s. 107). Mexico (Art. 149, Federal Penal Code 1931, amended up to 2009) also considers an offence to 'violate the duties of mankind on POWs'.

19 For a recent example in this regard, see G. Chavez Tafur, 'Using International Law to By-pass Domestic Legal Hurdles: On the Applicability of the Statute of Limitations in the Menéndez et al. Case', *Journal of International Criminal Justice*, Vol. 6, No. 5, 2008, at 1061–1075.

20 A number of States' Constitutions and penal codes establish that treaties/custom shall be part of the law of the land. Whether such reference would allow for direct application of international law by domestic courts is still uncertain.

21 While in Hungary the Constitutional Court accepted the direct application of the Geneva Conventions in domestic criminal courts (see Decision No. 53/1993), in France a similar contention was rejected by the *Cour de Cassation* (*In re Javor*, 26 March 1996, Criminal Bulletin No. 132).

persons or property, while addressing in others the means and methods of warfare. This in itself could make it extremely difficult to determine clearly the extent of a particular state's international obligation to penalize unlawful conduct.

Moreover, as already mentioned, the process of implementation could require the adoption of specific regulations and laws to be inserted throughout various legal texts (e.g., penal code, code of criminal procedure, code of military justice), and thus demand the involvement of different ministries, the legislature, the armed forces and other technical offices or bodies, as well as Red Cross/Red Crescent national societies and civil society. As is common in such situations, any action taken would need to be coordinated, and different objectives, levels of expertise and commitment to the final outcome would need to be reconciled.[22]

These challenges shed the proper light on the value of Article 8 ICCSt, the contribution of which to any process of implementation shall be discussed next.

3. Analysis of Article 8 of the Rome Statute

Against such diverse challenges that any process of domestic implementation of IHL must face, the development and final adoption of the Rome Statute and, in particular, of its Article 8 can only be seen as of significant importance, for several reasons.

First, Article 8 ICCSt represents the most comprehensive list of war crimes (including most of the 'grave breaches' provisions in the Geneva Conventions and Additional Protocol I) defined with sufficient clarity and specificity to be used directly by a court of law (primarily the ICC, of course) without major changes or amendments.[23] As discussed above, such quality makes the Statute relatively simple to 'import' into domestic law.

In this regard, particular praise must be attributed to the provisions dealing with non-international armed conflicts. While penalization of criminal conduct committed during an interstate war may be traced back almost a century, the same has not been the case for punishment of war crimes committed during an internal conflict.[24] Indeed, this may be seen from the fact that neither Article 3 common nor Additional Protocol II of 1977 (AP II), as opposed to the Geneva Conventions (GCs) and Additional Protocol I (AP I), contain a 'grave breaches' provision, nor do they establish a right or an obligation to search for suspected criminals and bring them to trial or extradite them.[25]

22 Such facilitator's role is often performed by IHL National Committees. ICRC documentation. Available at http://www.gva.icrc.priv/Web/Eng/siteeng0.nsf/htmlall/section_ihl_nat_national_committees?OpenDocument (visited 8 June 2009).

23 Partial precedents may be found in the Statutes of the International Criminal Tribunals for Former Yugoslavia and for Rwanda.

24 Before the Second World War, the definition of war crimes and their repression fell within the exclusive competence of states (see, for instance, Art. 28 and Art. 29 of the 1906 and 1929 Geneva Conventions, respectively). Only after the Nüremberg trials did international law develop to the stage where self-contained definitions of crimes began to be included into international instruments.

25 See generally Y. Sandoz et al. (eds), *Commentary on the Additional Protocols of 8 June 1977* (Martinus Nijhoff Publishers: Geneva 1987); and M. Bothe, 'War Crimes', in A. Cassese, P. Gaeta and J.R.W.D. Jones (eds), *The Rome Statute of the International Criminal Court: A Commentary* (Oxford: Oxford University Press, 2002), at 420. In his own words, 'the authors of the drafts of the Geneva Conventions of 1949 as well as considerable number of States represented at the Diplomatic Conference held in Geneva in 1974–1977 had wanted to [provide the Additional Protocol II with a "grave breaches" provision], but could not overcome the objections based on an argument of "sovereignty" put forward by other States'.

This has meant that, until quite recently, violations of IHL committed in internal armed conflicts were dealt with only by means of general application of provisions for common crimes (e.g., murder, rape, torture) found in domestic penal codes (with the shortcomings already discussed) or of some *ad hoc* definitions of war crimes adopted by individual states, or were not dealt with at all. Although Article 8 ICCSt is not the first international law provision to include non-international armed conflicts in its scope, it is unquestionably the first to do so in such a detailed fashion.[26]

Secondly, it must be borne in mind that Article 8 was extensively negotiated by some 150 states during the Rome Conference, which agreed to only include on the list of crimes prohibited conduct which, first, was considered to be already part of customary law, and second, the violation of which already entailed the criminal responsibility of individual perpetrators. These conditions would evidently confer Article 8 the special value of being, for most of its provisions, a codification of customary law. Such a result has led even states not parties to the Statute to engage in a revision of their domestic laws and regulations in order to take into additional consideration standards of IHL or international criminal law.[27]

Unfortunately, Article 8's shortcomings must also be noted. Indeed, for all its positive aspects, Article 8 remains far from exhaustively reflecting customary IHL on war crimes. It contains significant weaknesses and lacunae, some of which could be considered the unavoidable result of extensive political negotiations and compromises during the Rome Conference, while others stem from (mainly procedural) norms purposefully left aside due to their incompatibility with the object of the treaty itself, aimed at being a rulebook for an international criminal court. These will be reviewed below.

A. Lacunae for International Armed Conflicts

With regards to the provisions dealing with international armed conflicts, the first lacuna that needs to be mentioned is related to those grave breaches which – although found in Additional Protocol I and that may be argued as already being part of customary law[28] – were not included in the Statute. These involve the wilful launching of an attack against works or installations containing dangerous forces,[29] wilfully and unjustifiably delaying the repatriation of prisoners of war or civilians,[30] and apartheid or other inhuman and degrading practices based on racial discrimination.[31]

---

26 Other IHL instruments explicitly covering internal conflicts include the Amended Protocol II to the Convention on Certain Conventional Weapons (3 May 1996), the Second Protocol to the Convention for the Protection of Cultural Property (26 March 1999), and the Amended Art. 1 to the Convention on Certain Conventional Weapons (21 December 2001). Other treaties, such as the Ottawa Convention on anti-personnel mines (18 September 1997), the Chemical Weapons Convention (13 January 1993), the Optional Protocol to the Convention on the Rights of the Child (25 May 2000) and the Convention on Cluster Munitions (adopted on 4 December 2008), have been interpreted to apply in all armed conflicts.

27 Examples include Armenia's Criminal Code, adopted on 11 April 2003; and Rwanda's Law No. 33 *bis*/2003 repressing the crime of genocide, crimes against humanity and war crimes, entered into force on 1 November 2003.

28 Their customary status was acknowledged by the ICRC under Rule 156 of the CIHL Study. *Supra* note 1.

29 Art. 85(3)(c) AP I.

30 Art. 85(4)(b) AP I.

31 Art. 85(4)(c) AP I. It should be noted that the crime was included in the Statute as a crime against humanity. See Art. 7(1)(j) ICCSt.

The second major lacuna refers to means and methods of warfare, and in particular to the Annex mentioned in Article 8(2)(b)(xx), which was supposed to contain a list of prohibited weapons but was not drafted during the Conference or thereafter. Two conditions were agreed for the inclusion of weapons in such Annex, as mentioned in the provision's sub-paragraph: first, that any weapon, projectile, means or method of warfare to be considered would need to cause superfluous injury or unnecessary suffering, or to be inherently indiscriminate; and, second, that it should be the object of a 'comprehensive prohibition'.[32] While clearly the use of chemical and biological weapons would fulfil such conditions, the states present in Rome were still unable to reach consensus on their inclusion as during the negotiations such weapons were linked to nuclear weapons.[33] At present, only the use of poison or poisoned weapons, toxic gases and dum-dum bullets are prohibited under the Statute.[34] Other weapons acknowledged to be absolutely prohibited under customary law – such as exploding bullets,[35] non-detectable fragments[36] and blinding laser weapons specifically designed to cause permanent blindness[37] – as well as others the use of which is qualified, such as booby-traps,[38] anti-personnel mines[39] or cluster munitions,[40] were not considered at all.

B. Lacunae for Non-International Armed Conflicts

As for non-international armed conflicts, Article 8's lacunae are considerably more extensive. The provision lists the applicable war crimes in two paragraphs: the first refers to serious violations of Article 3 common,[41] while the second lists 'other serious violations of the laws and customs applicable in armed conflicts not of an international character, within the established framework of international law'.[42] The sub-paragraphs that follow, however, included very partially or completely excluded crimes already mentioned in several IHL conventions applicable to non-international armed conflicts and already considered to be part of customary international law. The fact that some war crimes were included in Article 8(2)(b) – that is, when committed in an international

32 Not much can be found in the *travaux préparatoires* on the meaning that should be attached to the expression 'comprehensive prohibition'. While some approached it from a quantitative point of view, in that a comprehensive prohibition entails that a treaty prohibiting the weapon be widely ratified, others would tend to argue that it refers to an absolute ban, as opposed to a qualified prohibition. See M. Cottier's commentary on Art. 8(2)(b)(xx) of the ICC Statute, in O. Triffterer (ed.), *Commentary on the Rome Statute of the International Criminal Court – Observers' Notes, Article by Article* (1st edn, Baden-Baden: Nomos Verlagsgesellschaft, 1999).

33 The debate was taken to the point of either including all three weapons or none at all. The result, as can be seen, was the latter option. See R. Clark, 'The Rome Statute of the International Criminal Court and Weapons of a Nature to Cause Superfluous Injury or Unnecessary Suffering, or Which are Inherently Indiscriminate', in J. Carey et al. (eds), *International Humanitarian Law: Challenges* (Ardsley: Transnational Publishers Inc., 2004), at 259–283.

34 Art. 8(2)(b) numerals (xvii), (xviii) and (xix), respectively.

35 Prohibited under customary law, according to Rule 78 of the CIHL Study.

36 See Rule 79 of the CIHL Study.

37 See Rule 86 of the CIHL Study.

38 See Rule 80 of the CIHL Study.

39 See Rule 81 of the CIHL Study.

40 Although too early to be considered customary law, the recently adopted Convention on Cluster Munitions (30 May 2008), with almost 90 State signatories, could be considered a step in this direction. It shall enter into force six months after the receipt of 30 ratifications.

41 Art. 8(2)(c) ICCSt.

42 Art. 8(2)(d) ICCSt.

armed conflict – but not included when it comes to non-international armed conflict, has raised the question why should such prohibitions be accepted by states when fighting foreign troops but not when facing their own nationals in an internal conflict. As stated by the ICTY in *Tadić*, victims certainly should deserve the same level of protection and assistance in all conflicts as 'what is inhumane and consequently proscribed in international wars, cannot but be inhumane and inadmissible in civil strife'.[43]

Further, the Statute does not provide for any weapons the prohibition of which has been accepted to apply in all conflicts or situations,[44] even when – i.e., the use of poison or poisoned weapons, toxic gases and dum-dum bullets already mentioned – they were included in the provisions applicable to international armed conflicts. In fact, discussions on and about the provisions concerning non-international armed conflicts did not tackle the issue of any prohibited weapon whatsoever.[45]

Thirdly, provisions relating to the conduct of hostilities were limited to a minimum. Numerous methods of warfare already considered to be prohibited in non-international armed conflict, such as carrying out indiscriminate attacks, starvation of civilians as a method of warfare, or attacks against civilian objects, were also excluded.[46]

C. Limitations

As for limitations inherent to the Statute as a whole, the first would be that it does not expressly require State Parties to incorporate Statute's crimes into their domestic legal systems. Although some states have indeed enacted war crimes legislation or modified their criminal codes since the adoption of the Statute, this has been done mainly to avoid or reduce the possibility of the Court

---

43 See *Tadić*, *supra* note 5, para. 119. The ICRC has also systematically regretted that some crimes were not included in the Rome Statute when dealing with non-international armed conflicts: 'the lack of specific provisions mentioning the use of famine, indiscriminate attacks and prohibited weapons is to be regretted. Is it not true that today we recognize that it is unacceptable to use against one's own people weapons which are banned from use against an external enemy?' See Statement by Mr Y. Sandoz, Head of Delegation of the ICRC at the Conference in Rome, United Nations Diplomatic Conference of Plenipotentiaries on the Establishment of an International Criminal Court, 18 July 1998, Final plenary meeting.

44 For examples, see *supra* note 26.

45 See United Nations Diplomatic Conference of Plenipotentiaries on the Establishment of an International Criminal Court, Rome, 15 June–17 July 1998, Official Records. Available at http://untreaty.un.org/cod/icc/index.html (visited 8 June 2009).

46 Although some would argue that certain of the excluded crimes could be inferred by those found in the Statute (for example, 'intentionally directing an attack against the civilian population' – Art. 8(2)(e)(i)), the full list of war crimes not included in the Statute would comprise (ICRC CIHL Study, Rule 156. *Supra* note 1):

- killing or wounding an adversary by resort to perfidy;
- using prohibited weapons;
- launching an indiscriminate attack resulting in death of civilians, or an attack in the knowledge that it will cause excessive incidental civilian loss;
- making non-defended localities and demilitarized zones the object of attack;
- using human shields;
- slavery (included only under the provisions on crimes against humanity);
- collective punishments;
- starvation of civilians as a method of warfare.

applying the complementarity principle and thus taking over cases of national concern.[47] In terms of implementation, it seems as if an important opportunity was lost.[48] A large number of States Parties to the ICC Statute have yet to adapt (or adopt) national legislation, which is an entirely voluntary process.

A second and perhaps the most important limitation to the role of Article 8 as a basis for implementation is the fact that it does not include or explicitly state the appropriate bases of jurisdiction applicable to the prosecution of war crimes as currently established under international law.[49] Perhaps irrelevant to the functioning of the Court (which has its own jurisdictional regime), this lacuna becomes an important element when states choose implementation by means of importing provisions included in the Statute, and not all that current IHL requires them to implement.

In sum, it should be clear that Article 8 has and will continue to provide states with specific provisions penalizing prohibited conduct, which undoubtedly facilitates implementation of IHL at the domestic level. However, it should also be clear that the need persists to overcome Article 8's limitations in order to fully incorporate states' IHL obligations with regards to serious violations in their domestic legal system. How to tackle such necessity, both at the national and international levels, shall be discussed in the next two sections.

4. An Integrated Approach to Implementation of IHL

In spite of its shortcomings, Article 8 remains a privileged starting point to any IHL implementation process. In that sense, adoption of an ICC act or equivalent legislation should remain the minimum standard for states, at least to penalize the crimes already included and defined in the Statute. However, any discussions at states level to apply the ICC complementarity principle should not take place in a vacuum, because of both practical and legal reasons. Rather, implementation should be put in the broader perspective of IHL obligations incumbent on states.

More precisely and as a first step, states should ensure that all *figurae criminis* derived from their international obligations to repress IHL violations – be they conventional or customary – be covered by their domestic legislation. This may include, depending on the case and the level of implementation already achieved, international crimes that have not been inserted in the ICC Statute in one way or another, as for example those above-mentioned grave breaches found in AP I.[50]

Also, states should seize the occasion of the Rome Statute's implementation exercise to verify to what extent the protection granted to victims in international armed conflict might be extended

47 Arts 17 and 19 ICCSt.

48 Indeed, only Preamble (6) ICCSt barely touches upon the subject, reminding states of their 'duty to exercise criminal jurisdiction over those responsible for international crimes'.

49 While Preamble (6) and (10) ICCSt only refer to states' 'criminal jurisdiction', Arts 17 and 19 ICCSt, dealing with admissibility issues, establish that the ICC may be barred from a case, if a state 'which has jurisdiction over it' genuinely carries out an investigation or prosecution. The term 'jurisdiction' is not defined in the ICC Statute.

50 'Unjustifiable delay in the repatriation of prisoners of war' (Art. 85(4)(b) AP I) might be the best example. Other breaches, such as the wilful launching of an attack against works or installations containing dangerous forces in the knowledge that such attack will cause excessive loss of life and the injury to civilians or damage to civilian objects, could be considered to be covered by letters (ii) and (iv) of Art. 8(2)(b) ICCSt, if these provisions have been already implemented. Finally the practice of apartheid and other inhuman and degrading practices involving outrages upon personal dignity based on racial discrimination, as noted *supra*, may be found under Art. 7 ICCSt on crimes against humanity.

to those suffering in non-international armed conflict and eliminate, if necessary, all obstacles in this regard.

Thirdly, it would be useful for states to adjust to the requirements of international law the general principles of criminal law often included in their primary legislation, at least when dealing with international crimes. In this regard, implementation measures should ensure: non-applicability of statutes of limitations, recognition of modes of liability involving the responsibility of commanders, non-applicability of the defence of obedience to superior orders, and non-recognition of amnesties for war criminals.

Finally, and most importantly, this process should also involve the adoption of extraterritorial bases of jurisdiction. As is commonly known, the last 60 years have seen important developments, in the form of several international treaties, state practice and scholarly opinions,[51] towards the admission that, for certain international crimes, the exercise of some forms of extraterritorial bases of jurisdiction, including universal jurisdiction, are not only permitted, but may be required. In this regard, one of the most striking examples is undoubtedly the 'grave breaches' regime found in the four 1949 Geneva Conventions and their Additional Protocol I, which provide for an obligation binding states to search for and initiate proceedings against suspected offenders present on their territory, regardless of their nationality or of where the offence was committed.[52] Although not all conventions include such provisions on jurisdiction and, if they do, often only provide for limited extraterritorial jurisdiction,[53] it is today commonly accepted that states have the right to vest any

51 See Redress, *Universal Jurisdiction Developments: January 2006–May 2009*. Available at http://www.redress.org/news/09-06-01Universal%20Jurisdiction%20Developments%202006-09.pdf (visited 8 June 2009); Princeton University Program in Law and Public Affairs, *The Princeton Principles on Universal Jurisdiction*, 2001; Institute of International Law, Seventeenth Commission 'Universal Criminal Jurisdiction with regard to the crimes of genocide, crimes against humanity and war crimes', Krakow Session, 26 August 2005; International Association of Penal Law, 'Universal Jurisdiction, Global Report' (Report), prepared by I. Blanco and published in the *Revue International de Droit Pénal*, Volume 79, 2008.

52 Arts 50, 51, 130 and 147, respectively, of the 1949 Geneva Conventions.

53 IHL treaties covering both international and non-international armed conflicts allow four different approaches to extraterritorial jurisdiction to be distinguished: the first of these and the most limited, found, for example, in the Biological Weapons Convention or the 1925 Gas Protocol, only extends the prohibition to acts occurring 'within the territory of such State, under its jurisdiction or under its control anywhere' (Art. 4), but without any specific provision on the nature of the national measures that ought to be taken or on bases of criminal jurisdiction proper. The second includes instruments such as the Ottawa Convention (Art. 9) and the Amended Protocol II to the Convention on Certain Conventional Weapons (Art. 14(1)), which do extend the obligation to take legal action against persons or acts committed in the territory under a State's jurisdiction or control. The third refers to conventions such as the Chemical Weapons Convention, which refers to acts committed in 'any place under [the State's] control' but also obliges every State, under the active personality principle, to 'extend its penal legislation … to any activity prohibited … under this Convention undertaken anywhere by natural persons, possessing [the forum State's] nationality, in conformity with international law' (Art. VII (1)(c)). In the fourth approach, instruments such as the Second Protocol to the Convention on the Protection of Cultural Property obliges States to take action when the offence is committed in their territory (thus acting under the territoriality principle), when the alleged offender is a national of the State (active personality principle) and, for certain types of offences, when the alleged offender is present in their territory (a form of universal jurisdiction) (Art. 16). In this last case, the Protocol further requires that, if the state does not extradite that person, it should 'submit, without exception whatsoever, and without undue delay, the case to its competent authorities, for the purpose of prosecution' (Art. 17). Human rights treaties such as the Convention Against Torture and Other Cruel, Inhuman or Degrading Treatment or Punishment and the International Convention for the Protection of All Persons from Enforced Disappearance adhere to the last approach.

form of jurisdiction – over war crimes, crimes against humanity, genocide and torture[54] – in their national courts.

5. The Role of the ICC and its First Review Conference

As described above, Article 8 of the ICC Statute, as it stands today, may be seen as a good basis for implementation of IHL by states. However, efforts spent in this endeavour at the domestic level should not overshadow measures that may also be taken internationally. As mentioned before, the incorporation of, and resort to, international law by domestic courts, on one hand, and the influence of state practice in the development of international law, on the other, can only be considered components of a cross-feeding cycle, each component exercising reciprocal influence on the other. The more a treaty adequately reflects IHL norms – in this case with regards to the repression of its serious violations – the more it can be expected that the law and practice which result from its implementation and application at the domestic level will be in compliance with IHL. It is precisely in this light that the first Review Conference of the ICC Statute, and most particularly the possibility of amending the Statute, should be seen and understood. Albeit not without risks and challenges, whether and how such an opportunity should be seized shall be discussed below.

The first issue to consider is that any modification to the Statute's crimes provisions would need to follow the strict procedure applicable under the Statute itself, and this is not a simple process.[55] Only States Parties may propose formal amendments to the text, and must submit them to the UN Secretary General no later than three months before an Assembly of States Parties.[56] Once received, the Secretary General must send the proposal for review to all parties to the Statute, who must then, during the Assembly, decide by a simple majority whether to deal with the proposal directly or to convene a Review Conference, if the issue involved so warrants. The Statute also expressly provides that the first amendments to the Statute may only be considered by means of a Review Conference to be convened no sooner than seven years after the treaty's entry into force.[57] Finally, the adoption of any amendment may only be achieved either by consensus or by a two-thirds majority of State Parties.[58] It is under such rules that a Review Conference has been scheduled for early 2010.

This means that if a state wishes to propose an amendment to one of the ICC's crimes provisions, at least this first time around, it shall first need to ensure that it gathers the necessary support of at least the majority of states at the Assembly of States Parties, and then even further support at the Review Conference.[59] Evidently, the building of such support takes time and, ideally, should

54 For the case of war crimes, see Rule 157, CIHL Study, *supra* note 1.

55 See Arts 121 and 123 ICCSt.

56 Last ordinary session of the Assembly before the 2010 Review Conference is currently scheduled for 18 November 2009.

57 Art. 123 ICCSt.

58 Art. 121 ICCSt. On the question of counting with two versions of the Statute, the original and the amended, the treaty establishes that the latter would only enter into force for the States who agreed to it one year after submitting their instruments of ratification or acceptance. For States Parties not agreeing to the amendment, the ICC would not be able to exercise its jurisdiction over the new crimes, if committed by a national or on the territory of those States (Art. 121(5), ICCSt).

59 The number of States Parties to other IHL instruments, the provisions of which might be the object of the amendments, could serve as a first indicator to measure the support that such amendments may generate.

carefully represent a geographical balance so as to avoid unnecessary and unwanted friction among ICC States Parties.

Secondly, it would also be necessary to take into account the position of non-States Parties, at least for two issues. First, questions may be raised on the fact that the Statute is silent on whether states wishing to accede to the ICC Statute would be able to choose, after a successful amendment process, between the original and the amended versions of the Statute. Although public international law favours an approach,[60] the issue would need to be settled during the amendment process, having in mind the preservation of the integrity of the Statute as a whole. A pick-and-choose approach by states would damage the *raison d'être* behind the amendment discussed, namely to bring the Statute closer to customary IHL.

In addition, any proposed amendment could potentially diminish or seriously hinder the possibility of non-States Parties moving closer towards accession, and thus handicap the universal character of the Statute.[61] While this would entirely depend on the nature and contents of the amendment, it could place *realpolitik* considerations at the centre stage of negotiations and reduce the attention of parties on the original objective, namely to improve provisions aimed at the protection of victims of armed conflicts and other situations of violence.

With these considerations in mind, and attentive of the need to promote a more effective implementation of IHL at the domestic level, it would be highly beneficial that the first Review Conference is not seen as the final opportunity for amendment of the Statute, or even worse, as the passing of judgement on what is and what is not considered to be customary IHL. Instead, much would be gained if it could be seen as part of an ongoing process towards the development and effective repression of IHL violations, of which the Statute and its Article 8 form only an important part. What is more, acceptance that such process might include different stages and that not all desirable modifications should be attempted in a one-shot operation would effectively reduce the risk of rejection of the amendment process *in toto*, with the undesired consequence of blocking or endlessly postponing not only the resolution of the most contentious suggestions but also the inclusion of the more consensual ones.

Even more concretely, it would be wise to regard the first Review Conference as an occasion for State Parties to restate their commitment to the fight against impunity in the following ways. First, states could wish to reiterate their commitment to national implementation processes of the ICC Statute, as well as their willingness to provide assistance and support to initiatives in other countries.[62] Secondly, a process of very selective amendments could be favoured, focused only on limited but strongly supported issues. A first example which, as seen, would possibly already be counting on the required international consensus could be the importance of initiating the move towards having victims of non-international armed conflicts benefit from the same protection as those suffering in international armed conflict.

Thirdly, even if the amendments proposed were strictly circumscribed with a view to generating the greatest possible support, it would still be necessary to regard this not as the final step, but

---

60 Art. 40(5)(a) Vienna Convention on the Law of Treaties, 1969, reads: 'Any State which becomes a party to the treaty after the entry into force of the amending agreement shall, failing an expression of a different intention by that State: (a) be considered as a party to the treaty as amended; and (b) be considered as a party to the un-amended treaty in relation to any party to the treaty not bound by the amending agreement.'

61 Albeit fully operational with 111 State Parties, the Court is still far from achieving universal acceptance.

62 See, in this regard, the EU Guidelines on promoting compliance with international humanitarian law (IHL), 23 December 2005, 2005/c 327/04. Available at http://www.unhcr.org/refworld/docid/4705f7462.html (visited 8 June 2009).

rather as a mechanism towards states accepting the need to engage in the identification of further improvements to bring the Statute closer to full compliance with customary IHL. In this sense, one realistic objective for the Conference could be to find the consensus to initiate further discussions and follow-up initiatives over the next years, design an effective strategy for more efficient engagement of states regarding the most contentious issues surrounding IHL crimes, and take full advantage of the momentum gathered by the Conference to remind states of their international obligation to implement, at a minimum, the prohibitions found in those treaties to which they are already bound. Although such strategy would obviously require clear procedure, deadlines and expected outcomes, it could effectively yield the desired results concerning the future development of IHL.

6. Conclusion

As discussed throughout this paper, the development of the current system of repression for international crimes is a two-tiered and interdependent process: on one hand, states agree on rules at the international level and their enforcement is, for the great majority of cases, a matter for domestic courts; on the other, developments in national case law often push, or at least assist in setting, the conditions for further consensus among states. In such a system, effective implementation of international rules into domestic law is of paramount importance and requires constant promotion.

In a few cases this interplay is more prominent than it is with regards to war crimes and Article 8 of the ICC Statute. Wide-ranging and easily mouldable to fit most penal legislations, the Statute should continue to provide an excellent starting point for any implementation process. Efforts should be made, of course, to recognize its shortcomings and omissions. Although the upcoming ICC Review Conference may indeed prove to be fertile ground for improvements in this regard, the real opportunity ahead shall depend on states' capacity to set up the conditions for a more inclusive and permanent forum for the development of an enhanced system of repression – both at national and international level – that contributes to the fight against impunity. There lies the real challenge.

Chapter 22
The 'Weapons Provisions' and its Annex: The Belgian Proposals

Roger S. Clark

1. Introduction

During the Seventh session (second resumption) of the Assembly of States Parties of the Rome Statute of the International Criminal Court, held in New York, 9–13 February 2009, Belgium introduced a pair of informal proposals to add a significant number of provisions concerning prohibited weapons to the Statute.[1] This is the first public draft of a set of proposals that will no doubt undergo significant development before they are discussed at the 2010 Review Conference on the Statute – if indeed they make it to the Conference. Nevertheless, these important suggestions are sufficiently developed to warrant some first comments.

The background to the proposals is this. Article 8(2)(b) of the Rome Statute deals with '[o]ther violations of the laws and customs applicable in international armed conflict, within the established framework of international law'. Among the particular 'acts' that it proscribes are the following:

> "(xvii) employing poison or poisoned weapons;
>
> (xviii) employing asphyxiating, poisonous or other gases, and all analogous liquids, materials or devices;
>
> (xix) employing bullets which expand or flatten easily in the human body, such as bullets with a hard envelope which does not entirely cover the core or is pierced with incisions."[2]

The subparagraph also refers to this:

> "(xx) Employing weapons, projectiles and material and methods of warfare which are of a nature to cause superfluous injury or unnecessary suffering or which are inherently indiscriminate in violation of the international law of armed conflict, provided that such weapons, projectiles and material and methods of warfare are the subject of a comprehensive prohibition and are included in an annex to this Statute, by an amendment in accordance with the relevant provisions set forth in Articles 121 and 123."[3]

---

1 Documents headed 'Belgian proposal, Annex to article 8 paragraph 2, b) xx of the Rome Statute – Version 3 – 4 February 2009 – 10:30', and 'Belgian proposal, Draft amendments to the Rome Statute, Version 3 – 4th of February 2009 – 10:30'.

2 Rome Statute of the International Criminal Court, Art. 8(2)(b)(xvii), (xviii) and (xix).

3 Rome Statute of the International Criminal Court, Art. 8(2)(b)(xx).

This latter provision was adopted against the background of discussion of including in the Statute's catalogue of war crimes, in addition to those in subparagraphs (xvii), (xviii) and (xix), the use of chemical weapons, biological weapons, nuclear weapons, anti-personnel land mines and the like. Some of these (chemical and biological weapons in particular) were regarded by most participants in 1998 as already 'subject of a comprehensive prohibition' by treaty or custom (or both). But agreement could not be reached to include them in the Statute in light of the refusal to include nuclear weapons.[4] A majority of the participants, perhaps a substantial majority, regarded nuclear weapons as also prohibited under international customary law, in accordance with the dissent in the Nuclear Weapons Advisory proceedings.[5] But an adamant group, composed mostly of the Permanent Five members of the Security Council (P5) and NATO members, believed the contrary. The language contained in Article 2(b) (xx) was thus a compromise, designed to flag the point that a consensus had not been arrived at to include a longer list of prohibited weapons, and perhaps to create a special procedural framework for adding to the list.

There is a long history in warfare of regarding some weapons as so barbaric that it is forbidden to use them.[6] The issue now addressed by Belgium is whether to revisit, and include as criminal in the Rome Statute, chemical, biological and nuclear weapons (often lumped together as 'weapons of mass destruction' or WMD),[7] along with other types of currently disfavoured weaponry. Some of these others, such as anti-personnel mines and blinding laser weapons, were also discussed during the drafting of the Rome Statute, but ultimately not included; others have emerged clearly as an issue in subsequent negotiations – cluster munitions, in particular. As a NATO member, 'protected' by the American nuclear umbrella, Belgium is an unlikely candidate to tackle the nuclear weapons issue and its proposal does not touch it. Indeed, the time is probably not ripe to revisit nuclear weapons and the best chance currently for a way forward on that front may be the Nuclear Non-Proliferation Treaty Review Conference, also scheduled for 2010.

A further question is whether the prohibitions should apply in non-international as well as international armed conflict. Belgium proposes that the same weapons be banned in both types of

4 See P.K. and J.T. Holmes, 'The Rome Conference on an International Criminal Court: The Negotiating Process', 93 *Am J. Int'l L.* (1999), 2, at 11 n. 32; R.S. Clark, 'The Rome Statute of the International Criminal Court and Weapons of a Nature to Cause Superfluous Injury or Unnecessary Suffering, or Which are Inherently Indiscriminate', in J. Carey, W.V. Dunlap and R.J. Pritchard (eds), *International Humanitarian Law: Challenges* (Ardsley, New York: Transnational Publishers, 2004), at 259.

5 The Legality of the Threat or Use of Nuclear Weapons, Advisory Opinion of July 8, 1996, 1996 I.C.J. 226 (dissenting opinions of Judges Koroma, Shahabudeen and Weeramantry). The Advisory Opinion focuses on state responsibility, but the issue of individual criminal responsibility was not far from the surface. As the Nüremberg Tribunal put it, '[c]rimes against international law are committed by men, not by abstract entities, and only by punishing individuals who commit such crimes can the provisions of international law be enforced'. 'Judgment of the International Military Tribunal for the Trial of Major German War Criminals', 41 *Am. J. Int'l L.* (1946), 172, at 221. The Tribunal was speaking specifically to individual criminal responsibility for breaches of the Kellogg-Briand Pact, a treaty that was silent on the subject. Of course, the 'abstract entities' we call states may also be liable (if not 'criminally' so) on the basis of principles of state responsibility.

6 J.-M. Henckaerts and L. Doswald-Beck, for International Committee of the Red Cross, *Customary International Humanitarian Law*, Vol. I (Cambridge: Cambridge University Press, 2005), at 243 (examples of weapons causing unnecessary suffering, beginning with barbed lances and barbed spears) and 249 (examples of indiscriminate weapons).

7 See generally, R.S. Clark, 'Weapons of Mass Destruction', in Weapons of Mass Destruction Commission (WMDC), *Weapons of Terror: Freeing the World of Nuclear, Biological and Chemical Arms* (Stockholm: WMDC, 2006). Available at http://www.enotes.com/genocide-encyclopedia/weapons-mass-destruction (visited 20 August 2009).

conflict.[8] This issue had been discussed in the preparations for Rome, but references to prohibited weapons in internal conflict contained in drafts of the Rome Statute had disappeared during the Rome Conference.[9] The Statute currently contains no provisions of the use of prohibited weapons in non-international armed conflict.

2. First Belgian Proposal, Addressing the 'Annex to Article 8 paragraph 2, b) xx of the Rome Statute'

The first Belgian proposal reads:

> The annex to article 8 paragraph 2, b) xx of the Rome Statute covers the use of weapons, projectiles and material and methods of warfare which are the subject of a comprehensive prohibition and committed in violation of
>
> - the Convention on the Prohibition of the Development, Production and Stockpiling of Bacteriological (Biological) and Toxin Weapons and on their Destruction, London, Moscow and Washington, 10 April 1972;[10]
> - the Convention on the Prohibition of the Development, Production, Stockpiling and Use of Chemical Weapons and on their Destruction, Paris, 13 January 1993;[11]
> - the Convention on the Prohibition of the Use, Stockpiling, Production and Transfer of Anti-Personnel Mines and on their Destruction, Ottawa, 18 September 1997.[12]

A large majority of those participating in the Rome Conference were parties to the first two of these treaties and many of them regarded the prohibitions as reflective also of international customary

---

8 The distinctions between what applies to the two types of conduct are slowly being eroded – but not entirely. See generally J.G. Stewart, 'Towards a Single Definition of Armed Conflict in international Humanitarian Law: A Critique of Internationalized Armed Conflict', 85 *IRRC* (2003), 313. In its decision on the interlocutory appeal in the *Tadic* case, the International Criminal Tribunal for the Former Yugoslavia discussed at some length how customary law had expanded the application of the norms of the 1925 Geneva Protocol on Asphyxiating Gases from international into non-international armed conflict. Decision on the Defence Motion for Interlocutory Appeal on Jurisdiction, *Tadic*, Case No. IT-94-1-AR72, 2 October 1995, paras 96–236. The same transformation may well have occurred for other forbidden weapons, but which ones is a hard judgement call.

9 Until 6 July 1998, proposals on the table for the provisions in the Statute dealing with non-international conflict included weapons prohibitions modelled on those in the provisions on international armed conflict. These disappeared in a Discussion Paper circulated by the Bureau of the Committee of the Whole in Rome, UN Doc. A/CONF.183/C.1/L. 53 (6 July 1998). They never returned and there appears to be no explanation of the deletion on the record. Some significant players must have regarded the matter as controversial.

10 The 1972 Convention does not explicitly forbid use, but its preamble has the parties '*Determined*, for the sake of all mankind, to exclude completely the possibility of bacteriological (biological) agents and toxins being used as weapons' (emphasis added). The implied ban must cover use in both international and non-international conflict.

11 Art. 1(1)(b) of this Convention contains an explicit ban on the use of chemical weapons as well as on the activities mentioned in its title. The ban on use must include use in international and non-international conflict.

12 Art. 1(1)(a) of this Convention also has an explicit ban on the use of these weapons in any circumstances.

law. The third had not yet come into force. As Belgium notes in its proposal,[13] the Bacteriological Weapons Convention had 164 parties as of 3 February 2009; the Chemical Weapons Convention had 186 parties on the same date; and the Anti-Personnel Mines Convention, still quite new in 1998, now has 156 parties.

The chapeau of this part of the Belgian proposals is worded cautiously: 'the annex ... covers' these items. Obviously, this includes some kind of determination that these items have become the 'subject of a comprehensive prohibition'.[14]

In a brief explanatory note, the Belgian Proposal asserts:

> The number of States Parties for each of these treaties reaches more than four fifth[s] of the States in the world, which could be sufficient to consider that they establish a "comprehensive prohibition" as foreseen in Article 8, paragraph 2, b) xx) of the Rome Statute.[15]

Beyond that, however, the proposal has carefully avoided addressing at this stage what will no doubt become a fundamental issue later down the road: what procedure must be followed to add something to the mysterious annex. I have addressed this at length elsewhere[16] and merely introduce the point here. Clearly, the treaty means something when it refers to the annex and that something probably has to do with the procedures for achieving content in the annex.

The problem arises from the last phrase of subparagraph (xx), 'by an amendment in accordance with the relevant provisions set forth in Articles 121 and 123.' The difficulty is that Articles 121 and 123 contemplate two different kinds of amending procedures and there is debate about which are 'the relevant provisions'. The normal rule in the Statute, contained in Article 121(4), is that once seven-eighths of the Parties accept an amendment, that amendment comes into force for all parties. On the other hand, Article 121(5) has a special rule for amendments 'to' Articles 5, 6, 7 and 8 of the Statute. It says that such an amendment 'shall enter into force for those States Parties which have accepted the amendment one year after the deposit of their instruments of ratification or acceptance'. Article 121(5) adds that '[i]n respect of a State Party which has not

---

13 Belgian proposal on weapons subject of a comprehensive prohibition, footnotes. There is a downside to the argument of a comprehensive prohibition in the case of the Anti-Personnel Mines Convention, that while the list of parties includes, for example, France, Japan and the United Kingdom, it does not include China, India, the Russian Federation and the United States.

14 See M. Cottier, 'Article 8(2)(b)(xx), Employment of Means or Methods of Warfare included in an Annex to this Statute', in Otto Triffterer (ed.), *Commentary on the Rome Statute of the International Criminal Court: Observers' Notes, Article by Article* (2nd ed., Munich: C.H. Beck, 2008), at 423 and 424: 'A comprehensive prohibition may exist under customary international law as evidenced by the *opinio juris* and practice of States, or under conventional international law, in particular when a treaty prohibiting the employment of a specific weapon has widely been ratified. In both cases, almost universally accepted treaties will generally be clear evidence of a comprehensive prohibition. It is not necessary that the treaty prohibiting this weapon be universally ratified or that all States without exception have ratified such treaty. The qualified majority of States Parties at a Review Conference or Assembly of States Parties will determine which weapons can be considered as subject to a comprehensive prohibition when considering adding further weapons under the jurisdiction of the ICC.'

15 Belgian proposal on Annex, at 1.

16 R.S. Clark, 'Article 8 (2)(b)(xx): Weapons and Methods of Warfare', *New Criminal Law Review* (2009), Vol. 12, No. 3 (symposium issue on suggestions for amending the Rome Statute). For some more general discussion of potential amendments, only a few of which are likely to be taken up at the 2010 Conference, see R.S. Clark, 'Possible Amendments for the First ICC Review Conference' (2007), 4 *New Zealand Yearbook of International Law* 103.

accepted the amendment, the Court shall not exercise its jurisdiction regarding a crime covered by the amendment when committed by that State Party's nationals or on its territory'. What is the effect of the phrase 'in accordance with' as used in Article 8(2)(b)(xx)?[17] Does it mean that all of Article 121 applies in the same manner as it would if a 'new' prohibition were being added as an 'amendment' to the Statute? On the plain language of Article 8(2)(b)(xx) a provision on weapons is obviously an 'amendment' to the Statute in some respects. It needs to be 'adopted' by the Assembly or a Review Conference pursuant to Article 121, paragraph 3.[18] So far so good. Is it, however, an amendment to which paragraph 4 applies, or one to which paragraph 5 applies? At the very least, it gives content to a now empty (and indeed completely notional) Annex.[19] Is that 'amending' Article 8 by creating a 'new' crime (or giving birth to a nascent one)? Certainly, it is not an amendment to Articles 5,[20] 6 or 7. However, is it an 'amendment' to Article 8? 'Amendment' normally implies that something is being changed or altered. One could contend strongly that it is not necessary to change the wording or effect of Article 8 in order to fulfil the expectations of the drafters. Article 8(2)(b)(xx) is arguably an example of a 'facilitative' or 'enabling' provision which is a condition to be met, rather than an obstacle that needs to be changed. Does it need to be 'applied' rather than 'amended'? Is the inclusion in an annex something in the nature of a 'completion' of, rather than an amendment to, Article 8? Is it filling an anticipated gap rather than changing something in the Statute? Compare, for example, adding a new subcategory of crime in armed conflict to the Statute, such as spreading terror among a civilian population,[21] which would surely be an amendment to Article 8.

While the matter is not entirely free from doubt, I believe that a reasonable argument can be made on the basis of the language and the preparatory work of the Statute that adding something to the Annex is not an amendment to Article 8 and is thus subject to the general seven-eighths

---

17 It will be noted that there is no verb before the words 'in accordance with'. (The same is true in at least the French and Spanish texts of the Statute.) One might have expected something like 'approved' or 'agreed upon'. In the case of Art. 5(2) on aggression, the language is 'once a provision is *adopted* in accordance with' (emphasis added). For a possible argument based on this, see *infra* note 18.

18 Paragraph 3 corresponds with the default rule for adoption of a text of a treaty at an international conference – a two-thirds vote unless otherwise agreed. The use of the identical word 'adopted' both in Art. 5(2) and in Art. 121(3) of the Statute opens up the possibility that nothing more than adoption by the Review Conference is required for completing the definition of aggression. Most participants in the process resist that interpretation and insist that more is needed, whether it is paragraph 4 or paragraph 5 that is the 'more' is hotly debated. The argument for applying either paragraph 4 or paragraph 5 has to accept that 'adopted' is used in different senses in Arts. 5(2) and 121(3), the latter being narrower. The argument for approval by the Review Conference alone is harder to make in the case of the Annex, since the word 'adopted' is not there in Art. 8(2)(b)(xx) to base it upon.

19 It does not yet exist at all, not even as an empty page headed 'Annex.'

20 It does not add a new category of offences to the list in Art. 5 – the category (war crimes) and a subcategory (forbidden weapons) already exist. Adding, say, a new category of 'terrorist' or 'drug' offences to the Statute, on the other hand, would entail an amendment to Art. 5 and thus apply only to the territory or nationals of those who accept it.

21 See Judgement, *Galic*, Case No. IT-98-29-A (5 December 2006) (spreading terror among the civilian population held to be a breach of customary law giving rise to individual criminal responsibility by a majority of the Appeals Chamber of the ICTY, even though that offence, while contemplated by Geneva Conventions and Protocols, is not subject to grave breach regime thereof). Adding such an offence to the list in Art. 8 seems fairly clearly to be governed by paragraph 5 of Art. 121. As an 'amendment to Article … 8' (by adding a new war crime within the jurisdiction of the Court), it must apply only to the territory or nationals of those parties 'which have accepted the amendment'.

rule.[22] It does not apply to any Party until seven-eighths agree, but once it comes into force, it is for everyone.

3. Second Belgian Proposal: Draft Amendments to the Rome Statute

None of the other additions to the Statute proposed by Belgium relate to the 'annex', and, certainly as currently presented, they all appear to be governed by the rules of Article 121(5), namely that they are applicable only to the citizens or territory of those States that become party to them. No contention is made by Belgium (although some might make a different calculation) that they have become the subject of a comprehensive prohibition. The treaty instruments on which some of these further proposed amendments are based have significantly fewer ratifications and accessions than the prohibitions on biological, chemical and anti-personnel weapons. These 'draft amendments', so described in the proposal, are six in number.

The first two of them relate to Article 8(2)(e) of the Statute which deals with offences in non-international armed conflict. Amendment No. 1 is on poison or poisoned weapons, asphyxiating, poisonous or other gases and bullets that flatten easily in the human body. Its language comes directly from the existing provisions on these subjects in Article 8(2)(b).[23] It simply extends the existing prohibition concerning international armed conflict to non-international armed conflict. Amendment No. 2 tracks the language proposed by Belgium for inclusion in the annex, dealing with biological weapons, chemical weapons and anti-personnel mines.[24] The effect of these two amendments is thus to introduce similar prohibitions in both international and non-international armed conflict.

Amendments 3 and 4 also track each other. Amendment No. 3 adds to Article 8(2)(b) on international armed conflict a reference to '[u]sing cluster munitions as prohibited by the Convention on Cluster Munitions, Dublin, 30 May 2008'. Belgium comments:

> The Dublin Convention has not yet entered into force and can not therefore be considered as creating a "comprehensive prohibition" as foreseen in Article 8, paragraph 2, b, xx) of the Statute. In order to extend the jurisdiction of the Court to these crimes in a case of international armed conflict, it is then necessary to adopt an amendment and not to include the Convention in the Annex to the Statute.[25]

Amendment No. 4 adds similar language to Article 8(2)(e) on non-international armed conflict.[26]

Amendments 5 and 6 are again parallel. They deal with weapons which would be incorporated into the provisions on international and non-international armed conflict respectively:

> Using weapons as prohibited by the Convention on Prohibitions or Restrictions on the Use of Certain Conventional Weapons Which May be Deemed to be Excessively Injurious or Have Indiscriminate Effects. Geneva, 10 October 1980, combined with:

22 Clark, *supra* note 16.

23 *Supra* note 2.

24 *Supra*, at notes 10–12.

25 Belgian proposal, Draft amendments to the Rome Statute, at 2.

26 The only 'Explanation' supplied by Belgium is 'same purpose than amendment no 3, but in the case of armed conflict not of an international character'. Ibid.

- Protocol on Non-Detectable Fragments (Protocol I). Geneva, 10 October 1980;
- Protocol on Prohibitions or Restrictions on the Use of Mines, Booby-Traps and Other Devices (Protocol II), Geneva, 10 October 1980, as amended on 3 May 1996;
- Protocol on Prohibitions or Restrictions on the Use of Incendiary Weapons (Protocol III). Geneva, 10 October 1980; or
- Protocol on Blinding Laser Weapons (Protocol IV to the 1980 Convention), 13 October 1995.[27]

The Belgian proposal notes that the Convention and the four additional protocols it mentions 'have been ratified by approximately half [the] States of the world (approx. 100 ratifications for each of them)'. It adds that they 'can not be considered as creating a 'comprehensive prohibition' as foreseen in Article 8. Thus, it concludes, to extend the jurisdiction of the Court here 'it is then necessary to adopt an amendment and not to include the Convention in the Annex to the Statute'.

Although it is not mentioned in the Belgian proposal, it should be noted, concerning Amendment No. 6, that the package of protocols adopted in 1980 originally applied only in international armed conflict. An amendment to the framework Convention (and thus the first four Protocols) in 2001 extended the prohibitions to non-international armed conflict.[28] There are currently 64 parties to this amendment.

4. Conclusion

The Belgian proposals are significant ones, designed in part to respond to regrettable omissions in the Statute that emerged from complex negotiations during the latter stages of the Rome Conference, and in part to reflect growing state practice in opposition to weapons of a nature to cause superfluous injury or unnecessary suffering or which are inherently indiscriminate. There will no doubt be some informal discussions of the proposals in New York and The Hague during 2009 and some more formal consideration at the Assembly of States Parties meeting later in the year. It is hoped that these initial comments will contribute to the necessary debate.

27 The 1980 Convention is a framework convention; the concrete prohibitions are in the protocols. The Belgian proposal notes, at 2, that Protocol I had 105 parties as of 3 February 2009; Protocol II (as amended) had 92 parties; Protocol III had 101 parties; and Protocol IV had 93 parties. There is a further protocol to the 1980 Convention not mentioned by Belgium, namely Protocol V on Explosive Remnants of War, adopted in 2003. It has only 49 parties at the time of writing which probably explains why Belgium has not included it in the proposals. There was some discussion of the 1980 Convention and its Protocols in the preparations for Rome and at Rome, but nothing from these instruments was ultimately included, a consensus on including them perhaps being unattainable at the time. Including the items in 1998 would have meant that they applied to everybody who ratified or acceded to the Statute. Including them now, in an amendment applicable only to those who agree to it, ought to be much less controversial.

28 Amendment to the Convention on Prohibitions or Restrictions on the Use of Certain Conventional Weapons which may be deemed Excessively Injurious or have Indiscriminate Effect, Doc. CCW/CONF.II/2 (2001).

SECTION II
The Crime of Aggression

Chapter 23

State Responsibility for Acts of Aggression Under the United Nations Charter: A Review of Cases

Edoardo Greppi

1. Aggression and Collective Security

A. General Features

In the international community there seems to be a shared opinion and a general agreement on the point that there cannot be individual responsibility for the crime of aggression unless the state concerned has international responsibility for aggression. A crime of aggression 'would be inconceivable under international law without a state or another entity having committed aggression'.[1] Individual liability (for war of aggression) and state responsibility (both for a war of aggression and for any other use of force which may be qualified as unlawful) 'exist cumulatively rather than alternatively'.[2]

From a certain perspective, the Security Council determination should be considered a precondition. This is the view of the International Law Commission (ILC): 'any criminal responsibility of an individual for an act or crime of aggression necessarily presupposes that a state had been held to have committed aggression, and such a finding would be for the Security Council acting in accordance with Chapter VII of the Charter to make.'[3] On the other hand, in the context of the International Criminal Court (ICC), the Security Council's power should not be considered exclusive, as other bodies, such as the General Assembly or the International Court of Justice, may determine the existence of aggression.[4]

Another shared opinion – which is strictly linked to this one on state responsibility – is that the crime of aggression is a leadership crime, the result of acts committed by state officials, in particular by those who are in a position of high political and/or military responsibility, putting them in a position of authority in the decision-making process.[5] In other words, aggression is a not a crime which can be committed by individuals acting in their private capacity, or by low-level politicians or low-ranking officers in the armed forces.

---

1 G. Gaja, 'The Respective Roles of the ICC and the Security Council in Determining the Existence of an Aggression', in M. Politi and G. Nesi, *The International Criminal Court and the Crime of Aggression* (Aldershot: Ashgate, 2004), at 121.

2 Y. Dinstein, *War, Aggression and Self-Defence* (Cambridge: Cambridge University Press, 2005), at 104.

3 ILC, *Report of the International Law Commission on the Work of its Forty-Sixth Session, Draft Statute of the International Criminal Court*, UN GAUR 49th Session, Supp. No. 10, at 86, UN Doc. A/49/10 (1994).

4 M.S. Stein, 'The Security Council, the International Criminal Court, and the Crime of Aggression: How Exclusive is the Security Council's Power to Determine Aggression?', *Ind. Int'l & Comp. Law Rev* (2005), at 1–36.

5 M. Politi, 'The Debate within the Preparatory Commission for the International Criminal Court', in Politi and Nesi, note 1 *supra*, at 46.

Moreover, aggression is prohibited by international law rules as a conduct of a state in relation to another state. In other words, only states can commit aggression and violate those rules. This original feature does not help much in cases in which an act is perpetrated by 'other entities', like those frequently appearing nowadays in international relations (armed organizations fighting in conflicts of non-international character, terrorist groups etc.).[6]

A first point to be underlined is therefore that we cannot talk about a 'crime of aggression' without having preliminarily established that there has been an 'act of aggression'.

This is the logical and necessary link between the Rome Statute and the UN Charter. The first deals with crimes, from the perspective of establishing individual criminal responsibility under international law. The second addresses state behaviour, from the perspective of the obligation of states to respect the general prohibition to use force against another state.

According to Article 2(5) of the Rome Statute:

> the Court shall exercise jurisdiction over the crime of aggression once a provision is adopted in accordance with Articles 121 and 123 defining the crime and setting out the conditions under which the Court shall exercise jurisdiction with respect to this crime. Such a provision shall be consistent with the relevant provisions of the Charter of the UN.

B. Historical Bases for a Definition

The United Nations Charter does not offer a definition of aggression, which is left in the heading of Chapter VII together with threats to peace and breaches of peace, which are undefined as well. The issue of a possible definition of aggression had already been dealt with in the period between the two World Wars, and had given origin to lengthy and unfruitful debates.

An attempt had been made in the Versailles Treaty, where in Article 227 '[t]he Allied and Associated Powers publicly arraign William II of Hohenzollern, formerly German Emperor, for a supreme offence against international morality and the sanctity of treaties'. It was a 'purely declaratory' statement, as the Treaty was expected to deal with rights and obligations of states, and at that time it was impossible to use terms such as 'aggression' because war was not considered to be against international law.[7] Moreover, the definitions are weak since they mention concepts which do not belong to international law, like 'morality' and 'sanctity'. The same Versailles Treaty, in Article 231, established Germany's responsibility 'for causing all the loss and damage to which the Allied and Associated Governments and their nationals have been subjected as a consequence of the war imposed upon them by the aggression of Germany and her allies'. This last is a very delicate issue. Heavy war reparations are devastating for a country which has lost a war, and may appear scarcely compatible with the respect of human rights of the civilian population.

This leads to the crucial issue of a possible state responsibility for international crimes. In the 1996 ILC Draft Code of Crimes Against the Peace and Security of Mankind, a reference can be found under Article 16 to the fact that the crime of aggression must be committed by a state. It is a peculiar element, since the Draft Code is supposed to deal with individual responsibility, which is done 'without prejudice to any question of responsibility of states under international law' (Article 4). Can a state be subject to criminal sanctions as such? The answer is yes, provided that we

6 E. Greppi, 'Terrorism and Rogue States. Some Reflections on International Law Issues', *La Comunità Internazionale* (2005), at 231.

7 W.A. Schabas, 'Origins of the Criminalization of Aggression: How Crimes Against Peace Became the "Supreme International Crime"', in Politi and Nesi, note 1 *supra*, at 21.

consider as penal sanctions measures which are diplomatic, economic or military. Attempts in this direction were made in the 1920s, but today they would possibly be considered inconsistent with the contemporary concern for human rights protection since this kind of sanction would be mainly imposed on human beings, in a sort of 'collective punishment'.[8]

Having left the Treaty of Versailles' first attempt aside, the real starting point of the efforts to define aggression was the one consisting of the adoption of the London Charter of 1945, followed by Control Council Law No. 10. In both these texts, the wording is 'war of aggression', together with 'acts of aggressive war'. One first remark is then that 'aggression' gives origin to international state responsibility, whereas 'war of aggression' is a concept which leads to the category of international crimes and, in particular, to those 'against peace' (as they were indicated in the Nüremberg Charter).

The Nüremberg Tribunal (IMT) described the Nuremberg Charter as an expression of existing international law rather than an arbitrary exercise of power by the victorious nations. The Tribunal considered the law of the Charter to be decisive and binding upon it. As far as 'crimes against peace' are concerned, the IMT mainly referred to the Briand-Kellogg Pact, which implied renunciation of war. The weakest link was the one between the illegality of war (for violation of the Briand-Kellogg Pact) and its criminalization (which was not that sure at the time): 'to initiate a war of aggression, therefore, is not only an international crime; it is the supreme international crime differing from the other war crimes in that it contains within itself the accumulated evil of the whole.'[9] We may conclude that in 1945, individual responsibility for an aggressive war was not declaratory of pre-existing customary international law, but rather innovative. Today, we have no more doubts since the existing positive international law reflects the Nüremberg Judgement.[10]

On the issue of the 'war of aggression', in response to arguments made by the prosecution and the defence, the Nüremberg Tribunal considered whether aggressive war had been a crime before the adoption of the Nüremberg Charter. The Tribunal concluded that war as an instrument of national policy was already a crime based on the 1928 General Treaty for the Renunciation of War (the Briand-Kellogg Pact):

> ... the solemn renunciation of war as an instrument of national policy necessarily involves the proposition that such a war is illegal in international law; and that those who plan and wage such a war, with its inevitable and terrible consequences, are committing a crime in so doing. War for the solution of international controversies undertaken as an instrument of national policy certainly includes a war of aggression, and such a war is therefore outlawed by the Pact.[11]

The Nüremberg Tribunal considered the following earlier solemn expressions of opinion in support of this interpretation, and based its judgement on the distinction between acts of aggression and aggressive wars:

(a) Article I of the 1923 draft Treaty of Mutual Assistance sponsored by the League of Nations, which declared that 'aggressive war is an international crime';

8 Y. Dinstein, *supra* note 2, at 111.

9 IMT, Judgement, 186. See also Lord Wright, 'War Crimes under International Law', *LQR*, 1946, at 47.

10 Y. Dinstein, *supra* note 2, at 121.

11 *Trial of the Major War Criminals Before the International Military Tribunal*, Nüremberg, 14 November 1945–1 October 1946, Volume 1, Official Documents (Nüremberg, 1947), at 220. Also available at http://www.loc.gov/rr/frd/Military_Law/NT_major-war-criminals.html (visited 20 August 2009) .

(b) the preamble to the 1924 League of Nations Protocol for the Pacific Settlement of International Disputes (unanimously recommended to members by the League of Nations Assembly but never ratified), which declared that 'a war of aggression ... is an international crime';
(c) the preamble to the 1927 declaration unanimously adopted by the League of Nations Assembly stating that 'a war of aggression can never serve as a means of settling international disputes, and is in consequence an international crime';
(d) the resolution adopted unanimously by 21 nations at the Pan-American Conference in 1928, declaring that 'war of aggression constitutes an international crime against the human species'.

The Nüremberg Tribunal then turned to the charges of acts of aggression against Austria and Czechoslovakia and acts of aggressive war against Poland; Denmark and Norway; Belgium, the Netherlands and Luxembourg; Yugoslavia and Greece; the Soviet Union; and the United States.[12]

Aggression – war of aggression: let us turn again on this alternative. Of course, one of the key questions is linked to the determination of what is 'war'. In the first place, we cannot consider any form of 'use of force' by a state as a 'war'. In other words, not all kinds of 'use of force' prohibited by Article 2, paragraph 4 of the UN Charter fall within the scope of the definition of war. A border skirmish or the exchange of fire between patrols on the riverside is not a war. The final decision at the San Francisco Conference was therefore to leave to the Security Council to decide, on a case by case basis.

C. The 1974 General Assembly Definition of Aggression

On 14 December 1974, the UN General Assembly adopted by consensus Resolution 3314 (XXIX) on the definition of aggression. It is a rather short text – 10 Articles with a long and detailed Preamble – the main feature of which is that it provides guidance, but does not interfere with the Security Council power and responsibility to determine under Article 39 whether each single situation might amount to acts of aggression. A short text with a long Preamble: this is typical of matters which are and remain controversial. The Preamble reflects radical opposition to the adoption of really shared definitions and concepts.

In addition, the Assembly adopted a number of resolutions concerning acts of aggression in situations involving Korea, Namibia, South Africa, the Middle East and Bosnia and Herzegovina. In some instances, the General Assembly declared that a particular conduct of a state constituted an act of aggression in terms of the Definition of Aggression.

Article 1 defines aggression as 'the use of armed forces by a state against the sovereignty, territorial integrity or political independence of another state, or in any other manner inconsistent with the Charter'. The General Assembly had also previously considered 'that armed intervention

---

12 *Trials of the Major War Criminals before the International Military Tribunal*, *supra* note 11, at 192–216. The Tribunal also observed: '*Mein Kampf* was no mere private diary in which the secret thoughts of Hitler were set down ... *Mein Kampf* is not to be regarded as a mere literary exercise, nor as an inflexible policy or plan incapable of modification. Its importance lies in the unmistakable attitude of aggression revealed throughout its pages.' Ibid., at 188

is synonymous with aggression'[13] and recognized that a war of aggression constituted a crime against peace.[14]

The Article 1 definition does not entirely reflect Article 2, para. 2 of the UN Charter. It excludes the simple threat of force; therefore force must be actual; force must be 'armed'; sovereignty is mentioned with territorial integrity and political independence; use of force is forbidden when inconsistent with the whole of the Charter and not only with its purposes.

Article 5 paragraph 2 of the Declaration distinguishes between aggression – which gives 'rise to international responsibility' – and 'war of aggression', which is a crime against international peace. This main distinction underlines that not every 'act of aggression' constitutes a crime against peace, but only a 'war of aggression' does.[15] This, of course, does not mean that to the state the rules on state responsibility do not apply.

Serious violations of the UN Charter prohibition to use force may still constitute an act of aggression 'short of war', and this is a relevant step forward from the 1945 London Charter and the 1974 Declaration. This step should be evaluated with regard to state practice.

Article 2 provides that the first use of armed force by a state in contravention of the Charter constitutes *prima facie* evidence of an act of aggression. However, the Security Council may conclude that the act does not constitute aggression based on other relevant circumstances, including the insufficient gravity of the act or its consequences; 'other relevant circumstances' leaves a certain margin to interpretation.

Article 3 sets forth a list of acts which, regardless of a declaration of war, qualify as an act of aggression subject to Article 2:

> (a) the invasion or attack by the armed forces of a State of the territory of another State, or any military occupation, however temporary, resulting from such invasion or attack, or any annexation by the use of force of the territory of another State or part thereof;
> (b) bombardment by the armed forces of a State against the territory of another State or the use of any weapons by a State against the territory of another State;
> (c) the blockade of the ports or coasts of a State by the armed forces of another State;
> (d) an attack by the armed forces of a State on the land, sea or air forces, or marine and air fleets of another State;
> (e) the use of armed forces of one State which are within the territory of another State with the agreement of the receiving State, in contravention of the conditions provided for in the agreement or any extension of their presence in such territory beyond the termination of the agreement;
> (f) the action of a State in allowing its territory, which it has placed at the disposal of another State, to be used by that other State for perpetrating an act of aggression against a third State;
> (g) the sending by or on behalf of a State of armed bands, groups, irregulars or mercenaries, which carry out acts of armed force against another State of such gravity as to amount to the acts listed above, or its substantial involvement therein.

13 Declaration on the Inadmissibility of Intervention in the Domestic Affairs of States and the Protection of Their Independence and Sovereignty, GA Res. 2131 (XX), 21 December 1965, at PP 7, adopted by a vote of 109 to none, with one abstention.

14 Declaration on Principles of International Law concerning Friendly Relations and Cooperation among States in accordance with the Charter of the United Nations, GA Res. 2625 (XXV), 24 October 1970, adopted without a vote.

15 Y. Dinstein, *supra* note 2, at 125.

Article 4 explicitly recognizes the non-exhaustive nature of this list, as well as the possibility for the Security Council to determine that other acts constitute aggression under the Charter.

Article 5, paragraph 1, provides that no consideration of whatever nature, whether political, economic, military or otherwise, may justify aggression, that is that even a good reason does not exclude illegality of the act.

In the field of definitions, the one adopted by the 1974 General Assembly Declaration is recognized and quoted as the 'authoritative and generally agreed upon definition of aggression',[16] even if – being a Declaration of Principles – it belongs to the broad category of Recommendations, that is non-binding legal acts. The General Assembly (GA) definition is 'the most widely (albeit not universally) recognised'.[17]

As already underlined, the real objective of the Resolution was to propose a definition which could be useful to the Security Council in its delicate and crucial function of determining if and when a certain situation can be qualified as an aggression by a state on another state. In practice, the definition was not much used by the Security Council.

In recent times, after the outbreak of the first Gulf War, the Security Council in its Resolution 674 (1990) reminded Iraq that 'under international law it is liable for any loss, damage or injury arising in regard to Kuwait and third states, and their nationals and corporations, as the result of the invasion and illegal occupation of Kuwait by Iraq'. Also, Resolution 687 (1991), which established the terms of the ceasefire, reiterated Iraq's liability under international law. As we can see, while the Versailles Treaty had made an explicit reference to German 'aggression', in the case of Iraq the Security Council only referred to 'invasion and illegal occupation', carefully avoiding qualifying this invasion as an aggression.

As far as state responsibility is concerned, the International Law Commission has established that the responsible state 'is under an obligation to make full reparation for the injury caused by the internationally wrongful act'.[18]

One last point is that of consent, which has sometimes been presented as a cause of justification. It offers examples of abuses, such as in the cases of Hungary (Soviet invasion, 1956) and of Afghanistan (Soviet intervention, 1979), or of Panama (US intervention, 1989). Alleged consent or invitation is to be carefully analysed, particularly when it comes from a puppet government.

2. The Role of the Security Council

The UN Charter gave the Security Council (SC) the primary responsibility for the maintenance of international peace and security and, for this purpose, the SC is called to determine the existence of a threat to the peace, breach of the peace or act of aggression (Article 39 UN Charter), and authorized to make recommendations or decide what measures shall be taken to maintain or restore international peace and security (Articles 41 and 42).

---

16 M.A. Shukri, 'Will Aggressors Ever be Tried Before the ICC?' in Politi and Nesi, *supra* note 1; M.M. Gomaa, 'The Definition of the Crime of Aggression and the ICC Jurisdiction over that Crime', 67, in Politi and Nesi, *supra* note 1.

17 Y. Dinstein, *supra* note 2, at 126.

18 Art. 31(1) Draft Articles on the 'Responsibility of States for Internationally Wrongful Acts', adopted by ILC at its 53rd session, and appearing as Annex to GA Res. 56/83, 12 December 2001 and A/56/49 (Vol.1)/Corr. 4. Available at http://untreaty.un.org/ilc/texts/instruments/english/draft%20articles/9_6_2001.pdf (visited 9 February 2009).

Aggression is one of the three 'pre-conditions' for the Security Council to be entitled to use its powers under Chapter VII of the UN Charter.[19] But this does not necessarily mean exclusiveness, which is the exclusive power to take the delicate decision on the existence of aggression, as exclusiveness may be in contrast with the principle of sovereign equality (Article 2, para. 1 UN Charter). Permanent Members have a veto right, which places them apart from all other Members. Exclusive determination would grant Permanent Members immunity, and in the long run would allow them to block legal proceedings against their political and military leaders, in serious violation of the principle of sovereign equality.[20]

Moreover, exclusiveness would give the Security Council a kind of judicial role, which would not be compatible with its political functions. Long practice shows that the Security Council evaluation has always been made according to political parameters, far away from legal and judicial ones. So the Council, as we will see, used the word aggression in cases regarding South Africa and Rhodesia and Israel, and not in the Iraq/Kuwait case, the most evident situation of an aggression in the last 50 years. Therefore, an Israel attack against the PLO headquarters in Tunis (1985) with 67 victims, and the 1988 attack with four victims, were condemned as aggression, whereas the invasion, occupation and pillage of Kuwait (which was even annexed to Iraq) was not qualified as an aggression. Last but not least, in cases affecting Permanent Members, the Security Council would permit states to be judges in their own case, in violation of a basic legal principle, with a veto power. In any event, states surely prefer to be called aggressors without important consequences (like Israel), rather than be accused of a breach of peace and have the Council impose sanctions on them (as in the Iraqi case).

In UN law and practice, the Security Council's exclusive power to determine aggression is only linked to that of adopting measures to suppress aggression, under Article 39 and the following under Chapter VII.

Another key element in our discussion is Article 51 and self-defence. This can be invoked when an 'armed attack occurs', until the Security Council 'has taken measures necessary to maintain international peace and security'. States are therefore allowed to determine whether an aggression has occurred, subject to review by the Security Council. Is the wording 'armed attack' in Article 51 to be considered equivalent to that of 'aggression' in Article 39?

This solution was the one adopted by the ICJ in the Nicaragua case,[21] and it seems consistent with the French text, in which 'armed attack' is *agression armée*. The Court equated armed attack with aggression in two parts of its judgement. In paragraph 195, it stated that the 'Definition of Aggression' in General Assembly Resolution 3314 'may be taken to reflect customary international law' on what constitutes an *armed attack*. Therefore, an armed attack includes 'the sending by or on behalf of a State of armed bands, groups, irregulars or mercenaries, which carry out acts of armed force of sufficient gravity against another State'. This sending amounts to an armed attack, the Court decided, because it is defined as *aggression* in General Assembly Resolution 3314. In paragraph 191, the Court referred to General Assembly Resolution 2625 (XXV),[22] and once again equated armed attack and aggression:

19 G. Gaja, *supra* note 1, at 123.

20 M.S. Stein, *supra* note 4, at 6.

21 ICJ, Judgment, *Military and Paramilitary Activities in and Against Nicaragua*, 27 June 1986. Available at http://www.icj-cij.org/docket/files/70/6503.pdf (visited 13 February 2009).

22 Declaration on Principles of International Law concerning Friendly Relations and Cooperation among States in accordance with the Charter of the United Nations, *supra* note 14.

> As regards certain particular aspects of the principle in question, it will be necessary to distinguish the most grave forms of the use of force (those constituting an armed attack) from other less grave forms. In determining the legal rule which applies to these latter forms, the Court can again draw on the formulations contained in the Declaration on Principles of International Law concerning Friendly Relations and Co-operation among States in accordance with the Charter of the United Nations. As already observed, the adoption by States of this text affords an indication of their *opinio juris* as to customary international law on the question. Alongside certain descriptions which may refer to aggression, this text includes others which refer only to less grave forms of the use of force.

As we can see, the terms -armed attack' and 'aggression' are used, interchangeably, to refer to more serious forms of the use of force, as opposed to less grave forms that do not constitute armed attack or aggression.[23] The same conclusions were reached both in the Oil Platform Case and in the *Armed Activities* case (Congo v. Uganda). In addition, in the Wall case the Court also underlined that 'armed attack' under Article 51 implies that the attack comes from another state.[24]

In this field of wording, there is a certain amount of confusion. The French *agression armée* looks similar to 'aggression'. 'Armed attack' of Article 51 is different from 'act of aggression' in Article 39, which is also different from 'crime of aggression' in the Rome Statute, which appears closer to the meaning of attack under Article 51 than to that of act of aggression under Article 39.[25] This appears also in the ICJ judgements.

The General Assembly is also concerned with the maintenance of international peace and security. Moreover, the paralysis of the Council caused by the lack of unanimity among the Permanent Members because of the abuse of the right to veto crucial and delicate decisions was at the very origin of Resolution *Uniting for Peace* in 1950.[26] Part A of the Resolution provides that if the Security Council fails to exercise its primary responsibility, the General Assembly shall consider the matter. In UN practice, this Resolution has been invoked in several cases, and allowed the convening of Emergency Special Sessions of the General Assembly, sometimes even at the initiative of the Security Council itself. A certain number of measures have been taken over time, and some recommendations have been adopted in the field of maintenance of peace and security.

The issue of primary responsibility was also addressed by the International Court of Justice, in particular in the case of *Certain Expenses of the United Nations*.[27] The ICJ observed that 'primary responsibility' does not necessarily mean 'exclusive responsibility'. The idea of 'primacy' has been conceived in order to ensure 'prompt and effective action', while exclusiveness applies only where measures which require coercive action against the aggressor are concerned. In other words, only the Security Council is entitled to trigger the power to make recommendations or decisions on a threat to international peace and security.

The Security Council and the ICJ are also entitled to perform their functions separately with respect to the same event. The Court ruled that 'the Council has functions of a political nature

---

23 M.S. Stein, *supra* note 4, at 21.

24 ICJ, Advisory Opinion, *Legal Consequences of the Construction of a Wall in the Occupied Palestinian Territory*, 9 July 2004, at 139. Available at http://www.icj-cij.org/docket/files/131/1671.pdf (visited 12 February 2009).

25 M.S. Stein, *supra* note 4, at 24.

26 GA Res. 377 (V) 3 November 1950. Available at http://daccessdds.un.org/doc/RESOLUTION (visited 5 February 2009).

27 ICJ, Advisory Opinion, *Certain Expenses of the United Nations*, 20 July 1962. Available at http://www.icj-cij.org/docket/files/49/5259.pdf (visited 5 February 2009).

assigned to it, whereas the Court exercises purely judicial functions'. Both organs can therefore perform their separate but complementary functions.

3. A Review of Cases. The Security Council

The Security Council addressed the issue of acts of aggression in a number of situations.[28]

A. Southern Rhodesia

The Security Council adopted several resolutions concerning Southern Rhodesia, condemning its various acts of aggression against other states, such as Angola, Botswana, Mozambique and Zambia.

In Resolution 326 (1973) the Security Council considered 'aggressive acts' against Zambia, and recalled its Resolution 232 (1966) determining that the situation in Southern Rhodesia constituted a threat to international peace and security; was convinced that 'the recent provocative and aggressive acts perpetrated by the illegal regime against Zambia' aggravated the situation; expressed deep shock and grief at 'the loss of human life and damage to property caused by the aggressive acts of the illegal regime in Southern Rhodesia and its collaborators against Zambia'.[29]

In its Resolutions 386 (1976) of 17 March 1976[30] and 411 (1977) of 30 June 1977, the Security Council considered acts of aggression committed by Southern Rhodesia against Mozambique. In Resolution 386 (1976), the Council condemned 'all provocative and aggressive acts, including military incursions, against the People's Republic of Mozambique by the illegal minority regime of Southern Rhodesia'. In Resolution 411 (1977) the Council expressed its indignation at 'the systematic acts of aggression', and found that the 'constant acts of aggression and threats against the sovereignty and territorial integrity' of Botswana and Zambia, aggravated the existing serious threat to the security and stability of the region; strongly condemned 'the illegal racist minority regime in Southern Rhodesia for its recent acts of aggression' against Mozambique.[31]

In its Resolution 424 (1978) of 17 March 1978,[32] the Security Council considered new acts of aggression committed by Southern Rhodesia against Zambia, including armed invasion, and expressed its grave concern at 'the numerous hostile and unprovoked acts of aggression by the illegal minority regime in Southern Rhodesia violating the sovereignty, airspace and territorial integrity of the Republic of Zambia'; strongly condemned 'the recent armed invasion perpetrated by the illegal racist minority regime in the British colony of Southern Rhodesia against the Republic of Zambia' in flagrant violation of its sovereignty and territorial integrity.

In its Resolution 445 (1979) of 8 March 1979,[33] the Security Council considered the armed invasion of Angola, Mozambique and Zambia perpetrated by Southern Rhodesia and expressed

---

28 The compilation *Historical Review of Developments Relating to Aggression*, Preparatory Commission for the International Criminal Court, Working Group on the Crime of Aggression, 24 January 2002, United Nations, PCNICC/2002/WGCA/L.I and Add. 1 is acknowledged to have provided an important contribution to the present work.

29 Resolution 326 (1973) was adopted by 13 votes to none, with two abstentions (UK and USA).

30 Resolution 386 (1976) was adopted unanimously.

31 Resolution 411 (1977) was adopted unanimously.

32 Resolution 424 (1978) was adopted unanimously.

33 Resolution 445 (1979) was adopted by 12 votes to none, with three abstentions (France, United Kingdom and United States).

its grave concern at 'the indiscriminate military operations undertaken by the illegal regime and the extension of its premeditated and provocative acts of aggression not only against neighbouring independent countries, but also against non-contiguous states, resulting in wanton killings of refugees and civilian populations'; reaffirmed that 'the existence of the illegal racist minority regime in Southern Rhodesia and the continuance of its acts of aggression against neighbouring independent states' constituted a threat to international peace and security; strongly condemned the recent armed invasions perpetrated by Southern Rhodesia against Angola, Mozambique and Zambia in flagrant violation of their sovereignty and territorial integrity.

In its Resolution 455 (1979) of 23 November 1979,[34] the Security Council considered further acts of aggression committed by Southern Rhodesia against Zambia, with the collusion of South Africa, and, again, expressed its grave concern at 'the numerous hostile and unprovoked acts of aggression committed by the illegal minority regime in Southern Rhodesia violating the sovereignty, airspace and territorial integrity of the Republic of Zambia'; strongly condemned Southern Rhodesia for the 'continued, intensified and unprovoked acts of aggression' against Zambia in flagrant violation of its sovereignty and territorial integrity.

B. South Africa

The Security Council adopted a number of resolutions condemning acts of aggression committed by South Africa against Angola, Botswana, Lesotho, Seychelles and other states in southern Africa.

From 1976 to 1987, the Security Council adopted several resolutions condemning acts of aggression committed by South Africa against Angola and the use by South Africa of the international Territory of Namibia to mount these aggressive acts. In its Resolution 387 (1976) of 31 March 1976,[35] the Council considered the armed invasion of Angola by South Africa and expressed its grave concern at the acts of aggression committed by South Africa against Angola in violation of its sovereignty and territorial integrity; and condemned South Africa's use of the international Territory of Namibia to mount that aggression.

Security Council Resolution 418 (1977), adopted unanimously on 4 November 1977, recognized that South Africa's military build-up and persistent acts of aggression against neighbouring states seriously disturbed their security; and strongly condemned South Africa for its attacks against neighbouring independent states; and Resolution 581 (1986), adopted unanimously on 13 February 1986,[36] strongly condemned South Africa for its threats to perpetrate acts of aggression against the front-line states and other states in southern Africa.

On 11 April 1980, the Council unanimously adopted Resolution 466 (1980) in which it did not refer to 'acts of aggression', but in paragraph 1 strongly condemned the racist regime of South Africa for 'its continued, intensified and unprovoked acts against the Republic of Zambia, which constitute a flagrant violation of the sovereignty and territorial integrity of Zambia'. It condemned South Africa's aggression against Angola.

In its Resolution 546 (1984) of 6 January 1984,[37] the Security Council considered the bombing and partial occupation of Angola by South Africa and expressed its grave concern at 'the renewed escalation of unprovoked bombing and persistent acts of aggression, including the military

34 Resolution 455 (1979) was adopted by consensus.

35 Resolution 387 (1976) was adopted by nine votes to none, with five abstentions (France, Italy, Japan, United Kingdom and United States), with one member not participating in the vote (China).

36 Adopted by 13 votes to none, with two abstentions (United Kingdom and United States).

37 Resolution 546 (1984) was adopted by 13 votes to none, with two abstentions (United Kingdom and United States).

occupation, committed by the racist regime of South Africa in violation of the sovereignty, airspace and territorial integrity of Angola'.

In its Resolution 571 (1985) of 20 September 1985,[38] the Security Council considered the renewed escalation of acts of aggression by South Africa against Angola, which formed a consistent and sustained pattern of violations, and expressed its grave concern at 'the further renewed escalation of hostile, unprovoked and persistent acts of aggression and sustained armed invasions' committed by South Africa in violation of the sovereignty, airspace and territorial integrity of Angola; and further expressed its grave concern that 'these wanton acts of aggression by South Africa form a consistent and sustained pattern of violations'.

In its Resolution 568 (1985) of 21 June 1985,[39] the Security Council considered the premeditated acts of aggression committed by South Africa against Botswana, including the military attack on its capital, and strongly condemned South Africa's aggression against Angola; expressed its grave concern that such acts of aggression could only aggravate the already volatile and dangerous situation in southern Africa; strongly condemned 'South Africa's recent unprovoked and unwarranted military attack on the capital of Botswana as an act of aggression against that country and a gross violation of its territorial integrity and national sovereignty'; and further condemned 'all acts of aggression, provocation and harassment, including murder, blackmail, kidnapping and destruction of property committed by the racist regime of South Africa against Botswana'.

In its Resolution 572 (1985) of 30 September 1985,[40] the Security Council, in paragraph 4, demanded that 'South Africa pay full and adequate compensation to Botswana for the loss of life and damage to property resulting from its act of aggression'.

In its Resolution 527 (1982) of 15 December 1982,[41] the Security Council, after condemning South Africa 'for its premeditated aggressive act against the Kingdom of Lesotho which constitut[ed] a flagrant violation of the sovereignty and territorial integrity of that country', demanded 'the payment by South Africa of full and adequate compensation to the Kingdom of Lesotho for the damage to life and property resulting from this aggressive act'. It also called upon South Africa to declare publicly that 'it will, in the future, comply with provisions of the Charter and that it will not commit aggressive acts against Lesotho either directly or through its proxies'; and demanded 'the payment by South Africa of full and adequate compensation to the Kingdom of Lesotho for the damage and loss of life resulting from this act of aggression'.

By its Resolution 496 (1981) of 15 December 1981,[42] the Security Council condemned the 'mercenary aggression [of 25 November 1981] against the Republic of Seychelles and the subsequent hijacking'. The Council adopted Resolution 507 (1982) of 28 May 1982,[43] in which it strongly condemned the mercenary aggression against Seychelles and commended Seychelles for successfully repulsing the mercenary aggression and defending its territorial integrity and independence.

38 Resolution 571 (1985) was adopted unanimously.
39 Resolution 568 (1985) was adopted unanimously.
40 Resolution 572 (1985) was adopted unanimously.
41 Resolution 527 (1982) was adopted unanimously.
42 Resolution 496 (1981) was adopted unanimously.
43 Resolution 507 (1982) was adopted unanimously.

C. Benin

In 1977, Benin was attacked by an invading force of mercenaries. In its Resolution 405 (1977) adopted on 14 April 1977,[44] the Security Council condemned the attack as an act of aggression. It strongly condemned 'the act of armed aggression perpetrated against the People's Republic of Benin on 16 January 1977'.

D. Tunisia

The Security Council on two separate occasions condemned attacks committed by Israel against Tunisia and characterized these attacks as unlawful acts of aggression.

In its Resolution 573 (1985) of 4 October 1985,[45] the Security Council considered the air raid perpetrated by Israel against Tunisia. It drew attention to the serious effect which 'the aggression carried out by Israel' could not but have on any Middle East peace initiative; and condemned 'vigorously the act of armed aggression perpetrated by Israel against Tunisian territory in flagrant violation of the Charter of the United Nations, international law and norms of conduct'.

In its Resolution 611 (1988) of 25 April 1988,[46] the Security Council considered the 'new act of aggression' committed by Israel against Tunisia and expressed grave concern regarding 'the act of aggression which constitutes a serious and renewed threat to peace, security and stability in the Mediterranean region'; and condemned 'vigorously the aggression perpetrated on 16 April 1988 against the sovereignty and territorial integrity of Tunisia in flagrant violation of the Charter of the United Nations, international law and norms of conduct'.

E. Falkland Islands

In Resolution 502 (1982) of April 3 1982, the Security Council was 'deeply disturbed' at reports of an invasion on April 2 1982 by armed forces of Argentina, and demanded 'an immediate cessation of hostilities', after having determined that it was a 'breach of the peace' in the region of the Falkland Islands'.

F. Iraq

Following the invasion of Kuwait on 2 August 1990 by the military forces of Iraq, the Security Council, acting under Articles 39 and 40 of the Charter, adopted Resolution 660 (1990),[47] in which it condemned 'the Iraq invasion of Kuwait'. In a number of subsequent resolutions, the Council, while condemning the 'invasion' and illegal 'occupation' of Kuwait by Iraq, did not use the term 'aggression' or 'act of aggression'.

In its Resolution 667 (1990) of 16 September 1990,[48] the Security Council strongly condemned 'aggressive acts perpetrated by Iraq against diplomatic premises and personnel in Kuwait, including the abduction of foreign nationals who were present in those premises'.

---

44 Resolution 405 (1977) was adopted by consensus.

45 Resolution 573 (1985) was adopted by 14 votes to none, with one abstention (the United States).

46 Resolution 611 (1988) was adopted by 14 votes to none, with one abstention (the United States).

47 Resolution 660 (1990) was adopted by 14 to none. One member (Yemen) did not participate in the vote.

48 Resolution 667 (1990) was adopted unanimously.

4. A Review of Cases. The General Assembly

The General Assembly, in accordance with Article 11 of the Charter, may discuss any questions relating to the maintenance of international peace and security brought before it by a Member State, the Security Council or a non-Member State. Some cases can be found in General Assembly practice.[49]

A. Korea

In its Resolution 498 (V), adopted on 1 February 1951, the General Assembly considered the intervention of China in Korea and concluded that China had engaged in aggression. The General Assembly: (a) noted that 'the Security Council, because of lack of unanimity of the permanent members, has failed to exercise its primary responsibility for the maintenance of international peace and security in regard to Chinese Communist intervention in Korea'; and (b) found that China, 'by giving direct aid and assistance to those who were already committing aggression in Korea and by engaging in hostilities against United Nations forces there, has itself engaged in aggression in Korea'.

B. Namibia

From the 1960s through the 1980s, the General Assembly adopted a series of resolutions condemning South Africa for its occupation of Namibia as an act of aggression, and its use of the international Territory of Namibia to commit aggression against independent African States. In 1963, the Assembly adopted Resolution 1899 (XVIII) on South West Africa, by which it considered that 'any attempt to annex a part or the whole of the Territory of South West Africa constitutes an act of aggression'. In Resolution S-9/2, adopted on 3 May 1978, the Assembly: (a) reiterated that 'South Africa's illegal occupation of Namibia constitutes a continued act of aggression against the Namibian people and against the United Nations'; and (b) stated that the 'aggressive policies of the South African occupation regime in Namibia are further reflected in its repeated acts of aggression against, military incursions into, and violations of the territorial integrity of the neighbouring states, in particular Angola and Zambia, causing considerable loss of life and damage to property'.

The General Assembly later declared that South Africa's illegal occupation of Namibia constituted an act of aggression in terms of the Definition of Aggression. In a number of resolutions, the General Assembly: (a) strongly reiterated that South Africa's continuing illegal and colonial occupation of Namibia, in defiance of repeated General Assembly and Security Council resolutions, constituted an act of aggression against the Namibian people and a challenge to the authority of the United Nations, which had direct responsibility for Namibia until independence; (b) declared that South Africa's illegal occupation of Namibia constituted an act of aggression against the Namibian people in terms of the Definition of Aggression; (c) strongly condemned South Africa for its use of the illegally occupied international Territory of Namibia as a staging ground for launching continuing armed attacks or as a spring board for perpetrating armed invasions, subversion, destabilization and aggression against independent African States, which had caused extensive loss of human life and destruction of economic infrastructures; (d) specifically denounced South Africa for its acts of aggression against Angola, Botswana, Mozambique, Zambia and Zimbabwe; (e) strongly condemned South Africa for its persistent and repeated unprovoked acts of aggression

49 See *Historical Review of Developments Relating to Aggression*, *supra* note 28.

against and invasion of Angola, including the continued occupation of part of its territory in gross violation of its sovereignty and territorial integrity.

C. South Africa

From the 1960s through the 1980s, the General Assembly adopted several resolutions condemning South Africa for its repeated acts of aggression against other African States. The Assembly in 1962 warned South Africa that any attempt 'to annex or encroach upon the territorial integrity of [Basutoland, Bechuanaland and Swaziland] shall be considered an act of aggression'.[50]

The General Assembly condemned: (a) South Africa's 1969 armed intervention in Southern Rhodesia as constituting an act of aggression; (b) its continuing acts of aggression, particularly its raid on Matola, Mozambique, in January 1981, its large-scale invasion of Angola since July 1981 and its invasion of Seychelles in November 1981; (c) its acts of military aggression against Angola, Botswana, Lesotho, Mozambique, Seychelles, Swaziland, Zambia and Zimbabwe, as well as its activities to recruit, train, finance and arm mercenaries for aggression against neighbouring states; (d) its continued occupation of parts of the territory of Angola, its acts of armed aggression against Lesotho, as well as its acts of aggression against Mozambique.

D. The Middle East

In 1947, the General Assembly adopted Resolution 181 (II) on the future government of Palestine, in which it requested the Security Council to take certain measures, including determining, 'as a threat to the peace, breach of the peace or act of aggression, in accordance with Article 39 of the Charter, any attempt to alter by force the settlement envisaged by this resolution'. In Resolution 3414 (XXX) of 1975, the Assembly indicated that it was guided by the purposes and principles of the Charter which considered 'any military occupation, however temporary, or any forcible annexation of such territory, or part thereof, as an act of aggression'.

In its Resolution 36/27, adopted on 13 November 1981, the General Assembly considered the Israeli attack against the Iraqi nuclear installations and (a) expressed 'its deep alarm over the unprecedented Israeli act of aggression against the Iraqi nuclear installations on 7 June 1981, which created a grave threat to international peace and security'; (b) strongly condemned 'Israel for its premeditated and unprecedented act of aggression in violation of the Charter of the United Nations and the norms of international conduct, which constitutes a new and dangerous escalation in the threat to international peace and security'; (c) issued 'a solemn warning to Israel to cease its threats and the commission of such armed attacks against nuclear facilities'. In paragraph 6 of the same Resolution, the General Assembly demanded that Israel, 'in view of its international responsibility for its act of aggression, pay prompt and adequate compensation for the material damage and loss of life suffered as a result of that act'. In its Resolution 37/18, adopted on 16 November 1982, the General Assembly further considered the attack on the Iraqi nuclear installations, and (a) expressed grave alarm at the dangerous escalation of Israel's acts of aggression in the region; and (b) strongly condemned 'Israel for the escalation of acts of aggression in the region'.

In 1981 and 1982, with regard to the situation in Lebanon,[51] the General Assembly (a) strongly condemned 'the Israeli aggression against Lebanon and the continuous bombardment

---

50 GA Res. 1954 (XVIII), 11 December 1963.

51 General Assembly Resolution 36/226 A, 17 December 1981 General Assembly Resolution 37/3, 3 December 1982.

and destruction of its cities and villages, and all acts that constitute a violation of its sovereignty, independence; (b) expressed its deep shock and alarm at the 'deplorable consequences of the Israeli invasion of Beirut on 3 August 1982'; and (c) strongly condemned the Israeli aggression against Lebanon in June 1982.

In a series of resolutions with regard to the situation of Palestinian people, adopted from 1981 to 1990, the General Assembly condemned 'Israel's aggression and practices against the Palestinian people in the occupied Palestinian territories and outside these territories, particularly in the Palestinian refugee camps in Lebanon, including the expropriation and annexation of territory, the establishment of settlements, assassination attempts and other terrorist, aggressive and repressive measures, which are in violation of the Charter and the principles of international law and the pertinent international conventions'.

The resolutions adopted at the 37th to 39th sessions referred particularly to Palestinians in Lebanon; subsequent resolutions contained no such reference. The resolutions adopted from the 38th to 46th sessions refer to Israel's '*aggression*, policies and practices'.

In 1982, the Security Council, taking into account its inability to exercise its primary responsibility for the maintenance of international peace and security because of the lack of unanimity of its Permanent Members, decided to call an emergency special session of the General Assembly to consider Israel's actions with respect to the Golan Heights. At its ninth emergency special session and subsequent sessions held from 1982 to 1990, the General Assembly considered Israel's occupation of the Golan Heights and (a) recalled Article 3, subparagraph (a), and Article 5, paragraph 1, of the Definition of Aggression; and (b) declared that Israel's continued occupation of the Golan Heights and its decision of 14 December 1981 to impose its laws, jurisdiction and administration on the occupied Syrian Golan Heights constituted an act of aggression under Article 39 of the Charter of the United Nations and the Definition of Aggression. In the resolutions adopted from the 38th to the 45th sessions, the Assembly declared that Israel's continued occupation of the Syrian Golan Heights (as well as its decision of 14 December 1981 to apply Israeli law to this occupied territory) constituted an act of aggression under Article 39 of the Charter and the Definition of Aggression, and similarly resolutions adopted from the 42nd to the 45th session deplored the aggression against the same territory.

E. Bosnia and Herzegovina

In its Resolutions 46/242 of 25 August 1992, and 47/121 of 18 December 1992, the General Assembly considered the situation in Bosnia and Herzegovina. The Assembly (a) deplored 'the grave situation in Bosnia and Herzegovina and the serious deterioration of the living conditions of the people there, especially the Muslim and Croat populations, arising from the aggression against the territory of the Republic of Bosnia and Herzegovina, which constitutes a threat to international peace and security'; (b) demanded that all forms of outside interference cease immediately and that the Yugoslav People's Army units and the Croatian Army be withdrawn, subjected to the authority of the Government of Bosnia and Herzegovina or disbanded and disarmed with their weapons placed under effective international monitoring; (c) condemned the violation of the sovereignty, territorial integrity and political independence of Bosnia and Herzegovina; and (d) demanded that Serbia and Montenegro and Serbian forces in Bosnia and Herzegovina immediately cease their aggressive acts and hostility and comply fully and unconditionally with the relevant resolutions of the Security Council.

F. Afghanistan

In Resolution ES-6/2, of 14 January 1980, the General Assembly reaffirmed that respect for the sovereignty, territorial integrity and political independence of every state is a fundamental principle of the Charter, and strongly deplored 'the recent armed intervention in Afghanistan, which is inconsistent with that principle'.

5. A Review of Cases. The International Court of Justice

The Court considered issues relating to aggression in three contexts, in relation to: (a) the functions of the principal organs of the United Nations; (b) requests for provisional measures to prevent alleged acts of aggression from exacerbating the situation giving rise to the legal dispute referred to the Court; and (c) a legal dispute involving an alleged unlawful use of force or act of aggression committed by a state which is the subject of a case referred to the Court. A few cases offered the Court the opportunity to address general issues on aggression.[52]

A. The Advisory Opinion on Certain Expenses of the United Nations

With regard to *Certain Expenses of the United Nations*, in an advisory opinion, the International Court of Justice (ICJ) considered the respective functions of the General Assembly and the Security Council under the Charter, particularly with respect to the maintenance of international peace and security. The Court stated that the responsibility conferred on the Security Council by Article 24 of the Charter is 'primary not exclusive'. The Court further stated that 'the primary responsibility is conferred upon the Security Council, which is given a power to impose an explicit obligation of compliance if for example it issues an order or command to an aggressor under Chapter VII. It is only the Security Council which can require enforcement by coercive action against an aggressor'.

This last sentence says that when 'action' is necessary the General Assembly shall refer the question to the Security Council. The word 'action' must mean such action as is solely within the province of the Security Council. The action which is solely within the province of the Security Council is that which is indicated by the title of Chapter VII of the Charter, namely 'action with respect to threats to the peace, breaches of the peace, and acts of aggression'.

B. The Contentious Case of the US Diplomatic and Consular Staff in Tehran

In the *United States Diplomatic and Consular Staff in Tehran* case, the Court considered its functions in relation to those of the Security Council:

> The Charter accordingly does not confer *exclusive* responsibility upon the Security Council for the purpose. While in Article 12 there is a provision for a clear demarcation of functions between the General Assembly and the Security Council in respect of any dispute or situation, that the former should not make any recommendation with regard to that dispute or situation unless the Security Council so requires, there is no similar provision anywhere in the Charter with respect to

52 See *Historical Review of Developments Relating to Aggression*, *supra* note 28.

the Security Council and the Court. The Council has functions of a political nature assigned to it, whereas the Court exercises purely judicial functions. (pp. 434–435)

C. The Provisional Measures in the Cases Concerning the Frontier Dispute (Burkina Faso/Mali) and the Land Maritime Boundary (Cameroon/Nigeria)

In the *Case concerning the Frontier Dispute (Burkina Faso/Mali)*, the Chamber of the Court formed to deal with a dispute concerning the delimitation of the common frontier of Burkina Faso and Mali was requested by both parties to order provisional measures to address their respective claims of armed attack and occupation by armed forces. The Chamber noted: that the armed actions had taken place within or near the disputed area; that the resort to force was irreconcilable with the principle of the peaceful settlement of international disputes; and that the armed actions within the disputed territory could destroy relevant evidence. The Chamber ordered both parties to ensure that no action was taken that might aggravate or extend the border dispute or prejudice the right of the other party to compliance with the eventual judgement; and to refrain from any act likely to impede the gathering of evidence material to the case; to withdraw their armed forces; and to observe the ceasefire.

In the *Case concerning the Land and Maritime Boundary between Cameroon and Nigeria*, Cameroon filed an application with the Court requesting the determination of its boundary with Nigeria and alleging that Nigeria had contested the boundary in the form of aggression by its troops which had occupied Cameroonian territory. Cameroon subsequently requested the Court to order provisional measures to address new armed attacks by Nigerian forces in the disputed territory. The Court noted that the armed actions within the disputed territory could jeopardize relevant evidence and aggravate or extend the dispute. The Court also noted the letters from the President of the Security Council addressed to the parties calling upon them to respect the ceasefire agreement and to return their forces to their positions before the dispute was submitted to the Court. The Court ordered the parties: to ensure that no action was taken, particularly by their armed forces, which might prejudice the rights of the other party with respect to the eventual judgement or aggravate or extend the dispute; to observe the ceasefire agreement; to ensure that the presence of their armed forces did not extend beyond their positions before the latest armed actions; and to take all necessary steps to conserve relevant evidence within the disputed area.

D. Legal Disputes Concerning the Use of Force or Aggression (Nicaragua and Congo Cases)

In the *Military and Paramilitary Activities in and against Nicaragua* case, Nicaragua alleged that the United States had violated the prohibition of the threat or use of force under Article 2, paragraph 4, of the Charter and had breached its obligation under general and customary international law by violating the sovereignty of Nicaragua through armed attacks carried out by air, land and sea. The United States did not participate in the proceedings on the merits because in its view the Court did not have jurisdiction over the case. Nonetheless the Court considered the arguments advanced by the United States to justify its action, which required a determination of the content of the right of self-defence. Even though Nicaragua did not allege that the United States had committed aggression, the Court considered certain aspects of the Definition of Aggression when determining the more serious violations of the prohibition of the use of force which constituted an armed attack for purposes of the right of self-defence. The Court stated that as regards certain particular aspects of the principle prohibiting the use of force embodied in Article 2, paragraph 4, of the Charter, it would be necessary to distinguish the most grave forms of the use of force, 'those constituting an armed attack', from other less grave forms. In determining the legal rules which applied to the less grave forms of the use of force, the Court drew on the formulations contained in the Declaration on Principles of International Law concerning Friendly Relations and Cooperation among states,[53] whereby, in its view, states by adopting it afforded 'an indication of their *opinio juris* as to customary international law on the question'. The Court further stated that '[a]longside certain descriptions [in the Friendly Relations Declaration] which refer to aggression, this text includes others which refer only to less grave forms of the use of force'. Referring to the Definition of Aggression, the Court concluded that an armed attack included not only action by regular armed forces across an international border, but also the sending by a state of armed bands which carry out, against another state, acts of armed force of such gravity as to amount to an actual attack conducted by regular forces. The Court indicated that the description of such action contained in Article 3, paragraph (g), of the Definition of Aggression 'may be taken to reflect customary international law'. The Court also made the following observation:

> The Court sees no reason to deny that, in customary law, the prohibition of armed attacks may apply to the sending by a State of armed bands to the territory of another State, if such an operation, because of its scale and effects, would have been classified as an armed attack rather than as a mere frontier incident had it been carried out by regular armed forces. But the Court does not believe that the concept of "armed attack" includes not only acts by armed bands where such acts occur on a significant scale but also assistance to rebels in the form of the provision of weapons or logistical or other support.

In the *Armed Activities on the Territory of the Congo* case, the Democratic Republic of the Congo alleged that Uganda had perpetrated acts of armed aggression on its territory within the meaning of Article 1 of the Definition of Aggression and contrary to Article 2, paragraph 4, of the Charter. The Democratic Republic of the Congo (DRC) asserted that Ugandan armed forces had conducted a surprise invasion, committed armed attacks and occupied the territory of the Congo. The Congo included an illustrative list of incidents to provide 'evidence of a deliberate policy operated by the Ugandan Government against the Democratic Republic of the Congo' and 'to demonstrate, moreover, the extent of the responsibility incurred by the leaders of the countries perpetrating the aggression'. The Congo considered the armed aggression by Uganda to be 'an established reality, since the Ugandan Government, having long denied the presence of its forces, is now imposing conditions for their withdrawal'. The Congo also asserted that '[t]his aggression was in reality the result of a clearly established common intent, formed in close collaboration with foreign powers, who provided the necessary financial backing and a large degree of logistic support'. Uganda challenged the allegations of the Democratic Republic of the Congo. The Court held that Uganda had violated the sovereignty and territorial integrity of the DRC, that Uganda's actions constituted an interference in the internal affairs of the DRC, and that:

> The unlawful military intervention by Uganda was of such a magnitude and duration that the Court considers it to be a grave violation of the prohibition on the use of force expressed in Art. 2 para. 4 of the Charter (§ 165). By sixteen votes to one, the Court finds that the Republic of Uganda, by engaging in military activities against the Democratic Republic of Congo on the latter's territory, by occupying Ituri and by actively extending military, logistic, economic and financial support to

53 GA Res. 2625 (XXV), 24 October 1970.

irregular forces having operated on the territory of the DRC, violated the principle of non-use of force in international relations and the principle of non-intervention.

In their separate opinions, Judges Elaraby and Simma argued that the actions of Uganda should have been adjudicated to amount to unlawful armed aggression.

6. Conclusion

In those cases in which the Security Council is able to fulfil its mandate and to decide that a state has committed aggression, we would have 'an ideal scenario' as the International Criminal Court would be in a position to prosecute and punish individuals for their role in the launching of an aggression.[54] But what about all those cases in which this ideal scenario is not likely to appear? If an aggression takes place, but the Security Council – because it is paralysed by a veto (and sometimes more than one) – is in a position where it is impossible for it to qualify a state as an aggressor, then an alternative body or authority has to be identified.

One way is to go back to the *Uniting for Peace* Resolution of 1950, that is to convene an Emergency Session of the General Assembly and pass a recommendation. A second way for the ICC could be to ask the General Assembly to submit the question to the International Court of Justice in order to get a ruling. In other words, the Court would be asked to give an advisory opinion (that is a legal assessment) as an alternative to the decision of the political body, the Security Council. The limit of this option is that the General Assembly is a political body as well. Therefore, in the case that the Assembly refuses to request the opinion (or in the case that – although it is less likely to happen – the ICJ refuses to give an opinion), the ICC should not be prevented from starting the procedure. A third and last possibility would be to leave to the ICC itself to rule in absence of determination by the Security Council. This last solution would cause a sort of overlapping of judicial and political functions, which would in a remarkable way alter the original perspective which was centred on the role of a political body – the Security Council – with extended discretionary powers to determine, under Article 39, that an act of aggression has taken place.

A balanced solution would be to give the ICC a specific competence in the field of preliminary determinations on the state responsibility issue from a strictly legal perspective, and avoid entering the sphere of politics and political assessments and evaluations. In *Tadić*, the International Criminal Tribunal for the Former Yugoslavia made determinations on the nature of the conflict (international or internal)[55] and dealt with general rules on state responsibility.[56]

The International Court of Justice should be given an even more relevant role, and be called to determine, in an abstract and general way who – in a given case – would be responsible to evaluate the behaviour of a state in terms of aggression. In other words, the Court should be asked to evaluate whether the functions of the Security Council are exclusive or not, and whether it would be necessary to establish the existence of an act of aggression by the Security Council before the ICC starts a procedure of indictment for a (individual) crime of aggression. The ICJ is a purely judicial body, and it has long and consolidated experience in the field of the use of force

54 S.M. Yengejeh, Reflections on the Role of the Security Council in determining an Act of Aggression, in Politi and Nesi, *supra* note 1, at 126.

55 ICTY, Judgment, *Dusko Tadic*, Appeals Chamber, 15 July 1999, paras 83–87.

56 Ibid., para. 105.

by states. The ICC Assembly of State Parties could therefore ask the General Assembly to seek a general advisory opinion from the ICJ in order to determine what is most compatible with the UN Charter.[57]

57 M.S. Stein, *supra* note 4, at 36.

Chapter 24
Individual Responsibility for the Crime of Aggression

Muhammad Aziz Shukri

1. Introduction

The concept of responsibility introduces in all national or international legal systems guarantees for the respect of obligations and sanctions for violations and refusals to comply with such obligations. Therefore, provisions on responsibility contribute largely to the balance of concurring and competing interests within a legal system and are regarded as the cornerstone in the establishment and prosperity of the system itself. Rules of law would be sterile and ineffective if not complemented by responsibility.

International legal responsibility arises out of actions or omissions by a state or any person contrary to obligations established under international law by customs, treaties or general principles of law. That should be the only basis for the liability and punishment of individuals under international law.

Aggression is the mother of international crimes as most other international crimes are carried out during its commission and because of it: it is the crime which has, throughout centuries, cost humanity an outrageous number of victims, dead, wounded, or impaired, not to mention the difficulty to determine material losses. Between 1816 and 1980 the world witnessed 118 international wars and 106 civil wars, which have claimed the lives of millions of people and left millions of others wounded and impaired. Human casualties during WWI reached roughly 10 million people. During WWII the number of casualties skyrocketed, as 54 million people died, 90 million people were wounded and 28 million became impaired. In addition, the material losses incurred amounted to 1.4 billion dollars, a sum that in the 1940s would have been more than sufficient to end all aspects of poverty in the international community.[1]

These facts make it apparent why it is imperative to criminalize the conduct of aggression and ensure the punishment of perpetrators and instigators thereof. Achieving this goal requires a comprehensive and effective legal system, which accurately defines the crime and concept; underlines its elements, forms and aspects; distinguishes it from the use of force in lawful situations; regulates sanctions so that persons responsible for aggression are appropriately punished; and does not allow for incomplete solutions. The power-based inequality of states should not be matched with inconsistencies in their legal status because this runs against the basis, essence and purpose of the principle of legality. As fighting aggression was one of the earliest missions in the mandate of the United Nations, efforts for a definition of aggression[2] in this context have been carefully aimed at having international sanctions properly inflicted upon aggressors.

1 M. Shadoud, *International Political Relations* [in Arabic] (Damascus: University of Damascus, 1986), at 102.

2 The term aggression was already used in the early stages of international relations, long before the establishment of the League of Nations, in several defence alliance treaties in the nineteenth century, such as the 1815 secret treaty of the defensive alliance between Britain, France and Austria. However, at that time the use of the term aggression did not bear any legal meaning.

The definition of aggression would serve the primary purpose of establishing a clear legal standard to settle mutual allegations between states during their international disputes. The years following the establishment of the League of Nations revealed the dire need for such a definition since the lack of a clear definition was one of the main impediments to the work of the Security Council, limiting its ability to perform its functions in accordance with the provisions of the Charter. It is worth noting here that there was no international and jurisprudential agreement regarding the need for a definition of aggression. Some asserted the importance of reaching a definition of aggression while others opposed it, warning that any definition would have dire consequences and serious effects, particularly on the development of international relations. Proponents of a definition were themselves divided, following different approaches to reach a definition.

In one option, a general definition should have allowed the Security Council and other UN-affiliated bodies to define aggression based on a general norm, all the while giving those bodies the discretion to assess each case in the circumstances. Such an approach would have been appropriate to confront evolving future circumstances. Others favoured defining the act of aggression in a descriptive or restrictive manner: by enumerating or describing situations constituting the crime of aggression, the aim would have been to prevent any ambiguity, while both regulating the act and facilitating the authority's mission to repress it. A third opinion supported a mixed and guiding definition, trying to combine the first two approaches by including a general definition followed by a list of recurrent cases or situations, while adding a general sentence which would have allowed the inclusion of other situations of the same nature.

There were many attempts to reach a clear and consensus definition of aggression. The General Assembly of the United Nations (UNGA) reached an agreement for the required definition when it approved the recommendation of the Sixth Committee which included the resolution for the definition of aggression;[3] the adoption of GA Resolution 3314 on 14 December 1974 is regarded as an essential contribution to efforts to establish responsibility for the illegal use of force in international relations. However, such definition does not impose obligations on states nor does it remedy legal gaps in the Charter, and it is flawed and incomplete. For instance, it is limited to the illegality of armed aggression, while not addressing other forms of aggression,[4] and also fails to mention the individual responsibility of instigators' of acts of aggression. Such gaps have undoubtedly limited the effectiveness of the international legal system as a whole. Failure to include individual responsibility for the crime of aggression in the 1974 Resolution is also one of the major obstacles which hindered the inclusion of the crime of aggression in the subject matter jurisdiction of the International Criminal Court (ICC), as critics indicated that the crime of aggression was 'not ... defined under customary international law for purposes of individual criminal responsibility'.[5]

Resolution 3314 (1974) did not have any effect on the discretionary power that the Security Council enjoys in accordance with the provisions of the UN Charter since it does not limit Security Council's authority to determine the existence of an act of aggression, but is rather a guideline for the exercise of such authority.

Article 5(2) of the Resolution defines aggression, stipulating that 'a war of aggression is a crime against international peace liable for international responsibility'. This is the basis for an act of aggression to give rise to a double international responsibility: on the one hand, the aggressor

3 UNGA, 29th Session, UN Charter N.A/9890-14 December 1974.

4 J. Stone, *Legal Controls of International Conflicts* (Holmes Beach: Gaunt and Sons Inc., 1974), at 224.

5 D. Scheffer, US Ambassador at large for war crimes and head of the American delegation to the 1998 UN Diplomatic Conference on the establishment of the permanent International Criminal Court. Statement before the Foreign Relations Commission at the United States Congress, Washington, 23 July 1998. Available at http://www.iccnow.org/documents/USScheffer_Senate23July98.pdf (visited on 4 July 2009).

state is held accountable for its act and is liable to have international sanctions inflicted upon it, and for compensations for the damages the war of aggression has caused; on the other hand, natural persons, such as military commanders or political leaders who caused the commission of the act would be liable for criminal prosecution.

Prominent jurists assert that a double legal international responsibility arises out of the commission of serious international crimes. Some confirm that 'the responsibility of a state is not merely restricted to financial compensations or punishment-like compensations since the state and the persons who act on its behalf bear the criminal responsibility for serious violations of international law, namely mercilessness and diminishment of human life in such a way that these violations are considered criminal acts in the common sense of the term.'[6] They also maintain that preparing and launching a war of aggression is considered a criminal act.[7] Others refer to the same meaning by asserting that contemporary international law tends to set another standard for international responsibility: the state's obligation to compensate for the damage, as well as to prosecute the perpetrators of unlawful acts when such acts also amount to an international crime.[8]

Thus, individual international responsibility for the crime of aggression is not restricted to the aggressing state – which could be liable for sanctions and has an obligation to compensate the damages resulting from aggression – but it also includes natural persons such as military commanders or political leaders who conspire, plan and execute acts to trigger a war of aggression. Further, the seriousness of the crime of aggression and the suffering it causes to humanity and peace require that all measures should be taken to eradicate it, including the imposition of serious punishment on perpetrators.

2. Individual Criminal Responsibility for Aggression Prior to the Rome Statute

Individual responsibility for the crime of aggression arises when a person commits an act which threatens an interest or value protected under the relevant provisions of international law. Like any other legal rule, the individual responsibility for the crime of aggression has witnessed several stages of evolution before agreement was reached to establish it by consensus.[9]

Calls to prosecute instigators of crimes of aggression and to apply rules of individual responsibility for the punishment of their acts have been common in the wake of every war of aggression. However, while such responsibility has been implemented in some cases, in others it has been either disregarded or misapplied. If the Nüremberg and Tokyo trials held after WWII represent an important and crucial phase in the establishment and activation of this legal rule, it should be acknowledged that earlier international attempts were made to define individual criminal responsibility for the crime of aggression.

6 L.F.L.Oppenheim, *International Law*, Vol. 1 – Peace, 8th edn (London: Lauterpacht, Longmans, Green and Co., 1954), at 355.

7 Ibid., at 366.

8 G. Schwarzenberger, 'International Responsibility in the Time of War', *BYBIL*, Vol. 14, 1965, at 15.

9 B.B. Ferencz, *The Evolution of International Criminal Law* (Hamburg: S & F Foundation, 28 November 1999), at 1–2. Available at http://www.benferncz.org/hamburg.htm (visited 3 April 2009).

A. The Rules of Traditional International Law

1. Responsibility and Pardon

Under traditional international law, the general rule was to disregard individual criminal responsibility for 'acts of states'. Collective responsibility was the only effect attached to the violation of international obligations by a state, as the aggressed state resorted to act of revenge and war. In turn, the classic doctrine of sovereignty required that acts of states could not be governed by another state and, thus, the jurisdiction of a state could not cover the criminal or civil jurisdiction of another state. Under this regime, individual criminal responsibility for the crime of aggression did not exist or was not implemented in practice. As an aspect of national sovereignty, waging war was a political act and, therefore, war itself was regarded as a lawful choice, thus making inadmissible any international criminal punishment. Atrocities committed by enemy soldiers in occupied territories were allowed as states committed all types of acts of cruelty and violence, whether against soldiers or civilians, in order to achieve victory. Upon those who declared a war of aggression or committed acts of cruelty and violence against civilians, acts of retribution were the only possible punishment.

The prevailing rule pursuant to the rule of traditional international law was that peace treaties signed in the wake of wars had to include specific provisions on a general and mutual pardon for all harmful acts committed for political motives by combatants, members of their armed forces or nationals during the war, including causing a war, acts of violence, vandalism, murder and similar acts. Such clauses were included in most peace treaties signed under traditional international law.

2. The Napoleon Bonaparte Precedent

A historical study of international relations highlights the Napoleon Bonaparte precedent which may well – given that it entailed an individual criminal responsibility for the crime of aggression – represent the first sign of the emergence of the concept of crime against peace. When Napoleon returned from the island of Elba and marched on France, in the 13 March 1815 Declaration[10] at the Vienna Conference allied European countries stated that they would prosecute Napoleon for the blood he spilled, the damage he caused to the whole of Europe for the 14 years of wars he had waged: Napoleon would not benefit from the protection of the law as he appeared unwilling to live in peace. Since Napoleon was considered an enemy of the world and a cause of disturbance and annoyance, he should have been reprimanded in a general manner, i.e., he had to be punished for his crimes against the international community. Thus, the Union of States and Powers bestowed upon itself a higher power which spoke in the name of the law and public order to compel the one who triggered the unjust war – the enemy of peace and international security of the world – to make amends and atone for his sins.

After his defeat in Waterloo, on 18 June 1815, Napoleon was not prosecuted, neither was he tied up to a block of wood and shot dead as Prussia intended, nor hung as Britain demanded. The Allies settled for denying Napoleon his civil and social rights and imprisoning him without a trial. The British government took it upon itself to guard him, and to choose the place to deport and detain him – the island of Saint Helena – pursuant to an agreement signed on 2 August 1815.

---

10 Available at http://www.napoleon-series.org/research/government/diplomatic/c_declaration.html (visited 4 July 2009).

Although the states which convened in Vienna accused Napoleon of committing a crime against Europe and disturbing their peace, they did not try him under due process to inflict an individual criminal sanction. Instead, they resorted to the power of the victor to take revenge over the defeated, and deported him. In spite of that, the Napoleon precedent – although incomplete and not set in conformity with sound judicial and legal procedures – represents the first sign of the system of individual responsibility for the crime of aggression and deserves to be assessed according to the norms and practice applicable at that time. In this perspective, the Napoleon precedent – at a time when the principle of sovereignty ranked at the highest level of international and national law, calling for unchecked discretion of choices made by states and their leaders – meant that triggering a war and disturbing peace was a crime which called for accountability, punishment and prosecution of the leader of the aggressing state.

However, the Napoleon precedent did not affect international events and acts of war and aggression that the world witnessed in the following years, as throughout the nineteenth century states held on to the old usage to consider war an expression of sovereignty without any supervision, punishment or criminal prosecution to those who cause it, whether the instigator of war is in the end victorious or defeated. In the same manner, imposition of victor's power on the defeated was a practice the international community did not abandon in its approach to prosecutions and trials, even more than a century after the Napoleon precedent, on the occasion of the 1919 Treaty of Versailles and the Nüremberg and Tokyo trials.

B. The Lesson of World War I

1. An Emerging Individual Responsibility

In the wake of WWI, the world realized that the atrocities of war impacted the entire world, civilians and soldiers alike, and gravely violated rules of international law. Treaties were breached, established states' neutralities were violated, civilians were deported and enslaved, innocent people were murdered, hostages were killed, cities, churches, libraries, artistic treasures and historical landmarks were destroyed, neutral ships and hospital ships were sunk, and toxic and asphyxiating gasses were used. In the European countries only, an estimated 8.5 million people died, were injured or mutilated.[11]

Given the gravity of these losses and damages, unanimous was the call for the punishment of war criminals or any person responsible for violations of the laws and customs of war. Resentment culminated in a claim to prosecute heads of states who caused the war, helped to launch it, aided in its execution or ordered war crimes to be committed.

Some states took several measures to ensure that people accused of waging a war of aggression or committing war crimes were prosecuted. In France, a decree was issued on 2 September 1914 to establish a committee responsible for investigating acts perpetrated by the enemy and contrary to the law of the people (*juris gentium*). Russia created an extraordinary committee for criminal investigation for the same purpose. On 14 January 1915, Deputy Fernand Engerand submitted a draft law to the French Senate stipulating new sanctions in addition to the existing ones to punish war criminals. In addition, on 5 May 1917, the French Prime Minister declared that after victory 'we will not call for revenge but for justice, because there must be no crimes without punishment'. Similarly, another French statement in 1918 held that with respect to the many violations of law

---

11 Complete statistics on casualties of WWI are available at http://en.wikipedia.org/wiki/World_War_I_casualties (visited 30 August 2009).

and humanity, perpetrators of these crimes and those who ordered them shall be held ethically, criminally and financially responsible. Also, the British Prime Minister Lloyd George declared that every perpetrator of a war crime should be punished regardless of his position and that the German Emperor deserved to be hung for starting the war.

It is clear that the Allies were advocating the necessity to implement the law rather than resort to revenge, departing from the precedent practice whereby the victor imposed conditions on the defeated. They also asserted the necessity to hold accountable for their acts those who started the war and committed an act of aggression against other states. Thus, individual responsibility of the natural person emerged for the very first time.

2. The William II of Hohenzollern Precedent

However, practically and legally implementing the rules of such responsibility was not an easy task, particularly since there was no international precedent in the criminalization of the war of aggression. That is why at the 25 January 1919 session of the Preparatory Conference on Peace in Paris held by the victorious Allies, the 'Commission on responsibilities and sanctions of war perpetrators' was established with the mandate to investigate the responsibilities for WWI (1914–1918), determine the 'responsibility of the authors of the war', and decide whether it was possible to implement the rules of individual criminal responsibility on individuals who launched the war of aggression. In particular, the Commission was to determine the responsibility of high military officers and officials, regardless of their position, and to study the possibility of establishing an international criminal court to prosecute them.

Although the Commission held Germany and its allies fully responsible for starting the war, its regulations could not legally hold the leaders of these countries individually and criminally responsible for the crime of initiating a war of aggression. Therefore, the Commission recommended that it was impossible to prosecute them for the crime of initiating a war, and ruled that acts of instigating a war cannot form the basis for prosecution before a criminal court. The final report indicated that 'a war of aggression cannot be considered a direct violation of national Law … and that … the responsibility of launching a war of aggression is an ethical responsibility due to the absence of a previous International Law which criminalizes it and sets criminal sanctions for it'. In order to fill this gap, it was recommended that this situation be taken into consideration in the future and that the commission of the crime of launching a war of aggression be penalized so that its perpetrators can in future be punished.[12]

However, such conclusions did not satisfy the increasing demands to prosecute those who caused the war, namely the German Emperor William II, particularly after British Prime Minister David Lloyd George's statement: 'hang the Kaiser for starting the war.'[13]

Consequently, the preparatory meeting of the Supreme War Council consulted jurists – the Dean of the Law School in Paris, Professor Larnaude, and Professor De la Pradelle, a professor at the same university – who submitted a report to the commissioners of the Allied Forces convening in Paris in January 1919. The report concluded that the crimes attributed to the German Emperor were international crimes, and that he had to be tried before an international court as an Emperor,

12 F.B. Schnick, 'International Criminal Law, Facts and Illusions', the *Modern Law Review*, Vol. II, 1948, at 290–291. M.A. Marin, 'The Evolution and Present Status of the Law of War', *RCADI*, Vol. II, 1975, at 92.

13 For a review of different positions of Europe's leaders on faith of the Kaiser in the aftermath of WWI, see http://www.historylearningsite.co.uk/treaty_of_versailles.htm (visited 4 July 2009).

as the Commander-in-Chief of the German Army, and as a war lord. The whole world demanded that he be punished for violating the law of war and the law of neutrality.

The report also indicated that the removed Emperor's motto – 'the Emperor's will absolves the law' – included in itself his legal responsibility for his acts, particularly for the war, which only he could declare under Article 11 of the 16 April 1871 German Empire's constitution: 'Emperor represents the Empire in international relations. He declares war and institutes peace in the name of the Empire.' Consequently, the Emperor had an individual criminal responsibility, as well as a civil responsibility, towards the German Empire.

The jurists believed it was impossible that an aggression, as an act against peace, went unpunished and that, therefore, such a crime had to be severely punished. It is clear that the report of jurists Larnaude and De la Pradelle confirmed the necessity to hold the German Emperor individually and criminally responsible for initiating the war of aggression, and acknowledged the Allies had the power and the legal authority to charge and prosecute him. The Allies did not disregard such conclusions and, under Article 227 of the Versailles Peace Treaty of 1919, provided that 'the Allied and Associated Powers publicly [charge] William II of Hohenzollern, former German Emperor, for a supreme offence against international morality and the sanctity of treaties'. The Allied Powers also agreed to establish 'a special tribunal' composed of judges appointed by the United States, Great Britain, France, Italy and Japan to try the accused, all the while preserving his right to a defence. The tribunal was to consider 'the highest motives of international policy, with a view to vindicating the solemn obligations of international undertakings and the validity of international morality'. The Allied Powers empowered the court to determine the sentence it deemed necessary. The Allied powers also agreed to submit a request to the government of the Netherlands for the former Emperor's surrender for purposes of prosecution.[14]

However, German Emperor William II resigned before the declaration of truce of 9 November 1919 and permanently abdicated the throne; while the Versailles conference was in session and before the Treaty was signed, William II sought and obtained asylum in the Netherlands, crossing the border with the Crown Prince, to be detained in the palace of Doorn. In January 1920, the Allies submitted an official plea to the government of the Netherlands, requesting that the German Emperor be turned over to them in preparation for his trial. One week later, the government of the Netherlands rejected the Allies' plea[15] arguing that the German Emperor had not committed any punishable act according to the 1858 Dutch penal code or the extradition treaty signed with the Allies, and adding that the charge against the German Emperor was political more than legal. Turning over the Emperor to be tried before an *ad hoc* tribunal did not in any way comply with the provisions of the Dutch law because the accused would have been tried by his enemies, whose sentence would have undoubtedly been unjust due to the abhorrence and hatred they had for him. In spite of all the guarantees given, the judges would have been opponents and referees at the same time. The Netherlands believed that the matter had to be addressed according to its penal code, and that theoretical doctrines were not enough to turn over the fugitive or to inflict a criminal sentence upon him. In spite of Allied states' attempts to resubmit the plea of surrender, the Dutch

14 E. Greppi, 'The Evolution of Individual Criminal Responsibility under International Law', *International Review of the Red Cross*, No. 835, 531–553, at 537.

15 B.B. Ferencz, *The Evolution of Individual Criminal Responsibility under International Law*, note 9 *supra*, at 538; C. Bassiouni, *International Criminal Law*, Vol. I, Crimes and Punishment (Leiden: Martinus Nijhoff Publishers, 1973), at 571.

government consistently refused to turn over the fugitive.[16] That prevented Article 227 from being implemented, and Emperor William II was neither held accountable for his acts, nor were the rules of individual responsibility for the crime of aggression ever applied to him, and he remained in the Netherlands until his death in 1941.

In spite of all the flaws, deficiencies and legal gaps which characterized this incomplete precedent, and which ended up being a mere moral condemnation akin to the one against Napoleon, its positive implications cannot be disregarded as it laid several new principles which paved the way for what was to come. The Versailles precedent is regarded as having established the:

(a) principle of individual criminal responsibility for international crimes;
(b) principle of responsibility of heads of states for the acts they commit;
(c) possibility to prosecute and try heads of states for their international crimes, including acts of aggression, thus going beyond the previous rule of full immunity, even when they committed the most heinous crimes against humanity.

Although Article 227 of the Treaty of Versailles was based on political, not legal grounds, it paved the way for the establishment of a new legal rule which could develop over time to be acknowledged in the international realm. The Versailles precedent warned states of the many gaps which characterized the legal system, particularly with respect to the non-criminalization of the war of aggression. For this reason, the League of Nations undertook several initiatives to attempt to criminalize aggression.

C. The Practice of Trials Following World War II

World War II was characterized by an increased number of human casualties and brutal crimes committed between states which violated all rules of international law and applicable international conventions. During the war, 54 million people were killed, roughly 90 million were injured and 28 million became impaired.

Given the gravity of these losses and the seriousness of the violations committed, repeated calls were made, even before the war was over, to try the persons who committed war crimes and crimes of aggression.[17] Among the others, the statement of US President Roosevelt on 22 October 1941: 'Terrorism and terror cannot bring peace to Europe. They merely sow the seeds of hatred which will eventually lead to a terrible punishment.' USSR Foreign Minister Molotov declared on 27 April 1942: 'Hitler's government and its accomplices will not escape responsibility and the punishment they deserve for their unique crimes.' All this paved the way for the trials which took place when the conflict was over.

The choice to prosecute war criminals was one of several alternatives suggested: some secretly called for summary executions, as soon as perpetrators had fallen into the hands of one of the Allied states; others believed that there was no need for trials, as accused could have been simply imprisoned for life – as it had been the case for Napoleon in 1815. But the solution finally adopted was the one heralded both by the United States and the USSR, which called for a trial that would

16 Allegations of several other reasons behind the Netherland's refusal to surrender the Kaiser included the kinship between the two ruling families, in the Netherlands and Germany, and the interference of Pope Benoit V on behalf of the Emperor.

17 E. Greppi, 'The Individual Criminal Responsibility Under International Law', *International Review of the Red Cross*, No. 835, 531–553, at 538.

set a historical example for generations to come, and through which condemnation would become international and public. And this was indeed what happened.

With the end of the war, after the Axis states were defeated and Germany surrendered, Allied governments did not want to miss the opportunity to try to punish the Nazi leaders for all the crimes they committed against humanity, including for the crime of aggression.

US Judge Robert Jackson's report represents an important phase in addressing responsibility for international crimes and consequently in including aggression in the list of crimes punishable under the Statutes of the Nüremberg and Tokyo Tribunals. Judge Jackson, a US Supreme Court of Justice judge who represented the US at the Moscow Conference of October 1943 and at its Joint Four-Nation Declaration, visited the European countries targeted by German acts of aggression and where the conflict took place. He listened to witnesses and prisoners of war, gathered all available evidence, and then filed his report to the President of the United States,[18] devising a procedure for the trials and outlining the crimes for which the accused should have been tried, including breaching international law by means of the invasion of other territories and initiating wars of aggression. Based on the above, Jackson concluded that the war of aggression was a crime and that the new international law had cancelled the old defence which absolved the responsibility of the persons who caused the crime of aggression. Therefore, the forces of the law should all unite in the best interest of peace and hold those who cause the crime of aggression accountable for their acts. This is exactly the position the Allies adopted – to try persons responsible for aggression as part of crimes against peace – by determining the mechanisms for such trials in the London Agreement on the prosecution of war criminals (8 August 1945) and the annexed Charter of the International Military Tribunal of Nüremberg (IMT). Article 6(a) IMT Charter determined the acts considered offences under the jurisdiction of the Tribunal and which entail an individual responsibility,[19] condemning 'crimes against peace, namely the planning, preparation, initiation or waging of aggression, or a war in violation of international law, treaties, agreements or assurances, or participation in a common plan or conspiracy for the accomplishment of any of the foregoing'. The 26 July 1945 Potsdam Declaration included a similar text for the establishment of the International Military Tribunal for the Far East (IMTFE or Tokyo Tribunal), stipulating that those responsible for the crime of aggression had to be tried.

Thus, the international regulation system raised, for the first time, the issues of individual responsibility for a crime of aggression and of the trial before an international tribunal of persons accused of instigating such a crime.

The above quoted wording of Article 6 IMT Charter makes it clear that the Allies enlarged the scope of accused of the crime of aggression: no longer limited to those who initiated, waged or planned a war of aggression, but also included those who conspired to commit such a crime. It must be noted that the Tribunal refused to punish the act of conspiracy for other crimes under its jurisdiction (war crimes and crimes against humanity), thus making conspiracy only punishable when specifically part of the crime of aggression. Thus, persons responsible for committing the crime of aggression included only those who prepare, plan, wage and initiate a war of aggression, as well as those who conspire to commit this crime.

---

18 R.H. Jackson, *Report to the President by Mr. Justice Jackson*, 6 June 1945. Available at http://avalon.law.yale.edu/subject_menus/jackson.asp (visited 4 July 2009).

19 B.B. Ferencz, *From Nüremberg to Rome, the Prosecution of International Crimes* (Bonn: The Development and Peace Foundation, 1998), at 2. Available at http://www.benferencz.org/artis.html (visited 3 April 2009).

1. Planning and Preparing to Commit the Crime of Aggression

Normally, aggression is preceded by several preparatory acts,[20] including providing the necessary military, economic and financial capacities to commit the act of aggression. The same preparations occur at the political level, as alliances are formed and political manoeuvres are executed to cover the preparation to commit aggression and conceal the state's real intention.

The Nüremberg Tribunal concluded that planning and preparing to commit aggression was a punishable act, if committed by persons in leadership positions, and accordingly charged some of the accused. The Göring indictment stated he had prepared all diplomatic endeavours for war, particularly his diplomatic manoeuvre preceding the war of aggression against Poland; Rosenberg, the Head of the Foreign Affairs Department in the Nazi party, was found responsible for the planning and preparation of aggression against Norway; Foreign Minister von Ribbentrop was held accountable because his diplomatic authority prepared for the aggression against Poland and the other countries; Walter Funk was charged with the crime of preparing aggression because he helped in the economic preparations which preceded the aggression against Poland and the Soviet Union; on the same count, however, Hjalmar Schacht was acquitted, although he had occupied a prominent position in the program of rearming Germany, because rearmament was not a crime in itself according to the IMT Statute and evidence was not given of his knowledge to contributing to a common plan to commit aggression.

2. Initiating the War of Aggression

Initiating the war of aggression means making the decision to commit the act of aggression. The power to make such a decision only pertains to state leaders and military commanders in positions of supreme power, when not reserved to the head of state. That is why the Nüremberg Tribunal considered initiating the war of aggression to be not only a crime under international law, but also the 'supreme international crime', although it did not prosecute anyone on this charge as it wanted to make Hitler the only one responsible for making the decision to initiate aggression.

3. Waging the War of Aggression

This conduct refers to the persons who are in charge of leading and guiding operations after the decision to initiate the aggression has been taken. Such persons make different military, political and economic decisions to secure the continuation and success of the act of aggression. The Tribunal charged Admiral Dönitz with this conduct because he was Commander-in-Chief of the German Navy from 30 January 1943 and head of state on 9 May 1945, and he ordered the Army to continue the war on the Eastern Front against the Soviet Union. The Tribunal also charged General Göring, Marshall Keitel and Marshall Jodl for a similar conduct.

It is worth noting that the Nüremberg Tribunal held only high-ranking officers and officials responsible for such crimes, while under Article 6 of the Nüremberg Charter a regular soldier also could have been responsible for the planning, preparation, initiation and waging of a war of

---

20 *Prepared by the Secretariat*, Preparatory Commission for the International Criminal Court, Working Group on the Crime of Aggression, 24 January 2002, United Nations PCNICC/2002/WGCA/L.1. at 27–39. Available at http://www.un.org/law/icc/prepcomm/apr2002/pcnicc 2002wgca11e.pdf (visited 3 April 2009).

aggression, while being also liable for other crimes – war crimes and crimes against humanity – which he might have committed during the war of aggression, such as killing of prisoners or wounded.

The IMT also convicted civilians for waging an aggressive war: Seyss-Inquart, Head of Administration in the Southern section of Poland, was held accountable for his civilian positions in territories occupied following wars of aggression, and for playing a major role in waging other aggressive wars.

4. Conspiring to Commit the Crime of Aggression

The Nüremberg Tribunal established a precedent by punishing conspiracy[21] to commit the crime of aggression, as conspiracy was previously unknown to international law. The purpose of prosecuting conspiracy was to allow the punishment of accomplices in conspiracy for aggression, even if the crime of aggression itself was not committed. As conspiracy is an earlier conduct, prohibiting and punishing it is intended to prevent the furtherance of a threat to the security of the international community through the subsequent acts of planning and preparation for aggression.

The IMT adopted a narrow concept of conspiracy – indicating that its Charter did not include a definition for it – which was to be defined and limited within the framework of its criminal objective as a conduct close to the determination and the act of aggression itself. Therefore, conspiracy could not be considered as existing just because there were political clauses related to it in the Nazi's program or in Hitler's book *Mein Kampf.* Instead, it had to be proven with the existence of a realistic plan for war and with evidence on the contribution of each accused who took part in it.

The Tribunal found that Hitler could not have waged an aggressive war by himself, but had to be assisted by accomplices, and that several government officials played such a role, whether as military commanders, diplomatic leaders or financiers and industrialists: by voluntarily offering Hitler their assistance, those persons became his accomplices in conspiracy to commit acts of aggression.

To hold accused accountable for conspiracy in the commission of aggression, the Tribunal had to prove the existence of a calculated and specific plan aimed at initiating aggressive war, although there is no requirement for the plan to be as comprehensive and detailed as to specify, for instance, the date and means for executing aggression. The objective of the plan must be the commission of the crime of aggression or of a war which is deemed a violation of international treaties and conventions.

Finally, it is worth noting that the perpetrator of the crime of aggression is not required to conspire in order to commit it. Conspirators can be non-executors. For this reason, the Nüremberg Tribunal convicted four accused of the crime of arranging and executing an aggressive war, but acquitted them of the count of conspiracy.

5. The Legacy of the International Military Tribunals

In spite of all the criticism that the Nüremberg trials endured, they do represent a international legal and judicial precedent unknown to the contemporary international regulatory system, particularly with respect to individual criminal responsibility for the crime of aggression. They confirmed the criminalization of aggression, putting an end to all speculations about it, and convicted all

---

21 Ibid., at 14–15.

participants in the planning, execution and conspiracy to commit the crime of aggression, thus establishing several rules which were no longer contentious.

The importance of these trials resides in the legal principles they created, enforced and which thereafter governed individual responsibility for international crimes in accordance with the rules of international law. Previous international precedents revealed that the international community lacked a mechanism to govern individual responsibility for the crime of aggression and other international crimes. This was apparent in the criticism of the previous trials, whether by states and opponents with interests during the proceedings of these trials, or by jurists who devoted themselves to the study of previous precedents in order to assess them and infer the legal principles which should regulate individual criminal responsibility. There was a dire need for such principles in order to achieve a legal system which included a fair and legitimate accountability for persons accused of the commission of the crime of aggression, and to overcome pre-existing arbitrariness, provided that such a system included legal principles to govern the issue of individual responsibility in international law on the one hand, and determine the judicial competence to try those accused of committing international crimes, on the other hand.

Previous international trials where characterized by the absence of a system for individual criminal responsibility under international law and by the inconsistency of such responsibility with the principles of state sovereignty, immunity of heads of states and the binding nature of their orders. Furthermore, these trials breached the principles of legality, violated the accused rights to a fair trial and raised questions on the legality of the establishment of these military tribunals, which went against several of the prevailing legal principles.

These trials and the legal system of these tribunals – whose judges enjoyed wide-ranging authority to determine the legal system to be used and the law to be implemented – were targeted by several legal criticisms. In addition, this sapped the rules of personal and regional jurisdiction. Those trials were originally based on what was then known as the justice of the victor, a concept which is far from the notion of justice based on the law. The outcome of war has nothing to do with the idea of justice, for under the law the strong one is not always right and the defeated one does not necessarily have to be a criminal. In WWII, the Allies were victorious, Hitler committed suicide, Mussolini was summarily executed and Rudolph Hess and his accomplices were tried. Had the outcome of the war been different, we probably would have seen Roosevelt, Churchill, Stalin or Charles de Gaulle being tried and the tribunals would have probably been established in Washington, London, Paris and Moscow instead of Nüremberg and Tokyo. So, the justice of the victor is not a legal principle because justice entails a final judgment independent of the outcome of the fight, and has nothing to do with the identity of the victor and the defeated. That is why it is always represented by the blindfolded lady.

In the wake of the WWII trials, there was a clear consensus among member states of the international community that it was necessary to strive to avoid the atrocities and tragedies of previous wars, and benefit from the trials which followed them in order to draw a legal system that included the principles governing individual responsibility for international crimes and to ensure trials for perpetrators. That was very clear, for instance, at the first UNGA meeting of 23 October 1946 in New York, when US President Truman indicated that '23 Member States of the United Nations have officially joined the Statute of the Nüremberg Tribunal which regarded the act of planning, preparation, initiation or waging of a war of aggression as a crime against humanity, the perpetrators of which, whether persons or states, could stand trial before the Tribunal of Nations'. The United Nations Secretary General Trygvie Lie, in his report dated 24 October 1946, recommended that the principles used in the Nüremberg trials be included in international law in order to ensure peace and protect mankind from new wars, so that those who instigate a new war be aware of the law and penalties for their crimes.

Consequently, the United States of America submitted, on 15 November 1946, to the UNGA a draft to codify and disseminate the set of legal rules which could be inferred from the Statute and judgment of the Nüremberg Tribunal. The Assembly approved the draft[22] by Resolution 95 of 11 December 1946, which confirmed the principles adopted by the Nüremberg Tribunal and regarded them as part of positive international law. It then assigned its International Law Commission (ILC), established on the same date by Resolution 94, to formulate these principles within a comprehensive code, including a definition of international crimes against peace and security.[23]

To facilitate this task, the General Assembly also assigned the ILC[24] to 'formulate the principles of International Law acknowledged in the Statute and in the judgment of the Nüremberg Tribunal': upon accomplishment of such mandate,[25] the Commission submitted its report to the GA at its Fifth Session, on 3 August 1950.

The 1950 ILC report included the formulation of seven Principles of International Law Recognized in the Charter of the Nuremberg Tribunal and in the Judgment of the Tribunal, which represented the legal basis to govern individual responsibility for international crimes, including for the crime of aggression. The principles set the basis and regulations of the punishment, and addressed the issue of legality by specifying international crimes, including crimes against peace, war crimes and crimes against humanity. Principle VI(a) on crimes against peace included the planning, preparation, initiation and waging of a war of aggression, or a war in violation of international treaties, agreements or assurances, or participation in a common plan or conspiracy for the accomplishment of any of the foregoing. The other six principles established the legal system which should govern the issue of individual responsibility for international crimes: personal liability, prevalence of international over national law, non-applicability of immunity to international crimes, irrelevance of execution of orders, right to fair trial and liability for participation in international crimes.

3. Individual Criminal Responsibility for Aggression Under the Rome Statute

After great efforts, and long decades of failure and disappointment, the International Criminal Court (ICC) became a reality when states finally agreed, at the United Nations Diplomatic Conference of Plenipotentiaries held in Rome, Italy, from 15 June till 17 July 1998, on the establishment of an International Criminal Court. The conference eventually gave birth to the ICC Statute, with 120 states voting in favour, 21 abstaining, and seven voting against (including the United States of America, China and Israel).

The threshold of 60 ratifications for the entry into force of the Statute was reached on 10 April 2002, with the deposit of 10 ratification instruments at the UN Headquarters. According to the alphabetical order, the Democratic Republic of the Congo was the sixtieth ratifying state to join the Rome Statute. Thus, under Article 126 ICCSt, the Statute entered into force on 1 July 2002.

---

22 Available at http://untreaty.un.org/ilc/texts/instruments/english/reports/1_4_1950.pdf (visited 3 April 2009).

23 GA Res. 95, 1st Session, UN Doc A/64/ Add. 1 (1946). Available at http://daccessdds.un.org/doc/RESOLUTION/GEN/NR0/033/46/IMG/NR003346.pdf?OpenElement (visited 29 January 2009).

24 GA Res. 177 of 21 November 1947.

25 Second session of the Commission, 5 June–29 July 1950.

Unlike the International Criminal Tribunal for Rwanda and the International Criminal Tribunal for the former Yugoslavia, the International Criminal Court is a permanent court which does not come into existence with and exhaust its mandate for only one incident. Great hopes and expectations hung on the ICC because, since 1945, 170 million people have been killed in conflicts, but no one has been held criminally accountable for their deaths.[26] Such impunity made Douglas Cassel describe the twentieth century as

> a good century for tyrants whereby Stalin killed millions, Pol Pot murdered over a million people and Idi Amin and Raoul Cédras got a comfortable retirement, while General Augusto Pinochet eluded trial due to legal complications and procedures. However, the establishment of the International Criminal Court gives justice a chance, makes the 21st century somewhat better and instills some fear in the tyrants of the 21st century …[27]

Therefore, the ICC Statute is expected to have, in the near future, a value which, perhaps, matches or exceeds the UN Charter itself. In fact, the UN Charter includes rules to regulate relations between states and Chapter VII 'political, economic and military sanctions', which can be imposed on a state when violating its international obligations and rules of international law. An aggressor state is supposed to be subjected to these sanctions, including the possibility of imposing on it lasting economic sanctions. However, while sanctions normally affect a high number of people among the weakest ones, the leading figures of the aggressor state – who initiated the aggression and ordered, allowed or disregarded war crimes, extermination and other crimes against humanity – remain remotely affected: leaders are not held accountable in spite of their responsibility for having involved their peoples in international crimes, wasted the resources of their countries and compromised the security and integrity of the entire international community.

Such an outcome appears to be unreasonable, illogical, contrary to basic principles of law and justice, as well as in violation of the principle of individuality of sanctions. The reason behind this is the absence of an international court competent for the trial of persons accused of committing such international crimes: perpetrators are not likely to be tried in their own country, where they hold the highest positions and are often regarded as national heroes for defending their country's interest, fending off and killing their enemies. They will also not be tried internationally because of the absence of a permanent and neutral international judicial body to handle this task in order to implement the rules of justice, and in the absence of sound legal logic, away from the lust for revenge and the desire to humiliate opponents and enemies alike. Contemporary international rules need to deal with this shortcoming and deficiency, as history of international relations reveals that, in spite of the thousands of wars of aggression waged and the millions of innocent people who fell victims of war crimes, genocide and crimes against humanity, no one was brought to justice, and no criminal was punished: criminals remained free, victims' rights violated and justice was not achieved throughout centuries.

In spite of all this, states did not agree on the jurisdiction of the International Criminal Court over the crime of aggression. On the contrary, aggression caused a wide-ranging legal and political debate and controversy before, during and after the Rome Conference. Up to now, aggression is still the main dilemma which has not seen any clear consensus, a fact which disappoints many who

26 B.B. Ferencz, 'Getting Aggressive about Preventing Aggression', *Brown Journal of World Affairs*, Winter/Spring 1999, Vol. VI, Issue 1, at 87. Available at http://www.igc.org/icc/html/ferencz1999 (visited 3 April 2009).

27 D. Cassel, 'Why We Need the International Court'. Available at http://www.religion-online.org/showarticle.asp?title=561 (visited 26 June 2009).

had hoped the establishment of the Court would be the most important step since the UN Charter itself to achieve security, stability and peace, as well as to uphold the rules of law and justice all over the world.

A. States in Favour of the ICC Jurisdiction Over the Crime of Aggression

During the 1998 Rome Diplomatic Conference most states expressed a strong will that the subject matter jurisdiction of the Court included the crime of aggression, both in their official statements before the Conference or during detailed discussions held in meetings of specialized committees. Arab states were at the forefront of those in favour of the jurisdiction of the Court over the crime of aggression. This position was asserted and adopted by the Syrian delegation in order to 'empower the Court to prosecute perpetrators of aggression as a crime against peace with accuracy and according to one norm'.[28] The same position was maintained by most Arab states as well.[29] Iran asserted steadfast support for the inclusion of aggression within the Court's jurisdiction, failing which the Court would have become more symbolic than effective and, thus, its existence compromised.[30]

During the meetings of the Committee on the Whole, France and Britain reiterated their support for including the crime of aggression in the jurisdiction of the Court provided that there was a clear and accurate definition, and that the Security Council's role in determining when aggression had occurred was preserved.[31] Belgium stated its strong support for including the crime of aggression in the Statute and raised the issue of reasonability of prosecutions of war crimes if the first crime triggering any armed conflict – the crime of aggression – was not prosecuted.[32] Likewise, the Russian Federation indicated that the inclusion of aggression within the jurisdiction of the Court was of great importance, and that crimes committed against humanity were often committed as part of wars of aggression.[33] Denmark stated that it was in favour of including the crime of aggression in the jurisdiction of the Court and that the Statute would be severely incomplete without such an inclusion.[34] Greece mentioned that the discussions held in the Preparatory Committee and during the general sessions of the Conference showed an evident increase in the number of states wishing the crime of aggression to be included in the jurisdiction of the Court: as it considered it illogical to ignore aggression and merely concentrate on its collateral effects (war crimes, crimes against humanity and genocide), Greece favoured the inclusion of aggression in the ICC jurisdiction.[35] Germany, the Republic of Korea, Costa Rica, Sweden, Slovakia, Japan, the Ivory Coast, Senegal,

---

28 From the Statement of the Saudi Arabian Delegation before the UN Diplomatic Conference of the Plenipotentiaries on the establishment of an International Criminal Court. Available at http://www.un.org/icc/speeches/616syr4.htm (visited 3 April 2009). See also Syria's position regarding the crime of aggression during the PrepCom: A/CONF.183/C.1/SR 25, 9–10; A/CONF.183/C.1/SR 33, 7.

29 See the Court's official website and the Rome Conference documents A/CONF. 183/C.1/SR 6, A/CONF.183/C.1/SR 34, A/CONF.183/C.1/SR 35.

30 A/CONF. 183/C.1/SR 6, 23.

31 A/CONF.183/C.1/SR 6, 18.

32 A/CONF. 183/C.1/SR 6, 11.

33 A/CONF. 183/C.1/SR 6, 17.

34 A/CONF.183/C.1/SR 6, 15.

35 A/CONF.183/C.1/SR 6, 12.

Ukraine, Thailand, Zambia, Vietnam, Italy, Ethiopia,[36] Jamaica, Azerbaijan, Poland,[37] Burundi, Indonesia, Tanzania and several other states[38] all had the same position.

Trinidad and Tobago, on behalf of the member states of the Caribbean Community (CARICOM), favoured the inclusion of aggression in the jurisdiction of the Court, provided that an acceptable definition was worked out.[39] The same position was taken by South Africa, on behalf of the South African Development Group, provided that there was a consensus definition and a clear outline of the Security Council's role.[40]

The foregoing clearly shows an overwhelming consensus at the Conference regarding the inclusion of aggression in the crimes within the jurisdiction of the Court. During the Preparatory Committee meetings, Germany had also stated that the establishment of an international criminal court that excluded the crime of aggression could represent a setback from the 1945 Nüremberg Charter, as well as from the 1950 Nüremberg Principles, the 1994 ILC draft Statute (Article 20) and the 1996 ILC Draft Code of Crimes against the Peace and Security of Mankind. It would also represent a failure to learn the proper lessons from modern history. The German delegation believed the inclusion of the crime of aggression was necessitated by reasons related to deterrence and prevention, and to reiterating more clearly that waging a war of aggression is a crime under international law.[41]

B. States with Reservations on the ICC Jurisdiction Over the Crime of Aggression

While the majority of states were in favour of an ICC jurisdiction over the crime of aggression, a minority had reservations on it, claiming that that would caused many legal and political difficulties, including with the role of the Security Council. The United States doubted that the Conference would be able to adopt a satisfactory definition for acknowledging individual responsibility and noted that GA Res. 3314 (1974) did not attempt to define aggression as an individual crime as it was, instead, a mere repetition of the Nüremberg Charter formulation.[42]

The same position was held by Israel, unconvinced of the necessity to include the crime of aggression in the subject matter jurisdiction of the ICC. Additionally, Israel made the point that the Statute of the Court stipulated sanctions as a punishment for criminal acts, and that criminal liability should be based on accurate and universally acknowledged definitions. At that time, such a definition for the crime of aggression was not stirring on the distant horizon, and the lack thereof could have lead to the use of definitions driven by political motives, which could have affected the independence and non-political character of the Court. It was also argued that aggressive acts committed by states against other states did not fall in the category of crimes committed by individuals violating international humanitarian law, while it was such acts that the Statute meant to deal with.[43]

Likewise, Brazil stated that it did not favour including aggression because of serious doubts about the possibility of reaching a wide agreement on the definition of aggression as a crime of

36 Positions of these states in A/CONF.183/C.1/SR 6, 17–23.
37 Positions of these states in A/CONF.183/C.1/SR 34.
38 Position of these states in A/CONF.183/C.1/SR 35.
39 A/CONF.183/C.1/SR 6, 13.
40 A/CONF.183/C.1/SR 6, 4.
41 A/AC. 249/1997/WG.1/DP.20, 11 December 1997.
42 A/CONF.183/C.1/SR 6, 16.
43 A/CONF.183/C.1/SR 6, 9.

individuals. It anticipated serious problems regarding the conflicting jurisdictions of the Security Council and of the ICC, which would have affected the independence of the Court.[44]

Similarly, Turkey indicated that there was no universally accepted definition of aggression, that there was no precedent regarding individual criminal responsibility for aggressive acts and that the competent body was the Security Council which deals with actions of states. It was, therefore, difficult to see how an act attributed to a state could be attributed to an individual.[45]

C. Assessing the Different Positions of States

What the above discussion clearly shows is that there was an overwhelming number of states from all regional groups and with different cultures, ideologies and political tendencies which supported the need to include the crime of aggression within the subject matter jurisdiction on the Court. In the words of professor Benjamin B. Ferencz: 'at the Rome Conference, most states, including the European Union, about 30 nations united in the Non-Aligned Movement, and the Arab Group insisted that the Court should have jurisdiction over the crime of aggression and that without the inclusion of aggression as a crime within the Statute, they would not be able to support the new court.'[46]

It is clear that this laudable tendency reflects the whole world's understanding of the seriousness and gravity of the crime of aggression – and of the damages and losses it brings – as well as the necessity to punish all those responsible for the commission of such a crime, which threatens the existence of the entire humankind. It would have been illogical for the Statute to include punishment for other crimes which, in spite of their gravity, are less harmful and serious than the crime of aggression, which is indeed the mother of crimes and the natural context in which most other crimes are committed. Consequently, it was understood to be of paramount importance to provide concretely for the punishment of the crime of aggression, and this chance had to be seized so as not to allow the Court's system be flawed by its inability to prosecute the most serious of international crimes.

However, states maintaining reservations on the inclusion of aggression within the jurisdiction of the Court based their position on the absence of a consensus definition of aggression. Other points of disagreement were related to: the role of the Security Council with respect to the commission of this crime; the claim that aggression is an act which gives rise to the responsibility of states and not of individuals; the absence of precedents related to individual criminal responsibility for the crime of aggression in international law.

Such arguments do not justify the exclusion of aggression from the Court's actual jurisdiction because, with respect to the definition of aggression, conferees had several alternatives and options.[47] These included General Assembly Resolution 3314 (1974) on the definition of aggression – which is the resolution most jurists believe 'has become an international custom acknowledged as such by doctrine and jurisprudence alike, particularly in the verdict of the International Court of Justice in the 1986 case of *Nicaragua vs. the United States*'.[48] Also, available for such task are the definition of aggression affirmed during the Nüremberg trials and the ILC efforts during the preparation of

---

44 A/CONF.183/C.1/SR 6, 22.

45 A/CONF.183/C.1/SR 6, 22.

46 B.B. Ferencz, 'Can Aggression be Deterred by Law?', 10 *Pace International Law Review*, Fall 1999. Available at www.benferencz.org/peacearti.htm (visited 3 April 2009).

47 See Art. 5 ICCSt, Doc. A/CONF. 183/2/ADD.1, Arabic, 12–15.

48 M.A. Shukri, *The Necessity of Ratification and Accession of Arab States to the Statute of the International Criminal Court*, research submitted to the Arab Legal Symposium on the Impact of Ratification

the 1996 Draft Code of Crimes Against the Peace and Security of Mankind.[49] Thus, aggression is not an undefined crime or a natural act impossible to define, and it appears to be illogical to resort to arguments used since the nineteenth century to justify violations of international law and elude punishment.

The maintenance of a position whereby disadvantages would prevail in allowing the ICC to exert its jurisdiction under Article 5 ICCSt over the crime of aggression does not take into account that aggression is not a political act by nature which justifies its exclusion from the jurisdiction of the Court.[50] It is the most serious of international crimes and all its elements are widely agreed upon. Consequently, the role of the law is not to submit, accept and acknowledge the politicization of this crime, but to deal with it as a clear and established international crime, and allow the jurisdiction of the Court to be triggered very much as it is for less serious international crimes.

As for the role of the Security Council, the current situation under the Statute is the outcome of the opposite positions of states on the prominence of the Security Council versus the independence of the Court. Some major states favoured maintaining full discretion in the political choices of the Council (United States), while others believed that the inclusion of aggression would have opened the door to veto rights and given aggressors the chance to elude punishment (Mexico).[51] The last argument, however, does not seem to take into account that the Court is independent from the Security Council. Consequently, the Court may very well represent a rare opportunity for the international community to correct its path and, by affirming the legal dimension of the act of aggression, overcome the flaws and negative aspects of the methods of work of the Security Council in determining whether aggression has occurred.

The arguments of some states that aggression is an act of states which does not entail individual responsibility are also objectionable. It would run against the principle of individuality of sanctions, which is the very basic principle in the concept of liability, to agree on the imposition of collective sanctions on the aggressing state – all the while accepting the negative effects on the masses that those sanctions entail – but then object to the prosecution of individuals personally and directly responsible for the commission of the crime of aggression.

Supporting the inclusion of aggression within the jurisdiction of the Court is not flawed by the limited number of international precedents or lack thereof, because individual responsibility for the crime of aggression was underlined and confirmed in the Nüremberg and Tokyo trials. Following the end of World War II, one of the major objectives and missions of the victorious Allies was to promote the role of international law in the maintenance of peace. In fact, the aggressions, invasions and heinous crimes perpetrated by Hitler's regime were so humiliating and atrocious that it was paramount to prosecute and try Nazi leaders so as not to allow them to elude punishment for the crimes of aggression they had committed. That is why Ferencz asserts that the greatest achievement of the Nüremberg trials was the condemnation and criminalization of aggressive war as the most dangerous international crime that could be committed.[52] The scarcity of international precedents is due to the absence of an international judicial body in charge of prosecuting those accused of committing international crimes: it is time to finally overcome such flaw in the international legal order by empowering the International Criminal Court with the actual jurisdiction over the crime

---

and Accession to the ICC Statute on legal commitments and national legislations in the Arab countries, Arab League, Cairo, 3–4 February 2002, at 6.

49 See Art. 15 of the Draft Code of Crimes against the Peace and Security of Mankind and the discussions about it, Yearbook of the International Law Commission, 1996, Vol. II, at 98 and 155–176.

50 A/CONF.183/C.1/SR 29, at 9.

51 A/CONF.183/C.1/SR 6, at 14.

52 B.B. Ferencz, "Can Law Deter Aggression?", *Peace International Law Review*, Fall 1999, at 2.

of aggression in order to promote the role of international law and preserve peace and stability in the whole world.

4. The Rome Compromise on the Crime of Aggression

Most states participating in the Rome Conference were in favour of the inclusion of aggression in the list of crimes within the jurisdiction of the International Criminal Court, but this was a very controversial topic and no final and conclusive agreement was reached regarding this subject, leading to the deletion of the crime of aggression from the draft Statute.[53] Such a proposal, submitted by the Conference Bureau two days before the end of the Diplomatic Conference, was rejected by most participating states and it almost caused the Conference to fail when several states threatened not to approve the Statute if it did not include the crime of aggression.

The Iranian delegate, on behalf of member states of the Non-Aligned Movement, expressed disappointment because the proposal of the Bureau did not include an option regarding the crime of aggression, and stated that many difficulties allegedly resulting from such inclusion appeared to be excuses to exclude the mother of all crimes, acknowledged by the Nüremberg Tribunal 50 years before the negotiations of the Statute. He added that the Conference had a duty towards future generations to ensure that aggression and the use of nuclear weapons were categorized as crimes in the Statute.[54] The Syrian delegation stated its strong support for the same position, shared by over 100 states, and added that the failure to find an agreed definition of the crime of aggression did not justify placing it on equal footing with 'treaty crimes' and that, should the crime of aggression not be included, the delegation would have had to reconsider its position regarding the Statute as a whole.[55]

Several states exerted huge efforts to re-include the crime of aggression in the Statute of the Court:[56] interventions of the Arab Group, the Non-Aligned Movement and some European countries resulted in the re-inclusion of aggression in the Article 5 Statute's list of the crimes within the jurisdiction of the Court, alongside genocide, crimes against humanity and war crimes,[57] only a few hours before the end of the Conference.

Consequently the final text of Article 5 of the Statute of the International Criminal Court under the title of 'crimes within the jurisdiction of the Court' was adopted as follows:

> 1. The jurisdiction of the Court shall be limited to the most serious crimes of concern to the international community as a whole. The court has jurisdiction in accordance with this Statute with respect to the following crimes:
>
> (a) The crime of genocide;
> (b) Crimes against humanity;
> (c) War crimes;
> (d) The crime of aggression.

---

53 Ibid.

54 M.A. Shukri, *The Crime of Aggression Between the Rome Statute and the Preparatory Commission*, a colloquium on IHL Reality and the Ambitions, Damascus, 4–5 November 2000, at 7.

55 A/CONF.183/C.1/SR 33, at 5.

56 M.A. Shukri, *The Crime of Aggression Between the Rome Statute and the Preparatory Commission*, note 54 *supra*, at 7.

57 A/CONF.183/C.1/SR 33, at 7.

> 2. The Court shall exercise jurisdiction over the crime of aggression once a provision is adopted in accordance with articles 121 and 123 defining the crime and setting out the conditions under which the Court shall exercise jurisdiction with respect to this crime. Such a provision shall be consistent with the relevant provisions of the Charter of the United Nations.

Article 5 includes the other categories of crimes which are already defined under Articles 6, 7 and 8 and, therefore, have been in the actual jurisdiction of the Court since the entry into force of the Statute. On the other hand, the crime of aggression will be defined and become enforceable only pursuant to the provisions of Articles 121 and 123 of the Statute: seven years after the entry into force of the Statute, the Secretary-General of the United Nations shall convene a Review Conference of States Parties[58] and at such Conference the proposed definition of aggression should be approved by consensus or require a two-third majority of States Parties.[59] The Court shall be able to exercise its jurisdiction over the crime of aggression one year after the deposit of instruments of ratification or acceptance by the States Parties which accepted it. However, the Court will not have jurisdiction over nationals or territory of States Parties which have not agreed on the definition of the crime of aggression.[60]

This regime entails that, should even a consensus definition of aggression be finally reached, the Court would still not be able to exercise its jurisdiction on the crime of aggression before at least 8 years from the entry into force of the Statute had elapsed: a lengthy period of time, during which the leaders of aggressing states would have continued to enjoy peace of mind and safety from any potential international prosecution.

Furthermore, the Article 5 regime contains several gaps and discrepancies, in particular whereby it gives States Parties the privilege of eluding prosecution for the crime of aggression: if a State Party to the Statute refuses to accept the definition of aggression, the Court shall not exercise its jurisdiction regarding this crime, whereas a state which accedes the Statute after the adoption of the definition would be bound by it, and would not be able to avoid the Court's jurisdiction regarding this crime.[61] This privilege does not seem to be justifiable, unless its purpose had been – in open contradiction with the purpose of international criminal justice itself – to encourage states to ratify and accede the Statute with the privilege of eluding prosecution for this crime, should they refuse the proposed definition: should such states be suspected of having committed aggression, they could not be referred to the Court and this would not be a deterrent for the continuation of such crime in future.

Paradoxically, previous drafts gave the Court competence to look into the crime of aggression with respect to a non-State Party (whenever this non-State Party had committed the crime of aggression on the territory of a State Party or non-State Party which had accepted the jurisdiction of the Court regarding this crime), whereas it is now impossible to prosecute a national of a State Party which has not accepted the definition of the crime of aggression.

---

58 See Art. 123(1) ICCSt.

59 See Art. 121(3) ICCSt.

60 See Art. 121(5) ICCSt. See also M. Aziz Shukri, *The Crime of Aggression Between the Rome Statute and the Preparatory Commission*, note 54 *supra*, at 7.

61 A.R.Y. Al Awadi, Consultant, International Criminal Court, *Complementarities and Validity of the Judgments Rendered by the National Justice System*, Research submitted to the Arab Legal Symposium on the Impact of Ratification and Accession to the ICC Statute on the legal commitments and national legislations in the Arab countries, Arab League, Cairo, 3–4 February 2002, at 8.

5. Elements for a Regime

In accordance with the UN Charter, the Court should have binding jurisdiction whenever the crime of aggression is committed. In the event of an aggression, the Security Council's intervention under Chapter VII of the Charter does not depend on the acceptance or will of the aggressor state. Likewise, the Court's prosecution of aggressor leaders – in order to avoid the gaps that so far allow them to elude punishment – should not depend on the acceptance and approval by the regimes they run. The immunity of aggressor leaders is not more important than that of the peoples, which is violated by the collective sanctions inflicted upon them. Therefore, the current provisions of the Statute regarding the crime of aggression seem to be disappointing and even depressing. It might have been more appropriate to allow States Parties to hold a Review Conference as soon as an agreement on the definition of aggression was reached, and not instead to defer it to the expiry of seven years, because such procedure has caused states to act slowly and postpone actions, sapping any true will to reach an agreement, as has been apparent throughout the work of the Preparatory Commission for the International Criminal Court (PrepCom) and of the Assembly of States Parties (ASP) on aggression. Also, once an agreement on aggression is reached, the Court should automatically have jurisdiction with respect to all States Parties, as it is illogical for it to have jurisdiction with respect to non-State Parties and not regarding State Parties just because these may have not accepted the definition of aggression. The principle of a state's consent cannot be used here because it has been wasted in favour of justice when holding a national of a non-State Party accountable before the Court: as consent of an aggressor non-State Party is not relevant, there is also no reason to consider relevant the consent of an aggressor State Party which has refused the definition of aggression.

Based on the above, it seems undeniable that, instead of facing it head on, the Statute tried to postpone the solution on aggression by adopting a political approach at the expense of international justice. For this reason, at the closing session of the 1998 Diplomatic Conference the Arab Group stated that it 'believed it was possible to include aggression as a defined crime within the Statute, that it was a shame that the Statute used general terms, and that we had to wait several years before the Court could, if ever, exercise its jurisdiction over the crime of aggression, the mother of international crimes'.[62] It was also made clear that the compromise provisions included in the Statute for the crime of aggression were the main reason why Arab states refrained from signing, not to mention ratifying, the Rome Statute.[63]

6. The Efforts of the Preparatory Commission

The Final Act of the 1998 Rome Conference included the establishment of a Preparatory Commission to finalize the Elements of Crimes within the ICC jurisdiction, as well as its Rules of Procedure and Evidence by 30 June 2000. It also mandated the PrepCom, without any deadline, to define the crime of aggression and elaborate the relationship agreement between the Court and the United Nations, as well as the headquarters' agreement between the Court and the host state. The UNGA adopted in its 53rd session on 23 December 1998 a resolution calling the PrepCom to convene and

62 Statement of the Arab Group at the closing session of the UN Diplomatic Conference on the establishment of the International Criminal Court, Arab League – Legal Department, at 37.

63 M.A. Shukri, *The Necessity of Ratification and Accession of Arab States to the International Criminal Court Statute*, note 48 *supra*, at 5.

included an additional directive to the PrepCom to study the requirements necessary to widen the acceptance and reinforce the effectiveness of the Court. The PrepCom began its meetings in 1999, holding three sessions that year, three in 2000, and two more in 2001. The last meeting was held during its ninth session in April 2002, a few days after the threshold number of ratifications for the entry into force of the Rome Statute was reached.

Although the Arab Group, supported by the Non-Aligned Movement and other states, had raised the issue of aggression, their demands were not heeded because the PrepCom was focused during its first meetings on the Elements of Crimes and on the Rules of Procedure and Evidence. Additional efforts allowed it to pay more attention to the issue of aggression, and at the second session of the PrepCom (13–26 August 1999) its President appointed a coordinator for the issue and encouraged concerned states to hold as many discussions as possible regarding this issue.[64]

During the PrepCom meetings, several options and alternatives were suggested in order to define aggression and to determine the role of the Security Council. Previous suggestions studied at the Rome Conference were reviewed. One of these was the Russian Federation's proposal which reads:

> for the purposes of this Statute and subject to a prior decision by the United Nations Security Council of an act of aggression by the state concerned, the crime of aggression means any of the following acts: planning, preparing, initiating or waging a war of aggression.[65]

The Russian proposal defines aggression, clarifying with one concise statement that the existence of an act of aggression is determined by the Security Council. It is a political definition which refers the decision on the existence of aggression to a political body, without determining its legal concept and content, nor determining the role of the Court: the definition would allow punishment of perpetrators responsible for planning, preparing, initiating and waging a war of aggression as defined by virtue of a Security Council resolution.

During the meetings of the 8th session of the PrepCom (23 September–5 October 2001), the coordinator for the crime of aggression reintroduced a discussion paper which included a unified text and suggestions, several options and alternatives for the definition or the conditions to exercise jurisdiction, and settled the relationship with the Security Council.[66] The coordinator's paper indicated that suggested options and alternatives included different points of view about whether the definition should be more general in nature – referring to what may be the essential characteristics of the crime of aggression – or instead include a more specific list of acts constituting the crime of aggression, or whether it would be possible to determine some acts listed in Resolution 3314 and add them to the general definition of the crime of aggression.[67] The coordinator also underlined two principles which seemed to be widely supported: the leadership nature of the crime, i.e., that aggression is committed by political leaders or military commanders; and the exclusion of criminalization of planning, preparing or ordering aggression when the act of aggression is not executed.[68] A series of options aimed at reconciling the prerogatives of the Security Council regarding the crime of aggression with the independence of the Court were also included in the coordinator's paper. However, disagreement remained unchanged on all these issues over the years.

---

64 M.A. Shukri, *The Crime of Aggression Between the Rome Statute and the Preparatory Commission*, note 54 *supra*, at 7.

65 PCNICC/1999/DP. 12, 29 July 1999.

66 PCNICC/2001/L.3/Rev. 1, at 14–18.

67 PCNICC/2001/L.3/Rev. 1, at 21.

68 PCNICC/2001/L.3/Rev. 1, at 18.

7. Searching for a Viable Option

The definition of aggression, on the one hand, and the role of the Security Council and conditions for the exercise of jurisdiction, on the other, should not be linked, but kept separated. Including both issues in one document under the heading 'definition of the crime of aggression' would create more problems and give fewer chances of reaching consensus, particularly since both issues are different in nature. Defining aggression means setting a norm for the Court when addressing criminal conducts. This has nothing to do with the role of the Security Council, which falls under the rules governing the jurisdiction. Nonetheless, several suggestions, options and alternatives, when defining aggression, focus on determining the role of the Security Council. A case in point is the German and Russian definition, as well as the options prepared by the coordinator and presented again during the 8th session of the PrepCom in September/October 2001, which always included the wording 'for the purposes of this Statute and subject to a decision by the United Nations Security Council'. This formulation would restrict and undermine the authority and competencies of the Court, while a definition of aggression should disregard how the Court shall exercise its jurisdiction. It is, thus, appropriate to concentrate first on a consensus definition of aggression in a separate Article, after which the role of the Security Council can be dealt with separately when addressing the rules governing the jurisdiction. Determining the role of the Security Council within the definition itself is not appropriate because it is neither the place nor domain to do so. The insistence for such an approach is an obstacle which will limit the possibility of reaching the objective, as many states will object to the definition because of what it does or does not include on the role of the Security Council.

The coordinator of the Arab Group on the crime of aggression stated that 'the real issue is not defining the word aggression, however important it may be, but the relationship between the International Criminal Court and the Security Council, should the Court ever want to exercise its jurisdiction over the crime of aggression'.[69] Therefore, in order to be able to deal with the dilemma the definition must focus on the legal dimension of the concept of aggression without digressing and wallowing in procedural and political issues, which would greatly impede and delay the process of reaching the desired definition.

The definition must focus on the scope of individual responsibility for the crime of aggression, i.e., determining the persons legally responsible for the commission of this crime. In the many proposals forwarded lie several alternatives and options which could achieve this purpose by focusing on the persons who are in a position to exercise power and direct political and military acts against other states. Consequently, the scope of such responsibility includes the planning preparation, order and execution for the purpose of committing aggression. It is worth noting here that planning, preparing and giving the order to wage an aggressive war should not be liable for punishment unless aggression is indeed carried out. This will prevent the Court from stepping into political allegations and accusations exchanged between states regarding the threat and preparation to wage war: only aggression actually committed calls for individual accountability, whereas threats and altercations between states should remain within the jurisdiction of the Security Council under Chapters VI and VII of the Charter.

The International Criminal Court needs to be exclusively rooted in legal and not political grounds, as well as to be run by judges known to be just and to believe in the law, and not submissive or influenced by political considerations or narrow affiliations. From this perspective the definition of

69 M.A. Shukri, *The Crime of Aggression Between the Rome Statute and the Preparatory Commission*, note 54 *supra*, at 11.

the crime of aggression should follow the mixed method: adopting a general definition would leave the Court sufficient discretion, all the while mentioning the directive cases and giving the Court the competence and power to assess the gravity of such acts or whether others would be prosecuted. This was the basis for the proposal of some Arab states, which included cases mentioned in Article 3 of GA resolution 3314 (1974). The list of cases contained in Res 3314 (1974), adopted after difficult and lengthy negotiations, reflects the most common cases of aggression, and is the result of a long and hard work which should not be discarded to go back to square one. However, it would be inappropriate to adopt for the Court the definition under Resolution 3314, as it includes an absolute affirmation of the authority of the Security Council to determine when aggression has occurred, which is inappropriate in the case of the Court's jurisdiction. It would also be illogical to hold on to the parts and paragraphs of the Resolution which we like and acknowledge as enjoying legal power, then disregard the alleged legal authority of the other paragraphs relative to the Security Council and which do not go along with our interest and our wish to prevent the Court from falling under the power of the Security Council.

A viable option includes the following definition, which draws on the positions of states regarding the definition of aggression, the drafts and proposals submitted in this respect, as well as the works of the PrepCom:

1. For the purposes of this Statute, the crime of aggression is committed by a person who is in a position enabling him to exercise control or who is capable of directing political/military operations in his State against another State, or depriving other peoples of their rights to self-determination, freedom and independence, in contravention of the Charter of the United Nations, by resorting to armed force to threaten or to violate the sovereignty, territorial integrity or political independence of the State, or the inalienable rights of these peoples.

2. Acts constituting aggression include the following:

(a) The invasion or attack by the armed forces of a State, on the territory of another State, or any military occupation, however temporary, resulting from such invasion or attack, or any annexation by the use of the force of the territory of another State or part thereof;
(b) The bombardment of the territory of a State by the armed forces of another State;
(c) The blockade of the ports or coasts of a State by the armed forces of another State;
(d) The attack by the armed forces of a State on the land, marine or air forces, or marine and air fleets of another State;
(e) The use of armed forces of one State which are within the territory of another State, with the consent of the receiving State in contravention of the conditions provided for in the agreement, or any extension of their presence in such territory beyond the termination of the agreement;
(f) The action of a State in allowing its territory, which it has placed at the disposal of another State, to be used by that other State for perpetrating an act of aggression against a third State;
(g) The sending by or on behalf of a State, of armed bands, groups, irregulars or mercenaries who carry out acts of armed force against another State of such gravity as to amount to the acts listed above, or its substantial involvement therein.

3. The International Criminal Court shall determine the gravity of any of the acts perpetrated and indicated in paragraph 2, and may criminalize any other act which the Court decides to be an act of aggression.

4. Shall the Court decide that the crime of aggression has been committed, the acts of:

(a) Planning;
(b) Preparing;
(c) Ordering the commission of this crime shall also constitute a crime of aggression.

5. Pursuant to the provision of Articles 11 and 24, the Court shall be able to look into continuing crimes of aggression.

It is worth noting here that this definition:

(a) is based on General Assembly Resolution 3314 (1974), and tries to reconcile as much as possible some proposals submitted to the Prep Com, particularly the Arab and German proposals;
(b) determines the scope of individual responsibility for the crime of aggression, by specifically determining the persons responsible for its commission;
(c) includes two very important issues regarding the crime of aggression, which other proposals failed to include:

(i) grants the Court discretion when determining the gravity of acts committed, as well as whether other non-listed acts also constitute aggression, which is required to take into account modern means of warfare;
(ii) covers crimes of aggression committed before the initial date of actual jurisdiction, and accompanied by ongoing acts of annexation or occupation.

8. Conclusion

Open questions remain: has individual responsibility for the crime of aggression become a reality? Will the leaders of states, high military commanders and high ranking political officials be brought before the International Criminal Court to be tried for this crime and for the losses and damage caused to all members of the international community? Has individual responsibility for the crime of aggression witnessed such a major development that it has become a legal principle established under international law?

In this respect, it seems that there are several developments worth mentioning, including that the principle of sovereignty shrank from a starting point where states were considered entitled to wage war and commit aggression without being held accountable or liable for punishment. The acknowledgment of the prevailing interests of justice and international peace over national sovereignty has finally led to the loss of the right to immunity of heads of states, military commanders and political leaders responsible for the commission of the crime of aggression.

Jurisdiction over the crime of aggression aims to hold leaders and heads of states, and only them, accountable. That is why developments for this crime were slow and cautious, compared to prosecutions for other heinous international crimes (such as war crimes, genocide and crimes against humanity), the perpetrators of which do not usually enjoy any sympathy, support or protection. On the other hand, alleged perpetrators of the crime of aggression may be considered heroes in their country for waging wars presented by appropriate publicity and propaganda as aimed at ensuring national interests, regaining historical rights, realizing religious prophecies, bringing wealth to the nationals, preserving the territorial integrity of the country and defending its national security. Particularly in the war of aggression, the line between truth and lies is blurred: accusations and allegations are exchanged in such a way that it becomes hard to know the truth.

The activation of individual responsibility for the crime of aggression represents also the natural, legal and just alternative to the system of unjust collective sanctions. There is a strong reason to link both subjects since the various international sanctions – political, economic and military – stipulated in Article 39 of the UN Charter are usually inflicted upon states for the commission of aggression or of other serious crimes of international concern. Such sanctions are meant to weaken and isolate the dominant political system in the targeted state, and to provoke its people to change and replace it. This happened, e.g., in the Federal Republic of Yugoslavia as a result of economic sanctions upon it in the wake of the Balkan war and of the military intervention of NATO which set the international and internal mood for the removal of Yugoslav President Slobodan Milosević by his people and for surrendering him to the International Criminal Tribunal for the Former Yugoslavia, in The Hague.

Unfortunately however, it is not often that such a result is reached. Moreover, these collective sanctions affect primarily innocent peoples and not directly the targeted rulers who are responsible for these sanctions as a result of their international crimes; perpetration of international crimes should be tried without waiting for collective sanctions to be inflicted and to negatively affect ordinary people. Activating the system of individual responsibility for the crime of aggression would reduce the resort to international collective sanctions and their harsh effects on peoples. Regardless of the embellished formulas with which they are presented, even 'intelligent sanctions' are eventually stupid, as long as they target and negatively affect the population of the targeted state.

Thus, when a state commits an act of aggression and military sanctions are inflicted upon it, the purpose of such sanctions should be two-fold: liberating the occupied territory or defending the aggressed territory and terminating the effects of aggression, on the one hand, and arresting and trying the persons responsible for the commission of the crime of aggression before the International Criminal Court, on the other hand. Achieving the first objective alone – followed by the imposition of collective economic sanctions in order to weaken a criminal political system and push its people to change it, something which often does not happen – is not enough. Collective economic sanctions (such as blockades and embargoes) often lead to a contradictory effect, as they weaken the people and the opposition while reinforcing the political establishment they targeted, because the establishment would maintain control over the limited economic resources available. It is thus illogical to violate basic human rights by affecting the population with these collective sanctions under the pretext of preserving its will according to principles of democracy. Instead, activating the system of individual responsibility for the crime of aggression may limit the resort to collective sanctions, particularly the economic ones, and can be an effective alternative.

Although international law is widely criticized for its failure and incapacity in several situations (e.g., in Iraq and Palestine), with respect to the responsibility for the commission of international crimes, including aggression, international law has achieved great success and it is rapidly growing and evolving. It is also effectively contributing to increasing the commitment of the international community to the rule of law. Suffice to say that over the last 15 years we have witnessed the establishment of many international tribunals for the prosecution of those accused of committing the most heinous and serious international crimes, which makes us hope, much like Douglas

Cassel, that justice is given a chance, that the twenty-first century becomes a better place, and that the tyrants of the twenty-first century have every reason to be fearful.[70]

70 See D. Cassel, 'Why We Need the International Court'. Available at http://mehr.org/why_ICC.htm (visited 26 June 2009).

Chapter 25

National Legislation on Individual Responsibility for Conduct Amounting to Aggression

Astrid Reisinger Coracini*

1. Preliminary Considerations

A. Indirect Enforcement of Crimes Under International Law and the Principle of Complementarity

When the International Law Commission (ILC) was about to finalize its Draft Code of Crimes against the Peace and Security of Mankind, it reported to the General Assembly 'that the crime of aggression was inherently unsuitable for trial by national courts and should instead be dealt with only by an international court'.[1] This view of some ILC members was expressed in the context of the question of whether or not a national court was able to adjudicate that a state had committed an act of aggression by using armed force against another state. Such a determination was considered to be contrary to the principle of international law *par in parem non habet iurisdictionem* and to bear serious implications for international relations and international peace and security.[2] Consequently, the 1996 ILC Draft Code introduced two jurisdictional regimes. It provided for concurrent jurisdiction of states and an international criminal court for genocide, crimes against humanity, war crimes, as well as crimes against United Nations and associated personnel, whereby states were obliged to establish universal jurisdiction under domestic law for these crimes.[3] Jurisdiction over the crime of aggression[4] was exclusively reserved to an international criminal court 'with the singular exception of the national jurisdiction of the state which has committed aggression over its own nationals'.[5] Only in this case national courts were not required to consider an act of aggression by another state. Prosecution of a state's own leaders who participated in an act of aggression was deemed useful, e.g., during a process of national reconciliation. Should these national court proceedings fail to meet the necessary standard of independence and impartiality, a

* The author wishes to thank The Planethood Foundation for having encouraged and supported research on national laws on aggression upon which this chapter is based.

1 Report of the International Law Commission on the work of its forty-seventh session, 2 May to 21 July 1995 (A/50/10), hereinafter '1995 ILC Report', at 39.

2 Draft Code of Crimes Against the Peace and Security of Mankind, Report of the International Law Commission on the work of its forty-seventh session, 6 May to 26 July 1996 (A/51/10), 9, hereinafter '1996 ILC Draft Code', at 49 to 50.

3 1996 ILC Draft Code, at 42.

4 Art. 16 1996 ILC Draft Code defined the crime of aggression as follows: 'An individual who, as leader or organizer, actively participates in or orders the planning, preparation, initiation or waging of aggression committed by a state shall be responsible for a crime of aggression.'

5 1996 ILC Draft Code, at 49.

subsequent trial by an international criminal court was not precluded according to the principle of *ne bis in idem* as defined in the 1996 ILC Draft Code.[6]

Different from that approach, the Rome Statute is based on the primary responsibility of states to prosecute crimes under international law. The crime of aggression, being listed as one category of crimes within the jurisdiction of the International Criminal Court (ICC or Court), does not require deviating procedures in respect of the Statute's general framework. This view has also been endorsed by the Special Working Group on the Crime of Aggression, which reached agreement that 'Articles 17, 18 and 19 were applicable in their current wording' to the crime of aggression.[7] States upon becoming a Party to the Statute have accepted the Court's jurisdiction for all crimes listed in Article 5 ICCSt.[8] Also in the case of aggression, the complementary jurisdiction of the Court only steps in if states do not genuinely exercise the *ius puniendi* of the international community as a whole.[9] In this context, the lacuna of Article 20(3) ICCSt should be kept in mind. While national trials for any crime under the jurisdiction of the ICC are barred once a person has been convicted or acquitted by the Court,[10] the current protection of *ne bis in idem* regarding subsequent trials before the ICC after national prosecutions is limited to conduct defined as genocide, crimes against humanity and war crimes.[11] Accordingly, the ICC would have a wider power to control and admit national cases regarding charges of aggression, even if none of the exceptions listed in Article 20(3) ICCSt applied. The Special Working Group on the Crime of Aggression however, clarified that once the provision of the crime of aggression is adopted, reference to this category of crime will need to be included into the chapeau of paragraph 3.[12]

Despite the applicability of the complementarity regime to charges of aggression, national prosecution may be precluded in specific cases by prerogatives of international law, political considerations or factual circumstances. In the language of Article 17 ICCSt, a state may often find itself 'unable or unwilling' to prosecute an individual for the crime of aggression.[13] For instance, a state may not be in a position to prosecute because its domestic criminal code does not provide for adequate offences and international law is not directly applicable. Even if customary international law forms part of a national legal system, courts may declare the matter as non-justiciable according

---

6 Art. 12(2)(a)(ii) 1996 ILC Draft Code.

7 Report of the Informal Inter-Sessional Meeting of the Special Working Group on the Crime of Aggression of the Assembly of States Parties of the International Criminal Court, Liechtenstein Institute for Self Determination, Woodrow Wilson School, at Princeton University, 21–23 June 2004, ICC-ASP/3/SWGCA/INF.1 (hereinafter '2004 Princeton Report'), para. 27.

8 Art. 12 ICCSt.

9 For details see O. Triffterer, 'Concluding Remarks', in Austrian Federal Ministry for Foreign Affairs/Salzburg Law School on International Criminal Law (eds), *The Future of the International Criminal Court – Salzburg Retreat, 25–27 May 2006* (2006). Available at http://www.sbg.ac.at/salzburglawschool/Retreat (visited 30 September 2009), 26, at 32; id., 'Preliminary Remarks: The Permanent International Criminal Court – Ideal and Reality', in O. Triffterer (ed.), *Commentary on the Rome Statute of the International Criminal Court. Observers' Notes, Article by Article* (2nd edn, Oxford: Hart Publishing, 2008), margin No. 60.

10 Art. 20(2) ICCSt.

11 Art. 20(3) ICCSt. For details see I. Tallgren and A. Reisinger Coracini, 'Article 20 – *Ne bis in idem*', in O. Triffterer (ed.), *Commentary on the Rome Statute of the International Criminal Court. Observers' Notes, Article by Article* (2nd edition, Oxford: Hart Publishing, 2008), margin No. 41.

12 2004 Princeton Report, para. 34.

13 W. A. Schabas, 'Origins of the Criminalization of Aggression: How Crimes Against Peace Became the "Supreme International Crime"', in M. Politi and G. Nesi (eds), *The International Criminal Court and the Crime of Aggression* (2004), 17, at 18, assesses that 'the complementarity regime … seems virtually inapplicable'.

to the political question doctrine.[14] Further potential obstacles to prosecution, in particular high officials of a foreign state, in a specific case may include difficulties in obtaining evidence or getting hold of the accused, or concern immunities under international law.[15] Even if it were in the position to carry out a prosecution, a victim state may refrain from trying alleged perpetrators for aggression out of fear of the aggressor state.[16] Lastly, national proceedings, if carried out, may not satisfy the plea to bring alleged perpetrators to justice. One may think of a sham trial conducted in an aggressor state against its former leaders,[17] or a victorious state that had previously been a victim of aggression and commences proceedings which are not being 'conducted independently or impartially', depriving an alleged perpetrator of his or her rights.[18] Despite these potential perils, states should not *a priori* be suspected of being unwilling to genuinely prosecute. As soon as a provision on aggression is adopted, their performance will be under the scrutiny of the Court, whose complementarity regime was established particularly to counter historic patterns of impunity and the detrimental consequences of victor's justice.[19]

This chapter will examine how existing national legislation fits into the framework according to which national prosecutions of the crime of aggression will be evaluated, once the Court will be able to exercise its jurisdiction over the crime of aggression.[20]

B. Method of Research

This research deals exclusively with statutory legislation. It does not tackle the question of whether or not the crime of aggression under customary international law forms an integral part of certain legal systems and may otherwise be directly applicable.[21] To collect material, some 90 national

---

14 See in this regard e.g. N. Strapatsas, 'Complementarity & Aggression: A Ticking Time Bomb?', Draft presented to the Marie Curie Research Course on International Criminal Law 2007, at 24 ff.; P. Wrange, 'The Principle of Complementarity under the Rome Statute and its Interplay with the Crime of Aggression', *supra* in this Volume.

15 The International Court of Justice held that immunities enjoyed under international law by an incumbent or former Minister for Foreign Affairs do not represent a bar to criminal prosecution in a foreign state only (1) when 'such persons enjoy no criminal immunity under international law in their own countries'; (2) 'if the State which they represent or have represented decides to waive that immunity'; and (3) 'after a person ceases to hold the office … in respect of acts committed prior or subsequent to his or her period of office, as well as in respect of acts committed during that period of office in a private capacity'. See International Court of Justice, Case Concerning the Arrest Warrant of 11 April 2000 (*Democratic Republic of the Congo v. Belgium*), Judgement of 14 February 2002, para. 61. Critically thereto, see e.g. Dissenting Opinion of Judge van den Wyngaert, paras 11 ff.; A. Cassese, 'When May Senior Officials Be Tried for International Crimes? Some Comments on the *Congo v. Belgium* Case', 13 *European Journal of International Law* (2002), at 853.

16 For this scenario see e.g. 2004 Princeton Report, para. 25.

17 Art. 17(2)(a) ICCSt.

18 Art. 17(2)(c) ICCSt; see also 2004 Princeton Report, para. 25.

19 See e.g. Preambular para. 5 ICCSt. For details on the principle of complementarity as applicable to the crime of aggression, see Wrange, *supra* note 14.

20 According to Art. 5(1) ICCSt, the ICC has jurisdiction over the 'most serious crimes of concern to the international community as a whole', including the crime of aggression. However, the Court can only exercise this jurisdiction, once a provision 'defining the crime [of aggression] and setting out the conditions under which the Court shall exercise jurisdiction with respect to this crime' will be adopted (Art. 5(2) ICCSt).

21 See thereto e.g. House of Lords in *R. v. Jones et al.*, Session 2005–2006, [2006] UKHL 16; see also T. Gut and M. Wolpert, 'Canada', in A. Eser, U. Sieber and H. Kreicher (eds), *National Prosecution*

criminal codes and criminal law acts were analysed.[22] Main sources were online information provided by national ministries of justice and databases of regional organizations and research institutions.[23] In addition, with regard to some countries, a study undertaken by the Max Planck Institute for Foreign and International Criminal Law in Freiburg on National Prosecution of International Crimes was relied upon.[24] This survey was particularly helpful to get an insight into national academic discourse and commentary literature. Due to language barriers and difficulties of acquiring reliable translations, a number of national codes could not be taken into account. Therefore, the survey has to be seen as illustrative, not exhaustive. Given the limited access to authentic sources and secondary literature, this chapter will not engage in a detailed analysis of every single national provision. It will instead give examples, provide an overview of the main features of relevant provisions and analyse them with a view to the definition of the crime of aggression under international law.[25]

---

of International Crimes (Berlin: Duncker & Humblot, 2005), at 33; generally, W.N. Ferdinandusse, *Direct Application of International Criminal Law in National Courts* (The Hague: TMC Asser Press, 2006).

22 These include sources from Albania, Argentina, Armenia, Australia, Austria, Azerbaidjan, Belarus, Belgium, Bolivia, Bosnia and Herzegovina (Federation, Brcko District and Republika Srpska), Brazil, Bulgaria, Canada, Chile, China, Colombia, Costa Rica, Côte d'Ivoire, Croatia, Cuba, Ecuador, El Salvador, England and Wales, Estonia, Fidji, Finland, France, Georgia, Germany, Greece, Guatemala, Guyana, Haiti, Honduras, Hong Kong, Hungary, India, Iran, Ireland, Iraq, Israel, Italy, Japan, Kazakhstan, Kiribati, Kosovo, Latvia, Liechtenstein, Luxemburg, Macedonia, Malta, Mexico, Moldova, Mongolia, Montenegro, Netherlands, New Zealand, Nicaragua, Nigeria, Norway, Panama, Papua New Guinea, Paraguay, Peru, Philippines, Poland, Portugal, Romania, Russian Federation, Schweiz, Scotland, Serbia, Slovakia, Slovenia, South Africa, Spain, Sweden, Tajikistan, Turkey, Ukraine, United States of America, Uruguay, Uzbekistan, Vanuatu, Venezuela, Yugoslavia and Zambia. References to Titles, Chapters or Sections of national criminal codes, if not otherwise indicated, relate to the respective code's Special Part.

23 E.g. Organization of American States. Available at http://www.oas.org/juridico/mla/en/index.html (visited 30 September 2009); OSCE Office for Democratic Institutions and Human Rights. Available at http://www.legislationline.org (visited 30 September 2009); University of Fribourg. Available at http://www.unifr.ch/ddp1/derechopenal/ley.htm (visited 30 September 2009); Academy of European Law. Available at http://www.era.int/domains/corpus-juris/public/texts/legal_text.htm (visited 30 September 2009); Eurojustice network. Available at http://www.eurojustice.org/member_states (visited 30 September 2009). For a compendium of over 60 national implementing laws see the International Criminal Court Legislation Database of the University of Nottingham's Human Rights Law Centre. Available at http://www.nottingham.ac.uk/law/hrlc/international-criminal-justice-unit/implementation-database.php (visited 30 September 2009); see also International Humanitarian Law/International Criminal Law database. Available at http://www.wihl.nl (visited 30 September 2009).

24 A. Eser, U. Sieber and H. Kreicker (eds), *Nationale Strafverfolgung völkerrechtlicher Verbrechen/National Prosecution of International Crimes*, Vol. 1: H. Gropengießer/H. Kreicker, 'Deutschland' (2003); Vol. 2: D. Frände, 'Finnland', E. Weigend, 'Polen', K. Cornils, 'Schweden' (2003); Vol. 3: P. Novoselec, 'Kroatien', I. Zerbes, 'Österreich', M. Škulić 'Serbien und Montenegro', D. Korošec, 'Slowenien' (2004); Vol. 4: A. B. Kouassi/S. Paulenz, 'Côte d'Ivoire', A. Gil Gil, 'España', J. Lelieur-Fischer, 'Frankreich', K. Jarvers/Ch. Grammer 'Italien', K. Ambos/E. Malarino, 'Lateinamerika' (2005); Vol. 5: T. Gut/M. Wolper, 'Canada', A. Parmas/T. Ploom, 'Estonia', M. G. Retalis, 'Greece', M. Kremnitzer/M. A. Cohen, 'Israel', E. Silverman, 'United States of America' (2005); Vol. 6: A. Biehler/Ch. Kerll, 'Australien', T. Richter, 'China', Ch. Rabenstein/R. Bahrenberg, 'England und Wales', S. Lammich, 'Russland und Weißrussland', S. Tellenbach, 'Türkei' (2005) (Berlin: Duncker & Humblot).

25 For the current state of negotiations see Report of the Informal Inter-Sessional Meeting of the Special Working Group on the Crime of Aggression of the Assembly of States Parties of the International Criminal

This chapter will first focus on states, which have implemented legislation in order to enforce the crime of aggression under customary international law before domestic courts, thereby aiming at protecting legal values of the international community as a whole. In that context, the respective national definitions will be scrutinized in the light of the current state of the negotiations on codifying the crime of aggression for adjudication before the ICC. Furthermore, it will be examined under what circumstances these states can establish jurisdiction to adjudicate and are actually in a position to prosecute this crime. Secondly, the chapter will deal with conduct criminalized under domestic law, primarily aiming at protecting national interests, which falls short of the crime of aggression under international law but includes aspects of its definition. Regarding the second category, the question, whether any of these crimes may contribute to national prosecution under the complementarity regime of the Rome Statute will be analysed.

With a view to the protected legal values, these two categories partly overlap. The crime of aggression, as all other crimes under international law, ultimately seeks to protect 'international peace and security' or, in the words of the Rome Statute, 'the peace, security and well-being of the world'.[26] Another facet of the crime of aggression is that it protects the 'sovereignty, territorial integrity or political independence'[27] of a state, interests which form the cornerstones of the international system. At the same time, every national state has a fundamental interest to protect its own sovereignty, territorial integrity and political independence. Accordingly, most states protect these values as *ultima ratio* also by means of criminal law. In that sense they can be considered as national legal values. The structure of this survey will follow the categorization introduced by national legislatures. It will be interesting to see that, as a consequence of the twofold nature of the protected legal values, similar conduct which is implemented as a crime under international law in some states is criminalized as a domestic crime in others.[28]

2. Norms Implementing the Crime of Aggression Under International Law

From 90 national criminal codes reviewed, statutory provisions relating to the crime of aggression under international law were detected in some 25 countries,[29] predominately Eastern European and Central Asian states. The relevant norms carry different designations. Many provisions are simply

Court, Liechtenstein Institute for Self Determination, Woodrow Wilson School, at Princeton University, 11–14 June 2007, ICC-ASP/6/SWGCA/INF.1, hereinafter '2007 Princeton Report'.

26 Preambular para. 3 ICCSt. On this changed formula of international legal interests see O. Triffterer, Preamble, in Triffterer (ed.), *Commentary on the Rome Statute of the International Criminal Court. Observers' Notes, Article by Article* (2nd edn, Oxford: Hart Publishing, 2008), margin No. 11.

27 See Art. 1 Definition of Aggression, UN GA Res. 3314 (XXIX), 1974. The question of subsidiary protection of individual interests is beyond the scope of this chapter. For details see A. Reisinger Coracini, 'Verbrechen gegen den Frieden' (21 *Leiden Journal of International Law 2009*, 699), at II.

28 See in this context, for instance, Title One of the Philippine criminal code, which merges 'crimes against national security and the law of nations'.

29 Armenia, Azerbaijan, Belarus, Bosnia and Herzegovina (criminal codes of the Federation, Brcko District and Republika Srpska), Bulgaria, Croatia, Estonia, Georgia, Hungary, Kazakhstan, Kosovo, Latvia, Macedonia, Moldova, Mongolia, Montenegro, Poland, Russian Federation, Serbia, Slovakia, Slovenia, Tajikistan, Ukraine, Uzbekistan. The relevant norms either implement the crime of aggression under international customary law, the treaty-based prohibition of propaganda of war, or both. Also the Portuguese criminal code, Chapter I of Title III, contained a crime of incitement to war (Art. 236) entitled 'dos crimes contra a paz'; the provision has, however, been renounced in 2004.

titled 'war of aggression', 'aggressive war',[30] or 'aggression'.[31] The Latvian criminal code uses the term 'crimes against peace'.[32] In the majority of cases the designation of the crime mentions particular modes of participation. These range from very specific acts, such as 'instigating an aggressive war',[33] 'incitement to war',[34] or 'stirring up of an armed conflict'[35] to the complete spectrum of 'planning, preparing, unleashing, or waging an aggressive war'.[36]

Provisions on the crime of aggression are located in such chapters of national criminal codes which comprise crimes under international law enforceable by domestic courts. The titles of these chapters mirror the international legal values they seek to protect. Chapter XIII of the Croatian Criminal Code, for instance, which also includes individual criminal responsibility for 'war of aggression' (Article 157), refers explicitly to 'criminal offences against values protected by international law'. Other criminal codes similarly refer to crimes against 'rights guaranteed under international law', crimes against the 'international legal order' or generally to crimes against 'international law'.[37] Frequently, references to the ILC Draft Code of 'crimes against the peace and security of mankind' can be found.[38] Next to 'peace' and 'security', the category 'humanity' is listed as a protected interest in some cases.[39] At least twice, the term 'crimes against humanity' serves as a generic denomination for crimes under international law, including crimes against peace.[40] Occasionally, the chapter headings simply list those crimes under international law which are subsequently defined.[41]

The majority of national criminal codes, however, do not contain the crime of aggression under international law. In same countries, respective legislative proposals were discussed[42] but rejected, e.g., in Sweden, due to lack of an agreed definition of the crime on the international level,[43] or in Finland, because aggression was understood as a matter between states.[44]

---

30 See Art. 384 Armenian criminal code; Art. 157 Croatian criminal code; Art. 442 Montenegrin criminal code; Art. 386 Serbian criminal code; Art. 395 Tajik criminal code.

31 Para. 91 Estonian criminal code; Art. 151 Uzbek criminal code.

32 Section 72 Latvian criminal code.

33 Art. 165 Bosnian federal criminal code; Art. 159 Bosnian criminal code (Brcko District); Art. 444 Bosnian criminal code (Republika Srpska); Art. 385 Slovenian criminal code.

34 Art. 114 Cuban criminal code; Section 153 Hungarian criminal code; former Art. 236 Portuguese criminal code.

35 Art. 297 Mongolian criminal code.

36 Art. 353 Russian criminal code. Similarly, e.g., Art. 139 Moldovan criminal code; Art. 156 Kazakh criminal code; Art. 117 (1) Polish criminal code; Art. 437 Ukrainian criminal code.

37 See, for instance, Chapter 35 Montenegrin criminal code; Chapter 34 Serbian criminal code; Chapter XXXV Slovenian criminal code; Chapter XX Ukrainian criminal code; Chapter XIV Kosovar criminal code; Title I, Chapter III Venezuelan criminal code.

38 Section 13, Chapter 33 Armenian criminal code; Chapter 4 Kazakh criminal code; Title 10, Chapter 30 Mongolian criminal code; Section XV Chapter 34 Tajik criminal code; Section 2, Chapter 8 Uzbek criminal code; Chapter 34 Russian criminal code.

39 Chapter XVI Bosnian federal criminal code; Chapter XIV Bulgarian criminal code; Chapter 8 Estonian criminal code.

40 Section 14 Georgian criminal code; Chapter XI Hungarian criminal code.

41 See, e.g., Chapter IX Latvian criminal code; Chapter I Moldovan criminal code; Chapter XVI Polish criminal code.

42 For the discussion in Canada in the context of the preparation of the ICC implementation act see Gut and Wolpert, *supra* note 24, at 34.

43 Cornils, *supra* note 24, at 220.

44 Frände, *supra* note 24, at 45.

A. Leadership Element

At first glance, it is striking that national provisions scarcely refer to the one component of the crime of aggression over which there seems to be a broad international consensus: the leadership element. Although there has been some discussion at the international level of whether the leadership element was an integral part of the definition of the crime (definitional element), or whether it was to be understood as restricting the jurisdiction of the ICC (jurisdictional element),[45] it is generally understood that only high-ranking officials, persons who are in a decision-making position in their country, shall bear responsibility for the crime of aggression.[46] The established qualification of a potential perpetrator of the crime of aggression as 'being in a position effectively to exercise control over or to direct the political or military action of a state' originates from the 2002 Discussion Paper and has since remained unchanged.[47]

None of those national norms, which strictly relate to conduct punishable under the Charter of the International Military Tribunals of Nuremberg and Tokyo,[48] expressly limits the circle of potential perpetrators to certain groups of individuals. Legal commentaries to these provisions offer the following guidelines for interpretation. First, since the national norm implements a crime under international law, it has to be read in accordance with the customary law definition of the crime. Second, a potential perpetrator of the crime of aggression has to be capable and in the position to carry out the *actus reus*. Therefore, it is suggested that only persons who have a leading position in the military or the political decision-making bodies are *per se* capable of perpetrating

---

45 This discussion arose following the circulation of a proposal for alternative language for the definition of the crime of aggression by the Chairman of the Special Working Group for the Crime of Aggression (SWGCA) at the fifth resumed session of the Assembly of States Parties. It suggested that '[t]he Court shall have jurisdiction with respect to the crime of aggression when committed by a person being in a position effectively to exercise control over or to direct the political or military action of a state' (Report of the Special Working Group on the Crime of Aggression, ICC-ASP/5/SWGCA/3 of 31 January 2997, Annex, at 7). Meanwhile, the question seems to have been settled with a vast majority of delegates expressing their understanding of the leadership element as an integral part of the definition of crime (2007 Princeton Report, para. 9). During the discussions some delegations voiced the opinion that they would not see a substantive change regarding the result of the two different formulations. This may be true regarding prosecutions before the ICC. However the question of whether the leadership element forms part of the customary definition of the crime may have an impact on domestic enforcement.

46 This consensus can also be illustrated by the drafting history for a provision on aggression. All but one proposal on the definition of the crime expressly refer to the leadership element and even PCNICC/1999/DP.12 (Russian Federation), introducing Art. 6 (a) IMT Charter, is to be understood as implicitly incorporating this element. See also e.g. C. Kress, 'The Crime of Aggression before the First Review of the ICC Statute', 20 *Leiden Journal of International Law* (2007), 851, at 855.

47 See Discussion paper proposed by the Coordinator, Report of the Preparatory Commission for the International Criminal Court, Addendum, Part II Proposals for a provision on the crime of aggression, PCNICC/2002/2/Add. 2 of 24 July 2002, 3, at I 1 and Discussion paper on the crime of aggression proposed by the Chairman, ICC-ASP/5/SWGCA/2 of 16 January 2007, at 3.

48 Agreement for the Prosecution and Punishment of the Major War Criminals of the European Axis, and Charter of the International Military Tribunal. London, 8 August 1945 (hereinafter 'IMT Charter' or 'Nüremberg Charter'); Special Proclamation of General MacArthur, the Supreme Commander for the Allied Powers, of 19 January, 1946 (hereinafter 'IMTFE Charter').

the crime of aggression, but not, for instance, persons at the bottom of the chain of command, who are executing military operations.[49]

An implicit reference to criminal responsibility of persons in a superior position can be found in the criminal codes of Montenegro and Serbia. Next to any person who 'calls for or instigates aggressive war', 'anyone who orders waging war'[50] is liable for punishment. Comparably, the Croatian criminal code specifies waging a war of aggression as 'commanding an armed action of one state against the sovereignty, territorial integrity or political independence of another state'. The conduct verbs 'order' and 'command' imply the existence of a hierarchical, superior-subordinate relationship and thus limit criminal responsibility to persons in a position to give such orders or commands.[51]

In addition, however, the Croatian Criminal Code provides equal punishment for a person who wages aggressive war and 'whoever acts according to a command for action from armed forces or para-military armed forces for the purpose of waging a war of aggression'.[52] This norm is consistent with the general principle of international criminal law according to which acting pursuant to an order of a government or of a superior does not relieve a person from criminal responsibility for the perpetration of a core crime.[53] Yet, if extended to anyone within a chain of command, the provision challenges the *ratio* behind the limitation of the circle of perpetrators for the crime of aggression on the international level, which is to exclude ordinary soldiers from criminal responsibility for acts they may not be in a position to judge as being in conformity with or against international law.[54]

The leadership element is more frequently referred to with regard to conduct going beyond the Nüremberg acts. Estonia, for instance, expressly punishes 'a representative of the state who threatens to start a war of aggression'.[55] Other states, in the context of the crime of war propaganda,

49 See e.g. Weigend, *supra* note 24, at 113; Parmas and Ploom, *supra* note 24, at 123. An Estonian Commentary bases individual criminal responsibility on 'strategic leadership in a war as a whole', a person giving orders and instructions for warfare on the highest state level (political and military governance). State representatives as well as other persons not belonging to the public service, but having nevertheless sufficient power to commit the crime (e.g. leaders of the political party currently in power or an influential business figure) similarly qualify as perpetrators. See para. 91 in J. Sootak and P. Pikamäe (eds), *Penal Code. The Commented Edition* (2nd edn, Tallinn: Juura, 2004), at 4.2 and 5.

50 Art. 442 Montenegrin criminal code; see also Art. 386 Serbian criminal code. Employment of the conduct verb 'order' has also been discussed on the international level, see in this sense, e.g., Art. 16 1996 Draft Code; 2002 Discussion Paper, at I 1; 2007 Discussion Paper I 1 Variant (a).

51 See, e.g., ICTR, Judgement, *Akayesu*, Chamber I, 2 September 1998, para. 483: 'Ordering implies a superior-subordinate relationship between the person giving the order and the one executing it. In other words, the person in a position of authority uses it to convince another to commit an offence'; see also ICTR, Judgement, *Rutaganda*, Trial Chamber, 6 December 1999, para. 39; ICTR, Judgement, *Musema*, Trial Chamber, 27 January 2000, para. 121.

52 Art. 157(3) Croatian criminal code.

53 See Art. 8 IMT Charter yet allowing for the mitigation of punishment, and Art. 33 ICCSt refining the applicable test.

54 Art. 33(1) ICCSt specifies that acting pursuant to an order may relieve a person under the legal obligation to obey such orders (*litera* a) from criminal responsibility, if the person did not know that the order was unlawful (*litera* b) and the order was not manifestly unlawful (*litera* c). According to Art. 33(2), only orders to commit genocide or crimes against humanity are 'manifestly unlawful'. The test for a subordinate under a legal obligation to obey an order with regard to the crime of aggression, therefore, would probably be whether the person knew that the order was unlawful.

55 Para. 91 Estonian criminal code.

public incitement, or calls for a war of aggression consider a perpetrator's high official position as an aggravating circumstance for punishment.[56]

The fact that a majority of national provisions on aggression lack explicit reference to the leadership element, as well as the suggested interpretation of national laws on aggression in accordance with international law, demands further consideration of its customary law nature.

The leadership element can barely be traced in definitions and draft definitions of the crime of aggression before the 1991 ILC Draft Code. The definition of crimes against peace in the International Military Tribunal (IMT) and the International Military Tribunal for the Far East (IMTFE) Charter did not restrict individual criminal responsibility to a certain circle of perpetrators.[57] Albeit, the Tribunals' jurisdiction was limited per definition to 'the trial and punishment of the major war criminals of the European Axis countries' and 'in the Far East' respectively.[58] To determine criminal responsibility for crimes against peace, the military Tribunals relied on the alleged perpetrator's high position in government, military, politics or as a state official. The determination of such high position, however, was not based on formal requirements, but foremost on a person's ability to actually exercise power in a leadership, policy- or decision-making, or otherwise influencing position.[59] These criteria do not necessarily constitute a limitation of the circle of perpetrators, but could equally be seen as a manifestation of the principle of personal guilt. Nonetheless, Control Council Law No. 10 subsequently confined responsibility for crimes against peace to persons who 'held a high political, civil or military (including General Staff) position in Germany or one of its Allies, cobelligerents or satellites or held high position in the financial, industrial or economic life of any such country'.[60]

---

56 '[T]he highest state authority' according to Art. 385 of the Armenian criminal code is to be understood as 'the President of the Republic of Armenia, the members of the Government of the Republic of Armenia, the members of the National Assembly of the Republic of Armenia', ibid., para. 3. Art. 405 of the Georgian criminal code refers to 'a person holding a statepolitical office'; see also references to an 'official holding a responsible position', Art. 156 Kazakh criminal code; 'civil servant' Art. 298 Mongolian criminal code; or 'holding a state position' Art. 396 Tajik criminal code.

57 See Art. 6(a) IMT Charter and Art. 5(a) IMTFE Charter respectively. The definitions of crimes against peace in these documents differ only in that Art. 5(a) specifies a war of aggression to be 'declared or undeclared'. Further references to Art. 6(a) IMT Charter are therefore understood as to comprise Art. 5(a) IMTFE Charter. The IMT judgement confirmed, '[t]he argument that such common planning cannot exist where there is complete dictatorship is unsound ... Hitler could not make aggressive war by himself. He had to have the cooperation of statesmen, military leaders, diplomats and businessmen', Trial of the Major War Criminals before the International Military Tribunal, Nüremberg, 14 November 1945–1 October 1946, Vol. I (1947), at 226.

58 Art. 1 IMT and IMTFE Charter.

59 For an overview, see Historical review of developments relating to aggression, PCNICC/2002/WGCA/L.1/Add.1 of 18 January 2002, at 32 ff.

60 Art II para. 2(f) Control Council Law No. 10. As occupation law, Control Council Law No. 10 is not a direct source of international law, but has frequently been invoked as one indicator in determining international customary law (see e.g. ICTY, *Tadic*, App. Ch. Judgement, 15 July 1999, para. 289). Given the exceptional appearance of the leadership element in this legal text, its customary nature cannot be assumed *per se*. Applying the 'high position' standard, e.g. in the *High Command* case, the accused were acquitted of the count of crimes against peace since '[t]he acts of commanders and staff officers below the policy level ... do not constitute the planning, preparation, initiation and waging of war or the initiation of invasion'; criminality was not determined by their rank or status, but by the defendants 'power to shape or influence the policy of his state' (*Trials of War Criminals before the Nüremberg Military Tribunals*. Vol. XI (1950), 462, at 490–491). The *I.G. Farben* case, though the accused were again acquitted for being followers rather

The ILC's formulation of the Nüremberg principles,[61] literally repeats the definition of crimes against peace in the Nüremberg Charter. It does not limit the circle of perpetrators, but the ILC Commentary explains that 'waging of a war of aggression' was understood as to 'refer only to high-ranking military personnel and high state officials'.[62] The 1951 and 1954 versions of the ILC Draft Code again do not restrict the group of perpetrators according to their position. Hence, they make clear that since aggression can only be committed by a state, only state officials qualify as principal offenders of the crime of aggression.[63] Nonetheless, private individuals could participate in the commission of the crimes as accessories.[64]

The discussion about the circle of perpetrators of the crime of aggression in the second phase of the ILC's elaboration of a draft code was dominated by the question of whether only government officials or also other persons bearing political and military responsibility or even private persons 'who place their economic or financial power at the disposal of the authors of the aggression' should be criminally responsible.[65] The question had not yet been resolved when the ILC provisionally adopted a draft Article on aggression in 1988.[66] With the lapidary explanation that 'the Commission either added an introductory paragraph or slightly recast the Articles to cover the question of attributing the crimes to individuals and of punishment',[67] the 1991 and the 1996 ILC Draft Code expressly limited individual criminal responsibility for the crime of aggression to leaders or organizers.[68] To appease critical voices,[69] the ILC Commentary clarified that the terms 'leaders' or 'organizers' 'must be understood in the broad sense, i.e., as referring, in addition to the members of a government, to persons occupying high-level posts in the military, the diplomatic corps, political parties and industry, as recognized by the Nüremberg Tribunal'.[70]

This overview shows that the leadership element has not necessarily constituted an explicit part of the definition of the crime of aggression. At the same time, it has evidently been understood from the very beginning as an implicit component of the definition of crime. The difficulty therefore lies in the codification of criteria exemplifying the personal authority or power of an offender to be in

---

then leaders, confirmed that economic leaders can be held accountable for crimes against peace (*Trials of War Criminals before the Nüremberg Military Tribunals*. Vol. VIII (1952), 1081, at 1126). For details on the applied 'shape or influence' test see K.J. Heller, 'Retreat from Nüremberg: The Leadership Requirement in the Crime of Aggression', *European Journal of International Law* 18 (2007), 477, at 482 ff.

61 Report of the International Law Commission on the work of its second session, 5 June to 29 July 1950, Yearbook of the International Law Commission 1950, Vol. II, at 374.

62 Ibid., at 376. The ILC did not intend that 'everyone in uniform who fought in a war of aggression' should be charged with waging such a war.

63 See Art. 2(1) Draft Code of Crimes Against the Peace and Security of Mankind, Report of the International Law Commission on the work of its third session, 16 May to 27 July 1951, *Yearbook of the International Law Commission 1951*, Vol. II, 134 ff., hereinafter '1951 Draft Code', and Art. 2(1) Draft Code of Crimes Against the Peace and Security of Mankind, Report of the International Law Commission on the work of its sixth session, 3 June to 28 July 1954 (A/2693), 462 ff., hereinafter '1954 ILC Draft Code'.

64 See, e.g., Art. 2(12), 1951 ILC Draft Code and Commentary thereto, ibid., at 137.

65 Report of the International Law Commission on the work of its fortieth session, 9 May to 29 July 1988, *Yearbook of the International Law Commission 1988*, Vol. II (Part 2), at 72.

66 See draft Art. 12(1), 1988 ILC Report, *supra* note 65, at 71.

67 Report of the International Law Commission on the work of its forty-third session, 29 April to 19 July 1991, *Yearbook of the International Law Commission 1991*, Vol. II (Part 2), at 93.

68 Art. 15 Draft Code of Crimes Against the Peace and Security of Mankind, 1991 ILC Report, *supra* note 67, 94 ff., hereinafter '1991 ILC Draft Code'.

69 See, e.g., 1995 ILC Report, at 35.

70 1996 ILC Draft Code, at 83.

a position potentially to play a decisive role in committing aggression without narrowing down the circle or perpetrators.[71] Pending the final outcome of the work of the Special Working Group on the Crime of Aggression and the adoption of a provision of aggression, the formulation of the leadership element, though certainly constituting a strong hint as to the scope of this element under customary law, may leave open a margin for states to enlarge the circle of perpetrators under domestic law, in particular with a view to the leadership requirement for secondary offenders.

B. The Individual's Conduct

Structurally, the examined national provisions define the crime of aggression as the participation of an individual perpetrator in an act of aggression by a state.[72] In that aspect, they correspond to the definition of crimes against the peace as contained in the IMT Charter and are in conformity with the ongoing negotiations on the international level.

As regards the definition of the individual's conduct, national laws to a large extent implement the modes of participation and stages of criminal responsibility contained in the IMT Charter. Again, this practice is in line with the international negotiations. Although the Preparatory Commission and the Special Working Group on the Crime of Aggression have been discussing various variants, late developments indicate a revival of the Nüremberg formula. By listing specific modes of perpetration in the definition of the crime itself, the provisions seem to follow what has been described as the 'monistic approach'.[73] However, despite the use of specific conduct verbs, none of the examined criminal codes expressly excludes the application of its general part. It is therefore assumed that the provisions of the respective general part apply and potential overlaps or contradictions, should they occur, would have to be sorted out by way of interpretation.[74]

In accordance with individual conduct criminalized by the IMT Charter,[75] a majority of states that have implemented the crime of aggression declare punishable the classic canon of 'planning,[76]

71 1996 ILC Draft Code, at 83. Critically whether the 'control or direct' test currently referred to would include all groups of perpetrators, see *Heller*, *supra* note 60, at 488.

72 For details on alternative terminology regarding the act of state, see *infra* C.

73 Whereas the differentiated approach would formulate the definition in a neutral way and regulate modes of participation in the General Part. See generally Discussion paper 1: The Crime of Aggression and Article 25, paragraph 3, of the Statute, Assembly of States Parties to the Rome Statute of the International Criminal Court, Fourth session, The Hague, 28 November to 3 December 2005, Official Records, ICC-ASP/4/32, Annex II.B, at 376; Informal Inter-sessional Meeting of the Special Working Group on the Crime of Aggression, held at the Liechtenstein Institute on Self-Determination, Woodrow Wilson School, Princeton University, United States of America, 8-11 June 2006, ICC-ASP/5/SWGCA/INF.1, hereinafter '2006 Princeton Report', paras 84 ff.

74 See in this direction also 2007 Princeton Report, para. 7.

75 Art. 6(a) IMT Charter defines crimes against peace as 'planning, preparation, initiation or waging of a war of aggression, or a war in violation of international treaties, agreements or assurances, or participation in a common plan or conspiracy for the accomplishment of any of the foregoing'. Art. 5(a) IMTFE Charter employs the same definition, though specifying the war of aggression as 'declared or undeclared'.

76 Art. 384(1) Armenian criminal code; Art. 409 Bulgarian criminal code; Art. 404(1) Georgian criminal code; Art. 156(1) Kazakh criminal code; Section 72 Latvian criminal code; Art. 139 Moldovan criminal code; Art. 353 Russian criminal code; Art. 396 Tajik criminal code; Art. 437 Ukrainian criminal code; Art. 151 Uzbek criminal code.

preparation,[77] initiation[78] or waging[79] of a war of aggression or a war in violation of international treaties, agreements or assurances'.[80] While many countries implemented all four modes of perpetration, others were selective.[81] In particular, it is noteworthy that some states do criminalize preparatory acts, but not the initiation or execution of an act of aggression as such. Fewer states included in their domestic definition of aggression 'participation in a common plan or conspiracy for the accomplishment of any of the foregoing'.[82] Yet, the absence of this mode of conduct is without prejudice to the application of a general conspiracy provision enshrined in the general part of a respective penal code.

In addition to the traditional modes of criminal responsibility for the crime of aggression, a number of states use conduct verbs going beyond the Nüremberg canon. The criminal codes of Montenegro and Serbia, for instance, provide punishment for a person who 'orders waging a war of aggression'.[83] Other criminal codes contain provisions criminalizing 'calls for',[84] 'instigation of',[85] 'public calls for',[86] or '(public) incitement of'[87] a war of aggression. The Latvian criminal code, for instance, incorporates instigation as an additional mode of participation in the definition

77 Art. 384(1) Armenian criminal code; Art. 409 Bulgarian criminal code; para. 91 Estonian criminal code; Art. 404(1) Georgian criminal code; Art. 156(1) Kazakh criminal code; s. 72 Latvian criminal code; Art. 139 Moldovan criminal code; Art. 117(2) Polish criminal code; Art. 353 Russian criminal code; Art. 396 Tajik criminal code; Art. 437 Ukrainian criminal code; Art. 151 Uzbek criminal code.

78 Different conduct verbs are used, e.g., 'starting' Art. 384(2) Armenian criminal code; 'unleashing', Art. 404(2) Georgian criminal code; Art. 139 Moldovan criminal code; Art. 353 Russian criminal code; Art. 396 Tajik criminal code; Art. 156(1) Kazakh criminal code; 'stirring up of an armed conflict', Art. 297 Mongolian criminal code; Art. 117(1) Polish criminal code; 'commencement', Art. 151 Uzbek criminal code.

79 Art. 409 Bulgarian criminal code; Art. 157(1) Croatian criminal code; Art. 404(2) Georgian criminal code; Art. 139 Moldovan criminal code; Art. 117(1) Polish criminal code; Art. 353 Russian criminal code; Art. 437 Ukrainian criminal code. Some translations use the term 'conduct', e.g. Art. 384(2) Armenian criminal code; Art. 156(1) Kazakh criminal code; Section 72 Latvian criminal code; Art. 396 Tajik criminal code; Art. 151 Uzbek criminal code.

80 Para. 91 Estonian criminal code; s. 72 Latvian criminal code; see *infra* C.

81 Art. 409 Bulgarian criminal code, for instance, punishes a person '[w]ho plans, prepares or wages aggressive war'; para. 91 Estonian criminal code limits criminal responsibility to 'leading or participating in preparations for a war of aggression'.

82 See in this regard, s. 72 Latvian criminal code; Art. 437 Ukrainian criminal code; Art. 151 Uzbek criminal code.

83 Art. 386 Serbian criminal code; Art. 442 Montenegrin criminal code. For implications on the leadership element see *supra* note 50.

84 Art. 165 Bosnian federal criminal code; Art. 157 para. 4 Croatian criminal code; Art. 405(1) Georgian criminal code; Art. 442 Montenegrin criminal code; Art. 386 Serbian criminal code; Art. 385 Slovenian criminal code.

85 E.g., Art. 165 Bosnian federal criminal code; Art. 408 Bulgarian criminal code; Art. 157 para. 4 Croatian criminal code; Art. 130 Kosovar criminal code; Art. 442 Montenegrin criminal code; Art. 386 Serbian criminal code; Art. 385 Slovenian criminal code.

86 E.g., Art. 385 Armenian criminal code; Art. 130 Kosovar criminal code; see also 'public appeals to unleash an aggressive war' Art. 354 Russian criminal code and Art. 396 Tajik criminal code.

87 E.g., s. 77 Latvian criminal code; Art. 117(3) Polish criminal code; former Art. 236 Portuguese criminal code. Art. 114 Cuban criminal code does not only cover incitement to a war of aggression; the provision equally provides punishment for instigating the public in favour of war during the course of diplomatic negotiations for the peaceful solution of an international conflict.

of the crime of aggression.[88] Usually, however, these modes of perpetration are implemented as distinct unlawful acts, which complement[89] or substitute the traditional definition of the crime of aggression.[90] As a distinct category of crime, these definitions usually criminalize instigation or incitement as an inchoate offence.[91] The respective Bulgarian provision, for instance, reads: 'Who, directly or indirectly, through publications, speeches, radio or in any other way aims at provoking armed attack by one country to another shall be punished for war instigation by imprisonment of three to ten years.'[92]

Closely related to instigating or inciting an act of aggression as an inchoate crime, a number of states punish propaganda of war as a crime under international law.[93] These national provisions also stem from an international treaty obligation. Article 20(1) of the International Covenant on Civil and Political Rights (ICCPR) requires states to prohibit by law any propaganda for war.[94] The obligation includes the provision of appropriate sanctions, although they do not necessarily need to be of a penal nature.[95] As of today, 164 states have ratified or acceded to the ICCPR.[96] However,

---

88 Section 72 Latvian criminal code holds accountable 'a person who commits crimes against peace, that is, commits planning, preparation or instigation of, or participation in, military aggression'. It should be kept in mind that instigation to war in some countries is codified as a treasonable offence (e.g. Chapter 12 s. 2 Finnish criminal code). For details see *infra* 3 B.

89 See, e.g., Art. 157 Croatian criminal code; Arts 404 and 405 Georgian criminal code; s. 72 Latvian criminal code; Arts 436 and 437 Ukrainian criminal code.

90 See, e.g., Art. 165 Bosnian federal criminal code; Art. 442 Montenegrin criminal code; Art. 386 Serbian criminal code. Section 153 Hungarian criminal code and former Art. 236 Portuguese criminal code expressly implement incitement to war as a crime against peace. For the Portuguese provision see, e.g., M. J. Antunes, 'Título III – Dos crimes contra a paz e a humanidade', in J. De Figueiredo Dias (ed.), *Comentário Conimbricense do Código Penal, Parte Especial, Tomo II* (Coimbra: Coimbra Edition, 1999), 599, at 559.

91 On the international level, instigation, as opposed to public incitement, is usually understood as a mode of participation in the crime, not an inchoate offence. See, e.g., '"Instigating" means prompting another to commit an offence' (ICTY, Judgement, *Krstic*, Trial Chamber, 2 August 2001, para. 601; ICTY, Judgement, *Blaskic*, Trial Chamber, 3 March 2000, para. 280); 'By urging or encouraging another person to commit a crime, the instigator may contribute substantially to the commission of the crime.' ICTR, Judgement, *Bagilishema*, Trial Chamber, 7 June 2001, para. 30). National criminal codes seem to use these notions interchangeably, at least as regards their English translation, see e.g. *infra* note 93.

92 Art. 408 Bulgarian criminal code.

93 E.g. Art. 407 Bulgarian criminal code; para. 92 Estonian criminal code; s. 153 Hungarian criminal code; Art. 157 Kazakh criminal code; Art. 140 Moldovan criminal code; Art. 298 Mongolian criminal code; Art. 436 Ukrainian criminal code; Art. 150 Uzbek criminal code. Art. 115 Cuban criminal code only criminalizes the distribution of *false* information with the purpose of disturbing international peace. The borders between instigation, incitement and war propaganda are permeable. In some cases these notions seem interchangeable in others they define distinct criminal acts. Para. 92. Estonian criminal code, for instance, defines 'propaganda for war' as 'any incitement to war'. The Bulgarian criminal code, on the other hand, contains separate provisions on propaganda of war (Art. 407) and war instigation (Art. 408).

94 GA Res. 2200A (XXI), of 16 December 1966. For details on Art. 20 ICCPR see M. Kearney, *The Prohibition of Propaganda for War in International Law* (Oxford: Oxford University Press, 2007). See in this context also, GA Resolution 380 (V) which condemns 'incitement to conflicts or acts of aggression' as 'propaganda against peace'. It should be noted in this regard, that some states have implemented their obligation under the ICCPR as a crime under national law, see *infra* 3 B.

95 See in this regard M. Nowak, *U.N. Covenant on Civil and Political Rights* (2nd edn, Oxford: Clarendon Press, 2005), at 474.

96 See http://www2.ohchr.org/english/bodies/ratification/4.htm (visited 26 January 2009).

several states have made reservations or declarations with regard to Article 20.[97] A possible criminalization of war propaganda was also discussed in the context of the ILC Draft Code. The ILC did not include propaganda for war as a separate offence in its early versions of the Draft Code but understood such conduct to be covered by the inchoate crime of incitement according to Article 2(12) ILC Draft Code.[98]

As regards the mental element, the examined criminal codes provide for no specific rules. The *actus reus*, therefore, is to be conducted with the default *mens rea* provided for in the respective criminal code. No deviating degree of *dolus*, purpose going beyond the realization of the material elements, is required to meet the definition of the crime of aggression.[99] Purpose becomes of relevance only where incitement or propaganda of war are punishable as inchoate offences. In these cases, which do not demand the occurrence of a result of the criminal conduct, the criminality manifests itself particularly in the perpetrator's *mens rea.*[100]

Finally, a different type of norm merits attention. They do not claim to implement the crime of aggression nor fit the particular structure of this crime. However, they criminalize *as crimes against international law* conduct which may lead to an international war.[101] The Hungarian criminal code, for instance, criminalizes as a crime against peace the attempt to recruit military personnel.[102] The Cuban criminal code contains a crime of conscription or hostile acts against another state, conducted without the authorization of the government, with the purpose of exposing Cuba to the danger of a war.[103] Persons, who on Cuban territory commit acts which infringe the independence of a foreign

97 Australia, Belgium, Denmark, Finland, France, Iceland, Ireland, Luxembourg, Malta, Netherlands, New Zealand, Norway, Sweden, Switzerland, Thailand, United Kingdom of Great Britain and Northern Ireland, United States of America. See http://www.unhchr.ch/pdf/report.pdf (visited 30 September 2009). For freedom of speech concerns reflected in the vote on the adoption of the ICCPR see Nowak, *supra* note 95, at 471.

98 In response to the 1954 ILC Report, several representatives spoke up for a future inclusion of the prohibition of war propaganda in the ILC Draft Code, e.g., Mongolia, Bulgaria, Afghanistan. See Analytical paper prepared pursuant to the request contained in para. 256 of the report of the Commission on the work of its forty-fourth session, UN Doc A/Cn.4/365, 25 March 1983, para. 89.

99 For the concept of *animus aggressionis* as requiring an alleged perpetrator of the crime of aggression to act with a specific intent see, e.g., S. Glaser, 'Culpabilité en droit international pénal', 99 *Recueil des Cours* (1960), 467, at 504 and A. Cassese, 'On Some Problematical Aspects of the Crime of Aggression', 20 *Leiden Journal of International Law* (2007), 841, at 848. However, international law sources do not reflect such an element. Accordingly, the current negotiations on the crime of aggression demand 'intent and knowledge' to commit the criminal conduct and 'knowledge' with regard to the existence of an act of aggression by the state; see, e.g., R. Clark. 'Rethinking Aggression as a Crime and Formulating Its Elements: The Final Work-Product of the Preparatory Commission for the International Criminal Court', 15 *Leiden Journal of International Law* (2002), 859, at 875 ff.

100 See, in particular, former Art. 236 Portuguese criminal code. The crime of 'incitement to war' was defined by 'inciting hatred against a people', Portuguese or other, with the specific intent to 'unleash a war'. For details see Antunes, *supra* note 90, at 562. Art. 5 Portuguese criminal code provided universal jurisdiction over this crime, see also *infra* note 135.

101 If such acts reach the necessary threshold of an act of aggression and are attributable to the state, conduct falling under the definition of these offences may come close to the crime of aggression. For details see *infra* 3.

102 Section 153 Hungarian criminal code refers to recruitment on Hungarian territory 'for military service, paramilitary service or for military training in a foreign armed organization'. See in this regard also former Art. 237 Portuguese criminal code which applied to the 'recruitment of elements of the Portuguese armed forces for a war against a foreign state or territory'. For details Antunes, *supra* note 90, at 563–565.

103 Art. 110(1) Cuban criminal code; see also Art. 111, ibid.

state, its territorial integrity, or the stability and authority of its government, are equally liable for punishment.[104] Similarly, Venezuelan nationals and foreigners who on Venezuelan territory prepare or commit hostile acts to attack or invade a friendly or neutral nation on land or sea are liable for punishment.[105] The respective Panamanian provision again prescribes unauthorized conscription, rearmament or other hostile acts against another state, which expose Panama to the danger of war or the rupture of international relations.[106] Although the last mentioned provisions are specified as crimes against international law, they are to be seen in the primary national context of protecting the existence of the state.[107] Comparable, explicitly domestic offences can be found in various national criminal codes; they will be dealt with in more detail under 3.

C. Act of Aggression by a State

The prerequisite act of aggression by a state, *conditio sine qua non* for the establishment of individual criminal responsibility for the crime of aggression, is referred to as 'war of aggression' or 'aggressive war' in the majority of national provisions.[108] Some states use the term 'war' without further specification.[109] Others refer to 'military aggression',[110] 'armed conflict'[111] or 'military operations'.[112]

In this context, a commentator on the Polish criminal code clarifies that the notion 'war of aggression' has remained part of Polish law, despite the fact that the term 'war' was replaced by 'armed aggression' in international law. Notwithstanding the use of the traditional name, it is generally understood that Article 117(1) Polish Criminal Code on the crime of aggression comprises the initiation and waging of *any international armed conflict in violation of international law*. Only minor, sporadic and isolated cross-border use of force is considered to fall short of the definition of the crime.[113]

The vast majority of national provisions do not provide for any definition of the prerequisite act of aggression by a state, which forms a major element of the definition of the crime. Commentary literature suggests an interpretation in conformity with international law and particularly refers

104 Art. 112 Cuban criminal code.

105 Art. 154 Venezuelan criminal code.

106 Art. 312 Panamanian criminal code.

107 Arts 110 and 112 Cuban criminal code fall under Title I 'delitos contra la seguridad del estado', Chapter III 'delitos contra la paz y el derecho internacional'; Art. 312 Panamanian criminal code can be found under Title IX 'de los delitos contra la personalidad jurídica del estado', Chapter III 'delitos contra la comunidad internacional'; and Art. 154 Venezuelan criminal code under Title I 'de los delitos contra la independencia y la seguridad de la nación', Chaper III 'de los delitos contra el derecho internacional'.

108 Art. 384 Armenian criminal code; Art. 165 Bosnian federal criminal code; Art. 409 Bulgarian criminal code; Art. 157 Croatian criminal code; § 91 Estonian criminal code, Art. 404 Georgian criminal code; Art. 156 Kazakh criminal code; Art. 130 Kosovar criminal code; Art. 442 Montenegrin criminal code; Art. 117 Polish criminal code; Art. 353 Russian criminal code; Art. 385 Slovenian criminal code; Art. 395 Tajik criminal code; Art. 437 Ukrainian criminal code, Art. 151 Uzbek criminal code.

109 Section 153 Hungarian criminal code; Art. 139 Moldovan criminal code.

110 Section 72 Latvian criminal code.

111 Art. 130 Kosovar criminal code; Art. 297 Mongolian criminal code; Art. 437 Ukrainian criminal code.

112 Art. 437 Ukrainian criminal code.

113 Weigend, *supra* note 24, at 112.

to General Assembly Resolution 3314.[114] In addition, Polish literature also cites the 1933 London Convention on the Definition of Aggression.[115] It is left to the competent national court to interpret the notion according to international law. Such judicial discretion is criticized by some authors as a rather atypical loophole in the light of the principle of legality.[116]

As a marginal hint, §91 of the Estonian criminal code specifies that a 'war of aggression' is 'directed by one state against another state'. A more detailed definition can only be found in Article 157(1) Croatian criminal code. This relatively new provision[117] combines a generic definition of an act of aggression by a state, which is based on Article 1 GA Resolution 3314, with a selection of acts listed in Article 3 of the same resolution:

> (1) Whoever, regardless of whether a war has previously been declared or not, wages a war of aggression by commanding an armed action of one state against the sovereignty, territorial integrity or political independence of another state, so that such an action is performed by invasion or by an armed attack on its territory, aircraft or ships, or by the blockading of ports or shores or by the military occupation of the territory, or in some other way which denotes the forcible establishment of rule over such a state, shall be punished by imprisonment for not less than ten years or by long-term imprisonment.
>
> (2) The same punishment as referred to in paragraph 1 of this Article shall be inflicted on whoever, for the purpose of waging a war of aggression of one state against another, commands or enables the sending of armed mercenary groups or other paramilitary armed forces into a state, so that these forces achieve the aims of a war of aggression.[118]

At first glance, Article 1 has similarities with a proposal on the definition of the crime of aggression that emerged as a potential compromise solution just before the Rome Conference.[119] However, the

---

114 GA Res. 3314 (XIXX), 14 December 1974. See, e.g., Weigend, *supra* note 24, at 113; Skulic, ibid., at 241.

115 See in this regard Weigend, *supra* note 24, at 113. The Convention for the Definition of Aggression of 3 July 1933 (LNTS 1934, 69) was signed by Afghanistan, Estonia, Latvia, Persia, Poland, Romania, the Soviet Union, Turkey and later Finland; it entered into force on 16 October 1933. See, e.g., B. Broms, 'The Definition of Aggression', *Recueil des Cours* 154 (1978), 301, at 389; B. Ferencz, *Defining International Aggression. The Search for World Peace. A Documentary History and Analysis (1975), Vol. I The Tradition of War and the Aspiration of Peace* (New York: Oceana Publications Inc., 1975), at 34. For details on the negotiations of the Disarmament Conference 1932–34 and the Litvinov-Politis proposal, see Reisinger Coracini, *supra* note 27, at III C 1.

116 See, e.g., Skulic, *supra* note 24, at 241; M. Hummrich, Der völkerrechtliche Straftatbestand der Aggression: historische Entwicklung, Geltung und Definition im Hinblick auf das Statut des Internationalen Strafgerichtshofes (Baden-Baden: Nomos, 2001), at 87.

117 Chapter XIII Croatian criminal code dealing with crimes under international law was amended in 2004 to bridge gaps between the existing definitions of crimes and the definition of core crimes in the Rome Statute. Above all, the former criminal code did not include crimes against humanity as a separate offence. For details see Novoselec, *supra* note 24, at 43. See also P. Novoselec, 'Substantive International Criminal Law Amendments of the Croatian Criminal Code of 15 July 2004', in I. Josipović (ed.), *Responsibility for War Crimes* (Zagreb: University Press, 2005), 255, at 260–261.

118 Art. 157(1) and (2) Croatian criminal code.

119 Revised proposal submitted by a group of interested states, including Germany, Preparatory Committee on the Establishment of an International Criminal Court, 16 March–3 April 1998, A/AC.249/1998/DP.12 of 1 April 1998; see also Informal Discussion Paper submitted by Germany, Preparatory Committee on

Croatian provision reaches further by reflecting acts of 'indirect aggression' according to Article 3(g) of the GA Definition of Aggression and including 'other ways' of establishment of forcible rule over a state. The latter may serve as a catch-all clause for those acts, listed in GA Resolution 3314, which are not expressly reflected, and also leaves open some space for interpretation regarding other potential ways to perform an act of aggression. By relying on GA Resolution 3314, Article 157 of the Croatian criminal code is in compliance with the ongoing negotiations on the international level. According to the Special Working Group's current approach all acts of aggression listed in Article 3 of the GA Definition of Aggression may qualify as a basis for individual criminal responsibility.[120]

Next to criminal responsibility for a war of aggression, §91 of the Estonian criminal code criminalizes participation in a 'war violating international agreements or security guarantees provided by the state'.[121] This additional basis for individual criminal responsibility enshrined in the IMT Charter has not received the same continuous attention as its counterpart 'war of aggression'.[122] The Nüremberg judgement did not invoke this basis for responsibility. But as the ILC elaborated, since the German war was judged as 'aggressive war', there was no need for the Tribunal to further examine whether it would also constitute a 'war in violation of international treaties, agreements, or assurances'.[123] Consequently, the ILC upheld the criminality of both acts of state in the Nüremberg principles.[124] In this context it is worthwhile to mention that Article 137 of the Bolivian criminal code similarly criminalizes the violation of certain types of international treaties, in particular agreements guaranteeing a truce, armistice or safe passage, as a crime against international law.[125]

With regard to the prerequisite act of state forming a basis for individual criminal responsibility for the crime of aggression, only Estonia goes beyond the acts enshrined in the Nüremberg Charter.

---

the Establishment of an International Criminal Court, 1–12 December 1997, Working Group on Definitions and Elements of Crime, A/AC.249/1997/WG.1/DP.20 of 11 December 1997.

120 See, e.g., 2007 Princeton Report, paras 36 ff.

121 Para. 91 Estonian criminal code; s. 72 Latvian criminal code similarly refers to 'war of aggression in violation of international treaties, agreements or assurances'.

122 Earlier, the aspect of individual criminal responsibility for the violation of certain international treaties as aggression can be traced to Art. 227 Versailles Peace Treaty, 28 June 1919, by which former German Emperor Wilhelm II was publicly arraigned 'for a supreme offence against international morality and the sanctity of treaties'. A major accusation of aggressive acts related to the violation international treaties guaranteeing the neutrality of Belgium and Luxembourg; for details see Commission on the Responsibilities of the Authors of the War and on Enforcement of Penalties, Report presented to the Preliminary Peace Conference, March 29 1919, printed in AJIL 14 (1920), 95, at 107, 112. For details on the principle *pacta sunt servanda* in the context of the crime of aggression, see Reisinger Coracini, *supra* note 27, at III B 2.

123 1950 ILC Report, at 376. See in this regard also Discussion paper proposed by the Coordinator, Preparatory Commission for the International Criminal Court, Working Group on the Crime of Aggression, PCNICC/1999/WGCA/RT.1 of 9 December 1999.

124 Principle VI (a)(i), 1950 ILC Report, at 376.

125 However, the provision has to be seen in the context of protecting state security (see Title I, Chapter IV Bolivian criminal code). See also *supra* text before note 107. Comparable offences can be found in Art. 220 Argentinian criminal code; Art. 113 Chilean criminal code; Art. 123 Ecuadorian criminal code; Art. 340 Peruvian criminal code. These norms criminalize domestically certain violations of international law, which at the same time constitute a danger for the peace and national security of a state, see e.g. for Chile, A. Etcheberry, *Derecho Penal* (3rd edn, Santiago: Editorial Juridica de Chile, 1997), at 110; for Argentina, E.A. Donna, *Derecho Penal, Parte Especial* (Tomo II-C, Madrid: Global Publisher, 2002), at 396–397.

Paragraph 91 of the Estonian criminal code renders liable 'a representative of the state who threatens to start a war of aggression'.[126]

D. Jurisdiction of Domestic Courts to Enforce the Crime of Aggression

The preceding examination has shown that a considerable number of states have implemented the crime of aggression under international law into domestic legislation. Relying on established drafting techniques, these definitions are formulated in a generic way. Read alone, they may appear applicable to any crime of aggression, committed by a national of any state, at any place. To evaluate the concrete ability of domestic courts to give effect to these norms, the following section takes a closer look at the provisions on the establishment of jurisdiction in those states which domestically criminalize the crime of aggression.

Since an act of aggression necessarily involves cross-border activities, a potential prosecution on charges of aggression may be based on various principles of jurisdiction. Every state, which is the victim of an act of aggression, may establish jurisdiction on the principle of territoriality.[127] At the same time, where available, the principle of passive nationality may apply if an act of aggression caused individual victims. In addition, a number of states provide for jurisdiction upon the protective principle, where that state's interests are violated.[128] An aggressor state may as well invoke jurisdiction upon the principle of territoriality where preparatory acts will have taken place on its territory.[129] It may usually also assume jurisdiction according to the basis of active personality.[130] Furthermore, such jurisdictional links may eventually also be established by a third state.

Only few states go beyond these traditional principles of jurisdiction and do not require a specific link to the offence. These criminal codes do not only criminalize the crime of aggression as a crime under international law, but also provide for the possibility of enforcing it universally. Bulgaria, Croatia and Moldova, for instance, establish a universal jurisdiction for the crime of aggression.[131] Bulgaria justifies its jurisdiction 'regarding foreigners who have committed abroad a crime against the peace and mankind' in that this affects the interests of another country or

---

126 Art. 16(2), 1991 ILC Draft Code, defined the crime of threat of aggression as 'declarations, communications, demonstrations of force or any other measures which would give good reason to the Government of a State to believe that aggression is being seriously contemplated against that State'; see also Art. 2(2), 1954 ILC Draft Code and generally GA Resolutions 2625 (XXV), 24 October 1970 and 42/22, 18 November 1987.

127 All examined states, which implement the crime of aggression, provide for jurisdiction on the principle of territoriality. See, e.g., Art. 14 Armenian criminal code; Art. 130 Bosnian federal criminal code; Article 13 Croatian criminal code; Art. 6 Estonian criminal code; Art. 4 Georgian criminal code; s. 4(3) Latvian criminal code.

128 For the passive personality or protective principle see, e.g., Art. 15(3)(2) Armenian criminal code; Art. 132 Bosnian criminal code (Brcko district); Art. 9 Estonian criminal code; Art. 5(3) Georgian criminal code; Art. 6 para. 4 Kazakh criminal code.

129 Very explicit in that regard, e.g., Art. 6 para. 2 Kazakh criminal code.

130 See, e.g., Art. 15(2) Armenian criminal code; Art. 132 Bosnian federal criminal code; Art. 14(2) Croatian criminal code; Art. 7 Estonian criminal code; Art. 5 Georgian criminal code; Section 3 Hungarian criminal code; Art. 6 Kazakh criminal code; Section 4(3) Latvian criminal code. Given the leadership nature of the crime of aggression and frequent restrictions of public employment to nationals, potential perpetrators of this crime will be nationals of the aggressor state in many cases.

131 But see also, e.g., s. 12.3. Azerbaijani criminal code.

foreign citizens.[132] The Moldovan criminal code equally provides universal jurisdiction for 'crimes against the peace and security of mankind and war crimes': 'Foreign citizens and persons without citizenship that do not have permanent domicile on the territory of the Republic of Moldova, who committed crimes outside the territory of the Republic of Moldova, are liable to criminal responsibility under the present Code and are subject to criminal responsibility on the territory of the Republic of Moldova', as long as they were not held criminally liable or convicted by a foreign state.[133] The Croatian criminal code establishes universal jurisdiction for all 'criminal offences against values protected by international law', including the crime of aggression, 'if the perpetrator is found within the territory of the Republic of Croatia and is not extradited to another state'.[134] Hungary also allows for universal jurisdiction for crimes against the peace, which are defined as incitement to a war of aggression.[135]

In addition, a number of criminal codes contain blanket universal jurisdiction clauses. They allow prosecution of non-nationals for crimes committed abroad against foreigners, if such crimes are proscribed by a recognized norm of international law or an international treaty binding upon that state.[136] Depending on the specific formulation and interpretation of such a clause, it may apply to the crime of aggression as a crime under customary law, or as a crime defined by treaty law, if the state in question is a party to the London Agreement or the Rome Statute.[137] In the latter case, the prerequisite prescription might already be met, since the Statute confirms the existence of individual criminal responsibility for the crime of aggression and lists it as one of the 'most serious crimes of concern to the international community as a whole' falling within the jurisdiction of the ICC. From a more cautious approach, complete international proscription may only be assumed, once a provision on aggression is adopted and binding upon a State Party. Some states, however, do not only require the international prescription of the crime in this context, but only accept the establishment of universal jurisdiction if explicitly foreseen by an international treaty obligation.[138]

National provisions on the crime of aggression have hardly been enforced by national prosecuting authorities. Apart from a number of national trials conducted in the aftermath of the Second World War, e.g., on the basis of Control Council Law No. 10, next to no prosecutions have

---

132 Art. 6(1) Bulgarian criminal code. The reference to another state's interests instead of the common interest of the international community as a whole brings this provision in vicinity of the principle of vicarious jurisdiction. See in this regard also, e.g., Art. 14 para. 4 Croatian criminal code. In relation to vicarious jurisdiction, some states expressly exclude the requirement of double criminality for the crime of aggression: see, e.g., Art. 15(2) Armenian criminal code.

133 Art. 11 Moldovan criminal code.

134 Art. 14 paras 4 and 5 Croatian criminal code. For details see Novoselec, *supra* note 117, at 262.

135 Section 4(1)(c) Hungarian criminal code states that 'Hungarian law shall also be applied to acts committed by non-Hungarian citizens abroad, if they are ... crimes against humanity (Chapter XI) or any other crime, the prosecution of which is prescribed by an international treaty', See in this regard also former Art. 5(1)(b) Portuguese criminal code which specified that this jurisdictional basis is only applicable if not banned by an international treaty, if the perpetrator is present on Portuguese territory and cannot be extradited.

136 Art. 15(3)(1) Armenian criminal code; para. 8 Estonian criminal code; Art. 5(2) and (3) Georgian criminal code; Art. 6 para. 4 Kazakh criminal code; Art. 15(2) Tajik criminal code.

137 In addition to the four signatory states of the London Agreement, France, the USSR, United Kingdom and United States of America, 19 states ratified or acceded to the Agreement: Australia, Belgium, Czechoslovakia, Denmark, Ethiopia, Greece, Haiti, Honduras, India, Luxembourg, Netherlands, New Zealand, Norway, Panama, Paraguay, Poland, Uruguay, Venezuela, Yugoslavia.

138 See in that regard, e.g., s. 4(3) Latvian criminal code; Art. 14.4. Mongolian criminal code; Art. 12(3) Russian criminal code.

been reported.[139] The crime of aggression, on the other hand, has played a significant role in some cases relating to civil obedience in relation to the Vietnam war, Iraq and Afghanistan.[140]

3. Norms Criminalizing Conduct, which Includes Elements of the Crime of Aggression

References to war or acts of aggression in domestic criminal legislation are not limited to norms that aim to implement the crime of aggression under international law. The same notions are also used to describe elements of definitions of other crimes. These crimes, contrary to the group of crimes dealt with under 2, were categorized by the national legislature as protecting primarily national legal values, in particular, the independence,[141] sovereignty,[142] security,[143] international personality,[144] existence[145] and authority of the state or the sovereign.[146] Where they protect peace, they are primarily concerned with the nation's peace rather than with international peace as such.[147]

Nonetheless, these national offences might play a role with regard to the ICC's potential exercise of complementary jurisdiction over the crime of aggression. Depending on the stage of a national proceeding, the Court determines the inadmissibility of a case before it if 'the case' is being investigated or prosecuted, has been investigated without the initiation of a prosecution or 'the person concerned has already been tried for conduct which is the subject of the complaint'.[148] The decisive criteria seem to be national allegations against the same individual for 'conduct also proscribed' in the definition of the crime in the Rome Statute.[149] Consequently, national offences based on the same criminal conduct as the crime of aggression constitute an obstacle for the

---

139 For the one judicial decision on Art. 80 German criminal code (*supra* 3 A) see L.G. Köln, NStZ, 1981, 261; for details G. Werle, *Völkerstrafrecht* (Tubingen: Mohr Siebeck, 2007), margin No. 1321. See in this regard also C. Kress, 'The German Chief Federal Prosecutor's Decision Not to Investigate the Alleged Crime of Preparing Aggression against Iraq', 2 JICJ (2004), 245.

140 For a rough overview of anti-war litigation before United States tribunals, see C. Villarino Villa, 'The Crime of Aggression before the House of Lords – Chronicle of a Death Foretold', 4 *Journal of International Criminal Justice* (2006), 866, at 876, note 53. On the House of Lords decision in *R. v Jones et al., supra* at 21, see, e.g., R. Clark, 'Aggression: A Crime Under Domestic Law?', *New Zealand Law Journal* (Oct. 2006), 349; R. Cryer, 'Aggression at the Court of Appeal', 10 *Journal of Conflict & Security Law* (2005), 209, at 230; D.M. Ferencz, 'Introductory Note to the United Kingdom House of Lords: *R v. Jones et al.*', 45 *International Legal Materials* (2006), 988; Villarino Villa op. cit.

141 E.g., s. 1 Albanian criminal code; Chapter 8 Norwegian criminal code; Art. 266 Swiss criminal code.

142 E.g., s. 1 Finnish criminal code; Title I Uruguayan criminal code.

143 E.g., Title IX Argentinian criminal code; Title I Bolivian criminal code; Title I Cuban criminal code; Title XI Guatemalan criminal code; Chapter 8 Norwegian criminal code; Chapter 19 Swedish criminal code.

144 E.g., Title I, Chapter 1 Italian criminal code, Title IX, Chapter 1 Panamanian criminal code.

145 E.g., Title VII, Chapter I Paraguayan criminal code.

146 E.g., Division 1, Chapter VII Fijian criminal code (the same division contains the crime of genocide in Chapter VIII); Chapter VI Indian criminal code.

147 See, e.g., Title IX, Chapter II Argentinian criminal code ('delitos que comprometen la paz y la dignidad de la Nacíon'); Art. 546 Nicaraguan criminal code ('delito contra la paz de la República'); Chapter 1 German criminal code ('Friedensverrat, Hochverrat und Gefährdung des demokratischen Rechtsstaates').

148 See Art. 17(1)(a) to (c) ICCSt.

149 See also Art. 20(3) ICCSt. For details see Tallgren and Reisinger Coracini, *supra* note 11, at margin No. 39 ff.

admissibility of an aggression case before the ICC, if none of the exceptions of Articles 17 and 20(3) applies.

The following section will examine national norms containing elements, which are also components of the crime of aggression under international law, and will analyse in what way, if any, the relevant national crime might be an alternative to prosecution of the crime of aggression before the ICC.

Beforehand, it should be mentioned that none of the following criminal provisions limits individual criminal responsibility to persons 'being in a position effectively to exercise control over or to direct the political or military action of a state'. However, none of the definitions of crimes *per se* excludes the prosecution of such persons. Given the lack of an express qualification of the perpetrator of the crime of aggression in those national provisions which implement it into domestic law,[150] such missing component of the definition does not create an obstacle to the potential suitability of one of the following norms.

A. Preparation of a War of Aggression

Germany and Paraguay criminalize, as a domestic crime, conduct which seems to originate directly from international law sources: the preparation of a war of aggression.[151] The relevant provision of the German criminal code requires two conditions, which strictly link its scope of application to Germany. It is expressly limited to the preparation of a war of aggression with *German participation* and it demands the creation of a *danger of war for Germany*. A war of aggression which does not involve Germany does not fall within the definition of the crime. Section 80 provides: '[w]hoever prepares a war of aggression (Art. 26 subsection (1), of the Basic Law) in which the Federal Republic of Germany is supposed to participate and thereby creates a danger of war for the Federal Republic of Germany, shall be punished with imprisonment for life or for not less than ten years.'[152] In light of this restrictive definition, section 80 is understood as primarily protecting the external security of Germany.[153] Therefore, the crime has been embedded within the section of 'crimes against peace, high treason and endangering the democratic rule of law'.[154] According to the prevailing opinion, the requested type of participation includes the preparation of a war of aggression in which Germany would be the aggressor, as well as a war of aggression against Germany.[155] However, based on a teleological argumentation, a further limitation of the application of this norm to wars in which Germany participates as an aggressor has also been

150 For details see *supra* 2 A.

151 For details see *supra* 2 B.

152 Sections 80 and 80a of the German criminal code were introduced in 1968 to implement a constitutional law obligation, Art. 26(1) German Basic Law. It declares unconstitutional acts which may disturb the peaceful coexistence of peoples, in particular, the preparation of a war of aggression, and obliges the German legislature to criminalize such conduct under domestic law. Since this prohibition is not limited to the preparation of a war of aggression in which Germany would be participating, the constitutional obligation has only been partly fulfilled by s. 80 of the German criminal code. For details see, e.g., Gropengießer/Kreicker, *supra* note 24, at 242–244.

153 For divergent opinions regarding the legal values protected by s. 80 of the German criminal code, see e.g., Gropengießer/Kreicker, *supra* note 24, at 245, note 1026; C. Kress, 'Strafrecht und Angriffskrieg im Licht des "Falles Irak"', 115 *Zeitschrift für die gesamte Strafrechtswissenschaft* (2003), 294, at 337–339.

154 See *supra* note 147.

155 See e.g., Werle, *supra* note 139, margin No. 1322, with further references in note 123.

voiced.[156] Paragraph 5(1) German criminal code extends the application of this norm to criminal acts of non-nationals committed abroad.[157]

Article 271 of the Paraguayan criminal code is clear with regard to its scope of application. It applies exclusively to the preparation of wars of aggression in which the Republic of Paraguay would be the aggressor: 'El que preparara una guerra de agresión en la cual la República sea la agresora, será castigado con pena privativa de libertad de hasta diez años'.[158] Criminal acts perpetrated on Paraguayan territory, as well as abroad, are equally covered by the provision and may be prosecuted before domestic courts.[159] The provision is categorized as a criminal act against the state, in particular, against the existence of the state.[160]

The aforementioned provisions cover only part of the *actus reus* of the crime of aggression. They criminalize preparatory acts, irrespective of whether an act of aggression occurs or not. However, the initiation and the actual waging of a war of aggression are not covered by the definition of the crime. The provisions are further limited by demanding participation of the proscribing state in the act of aggression, either as the aggressor or as the attacked state. Given the required link to the proscribing state and the limited criminalization of individual conduct, these provisions can only play an auxiliary role within the Rome Statute's complementary system. The ICC will only be competent to adjudicate in the case of individuals for the crime of aggression when an act of aggression has been executed. In that case, however, it is assumed that the Court would also have jurisdiction over related preparatory acts. National prosecutions based on the crime of preparation of aggression cannot cover the very core of the crime of aggression – the actual waging of an act of aggression. Therefore, it would be preferable to have a complete investigation of all modes of participation before the ICC. However, even if national proceedings take place, the Court would not be hampered to proceed with its own case based on charges of initiating and waging an act of aggression.[161] National provisions on preparatory acts might be an asset, if an alleged perpetrator, for practical or policy reasons, is not charged before the ICC. In such a case it might be preferable to at least hold a person accountable for preparatory acts if there is no other possibility of prosecuting for the crime of aggression in its entirety. In any case, the strict preconditions of the definition of the crime and for the establishment of jurisdiction must be fulfilled.

The Japanese criminal code contains a comparable norm, directed at protecting Japanese foreign relations.[162] Article 93 of the Japanese criminal code provides punishment for 'a person who prepares or plots to wage war privately upon a foreign state'. This definition contains an additional element, by requiring the waging of war to be conducted 'privately'. However, an armed attack against a foreign state conducted privately, without the authorization or acknowledgment of a state, in principle, does not qualify as an act of aggression by that state. Such acts, therefore, are unlikely to reach the threshold of the definition of the crime of aggression for the ICC. One rather

156 See e.g., Werle, *supra* note 139, margin No. 1322; see also Kress, *supra* note 153, at 344-8.

157 For details see Gropengießer/Kreicker, *supra* note 24, at 244, with further references in note 1021.

158 Art. 271(1) Paraguayan criminal code; its para. 2 establishes criminal responsibility also for attempt to prepare a war of aggression.

159 Art. 7(1) Paraguayan criminal code.

160 Title VII, Chapter I Paraguayan criminal code.

161 Additional charges of preparing an act of aggression are likely to be inadmissible according to Art. 17 ICCSt. Similarly, if the alleged perpetrator has already been tried the Court might proceed with its case in relation to conduct which forms the basis for the charge of initiation and the waging of aggression, though charges based on conduct relative to the preparation of such acts would be inadmissible. See Art. 20(3) ICCSt, if applicable for the crime of aggression, and *supra* 1A.

162 Chapter IV Japanese criminal code.

hypothetical scenario in which this provision might overlap with individual criminal responsibility for the crime of aggression might be that the private acts can be imputed upon a state: for instance, a state organ in a decision-making position that 'privately' prepares an act of aggression and eventually orders elements of the armed forces to attack a foreign state.

B. Incitement to a War of Aggression and Propaganda of War

While a number of states classify acts, such as instigation (public) incitement to war, or war propaganda as a crime under international law,[163] others criminalize comparable conduct as a domestic crime, usually within the categories of crimes against national security or treasonable offences.[164]

Section 80a of the German criminal code defines the crime of 'incitement to a war of aggression' by 'public incitement ... in a meeting or through the dissemination of writings ... in the territorial area of application of this law'. The term 'war of aggression' has to be interpreted in accordance with section 80 of the German criminal code, ultimately, in accordance with international law.[165] As in the case of preparation of a war of aggression, the definition of the crime requires a link to Germany. Incitement only falls within the definition of section 80a when committed on German territory.[166]

Romanian citizen and residents who get in contact with a foreign power 'in order to suppress or undermine the state unity, indivisibility, sovereignty or independence, by actions instigating a war against the country or facilitating foreign military occupation' are responsible according to Article 271 of the Romanian criminal code. The same criminal conduct can be performed by foreign citizens and non-residents as a 'hostile act against the Romanian state'.[167] With prior authorization by the general prosecutor, Romanian courts may establish jurisdiction for relevant acts committed outside Romanian territory.[168] In addition, the category of crimes against national security contains the offence of 'dissemination of false information in order to cause a war'.[169]

Finland criminalizes various acts when committed 'during an ongoing or imminent military crisis or international political crisis, for the purpose of causing Finland to be at war or the target of a military operation' under the heading of 'warmongering'.[170] Two of these acts relate to incitement to and propaganda of war. Paragraph 1 criminalizes a person who 'publicly exhorts a foreign state to carry out an offensive against Finland or Finland to carry out an offensive against a foreign state'. Paragraph 2 concerns the public dissemination of statements or other propaganda 'intended to turn the public opinion in favour of the carrying out of offensives'. The proscribed conduct

163 For details see *supra* 2B.

164 See e.g. Chapter 5 Australian criminal code; Chapter 12 Finnish criminal code; Chapter 1 German criminal code, *supra* note 154; Title XIII Chapter I Nicaraguan criminal code; Chapter 6 Nigerian criminal code.

165 See *supra* note 152.

166 No extraterritorial application of the German criminal code is provided for in s. 80a; compare *supra* note 157.

167 Art. 274 Romanian criminal code. The two norms are based on a constitutional obligation. Art. 30 para. 7 Romanian Constitution provides *inter alia*, that 'any instigation to a war of aggression, ... shall be prohibited by law'. See in this regard also Art. 356 Romanian criminal code of 1969, which however categorized propaganda of war as a crime against peace.

168 Art. 12 Romanian criminal code.

169 Art. 276 Romanian criminal code. See in this regard also Art. 115 Cuban criminal code, *supra* note 93.

170 Section 2 Finnish criminal code falls within Chapter 12 on treasonable offences. See also *infra* 3D1.

only falls within the definition of the crime when committed on Finnish territory or by a Finnish citizen outside of Finland. Criminal responsibility is further limited to situations of an ongoing or imminent military or political crisis. Lastly, all acts must be committed for the purpose of causing war. However, if these preconditions are met, the crime covers instigation of and propaganda for military operations undertaken by Finland against another state, as well as against Finland.

The Australian criminal code, for instance, defines as an act of treason the instigation by 'a person who is not an Australian citizen to make an armed invasion of the Commonwealth or a Territory of the Commonwealth'.[171] The comparable Nigerian provision criminalizes 'any person who instigates any foreigner to invade Nigeria with an armed force'.[172] The Nicaraguan criminal code provides punishment for individuals who: '[i]nciten a una potencia extranjera a hacer la guerra a Nicaragua o se concierten con ella para tal objeto'.[173]

Individual conduct as defined in the examined national provisions of incitement to war or propaganda of war is not significantly different as regards norms which intend to implement a crime under international law and those which primarily aim to protect national legal values. Nevertheless, the scope of application of the latter is limited. The vast majority of states restrict the definition of crime in order to exclusively protect their own security. The German and Finnish provisions, which apply also to incitement of acts of aggression against a foreign state, are exceptional. As regards incitement as a treasonable offence, the aspect of international aggression is strongly overlapped by criminalizing a citizen's behaviour against its own government.[174] The reach over persons not aligned with the proscribing state is rather exceptional. In such cases, the definitions of crime tend to be restricted to acts conducted on national territory.

The definition of the crime of aggression under the Rome Statute most probably will not comprise instigation and propaganda of war as specific criminal acts. National prosecutions simply on these charges, therefore, will unlikely bar a prosecution for the crime of aggression before the ICC. Even if some aspects of instigation and propaganda of war were understood as preparatory acts, conduct potentially constituting a common basis for prosecution on the national as well as on the international level would be very restricted.[175]

C. Waging a War, Conspiracy and Other Treasonable Offences

The Indian criminal code contains provisions to protect itself as well as its allies from outside attacks. Its Article 121 criminalizes the waging of war against the Government of India as an

171 Division 80.1 (1)(g) Australian criminal code.

172 Para. 38 Nigerian criminal code; see also, e.g., for Ireland, Treason Act 1939 (based on Art. 39 Irish Constitution); s. 53 (c) Fijian criminal code; Art. 315 Guyanese Criminal Law (Offence) Act; s. 48 criminal code of Kiribati; Art. 37(g) Papua New Guinean criminal code; Section 73(d) Crimes Act 1961 of New Zealand; Art. 115 Philippine criminal code; Section 38 Nigerian criminal code; s. 3 Treason Felony Act 1848 of the United Kingdom ('to move or stir any foreigner or stranger with force to invade the United Kingdom or any other of her Majesty's dominions or countries under the obeisance of her Majesty'); s. 59(1)(c) criminal code of Vanuatu; s. 43(1)(e) Zambian criminal code.

173 Art. 528 para. 5 Nicaraguan criminal code; see also, e.g., Art. 123 para. XI Mexican criminal code; Art. 581 Spanish criminal code. Art. 315(2) Argentinian criminal code contains a similar provision, which however is only applicable during times of war. In that case it would, for instance, cover the incitement of a third state to enter the war against Argentina. See in this sense Donna, *supra* note 125, at 380–381. For a definition of propaganda of war see, e.g., Art. 22 III Brazilian Lei de Segurança Nacional (1983).

174 For details see *infra* C.

175 For details see *supra* A.

offence against the state. Criminal responsibility is also provided for attempting, abetting and conspiring to wage such war.[176] In a comparable way, punishment is prescribed for 'whoever wages war against the Government of any Asiatic Power in alliance or at peace with the Government of India or attempts to wage such war, or abets the waging of such war'.[177]

'Levying war' against the prescribing state,[178] 'the Queen and Head of State'/'Her Majesty',[179] or 'the Commonwealth'[180] is defined as a treasonable offence (high treason) in all examined states of the Anglo-Saxon legal tradition. In many cases conspiracy to levy war,[181] preparatory acts[182] or forms of aiding and abetting[183] are expressly listed as criminal acts. Criminal responsibility for such conduct dates back to the earliest English treason legislation of 1351.[184] It may be established as early as the formation of a respective purpose or design of the mind manifested by an overt act.[185] The definitions of crimes generally cover conduct 'within' as well as 'without' the prescribing state.[186] The statutory definition may confine individual criminal responsibility to persons owing allegiance to the prescribing state (or head of state), sometimes including a protective power, in any event[187] or only in cases where the crime was committed abroad.[188]

Treason is a common offence in national criminal laws, though with deviating definitions and scope of application. Many states use this category of crime or criminalize similar conduct to

---

176 Art. 121 and Art. 121A Indian criminal code. For details see B.M. Gandhi, *Indian Penal Code* (Lucknow: Eastern Book, 1996), at164; R. Ranchhoddas and D. K. Thakore, *The Indian Penal Code* (28th edn, Delhi: Wadhwa and Company, 1997), at 161.

177 Art. 125 Indian criminal code.

178 Section 46(1)(b) Canadian criminal code; Irish Treason Act 1939 (implementing Art. 39 Irish Constitution); s. 73(b) Crimes Act 1961 of New Zealand; s. 37(1) Nigerian criminal code; s. 2381 United States Code (18USC2381).

179 Section 53(b) Fijian criminal code; para. 37 (e) Papua New Guinean criminal code.

180 Section 80.1(d) Australian criminal code.

181 See, e.g., Irish Treason Act 1939; Art. 115 Philippine criminal code; s. 73(f) Crimes Act 1961 of New Zealand; s. 37(2) Nigerian criminal code; s. 59(1)(e) criminal code of Vanuatu.

182 See, e.g., s. 80.1(d) Australian criminal code; s. 46(1)(b) Canadian criminal code.

183 See, e.g., Irish Treason Act 1939; Art. 114 Philippine criminal code; s. 2381 United States Code (18USC2381).

184 See Treason Act 1351, which enacted a common law offence: 'if a Man do levy War against our Lord the King in his Realm, or be adherent to the King's Enemies in his Realm, giving to them Aid and Comfort in the Realm, or elsewhere, and thereof be [probably] attainted of open Deed by [the People] of their Condition.' Before that treason was a common law offence. For details see, e.g., M.E.J. Black, 'Five Approaches to Reforming the Law: 650 Years of Treason and Sedition'. Keynote Address at the Australasian Law Reform Agencies Conference 2006. Available at http://www.alrc.gov.au/events/events/alrac/Presentations/BlackCJ.pdf, at 4 (visited 26 March 2009).

185 See, in particular, s. 3 Treason Felony Act 1848 of the United Kingdom; for details see W. Blackstone, *Commentaries on the Laws of England* (1765–1769), Book IV, Chapter 6 (Chicago and London: University of Chicago Press, 1979), at 78. See also, e.g., s. 80.1(h) Australian criminal code; s. 53 Fijian criminal code; s. 50 criminal code of Kiribati; s. 41 Nigerian criminal code.

186 Section 1(1) and (2) Irish Treason Act 1939; s. 3 Treason Felony Act 1848 of the United Kingdom; s. 73 Crimes Act 1961 of New Zealand; Art. 114 Philippine criminal code; s. 2381 United States Code (18USC2381); s. 59 (1)(e) criminal code of Vanuatu. Sections 80.4 and 15.4 Australian criminal code provide extended geographical jurisdiction for treason. See also, e.g., Gandhi, *supra* note 176, at 165.

187 Art. 114 Philippine criminal code ('allegiance to (the United States or) the Government of the Philippine Islands'); s. 73 Crimes Act 1961 of New Zealand; s. 2381 United States Code (18USC2381); s. 59 (1)(e) criminal code of Vanuatu.

188 Section 46 Canadian criminal code; s. 1(2) Irish Treason Act 1939; s. 43(3) Zambian criminal code.

protect the existence of the state not only from internal uprising, but also from outside dangers. Offences to this end include conspiracy, agreement or negotiation with a foreign power aiming at declaring war or undertaking armed intervention against the prescribing state[189] or the seceding or transfer of territory.[190] Criminal responsibility is often restricted per definition to acts committed on the territory of the prescribing state[191] or to its nationals.[192] However, criminal responsibility for the actual waging of a war is rarely found outside the common law tradition. A Cuban provision safeguarding the state's external security comes close, but protects more generally against acts committed in the interest of a foreign power and which violate its independence and territorial integrity.[193] Similarly, the Iraqi criminal code provides punishment for '[a]ny person who, in a foreign country or in association with it or with a person who is working on its behalf, attempts to commit hostile acts against Iraq that may lead to the outbreak of war or the severing of diplomatic relations or who provides it with the means to that end'.[194]

National treason laws and other crimes protecting the state may provide a wide variety of conduct which is also reflected in the definition of the crime of aggression under international law: the waging of war, conspiracy and preparation to commit this crime, as well as aiding and abetting in its execution. In some cases, all modes of perpetration contained in the Nüremberg Charter are reflected in national laws. However, given the legal values protected by these norms, they are mainly concerned with attacks against the prescribing state (in some cases this protection is extended to allies[195]). In addition, treason is a crime which builds upon the specific relationship between a citizen (or person otherwise owing allegiance to) and its state.[196] These definitional restrictions almost nullify the possibility of treason provisions countering cases of aggression. For a limited scope of application, one may think of, e.g., a high-level official of state A playing a significant role in state B's act of aggression against state A. Furthermore, it is questionable whether treason laws, which have been dormant in many states, should be reactivated. The definition of these crimes is often rather wide and open to abuse.[197] The very aim of some treason provisions, in

189 See, e.g., Art. 212 Albanian criminal code; Art. 8 Brazilian Lei de Segurança Nacional (1983); Art. 106 Chilean criminal code; Art. 115 Ecuadorian criminal code; Art. 139 Greek criminal code; Art. 362 Guatemalan criminal code; Art. 114 Luxembourgian criminal code; Art. 528 para. 5 Nicaraguan criminal code; Art. 266 Swiss criminal code.

190 Art. 208 Albanian criminal code; para. 242 Austrian criminal code; Chapter 12, s. 1 Finnish criminal code; Art. 528(3) Nicaraguan criminal code.

191 Art. 115 Ecuadorian criminal code; Art. 106 Chilean criminal code.

192 Art. 362 Guatemalan criminal code.

193 Art. 91 Cuban criminal code reads: 'El que, en interés de un Estado extranjero, ejecute un hecho con el objeto de que sufra detrimento la independencia del Estado cubano o la integridad de su territorio, incurre en sanción de privación de libertad de diez a veinte años o muerte.'

194 Para. 158 Iraqi criminal code. Para. 9 Iraqi criminal code confirms extraterritorial jurisdiction of Iraqi courts for offences affecting the internal or external security of the state. The threshold for such countermeasures seems to be rather low, since they would be invoked solely 'for attempts to commit hostile acts against Iraq'.

195 See, e.g., s. 80.1(d) Australian criminal code; Art. 139 Greek criminal code; Art. 125 Indian criminal code.

196 See e.g. Donna, *supra* note 125, at 373; Etcheberry, *supra* note 125, at 99.

197 In the sixteenth century, the broadening of the statutory treason provisions in the United Kingdom through judicial interpretation was known as 'constructive treason', Black, *supra* note 184, at 8. In this context, serious forms of public protest, such as insurrection against a Statute of Labourers, were understood as a 'constructive levying of war', ibid., at 11.

particular where they expand responsibility to early stages of criminal conduct, has to be judged critically in modern democratic states.[198]

D. Hostile Acts

Several states criminalize acts which may provoke an armed intervention or expose the nation to war. Such crimes, often referred to as 'hostile acts', do not primarily aim to safeguard the sovereignty, territorial integrity and political independence of the attacked state, but rather relate to protecting the perpetrator's own state from the danger of war.[199] These crimes are generally categorized as offences against the external security,[200] the peace,[201] or the independence and integrity of the state,[202] or as treasonable offences.[203]

The structure of crimes involving 'hostile acts' is comparable. Certain acts are committed, usually by a national or from the territory of the prescribing state, against another state and may or do provoke a reaction by the targeted state which amounts to the use of armed force. However, specific elements of the definitions of crimes describing 'hostile acts' vary. They may require conduct with a specific intent to bring about a danger of war (*infra* at 1). In other states, the mere act that may cause such danger suffices (*infra* at 2). A third group of crimes specifies that the acts in question are to be conducted against the will of the government (*infra* at 3).

1. Acts Committed With the Intent to Provoke War

Article 211 of the Albanian criminal code defines 'provocation of war' as '[c]ommitting acts which intend to provoke war or make the Republic of Albania face the danger of a (military) intervention from foreign powers'. A comparable provision can be found in the Cuban criminal code, and which relates to the encouragement of armed aggression against Cuba.[204] Both provisions are applicable to acts committed on each country's respective territory, as well as to acts committed abroad by nationals or foreigners.[205]

El Salvador confines the definition of provoking war, reprisals or international hostilities to acts committed on Salvadorian territory.[206] It has been noted in this context that hostile acts against

198 See in this regard, e.g., the current Guardian's campaign at http://www.guardian.co.uk/Archive/Article/0,4273,4358082,00.html (visited 30 September 2009); see also Law Commission of England and Wales, Working Paper Number 72, Second Programme Item XVIII, Codification of the Criminal Law: Treason, Sedition and Allied Offences (1977), at 32.

199 Ambos and Malarino, *supra* note 24, at 476, note 19.

200 See, e.g., Title I Chapter I Cuban criminal code; Title I Chapter I Bolivian criminal code; Title I Chapter I Italian criminal code ('dei delitti contro la personalitá internazionale dello stato').

201 See, e.g., Title IX Chapter II Argentinian criminal code; Title VIII Chapter II Nicaraguan criminal code; Title XXIII Chapter II Spanish criminal code.

202 E.g., Art. 211 Albanian criminal code; Title XXIII Chapter II Spanish criminal code; Title I Uruguayan criminal code.

203 E.g., Chapter 12 Finnish criminal code; Art. 305 Honduran criminal code.

204 See Art. 92 Cuban criminal code: 'El que ejecute un hecho dirigido a promover la guerra o cualquier acto de agresión armada contra el Estado cubano, incurre en sanción de privación de libertad de diez a veinte años o muerte'.

205 See Art. 7(b) Albanian criminal code; Art. 5(1)(3) Cuban criminal code.

206 'El que realizare *en territorio salvadoreño* reclutamiento u otro acto hostil contra un Estado extranjero de modo que expandiere al Estado salvadoreño al peligro de una guerra'. Art. 354 Salvadorian criminal code (emphasis added).

a foreign state, as required in Article 354 of the Salvadorian criminal code, can be understood as acts against the sovereignty, territorial integrity and political independence of a state according to Resolution 3314.[207] While acts which expose the state to the danger of a war are sanctioned with five to ten years imprisonment, the penalty rises to 10 to 20 years in the case of an actual outbreak of a war.[208] Honduras, on the other hand, restricts criminal responsibility to its own nationals, certain residents and former nationals. Any acts have to be committed with the purpose of provoking aggression or hostilities against Honduras.[209]

The Finnish criminal code requires that 'a person in Finland or a Finnish citizen outside of Finland, during an ongoing or imminent military crisis or international political crisis, for the purpose of causing Finland to be at war or the target of a military operation ... unlawfully commits a violent act against a foreign state or the representative, territory or property of a foreign state so that the act evidently increases the danger of Finland being at war or the target of a military operation, that person shall be sentenced for warmongering to imprisonment for at least one and at most ten years' to fulfil the definition of warmongering as a treasonable offences.[210] This definition contains several distinct elements. In particular, the violent acts have to be committed unlawfully, specifically targeted and need to evidently increase the danger of war for Finland.

2. Acts That Cause or May Lead to the Outbreak of War

Some national criminal codes contain similar offences as discussed under D1, which differ insofar as they do not require the hostile act to be particularly directed or intended to provoke a war. The definitions of these crimes are fulfilled when the act is able to cause war or actually leads to the outbreak of war.

The Swedish criminal code provides for punishment of '[a] person who by violent means or foreign aid causes a danger of the Realm being involved in war or other hostilities' for high treason or for instigating war.[211] Similarly, Norway criminalizes '[a]ny person who unlawfully causes or is accessory to causing an outbreak of war or hostilities'.[212] This norm expressly requires the acts causing the outbreak of a war to be unlawful. Furthermore, it does not only protect Norway from becoming the target of hostilities, but also 'any state allied with Norway in time of war'.[213]

3. Acts Not Authorized by the Government

The majority of national codes, which invoke individual criminal responsibility for 'hostile acts', rely upon an additional element of the definition of crime. To apply these norms, two conditions usually need to be established. First, the acts against a foreign nation must be qualified as being

207 Ambos and Malarino *supra* note 24, at 476, note 19.

208 Art. 354 Salvadorian criminal code. A lesser penalty is foreseen for acts which (only) disturb external relations or provoke internal disturbances or reprisals, *ibid.*

209 See Art. 305 Honduran criminal code: 'El Hondureno, aunque haya perdido su nacionalidad, o el extranjero que deba obediencia a Honduras a causa de su empleo o función pública, quien con el propósito de provocar contra Honduras agresíon u hostilidades de una u otras naciones, ejecutare actos que tiendan directamente a ese fin, sufrirá reclusión de diez a quince anos.' Again, the actual waging of aggression or hostilities lifts the penalty frame, ibid. Art. 312 expands liability to acts against allied states.

210 Chapter 12, s. 2 para. 4 Finnish criminal code; see also *supra* text around note 170.

211 Chapter 19, s. 2 Swedish criminal code.

212 Para. 84 Norwegian criminal code.

213 Ibid.

'not approved' or 'against the will' of the government.[214] Secondly, they must create or increase the danger of counter-acts by that foreign state, which may take different appearances and intensities:[215] they may concern the aggravation or rupture of diplomatic relations,[216] a risk or danger of a declaration of war,[217] a risk or danger of war,[218] a declaration of war,[219] reprisals,[220] or they may actually provoke a war or the outbreak of hostilities.[221] If the definition of crime relates primarily to the causing of a certain danger, punishment generally increases if the hostile acts result in the materialization of that danger.[222] Accordingly, in cases where the definition of crime demands a result, lower penalties may be provided if the intended result does not occur.[223] Different penalties may be foreseen for public officers or employees and private individuals.[224]

The Greek provision does not only protect Greece from exposure to the risk of war or hostilities, but also any of its allies.[225] Uruguay specifies the acts which are able to expose the Republic to the danger of war as 'levantare tropas contra un gobierno extranjero, o ejercitare otros actos susceptibles, por su naturaleza, de exponer a la República al peligro de una guerra'.[226] Similarly, the Italian provision mentions 'fa arruolamenti o compie altri atti ostili'.[227]

In some cases the definitions of crime limit accountability to citizens[228] or to acts committed on the prescribing state's territory.[229] The majority of definitions are formulated in a neutral way as regards the nationality of the perpetrator or the territory of the offence. They may be subject

214 See, e.g., Art. 219 Argentinian criminal code; Art. 114 Bolivian criminal code; Art. 339 Peruvian criminal code; Art. 118 Philippine criminal code; see also, e.g., former Art. 311 Portuguese criminal code.

215 These levels of intensity are also mirrored in the applicable penalties; see, e.g., the different penalty frames in Art. 244 Italian criminal code.

216 E.g. Art. 219 Argentinian criminal code; Art. 114 Bolivian criminal code; Art. 546 Nicaraguan criminal code; Art. 312 Panamanian criminal code; Art. 339 Peruvian criminal code ('friendly relations').

217 E.g. Art. 114 Bolivian criminal code; Art. 546 Nicaraguan criminal code; Art. 339 Peruvian criminal code.

218 E.g. Art. 140 Greek criminal code; Art. 244 Italian criminal code; Art. 312 Panamanian criminal code; Art. 133 Uruguayan criminal code.

219 E.g. Art. 151(1) criminal code of Cote d'Ivoire; Art. 590 Spanish criminal code.

220 E.g. Art. 219 Argentinian criminal code; Art. 114 Bolivian criminal code; Art. 151(1) criminal code of Cote d'Ivoire; Art. 546 Nicaraguan criminal code; Art. 339 Peruvian criminal code; Art. 590 Spanish criminal code; Art. 133 Uruguayan criminal code.

221 Art. 118 Philippine criminal code.

222 See, e.g., Art. 219 Argentinian criminal code; Art. 114 Bolivian criminal code; Art. 244 Italian criminal code; Art. 140 Greek criminal code; Art. 313 Honduran criminal code; Art. 339 Peruvian criminal code.

223 See, e.g., Art. 590 Spanish criminal code.

224 See, e.g., Art. 118 Philippine criminal code; Art. 590 Spanish criminal code.

225 Art. 140 Greek criminal code.

226 Art. 133 Uruguayan criminal code. See in this regard also Art. 123 para. V Mexican criminal code and Art. 312 Panamanian criminal code, which is however categorized as a crime against the international community (see *supra* 2 B).

227 Art. 244 Italian criminal code. The Italian military code contains a similar provision for military leaders. For details see Jarvers and Grammer, *supra* note 24, at 378.

228 See, e.g., Art. 133 Uruguayan criminal code.

229 E.g. Art. 312 Panamanian criminal code; Art. 354 Salvadorian criminal code.

to general jurisdictional limitations.[230] However, several states provide for various forms of extraterritorial jurisdiction when it comes to offences against the security of the state.[231]

Hostile acts as described under (D) cover a wide variety of criminal acts. They may include the expression of intimidating views against a foreign state in periodicals or other publications,[232] the recruitment of armed forces,[233] as well as acts of war.[234] Despite the fact that this type of crime primarily protects national legal interests, a hostile act, which attains a level of seriousness, constitutes a violation of the sovereignty of the state against which these acts were directed. If such an act was attributable to a state, it would depend on its intensity and scale whether the act could be regarded as a violation of the prohibition of intervention, the use of force, or an act of aggression at the international level. In case the intensity and scale of the act are those of an act of aggression, the conduct falling under the definition of hostile acts on the national level could at the same time constitute the basis for the crime of aggression under international law.

A specific problem arises where the definition of crime requires that the hostile acts in question were not authorized by the government or state.[235] Since the existence of an act of aggression by a state is a precondition for individual criminal responsibility for the crime of aggression, the question arises whether or not an unauthorized act could be attributable to a state. As elaborated above,[236] such a scenario is most unlikely to achieve practical importance.

4. Conclusion

It is noteworthy that a considerable number of states have implemented the crime of aggression under international law into domestic criminal law. These norms are directly interrelated with international law as the source of criminalization. By enabling national courts to enforce this crime, states contributed to the protection of the legal values of the international community as a whole. The relevant provisions usually date from a time before the negotiation of the Rome Statute and were not introduced in the process of implementing the Rome Statute.

National norms relating to aggression reflect two main sources of international law. On the one hand, the customary crime of aggression, which originates from Article 6(a) of the Nüremberg Charter, and, on the other hand, the prohibition of any propaganda for war according to the International Covenant on Civil and Political Rights. In some cases it is notable that states seem to understand these provisions as components of one crime under international law.

With regard to the customary crime of aggression, national definitions of the crime draw largely upon the definition of crimes against peace in the Nüremberg Charter. However, it is clearly understood that this blanket, and rather rudimentary, definition has to be interpreted in the light of subsequent developments. National definitions are therefore apt to take into account customary

---

230 Art. 1 Argentinian criminal code, e.g,. limits the scope of application to Argentinian territory and to acts committed abroad by state officials.

231 See e.g. Art. 1 para. 4 Bolivian criminal code; Art. 7(1) Italian criminal code.

232 Art. 339 Peruvian criminal code does not criminalize the mere expression of such views, but only when they result in one of the described reactions by a third state, see, e.g., G. Calderón, *Código Penal* (3rd edn, Madrid: Universidad Complutense, reprinted 1997), at 516.

233 See *supra* notes 226 and 227.

234 Donna, *supra* note 125, at 393.

235 Authorization is to be understood as the express or implicit approval by the competent national organ. See in this sense, e.g., Donna, *supra* note 125, at 394.

236 See *supra* 3A, text after note 162.

developments with regard to the crime of aggression under international law, as long as they do not contradict the implemented legislation.

In the light of the Nüremberg Charter, most national definitions do not limit the circle of perpetrators of the crime of aggression. However, should the leadership element be understood as an integral element of the definition of the crime under customary international law, national norms may be interpreted and warrant an interpretation reflecting this element. The final outcome of the work of the Special Working Group on the Crime of Aggression will certainly be a strong indication as regards the customary status of the leadership element.

With regard to individual conduct, most states rely on the Nüremberg precedent. However, some states chose a selective approach or went beyond, introducing additional modes of liability. Despite the incorporation of specific modes of perpetration in the definition of the crime, no national criminal code expressly excludes the application of its general part. Potential conflicts of norms, therefore, need to be solved by way of interpretation.

The definition of the act of aggression by a state, *conditio sine qua non* for individual criminal responsibility for the crime of aggression, remains rudimentary in national provisions. Most states implement parts of the wording of the Nüremberg Charter and criminalize a 'war of aggression'. However, national commentaries underline that this notion has to be interpreted in the light of customary law developments, in particular, with regard to GA Resolution 3314. In some cases the use of this term has been criticized for its lack of legal certainty in the light of the principle of legality. Only one national legislation contains a specific definition of the prerequisite act of aggression by a state. The Croatian criminal code relies on a combination of a generic definition and the reference to specific criminal acts, in accordance with Articles 1 and 3 of GA Definition of Aggression.

In short, national provisions on the crime of aggression are largely orientated alongside a well-established definition under customary international law and are formulated flexibly enough to incorporate subsequent customary law developments. They will presumably be in compliance with the final proposal elaborated by the Special Working Group on the Crime of Aggression, which will serve as a basis for a provision on aggression enabling the ICC to exercise its jurisdiction over this crime, or may be interpreted accordingly.

In light of the ongoing negotiations to define the crime of aggression on the international level, some aspects of national definitions merit particular attention. First of all, one may observe that domestic provisions on the crime of aggression do not reflect the leadership element in the definition of crime. Secondly, national laws do not appear to have any difficulty in applying the general part of the national criminal code to a definition of crime which itself contains specific modes of perpetration. Last but not least, the definition of the crime of aggression in Article 157 of the Croatian criminal code provides an interesting example of innovative codification.

Despite the international character of the crime of aggression, only a few states provide for its enforcement on the basis of universal jurisdiction. The vast majority of states base their jurisdiction on the establishment of one of the traditional jurisdictional links between the criminal act and a state's territory, its nationals or interests.

In addition to national provisions implementing the crime of aggression under customary law, other national norms also refer to acts of aggression. These provisions – usually crimes against the existence, sovereignty, territorial integrity, independence, security of the state or treasonable offences – aim primarily at protecting national legal values. Nevertheless, some definitions of crimes only differ from certain forms of implementing laws because they are not formally identified as protecting international legal values.

Some of these offences cover only parts of the material elements of the crime of aggression. Others define a lower threshold as to the scale and gravity of the unlawful act, which however would not exclude their relevance in more severe cases. Often, they can be distinguished in that the definitions of these crimes are specifically linked to nationals or to the territory of the respective state. They may only cover situations in which the prescribing state is involved in aggressive acts, or they may aim to protect the state from outside aggression. In some instances, protection is expanded to third states. The relevance of these national offences in cases involving the crime of aggression is limited. However, when the strict definitional confinements are met, national *bona fide* prosecutions may limit or bar a case before the ICC – if the general complementarity framework will apply to the crime of aggression. In addition, national provisions covering specific aspects of the crime of aggression might also play a role in order to ensure the prosecution of persons who might not be prosecuted by the ICC, e.g., lower-level perpetrators or accessories.

However, if states desire to enforce the crime of aggression under international law on the national level, it is advisable to fully implement this crime into national legislation. Only then, they will ensure that the complete range of criminal acts can be prosecuted before national courts and that all aspects of this crime are adequately taken into account by national judges. Such implementation would serve various aims. States would foster their ability to exercise primary responsibility under the Rome Statute's complementarity regime. They would contribute to the endeavours of the international community to ensure that the most serious crimes do not go unpunished. Furthermore, national provisions on aggression may serve as a deterrent for states against outside aggression.

Chapter 26
The Crime of Aggression before the First Review of the ICC Statute*

Claus Kreß

The ultimate step in avoiding periodic wars, which are inevitable in a system of international lawlessness, is to make statesmen responsible to law. And let me make clear that while this law is first applied against German aggressors, the law includes, and if it is to serve a useful purpose it must condemn, aggression by any other nations, including those which sit here now in judgment.

Robert Jackson**

1. Introduction

There seems to be a paradox under the Rome Statute: the third preambular paragraph of the Statute[1] recalls that the peace and the security of the world is the paramount collective value that the ICC is to protect;[2] at the same time, the Court – under Article 5(2) of its Statute – is prevented from exercising its jurisdiction over precisely the crime that directly violates this value.

---

* This chapter is a slightly updated and footnoted version of the presentation made at the Turin *Conference on International Criminal Justice* on 15 May 2007, which has thereafter been published in the *Leiden Journal of International Law* 20 (2007), 851–865 and further updated, while the main points in law and legal policy remain valid.

** Opening speech of the American Chief Prosecutor in Nüremberg, reprinted in: *Trial of German Major War Criminals by the International Military Tribunal Sitting at Nuremberg Germany* (Buffalo, New York: William S. Hein & Co., 2001), 45.

1 Rome Statute of the International Criminal Court, A/CONF.183/9, 17 July 1998, corrected by process-verbaux on 10 November 1998, 12 July 1999, 30 November 1999, 8 May 2000, 17 January 2001 and 16 January 2002 (entry into force: 1 July 2002).

2 Focus on the protection of international peace and security is firmly entrenched in the tradition: cf. V.V. Pella, *La guerre-crime et les criminels de guerre* (Geneva/Paris: A. Sottile/Éditions A. Pedone, 1946), 15 ff. For a more recent restatement of the same focus, cf. the title of the 1996 ILC Draft Code of Crimes Against the Peace and Security of Mankind, A/51/10, 26 July 1996. In his recent study, M. Schuster argues that 'it should be acknowledged that the world has changed in the last fifty years. Whereas State sovereignty was almost unlimited at the time of the Nüremberg judgment, and human rights concerns relegated to the sidelines, this situation has now fundamentally changed.' 'The Rome Statute and the Crime of Aggression: A Gordian Knot in Search of a Sword', 14 *Criminal Law Forum* (2003), 14. This statement is correct in its reference to the grown importance of international human rights standards. But Schuster is wrong to imply that, as a result thereof, the value of international peace and security has lost its significance. While the latter remains a core international value to be protected by a rule of international criminal law, the coming into existence of international human rights standards adds another dimension to this rule in that soldiers' rights to life and physical integrity enter into the picture.

Also, there is a sad historic irony: the Nüremberg Tribunal recognized the crime of waging a war of aggression as the supreme international crime[3] and the most fundamental promise made in Nüremberg applies above all to this crime: the promise of equal application of the law in the future as cited above in the form of Robert Jackson's powerful words. Yet, the first permanent International Criminal Court in history has begun its work with the stated painful disability regarding the crime of aggression.

Why those reminders? Just to highlight right from the outset why the crime of aggression cannot but receive the greatest measure of attention at the upcoming first Review Conference. And just to indicate why it would be seriously mistaken to confuse, in that context, the crime of aggression with – say – the crime of trafficking in drugs.[4] Whether drug trafficking will and should ever rise to the level of a crime under general customary international law is questionable, but remains to be seen.[5] The crime of aggression, for its part, has already risen to this level[6] and the British House

---

3 'To initiate a war of aggression, therefore, is not only an international crime, it is the supreme crime', Judgment of the International Military Tribunal (IMT) for the Trial of German Major War Criminals in Nüremberg September 30 and October 1, Miscellaneous No. 12 (London: Her Majesty's Stationary Office, 1946), 13. M. Schuster, *supra* note 2: 'Even if aggression was once the supreme crime, then its importance in a legal context has certainly faded by now, as the other Nüremberg crimes have risen to the undisputed status of customary international law.' There is certainly room for doubt as to whether the crime of aggression is 'the supreme crime under international law'. This, however, is a question of secondary importance. What matters is that, contrary to Schuster's claim, the crime of aggression has not lost its importance as a result of international criminal law's evolution in other respects.

4 It is of course true that Resolution E adopted by the Rome Conference (United Nations Diplomatic Conference of Plenipotentiaries on the Establishment of an International Criminal Court, Official Records, Vol. I, Final Documents, Annex I) recommends that a Review Conference pursuant to Art. 123 of the ICCSt consider the crimes of terrorism and drug crimes with a view to arriving at an acceptable definition, and their inclusion in the list of crimes within the jurisdiction of the Court.

5 On the non-inclusion of a number of so-called 'treaty crimes' or 'transnational crimes', A. Zimmermann states: 'The main reason was that not all of the conventions providing the basis for such "treaty crimes" have found sufficient international acceptance and thus could not be considered as reflecting customary international law.' – Article 5, *Commentary on the Rome Statute of the International Criminal Court*, O. Triffterer (ed.) (2nd edn, München/Oxford/Baden-Baden: C.H. Beck/Hart/Nomos, 2008), 130 (hereinafter, Triffterer's 2nd edn). On drug trafficking, in particular, the same author notes at 132: 'However, most delegations took the position that such acts, notwithstanding their criminal nature under domestic criminal law, were not of the same nature as those now listed in Article 5.'

6 The ILC confirmed this legal status of the crime of aggression by including it in its 1996 Draft Code, *supra* note 2. In her recent textbook treatise of the subject, E. Wilmshurst, former British negotiator for the ICCSt, states: 'Aggression is widely regarded as a crime under customary international law' in R. Cryer, H. Friman, D. Robinson and E. Wilmshurst, *An Introduction to International Criminal Law and Procedure* (Cambridge: Cambridge University Press, 2007), 262 (hereinafter, Wilmshurst). This view is correct. See for example K. Ambos, 'Strafrecht und Krieg: strafbare Beteiligung der Bundesregierung am Irak-Krieg?', *Menschengerechtes Strafrecht: Festschrift für Albin Eser zum 70. Geburtstag*, J. Arnold et al. (eds) (München: Verlag C.H. Beck, 2005), 674; M.C. Bassiouni and B.B. Ferencz, *International Criminal Law: Crimes*, (2nd edn, New York: Transnational Publishers Inc., 1999), 313 ff.; I. Brownlie, *Principles of Public International Law* (6th edn, Oxford: Oxford University Press, 2003), 561 ff.; A. Cassese, *International Criminal Law* (Oxford: Oxford University Press, 2003), 113; P. Daillier and A. Pellet, *Droit international public* (Paris: LGDJ, 1999), 677; Y. Dinstein, *War, Aggression and Self-Defence* (3rd edn, Cambridge: Cambridge University Press, 2001), 113 ff.; M. Dumée, Le crime d'agression, in H. Ascensio, E. Decaux and A. Pellet (eds), *Droit International Pénal*, (Paris: Éditions A. Pedone, 2000), 251 ff.; G. Gaja, 'The Long Journey towards Repressing Aggression', in A. Cassese, P. Gaeta and J.R.W.D. Jones (eds), *The Rome Statute of the International Criminal Court: A*

of Lords is to be commended for its recent – unanimous – confirmation of this fact.[7] This basic truth explains why the crime of aggression – unlike the crime of trafficking in drugs – already forms part of the ICC's list of so-called 'core crimes'.[8] And it explains why Article 5(2) ICCSt, in conjunction with Article 5(1)(d) ICCSt, calls upon States Parties to work towards a definition of the crime so as to allow the Court to activate its jurisdiction.[9] Against this background, it may be formally true to say that the inclusion of a definition of this crime of aggression into the ICCSt will require an amendment to the latter.[10] In substance, though, States are not being invited to traverse new legal ground. Rather, the ICCSt simply calls for its own completion by finishing the job – left unfinished in Rome to the profound regret of so many – of fully transposing the customary *acquis* of international criminal law into the form of a treaty text.

Commentary, Vol. 1, (Oxford: Oxford University Press, 2002), 430 ff.; E. Greppi, 'The Evolution of Individual Criminal Responsibility under International Law', 835 *International Review of the Red Cross* 531 ff.; R.L. Griffiths, 'International Law, the Crime of Aggression and the *Ius Ad Bellum*', 2 *International Criminal Law Review* (2002), 308; M. Hummrich, *Der völkerrechtliche Straftatbestand der Aggression* (Baden-Baden: Nomos Verlagsgesellschaft, 2001), 90 ff.; C. Kreß, 'Strafrecht und Angriffskrieg im Licht "des Falles Irak"', 115 *Zeitschrift für die gesamte Strafrechtswissenschaft* (2003), 295 ff.; T. Meron, 'Defining Aggression for the International Criminal Court', 1 *Suffolk Transnational Law Review* (2001), 6; I.K. Müller-Schieke, 'Defining the Crime of Aggression Under the Statute of the International Criminal Court', 14 *Leiden Journal of International Law* (2001), 414; D.D. Nsereko, 'Defining the Crime of Aggression: An Important Agenda Item for the Assembly of States Parties to the Rome Statute of the International Criminal Court', *Acta Juridica* (2003), 266; L. Sadat and S.R. Carden, 'The New International Criminal Court: An Uneasy Revolution', 88 *Georgetown Law Journal* 437 (note 341); M. Aziz Shukri, 'Will Aggressors Ever be Tried Before the ICC?', in M. Politi and G. Nesi (eds), *The International Criminal Court and the Crime of Aggression*, (Aldershot: Ashgate Publishing Ltd., 2004), 35 (Politi & Nesi) and, ibid, E. Wilmshurst, 'Definition of the Crime of Aggression: State Responsibility or Individual Criminal Responsibility?', at 95; O. Triffterer, 'Establishment of the Court', in O. Triffterer (ed.), *Commentary on the Rome Statute of the International Criminal Court* (Baden-Baden, Nomos Verlagsgesellschaft, 1999) (hereinafter, Triffterer's 1st edn); G. Werle, *Principles of International Criminal Law* (The Hague: T.M.C. Asser Press, 2005), 393; G. Westdickenberg and O. Fixson, 'Das Verbrechen der Aggression im Römischen Statut des Internationalen Strafgerichtshofes', in J.Abr. Frowein et al. (eds), *Verhandeln für den Frieden: Liber Amicorum Tono Eitel* (Berlin: Springer, 2003), 500 ff. For a different view, M. Schuster, *supra* note 2 at 13.

7 *R. v. Jones et al.*, [2006] UKHL 16, paras 12, 19 (Lord Bingham); paras 44, 59 (Lord Hoffmann); para. 96 (Lord Rodger); para. 97 (Lord Carswell); para. 99 (Lord Mance).

8 With respect to the crime of aggression, it is therefore a little bit misleading to speak of the inclusion of a 'new' crime as Rolf Fife does in 'Criminalizing Individual Acts of Aggression by States', in M. Bergsmo (ed.), *Human Rights and Criminal Justice for the Downtrodden. Essays in Honour of Asbjorn Eide* (Leiden/Boston: Martinus Nijhoff Publishers, 2003), 73.

9 Accordingly, Resolution F adopted by the Rome Conference is formulated in mandatory terms: 'The [Preparatory] Commission shall prepare proposals for a provision on aggression' (United Nations Diplomatic Conference of Plenipotentiaries on the Establishment of an International Criminal Court, Official Records, Vol. I, Final Documents, Annex I) 72.

10 For a summary of the debate within the Special Working Group on how to 'adopt a provision in accordance with articles 121 and 123 defining the crime and setting out the conditions under which the Court shall exercise jurisdiction', see ICC-ASP/8/INF.2, paras 32 ff.; ICC-ASP/7/20/Add. 1, paras 6 ff.; ICC-ASP/3/25, 344 and ICC-ASP/4/32, 359 ff.

2. Building a Definition and a Procedure

The Special Working Group for the Crime of Aggression[11] has gone a very long way to prepare the ground for that transposition. Scholars, criminal law scholars in particular, tend to possess a degree of suspicion when crimes are being defined by diplomats. There is a fear that diplomats may not always be sensitive enough to the peculiarities and technical subtleties of criminal law. Such a suspicion, however, was not justified in respect of those who worked together in the Special Working Group. Quite the contrary, the following are indicators of the intensive, thorough, and sincere work conducted within the Group over six years: first, there is probably no other crime in the ICCSt, the formulation of which has received greater attention than the crime of aggression; second, as a result thereof, there has been no time in the century-long process of reflecting about the crime of aggression[12] that its special structure has been more fully explored and understood than now.[13] This general appraisal is specified below in light of the three main baskets of problems that the Group has addressed in its recent work.[14]

3. The Individual Responsibility

Regarding the position and the conduct of the individual perpetrator, there continues to be a very solid consensus on the absolute[15] leadership nature of the crime of aggression as established in Nüremberg and Tokyo.[16]

The most recent debate has been about the possible interplay between the general principles of criminal law as crystallized in Part 3 ICCSt, and the definition of the crime. The clear and dominant view is to deviate as little as possible from the solutions contained in Part 3. To my own surprise, this view has been maintained even in respect of the forms of individual participation that are listed

---

11 The Special Working Group was established by Resolution ICC-ASP/1/Res.1 adopted by consensus at the 3rd Plenary Meeting on 9 September 2002, ICC-ASP/1/3, 328.

12 For a monumental study of the aggression debate from 1920 to 1975, see B.B. Ferencz, *Defining International Aggression –The Search for World Peace: A Documentary History and Analysis*, 2 Volumes (Dobbs Ferry, New York: Oceana Publications Inc., 1975). For a useful and more recent account, United Nations (ed.), *Historical Review of Developments relating to Aggression* (New York: United Nations Publications, 2003).

13 As early as in 2002, R.S. Clark welcomed the existence of a 'now substantial focus on the "technical", "criminal law" aspects of the endeavour', 'Rethinking Aggression as a Crime and Formulating Its Elements: The Final Work-Product of the Preparatory Commission for the International Criminal Court', 15 *Leiden Journal of International Law* (2002), 886. R.S. Clark has been participating for a very long time in the negotiations on the crime of aggression and has made many significant contributions to them.

14 These three 'baskets' are clearly distinguished in the 2007 Report of the Special Working Group on the Crime of Aggression, ICC-ASP/5/35, 9 ff. under the following headings: (1) 'The crime of aggression – defining the individual's conduct'; (2) 'The act of aggression – defining the conduct of the State'; and (3) 'Conditions for the exercise of jurisdiction'. For an excellent analysis of the complementarity issue, see P. Wrange, 'The crime of Aggression and Complementarity', in this Volume.

15 By 'absolute' I mean that the leadership requirement applies to *all* forms of participation in the crime.

16 In the Draft Resolution to be adopted by Review Conference on the Crime of Aggression, ICC-ASP/7/ 20/Add. 1, Appendix I, 30, the words intended to restate the Nüremberg *acquis* are as follows: 'a person in a position effectively to exercise control over or to direct the political or military action of a State.' There is a question mark as to whether that formula is broad enough: see '2007 Report of the Special Working Group on the Crime of Aggression', ICC-ASP/5/35, 10 (para. 13) (2007 SWG Report).

in Article 25(3)(a) to (d) ICCSt. As a consequence, a lot of thought has gone into the formulation of what I have called the 'differentiated approach', i.e., the legal recognition of all different forms of individual participation in the crime of aggression.[17] It would now seem that a solution that uses language almost mirroring that of the Nüremberg and Tokyo judgment has been reached.[18]

4. The Act of Aggression

The Group has also made tremendous progress regarding the definition of the state act of aggression.[19] The greatest achievement of the Draft Resolution on the Crime of Aggression[20] is that it reflects the wish of the Group to no longer confuse the substantive definition of the state act with the procedural issue of a possible role for the Security Council in the early stages of the proceedings.[21]

In the second place, the proposed solution reflects the wish of an overwhelming majority of delegations to see the definition based on the Annex to General Assembly Resolution 3314 (XXIX) of 14 December 1974.[22] This again constitutes a major clarification of the overall picture, even though I had personally favoured a different approach.[23] The '3314 approach' has not been spelled out in such detail and with such precision as would have been desirable. Yet, the wording suggested in the Draft Resolution allows for a sensible approach that respects the simple, but important, fact that the General Assembly text has been written as a guide for a political organ, the Security Council of the United Nations, to assist that organ in its application of Article 39 of the

17 I have tried to set out in detail the distinction between the 'monistic approach' suggested in the Coordinator's 2002 'Discussion Paper', ICC-ASP/2/10, 234 (sub. I.1 and I.3), and the 'differentiated approach' in my Sub-coordinator, 'Discussion Paper 1: The Crime of Aggression and Article 25, paragraph 3, of the Statute', ICC-ASP/4/32, 376 ff.

18 The suggested solution reads: 'For the purpose of this Statute, "crime of aggression" means the planning, preparation, initiation or execution of an act of aggression.' ICC-ASP/7/20/Add.1, 30.

19 At no point in the debate has there been an appreciable degree of support to extend the definition to non-State acts of aggression. This is in line with existing customary international law: see Wilmshurst, note 6 *supra*, at 272.

20 ICC-ASP/7/20/Add.1, 30.

21 This distinction is not only required under sound principles of criminal law, but it is also envisaged by the wording of Art. 5(2) of the ICCSt. Conversely, the Coordinator's 2002 Discussion Paper, *supra* note 19 at sub I.2, confused substance and procedure. For a pertinent critique, see D.D. Nsereko, *supra* note 7, at 278.

22 GAOR (Official Records of the General Assembly), 20th Session, Supplement 31, 142 ff.

23 My view is based on doubts about whether all of the acts listed in Article 3 of the Annex to Resolution 3314 reflect customary international criminal law; I have set out some arguments supporting those doubts in C. Kress, 'The German Chief Federal Prosecutor's Decision Not to Investigate the Alleged Crime of Preparing Aggression against Iraq', 2 *Journal of International Criminal Justice* (2004), 249 ff.; for a similar scepticism, see Wilmshurst, note 6 *supra*, at 272 ff. Perhaps it can be argued that the '3314 approach' could *crystallize* into custom through a broad consensus among States taking part in the negotiations.

United Nations Charter.[24] This caveat applies, in particular, to Articles 2[25] and 4[26] of the annex to Resolution 3314, as well as to one passage in the chapeau of Article 3.[27]

The third noteworthy aspect of the debate on the definition of the state act of aggression relates to the so-called qualifier. There is now a very substantial measure of support for limiting the definition of the state act as part of the definition of the crime to an instance of the use of armed force[28] 'which, by its character, gravity, and scale, constitute a manifest violation of the Charter of the United Nations'.[29] This is a clear and crucial signal that the Special Working Group is fully aware of the reality of the present-day *jus contra bellum*. One essential aspect of this reality is the fact that, regrettably, there is a grey area in the international legal framework, i.e., an area where reasonable international lawyers may legitimately disagree in their assessment of the *lex lata*, depending *inter alia* on how the more recent international practice is seen and weighed.[30] It should not be seen as the expression of an unprincipled realism if the Special Working Group were to have the ICC stay away from that grey zone.[31] It is, quite to the contrary, fully in line with the overall thrust that guided the negotiators of the ICCSt, i.e., to confine the Court's jurisdiction to atrocious behaviour

---

24 See in particular para. 4 of Resolution 3314; E. Wilmshurst concurring, ibid., at 272 ff.

25 Art. 2 reads: 'The first use of armed force by a State in contravention of the Charter shall constitute *prima facie* evidence of an act of aggression although the Security Council may, in conformity with the Charter, conclude that a determination that an act of aggression has been committed would not be justified in the light of other relevant circumstances, including the fact that the acts concerned or their consequences are not of sufficient gravity.' Making this provision part of the definition of the State act of aggression would not only pose a serious problem in respect of Art. 67(1)(i) of the ICCSt ('Not to have imposed on him or her any reversal of the burden of proof or any onus of rebuttal'), but it would also undo the necessary distinction between substance and procedure by making the existence of an act of aggression dependant on the *ex post facto* decision of the Security Council.

26 Art. 4 reads: 'The acts enumerated above are not exhaustive and the Security Council may determine that other acts constitute aggression under the provisions of the Charter.' Apart from a serious question pertaining to the legality principle, the incorporation of this provision would again entail a complete confusion between substance and procedure.

27 The chapeau of Art. 3 reads: 'Any of the following acts, regardless of a declaration of war, shall, *subject to and in accordance with provisions of Article 2*, qualify as an act of aggression' (emphasis added). The italicized words are open to the same critique as has been set out in note 28 *supra*.

28 Draft Resolution, ICC-ASP/7/20/Add.1, 30; the wording of the qualifier has a noteworthy resemblance to the language used by the ICJ in para. 165 of its Judgment of 19 December 2005 in the *Case Concerning Armed Activities on the Territory of the Congo (Democratic Republic of Congo v. Uganda)* where the Court speaks of a military intervention 'of such magnitude and duration that the Court considers it to be a grave violation of the prohibition on the use of force expressed in Article 2, paragraph 4, of the Charter'; it is certainly not a far-fetched assumption that the Court used this language with the term 'act of aggression' in mind while stopping short of calling a spade a spade (for a critique of the latter failure, see para. 2 of the Separate Opinion of Judge Simma).

29 Numerous efforts have been made to further specify the qualifier through a formulation of a 'specific collective intent' (for the position of this author, see *supra* note 15, at 258 ff.) to pinpoint the criminal *noyeau dur*; while those efforts should be pursued further by scholars, it has proven overly ambitious to agree on a specific wording as part of the definition; for precisely this reason, it would seem to overstretch the requirements flowing from the legality principle to demand the inclusion of such a wording into the definition instead of using the qualifier mentioned in the above text.

30 For a succinct and fair presentation of this grey area, see Wilmshurst, note 6 *supra*, at 268 ff.

31 At the same time, the qualifier excludes *minor* uses of armed force from the international criminalization; this is, of course, without prejudice to the question of state responsibility where the use of force is illegal.

that indisputably violates general customary international law.[32] In a thought-provoking article on the crime of aggression, Rolf Fife cautioned against developing the international law on the use of force through the back door of international criminal law.[33] The so-called qualifier contained in the Draft Resolution reflects this fundamental concern. By the same token, it constitutes the wise recognition of the fact that international criminal law is ill-equipped to decide major controversies about the content of existing legal rules.[34]

5. The Role of the Security Council

This brings me to the procedural question of the possible role of the Security Council. The different positions are too well known to require any restatement.[35]

While it is not difficult to find a solution for this problem in terms of drafting, it is obvious that the Security Council issue remains the political question of questions on the crime of aggression, and every participant in the negotiations in Rome will recognize a certain parallel between this and the jurisdiction issue that was finally settled in the form of Article 12 of the ICCSt.[36] In light of this, it would be a little naive to expect a consensus on this issue emerging long before Kampala. This is worth stating because it reveals how seriously mistaken it would be to say that the crime of aggression should be placed on the first Review Conference's agenda only if agreement on this last issue has been reached before that conference begins. The contrary is true: if one is serious about reaching agreement on the crime of aggression, one will give the Review Conference the procedural framework and the necessary time to make the final choice. The Special Working Group can claim to have, as much as possible, prepared the technical ground for the political decision that remains to be made. Draft Article 15 bis, as proposed in the Draft Resolution, sets up a workable jurisdictional and procedural regime that can be quickly completed by legal experts once the necessary political guidance has been provided.

I shall not speculate on what the final choice will look like. However, as a scholar of international criminal law, I wish to state my firm and considered belief about what the final solution must *not* look like: any rule that would invariably subject international judicial proceedings for an alleged

32 This general thrust is probably best expressed in para. 1 of the 'Introduction' to the Elements of the Crimes Against Humanity, which reads: 'Since article 7 pertains to international criminal law, its provisions, consistent with article 22, must be strictly construed, taking into account that crimes against humanity as defined in article 7 are among the most serious crimes of concern to the international community as a whole, warrant and entail international criminal responsibility, and require conduct which is impermissible under generally applicable international law, as recognized by the principal legal systems of the world.' This reasonable statement must apply to the crime of aggression *mutatis mutandis*.

33 'The Court needs to be well integrated in the existing system of peace and security of the international community. This system is certainly imperfect, and legitimate reasons speak in favour of its strengthening. However, it seems a dangerous illusion to believe that it could be revised through international criminal law', R. Fife, *supra* note 8, at 73.

34 If States agreed on the inclusion of the qualifier into the definition, Rolf Fife's (*supra* note 8, at 73) two central and very stringent demands would clearly be met: the crime of aggression would 'rest on rock-solid foundations' and the 'discussion of crimes against the peace [would] not lead to a continuation of politics in a legal forum'.

35 See the list of options contained in the Draft Resolution ICC-ASP/7/20/Add.1, 31 (Art. 15 bis, para. 4).

36 For a detailed account of the negotiations leading to the final vote on the ICC's jurisdiction regime, see H.P. Kaul and C. Kreß, 'Jurisdiction and Cooperation in the Rome Statute on the International Criminal Court: Principles and Compromises', 2 *Yearbook of International Humanitarian Law* (1999), 143 ff.

crime of aggression to the veto power of each of the Permanent Members of the Security Council must be considered as fundamentally flawed. This position is not only based on the now well-known fact that there is no legal requirement – especially not one flowing from Article 39 of the United Nations Charter[37] – to vest the Security Council with such a decisive role.[38] More

37 E. Wilmshurst correctly notes: 'It is clear that the Council does not have *exclusive* responsibility with regard to threats to international peace and security. Its responsibility is exclusive only for the purpose of its powers under Chapter VII which include deciding upon economic sanctions and other responses to breaches of the peace.' Wilmshurst, note 6 *supra*, at 277. As early as 1984, the ICJ clarified the limited scope of Art. 39 of the United Nations Charter and stated: 'The Council has functions of a political nature assigned to it, whereas the Court exercises purely judicial functions. Both organs perform their separate but complementary functions with respect to the same events.' *Case Concerning Military and Paramilitary Activities in and against Nicaragua (Nicaragua v. US)*, ICJ Reports (1984), 392 (para. 95). For an extensive and illuminating analysis of this decision, see C. McDougall, 'When Law and Reality Clash – the Imperative of Compromise in the Context of the Accumulated Evil of the Whole: Conditions for the Exercise of the International Criminal Court's Jurisdiction over the Crime of Aggression', in 7 *International Criminal Law Review* (2007). The logic set out in 'Nicaragua 1984' as cited above applies *a fortiori* to the Security Council and the ICC, as the latter is an international legal person independent from the United Nations. For a mistaken position ignoring this basic fact, see, however, M. Schuster, *supra* note 2, at 37.

38 Again one can only agree with Wilmshurst, note 6 *supra*, at 278: 'The *legal* reasons for the proposal that the Security Council should make a prior determination, as outlined above, are weak.' For a particularly detailed reason analysis to support this view, see C. McDougall, *supra* note 37; this author concludes as follows: 'As Article 5(2) of the Rome Statute is inconclusive, any legal restriction on the ability of other entities to make such a determination would have to be found in the UN Charter. An analysis of the Charter finds no such restriction'; as early as 2001, M. Hummrich, *supra* note 6, at 222 ff. arrived at the same result on the basis of a similarly detailed analysis; for another rather comprehensive recent analysis supporting the same view, see M. Stein, 'The Security Council, The International Criminal Court, and the Crime of Aggression: How Exclusive is the Security Council's Power to Determine Aggression?', 16 *Indiana International & Comparative Law Review* (2005), 5 ff. For a selection of views concurring with which is clearly the prevailing positions in international legal scholarship, see A. Cassese, *International Criminal Law*, note 6 *supra*, at 117; L. Condorelli, 'Conclusions Générales', Politi & Nesi, note 6 *supra*, 159 ff.; P. Escarameia, 'The ICC and the Security Council on Aggression: Overlapping Competencies?', ibid., at 139 ff.; G. Gaja, 'The Respective Roles of the ICC and the Security Council in Determining the Existence of Aggression', ibid., at 121 ff.; S.M. Yengejeh, 'Reflections on the Role of the Security Council in Determining an Act of Aggression', ibid., at 125; M. Lehto, 'The ICC and the Security Council: About the Argument of Politicization', ibid., at 148 ff.; G. Gaja, *supra* note 7, at 433 ff.; C. Kress, 'Versailles, Nüremberg, The Hague: Germany and International Criminal Law', 40 *The International Lawyer* (2005), 38; M.E. Kurth, *Das Verhältnis des Internationalen Strafgerichtshofes zum UN Sicherheitsrat* (Baden-Baden: Nomos-Verlagsgesellschaft, 2006), 216 ff.; I.K. Müller-Schieke, *supra* note 6, at 425 ff.; D.D. Nsereko, *supra* note 6, at 285 ff.; A. Paulus, 'Peace through Justice? The Future of the Crime of Aggression in a Time of Crisis', 50 *Wayne Law Review* (2004), 21 ff.; L.J. Springrose, 'Aggression as a Core Crime in the Rome Statute Establishing an International Criminal Court', 5 *St. Louis-Warsaw Transatlantic Law Journal* (1999), 167. For a somewhat weak albeit detailed effort to argue the opposite case *on the basis of the United Nations Charter*, see M. Schuster, *supra* note 2, at 35 ff. For the same view, but without as much reasoning, see B.B. Ferencz, 'Enabling the International Criminal Court to Punish Aggression', 6 *Washington University Global Studies Law Review* (2006), 13. For an equally unconvincing view to the same effect *based on Article 5(2) of the ICCSt*, see A. Zimmermann, 'Article 5', Triffterer's 1st edn, note 6 *supra*, 106 (Zimmermann has appreciably qualified his position in the Triffterer's 2nd edn, note 5 *supra*, 140 (marginal note 37). It is true that the United Kingdom has interpreted Art. 5(2) of the ICCSt this way, A/CONF.183/13[Vol.II], 124: 'Sir Franklin Berman (United Kingdom of Great Britain and Northern Ireland) said that the United Kingdom interpreted the reference to aggression in article 5 and, in particular, the last sentence of paragraph 2 of that article, which mentioned the Charter of United Nations

fundamentally, my position is based on the minimum requirements of legitimacy in international criminal justice. In this respect, it has been said by some that the ICC needs the political backing of the Security Council in aggression proceedings. I wholeheartedly agree that the Security Council can lend the ICC – here, as in all its proceedings – its most precious support. This support may, of course, include a referral under Article 13(b) ICCSt. It will not help the ICC, though, if each Permanent Member of the Security Council is empowered to prevent the Court from exercising its jurisdiction over the crime of aggression.[39] Such a power would instead adversely affect the Court's legitimacy, as it would fly in the face of the absolutely essential aspiration of equal application of the law.[40] As a great jurist, Robert Jackson could not avoid developing an intimate feeling for that basic truth when he made his above-cited famous promise in Nüremberg. One should remain confident that the political leadership in France, the United Kingdom, Russia, and – certainly not least – the United States will recall that the noble promise to ensure equality before the law forms an integral part of their precious Nüremberg and Tokyo legacy.[41]

6. Conclusion

A frightening number of brackets around draft proposals were to be eliminated at the Rome Conference: if this state of play before the Rome Conference is compared with the situation before the first Review Conference, then there is ample reason to be optimistic.

[sic], as a reference to the requirement of prior determination by the Security Council that an act of aggression had occurred.' (For a restatement of this view, see F. Berman, 'The Relationship between the International Criminal Court and the Security Council', in H.A.M. von Hebel, J.G. Lammers and J.J.Schukkina (eds), *Reflections on the International Criminal Court: Essays in Honour of Adriaan Bos* (The Hague: T.M.C. Asser Press, 1999), 178). It is equally true, though, that this statement does not reflect a *shared* understanding; for extensive and persuasive arguments to the same effect, see M. Hummrich, *supra* note 6, at 231 ff.; C. McDougall, *supra* note 37.

39 It is the wisdom of the underlying compromise in Art. 16 of the ICCSt that no such veto power is granted.

40 One may well go one step further and ask the question whether the Security Council acts legally if it allows its Permanent Members 'to sit in judgment in their own cause'. E. de Wet makes a powerful case that the Security Council must satisfy the requirements of 'independence, impartiality and even-handedness' where it acts in relation to criminal proceedings: *The Chapter VII Powers of the United Nations Security Council* (Oxford and Portland Oregon: Hart Publishing, 2004), 348 ff.

41 For an impressive appeal to his government, see the remarks of H.T. King, former Nüremberg war crimes Prosecutor, at the American Bar Association's Commemoration of the 60th Anniversary of the Nüremberg Trials, November 11, 2005, Georgetown School of Law, Washington, DC, 40 *The International Lawyer* (2006), 5: 'Nüremberg is sometimes viewed as a legend in today's world, but its legacy is with the people of the world. We must honor the actuality of Nüremberg while respecting its symbolism so that the Nüremberg principles, which are indeed far-reaching, become the universal rule of law in the world.' The example of Germany demonstrates that a government may be wise enough to reconsider its own position based on sound principles. In 1980, Germany spoke in favour of having the Security Council determine the existence of an act of aggression before starting international criminal proceedings, A/C.6/35/Sr. 12, 7 October 1980, 7 ff. At a formal meeting of the Assembly of States Parties in 2007, however, the German delegation stated the following: 'We have been following the debate on this issue very carefully throughout the years. We came to the conclusion that, under international law, the exercise of the ICC's jurisdiction should not be dependent on the authorization by any other body, such as the Security Council. Therefore, like many delegations who spoke before us, we are in favour of Option 1 in paragraph 5 of your paper.'

The fact that in the future there will be more Review Conferences to follow the first is to be understood as further opportunities for possible amendments to the ICC's law of procedure. In that respect, I fully agree with the implication that the early practice of the Court has not yet have yielded sufficient experience by the time of the first Review Conference to allow for considered decisions to be made about procedural amendments. The case of the crime of aggression, however, is quite different and this difference does not only lie in the fact that, by fulfilling their mandate under Article 5(2) ICCSt, States Parties will, in substance, complete the Rome Statute rather than proceed to its amendment. The crucial difference, as was frequently pointed out by the successful coordinator of the Special Working Group on the Crime of Aggression, Ambassador Christian Wenaweser, is that the negotiations on the crime of aggression possess a momentum and have reached the point where political leaders must decide whether or not they wish to take advantage of the large and distinct window of opportunity that has been created. Few who have studied the century-long effort to come to terms with the 'supreme international crime' will doubt that political leaders have before them a historic opportunity.[42] The world's civil society and certainly the Coalition for the ICC[43] may be expected to signal to those leaders that it would be more than sad to let this opportunity pass. Two principles should guide the final decision-making are as follows:

> (i) the substantial definition of the state act of aggression must stay within the legitimate limits of international criminal justice by not exceeding undisputable general customary international law; on the basis of the '3314 approach', the so-called qualifier is of paramount importance to guarantee that this principle will be observed;
> (ii) a special procedural regime that includes a carefully articulated role for the Security Council may well be devised and it should be drafted with a close view to the applicable amendment procedure and the latter's jurisdictional consequences. Such a regime must not, however, defy fundamental principles of international criminal justice and must not, in particular, have the practical effect of placing the Permanent Members of the Security Council (and their friends and partners in trade) beyond the reach of the law.

---

42 Those who are less familiar with the subject may wish to listen to B.B. Ferencz, a *grandseigneur* of international criminal justice who acted as the American Chief Prosecutor in the *Einsatzgruppen* case and remains dedicated enough to allow the Special Working Group to benefit from his experience and wisdom: 'The most important achievement of the Nüremberg trials, after over 40 million people had died in World War Two, was the confirmation that war-making was no longer a national right but had become, and henceforth would be condemned, as an international crime. That great historical step forward toward a more rational and human world order under law must not be allowed to perish', *supra* note 38, at 15. For a (rare) radical view to the contrary, see M. Schuster, *supra* note 2, at 51, who advocates for the deletion of the crime of aggression from the ICC list of crimes.

43 The Coalition must be commended for its support of the ongoing negotiations by involving a number of highly competent legal experts in the process. One is, however, surprised by the conspicuous silence of organizations such as Amnesty International and Human Rights Watch. Even from the narrowest perspective of human rights protection, one would expect such organizations to be concerned about the right to life of soldiers exposed to death in conflicts arising from criminal acts of aggression.

Adherence to these two principles will require a spirit of compromise from almost all[44] sides. Let us hope that a so inspired political leadership assumes its responsibility and closes, ideally by consensus, the Statute's most prominent lacuna before it turns into a legitimacy gap.

44 Conversely, contrary to what that author pretends, the proposal submitted by C. McDougall, *supra* note 37, calls for a spirit of compromise from only one side, that is, from the vast majority opposing an exclusive power of the Security Council. McDougall's suggestion 'that the ability of the P5 to exercise their veto is a necessary component of any compromise solution that is to be successful' amounts to much the same as saying that the five Permanent Members of the Security Council need not compromise. It is deplorable to note that McDougall, following a legal and legal policy analysis of outstanding quality, decides to bow to the alleged demands of *realpolitik*. Contrary to McDougall, the author of this chapter believes that international criminal justice must not sacrifice its legitimacy at the altar of *realpolitik* if it is to endure.

Chapter 27
The Crime of Aggression and Complementarity*

Pål Wrange

1. Introduction

The focus of this article is not the law as it is (*de lege lata*), nor how one would wish it to be (*de lege ferenda*). Both de *lege lata* and *de lege ferenda* are proper *modi* for a government to speak in. However, governments rarely speculate about what the law *might* be, but that is an approach that suits my personal temperament and interests quite well.[1]

I will take a cue here from an important statement made by an eminent lawyer from Northern Italy, Judge Politi of Trento, who already in the Preparatory Commission of the International Criminal Court (ICC) in 2000 advised us to think about aggression and complementarity.[2] I will therefore deal with the legal principle of complementarity as provided for in the Preamble, in Article 1 and in Articles 17–19 of the Rome Statute, i.e., briefly that the Court shall exercise its jurisdiction only when there is no state that is willingly and ably investigating or prosecuting the case. But I shall also reflect on the idea of complementarity in a broader sense, namely that international criminal law should be developed and exercised in interplay between domestic and international jurisdictions, and what are the implications of this idea on other issues before the Special Working Group on the Crime of Aggression (SWGCA) of the Assembly of States Parties (ASP). I will venture to speculate a bit about how domestic legislators and jurisdictions might react with or without one or more agreed provisions on the crime of aggression after the Review Conference in 2010.

2. Complementarity

The principle of complementarity was not embraced by everyone when it entered the Rome Statute. In fact, many saw it as a way of weakening the Statute of the new Court.[3] However, I believe it fair to say that there is now broad agreement that the principle is a useful and even necessary feature of the Statute. This principle provides a connection between, at one end, national, and at the other

---

* The author wishes to thank Claus Kress, Håkan Friman, Jutta Bertram-Nothnagel, Christian Wenaweser, Don Ferencz (for his analysis of the judgment in the House of Lords, herewith in note 42) and, most of all, Christina Villarino Villo and Nicolaos Strapatsas, for helpful comments. Though the author holds different views on the matter, N. Strapatsas's paper 'Complementarity & Aggression: A Ticking Time Bomb?' (Draft Presented to the Marie Curie Research Course on International Criminal Law, 2007) – thorough and thought-provoking as all of his work – has been useful for the elaboration of this piece, even when not cited below.

1 However, the notes include an occasional comment *de lege lata*.

2 PCNICC/2000/WGCA/DP.3, at 3.

3 See J.T. Holmes, 'Complementarity: National Courts versus the International Criminal Court', in A. Cassese, P. Gaeta and J.R.W.D. Jones (eds), *Rome Statute of the International Criminal Court* (Oxford: Oxford University Press, 2002), 672 note (hereinafter, Cassese, Gaeta and Jones).

end, international – or supranational – jurisdictions. It is the link that forces the ICC and national legal systems to engage with one another, at the judicial as well as – sometimes – at the political level. Hence, the most important effect of the provision on the crime of aggression might not be prosecutions in The Hague, but prosecutions, and threat of prosecutions, in local jurisdictions.[4]

Now, if a provision on the crime of aggression were to be adopted in accordance with Article 5(2) of the Rome Statute, how would it play out with regard to the principle of complementarity?

To my knowledge, the SWGCA has discussed the principle of complementarity only during the informal meeting at the Liechtenstein Institute at Princeton University in 2004, as I will refer to shortly.[5] The general feeling of the group was that there was no need for any special provisions on complementarity in relation to the crime of aggression. I agree with that conclusion. But that does not mean that the issue is unproblematic.

The questions I would like to ask in this context are if and under what conditions domestic prosecutions might take place in either of three scenarios, and what might be the problems and issues associated with each of them:

I. The scenario where there is a provision on the crime of aggression and the Court is exercising or is ready to exercise jurisdiction over the situation, but a domestic process is under way.

II. The scenario where there is a provision on the crime of aggression, and that clause provides that the ICC can exercise its jurisdiction only after a decision by the UN Security Council (SC) or some other body, and no such decision is forthcoming. This means that the ICC cannot exercise jurisdiction in such a situation.

III. The scenario where there is no provision on the crime of aggression in the Rome Statute, i.e., a situation in which the ICC is never allowed to exercise its jurisdiction over that crime and when there is no agreed definition.

So, the first two situations occur in a hypothetical world after the Review Conference, when a provision on the crime of aggression has been adopted and such a provision has entered into force, while the third scenario is when no such provision is in force, but states still might exercise national jurisdiction over the crime of aggression. Legislators will encounter issues, of course, in drafting and adopting domestic provisions relating to the crime of aggression. But judges and other officials of a court may also be faced with questions, even when there is a national statutory provision: the scope of the domestic provision may be unclear; the domestic statute on the crime of aggression may be challenged as unlawful under international law; and a defendant or others might bring forward arguments for why a national court should not exercise its jurisdiction. What attitudes might national institutions take under these scenarios? In my efforts to answer these questions, I will address several legal issues, such as:

1. whether there are sovereignty or legal policy related bars, like the act of state doctrine or the political questions doctrine;
2. whether there is universal jurisdiction over the crime of aggression or any other ground to prosecute a foreigner for the crime of aggression;

---

4 Prosecutor Luis Moreno Ocampo has even stated that the best outcome of the ICC would be if it had no work at all, due to national jurisdictions doing their job. 'Paper on some policy issues before the Office of the Prosecutor', II (1), at 4.

5 ICC-ASP/3/25, at 345.

3. whether it is probable that domestic courts might find themselves compelled to wait for a decision by the Security Council; and
4. whether the crime is sufficiently clear in international law when there is no definition in the Rome Statute.

Some of these questions – such as 1 and 2 – will arise under all scenarios, but I will deal with each under the scenario under which the respective question likely will be most prominent.[6]

3. Scenario I: The ICC is Ready to Exercise Jurisdiction, but National Authorities are Seized of the Case

A. Conditions of Scenario I

Under this scenario there is a provision on the crime of aggression in the Statute, and either there are no special conditions for the exercise of jurisdiction, or those conditions have been met. Consequently, this is the situation where the Court is ready to go, but there are domestic processes in motion. If the Court is investigating or planning to investigate a case, then it has to consider whether the domestic proceedings would be an obstacle to admissibility under the principle of complementarity. Article 17(a) of the Rome Statute provides that a case is inadmissible when '[t]he case is being investigated or prosecuted by a State which has jurisdiction over it, unless the State is unwilling or unable genuinely to carry out the investigation or prosecution', and the same criteria of willingness and ability applies to the situation where a domestic trial has already taken place or a decision has been taken not to prosecute. Hence, issues would arise at the domestic level as well as at the level of the ICC.

B. Issues before National Jurisdictions

The first issue is whether domestic courts really have *prima facie* jurisdiction, including *ratione materiae* and *ratione personae*. Under this scenario, where the crime is in the Statute, the issue of national jurisdiction *ratione materiae* might not be controversial. The jurisdiction *ratione personae* might be challenged, in particular in claims to universal jurisdiction, but it might also be well accepted when the crime has the imprimatur of a definition in the Rome Statute. It will probably be assumed that aggression is an international crime, and that the same rules on jurisdiction apply as for the other international crimes, i.e., universal jurisdiction. At any rate, I will deal with both of those issues below. But there will be other difficulties.

1. Immunities

The crime of aggression is a leadership crime, so the people prosecuted for the crime of aggression will be leaders, i.e., most likely present or former high public officials of a state.[7] For leaders, the

---

6 This is, of course, difficult to predict. For instance, under scenario 3, it is obvious that the lack of an agreed definition will feature prominently in the discussion, but it might very well turn out that the most contentious issue is whether a certain person is covered by procedural immunities or not.

7 Though not necessarily only government officials, unless the precedents from Nüremberg are being restricted. K.J. Heller, 'Retreat from Nüremberg: The Leadership Requirement in the Special Working Group's Definition of Aggression', 18 *European Journal of International Law* (2007), at 477–497.

issue of immunity from domestic prosecutions in foreign courts[8] will likely be raised. Immunities generally come under two rubrics: substantive (or functional) immunity and procedural (or personal) immunity.[9] The first one means that officers of the state shall never be liable individually for state acts. Domestic courts will probably not feel that this applies to international crimes.[10]

The second type of immunity is the procedural immunity, which entails that some types of officials are immune as long as they hold a certain office, for instance that of a foreign minister or a diplomat posted in a certain country. This type of immunity will normally prevent a state from prosecuting, even for international crimes. In the *Arrest Warrant* case before the International Court of Justice (ICJ), the Court concluded that the then Foreign Minister of the Democratic Republic of the Congo, Abdulaye Yerodia Ndombasi, was immune before Belgian Courts. The ICJ judgment is correct and authoritative in this respect.[11] Of course, there is no immunity in the ICCSt, but the renunciation of immunity *inter partes* in the Rome Statute most likely only applies before the ICC. National jurisdictions typically accept procedural immunity, which thus trumps any right or obligation to prosecute international crimes.

In domestic jurisdictions there might also be national immunities, which protect officials from prosecutions before their *own* courts. As distinct from procedural immunity for foreign officials, however, domestic immunity is not a valid excuse under international law to not prosecute in cases where there is an international duty to do so.

So, suspects of crimes of aggression may in many cases be protected by immunities. However, even if so protected, prosecutions – or fear of prosecution – will still have effects on the suspect, who will cautiously refrain from travelling to many places, fearing that there might be an international arrest warrant waiting in a particular country, and not knowing whether the local authorities in that country will or will not accept the traditional notion of procedural immunity that usually

---

8 I.e., typically courts other than the courts which have jurisdiction based on the nationality principle.

9 The Latin terms are *ratione materiae* and *ratione personae* respectively. C. Wickremasinghe, 'Immunities Enjoyed by Officials of States and International Organizations', in M.D. Evans (ed.), *International Law* (2nd edn, Oxford: Oxford University Press, 2006), 395–422, at 397; R. Cryer, H. Friman, D. Robinson and E. Wilmshurst, *International Criminal Law and Procedure* (Cambridge: Cambridge University Press, 2007), 423. See also N. Strapatsas, 'Complementarity & Aggression: A Ticking Time Bomb?' (Draft Presented to the Marie Curie Research Course on International Criminal Law, 2007).

10 Principle 5 of the Princeton Principles provides that for 'serious crimes under international law', including crimes against peace, the official position shall not relieve a person of criminal responsibility. 'The Princeton Principles on Universal Jurisdiction', reprinted in S. Macedo (ed.), *Universal Jurisdiction: National Courts and the Prosecution of Serious Crimes Under International Law* (Philadelphia: University of Pennsylvania Press, 2004), 18–25, at 22. See also A.H. Butler, 'The Growing Support for Universal Jurisdiction in National Legislation', in S. Macedo (ed.), ibid., at 76; R. Cryer et al., *supra* note 9, at 432; V. Koivu, 'Head of State Immunity v. Individual Criminal Responsibility', XII *Finnish Yearbook of International Law* (2001), 305–330, at 330. Wickremasinghe is a bit more cautious; C. Wickremasinghe, 'Immunities Enjoyed by Officials of States and International Organizations', in M.D. Evans (ed.), *International Law* (2nd edn, Oxford: Oxford University Press, 2006), 395–422, at 416. The ICJ's conservative assertion in the *Arrest Warrant* Case that *e contrario* seems to confirm functional immunity *tout court* (Judgment, *Arrest Warrant of 11 April 2000* (*Democratic Republic of the Congo v. Belgium*), 14 February 2002, para. 61) has been widely and rightly criticized, and could probably be set aside as an *obiter dictum* with less authority than the *stare decisis*. R. Cryer et al., *supra* note 9, at 437; D. Akande, 'International Law Immunities and the International Criminal Court', *The American Journal of International Law* (2004), 407–433, at 413.

11 See *supra* note 10, at para. 58. For a slightly different perspective, see V. Koivu, 'Head of State Immunity v. Individual Criminal Responsibility', XII *Finnish Yearbook of International Law* (2001), 305–330, at 311.

shields leaders. Further, an incumbent leader will know that the chances of avoiding prosecution will be much slimmer when he or she is no longer in office. A prosecution will also have political consequences. A prosecuted leader will lose legitimacy, and if he or she is unable to travel freely, that will inevitably affect her or his ability to function as a leader.

In addition to immunity, there are other 'avoidance techniques' – as Hazel Fox has called them – that might be invoked to prevent a court from exercising its jurisdiction.[12]

2. The Act of State Doctrine

The act of state doctrine builds on the same rational as state immunity, namely that one sovereign should not sit in judgment of another one (*par in parem imperium non habet*). Thus, it protects foreign sovereigns. This doctrine probably applies only to acts committed within the territory of that state,[13] but it is not clear whether an act of aggression corresponds to that requisite. The decision to initiate an act of aggression will most likely be made within the foreign state – in its capital – but, on the other hand, that decision will take effect abroad, and I therefore expect that the doctrine would not apply. At any event, in the US, the act of state doctrine seems not to have provided a bar to court proceedings in cases of international crimes or breaches of *jus cogens*, and this has been the case also in other jurisdictions, such as the UK.[14] And, of course, the rationale of the act of state doctrine was refuted so elegantly by the Nüremberg Tribunal, when they reminded us that crimes against international law are committed by men, not by abstract entities.[15]

3. The Political Question Doctrine

Another 'avoidance technique' is the political questions doctrine, which comes in many shapes, and is sometimes called 'executive privilege', 'non-justiciability' or 'judicial restraint'.[16] This doctrine says that some issues are not appropriate for judges to handle. It is often applied to matters of foreign policy, and it essentially serves to protect the own sovereign from embarrassment, since the effect is that judges will refrain from entering into areas that the executive usually wants to have reserved for itself.[17]

---

12 See generally and interestingly, H. Fox, 'International Law and Restraints on the Exercise of Jurisdiction by National Courts of States', in M.D. Evans (ed.), *International Law* (2nd edn, Oxford: Oxford University Press, 2006), 361–391; N. Strapatsas, *supra* note 10.

13 H. Fox, *supra* note 12, at 383.

14 N. Strapatsas, *supra* note 10, at 22–23. Please note that when I refer to the act of state doctrine, I mean what Strapatsas calls 'the second variant' of that doctrine, namely that 'courts of one state will generally refrain from sitting in judgment on acts of a governmental character done by a foreign state within its territory and applicable there' (ibid., at 21).

15 Judgment of the International Military Tribunal, cited. Available at http://avalon.law.yale.edu/imt/judlawch.asp (visited 1 February 2009).

16 See H. Fox, *supra* note 12, at 384 and N. Strapatsas, *supra* note 10, at 24–28. For an interesting plea for judicial restraint or 'reluctance' – mainly built on policy – see M. Kirby, 'Universal Jurisdiction and Judicial Reluctance: A New "Fourteen Points"', in S. Macedo (ed.), *Universal Jurisdiction: National Courts and the Prosecution of Serious Crimes Under International Law* (Philadelphia: University of Pennsylvania Press, 2004), at 240–259.

17 It has also been questioned whether it is right to second-guess very difficult decisions of political leaders, decisions taken by people who voluntarily have taken on the arduous task of making difficult choices on our behalf. But the same could be said with even more relevance of military commanders, who often have very little time for deliberation in situations which ultimately might render accusations of war crimes.

These two doctrines – act of state and political questions – are usually based on comity rather than on legal obligations. They frequently interact, and I have no intention of analysing them in any detail since they are domestic doctrines which look different in different countries. I will, however, briefly cover a few arguments that likely would underpin their application.

It has often been said that the crime of aggression is the most controversial and politically charged crime. This consideration might speak against independent national prosecutions, particularly in cases where there is no authoritative international decision by an international organ, be it the ICC or the SC. (If, on the other hand, there is an international decision to the effect that an act of aggression has occurred, then the burden on the domestic body would be less heavy, and perhaps it would be emboldened to disregard these doctrines.) We can all imagine events in recent history that could have been subjected to prosecution in The Hague if the Court had been able to exercise jurisdiction, and we can all also imagine that such prosecutions might have produced great political havoc. But is that unique to the crime of aggression? Is it really true that, for instance, the 2007 judgment in the ICJ between Bosnia & Herzegovina and Serbia on the matter of genocide was any less politically and emotionally charged than the dispute between the Democratic Republic of the Congo and Uganda on aggression, adjudicated by the World Court little more than a year earlier?[18] Has not 'the genocide word' been used lately with even more force than 'aggression'? Was not genocide called 'the crime of crimes' by the ICTR?[19]

Further, even if it were true that aggression is committed only (or mainly) by states (see *infra*) – which necessitates implications at the highest governmental level – that might not be so unique. First of all: all acts of genocide that have been committed, or have allegedly been committed, in recent years have a clear state nexus. The genocide in Rwanda was planned and ordered by the then Government of Rwanda. The alleged genocide in Darfur appears to come under the responsibility of the Sudanese Government, or at least that is the necessary conclusion of recent decisions by the Prosecutor and the Pre-Trial Chamber of the ICC.[20] Secondly, it has been held by some commentators that an armed attack and an act of aggression can be committed also by a non-state armed group, be it al-Qaida or Hezbollah.[21] For sure, there is no state practice whatsoever for

18 ICJ, Judgment, *Application of the Convention on the Prevention and Punishment of the Crime of Genocide* (*Bosnia and Herzegovina v. Serbia and Montenegro*), 26 February 2007; ICJ, Judgment, *Armed Activities on the Territory of the Congo* (*Democratic Republic of the Congo v. Uganda*), 19 December 2005. Both available at http://www.icj-cij.org (visited 16 January 2008).

19 ICTR, Judgment (sentence), *Jean-Paul Akayesu*, Case No. ICTR–96–4–T, 2 October 1998. Available at http://www.ictr.org (visited 16 January 2008).

In Nüremberg, the judges said that '[t]o initiate a war of aggression … is the supreme international crime … [which] contains within itself the accumulated evil of the whole.' Cited from B.B. Ferencz, 'The Crime of Aggression' in G.K. McDonald and O. Swaak-Goldman (eds), *Substantive and Procedural Aspects of International Criminal Law: The Experience of International and National Courts* (The Hague: Kluewer Law International, 2000), 37–62 at 37 and R. Cryer, H. Friman, D. Robinson and E. Wilmshurst, *supra* note 9, at 267. Is the crime of aggression still the mother of all crimes, as it was in 1939? Most mass killings today take place in the context of internal armed conflict, in which there is no aggressor, per definition. Wilmshurst wisely asserts that 'there cannot be any need to engage in an abstract competition for the dreadful title of the worst international crime'. Ibid.

20 ICC, Decision (Warrant for Arrest), *Ahmad Harun*, Pre-Trial Chamber, ICC-02/05-01/07, 27 April 2007, p. 5. Harun is charged with crimes against humanity and war crimes, not genocide, before the ICC, but the acts which are the subject of the prosecution are the same as those that some commentators would judge to constitute genocide.

21 For that view, see Mark S. Stein, 'The Security Council, the International Criminal Court, and the Crime of Aggression: How Exclusive is the Security Council's Power to Determine Aggression?', 16 *Indiana*

criminal responsibility for non-state aggression, and it might therefore be difficult or impossible to criminalize such conduct as aggression in the Rome Statute (it is, of course, already criminalized in many other ways). However, this notion is still significant for its implications on the idea that there is a necessary and unique state nexus for the crime of aggression.

4. Gathering the Evidence

Hence, there are a number of more or less surmountable legal hurdles for foreign national prosecutions, most prominently personal immunity. A practical problem that national authorities might face is the lack of evidence. A state that wants to prosecute a foreign national may encounter difficulties in finding evidence of that person's involvement in the aggression. This holds true for all international crimes, but the crime of aggression is still a bit different, in that it is more likely that perpetrators will be far removed from the scene of the crime, as well as that much of the evidence will lie in protocols, minutes and other documents in governmental quarters, as the Nüremberg judgments bear out. Nevertheless, in some situations that involvement will be so obvious that a prosecution can take place even in the absence of such documentation.[22]

What would be the complementarity issues before the ICC? Well, by and large they would be the same as would normally arise before the Court for the other crimes. If a state is unable to prosecute because of immunities or other procedural bars, then complementarity could probably not be successfully raised as a bar to admissibility (even if that does not follow explicitly from the Statute). The same applies if the domestic authorities have been unable to acquire necessary evidence to prosecute. These issues have not been debated in the SWGCA.

An issue that was raised during the informal Princeton meeting of the Working Group is that a victorious nation might prosecute without due regard to the rights of the victim, or that, conversely, a 'victim' state might be intimidated by a more powerful state from prosecuting. Either of those eventualities might – perhaps, but for different reasons – justify an intervention by the ICC, and they might both be more likely in connection with a crime of aggression.[23] However, both situations

---

International and Comparative Law Review (2005), 1–36, at 4; Grant M. Dawson, 'Defining Substantive Crimes within the Subject Matter Jurisdiction of the International Criminal Court: What is the Crime of Aggression?', 19 *New York Law School Journal of International and Comparative Law* (2000), 413–452, at 444. Cf. also R.E. Fife, 'Criminalizing Individuals for Acts of Aggression Committed by States' in *Human Rights and Criminal Justice for the Downtrodden: Essays in Honour of Asbjorn Eide* (Leiden. Brill, 2003), 53–74, at 72. This, of course, builds on the assumption that the September 11th attacks indeed constituted an armed attack (that could, but does not have to be inferred from SC Res 1368), and that 'armed attack' is the same thing as 'aggression', following Bengt Broms. B. Broms, 'The Definition of Aggression', 154 *Recueil des Cours* (1977), 301–399, at 370. *Contra*, R. Cryer et al., *supra* note 9, at 267 and 274.

22 A legal-technical problem, when it comes to the criminalization in domestic law of the crime of aggression, is that the general principles in Part 3 of the Rome Statute, like Art. 25(3)(f) on attempts, might not apply fully to the crime of aggression, as has been discussed in the SWGCA in quite some detail. See Report on Informal Inter-sessional Meeting of the Special Working Group on the Crime of Aggression, held at the Liechtenstein Institute on Self-Determination, Woodrow Wilson School, at Princeton University, New Jersey, United States, from 21–23 June 2004, ICC-ASP/3/SWGCA/INF.1, paras 20–27.

That is a problem that will likely be resolved by legislators, once the Rome Statute has been amended, but it will be resolved differently in different jurisdictions, since legislators have chosen different techniques to incorporate international crimes in their jurisdictions.

23 Several commentators emphasize, though, that it was not the intention of the Statute to monitor the respect for the right to a fair trial and other human rights standards in domestic trials. Robert Cryer et al., *supra* note 9, at 129.

may appear with regard to other crimes, too, and the meeting felt that these problems could be dealt with within the existing language of the Rome Statute.[24]

The informal Princeton meeting also discussed the case where an act may fall under more than one heading. What if something is prosecuted nationally as a crime against humanity or a war crime when the same concrete acts – though viewed from another perspective, as an aggregate – might constitute an act of aggression? That possibility is also not unique for the crime of aggression; there are many examples from the jurisprudence of the international criminal Tribunals where the same act might, for instance, constitute both a crime against humanity and a war crime. Article 20(3) ICCSt on *ne bis in idem* refers to the more concrete term 'conduct' rather than the abstract juristic concept of 'crime',[25] and that was confirmed in the *Thomas Lubanga* case, where the Pre-Trial Chamber of the ICC referred to the conduct of Lubanga, not the crime, in its deliberation of complementarity.[26]

So, the general rules on admissibility in the Rome Statute would seem to apply without effort to the crime of aggression (and, as we have seen, the same applies to other procedural issues relevant to domestic prosecutions). However, perhaps the process leading up to the determination of admissibility is more significant for aggression than for the other crimes. According to Article 53, the Prosecutor must assess complementarity before initiating an investigation and Article 17 provides that the Court shall consider the same factors. This will inevitably involve a certain amount of interaction between the Court and national authorities, which might be more significant for a crime that is not very established in international and domestic jurisprudence (see *infra*). But it is far from certain that such interaction will be possible, and that leads me to the second scenario.

4. Scenario II: The ICC Cannot Exercise Jurisdiction *In Casu*

This is the situation where there is a provision on aggression, and that provision includes special conditions – such as a decision by the Security Council or some other organ – and such condition has not been met.

Under this scenario, the issue of complementarity will not arise since the ICC will not be able to exercise jurisdiction. Instead, here it is domestic courts that might be complementing the ICC, as it were.

The issues discussed above that domestic authorities might face will be relevant here too, like immunities, the act of state doctrine and the political questions doctrine, and they will probably be even more acute, since in this situation the question is probably not *where* the suspect will be prosecuted but *if* he will be prosecuted at all because the ICC will no longer be an alternative. Nevertheless, from a strictly legal perspective these issues will not be different under this scenario than under the former one.

---

24 *Supra* note 5, at paras 25 and 26.

25 *Supra* note 5, at paras 30–31. The Review Conference will further have to deal with the fact that Art. 20(3) at present does not cover the crime of aggression (ibid., at 29). That does not seem to be a problem for the situation discussed here, though.

26 ICC, Decision (Warrant of Arrest), *Lubanga Dylo*, Pre-Trial Chamber 10 February 2006, ICC-01/04-01/06, paras 37–39. Therefore, the situation could arise that a national court is trying a person for war crimes amounting to an indiscriminate bombing campaign that also constitutes an act of aggression that the ICC Prosecutor is looking into.

The same goes for the issue of jurisdiction. I have, however, chosen to deal with it under this rubric since it is connected to the problem of the Security Council – if I may put it like that – which is particularly relevant for this scenario, and which will be treated a bit later.

It shouldn't be necessary to inform the readers of this text that international law recognizes several grounds for criminal jurisdiction: territoriality, the nationality of the perpetrator, as well as – more controversially – of the victim, national security and other vital national interests and universal interest – the principle of universality. Jurisdiction on the basis of the principle of nationality and the principle of territoriality are absolutely uncontroversial, at least if they coincide. That is, no state would protest if the aggressor state itself prosecutes persons responsible for an act of aggression that that state has committed. Further, jurisdiction by the victim state over the aggressor's nationals would probably not be challenged even if the relevant concrete conduct by that individual (such as an order) took place on the territory of the aggressor.

The interesting question to ask is can domestic courts can go further? In the 1996 Draft Code of Crimes against the Peace and Security of Mankind, the International Law Commission (ILC) proposed in Article 8 that only the ICC and the home state of the aggressor state should have jurisdiction over the crime of aggression. That seems to be a more restricted view than the one I just presented. However, if one reads the Commentary to Article 8, one finds that it does not build on existing state practice.[27] Except for a very general invocation of the principle *par in parem imperium non habet*, the Commentary only refers to what the Commission finds proper and practical. In fact, it appears, it was referring to what some members of the Commission thought proper and practical. Hence, the ILC was in this particular instance involved in progressive (or perhaps retrogressive) development rather than codification of positive international law.

In fact, as shown by Nicolaos Strapatsas, the 1996 Draft Code of Crimes does not correspond to state practice.[28] In addition to the countries that now have the crime against peace or the crime of aggression in their criminal codes – I will mention some of them *infra* – after WWII a number of Allied countries, and a couple of countries that had been on the side of the Axis powers, adopted laws for the prosecution of crimes against peace against the recent aggressors, and a couple of states also did pursue such prosecutions. Furthermore, in addition to the Nüremberg Tribunal, which was quasi-international – if you will – there were also prosecutions in the US and French zones for the crime against peace, and neither of those countries had even been the subject of aggression by Germany, according to the Nüremberg Tribunal.

I guess that many countries would be prone to say that if they are victims of aggression, they could assert jurisdiction too, just like several Allied powers did after WWII. They could base that either on the principle of territoriality – which might extend to the consequences of the individual crime of aggression, which takes effect on the territory of the victim state or on the principle of security, i.e., that states have jurisdiction over crimes that affect their national security.

Is there also universal jurisdiction? Many commentators – such as Yoram Dinstein – believe that the crime of aggression already is an international crime with individual responsibility,[29] and

---

27 *Yearbook of the International Law Commission*, Volume II, Part II (1996) A/CN.4/SER.A/1996/Add. 1 (Part 2), at 30.

28 N. Strapatsas, *supra* note 10, at 5–6.

29 Y. Dinstein, *War, Aggression and Self-Defence* (4th edn, Cambridge: Cambridge University Press, 2005), 123; *Rolf Einar Fife*, 'Criminalizing Individuals for Acts of Aggression Committed by States' in *Human Rights and Criminal Justice for the Downtrodden: Essays in Honour of Asbjorn Eide* (Leiden: Brill, 2003), 53–74, at 53; I.K. Müller-Schieke, 'Defining the Crime of Aggression Under the Statute of the International Criminal Court', 14 *Leiden Journal of International Law* (2001), 409–430, at 414–415; R. Cryer et al., *supra* note 9, at 262. That point is argued in detail also in the contribution to this Volume by M.A. Shukri.

that courts therefore may judge a national of a foreign state for that crime, even under universal jurisdiction.[30] Others would be more cautious and say that given the lack of state practice, apart from that post-World War II, it is difficult to confirm whether there is really universal jurisdiction.[31] But a domestic institution that would like to exercise universal jurisdiction would probably invoke the Nüremberg precedent, as well as a number of domestic examples just alluded to.

As already mentioned, another issue that will be at the forefront under this scenario is the role of the Security Council. It is well known that one of the most difficult issues in the discussions on the crime of aggression, probably *the* most difficult, is the role of the Council. Will the ICC be able to function independently of the SC or is it necessary that the Council determine that an act of aggression has occurred or otherwise agree to a prosecution before the Court may proceed?[32]

---

30 Y. Dinstein, *War, Aggression and Self-Defence* (4th edn, Cambridge: Cambridge University Press, 2005), 145; A.R. Brotóns, 'Aggression, Crime of Aggression, Crime without Punishment', Working Paper No. 10 (Madrid: Fundación para las Relaciones Intemacionales y el Diálogo Exterior (FRIDE), 2005), 16. See also Principles 1 and 2 of 'The Princeton Principles on Universal Jurisdiction', reprinted in S. Macedo (ed.), *Universal Jurisdiction: National Courts and the Prosecution of Serious Crimes Under International Law* (Philadelphia: University of Pennsylvania Press, 2004), 18–25, at 21. See further the resolution adopted by the *Institut de droit international* in 2005, 'Universal criminal jurisdiction with regard to the crime of genocide, crimes against humanity and war crimes', available at http://www.idi-iil.org/idiE/resolutionsE/2005_kra_03_en.pdf, which, however, explicitly does not address the crime of aggression, as well as 'The Cairo – Arusha Principles On Universal Jurisdiction In Respect Of Gross Human Rights Offences: An African Perspective', available at http://www.kituochakatiba.co.ug/cairo-arusha.htm, which only cover gross human rights abuses and similar offences, not the crime of aggression (both Internet addresses above visited 9 February 2009). See also C. Kreß, 'Universal Jurisdiction Over International Crimes and the *Institut de droit international*', *Journal of International Criminal Justice* (2006), 1–25, at 15, which suggests the presumption that there is universal jurisdiction for any crime under international customary law. I will here leave aside the difficult and important issue of whether universal jurisdiction can be exercised *in absentia* and, if so, to what degree. As is well known, that was one of the key issues in the *Arrest Warrant* case.

31 G. Gaja, 'The Long Journey towards Repressing Aggression', in Cassese, Gaeta and Jones, *supra* note 3, at 427–441, at 432.

32 The real problem, as many negotiators would see it (including this one), is how to pay respect to the SC as a *body* without vesting each Permanent Member with a veto. There is no magic formula on the table yet. In principle, one can approach it from either of two angles: 1. Accept that there will have to be some sort of affirmative decision by the SC, but make it as hard as possible for the Council to not agree to a prosecution and as easy for it as possible to say yes. Various ideas have been put on the table, including a proposal that the SC could give a 'green light' to prosecutions without having to pronounce itself on the substance, namely whether an act of aggression has occurred or not. To put the matter before the SC as late as possible in the proceedings is another option, since the pressure on the Council would be greater if the Prosecutor has already found there to be a *prima facie* case. Another theoretically possible way to get around the veto might be to seize upon the last words of Art. 27(3) of the Charter, namely that a member of the Council that is a party to a dispute shall not participate in decisions under Chapter VI. The States Parties could in one way or another remind the Council of this. Of course, this assumes that a crime of aggression situation could be labelled a 'dispute' or a 'situation' under Chapter VI (see Arts 33 and 34 of the Charter) which is not certain. 2. Do not give the P5 (the five Permanent Members) a veto, but make it as hard as possible for the Court to proceed without an affirmative SC decision. The extra judicial filter through a 'Grand Pre-Trial Chamber' (my words) proposed by Belgium (ICC-ASP/5/SWGCA/WP.1) is one such means; another is to have a long waiting period before the Court may proceed in the absence of a SC decision. One possible way to get around the objection that it is the SC that has the mandate to deal with aggression (Art. 39 of the Charter) might be to accept, as 'a second best', a permissive decision by the UN General Assembly under the Uniting for Peace formula. The Uniting for Peace mechanism (GA Resolution 377 (V)) acknowledges the Council's primary responsibility, but gives

During the discussions, organs other than the SC have been mentioned as well, namely the UN General Assembly, the International Court of Justice and the ICC Assembly of States Parties. Nevertheless, since it is the Council that has been the focus of the discussions, I, too, will focus on the possible role of this organ.

Can domestic prosecutions take place only after the Security Council has made a decision? To my knowledge, that issue has lately been discussed seriously by States Parties only informally, during the aforementioned 2004 inter-sessional meeting at Princeton, and even then not at any great length. The records of the meeting are a bit Delphic: 'It was emphasized that the issue of complementarity and admissibility was closely related to the definition of aggression and the role of the Security Council.' Some delegations found that a decision by the SC 'would not be needed for the application of national legislation on aggression'. However, '[o]ther delegations expressed the view that national legislation should be consistent with applicable international law'.[33] On its face, the latter statement seems superfluous; national legislation always has to conform to international law, or at least that is how we international lawyers would like to see things. However, for those who have followed the crime of aggression negotiations, phrases like 'consistency with applicable international law' are familiar code words for a reference to Article 39 of the Charter which, in the view of some delegations, provides that it is only the SC that may determine when an act of aggression has occurred.[34]

Most states that have found that the domestic authorities have *prima facie* jurisdiction – as I will deal with later on – will probably not feel duty-bound under international law to wait for a decision by the Council. However, some states have held that an individual crime of aggression has occurred only subject to a prior determination of the state act of aggression by the SC in accordance with Article 39 of the UN Charter. According to one old proposal, the crime of aggression should be defined that way, namely that an act of aggression is whatever the SC determines to be an act of aggression, and only that. That proposal has considerably less support now.[35] At any rate, states

the Assembly the possibility to deal with a matter if the Council 'fails to exercise its primary responsibility for the maintenance of international peace and security' (though not explicit Chapter VII powers). Hence, to avail oneself of this mechanism would not mean a new by-pass of the Council, but merely the use of a procedure that has been established and continuously used for more than half a century.

33 *Supra* note 5, paras 22 and 23, respectively.

34 The formula in the Statute itself is 'consistent with the relevant provisions of the Charter of the United Nations' (Art. 5(2)). See V. Gowlland-Debbas, 'The Functions of the United Nations Security Council in the International Legal System', in M. Byers (ed.), *The Role of Law in International Politics: Essays in International Relations and International Law* (Oxford: Oxford University Press, 2000), 277–314, at 298; C. McDougall, 'When Law And Reality Clash – the Imperative of Compromise in the Context of the Accumulated Evil of the Whole: Conditions for the Exercise of the International Criminal Court's Jurisdiction over the Crime of Aggression', 7 *International Criminal Law Review* (2007), 277–333, at 278–279.

35 The legal argument for that view is weak, and doctrinal writers are generally quite sceptic, to make an understatement. R. Cryer et al., *supra* note 9, at 278 (that section was written by E. Wilmshurst); V. Gowlland-Debbas, *supra* note 34, at 299; I.K. Müller-Schieke, 'Defining the Crime of Aggression Under the Statute of the International Criminal Court', 14 *Leiden Journal of International Law* (2001), 409–430, at 425–427; M.S. Stein, 'The Security Council, the International Criminal Court, and the Crime of Aggression: How Exclusive is the Security Council's Power to Determine Aggression?', 16 *Indiana International and Comparative Law Review* (2005), 1–36; A.R. Brotóns, 'Aggression, Crime of Aggression, Crime without Punishment', Working Paper No. 10 (Madrid: Fundación para las Relaciones Intemacionales y el Diálogo Exterior (FRIDE), 2005), 14; D.D.N. Nsereko, 'Bringing Aggressors to Justice: From Nüremberg to Rome', 2 *University of Botswana Law Journal* (2005), 4–32, at 25–31; C. McDougall, *supra* note 34. See also R.S. Clark, 'Rethinking Aggression as a Crime and Formulating Its Elements: The Final Work-Product of the Preparatory

who do not feel that Article 39 gives the SC global and exclusive competence to determine acts of aggression will likely not feel obliged to implement such a definition of the crime in their domestic legislations.

The (old?) view that the SC determination is a part of the definition means that the Council's role is in the substance, i.e., a requisite of the crime. However delegations that today want to introduce a decision by the SC as a necessary requirement generally hold such a decision as a procedural condition. That is, the role of the Council, as contemplated by the SWGCA, is in jurisdiction, not in substance. Could it be argued that a decision by the SC is a procedural condition also for domestic prosecutions?

It would be quite difficult to argue that current international law requires that a SC decision is a procedural condition for states to prosecute the crime of aggression. There is some logic – though deficient and built on mistaken premises, in my already implied view[36] – to the claim that a SC determination is a part of the definition of the crime, that is, that such a determination is a substantive requirement. However, I cannot really see how one could formulate an argument that it would be an existing procedural requirement for domestic prosecutions. Either national legal systems have jurisdiction, or they do not; general international law cannot possibly require that states defer to an institution created by a treaty. And the treaty itself – the UN Charter – does not so provide, or at least I have not been able to find such a provision. Hence, if the basic jurisdiction were there, with regard to the crime of aggression, states would most likely not feel that international law requires them to wait for a SC determination before their national authorities may proceed. Moreover, many if not most legislators and judges would feel great unease at the idea of being themselves subjected to or involved in such a political procedure.

Nevertheless, states could surely agree between themselves to restrict a right to exercise jurisdiction. Article 20(3) of the Rome Statute on *ne bis in idem* provides that '[n]o person shall be tried by another court for a crime referred to in Article 5 for which that person has already been convicted or acquitted by the Court'. This is a restriction of States Parties' right to prosecute, which goes beyond the common *ne bis in idem* provisions under human rights law, which only prohibit multiple prosecutions in the *same* domestic jurisdiction, not multiple prosecutions in *different* jurisdictions.[37] Further, Article 15(5) of the 1991 Draft Code of Crimes proposed – within square brackets, curiously enough – that any determination by the SC as to the existence of an act of

---

Commission for the International Criminal Court', 15 *Leiden Journal of International Law* (2002), 859–890, at 869–872; C. Antonopolous, 'Whatever Happened to Crimes against Peace?', 6 *Journal of Conflict and Security Law* (2001), 33–62, at 48–52; N. Blokker, 'The Crime of Aggression and the United Nations Security Council', 20 *Leiden Journal of International Law* (2007), 867–894. One writer leaves the door open to 'the P5 view', however; K. Kittichaisaree, *International Criminal Law* (Oxford: Oxford University Press, 2001), 219–220. One particularly strong argument against 'the P5 view' is that it would impinge in the rights of the defendant since the ICC would be bound by the Security Council's decision (how could the right to 'determine the existence of … an act of aggression' otherwise be exclusive?) and hence would be unable to defend herself on the ground that the act in question did not amount to an act of aggression. That problem has been pointed out by many delegations (including my own from the year 2000), and has been noted also in literature. I.K. Müller-Schieke, 'Defining the Crime of Aggression Under the Statute of the International Criminal Court', 14 *Leiden Journal of International Law* (2001), 409–430 at 427; R. Cryer et al., *supra* note 9, 278.

36 I here felt it necessary to depart from my chosen course not to speak *de lege lata* even in the main text. For references to the arguments against this deficient logic, see *supra* note 35.

37 W.A. Schabas, *An Introduction to the International Criminal Court* (2nd edn, Cambridge: Cambridge University Press, 2004), 89.

aggression would be binding on national courts. Hence, it would not be totally unheard of if states put such a restriction on themselves.

So, States Parties to the Rome Statute can restrict the rights of domestic jurisdictions. All calls for caution with regard to this potentially politicized crime might be held to apply with greater force to foreign domestic jurisdictions than to the ICC, which is a creation of 108 states with 18 judges from 18 different countries. But then again, a restriction of an existing right to prosecute nationally would require a positive decision by States Parties, and would have to be adopted in accordance with Article 121 of the Statute. That would be possible, but I leave it to others to determine whether it is likely.[38] At any rate, such a restriction would only be binding *inter partes*.

In addition to a statutory restriction, one could also imagine a decision by the SC that would restrict the right to prosecute nationally. That would not be a decision under Article 16 of the Rome Statute, since Article 16 only pertains to the ICC, not to domestic courts. Instead, it would be a decision under the general competence of the Council under Chapter VII of the UN Charter. The SC has previously taken decisions with broad, horizontal effect. In Resolutions 1422 and 1487, the SC very controversially immunized all peacekeepers from the jurisdiction of the ICC.[39] The Council has also adopted resolutions that have been called law-making, such as Resolutions 1373 and 1540. While these resolutions were welcomed widely for their political usefulness in the fight against terrorism, they have also been questioned as to their legal effect and as to the appropriateness of the Council taking on the role of adopting binding resolutions that apply not only to specific situations, but have general, law-making application. The SC could further pass situation-specific resolutions, like Resolution 1497 on Liberia, which put peacekeepers in Liberia from non-parties to the Rome Statute under the exclusive jurisdiction of their home states, thus restricting the universal jurisdiction for international crimes by state. However, I believe it unlikely that it would be possible to muster the necessary majority in the SC to adopt a resolution limiting the right to prosecute for the crime of aggression.

So, it is unlikely that national authorities will become or feel duty-bound to refrain from proceeding in the absence of a Security Council decision. Nevertheless, states and domestic legal authorities might feel that they need some political legitimacy for the quite bold step of exercising jurisdiction over the most politically charged crime, the crime of aggression. A state might therefore unilaterally take a cautious approach, if lacking the backing of the Council. Caution in this situation can be required under judicial doctrine – such as the act of state or the political questions doctrine. But it might also be provided for by statutory law. The Swedish Code of Crimes requires, in general, that the government give its consent to prosecution of foreign officials for conduct abroad.[40] Such consent might be given more reluctantly if there is no green light from the SC.

The result of this discussion is that it is highly unlikely that it will be possible to limit what most would perceive to be legal freedom for states to prosecute for the crime of aggression. However, states – legislators or judges – might still feel a political or legal policy need for restraint.

I now come to the third case.

---

38 Gaja does not find it unlikely. G. Gaja, 'The Long Journey towards Repressing Aggression', in Cassese, Gaeta and Jones, *supra* note 3, at 427–441, at 440.

39 When Resolution 1487 was up for renewal in 2004, the US was unable to garner anything close to a majority, not counting the likely vetoes from some Permanent Members of the Council.

40 See in particular ss 7 a and 7 b, Chapter 2, the Swedish Penal Code. Available in English at http://www.sweden.gov.se/sb/d/108/a/1536 (visited 16 January 2008).

5. Scenario III: There is No Provision on the Crime of Aggression

Under this scenario, the ICC can not act at all, and there is not even a definition of the crime in the Statute. In this situation, all of the aforementioned problems related to domestic prosecutions will apply, but there will be an added one, which we have not yet dealt with, that will feature very prominently, namely the lack of an agreement on what acts are covered by the crime: what is the definition of the crime? Some might even question whether aggression is an international crime under domestic jurisdiction. In addition, in those states that already have provisions on the crime of aggression or similar crimes, judges might regret the lack of international authority from the Rome Statute to help them interpret the domestic provisions on those crimes.

Many, if not all, lawyers would probably say that the crime of aggression is already under domestic jurisdiction. The crime of aggression is on the book, as one of four crimes in Article 5, and as mentioned the Preamble claimed 'that it is the duty of every State to exercise its criminal jurisdiction over those responsible for international crimes'.[41] The *Court* is currently prevented from exercising its jurisdiction with regard to this crime, but that does not mean that *states* are prevented from doing so.

This conclusion seems to have been corroborated recently in a judgment by the House of Lords. In that case, five peace activists, who had caused damage on a Royal Air Force base in the UK, had claimed that their acts were legally justified since they sought to prevent an alleged crime of aggression (the 2003 invasion of Iraq). The crux of the matter was therefore whether the crime of aggression was a crime under British law. The Law Lords held, very briefly, that there was indeed such a crime under international law, but that it was not a part of domestic law.[42] The upshot seems to be that Great Britain and any other country has the authority to prosecute such crimes, but that the UK has not taken advantage of this opportunity, since it has not incorporated the crime of aggression into its criminal law. This is further confirmed by a number – admittedly not very high – of provisions in domestic statutes, the most famous one being Article 353 in the Russian Criminal Code, but also the criminal codes of Poland, Croatia, Germany and several other states.[43]

41 Perhaps one should not draw to far-reaching conclusions from that preambular statement. See R. Cryer et al., *supra* note 9, at 133. In general, on the possibility of exercising domestic jurisdiction over individual crime of aggression at present, see A. Cassese, 'On Some Problematical Aspects of the Crime of Aggression', 20 *Leiden Journal of International Law* (2007), at 841–849.

42 House of Lords, Judgment, *R v. Jones* (Appellant) [2006] UKHL 16. The opinion observes that the core elements of the crime of aggression have been understood since 1945 and that current efforts to statutorily define it for purposes of the exercise of personal jurisdiction by the ICC do not obscure such historic elements. Lord Bingham's opinion cites, *inter alia*, the Preamble and Art. 2(4) of the Charter of the United Nations, the Charters of the Nüremberg and Tokyo Tribunals, General Assembly Resolution 3314 (XXIX), and the 1954 and 1996 reports of the International Law Commission on the Draft Code of Offences against the Peace and Security of Mankind. See ibid., at paras 11–18. See also Lord Hoffman's opinion at para. 59. Lord Mance observes 'there is under public international law a crime of aggression which is, as history confirms, sufficiently certain to be capable of being prosecuted in international tribunals.' See ibid, at para. 99. A summary analysis of the case by Donald Ferencz, as well as the full text of the *Jones* judgment itself, may be found in 45 *International Legal Materials* (July 2006), 988–1014.

43 See H. Gropengießer and H. Kreicker, *Deutschland*, in the series Albin Eser and Helmut Kreicker (eds), *Nationale Strafverfolgung Völkerrechtlicher Verbrechen (*Freiburg im Breisgau: Edition Juscrim, 2003) as well as other volumes in that series. See also the contribution by A. Reisinger Coracini in this Volume, and Alberto L. Zuppi, 'Aggression as International Crime: Unattainable Crusade or Finally Conquering the Evil?', 26 *Penn State International Law Review* (2007), 1–36, quoted from p. 37 of draft, on file with author; N. Strapatsas, *supra* note 10, at 5.

However, the domestic laws containing the crime of aggression are still few in number. States have probably felt that customary law might have to be clarified. Ten years of negotiations on the crime of aggression show that the matter is not universally agreed. Here are a few of the issues:

1. Does every illegal use of force constitute an act of aggression?
2. Do all acts of aggression by states correspond to crimes of aggression at the level of individuals? Is there a threshold?
3. Does the crime of aggression only cover 'traditional' military action, such as military invasions or the other acts enumerated in Article 3 of the 1974 Definition of Aggression, or should the definition be open also to postmodern means of coercion and destruction, such as computer network attacks (or cyber war), which can create just as much death and destruction as old-fashioned kinetic attacks?[44]

Nevertheless, even in this far from clear-cut legal situation legislators and judges could conservatively and safely proceed from the Nüremberg precedent and the concept of war of aggression, which at least covers the penumbra of violent acts that are universally accepted as being acts of aggression. The House of Lords found that there were core elements of the crime, understood since 1945. Another possibility would be to take the current state of the discussions in the Special Working Group as a starting point; recent records show that the differences have been narrowed down quite a bit. Courts and domestic legislators might not feel it necessary to wait for States Parties do adopt a definition. An indication of what customary law says might suffice, were it to be supplied by the *opinio juris* expressed by the learned delegates of states participating in the Assembly of States Parties' SWGCA.

A preliminary conclusion here is that states might feel free to criminalize and prosecute for the crime of aggression at the domestic level, even without a provision on the crime of aggression in the Rome Statute, and the same applies to the event that there is such a provision, but the decision by the SC called for by such a hypothetical provision is not forthcoming. In other words, domestic legislators and authorities might feel authorized to criminalize and prosecute for crimes of aggression in situations where neither the ICC nor the Security Council has taken any form of decision on the matter. Whether that is likely to happen or not is impossible to say. The propensity to do so is not very widespread today, but things may change.

6. Conclusion

Some people find it dangerous to believe that the world could be changed through international criminal law. For sure, one should be realistic. But being realistic also means not to underestimate the power of law.[45] Law is (in general) a force for peace and justice, but it must always be exercised with prudence.

There are, as always, good arguments for domestic prosecutions. They are generally cheaper and quicker, and they might take place closer to the site of the crime. Furthermore, it is often better

44 It is my view that cyber attacks may be covered by the word 'attack' in Art. 3 of the Definition of Aggression, annexed to GA Res 3314 (XXIX).

45 For this argument see, briefly as regards international criminal law, F. Mégret, 'Three Dangers for the International Criminal Court', XII *Finnish Yearbook of International Law* (2001), 193–248, at 198.

for a people that has been implicated in aggression and other crimes of the highest order, that it cleanse itself, through national trials.

There have been many calls for caution with regard to the criminalization and prosecution of the crime of aggression – as well as other international crimes, in particular, system crimes – in both domestic and international fora. But it appears to me that caution should be even greater in the domestic than in the international arena.[46] This applies both to foreign national courts and to courts of the state of nationality of the alleged perpetrator; a person responsible for aggression will most likely not be prosecuted in his or her own state while that person is in power, so the prosecution will take place under another, new regime, which might have its reasons for not allowing a completely impartial trial.[47]

No doubt, many domestic courts and legal authorities will be able to handle prosecutions of the crime of aggression in a professional and impartial manner. Courts in many countries have displayed courage and integrity in difficult circumstances. Nevertheless, controversial cases can sometimes be dealt with in a more effective and legitimate manner in an international than in a domestic court. Further, many states that may wish to prosecute the crime of aggression will feel the need for support from the ICC through the interaction between the ICC and domestic courts that is called for by the principle of complementarity. The ICC might be taking over the case, but it might also just be overlooking the domestic process in order to assess the admissibility situation, after having made out a *prima facie* case for a crime aggression, and that might actually help domestic legal authorities in their own pursuit of the case. And even when national prosecutions are being carried out professionally and impartially, it will be useful to have the legal guidance that a definition in the Rome Statute and judicial practice from the Court can provide, which is particularly important for a crime that has not been developed in the rich jurisprudence from which the other international crimes benefit.

The SC may provide political backing, and will always have the freedom to do so, regardless of what provision the States Parties to the Rome Statute eventually adopt. However, the Council will not be available to provide legal guidance. The SC is not a court of law, and, at any rate, those states that are sceptical of the Security Council will probably never accept having their freedom to prosecute circumscribed by the Council. The only viable alternative is to let the ICC do the job that was intended for it. The practical outcome of this argument is, it appears to me, that it is very important that the States Parties agree on a viable definition, and secondly also agree on a provision to let the ICC exercise jurisdiction.[48] This would give the ICC an opportunity to perform its guiding role.

The domestic prosecution of the crime of aggression is not about protecting, or infringing on, another nation's sovereignty. It is a matter of balancing and accommodating different sovereign rights: those of the state that wants to exercise jurisdiction and those of the other states involved. As the much criticized but still interesting Lotus judgment of the Permanent Court of International Justice from 1927 makes clear, jurisdiction is about the potential collision of sovereign rights. On

46 C.L. Sriram, 'Universal Jurisdiction: Problems and Prospects of Externalizing Justice', XII *Finnish Yearbook of International Law* (2001), 47–70. The discussion in F. Mégret, 'Three Dangers for the International Criminal Court', XII *Finnish Yearbook of International Law* (2001), 193–248 could also, *mutatis mutandis*, be applied to universal jurisdiction.

47 Some doubt that a new regime would be interested at all, since such a trial would implicate the whole nation. A.R. Brotóns, 'Aggression, Crime of Aggression, Crime without Punishment', Working Paper No. 10 (Madrid: Fundación para las Relaciones Intemacionales y el Diälogo Exterior [FRIDE], 2005), 16.

48 On the current negotiations, see C. Kress, 'The Crime of Aggression before the First Review of the ICC Statute', 20 *Leiden Journal of International Law* (2007), 851–865.

the one hand, the right to exercise jurisdiction on one's own soil, and on the other hand, the right to protect one's nationals or the right to have one's sovereign acts respected. It seems to me that all states would have an interest in authorizing an impartial arbiter to handle or overlook such conflicts, in particular when it comes to a crime in which the international interest is so strong.

Chapter 28

A Pragmatic Approach to the Crime of Aggression*

David Scheffer

1. Introduction

In an effort to achieve a compromise in the examination by the Special Working Group on the Crime of Aggression (SWGCA)[1] concerning the jurisdictional and definitional requirements for activating the crime of aggression in the Rome Statute of the International Criminal Court (ICC),[2] I advance a proposal that offers two options. Options I (judicial green light) and II (soft green light), set forth below, enable negotiators and governments to consider a range of opportunities by which to argue the merits of sustaining some form of UN Security Council engagement in the jurisdictional filter and yet to do so within a singular approach to the personal jurisdiction and subject matter jurisdiction requirements of the crime of aggression. In accordance with the framework of the May 2008 Chairman's Proposal of the SWGCA,[3] I have structured my proposal so that the definition of the crime of aggression is found in new Article 8bis and the jurisdictional filter is found in new Article 15bis.

The following discussion recognizes the utility of, and broad support that might be obtained from, recognition of the opportunity afforded by Article 121(5) of the Rome Statute. Under this amendment provision, any State Party (and, I would argue as a matter of logic, any non- State Party unless covered by a Security Council Chapter VII referral resolution pursuant to Article 13(b) of the Rome Statute) can opt-in to any amendment on the crime of aggression. The use of the opt-in right may constitute the ultimate compromise between the Permanent Five (United States, France, United Kingdom, People's Republic of China and Russia) and other governments before the crime of aggression can be operationalized in the Rome Statute. Another lawyer's proposal, seeks an amendment to Article 12 of the Rome Statute that merit serious consideration.[4]

---

* This chapter is an updated and footnoted version of the presentation made at the 2007 Turin *Conference on International Criminal Justice*, which has thereafter been published in 41 *Case Western Reserve Journal of International Law* (2009), 397–411. The author wishes to thank Ms Kristen Knapp, a student at Northwestern University School of Law, for her expert assistance with this chapter.

1 See International Criminal Court, Assembly of State Parties, *Report of the Special Working Group on the Crime of Aggression*, ICC-ASP/7/SWGCA/2, 20 February 2009. Available at http://www.icc-cpi.int/iccdocs/asp_docs/ICC-ASP-7-SWGCA-2%20English.pdf (visited 20 September 2009).

2 Rome Statute of the International Criminal Court. UN doc. A/CONF.183/9, 17 July 1998, reprinted in 37 ILM 99 (1998). Available at http://www.iccnow.org/documents/rome-e.pdf (visited 20 September 2009) (hereinafter Rome or ICC Statute).

3 International Criminal Court, Discussion Paper on the Crime of Aggression Proposed by the Chairman (Revision June 2008, ICC-ASP/6/SWGCA/2, 14 May 2008 (hereinafter May 2008 Chairman's Proposal). Available at http://www2.icc-cpi.int/NR/rdonlyres/2AE911B2-15AA-4276-8F23-5D6818907007/146570/ICCASP6SWGCA2English1.pdf (visited 20 September 2009).

4 R. Manson, *The ICC, the U.N. and Crimes of Aggression*, BEPJ, 1 March 2007. Available at http://www.bepj.org.uk/icc-un-crimes-of-aggression (visited 20 September 2009); see *also* ICC Statute, *supra* note 2, at sect. 12.

2. New Article 8*bis*

In my proposal, new Article 8bis is common to both options, but differs somewhat from the May 2008 Chairman's Proposal. I have omitted any effort to define an 'act of aggression', as the SWGCA sought to do in its Article 8bis(2) with liberal application of UN General Assembly Resolution 3314 (GA Res. 3314).[5] I propose a definition of the crime of aggression that avoids reference to an 'act of aggression' because the Security Council and the International Court of Justice have not in the past, and would not in the future, consider themselves bound to UNGA resolution 3314 when determining the existence of an act of aggression. Neither should the ICC when adjudicating the crime of aggression against an individual (or an act of aggression if given the chance under Option 1 below). However, I propose that the elements of the crime of aggression (when drafted) should draw (but not exclusively) upon the acts listed in Article 3 of UNGA Resolution 3314.[6] This keeps UNGA Res. 3314 'in the game', but in a far more realistic and practical manner than, in my humble view, was contemplated by the SWGCA.

Within my definition of the crime of aggression in new Article 8(1), I have narrowed the crime (for purposes of individual criminal responsibility) to military interventions of a specific character, with caveats that reflect the reality of UNSC authorizations, the Uniting for Peace option, and Article 51 exercises of the right of individual or collective self-defence. (Bear in mind that in Article 15bis of my proposal, the Security Council, General Assembly, ICC, or the International Court of Justice (ICJ) (depending on what option is used), can override a state's initial invocation of Article 51 and determine that in fact an act of aggression has occurred despite the state's plea of self-defence, and thus launch the ICC into individual criminal accountability.) I have incorporated much of what is in the SWGCA draft, but also focused on Article 2(4) of the United Nations Charter as an alternative to the broader and far more indeterminate (for criminal purposes) scope of the Charter of the United Nations.

---

5 *May 2008 Chairman's Proposal*, *supra* note 3, Art. 8 bis, 2; G.A. Res. 3314 (XXIX), U.N. Doc. A/9619, 14 December 1974.

6 G.A. Res. 3314, *supra* note 5, Art. 3, which states:

'Any of the following acts, regardless of a declaration of war, shall, subject to and in accordance with the provisions of article 2, qualify as an act of aggression:

(a) The invasion or attack by the armed forces of a State of the territory of another State, or any military occupation, however temporary, resulting from such invasion or attack, or any annexation by the use of force of the territory of another State or part thereof,
(b) Bombardment by the armed forces of a State against the territory of another State or the use of any weapons by a State against the territory of another State;
(c) The blockade of the ports or coasts of a State by the armed forces of another State;
(d) An attack by the armed forces of a State on the land, sea or air forces, or marine and air fleets of another State;
(e) The use of armed forces of one State which are within the territory of another State with the agreement of the receiving State, in contravention of the conditions provided for in the agreement or any extension of their presence in such territory beyond the termination of the agreement;
(f) The action of a State in allowing its territory, which it has placed at the disposal of another State, to be used by that other State for perpetrating an act of aggression against a third State;
(g) The sending by or on behalf of a State of armed bands, groups, irregulars or mercenaries, which carry out acts of armed force against another State of such gravity as to amount to the acts listed above, or its substantial involvement therein.'

Furthermore, Article 8bis (1) of my proposal limits the definition of the crime of aggression to those acts that are 'of such a character, gravity, and scale that it constitutes a manifest violation of the prohibition on the use of force under article 2(4) of the United Nations Charter …'. This definition conforms to the gravity, duration and context confirmed by the ICJ in the *Democratic Republic of the Congo v. Uganda* judgment (2005).[7] Given the important gravity and contextual requirements associated with genocide, crimes against humanity and war crimes under the Rome Statute, there is an obvious need to establish some general threshold for the use of armed force which would qualify it as the crime of aggression. The language I have chosen to express that threshold is open to interpretation, as are the other crimes subject to magnitude conditionality under the Rome Statute. But it is a calculation that the ICC, once seized with an investigation into an act of aggression, should be capable of making.

3. Article 15*bis*: Language Common to Both Options

Both of the options for Article 15bis, sections 1 and 2, mirror the language from the May 2008 Chairman's Proposal for Article 15bis, sections 1 and 2.[8] This initial jurisdictional filter would require that 'the Security Council has made a determination of an act of aggression committed by the State concerned'. This reflects the longstanding proposal of the five Permanent Members of the Security Council and other nations which would minimize any concerns about contravening the UN Charter because the Security Council has clear, and some would argue sole, authority to make such a determination pursuant to Article 39 of the Charter.[9] Once such a determination on aggression is made by the Council, then the ICC Prosecutor could investigate any individual who might be responsible in a criminal context for such act of aggression identified by the Council. Most proponents of much broader jurisdictional filters for the crime of aggression still embrace the logic of including this procedure of the Security Council's determination on aggression as one of several ways to trigger ICC jurisdiction, and the May 2008 Chairman's Proposal reflects it.[10] Thus,

7 'In relation to the first of the DRC's final submissions, the Court accordingly concludes that Uganda has violated the sovereignty and also the territorial integrity of the DRC. Uganda's actions equally constituted an interference in the internal affairs of the DRC and in the civil war there raging. The unlawful military intervention by Uganda was of such a magnitude and duration that the Court considers it to be a grave violation of the prohibition on the use of force expressed in Article 2, paragraph 4, of the Charter.' ICJ, *Case Concerning Armed Activities on the Territory of the Congo (Democratic Republic of the Congo v. Uganda)*, 2005, 57, at 165.

8 *May 2008 Chairman's Proposal* at 4.

9 Informal Inter-Sessional Meeting of the Special Working Group on the Crime of Aggression, ICC-ASP/6/SWGCA/INF.1, 25 July 2007, paras 25 and 30; Report of the Special Working Group on the Crime of Aggression, ICC-ASP/5/35, 29 January–1 February 2007, para. 26; Informal Inter-Sessional Meeting of the Special Working Group on the Crime of Aggression, ICC-ASP/5/SWGCA/INF.1, 23 November–1 December 2006, para. 57; Informal Inter-Sessional Meeting of the Special Working Group on the Crime of Aggression, ICC-ASP/4/32, 13–15 June 2005, para. 66–67; M. Politi and G. Nesi (eds), *The International Criminal Court and the Crime of Aggression* (Aldershot: Ashgate Publishing Limited, 2004), 121–150.

10 See *May 2008 Chairman's Proposal*, *supra* note 3, and also Informal Inter-Sessional Meeting of the Special Working Group on the Crime of Aggression. ICC-ASP/6/SWGCA/INF.1, 25 July 2007. While some participants argued that 'the Statute did not require a prior determination by the Security Council' and others supported additional trigger mechanisms, such as determinations by the General Assembly or the ICJ, none of the members of the Special Working Group on the Crime of Aggression proposed removing entirely the role of the Security Council as an option in the determination on aggression.

I position it as the first of two alternative means to establish ICC jurisdiction. The reality, however, is that the Security Council rarely makes such an emphatic decision on an act of aggression.[11] The question governments confront is whether there should be a continued role for the Security Council in the jurisdictional framework in the absence of an explicit decision by the Council on aggression, and whether that role should reflect the reality of how the Council actually operates.

Similarly, the language of section 3(a) is drawn from Article 15bis Alternative 1, Option 2 (green light) of the May 2008 Chairman's Proposal,[12] which simply incorporates what already is permitted under Rome Statute Article 13(b), namely, referrals by the Security Council under Chapter VII of the UN Charter.

A. Option I: Judicial Green Light

Option I steers the jurisdictional filter away from political determinations of aggression *per se* and towards a more pragmatic methodology in terms of how the UN Security Council operates. The substance of Option I, which is set forth in its entirety in the Annex to this article, is as follows.

The new Article 15(3)(b) of Option I would require a Security Council Chapter VII resolution determining a breach of the peace resulting from the use of armed force (and lacking any conditionality prohibiting Court interference), which then triggers a judicial option for the ICC or the ICJ to determine whether an act of aggression has occurred. This option invites a judicial consideration, provided the Security Council has not prohibited it by the terms of the Chapter VII resolution (which could arise, for example, if it is simply a follow-on sanctions resolution and the Council determines that ICC intervention at that stage would be too disruptive of peace and security priorities).

If the jurisdictional filter requires a continued role for the Security Council – an outcome that may be necessary in order to reach a broad consensus on the crime of aggression for the Rome Statute – then new Article 15(3)(b) of Option I provides that when the Security Council makes a determination about the existence of any breach of the peace — which it is empowered to make, but which may or may not describe an actual act of aggression – then an international court of law has the opportunity to determine whether an act of aggression in fact has occurred. I have bracketed both judicial options to invite consideration whether the SWGCA wants to resort only to the ICC, only to the ICJ, or to either option.

The proposed language narrows the scope for action to those situations which are 'the result of the use of armed force between States …'. I have structured the proposal in this vein in order to achieve common ground on the character of state-on-state aggression that all governments can agree would constitute the context within which an individual should be subject to investigation and, if merited, prosecution for the crime of aggression under customary international law. The use of armed force is a requirement for the definition of aggression as set forth in Articles 1, 2, and 3 of General Assembly Resolution 3314 (14 December 1974)[13] and therefore the proposal embraces

---

11 United Nations, Security Council Resolutions. Available at http://www.un.org/documents/scres.htm (visited 20 September 2009).; See also K.E. Puls, Book Review, 12 B.U. Int'l L.J. 139, 142 (1994) (noting the relative absence of explicit decisions by the Security Council).

12 *May 2008 Chairman's Proposal*, *supra* note 3, Art. 15bis, Option 2.

13 '*Article 1* – Aggression is the use of armed force by a State against the sovereignty, territorial integrity or political independence of another State, or in any other manner inconsistent with the Charter of the United Nations, as set out in this Definition. *Explanatory note*: In this Definition the term "State": (a) Is used without prejudice to questions of recognition or to whether a State is a member of the United Nations; (b) Includes the concept of a "group of States" where appropriate.

the core principles of that key resolution which many governments rely on to help frame their own positions regarding the crime of aggression of the Rome Statute. Furthermore, this formulation complements the language suggested for Article 8bis.

Absent from this determination by the Security Council would be strictly 'economic aggression' (such as economic sanctions or punitive trade measures) or 'political aggression' (such as diplomatic sanctions or immigration restrictions) or any other alleged aggression that occurs without the use of armed force. One can always make the argument that the Security Council can find such non-military forms of aggression to be threats to international peace and security and act accordingly, but that need not throw the situation into the lap of the ICC for criminal investigations and prosecutions. That extreme measure – at this point in history and in the development of customary international law – should be reserved for aggression that arises from the threat or use of armed force.

I have bracketed two sub-options pursuant to which a judicial body would make the determination of state-on-state aggression in the event the Security Council does not explicitly do so as described in new Article 15(3)(b) of Option I. The first sub-option would designate the Pre-Trial Chamber of the ICC as the judicial body empowered to make a judgment about an act of aggression having been committed. Some may find this option too problematic and risky because the ICC judges' primary expertise likely will be in national or international criminal law and not the international law jurisprudence and theory typically associated with judgments about state-on-state acts of aggression.

The latter kind of expertise would be found in the second sub-option, whereby the ICJ would deliver a judgment on aggression pursuant to either: (1) a contentious case between states, or (2) a formal request by the Security Council or the UN General Assembly. Advisory opinions often can be delivered within relatively short periods of time compared to judgments in contentious cases,[14] and such a procedure might lend itself to the need to act in a timely manner to deter alleged aggressors from continuing with plans or actions relating to aggression.

Article 2 – The first use of armed force by a State in contravention of the Charter shall constitute *prima facie* evidence of an act of aggression although the Security Council may, in conformity with the Charter, conclude that a determination that an act of aggression has been committed would not be justified in the light of other relevant circumstances, including the fact that the acts concerned or their consequences are not of sufficient gravity.

Article 3 – Any of the following acts, regardless of a declaration of war, shall, subject to and in accordance with the provisions of article 2, qualify as an act of aggression. (a) The invasion or attack by the armed forces of a State of the territory of another State, or any military occupation, however temporary, resulting from such invasion or attack, or any annexation by the use of force of the territory of another State or part thereof; (b) Bombardment by the armed forces of a State against the territory of another State or the use of any weapons by a State against the territory of another State; (c) The blockade of the ports or coasts of a State by the armed forces of another State; (d) An attack by the armed forces of a State on the land, sea or air forces, or marine and air fleets of another State; (e) The use of armed forces of one State which are within the territory of another State with the agreement of the receiving State, in contravention of the conditions provided for in the agreement or any extension of their presence in such territory beyond the termination of the agreement; (f) The action of a State in allowing its territory, which it has placed at the disposal of another State, to be used by that other State for perpetrating an act of aggression against a third State; (g) The sending by or on behalf of a State of armed bands, groups, irregulars or mercenaries, which carry out acts of armed force against another State of such gravity as to amount to the acts listed above, or its substantial involvement therein.' GA Res. 3314 (XXIX), 14 December 1974, Annex.

14 Of the 24 ICJ advisory opinions since 1947, 62.5% (14) were rendered within eight months of their respective filings. ICJ, List of Advisory Proceedings Referred to the Court Since 1946 by Date of Culmination. Available at http://www.icj-cij.org/docket/index.php?p1=3&p2=4&sort=2&p3=0 (visited 20 September 2009).

Provided the jurisdictional filter can be established as set forth in Article 15(3)(b) of Option I, the ICC will need to (and Article 5(2) of the Rome Statute requires that the ICC) have a defined crime of aggression for which individuals can be investigated and, if merited, prosecuted. This requirement is fulfilled by Article 8bis described above, specifically Article 8(1).

Article 8bis establishes a leadership criterion for the commission of the crime, namely, 'a person in a position effectively to exercise control over or to direct the political or military action (in whole or in substantial part) of a state, of an unlawful military intervention by one state into the territory (land, sea, or air) of another state of such character, gravity and scale that it constitutes a manifest violation of the prohibition on the use of force under Article 2(4) of the United Nations Charter …'. This does not preclude the further requirement, set forth in new Article 15(3)(b) of Option I, that the decision of the Security Council on a use of armed force still requires a further decision on an act of aggression by either the ICC or the ICJ (depending on whether one or both bracketed options would be agreed to by negotiators and States Parties to the Rome Statute). This definitional provision ensures that the individual who is or has been in a leadership position holds that post in the state that is determined to be the aggressor state.

The Security Council rarely resorts to 'aggression' terminology and the examples of the now distant past demonstrate that the Council has used the term to describe relatively minor uses of military force while using other UN Charter terminology (threats to or breaches of international peace and security, unlawful use of force, etc.) to describe far more significant uses of military force classically regarded as aggression.[15] Once the Security Council determines that a breach of the peace has occurred, often by condemning it, that determination memorialized in a resolution should be sufficient to trigger a process that can determine whether an act of state-on-state aggression *per se* has occurred, which then would enable the ICC to investigate persons for purposes of individual criminal culpability.

Permanent Members of the Security Council concerned that this methodology too easily would open the door to determinations of state-on-state aggression, which arguably only the Security Council should make pursuant to Article 39 of the UN Charter, could remain confident that any determination or condemnation regarding a breach of the peace as a result of the use of armed force, which is adopted by the Security Council in a resolution, likely will not condemn any one of them. Of course, such a result understandably will be of concern to other governments resentful of the powers and protection that the Permanent Members enjoy under the UN Charter. But the advantage of the proposal is that it realistically would open up most (perhaps all if the Permanent Five refrain from aggression) situations of aggression in the future to scrutiny by the ICC if the Security Council or, depending on which bracketed option is chosen, the ICC or the ICJ reaches the preliminary decision that state-on-state aggression has occurred following a determination by the Security Council that a breach of the peace has occurred.

This kind of determination (breach of the peace) constitutes the *raison d'être* of the Security Council and necessarily will remain the bread and butter of Council work. In other words, addressing threats to international peace and security is the Council's primary job and it is unavoidable. My proposal accepts that reality and uses it to open a logical door to determination of whether state-on-state aggression has occurred. I would argue that the equality of states principle[16] remains intact

---

15 See J.A. Frowein and N. Krisch, 'Article 39', in B. Simma (ed.), *The Charter of the United Nations: A Commentary* (2nd edn, Oxford: Oxford University Press, 2002), 718–729. See also Y. Dinstein, *War, Aggression and Self-Defence* (4th edn, Cambridge: Cambridge University Press, 2005), 214–215.

16 L.F. Damrosch et al., *International Law Cases and Materials* (4th edn, St. Paul, MN: West Group, 2001), 106–107, 350 and 428; E. Dickinson, *The Equality of States in International Law* (Cambridge: Harvard University Press, 1920); GA Res. 2625 (XXV), 24 October 1970, Annex, U.N. Doc. A/8082 (1970).

because this process conforms to the UN Charter. It remains possible that aggression allegedly committed by a Permanent Member of the Security Council could be adjudicated by the ICJ if the jurisdictional requirements of that Court are met. It would be difficult to argue that somehow the existing procedures of the ICJ challenge the equality of states principle less than would the procedures I have proposed with respect to the ICC's jurisdiction over the crime of aggression.

There has been commentary within the Special Working Group with respect to this approach, namely that 'a Council decision might be interpreted as *de facto* determination of an act of aggression, irrespective of the Council's intention. It might therefore have a negative impact on the decision-making within the Council, which might adjust the way it used certain terms. It was argued that this option would also create a subordinate relationship between the Court and the Council'.[17] This merits a response.

Under Option I as I have drafted it, an act of *aggression* must still be determined to have been committed following the initial Security Council determination of 'the existence a breach of the peace as a result of the use of armed force between States …'. Security Council members would know that their determination alone does not trigger ICC jurisdiction. Rather, a subsequent decision by an international court, either the ICC or the ICJ (depending on which bracketed option is chosen), would be required. One might argue that such a prospect alone would cause havoc within Council deliberations, such that both Permanent and non-Permanent Members of the Council would seek to find alternative formulations or decide not to decide in order to avoid potential ICC jurisdiction over the crime of aggression. While that concern is understandable, I do not believe it has as much currency as might be presumed.

First, the UN Charter does not provide any flexibility to arrive at decisions in the Security Council other than with respect to and in the context of issues of international peace and security, however they may be described. Option I captures the ambit of Council decision-making. The Council would have an easy supplemental choice if it wishes to adopt a resolution that forecloses the possibility of ICC jurisdiction in a particular matter. The Council either (i) could use wording that conforms to the requirements of Article 16 of the Rome Statute[18] or (ii) adopt a Chapter VII resolution that would narrowly focus potential ICC jurisdiction. Alternative (i) was used in Security Council Resolutions 1422 (2002)[19] and 1487 (2003).[20] Despite the controversy generated by these resolutions, which ensured that the second one would not be renewed in 2004, the Council has demonstrated its ability to take such a step. Alternative (ii) was used in Security Council Resolution 1593 (2005)[21] referring the Darfur situation to the ICC and in other Chapter VII resolutions pertaining to the International Criminal Tribunals established by the Security Council.[22]

There might be some dispute over the extent of the Council's powers to establish the scope of the ICC's jurisdiction in a particular situation, but in the end the ICC likely would give great deference to any limitations that the Council might impose under Chapter VII authority. The alternative – to

17 Informal Inter-Sessional Meeting of the Special Working Group on the Crime of Aggression, 25 July 2007, para. 30, *supra* note 9.

18 Art. 16 ICCSt: 'No investigation or prosecution may be commenced or proceeded with under this Statute for a period of 12 months after the Security Council, in a resolution adopted under Chapter VII of the Charter of the United Nations, has requested the Court to that effect; that request may be renewed by the Council under the same conditions.'

19 SC Res. 1422 (2002), 12 July 2002.

20 SC Res. 1487 (2003), 12 June 2003.

21 SC Res. 1593 (2005), 31 March 2005.

22 SC Res. 827 (1993), SC Res. 955 (1994), SC Res. 1315 (2000) and SC Res. 1400 (2002), Sc Res. 1757 (2007).

require an explicit Security Council determination on aggression *per se* – invites the predicament that the Security Council may never again make such a determination. If it does not, the issue arises whether that indecision unleashes non-Security Council options on the crime of aggression for the ICC that have been proposed, but also have proven so intractable in the Special Working Group negotiations. Option I embraces the obvious reality that nostalgic adherence to the term 'aggression' creates a gridlock that defies the actual practice of the Council and how the modern world describes what is occurring in the field, namely as breaches of the peace which sometimes – although likely infrequently – would embrace the classic understanding of aggression and yet more often would be defined as uses of armed force falling short of aggression.

Second, the Rome Statute already recognizes a *de facto* 'subordinate relationship' between the ICC and the Security Council in Article 16 of the Rome Statute and in the limitations that the Council itself might impose in a referral under Article 13(b) of the Rome Statute. It is a very limited and practical (*de facto*) subordinate relationship, but one that was well recognized in the drafting of those provisions. Article 5(2) of the Rome Statute also leaves the door open for a limited subordinate relationship when it requires that the crime of aggression 'provision shall be consistent with the relevant provisions of the Charter of the United Nations'. Option I avoids what some governments might view as the extreme position of requiring a Security Council determination of 'aggression' *per se*, which creates a far more radical subordinate relationship to the Council on the crime of aggression; it also avoids, however, the other extreme position that simply includes the Council as one of several different means to initiate a determination that an act of aggression has occurred. In Option I, the Council at least has to be engaged in order to determine that a breach to international peace and security is present, following which another designated body may determine that, within the context established by the Council, an act of aggression between one state and another state has occurred.

The result is the proverbial 'you can't please everybody' compromise. In my opinion, there is far greater risk in challenging the authority of the Security Council and triggering dangerous confrontations between the Council and the ICC if even the Council's authority with respect to breaches to international peace and security, much less aggression, is ignored by the Rome Statute. Fears that the Council will feel constrained by Option I pale in comparison to how the Council will react if the ICC moves forward on the crime of aggression without any deference to the Council's overall Charter authority with respect to breaches of the peace, which in any practical sense would first have to be established before determinations regarding acts of aggression could be credibly examined by any other UN body. If the ICC could act upon a non-Council determination that an act of aggression has occurred without any initial determination by the Security Council that a breach of the peace has occurred, then potentially destructive jurisdictional battles would be fought between the Council and the ICC, probably to the detriment of both peace and justice.

A further advantage to Option I is that it avoids, at least in significant part, the debate that predictably would arise as to whether a particular use of armed force constitutes an exception to the UN Charter Article 2(4) prohibition on 'the threat or use of force against the territorial integrity or political independence of any state, or in any other manner inconsistent with the Purposes of the United Nations'. If the Security Council determines that a breach of the peace has occurred and has identified the offending state in a Chapter VII resolution embodying the determination, then the Council for all intents and purposes has denied the legitimacy of any rationale for the use of armed force by the offending state in the particular situation (including self-defence, humanitarian intervention, protection of nationals, counterterrorism, or advancement of democracy). If, however, negotiators turn to non-Council formulas to trigger ICC jurisdiction over the crime of aggression, then any of those rationales for the use of armed force, such as self-defence, could be employed by governments, defence counsel, scholars and the media to challenge the ICC's jurisdiction. The Security Council can pre-emptively sideline those arguments by using wording and a procedure that establish an unlawful use of armed force and, perhaps, an act of aggression for which there is no justifiable rationale under international law.

B. Option II: Soft Green Light

Option II preserves a significant role for the Security Council but, at the discretion of the Council, offers the option of sharing the final determination of whether aggression has occurred with certain other designated UN organs or the ICC itself. It recognizes that the Security Council may not, indeed probably will not, want to make an immediate determination about aggression, but may be willing to initiate a process that enables another UN organ, or the ICC, to make that call. It is 'passing the buck' to other bodies, but in a way that remains within the initial control of the Security Council.

Under New Article 15(3)(b) of Option II, the wording of which is set forth in the annex to this chapter, I propose a formula that retains more control with the Security Council by requiring that the Security Council must first refer a breach of the peace situation to the Prosecutor who can then launch an investigation in one of two situations. Either the General Assembly must have adopted a resolution determining that an act of aggression has occurred or the ICJ must have delivered a judgment or an advisory opinion ruling that an act of aggression has occurred. Under this proposal, the Security Council steers the decision-making process into the institution of its choosing if the Council has chosen not to make the decision itself.

My hope is that negotiators will recognize the considerable latitude afforded the Security Council in these proposals, such that a far broader range of situations which may constitute state-on-state aggression can, in fact, be brought before the ICC for investigation of individual criminal culpability. This bridge, between those governments which believe in a central role for the Security Council and those governments which reject that view, is intended to establish a very pragmatic but disciplined process. I purposely do not include within any definitional structure acts of strictly internal aggression or terrorist or militia acts unconnected to state authority. That is a bridge too far for customary international law and for the ICC's criminal jurisdiction at this stage, in my view. I also think moving in that direction would break the back of the entire exercise.

4. Conclusion

I readily concede that the straightforward SWGCA green light jurisdictional procedure, coupled with an opt-in procedure for the crime of aggression, may be the ideal formula for the Permanent Five and some other UN Members. However, the objective of this chapter is to present two additional options that may be necessary to consider to bridge the gap between the Permanent Five and a number of other governments, the latter of which are seeking some alternative to an exclusive Security Council filter.

Annex: Scheffer Proposal

New Article 8bis of the Rome Statute

Crime of aggression

1. For the purpose of this Statute, 'crime of aggression' means the planning, preparation, initiation or execution, by a person in a position effectively to exercise control over or to direct the political or military action (in whole or substantial part) of a State, of an unlawful military intervention by one State into the territory (land, sea, or air) of another State of such character, gravity, and scale that it constitutes a manifest violation of the prohibition on the use of force under Article 2(4) of the United Nations Charter, provided that the lawful deployment or use of armed force undertaken pursuant to Security Council authorization, United Nations General Assembly Resolution 377(V) of 3 November 1950, or Article 51 of the United Nations Charter shall be excluded from such definition.
2. The elements of the crime of aggression shall draw, *inter alia*, from Articles 2 and 3 of United Nations General Assembly Resolution 3314 (XXIX) of 14 December 1974 to establish the character of an act of aggression for purposes of criminal responsibility under this Statute.

Option 1 (judicial green light)

New Article 15bis of the Rome Statute

Exercise of jurisdiction over the crime of aggression

1. The Court may exercise jurisdiction over the crime of aggression in accordance with Article 13, subject to the provisions of this article.
2. Where the Prosecutor concludes that there is a reasonable basis to proceed with an investigation in respect of a crime of aggression, he or she shall first ascertain whether the Security Council has made a determination of an act of aggression committed by the State concerned. The Prosecutor shall notify the Secretary-General of the United Nations of the situation before the Court, including any relevant information and documents.
3. In the absence of such a determination, the Prosecutor may not proceed with the investigation in respect of a crime of aggression unless:

(a) the Security Council has, in a resolution adopted under Chapter VII of the Charter of the United Nations, requested the Prosecutor to proceed with the investigation in respect of an act of aggression committed by the State concerned and any crime of aggression that arises thereunder, or
(b) the Security Council has, in a resolution adopted under Chapter VII of the Charter of the United Nations and which lacks any conditionality regarding the Court, determined the existence of a breach of the peace as the result of the use of armed force between States and thereafter, with respect to that situation, [the Pre-Trial Chamber has determined at the request of the Prosecutor, a State Party, or the Security Council that an act of aggression has been committed by the State concerned] [or] [the International Court of

Justice has delivered a judgment in a contentious case or an advisory opinion, pursuant to the request of the General Assembly or the Security Council, which determines that an act of aggression has been committed by the State concerned].
4. This article is without prejudice to the provisions relating to the exercise of jurisdiction with respect to other crimes referred to in Article 5.

Option II (soft green light)

Article 15bis

Exercise of jurisdiction over the crime of aggression

1. The Court may exercise jurisdiction over the crime of aggression in accordance with Article 13, subject to the provisions of this article.
2. Where the Prosecutor concludes that there is a reasonable basis to proceed with an investigation in respect of a crime of aggression, he or she shall first ascertain whether the Security Council has made a determination of an act of aggression committed by the State concerned. The Prosecutor shall notify the Secretary-General of the United Nations of the situation before the Court, including any relevant information and documents.
3. In the absence of such a determination, the Prosecutor may not proceed with the investigation in respect of a crime of aggression unless:

(a) the Security Council has, in a resolution adopted under Chapter VII of the Charter of the United Nations, requested the Prosecutor to proceed with the investigation in respect of an act of aggression committed by the State concerned and any crime of aggression that arises thereunder, or
(b) the Security Council has, in a resolution adopted under Chapter VII of the Charter of the United Nations, referred to the Prosecutor a situation regarding the existence of a breach of the peace as a result of the use of armed force between States but about which the Security Council has not determined that an act of aggression has occurred, and provided thereafter that the General Assembly has determined by resolution or the International Court of Justice has delivered a judgment in a contentious case or an advisory opinion, pursuant to the request of the General Assembly or the Security Council, determining that an act of aggression has been committed by the State concerned in respect of such situation.
4. This article is without prejudice to the provisions relating to the exercise of jurisdiction with respect to other crimes referred to in Article 5.

For both Option I and Option II:

New Article 25 (3bis)

In respect of the crime of aggression, the provisions of this article shall apply only to persons in a position effectively to exercise control over or to direct the political or military action (in whole or substantial part) of a State.

Chapter 29

Against the Odds: The Results of the Special Working Group on the Crime of Aggression*

Stefan Barriga

1. Introduction

On Friday 13 February 2009 the Special Working Group on the Crime of Aggression (SWGCA) concluded its work of almost five and a half years.[1] It submitted 'proposals for a provision on aggression'[2] to the Assembly of States Parties (ASP) of the International Criminal Court and thereby fulfilled the mandate established at the very first ASP meeting in September 2002.[3]

This chapter is intended to provide insights into the negotiation process that led to the successful conclusion of the SWGCA's work, as well as a preliminary analysis of the text submitted by the Group, which is annexed for ease of reference. At the same time, it should be borne in mind that the negotiations are far from over and likely to continue to the final day of the 2010 Review Conference in Kampala (Uganda). The reader should thus not expect a tell-all tale of diplomatic haggling or political intrigue, despite the fact that the process is, in essence, about the political question of the illegal war. For one, it would be imprudent to attempt to tell it all during the final stretch of a delicate negotiation process. But more importantly, so far, this is a story of constructive engagement by legal experts from countries with different and sometimes diametrically opposed political interests. It led, rather surprisingly, to the consensual adoption of 'proposals' (note the plural, though) for a provision on aggression more than one year in advance of the actual Review Conference. Divergent views remain and must be overcome only with respect to a small portion of the text, albeit the politically most difficult.

2. The Princeton Process on the Crime of Aggression

The controversy over the inclusion of the crime of aggression in the Rome Statute was responsible for much of the drama prior to and during the 1998 Diplomatic Conference.[4] As a final compromise, aggression was included as one of the four core crimes in Article 5 ICCSt, but was not yet activated. A provision was to be adopted at a later stage, at a Review Conference, 'defining

* Much appreciated comments and suggestions on a draft version of this text were provided by Roger Clark, Jutta Bertram-Nothnagel, Claus Kress, Susanna Blancke and Shantha Rau Barriga.

1 The SWGCA met for the first time during the 2nd ASP session from 8–12 September 2003 in New York. No written report was adopted.

2 February 2009 SWGCA Report, ICC-ASP/7/SWGCA/2, Annex I.

3 ICC-ASP/1/Res.1, *Continuity of work in respect of the crime of aggression.*

4 A. Zimmermann, 'Article 5. Crimes within the Jurisdiction of the Court', in O. Triffterer (ed.), *Commentary on the Rome Statute of the International Criminal Court* (Munich: C.H. Beck, 2008), 22–25.

the crime and setting out the conditions under which the Court shall exercise jurisdiction'.[5] The Rome Conference then mandated the Preparatory Commission (PrepCom) to draft proposals for a provision on aggression, 'including the definition and Elements of Crimes of aggression and the conditions under which the International Criminal Court shall exercise its jurisdiction with regard to this crime'.[6] The PrepCom made some progress, but still did not get past a rather preliminary discussion of aggression, reflected in a Coordinator's paper and some written proposals submitted by delegations.[7] By the time the PrepCom came to a close in July 2002, the first Review Conference was still many years into the future,[8] and a number of other issues needed to be resolved more urgently. The PrepCom therefore deferred consideration of this issue to a Special Working Group on the Crime of Aggression,[9] open to participation by all states, established by the first meeting of the Assembly of States Parties in September 2002.

The SWGCA met for the first time in September 2003, but the discussions on aggression were once again relegated to second tier matters in light of other, more immediately pressing issues. The Chairman of the Group, Ambassador Christian Wenaweser of Liechtenstein, therefore suggested an alternative avenue to get the work rolling: informal, inter-sessional meetings, focused exclusively on the crime of aggression, and held away from UN Headquarters. Similar informal meetings had been held for the purpose of advancing work on the definition of crimes prior to the Rome Conference, albeit in a smaller setting, in Siracusa (Italy).[10] The formula of taking delegates to an academic environment to discuss difficult topics seemed promising for the crime of aggression as well. Four such meetings were subsequently organized from 2004 to 2007 at Princeton University, under the auspices of the Liechtenstein Institute on Self-Determination at the Woodrow Wilson School.[11] These intense working sessions compensated for the lack of formal meeting time allocated to the SWGCA during the actual ASP. The Princeton Process was also a crucial catalyst that brought the crime of aggression back to the centre of the ASP's attention. In December 2005, the ASP decided on a roadmap[12] for the future work on aggression that finally devoted enough formal meeting time to the discussions on this topic, mostly at UN Headquarters in New York.[13] But the spirit of Princeton that had infused the work of the SWGCA remained a constant companion until the conclusion of the Group's work in February 2009.

---

5 Article 5(2) ICCSt.

6 Resolution F, Final Act of the United Nations Diplomatic Conference of Plenipotentiaries on the Establishment of an International Criminal Court, U.N. Doc. A/CONF.183/10*.

7 The Coordinator's Paper and a list of proposals and documents relating to the crime of aggression are contained in PCNICC/2002/2/Add.2. See also R.S. Clark, 'Rethinking Aggression as a Crime and Formulating Its Elements: The Final Work-Product of the Preparatory Commission for the International Criminal Court', 15 *Leiden Journal of International Law* (2002), 859–890.

8 Seven years after the entry into force of the Rome Statute, see Article 123 ICCSt.

9 PCNICC/2002/WGCA/L.2/Rev.1.

10 S.A. Fernández de Gurmendi, 'The Process of Negotiations', in R.S. Lee (ed.), *The International Criminal Court. The Making of the Rome Statute* (The Hague: Kluwer Law International, 1999), 217–227, at 218. Further such meetings took place after the Rome Conference to work on the Elements of Crimes.

11 These discussions are reflected in four reports: June 2007 Princeton Report, ICC-ASP/6/SWGCA/INF.1; June 2006 Princeton Report, ICC-ASP/5/SWGCA/INF.1; June 2005 Princeton Report, ICC-ASP/4/32; June 2004 Princeton Report, ICC-ASP/3/SWGCA/INF.1.

12 Resolution ICC-ASP/4/Res.4.

13 The discussions of the SWGCA in its official meetings are reflected in the following reports: February 2009 SWGCA Report, ICC-ASP/7/SWGCA/2; November 2008 SWGCA Report, ICC-ASP/7/SWGCA/1*; June 2008 SWGCA Report, ICC-ASP/6/20/Add.1; December 2007 SWGCA Report, ICC-ASP/6/SWGCA/1;

What did the Princeton Process achieve, and how? In general terms, it is safe to say that the Princeton Process was to a great extent responsible for the successful conclusion of the SWGCA, as evidenced by both the length and content of the Princeton reports, compared to the regular reports of the SWGCA meeting in formal session. Many of the understandings and compromises reached in February 2009 originated in Princeton. The Princeton Process therefore contributed greatly to the SWGCA's final proposals, which were adopted by consensus. This text is not equivalent to a final negotiated outcome ready for adoption by the Review Conference, but it does come very close. The technical quality of the draft, compared to the 2002 Coordinator's Paper, is one yardstick to measure the significant progress made by the SWGCA. An even more important one is the limited number of open issues remaining in the text.

A. Issues Remaining Open for Future Discussion

On the face of it, only two issues remain to be resolved. The first is whether the provisions on aggression should only be binding upon those States Parties that have accepted the amendment (Article 121(5) ICCSt), or whether the amendment would enter into force for all States Parties once ratified by seven-eighths of them (Article 121(4) ICCSt).[14] The second is the question of the role of the Security Council, and implicitly the role of the Permanent Members of the Council. On this eminently political issue, the SWGCA was not able to bridge the gap, but instead provided a number of technically well-drafted alternatives and options contained in Draft Article 15 bis (4). These will form the basis of the remaining negotiations until the Review Conference. Nevertheless, and despite the relatively clean set of proposals on aggression, it would be inaccurate to claim that the SWGCA left only two issues open. For one, the Group did not elaborate a set of Elements of Crimes. This exercise was regarded as premature by some, even though there was general agreement that it would be useful to have the Elements adopted directly at the Review Conference.[15] In addition, the final report of the SWGCA makes it clear that the Group worked on the basis of the principle 'nothing is agreed until everything is agreed'.[16] Surprises can therefore not be excluded during the course of the remaining negotiations. Indeed, the report reflects the comments and concerns of delegations with respect to numerous elements of the proposals on aggression that did not have to be reflected with brackets or footnotes in the outcome of the SWGCA. But some of these may at a later stage, and depending on the further discussions on the big issues, cause problems. The most notable of these issues concerns the threshold clause contained in Draft Article 8 bis (1), which would limit the Court's jurisdiction to clear cases of aggression, thereby excluding borderline situations, and possibly addressing the thorny question of humanitarian interventions. At this point, these issues could be regarded as contained, but not necessarily as resolved.

B. Factors Contributing to the Success of the Princeton Process

The fact that more than one year prior to the Review Conference there is no full agreement on the provisions on aggression should come as no surprise to any observer. It should also not be seen as a stain on the SWGCA's record, at least not yet. Instead, the fact that the Group was able to agree on such a relatively clean text must be seen as a success, which can be attributed

January 2007 SWGCA Report, ICC-ASP/5/35; November 2006 SWGCA Report, ASP/5/SWGCA/1; November/December 2005 SWGCA Report, ASP/4/SWGCA/1.

14 February 2009 SWGCA Report, *supra* note 2, Draft Resolution, para. 1.

15 November 2008 SWGCA Report, *supra* note 13, paras 30–34.

16 February 2009 SWGCA Report, *supra* note 13, para. 4.

to a number of factors. The first one is the Princeton Process itself. With all due respect to the windowless conference rooms in the basement of the UN Headquarters in New York, the serene environment at the campus of Princeton University (New Jersey) contributed greatly to the friendly and constructive atmosphere, as well as the sense of historic purpose that marked the work on this issue over the last years. Professor Wolfgang Danspeckgruber, Director of the Liechtenstein Institute, proved to be an enthusiastic host, whose addresses were only surpassed in passion and motivational effect by those of Ben Ferencz, former Prosecutor at the Nüremberg Trials, who regularly spoke to the conscience of all participating delegates. Furthermore, interventions made during the Princeton meetings were usually not based on formal instructions. For the most part, they were individual contributions to unfolding discussions and were generally understood not to be binding on the government that nominated the respective participant, but having been made with that government's interests in mind.[17] In addition, the informal character of the Princeton meetings greatly facilitated the active involvement of NGO representatives, beyond the customary time reserved to NGO statements in the work of the ASP. Several NGO representatives with great expertise in the matter at hand participated on an equal basis with government delegates in the discussions, thereby elevating the quality of the exchange. In between sessions, SWGCA members communicated by way of an electronic mailing list. The so-called Virtual Working Group[18] contributed significantly to the substantive preparation of the Group's sessions, rendering them more efficient and reinforcing the informal and friendly tone of the discussions. Over time, the Group developed a sense of camaraderie that can rarely be found in negotiation processes on such sensitive issues, and that had a direct impact on the manner in which discussions were conducted: namely more interactive, focused, open and frank than is otherwise the custom. It may not be possible to scientifically determine the exact impact of the positive atmosphere thus created, but its effect cannot be denied.

Another important factor that contributed to the continuous momentum of the SWGCA towards compromise and agreement on a number of issues was the pro-active approach taken by its Chairman. Based on the 2002 Coordinator's paper,[19] Ambassador Wenaweser steered the discussions by submitting several very informal non-papers on topical issues, as well as a number of Chairman's papers reflecting the status of the discussions.[20] In the early stages of the Group's work, the Chairman was furthermore assisted by three facilitators who submitted questionnaires to delegations and then suggested a way forward on the issues assigned to them.[21] The Chairman's papers allowed the Group to build upon past progress and to focus its work on formulations around which consensus began to emerge, rather than get distracted by individual proposals far from the mainstream. The several revisions of the Chairman's papers also helped leave past discussions behind, cement sometimes fragile agreements and forge new compromises. Consequently, the drafting of these Chairman's papers involved difficult balancing acts. Which suggestions were ripe for inclusion in the paper? Which compromises should the Chairman push for? What language

---

17 The earlier reports of the Princeton meetings explicitly stated that they do 'not necessarily represent the views of the Governments that the participants represent', see June 2004 Princeton Report, *supra* note 11, para. 3, and June 2005 Princeton Report, *supra* note 11, para. 3.

18 Ibid., para. 91.

19 *Supra* note 7.

20 The various non-papers and Chairman's paper are all contained in the respective reports of SWGCA sessions during which they were discussed.

21 The three so-called baskets were: The crime of aggression and Article 25(3) ICCSt (coordinated by Claus Kress); Conditions for the exercise of jurisdiction (coordinated by Pal Wrange); The definition of aggression (coordinated by Phani Dascalopoulou-Livada). See ICC-ASP/4/32, Annex II.

should no longer be included because it was considered discussed, but rejected – albeit not explicitly so? On several occasions, the Chairman tested new formulations through informal non-papers, before including them later (or not) in a revised Chairman's paper.[22] Overall, the discussions were thus focused on the papers drafted under the sole authority of the Chairman, but understood to reflect, to a reasonable extent, the variety of views in the room. This approach saved the Group from working on the basis of the dreaded Christmas tree drafts containing each and every proposal in a maze of brackets. At the same time, this approach required a certain spirit of compromise, or at least a willingness to choose their battles, on behalf of delegations who found themselves in minority positions. Obviously, the biggest battle in this process, over the role of the Security Council, is yet to come.

One further success factor needs to be mentioned: the Rome Statute itself. In the early stages of the SWGCA's work, delegations increasingly realized that their task was to some extent easier than what it was during and before the Rome Conference. This was due to the fact that many of the variables that were still unclear before 17 July 1998 were now set. The existing Rome Statute, in particular Part 3 (General Principles of Criminal Law), as well as the definitions of crimes in Articles 6, 7 and 8 provided valuable guidance and spared the Group a number of difficult questions. Early in its work, the SWGCA took the approach that the provisions on the crime of aggression should fit into the Rome Statute as smoothly as possible, and that general provisions applicable to other crimes in the Statute should, as a default rule, also apply to the crime of aggression. As a result, the Group soon focused its work on the core issues of the definition of crime of aggression and the specific conditions for the exercise of jurisdiction, rather than on ancillary issues. The understanding that all relevant provisions of the Statute would in principle apply to the crime of aggression spared the Group from a whole set of further complicated discussions. This understanding was reached gradually, after examining a number of existing articles in detail and questioning whether they should indeed be applicable to the crime of aggression. In almost all instances, the Group came to the conclusion that there was no reason to treat the crime of aggression differently from other crimes, e.g., with respect to the application of Article 30 ICCSt (Mental Element) or Article 32 (Mistake of Fact or Mistake of Law).[23] The fact that the Rome Statute provided a comprehensive context for the provisions on the crime of aggression thus greatly facilitated the discussions.

3. The Outcome of the SWGCA: A Watershed in the Negotiations on Aggression

As alluded to in the Introduction, the status and significance of the 'proposals for a provision on aggression' adopted by the SWGCA are somewhat ambivalent. On the one hand, the text itself marks two important issues explicitly as not agreed yet, and the accompanying report refers to the principle of 'nothing is agreed until everything is agreed', explaining in detail the criticisms voiced in respect of these and several other parts of the text.[24] On the other hand, the fact that the SWGCA was able to adopt a single, substantially clean text builds a strong perception that changes to unmarked parts of the text would be very difficult to achieve. The SWGCA proposals

22 This also illustrates the main difference between these informal non-papers and the Chairman's papers. The former were more preliminary in nature and served to introduce new ideas, whereas the latter were intended to reflect the status of the negotiations.

23 Other examples are the issues of complementarity and admissibility (June 2004 Princeton Report, *supra* note 11, para. 27), *ne bis in idem* (ibid., para. 33), as well as investigation and prosecution in accordance with Part 5 ICCSt (June 2005 Princeton Report, *supra* note 11, para. 52).

24 *Supra* note 16.

thus represent a clear watershed in the negotiations on the crime of aggression, allowing the future process to focus on those issues that have been most clearly marked as still controversial.

In light of the fact that the SWGCA was open to States Parties and non-States Parties on an equal footing, its consensual outcome is also highly significant in a more general way: given the controversy over the question of aggression at the Rome Conference, the SWGCA's process and outcome reflect a remarkable acceptance of the notion that the ICC could one day effectively exercise jurisdiction over this crime, far beyond the group of States that voted in favour of, signed or ratified the Statute. At no point during the Group's work was the mandate and ultimate goal of the process put into question by any of the delegations. Indeed, with the conclusion of the SWGCA as an open platform for all governments and the passing of the torch back to the Assembly of States Parties and the Review Conference,[25] any non-State Party that would actually be opposed, as a matter of principle, to the Court's exercising jurisdiction over the crime of aggression has clearly missed the best moment for objection.[26] The SWGCA's proposals make it clear that the remaining process is not about whether to include provisions on the crime of aggression in the Statute, but how.

The SWGCA's proposals consist of a short draft for an enabling resolution to be adopted by the Review Conference, accompanied by an appendix with six draft amendments to the Rome Statute. The first amendment would delete current Article 5(2) ICCSt, on the assumption that that provision would become obsolete. The second amendment contains the actual definition of the crime of aggression, including the definition of the State act of aggression, to be inserted into the Statute as a new Article 8 bis. The third amendment contains a new draft Article 15 bis, dealing with the conditions for the exercise of jurisdiction, and in particular the role of the Security Council. The fourth amendment would add a new paragraph to Article 25 ICCSt in order to limit individual criminal responsibility to leaders only. Amendments five and six contain consequential changes to the Rome Statute that would be necessitated by the insertion of a new Article 8 bis.[27] As a whole, this document reflects the current state of the negotiation process on the crime of aggression, and its main substantive features are analyzed below.

A. The Definition of the Individual's Crime of Aggression

One of the major achievements of the SWGCA is to be found in its draft Article 8 bis, containing the definition of the crime of aggression. In the course of its work, the Group consistently kept a clear distinction between the 'crime' of aggression as the individual's conduct triggering criminal responsibility, and the State 'act' of aggression.[28] The definition of the individual's conduct is contained in the first paragraph of draft Article 8 bis and constitutes the core of the provisions on aggression:

> 1. For the purpose of this Statute, "crime of aggression" means the planning, preparation, initiation or execution, by a person in a position effectively to exercise control over or to direct the political

25 While the SWGCA was open to all States on an equal footing, non-States Parties do not have the right to vote in ASP meetings; see ASP Rules of Procedure, ICC-ASP/1/3; the same is true for the Review Conference, see Article 123(1) ICCSt.

26 It should be noted, however, that the United States did not participate in the SWGCA.

27 The changes would affect Articles 9(1) and 20(3) ICCSt and would simply add a reference to the new Article 8 bis.

28 See, e.g., the structure of the June 2006 Princeton Report, *supra* note 11.

or military action of a State, of an act of aggression which, by its character, gravity and scale, constitutes a manifest violation of the Charter of the United Nations.

1. A Smooth Embedding in the Rome Statute

The wording and structure of this paragraph closely resembles the manner in which the other core crimes have been defined in Articles 6 to 8 ICCSt, and purposefully so.[29] The SWGCA held extensive discussions over the question of whether the criminalized individual conduct could be described in such a manner that Part 3 of the Rome Statute, containing general principles of criminal law, would fully apply to the crime of aggression. The definition of the crime of aggression would thus not include references to the required intent and knowledge or the various forms of participation in the crime.[30] This so-called 'differentiated approach'[31] ultimately prevailed, and it is thus clear that the Rome Statute's general principles of criminal law would fully apply to the crime of aggression.[32] The mental element would thus have to be established, as with any other core crime, in accordance with Article 30 ICCSt (requiring intent and knowledge).[33] Also, the various forms of participation foreseen in Article 25 would fully apply to the crime of aggression, with one caveat relating to the leadership nature of the crime addressed below. The Group's agreement on such an approach constituted a complete turnaround from the 2002 Coordinator's paper. That document was based on the so-called monistic approach, which attempted to include the mental element as well as the forms of participation in the definition of the crime itself,[34] and which would have explicitly excluded the corresponding provisions of Part 3, such as Article 25(3) ICCSt. Moving from the monistic to the differentiated approach was overall considered a rather technical matter, but it spared the Group difficult discussions on how to define aggression-specific mental elements and forms of participation. This approach furthermore had the advantage that the SWGCA could largely align its draft to the Nüremberg language on the crime of aggression, namely by describing the actions of the principal perpetrator as the 'planning, preparation, initiation or execution' of an act of aggression.[35] The word 'execution' could be seen as the odd sibling among these words, as all the others describe the typical activity of the leader, whereas it is usually the soldier who executes

29 June 2007 Princeton Report, *supra* note 11, para. 8.

30 The 2002 Coordinator's paper, *supra* note 7, by contrast, still included the phrase 'intentionally and knowingly' in its definition of aggression.

31 The notion of the differentiated versus the monistic approach was introduced in the 2005 Discussion Paper by Claus Kress, *supra* note 21.

32 February 2009 SWGCA Report, *supra* note 2, para. 15.

33 Taking into account the yet to be drafted Elements of Crime in this respect.

34 The relevant part reads: '... a person commits a "crime of aggression" when, being in a position effectively to exercise control over or to direct the political or military action of a State, that person intentionally and knowingly orders or participates actively in the planning, preparation, initiation or execution of an act of aggression ...', PCNICC/2002/2/Add.2.

35 Article 6 of the Charter of the International Military Tribunal actually uses the phrase '... planning, preparation, initiation or *waging* of a war of aggression ...' (emphasis added), rather than 'execution'. Earlier rounds of the SWGCA had struggled with the search for an action word that accurately described, under the differentiated approach, what the leader actually does in relation to the State act of aggression, while avoiding overlap with the secondary forms of participation under Article 25(3) ICCSt, such as 'orders, solicits or induces', 'aids, abets or otherwise assists' or 'contributes'. One suggestion that got considerable traction in the Group was to refer to a leader who 'directs' an act of aggression. Such a description of the principal form of perpetration would then have been easy to connect with the verbs describing the various forms of participation of Article 25(3): The principal perpetrator would 'commit' the crime, i.e., the directing of a State act of

an act of aggression by actively engaging in combat. Then again, modern warfare would allow a leader to execute a devastating act of armed force by a simple push of a button. There was little worry that the phrase 'planning, preparation, initiation or execution' could imply the responsibility of individual soldiers, as the draft provides for double assurance that the Court could only hold leaders accountable, as will be considered next.

2. The Leadership Element

One of the few elements of the 2002 Coordinator's paper that made their way unchanged to the SWGCA's 2009 proposals is the leadership clause, which was even granted two appearances. First, it appears as a qualification to the description of the principal conduct in draft Article 8 bis (1), where the crime of aggression is defined as the planning, preparation, initiation or execution of an act of aggression 'by a person in a position effectively to exercise control over or to direct the political or military action of a State'. Despite its straightforward wording, that clause alone would not guarantee that the Court could only prosecute leaders so described. Theoretically, any person who simply assists the leader in the commission of the crime could be held liable as a secondary perpetrator. Article 25(3)(c) ICCSt could trigger the criminal responsibility of, e.g., the leader's personal assistant, who could – conceivably with full knowledge and intent – 'aid, abet or otherwise assist' in the commission of the crime. The SWGCA's draft therefore repeats the leadership clause as a new paragraph 3 bis to Article 25 ICCSt (Individual Criminal Responsibility), clarifying that the article 'shall apply only to persons in a position effectively to exercise control over or to direct the political or military action of a State'. The leadership requirement would thus not only apply to the principal perpetrator, but to all forms of participation.[36]

There has been some criticism that the leadership clause would constitute a retreat from Nüremberg in that it envisages a rather narrow circle of potential perpetrators.[37] There had indeed been suggestions in the SWGCA to refer to persons who 'shape or influence' the political or military action of a State, rather than to those who exercise control over or direct that action. But there was concern that this formula would open the doors too far, especially in relation to democracies where a very large circle of persons could be said to 'shape or influence' the State's action.[38] At the same time, there was an understanding in the SWGCA that the language used was not intended to retreat from the Nüremberg precedent that included criminal responsibility for industrialists, albeit without using the exact same words.[39] In any event, the SWGCA's draft certainly does not explicitly require that a leader be part of the formal government.[40]

3. The Threshold of a 'Manifest Violation' of the UN Charter

The definition of the crime of aggression in draft Article 8 bis (1) contains one further qualification that has been referred to as the 'threshold clause'. Without touching the actual definition of a State act of aggression in paragraph 2, this clause would effectively limit the Court's jurisdiction to those

aggression, whereas secondary perpetrators would, e.g., 'aid' the directing of an act of aggression. There was, however, a significant level of discomfort in taking the differentiated approach to its ultimate consequence.

36 June 2008 Princeton Report, *supra* note 11, para. 18.

37 K.J. Heller, 'Retreat from Nüremberg: The Leadership Requirements in the Special Working Group's Definition of Aggression', 18 *EJIL* (2007), 477–97.

38 June 2007 Princeton Report, *supra* note 11, para. 12.

39 February 2009 SWGCA Report, *supra* note 2, para. 25.

40 The issue could possibly be further clarified in the Elements of Crimes.

cases where the act of aggression 'by its character, gravity and scale, constitutes a manifest violation of the Charter of the United Nations'. The threshold clause had formed part of the SWGCA's text from the beginning, but a number of concerns about it remained until the end. The proponents of the threshold clause argue that it would be an important safeguard, as it would prevent the Court from addressing borderline cases of various kinds. Arguably, the requirement that the character, gravity and scale of an act of aggression amount to a manifest violation of the Charter would ensure that a minor border skirmish would not be a matter for the Court to take up – in addition to other safeguards that limit the Court's exercise of jurisdiction to the 'most serious crimes of international concern'.[41] Some of those delegations opposed to the threshold clause regard it as unnecessary at best and as establishing two kinds of acts of aggression at worst: those worth prosecuting and those not.[42] Some also regard the threshold clause as the entrance door for the legalization of humanitarian interventions without Security Council authorization, whereas others regret that it is not.[43] It can therefore not be excluded that the threshold clause could cause further problems in the remaining negotiations. At the same time, it should be borne in mind that some delegations made it very clear that the threshold clause was the main reason why they did not object to the use of GA Resolution 3314 (XXIX) as the basis for the definition of the State act of aggression – an important concession that allowed the Group to take a major step forward.[44] Those delegations would probably be strongly opposed to any further weakening or even deletion of the clause in the run-up to the Review Conference.

B. The Definition of the State 'Act' of Aggression

When the SWGCA started to take up its mandate in 2003, few would have thought that it would actually be able to agree on a definition of the State act of aggression as the basis of the definition of the crime. But draft Article 8 bis (2) contains just that:

> For the purpose of paragraph 1, "act of aggression" means the use of armed force by a State against the sovereignty, territorial integrity or political independence of another State, or in any other manner inconsistent with the Charter of the United Nations. Any of the following acts, regardless of a declaration of war, shall, in accordance with United Nations General Assembly resolution 3314 (XXIX) of 14 December 1974, qualify as an act of aggression: (a) The invasion or attack by the armed forces of a State of the territory of another State, or any military occupation, however temporary, resulting from such invasion or attack, or any annexation by the use of force of the territory of another State or part thereof; (b) …[45]

1. GA Resolution 3314 (XXIX): The Basis for the Definition of the Act of Aggression

The SWGCA's definition of the act of aggression is based on GA Resolution 3314 (XXIX), which contains in its annex a 'Definition of Aggression'. That definition, adopted by the UN General

41 June 2006 Princeton Report, *supra* note 11, para. 19.

42 February 2009 SWGCA Report, *supra* note 2, para. 13.

43 An earlier version of the threshold clause would have required a 'flagrant' violation of the Charter and thereby, some delegations thought, would have set the bar slightly higher. June 2006 Princeton Report, *supra* note 11, paras 18–20.

44 December 2007 SWGCA Report, *supra* note 13, para. 13; June 2007 Princeton Report, *supra* note 11, para. 37.

45 See the full text of the provision in the Annex to this article.

Assembly in 1974, was intended to serve as guidance for the Security Council in determining the existence of an act of aggression by a State in accordance with Article 39 UN Charter.[46] The resolution, the culmination of some 20 years of negotiations, was seen by most delegations in the SWGCA as the appropriate basis for the definition of aggression in the Statute, given the fact that it constituted a consensual and time-tested document adopted by the General Assembly on this extremely delicate topic.[47] An alternative approach was also considered for some time, namely to draft a definition of the act of aggression in a more generic manner,[48] without recourse to a GA resolution that had been drafted for a quite different purpose.[49] But the appeal of GA Resolution 3314 (XXIX) turned out to be irresistible, and as of November 2007 the SWGCA focused on the remaining challenge, namely how exactly to make use of the resolution in this new context.[50] One important criterion was to preserve the integrity of GA Resolution 3314 (XXIX) as a comprehensive and delicately balanced text, and therefore a simple reference to Articles 1 and 3 (containing the actual definition of acts of aggression) was rejected as 'pick and choose'. At the same time, one could also not simply refer to GA Resolution 3314 (XXIX) in its entirety, without quoting from its text, nor do the opposite, namely incorporate the lengthy definition into the Rome Statute as a whole, including some of its articles that only make sense in the context of the resolution's original purpose.[51] The solution was not to refer to the numbers of, but to directly incorporate language from the resolution's most relevant Articles 1 and 3 and to link these quotes to the resolution in its entirety through the phrase 'in accordance with United Nations General Assembly resolution 3314 (XXIX) of 14 December 1974'. The definition of the act of aggression would therefore have to be read in conjunction with other parts of the resolution that address relevant issues, such as statehood (Article 1),[52] self-determination (Article 7),[53] and the principle that the provisions of the resolution are interrelated and must be read together (Article 8).[54]

---

46 See para. 4 of GA Resolution 3314 (XXIX).

47 June 2006 Princeton Report, *supra* note 11, paras 32–35;

48 That approach was based on the concept of an 'armed attack' in contravention of the UN Charter. Those delegations that preferred that approach underlined that they could be flexible provided that the threshold clause would remain in the text. See June 2007 Princeton Report, *supra* note 11, para. 37.

49 January 2007 SWGCA Report, *supra* note 11, para. 22.

50 December 2007 SWGCA Report, *supra* note 13, para. 13; January 2007 SWGCA Report, *supra* note 11, paras 19–21.

51 The various positions and arguments are amply reflected in the June 2007 Princeton Report, *supra* note 11, paras 38–43, as well as in the December 2007 SWGCA Report, *supra* note 13, paras 14–15.

52 The explanatory note to Article 1 of GA Resolution 3314 (XXIX) would therefore have to be taken into account. It reads: 'In this Definition the term "State": (a) is used without prejudice to questions of recognition or to whether a State is a member of the United Nations; (b) Includes the concept of a "group of States" where appropriate.'

53 The strong references contained in Article 7 of GA Resolution 3314 (XXIX) to self-determination were an important reason for the appeal of that resolution as a basis for the definition and for calls to refer to that resolution in its entirety. The Article reads: 'Nothing in this Definition, and in particular article 3, could in any way prejudice the right of self-determination, freedom and independence, as derived from the Charter, of peoples forcibly deprived of that right and referred to in the Declaration on Principles of International Law concerning Friendly Relations and Co-operation among States in accordance with the Charter of the United Nations, particularly peoples under colonial and racist régimes or other forms of alien domination; nor the right of these peoples to struggle to that end and to seek and receive support, in accordance with the principles of the Charter and in conformity with the above-mentioned Declaration.'

54 Article 8 of GA Resolution 3314 (XXIX) reads: 'In their interpretation and application the above provisions are interrelated and each provision should be construed in the context of the other provisions.'

Using GA Resolution 3314 (XXIX) as the basis for the definition became at some point an inevitable choice, despite the fact that some delegations considered the resolution to be rather outdated, or not fully reflective of customary international law.[55] Suggestions were made to include non-conventional means of aggression beyond the use of armed force, such as cyber-attacks or economic embargoes.[56] Nevertheless, there was no desire to open the proverbial can of worms, and the great majority of delegations considered the limitation to the use of armed force as appropriate for the purpose of individual criminal justice.[57]

2. The List of Acts of Aggression: Open or Closed?

The definition of the act of aggression in draft Article 8 bis (2) consists of two parts. The opening phrase defines an act of aggression in general terms, using the exact formulation of Article 1 of GA Resolution 3314 (XXIX), which in turn is based almost word for word on Article 2(4) UN Charter, referring to the 'use of armed force by a State against the sovereignty, territorial integrity or political independence of another State, or in any other manner inconsistent with the Charter of the United Nations'. Subsequently, the definition quotes the list of acts contained in Article 3 of GA Resolution 3314 (XXIX): 'Any of the following acts shall … in accordance with United Nations General Assembly resolution 3314 (XXIX) of 14 December 1974, qualify as an act of aggression: …'. The exact nature and legal consequence of the list of acts that follows was amply discussed in the SWGCA, though not in a conclusive manner.[58] Some considered that the list was and indeed should be open rather than exhaustive, in particular as Article 4 of GA Resolution 3314 (XXIV) explicitly states: 'The acts enumerated above are not exhaustive and the Security Council may determine that other acts constitute aggression under the provisions of the Charter.' Others pointed to the fact that the wording of the list in the SWGCA's draft itself does not clearly mark it as open, and rejected suggestions that its open nature be made more explicit. They argued that the principle of legality required that the list be read as closed; Article 4 might say that the Security Council may determine other acts as aggression, but such unfettered discretion could not possibly apply to a criminal court. The discussion over the nature of the list was, however, somewhat tempered by the fact that in any event an act of aggression would have to satisfy the criteria outlined in the opening sentence of draft Article 8 bis (2) and at least constitute a use of armed force by one State against another that is inconsistent with the UN Charter. Some therefore argued that the list was semi-open (or semi-closed): acts similar to those listed could also constitute aggression, provided that they would satisfy those criteria. As an additional safeguard, the threshold clause contained in draft Article 8 bis (1) would ensure that the bar would not be put too low.

In the end, there was a very solid acceptance of the wording of draft Article 8 bis (2) as suggested by the Chairman, despite some divergence in its interpretation. Nevertheless, it would probably not be justified to consider that wording a case of constructive ambiguity, given that it would eventually be part of the Rome Statute and would therefore have to be interpreted by the organs of the Court in accordance with the Statute's rules of interpretation. This includes in particular the

55 June 2007 SWGCA Report, *supra* note 13, para. 46.

56 February 2009 SWGCA Report, *supra* note 2, para. 17; June 2008 SWGCA Report, *supra* note 13, para. 35.

57 While the SWGCA reports do not further reflect on the issue of attacks on computer networks as a means of warfare, it could be argued that a contemporary interpretation of the term armed force could, under some circumstances, include the use of computer networks as weapons.

58 December 2007 SWGCA Report, *supra* note 13, paras 18–23; June 2007 Princeton Report, *supra* note 11, paras 46–53.

requirement to strictly construe the definition of a crime (Article 22 ICCSt). That is not necessarily the standard always used by government delegates arguing for one position or another, but a necessary component of a definition of aggression that satisfies the principle of legality.

C. The Conditions for the Exercise of Jurisdiction: The Role of the Security Council

The single most difficult aspect of the negotiations on the crime of aggression was and remains what Article 5(2) ICCSt calls 'the conditions under which the Court shall exercise jurisdiction with respect to this crime'. The Article continues that the provisions on aggression 'shall be consistent with the relevant provisions of the Charter of the United Nations', thereby not just stating the obvious, but implicitly referring to the most contentious: the question of the role of the Security Council. The SWGCA's proposals address the conditions for the exercise of jurisdiction in a new draft Article 15 bis, and the various alternatives and options marked in bold in its paragraph 4 leave no doubt that this continues to be the crux of the matter. Some delegations, among them Permanent Members of the UN Security Council, insist that the Court may only prosecute a crime of aggression once the Council has made a determination of aggression in accordance with Article 39 UN Charter. Others reject the notion that the Security Council would have absolute priority[59] in determining an act of aggression, and are ready to consider a number of alternatives. While this is an ongoing and ultimately very political debate,[60] draft Article 15 bis also contains a number of agreed paragraphs that are related to this debate and reflect significant progress. These will be considered first.

1. An Agreed Trigger for the Crime of Aggression

The discussion over the role of the Security Council is often equated with a discussion over the trigger mechanism. It is true that this discussion is indeed linked to the question as to who can trigger the Court's investigation into a crime of aggression, but that specific question has been settled by the SWGCA. Draft Article 15 bis (1) states that the 'Court may exercise jurisdiction over the crime of aggression in accordance with article 13, subject to the provisions of this article'. Article 13 ICCSt in turn refers to the existing trigger mechanisms, which would therefore apply to the crime of aggression. In other words: the SWGCA has already agreed that the Security Council would not be the only organ that could provide the Court with a basis for its exercise of jurisdiction. That basis could also be a State referral[61] as well as an investigation initiated by the Prosecutor *proprio motu*.[62] The controversial question of the Security Council determination of aggression comes into play at a later stage: when the Prosecutor concludes that there is a reasonable basis to proceed with an investigation, but the Security Council does not follow-up with a determination of

59 The SWGCA reports usually refer to arguments about the 'exclusive' competence of the Security Council to determine aggression, but in light of the evolution of its discussions it would be more appropriate to refer to the Council's 'priority' competence. Draft Article 15 bis (5) implies that even if the Security Council would ultimately be given the strongest role currently envisaged in the text (Draft Article 15 bis (4), Alternative 1), there would still be a competence for the Court to determine aggression by its own standards. This draft provision is not disputed, and it seems incompatible with the notion of an 'exclusive' competence for the Security Council.

60 See in particular the discussions reflected in the June 2008 SWGCA Report, *supra* note 13, paras 38–48; and the June 2007 Princeton Report, *supra* note 11, paras 14–35.

61 Article 13(a) ICCSt.

62 Article 13(c) ICCSt.

aggression by one State against another. The question of the role of the Security Council is therefore not (or not anymore) a question of the trigger mechanism, but a question of a jurisdictional filter. The ways in which the Court could be seized with a situation involving a crime of aggression would be the same as for the other crimes. It is an important achievement for the SWGCA to have clarified this question.

2. ICC Not Bound by a Determination of Aggression by the Security Council

Draft Article 15 bis (5) states in unequivocal terms that 'a determination of an act of aggression by an organ outside the Court shall be without prejudice to the Court's own findings under this Statute'. This draft provision reflects an understanding that the SWGCA reached gradually, beginning with discussions over the consequences of a Security Council determination of aggression for due process, and later in the context of the discussions over GA Resolution 3314 (XXIX).[63] The resolution states in its Article 4 that the '… Security Council may determine that other acts constitute aggression under the provisions of the Charter'. This provision is difficult to reconcile with the principle of legality required for individual criminal justice, especially where the Security Council might make a rather creative determination of aggression, or where a determination of aggression may have been, for whatever reason, simply erroneous. Draft Article 15 bis (5), however, confirms the independence of the Court in its judicial decisions and thereby safeguards the rights of the accused. It would thus be conceivable that the Court would disagree with a Security Council determination of aggression, in particular after having considered the arguments and evidence provided by the accused.[64]

This paragraph also confirms an important underlying premise of the work on aggression, according to which the definition would only serve the purposes of individual criminal justice under the Rome Statute[65] and not affect the manner in which the Security Council or any other organ determines aggression. The clear understanding that the Security Council will not be bound by the definition of aggression in the Rome Statute, and that in turn the Court will not be bound by a determination of aggression by the Security Council, greatly facilitated the discussions on the definition of an act of aggression in draft Article 8 bis (2). It reconciled two interests that were often seen as competing: on the one hand, the principle of legality and the rights of the accused, and, on the other hand, the power and authority of the Security Council.

3. Prosecution of Other Crimes Proceeds Irrespective of the Crime of Aggression

Draft Article 15 bis (6) states that the Court's exercise of jurisdiction is 'without prejudice to the provisions relating to the exercise of jurisdiction with respect to other crimes referred to in article 5'. This is a significant statement, since any case of aggression is very likely to also include the commission of other crimes, in particular war crimes. This provision would thus ensure that an investigation into such other crimes could move forward, even if the Court's proceedings might ultimately be dependent on a Security Council determination as a jurisdictional filter, and where the Council does not make such a determination. Ben Ferencz has frequently pointed to the

63 June 2005 Princeton Report, paras 60–62; June 2006 Princeton Report, paras 70–72; June 2007 Princeton Report, para. 54 (all *supra* note 11).

64 It also confirms that the link to GA Resolution 3314 (XXIX) does not imply that the Security Council could effectively 'amend' the future provisions on aggression in the Rome Statute by determining acts of aggression that would clearly go beyond those envisaged in the resolution.

65 See also the opening phrase of draft Article 8 bis: 'For the purpose of this Statute …'.

importance of this provision, as it could allow the Court to continue the process of investigation and revelation of the truth, thereby putting pressure on the Council to acknowledge an alleged case of aggression.[66] Whether that prospect alone would eventually satisfy those delegations opposed to an exclusive role for the Security Council as jurisdictional filter need not be answered here. In any event, this provision was not controversial in the SWGCA.[67]

4. What if the Security Council Does Not Make a Determination of Aggression?

The relationship between the Court and the Security Council as regards the crime of aggression is addressed in several paragraphs of draft Article 15 bis. Paragraphs 1 to 3 envisage the procedure for the best-case scenario, in which the Court and the Security Council proceed in tandem: the Court is seized with a situation (via State referral, *proprio motu*, or via a Security Council referral that does or does not include a determination of aggression), the Prosecutor initiates the investigation and concludes on the basis of the evidence available that there is a reasonable basis to assume that a crime of aggression was committed. At that stage, he or she will notify the Secretary General of the United Nations, who will in turn inform the Security Council about the status of the investigation.[68] If the Security Council has not yet done so before, this is the moment for it to determine the existence of an act of aggression (applying the Council's own standards for the determination of aggression, not necessarily those of the Rome Statute), and thereafter the Prosecutor can proceed.

But what if the Security Council does not make a determination of aggression, especially if the cause for the Council's inaction is not the absence of aggression? That is the big question, to which draft Article 15 bis (4) provides a whole menu of possible answers, presented as two sets of several options under Alternatives 1 and 2.

Alternative 1 contains only two options, both of which leave the fate of the investigation entirely in the hands of the Security Council and thus in the hands of any Permanent Member of the Council. Option 1 simply prevents the Prosecutor from proceeding in the absence of a substantive determination by the Security Council that an act of aggression has been committed. That option is favoured, in particular by Permanent Members of the Security Council who argue that the Council is the only[69] organ that has the competence to determine aggression, as evidenced by Article 39 UN Charter.[70] Some also argue that the Court would be protected from any perception of politicization if the question of aggression at the State level was outsourced to the Security Council.[71] Option 2 provides a slightly lower threshold for the Prosecutor to proceed. Instead of a substantive determination of an act of aggression, the Security Council would only be required to give the green light for the Court's proceeding. While this option still preserves the Security Council's full control, it lowers the bar for the Council's decision-making and increases the potential for cases of aggression to proceed at the Court.[72] It would also constitute an additional policy option for the Council, since it could choose not to make a substantive determination of aggression, but instead pass the buck to the Court.

---

66 See the transcript of a statement by Ben Ferencz in the SWGCA on 5 June 2008. Available at http://www.benferencz.org/arts/95.html (visited 28 March 2009).

67 June 2007 Princeton Report, *supra* note 11, para. 18.

68 In accordance with the Relationship Agreement between the International Criminal Court and the United Nations, 2283 UN Treaty Series (2004).

69 See however the argument in note 59.

70 June 2005 Princeton Report, *supra* note 11, para. 66;

71 June 2007 Princeton Report, *supra* note 11, para. 25.

72 Ibid., paras 27–29.

Alternative 2 lists a number of options that still grant the Security Council the right to take the first shot at a determination of aggression, but that do not simply defer to the Council's inaction. After a certain period of time (the text mentions six months, largely a placeholder), the Court could thus proceed – under Option 1 even without any further conditions. Option 2 would require the Pre-Trial Chamber to specifically authorize the investigation into the crime of aggression and would thus serve as a judicial filter in the same way as its authorization is currently required for *proprio motu* investigations into other crimes.[73] This option thus follows the rationale for Article 15 ICCSt as a check on the Prosecutor's *proprio motu* powers and applies the same checks to the Prosecutor's investigations into the crime of aggression, in particular in case of a State referral.[74] Option 3 would allow the Court to proceed once the General Assembly has made a determination of aggression, an option inspired by the Assembly's powers under the Uniting for Peace formula. Finally, Option 4 would allow the Court to proceed where the ICJ has made a determination of aggression, either through its advisory or its contentious powers.

While draft Article 15 bis (4) may look rather hopeless in that some of the alternatives and options are simply diametrically opposed to each other, the SWGCA managed at least to bundle the multitude of approaches to a concise text that reflects the positions of all delegations. It is clearly understood by all that this paragraph requires 'further discussion, including on the basis of new ideas and suggestions'.[75] The future of draft Article 15 bis (4) is linked to another issue, namely the question of the relevant entry into force procedure for the amendments on aggression, to be discussed next. The outlook on both of these issues will therefore be discussed further below in the final section on the remaining challenges.

D. Entry into Force Procedures for the Amendment on Aggression

The second issue clearly marked as still open for discussion, besides draft Article 15 bis (4), can be found at the very beginning of the SWGCA's proposals in the draft resolution. The draft resolution contains the text of the actual decision to be taken by the Review Conference, namely to 'adopt the amendments to the Rome Statute of the International Criminal Court … contained in the annex to the present resolution, which are subject to ratification or acceptance and shall enter into force in accordance with article 121, paragraph [4/5] of the Statute'. The two options referred to in square brackets are fundamentally different, and both have attracted substantial support. So far, any attempts to consider the two provisions as complementary rather than mutually exclusive have been rejected,[76] and it is thus likely that in the final decision on the matter, the Review Conference will simply have to choose one or the other option. These are:

1. Article 121(4) ICCSt: A Unified Regime for All States Parties

According to Article 121(4) ICCSt, the amendment on aggression would enter into force for all States Parties at the same time, namely once seven-eighths of them have ratified or accepted

73 November 2006 SWGCA Report, *supra* note 11, para. 9; December 2007 SWGCA Report, *supra* note 11, paras 31–34.

74 The Pre-Trial Chamber's authorization would also be required in case of a Security Council referral that did not already include a determination of aggression. In case of *proprio motu* proceedings, the authorization would already be necessary by virtue of the existing Article 15 ICCSt, even if the draft provision was not adopted.

75 February 2009 SWGCA Report, *supra* note 13, para. 19.

76 February 2009 SWGCA Report, *supra* note 2, para. 8.

the amendment.[77] This would lead to a unified regime on the crime of aggression among States Parties, and would potentially extend the Court's exercise of jurisdiction to nationals of States Parties that would be opposed to the amendment, as well as non-States Parties.[78] Nevertheless, the ratification process required for the entry into force of the amendment could take a long time until the threshold of seven-eighths is reached. The proponents of such a solution argue that the crime of aggression should be treated equally to all other crimes under the Statute and be subject to a unified jurisdictional regime, thus avoiding double standards.[79] Some delegations argue in this context that the plain language of the Statute requires that Article 121(4) ICCSt be applied to the amendment on aggression, since it is the default provision applicable to amendments. The exception to this default provision, contained in Article 121(5) ICCSt, only applies to amendments to Articles 5, 6, 7 and 8. It is then noted that the draft amendments adopted by the SWGCA mainly contain new Articles (8 bis, 15 bis) and changes to other existing Articles (9, 20, 25).[80] Those who argue in favour of such a unified regime also frequently point out that defining the crime of aggression is a different exercise than amending existing definitions of crimes or adding entirely new crimes (such as drug crimes or acts of terrorism): it is the process of completing the Rome Statute on an issue that was left over at the Rome Conference, at which there was already agreement that Court should have jurisdiction over the crime of aggression. Allowing some States Parties to ultimately not opt into the amendment on aggression to be adopted by the Review Conference would thus constitute a step back from the principle of automatic jurisdiction over the crimes referred to in Article 5 ICCSt.[81]

2. Article 121(5) ICCSt: An Opt-In Regime for States Parties Accepting the Amendment

Under the alternative approach, contained in Article 121(5) ICCSt, the amendment on aggression would enter into force only for those States Parties that have accepted it and thus allow States Parties to choose to be bound or not.[82] Those who favour this approach argue that Article 121(5) ICCSt is the applicable provision for amendments to the core crimes under the Statute, and furthermore refers specifically to Article 5 ICCSt, which contains the Statute's only current provision on aggression.[83] The fact that most of the draft amendments do not make changes to Articles 5, 6, 7 and 8 as such is not seen as relevant in this context since that was mainly a structural decision aimed at integrating the provisions on aggression smoothly into the Statute. Alternatively, all these provisions could have been packed into Article 5 ICCSt itself, thereby removing any doubt as to

77 Article 121(4) ICCSt reads: 'Except as provided in paragraph 5, an amendment shall enter into force for all States Parties one year after instruments of ratification or acceptance have been deposited with the Secretary-General of the United Nations by seven-eighths of them.'

78 Only potentially, since that would depend on how the other provisions on the exercise of jurisdiction are finally agreed upon.

79 June 2008 SWGCA Report, *supra* note 13, paras 13–14.

80 Only the deletion of Article 5(2) ICCSt, which is envisaged in the SWGCA's proposals as a way of cleaning up after the inclusion of the provisions on aggression, is conceded to possibly constitute an amendment to Articles 5, 6, 7 and 8. Nevertheless, the deletion of Article 5(2) ICCSt is not regarded as a central element of the package, and indeed one that could be left out altogether.

81 February 2009 SWGCA Report, *supra* note 2, para. 9.

82 Article 121(5) ICCSt reads: 'Any amendment to articles 5, 6, 7 and 8 of this Statute shall enter into force for those States Parties which have accepted the amendment one year after the deposit of theirs instruments of ratification or acceptance. In respect of a State Party which has not accepted the amendment, the Court shall not exercise its jurisdiction regarding a crime covered by the amendment when committed by that State Party's national or on its territory.'

83 June 2008 SWGCA Report, *supra* note 13, para. 9.

the applicability of Article 121(5) ICCSt. It is further argued that Article 121(5) ICCSt would lead to a much earlier entry into force of the provisions on aggression and would prevent the scenario in which some States Parties might consider withdrawing from the Statute.[84]

Those who argue in favour of the opt-in approach of Article 121(5) ICCSt have their lives greatly complicated by the wording of the second sentence of that paragraph, which reads: 'In respect of a State Party which has not accepted the amendment, the Court shall not exercise its jurisdiction regarding a crime covered by the amendment when committed by that State Party's national or on its territory.' That sentence, taken at face value, would have a number of serious and potentially overreaching implications for the Court's exercise of jurisdiction over the crime of aggression. One implication could be that an alleged aggressor State Party, by not ratifying the amendment, could effectively shield its nationals from prosecution for a crime of aggression committed against a victim State Party, even if the latter has accepted the amendment. That shield would not be available for an aggressor non-State Party – a circumstance which the SWGCA has already identified as discrimination that should be avoided.[85] There are, however, two ways of avoiding such discrimination: by either providing the shield to both non-States Parties and State Parties that have not accepted the amendment – or removing the shield from both categories of States.[86] The SWGCA started looking at the potential implications of this sentence only during its last two meetings and discussed a number of draft 'understandings' that could serve as authoritative interpretations to be adopted simultaneously with the amendments on aggression to avoid discriminatory or absurd results. It would go beyond the scope of this chapter to address these issues in detail; suffice it to say that the discussion indicated that it could be technically manageable to tailor the implications of the wording of the second sentence of Article 121(5) ICCSt for a package on aggression to be adopted by the Review Conference.

4. The Remaining Challenge: Jurisdiction Over Dissenting States

The dispute over the application of either paragraph 4 or 5 of Article 121 ICCSt may be mostly carried out with arguments over the correct interpretation of the Statute, but in its essence the various positions are closely linked to the elusive question of the 'conditions for the exercise of jurisdiction'. Under paragraph 5, combined with a rather literal interpretation of its second sentence, it would be a condition for the Court's exercise of jurisdiction that the aggressor State have accepted the amendment on aggression[87] – an approach obviously favoured by those worried about State sovereignty. If paragraph 4 were chosen, the consent of an aggressor State would not necessarily be relevant for the exercise of jurisdiction. Under both paragraphs, a strong role for the Security Council could effectively introduce another layer of consent required for the exercise of

84 Article 127 ICCSt.

85 November 2008 SWGCA Report, *supra* note 13, para. 15. The somewhat cynical argument could also be made that such an effect of the second sentence of Article 121(5) would simply constitute an incentive to join the Rome Statute prior to the adoption of the amendment on aggression.

86 February 2009 SWGCA Report, *supra* note 2, paras 31–37.

87 Except if the Court's jurisdiction is based on a Security Council referral: there is agreement in the SWGCA that – once the amendment enters into force – the Court may exercise jurisdiction on the basis of a Security Council referral irrespective of whether the State concerned has accepted the Court's jurisdiction with respect to the crime of aggression. In order to ensure that this interpretation prevails despite the wording of the second sentence of Article 121(5) ICCSt, the Review Conference might have to adopt an explicit 'understanding' on this matter. See February 2009 SWGCA Report, *supra* note 2, paras 28–29.

jurisdiction – namely the consent of at least each Permanent Member of the Security Council in any given case.

The search for agreement on these two issues – entry into force procedure as well as the role of the Security Council – remains the core challenge for the remaining negotiations. These two issues, both of which have several subsidiary aspects, are strongly interlinked. Ultimately, they boil down to the question of how to deal with States that do not accept the Court's jurisdiction over the crime of aggression. Should the amendments on aggression allow the Court to exercise jurisdiction with respect to alleged aggression committed by such dissenting States, be they parties to the Rome Statute or not?[88] For less powerful States, that would obviously constitute the central value added of the protective shield provided by the future provisions on aggression. However, such an approach could lead to serious alienation and possibly retaliation on behalf of the dissenters if they feel that they have good reason not to agree to the Court's active jurisdiction over this crime, e.g., because they disagree with the crime's definition or with other aspects, such as the degree of deference to the Permanent Members of the Security Council (either too much or too little).

The question can, cautiously, be narrowed down even further: the SWGCA proposals indicate, in principle, agreement that the Court should be allowed to exercise jurisdiction in respect of a dissenting State if the Security Council has determined that the State has committed an act of aggression. The question remains, however, how to deal with an investigation into a crime of aggression that has not received the Council's stamp of approval – a scenario that is particularly relevant for State referrals and *proprio motu* investigations.[89] To pick the latter scenario: if the Prosecutor has reason to believe that an act of aggression has been committed against a State Party that has accepted the amendment on aggression by a State that has not, should some form of consent of the latter State be required for the Prosecutor to proceed (provided the Security Council is not 'helping' either)? Three main approaches can be identified to answer the question:

(1) Yes, consent should be required in some cases, namely, if the State in question is a Permanent Member of the Security Council. In practice, that privilege would probably also extend to friends and allies of Permanent Members. This is the answer reflected in draft Article 15 bis (4), Alternative 1. It is the answer that some consider to be in line with the reality of the UN Charter, and that others consider to be incompatible with the principle of equality of all before the law;

(2) No, consent should not be required. All States, including Permanent Members of the Council that are non-States Parties or that do not accept the amendment on aggression, should be subject to a procedure that is not entirely and in all situations dependent on their consent, similar to the current system[90] with respect to other crimes under the Rome Statute. This is essentially the answer contained in draft Article 15 bis (4), Alternative 2. That approach would still give the

88 The Court would of course only try individuals and not States, but incidentally the Court would have to pronounce itself over the question whether the State committed an act of aggression.

89 It seems unlikely that the Security Council would refer a situation to the Court that could involve a crime of aggression, without the Council being aware of that possibility and indeed being willing to determine, albeit possibly at a later stage, that an act of aggression has been committed.

90 Under Article 12(2)(a) ICCSt it is a sufficient precondition for the Court's exercise of jurisdiction that the criminal conduct take place on the territory of a State Party. It is therefore not required that the perpetrator be a national of a State Party. There was general support in the SWGCA for the view that the crime of aggression is typically committed on the territories of both the aggressor and the victim State. The leader's criminal conduct may take place on the territory of the aggressor State, but the consequences of the conduct are felt on the territory of the victim State and are equally relevant for the purposes of establishing territoriality. See February 2009 SWGCA Report, *supra* note 2, paras 38–39; November 2008 SWGCA Report, *supra* note 13, paras 28–29.

Security Council priority in determining the existence of aggression in accordance with Article 39 UN Charter, but inaction on behalf of the Council over a significant period of time would not in itself prevent the Court from proceeding. No individual person accused of having committed the crime of aggression would be able to rely on his or her country of nationality alone as a shield from prosecution by the Court;

(3) Yes, consent should be required in all cases. This possibility is currently not very explicitly reflected in the text,[91] but it could result from the conflict between the first and the second approach: if those arguing for equality for all are not able to get a solution that dispenses with the Permanent Members' privilege to shield their nationals from the Court's jurisdiction, then one logical fall-back position would be to ask that this privilege be extended to all States.[92] That could be achieved by choosing Article 121(5) ICCSt as the procedure for entry into force of the amendment, combined with an understanding by the States Parties that this provision effectively 'prevents the Court from exercising jurisdiction in respect of an act of aggression committed by any State that has not accepted the amendment'.[93] One further option would be to require a determination of an act of aggression by the ICJ under its consent-based contentious jurisdiction.[94] Another way of achieving a similar result would be to limit the Court's jurisdiction to situations involving alleged acts of aggression committed by States that actively accept the Court's jurisdiction by way of a declaration.[95] Such approaches have barely been explored so far, as the main focus of the discussion had been the role of the Security Council. But if other ways of addressing sovereignty concerns would receive greater attention, the dynamics of the discussion might change considerably – both with respect to the role of the Security Council[96] and with respect to the applicable entry into force procedure.[97]

In the search for a solution, these three general approaches for dealing with the question of the dissenting State could be dissected even further. One possibility would be to look at the three trigger mechanisms separately and come to different solutions for each of them:[98] if a situation reaches the Court because of a Security Council referral, why not allow the Council to insist that the Court should only proceed with an investigation into the crime of aggression if the Council explicitly agrees?[99] After

91 See however the discussion in the February 2009 SWGCA Report, *supra* note 2, para. 9.

92 It could, however, also lead those countries to challenge the already agreed notion that a Security Council determination of aggression is a sufficient condition for the Court to proceed.

93 February 2009 SWGCA Report, *supra* note 2, paras 36 and 37.

94 Draft Article 15 bis (4), Alternative 2, Option 4 currently does not distinguish between the ICJ's powers in advisory and contentious matters.

95 February 2009 SWGCA Report, *supra* note 2, para. 9.

96 Since such a declaration-based system would allow any State to shield its nationals from the Court's jurisdiction, Permanent Members of the Security Council might possibly no longer insist on an exclusive role for the Security Council as a jurisdictional filter in cases of *proprio moto* investigations and State referrals, in particular if combined with a solution that still allows the Security Council to remain in control of the issue of aggression in case of Security Council referrals that are not accompanied by a determination of aggression (as explained in the following paragraph).

97 Delegations with a strong preference for the application of Article 121(5) ICCSt could possibly be more flexible on the issue of entry into force procedures if their sovereignty concerns would effectively be taken care of through other means.

98 Briefly alluded to in the June 2006 Princeton Report, *supra* note 11, para. 61.

99 Either by making a determination of an act of aggression (Draft Article 15 bis (4), Alternative 1, Option 1), or by allowing the Court to proceed without a Security Council determination of aggression (Draft Article 15 bis (4), Alternative 1, Option 2).

all, the Council could alternatively simply choose not to refer the situation to the Court and therefore already has all the cards in its hands.[100] Another scenario that might deserve a separate solution could be the self-referral of a State that has committed aggression: why not allow that State, probably only after a new government has come to power, to refer its own situation to the Court without approval from any other organ? After all, that State would have every right to prosecute its own former leader domestically. No sovereignty concerns should arise if the new government chooses to voluntarily entrust an international court with the proceedings as a form of 'technical assistance'.

Still, a *proprio motu* investigation or a regular State referral involving a case of aggression committed by a non-State Party or by a State Party that has not accepted the amendment on aggression remains a difficult scenario to resolve.

5. Conclusion

The proposals for a provision on aggression elaborated by the SWGCA represent a watershed in the negotiations on the crime of aggression. Never before has the concept of the crime of aggression been better analysed and understood in an intergovernmental process. The SWGCA has drafted provisions on aggression that could be smoothly embedded into the Rome Statute. In doing so, the SWGCA has agreed *inter alia*:

- on a definition of the individual's conduct that fits with the Statute's Part 3 on General Principles of Criminal Law;
- on a clause reflecting the leadership nature of the crime;
- on a definition of the State act of aggression on the basis of GA Resolution 3314 (XXIX);
- on the use of all three existing trigger mechanisms in accordance with Article 13 ICCSt;
- that the ICC would – for reasons of due process – not be bound by a determination of aggression by any organ outside the Court.

More generally, the SWGCA's work reflects a general acceptance of the notion that the ICC could one day effectively exercise jurisdiction over this crime, while there are still open questions as to the conditions for the exercise of jurisdiction. To come to an agreement on this issue will require intense efforts on behalf of all parties at the negotiating table. The underlying issues are both complex and polarizing, and a consensual solution at the Review Conference is still a long shot. But if the previous work of the SWGCA is any indication, one should expect that the remaining negotiations would be driven by a sense of purpose and a willingness to engage on the outstanding issues in good faith. A number of avenues that could lead to a negotiated solution on these issues are still waiting to be explored in depth. Based on the groundbreaking preparatory work conducted by the SWGCA, the delegates in Kampala will have a historic chance to beat the odds once again.

100 A reverse argument could also be made: if the Security Council were not to be given control over the question of aggression in the context of its own referrals to the Court, it might be more reluctant to make such referrals – even where it would otherwise have agreed to refer a situation with respect to the other crimes under the Statute.

Annex: Proposals for a provision on aggression elaborated by the Special Working Group on the Crime of Aggression

Draft resolution

(to be adopted by the Review Conference)

The Review Conference,

(insert preambular paragraphs)

1. *Decides* to adopt the amendments to the Rome Statute of the International Criminal Court (hereinafter: 'the Statute') contained in the annex to the present resolution, which are subject to ratification or acceptance and shall enter into force in accordance with article 121, paragraph [4/5] of the Statute;

(add further operative paragraphs as needed)

Appendix: Draft amendments to the Rome Statute of the International Criminal Court on the Crime of Aggression

1. Article 5, paragraph 2, of the Statute is deleted.

2. The following text is inserted after article 8 of the Statute:

Article 8 bis

Crime of aggression

1. For the purpose of this Statute, 'crime of aggression' means the planning, preparation, initiation or execution, by a person in a position effectively to exercise control over or to direct the political or military action of a State, of an act of aggression which, by its character, gravity and scale, constitutes a manifest violation of the Charter of the United Nations.

2. For the purpose of paragraph 1, 'act of aggression' means the use of armed force by a State against the sovereignty, territorial integrity or political independence of another State, or in any other manner inconsistent with the Charter of the United Nations. Any of the following acts, regardless of a declaration of war, shall, in accordance with United Nations General Assembly resolution 3314 (XXIX) of 14 December 1974, qualify as an act of aggression:

(a) The invasion or attack by the armed forces of a State of the territory of another State, or any military occupation, however temporary, resulting from such invasion or attack, or any annexation by the use of force of the territory of another State or part thereof;
(b) Bombardment by the armed forces of a State against the territory of another State or the use of any weapons by a State against the territory of another State;

(c) The blockade of the ports or coasts of a State by the armed forces of another State;
(d) An attack by the armed forces of a State on the land, sea or air forces, or marine and air fleets of another State;
(e) The use of armed forces of one State which are within the territory of another State with the agreement of the receiving State, in contravention of the conditions provided for in the agreement or any extension of their presence in such territory beyond the termination of the agreement;
(f) The action of a State in allowing its territory, which it has placed at the disposal of another State, to be used by that other State for perpetrating an act of aggression against a third State;
(g) The sending by or on behalf of a State of armed bands, groups, irregulars or mercenaries, which carry out acts of armed force against another State of such gravity as to amount to the acts listed above, or its substantial involvement therein.

3. The following text is inserted after article 15 of the Statute:

Article 15 bis

Exercise of jurisdiction over the crime of aggression

1. The Court may exercise jurisdiction over the crime of aggression in accordance with article 13, subject to the provisions of this article.
2. Where the Prosecutor concludes that there is a reasonable basis to proceed with an investigation in respect of a crime of aggression, he or she shall first ascertain whether the Security Council has made a determination of an act of aggression committed by the State concerned. The Prosecutor shall notify the Secretary-General of the United Nations of the situation before the Court, including any relevant information and documents.
3. Where the Security Council has made such a determination, the Prosecutor may proceed with the investigation in respect of a crime of aggression.
4. **(Alternative 1)** In the absence of such a determination, the Prosecutor may not proceed with the investigation in respect of a crime of aggression,

***Option 1** – end the paragraph here.*
Option 2 – add: unless the Security Council has, in a resolution adopted under Chapter VII of the Charter of the United Nations, requested the Prosecutor to proceed with the investigation in respect of a crime of aggression.

4. **(Alternative 2)** Where no such determination is made within [6] months after the date of notification, the Prosecutor may proceed with the investigation in respect of a crime of aggression,

***Option 1** – end the paragraph here.*
Option 2 – add: provided that the Pre-Trial Chamber has authorized the commencement of the investigation in respect of a crime of aggression in accordance with the procedure contained in article 15;
Option 3 – add: provided that the General Assembly has determined that an act of aggression has been committed by the State referred to in article 8 bis;

Option 4 – add: provided that the International Court of Justice has determined that an act of aggression has been committed by the State referred to in article 8 bis.

5. A determination of an act of aggression by an organ outside the Court shall be without prejudice to the Court's own findings under this Statute.
6. This article is without prejudice to the provisions relating to the exercise of jurisdiction with respect to other crimes referred to in article 5.

4. The following text is inserted after article 25, paragraph 3 of the Statute:

3 bis. In respect of the crime of aggression, the provisions of this article shall apply only to persons in a position effectively to exercise control over or to direct the political or military action of a State.

5. The first sentence of article 9, paragraph 1 of the Statute is replaced by the following sentence:

1. Elements of Crimes shall assist the Court in the interpretation and application of articles 6, 7, 8 and 8 bis.

6. The chapeau of article 20, paragraph 3 of the Statute is replaced by the following paragraph; the rest of the paragraph remains unchanged:

3. No person who has been tried by another court for conduct also proscribed under article 6, 7, 8 or 8 bis shall be tried by the Court with respect to the same conduct unless the proceedings in the other court: [.]

Index

For Product Safety Concerns and Information please contact our EU representative GPSR@taylorandfrancis.com Taylor & Francis Verlag GmbH, Kaufingerstraße 24, 80331 München, Germany

Batch number: 10726296

Printed by Printforce, the Netherlands